AF814299

NAVIGATOR SERIES

2000+ PROBLEMS

JEE Main & Advanced

Optics & Modern Physics

PRADEEP BENIWAL

IIT Kharagpur

arihant

SUCCESS AND NOTHING LESS

arihant
SUCCESS AND NOTHING LESS

ARIHANT PRAKASHAN (Series), MEERUT

- **Administrative & Production Offices**

  Regd. Office
  'Ramchhaya' 4577/15, Agarwal Road, Darya Ganj, New Delhi -110002
  Tele: 011- 47630600, 43518550

  Head Office
  Kalindi, TP Nagar, Meerut (UP) - 250002
  Tel: 0121-7156203, 7156204

- **Sales & Support Offices**
  Agra, Ahmedabad, Bengaluru, Bareilly, Chennai, Delhi, Guwahati, Hyderabad, Jaipur, Jhansi, Kolkata, Lucknow, Nagpur & Pune.

- **PRICE :** ₹395.00

- **PO No :** TXT-XX-XXXXXXX-X-XX

  Published by Arihant Publications (India) Ltd.

  For further information about the books published by Arihant, log on to www.arihantbooks.com or e-mail at info@arihantbooks.com

  Follow us on

PREFACE

Physics is a subject that requires a lot of practice to master it and the best way to practice Physics is to solve more & more problems right from the beginner's level to the most complex ones. That's why the search for a good Physics Problems book has always been the top notch task of each good student.

During the last 15 Years while teaching & mentoring thousands of students preparing for JEE Main, JEE Advanced, KVPY, Olympiads etc. I always felt the need of such a book that can offer quality problems of Physics for all the topics of different chapters. There are many problems books available in the market but unfortunately none of them serve the purpose perfectly.

To fulfil the need of a good Physics Problems book, I have prepared the book **JEE Navigator, Optics & Modern Physics**. All the problems given in this book are arranged conceptually and systematically in order to test the conceptual understanding & analytical ability of the students.

All the problems given in each chapter of this book have been developed with the utmost care and arranged in a way to enhance the problem-solving skills of the students & to boost their confidence to tackle complex JEE Problems.

The Points given below will help you to learn the basic structure of the book;

- Each chapter is divided into three major heads; **Level 1 'Starter Level', Level 2 'JEE Main Level' & Level 3 'JEE Advanced Level'.**
- **Level 1 'Starter Level'** consists of preliminary questions that test basic concepts. After completing this level student will have a solid understanding of fundamentals of the chapter necessary to solve the problems.
- **Level 2 'JEE Main Level'** has single choice correct questions and numerical value questions aimed especially for JEE Main.
- **Level 3 'JEE Advanced Level'** consists of various types of questions; MCQ with one or more than one correct answer, Comprehension Based Questions, Match the Columns and Numerical Value problems as per JEE Advanced Pattern.
- The problems given in JEE Advanced Level are made to be conceptually challenging resulting in practical and relevant practice for JEE Advanced.
- Detailed solutions to all the problems have been provided at the end of every chapter just to help the students in case they stuck somewhere while solving some questions.

At the end, I can say confidently that if you rigorously practice the problems given in this book then surely you will get an edge in Physics and will increase your chance of getting good JEE Score.

However, I have taken the utmost care while writing this book but if any error or whatsoever has skipped my attention then please bring it to my notice so that it can be rectified. I would also like to appeal all my fellow Physics Teachers to have a look at the book and share their valuable suggestions for its further improvement.

Pradeep Beniwal
B.Tech, IIT Kharagpur
problemsinphysics@yahoo.com

CONTENTS

CHAPTER~01

REFLECTION AT PLANE AND SPHERICAL SURFACE

LEVEL 01 Starter Level

1.1 Reflection from Plane Mirror

1 Find the angle of deviation (both clockwise and anti-clockwise) suffered by a ray incident on a plane mirror, at an angle of incidence 30°.

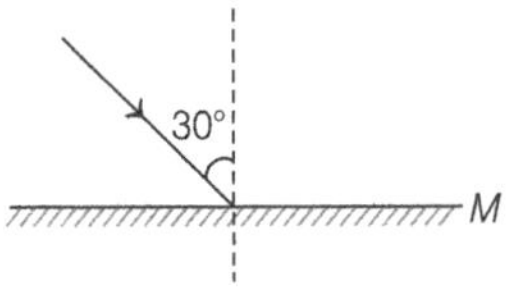

2 A ray of light incident on a plane mirror at an angle 10° with horizontal. After reflection from mirror the reflected ray becomes vertical as shown. Find the angle θ made by the plane mirror with horizontal.

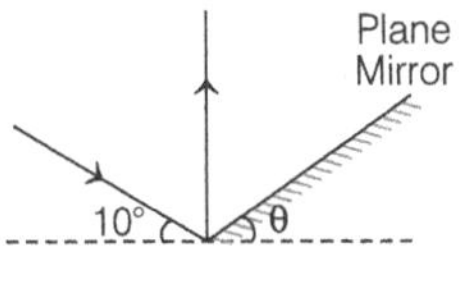

3 Figure shows a plane mirror onto which a light ray is incident. If the incident light ray is turned by 10° and the mirror by 20°, as shown, find the angle turned by the reflected ray.

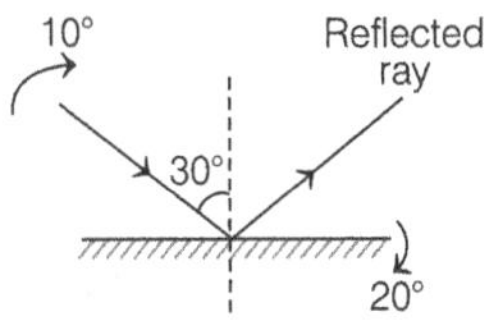

4 Two plane mirrors are inclined at angle θ as shown in figure. If a ray parallel to OB strikes the other mirror at P and finally emerges parallel to OA after two reflections, then find θ.

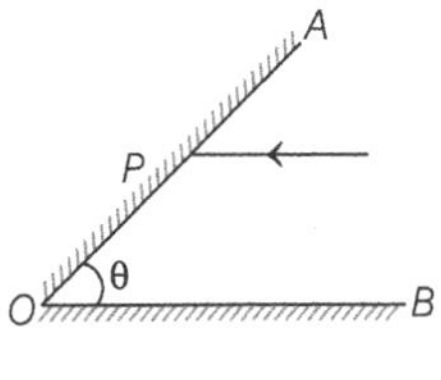

5. A light ray is incident on a plane mirror, which after getting reflected strikes another plane mirror, as shown in figure. The angle between the two mirrors is 70°. Find the angle θ shown in figure.

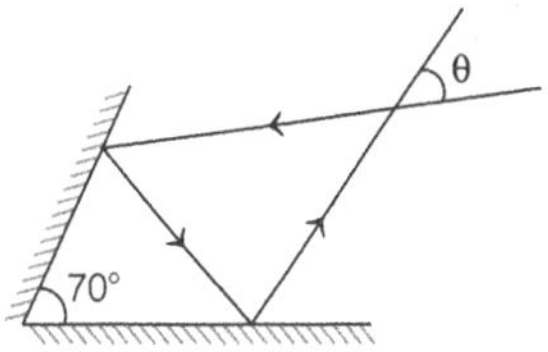

6 A ray of light is incident on a plane mirror along a vector $\hat{i} + 2\hat{j} - 2\hat{k}$. The normal on incidence point is along $\hat{i} + \hat{j}$. Find the unit vector along the reflected ray.

1.2 Image Formation by a Plane Mirror

1 An object is placed at (0, 0) and a plane mirror is placed, inclined 30° with the X-axis as shown in figure. Find the position of image.

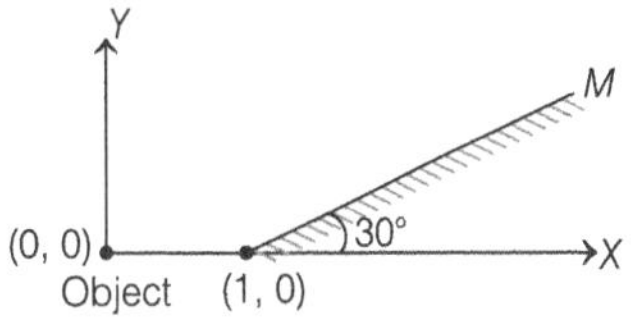

2 An object is kept in front of plane mirror as shown in figure. Draw its image.

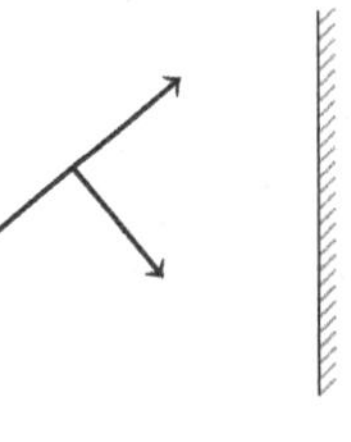

1.3 Image Formation by Two Plane Mirrors

1 Figure shows two plane mirrors parallel to each other and an object O placed between them. Find the distance of the first three images from the mirror M_2.

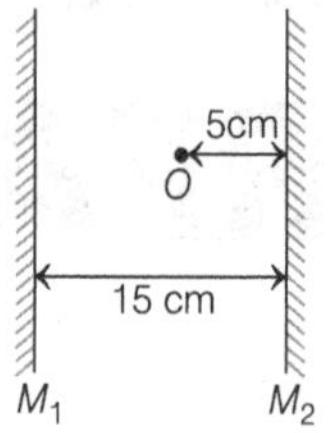

2 An object O is kept between two inclined plane mirrors as shown in each figure. Find the number of distinct images formed in each case.

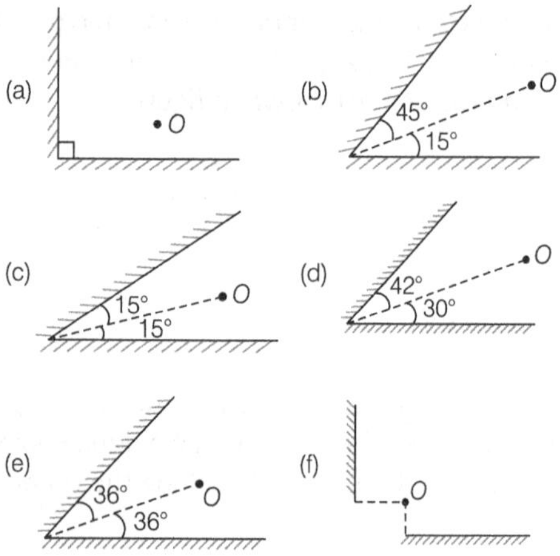

1.4 Field of View

1 Find the region on Y-axis in which reflected rays are present. Object is at A (2, 0) and MN is a plane mirror, as shown.

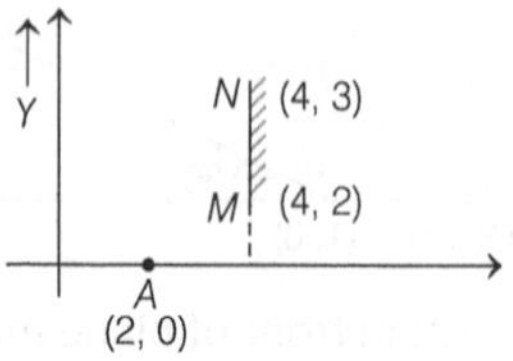

2 Show that the minimum size of a plane mirror, required to see the full image of an observer is half the size of that observer.

3 A point source of light S is placed at a distance L in front of the centre of a mirror of width d hung vertically on a wall. A man walks in front of the mirror along a line parallel to the mirror at a distance $2L$ from it as shown. Find the greatest distance over which he can see the image of the light source in the mirror.

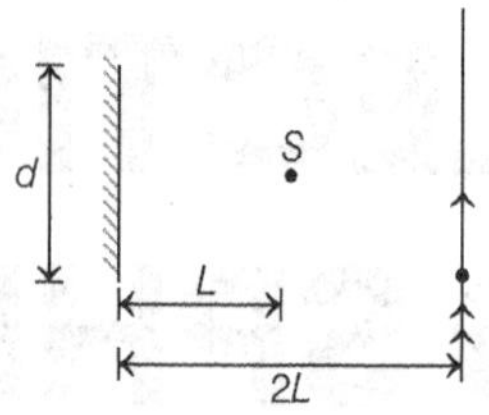

4 In figure shown AB is a plane mirror of length 40 cm placed at a height 40 cm from ground. There is a light source S at a point on the ground. Find the minimum and maximum height of a man (eye height) required to see the image of the source if he is standing at a point A on ground shown in figure.

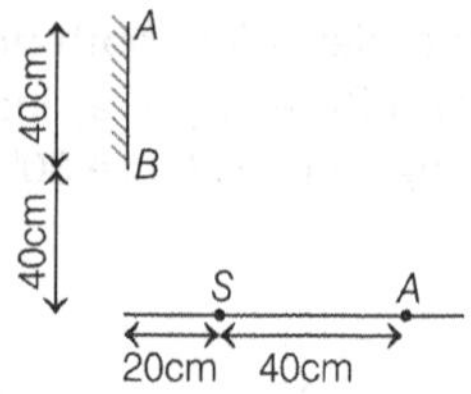

1.5 Velocity of Image in Plane Mirror

1 Image of the object is formed as shown in figure. If the mirror starts moving towards the object with velocity v, then what is the velocity of image?

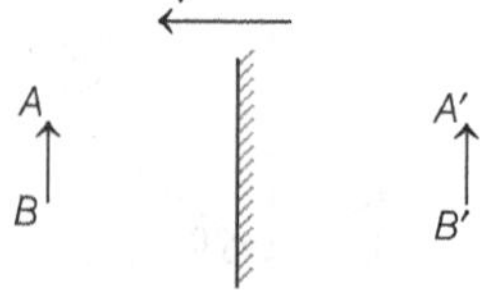

2 An object moves with 5 m/s towards right while the mirror moves with 1 m/s towards the left as shown. Find the velocity of image.

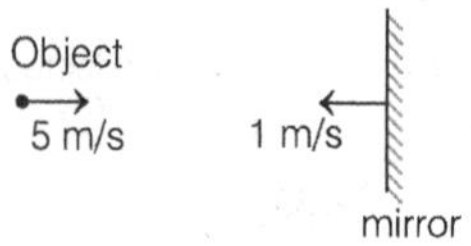

3 In the situation shown in figure, find the velocity of image.

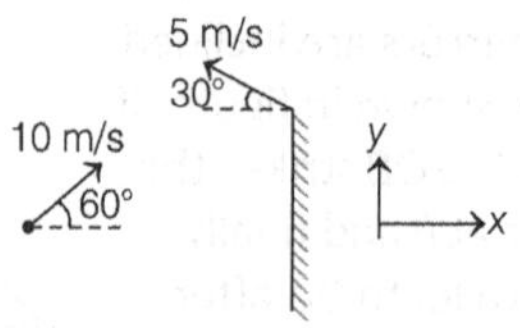

1.6 Spherical Mirror

1 A light ray AB, parallel to the principal axis is incident on a concave mirror as shown in figure. Find the angle of incidence (i) of the ray for which it passes through the pole.

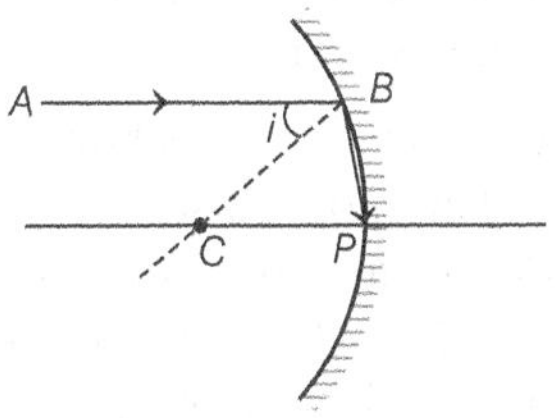

2 Find the distance CQ if incident light ray parallel to principal axis is incident at an angle i on a concave mirror of radius of curvature R. Also find the distance CQ if $i \rightarrow 0$.

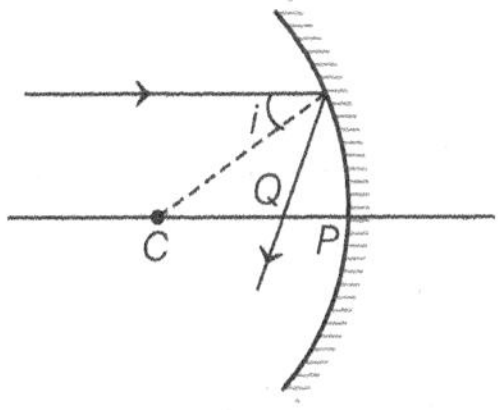

3 Figure shows a spherical concave mirror with its pole at (0, 0) and principal axis along X-axis. There is a point object at (−15 cm, 1 cm), find the position of image.

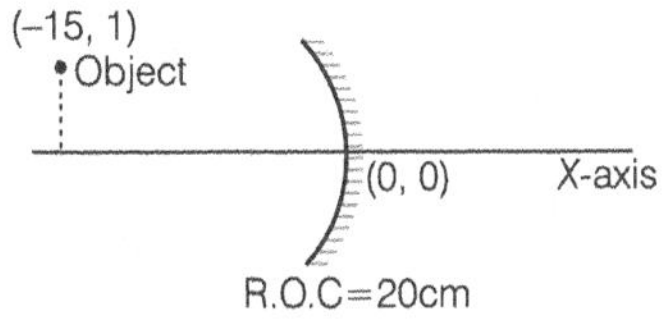

4 Find the diameter of the image of the moon formed by a spherical concave mirror of focal length 11.4 m. The diameter of the moon is 3450 km and the distance between the earth and the moon is 3.8×10^5 km.

5. A concave mirror forms an image of 20 cm high object on a screen placed 5.0 m away from the mirror. The height of the image is 50 cm. Find the focal length of the mirror and the distance between the mirror and the object.

6 A candle flame 1.6 cm high is imaged in a ball bearing of diameter 0.4 cm. If the ball bearing is 20 cm away from the flame, find the location and the height of the image.

7 A 1 cm object is placed perpendicular to the principal axis of a convex mirror of focal length 7.5 cm. Find its distance from the mirror if the image formed is 0.6 cm in size.

8 A concave mirror has a focal length of 20 cm. Find the position or positions of an object for which the image size is double of the object size.

9 A person looks into a spherical mirror. The size of image of his face is twice the actual size of his face. If the face is at a distance 20 cm, then find the nature and radius of curvature of the mirror.

10 An image of a candle on a screen is found to be double its size. When the candle is shifted by a distance 5 cm, then the image becomes triple its size. Find the nature and ROC of the mirror.

11 A U-shaped wire is placed before a concave mirror having radius of curvature 20 cm as shown in figure. Find the total length of the image.

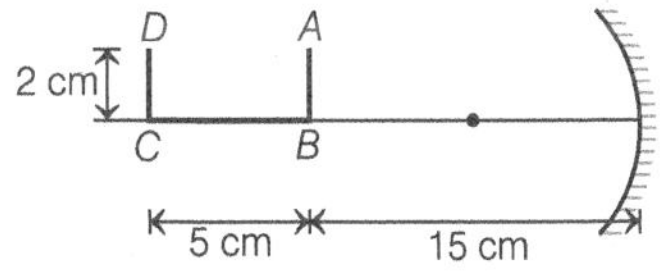

12 A thin rod of length $d/3$ is placed along the principal axis of a concave mirror of focal length $= d$ such that its image, which is real and elongated, just touches the rod. Find the length of the image.

13 Converging rays are incident on a convex spherical mirror, so that their extensions intersect 30 cm behind the mirror on the optical axis. The reflected rays form a diverging beam, so that their extensions intersect the optical axis 1.2 m from the mirror. Determine the focal length of the mirror.

14 The principal axis of a spherical mirror is shown by dotted line. O is the point object whose real image is I. Find the distance of the pole and centre of curvature of the mirror from object measured along principal axis by drawing ray diagram.

1.7 Velocity of Image in Spherical Mirror

1 A point object is placed on the principal axis at 60 cm in front of a concave mirror of focal length 40 cm on the principal axis. Find the velocity of image if the object is moved with a velocity of 10 cm/s

(a) along the principal axis

(b) perpendicular to the principal axis

2 An object is present on the principal axis of a concave mirror of focal length 15 cm. Object is at a distance of 20 cm from mirror. If velocity of object is 5 cms^{-1} towards mirror and velocity of mirror is 5 cms^{-1} towards object, then find velocity of image in mirror.

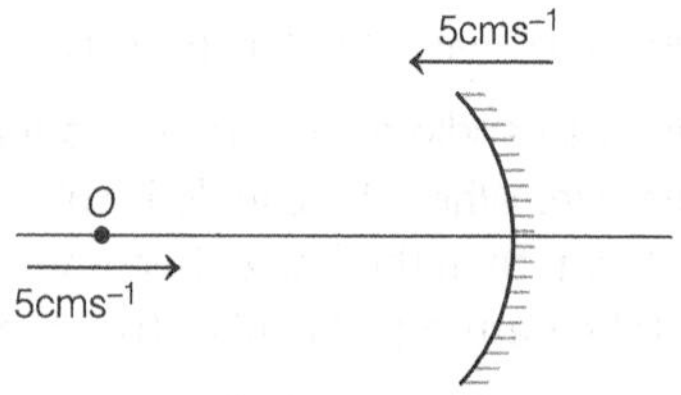

3 A point source *S* is moving with a speed of 10 m/s in *XY*-plane as shown in the figure. The radius of curvature of the concave mirror is 4 m. Determine the velocity vector of the image formed by paraxial rays.

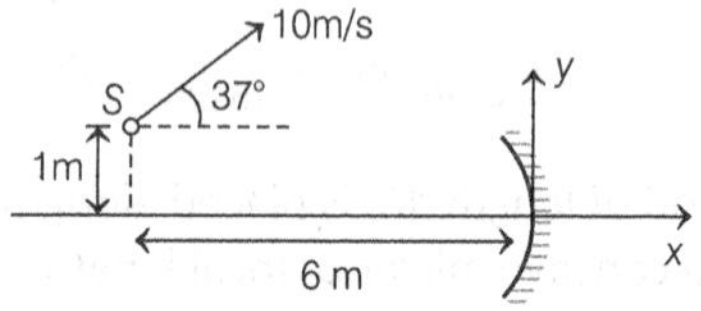

4 A point object is placed 60 cm from pole of a concave mirror of focal length 10 cm on the principal axis. If object is shifted 1 mm towards the mirror along principal axis find the shift in image.

1.8 Combination of Mirrors

1 A point object O is placed between two mirrors as shown. Find the position of final image after three successive reflections taking first reflection on M_1 in each case.

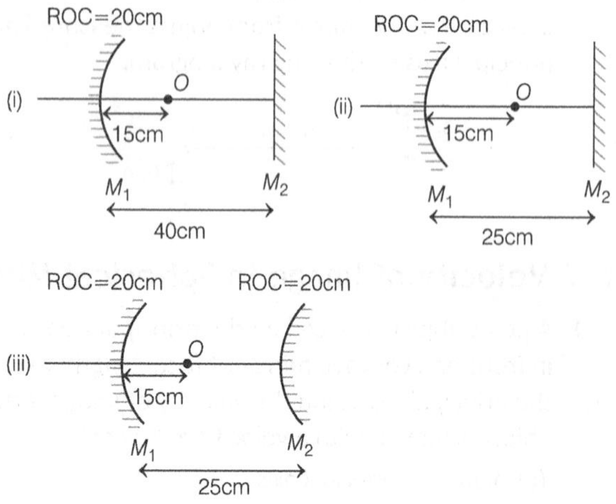

2 An object is placed exactly mid-way between a concave mirror of radius of curvature 40 cm and a convex mirror of radius of curvature 30 cm. The mirrors face each other and are 50 cm apart. Determine the position of the image formed by the successive reflections, first at the concave mirror and then at the convex mirror.

3 In the figure shown, *S* is a tiny bulb and on the far right side is a flat mirror. Black paint on right surface of bulb blocks any light from the bulb reaching the flat mirror directly. When the concave mirror ($f = 40$ cm) is at a distance of 60 cm from the bulb, the real image of the bulb formed after one reflection from the concave mirror and then from flat mirror coincides with the bulb. Find the distance between the bulb and flat mirror.

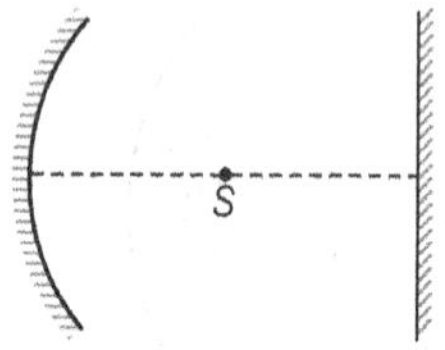

4 A point source *S* is placed mid-way between two converging mirrors having equal focal length *f* as shown in figure. Find the values of *d* for which only one image is formed.

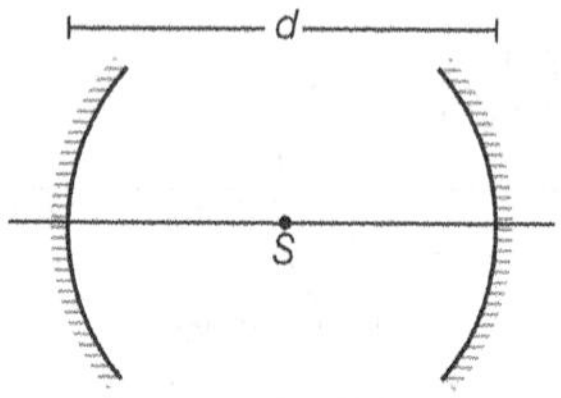

5 A convex mirror and a concave mirror are placed coaxially. An object is placed 15 cm from the concave mirror as shown in figure. Find the separation between the two mirrors, so that the final image (after taking first reflection on the concave mirror) is formed on the object itself.

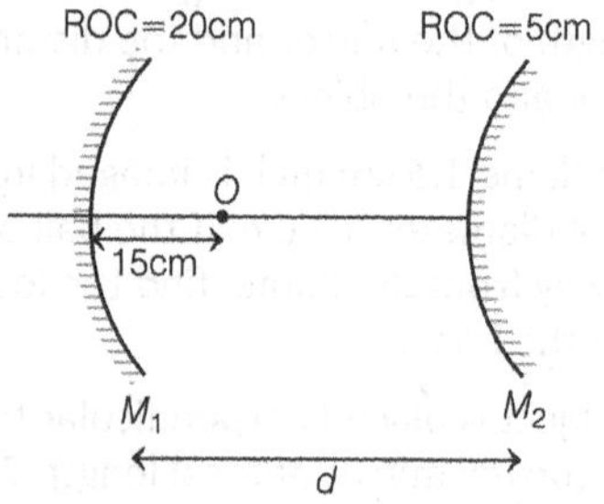

LEVEL 02 JEE Main Level

Single Choice Correct Questions

1 Two plane mirrors are inclined at 70°. A ray incident on one mirror at an angle θ, after reflection falls on the second mirror and is reflected from there parallel to the first mirror, θ is

(a) 50° (b) 45° (c) 30° (d) 55°

2 Two mirrors are inclined at an angle θ as shown in figure. Light ray is incident parallel to one of the mirrors. The ray will start retracing its path after third reflection if

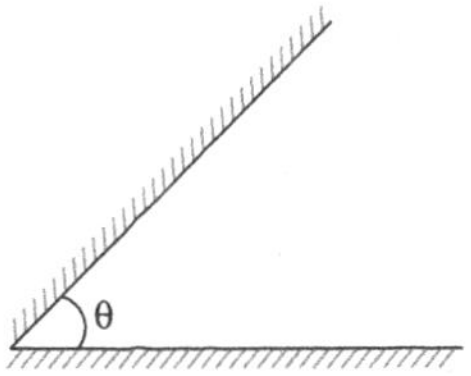

(a) $\theta = 45°$ (b) $\theta = 30°$ (c) $\theta = 60°$ (d) All three

3 Two plane mirrors are inclined to each other at 30°. A ray is incident on M at 40°. Find deviation produced in it by three successive reflections due to mirrors.

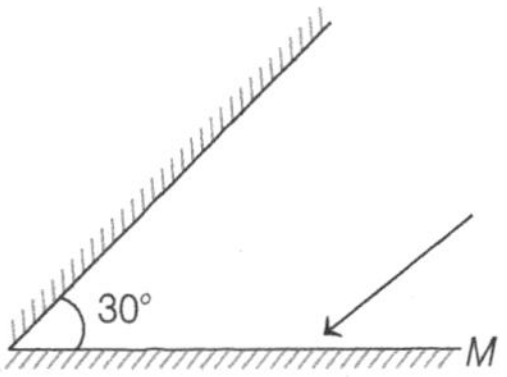

(a) 60° clockwise (b) 120° clockwise
(c) 150° clockwise (d) 160° clockwise

4 By what angle mirror M_2 is rotated, so that the light ray after reflection from both the mirrors become horizontal?

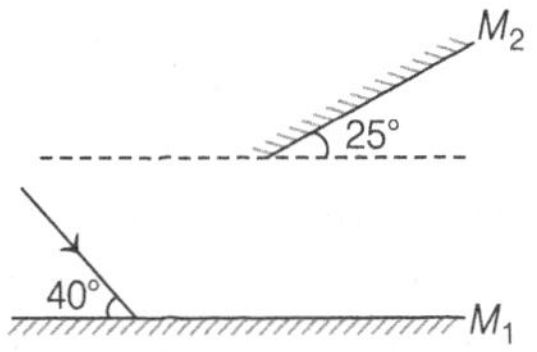

(a) 95° clockwise (b) 75° anti-clockwise
(c) 5° clockwise (d) 15° clockwise

5 Two plane mirrors A and B are aligned parallel to each other, as shown in the figure. A light ray is incident at an angle of 30° at a point just inside one end of A. The plane of incidence coincides with the plane of the figure. The maximum number of times the ray undergoes reflections (including the first one) before it emerges out is

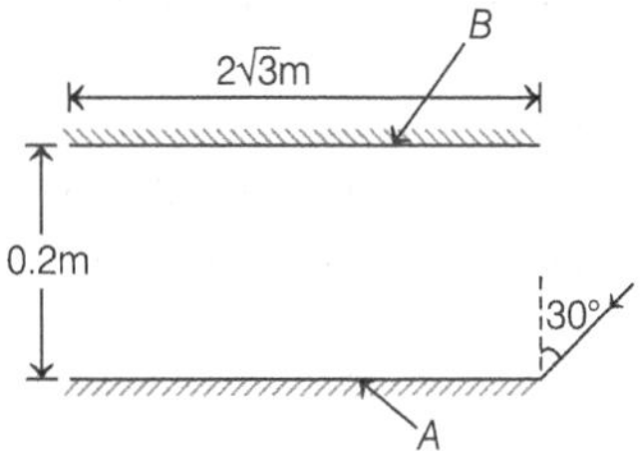

(a) 28 (b) 30 (c) 32 (d) 34

6 An unnumbered wall clock shows time 04:25:37, where 1st term represents hours, 2nd represents minutes and the last term represents seconds. What time will its image in a plane mirror show?

(a) 08:35:23 (b) 07:35:23
(c) 07:34:23 (d) None of these

7 Two mirrors labelled L_1 for left mirror and L_2 for right mirror in the figure are parallel to each other and 3.0 m apart. A person standing 1.0 m from the right mirror (L_2) looks into this mirror and sees a series of images. The second nearest image seen in the right mirror is situated at a distance

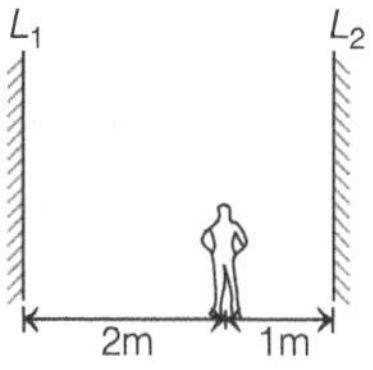

(a) 2.0 m from the person (b) 4.0 m from the person
(c) 6.0 m from the person (d) 8.0 m from the person

8 A point object is placed mid-way between two plane mirrors distance a apart. The plane mirrors form an infinite number of images due to multiple reflections. The distance between nth order images formed in the two mirrors is

(a) na (b) $2na$ (c) $na/2$ (d) $4na$

9 A person's eye is at a height of 1.5 m. He stands in front of a 0.3m long plane mirror which is 0.8 m above the ground. The length of the image he sees of himself is

(a) 1.5 m (b) 1.0 m (c) 0.8 m (d) 0.6 m

10 A point source of light S is placed in front of two large mirrors as shown. Which of the following observers will see only one image of S?

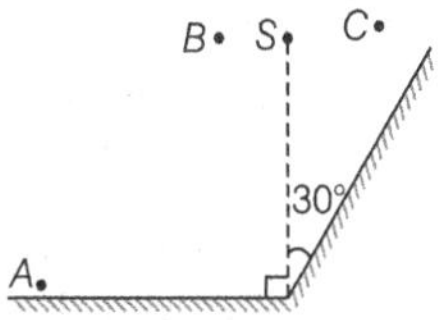

(a) only A (b) only C
(c) Both A and C (d) Both B and C

11 The image formed by a plane mirror

(a) is always virtual (b) is always real
(c) may be real (d) is never real

12 Two plane mirrors of length L are separated by distance L and a man M_2 is standing at distance L from the connecting line of mirrors as shown in figure. A man M_1 is walking in a straight line at distance $2L$ parallel to mirrors at speed u, then man M_2 at O will be able to see image of M_1 for time

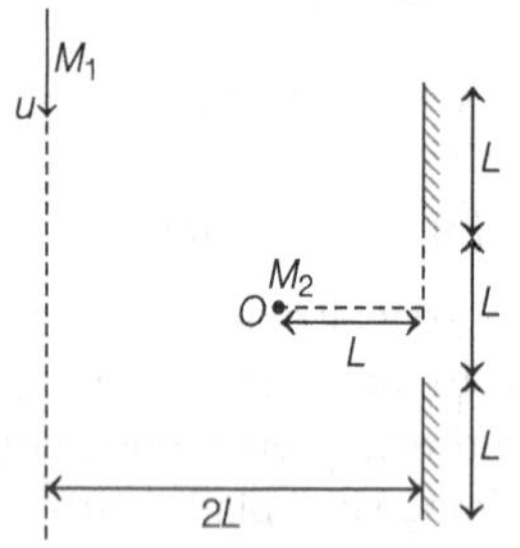

(a) $\frac{4L}{u}$ (b) $\frac{3L}{u}$ (c) $\frac{6L}{u}$ (d) $\frac{9L}{u}$

13 A boy of height H is standing in front of mirror, which has been fixed on the ground as shown in figure. What length of his body can the man see in the mirror? The length of the mirror is $(H/2)$

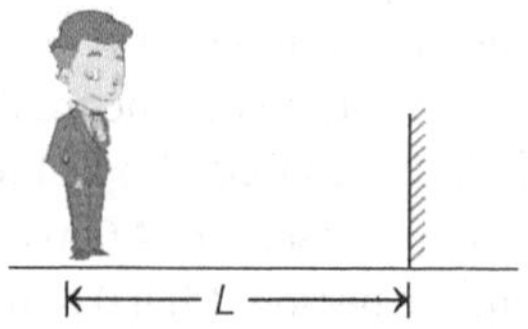

(a) H (b) $\frac{H^2}{(H^2+L^2)^{1/2}}$

(c) zero (d) $\frac{2H^2}{L}$

14 A person runs with a speed u towards a bicycle moving away from him with speed v. The person approaches his image in the plane mirror fixed at the rear of bicycle with a speed of

(a) $u-v$ (b) $u-2v$
(c) $2u-v$ (d) $2(u-v)$

15 A plane mirror is moving with velocity $4\hat{i}+5\hat{j}+8\hat{k}$. A point object in front of the mirror moves with a velocity $3\hat{i}+4\hat{j}+5\hat{k}$. Here $\hat{k}$ is along the normal to the plane mirror and facing towards the object. The velocity of the image is

(a) $-3\hat{i}-4\hat{j}+5\hat{k}$ (b) $3\hat{i}+4\hat{j}+11\hat{k}$
(c) $-3\hat{i}-4\hat{j}+11\hat{k}$ (d) $7\hat{i}+9\hat{j}+11\hat{k}$

16 There are two plane mirror with reflecting surfaces facing each other. Both the mirrors are moving with speed v away from each other. A point object is placed between the mirrors. The velocity of the image formed due to nth reflection will be

(a) nv (b) $2nv$ (c) $3nv$ (d) $4nv$

17 The reflecting surface of a plane mirror is vertical. A particle is projected in a vertical plane which is also perpendicular to plane of the mirror. The initial velocity of the particle is 10 m/s and the angle of projection is 60°. The point of projection is at a distance 5 m from the mirror. The particle moves towards the mirror. Just before the particle touches the mirror, the velocity of approach of the particle and its image is

(a) 10 m/s (b) 5 m/s (c) $10\sqrt{3}$ m/s (d) $5\sqrt{3}$ m/s

18 A boy is walking under an inclined mirror at a constant velocity v along the X-axis as shown in figure. If the mirror is inclined at an angle θ with the horizontal, then what is the velocity of the image?

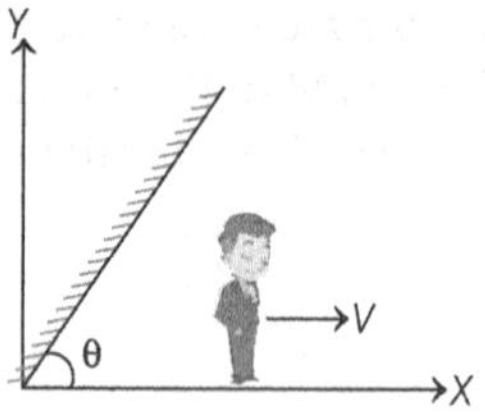

(a) $v\sin\theta\,\hat{i}+v\cos\theta\,\hat{j}$ (b) $v\cos\theta\,\hat{i}+v\sin\theta\,\hat{j}$
(c) $v\sin 2\theta\,\hat{i}+v\cos 2\theta\,\hat{j}$ (d) $v\cos 2\theta\,\hat{i}+v\sin 2\theta\,\hat{j}$

19 A ray of light is incident on a plane mirror along a vector $\hat{i}+\hat{j}-\hat{k}$. The normal on incidence point is along $\hat{i}+\hat{j}$. Unit vector along reflected ray is

(a) $\frac{1}{\sqrt{3}}(\hat{i}+\hat{j}-\hat{k})$ (b) $-\frac{1}{\sqrt{3}}(\hat{i}+\hat{j}-\hat{k})$
(c) $\frac{1}{\sqrt{3}}(\hat{i}+\hat{j}+\hat{k})$ (d) $-\frac{1}{\sqrt{3}}(\hat{i}+\hat{j}+\hat{k})$

20 A point object is kept in front of a plane mirror. The plane mirror is doing SHM of amplitude 2 cm. The plane mirror moves along the X-axis and X-axis is normal to the mirror. The amplitude of the mirror is such that the object is always infront of the mirror. The amplitude of SHM of the image is

(a) zero (b) 2 cm
(c) 4 cm (d) 1 cm

21 A beam of convergent light converges to a point 0.5 m in front of the mirror after reflection at a convex mirror but in the absence of the mirror the beam converges to a point 0.2 m behind the mirror. The radius of curvature of the mirror is

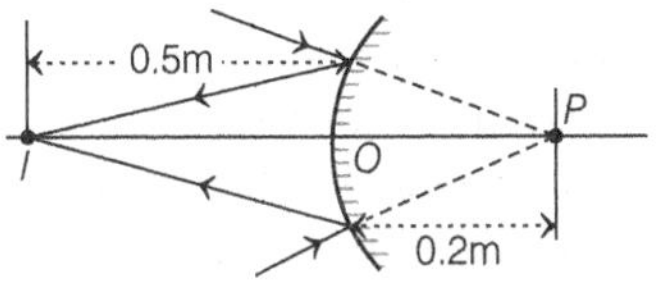

(a) 20 cm (b) 50 cm (c) 66.67 cm (d) 28.57 cm

22 An object of height 1 cm is kept perpendicular to the principal axis of a convex mirror of radius of curvature 20 cm. If the distance of the object from the mirror is 20 cm, then the distance (in cm) between heads of the image and the object will be

(a) $\sqrt{\frac{6404}{9}}$ (b) $\sqrt{\frac{6414}{9}}$ (c) $\frac{40}{3}$ (d) None

23 A concave mirror has a focal length 20 cm. The distance between the two positions of the object for which the image size is double the object size is

(a) 20 cm (b) 40 cm (c) 30 cm (d) 60 cm

24 A spherical mirror forms an erect image three times the linear size of the object. If the distance between the object and the image is 80 cm, the focal length of the mirror is

(a) 15 cm (b) 20 cm (c) 30 cm (d) 40 cm

25 When an object is placed at a distance of 25 cm from a concave mirror, the magnification is m_1. The object is moved 15 cm further away with respect to the earlier position, and the magnification becomes m_2. If $m_1 = 4m_2$ the focal length of the mirror is (Assume image is real. m_1, m_2 are numerical values)

(a) 10 cm (b) 30 cm (c) 15 cm (d) 20 cm

26 A candle flame 3 cm high is placed at distance of 3m from a wall. How far from the wall must a concave mirror be placed in order that it may form an image of the flame 9 cm high on the wall ?

(a) 3.5 m (b) 4 m (c) 4.5 m (d) 5.5 m

27 The distance between an object and its doubly magnified image by a concave mirror is [Assume f = focal length]

(a) $\frac{3f}{2}$ (b) $\frac{2f}{3}$ (c) $3f$

(d) depends on whether the image is real or virtual.

28 An infinitely long rod lies along the axis of a concave mirror of focal length f. The near end of the rod is at a distance $u > f$ from the mirror. Its image will have a length

(a) $\frac{f^2}{u-f}$ (b) $\frac{uf}{u-f}$ (c) $\frac{f^2}{u+f}$ (d) $\frac{uf}{u+f}$

29 The distance of an object from the focus of a convex mirror of radius of curvature a is b. Then, the distance of the image from the focus is

(a) $\frac{b^2}{4a}$ (b) $\frac{a}{b^2}$ (c) $\frac{a^2}{4b}$ (d) $\frac{4b}{a^2}$

30 A point object at 15 cm from a concave mirror of radius of curvature 20 cm is made to oscillate along the principal axis with amplitude 2 mm. The amplitude of its image will be

(a) 2 mm (b) 4 mm
(c) 8 mm (d) 16 mm

31 A metal wire AB of length 10 cm is placed in front of a concave mirror of focal length 15 cm as shown in figure. Find the length of the image of the wire.

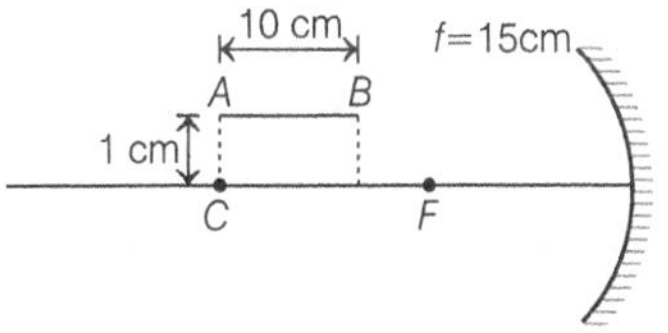

(a) 30 cm (b) $\sqrt{904}$ cm
(c) $\sqrt{909}$ cm (d) None of these

32 A virtual erect image in a concave mirror is represented, in the given figure, by

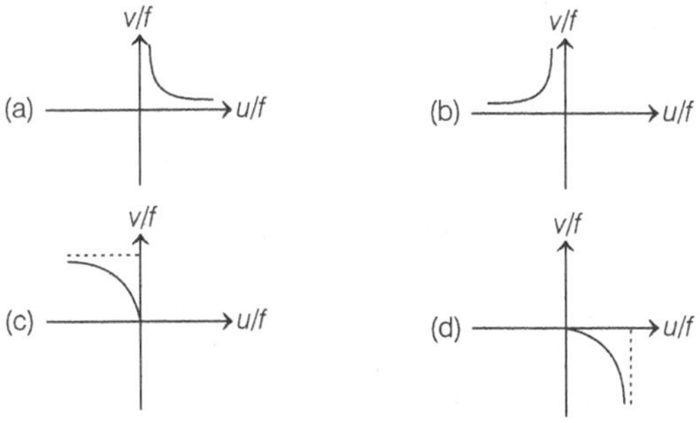

33 The distance of an object from the pole of a concave mirror is equal to its radius of curvature. The image must be

(a) real (b) inverted
(c) same sized (d) erect

34 A concave mirror is used to form image of the sun on a white screen. If the lower half of the mirror were covered with an opaque card, the effect on the image on the screen would be

(a) negligible
(b) to make the image less bright than before
(c) to make the upper half of the image disappear
(d) to make the lower half of the image disappear

35 In the figure shown, the image of a real object is formed at point I. AB is the principal axis of the mirror. The mirror must be

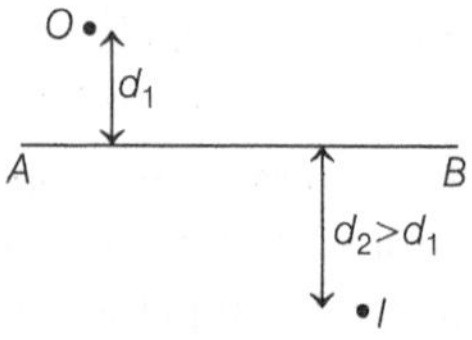

(a) concave and placed towards right of I
(b) concave and placed towards left of O
(c) convex and placed toward right of I
(d) convex and placed towards left of I

36 A particle is moving towards a fixed spherical mirror. The image
(a) must move away from the mirror
(b) must move towards the mirror
(c) may move towards the mirror
(d) will move towards the mirror, only if the mirror is convex

37 The origin of x and y coordinates is the pole of a concave mirror of focal length 20 cm. The X-axis is the optical axis with $x > 0$ being the real side of mirror.

A point object at the point (25 cm, 1 cm) is moving with a velocity 10 cm/s in positive X-direction. The velocity of the image in cm/s is approximately
(a) $-80\hat{i} + 8\hat{j}$ (b) $160\hat{i} + 8\hat{j}$
(c) $-160\hat{i} + 8\hat{j}$ (d) $160\hat{i} - 4\hat{j}$

38. A convex and a concave mirror of radii 10 cm each are facing each other and 15 cm apart. A point object is placed mid-way between them. Then, the position of the final image if the reflection first takes place at the concave mirror and then in the convex mirror is
(a) at the pole of the concave mirror
(b) at the pole of the convex mirror
(c) coincident with the object itself
(d) 5 cm behind the convex mirror

39 An object is placed in front of a convex mirror at a distance of 50 cm. A plane mirror is introduced covering the lower half of the convex mirror. If the distance between the object and the plane mirror is 30 cm , it is found that there is no gap between the images formed by the two mirrors. The radius of the convex mirror is
(a) 12.5 cm (b) 25 cm
(c) 50 cm (d) 100 cm

40 A point object is kept between a plane mirror and a concave mirror facing each other. The distance between the mirrors is 22.5 cm. Plane mirror is placed perpendicular to principal axis of concave mirror. The radius of curvature of the concave mirror is 20 cm. What should be the distance of the object from the concave mirror so that after two successive reflections the final image is formed on the object itself ? (Consider first reflection from concave mirror)
(a) 5 cm (b) 15 cm (c) 10 cm (d) 7.5 cm

41 In the figure shown find the total magnification after two successive reflections first on M_1 and then on M_2.

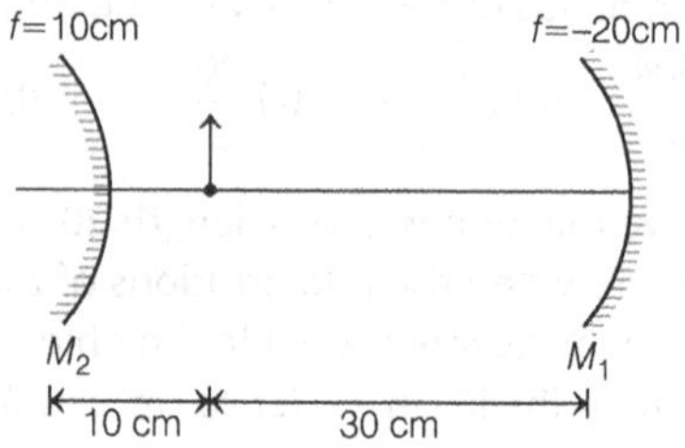

(a) +1 (b) −2 (c) +2 (d) −1

Numerical Value Questions

1 A plane mirror 50 cm long, is hung on a vertical wall of a room, with its lower edge 50 cm above the ground. A man stands infront of the mirror at a distance 2 m away from the mirror. If his eyes are at a height 1.8 m above the ground, find the length (distance between the extreme points of the visible region) of the floor (perpendicular to the mirror), visible to him reflected from the mirror. (in m)

2 Fig. shows a torch producing a straight light beam falling on a plane mirror at an angle 60°. The reflected beam makes a spot P on the screen along Y-axis. If at $t = 0$, mirror starts rotating about the hinge A with an angular velocity $\omega = 1°$ per second clockwise, the speed of the spot on the screen after time $t = 15$s is $\frac{2\pi}{N}$ m/s,then find N.

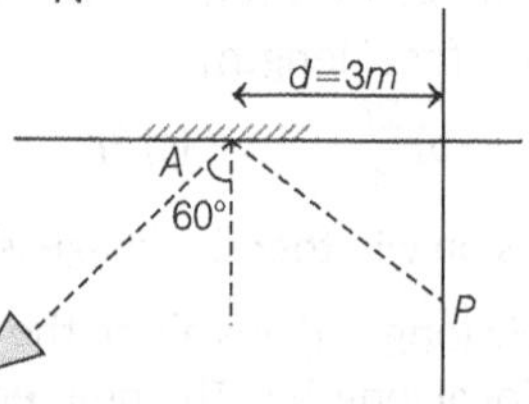

3 An elevator at rest which is at 10th floor of a building is having a plane mirror fixed to its floor. A particle is projected with a speed $\sqrt{2}$ m/s and at 45° with the horizontal as shown in the figure. At the very instant of projection, the cable of the elevator breaks and the elevator starts falling freely. What will be the separation (in m) between the particle and its image 0.5 s after the instant of projection?

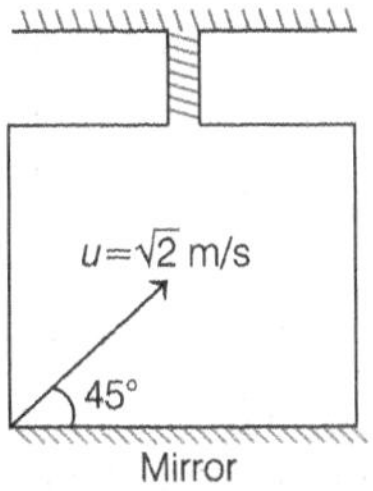

4 A point object is moving with a speed of 5 m/s infront of a mirror moving with a speed of 2.5 m/s as shown in figure. If the velocity of image of the object with respect to ground is $\sqrt{x}$ m/s, then find x.

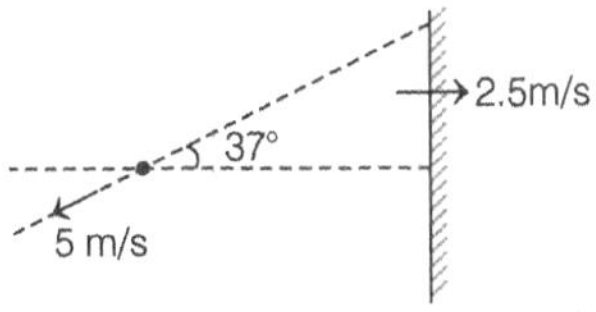

5 A balloon is rising up along the axis of a concave mirror of radius of curvature 20 m. A ball is dropped from the balloon at a height 15 m from the mirror, when the balloon has velocity 20 m/s. Find the speed (in m/s) of the image of the ball formed by concave mirror after 4 s? [Take: $g = 10\ m/s^2$]

6 A cube of side length 1 mm is placed on the axis of a concave mirror at a distance of 45 cm from the pole as shown in the figure. One edge of the cube is parallel to the axis. The focal length of the mirror is 30 cm. Find approximate volume (in mm^3) of the image.

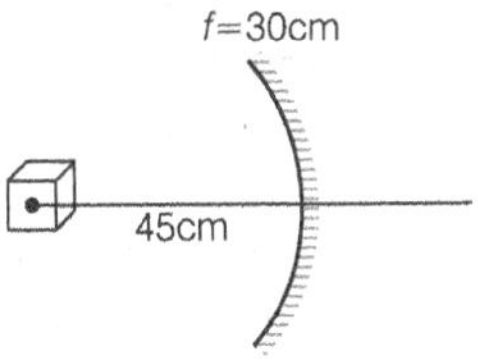

7 The image produced by a concave mirror is one quarter the size of the object. If the object is moved by 5 cm along the principal axis, the image will only be half the size of the object. Find the radius of curvature (in cm) of the mirror.

8 A concave spherical mirror produces an inverted image of an object. The distance between object and image is $d = 12$ cm and lateral magnification is 2. Then, find the radius of curvature (in cm) of mirror.

9 A concave mirror forms a real image on a screen of thrice the linear dimension of the real object. Object and screen are moved until the image is twice the size of the object. If the shift of the object is 6 cm, find focal length (in cm) of the mirror.

10 Two spherical mirrors (convex and concave) having the same focal length of 36 cm are arranged as shown in figure so that their optical axes coincide. The separation between the mirrors is 1 m. At what distance (in cm) from the concave mirror should an object be placed so that its images formed by the concave and convex mirrors independently are identical in size?

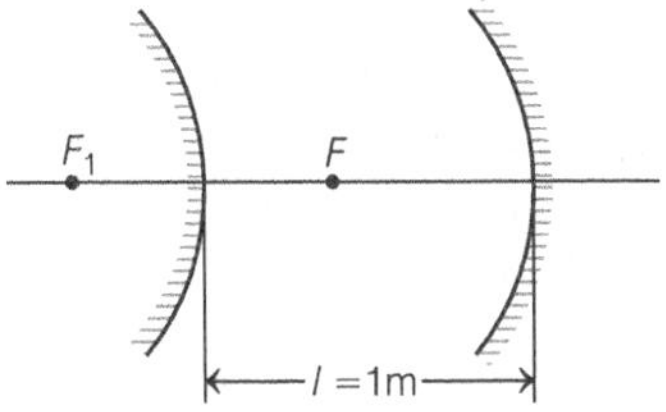

LEVEL 03 JEE Advanced Level

Single Choice Correct Questions

1 Two plane mirrors AB and AC are inclined at an angle $\theta = 20°$. A ray of light starting from point P is incident at point Q on the mirror AB, then at R on mirror AC and again on S on AB.

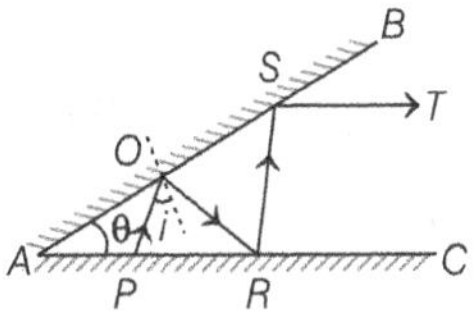

Finally the ray ST goes parallel to mirror AC. The angle which the ray makes with the normal at point Q on mirror AB is

(a) 20° (b) 30° (c) 40° (d) 60°

2 A light ray I is incident on a plane mirror M. The mirror is rotated in the direction as shown in the figure by an arrow at frequency $\frac{9}{\pi}$ rev/s. The light reflected by the mirror is received on the wall W at a distance 10 m from the axis of rotation. When the angle of incidence becomes 37°, the speed of the spot (a point) on the wall is

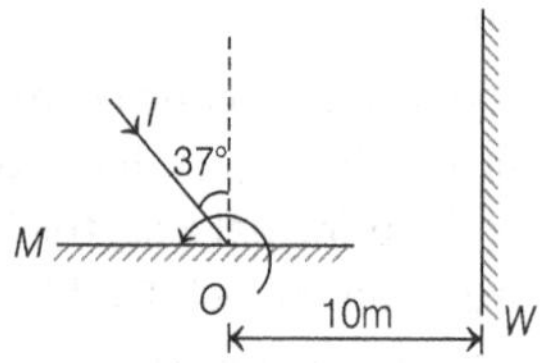

(a) 10 m/s (b) 1000 m/s
(c) 360 m/s (d) None of these

3 As shown in the figure a particle is placed at O in front of a plane mirror M. A man at P can move along path PY and PY', then which of the following is true?

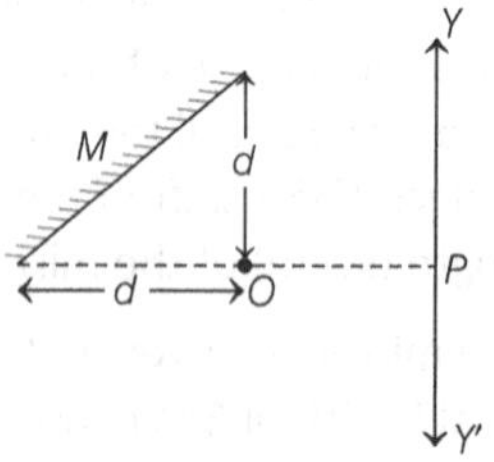

(a) for all points on PY, man can see the image of O
(b) for all points on PY' man can see the image, but for no point on PY he can see the image of O
(c) for all points on PY' he can see the image but on PY he can see the image only upto distance d
(d) he can see the image only upto a distance d on either side of P

4 A two eyed man is looking at the junction of two large mutually perpendicular mirrors from a far off distance. Assume no reflection to occur from the edge. Then, if both the eyes are open,

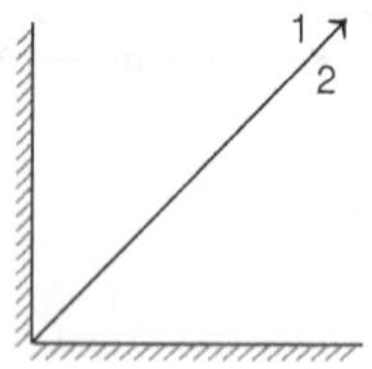

(a) the eye 1 of man can see image of both eye 1 and eye 2.
(b) the eye 1 can see image of eye 1 only and eye 2 see image of eye 2 only.
(c) the eye 1 can see image of eye 2 only and eye 2 can see image of eye 1 only.
(d) All the above statements are false.

5 A plane mirror of length 2 m is kept along the line $y = -x$ as shown in the figure. An insect having velocity of $4\hat{\mathbf{i}}$ cm/s is moving along the X-axis from far away.

The time span for which the insect can see its image will be

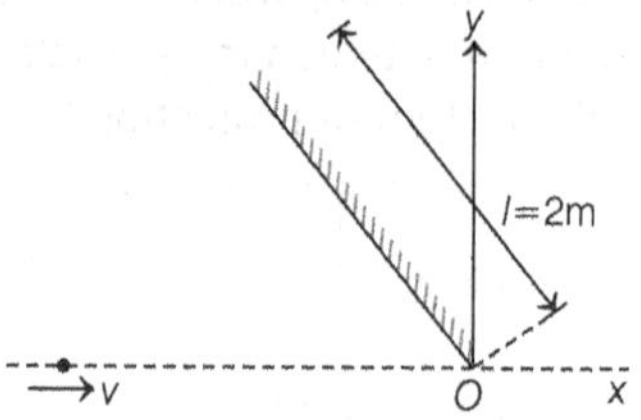

(a) 50 s (b) 25 s (c) $25\sqrt{2}$ s (d) $50\sqrt{2}$ s

6 A child is standing in front of a vertical plane mirror. His father is standing behind him, as shown in the figure. The height of the father is $2H$. The height of the eye level of the child is H. What is the minimum height of the mirror required so, that the child can completely see his own and his father's image in the mirror?

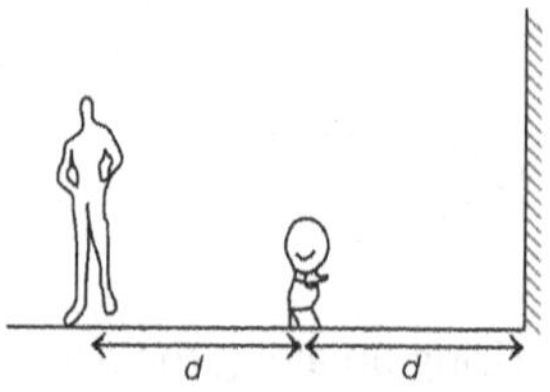

(a) $\frac{H}{2}$ (b) $\frac{5H}{6}$
(c) $\frac{3H}{2}$ (d) None of these

7 The angle between two mirrors is 60° and is kept fixed. A ray is incident on one mirror at an angle i as shown in figure. The angle i is slowly increased from 0° to 90°. The net deviation suffered by the ray after two reflections is D. Which of the following plots for D versus i is correct?

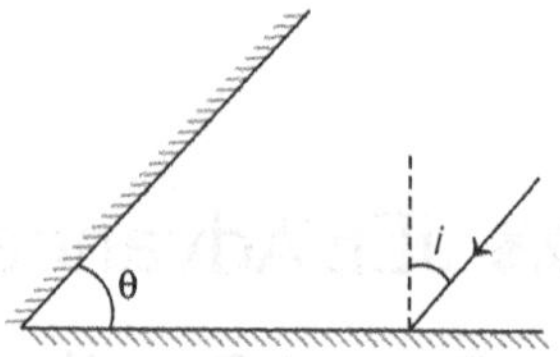

(a)
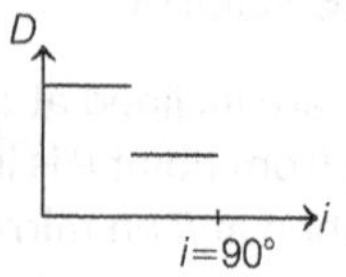

(b)
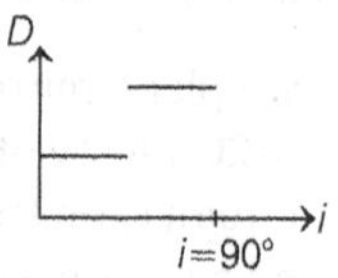

(c)
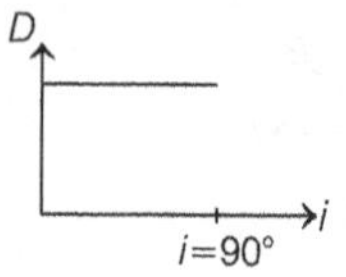

(d) None of these

8 The reflecting surfaces of two intersecting flat mirrors are at an angle $\theta(0° < \theta < 90°)$, as shown in Figure. For a light ray that strikes the horizontal mirror, the emerging ray intersects the incident ray at an angle β. If one of the mirrors is rotated at $\frac{d\theta}{dt} = 1°/s$, then the angle β changes at the rate of

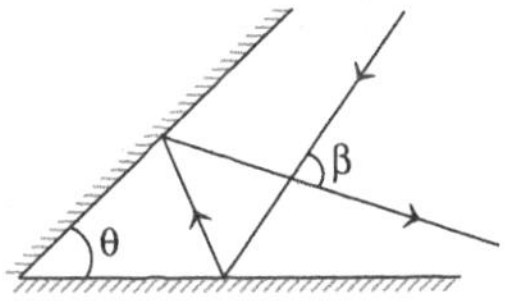

(a) 1°/s (b) 2°/s (c) −1°/s (d) −2°/s

9 A point source of light *S* is located on a wall. A plane mirror *M* having length *l* is moving parallel to the wall with constant velocity *v*. The bright patch formed on the wall by reflected light will

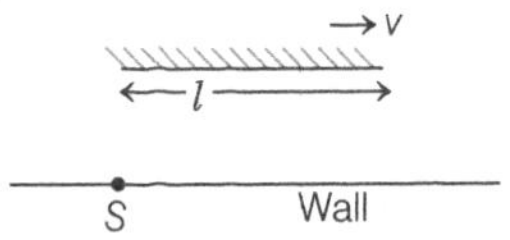

(a) move with uniform velocity *v* and will have a length 2*l*.
(b) move with uniform velocity 2*v* and will have a length *l*.
(c) move with uniform velocity 2*v* and will have a length 2*l*.
(d) move with uniform velocity but will have a changing length.

10 A point source of light *S* at a distance *d* from the screen *A* produces light intensity I_0 at the centre of the screen. If a completely reflecting mirror *M* is placed at a distance *d* behind the source as shown in the figure, find the intensity at the centre of the screen

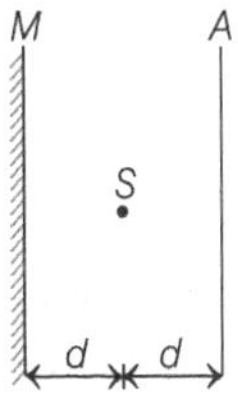

(a) $\frac{9}{10}I_0$ (b) $\frac{10}{9}I_0$ (c) $\frac{8}{9}I_0$ (d) $\frac{9}{8}I_0$

11 Rear window of a car has a size of $120 \times 45\ cm^2$. The driver sits at a distance $L = 2$ m from the rear window. What should be the minimum size of flat mirror, hanging at a distance of 0.5 m in front of the driver so that he has the best view of road situation behind the car?

(a) (24 cm × 9 cm) (b) (30 cm × 11.25 cm)
(c) (40 cm × 15 cm) (d) (20 cm × 7.5 cm)

12 A cubical room is formed with 6 plane mirrors. An insect moves along the diagonal of the floor with uniform speed. The velocity of its image in two adjacent walls (seen by insect) is 20 cm/s. Then, the velocity of image formed in the roof is

(a) 20 cm/s (b) 40 cm/s
(c) $20\sqrt{2}$ cm/s (d) $10\sqrt{2}$ cm/s

13 Two blocks each of mass *m* lie on a smooth table. They are attached to two other masses as shown in the figure. The pulleys and strings are light. An object *O* is kept at rest on the table. The sides *AB* and *CD* of the two blocks are made reflecting. The acceleration of two images formed in those two reflecting surfaces w.r.t. each other is

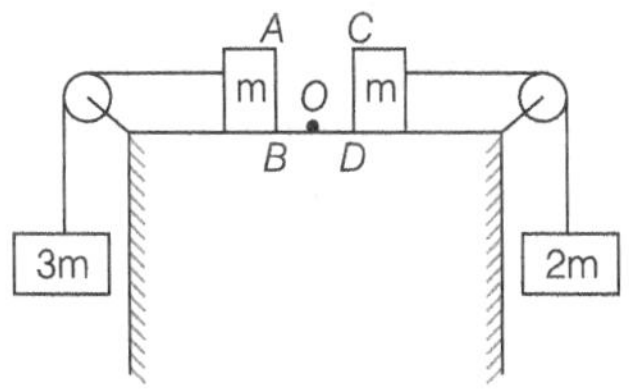

(a) $\frac{5g}{6}$ (b) $\frac{5g}{3}$ (c) $\frac{g}{3}$ (d) $\frac{17g}{6}$

14 Mirror is moving towards the particle with speed 2 cm/s. Speed of *A* and *B* are $10\sqrt{2}$ cm/s and 5 cm/s, respectively in the directions shown in figure. Magnitude of velocity of image of the particle *B* with respect to image of *A*.

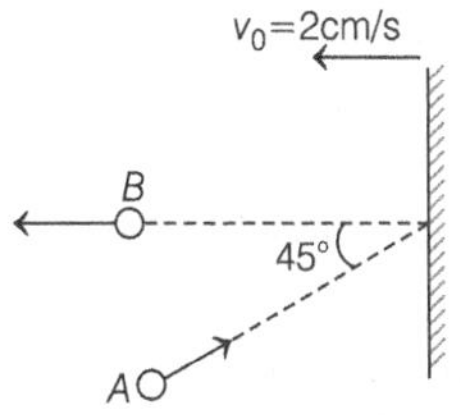

(a) $\sqrt{325}$ cm/s (b) 15 cm/s
(c) 13 cm/s (d) $\sqrt{269}$ cm/s

15 In the diagram shown, all the velocities are given with respect to earth. What is the relative velocity of the image in mirror (1) with respect to the image in the mirror (2)? The mirror (1) forms an angle β with the vertical.

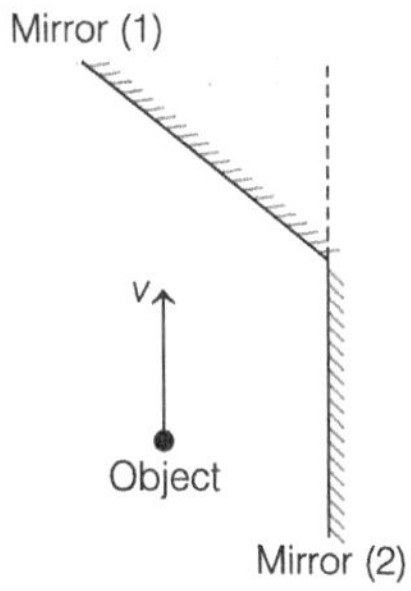

(a) $2v\sin 2\beta$
(b) $2v\sin\beta$
(c) $\frac{2v}{\sin 2\beta}$
(d) None of the above

16 A particle is projected with speed 25 m/s at angle 53° from horizontal in front of an inclined plane mirror as shown in figure. After how much time speed of image w.r.t object will be minimum? ($g = 10\ \text{m/s}^2$)

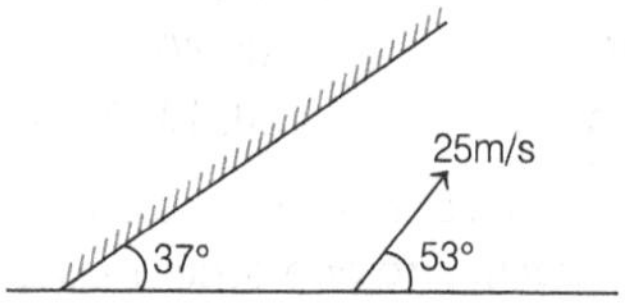

(a) $\frac{7}{8}$ s (b) $\frac{5}{3}$ s (c) $\frac{4}{5}$ s (d) 1 s

17 A beam of light strikes one mirror of a right angle mirror assembly at an angle of incidence 45° as shown in the figure. The right angle mirror assembly is rotated such that the angle of incidence becomes 60°. Which of the following statement is correct about the emerging light beam?

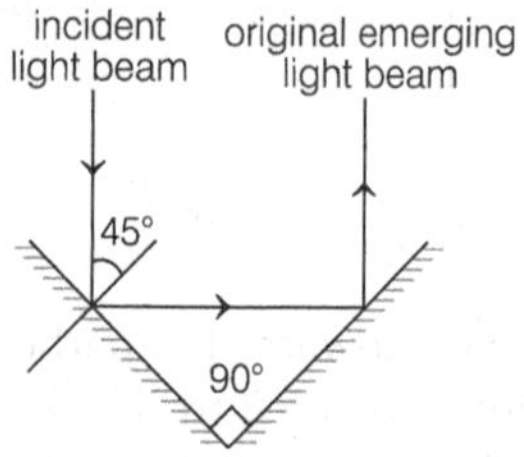

(a) It will move through an angle of 15° w.r.t. the original emerging beam.
(b) It will move through an angle of 30° w.r.t. the original emerging beam.
(c) It will move through an angle 45° w.r.t. the original beam.
(d) It will emerge parallel to the original emerging beam.

18 An insect of negligible mass is sitting on a block of mass M, tied with a spring of force constant K. The block performs simple harmonic motion with amplitude A infront of a plane mirror placed as shown. The maximum speed of insect relative to its image will be

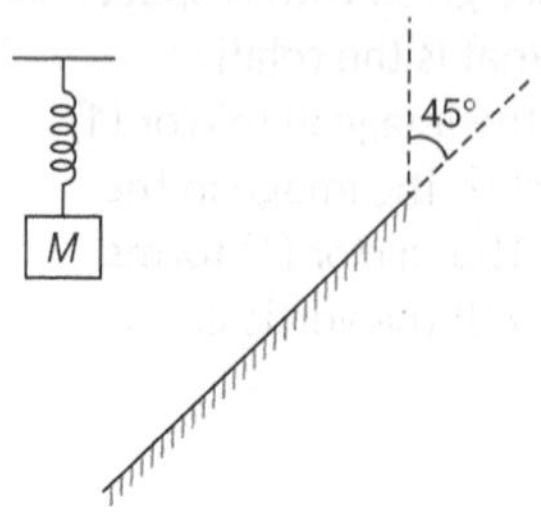

(a) $A\sqrt{\frac{K}{M}}$ (b) $\frac{A}{\sqrt{2}}\sqrt{\frac{K}{M}}$ (c) $A\sqrt{2}\sqrt{\frac{K}{M}}$ (d) $A\sqrt{\frac{M}{K}}$

19 Area of triangle formed by S and its two images is

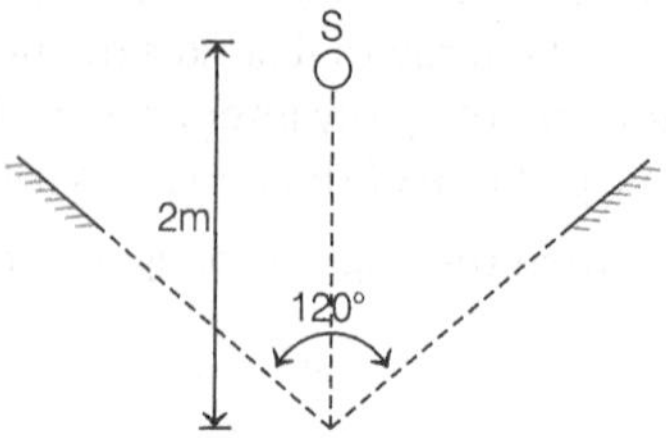

(a) $3\sqrt{3}\ \text{m}^2$ (b) $\frac{3\sqrt{3}}{4}\ \text{m}^2$

(c) $\frac{4}{3\sqrt{3}}\ \text{m}^2$ (d) can't be determined

20 A light ray parallel to the X-axis strikes the outer reflecting surface of a sphere at a point (2, 2, 0). Its center is at the point (0, 0, −1). The unit vector along the direction of the reflected ray is $x\hat{\mathbf{i}} + y\hat{\mathbf{j}} + z\hat{\mathbf{k}}$. Find the value of $\frac{yz}{x^2}$.

(a) 8 (b) 16 (c) 32 (d) 40

21 A parallel beam of light ray parallel to the X-axis is incident on a parabolic reflecting surface $x = 2by^2$ as shown in the figure. After reflecting, it passes through focal point F. The focal length of the reflecting surface is

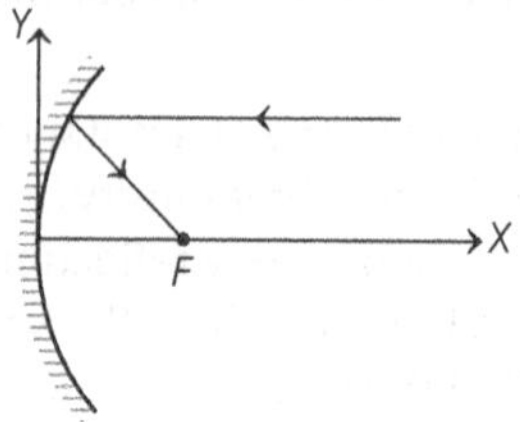

(a) $\frac{1}{8b}$ (b) $\frac{1}{4b}$

(c) $\frac{1}{b}$ (d) None of these

22 A square $ABCD$ of side 1 mm is kept at distance 15 cm infront of the concave mirror as shown in the figure. The focal length of the mirror is 10 cm. The length of the perimeter of its image will be (nearly)

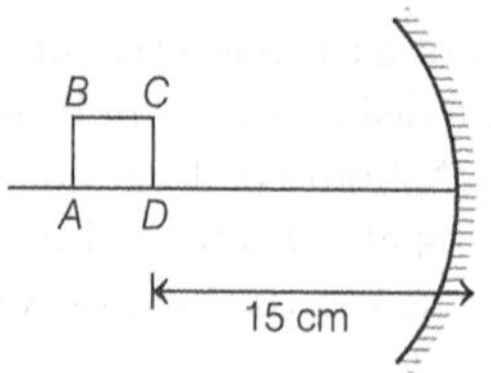

(a) 8 mm (b) 2 mm
(c) 12 mm (d) 6 mm

23 A spherical mirror is polished on both sides. When the convex side is used as a mirror, the image is erect with magnification 1/4. What is the magnification, when the concave side is used as a mirror, the object remaining the same distance from the mirror?

(a) $-\frac{1}{4}$ (b) $-\frac{1}{2}$ (c) $-\frac{1}{3}$ (d) $+\frac{1}{4}$

24 A converging beam of light having angle of convergence 4° is incident upon a convex mirror as shown. Find the angle of convergence after reflection.

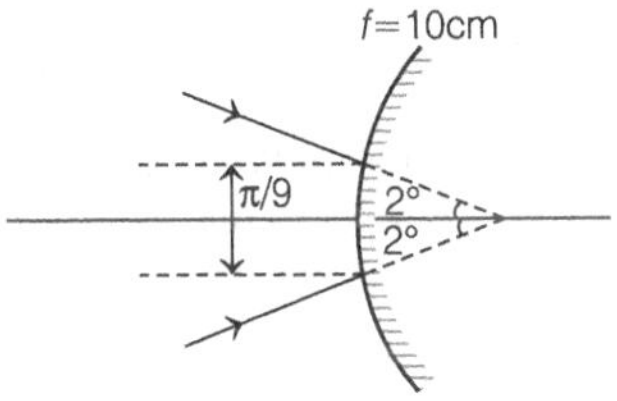

(a) 0.5° (b) 1° (c) 1.5° (d) 2°

25 A ray of light is incident on a concave mirror. It is parallel to the principal axis and its height from principal axis is equal to the focal length of the mirror. The ratio of the distance of point B to the distance of the focus from the centre of curvature is (AB is the reflected ray)

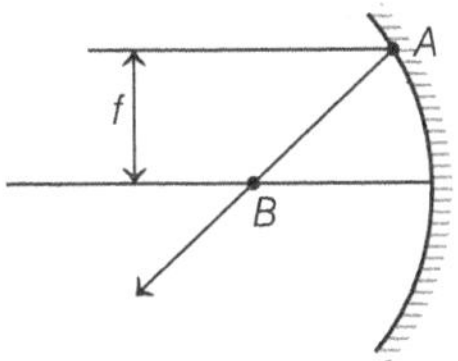

(a) $\frac{2}{\sqrt{3}}$ (b) $\frac{\sqrt{3}}{2}$ (c) $\frac{2}{3}$ (d) $\frac{1}{2}$

26 A point source is situated at a distance $x < f$ from the pole of the concave mirror of focal length f. At time $t = 0$, the point source starts moving away from the mirror with constant velocity. Which of the graphs below represents best, variation of image distance $|v|$ with the distance x between the pole of mirror and the source?

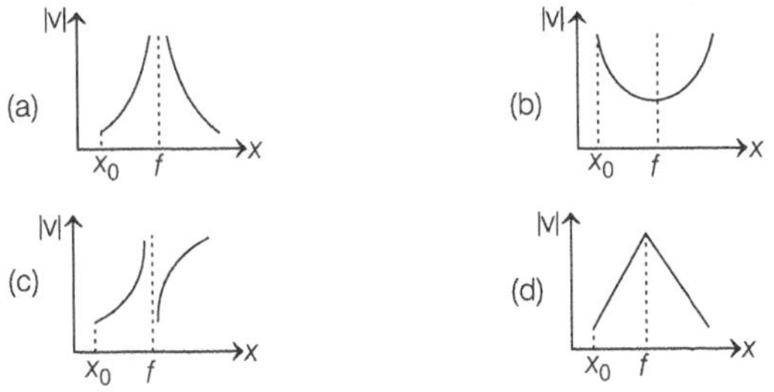

27 In the figure shown a thin parallel beam of light is incident on a plane mirror M_1 at small angle θ. M_2 is a concave mirror of focal length f. After three successive reflections of this beam, the x and y coordinates of the image is

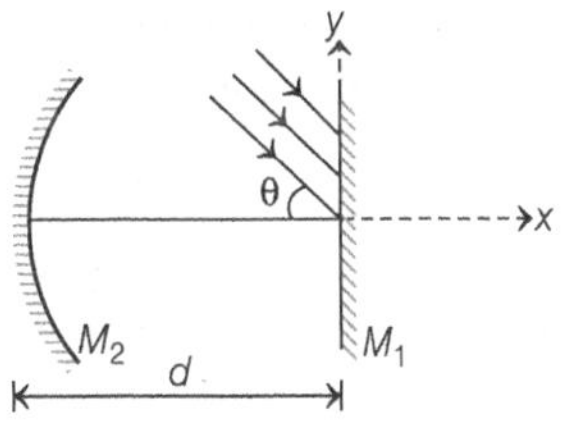

(a) $x = f - d, y = f\theta$ (b) $x = d + f, y = f\theta$
(c) $x = f - d, y = -f\theta$ (d) $x = d - f, y = -f\theta$

28. An object O is placed in front of a plane mirror and concave mirror as shown in fig. If f is the focal length of concave mirror, then the separation between the two mirrors so that image obtained after two reflections coincides with object O is

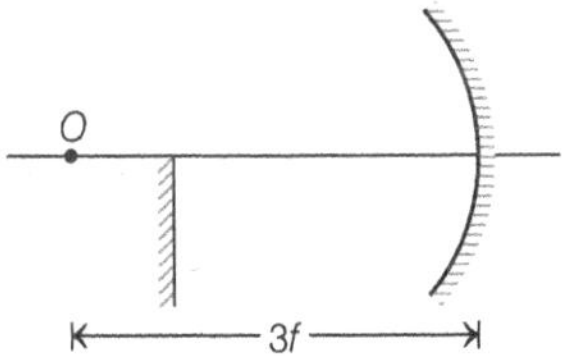

(a) $\frac{9f}{4}$ (b) $\frac{7f}{4}$ (c) f (d) None

29 A body of mass 100 g is tied to one end of spring of constant 20 N/m. It is released with spring unelongated. The distance between pole of mirror and mean position of the body is 20 cm. The focal length of convex mirror is 10 cm. The length over which vibration of image takes place is

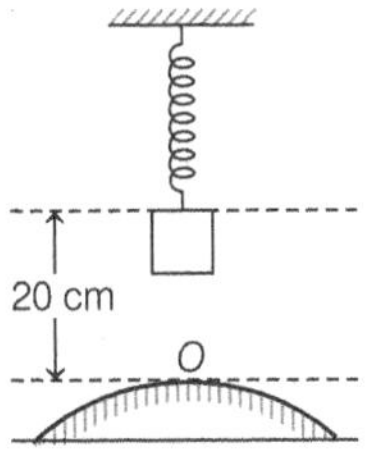

(a) 10 cm (b) 50 cm (c) 1.14 cm (d) 0.33 cm

30 A linear object AB is placed along the axis of a concave mirror. The object is moving towards the mirror with speed v. The speed of the image of the point A is $4v$ and the speed of the image of B is also $4v$. If centre of the line AB is at a distance L from the mirror, then length of the object AB will be

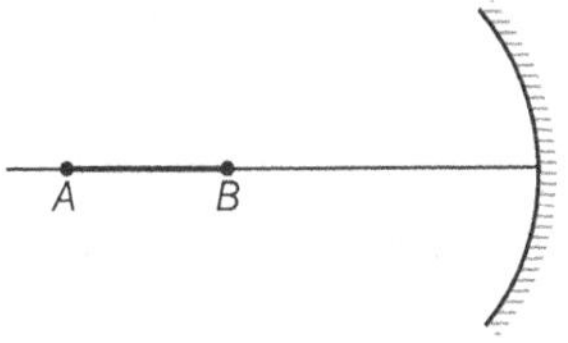

(a) $\frac{3L}{2}$ (b) $\frac{5L}{3}$ (c) L (d) $\frac{4L}{3}$

31. Radius of curvature of a concave mirror varies as $R = \left|\dfrac{6}{t^2 - 5t + 6}\right|$ cm. Initially the object was at a distance 100 cm from the pole as shown. At $t = 0$ the object started moving with velocity $v = 2t\,\hat{\mathbf{i}}$ (cm/s). Find the speed of image at time $t = 3$ s. Mirror is moving with constant velocity $(-3\,\hat{\mathbf{i}})$ cm/s.

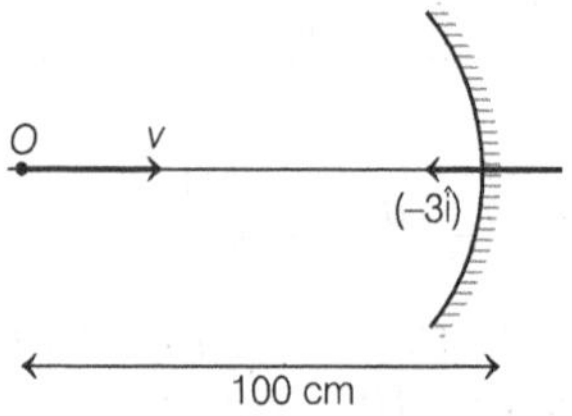

(a) 12 cm/s (b) 20 cm/s (c) 5 cm/s (d) 24 cm/s

32 A point object located at a distance of 15 cm from the pole of a concave mirror of focal length 10 cm on its principal axis is moving with velocity $(8\hat{\mathbf{i}} + 11\hat{\mathbf{j}})$ cm/s and velocity of mirror is $(4\hat{\mathbf{i}} + 2\hat{\mathbf{j}})$ cm/s as shown. If **v** is the velocity of image then find $|\mathbf{v}|$.

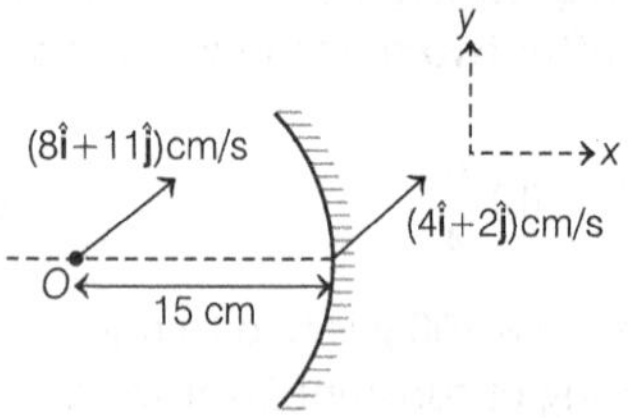

(a) 10 cm/s (b) 20 cm/s (c) 30 cm/s (d) 40 cm/s

33 Two spherical mirrors, one convex and the other concave, each of same radius of curvature R are arranged coaxially at a distance of $2R$ from each other. A small circle of radius a is drawn on the convex mirror as shown in figure. What is the radii of first two images of the circle?

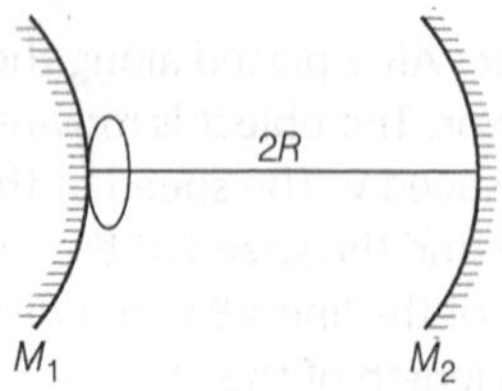

(a) $\dfrac{a}{3}, \dfrac{a}{11}$ (b) $\dfrac{a}{6}, \dfrac{a}{2}$ (c) $\dfrac{a}{3}, \dfrac{a}{4}$ (d) $\dfrac{a}{12}, \dfrac{a}{4}$

34 In the shown figure M_1 and M_2 are two concave mirrors of the same focal length 10 cm. AB and CD are their principal axes respectively. A point object O is kept on the line AB at a distance 15 cm from M_1. The distance between the mirrors is 20 cm. Considering two successive reflections first on M_1 and then on M_2, the distance of final image from the line AB is

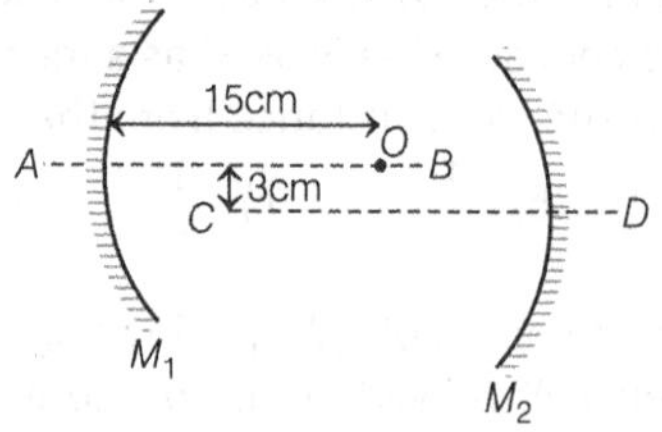

(a) 3 cm (b) 1.5 cm (c) 4.5 cm (d) 1 cm

Multiple Choice(s) Correct Questions

1 A man of height 170 cm wants to see his complete image in a plane mirror (while standing). His eyes are at a height of 160 cm from the ground.

(a) Minimum length of the mirror = 80 cm
(b) Minimum length of the mirror = 85 cm.
(c) Bottom of the mirror should be at a height 80 cm or less
(d) Bottom of the mirror should be at a height 85 cm.

2 A flat mirror M is arranged parallel to a wall W at a distance l from it. The light produced by a point source S kept on the wall is reflected by the mirror and produces a light spot on the wall. The mirror moves with velocity v towards the wall.

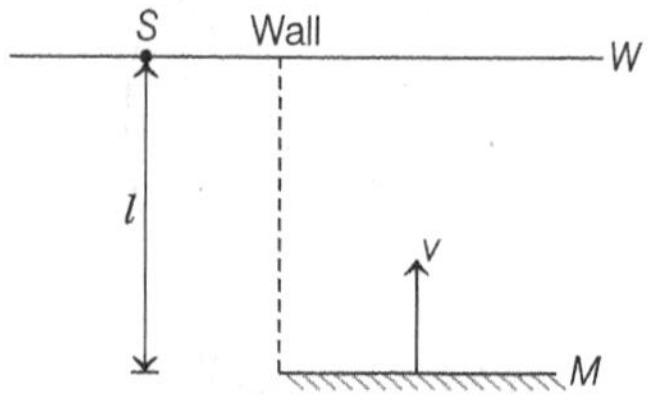

(a) The spot of light will move with the speed v on the wall.
(b) The spot of light will not move on the wall.
(c) As the mirror comes closer, the spot of light will become larger and shift away from the wall with speed larger, than v.
(d) The size of the light spot on the wall remains the same.

3 A reflecting surface is represented by the equation $Y = \dfrac{2L}{\pi}\sin\left(\dfrac{\pi x}{L}\right), 0 \le x \le L$.

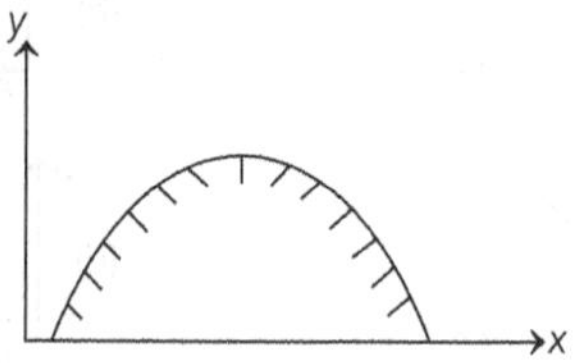

A ray travelling horizontally becomes vertical after reflection. The coordinates of the point(s) where this ray is incident is

(a) $\left(\frac{L}{4}, \frac{\sqrt{2}L}{\pi}\right)$ (b) $\left(\frac{L}{3}, \frac{\sqrt{3}L}{\pi}\right)$

(c) $\left(\frac{3L}{4}, \frac{\sqrt{2}L}{\pi}\right)$ (d) $\left(\frac{2L}{3}, \frac{\sqrt{3}L}{\pi}\right)$

4 Two plane mirrors at an angle such that a ray incident on a mirror undergoes a total deviation of 240° after two reflections

(a) the angle between the mirrors is 60°

(b) the number of images formed by this system will be 5, if an object is placed symmetrically between the mirrors

(c) the number of images will be 5 if an object is kept unsymmetrically between the mirrors

(d) a ray will retrace its path after 2 successive reflections, if the angle of incidence on one mirror is 60°

5 A spherical mirror forms image of a real object as shown, choose the correct option(s)

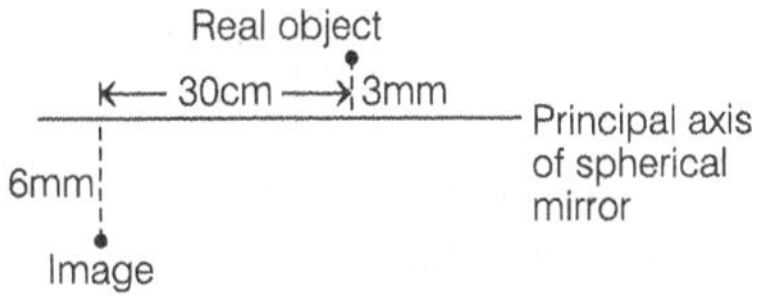

(a) Mirror is concave of radius 40 cm.

(b) Mirror is convex of radius 40 cm.

(c) Mirror is 30 cm from object along the principal axis.

(d) Mirror is 60 cm from image along the principal axis.

6. For a concave mirror, graph of square of magnification and image distance from pole is given for real object. Choose the correct statements(s).

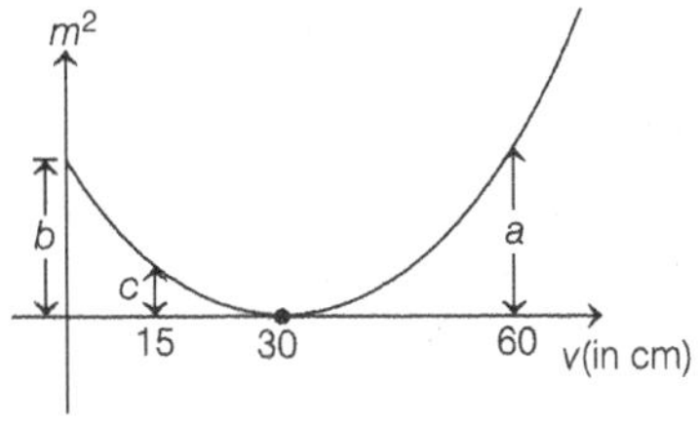

(a) This graph is hyperbola.

(b) Length a must be equal to length *b*.

(c) Radius of curvature of concave mirror is 60 cm.

(d) The length c will be half of length *a*.

7 A point object is placed on the axis of a concave mirror of focal length 24 cm such that the image is formed at a distance of 48 cm from the pole. Distance of the object from pole may be

(a) 48 cm (b) 16 cm (c) 32 cm (d) 20 cm

8 You are required to design a little dentist's mirror to be fixed at the end of a shaft for use in someone's mouth. The image should be erect and when held at 1.5 cm from a tooth, it should produce an image twice the size of the tooth.

(a) The mirror is convex with $|f| = 3$ cm

(b) The mirror is concave with $|f| = 3$ cm

(c) The image of this tooth is 3 cm behind the mirror

(d) The image of this tooth is 3 cm in front of the mirror.

9 Point $A(0, 1)$ and $B(12, 5)$ are object image pair (one of the point acts as object and the other point as image) X-axis is the principal axis of the mirror. Then, this object image pair is

(a) due to a convex mirror of focal length 2.5 cm

(b) due to a concave mirror having its pole at (2,0)

(c) real virtual pair

(d) data is insufficient for options (a) and (b)

10 Velocity of object and concave mirror are shown in the diagram. At the given instant choose the CORRECT statement(s)

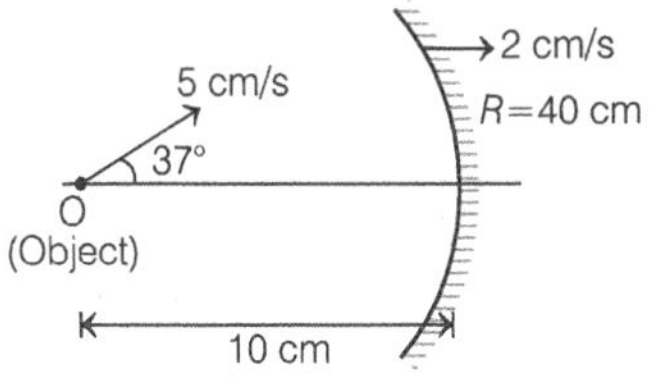

(a) Angle between velocity of image and velocity of object is 98°.

(b) Velocity of image with respect to object is $\sqrt{109}$ cm/s.

(c) Velocity of image with respect to object is $\sqrt{72}$ cm/s.

(d) Velocity of image is in the direction of velocity of plane mirror.

11. Which of the following statements are incorrect for spherical mirrors?

(a) A concave mirror forms only virtual images for any position of real object

(b) A convex mirror forms only virtual images for any position of a real object

(c) A concave mirror forms only a virtual diminished image of an object placed between its pole and the focus

(d) A convex mirror forms a virtual enlarged image of an object if it lies between its pole and the focus.

12 A real object is infront of a convex mirror. It moves towards the mirror, the image also moves. If v_i = speed of image and v_o = speed of the object, then

(a) $v_i < v_o$ if $0 < |u| < |f|$ (b) $v_i > v_o$ if $|u| > |f|$

(c) $v_i < v_o$ if $|u| > |f|$ (d) $v_i = v_o$ if $|u| = |f| \neq 0$

13 Converging rays strike a spherical convex mirror such that they can form the image in the absence of a mirror between pole and focus. Which of the following is a characteristic of the final image formed by the mirror?

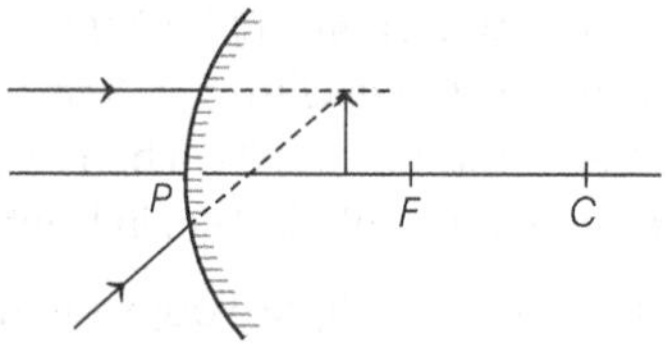

(a) Real (b) Virtual (c) Erect (d) Inverted

14 In the figure shown consider the first reflection at the plane mirror and second at the convex mirror. AB is object. C is the centre of curvature of the convex mirror.

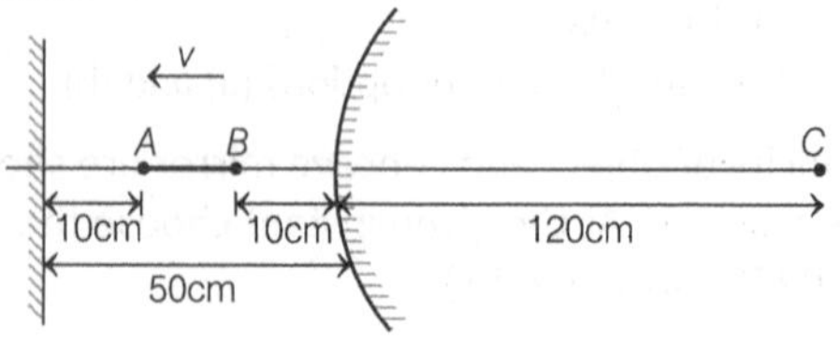

(a) The second image is real, inverted of 1/5 th magnification w.r.t AB
(b) The second image is virtual and erect with magnification 1/5 w.r.t AB
(c) The second image moves towards the convex mirror
(d) The second image moves away from the convex mirror.

Comprehension Based Questions

Comprehension-1

A man is standing in a room and a plane mirror is fixed on the wall in front of him. The height of the wall is H. Man has to see the complete image of wall behind him at a time.

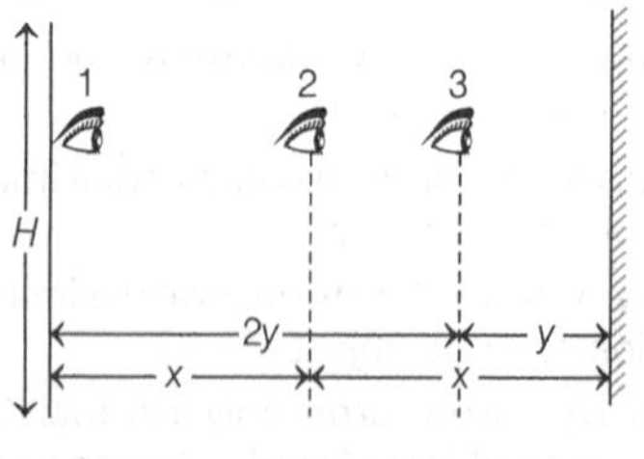

1 When the man is standing near wall i.e., at position 1, the minimum length of the mirror required is

(a) H (b) $\frac{H}{2}$ (c) $\frac{H}{3}$ (d) $\frac{H}{4}$

2 When the man is standing at the middle of the room i.e., at position 2, the minimum length of the mirror required is

(a) H (b) $\frac{H}{2}$ (c) $\frac{H}{3}$ (d) $\frac{H}{4}$

3 When the man is at position 3, the minimum length of the mirror required is

(a) H (b) $\frac{H}{2}$ (c) $\frac{H}{3}$ (d) $\frac{H}{4}$

Comprehension-2

A projectile is projected at an angle ϕ, with a speed u in the vertical plane and there is a plane mirror OM, in which image of the projectile is observed.

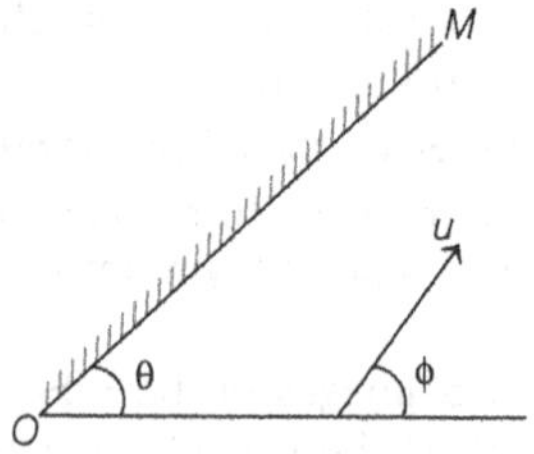

4 At a particular instant, image of the projectile appears to be at rest with respect to object. At this moment speed of the projectile is

(a) $\frac{u\sin\theta}{\sin\phi}$ (b) $\frac{u\sin(\theta+\phi)}{\sin(\theta-\phi)}$
(c) $\frac{u\sin\phi}{\sin\theta}$ (d) $\frac{u\cos\phi}{\cos\theta}$

5 The image will have maximum velocity with respect to object, when the particle has speed

(a) $\frac{u\cos(\theta+\phi)}{\cos(\phi-\theta)}$ (b) $\frac{u\cos\phi}{\sin\theta}$
(c) $\frac{u\sin\phi}{\cos\theta}$ (d) $\frac{u\sin\theta}{\cos\phi}$

6 The path of the image as seen by the projectile will be

(a) straight line (b) parabola
(c) circle (d) ellipse

Comprehension-3

The figure shows time varying θ can be given by equations is $\theta = (2 + 6t^2)$. The mirror is rotating about a horizontal axis in clockwise direction.

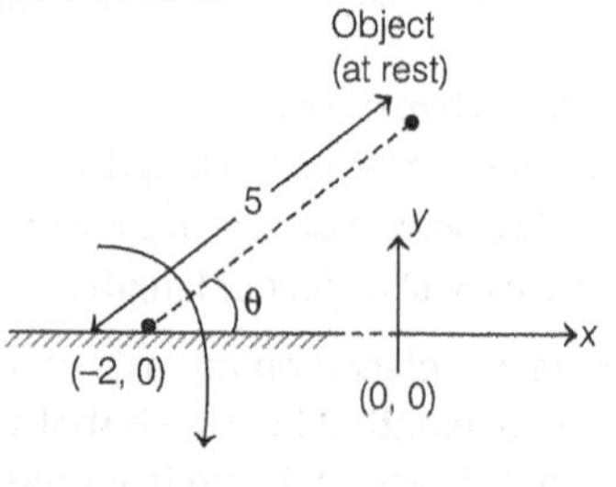

7 Locus of the image is

(a) $x^2 + y^2 = 5^2$ (b) $(x+2)^2 + y^2 = 5^2$
(c) $(x-2)^2 + y^2 = 5^2$ (d) $x^2 + (y-2)^2 = 5^2$

8 Angular velocity of the image at $t = 2$ s is
(a) 12 rad/s (b) 24 rad/s
(c) 36 rad/s (d) 48 rad/s

9 Acceleration of the image at $t = 0$ is
(a) 100.2 m/s^2 (b) 120 m/s^2
(c) 131.4 m/s^2 (d) 144.4 m/s^2

Comprehension-4

A balloon is moving upwards from ground with a constant speed of 10 m/s at a distance of 5 m infront of a plane mirror of length 2 m as shown in figure. A source S is placed symmetrically before plane mirror. The plane mirror is placed at a height $H = 15$ m above the surface of ground.

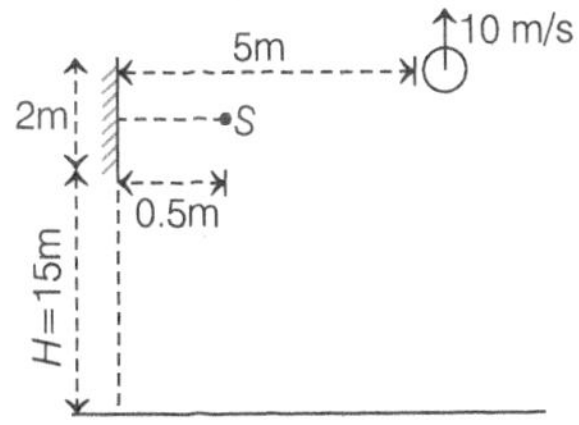

10 The maximum time interval during which a man inside the balloon can see the image of the source in the mirror is
(a) 2.2 s (b) 1.7 s (c) 4.6 s (d) 0.5 s

11 When the balloon is at a height of 17 m from ground, the man drops himself from the balloon. The greatest distance over which he can see the image of source in the plane mirror during free fall and corresponding time duration are respectively
(a) 22 m, 2.2 s (b) 17 m, 2.84 s
(c) 12 m, 1.7 s (d) 2m, 2s

12 If the balloon is moving upwards with a speed of 20 m/s, the man drops himself from the balloon at a height of 17 m from ground. The time duration for which he will see the image of source in the mirror is
(a) 2.2 s (b) 1.7 s (c) 1 s (d) 2.84 s

Comprehension-5

A concave mirror forms a real image of twice the linear dimension of the object on a screen. The object and the screen are then moved until the image is three times the linear size of the object. The shift of the screen is 25 cm.

13 Focal length of the mirror is
(a) 25 cm (b) 30 cm
(c) 35 cm (d) 40 cm

14 Shift of the object is
(a) 1.17 cm (b) 2.17 cm
(c) 3.17 cm (d) 4.17 cm

Comprehension-6

Two concave mirrors of equal radii of curvature R are fixed on a stand facing opposite directions. The whole system has a mass m and is kept on a frictionless horizontal table (see fig). Two blocks A and B each of mass m are placed on the two sides of the stand. At $t = 0$, the separation between A and the mirror is $2R$ and also the separation between B and the mirror is $2R$. The block B moves towards the mirror at a speed v. All collisions which take place are elastic. Taking the original position of the mirror stand system to be $x = 0$ and X-axis along AB.

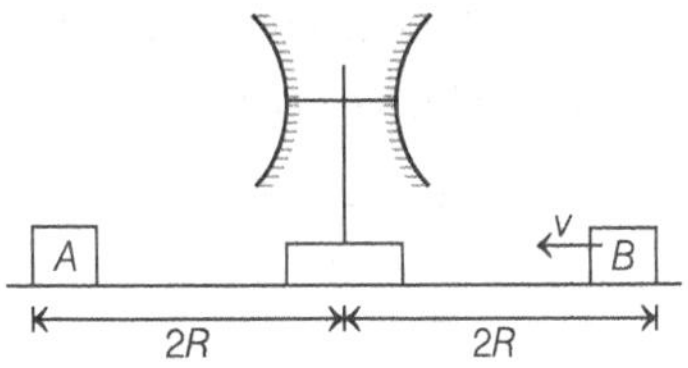

15 The position of image of A and B at $t = \frac{3R}{v}$
(a) $-\frac{2R}{3}, R$ (b) $-2R, 0$
(c) $-3R, -\frac{4R}{3}$ (d) $-\frac{4R}{3}, -3R$

16 Velocity of the image of A at $t = \frac{3R}{v}$
(a) zero (b) v (c) $2v$ (d) $\frac{2v}{3}$

17 Position of the images of A and B at $t = \frac{5R}{v}$
(a) $-2R, -R$ (b) $-3R, -R$ (c) $-R, -2R$ (d) $-3R, -\frac{4R}{3}$

Comprehension-7

A concave mirror of radius of curvature 20 cm is shown in the figure. A thin circular disc of diameter 1 cm is placed on the principal axis of mirror with its plane perpendicular to the principal axis at a distance 15 cm from the pole of the mirror. The radius of disc is increasing according to the law $r = (0.5 + 0.1t)$ cm/s.

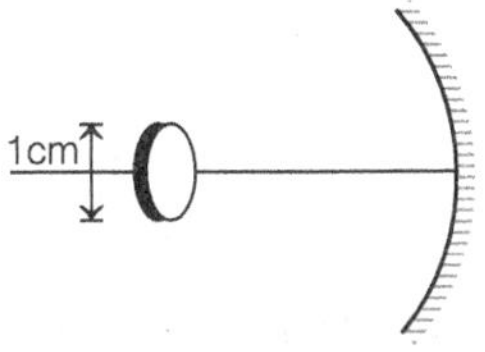

18 The image formed by the mirror will be in the shape of a
(a) circular disc
(b) elliptical disc with major axis horizontal
(c) elliptical disc with major axis vertical
(d) distorted disc

19 The area of image of the disc at $t = 1$ s is
(a) $1.2\,\pi\ cm^2$ (b) $1.44\,\pi\ cm^2$
(c) $1.52\,\pi\ cm^2$ (d) None of these

20. What will be the rate at which the radius of image will be changing?
(a) 0.2 cm/s, increasing (b) 0.2 cm/s, decreasing
(c) 0.4 cm/s, increasing (d) 0.4 cm/s, decreasing

Comprehension-8

Spherical aberration in spherical mirrors is a defect which is due to dependence of focal length f on angle of incidence θ as shown in figure is given by $f = R - \frac{R}{2}\sec\theta$

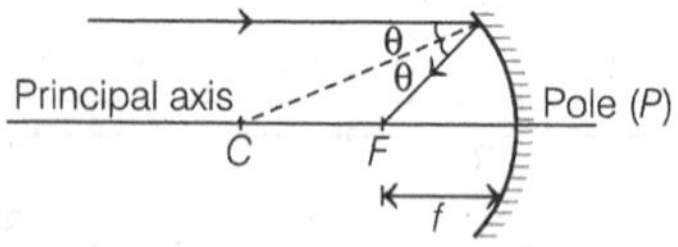

where R is radius of curvature of mirror and θ is the angle of incidence. The rays which are closed to principal axis are called paraxial rays and the rays far away from principal axis are called marginal rays. As a result of above dependence different rays are brought to focus at different points and the image of a point object is on a point.

21 If f_p and f_m represent the focal length of paraxial and marginal rays respectively, then correct relationship is
(a) $f_p = f_m$ (b) $f_p > f_m$
(c) $f_p < f_m$ (d) None of these

22 If angle of incidence is 60°, then focal length of this ray is
(a) R (b) $\frac{R}{2}$ (c) $2R$ (d) 0

23 The total deviation suffered by the ray falling on mirror at an angle of incidence equal to 60° is
(a) 180° (b) 90°
(c) Can't be determined (d) None of these

24 For paraxial rays, focal length approximately is
(a) R (b) $\frac{R}{2}$
(c) $2R$ (d) None of these

25 Which of the following statements is correct regarding spherical aberration?
(a) It can be completely eliminated
(b) It can't be completely eliminated but it can be minimized by allowing either paraxial or marginal rays to hit the mirror
(c) It is reduced by taking large aperture mirrors.
(d) None of the above

Comprehension-9

A spherical concave mirror of radius of curvature 40 cm is moving with a constant velocity 2 cm/s along positive X-axis as shown. A point object P located at a distance 30 cm left to the pole of the concave mirror is also moving with a velocity of 4 cm/s along positive X-axis at a height of 0.2 cm above the principal axis as shown in figure.

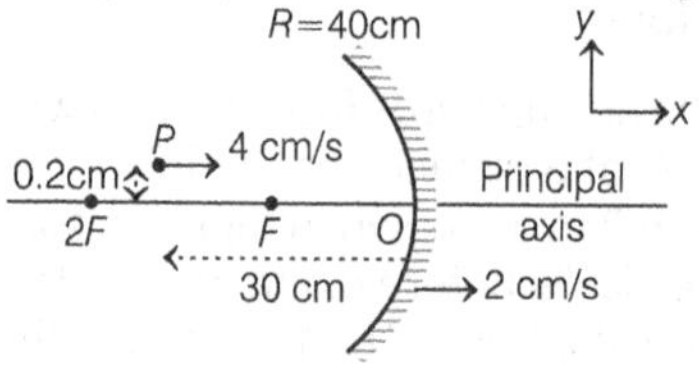

26 The velocity of image along X-axis is
(a) – 4 cm/s (b) – 6 cm/s (c) 4 cm/s (d) 6 cm/s

27 The velocity of image along Y-axis is
(a) 0 (b) $\frac{2}{25}$ cm/s
(c) $-\frac{2}{25}$ cm/s (d) $-\frac{4}{25}$ cm/s

Match the Columns Questions

1 Angle between two mirrors is θ and location of object is given in column I and some possible number of images are given in column II. Match the two columns.

Column I	Column II
A. $\theta = 60°$ and object is not on bisector	1. 4
B. $\theta = 72°$ and object is on bisector	2. 5
C. $\theta = 45°$ and object is on bisector	3. 7
D. $\theta = 50°$ and object is on bisector	4. 8

2 A beam of light appears to converge at a point O, x distance behind a convex mirror of focal length 10 cm. Determine nature of image if

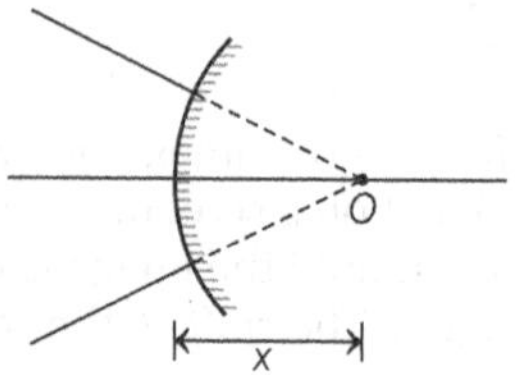

Column I	Column II
A. $x = 6$ cm	1. Real
B. $x = 11$ cm	2. Virtual
C. $x = 16$ cm	3. Magnified
D. $x = 30$ cm	4. Diminished

3 Consider a linear extended object that could be real or virtual with its length at right angles to the principal axis of a spherical mirror. With regards to image formation by spherical mirror, match column I with column II.

Column I		Column II	
A.	Image of the same size as the object is possible	1.	for concave mirror in case of real object
B.	Virtual image of a size greater, than that of object is possible	2.	for convex mirror in case of real object
C.	Real image of a size smaller, than that object is possible	3.	for concave mirror in case of virtual object
D.	Real and erect image is possible	4.	for convex mirror in case of virtual object

4 In Column I possible instantaneous velocity vector of the image with respect to ground are shown. These are corresponding to the situations shown in Column II. Match Column I with the situations shown in column-II.

Column I		Column II	
A.		1.	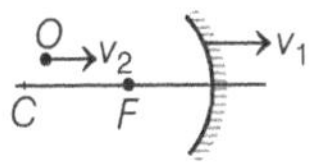
B.		2.	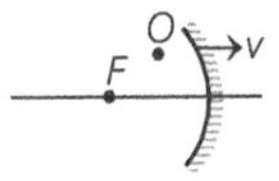
C.		3.	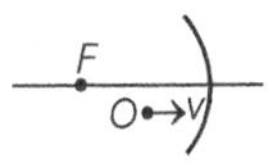
D.		4.	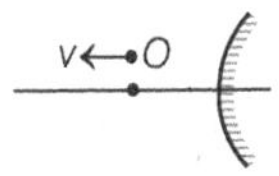
		5.	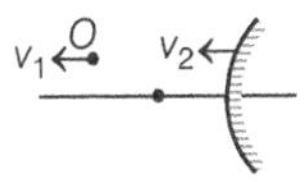

Numerical Value Questions

1 A fluorescent lamp of length 1 m is placed horizontally at a depth of 1.2 m below a ceiling. A plane mirror of length 0.6 m is placed below the lamp parallel to and symmetric to the lamp at a distance 2.4 m from it. Find the length (distance between the extreme points of the visible region along X-axis) of the reflected patch of light on the ceiling. (in m).

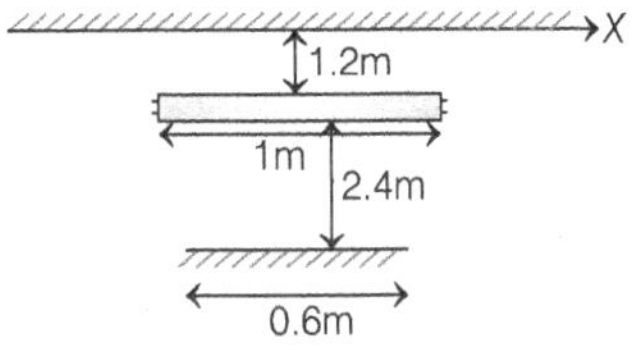

2 Two rays are incident on a spherical mirror of radius $R = 5$ cm parallel to its optical axis at the distance $h_1 = 0.5$ cm and $h_2 = 3$ cm. Find the distance Δx (in mm) between the points at which these rays intersect the optical axis after being reflected at the mirror.

3 A concave mirror of focal length 20 cm is cut into two parts from the middle and the two parts are moved perpendicularly by a distance 1 cm from the previous principal axis AB. Find the distance (in cm) between the images formed by the two parts

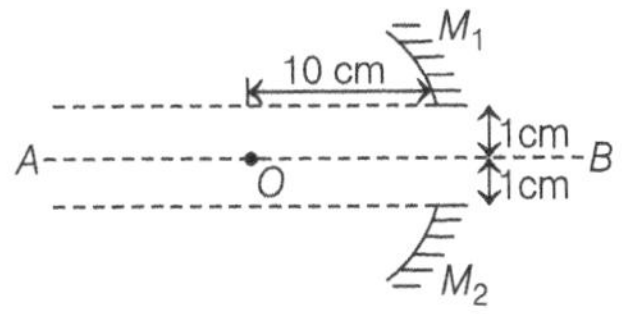

4 A thief is running away in a car with velocity of 20 m/s. A police jeep is following him, which is sighted by thief in his rear view mirror which is a convex mirror of focal length 10 m. He observes that the image of jeep is moving towards him with a velocity of 1 cm/s. The magnification of the mirror for the jeep at that time is 1/10. Find rate (per second) at which magnification is changing. Assume that police jeep is on the axis of the mirror. (answer in multiple of 10^{-3})

5 A particle is travelling along the principal axis of a concave mirror with a constant velocity of 5 cm/s. Find the acceleration of image (in cm/s^2), when the particle is at a distance of 40 cm from the pole as seen by a stationary observer. Focal length = 30 cm.

6 A rod of length l is moving with constant speed 9 m/s towards the pole of a concave mirror of focal length l. Find the rate of change in length of the image of the rod (in m/s) at the moment centre of the rod coincides with the centre of curvature of the mirror.

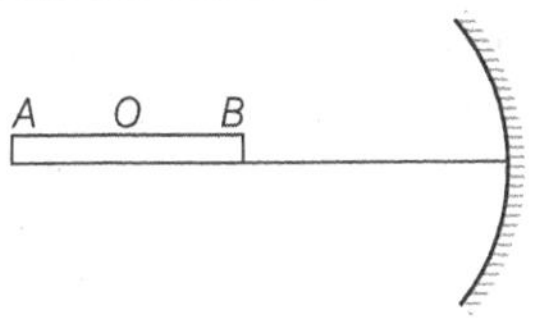

7 A particle is dropped along the axis from a height $\frac{f}{2}$ on a concave mirror of focal length f as shown in the figure. The acceleration due to gravity is g. If the maximum speed of image is $\frac{3}{4}\sqrt{nfg}$, then find n.

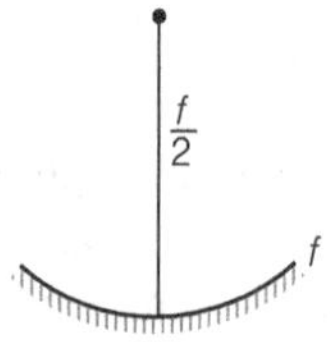

8 A point object is placed at the centre of curvature of a concave mirror (taken as origin). A plane mirror is also placed at a distance of 10 cm from the object as shown. Consider two reflections first at plane mirror and then at concave mirror. If the coordinates of the image thus formed are (x_0, y_0), then find the value of $\frac{\pi x_0}{y_0}$.

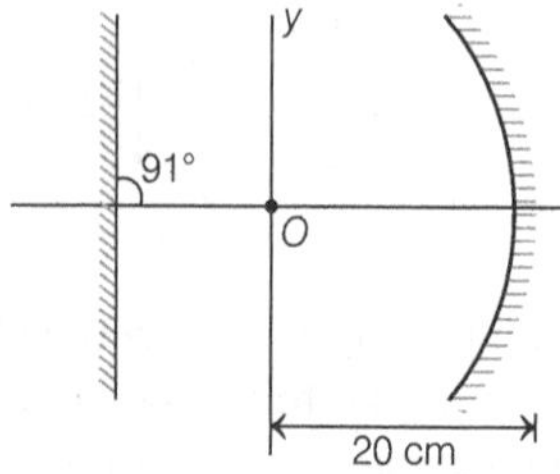

9 Consider a concave mirror kept at origin with focal length 40 cm. Parallel rays which subtend an angle $\theta = \frac{1}{40}$ rad are incident on it. A convex mirror is kept at a distance 25 cm from the first mirror as shown. Find the Y-coordinate of the image (in cm) formed by the system of mirrors after two reflections.

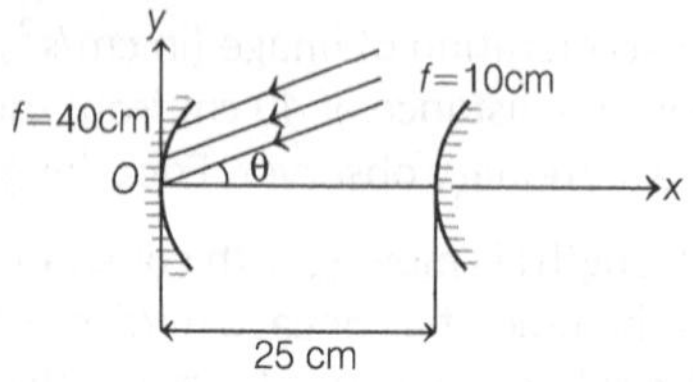

10. Two concave mirrors each of radius of curvature 40 cm are placed such that their principal axes are parallel to each other and at a distance of 1 cm to each other. Both the mirrors are at a distance of 100 cm to each other. Consider first reflection at M_1 and then at M_2. Take location of object as the origin. If the coordinates of the image thus formed are $(x_0, -y_0)$, then find the value $\frac{x_0}{y_0}$.

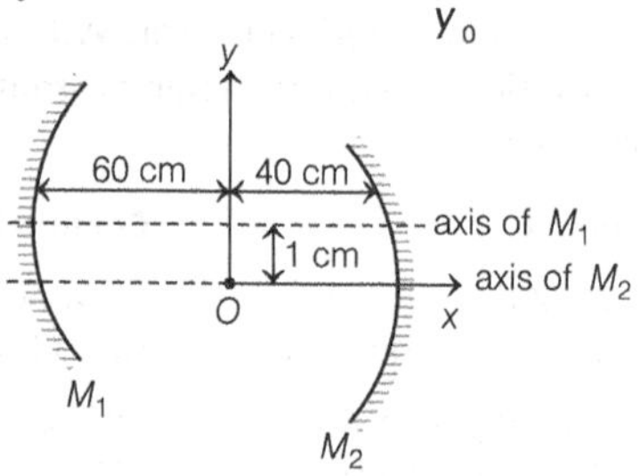

Previous Year's Questions

JEE Main

1 A convex mirror of radius of curvature 30 cm forms an image that is half the size of the object. The object distance is **[2024, 29 Jan Shift-I]**

(a) – 45 cm (b) 15 cm (c) 45 cm (d) –15 cm

2 If the distance between object and its two times magnified virtual image produced by a curved mirror is 15 cm, the focal length of the mirror must be **[2024, 29 Jan Shift-II]**

(a) –12 cm (b) (10/3) cm
(c) –10 cm (d) 15 cm

3 An object is placed at a distance of 12 cm infront of a plane mirror. A virtual and erect image is formed by the mirror. Now, the mirror is moved by 4 cm towards the stationary object. The distance by which the position of image would be shifted, will be **[2023, 10 April Shift-I]**

(a) 4 cm towards mirror (b) 8 cm away from mirror
(c) 2 cm towards mirror (d) 8 cm towards mirror

4 When one light ray is reflected from a plane mirror with 30° angle of reflection, the angle of deviation of the ray after reflection is **[2023, 11 April Shift-II]**

(a) 140° (b) 110° (c) 120° (d) 130°

5 The light rays from an object have been reflected towards an observer from a standard flat mirror, the image observed by the observer are

A. real B. erect
C. smaller in size then object
D. laterally inverted

Choose the most appropriate answer from the options given below. **[2023, 25 Jan Shift-II]**

(a) B and C Only (b) B and D Only
(c) A, C and D Only (d) A and D Only

6 Two objects A and B are placed at 15 cm and 25 cm from the pole in front of a concave mirror having

radius of curvature 40 cm. The distance between images formed by the mirror is ....
[2023, 1 Feb Shift-II]

(a) 60 cm (b) 40 cm (c) 160 cm (d) 100 cm

7 Two vertical parallel mirrors A and B are separated by 10 cm. A point object O is placed at a distance of 2 cm from mirror A. The distance of the second nearest image behind mirror A from the mirror A is .... cm. [2023, 8 April Shift-I]

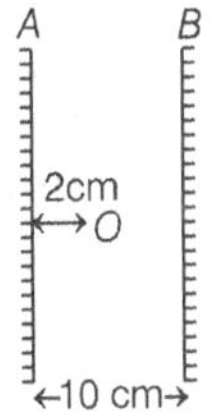

8 A thin cylindrical rod of length 10 cm is placed horizontally on the principle axis of a concave mirror of focal length 20 cm. The rod is placed in such a way that mid-point of the rod is at 40 cm from the pole of mirror. The length of the image formed by the mirror will be $x/3$ cm. The value of x is ....
[2023, 1 Feb Shift-I]

9 An object O is placed at a distance of 100 cm infront of a concave mirror of radius of curvature 200 cm as shown in the figure. The object starts moving towards the mirror at a speed 2 cm/s. The position of the image from the mirror after 10 s will be at .... cm. [2022, 28 July Shift-II]

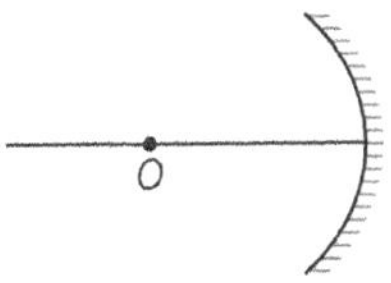

10 A light ray is incident at an incident angle θ_1, on the system of two plane mirrors M_1 and M_2 having an inclination angle 75° between them (as shown in figure). After reflecting from mirror M_1, it gets reflected back by the mirror M_2 with an angle of reflection 30°. The total deviation of the ray will be .... degree. [2022, 26 June Shift-I]

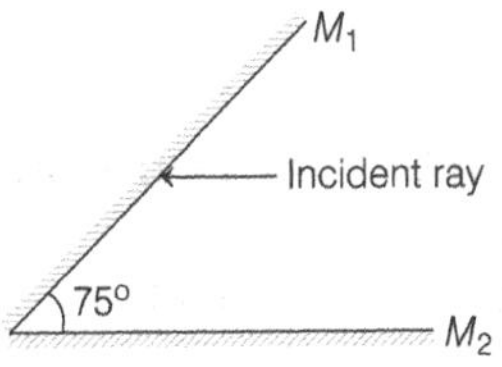

11 A point source of light S, placed at a distance 60 cm in front of the centre of a plane mirror of width 50 cm, hangs vertically on a wall. A man walks in front of the mirror along a line parallel to the mirror at a distance 1.2 m from it (see in the figure). The distance between the extreme points, where he can see the image of the light source in the mirror is .... cm. [2021, 26 Feb Shift-II]

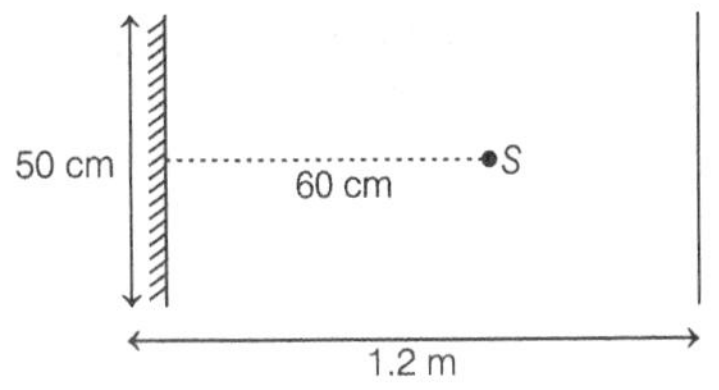

12 Two plane mirrors M_1 and M_2 are at right angle to each other shown. A point source P is placed at a and $2a$ meter away from M_1 and M_2, respectively. The shortest distance between the images thus formed is (Take, $\sqrt{5} = 2.3$) [2021, 31 Aug Shift-I]

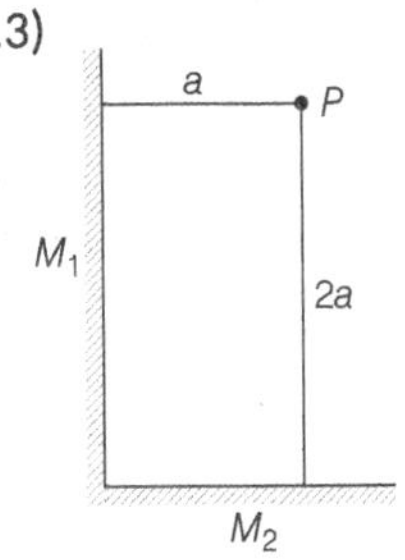

(a) $3a$ (b) $4.6\,a$ (c) $2.3\,a$ (d) $2\sqrt{10}\,a$

13 An object is placed beyond the centre of curvature C of the given concave mirror. If the distance of the object is d_1 from C and the distance of the image formed is d_2 from C, the radius of curvature of this mirror is [2021, 27 Aug Shift-I]

(a) $\dfrac{2d_1d_2}{d_1-d_2}$ (b) $\dfrac{2d_1d_2}{d_1+d_2}$ (c) $\dfrac{d_1d_2}{d_1+d_2}$ (d) $\dfrac{d_1d_2}{d_1-d_2}$

14 Car B overtakes another car A at a relative speed of 40 ms^{-1}. How fast will the image of car B appear to move in the mirror of focal length 10 cm fitted in car A, when the car B is 1.9 m away from the car A?
[2021, 26 Aug Shift-I]

(a) 4 ms^{-1} (b) 0.2 ms^{-1} (c) 40 ms^{-1} (d) 0.1 ms^{-1}

15 The incident ray, reflected ray and the outward drawn normal are denoted by the unit vectors $\mathbf{a}$, $\mathbf{b}$ and $\mathbf{c}$, respectively. Then, choose the correct relation for these vectors. [2021, 26 Feb Shift-II]

(a) $\mathbf{b} = \mathbf{a} + 2\mathbf{c}$ (b) $\mathbf{b} = 2\mathbf{a} + \mathbf{c}$
(c) $\mathbf{b} = \mathbf{a} - 2(\mathbf{a}\cdot\mathbf{c})\mathbf{c}$ (d) $\mathbf{b} = \mathbf{a} - \mathbf{c}$

JEE Advanced

1. An object and a concave mirror of focal length $f = 10$ cm both move along the principal axis of the mirror with constant speeds. The object moves with speed $v_0 = 15$ cm s^{-1} towards the mirror with respect to a laboratory frame. The distance between the object and the mirror at a given moment is denoted by u. When $u = 30$ cm, the speed of the mirror v_m is such that the image is instantaneously at rest with respect to the laboratory frame and the object forms a real image. The magnitude of v_m is .... cm s^{-1}. **(2022 Adv.)**

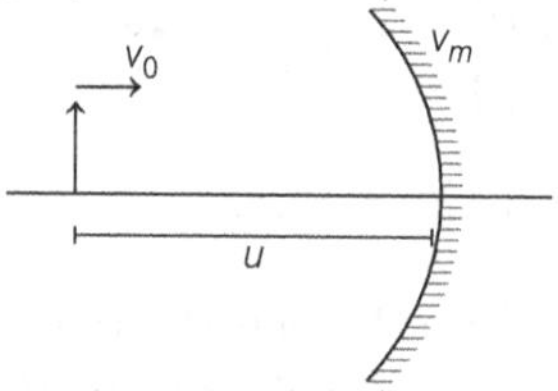

2. Three plane mirrors form an equilateral triangle with each side of length L. There is a small hole at a distance $l > 0$ from one of the corners as shown in the figure. A ray of light is passed through the hole at an angle θ and can only come out through the same hole. The cross-section of the mirror configuration and the ray of light lie on the same plane. **(2022 Adv.)**

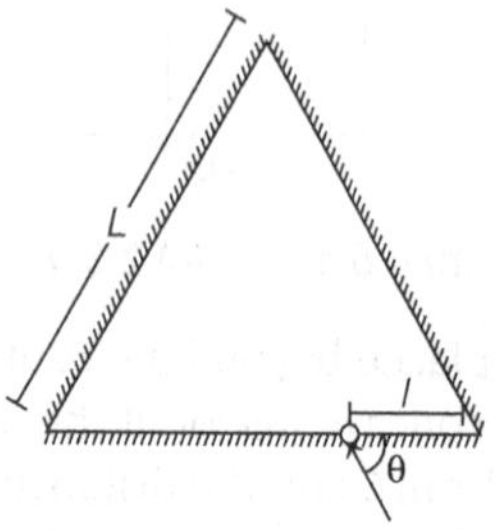

Which of the following statement(s) is(are) correct?

(a) The ray of light will come out for $\theta = 30°$, for $0 < l < L$.

(b) There is an angle for $l = \frac{L}{2}$ at which the ray of light will come out after two reflections.

(c) The ray of light will never come out for $\theta = 60°$, and $l = \frac{L}{3}$.

(d) The ray of light will come out for $\theta = 60°$, and $0 < l < \frac{L}{2}$ after six reflections.

3. A wire is bent in the shape of a right angled triangle and is placed in front of a concave mirror of focal length f as shown in the figure. Which of the figures shown in the four options qualitatively represent(s) the shape of the image of the bent wire? (These figures are not to scale.) **(2018 Adv.)**

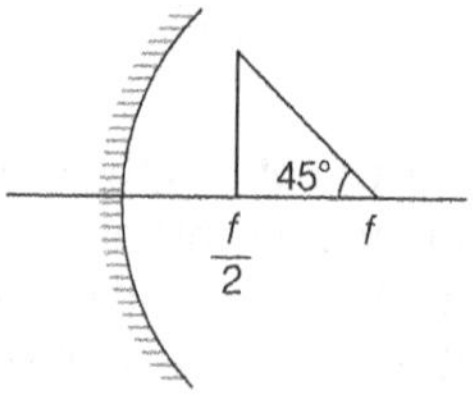

(a) 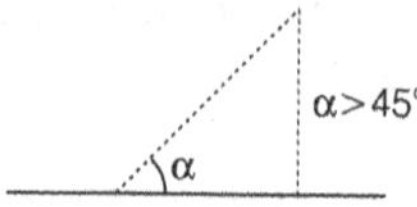

(b) 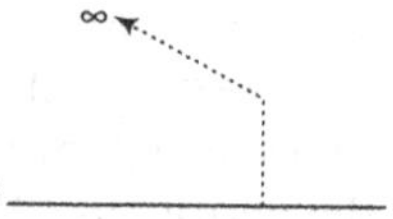

(c) 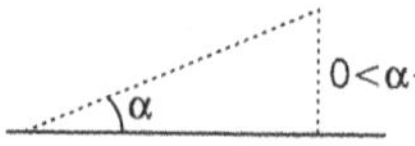

(d) 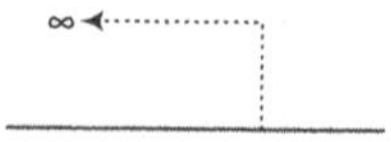

4. A ray of light travelling in the direction $\frac{1}{2}(\hat{\mathbf{i}} + \sqrt{3}\,\hat{\mathbf{j}})$ is incident on a plane mirror. After reflection, it travels along the direction $\frac{1}{2}(\hat{\mathbf{i}} - \sqrt{3}\,\hat{\mathbf{j}})$. The angle of incidence is **(2013 Adv.)**

(a) 30° (b) 45° (c) 60° (d) 75°

Answer Key

Level 1

1.1 Reflection from Plane Mirror

1. 120° anti-clockwise and 240° clockwise
2. 40°
3. 30° clockwise
4. 60°
5. 40°
6. $-\frac{(2\hat{i} + \hat{j} + 2\hat{k})}{3}$

1.2 Image Formation by a Plane Mirror

1. Position of image = (1 cos 60°, − 1 sin 60°)
2. 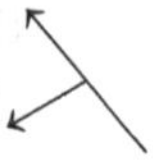

1.3 Image Formation by Two Plane Mirrors

1. 5 cm, 25 cm, 35 cm
2. (a) 3 (b) 5 (c) 11 (d) 5 (e) 4 (f) 2

1.4 Field of View

1. $P \equiv (0, 6)$, $Q \equiv (0, 9)$. PQ is the region on Y-axis in which reflected rays are present
3. $3d$
4. 160 cm, 320 cm

1.5 Velocity of Image in Plane Mirror

1. $2v$ towards left
2. 7 m/s towards left
3. $-5(1+\sqrt{3})\,\hat{i} + 5\sqrt{3}\,\hat{j}$ m/s

1.6 Spherical Mirror

1. 60°
2. $CQ = \frac{R}{2\cos i}$. If $i \to 0$, then $CQ = R/2$
3. (- 30 cm, - 2 cm)
4. 10.35 cm
5. 1.43 m, 2.0 m
6. 1.0 mm inside the ball bearing, 0.08 mm
7. 5 cm
8. 10 cm or 30 cm from the mirror
9. R.O.C. = 80 cm (concave)
10. R.O.C. = 60 cm (concave)
11. 16 cm
12. $d/2$
13. $f = 24$ cm
14. 20 cm from object, 20/3 cm from object

1.7 Velocity of Image in Spherical Mirror

1. (a) 40 cm/s opposite to the velocity of object, (b) 20 cm/s opposite to the velocity of object
2. 95 cms^{-1} towards left
3. $-2\hat{i} - 4\hat{j}$
4. 0.04 mm away from the mirror

1.8 Combination of Mirrors

1. (i) 12.5 cm right of M_1 (ii) 20 cm right of M_1 (iii) 30 cm right of M_1
2. 21.43 cm left of convex mirror
3. 30 cm
4. $2f, 4f$
5. 25 cm and 30 cm

Level 2

Single Choice Correct Questions

1. (a)	2. (b)	3. (d)	4. (c)	5. (b)
6. (c)	7. (c)	8. (b)	9. (d)	10. (b)
11. (c)	12. (c)	13. (c)	14. (d)	15. (b)
16. (b)	17. (a)	18. (d)	19. (d)	20. (c)
21. (c)	22. (a)	23. (a)	24. (c)	25. (d)
26. (c)	27. (a)	28. (a)	29. (c)	30. (c)
31. (b)	32. (d)	33. (a)	34. (b)	35. (b)
36. (c)	37. (c)	38. (b)	39. (b)	40. (b)
41. (c)				

Numerical Value Questions

1. 1.73	2. 15	3. 1	4. 90	5. 80
6. 16	7. 5	8. 16	9. 36	10. 86

Level 3

Single Choice Correct Questions

1. (b)	2. (b)	3. (c)	4. (c)	5. (d)
6. (b)	7. (c)	8. (d)	9. (c)	10. (b)
11. (d)	12. (d)	13. (d)	14. (a)	15. (b)
16. (a)	17. (d)	18. (c)	19. (a)	20. (c)
21. (a)	22. (c)	23. (b)	24. (d)	25. (a)
26. (a)	27. (d)	28. (a)	29. (c)	30. (c)
31. (a)	32. (b)	33. (a)	34. (b)	

Multiple Choice(s) Correct Questions

1. (b, c)	2. (b, d)	3. (b, d)	4. (a,b,c,d)
5. (a, c, d)	6. (b, c)	7. (a, b)	8. (b, c)
9. (a, b, c)	10. (a, b)	11. (a, c, d)	12. (a, c)
13. (a, c)	14. (b, c)		

Comprehension Based Questions

1. (b)	2. (c)	3. (d)	4. (d)	5. (b)
6. (a)	7. (b)	8. (d)	9. (b)	10. (a)
11. (b)	12. (b)	13. (a)	14. (d)	15. (b)
16. (c)	17. (d)	18. (a)	19. (b)	20. (a)
21. (b)	22. (d)	23. (a)	24. (b)	25. (b)
26. (b)	27. (c)			

Match the Columns Questions

1. A → 2; B → 2; C → 3; D → 4
2. A → 1,3; B → 2, 3; C → 2,3; D → 2,4
3. A → 1,2,3,4; B → 1,4; C → 1,3; D → 3,4
4. A → 1,2; B → 3,5; C → 1,5; D → 1,4,5

Numerical Value Questions

1. 3	2. 6.25	3. 2	4. 1	5. 45
6. 32	7. 3	8. 180	9. 2	10. 20

Previous Year's Questions

JEE Main

1. (d)	2. (c)	3. (d)	4. (c)	5. (b)
6. (c)	7. (18)	8. (32)	9. (400)	10. (210)
11. (150)	12. (b)	13. (a)	14. (d)	15. (c)

JEE Advanced

1. (3)	2. (a, b)	3. (d)	4. (a)

SOLUTIONS

Level

1.1 Reflection from Plane Mirror

1. Deviation, $\delta = 180° - 2i = 180° - 2(30°)$

$= 120°$ anti-clockwise or $240°$ clockwise

2.

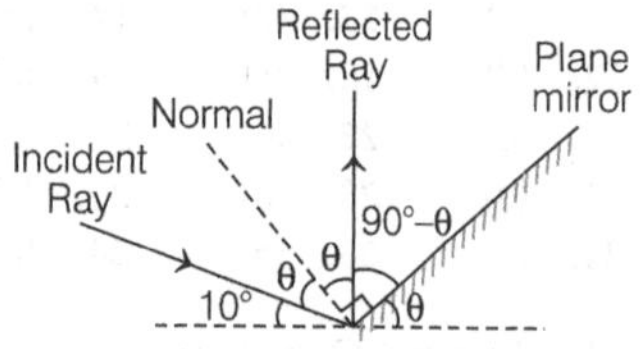

$\theta + \theta + 10° = 90° \Rightarrow \theta = 40°$

3. If the incident ray turns by an angle θ towards the normal, then the reflected ray also turns towards the normal by the same angle θ. If the mirror is rotated by an angle θ, then the reflected ray rotates by an angle 2θ.

So, angle turned by the reflected ray

$= 10°$ (anti-clockwise) $+ 2 \times 20°$ (clockwise)

$= 30°$ (clockwise)

4.

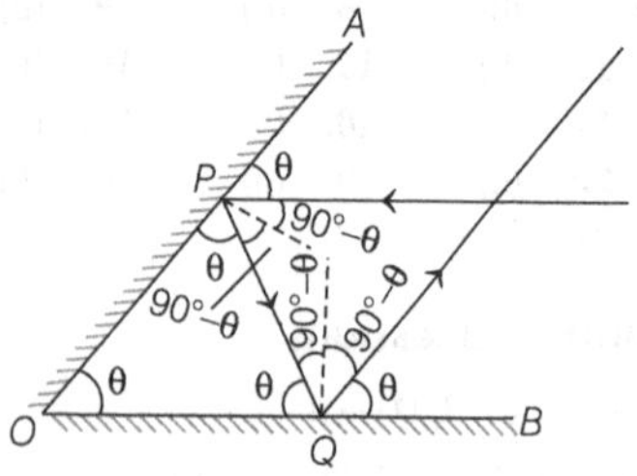

In ΔOPQ, $\theta + \theta + \theta = 180°$

$\Rightarrow$ $3\theta = 180° \Rightarrow \theta = 60°$

5.

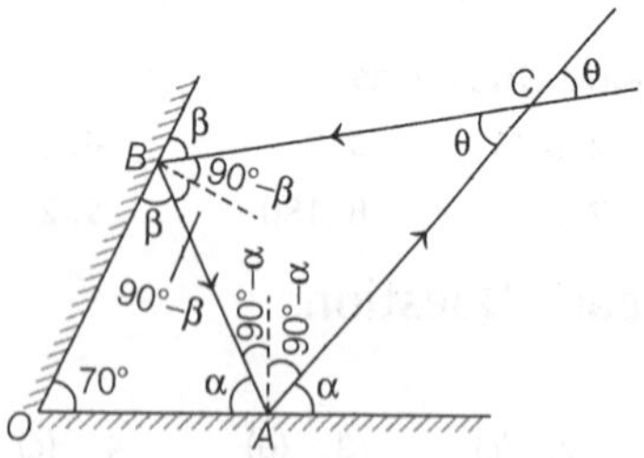

In ΔOAB, $\alpha + \beta + 70° = 180°$

$\Rightarrow$ $\alpha + \beta = 110°$

In ΔABC, $2(90° - \alpha) + 2(90° - \beta) + \theta = 180°$

$\Rightarrow$ $\theta = 2(\alpha + \beta) - 180°$

$= 2(110°) - 180° = 40°$

6. Unit vector along the incident ray, $\hat{\mathbf{a}} = \dfrac{\hat{i} + 2\hat{j} - 2\hat{k}}{3}$

Unit vector along the normal, $\hat{\mathbf{n}} = \dfrac{\hat{i} + \hat{j}}{\sqrt{2}}$

Let unit vector along the reflected ray be $\hat{\mathbf{b}}$.

So, $\mathbf{b} = \mathbf{a} - 2(\hat{\mathbf{a}} \cdot \hat{\mathbf{n}})\hat{\mathbf{n}}$

$$= \frac{\hat{i} + 2\hat{j} - 2\hat{k}}{3} - 2\left[\left(\frac{\hat{i} + 2\hat{j} - 2\hat{k}}{3}\right) \cdot \left(\frac{\hat{i} + \hat{j}}{\sqrt{2}}\right)\right]\frac{\hat{i} + \hat{j}}{\sqrt{2}}$$

$$= \frac{-(2\hat{i} + \hat{j} + 2\hat{k})}{3}$$

1.2 Image Formation by a Plane Mirror

1. Perpendicular distance of object from the mirror is $1 \sin 30°$.

So, image will be formed same distance behind the mirror.

$OI = 1 \sin 30° + 1 \sin 30°$

$= 2 \sin 30° = 1$

So, coordinates of image

$= (OI \cos 60°, - OI \sin 60°)$

$= (1 \cos 60°, - 1 \sin 60°)$

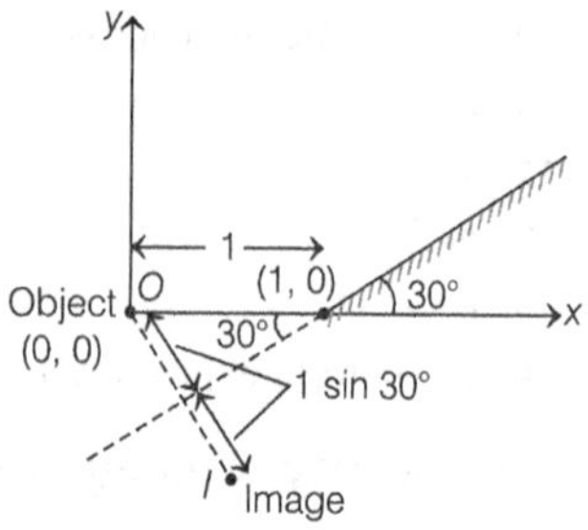

2.

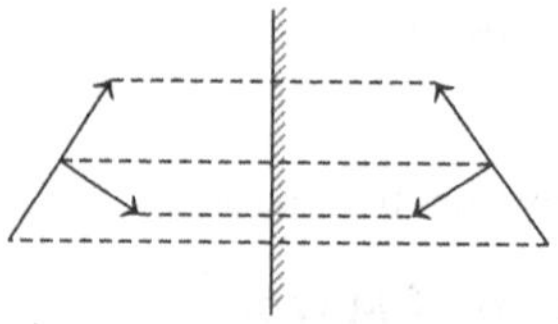

1.3. Image Formation by a Two Plane Mirrors

1.

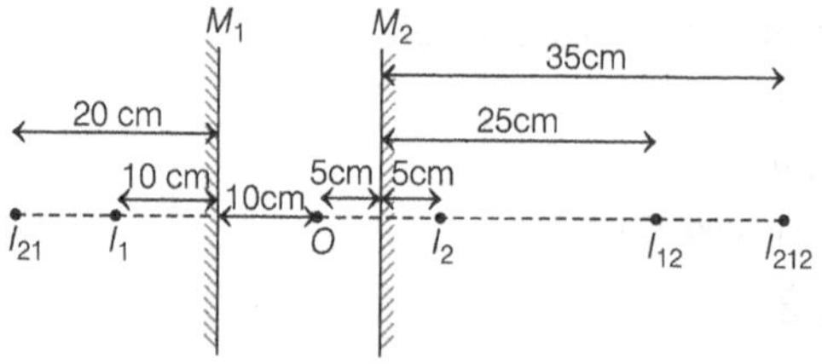

Distance of first three images from the mirror M_2 are 5 cm, 25 cm and 35 cm.

2. (a) $n = \dfrac{360°}{\theta} - 1 = \dfrac{360°}{90°} - 1 = 3$

(b) $n = \dfrac{360°}{\theta} - 1 = \dfrac{360°}{60°} - 1 = 5$

(c) $n = \dfrac{360°}{\theta} - 1 = \dfrac{360°}{30°} - 1 = 11$

(d) $n = \dfrac{360°}{\theta} = \dfrac{360°}{72°} = 5$

(e) $n = \dfrac{360°}{\theta} - 1 = \dfrac{360°}{72°} - 1 = 4$

(f) Each mirror forms one image of the object. Rays reflected from one mirror don't get reflected from other mirror. So, image of image won't be formed. Hence, total number of images = 2.

1.4 Field of View

1. $\tan\alpha = \frac{2}{2} = \frac{y_1}{4}$

$\Rightarrow \quad y_1 = 4$

$\tan\beta = \frac{3}{2} = \frac{y_2}{4}$

$\Rightarrow \quad y_2 = 6$

Reflected rays are present in the region PQ on the Y-axis.

Coordinates of $P = (0, 6)$

Coordinates of $Q = (0, 9)$

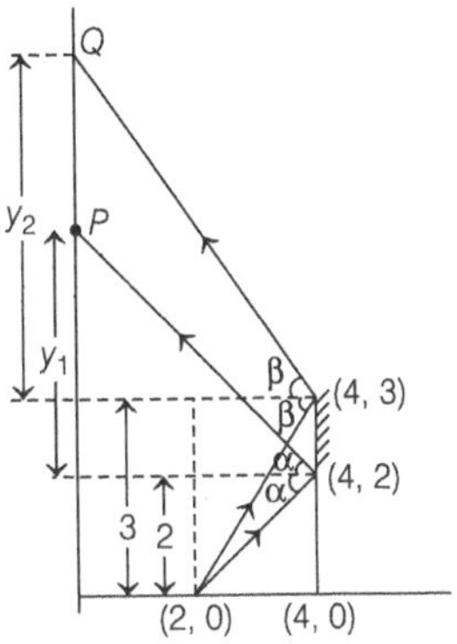

2. Height of person

$= 2(x + y) = H$

$\Rightarrow \quad x + y = \frac{H}{2}$

Size of mirror $= x + y = \frac{H}{2}$

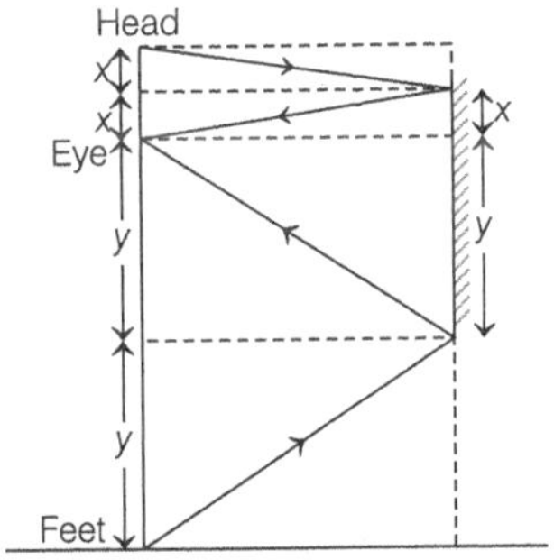

3. $\tan i = \frac{\frac{d}{2}}{L} = \frac{y}{2L}$

$\Rightarrow \quad y = d$

So, $\quad PQ = d + d + d = 3d$

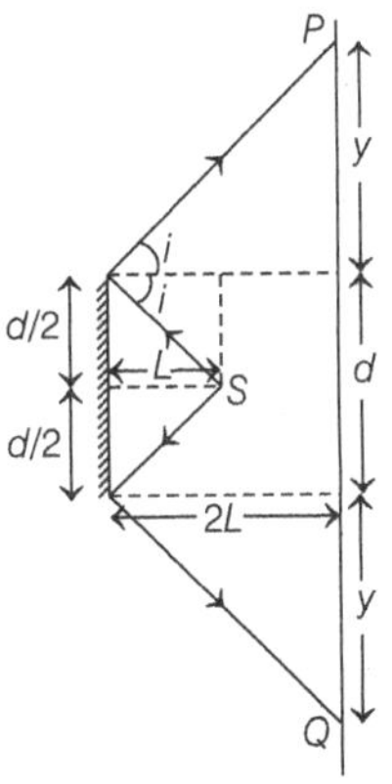

4. $\tan\alpha = \frac{40}{20} = \frac{y_1}{60}$

$\Rightarrow \quad y_1 = 120$ cm

$\tan\beta = \frac{80}{20} = \frac{y_2}{60}$

$\Rightarrow \quad y_2 = 240$ cm

So, minimum height of person

$= y_1 + 40$

$= 160$ cm

Maximum height of person

$= y_2 + 80$

$= 320$ cm

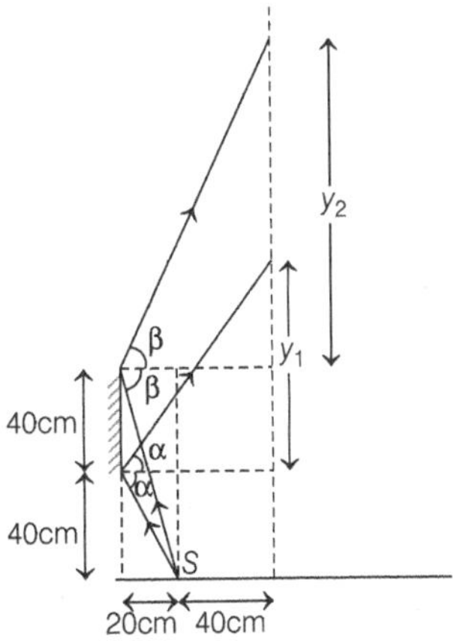

1.5 Velocity of image in Plane Mirror

1. $(v_{im})_x = -(v_{om})_x$

$\Rightarrow \quad v_i - v_m = -(v_o - v_m)$

$\Rightarrow \quad v_i - (-v) = -(0 - (-v))$

$\Rightarrow \quad v_i = -2v = 2v$ towards left

2. $(v_{im})_x = -(v_{om})_x$

$\Rightarrow \quad v_i - v_m = -(v_o - v_m)$

$\Rightarrow \quad v_i - (-1) = -(5 - (-1))$

$\Rightarrow \quad v_i = -7 = 7$ m/s towards left

3. $\mathbf{v}_o = 10\cos 60°\,\hat{\mathbf{i}} + 10\sin 60°\,\hat{\mathbf{j}} = 5\hat{\mathbf{i}} + 5\sqrt{3}\,\hat{\mathbf{j}}$

$\mathbf{v}_m = -5\cos 30°\,\hat{\mathbf{i}} + 5\sin 30°\,\hat{\mathbf{j}} = -2.5\sqrt{3}\,\hat{\mathbf{i}} + 2.5\hat{\mathbf{j}}$

Along x-direction,

$(v_{im})_x = -(v_{om})_x$

$\Rightarrow \quad v_i - v_m = -(v_o - v_m)$

$\Rightarrow \quad (v_i)_x - (-2.5\sqrt{3}) = -(5 - (-2.5\sqrt{3}))$

$\Rightarrow \quad (v_i)_x = -5(1 + \sqrt{3})$

Along y-direction,

$(v_i)_y = (v_o)_y$

$\Rightarrow \quad (v_i)_y = 5\sqrt{3}$

$\therefore \quad \mathbf{v}_i = -5(1 + \sqrt{3})\hat{\mathbf{i}} + 5\sqrt{3}\,\hat{\mathbf{j}}$

1.6. Spherical Mirror

1. $AB \,||\, CP$

$\Rightarrow \quad \angle BCP = \angle ABC = i$

From law of reflection, $i = r$

ΔBCP is an isosceles triangle since $\quad BC = CP$

So, $\quad \angle CPB = \angle CBP = r$

In ΔBCP, $i + r + r = 180°$

$\Rightarrow \quad i + i + i = 180°$

$\Rightarrow \quad 3i = 180° \Rightarrow i = 60°$

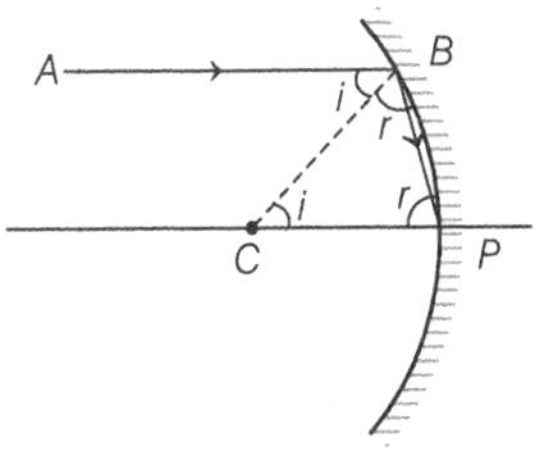

2. ΔBQC is an isoscles triangle. From Q, drop a perpendicular on the base BC. D is mid-point of the base BC.

$\therefore \quad CD = \frac{BC}{2} = \frac{R}{2}$

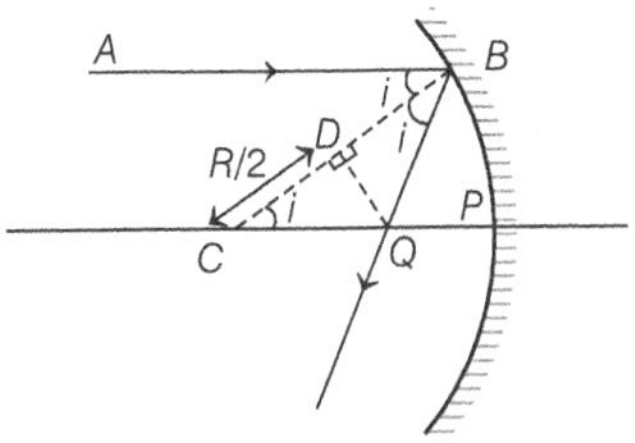

In ΔCDQ,

$\cos i = \frac{\frac{R}{2}}{CQ} \Rightarrow CQ = \frac{R}{2\cos i}$

If $i \to 0$, $\quad CQ = \frac{R}{2\cos 0°} = \frac{R}{2}$

3. $\frac{1}{v}+\frac{1}{u}=\frac{1}{f} \Rightarrow \frac{1}{v}+\frac{1}{(-15)}=\frac{1}{(-10)}$

$\Rightarrow \quad v=-30\text{ cm}$

$$m=\frac{h_i}{h_o}=-\frac{v}{u} \Rightarrow \frac{h_i}{1}=-\frac{(-30)}{(-15)}$$

$\Rightarrow \quad h_i=-2\text{ cm}$

So, position of image $=(-30\text{ cm}, -2\text{ cm})$

4. Since, $u >> f, v=f=-11.4\text{ m}$

$$m=\frac{h_i}{h_o}=-\frac{v}{u}$$

$$\Rightarrow \frac{h_i}{(3450\text{ km})}=\frac{-(-11.4\text{ m})}{(-3.8\times 10^5\text{ km})}$$

$\Rightarrow \quad h_i=-10.35\text{ cm}$

So, diameter of image $=10.35$ cm

5. $m=\frac{h_i}{h_o}=-\frac{v}{u} \Rightarrow \frac{(-50)}{20}=-\frac{(-5)}{u}$

$\Rightarrow \quad u=-2\text{ m}$

$$\frac{1}{v}+\frac{1}{u}=\frac{1}{f}$$

$$\Rightarrow \frac{1}{(-5)}+\frac{1}{(-2)}=\frac{1}{f} \Rightarrow f=-\frac{10}{7}\text{m}=-1.43\text{ m}$$

6. $R=\frac{d}{2}=0.2\text{ cm}, \quad f=\frac{R}{2}=0.1\text{ cm}$

$$\frac{1}{v}+\frac{1}{u}=\frac{1}{f} \Rightarrow \frac{1}{v}+\frac{1}{(-20)}=\frac{1}{(0.1)}$$

$\Rightarrow \quad v=0.1\text{ cm}=1\text{ mm}$

$$m=\frac{h_i}{h_o}=-\frac{v}{u} \Rightarrow \frac{h_i}{1.6}=-\left(\frac{0.1}{-20}\right)$$

$\Rightarrow \quad h_i=0.008\text{ cm}=0.08\text{ mm}$

7. $m=\frac{h_i}{h_o}=\frac{0.6}{1}$

Also, $\quad m=\frac{f}{f-u} \Rightarrow 0.6=\frac{7.5}{7.5-u} \Rightarrow u=-5\text{ cm}$

8. $m=\frac{f}{f-u} \Rightarrow \pm 2=\frac{-20}{-20-u}$

$\Rightarrow \quad u=-10\text{ cm or }-30\text{ cm}$

9. $m=\frac{f}{f-u} \Rightarrow +2=\frac{f}{f-(-20)} \Rightarrow f=-40\text{ cm}$

So, radius of curvature $=80$ cm (concave)

10. $m=\frac{f}{f-u} \Rightarrow -2=\frac{f}{f-u}$ ... (i)

Since, the magnitude of magnification increases, the object should be shifted towards the mirror.

$$-3=\frac{f}{f-(u+5)} \quad \text{...(ii)}$$

Solving Eqs. (i) and (ii), we get

$$f=-30\text{ cm}$$

So, radius of curvature $=60$ cm (concave)

11. For B, $\frac{1}{v}+\frac{1}{u}=\frac{1}{f}$

$$\Rightarrow \frac{1}{v}+\frac{1}{(-15)}=\frac{1}{-10}$$

$\Rightarrow \quad v=-30\text{ cm}$

For C, $\frac{1}{v}+\frac{1}{u}=\frac{1}{f}$

$$\Rightarrow \frac{1}{v}+\frac{1}{-20}=\frac{1}{-10}$$

$\Rightarrow \quad v=-20\text{ cm}$

For AB, $m=\frac{h_i}{h_o}=-\frac{v}{u}$

$$\Rightarrow \frac{h_i}{2}=-\frac{(-30)}{(-15)} \Rightarrow h_i=-4\text{ cm}$$

For CD, $m=\frac{h_i}{h_o}=-\frac{v}{u}$

$$\Rightarrow \frac{h_i}{2}=-\frac{(-20)}{(-20)} \Rightarrow h_i=2\text{ cm}$$

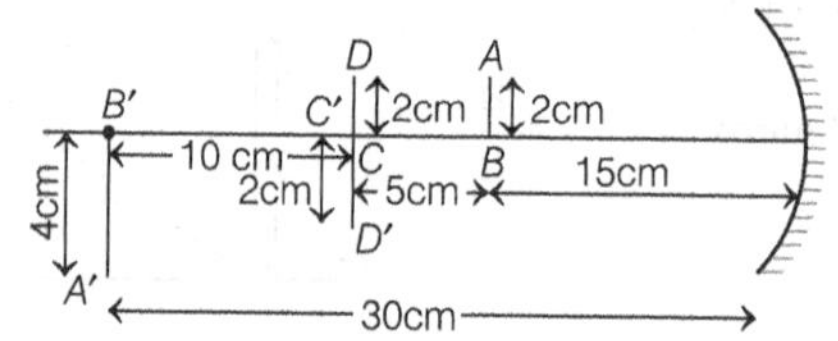

So, total length of image $(A'B'C'D')=B'C'+A'B'+C'D'$
$=(30-20)+4+2$
$=16$ cm

12. Since, the image just touches the rod, one end of the rod will be placed at the centre of curvature. The other end of the rod will be between C and F, since image is elongated.

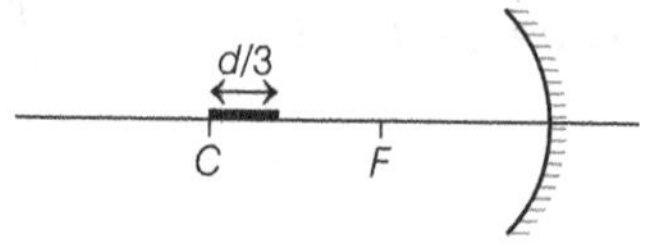

For the other end of the rod,

$$\frac{1}{v}+\frac{1}{u}=\frac{1}{f} \Rightarrow \frac{1}{v}+\frac{1}{-\left(2d-\frac{d}{3}\right)}=\frac{1}{-d}$$

$$\Rightarrow \quad v=-\frac{5d}{2}$$

Length of image $=\frac{5d}{2}-2d=\frac{d}{2}$

13.

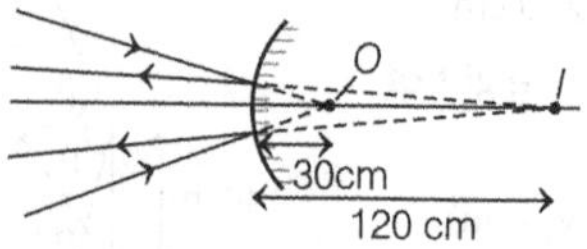

$u=+30\text{ cm}, \quad v=+120\text{ cm}$

$$\frac{1}{v}+\frac{1}{u}=\frac{1}{f} \Rightarrow \frac{1}{120}+\frac{1}{30}=\frac{1}{f}$$

$\Rightarrow \quad f=24\text{ cm}$

14.

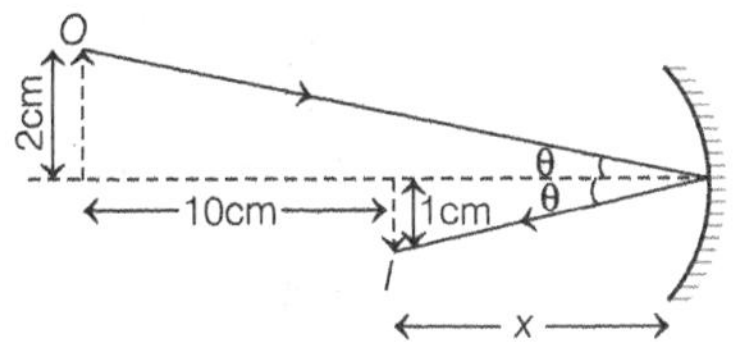

$$\tan\theta = \frac{2}{10+x} = \frac{1}{x} \Rightarrow x = 10 \text{ cm}$$

Distance of object from the pole

$$= 10 + x = 20 \text{ cm}$$

Using mirror formula, $\frac{1}{v}+\frac{1}{u}=\frac{1}{f}$

$$\Rightarrow \frac{1}{-10}+\frac{1}{-20}=\frac{1}{f} \Rightarrow f = -\frac{20}{3}\text{ cm}$$

So, radius of curvature $= 2\left(\frac{20}{3}\right) = \frac{40}{3}$cm

Distance of centre of curvature from object

$$= 20 - \frac{40}{3} = \frac{20}{3}\text{ cm}$$

1.7 Velocity of Image in Spherical Mirror

1. (a) $\frac{1}{v}+\frac{1}{u}=\frac{1}{f}$

$$\Rightarrow \frac{1}{v}+\frac{1}{-60}=\frac{1}{-40} \Rightarrow v = -120 \text{ cm}$$

$$(v_{im})_x = -\frac{v^2}{u^2}(v_{om})_x$$

$$\Rightarrow v_i - v_m = -\frac{v^2}{u^2}(v_o - v_m)$$

$$\Rightarrow (v_i)_x - 0 = -\left(\frac{-120}{-60}\right)^2 (10-0)$$

$$\Rightarrow (v_i)_x = -40 \text{ cm/s}$$

= 40 cm/s, opposite to the velocity of object

(b) $(v_i)_y = -\frac{v}{u}(v_o)_y$

$$\Rightarrow (v_i)_y = -\frac{(-120)}{(-60)}(10) \Rightarrow (v_i)_y = -20 \text{ cm/s}$$

= 20 cm/s, opposite to the velocity of object

2. $\frac{1}{v}+\frac{1}{u}=\frac{1}{f}$

$$\Rightarrow \frac{1}{v}+\frac{1}{(-20)}=\frac{1}{(-15)} \Rightarrow v = -60 \text{ cm}$$

$$(v_{im})_x = -\frac{v^2}{u^2}(v_{om})_x \Rightarrow v_i - v_m = -\frac{v^2}{u^2}(v_o - v_m)$$

$$\Rightarrow v_i - (-5) = -\left(\frac{-60}{-20}\right)^2 [5-(-5)]$$

$$\Rightarrow v_i = -95 \text{ cm/s} = 95 \text{ cm/s towards left}$$

3. $\frac{1}{v}+\frac{1}{u}=\frac{1}{f} \Rightarrow \frac{1}{v}+\frac{1}{(-6)}=\frac{1}{-2} \Rightarrow v = -3$ m

Along X-axis,

$$(v_{im})_x = -\frac{v^2}{u^2}(v_{om})_x$$

$$\Rightarrow (v_i)_x - (v_m)_x = -\frac{v^2}{u^2}[(v_o)_x - (v_m)_x]$$

$$\Rightarrow (v_i)_x - 0 = -\left(\frac{-3}{-6}\right)^2 (10\cos 37°-0)$$

$$\Rightarrow (v_i)_x = 2 \text{ m/s}$$

Along Y-axis,

$$m = \frac{h_i}{h_o} = \frac{f}{f-u} \Rightarrow h_i = \frac{f h_o}{f-u}$$

$$\Rightarrow \frac{dh_i}{dt} = \left(\frac{f}{f-u}\right)\frac{dh_o}{dt} + fh_o\frac{-1}{(f-u)^2}\left(\frac{-du}{dt}\right)$$

$$\Rightarrow (v_i)_y = \left(\frac{f}{f-u}\right)(v_o)_y + \frac{fh_o}{(f-u)^2}(v_o)_x$$

$$= \left[\frac{-2}{-2-(-6)}\right](10\sin 37°) + \frac{(-2)(1)}{(-2-(-6))^2}(10\cos 37°)$$

$$= -4 \text{ m/s}$$

$$\therefore \quad \mathbf{v}_i = -2\hat{\mathbf{i}} - 4\hat{\mathbf{j}}$$

4. $\frac{1}{v}+\frac{1}{u}=\frac{1}{f}$

Differentiating both side w.r.t. t,

$$-\frac{1}{v^2}\frac{dv}{dt} - \frac{1}{u^2}\frac{du}{dt} = 0$$

$$\Rightarrow dv = -\left(\frac{v^2}{u^2}\right)du$$

$$\Rightarrow dv = -\left(\frac{f}{f-u}\right)^2 du = -\left[\frac{-10}{-10-(-60)}\right]^2 (1 \text{ mm})$$

$$= -\frac{1}{25}\text{ mm} = -0.04 \text{ mm}$$

So, the image will be shifted 0.04 mm away from the mirror.

1.8 Combination of Mirrors

1. (i) For first reflection on M_1,

$$\frac{1}{v}+\frac{1}{u}=\frac{1}{f}$$

$$\Rightarrow \frac{1}{v}+\frac{1}{(-15)}=\frac{1}{(-10)} \Rightarrow v = -30 \text{ cm}$$

For second reflection on M_2,

Object distance = 40 – 30 = 10 cm

So, image will be formed 10 cm behind the plane mirror.

For third reflection on M_1,

$$u = -(40+10) = -50 \text{ cm}$$

$$\frac{1}{v}+\frac{1}{u}=\frac{1}{f} \Rightarrow \frac{1}{v}+\frac{1}{(-50)}=\frac{1}{(-10)}$$

$$\Rightarrow v = -12.5 \text{ cm}$$

So, the image is 12.5 cm right of M_1.

(ii) For first reflection on M_1,

$$\frac{1}{v}+\frac{1}{u}=\frac{1}{f} \Rightarrow \frac{1}{v}+\frac{1}{(-15)}=\frac{1}{-10} \Rightarrow v=-30\text{ cm}$$

For second reflection on M_2,

Object is $30-25=5$ cm behind the plane mirror. So, its image will be 5 cm infront of the plane mirror.

For third reflection on M_1,

$$u=-(25-5)=-20\text{cm}$$

$$\frac{1}{v}+\frac{1}{u}=\frac{1}{f} \Rightarrow \frac{1}{v}+\frac{1}{-20}=\frac{1}{-10}$$

$$\Rightarrow \quad v=-20\text{ cm}$$

So, the image is 20 cm right of M_1.

(iii) For first reflection on M_1,

$$\frac{1}{v}+\frac{1}{u}=\frac{1}{f} \Rightarrow \frac{1}{v}+\frac{1}{-15}=\frac{1}{-10} \Rightarrow v=-30\text{ cm}$$

For second reflection on M_2,

$$u=30-25=+5$$

$$\frac{1}{v}+\frac{1}{u}=\frac{1}{f} \Rightarrow \frac{1}{v}+\frac{1}{5}=\frac{1}{10} \Rightarrow v=-10\text{ cm}$$

For third reflection on M_1,

$$u=-(25-10)=-15\text{ cm}$$

$$\frac{1}{v}+\frac{1}{u}=\frac{1}{f} \Rightarrow \frac{1}{v}+\frac{1}{(-15)}=\frac{1}{(-10)} \Rightarrow v=-30\text{ cm}$$

So, the image is 30 cm right of M_1.

2. For first reflection at concave mirror

$$u=-25\text{ cm},\ f=-20\text{ cm}$$

$$\frac{1}{v}+\frac{1}{u}=\frac{1}{f} \Rightarrow \frac{1}{v}+\frac{1}{-25}=\frac{1}{-20}$$

$$\Rightarrow \quad v=-100\text{ cm}$$

For second reflection at convex mirror,

$$u=+(100-50)=+50\text{cm},\ f=+15\text{ cm}$$

$$\frac{1}{v}+\frac{1}{u}=\frac{1}{f} \Rightarrow \frac{1}{v}+\frac{1}{50}=\frac{1}{15} \Rightarrow v=21.43\text{ cm}$$

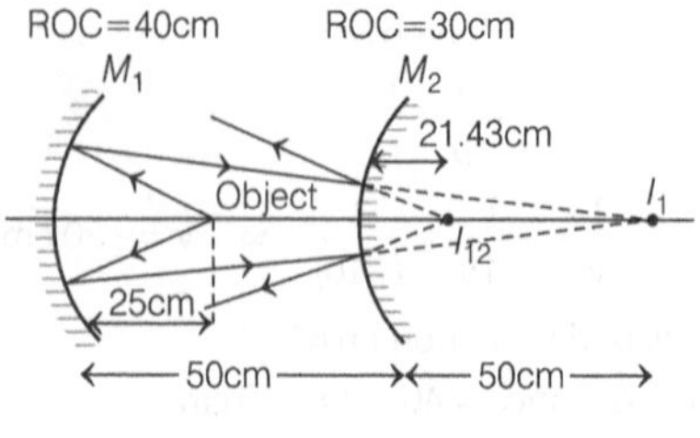

3.

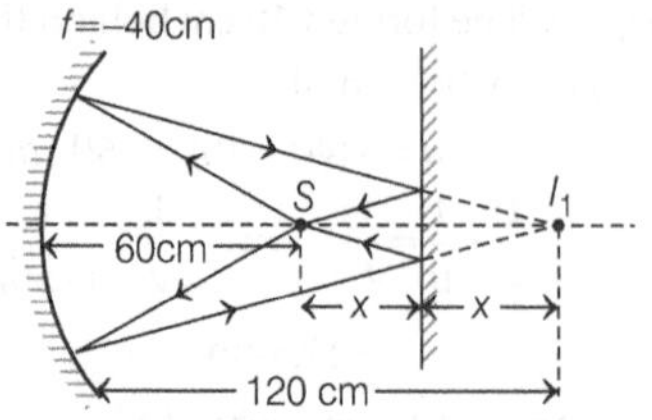

Let the distance between bulb and flat mirror be x.

For the first reflection on the concave mirror,

$$\frac{1}{v}+\frac{1}{u}=\frac{1}{f} \Rightarrow \frac{1}{v}+\frac{1}{(-60)}=\frac{1}{(-40)} \Rightarrow v=-120\text{ cm}$$

For second reflection on the flat mirror, image of I_1 should form on S.

$$\therefore \quad 60+x+x=120 \Rightarrow x=30\text{ cm}$$

4. **Case I** When the sources is at distance $2f$ from each mirror i.e., the source is at the centre of curvature of the mirrors, the image will be produced at the same point S.

So, $\quad d=2f+2f=4f$

Case-II When the source S is at distance f from each mirror, the rays from the source after reflecting from one mirror will become parallel and so these parallel rays after getting reflected from the other mirror will meet on the object itself.

So, $\quad d=f+f=2f$

5. **Case-I** For first reflection on the concave mirror,

$$\frac{1}{v}+\frac{1}{u}=\frac{1}{f} \Rightarrow \frac{1}{v}+\frac{1}{(-15)}=\frac{1}{-10} \Rightarrow v=-30\text{ cm}$$

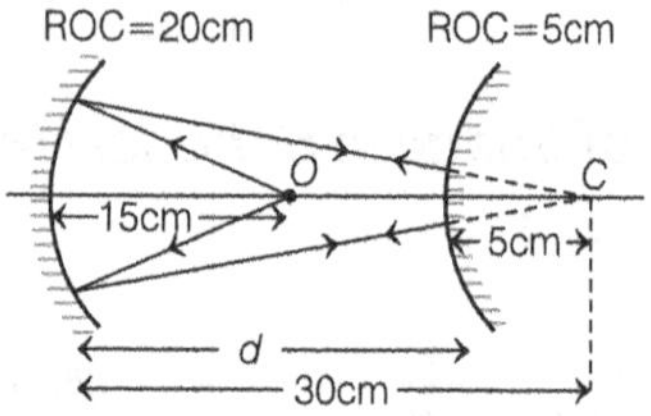

If the reflected rays from the concave mirror are normally incident on the convex mirror, the rays will retrace their path and final image will be formed on the object itself.

So, $\quad d+5=30 \Rightarrow d=25\text{ cm}$

Case II The other possibility is that the rays reflected from the concave mirror are incident on the pole of the convex mirror.

So, $\quad d=30\text{ cm}$

Level 2

Single Choice Correct Questions

1.

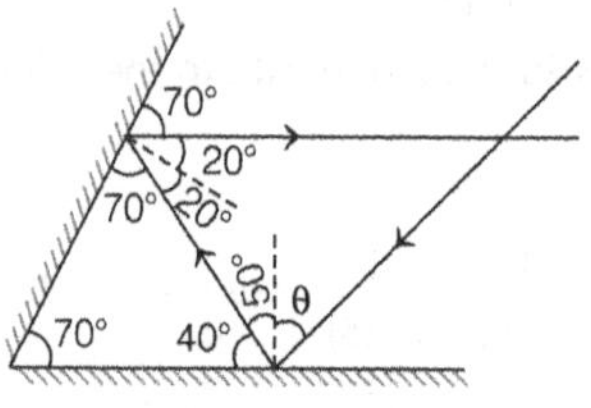

$\theta=50°$

2.

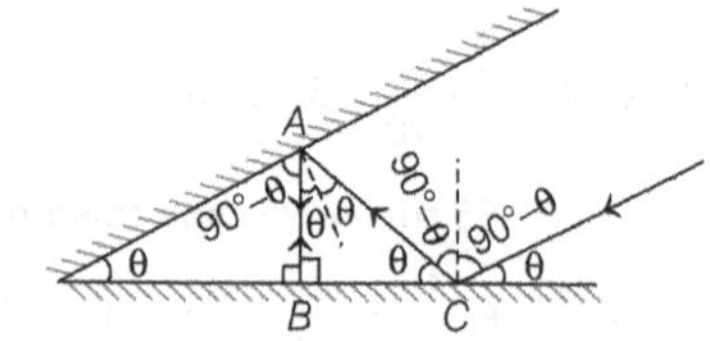

Light will retrace its path after third reflection if after second reflection it is incident normally on the horizontal mirror.

In $\Delta ABC, \theta + 2\theta + 90° = 180° \quad \Rightarrow \quad \theta = 30°$

3. $\delta = 180° - 2i$

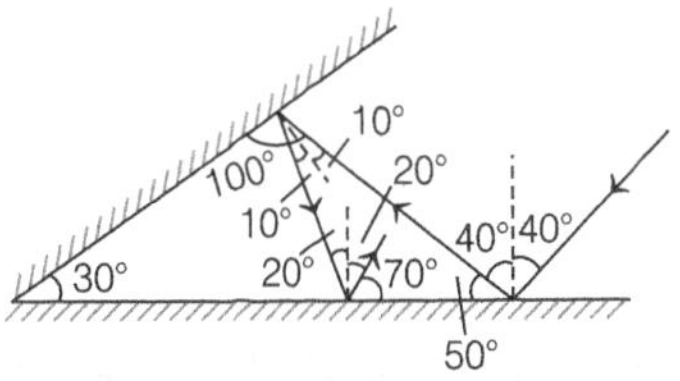

$\delta_1 = 180° - 2(40°) = 100°$ clockiwse

$\delta_2 = 180° - 2(10°) = 160°$ anti-clockwise

$\delta_3 = 180° - 2(20°) = 140°$ anti-clockwise

$\delta = \delta_1 + \delta_2 + \delta_3$

$= 200°$ anti-clockwise or $160°$ clockwise

4.

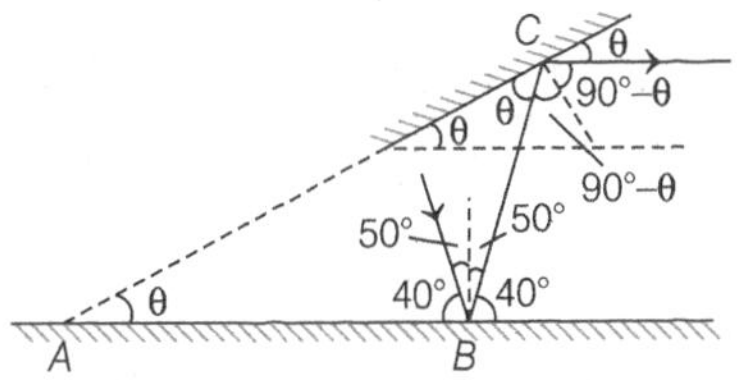

In $\Delta ABC, \theta + \theta + (50° + 50° + 40°) = 180°$

$\Rightarrow \theta = 20°$

So, M_2 should be rotated by $25° - 20° = 5°$ clockwise

5. Let, the distance covered by the ray after reflection from a surface be d.

From the figure, $\tan 30° = \frac{d}{0.2} \quad \Rightarrow \quad d = \frac{0.2}{\sqrt{3}}$ m

The ray will not undergo reflection after it emerges out of the arrangement i.e., after the ray covers $2\sqrt{3}$m.

Therefore, the maximum number of reflections that occur

$$= \frac{2\sqrt{3}}{\left(\frac{0.2}{\sqrt{3}}\right)} = 30$$

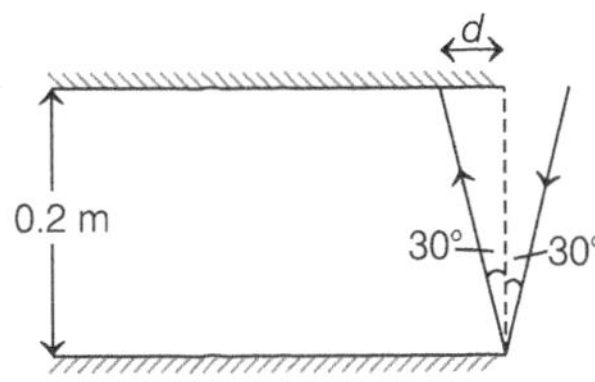

6. The hour hand is between 4 and 5. So, hour hand of image will be between 7 and 8.

Minute hand is between 25 and 26. So, minute hand of image will be between 34 and 35.

Second hand is at 37. So, second hand image will be at 23.

$\therefore$ Time shown by image = 07 : 34 : 23

7.

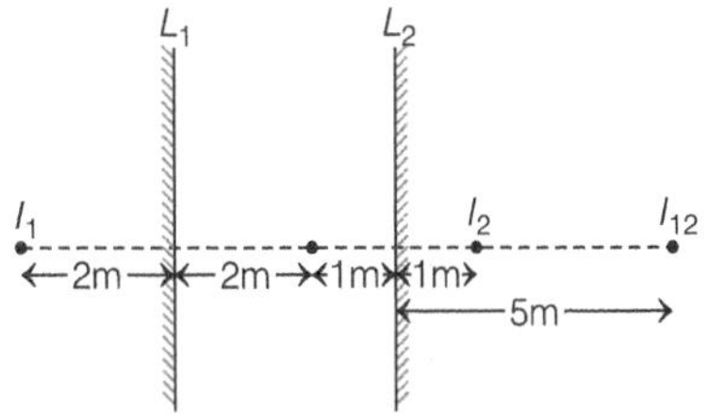

The second nearest image from L_2 is I_{12}.

Distance of I_{12} from the person $= 5 + 1 = 6$ m

8.

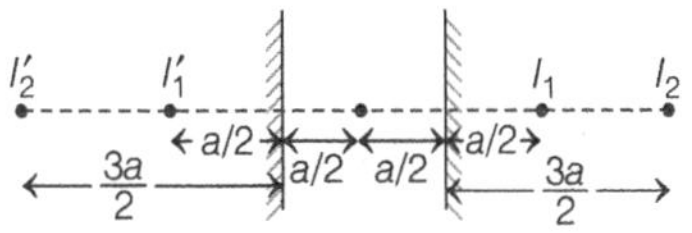

The distance between first order images (I_1 and I_1')

$$= \frac{a}{2} + \frac{a}{2} + a = 2a$$

The distance between second order images (I_2 and I_2')

$$= \frac{3a}{2} \times 2 + a = 4a$$

Similarly, the distance between nth order images.

$$= \frac{(2n-1)a}{2} \times 2 + a = 2na$$

9. Length of image he sees of himself $= DE$

ΔABC and ΔADE are similar triangles. So,

$$\frac{AB}{AD} = \frac{BC}{DE}$$

$$\Rightarrow \quad \frac{l}{2l} = \frac{0.3}{DE}$$

$$\Rightarrow \quad DE = 0.6 \text{ m}$$

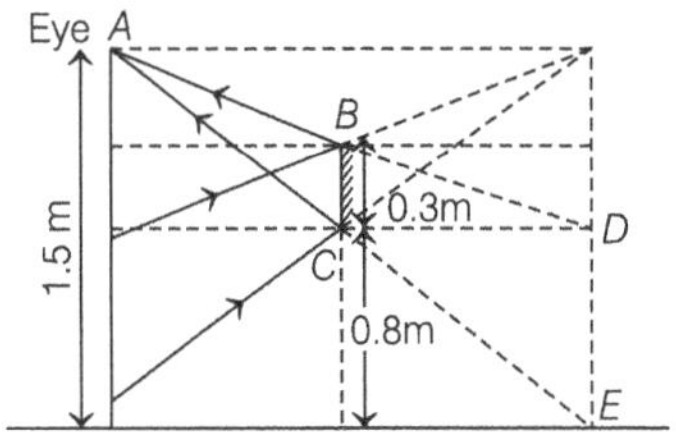

10. A and B lie in the field of view of both the mirrors. So, A and B will see image formed by each mirror. C lies in the field of view of only the inclined mirror. So, C can't see the image formed by the horizontal mirror.

11. A plane mirror forms virtual image of a real object and real image of a virtual object.

12. $\tan\alpha = \frac{L/2}{L} = \frac{y_1}{2L}$

$\Rightarrow \quad y_1 = L$

$\tan\beta = \frac{3L/2}{L} = \frac{y_2}{2L}$

$\Rightarrow \quad y_2 = 3L$

Distance travelled by M_1 for which M_2 can see M_1

$= 2y_2 = 6L$

Time for which M_2 can see M_1

$$= \frac{\text{Distance}}{\text{Speed}} = \frac{6L}{u}$$

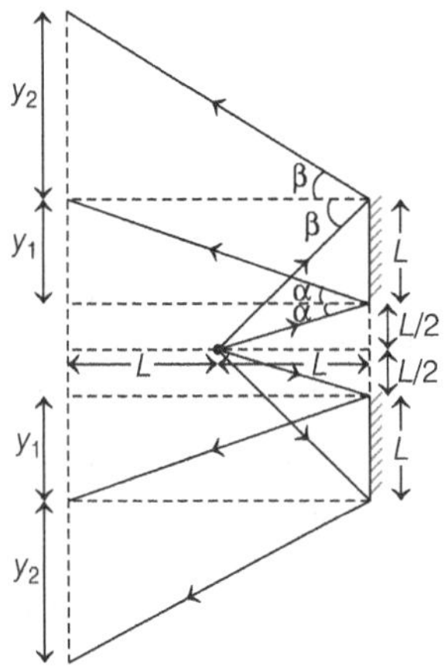

13.

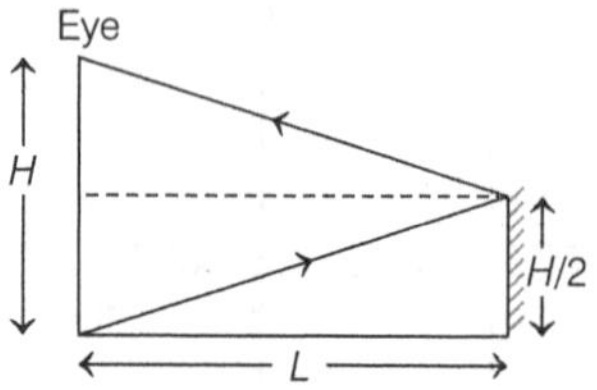

The boy can't see himself in the mirror.

14.

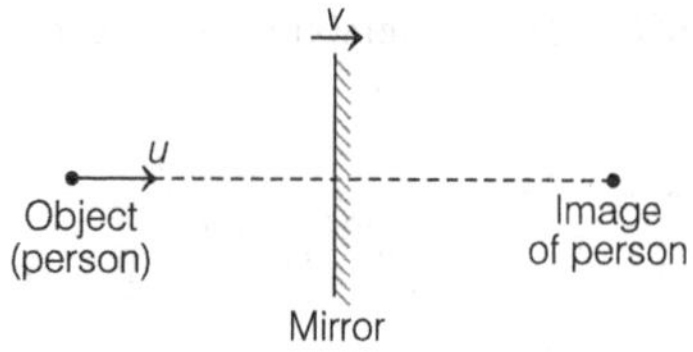

$$(v_{im})_x = -(v_{om})_x$$

$\Rightarrow \quad v_i - v_m = -(v_o - v_m) \Rightarrow v_i - v = -(u - v)$

$\Rightarrow \quad v_i = 2v - u$

$$v_{\text{object, image}} = v_o - v_i = u - (2v - u) = 2(u - v)$$

15. Velocity along normal changes but velocity perpendicular to normal remains unaffected.

$$(v_{im})_z = -(v_{om})_z$$

$\Rightarrow \quad (v_i)_z - (v_m)_z = -[(v_o)_z - (v_m)_z]$

$\Rightarrow \quad (v_i)_z - 8 = -(5 - 8)$

$\Rightarrow \quad (v_i)_z = 11$

$\therefore \quad \mathbf{v}_i = 3\hat{\mathbf{i}} + 4\hat{\mathbf{j}} + 11\hat{\mathbf{k}}$

16.

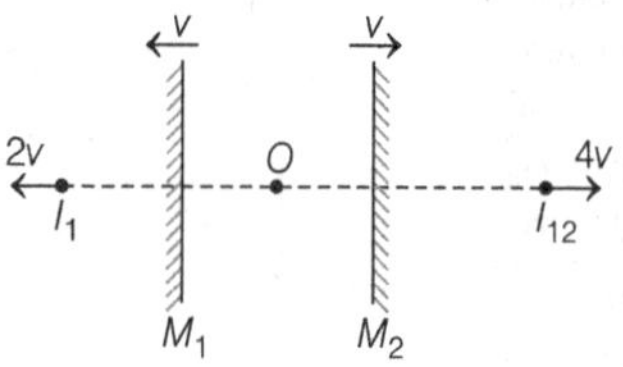

For the first reflection on M_1,

$$(v_{im})_x = -(v_{om})_x$$

$\Rightarrow \quad v_i - v_m = -(v_o - v_m)$

$\Rightarrow \quad v_i - (-v) = -(0 - (-v))$

$\Rightarrow \quad v_i = -2v$

For second reflection on M_2,

$$v_{im} = -v_{om}$$

$\Rightarrow \quad v_i - v_m = -(v_o - v_m)$

$\Rightarrow \quad v_i - v = -(-2v - v)$

$\Rightarrow \quad v_i = 4v$

Similarly, speed of image for 3rd reflection $= 6v$

and speed of image for nth reflection $= 2nv$

17. At any instant,

Velocity of particle $= 10\cos 60^\circ\,\hat{\mathbf{i}} + v_y\hat{\mathbf{j}}$

Velocity of image of particle $= -10\cos 60^\circ\,\hat{\mathbf{i}} + v_y\hat{\mathbf{j}}$

Velocity of approach of the particle and its image

$= \mathbf{v}_{\text{particle}} - \mathbf{v}_{\text{image}}$

$= (10\cos 60^\circ\,\hat{\mathbf{i}} + v_y\hat{\mathbf{j}}) - (-10\cos 60^\circ\,\hat{\mathbf{i}} + v_y\hat{\mathbf{j}})$

$= 10\hat{\mathbf{i}}$

18.

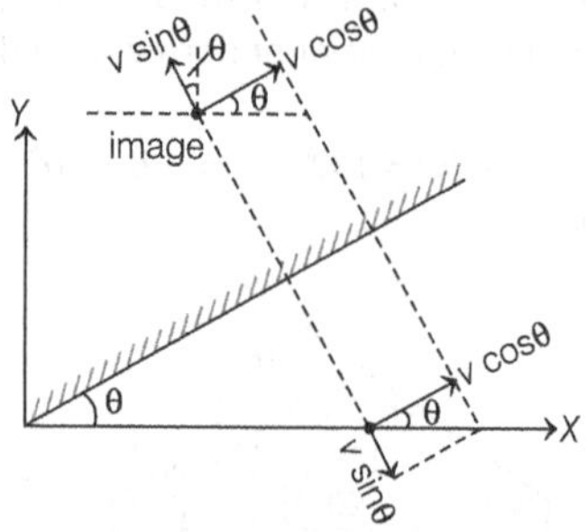

Component of velocity parallel to mirror remains unchanged while component of velocity perpendicular to mirror gets reversed.

$$\mathbf{v}_{\text{image}} = [(v\cos\theta)\cos\theta - (v\sin\theta)\sin\theta]\,\hat{\mathbf{i}}$$

$$+ [v\cos\theta\sin\theta + v\sin\theta\cos\theta]\hat{\mathbf{j}}$$

$$= v(\cos^2\theta - \sin^2\theta)\hat{\mathbf{i}} + v(2\sin\theta\cos\theta)\hat{\mathbf{j}}$$

$$= v\cos 2\theta\,\hat{\mathbf{i}} + v\sin 2\theta\,\hat{\mathbf{j}}$$

19. $\hat{\mathbf{r}} = \hat{\mathbf{i}} - 2(\hat{\mathbf{i}}\cdot\hat{\mathbf{n}})\hat{\mathbf{n}} = \left(\dfrac{\hat{\mathbf{i}}+\hat{\mathbf{j}}-\hat{\mathbf{k}}}{\sqrt{3}}\right) - 2\left[\left(\dfrac{\hat{\mathbf{i}}+\hat{\mathbf{j}}-\hat{\mathbf{k}}}{\sqrt{3}}\right)\cdot\left(\dfrac{\hat{\mathbf{i}}+\hat{\mathbf{j}}}{\sqrt{2}}\right)\right]\left(\dfrac{\hat{\mathbf{i}}+\hat{\mathbf{j}}}{\sqrt{2}}\right)$

$$= -\frac{1}{\sqrt{3}}(\hat{\mathbf{i}} + \hat{\mathbf{j}} + \hat{\mathbf{k}})$$

20. Let the initial distance of object from mirror be x

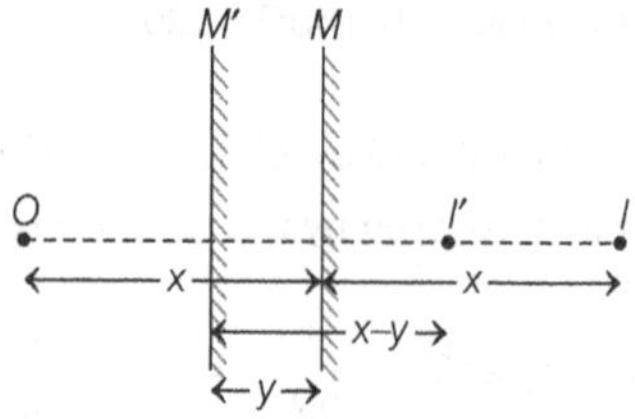

Lets displace the mirror by a distance y towards the object

New object distance $= x - y$

$\therefore$ New image distance $= x - y$

Shift of image $= (x + y) - (x - y) = 2y$

Therefore, if amplitude of mirror is 2 cm, amplitude of image will be 4 cm.

21. $u = +0.2$ m, $v = -0.5$ m

$$\frac{1}{v} + \frac{1}{u} = \frac{1}{f} \Rightarrow \frac{1}{-0.5} + \frac{1}{0.2} = \frac{1}{f} \Rightarrow f = \frac{1}{3}\text{m}$$

$\therefore$ Radius of curvature $= 2f = \dfrac{2}{3}\text{m} = 66.67$ cm

22. $u = -20$ cm, $f = 10$ cm

$$\frac{1}{v} + \frac{1}{u} = \frac{1}{f} \Rightarrow \frac{1}{v} + \frac{1}{-20} = \frac{1}{10} \Rightarrow v = \frac{20}{3}\text{cm}$$

$$m = \frac{h_i}{h_o} = -\frac{v}{u}$$

$$\Rightarrow \quad \frac{h_i}{1} = -\frac{\left(\frac{20}{3}\right)}{-20} \Rightarrow h = \frac{1}{3}\text{ cm}$$

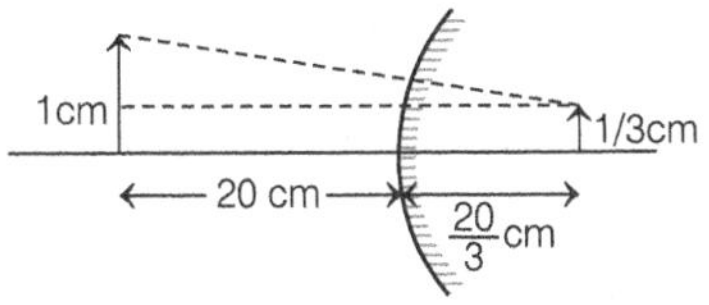

Distance between heads of the image and the object.

$$= \sqrt{\left(20 + \frac{20}{3}\right)^2 + \left(1 - \frac{1}{3}\right)^2} = \sqrt{\frac{6404}{9}} \text{ cm}$$

23. $m = \dfrac{f}{f-u}$

$\Rightarrow \qquad \pm 2 = \dfrac{-2}{-20-u}$

$\Rightarrow \qquad u = -10 \text{ cm} \quad \text{and} \quad u = -30 \text{ cm}$

Distance between the two positions of the object

$$= 30 - 10 = 20 \text{ cm}$$

24. $m = -\dfrac{v}{u}$

$\Rightarrow \qquad +3 = -\dfrac{v}{(-x)} \Rightarrow v = 3x$

$v + |u| = 80$

$\Rightarrow \qquad 3x + x = 80 \Rightarrow x = 20 \text{ cm}$

$\dfrac{1}{v} + \dfrac{1}{u} = \dfrac{1}{f}$

$\Rightarrow \qquad \dfrac{1}{60} + \dfrac{1}{(-20)} = \dfrac{1}{f} \Rightarrow f = -30 \text{ cm}$

25. $m = \dfrac{f}{f-u}$

When object is 25 cm from mirror,

$$m_1 = \frac{f}{f-(-25)} = \frac{f}{f+25}$$

When object is $25 + 15 = 40$ cm from mirror,

$$m_2 = \frac{f}{f-(-40)} = \frac{f}{f+40}$$

$m_1 = 4m_2$

$\Rightarrow \qquad \dfrac{f}{f+25} = 4\left(\dfrac{f}{f+40}\right)$

$\Rightarrow \qquad f = -20 \text{ cm}$

26.

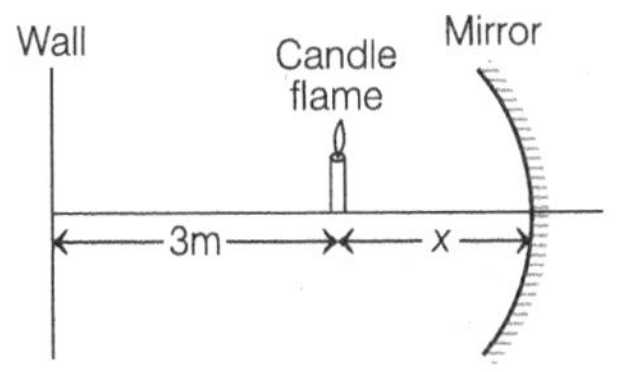

$m = \dfrac{h_i}{h_o} = -\dfrac{v}{u} \Rightarrow \dfrac{-9}{3} = -\left[\dfrac{-(x+3)}{-x}\right]$

$\Rightarrow \qquad x = 1.5 \text{ m}$

$\therefore$ Distance between the wall and the candle $= 3 + x$

$$= 3 + 1.5 = 4.5 \text{ m}$$

27. If image is real,

$$m = -\frac{v}{u} = -2 \Rightarrow v = 2u$$

$$\frac{1}{v} + \frac{1}{u} = \frac{1}{f} \Rightarrow \frac{1}{2u} + \frac{1}{u} = \frac{1}{f} \Rightarrow u = \frac{3f}{2}$$

$\therefore \qquad v = 2u = 3f$

Distance between object and its image $= v - u = \dfrac{3f}{2}$

If image is virtual,

$$m = -\frac{v}{u} = +2 \Rightarrow v = -2u$$

$$\frac{1}{v} + \frac{1}{u} = \frac{1}{f} \Rightarrow \frac{1}{(-2u)} + \frac{1}{u} = \frac{1}{f} \Rightarrow u = \frac{f}{2}$$

$\therefore \qquad v = -2u = -f$

Distance between object and its image $= |v - u| = \dfrac{3f}{2}$.

28. Image of end B will form at focus since it is at infinity. Image of A will be at A' which can be calculated using mirror formula.

$$\frac{1}{v} + \frac{1}{u} = \frac{1}{f} \Rightarrow \frac{1}{v} + \frac{1}{(-u)} = \frac{1}{(-f)}$$

$\Rightarrow \qquad v = \dfrac{fu}{f-u} = -\left(\dfrac{fu}{u-f}\right)$

$\therefore$ Image Length $= v - f = \dfrac{fu}{u-f} - f = \dfrac{f^2}{u-f}$

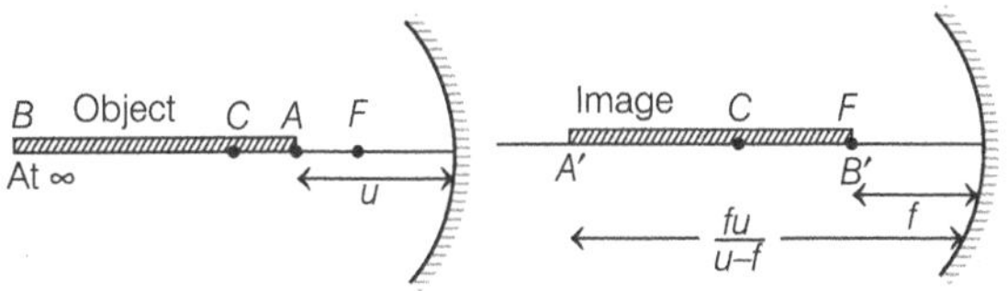

29. Using Newton's Mirror formula,

$$xy = f^2 \Rightarrow by = \left(\frac{a}{2}\right)^2 \Rightarrow y = \frac{a^2}{4b}$$

30. $\dfrac{1}{v} + \dfrac{1}{u} = \dfrac{1}{f} \Rightarrow \dfrac{1}{v} + \dfrac{1}{-15} = \dfrac{1}{-10}$

$\Rightarrow \qquad v = -30 \text{ cm}$

$$dv = -\frac{v^2}{u^2} du = -\left(\frac{-30}{-15}\right)^2 (2\text{mm}) = 8 \text{ mm}$$

31. For A, $\dfrac{1}{v} + \dfrac{1}{u} = \dfrac{1}{f}$

$\Rightarrow \qquad \dfrac{1}{v} + \dfrac{1}{-30} = \dfrac{1}{-15} \Rightarrow v = -30 \text{ cm}$

$\Rightarrow \qquad m = \dfrac{h_i}{h_o} = -\dfrac{v}{u} \Rightarrow \dfrac{h_i}{1} = -\left(\dfrac{-30}{-30}\right)$

$\Rightarrow \qquad h_i = -1 \text{ cm}$

For B, $\dfrac{1}{v} + \dfrac{1}{u} = \dfrac{1}{f} \Rightarrow \dfrac{1}{v} + \dfrac{1}{-20} = \dfrac{1}{-15}$

$\Rightarrow \qquad v = -60 \text{ cm}$

$$m = \frac{h_i}{h_o} = -\frac{v}{u} \Rightarrow \frac{h_i}{1} = -\left(\frac{-60}{-20}\right)$$

$$\Rightarrow \qquad h_i = -3 \text{ cm}$$

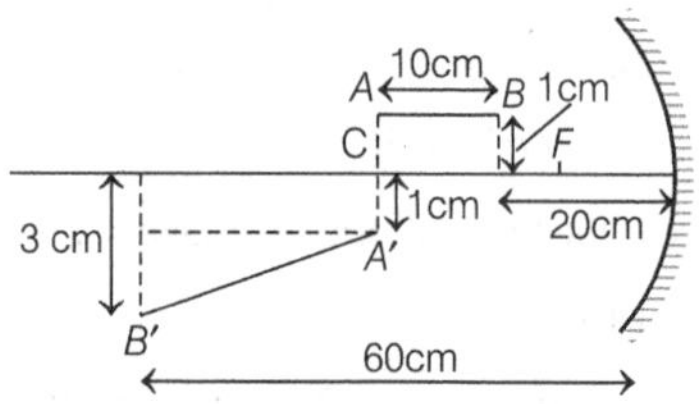

Length of image $= \sqrt{(30)^2 + (2)^2} = \sqrt{904}$ cm

32. For virtual erect image,
v is positive and u is negative.
$\therefore \frac{v}{f}$ is negative and $\frac{u}{f}$ is positive.

$$\frac{1}{v} + \frac{1}{u} = \frac{1}{f} \Rightarrow \frac{1}{\left(\frac{v}{f}\right)} + \frac{1}{\left(\frac{u}{f}\right)} = 1$$

$$\Rightarrow \frac{1}{y} + \frac{1}{x} = 1 \Rightarrow y = \frac{x}{x-1}$$

$$\lim_{x \to 0} y = 0, \qquad \lim_{x \to 1} y = \infty$$

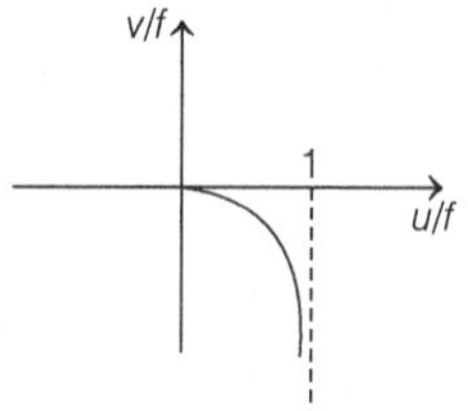

33. If the object is real, $u = -R$

$$\frac{1}{v} + \frac{1}{u} = \frac{1}{f} \Rightarrow \frac{1}{v} + \frac{1}{-R} = \frac{1}{\left(-\frac{R}{2}\right)} \Rightarrow v = -R$$

$$m = -\frac{v}{u} = -1$$

So, the image will be real, inverted and of same size.
If the object is virtual, $u = +R$

$$\frac{1}{v} + \frac{1}{u} = \frac{1}{f} \Rightarrow \frac{1}{v} + \frac{1}{(+R)} = \frac{1}{\left(-\frac{R}{2}\right)} \Rightarrow v = -\frac{R}{3}$$

$$m = -\frac{v}{u} = -\left(\frac{-\frac{R}{3}}{R}\right) = \frac{1}{3}$$

So, the image will be real, erect and diminished.
Therefore, we can say that image must be real.

34. Due to covering of lower half of the mirror, reflection will not take place from the lower half. So, amount of light getting reflected will decrease and therefore image will be less brighter.

35. Since, the image is real, enlarged and inverted, the object should be present between F and C and image formed beyond C. So, the concave mirror must be placed towards left of O.

36. $v_{\text{image}} = \left(-\frac{v^2}{u^2}\right) v_{\text{object}}$

So, the velocity of image and velocity of object are in opposite directions.
If the image is real, it will be formed infront of the mirror and moves away from the mirror.
If the image is virtual, it will be formed behind the mirror and moves towards the mirror.

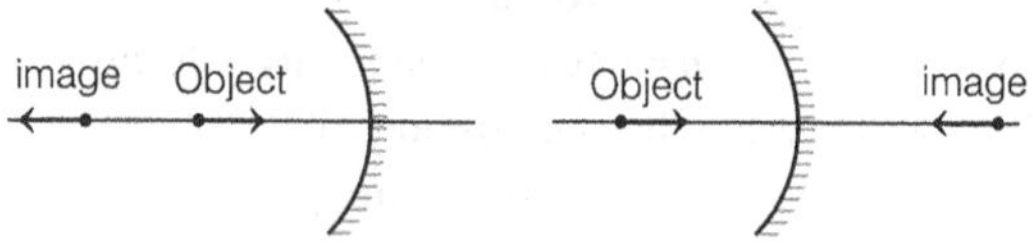

37. $u = -25$ cm, $f = -20$ cm

$$\frac{1}{v} + \frac{1}{u} = \frac{1}{f} \Rightarrow \frac{1}{v} + \frac{1}{-25} = \frac{1}{-20}$$

$$\Rightarrow \qquad v = -100 \text{ cm}$$

Along X-axis,

$$(v_i)_x = -\frac{v^2}{u^2}(v_o)_x = -\left(\frac{-100}{-25}\right)^2 (10) = -160 \text{ cm/s}$$

Along Y-axis,

$$m = \frac{f}{f-u} \Rightarrow \frac{dm}{dt} = -\frac{f}{(f-u)^2}\left(-\frac{du}{dt}\right) = -8$$

$$m = \frac{h_i}{h_o} \Rightarrow h_i = mh_o$$

$$\Rightarrow \qquad \frac{dh_i}{dt} = \frac{dm}{dt} h_o = (-8)(1) = -8 \text{ cm/s}$$

$$(v_i)_y = -\frac{dh_i}{dt} = -(-8) = 8 \text{ cm/s}$$

$$\therefore \qquad \mathbf{v}_i = -160\hat{\mathbf{i}} + 8\hat{\mathbf{j}}$$

38. For the first reflection,

$$\frac{1}{v} + \frac{1}{u} = \frac{1}{f} \Rightarrow \frac{1}{v} + \frac{1}{-7.5} = \frac{1}{-5} \Rightarrow v = -15 \text{ cm}$$

So, the first image is formed at the pole of the convex mirror.
For second reflection, $u = 0 \Rightarrow v = 0$
So, the second image will also be formed at the pole of the convex mirror.

39. For plane mirror,
Image distance = Object distance = 30 cm
So, the image is formed 30 cm behind the plane mirror or 10 cm behind the convex mirror.
For convex mirror,

$$\frac{1}{v} + \frac{1}{u} = \frac{1}{f} \Rightarrow \frac{1}{+10} + \frac{1}{-50} = \frac{1}{f}$$

$$\Rightarrow \qquad f = 12.5 \text{ cm}$$

$\therefore$ Radius of the convex mirror $= 2f = 25$ cm

40. Let the distance of the object from the concave mirror be x.

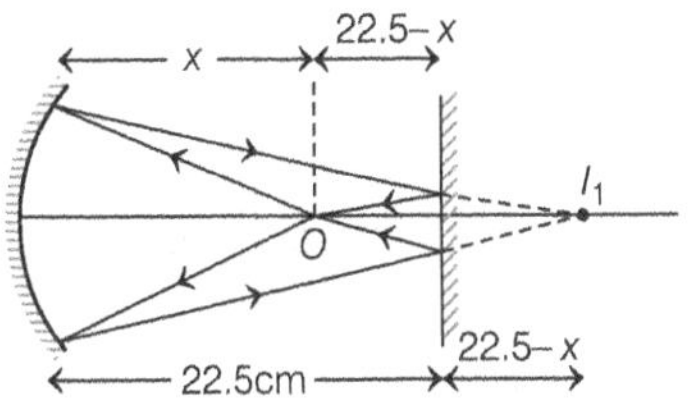

For concave mirror,

$$u = -x, v = -[22.5 + (22.5 - x)] = -(45 - x)$$

$$\frac{1}{v} + \frac{1}{u} = \frac{1}{f} \Rightarrow \frac{1}{-(45-x)} + \frac{1}{-x} = \frac{1}{-10}$$

$$\Rightarrow x = 15 \text{ cm}$$

41. For first reflection,

$$u = -30 \text{ cm}, f = -20 \text{ cm}$$

$$\frac{1}{v} + \frac{1}{u} = \frac{1}{f} \Rightarrow \frac{1}{v} + \frac{1}{-30} = \frac{1}{-20}$$

$$\Rightarrow v = -60 \text{ cm}$$

$$m_1 = -\frac{v}{u} = -\left(\frac{-60}{-30}\right) = -2$$

For 2nd reflection,

$$u = 60 - 40 = +20, f = +10 \text{ cm}.$$

$$\frac{1}{v} + \frac{1}{u} = \frac{1}{f} \Rightarrow \frac{1}{v} + \frac{1}{20} = \frac{1}{10}$$

$$\Rightarrow v = 20 \text{ cm}$$

$$m_2 = -\frac{v}{u} = -\left(\frac{+20}{+20}\right) = -1$$

$$\therefore m = m_1 m_2 = (-2)(-1) = +2$$

Numerical Value Questions

1. $\tan\alpha = \frac{0.5}{x} = \frac{1.3}{2}$

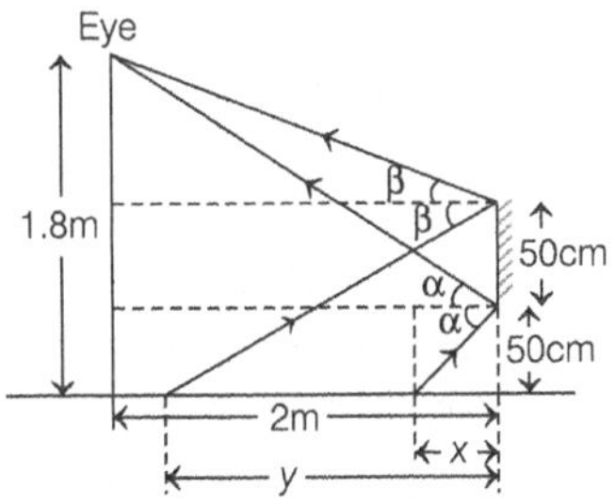

$$\Rightarrow x = \frac{10}{13} \text{ m}$$

$$\tan\beta = \frac{0.8}{2} = \frac{1}{y}$$

$$\Rightarrow y = \frac{5}{2} \text{ m}$$

Length of floor visible to person $= y - x$

$$= \frac{5}{2} - \frac{10}{13} = \frac{45}{26} \text{ m} = 1.73 \text{ m}$$

2.

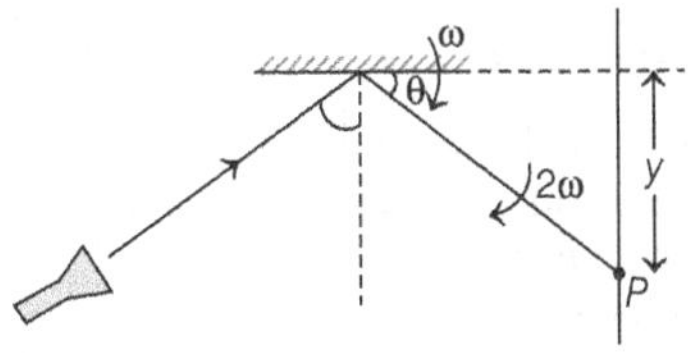

If the mirror rotates by an angle θ, the reflected rotates by an angle of 2θ. Therefore, if angular speed of mirror is ω, then angular speed of the reflected ray will be 2ω

$$\tan\theta = \frac{y}{3} \Rightarrow y = 3\tan\theta$$

$$\Rightarrow \frac{dy}{dt} = 3\sec^2\theta \frac{d\theta}{dt}$$

In 15 s, the reflected ray will rotate by an angle of 2° per second ×15 s = 30°.

So, $\theta = 30° + 30° = 60°$

$\therefore$ Speed of the spot $= \frac{dy}{dt} = (3\sec^2 60°)\, 2\left(\frac{\pi}{180}\right) = \frac{2\pi}{15}$ m/s

3. In y-direction, relative acceleration of the particle w.r.t. the mirror is zero since each has acceleration g downward.

$$s_{rel} = u_{rel}t + \frac{1}{2}a_{rel}t^2 \Rightarrow s_{rel} = (\sqrt{2}\sin 45°)(0.5) = 0.5 \text{ m}$$

So, w.r.t. the mirror, the particle is 0.5 m above it. Therefore, the image will be 0.5m below the mirror.

Separation between the particle and its image

$= 0.5 + 0.5 = 1$ m

4.

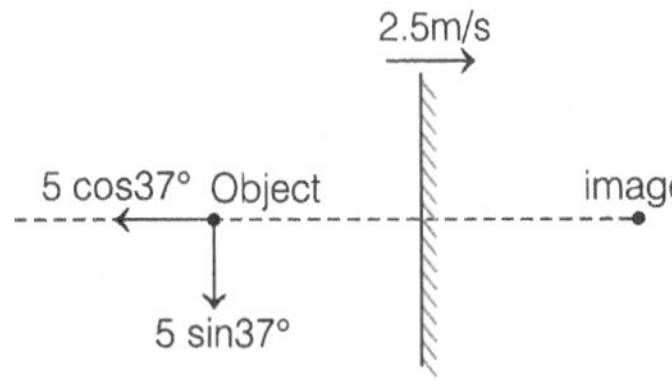

$$(v_{im})_x = -(v_{om})_x$$

$$\Rightarrow (v_i - v_m)_x = -(v_o - v_m)_x$$

$$\Rightarrow (v_i)_x - 2.5 = -(-5\cos 37° - 2.5)$$

$$\Rightarrow (v_i)_x = 9 \text{ m/s}$$

$$\Rightarrow (v_i)_y = (v_o)_y$$

$$\Rightarrow (v_i)_y = 5\sin 37° = 3 \text{ m/s}$$

$\therefore$ Velocity of image $= \sqrt{9^2 + 3^2} = \sqrt{90}$ m/s

5. At $t = 4$ s,

$$v_y = u_y + a_y t = 20 + (-10)(4) = -20 \text{ m/s}$$

$$s_y = u_y t + \frac{1}{2}a_y t^2 = 20(4) + \frac{1}{2}(-10)(4)^2 = 0$$

So, object distance $= u = -15$ m

$$\frac{1}{v} + \frac{1}{u} = \frac{1}{f} \Rightarrow \frac{1}{v} + \frac{1}{-15} = \frac{1}{-10}$$

$$\Rightarrow v = -30 \text{ m}$$

Velocity of image $= -\frac{v^2}{u^2}$ (Velocity of object)

$$= -\left(\frac{-30}{-15}\right)^2(-20) = 80 \text{ m/s}$$

6. $\frac{1}{v} + \frac{1}{u} = \frac{1}{f} \Rightarrow \frac{1}{v} + \frac{1}{(-45)} = \frac{1}{(-30)}$

$$\Rightarrow v = -90 \text{ cm}$$

Along the axis, $dv = -\frac{v^2}{u^2}du = -\left(\frac{-90}{-45}\right)^2(1) = -4$ mm

Along perpendicular to axis, $dv = -\frac{v}{u}du$

$$= -\left(\frac{-90}{-45}\right)(1) = -2 \text{ mm}$$

$\therefore$ Volume of the image $= 4 \times 2 \times 2 = 16 \text{ mm}^3$

7. $$m = \frac{f}{f-u} \Rightarrow -\frac{1}{4} = \frac{f}{f-u} \quad \text{...(i)}$$

Since, magnitude of magnification is increasing, the object should have been shifted towards the mirror

$$\therefore \quad -\frac{1}{2} = \frac{f}{f-(u+5)} \quad \text{...(ii)}$$

Solving Eqs. (i) and (ii), we get

$$f = -2.5 \text{ cm}$$

$\therefore$ Radius of curvature $= 2f = 5$ cm

8. Let, the distance of object from mirror be x.

$$m = -\frac{v}{u} \Rightarrow -2 = -\left[\frac{-(12+x)}{(-x)}\right]$$

$$\Rightarrow \quad x = 12 \text{ cm}$$

$$\frac{1}{v} + \frac{1}{u} = \frac{1}{f} \Rightarrow \frac{1}{(-24)} + \frac{1}{(-12)} = \frac{1}{f} \Rightarrow f = -8 \text{ cm}$$

Radius of curvature $= 2f = 16$ cm

9. $$m = \frac{f}{f-u} \Rightarrow -3 = \frac{f}{f-u} \quad \text{...(i)}$$

Since, the magnitude of magnification decreases, the object should be shifted away from the mirror

$$m = -2 = \frac{f}{f-(u-6)} \quad \text{...(ii)}$$

Solving Eqs. (i) and (ii) , we get

$$f = -36 \text{ cm}$$

10. Let the distance of object from the concave mirror be x cm.

For concave mirror, $m_1 = \frac{f}{f-u} = \frac{-36}{-36-(-x)}$

For convex mirror, $m_2 = \frac{f}{f-u} = \frac{36}{36-[-(100-x)]}$

$$|m_1| = |m_2|$$

$$\Rightarrow \quad \left|\frac{-36}{-36+x}\right| = \left|\frac{36}{136-x}\right| \Rightarrow x = 86 \text{ cm}$$

Level 3

Single Choice Correct Questions

1.

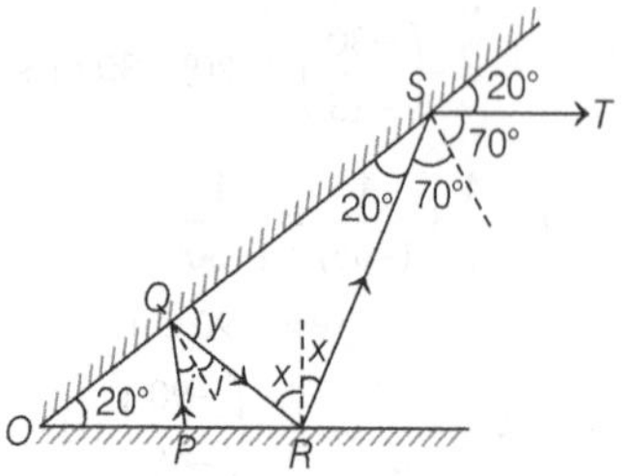

In ΔORS, $20° + (90° + x) + 20° = 180°$

$$\Rightarrow \quad x = 50°$$

In ΔQRS, $y + 2x + 20° = 180°$

$$\Rightarrow \quad y = 60°$$

$$\therefore \quad i = 90 - y = 90° - 60° = 30°$$

2. $\omega_{mirror} = 2\pi f = 2\pi\left(\frac{9}{\pi}\right) = 18$ rad/s

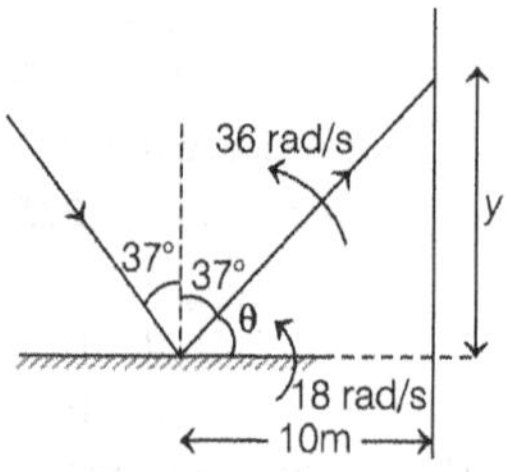

$\omega_{reflected\ ray} = 2\omega_{mirror} = 36$ rad/s

$$\tan\theta = \frac{y}{10}$$

$$\Rightarrow \quad y = 10\tan\theta$$

$$\Rightarrow \quad \frac{dy}{dt} = 10\sec^2\theta\frac{d\theta}{dt}$$

$\Rightarrow$ Speed of spot $= 10\sec^2 53°(36) = 1000$ m/s

3. Field of view of image is decided by the reflected rays. As we can see that the reflected rays from the extreme end points of mirror are at a height d above P and below P all points on PY'.

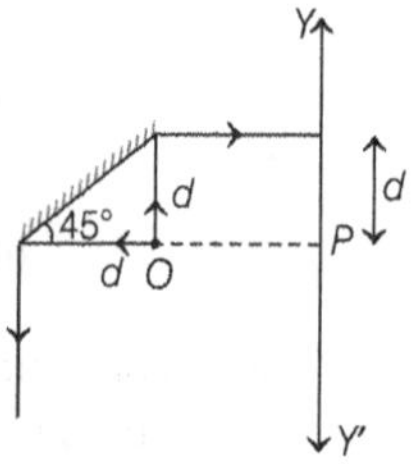

4.

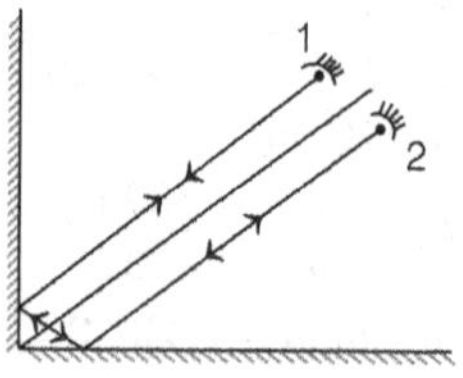

The eye 1 can see image of eye 2 only and eye 2 can see image of eye 1 only.

5. $\cos 45° = \frac{BC}{AC}$

$$\Rightarrow \frac{1}{\sqrt{2}} = \frac{2}{AC}$$

$\Rightarrow AC = 2\sqrt{2}$ m

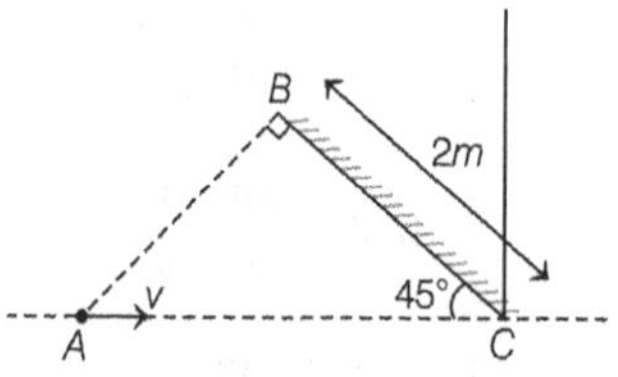

Length of field of view of image of insect is AC.

$$\therefore \quad \text{Time Span} = \frac{\text{Distance}}{\text{Speed}} = \frac{2\sqrt{2} \times 100}{4} = 50\sqrt{2} \text{ s}$$

6. For the child to see its full image, the length of mirror required is $\frac{H}{2}$. But, to see the full image of his father, the child requires an extra length x of the mirror as shown in figure. Also from the geometry it is clear that no extra mirror is required for the child to see the image of his father's feet.

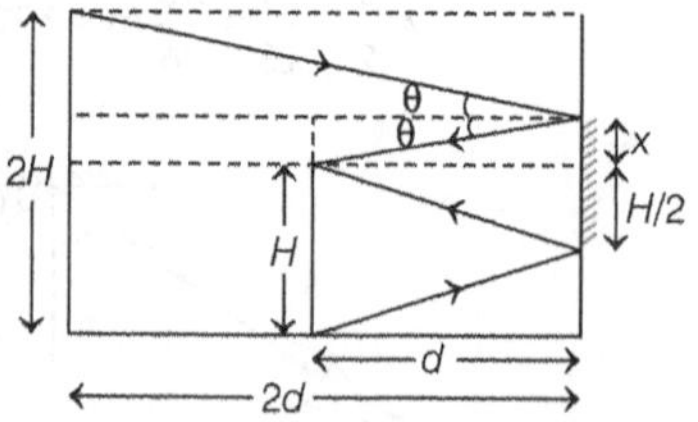

$$\tan\theta = \frac{x}{d} = \frac{H-x}{2d} \Rightarrow x = \frac{H}{3}$$

So, total length of mirror required

$$= x + \frac{H}{2} = \frac{H}{3} + \frac{H}{2} = \frac{5H}{6}$$

7.

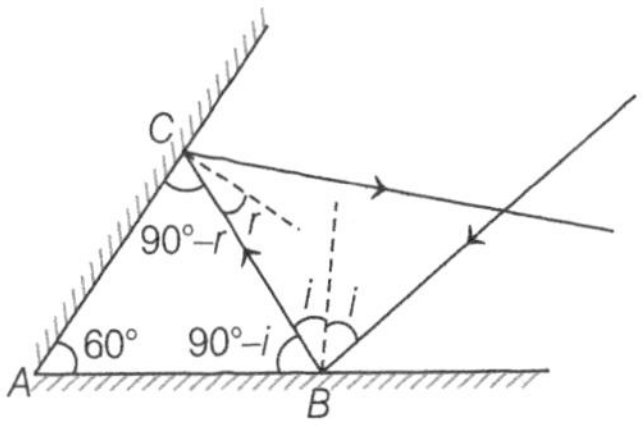

In $\Delta ABC, 60° + (90° - i) + (90° - r) = 180°$

$\Rightarrow \quad i + r = 60°$

$$\delta = \delta_1 + \delta_2 = (180° - 2i) + (180° - 2r) = 360° - 2(i + r)$$
$$= 360° - 2(60°) = 240°$$

So, deviation after two reflections is constant.

8.

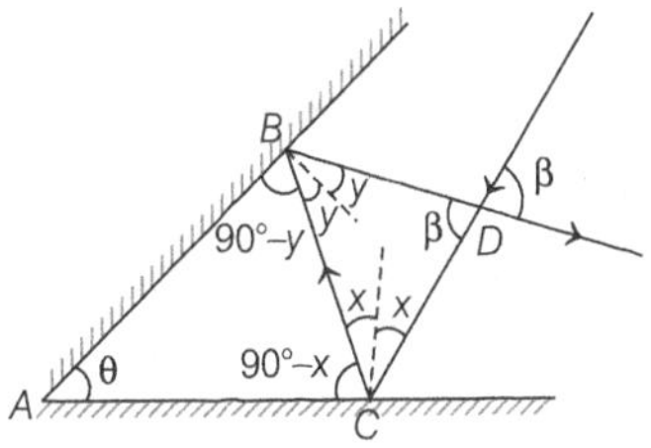

In $\Delta ABC, \theta + (90° - x) + (90° - y) = 180°$

$\Rightarrow \quad x + y = \theta$

In $\Delta BCD, 2x + 2y + \beta = 180°$

$\Rightarrow \quad \beta = 180° - 2(x + y) \Rightarrow \beta = 180° - 2\theta$

$$\therefore \quad \frac{d\beta}{dt} = -2\frac{d\theta}{dt} = -2\,(1°/s) = -2°/s$$

9.

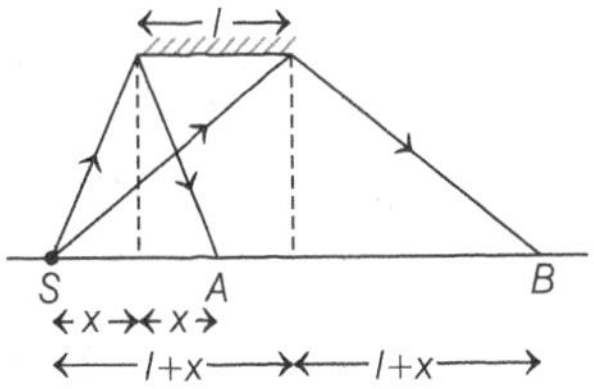

Length of spot $AB = 2(l + x) - 2x = 2l$

Velocity of spot $= \frac{d}{dt}(2x) = 2\frac{dx}{dt} = 2v$

10.

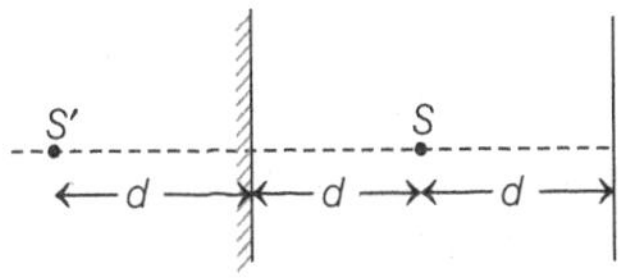

Intensity due to a point source of light $= \frac{P}{4\pi r^2}$

$$\therefore \quad I_o = \frac{P}{4\pi d^2}$$

After introduction of mirror,

$$I = I_1 + I_2 = \frac{P}{4\pi d^2} + \frac{P}{4\pi (3d)^2} = I_o + \frac{I_o}{9} = \frac{10 I_o}{9}$$

11.

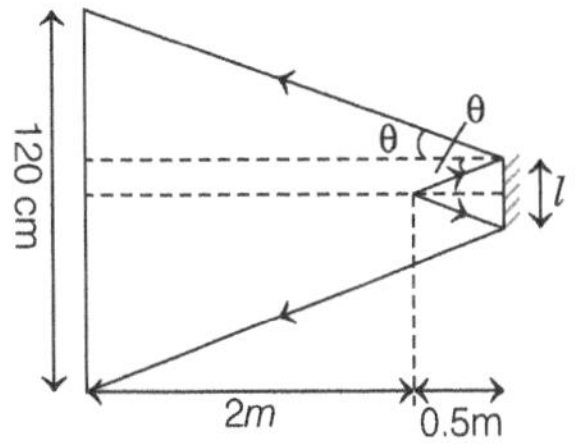

$$\tan\theta = \frac{60 - \frac{l}{2}}{2.5} = \frac{\frac{l}{2}}{0.5} \Rightarrow l = \frac{120}{6}\text{ cm} = 20\text{ cm}$$

Similarly, we can find width of mirror

Width, $w = \frac{45}{6} = 7.5$ cm

12. Let, velocity of the insect along the diagonal be v.

In adjacent mirrors,

$$v_{\text{image, insect}} = 20\text{ cm/s}$$
$$\Rightarrow \quad 2v\cos 45° = 20$$
$$\Rightarrow \quad v = 10\sqrt{2}\text{ cm/s}$$

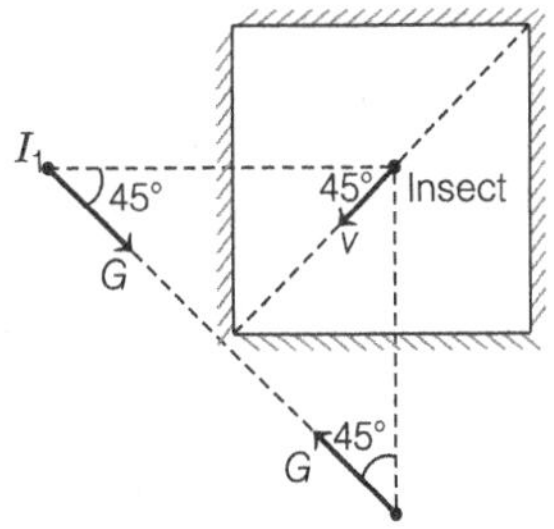

$\therefore$ Velocity of image in the roof $= v = 10\sqrt{2}$ cm/s

13. Acceleration of left side blocks

$$= \frac{\text{Net pulling force}}{\text{Total mass}} = \frac{3mg}{3m + m} = \frac{3g}{4}$$

Acceleration of right side blocks $= \frac{2mg}{2m + m} = \frac{2g}{3}$

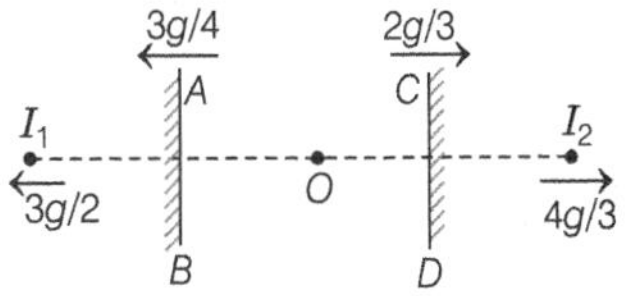

Acceleration of image $I_1 = 2\left(\frac{3g}{4}\right) = \frac{3g}{2}$

Acceleration of image $I_2 = 2\left(\frac{2g}{3}\right) = \frac{4g}{3}$

Relative acceleration of I_1 w. r. t. I_2

$$= \frac{3g}{2} - \left(-\frac{4g}{3}\right) = \frac{17g}{6}$$

14. For B, $(v_{im})_x = -(v_{om})_x$

$\Rightarrow \quad v_i - v_m = -(v_o - v_m)$

$\Rightarrow \quad (v_i)_x - (-2) = -[-5-(-2)] \quad \Rightarrow \quad (v_i)_x = 1 \text{ cm/s}$

For A, $\quad (v_{im})_x = -(v_{om})_x$

$\Rightarrow \quad v_i - v_m = -(v_o - v_m)$

$\Rightarrow \quad (v_i)_x - (-2) = -[10\sqrt{2}\cos 45° - (-2)]$

$\Rightarrow \quad (v_i)_x = -14 \text{ cm/s}$

$(v_i)_y = (v_o)_y \quad \Rightarrow \quad (v_i)_y = 10\sqrt{2}\sin 45° = 10 \text{ cm/s}$

Magnitude of relative velocity of image of B w. r. t. image of $A = \sqrt{[1-(-14)]^2 + (10)^2} = \sqrt{325}$ cm/s

15.

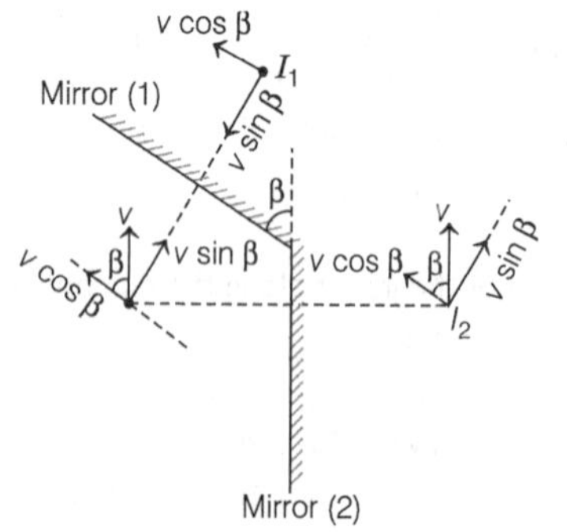

Relative velocity of I_1 w.r.t. $I_2 = 2v\sin\beta$

16. Speed of image w.r.t. object will be minimum when velocity of the object is parallel to the mirror, i.e. velocity of object makes an angle of 37° w.r.t. horizontal.

$$\tan\phi = \frac{u\sin\theta - gt}{u\cos\theta} \quad \Rightarrow \quad \tan 37° = \frac{25\sin 53° - 10t}{25\cos 53°}$$

$$\Rightarrow \quad t = \frac{7}{8} \text{ s}$$

17.

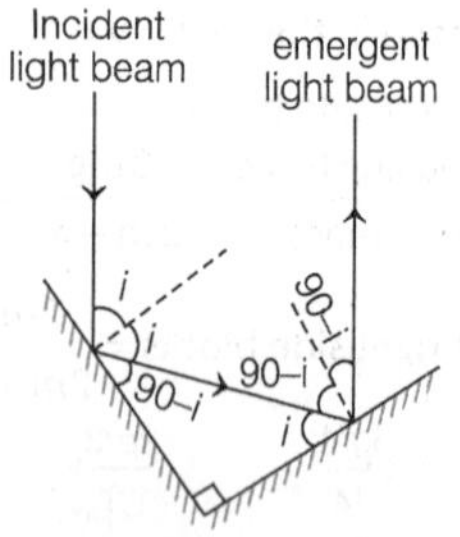

Emergent light beam is parallel to the incident light beam irrespective of the angle of incidence.

18. Maximum speed of insect $= A\omega = A\sqrt{\dfrac{k}{m}}$

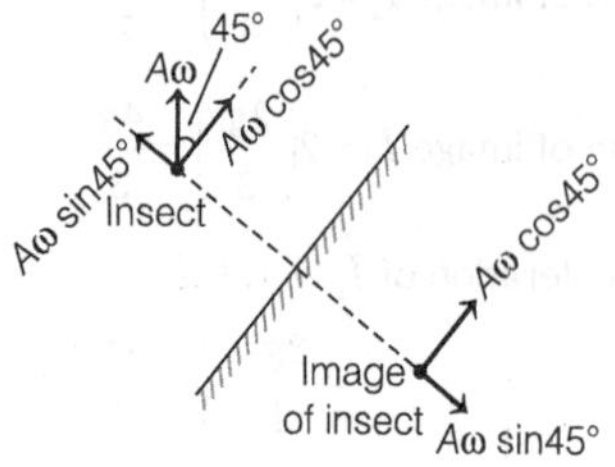

Maximum speed of insect relative to its image

$$= 2A\omega\sin 45° = \sqrt{2}\,A\omega = \sqrt{2}\,A\sqrt{\frac{k}{m}}$$

19.

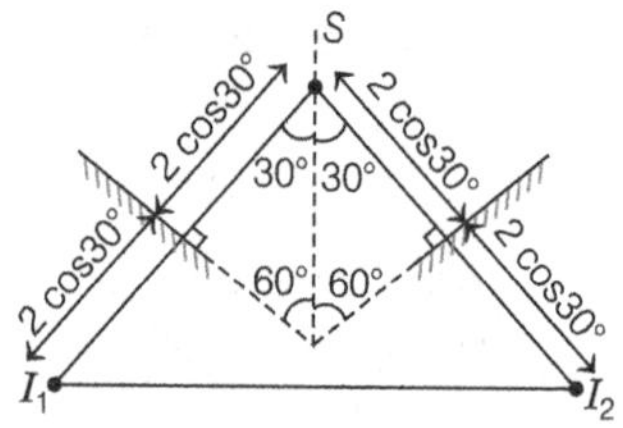

ΔSI_1I_2 is an equilateral triangle of side

$2(2\cos 30°) = 2\sqrt{3}$ m

Area of $\Delta SI_1I_2 = \dfrac{\sqrt{3}}{4}(2\sqrt{3})^2 = 3\sqrt{3}\text{ m}^2$

20. Unit vector along the incident ray, $\mathbf{I} = \hat{\mathbf{i}}$

Unit vector along the normal, $\hat{\mathbf{N}}$

$$= \frac{(2-0)\hat{\mathbf{i}} + (2-0)\hat{\mathbf{j}} + (0-(-1))\hat{\mathbf{k}}}{\sqrt{2^2+2^2+1^2}} = \frac{2\hat{\mathbf{i}} + 2\hat{\mathbf{j}} + \hat{\mathbf{k}}}{3}$$

$\hat{\mathbf{r}}$ = unit vector along the reflected ray

$\hat{\mathbf{r}} = \hat{\mathbf{i}} - 2(\hat{\mathbf{i}}\cdot\hat{\mathbf{n}})\hat{\mathbf{n}}$

$$= \hat{\mathbf{i}} - 2\left(\hat{\mathbf{i}}\cdot\left(\frac{2\hat{\mathbf{i}} + 2\hat{\mathbf{j}} + \hat{\mathbf{k}}}{3}\right)\right)\left(\frac{2\hat{\mathbf{i}} + 2\hat{\mathbf{j}} + \hat{\mathbf{k}}}{3}\right) = \frac{1}{9}\hat{\mathbf{i}} - \frac{8}{9}\hat{\mathbf{j}} - \frac{4}{9}\hat{\mathbf{k}}$$

So, $x = \dfrac{1}{9}, y = -\dfrac{8}{9}$ and $z = -\dfrac{4}{9}$

$\therefore \quad \dfrac{yz}{x^2} = 32$

21. General equation of parabola, $y^2 = 4ax$ where a is the focal length.

$$y^2 = \left(\frac{1}{2b}\right)x \quad \Rightarrow \quad 4a = \frac{1}{2b} \quad \Rightarrow \quad a = \frac{1}{8b}$$

22. $\dfrac{1}{v} + \dfrac{1}{u} = \dfrac{1}{f} \quad \Rightarrow \quad \dfrac{1}{v} + \dfrac{1}{-15} = \dfrac{1}{-10} \quad \Rightarrow \quad v = -30$ cm

Longitudinal magnification $= \dfrac{dv}{du} = -\dfrac{v^2}{u^2}$

$$\Rightarrow \quad \frac{dv}{(1\text{ mm})} = -\left(\frac{-30}{-15}\right)^2 \quad \Rightarrow \quad dv = -4\text{ mm}$$

So, length of images of AD and BC will be 4 mm each.

Transverse magnification $= -\dfrac{v}{u}$

$$\Rightarrow \quad \frac{h_i}{(1\text{ mm})} = -\frac{(-30)}{(-15)} \quad \Rightarrow \quad h_i = -2\text{ mm}$$

So, length of images of AB and CD will be 2mm each.

$\therefore$ Perimeter of image $= 4 + 4 + 2 + 2 = 12$ mm

23. For convex mirror, $m = \dfrac{f}{f-u}$

$$\Rightarrow \quad +\frac{1}{4} = \frac{f}{f-u} \quad \Rightarrow \quad u = -3f$$

For concave mirror, $m = \frac{f}{f-u} = \frac{(-f)}{(-f)-(-3f)} = -\frac{1}{2}$

24. In ΔOAP, $\tan\left[2\left(\frac{\pi}{180}\right)\right] = \frac{\frac{\pi}{18}}{u}$

$\Rightarrow \quad 2\left(\frac{\pi}{180}\right) = \frac{\pi}{18u}$

$\Rightarrow \quad u = 5$ cm

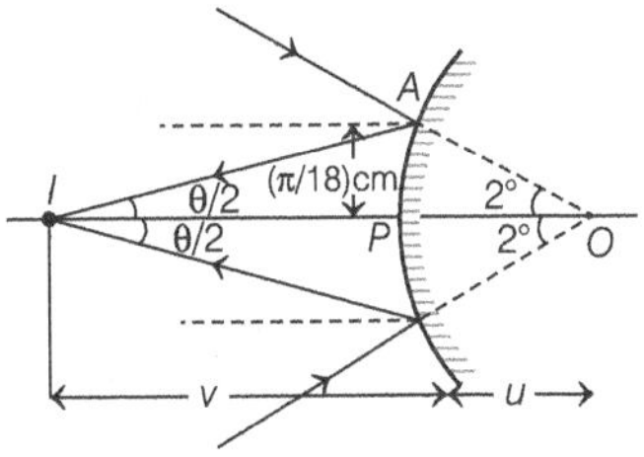

$\frac{1}{v} + \frac{1}{u} = \frac{1}{f}$

$\Rightarrow \quad \frac{1}{v} + \frac{1}{5} = \frac{1}{10}$

$\Rightarrow \quad v = -10$ cm

In ΔAPI, $\tan\left(\frac{\theta}{2}\right) = \frac{\frac{\pi}{18}}{v}$

$\Rightarrow \quad \frac{\theta}{2} = \frac{\pi}{18 \times 10} \quad \Rightarrow \quad \theta = \frac{\pi}{90}$ rad

$\Rightarrow \quad \theta = \frac{\pi}{90} \times \frac{180}{\pi} = 2°$

25. $\sin i = \frac{AP}{AC}$

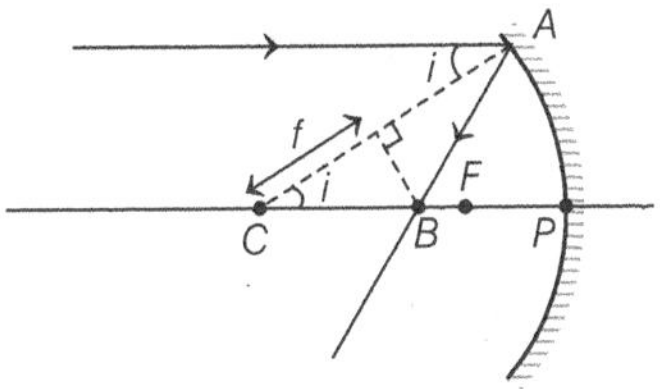

$\Rightarrow \quad \sin i = \frac{f}{2f}$

$\Rightarrow \quad i = 30°$

$BC = f \sec i = \frac{2f}{\sqrt{3}}$

$\frac{BC}{CF} = \frac{2f/\sqrt{3}}{f} = \frac{2}{\sqrt{3}}$

26. $\frac{1}{v} + \frac{1}{u} = \frac{1}{f}$

1. Equation shows that when $u = f$, $v = \infty$
2. As x approaches ∞, $|v|$ tends to be f.

Both the conditions are depicted by option (a).

27.

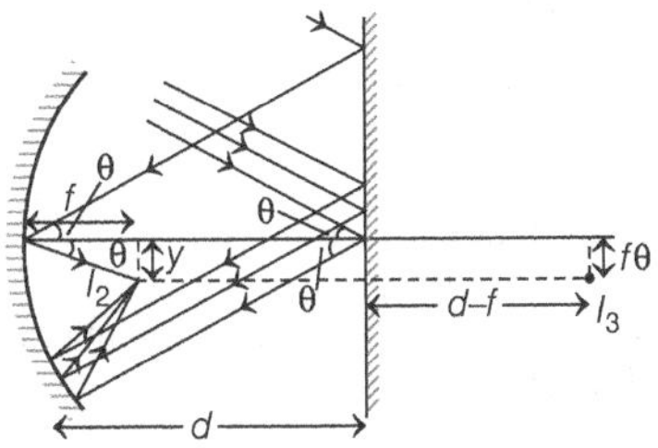

After reflection from concave mirror, image will formed in its focal plane.

$\tan\theta \approx \theta = \frac{y}{f} \quad \Rightarrow \quad y = f\theta$

After third reflection, coordinates of image

$\equiv (x = d - f, y = -f\theta)$

28. For concave mirror,

$u = -3f, v = -[d - (3f - d)]$

$= -(2d - 3f)$

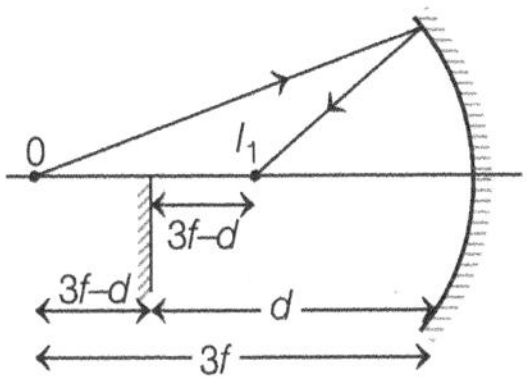

$\frac{1}{v} + \frac{1}{u} = \frac{1}{f}$

$\Rightarrow \quad \frac{1}{-(2d-3f)} + \frac{1}{(-3f)} = \frac{1}{-f}$

$\Rightarrow \quad d = \frac{9f}{4}$

29. Amplitude of motion,

$\frac{mg}{k} = \frac{0.1 \times 10}{20} = 0.05 \text{ m} = 5 \text{ cm}$

When the body is at the upper extreme position (spring unelongated),

$u = -(20 + 5) = -25$ cm

$\frac{1}{v} + \frac{1}{u} = \frac{1}{f} \quad \Rightarrow \quad \frac{1}{v} + \frac{1}{(-25)} = \frac{1}{10}$

$\Rightarrow \quad v = \frac{50}{7}$ cm

When, the body is at the lower extreme position,

$u = -(20 - 5) = -15$ cm

$\frac{1}{v} + \frac{1}{u} = \frac{1}{f} \quad \Rightarrow \quad \frac{1}{v} + \frac{1}{(-15)} = \frac{1}{10}$

$\Rightarrow \quad v = 6$ cm

The length over which image vibrates $= \frac{50}{7} - 6$

$= \frac{8}{7}$ cm $= 1.14$ cm

30. Let the length of object AB be $2a$,

$v_i = -\left(\frac{f}{f-u}\right)^2 v_o,$

$u_A = -(L + a),$

$u_B = -(L - a)$

Velocity of the image of point A,

$v_A = -\left(\frac{f}{f - (-(L+a))}\right)^2 v = -4v \quad$ ...(i)

Velocity of the image of point B,

$v_B = -\left(\frac{f}{f - [-(L-a)]}\right)^2 v = -4v \quad$ ...(ii)

From Eqs. (i) and (ii), we get

$\left(\frac{1}{f+L+a}\right)^2 = \left(\frac{1}{f+L-a}\right)^2$

$\Rightarrow \quad \left|\frac{1}{f+L+a}\right| = \left|\frac{1}{f+L-a}\right|$

If $f + L + a = f + L - a$

$\Rightarrow a = 0$; not possible

If $\quad f + L + a = -(f + L - a)$

$\Rightarrow \quad f = -L$

Substituting $f = -L$ in Eq. (i),

$$-\left(\frac{-L}{-L+L+a}\right)^2 v = -4v$$

$\Rightarrow \quad 2a = L$

So, length of object $AB = 2a = L$

31. At $t = 3, R = \left|\frac{6}{3^2 - 5(3) + 6}\right| = \infty$

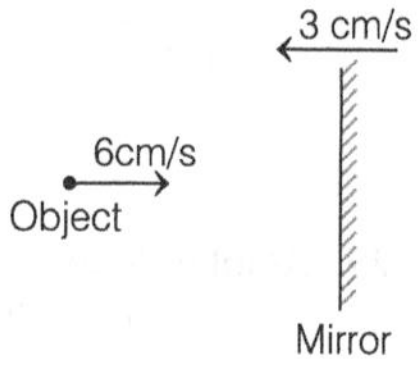

So, the concave mirror will act as a plane mirror.

At $t = 3$, velocity of object $= 2(3) = 6$ cm/s

$$v_{im} = -v_{om}$$

$\Rightarrow \quad v_i - v_m = -(v_o - v_m)$

$\Rightarrow \quad v_i - (-3) = -[6 - (-3)]$

$\Rightarrow \quad v_i = -12$ cm/s

32. Along X-axis,

$$(v_{im})_x = -\left(\frac{f}{f-u}\right)^2 (v_{om})_x$$

$\Rightarrow \quad v_i - v_m = -\left(\frac{f}{f-u}\right)^2 (v_o - v_m)$

$\Rightarrow \quad (v_i)_x - 4 = -\left[\frac{-10}{-10-(-15)}\right]^2 (8-4)$

$\Rightarrow \quad (v_i)_x = -12$ cm/s

Along Y-axis,

$$(v_{im})_y = \left(\frac{f}{f-u}\right)(v_{om})_y$$

$\Rightarrow \quad v_i - v_m = \left(\frac{f}{f-u}\right)(v_o - v_m)$

$\Rightarrow \quad (v_i)_y - 2 = \left[\frac{-10}{-10-(-15)}\right](11-2)$

$\Rightarrow \quad (v_i)_y = -16$ cm/s

$\therefore \quad \mathbf{v} = -12\hat{\mathbf{i}} - 16\hat{\mathbf{j}}$

$$|\mathbf{v}| = \sqrt{(12)^2 + (16)^2} = 20 \text{ cm/s}$$

33. First image is formed by the concave mirror.

$$\frac{1}{v} + \frac{1}{u} = \frac{1}{f}$$

$\Rightarrow \quad \frac{1}{v} + \frac{1}{(-2R)} = \frac{1}{\left(-\frac{R}{2}\right)} \Rightarrow v = -\frac{2R}{3}$

Magnification, $m_1 = -\frac{v}{u} = -\frac{\left(-\frac{2R}{3}\right)}{(-2R)} = -\frac{1}{3}$

Size of image $= m_1 \times$ size of object

$\therefore$ Radius of first image $= \frac{1}{3} \times a = \frac{a}{3}$

Now, this first real image acts as an object for the convex lens.

$$u = -\left(2R - \frac{2R}{3}\right) = -\frac{4R}{3}$$

$\frac{1}{v} + \frac{1}{u} = \frac{1}{f} \quad \Rightarrow \quad \frac{1}{v} + \frac{1}{\left(-\frac{4R}{3}\right)} = \frac{1}{\left(\frac{R}{2}\right)}$

$\Rightarrow \quad v = \frac{4R}{11}$

$$m_2 = -\frac{v}{u} = -\frac{\left(\frac{4R}{11}\right)}{\left(-\frac{4R}{3}\right)} = \frac{3}{11}$$

Radius of second image $= m_2 \times$ Radius of first image

$$= \frac{3}{11}\left(\frac{a}{3}\right) = \frac{a}{11}$$

34. For first reflection on M_1,

$\frac{1}{v} + \frac{1}{u} = \frac{1}{f} \quad \Rightarrow \quad \frac{1}{v} + \frac{1}{(-15)} = \frac{1}{-10}$

$\Rightarrow \quad v = -30$ cm

This image will act as an object for mirror M_2.

$$u = +(30 - 20) = +10 \text{ cm}$$

$\frac{1}{v} + \frac{1}{u} = \frac{1}{f} \quad \Rightarrow \quad \frac{1}{v} + \frac{1}{10} = \frac{1}{-10}$

$\Rightarrow \quad v = -5$ cm

Magnification, $m = -\frac{v}{u} = -\frac{(-5)}{+10} = \frac{1}{2}$

Distance of final image from $AB = \frac{1}{2}(3) = 1.5$ cm

Multiple Choice (s) Correct Questions

1.

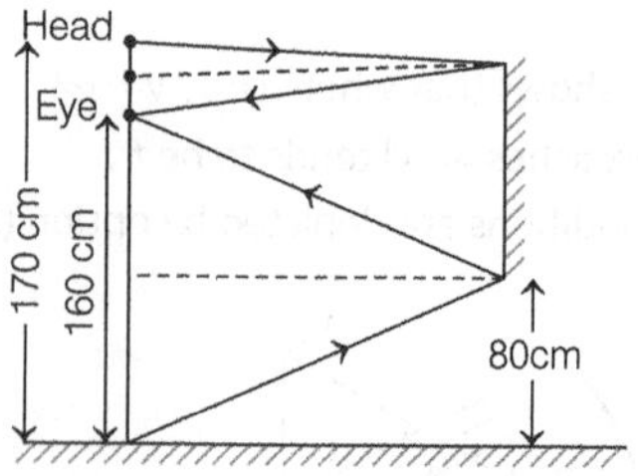

Minimum length of mirror required $= \frac{H}{2} = \frac{170}{2} = 85$ cm

To see image of his feet, bottom of the mirror should be at a height of 80 cm or less.

2.

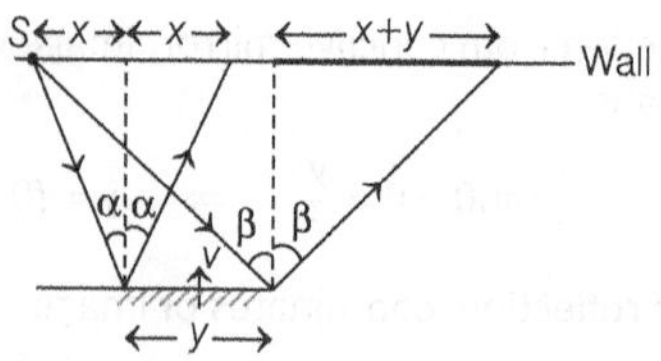

We can see from geometry that as the mirror moves towards the wall, the spot of light doesn't move on the wall.

Width of light spot $= 2(x + y) - 2x = 2y =$ constant

3.

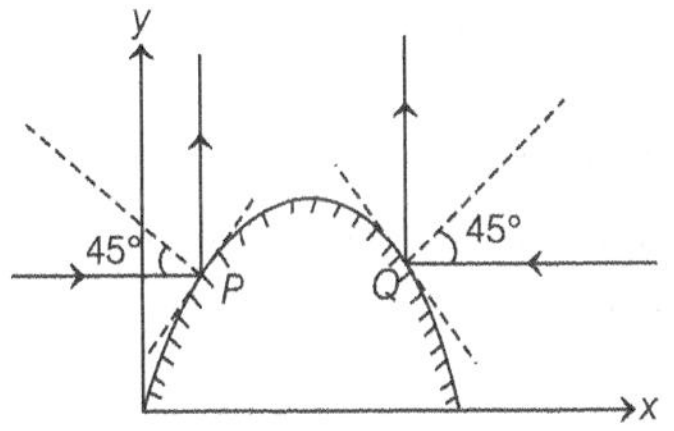

At P, tangent to the reflecting surface makes an angle of 45° with X-axis.

$$\frac{dy}{dx} = \frac{2L}{\pi}\left[\cos\left(\frac{\pi x}{L}\right)\right]\left(\frac{\pi}{L}\right) = \tan\left(\frac{\pi}{4}\right)$$

$$\Rightarrow \quad \cos\left(\frac{\pi x}{L}\right) = \frac{1}{2} \quad \Rightarrow \quad \frac{\pi x}{L} = \frac{\pi}{3}$$

$$\Rightarrow \quad x = \frac{L}{3}$$

At θ, tangent to the reflecting surface makes an angle of 135° with Y-axis.

$$\frac{dy}{dx} = \frac{2L}{\pi}\left[\cos\left(\frac{\pi x}{L}\right)\right]\left(\frac{\pi}{L}\right) = \tan\left(\frac{3\pi}{4}\right)$$

$$\Rightarrow \cos\left(\frac{\pi x}{L}\right) = -\frac{1}{2} \quad \Rightarrow \quad \frac{\pi x}{L} = \frac{2\pi}{3}$$

$$\Rightarrow \quad x = \frac{2L}{3}$$

4.

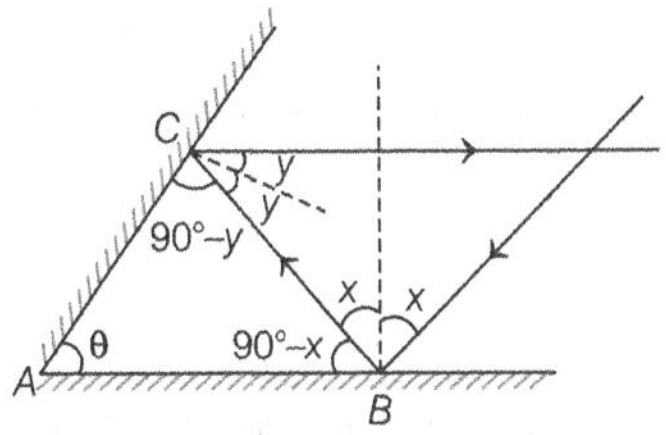

In $\Delta ABC, \theta + (90° - x) + (90° - y) = 180°$

$$\Rightarrow \quad x + y = \theta$$

$$\delta = \delta_1 + \delta_2 = (180° - 2x) + (180° - 2y) = 240°$$

$$\Rightarrow \quad 360° - 2(x + y) = 240°$$

$$\Rightarrow \quad 360° - 2\theta = 240°$$

$$\Rightarrow \quad \theta = 60°$$

Number of images

$$= \frac{360°}{\theta} - 1 = \frac{360°}{60°} - 1 = 5$$

Since, $\frac{360°}{\theta}$ is even integer, number of images will be 5 irrespective of the position of the object.

If angle of incidence on one mirror is 60°, the reflected ray strikes the other mirror normally. So, the ray will retrace its path.

5. Since, the image is enlarged, the mirror will be concave.

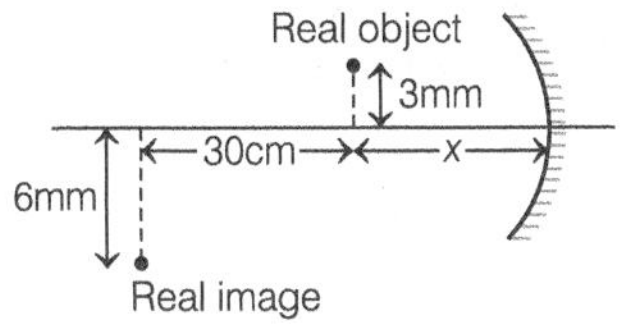

Magnification, $\quad m = \frac{h_i}{h_o} = -\frac{v}{u}$

$$\Rightarrow \quad \frac{-6}{3} = -\left[\frac{-(30 + x)}{-x}\right] \quad \Rightarrow \quad x = 30 \text{ cm}$$

$$\frac{1}{v} + \frac{1}{u} = \frac{1}{f} \quad \Rightarrow \quad \frac{1}{(-60)} + \frac{1}{(-30)} = \frac{1}{f}$$

$$\Rightarrow \quad f = -20 \text{ cm}$$

$\therefore$ Radius of curvature $= 2f = 40$ cm

6. $\frac{1}{v} + \frac{1}{u} = \frac{1}{f} \quad \Rightarrow \quad u = \frac{vf}{v - f}$

$$m = -\frac{v}{u} = -\frac{v}{\left(\frac{vf}{v-f}\right)} = 1 - \frac{v}{f}$$

$$m^2 = \left(1 - \frac{v}{f}\right)^2$$

So, the graph will be parabola.

For $v = 30$ cm, $m^2 = 0$

$$\Rightarrow \quad 0 = \left(1 - \frac{30}{f}\right)^2 \quad \Rightarrow \quad f = 30 \text{ cm}$$

$\therefore$ Radius of curvature $= 60$ cm

For $v = 0, m^2 = b$

$$\Rightarrow \quad b = (1 - 0) \quad \Rightarrow \quad b = 1$$

For $v = 15, m^2 = c$

$$\Rightarrow \quad c = \left(1 - \frac{15}{30}\right)^2 \quad \Rightarrow \quad c = \frac{1}{4}$$

For $v = 60, m^2 = a$

$$\Rightarrow \quad a = \left(1 - \frac{60}{30}\right)^2$$

$$\Rightarrow \quad a = 1$$

7. $v = \pm 48$ cm, $f = -24$ cm

$$\frac{1}{v} + \frac{1}{u} = \frac{1}{f} \quad \Rightarrow \quad \frac{1}{\pm 48} + \frac{1}{u} = \frac{1}{-24}$$

$$\Rightarrow \quad u = -48 \text{ cm} \quad \text{or} \quad u = -16 \text{ cm}$$

8. $m = \frac{f}{f - u} \quad \Rightarrow \quad +2 = \frac{f}{f - (-1.5)} \quad \Rightarrow \quad f = -3$ cm

So, the mirror is concave with $|f| = 3$ cm.

$$m = -\frac{v}{u} \quad \Rightarrow \quad +2 = -\frac{v}{(-1.5)}$$

$$\Rightarrow \quad v = 3 \text{ cm}$$

So, the image of the tooth is 3 cm behind the mirror.

9. (a)

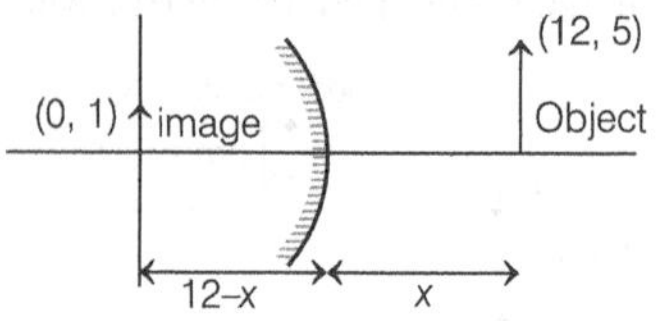

$$m = \frac{h_i}{h_o} = -\frac{v}{u} \Rightarrow \frac{1}{5} = -\frac{(12-x)}{(-x)}$$

$$\Rightarrow \quad x = 10 \text{ cm}$$

$$\frac{1}{v} + \frac{1}{u} = \frac{1}{f} \Rightarrow \frac{1}{2} + \frac{1}{(-10)} = \frac{1}{f} \Rightarrow f = 2.5 \text{ cm}$$

(b)

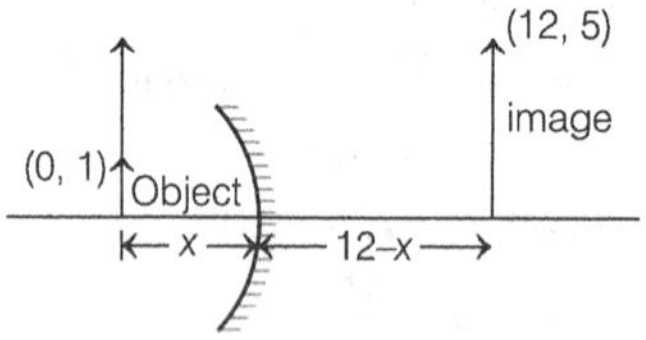

$$m = \frac{h_i}{h_o} = -\frac{v}{u} \Rightarrow \frac{5}{1} = -\frac{(12-x)}{-x}$$

$$\Rightarrow \quad x = 2 \text{ cm}$$

So, pole of concave mirror is at (2, 0).

(c) If object is real, image is virtual. If object is virtual, image is real.

10. $\frac{1}{v} + \frac{1}{u} = \frac{1}{f} \Rightarrow \frac{1}{v} + \frac{1}{-10} = \frac{1}{-20} \Rightarrow v = 20 \text{ cm}$

Along X-axis, $(v_{im})_x = -\frac{v^2}{u^2}(v_{om})_x$

$$\Rightarrow \quad v_i - v_m = -\frac{v^2}{u^2}(v_o - v_m)$$

$$\Rightarrow \quad (v_i)_x - 2 = -\frac{(20)^2}{(-10)^2}(5\cos 37° - 2)$$

$$\Rightarrow \quad (v_i)_x = -6 \text{ cm/s}$$

Along Y-axis,

$$(v_i)_y = -\frac{v}{u}(v_o)_y$$

$$\Rightarrow \quad (v_i)_y = -\frac{20}{(-10)}(5\sin 37°) = 6 \text{ cm/s}$$

$$\therefore \quad \mathbf{v}_i = -6\hat{\mathbf{i}} + 6\hat{\mathbf{j}}$$

Velocity of image w.r.t. object $= \mathbf{v}_i - \mathbf{v}_o$

$$\Rightarrow \quad \mathbf{v}_{io} = (-6\hat{\mathbf{i}} + 6\hat{\mathbf{j}}) - (4\hat{\mathbf{i}} + 3\hat{\mathbf{j}})$$

$$\Rightarrow \quad \mathbf{v}_{io} = -10\hat{\mathbf{i}} + 3\hat{\mathbf{j}}$$

$$\therefore \quad |\mathbf{v}_{io}| = \sqrt{(10)^2 + 3^2} = \sqrt{109} \text{ cm/s}$$

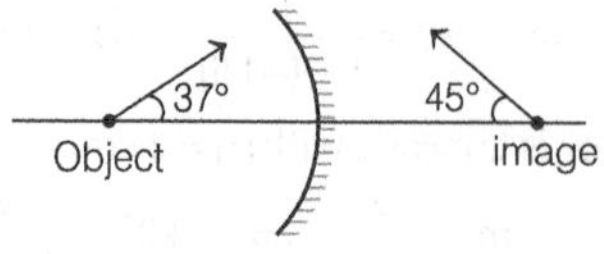

Angle between velocity of image and object

$$= 180° - 37° - 45° = 98°$$

11. (a, c, d)

12. $v_i = -\left(\frac{f}{f-u}\right)^2 v_o$

f is positive for convex mirror. Since, the object is in front of the convex mirror, u is negative. So, $|v_i| < |v_o|$.

13. $\frac{1}{v} + \frac{1}{u} = \frac{1}{f} \Rightarrow \frac{1}{v} = \frac{1}{f} - \frac{1}{u}$

Since, $u < f$, $v < 0$

The image is formed in front of the mirror.

So, it will be real image.

$$m = -\frac{v}{u}$$

$$\because \quad v < 0, u > 0 \Rightarrow m > 0$$

Hence, the image is erect.

14. Length of object AB is $(50 - 20) = 30$ cm

After first reflection from plane mirror, AB is inverted to B_1A_1 with distance from convex mirror as shown in figure.

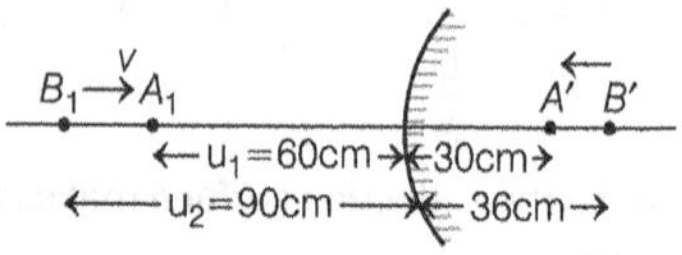

For A_1, $\frac{1}{v} + \frac{1}{u} = \frac{1}{f} \Rightarrow \frac{1}{v_1} + \frac{1}{-60} = \frac{1}{+60} \Rightarrow v_1 = 30$ cm

For B_1, $\frac{1}{v} + \frac{1}{u} = \frac{1}{f} \Rightarrow \frac{1}{v_2} + \frac{1}{-90} = \frac{1}{+60}$

$$\Rightarrow \quad v_2 = 36 \text{ cm}$$

Length of $A'B' = 36 - 30 = 6$ cm

$$\text{Magnification} = \frac{A'B'}{AB} = \frac{6}{30} = \frac{1}{5}$$

So, the second image is virtual and erect with magnification $\frac{1}{5}$ w.r.t. AB.

$$v_i = -\frac{v^2}{u^2} v_o$$

So, velocity of image and velocity of object are in opposite direction. Since, A_1B_1 is moving towards the convex mirror, $A'B'$ will also move towards the mirror.

Comprehension Based Questions

1.

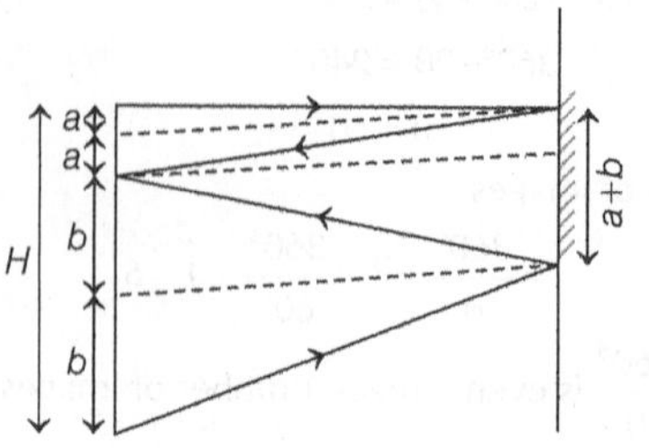

$$2a + 2b = H \Rightarrow a + b = \frac{H}{2}$$

$$\text{Length of mirror} = a + b = \frac{H}{2}$$

2.

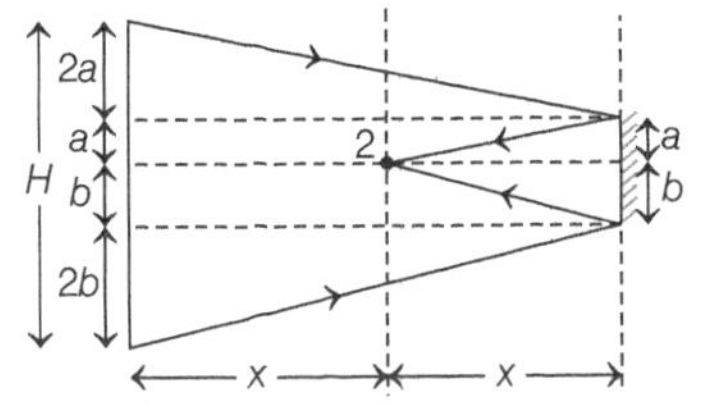

$$2a + a + b + 2b = H \quad \Rightarrow \quad a + b = \frac{H}{3}$$

Length of mirror $= a + b = \frac{H}{3}$

3.

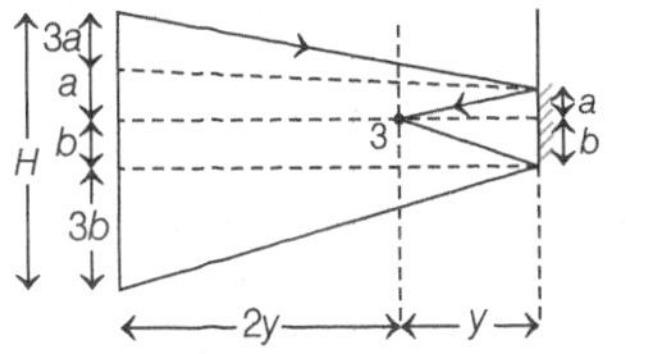

$$3a + a + b + 3b = H \quad \Rightarrow \quad a + b = \frac{H}{4}$$

Length of mirror $= a + b = \frac{H}{4}$

4. Velocity of image w.r.t. object will be zero, when velocity of object will be parallel to the mirror i.e., velocity of object makes an angle of θ with horizontal.

Horizontal component of velocity remains constant in projectile motion.

$$\Rightarrow \quad u\cos\phi = v\cos\theta \quad \Rightarrow \quad v = \frac{u\cos\phi}{\cos\theta}$$

5. The image will have maximum velocity with respect to object, when velocity of object is perpendicular to the mirror i.e., velocity of object makes an angle of $90° - \theta$ with horizontal.

$$\therefore \quad u\cos\phi = v\cos(90° - \theta) \quad \Rightarrow \quad v = \frac{u\cos\phi}{\sin\theta}$$

6. $a_{\text{image, object}} = a_{\text{image}} - a_{\text{object}} = g - g = 0$

Since, relative acceleration is zero, relative velocity will be constant and path will be straight line.

7. Let coordinates of the image be (x, y).

Distance between (x, y) and $(-2, 0) = 5$

$$\Rightarrow \quad \sqrt{[x - (-2)]^2 + (y - 0)^2} = 5$$

$$\Rightarrow \quad (x + 2)^2 + y^2 = 5^2$$

8. Angular velocity of mirror $= \frac{d\theta}{dt} = 12t$

Angular velocity of the reflected ray $= 2\left(\frac{d\theta}{dt}\right) = 24t$

At $t = 2$, angular velocity of image $= 24(2) = 48$ rad/s

9. Centripetal acceleration of image $= \omega^2 r = (24(0))^2 5 = 0$

Tangential acceleration of image $= r\alpha = r\frac{d\omega}{dt}$

$$= 5(24) = 120 \text{ m/s}^2$$

So, net acceleration $= \sqrt{a_c^2 + a_T^2} = 120 \text{ m/s}^2$

10.

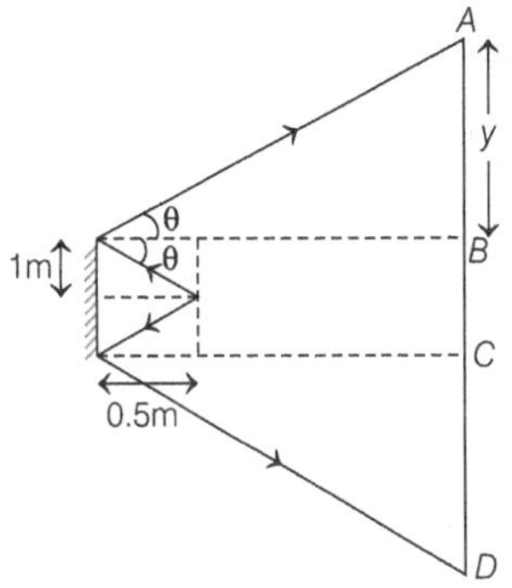

$$\tan\theta = \frac{1}{0.5} = \frac{y}{5} \quad \Rightarrow \quad y = 10 \text{ m}$$

$$AD = 10 + 2 + 10 = 22 \text{ m}$$

$$\text{Time interval} = \frac{\text{Distance}}{\text{Speed}} = \frac{22}{10} = 2.2 \text{ s}$$

11. Initial velocity of man will be same as that of the balloon i.e., 10 m/s upwards.

$$H_{\max} = \frac{u^2}{2g} = \frac{(10)^2}{2(10)} = 5 \text{ m}$$

The greatest distance over which man can see image of source $= H_{\max} + BD = 5 + 12 = 17$ m

To find time duration, $s_y = u_y t + \frac{1}{2}a_y t^2$

$$\Rightarrow \quad -12 = 10t + \frac{1}{2}(-10)t^2$$

$$\Rightarrow \quad 5t^2 - 10t - 12 = 0$$

$$t = \frac{10 \pm \sqrt{100 + 240}}{10} = 2.84 \text{ s}$$

12. $H_{\max} = \frac{u^2}{2g} = \frac{(20)^2}{2(10)} = 20$ m

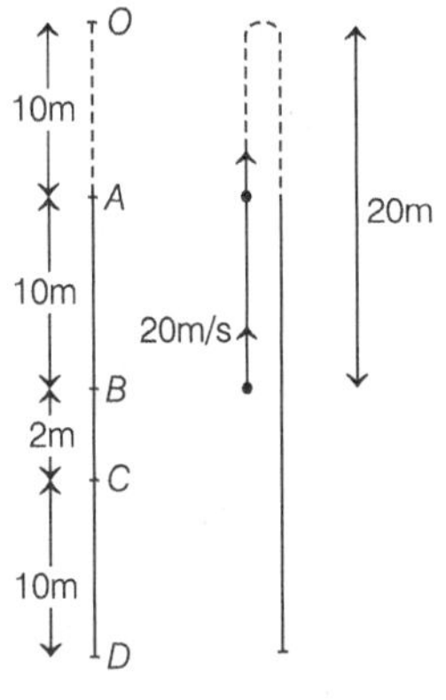

To find speed at A,

$$v^2 = u^2 + 2as$$

$$\Rightarrow \quad v^2 = (20)^2 + 2(-10)(+10)$$

$$\Rightarrow \quad v = 10\sqrt{2} \text{ m/s}$$

To find time taken from A to O and O to A,

$$t_1 = \frac{2u}{g} = \frac{2(10\sqrt{2})}{10}$$

$$= 2\sqrt{2} = 2.82 \text{ s}$$

To find time taken from B to D,

$$s = ut + \frac{1}{2}at^2$$

$$\Rightarrow \quad -12 = 20t_2 + \frac{1}{2}(-10)t_2^2$$

$$\Rightarrow \quad t_2 = 4.52 \text{ s}$$

Time duration for which the man can see image

$$= t_2 - t_1 = 4.52 - 2.82 = 1.7 \text{ s}$$

13. Magnification, $m = -\frac{v}{u} = 1 - \frac{v}{f}$

$m_1 = -2 \Rightarrow -2 = 1 - \frac{v_1}{f} \Rightarrow v_1 = 3f$

$m_2 = -3 \Rightarrow -3 = 1 - \frac{v_2}{f} \Rightarrow v_2 = 4f$

Shift of the screen = 25 cm

$\Rightarrow \quad |v_2| - |v_1| = 25 \Rightarrow f = 25$ cm

14. Magnification, $m = -\frac{v}{u}$

$m_1 = -2 \Rightarrow -2 = -\frac{3f}{u_1} \Rightarrow u_1 = \frac{3f}{2}$

$m_2 = -3 \Rightarrow -3 = -\frac{4f}{u_2} \Rightarrow u_2 = \frac{4f}{3}$

Shift of the object $= |u_1| - |u_2| = \frac{f}{6} = 4.17$ cm

15. At $t = \frac{2R}{v}$, block B collides elastically with the mirror stand.

Block B comes to rest and the mirror stand starts moving with velocity v.

At $t = \frac{3R}{v}$, positions of blocks and mirror stand are shown in the figure.

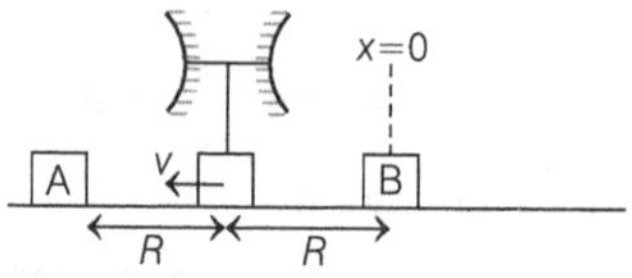

Each block lies at the centre of curvature of respective mirrors. So, their images will also be formed at their respective centres of curvature.

16. For A, $(v_{im})_x = -\frac{v^2}{u^2}(v_{om})_x$

$\Rightarrow \quad v_i - v_m = -\frac{v^2}{u^2}(v_o - v_m)$

$\Rightarrow \quad v_i - (-v) = -\left(\frac{-R}{-R}\right)^2 [0 - (-v)]$

$\Rightarrow \quad v_i = -2v$

17. At $t = \frac{4R}{v}$, the mirror stand collides elastically with block A and they exchange their velocities.

At $t = \frac{5R}{v}$,

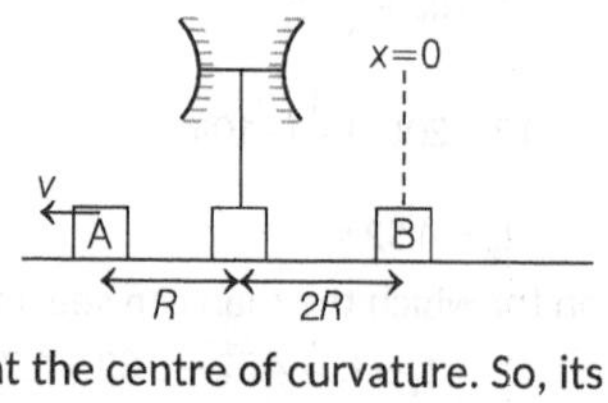

Block A is at the centre of curvature. So, its image will also be formed at the centre of curvature. So, $x_i = -3R$.

For block B, $\frac{1}{v} + \frac{1}{u} = \frac{1}{f}$

$\Rightarrow \quad \frac{1}{v} + \frac{1}{-2R} = \frac{1}{\left(\frac{-R}{2}\right)} \Rightarrow v = -\frac{2R}{3}$

So, position of image of

$B = -\left(2R - \frac{2R}{3}\right) = -\frac{4R}{3}$

18. All dimensions of the disc are perpendicular to the principal axis. Hence, all dimensions are equally magnified resulting in an image in the shape of a circular disc.

19. $m = \frac{f}{f-u} = \frac{-10}{-10-(-15)} = -2$

Radius of image = $(m) \times$ Radius of object

$= 2 \times 0.6 = 1.2$ cm

Area of image of disc $= \pi(1.2)^2 = 1.44\pi$ cm^2

20. $r_{image} = 2r_{object}$

$\Rightarrow \quad \frac{dr_{image}}{dt} = 2\frac{dr_{object}}{dt} = 2(0.1) = 0.2$ cm/s, increasing

21. $f = R - \frac{R}{2}\sec\theta$

For paraxial rays, angle of incidence (θ) is smaller compared to the angle of incidence for marginal rays.

$\because \quad \theta_p < \theta_m \Rightarrow f_p > f_m$

22. $f = R - \frac{R}{2}\sec 60° = 0$

23.

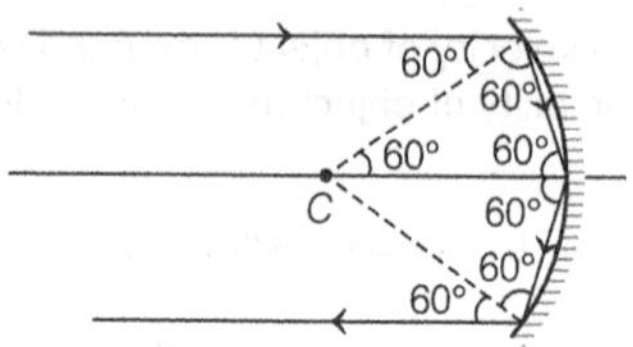

Total deviation = 180°

24. For paraxial rays, $\theta = 0°$

$\Rightarrow \quad f_p = R - \frac{R}{2}\sec 0° = \frac{R}{2}$

25. (b)

26. $\frac{1}{v} + \frac{1}{u} = \frac{1}{f} \Rightarrow \frac{1}{v} + \frac{1}{-30} = \frac{1}{-20}$

$\Rightarrow \quad v = -60$ cm

Along X-axis, $(v_{im})_x = -\frac{v^2}{u^2}(v_{om})_x$

$\Rightarrow \quad v_i - v_m = -\frac{v^2}{u^2}(v_o - v_m)$

$\Rightarrow \quad (v_i)_x - 2 = -\left(\frac{-60}{-30}\right)^2 (4-2)$

$\Rightarrow \quad (v_i)_x = -6$ cm/s

27. Along Y-axis, $m = \frac{h_i}{h_o} = \frac{f}{f-u}$

$$\Rightarrow \qquad h_i = \frac{fh_o}{f-u}$$

Differentiating both sides w.r.t. t,

$$\frac{dh_i}{dt} = fh_o\left[-\frac{1}{(f-u)^2}\right]\left(-\frac{du}{dt}\right)$$

$$\Rightarrow \qquad (v_i)_y = \frac{(-20)(0.2)}{[-20-(-30)]^2}(4-2) = -\frac{2}{25}\text{ cm/s}$$

Match the Columns Questions

1. (A) $\frac{360^\circ}{\theta}$ = even integer,

So, number of images $= n = \frac{360^\circ}{60^\circ} - 1 = 5$

(B) $\frac{360^\circ}{\theta}$ = odd integer and object kept symmetrically,

So, number of images $= \frac{360^\circ}{72^\circ} - 1 = 4$

(C) $\frac{360^\circ}{\theta}$ = even integer

So, number of images $= \frac{360^\circ}{45^\circ} - 1 = 7$

(D) $\frac{360^\circ}{\theta}$ = fraction and object kept symmetrically

So, number of images = Nearest even integer of $\frac{360^\circ}{\theta}$

$$= \left[\frac{360^\circ}{50^\circ}\right] = 8$$

2. (A) $\frac{1}{v}+\frac{1}{u}=\frac{1}{f} \Rightarrow \frac{1}{v}+\frac{1}{6}=\frac{1}{10}$

$\Rightarrow \qquad v = -15$ cm

$$m = -\frac{v}{u} = -\frac{(-15)}{(+6)} = 2.5$$

Since, image is formed in front of the mirror, it will be real image. Magnitude of magnification is greater than 1. So, it will be magnified image.

(B) $\frac{1}{v}+\frac{1}{u}=\frac{1}{f}$

$\Rightarrow \qquad \frac{1}{v}+\frac{1}{11}=\frac{1}{10} \quad \Rightarrow \quad v = 110$ cm

$$m = -\frac{v}{u} = -\frac{110}{11} = -10$$

Since, image is formed behind the mirror, it will be virtual image. Image will be magnified as explained above.

(C) $\frac{1}{v}+\frac{1}{u}=\frac{1}{f}$

$\Rightarrow \qquad \frac{1}{v}+\frac{1}{16}=\frac{1}{10} \quad \Rightarrow \quad v = \frac{80}{3}$ cm

$$m = -\frac{v}{u} = -\left(\frac{\frac{80}{3}}{16}\right) = -\frac{5}{3}$$

Image will be virtual and magnified.

(D) $\frac{1}{v}+\frac{1}{u}=\frac{1}{f} \quad \Rightarrow \quad \frac{1}{v}+\frac{1}{30}=\frac{1}{10}$

$\Rightarrow \qquad v = 15$ cm

$$m = -\frac{v}{u} = -\frac{15}{30} = -\frac{1}{2}$$

Image will be virtual and diminished.

3. A ⟶ 1, 2, 3, 4, B ⟶ 1, 4, C ⟶ 1, 3, D ⟶ 3, 4

4. A ⟶ 1, 2, B ⟶ 3, 5, C⟶ 1, 5, D⟶ 1, 4, 5

Numerical Value Questions

1.

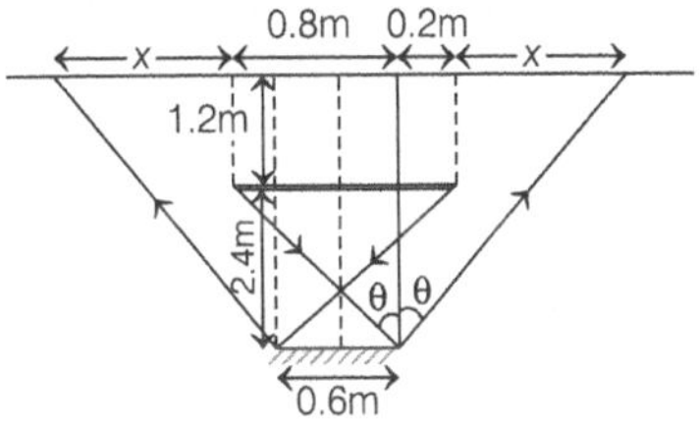

$$\tan\theta = \frac{0.8}{2.4} = \frac{x+0.2}{3.6} \quad \Rightarrow \quad x = 1\text{ m}$$

So, length of the reflected path of light on the ceiling

$$= 1+1+1 = 3\text{ m}$$

2.

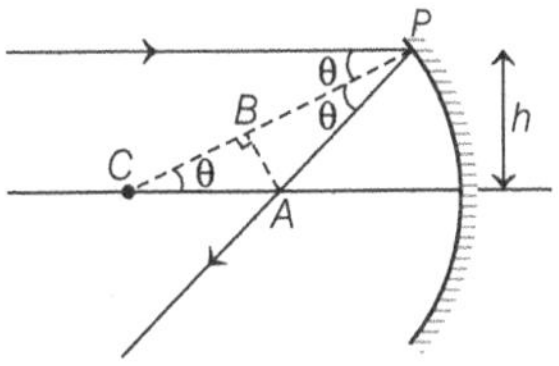

When $h_1 = 0.5\text{cm}, \sin\theta_1 = \frac{h_1}{R} = \frac{0.5}{5} = \frac{1}{10}$

or $\qquad \cos\theta_1 = \frac{\sqrt{99}}{10} \simeq 1$

When $h_2 = 3\text{cm}, \sin\theta_2 = \frac{h_2}{R} = \frac{3}{5}$

or $\qquad \cos\theta_2 = \frac{4}{5}$

$$AC = \frac{R}{2\cos\theta}$$

$$\therefore \quad \Delta x = \frac{R}{2}\left(\frac{1}{\cos\theta_2} - \frac{1}{\cos\theta_1}\right) = \frac{5}{2}\left(\frac{5}{4}-1\right)$$

$$= 0.625\text{ cm} = 6.25\text{ mm}$$

3. $\frac{1}{v}+\frac{1}{u}=\frac{1}{f} \quad \Rightarrow \quad \frac{1}{v}+\frac{1}{-10}=\frac{1}{-20}$

$\Rightarrow \qquad v = 20$ cm

$$m = -\frac{v}{u} = -\frac{20}{(-10)} = +2$$

For M_1, object O is 1 cm below its principal axis. So, image formed by M_1 will be 2 cm below the principal axis i.e., 1 cm below line AB.

Similarly image formed by M_2 will be 1 cm above line AB.

$\therefore$ Separation between the two images $= 1 + 1 = 2$ cm.

4. $\dfrac{dv}{dt} = -m^2 \dfrac{du}{dt}$

$$\Rightarrow \quad -\frac{1}{100} = -\left(\frac{1}{10}\right)^2 \frac{du}{dt} \quad \Rightarrow \quad \frac{du}{dt} = 1 \text{ m/s}$$

$$m = \frac{f}{f-u}$$

$$\Rightarrow \quad \frac{dm}{dt} = \frac{f}{(f-u)^2}\frac{du}{dt} = \frac{m^2}{f}\frac{du}{dt} = \frac{\left(\frac{1}{10}\right)^2}{10}(1) = 1 \times 10^{-3} \text{ / s}$$

5. $v_i = -\left(\dfrac{f}{f-u}\right)^2 v_o$

$$\Rightarrow \quad \frac{dv_i}{dt} = -\frac{2f^2 v_o}{(f-u)^3}\frac{du}{dt} = -\frac{2(-30)^2(5)}{[-30-(-40)]^3}(5)$$

$$= 45 \text{ cm/s}^2$$

So, acceleration of image is 45 cm/s^2.

6. $\dfrac{1}{v_1} + \dfrac{1}{u_1} = \dfrac{1}{f} \quad \Rightarrow \quad v_1 = \dfrac{u_1 f}{u_1 - f}$

$$\Rightarrow \quad \frac{1}{v_2} + \frac{1}{u_2} = \frac{1}{f} \quad \Rightarrow \quad v_2 = \frac{u_2 f}{u_2 - f}$$

$$\Delta v = v_1 - v_2 = \frac{u_1 f}{u_1 - f} - \frac{u_2 f}{u_2 - f} = \frac{(u_2 - u_1)f^2}{(u_1 - f)(u_2 - f)}$$

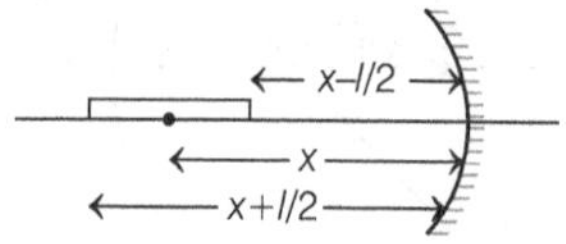

Let distance of centre of rod from mirror be x at any instant.

$$\therefore \; u_1 = -\left(x - \frac{l}{2}\right), \; u_2 = -\left(x + \frac{l}{2}\right), f = -l$$

$$\Delta v = \frac{(u_2 - u_1)f^2}{(u_1 - f)(u_2 - f)} = \frac{4l^3}{(3l - 2x)(l - 2x)}$$

$$\Rightarrow \quad \frac{d(\Delta v)}{dt} = \frac{-4l^3\left[(3l-2x)\left(-2\frac{dx}{dt}\right) + (l-2x)\left(-2\frac{dx}{dt}\right)\right]}{(3l-2x)^2(l-2x)^2}$$

$$= \frac{32}{9}\frac{dx}{dt} = \frac{32}{9} \times 9 = 32 \text{ m/s}$$

7. Velocity of particle at any instant $= gt$

Displacement of particle at any instant $= \dfrac{1}{2}gt^2$

$$v_i = -\left(\frac{f}{f-u}\right)^2 v_o \;\Rightarrow\; v_i = -\frac{(-f)^2}{\left[-f - \left\{-\left(\frac{f}{2} - \frac{1}{2}gt^2\right)\right\}\right]^2}(gt)$$

$$\Rightarrow v_i = -\frac{4f^2 gt}{(f + gt^2)^2}$$

To maximize velocity of image, $\dfrac{dv_i}{dt} = 0$

$$\frac{dv_i}{dt} = -4f^2 g\left[\frac{(f+gt^2)^2(1) - (t)2(f+gt^2)(2gt)}{(f+gt^2)^4}\right] = 0$$

$$\Rightarrow \quad t = \sqrt{\frac{f}{3g}}$$

$$\therefore \quad (v_i)_{max} = \frac{4f^2 g\sqrt{\frac{f}{3g}}}{\left[f + g\left(\frac{f}{3g}\right)\right]^2} = \frac{3}{4}\sqrt{3fg}$$

8.

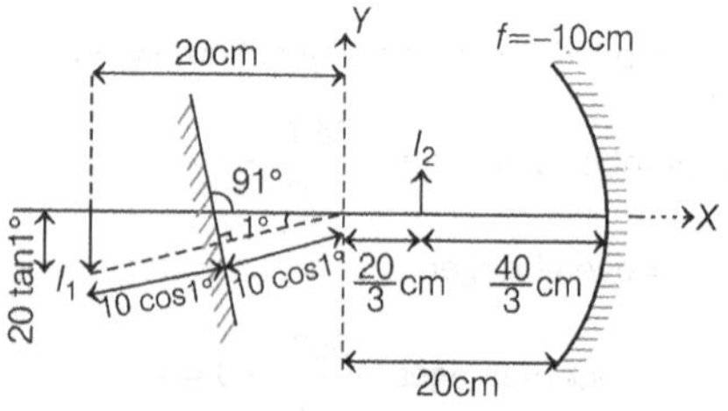

I_1 is the image formed by the plane mirror.

For concave mirror.

$$u = -(20 + 20) = -40 \text{ cm}, \; f = -10 \text{ cm}$$

$$\frac{1}{v} + \frac{1}{u} = \frac{1}{f} \quad \Rightarrow \quad \frac{1}{v} + \frac{1}{-40} = \frac{1}{-10}$$

$$\Rightarrow \quad v = -\frac{40}{3} \text{ cm}$$

Magnification, $m = -\dfrac{v}{u}$

$$\Rightarrow \quad \frac{h_i}{(-20 \tan 1^\circ)} = -\frac{\left(-\frac{40}{3}\right)}{-40}$$

$$\Rightarrow \quad h_i = \frac{20}{3}\tan 1^\circ = \frac{20}{3} \times 1 \times \frac{\pi}{180} = \frac{\pi}{27}$$

$$\therefore \quad x_o = 20 - \frac{40}{3} = \frac{20}{3} \text{ and } y_o = \frac{\pi}{27}$$

$$\therefore \quad \frac{\pi x_o}{y_o} = \frac{\pi\left(\frac{20}{3}\right)}{\frac{\pi}{27}} = 180$$

9. Parallel beam incident on the concave mirror would have met in its focal plane if the convex mirror were not there. So, for concave mirror,

$$v = f = -40 \text{ cm}, h_i = f\theta = 40\left(\frac{1}{40}\right) = 1 \text{ cm}$$

For convex mirror,

$$u = +(40 - 25) = +15 \text{ cm}, \; f = 10 \text{ cm}$$

$$\frac{1}{v} + \frac{1}{u} = \frac{1}{f} \quad \Rightarrow \quad \frac{1}{v} + \frac{1}{15} = \frac{1}{10}$$

$$\Rightarrow \quad v = 30 \text{ cm}$$

$$m=-\frac{v}{u}=-\left(\frac{30}{15}\right)=-2$$

$\therefore$ $$m=\frac{h'_i}{h_o}=-2 \Rightarrow \frac{h'_i}{-1}=-2$$

$\Rightarrow$ $$h'_1=2\text{ cm}$$

10. For first reflection,

$$u=-60\text{ cm}, f=-20\text{ cm}$$

$$\frac{1}{v}+\frac{1}{u}=\frac{1}{f} \Rightarrow \frac{1}{v}+\frac{1}{-60}=\frac{1}{-20}$$

$\Rightarrow$ $$v=-30\text{ cm}$$

$$m=-\frac{v}{u} \Rightarrow m=-\frac{(-30)}{(-60)}=-\frac{1}{2}$$

$$m=\frac{h_i}{h_o} \Rightarrow -\frac{1}{2}=\frac{h_i}{(-1)} \Rightarrow h_i=0.5\text{ cm}$$

For second reflection,

$$u=-(100-30)=-70\text{ cm}, f=-20\text{ cm}$$

$$\frac{1}{v}+\frac{1}{u}=\frac{1}{f}$$

$\Rightarrow$ $$\frac{1}{v}+\frac{1}{-70}=\frac{1}{-20}$$

$\Rightarrow$ $$v=-28\text{ cm}$$

$$m=\frac{h_i}{h_o}=-\frac{v}{u}$$

$\Rightarrow$ $$\frac{h'_i}{1.5}=-\frac{(-28)}{(-70)}$$

$\Rightarrow$ $$h'_i=-0.6\text{ cm}$$

$\therefore$ $x_o=(40-28)=12$ cm and $y_o=0.6$ cm

$\therefore$ $$\frac{x_o}{y_o}=\frac{12}{0.6}=20$$

Previous Year's Questions

JEE Main

1. $$R=30\text{ cm}$$

$$f=\frac{R}{2}=\frac{30}{2}=+15\text{ cm}$$

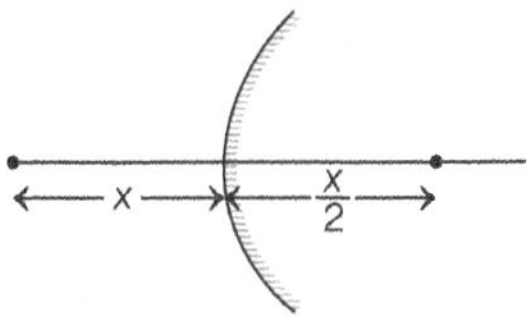

Magnification $(m)=\pm\frac{1}{2}$

For convex mirror, virtual image is formed for real object.

Therefore, m is + ve

$$m=\frac{f}{f-u} \Rightarrow +\frac{1}{2}=\frac{f}{f-u}$$

$\Rightarrow$ $$+\frac{1}{2}=\frac{15}{15-u}$$

$$15-u=30$$

$$15-30=u$$

$\Rightarrow$ $$u=-15\text{ cm}$$

2. Given,

Image distance, $v=15$ cm

Here, $m=2$

i.e., $$\frac{-v}{-u}=2$$

$$v=2u$$

Distance between object and image

$$u+v=15\text{ cm}$$

$$u+2u=15\text{ cm}$$

$$u=5\text{ cm}$$

$\therefore$ $$v=2\times5=10\text{ cm}$$

Using mirror formula,

$\Rightarrow$ $$\frac{1}{f}=\frac{1}{v}+\frac{1}{u}$$

$\therefore$ $$\frac{1}{f}=\frac{1}{10}+\frac{1}{-5}=-\frac{1}{10}$$

$$f=-10\text{ cm}$$

3. In a plane mirror, image is always at same distance from object.

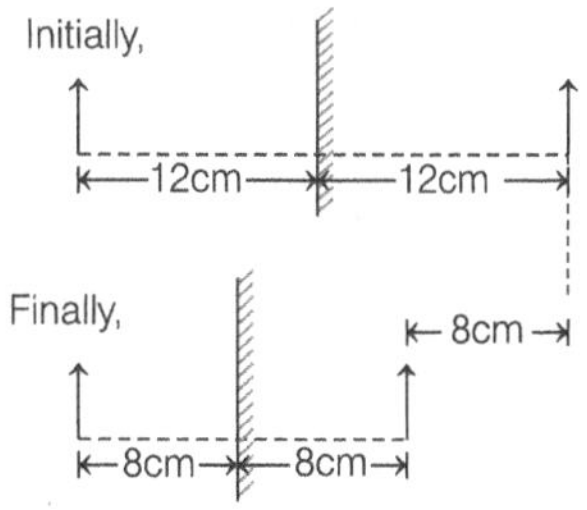

From above diagrams, distance by which image moved is 8 cm towards mirror (from it's previous position).

4. Given, $i=30°$

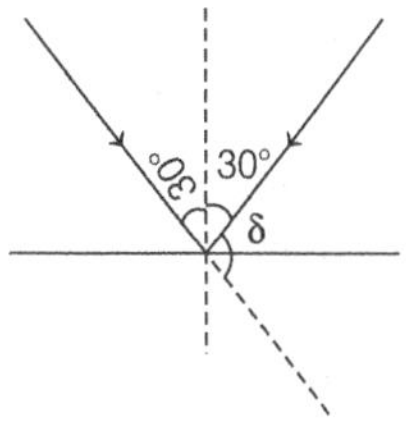

$$\delta=180°-2i=180-2\times30°$$

$$=180-60°=120°$$

5. When the light rays from an object have been reflected towards an observer from a standard flat mirror is the image observed by the observer is virtual, **erect**, same size as the object and **laterally inverted**.

6. The given situation in question is as follows.

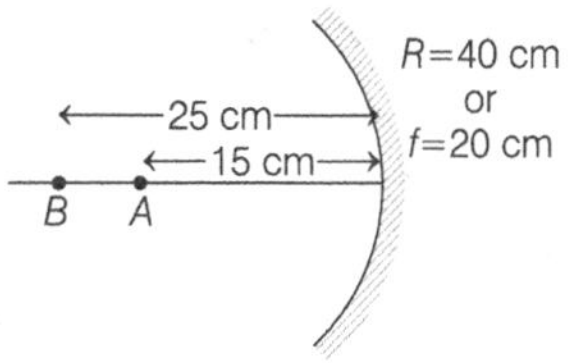

Using mirror formula, $\frac{1}{v}+\frac{1}{u}=\frac{1}{f}$

For point A, $u=-15$ cm, $f=-20$ cm

$$\frac{1}{v_A}+\frac{1}{-15}=\frac{1}{-20}$$

$$\frac{1}{v_A}=\frac{1}{15}-\frac{1}{20}=\frac{4-3}{60}=\frac{1}{60}$$

$$v_A=+60 \text{ cm}$$

For point B, $u=-25$ cm, $f=-20$ cm

$$\frac{1}{v_B}+\frac{1}{-25}=\frac{1}{-20}$$

$$\Rightarrow \quad \frac{1}{v_B}=\frac{1}{25}-\frac{1}{20}=\frac{4-5}{100}=-\frac{1}{100}$$

$$\Rightarrow \quad v_B=-100 \text{ cm}$$

Since, the sign of image formed by concave mirror is opposite i.e., both images lie opposite to pole.

Hence, the distance between images formed by the mirror is

$$d=|v_A-v_B|=|60-(-100)|$$

$$\Rightarrow \quad d=160 \text{ cm}$$

7.

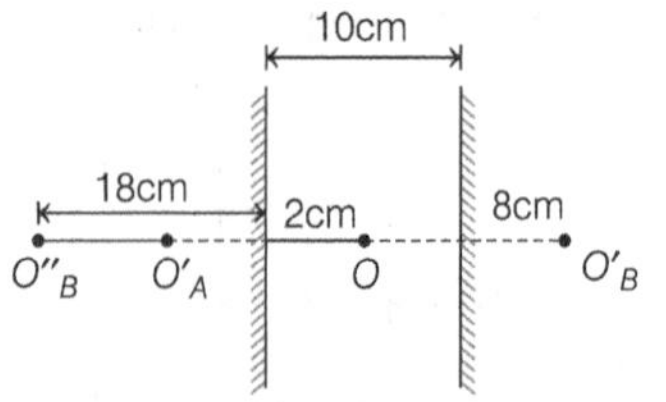

Reflection of O in mirror B is image $O'B$ at a distance of 18 cm from A.

Image of $O'B$ is at $O''B$ which is also at a distance of 18 cm from A.

8. Given that $l=10$ cm

$$f=20 \text{ cm},$$

$$d=40 \text{ cm}$$

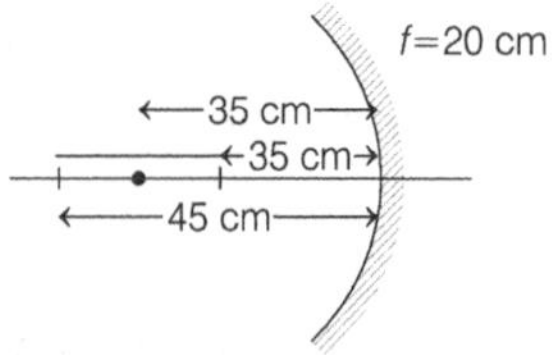

According to question,

Let, the image of AB rod be $A'B'$ and distance of point A' and B' from mirror be v_A' and v_B' respectively.

From mirror formula,

For point A, $\frac{1}{v_A'}+\frac{1}{(-45)}=\frac{1}{-20}$

$$\frac{1}{v_A'}-\frac{1}{45}=\frac{1}{-20} \Rightarrow v_A'=-36 \text{ cm}$$

For point B,

$$\frac{1}{v_B'}+\frac{1}{(-35)}=\frac{1}{-20}$$

$$\Rightarrow \quad \frac{1}{v_B'}-\frac{1}{35}=\frac{1}{-20}$$

$$\Rightarrow \quad v_B'=\frac{-140}{3} \text{ cm}$$

Length of rod $=|v_A'-v_B'|=\left|-36+\frac{140}{3}\right|=\frac{32}{3}$ cm

So, $x=32$

9. Given, $u=100$ cm

$$R=-200 \text{ cm}$$

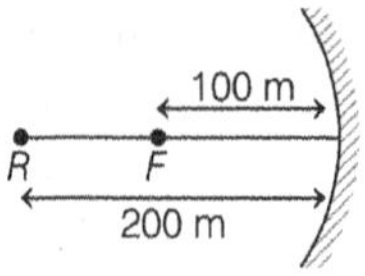

$$\therefore \quad f=\frac{R}{2}=-100 \text{ cm}$$

Speed of object $=2$ cm / s

After 10 s distance moved by object towards mirror,

$$s=v\times t=2\times 10=20 \text{ cm}$$

Distance of object,

$$u'=100-20=80 \text{ cm}$$

$$\Rightarrow \quad \frac{1}{v}+\frac{1}{u}=\frac{1}{f}$$

$$\Rightarrow \quad -\frac{1}{100}=\frac{1}{v}+\frac{1}{-80}$$

$$\Rightarrow \quad \frac{-1}{100}+\frac{1}{80}=\frac{1}{v} \Rightarrow v=400 \text{ cm}$$

10. Let us draw normals on M_1 and M_2 for convenience

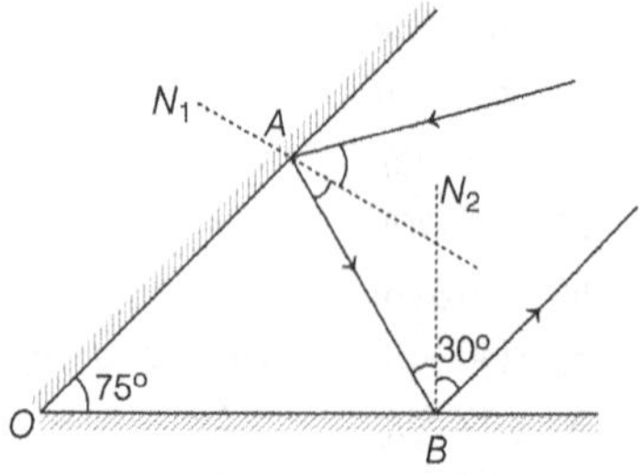

Given that the ray is finally reflected by 30° at point B.

Therefore, $\angle ABO=90°-30°=60°$

Hence, $\angle BAO=180°-75°-60°=45°$

Now to calculate total deviation, the angle between incident ray and reflected ray is obtained as,

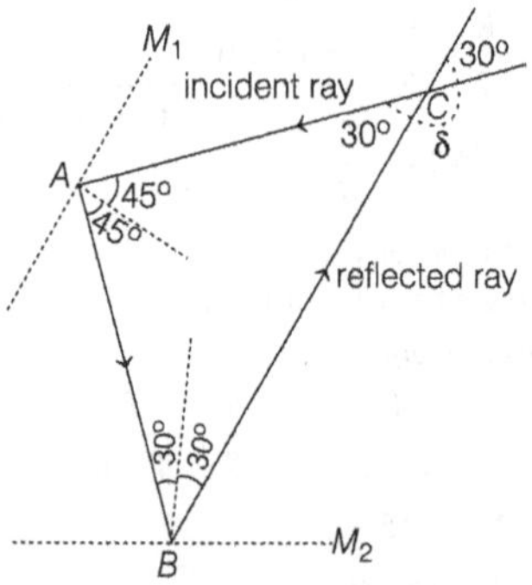

Total deviation $(\delta)=180°+30°=210°$

11. Given, length of mirror, $m=50 \text{ cm}=50\times 10^{-2}$ m

Distance of source from mirror, $d=60 \text{ cm}=60\times 10^{-2}$ m

Distance of man from mirror, $d_m=1.2$ m

By using the concept of ray diagram of plane mirror shown below

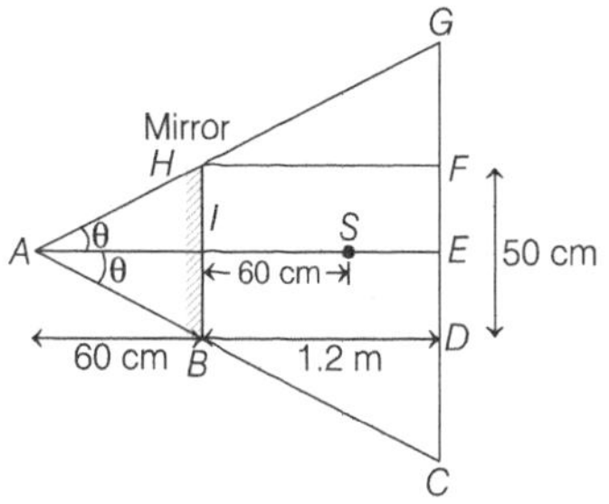

Now, using the concept of similar triangle,

$\Delta HAI \sim \Delta GAE$ and $\Delta BAI \sim \Delta CAE$

$$\therefore \quad \frac{AI}{AE} = \frac{HI}{EG} \Rightarrow \frac{0.60}{1.8} = \frac{0.25}{EG} \qquad (\because AI = IS)$$

$$\Rightarrow \quad EG = 0.25 \times \frac{1.8}{0.6} = 0.25 \times 3 = 0.75 \text{ m}$$

As, $CG = 2EG$

$$\Rightarrow \quad CG = 0.75 \times 2 = 1.50 \text{ m}$$

12. According to the given figure, we have two plane mirror, placed at 90° to each other.

Let I_1 is the image of P due to mirror M_1 and I_2 is the image of P due to mirror M_2

Therefore, the shortest distance between images i.e., between I_1 and I_2

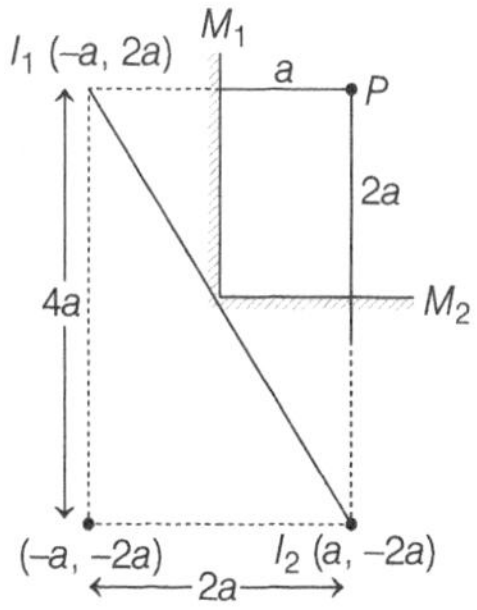

$$I_1I_2 = \sqrt{(4a)^2 + (2a)^2}$$

$$= \sqrt{16a^2 + 4a^2} = a\sqrt{20}$$

$$= a2\sqrt{5} = a \times 2 \times 2.3 = 4.6a$$

13. The given situation is shown in the following ray diagram.

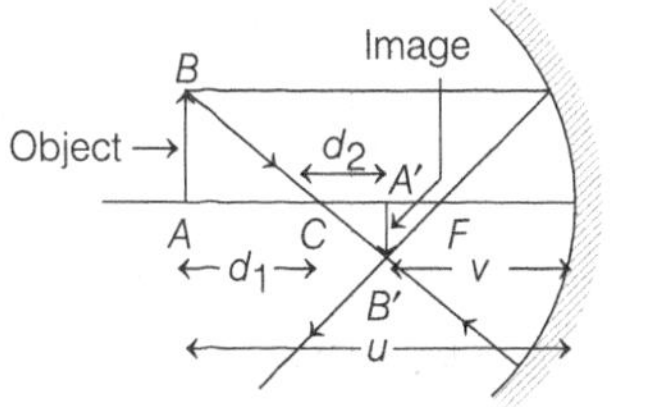

Consider radius of curvature of mirror is R.

Object distance, $u = -(R + d_1)$

Image distance, $v = -(R - d_2)$

Focal length of mirror, $f = \dfrac{-R}{2}$

Now, from mirror formula, we have

$$\frac{1}{f} = \frac{1}{v} + \frac{1}{u} = \frac{u+v}{uv} \Rightarrow uv = f(u+v)$$

On substituting the values in above expression, we get

$$[-(R + d_1)][-(R - d_2)] = -\frac{R}{2}(R + d_1 + R - d_2)$$

$$\Rightarrow 2(R^2 - d_2R + d_1R - d_1d_2) = 2R^2 + d_1R - d_2R = 2d_1d_2$$

$$\Rightarrow \quad R = \frac{2d_1d_2}{d_1 - d_2}$$

14. According to the question,

Velocity of car B w.r.t. mirror of car A,

$$v_{BM} = 40 \text{ m/s}$$

Distance of car B from mirror of car A,

$$u = 1.9 \text{ m} = 190 \text{ cm}$$

Focal length of mirror, $f = 10$ cm

We have to find the velocity of image of car B in the mirror, i.e. v_{IM}

We know that

$$v_{IM} = -m^2 v_{BM} \qquad \text{...(i)}$$

Where, m is the magnification produced by mirror of car A,

$$\Rightarrow \quad m = \frac{f}{f-u} = \frac{10}{10-(-190)} = \frac{10}{200} = \frac{1}{20}$$

On substituting the values in Eq. (i), we get

$$v_{IM} = -\left(\frac{1}{20}\right)^2 \times 40 = -\frac{1}{400} \times 40 = -0.1 \text{ m/s}$$

Here, negative sign shows that, the speed of image w.r.t. mirror of car A is in opposite direction.

15. Taking component of **a**, **b** and **c** along $\hat{\mathbf{i}}, \hat{\mathbf{j}}$ and $\hat{\mathbf{k}}$.

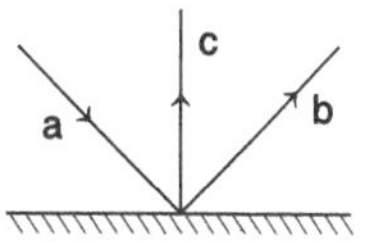

$$\therefore \quad \mathbf{a} = \sin\theta\hat{\mathbf{i}} - \cos\theta\hat{\mathbf{j}}, \;\; \mathbf{b} = \sin\theta\hat{\mathbf{i}} + \cos\theta\hat{\mathbf{j}}, \;\; \mathbf{c} = \hat{\mathbf{j}}$$

Now, on solving option (c), we get

$$\mathbf{a} - 2(\mathbf{a}\cdot\mathbf{c})\mathbf{c} = (\sin\theta\hat{\mathbf{i}} - \cos\theta\hat{\mathbf{j}}) - 2[(\sin\theta\hat{\mathbf{i}} - \cos\theta\hat{\mathbf{j}})\cdot\hat{\mathbf{j}}]\hat{\mathbf{j}}$$

$$= \sin\theta\hat{\mathbf{i}} + \cos\theta\hat{\mathbf{j}} = \mathbf{b}$$

JEE Advanced

1.

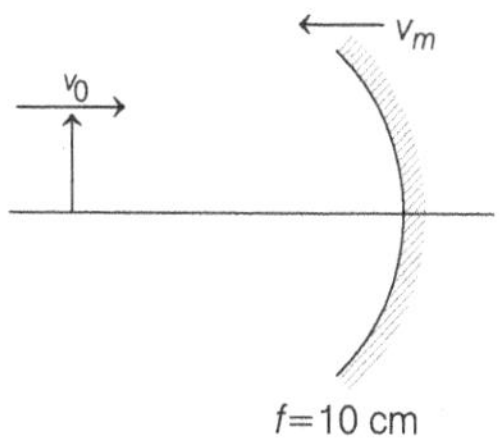

Let

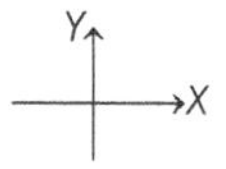

$$u = -30 \text{ cm}, \quad f = -10 \text{ cm}$$

$$\therefore \quad \frac{1}{v} + \frac{1}{u} = \frac{1}{f} \Rightarrow \frac{1}{v} - \frac{1}{30} = \frac{1}{-10} \quad \text{or} \quad v = -15 \text{ cm}$$

Further, $\dfrac{1}{v} + \dfrac{1}{u} = \dfrac{1}{f}$

Differentiating w.r.t. time, we get

$$\frac{du}{dt} = -\frac{v^2}{u^2}\frac{du}{dt}$$

$$\mathbf{v}_{IM} = -\left(\frac{v}{u}\right)^2 \mathbf{v}_{OM}$$

Given, $\mathbf{v}_I = 0$

$$\mathbf{v}_I - \mathbf{v}_M = -\left(\frac{-15}{-30}\right)^2 (\mathbf{v}_{OM})$$

$$\mathbf{v}_I - \mathbf{v}_M = -\frac{1}{4}\mathbf{v}_0 + \frac{1}{4}\mathbf{v}_M$$

$$\mathbf{v}_0 = 15 \text{ cm/s } \hat{\mathbf{i}}$$

$$\mathbf{v}_I = 0$$

$$\frac{5}{4}\mathbf{v}_M = \frac{\mathbf{v}_0}{4}$$

$$\mathbf{v}_M = \frac{\mathbf{v}_0}{4} = \frac{15 \text{ cm / s } \hat{\mathbf{i}}}{5} = 3 \text{ m/s } \hat{\mathbf{i}}$$

$$|\mathbf{v}_M| = 3$$

2.

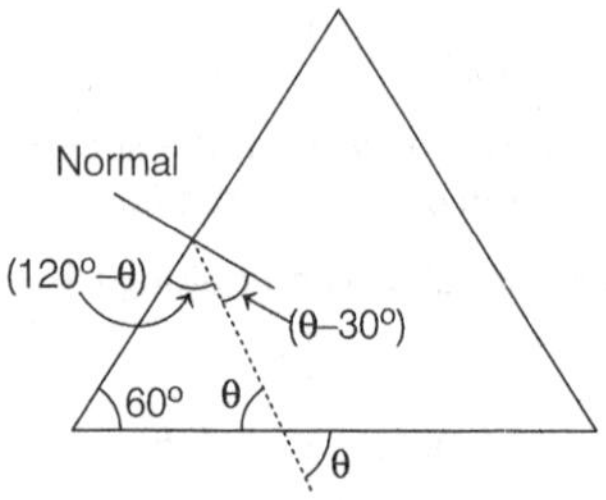

As we can see, for $\theta = 30°$, the ray will incident normally and hence, will retrace its path.

$\Rightarrow$ Option (a) is correct.

Considering the symmetry of the situation, we can have

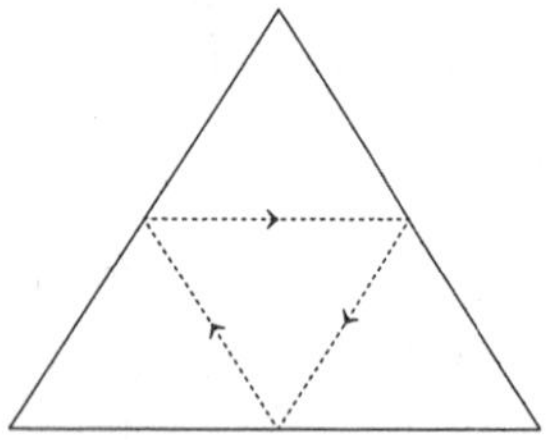

$\Rightarrow$ Option (b) is correct.

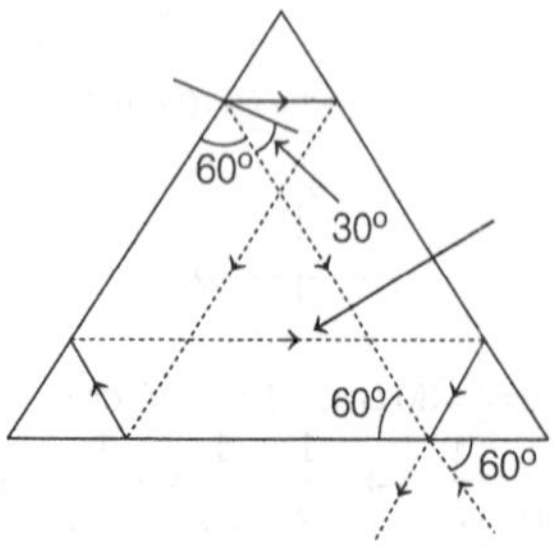

As it clear from the above diagram, ray comes out.

$\Rightarrow$ Option(c) is not correct.

Also, as is clear from the above diagram, total number of reflections = 5

$\Rightarrow$ Option (d) is not correct.

3. Image of point A

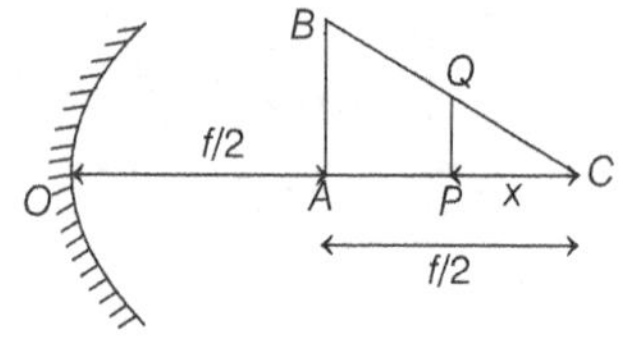

$$\frac{PQ}{x} = \frac{AB}{f/2}$$

$$\Rightarrow \quad PQ = \frac{2(AB)x}{f}$$

For A :

$$\frac{1}{v} + \frac{1}{[-(f/2)]} = \frac{1}{-f}$$

$$\Rightarrow \quad v = f$$

$$\Rightarrow \quad \frac{I_{AB}}{AB} = -\frac{v}{u} = -\frac{f}{\left(-\frac{f}{2}\right)}$$

$$\Rightarrow \quad I_{AB} = 2\,AB$$

For height of PQ,

$$\frac{1}{v} + \frac{1}{-[(f-x)]} = \frac{1}{-f}$$

$$\Rightarrow \quad \frac{1}{v} = \frac{1}{(f-x)} - \frac{1}{f}$$

$$\Rightarrow \quad v = \frac{f(f-x)}{x}$$

$$\Rightarrow \quad \frac{I_{PQ}}{PQ} = -\frac{v}{u} = \frac{f(f-x)}{x[(f-x)]} = \left(\frac{f}{x}\right)$$

$$\Rightarrow \quad I_{PQ} = \frac{f}{x}PQ = \left(\frac{f}{x}\right)\left(\frac{2(AB)x}{f}\right) \qquad \left[\because PQ = \frac{2(AB)x}{f}\right]$$

$$I_{PQ} = 2AB$$

(Size of image is independent of x. So, final image will be of same height terminating at infinity.)

4.

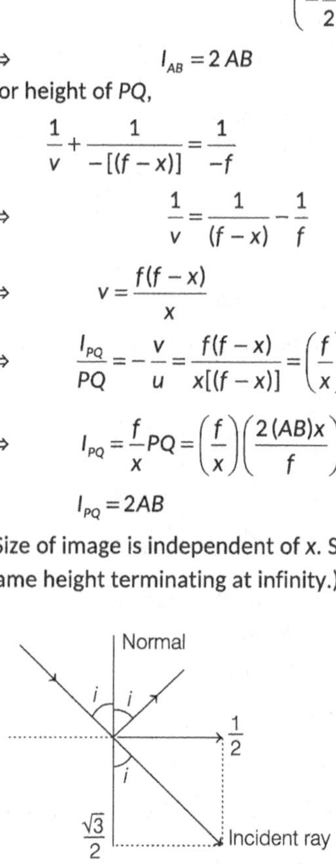

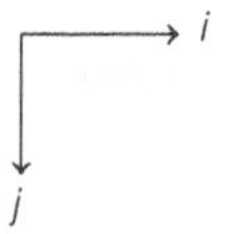

$$\tan i = \frac{1/2}{\sqrt{3}/2} = \frac{1}{\sqrt{3}}$$

$$\Rightarrow \quad i = 30°$$

CHAPTER~02

REFRACTION AT A PLANE SURFACE

LEVEL 01 Starter Level

2.1 Snell's Law

1 If μ_{ij} represents the refractive index, when a ray of light goes from medium i to medium j, then find value of $\mu_{12} \times \mu_{23} \times \mu_{34}$.

2 Find the speed of light in medium a, if speed of light in medium b is $c/3$, where c = speed of light in vacuum and light refracts from medium a to medium b making 45° and 60° respectively with the normal.

3 A ray of light AO is incident on the surface of oil. Reflected part of this ray OB and refracted part OC are mutually perpendicular as shown. Find refractive index of oil.

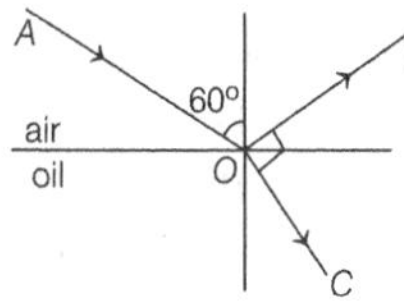

4 In the figure shown, find the angle made by the light ray with the normal in the medium of refractive index $\sqrt{2}$.

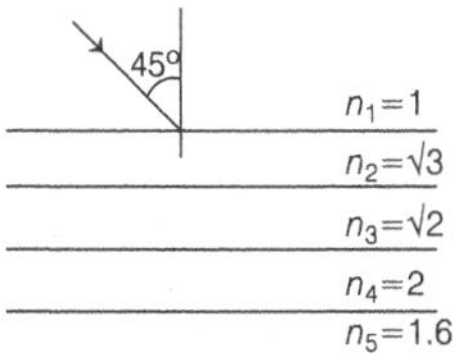

5 A ray of light falls on a transparent sphere with centre at C as shown in figure. The ray emerges from the sphere parallel to line AB. Find the refractive index of the sphere.

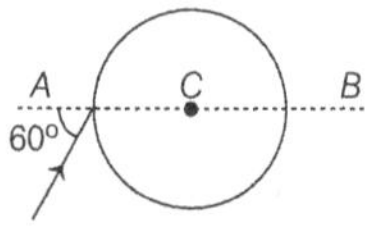

6 A pole of length 2.00 m stands half dipped in a swimming pool with water level 1 m higher than the bed. The refractive index of water is 4/3 and sunlight is coming at an angle of 37° with the vertical. Find the length of the shadow of the pole on the bed. [Use $\sin^{-1}(0.45) = 26.8°$, $\tan(26.8°) = 0.5$]

7 A cylindrical vessel, whose diameter and height both are equal to 30 cm, is placed on a horizontal surface and a small particle P is placed in it at a distance of 5.0 cm from the centre. An eye is placed at a position such that the edge of the bottom is just visible (see figure). The particle P is in the plane of drawing. Up to what minimum height should water be poured in the vessel to make the particle P visible?

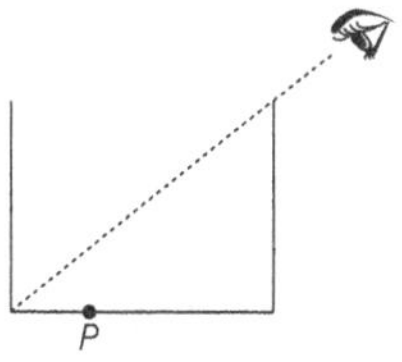

8 The XY-plane is the boundary between two transparent media. Medium-1 with $z > 0$ has refractive index $\sqrt{2}$ and medium-2 with $z < 0$ has a refractive index $\sqrt{3}$. A ray of light in medium-1 given by the vector $\mathbf{A} = 6\sqrt{3}\hat{\mathbf{i}} + 8\sqrt{3}\hat{\mathbf{j}} - 10\hat{\mathbf{k}}$ is incident on the plane of separation. Find the unit vector in the direction of refracted ray in medium-2.

2.2 Lateral Shift due to Parallel Glass Slab

1 A light ray falling at an angle of 60° with the surface of a clean slab of ice of thickness 1.0 m is refracted into it at an angle of 15°. Calculate the time taken by the light rays to cross the slab. Speed of light in vacuum $= 3 \times 10^8$ m/s.

2 A light ray is incident at 45° on a glass slab. The slab is 3 cm thick and the refractive index of the glass is 1.5. What will the lateral displacement of the ray be as a result of its passage through the slab? At what angle will the ray emerge from the slab?

2.3 Apparent Depth and Height

1 An observer in air ($n = 1$) sees the bottom of a beaker filled with water ($n = 4/3$) upto a height of 40 cm. What will be the depth felt by this observer?

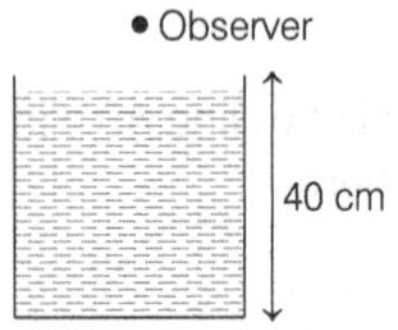

2 See the figure and answer the following questions.

(i) Find apparent height of the bird.
(ii) Find apparent depth of fish.
(iii) At what distance will the bird appear to the fish?
(iv) At what distance will the fish appear to the bird?

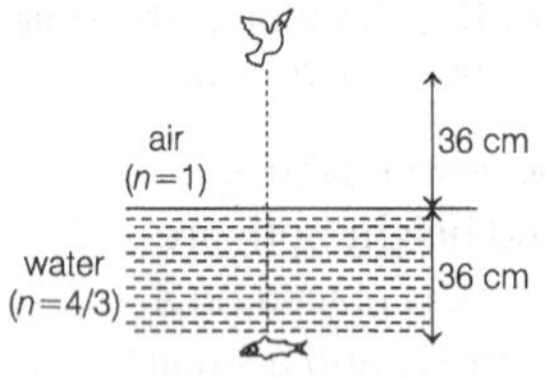

3 Find the apparent depth of the object seen below surface *AB* by the observer.

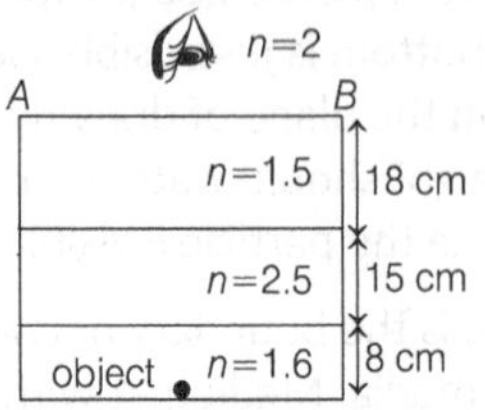

4 In the figure, an observer watches a fish through a 3.0 cm. The observer is in level with the fish, the index of refraction of the glass is 8/5 and that of the water is 4/3.

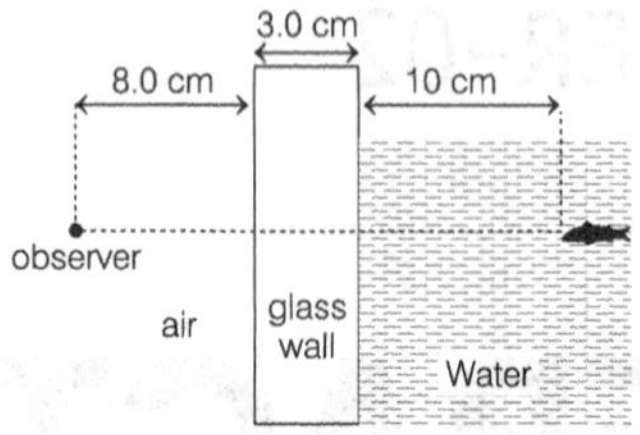

(a) To the fish, how far away does the observer appear to be?

(b) To the observer, how far away does the fish appear to be?

5 A concave mirror of radius *R* is kept on a horizontal table (figure). Water (refractive index $= \mu$) is poured into it upto a height *h*. Where should an object be placed (its distance from the water surface), so that its final image is formed on itself?

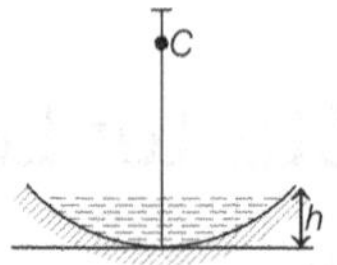

6 Rays incident on an interface would converge 10 cm below the interface, if they continued to move in straight lines without bending. But due to refraction, the rays will bend and meet some where else. Find the distance of meeting point of refracted rays below the interface, assuming the rays to be making small angles with the normal to the interface.

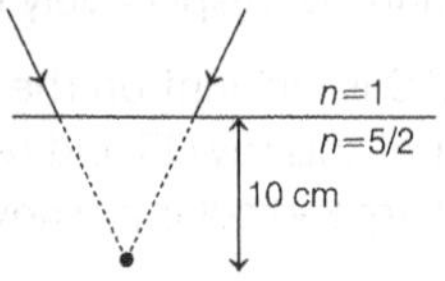

7 A concave mirror is placed inside water with its shining surface upwards and principal axis vertical as shown. Rays are incident parallel to the principal axis of concave mirror. Find the position of final image.

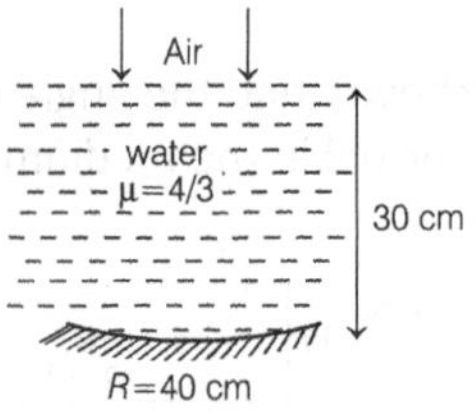

8 A fish is rising up vertically inside a pond with velocity of 4 cm/s and notices a bird, which is diving vertically downward and its velocity appears to be 16 cm/s (to the fish). What is the real velocity of the diving bird, if refractive index of water is 4/3?

2.4 Longitudinal Shift due to Parallel Glass Slab

1 A glass (RI = 1.5) slab having thickness 6 cm is placed infront of a concave mirror of focal length 20 cm as shown. A point object O is placed on the axis of mirror at a distance of 27 cm from the pole. Find the distance of final image from P.

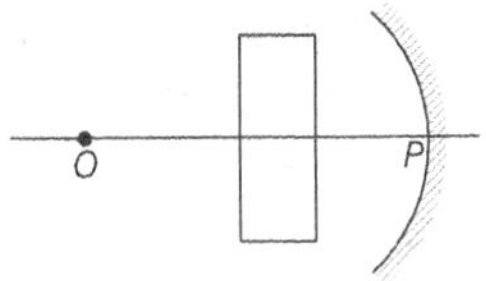

2 One face of a rectangular glass slab of thickness 6 cm and refractive index 1.5 is silvered. An object is held 8 cm in front of the front face as shown in figure. Find the distance of final image formed from the silvered face.

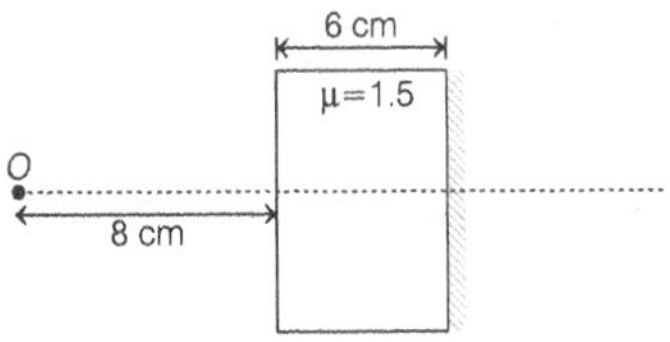

2.5 Total Internal Reflection

1 Find the maximum angle that can be made in glass medium ($\mu = 1.5$), if a light ray is refracted from glass to vacuum.

2 Find the angle of refraction in a medium ($\mu = 2$), if light is incident in vacuum, making angle equal to twice the critical angle.

3 Light goes from glass ($\mu = 1.5$) to air. Find the angle of incidence for which the angle of deviation is 90°.

4 A fish looking up through the water sees the outside world contained in a circular horizon. If the refractive index of water is 4/3 and fish is 12 cm below the surface, find the radius of the circle.

5 A point source is placed at a depth h below the surface of water (refractive index $= \mu$). The medium above the surface of water is air ($\mu = 1$). Find the area on the surface of water through which light comes in air from water.

6 A ray of light is incident normally on a prism of refractive index 3/2, as shown. The prism is immersed in water (refractive index $= 4/3$). Find the largest value of the θ, so that the ray is totally reflected at the face AC.

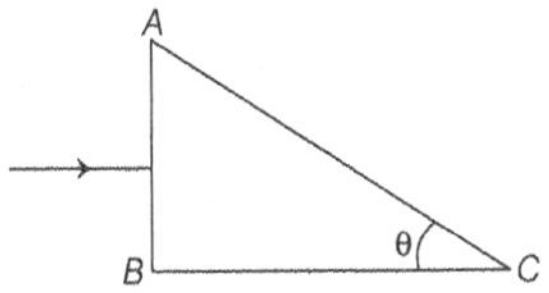

7 A long solid cylindrical glass rod of refractive index 3/2 is immersed in a liquid of refractive index $\frac{3\sqrt{3}}{4}$. A ray of light enters one end of the rod at the central axis as shown in the figure. Find the maximum value of angle θ for which total internal reflection occurs inside the rod?

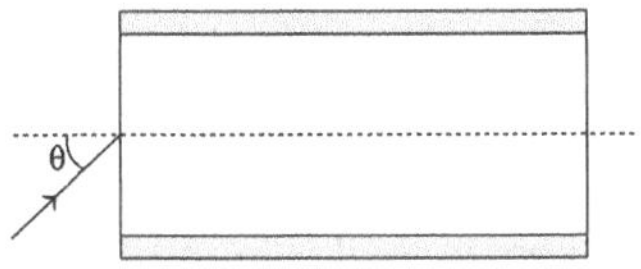

2.6 Variable Refractive Index

1 A ray of light travelling in air is incident at grazing angle (incidence angle = 90°) on a medium whose refractive index depends on the depth of the medium. The trajectory of the light in the medium is a parabola, $y = 2x^2$. Find, at a depth of 1 m in the medium

(i) the refractive index of the medium and

(ii) angle of incidence ϕ.

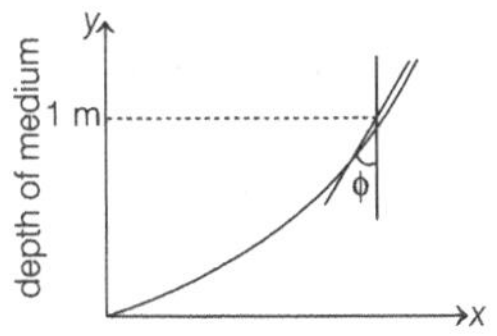

2 A ray of light travelling in air is incident at grazing angle (incident angle = 90°) on a long rectangular slab of a transparent medium of thickness $t = 1.0$ m (see figure). The point of incidence is the origin $A(0,0)$. The medium has a variable index of refraction $n(y)$ given by

$n(y) = [ky^{3/2} + 1]^{1/2}$, where $k = 1.0\ \text{m}^{-3/2}$.

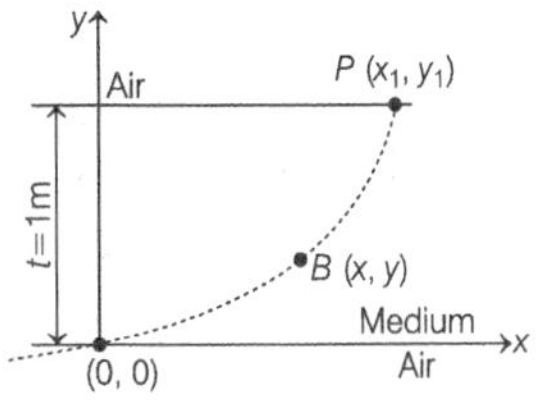

The refractive index of air is 1.0.

(i) Obtain an equation for the trajectory $y(x)$ of the ray in the medium.

(ii) Determine the coordinates (x_1, y_1) of the point P, where the ray intersects the upper surface of the slab-air boundary.

2.7 Prism

1 Draw a graph to show the angle of deviation δ with variation of the angle of incidence i for a monochromatic ray of light passing through a prism of refracting angle A. Deduce the relation

$$\mu = \frac{\sin\left(\frac{(A+\delta_{min})}{2}\right)}{\sin\left(\frac{A}{2}\right)}.$$

2 For a prism kept in air it is found that for an angle of incidence 60°, the angle of refraction A, angle of deviation δ and angle of emergence e become equal. Find the refractive index of the prism.

3 A prism of refractive index $\sqrt{2}$ has refracting angle 60°. In order that a ray suffers minimum deviation, what angle should it be incident at?

4 On an equilateral prism, it is observed that a ray strikes grazingly at one face and if refractive index of the prism is 2, then find the angle of deviation.

5 A ray of light is incident at an angle of 60° on one face of a prism which has an angle of 30°. The ray emerging out of the prism makes an angle of 30° with the incident ray. Show that the emergent ray is perpendicular to the face through which it emerges and calculate the refractive index of the material of the prism.

6 One face of a prism with a refracting angle of 30° is coated with silver. A ray incident on other face at an angle of 45° is refracted and reflected from the silvered coated face and retraces its path. Find the refractive index of the prism.

7 See the figure. Find the deviation caused by a thin prism having refracting angle 4° and refractive index 3/2.

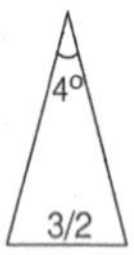

2.8 Dispersion

1 The refractive indices of flint glass for red and violet light are 1.613 and 1.632, respectively. Find the angular dispersion produced by a thin prism of flint glass having refracting angle 5°.

2 Calculate the dispersive power for crown glass from the following data $\mu_V = 1.523$ and $\mu_R = 1.515$.

3 If two prisms are combined, as shown in figure. Find the total angular dispersion and angle of deviation suffered by a white ray of light incident on the combination.

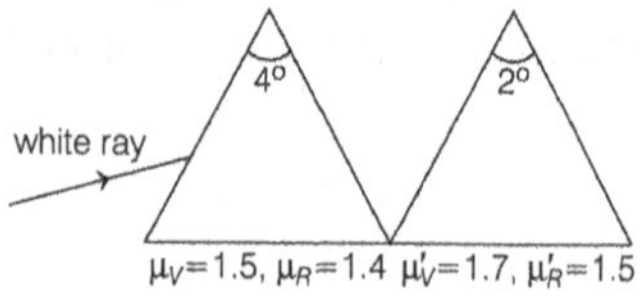

4 Two thin prisms are combined to form an achromatic combination.

For I prism $A = 4°, \mu_R = 1.35, \mu_Y = 1.40, \mu_V = 1.42$, for II prism $\mu_R' = 1.7, \mu_Y' = 1.8$ and $\mu_V' = 1.9$. Find the prism angle of II prism and the net mean deviation.

5 The refractive indices of the crown glass for blue and red light are 1.51 and 1.49 respectively and those of the flint glass are 1.77 and 1.73 respectively. An isosceles prism of angle 6° is made of crown glass. A beam of white light is incident at a small angle on this prism. The other flint glass isosceles prism is combined with the crown glass prism such that there is no deviation of the incident light.

(i) Determine the angle of the flint glass prism.

(ii) Calculate the net dispersion of the combined system.

LEVEL 02 JEE Main Level

Single Choice Correct Questions

1 A ray of light passes from vacuum into a medium of refractive index n. If the angle of incidence is twice the angle of refraction, then the angle of incidence is

(a) $\cos^{-1}\left(\frac{n}{2}\right)$ (b) $\sin^{-1}\left(\frac{n}{2}\right)$

(c) $2\cos^{-1}\left(\frac{n}{2}\right)$ (d) $2\sin^{-1}\left(\frac{n}{2}\right)$

2 A ray of light is incident on a parallel slab of thickness t and refractive index n. If the angle of incidence θ is small, then the displacement in the incident and emergent ray will be

(a) $\frac{t\theta(n-1)}{n}$ (b) $\frac{t\theta}{n}$

(c) $\frac{t\theta n}{n-1}$ (d) None of these

3 A ray incident at a point at an angle of incidence of 60° enters a glass sphere of $\mu = \sqrt{3}$ and it is reflected and refracted at the farther surface of the sphere. The angle between reflected and refracted rays at this surface is

(a) 50° (b) 90° (c) 60° (d) 40°

4 A ray of light passes through four transparent media with refractive indices μ_1, μ_2, μ_3 and μ_4 as shown in the figure. The surfaces of all media are parallel. If the emergent ray *CD* is parallel to the incident ray AB, we must have

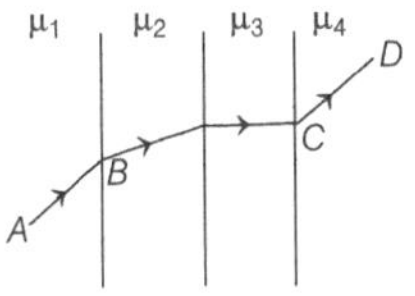

(a) $\mu_1 = \mu_2$ (b) $\mu_2 = \mu_3$
(c) $\mu_3 = \mu_4$ (d) $\mu_4 = \mu_1$

5 A ray of light is incident at the glass-water interface at an angle *i*, it emerges finally parallel to the surface of water, then the value of μ_g would be

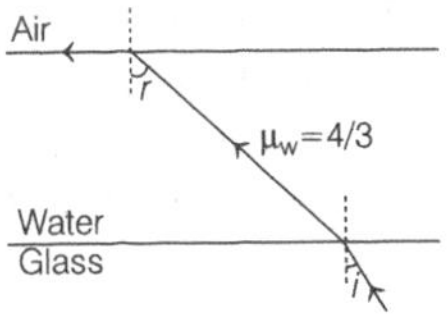

(a) $\left(\frac{4}{3}\right)\sin i$ (b) $\frac{1}{\sin i}$

(c) $\frac{4}{3}$ (d) 1

6 A ray of light moving along the vector $(-\hat{i} - 2\hat{j})$ undergoes refraction at an interface of two media, which is the *XZ*-plane. The refractive index for $y > 0$ is 2 while for $y < 0$, it is $\frac{\sqrt{5}}{2}$. The unit vector along which the refracted ray moves is

(a) $\frac{(-3\hat{i} - 5\hat{j})}{\sqrt{34}}$ (b) $\frac{(-4\hat{i} - 3\hat{j})}{5}$

(c) $\frac{(-3\hat{i} - 4\hat{j})}{5}$ (d) None of these

7 How much water should be filled in a container of 21 cm in height, so that it appears half filled when viewed from the top of the container? (Assume near normal incidence and $\mu_w = \frac{4}{3}$)

(a) 8.0 cm (b) 10.5 cm
(c) 12.0 cm (d) 14.0 cm

8 A tiny air bubble in a glass slab ($\mu = 1.5$) appears from one side to be 6 cm from the glass surface and from other side, 4 cm. The thickness of the glass slab is

(a) 10 cm (b) 6.67 cm
(c) 15 cm (d) None of these

9 A small rod *ABC* is put in water $\left(\mu_w = \frac{4}{3}\right)$ making an angle 6° with vertical. If it is viewed paraxially from above, it will look like bent shaped *ABC′*. The angle of bending ($\angle CBC'$) will be

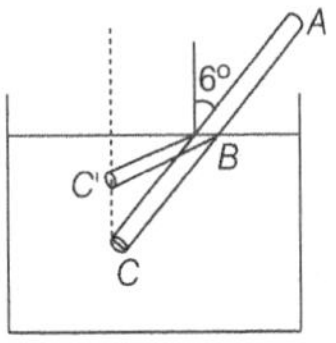

(a) 2° (b) 3° (c) 4° (d) 4.5°

10 What is the length of the image of the rod in mirror, according to the observer in air?

(The refractive index of liquid is μ)

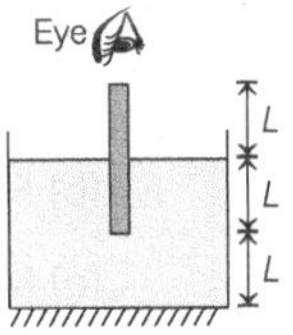

(a) $\mu L + L$ (b) $L + \frac{L}{\mu}$

(c) $\mu L + \frac{L}{\mu}$ (d) None of these

11 A fish rising vertically at the rate on 3 m/s, towards the surface of water observed a bird above the water, diving vertically towards it at the rate of 9 m/s. The refractive index of water is 4/3. Calculate the actual velocity (velocity w.r.t ground) of bird

(a) 1.5 m/s (b) 6 m/s (c) 12 m/s (d) 4.5 m/s

12 In the given figure, the image of point *P* when viewed from top of the slabs will be

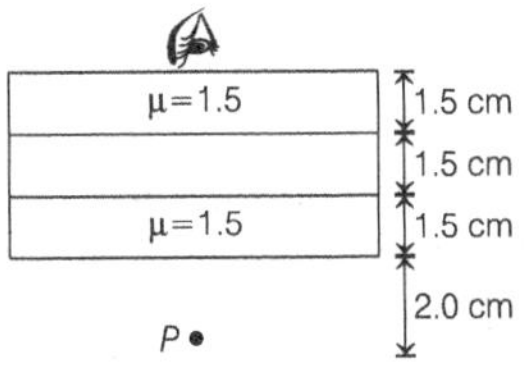

(a) 2.0 cm above *P* (b) 1.5 cm above *P*
(c) 2.0 cm below *P* (d) 1 cm above *P*

13 A vessel of depth *H* is filled with a non-homogeneous liquid whose refractive index varies with the depth *y* as $\mu = \left(1 + \frac{y}{H}\right)$. The apparent depth as seen by an observer from above is

(a) 0.693 *H* (b) 0.667 *H*
(c) 0.75 *H* (d) 0.500 *H*

14 A container is filled with water ($\mu = 1.33$) upto a height of 33.25 cm. A concave mirror is placed 15 cm above the water level and the image of an object placed at the bottom is formed 25 cm below the water level. The focal length of the mirror is

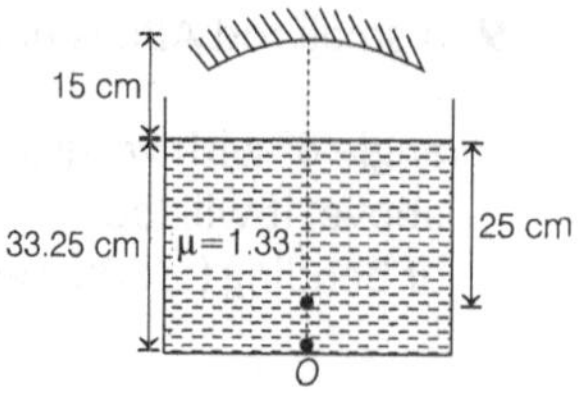

(a) 10 cm (b) 15 cm (c) 18.3 cm (d) 25 cm

15 A ray of light travelling in air is incident at grazing angle on a slab with variable refractive index, $n(y) = [ky^{3/2} + 1]^{1/2}$, where $k = 1\,\text{m}^{-3/2}$ and follows path as shown. What is the total deviation produced by slab, when the ray comes out?

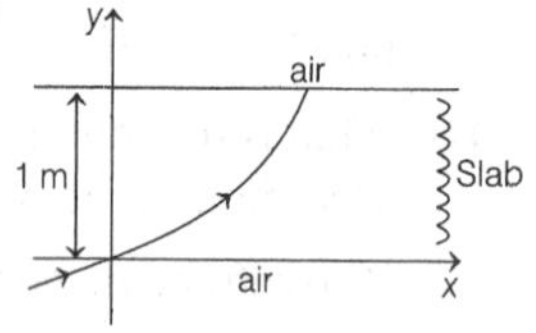

(a) 60° (b) 53°

(c) $\sin^{-1}\left(\frac{4}{9}\right)$ (d) No deviation at all

16 An observer can see through a pinhole the top end of a thin rod of height h, placed as shown in the figure. The beaker height is $3h$ and its radius h. When the beaker is filled with a liquid up to a height $2h$, he can see the lower end of the rod. Then, the refractive index of the liquid is

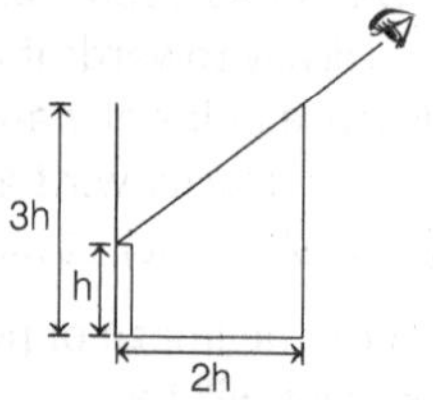

(a) $\frac{5}{2}$ (b) $\sqrt{\frac{5}{2}}$ (c) $\sqrt{\frac{3}{2}}$ (d) $\frac{3}{2}$

17 Two mirrors, placed perpendicularly, form two sides of a vessel filled with water. A light ray is incident on the water surface at an angle α and emerges at an angle β after getting reflected from both the mirrors inside. The relation between α and β is expressed as

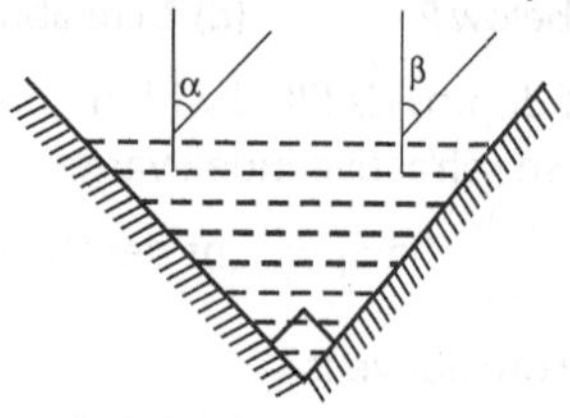

(a) $\alpha = \beta$ (b) $\alpha > \beta$ (c) $\alpha < \beta$

(d) All are possible, depending upon α

18 A diverging beam of light from a point source S having divergence angle α, falls symmetrically on a glass slab as shown. The angles of incidence of the two extreme rays are equal. If the thickness of the glass slab is t and the refractive index n, then the divergence angle of the emergent beam is

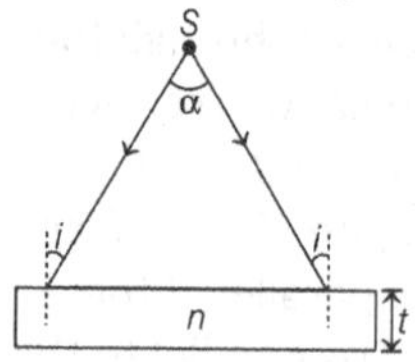

(a) zero (b) α

(c) $\sin^{-1}\left(\frac{1}{n}\right)$ (d) $2\sin^{-1}\left(\frac{1}{n}\right)$

19 An object is placed 30 cm (from the reflecting surface) in front of a block of glass 10 cm thick having its farther side silvered. The image is found to be at 23.2 cm behind the silvered face, by an observer infront of the block. The refractive index of glass is

(a) 1.41 (b) 1.46 (c) $\frac{200}{132}$ (d) 1.61

20. A beam of light is converging towards a point. A plane parallel plate of glass of thickness t refractive index μ is introduced in the path of the beam. The convergent point is shifted by (assume near normal incidence)

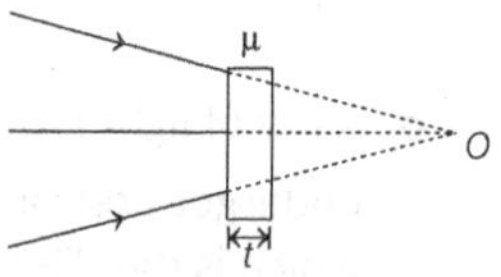

(a) $t\left(1 - \frac{1}{\mu}\right)$ away (b) $t\left(1 + \frac{1}{\mu}\right)$ away

(c) $t\left(1 - \frac{1}{\mu}\right)$ nearer (d) $t\left(1 + \frac{1}{\mu}\right)$ nearer

21 Inside a 6 cm thick glass slab, a rectangular cavity is made as shown.On one face of slab, a cross is marked. On other side, an observer is looking on the slab. Find the shift of cross as seen by the man.

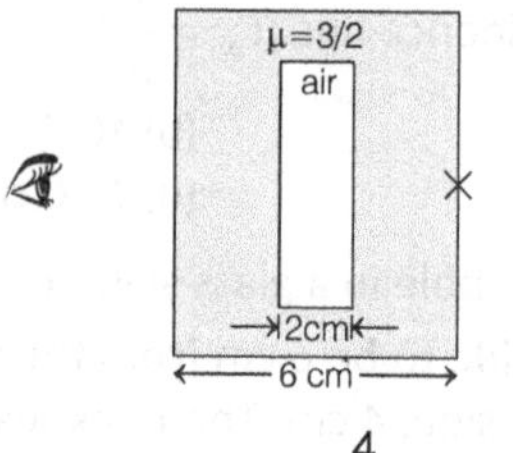

(a) $\frac{2}{3}$ cm (b) $\frac{4}{3}$ cm

(c) $\frac{8}{3}$ cm (d) None of these

22 A ray of sunlight enters a spherical water droplet $\left(n = \frac{4}{3}\right)$ at an angle of incidence 53° measured with respect to the normal to the surface. It is reflected from the back surface of the droplet and re-enters into air. The angle between the incoming and outgoing ray is [Take sin 53° = 0.8]

(a) 15° (8) 34° (c) 138° (d) 30°

23 The critical angle of light going from medium *A* to medium *B* is θ. The speed of light in medium *A* is *v*. The speed of light in medium *B* is

(a) $\frac{v}{\sin\theta}$ (b) $v\sin\theta$ (c) $v\cot\theta$ (d) $v\tan\theta$

24 A small source of light is 4 m below the surface of a liquid of refractive index 5/3. In order to cut-off all the light coming out of liquid surface, minimum diameter of the disc placed on the surface of liquid is

(a) 3 m (b) 4 m (c) 6 m (d) ∞

25 A fish looking up through the water sees the outside world contained in a circular horizon. If the refractive index of water is 4/3 and the fish is 12 cm below the surface, the radius of this circle is

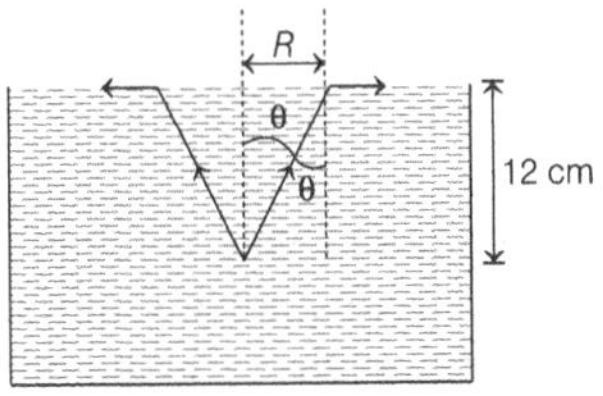

(a) $36\sqrt{5}$ cm (b) $4\sqrt{5}$ cm

(c) $36\sqrt{7}$ cm (d) $\frac{36}{\sqrt{7}}$ cm

26 A ray of light from a denser medium strikes a rarer medium at an angle of incidence *i* (see figure). The reflected and refracted rays make an angle of 90° with each other. The angles of reflection and refraction are *r* and *r′*. The critical angle is

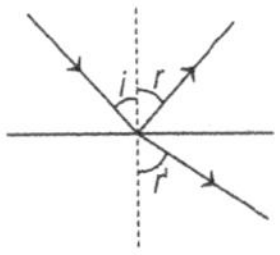

(a) $\sin^{-1}(\tan r)$ (b) $\sin^{-1}(\cot i)$

(c) $\sin^{-1}(\tan r')$ (d) $\tan^{-1}(\sin i)$

27 A ray of light traveling in water is incident on its surface open to air. The angle of incidence is θ, which is less than the critical angle. Then, there will be

(a) only a reflected ray and no refracted ray

(b) only a refracted ray and no reflected ray

(c) a reflected ray and a refracted ray and the angle between them would be less than $180° - 2\theta$

(d) a reflected ray and a refracted ray and the angle between them would be greater than $180° - 2\theta$.

28 A ray of light travelling in glass $\left(\mu_g = \frac{3}{2}\right)$ is incident on a glass air surface at the critical angle. If a thin layer of water $\left(\mu_w = \frac{4}{3}\right)$ is now poured on the glass air surface, at what angle will the ray of light emerge into air at the water air surface?

(a) 60° (b) 30° (c) 45° (d) 90°

29 A ray of light travels from an optical denser medium to rarer medium. The critical angle for the two media is *C*. The maximum possible deviation of the refracted light ray can be

(a) $\pi - C$ (b) $2C$ (c) $\pi - 2C$ (d) $\frac{\pi}{2} - C$

30 A rectangular glass slab *ABCD*, of refractive index n_1, is immersed in water of refractive index $n_2 (n_1 > n_2)$. A ray of light is incident at the surface *AB* of the slab as shown. The maximum value of the angle of incidence α_{max}, such that the ray comes out only from the other surface *CD* is given by

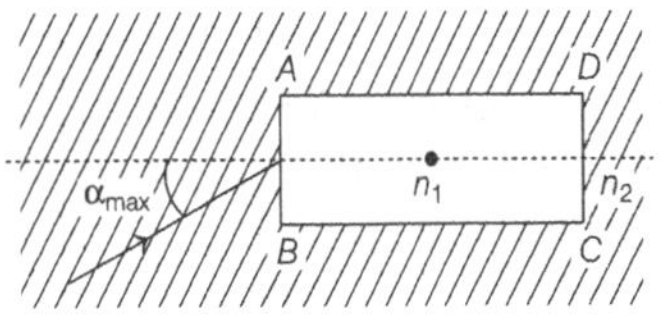

(a) $\sin^{-1}\left[\frac{n_1}{n_2}\cos\left(\sin^{-1}\frac{n_2}{n_1}\right)\right]$

(b) $\sin^{-1}\left[n_1\cos\left(\sin^{-1}\frac{1}{n_2}\right)\right]$

(c) $\sin^{-1}\left(\frac{n_1}{n_2}\right)$ (d) $\sin^{-1}\left(\frac{n_2}{n_1}\right)$

31 A ray R_1 is incident on the plane surface of the glass slab (kept in air) of refractive index $\sqrt{2}$ at angle of incidence equal to the critical angle for this air glass system. The refracted ray R_2 undergoes partial reflection and refraction at the other surface. The angle between reflected ray R_3 and the refracted ray R_4 at the surface is

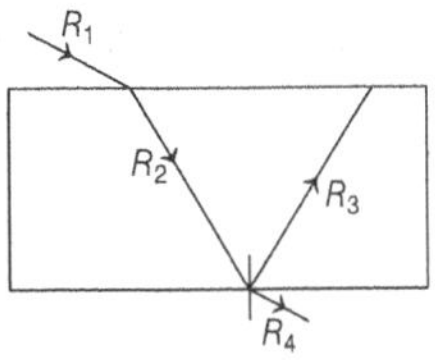

(a) 45° (b) 135°

(c) 105° (d) 75°

32 The observer at *O* views two closely spaced spots on a vertical wall through an angled glass slab as shown. As seen by observer, the spots appear

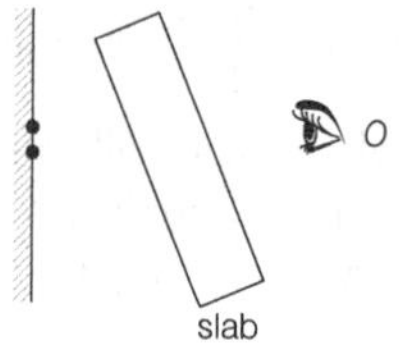

(a) shifted upward, such that distance between them remains same.
(b) shifted downward, such that distance between them remains same.
(c) spaced farther apart
(d) spaced closer together

33 A ray of light is incident on one face of a transparent slab of thickness 15 cm. The angle of incidence is 60°. If the lateral displacement of the ray on emerging from the parallel plane is $5\sqrt{3}$ cm, the refractive index of the material of the slab is
(a) 1.414 (b) 1.532
(c) 1.732 (d) None of these

34 The angle of incidence *i* for an equilateral prism of refractive index $\sqrt{3}$ so that the ray is parallel to the base inside the prism is
(a) 30° (b) 45°
(c) 60° (d) either 30° or 60°

35 A ray of monochromatic light is incident on one refracting face of a prism of angle 75°. It passes through the prism and is incident on the other face at the critical angle. If the refractive index of the material of the prism is $\sqrt{2}$, the angle of incidence on the first face of the prism is
(a) 30° (b) 45° (c) 60° (d) 0°

36 A certain prism is found to produce a minimum deviation of 38°. It produces a deviation of 44°, when the angle of incidence is either 42° or 62°. What is the angle of incidence, when it is undergoing minimum deviation?
(a) 45° (b) 49° (c) 40° (d) 55°

37 On an equilateral prism, it is observed that a ray strikes grazingly at one face and if refractive index of the prism is 2, then the angle of deviation is
(a) 60° (b) 120° (c) 30° (d) 90°

38 For a prism of apex angle 45°, it is found that the angle of emergence is 45° for grazing incidence. Calculate the refractive index of the prism.
(a) $(2)^{1/2}$ (b) $(3)^{1/2}$ (c) 2 (d) $(5)^{1/2}$

39 A prism has a refractive index $\sqrt{\frac{3}{2}}$ and refracting angle 90°. Find the minimum deviation produced by prism.
(a) 40° (b) 45° (c) 30° (d) 49°

40 A light ray is incident on face *AB* of an equilateral glass prism *ABC*. After refraction at *AB*, the ray is incident on face *BC* at the critical angle, so that it gets reflected from face *BC* and finally emerges out from face *AC*. Net deviation angle of the ray is 112° anti-clockwise. The angle of incidence *i* has value

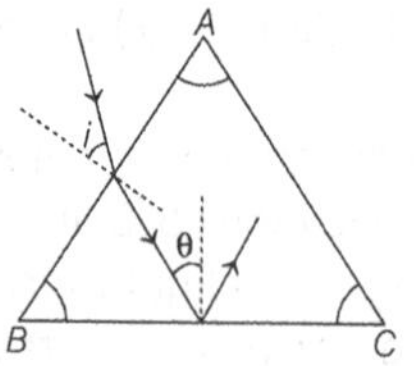

(a) 22° (b) 24° (c) 26° (d) 28°

41 One of the refractive surfaces of a prism of angle 30° is silvered. A ray of light incident at an angle of 60° retraces it path. The refractive index of the material of prism is

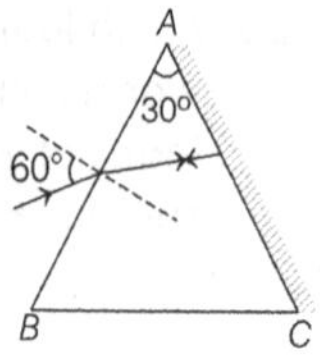

(a) $\sqrt{2}$ (b) $\sqrt{3}$
(c) 3/2 (d) 2

42 What is the minimum value of refractive index of a prism, having refracting angle *A* so that there is no emergent ray irrespective of angle of incidence?
(a) $\text{cosec}\left(\frac{A}{4}\right)$ (b) $\sin\left(\frac{A}{4}\right)$
(c) $\text{cosec}\left(\frac{A}{2}\right)$ (d) $\sin\left(\frac{A}{2}\right)$

43 A glass prism $\left(\mu_g = \frac{3}{2}\right)$ is immersed in water $\left(\mu_w = \frac{4}{3}\right)$. Now a beam of light is incident normally at face *AB* of a glass prism. The largest value for the angle ϕ, so that the ray is totally reflected at face *AC* is

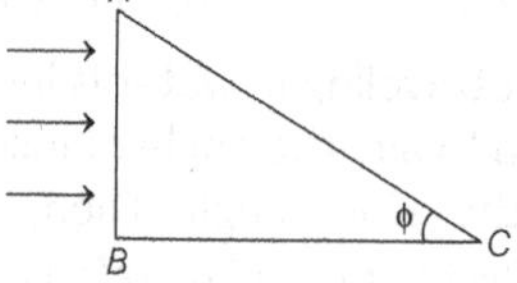

(a) $\cos^{-1}\left(\frac{2}{3}\right)$ (b) $\cos^{-1}\left(\frac{8}{9}\right)$
(c) $\cos^{-1}\left(\frac{3}{2}\right)$ (d) $\cos^{-1}\left(\frac{9}{8}\right)$

44 An isosceles prism of angle 120° has a refractive index 1.44. Two parallel rays of monochromatic light enter the prism parallel to each other in air as shown. The rays emerge from the opposite face

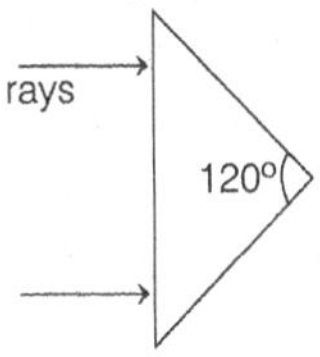

(a) are parallel to each other
(b) are diverging
(c) make an angle $2[\sin^{-1}(0.72) - 30°]$ with each other
(d) make an angle $2\sin^{-1}(0.72)$ with each other

45 A beam of light, consisting of red, green and blue colours, is incident on a right angled prism, as shown. The refractive indices of the material of the prism for the above red, green and blue wavelengths are 1.39, 1.44 and 1.47 respectively. The prism will

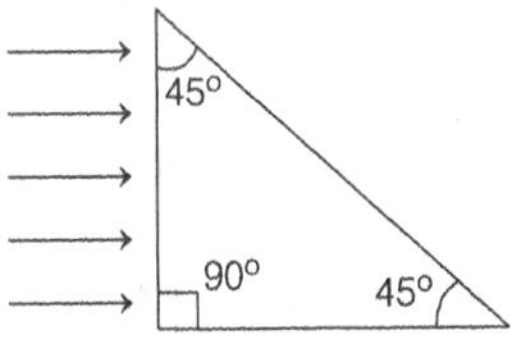

(a) separate part of the red colour from the green and blue colours
(b) separate part of the blue colour from the red and green colours
(c) separate all the three colours from one another
(d) not separate even partially any colour from the other two colours

46 The ratio of angle of minimum deviation produced by a thin prism $\left(\mu = \frac{3}{2}\right)$ in air to that in water is $\left[\mu_w = \frac{4}{3}\right]$

(a) $\frac{3}{4}$ (b) 2 (c) 4 (d) $\frac{1}{4}$

47 A ray of light strikes a plane mirror at an angle of incidence 45° as shown in the figure. After reflection, the ray passes through a prism of refractive index 1.5, whose apex angle is 4°. The angle through which the mirror should be rotated if the total deviation of the ray is to be 90° is

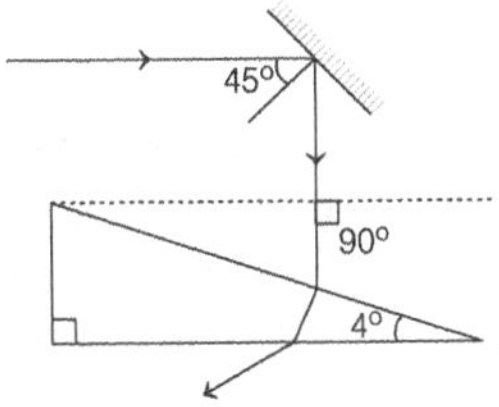

(a) 1° clockwise (b) 1° anti-clockwise
(c) 2° clockwise (d) 2° anti-clockwise

48 A ray of light is coming from air to water. Which of the following figure shows dispersion of light?

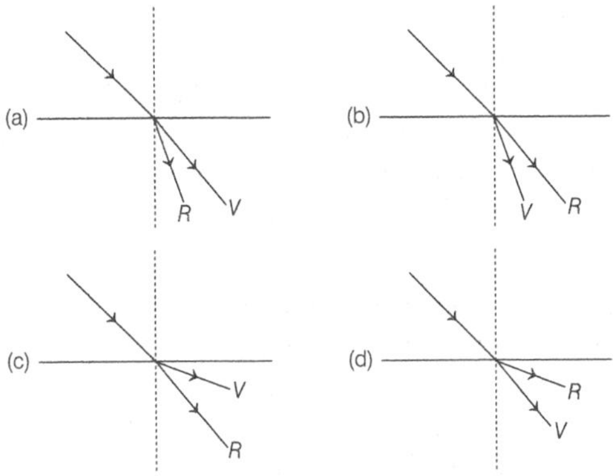

49 A ray of light passes through a prism whose refracting angle is 5° and dispersive power is 0.03. The refractive index for the mean ray in a spectrum is 1.62. The mean deviation and angle of dispersion respectively are

(a) 3.1°, 0.077° (b) 3.1°, 0.093°
(c) 6.2°, 0.093° (d) 6.2°, 0.077°

50 A thin prism P_1 with angle 4° and made from glass of refractive index 1.54 is combined with another thin prism P_2 made from glass of refractive index 1.72 to produce dispersion without deviation. The angle of the prism P_2 is

(a) 5.33° (b) 4° (c) 3° (d) 2.6°

51 Two prisms of different materials (one made of crown glass and other made of flint glass) and different angles (A_C and A_F) are combined in opposite manner. The condition to obtain deviation without dispersion is

(a) $\frac{\omega_C}{\omega_F} = -\frac{\delta_{FY}}{\delta_{CY}}$ (b) $\frac{\omega_C}{\omega_F} = \frac{\delta_{FY}}{\delta_{CY}}$

(c) $\frac{\omega_F}{\omega_C} = \frac{\delta_{FY}}{\delta_{CY}}$ (d) $\frac{\omega_F}{\omega_C} = -\frac{\delta_{FY}}{\delta_{CY}}$

52 Three thin prisms are combined as shown in figure. The refractive indices of the crown glass for red and violet rays are μ_r and μ_v respectively and those for the flint glass are μ_r' and μ_v' respectively. The ratio $\frac{A'}{A}$ for which there is no net angular dispersion is

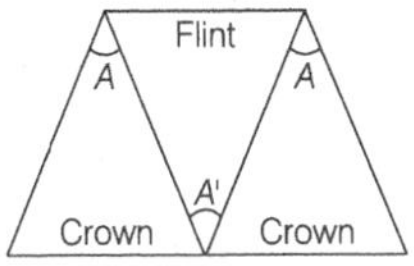

(a) $\frac{\mu_v - \mu_r}{2(\mu_v' - \mu_r')}$ (b) $\frac{2(\mu_v - \mu_r)}{\mu_v' - \mu_r'}$

(c) $\frac{\mu_v - \mu_r}{\mu_v' - \mu_r'}$ (d) None of these

Numerical Value Questions

1 A small piece of wood is floating on the surface of a $\sqrt{7}$ m deep lake. When the sun is vertically above the piece, its shadow is formed at *A*. When the sun is just setting, the shadow of the piece is formed at *B*. If the refractive index of water is 4/3, then find the distance (in m) between *A* and *B*.

2 A particle lies on the bottom of a tank *T* filled with water upto a height of 90 cm. The medium above the surface of water is of RI = 1.2 above which there is mirror *M*. Beyond the mirror *M* the region contains air ($\mu = 1$).

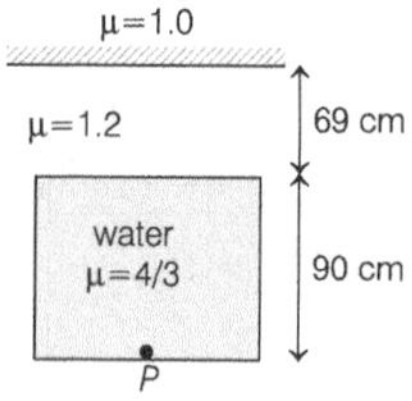

The distance of the image formed by the mirror after reflection of the rays coming from *P* is .... cm (w.r.t. mirror).

3 A concave mirror of radius of curvature 40 cm is filled with water $\left(n = \frac{4}{3}\right)$ upto a height of 12 cm. A point object *O* is kept on the principal axis of the mirror at height 13.5 cm from the water surface. Find the position (in cm) of the final image formed from water surface after refraction at water surface, reflection at mirror and again refraction at water surface in succession.

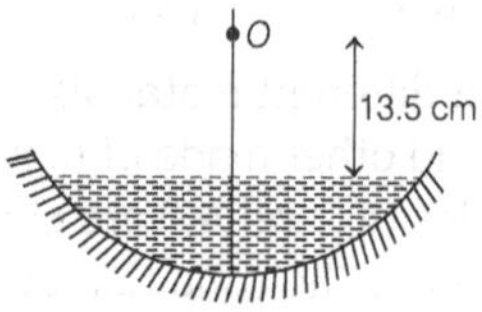

4 A rod of glass ($\mu = 1.5$) and square cross-section is bent into the shape as shown. A parallel beam of light falls perpendicularly on the flat surface *A*. *d* is width of a side and *R* is the radius of inner semicircle. Find the minimum value of $\left(\frac{R}{d}\right)$, so that all light entering the glass through *A* emerge from glass through *B*.

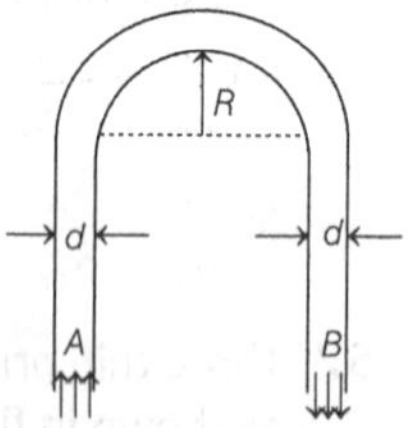

5 A transparent solid cube of side *a* has refractive index 3/2. A point source of light is embedded in it at its centre. If the minimum area of the surface of the cube which must be painted black, so that the source is not visible from outside is $n\pi a^2$, then find *n*.

6 Mirror in the arrangement shown in figure is moving up with speed 4 cm/s. Find the speed of final image of object *O* (in cm/s) formed after two refractions and one reflection.

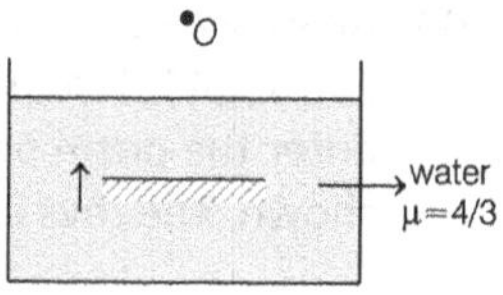

7 *AB* and *CD* are two slabs. The medium between the slabs has refractive index 2. Find the minimum angle (in degrees) of incidence of *Q*, so that the ray is totally reflected by both the slabs.

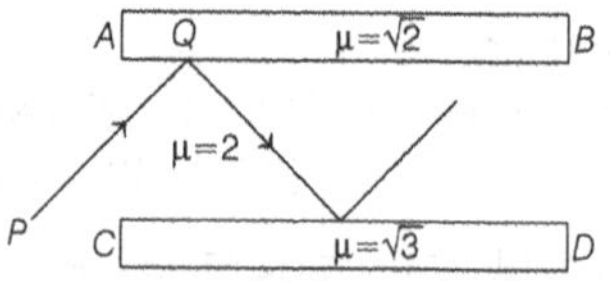

8 A composite slab consisting of different media is placed infront of a concave mirror of radius of curvature 150 cm. The whole arrangement is placed in water.

An object *O* is placed at a distance 20 cm from the slab. The RI of different media are given in the diagram. Find the distance of the final image formed by the system from the object.

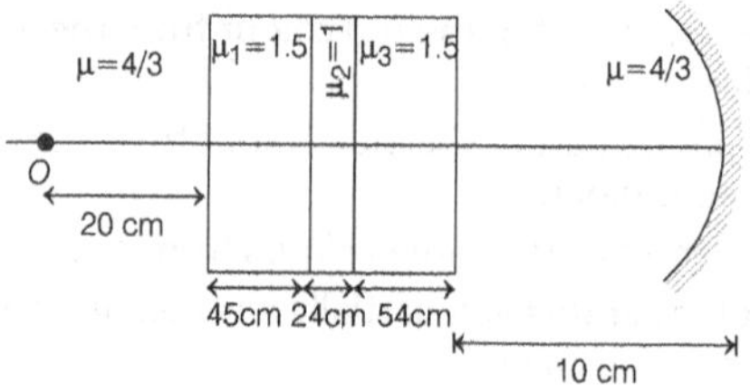

9 Find the speed of bird with respect to fish (in m/s) at given instant, if water surface is moving downward 2 m/s at this time

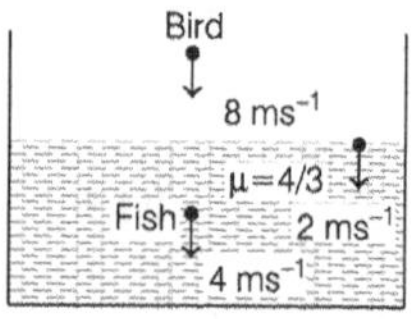

10 A ray of light enters at grazing angle of incidence into an assembly of three isosceles right angled prisms having refractive indices $\mu_1 = \sqrt{2}, \mu_2 = \sqrt{x}$ and $\mu_3 = \sqrt{3}$. If finally emergent light ray also emerges at grazing angle, then calculate *x*.

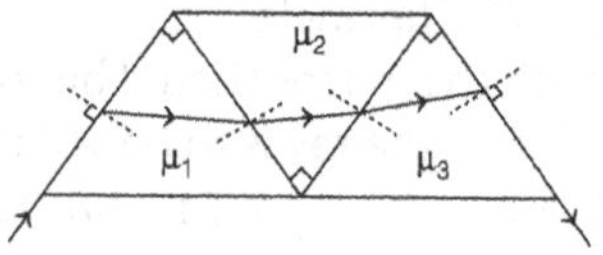

LEVEL 03 JEE Advanced Level

Single Choice Correct Questions

1 Light passes from air into flint glass with index of refraction n. What angle of incidence must the light have, so that the component of its velocity perpendicular to the interface remains same in both medium?

(a) $\tan^{-1}\left(\frac{1}{n}\right)$ (b) $\sin^{-1}\left(\frac{1}{n}\right)$

(c) $\cos^{-1}\left(\frac{1}{n}\right)$ (d) $\tan^{-1} n$

2 A ray of light is incident at an angle of 75° into a medium having refractive index μ. The reflected and the refracted rays are found to suffer equal deviations in opposite directions. μ equals

(a) $\frac{\sqrt{3}+1}{\sqrt{3}-1}$ (b) $\frac{\sqrt{3}+1}{2}$

(c) $\frac{2\sqrt{2}}{\sqrt{3}+1}$ (d) None of these

3 A monochromatic beam of width t is incident at 45° on an air water interface as shown in the figure. The refractive index of water is μ and that of air is 1. The width of the beam in water is

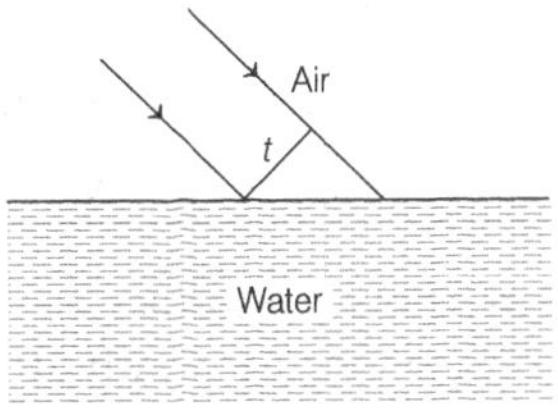

(a) $(\mu - 1)\,t$ (b) μt (c) $\frac{\sqrt{\mu^2-1}}{\mu}t$ (d) $\frac{\sqrt{2\mu^2-1}}{\mu}t$

4 A ray of light is incident on the surface of a sphere of refractive index $\frac{\sqrt{7}}{2}$. Other half of sphere is silvered. After refraction it is reflected and then refracted out of sphere again such that the total deviation is minimum, then total deviation of the ray will be $\left(\sin 41° = \sqrt{\frac{3}{7}}\right)$

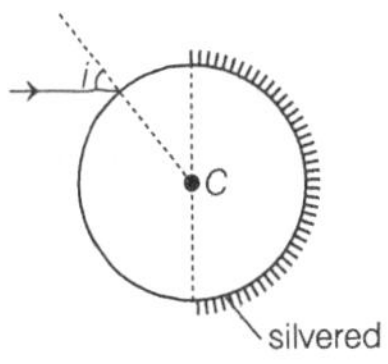

(a) 102° (b) 98° (c) 136° (d) 163°

5 In a vessel, as shown in fig, point P is just visible when no liquid is filled in vessel through a telescope in the air. When liquid is filled in the vessel completely, point Q is visible without moving the vessel or telescope. Find the refractive index of the liquid.

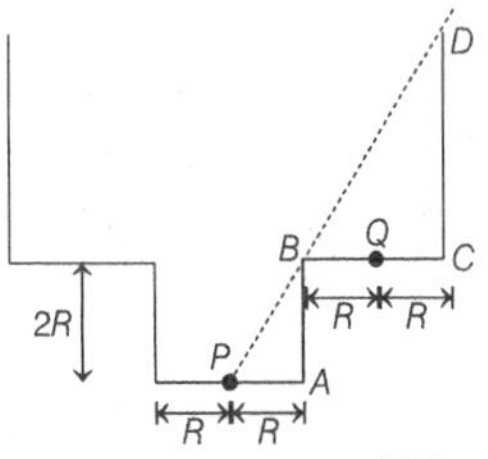

(a) $\sqrt{2}$ (b) $\sqrt{3}$ (c) $\frac{\sqrt{14}}{3}$ (d) $\frac{\sqrt{85}}{5}$

6 A cylinder is filled with a liquid of refractive index μ. The radius of the cylinder is decreasing at a constant rate K. The volume of the liquid inside the container remains constant at V. The observer and the object O are in a state of rest at a distance L from each other. When radius of cylinder is r, the apparent velocity of the object as seen by the observer is

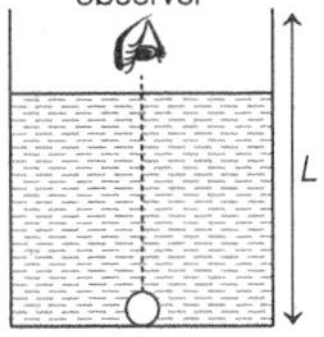

(a) $\frac{(1-\mu)\,2KV}{\pi\mu r^3}$ (b) $\frac{(1-\mu)\,2KV}{\pi\mu L r^2}$

(c) $\frac{(1-\mu)\,2K}{\pi}$ (d) $\frac{(1-\mu)\,K}{2\mu}$

7 A man observes a coin placed at the bottom of a beaker which contains two immiscible liquids of refractive indices 1.2 and 1.4 as shown in the figure. A plane mirror is also placed on the surface of liquid. The distance of image (from mirror) of coin in mirror as seen from medium B by an observer just below the boundary of the two media is

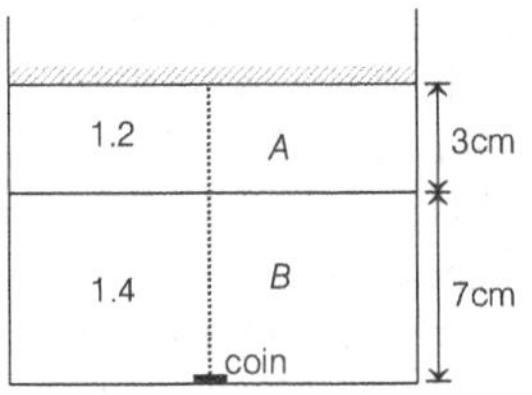

(a) 9 cm (b) 11 cm

(c) 14 cm (d) None of these

8 The flat bottom of cylinder tank is silvered and water $\left(\mu = \frac{4}{3}\right)$ is filled in the tank upto a height h. A small bird is hovering at a height $3h$ from the bottom of the tank. When a small hole is opened near the bottom of the tank, the water level falls at the rate of 1 cm/s. The bird will perceive that his image's velocity is

(a) 0.5 cm/s, upward (b) 1 cm/s, downwards
(c) 0.5 cm/s, downwards (d) None of these

9 Consider the situation sketched. An illuminated object lies 40 cm under the surface of water $\left(n = \frac{4}{3}\right)$, 80 cm above a concave spherical mirror whose radius of curvature is 120 cm. An observer looking down from above in the air ($n = 1.00$) sees two images. The distance between these two images is

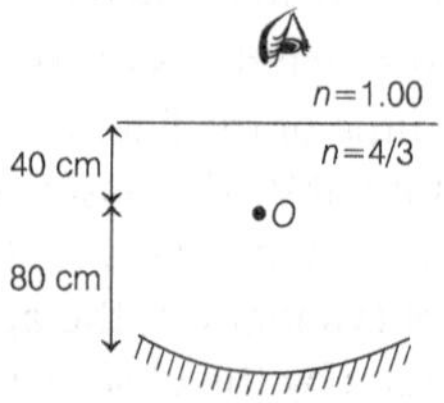

(a) 60 cm (b) 90 cm (c) 120 cm (d) 150 cm

10 A convex mirror of focal length 10 cm is kept 16 cm away from a point object on its principal axis. A slab of thickness 3 cm and refractive index 1.5 is kept between the object and the mirror. It is seen that the image formed due to partial reflection from the front face of the slab coincides with the final image formed from slab mirror combination. The separation between the front face of the slab and the object is

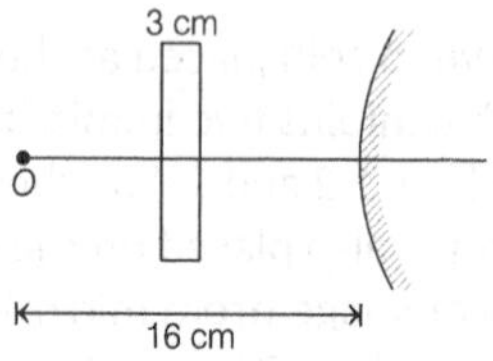

(a) 5 cm (b) 7.5 cm (c) 10.5 cm (d) 12 cm

11 A beaker is filled with water as shown. The bottom surface of the beaker is a concave mirror of large radius of curvature and small aperture. The height of water is $h = 40$ cm. It is found that, when an object is plaeed 4 cm above the water surface, the image coincides with the object. Now the water level h is reduced to zero (there will still be water left in the concave part of the mirror). The new height of the object above the new water surface, so that the image again coincides with the object, will be (refractive index of water = 4/3)

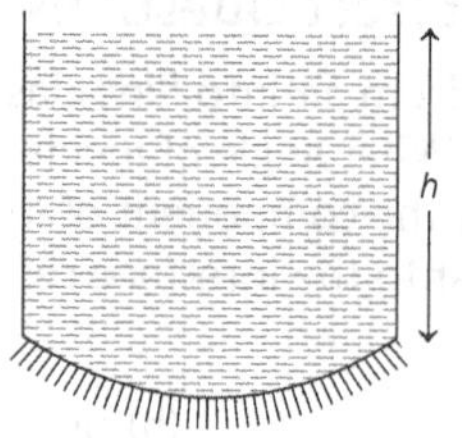

(a) 34 cm (b) 10 cm (c) 74 cm (d) zero

12 In a thick glass slab of thickness l, and refractive index n_1, a cuboidal cavity of thickness m is carved as shown in the figure and is filled with a liquid of refractive index n_2 ($n_1 > n_2$). The ratio of l/m, so that shift produced by this slab is zero, when an observer A observes an object B with paraxial rays is

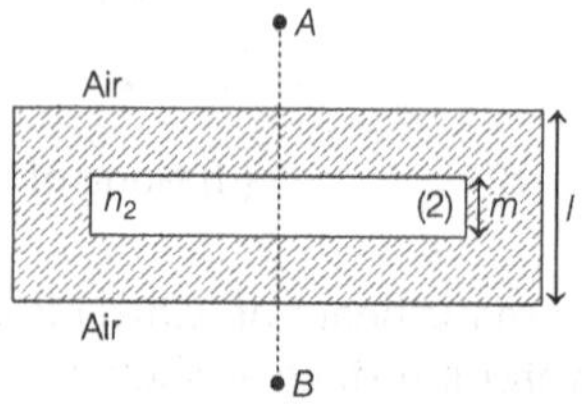

(a) $\frac{n_1 - n_2}{n_2 - 1}$ (b) $\frac{n_1 - n_2}{n_2(n_1 - 1)}$ (c) $\frac{n_1 - n_2}{n_1 - 1}$ (d) $\frac{n_1 - n_2}{n_1(n_2 - 1)}$

13 A man looks down on a fish of length 20 cm. His eye is 2 m above the surface of the water $\left(\mu = \frac{4}{3}\right)$ and the fish is 2 m below the surface as shown in the figure. The ratio of angular width $\Delta\theta$ of the fish as seen by the man in presence of water to the $\Delta\theta'$ in the absence of water is

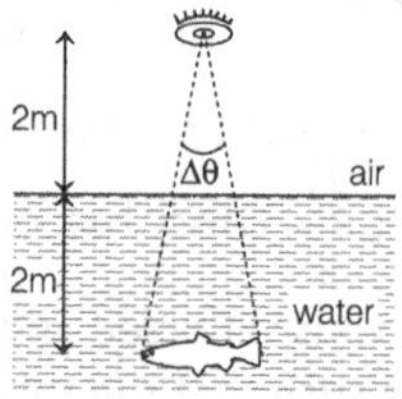

(a) $\frac{6}{5}$ (b) $\frac{5}{6}$ (c) $\frac{7}{8}$ (d) $\frac{8}{7}$

14 A bird is flying up at an angle $\sin^{-1}\left(\frac{3}{5}\right)$ with the horizontal. A fish in a pond looks at that bird, when it is vertically above the fish. The angle at which the bird appears to fly (to the fish) is $\left[n_{water} = \frac{4}{3}\right]$

(a) $\sin^{-1}\left(\frac{3}{5}\right)$ (b) $\sin^{-1}\left(\frac{4}{5}\right)$ (c) 45° (d) $\sin^{-1}\left(\frac{9}{16}\right)$

15 Bottom face of the glass cube is silvered as shown. A ray of light is incident on top face of the cube as shown. Find the deviation of the ray, when it comes out of the glass cube

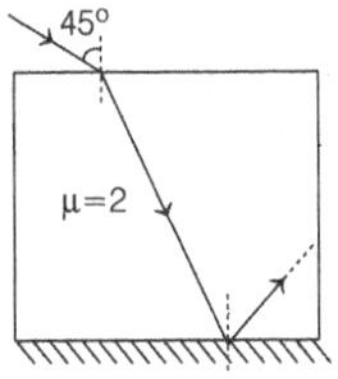

(a) 0 (b) 90° (c) 180° (d) 270°

16 A point source S is placed at the bottom of different layers as shown in the figure. The refractive index of bottommost layer is μ_0. The refractive index of any other upper layer is $\mu(n) = \mu_0 + \dfrac{\mu_0}{4n - 18}$

A ray of light with angle $i = 30°$ starts from the source S. Total internal reflection takes place at the upper surface of layer having n equal to

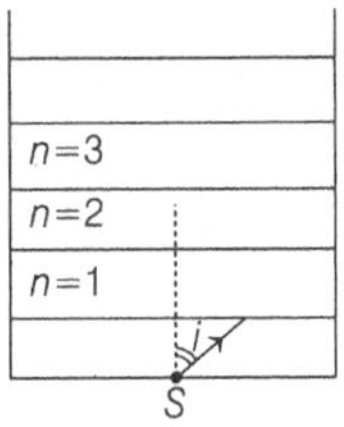

(a) 3 (b) 5 (c) 4 (d) 6

17 A light beam is traveling from Region I to Region IV (Refer Figure). The refractive index in Regions I, II, III and IV are $n_0, \dfrac{n_0}{2}, \dfrac{n_0}{6}$ and $\dfrac{n_0}{8}$, respectively. The angle of incidence θ for which the beam just misses entering Region IV is

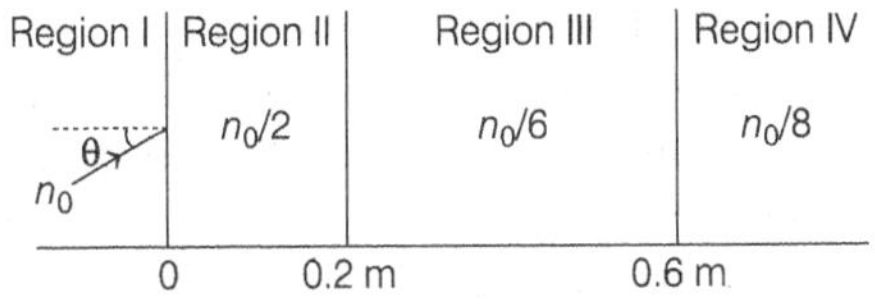

(a) $\sin^{-1}\left(\dfrac{3}{4}\right)$ (b) $\sin^{-1}\left(\dfrac{1}{8}\right)$

(c) $\sin^{-1}\left(\dfrac{1}{4}\right)$ (d) $\sin^{-1}\left(\dfrac{1}{3}\right)$

18 A cubical block of glass of refractive index n_1 is in contact with the surface of water of refractive index n_2. A beam of light is incident on vertical face of the block (see figure). After refraction, a total internal reflection at the base and refraction at the opposite vertical face, the ray emerges out at an angle θ. The value of θ is given by

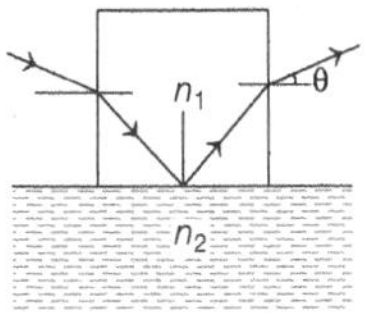

(a) $\sin\theta < \sqrt{n_1^2 - n_2^2}$ (b) $\tan\theta < \sqrt{n_1^2 - n_2^2}$

(c) $\sin\theta < \dfrac{1}{\sqrt{n_1^2 - n_2^2}}$ (d) $\tan\theta < \dfrac{1}{\sqrt{n_1^2 - n_2^2}}$

19 A man of height 2 m stands on a straight road on a hot day. The vertical temperature in the air results in a variation of refractive index with height y as $\mu = \mu_0\sqrt{(1 + ay)}$, where μ_0 is the refractive index of air near the road and $a = 2 \times 10^{-6}$/m. What is the actual length of the road, man is able to see?

(a) 2000 m (b) 390 m

(c) Infinite distance (d) None of these

20 A ray of light enters into a thick glass slab from air as shown in figure. The refractive index of the glass slab varies with the depth x from the top most surface of the slab as $\mu = \sqrt{3} - \dfrac{1}{\sqrt{3}}x$, where x is in metres. Slab is of sufficiently large thickness. Find the maximum depth reached by the ray inside the slab.

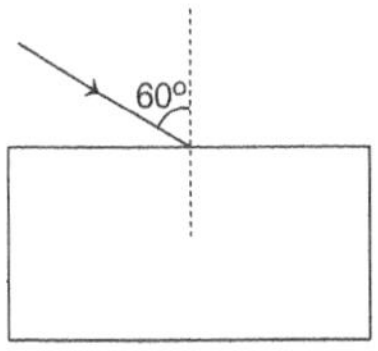

(a) 3 m (b) 1.5 m (c) 1 m (d) 0.5 m

21 An equilateral prism (side length $a = 15$ m) is arranged with its shown cross-section parallel to XY-plane. The refractive index of the material only varies along x is given by $n(x) = \sqrt{1 + x^{2/3}}$. A light ray is incident at origin (near-grazing incidence). Find the location at which the ray touches the edge BC for the first time.

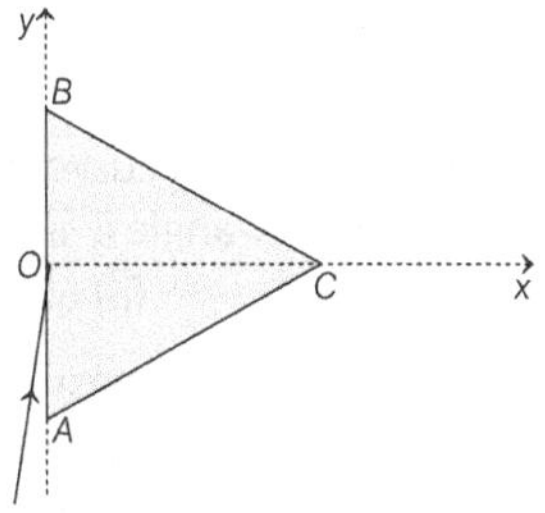

(a) $\left(\sqrt{3}, \dfrac{3^{4/5}}{2}\right)$ (b) $(\sqrt{3}, 3^{4/3})$

(c) $\left(3\sqrt{3}, \dfrac{9}{2}\right)$ (d) $(3\sqrt{3}, 9)$

22 A long rectangular slab of transparent medium is placed on a horizontal table with its length parallel to the X-axis and width parallel to the Y-axis as shown in the figure. A ray of light travelling in air makes a normal incidence on the slab. The refractive index μ of the medium varies as $\dfrac{\mu_0}{1-\left(\dfrac{x}{r}\right)}$, where μ_0 and $r\,(> d)$ are constants. The incident ray

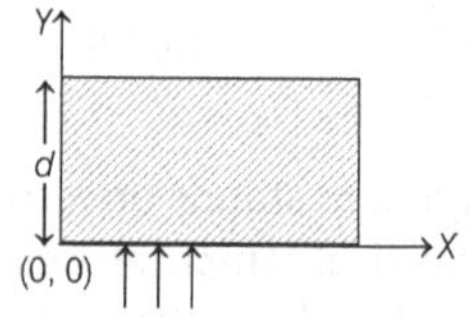

(a) travels in parabolic path inside the slab.
(b) travels in hyperbolic path inside the slab.
(c) travels in circular path inside the slab.
(d) travels in elliptical path inside the slab.

23 For a prism, $A = 60°$, $n = \sqrt{\dfrac{7}{3}}$. Find the minimum possible angle of incidence, so that the light ray is refracted from the second surface.
(a) 30° (b) 45° (c) 60° (d) 0°

24 The curve of angle of incidence *versus* angle of deviation shown has been plotted for prism. The value of refractive index of the prism used is

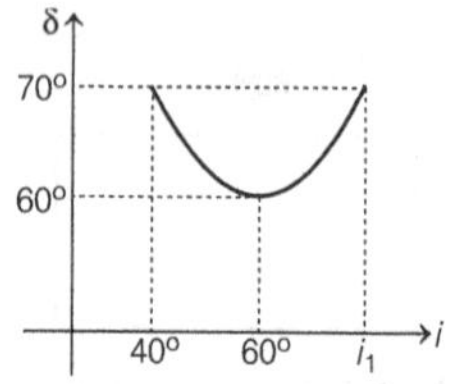

(a) $\sqrt{3}$ b) $\sqrt{2}$ (c) $\dfrac{\sqrt{3}}{\sqrt{2}}$ (d) $\dfrac{2}{\sqrt{3}}$

25 In the given curve of the above question, find the value of angle i_1 in degrees.
(a) 40° (b) 60° (c) 70° (d) 90°

26 A ray of light passes through a prism in a principle plane, the deviation being equal to angle of incidence which is equal to 2α. It is given that α is the angle of prism and μ is the refractive index of the material of prism, then

(a) $\cos\alpha = \sqrt{\dfrac{\mu^2-1}{2}}$ (b) $\cos\alpha = \sqrt{\dfrac{\mu^2-1}{8}}$

(c) $\sin\alpha = \sqrt{\mu^2-1}$ (d) $\sin\alpha = \sqrt{\dfrac{\mu^2-1}{8}}$

27 In the given figure ABC is a right angled isosceles prism kept in air. A ray of light is incident on it normally as shown in figure. Refractive index of prism is varying with time t as $\mu = (1 + 0.4t)$, here t is in seconds. The angular velocity of the emergent ray at $t = 1$ s is

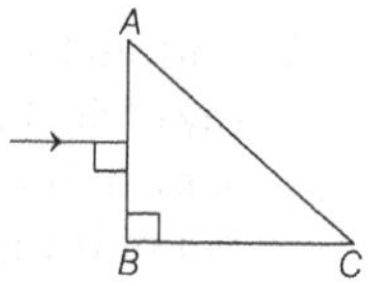

(a) 1.2 rad/s (b) 1 rad/s (c) 2 rad/s (d) 1.5 rad/s

28 Consider an equilateral prism ABC as shown in the figure. A ray of light is incident on the face AB and gets transmitted through the prism. Then, total internal reflection takes place at the face BC and the ray comes out of prism through the face AC. The total angle of deviation is 120°. Minimum value of refractive index μ of the material of the prism should be

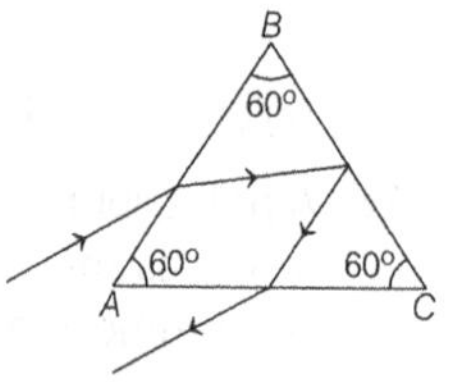

(a) $\sqrt{\dfrac{4}{3}}$ (b) $\sqrt{2}$ (c) $\sqrt{\dfrac{5}{3}}$ (d) $\sqrt{\dfrac{7}{3}}$

29 A ray of light from a liquid ($\mu = \sqrt{3}$) is incident on a system of two right angled prism of refractive indices $\sqrt{3}$ and $\sqrt{2}$ as shown. The ray suffers zero deviation, when emerges into air from CD. The angle of incidence i is

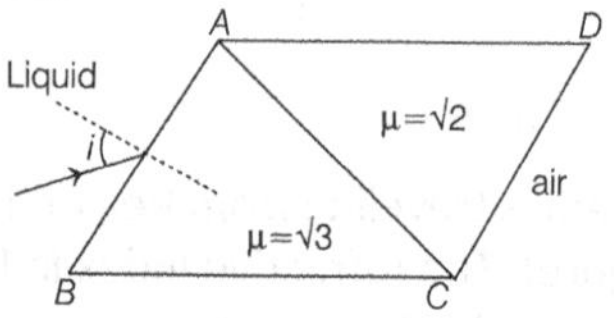

(a) 30° (b) 45° (c) 60° (d) 90°

30 An isosceles glass prism PQR having refractive index μ has one of its faces PR coated with silver. A ray of light is incident normally on the other face PQ as shown in figure ($PQ = PR$). The ray of light upon reflection from PR, then undergoes TIR at face PQ and finally emerges through the base of the prism perpendicularly. Then, angles of prism are

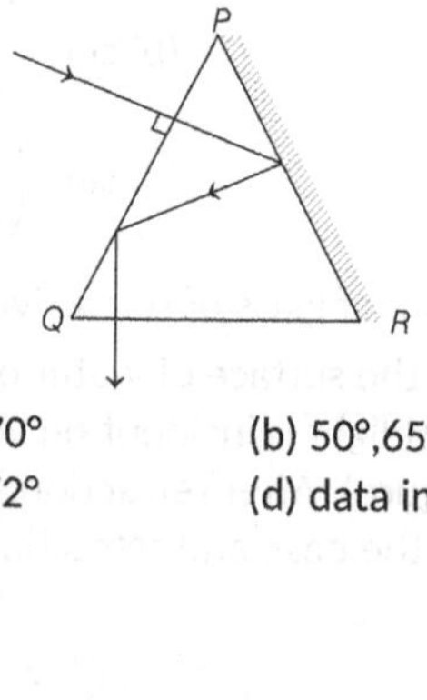

(a) 40°, 70°, 70° (b) 50°,65°,65°
(c) 36°, 72°, 72° (d) data insufficient

31 A ray incident on the solid at an angle of incidence equals to 53° on the vertical face of the solid. The ray just fails to emerge from the prism, if refractive index of prism is $\sqrt{3}$, then refractive index of the solid will be

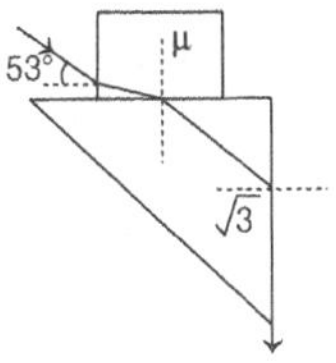

(a) $\sqrt{\frac{3}{2}}$ (b) $\frac{4}{3}$ (c) $\frac{5}{\sqrt{21}}$ (d) $\frac{\sqrt{66}}{5}$

32 A right angled triangular prism of refractive index μ_1 is kept floating on a liquid (surface) having refractive index μ_2. The condition such that light incident normally passes through base of prism as shown in figure.

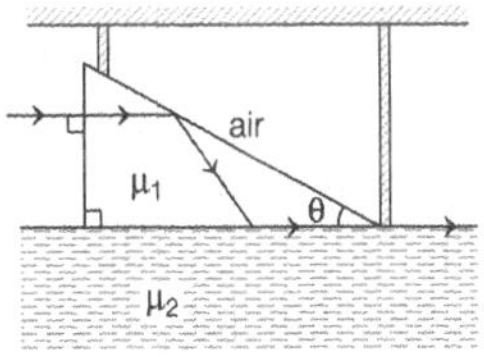

(a) $\mu_1 = \frac{\cos 2\theta}{\cos\theta}$ (b) $\mu_2 = \frac{\cos 2\theta}{\cos\theta}$

(c) $\mu_1 = \frac{\sin 2\theta}{\sin\theta}$ (d) $\mu_2 = \frac{\sin 2\theta}{\sin\theta}$

33 A ray of light is incident normally on the first refracting face of the isosceles prism of refracting angle A. The ray of light comes out at grazing emergence. If one half of the prism (shaded position) is knocked off, the same ray will

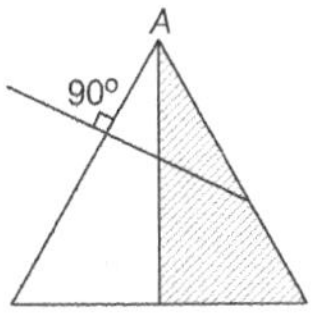

(a) emerge at an angle of emergence $\sin^{-1}\left(\frac{1}{2}\sec\frac{A}{2}\right)$

(b) not emerge out of the prism

(c) emerge at an angle of emergence $\sin^{-1}\left(\frac{1}{2}\sec\frac{A}{4}\right)$

(d) None of these

34 A horizontal ray of light passes through a prism of refractive index 1.5 whose apex angle is 4° and then strikes a vertical mirror M as shown in the figure. In order to have total deviation equal to 180°, the angle through which the mirror should be rotated is

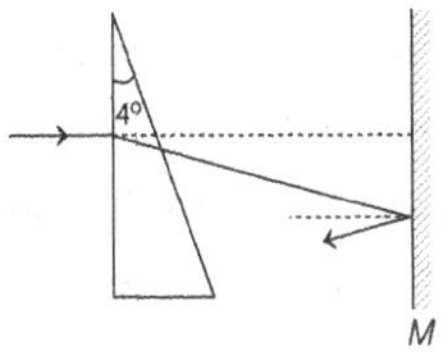

(a) 1° (b) 2° (c) 3° (d) 4°

35 A parallel beam of light is incident on the upper part of a prism of angle 1.8° and RI 3/2. The light coming out of the prism falls on a concave mirror of radius of curvature 20 cm. The distance of the point (where the rays are focused after reflection from the mirror) from the principal axis is

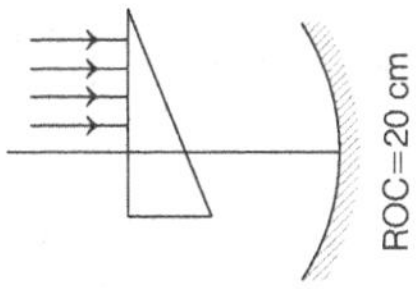

(a) 9 cm (b) 0.157 cm

(c) 0.314 cm (d) None of these

36 Two identical thin isosceles prisms of refracting angle A and refractive index m are placed with their bases touching each other. Two parallel rays of light are incident on this system as shown. The distance of the point, where the rays converge from the prism is

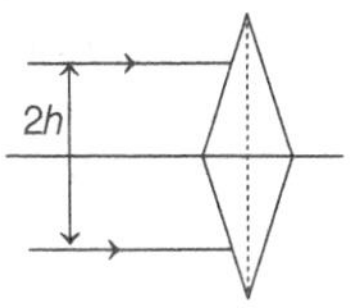

(a) $\frac{h}{\mu A}$ (b) $\frac{h}{A}$ (c) $\frac{h}{(\mu-1)A}$ (d) $\frac{\mu h}{(\mu-1)A}$

37 A beam of light has a small wavelength spread $d\lambda$ about a central wavelength λ. The beam travels in vacuum until it enters a glass plate at an angle θ relative to the normal to the plate, as shown in figure. The index of refraction of the glass is given by $n(\lambda)$. The angular spread $\delta\theta'$ of the refracted beam is given by

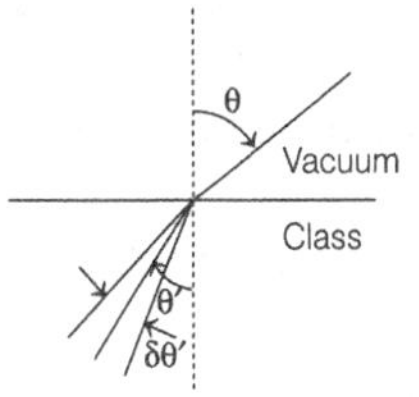

(a) $\delta\theta' = \left|\frac{1}{n}\delta\lambda\right|$ (b) $\delta\theta' = \left|\frac{dn(\lambda)}{d\lambda}\delta\lambda\right|$

(c) $\delta\theta' = \left|\frac{\tan\theta'}{n}\frac{dn(\lambda)}{d\lambda}\delta\lambda\right|$ (d) $\delta\theta' = \left|\frac{\sin\theta}{\sin\theta'}\frac{\delta\lambda}{\lambda}\right|$

38 The diagram shows five isosceles right angled prisms. A light ray incident at 90° at the first face emerges at same angle with the normal from the last face. Which of the following relations will hold regarding the refractive indices?

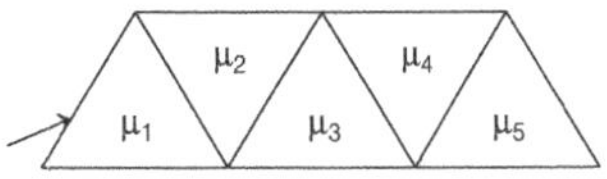

(a) $\mu_1^2 + \mu_3^2 + \mu_5^2 = \mu_2^2 + \mu_4^2$

(b) $\mu_1^2 + \mu_3^2 + \mu_5^2 = 1 + \mu_2^2 + \mu_4^2$

(c) $\mu_1^2 + \mu_3^2 + \mu_5^2 = 2 + \mu_2^2 + \mu_4^2$

(d) None of the above

Multiple Choice(s) Correct Questions

1 A ray of light is incident upon an air/water interface (it passes from air into water) at an angle of 45°. Which of the following quantities change as the light enters the water?

(a) Wavelength (b) Frequency
(c) Speed of propagation (d) Direction of propagation

2 A ray of monochromatic light is incident on the plane surface of separation between two media *x* and *y* with angle of incidence *i* in the medium *x* and angle of refraction *r* in the medium *y*. The graph shows the relation between sin *r* and sin *i*.

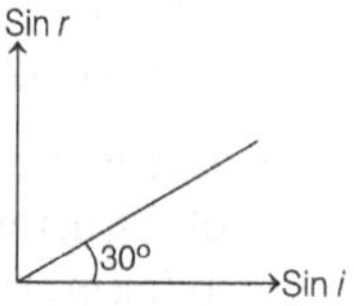

(a) The speed of light in the medium *y* is $(3)^{1/2}$ times, than in medium *x*.
(b) The speed of light in the medium *y* is $\left(\frac{1}{3}\right)^{1/2}$ times, than in medium *x*.
(c) The total internal reflection can take place when the incidence is in *x*.
(d) The total internal reflection can take place when the incidence is in *y*.

3 A small air bubble is trapped inside a transparent cube of size 12 cm. When viewed from one of the vertical faces, the bubble appears to be at 5 cm from it. When viewed from opposite face, it appears at 3 cm from it.

(a) The distance of the air bubble from the first face is 7.5 cm.
(b) The distance of the air bubble from the first face is 9 cm.
(c) Refractive index of the material of the prism is 2.0.
(d) Refractive index of the material of the prism is 1.5.

4 A fish, *F* in the pond is at a depth of 0.8 m from the water surface and is moving vertically upwards with velocity 2 m/s. At the same instant, a bird *B* is at a height of 6 m from the water surface and is moving downwards with velocity 3 m/s.

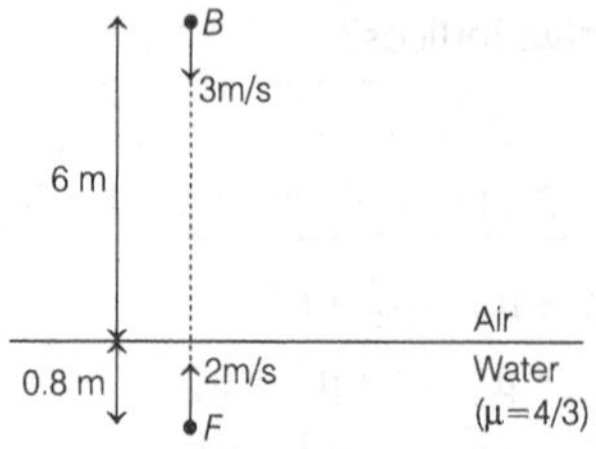

At this instant, both are on the same vertical line as shown in the figure. Which of the following statements are correct ?

(a) Depth of *F*, observed by *B* (from itself) is equal to 6.60 m
(b) Height of *B*, observed by *F* (from itself) is equal to 8.80 m
(c) Velocity of *B*, observed by *F* (relative to itself), is equal to 6 m/s.
(d) Velocity of *F*, observed by *B* (relative to itself), is equal to 4.50 m/s.

5 A ray of light travelling in a transparent medium falls on a surface separating the medium from air at an angle of incidence 45°. The ray undergoes total internal reflection. If *n* is the refractive index of the medium with respect to air, select the possible value(s) of *n* from the following

(a) 1.3 (b) 1.4 (c) 1.5 (d) 1.6

6 In the figure light is incident at an angle θ which is slightly greater than the critical angle. Now, keeping the incident fixed a parallel slab of refractive index n_3 is placed on surface *AB*. Which of the following statements are correct?

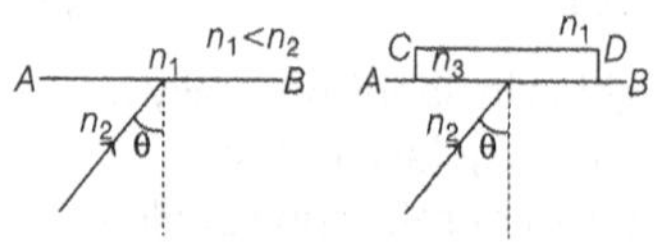

(a) Total internal reflection occurs at *AB* for $n_3 < n_1$
(b) Total internal reflection occurs at *AB* for $n_3 > n_1$
(c) The ray will return back to the same medium for all values of n_3
(d) Total internal reflection occurs at *CD* for $n_3 < n_1$

7 A light ray is incident on lower medium boundary at an angle 30° with the normal. Which of following statement is/are true?

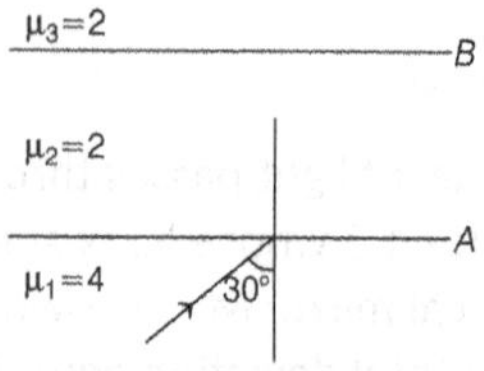

(a) If $\mu_2 > 2$, then total deviation is 60°
(b) If $\mu_2 < 2$, then total deviation is 60°
(c) If $\mu_2 > 2$, then total deviation is 120°
(d) If $\mu_2 < 2$, then total deviation is 120°

8 Two glass slabs of thickness t_1 and t_2 are joined to make *L* shape as shown in the figure. The refractive indices of both glass slabs are same.

A light ray is incident at point P with an angle of incidence θ as shown in the figure. It is assumed that refraction takes place from both the glass slabs. Then choose the correct option(s).

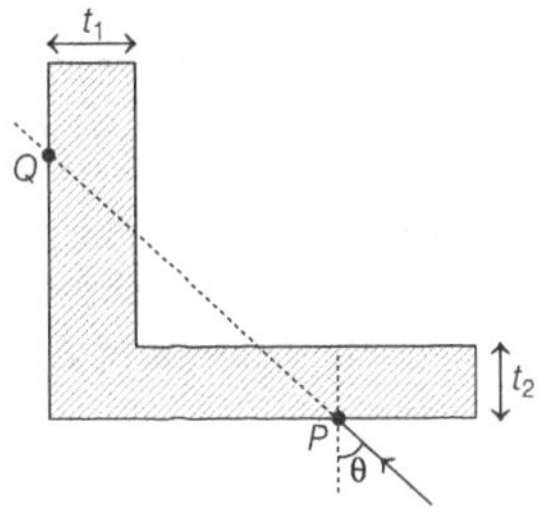

(a) Emergent ray doesn't pass from Q if $t_1 = t_2, \theta = 45^\circ$
(b) Emergent ray passes from Q if $t_1 = t_2, \theta = 45^\circ$
(c) Emergent ray passes above Q if $t_2 > t_1, \theta = 45^\circ$
(d) Emergent ray passes below Q if $t_2 < t_1, \theta = 45^\circ$

9 A ray of light is incident normally on one face of $30^\circ - 60^\circ - 90^\circ$ prism of refractive index 5/3 immersed in water of refractive index 4/3 as shown in figure.

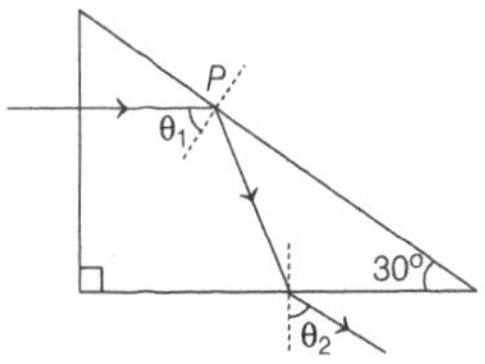

(a) The exit angle θ_2 of the ray is $\sin^{-1}\left(\frac{5}{8}\right)$
(b) The exit angle θ_2 of the ray is $\sin^{-1}\left(\frac{5}{4\sqrt{3}}\right)$
(c) Total internal reflection at point P ceases if the refractive index of water is increased to $\frac{5}{2\sqrt{3}}$ by dissolving some substance
(d) Total internal reflection at point P ceases if the refractive index of water is increased to $\frac{5}{6}$ by dissolving some substance

10 The refracting angle of a prism is 90°. If γ is the angle of minimum deviation, β is the deviation of ray which enters at grazing incidence and μ is refractive index of material of the prism, then which of the following(s) is correct?
(a) $\sin\gamma = \sin^2\beta$
(b) $\sin\gamma = \cos^2\beta$
(c) $\sin\gamma = \mu^2 - 1$
(d) $\sin\beta = \mu^2 - 1$

11 A monochromatic light is incident on a prism as shown. Deviation suffered by ray varies with angle of incidence as shown. Assuming refraction takes place at 1 and 2.

Choose the correct alternative(s).

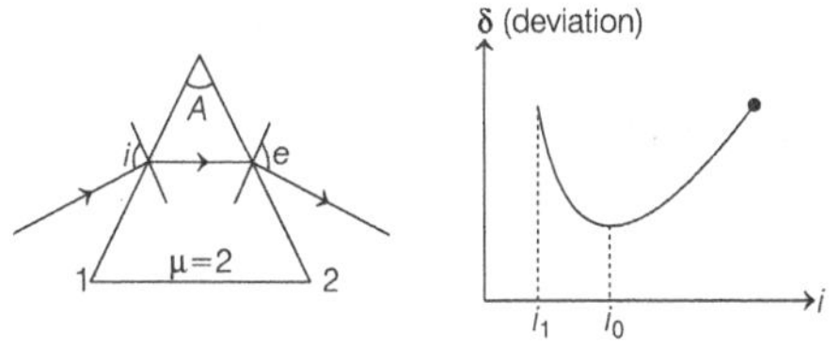

(a) i_1 can be equal to zero if $A = 30^\circ$
(b) If angle of incidence is increased by 2°, then angle of emergence may decrease by less than 2°.
(c) If angle of incidence is increased by 2°, then angle of emergence may decrease by more than 2°.
(d) If angle of incidence is increased by 2°, then angle of emergence may increase by equal to 2°.

12 A glass prism is immersed in a hypothetical liquid. The curves showing the refractive index n as a function of wavelength λ, for glass and liquid are as shown in the figure. When a ray of white light is incident on the prism parallel to the base

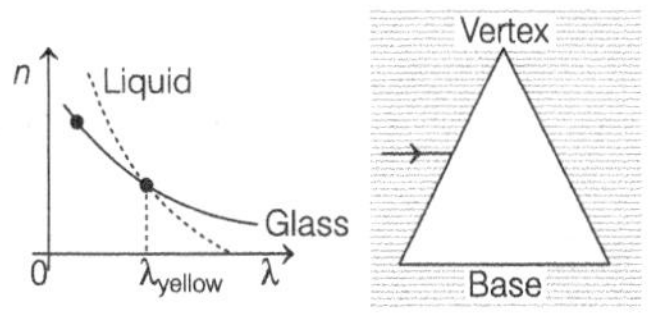

(a) yellow ray travels without deviation
(b) blue ray is deviated towards the vertex
(c) red ray is deviated towards the base
(d) there is no dispersion

13 Two prisms one made of crown glass ($\mu_{V_1} = 1.58$, $\mu_{R_1} = 1.52$) and second made of flint glass ($\mu_{V_2} = 1.48$, $\mu_{R_2} = 1.42$) are arranged as shown. Angle of prism for crown glass prism is given 9°. Now choose the correct statements

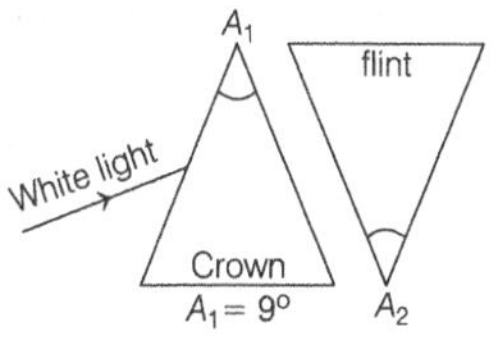

(a) For zero deviation of light ray, A_2 should be equal to 11° (Approx)
(b) For zero dispersion of light ray, A_2 should be equal to 9° (Approx)
(c) For zero deviation of light ray, A_2 should be equal to 9° (Approx)
(d) For zero dispersion, A_2 should be equal to 11° (Approx).

Comprehension Based Questions

Comprehension-1

The figure shows a ray incident at an angle $i = \frac{\pi}{3}$. The plot drawn shows the variation of $|r - i|$ *versus* $\frac{\mu_1}{\mu_2} = k$.

(r = angle of refraction)

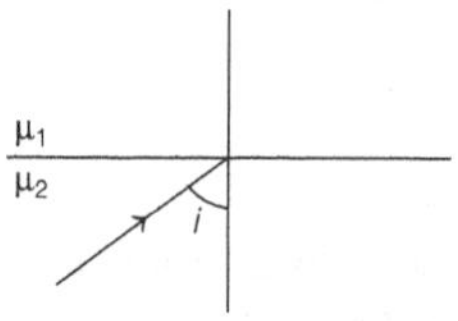

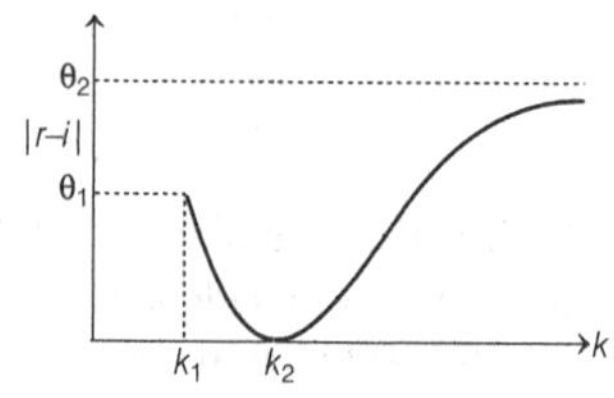

1 The value of k_1 is

(a) $\frac{2}{\sqrt{3}}$ (b) 1 (c) $\frac{1}{\sqrt{3}}$ (d) $\frac{\sqrt{3}}{2}$

2 The value of θ_1 is

(a) $\frac{\pi}{3}$ (b) $\frac{\pi}{2}$ (c) $\frac{\pi}{6}$ (d) zero

3 The value of k_2 is

(a) 1 (b) 2
(c) $\frac{1}{2}$ (d) None of these

Comprehension-2

A point object is placed on principal axis of a concave mirror (of focal length 15 cm) at a distance $u = 61$ cm from pole. A slab of thickness $t = 3$ cm and refractive index $\mu = 1.5$ is placed with two sides perpendicular to principal axis, such that its nearest face is x_0 cm from pole. The final image of object is to be considered after refraction by slab, reflection by mirror and final refraction by slab.

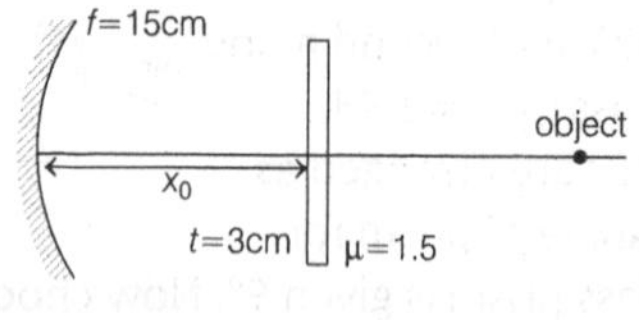

4 If $x_0 = 30$ cm, then the distance of final image from pole is

(a) 19 cm (b) 21 cm (c) 23 cm (d) 24 cm

5 If the slab is shifted parallel to itself by 3 cm, then the final image

(a) shifts towards left
(b) shifts towards right
(c) may shift towards left or right
(d) does not shift

6 If $x_0 = 30$ cm and the object is given velocity 18 m/s towards left, then the speed of image at that instant is

(a) 2 m/s (b) 6 m/s
(c) 9 m/s (d) 162 m/s

Comprehension-3

An equilateral prism ABC is placed in air with its base side BC lying horizontally along X-axis as shown in the figure. A ray given by $\sqrt{3}z + x = 10$ is incident at a point P on face AB of the prism.

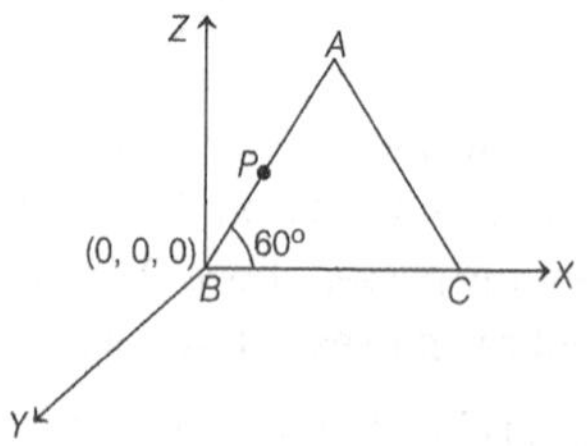

7 The value of μ for which the ray grazes the face AC is

(a) $\frac{1}{\sqrt{2}}$ (b) $\frac{2}{\sqrt{3}}$
(c) $\frac{\sqrt{3}}{2}$ (d) $\frac{1}{\sqrt{3}}$

8 Find the direction of the finally refracted ray if $\mu = \frac{3}{2}$

(a) at 45° to X-axis (b) parallel to Z-axis
(c) at 30° to Z-axis (d) None of these

9 Find the equation of ray coming out of prism if bottom BC is silvered for $\mu = \frac{3}{2}$

(a) $z + \sqrt{3}x = 10$ (b) $z + x = 10$
(c) $\sqrt{3}z + x = 10$ (d) None of these

Comprehension-4

A prism of refractive index n_1 and another prism of refractive index n_2 are stuck together with a gap as shown in the figure. The angles of the prism are as shown. n_1 and n_2 depend on λ, the wavelength of light according to

$n_1 = 1.20 + \frac{10.8 \times 10^4}{\lambda^2}$ and $n_2 = 1.45 + \frac{1.80 \times 10^4}{\lambda^2}$, where λ is in nm

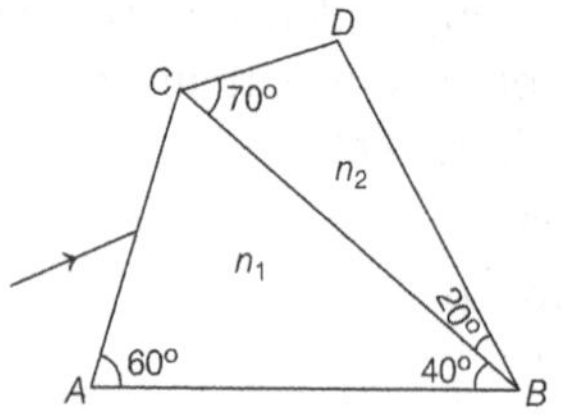

10 Calculate the wavelength λ_0 for which rays incident at any angle on the interface BC pass through without bending at that interface.

(a) 200 nm (b) 300 nm (c) 500 nm (d) 600 nm

11 For light of wavelength λ_0, find the angle of incidence i on the face AC such that the deviation produced by the combination of prisms is minimum.

(a) $\sin^{-1}\left(\frac{2}{3}\right)$ (b) $\sin^{-1}\left(\frac{3}{4}\right)$

(c) $\sin^{-1}\left(\frac{4}{5}\right)$ (d) $\sin^{-1}\left(\frac{3}{5}\right)$

Match the Columns Questions

1 A bird in air is diving vertically over a tank with speed 5 cm/s. Base of tank is silvered. A fish in the tank is rising upward along the same line with speed 2 cm/s. Water level is falling at rate of 2 cm/s.
$\left[\text{Take } \mu_{\text{water}} = \frac{4}{3}\right]$

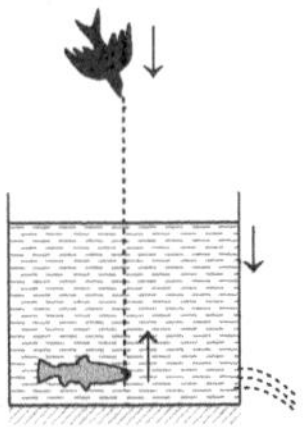

Column I	Column II
A. Speed of the image of fish as seen by the bird directly	1. 8 cm/s
B. Speed of the image of fish formed after reflection in the mirror as seen by the bird	2. 6 cm/s
C. Speed of image of bird relative to the fish looking upwards	3. 3 cm/s
D. Speed of image of bird relative to the fish looking downwards in the mirror	4. 4 cm/s

2 A white light ray is incident on a glass prism and it creates four refracted rays A, B, C and D. Match the refracted rays with the colours given (1 and D are rays due to total internal reflection)

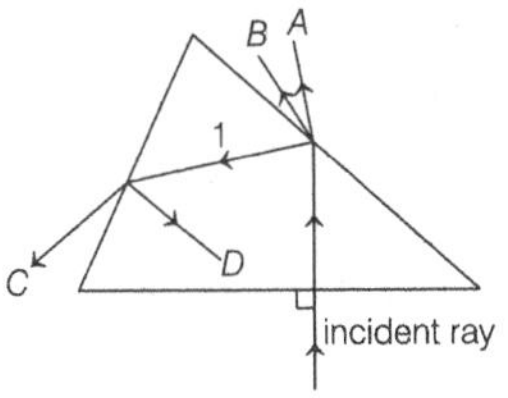

Column I (Ray)	Column II (Colour)
A. A	1. Red
B. B	2. Green
C. C	3. Yellow
D. D	4. Blue

3 Light is incident at surface PQ of prism as shown in Column I then match the Column I with column II (Surrounding medium is air in all cases)

Column I	Column II
A. 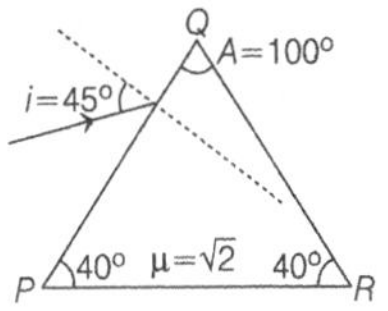	1. Total internal reflection takes place at surface QR.
B. 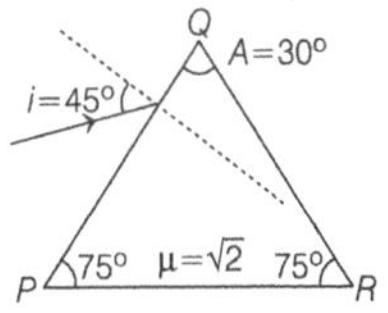	2. Light emerges normally from the surface QR.
C. 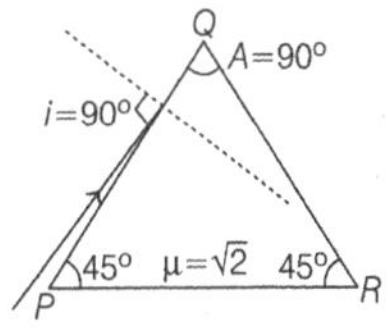	3. Light emerges parallel to surface QR.
	4. When light ray passes through the prism it is parallel to the base PR.

Numerical Value Questions

1 A ray of light is incident from air to a glass rod at point A. The angle of incidence being 45°. If the minimum value of refractive index of the material of the rod so that TIR takes place at B is $\sqrt{n}$, then find n.

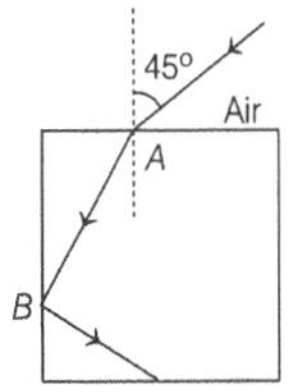

2 A man places his eye parallel to rim of a cylinder. When the cylinder is empty, the man cannot see anything inside the cylinder. Now, the cylinder is filled by two immiscible liquids to the top. Both the liquid layers have the same width. Now from the same position, the observer can just see the base of the cylinder. The upper layer has refractive index $\sqrt{2}$. The height of the cylinder is $2H$ and the diameter of the base is $3H$. If the refractive index of the lower layer is $\sqrt{n}$, then find n.

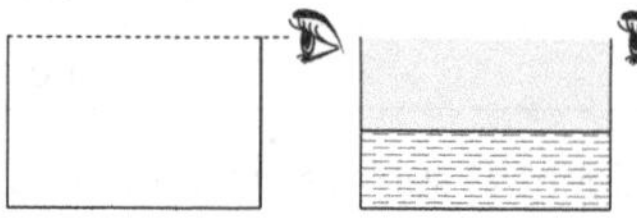

3 An insect at point P sees its two images in the water-mirror system as shown in the figure. One image is formed due to direct reflection from water surface and the other image is formed due to refraction, reflection and again refraction by water mirror system in order. Find the separation (in cm) between the two images. Mirror has focal length of 60 cm. $\left(\mu_w = \frac{4}{3}\right)$

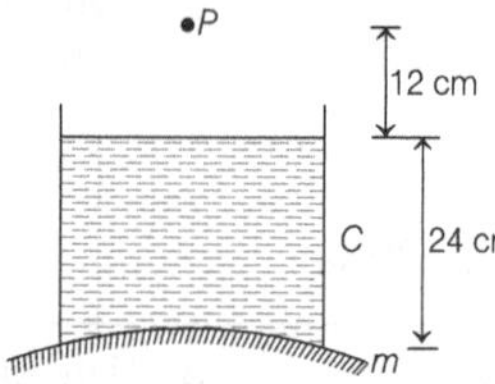

4 A fly F is sitting on a glass slab S 45cm thick and of refractive index 3/2. The slab covers the top of a container C containing water (RI 4/3) upto a height of 20 cm. Bottom of container is closed by a concave mirror M of radius of curvature 40 cm. Find the distance (in cm) of the final image from the upper surface of the glass slab formed by all refractions and reflection assuming paraxial rays.

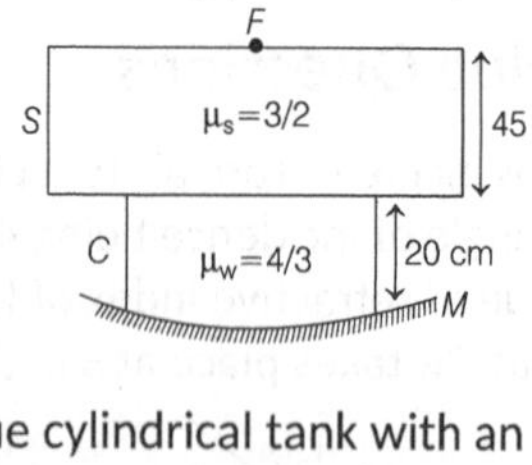

5 An opaque cylindrical tank with an open top has a diameter of 3 m and is completely filled with water $\left(\mu_w = \frac{4}{3}\right)$. When the setting sun reaches an angle of 37° above the horizon, sunlight ceases to illuminate any part of the bottom of the tank. How deep is tank in metre?

6 The figure shows the path of a ray passing through an equiangular prism PQR. It is incident on face PR at the critical angle (slightly greater than C) for total internal reflection. The angle (α) shown in the figure is 30°. If the refractive index of the material of the prism is $\sqrt{\frac{n}{3}}$, then find n.

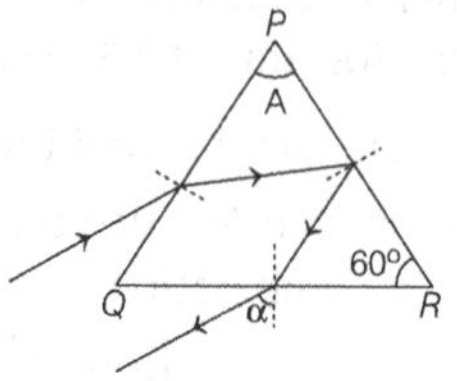

7 An equilateral prism deviates a ray through 23° for two angles of incidence differing by 23°. If refractive index of the prism is $\sqrt{\frac{43}{N}}$, find the value of N.

8 A ray of light travels from a medium of refractive index $\mu = 2$ to air. Its angle of incidence in the medium is i, measured from the normal to the boundary, and its angle of deviation is δ. δ is plotted against i as shown in figure. Find the value of $\left[\frac{\sin(\delta_2 - \delta_1)}{\sin\phi}\right]^2$.

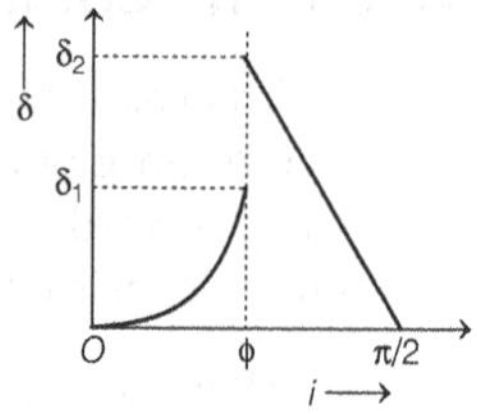

9 A direct vision prism is made out of three prisms, each with a refracting angle of 60°, attached to each other as shown in the figure. Light of a certain wavelength is incident on the first prism. The angle of incidence is 30° and the ray leaves the third prism parallel to the direction of incidence. The refractive index of the glass of the first and third prisms is 1.5. Find the refractive index of the material of the middle prism. ($\sqrt{6} = 2.45$)

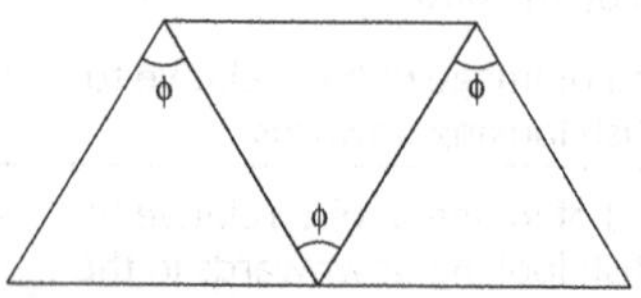

10 O is a point object kept on the principal axis of a concave mirror M of radius of curvature 20 cm. P is a prism of angle $\alpha = 1.8°$. Light falling on the prism (at small angle of incidence) get refracted through the prism and then fall on the mirror. Refractive index of prism is 3/2. Find the distance (in mm) between the images formed by the concave mirror due to this light.

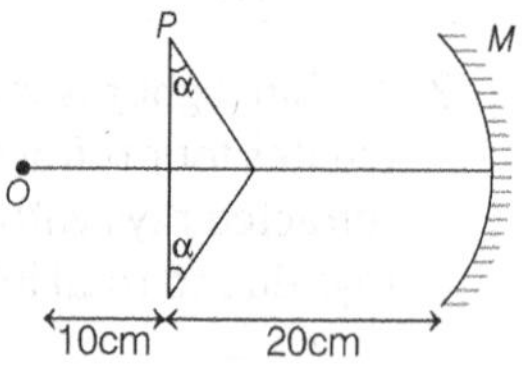

Previous Year's Questions

JEE Main

1 If the refractive index of the material of a prism is $\cot\left(\frac{A}{2}\right)$, where A is the angle of prism, then the angle of minimum deviation will be [2024, 27 Jan Shift-I]

(a) $\pi - 2A$ (b) $\frac{\pi}{2} - A$ (c) $\pi - A$ (d) $\frac{\pi}{2} - 2A$

2 Two immiscible liquids of refractive indices $\frac{8}{5}$ and $\frac{3}{2}$ respectively are put in a beaker as shown in the figure. The height of each column is 6 cm. A coin is placed at the bottom of the beaker. For near normal vision, the apparent depth of the coin is $\frac{\alpha}{4}$ cm. The value of α is .... [2024, 27 Jan Shift-I]

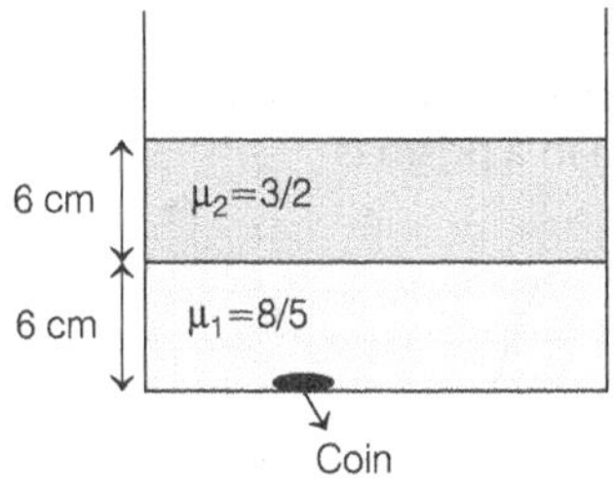

3 The refractive index of a prism with apex angle A is $\cot\frac{A}{2}$. The angle of minimum deviation is [2024, 31 Jan Shift-I]

(a) $\delta_m = 180° - 3A$ (b) $\delta_m = 180° - A$
(c) $\delta_m = 180° - 2A$ (d) $\delta_m = 180° - 4A$

4 As shown in the figure, a plane mirror is fixed at a height of 50 cm from the bottom of tank containing water $\left(\mu = \frac{4}{3}\right)$. The height of water in the tank is 8 cm. A small bulb is placed at the bottom of the water tank. The distance of image of the bulb formed by mirror at the bottom of the tank is .... cm. [2023, 11 April Shift-II]

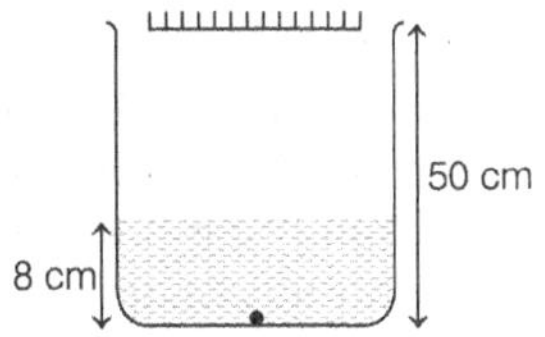

5 A monochromatic light wave with wavelength λ_1 and frequency ν_1 in air enters another medium. If the angle of incidence and angle of refraction at the interface are 45° and 30° respectively, then the wavelength λ_2 and frequency ν_2 of the refracted wave are [2023, 6 April Shift-I]

(a) $\lambda_2 = \lambda_1, \nu_2 = \sqrt{2}\nu_1$ (b) $\lambda_2 = \sqrt{2}\lambda_1, \nu_2 = \nu_1$

(c) $\lambda_2 = \frac{1}{\sqrt{2}}\lambda_1, \nu_2 = \nu_1$ (d) $\lambda_2 = \lambda_1, \nu_2 = \frac{1}{\sqrt{2}}\nu_1$

6 The critical angle for a denser-rarer interface is 45°. The speed of light in rarer medium is 3×10^8 m/s. The speed of light in the denser medium is [2023, 11 April Shift-I]

(a) 5×10^7 m/s (b) 2.12×10^8 m/s
(c) $\sqrt{2} \times 10^8$ m/s (d) 3.12×10^7 m/s

7 A microscope is focussed on an object at the bottom of a bucket. If liquid with refractive index $5/3$ is poured inside the bucket, then microscope have to be raised by 30 cm to focus the object again. The height of the liquid in the bucket is [2023, 31 Jan Shift-II]

(a) 75 cm (b) 50 cm
(c) 12 cm (d) 18 cm

8 A thin prism P_1 with an angle 6° and made of glass of refractive index 1.54 is combined with another prism P_2 made from glass of refractive index 1.72 to produce dispersion without average deviation. The angle of prism P_2 is [2023, 30 Jan Shift-II]

(a) 4.5° (b) 1.3°
(c) 7.8° (d) 6°

9 A pole is vertically submerged in a swimming pool, such that it gives a length of shadow 2.15 m within water when sunlight is incident at an angle of 30° with the surface of water. If swimming pool is filled to a height of 1.5 m, then the height of the pole above the water surface in centimeters is ($n_W = 4/3$) .... [2023, 6 April Shift-I]

10 The refractive index of a transparent liquid filled in an equilateral hollow prism is $\sqrt{2}$. The angle of minimum deviation for the liquid will be .... [2023, 15 April Shift-I]

11 The difference of speed of light in the two media A and B, $(v_A - v_B)$ is 2.6×10^7 m/s. If the refractive index of medium B is 1.47, then the ratio of refractive index of medium B to medium A is
(Given : speed of light in vacuum $c = 3 \times 10^8$ ms^{-1}) [2022, 25 June Shift-I]

(a) 1.303 (b) 1.318
(c) 1.13 (d) 0.12

12 If a wave gets refracted into a denser medium, then which of the following is true? [2022, 27 June Shift-II]

(a) Wavelength, speed and frequency decreases.
(b) Wavelength increases, speed decreases and frequency remains constant.
(c) Wavelength and speed decrease but frequency remains constant.
(d) Wavelength, speed and frequency increases.

13 Consider a light travelling in air is incident into a medium of refractive index $\sqrt{2n}$. The incident angle is twice that of refracting angle. Then, the angle of incidence will be **[2022, 27 June Shift-I]**

(a) $\sin^{-1}(\sqrt{n})$ (b) $\cos^{-1}\left(\sqrt{\frac{n}{2}}\right)$

(c) $\sin^{-1}(\sqrt{2n})$ (d) $2\cos^{-1}\left(\sqrt{\frac{n}{2}}\right)$

14 Light enters from air into a given medium at an angle of 45° with interface of the air-medium surface. After refraction, the light ray is deviated through an angle of 15° from its original direction. The refractive index of the medium is **[2022, 29 July Shift-II]**

(a) 1.732 (b) 1.333
(c) 1.414 (d) 2.732

15 Light travels in two media M_1 and M_2 with speeds 1.5×10^8 ms^{-1} and 2.0×10^8 ms^{-1}, respectively. The critical angle between them is **[2022, 26 July Shift-II]**

(a) $\tan^{-1}\left(\frac{3}{\sqrt{7}}\right)$ (b) $\tan^{-1}\left(\frac{2}{3}\right)$ (c) $\cos^{-1}\left(\frac{3}{4}\right)$ (d) $\sin^{-1}\left(\frac{2}{3}\right)$

16 The speed of light in media A and B are 2.0×10^{10} cm/s and 1.5×10^{10} cm/s, respectively. A ray of light enters from the medium B to A at an incident angle θ. If the ray suffers total internal reflection, then **[2022, 29 June Shift-II]**

(a) $\theta = \sin^{-1}\left(\frac{3}{4}\right)$ (b) $\theta > \sin^{-1}\left(\frac{2}{3}\right)$

(c) $\theta < \sin^{-1}\left(\frac{3}{4}\right)$ (d) $\theta > \sin^{-1}\left(\frac{3}{4}\right)$

17 The refracting angle of a prism is A and refractive index of the material of the prism is $\cot A/2$. Then the angle of minimum deviation will be: **[2022, 28 June Shift-I]**

(a) $180° - 2A$ (b) $90° - A$ (c) $180° + 2A$ (d) $180° - 3A$

18 A light wave travelling linearly in a medium of dielectric constant 4, incident on the horizontal interface separating medium with air. The angle of incidence for which the total intensity of incident wave will be reflected back into the same medium will be (Given, relative permeability of medium, $\mu_r = 1$) **[2022, 25 June Shift-I]**

(a) 10° (b) 20° (c) 30° (d) 60°

19 A ray of light is incident at an angle of incidence of 60° on a glass slab of refractive index $\sqrt{3}$. After refraction, the light ray emerges out from other parallel faces and lateral shift between incident ray and emergent ray is $4\sqrt{3}$ cm. The thickness of the glass slab is ...... cm. **[2022, 24 June Shift-II]**

20 A glass tumbler having inner depth of 17.5 cm is kept on a table. A student starts pouring water ($\mu = 4/3$) into it while looking at the surface of water from above. When he feels that the tumbler is half filled, he stops pouring water. Up to what height, the tumbler is actually filled? **[2021, 1 Sep Shift-II]**

(a) 11.7 cm (b) 10 cm (c) 7.5 cm (d) 8.75 cm

21 A ray of light passes from a denser medium to a rarer medium at an angle of incidence i. The reflected and refracted rays make an angle of 90° with each other. The angle of reflection and refaction are respectively r and r'. The critical angle is given by **[2021, 22 July Shift-II]**

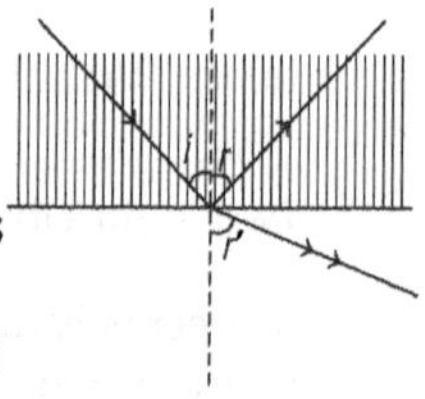

(a) $\sin^{-1}(\tan r')$ (b) $\tan^{-1}(\sin i')$
(c) $\sin^{-1}(\tan r)$ (d) $\sin^{-1}(\cot r)$

22 The expected graphical representation of the variation of angle of deviation δ with angle of incidence i in a prism is **[2021, 27 July Shift-II]**

(a)
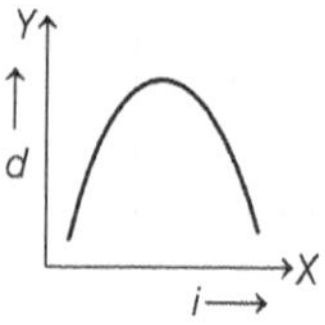

(b)
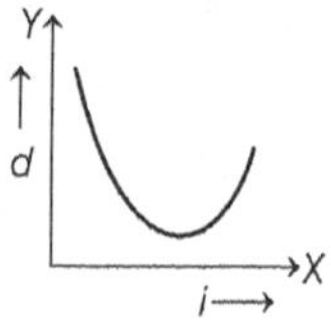

(c)
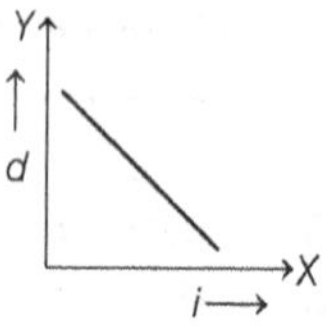

(d)
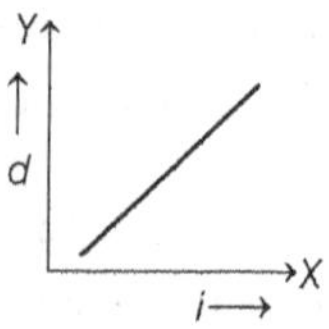

23 A ray of laser of a wavelength 630 nm is incident at an angle of 30° at the diamond-air interface. It is going from diamond to air. The refractive index of diamond is 2.42 and that of air is 1. Choose the correct option. **[2021, 25 July Shift-I]**

(a) Angle of refraction is 24.41°
(b) Angle of refraction is 30°
(c) Refraction is not possible
(d) Angle of refraction is 53.4°

24 Three rays of light, namely red (R), green (G) and blue (B) are incident on the face PQ of a right angled prism PQR as shown in figure

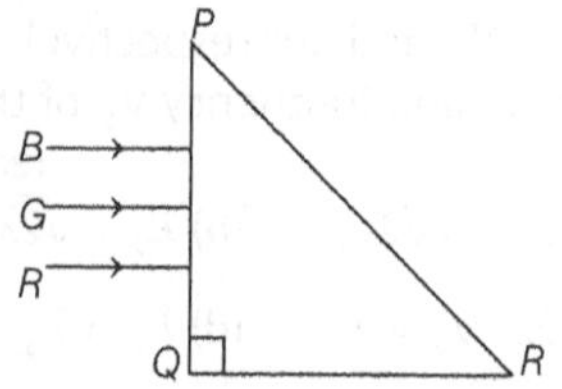

The refractive indices of the material of the prism for red, green and blue wavelength are 1.27, 1.42 and 1.49, respectively. The colour of the ray(s) emerging out of the face PR is **[2021, 18 March Shift-II]**

(a) green (b) red
(c) blue and green (d) blue

25 The angle of deviation through a prism is minimum when

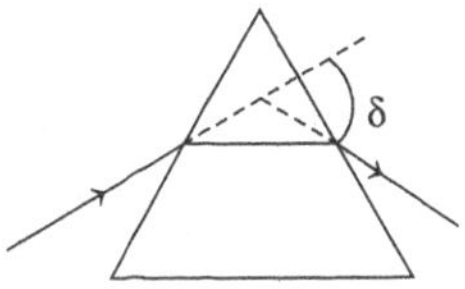

A. incident ray and emergent ray are symmetric to the prism
B. the refracted ray inside the prism becomes parallel to its base
C. angle of incidence is equal to that of the angle of emergence
D. angle of emergence is double the angle of incidence

Choose the correct answer from the options given below. **[2021, 16 March Shift-I]**

(a) Statements (A), (B) and (C) are true.
(b) Only statement (D) is true.
(c) Only statements (A) and (B) are true.
(d) Statements (B) and (C) are true.

26 Red light differs from blue light as they have **[2021, 16 March Shift-II]**

(a) different frequencies and different wavelengths
(b) different frequencies and same wavelengths
(c) same frequencies and same wavelengths
(d) same frequencies and different wavelengths

JEE Advanced

1 A plane polarised blue light ray is incident on a prism such that there is no reflection from the surface of the prism. The angle of deviation of the emergent ray is $\delta = 60°$ (see Fig. 1). The angle of minimum deviation for red light from the same prism is $\delta_{min} = 30°$ (see Fig. 2).

The refractive index of the prims material for blue light is $\sqrt{3}$. Which of the following statement(s) is/are correct? **(2023 Adv.)**

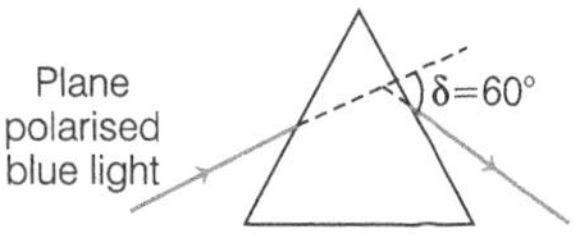

Fig. 1

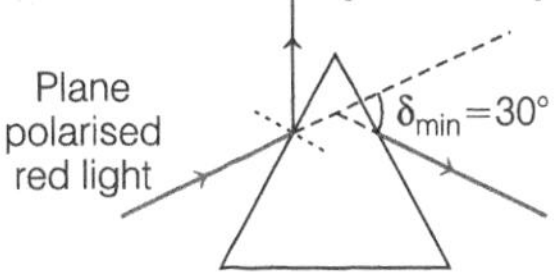

Fig. 2

(a) The blue light is polarised in the plane of incidence
(b) The angle of the prism is 45°
(c) The refractive index of the material of the prism for red light is $\sqrt{2}$
(d) The angle of refraction for blue light in air at the exit plane of the prism is 60°

2 A monochromatic light wave is incident normally on a glass slab of thickness d, as shown in the figure. The refractive index of the slab increases linearly from n_1 to n_2 over the height h. Which of the following statement(s) is (are) true about the light wave emerging out of the slab? **(2023 Adv.)**

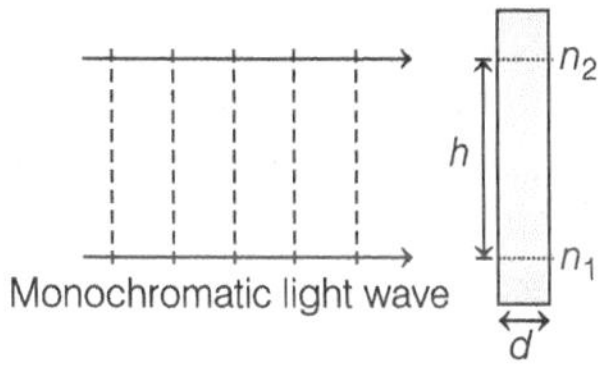

(a) It will deflect up by an angle $\tan^{-1}\left[\frac{(n_2^2 - n_1^2)\,d}{2h}\right]$

(b) It will deflect up by an angle $\tan^{-1}\left[\frac{(n_2 - n_1)\,d}{h}\right]$

(c) It will not deflect

(d) The deflection angle depends only on $(n_2 - n_1)$ and not on the individual values of n_1 and n_2.

3 Consider a configuration of n identical units, each consisting of three layers. The first layer is a column of air of height $h = \frac{1}{3}$ cm and the second and third layers are of equal thickness $d = \frac{\sqrt{3}-1}{2}$ cm and refractive indices $\mu_1 = \sqrt{3/2}$ and $\mu_2 = \sqrt{3}$, respectively. A light source O is placed on the top of the first unit, as shown in the figure. A ray of light from O is incident on the second layer of the first unit at an angle of $\theta = 60°$ to the normal.

For a specific value of n, the ray of light emerges from the bottom of the configuration at a distance $l = \frac{8}{\sqrt{3}}$ cm, as shown in the figure. The value of n is .... **(2022 Adv.)**

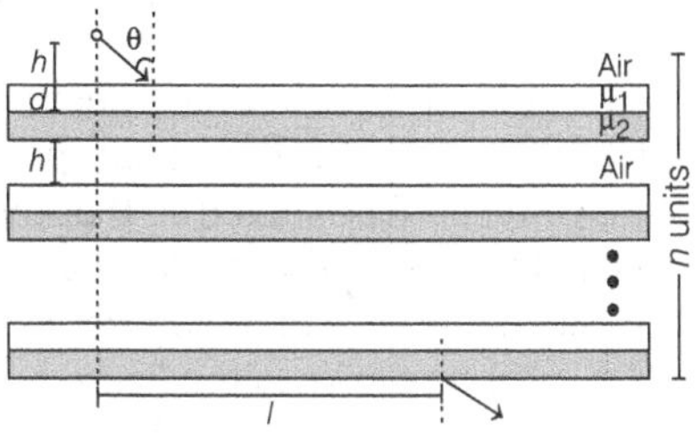

4 A wide slab consisting of two media of refractive indices n_1 and n_2 is placed in air as shown in the figure. A ray of light is incident from medium n_1 to n_2 at an angle θ, where $\sin\theta$ is slightly larger than $1/n_1$. Take, refractive index of air as 1. Which of the following statement(s) is(are) correct? **(2021 Adv.)**

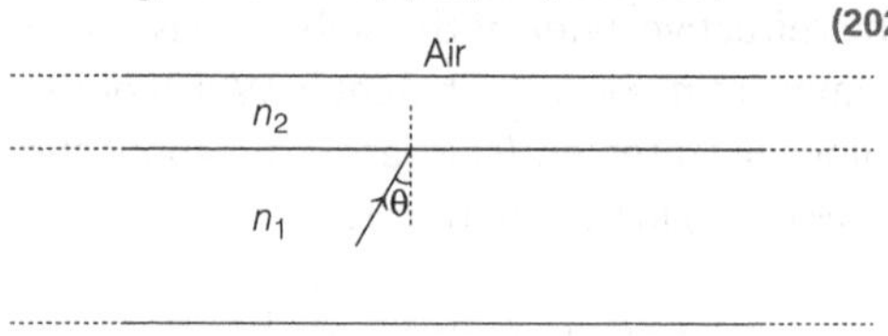

(a) The light ray enters air if $n_2 = n_1$

(b) The light ray is finally reflected back into the medium of refractive index n_1 if $n_2 < n_1$

(c) The light ray is finally reflected back into the medium of refractive index n_1 if $n_2 > n_1$

(d) The light ray is reflected back into the medium of refractive index n_1 if $n_2 = 1$

5 For a prism of prism angle $\theta = 60°$, the refractive indices of the left half and the right half are, respectively, n_1 and $n_2 (n_2 \geq n_1)$ as shown in the figure. The angle of incidence i is chosen such that the incident light rays will have minimum deviation if $n_1 = n_2 = n = 1.5$. For the case of unequal refractive indices, $n_1 = n$ and $n_2 = n + \Delta n$ (where, $\Delta n << n$), the angle of emergence $e = i + \Delta e$. Which of the following statement(s) is(are) correct? **(2021 Adv.)**

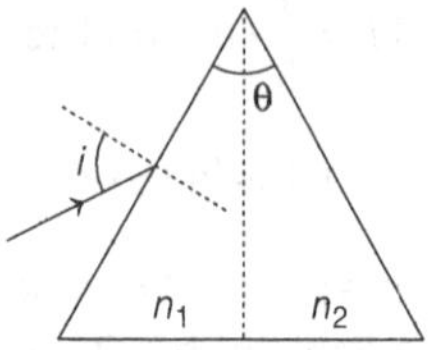

(a) The value of Δe (in radians) is greater than that of Δn.

(b) Δe is proportional to Δn.

(c) Δe lies between 2.0 and 3.0 milliradians, if $\Delta n = 2.8 \times 10^{-3}$.

(d) Δe lies between 1.0 and 1.6 milliradians, if $\Delta n = 2.8 \times 10^{-3}$.

6 A beaker of radius r is filled with water $\left(\text{refractive indexd } \frac{4}{3}\right)$ up to a height H as shown in the figure on the left. The beaker is kept on a horizontal table rotating with angular speed ω. This makes the water surface curved so that the difference in the height of water level at the center and at the circumference of the beaker is $h(h << H, h << r)$, as shown in the figure on the right. Take this surface to be approximately spherical with a radius of curvature R. Which of the following is/are correct? (g is the acceleration due to gravity) **(2020 Adv.)**

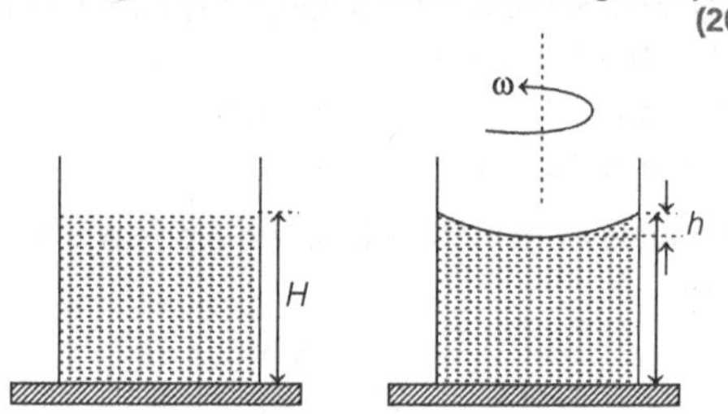

(a) $R = \dfrac{h^2 + r^2}{2h}$ (b) $R = \dfrac{3r^2}{2h}$

(c) Apparent depth of the bottom of the beaker is close to $\dfrac{3H}{2}\left(1 + \dfrac{\omega^2 H}{2g}\right)^{-1}$

(d) Apparent depth of the bottom of the beaker is close to $\dfrac{3H}{4}\left(1 + \dfrac{\omega^2 H}{4g}\right)^{-1}$

7 A large square container with thin transparent vertical walls and filled with water (refractive index $\frac{4}{3}$) is kept on a horizontal table. A student holds a thin straight wire vertically inside the water 12 cm from one of its corners, as shown schematically in the figure. Looking at the wire from this corner, another student sees two images of the wire, located symmetrically on each side of the line of sight as shown. The separation (in cm) between these images is ____________. **(2020 Adv.)**

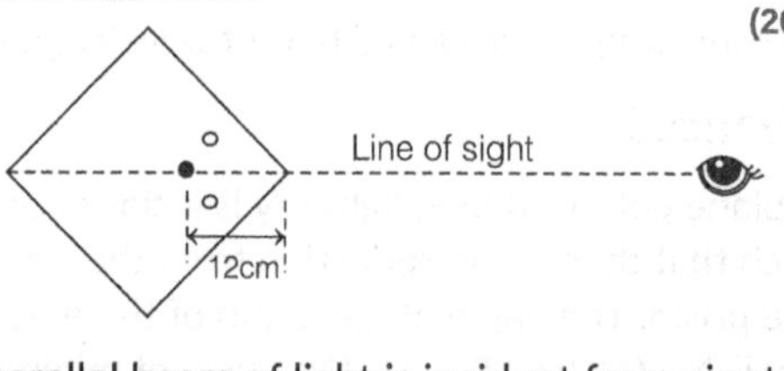

8 A parallel beam of light is incident from air at an angle α on the side PQ of a right angled triangular prism of refractive index $n = \sqrt{2}$. Light undergoes total internal reflection in the prism at the face PR when α has a minimum value of 45°.

The angle θ of the prism is **(2016 Adv.)**

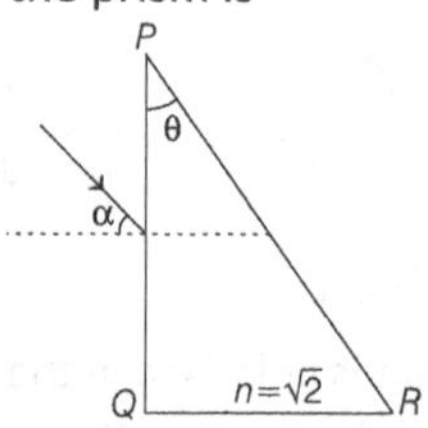

(a) 15° (b) 22.5° (c) 30° (d) 45°

Directions (Q.Nos. 9 to 10) Read the following passage and answer the questions.

Light guidance in an optical fibre can be understood by considering a structure comprising of thin solid glass cylinder of refractive index n_1 surrounded by a medium of lower refractive index n_2. The light guidance in the structure takes place due to successive total internal reflections at the interface of the media n_1 and n_2 as shown in the figure. All rays with the angle of incidence i less than a particular value i_m are confined in the medium of refractive index n_1. The numerical aperture (NA) of the structure is defined as $\sin i_m$. **(2015 Adv.)**

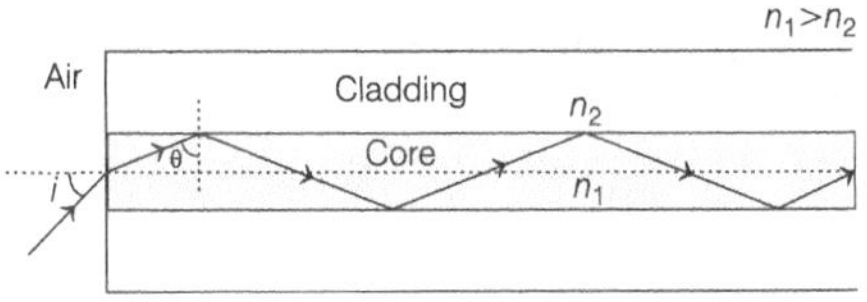

9 For two structures namely S_1 with $n_1 = \frac{\sqrt{45}}{4}$ and $n_2 = \frac{3}{2}$, and S_2 with $n_1 = \frac{8}{5}$ and $n_2 = \frac{7}{5}$ and taking the refractive index of water to be $\frac{4}{3}$ and that to air to be 1, the correct options is/are

(a) NA of S_1 immersed in water is the same as that of S_2 immersed in a liquid of refractive index $\frac{16}{3\sqrt{15}}$

(b) NA of S_1 immersed in liquid of refractive index $\frac{6}{\sqrt{15}}$ is the same as that of S_2 immersed in water

(c) NA of S_1 placed in air is the same as that S_2 immersed in liquid of refractive index $\frac{4}{\sqrt{15}}$

(d) NA of S_1 placed in air is the same as that of S_2 placed in water

10 If two structures of same cross-sectional area, but different numerical apertures NA_1 and NA_2 ($NA_2 < NA_1$) are joined longitudinally, the numerical aperture of the combined structure is

(a) $\frac{NA_1 NA_2}{NA_1 + NA_2}$ (b) $NA_1 + NA_2$

(c) NA_1 (d) NA_2

Answer Key

Level 1

2.1 Snell's Law

1. μ_{14} 2. $\frac{\sqrt{2}c}{3\sqrt{3}}$ 3. $\sqrt{3}$ 4. 30° 5. $\sqrt{3}$

6. 1.25 m 7. $\left(\frac{10\sqrt{23}}{\sqrt{23}-3}\right)$ cm 8. $\frac{3}{5\sqrt{2}}\hat{i} + \frac{2\sqrt{2}}{5}\hat{j} - \frac{1}{\sqrt{2}}\hat{k}$

2.2 Lateral Shift due to Parallel Glass Slab

1. $\frac{2}{3} \times 10^{-8}$ s 2. $3\left(\frac{1}{\sqrt{2}} - \frac{1}{\sqrt{7}}\right)$ cm $= 9.9$ mm, 45°

2.3 Apparent Depth and Height

1. 30 cm 2. (i) 48 cm (ii) 27 cm (iii) 84 cm (iv) 63 cm

3. 46 cm 4. (a) 139/6 cm (b) 139/8 cm 5. $\frac{(R-h)}{\mu}$

6. 25 cm 7. 7.5 cm below water surface 8. 9 cm/s

2.4 Longitudinal Shift due to Parallel Glass Slab

1. 102 cm (b) 10 cm

2.5 Total Internal Reflection

1. $\sin^{-1}\left(\frac{2}{3}\right)$ 2. $\sin^{-1}\left(\frac{\sqrt{3}}{4}\right)$ 3. 45° 4. $\frac{36}{\sqrt{7}}$ cm

5. $\frac{\pi h^2}{\mu^2 - 1}$ 6. $\cos^{-1}\left(\frac{8}{9}\right)$ 7. $\sin^{-1}\left(\frac{1}{\sqrt{3}}\right)$

2.6 Variable Refractive Index

1. $\mu = 3, \sin^{-1}\left(\frac{1}{3}\right)$

2.7 Prism

2. $\sqrt{3}$ 3. 45° 4. 120° 5. $\sqrt{3}$ 6. $\sqrt{2}$ 7. 2°

2.8 Dispersion

1. 0.095° 2. 0.0154 3. $\theta = 0.8°, \delta = 3.0°$

4. $A' = 1.4°, \delta_{net} = 0.48°$ 5. (i) 4°, (ii) – 0.04°

Level 2

Single Choice Correct Questions

1. (c)	2. (a)	3. (b)	4. (d)	5. (b)
6. (b)	7. (d)	8. (c)	9. (a)	10. (b)
11. (d)	12. (d)	13. (a)	14. (c)	15. (d)
16. (b)	17. (a)	18. (b)	19. (c)	20. (a)
21. (b)	22. (c)	23. (a)	24. (c)	25. (d)
26. (a)	27. (c)	28. (d)	29. (d)	30. (a)
31. (c)	32. (a)	33. (c)	34. (c)	35. (b)

36. (b)	37. (b)	38. (d)	39. (c)	40. (c)
41. (b)	42. (c)	43. (b)	44. (c)	45. (a)
46. (c)	47. (b)	48. (b)	49. (b)	50. (c)
51. (b)	52. (b)			

Numerical Value Questions

1. 3	2. 150	3. 36	4. 2	5. 1.2
6. 6	7. 60	8. 0	9. 6	10. 3

Level 3

Single Choice Correct Questions

1. (d)	2. (b)	3. (d)	4. (c)	5. (d)
6. (a)	7. (b)	8. (c)	9. (c)	10. (c)
11. (a)	12. (b)	13. (d)	14. (c)	15. (c)
16. (a)	17. (b)	18. (a)	19. (a)	20. (b)
21. (c)	22. (c)	23. (a)	24. (a)	25. (d)
26. (b)	27. (c)	28. (d)	29. (b)	30. (c)
31. (d)	32. (b)	33. (a)	34. (b)	35. (b)
36. (c)	37. (c)	38. (b)		

Multiple Choice(s) Correct Questions

1. (a, c, d)	2. (b, d)	3. (a, d)	4. (a,b,c,d)	
5. (c, d)	6. (a, c)	7. (a, d)	8. (b, c, d)	
9. (a, c)	10. (a, c)	11. (a, b, c)	12. (a, b, c)	13. (a, b)

Comprehension Based Questions

1. (d)	2. (c)	3. (a)	4. (b)	5. (d)
6. (a)	7. (b)	8. (b)	9. (c)	10. (d)
11. (b)				

Match the Columns Questions

1. A → 2, B → 3, C → 1, D → 4
2. A → 1, B → 3, C → 2, D → 4
3. A → 1, B → 2, C → 3,4

Numerical Value Questions

1. 1.5	2. 1.25	3. 24	4. 22.5	5. 4
6. 7	7. 5	8. 3	9. 1.95	10. 1.57

Previous Year's Questions

JEE Main

1. (a)	2. (31)	3. (c)	4. (48)	5. (c)
6. (b)	7. (a)	8. (a)	9. (50)	10. (30)
11. (c)	12. (c)	13. (d)	14. (c)	15. (a)
16. (d)	17. (a)	18. (d)	19. (12)	20. (b)
21. (c)	22. (b)	23. (c)	24. (b)	25. (a)
26. (a)				

JEE Advanced

1. (a, c, d)	2. (b, d)	3. (4)	4. (b, c, d)	5. (b, c)
6. (a, d)	7. (*)	8. (a)	9. (a, c)	10. (d)

SOLUTIONS

Level 1

2.1 Snell's Law

1. $\mu_{12} \times \mu_{23} \times \mu_{34} = \dfrac{\mu_1}{\mu_2} \times \dfrac{\mu_2}{\mu_3} \times \dfrac{\mu_3}{\mu_4} = \dfrac{\mu_1}{\mu_4} = \mu_{14}$

2. Using Snell's law,

$$\mu_1 \sin 45° = \mu_2 \sin 60°$$

$$\Rightarrow \quad \frac{\mu_1}{\mu_2} = \frac{\sqrt{3}}{\sqrt{2}}$$

Refractive index, $\mu = \dfrac{c}{v}$

$$\therefore \quad \frac{\mu_1}{\mu_2} = \frac{v_2}{v_1} \Rightarrow \frac{\sqrt{3}}{\sqrt{2}} = \frac{c/3}{v_1}$$

$$\Rightarrow \quad v_1 = \frac{\sqrt{2}\,c}{3\sqrt{3}}$$

3.

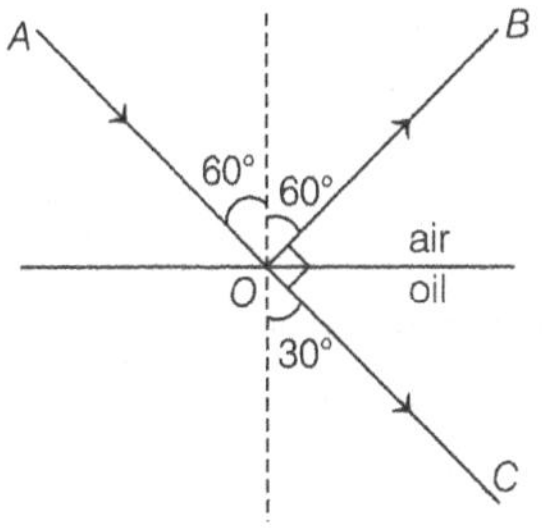

Using Snell's law

$$\mu_1 \sin i = \mu_2 \sin r$$

$$\Rightarrow \quad 1 \sin 60° = \mu_{\text{oil}} \sin 30°$$

$$\Rightarrow \quad \mu_{\text{oil}} = \sqrt{3}$$

4. Using Snell's law for medium 1 and medium 3,

$$\mu_1 \sin i = \mu_3 \sin r$$

$$\Rightarrow \quad 1 \times \sin 45° = \sqrt{2} \sin r$$

$$\Rightarrow \quad \sin r = \frac{1}{2} \Rightarrow r = 30°$$

5.

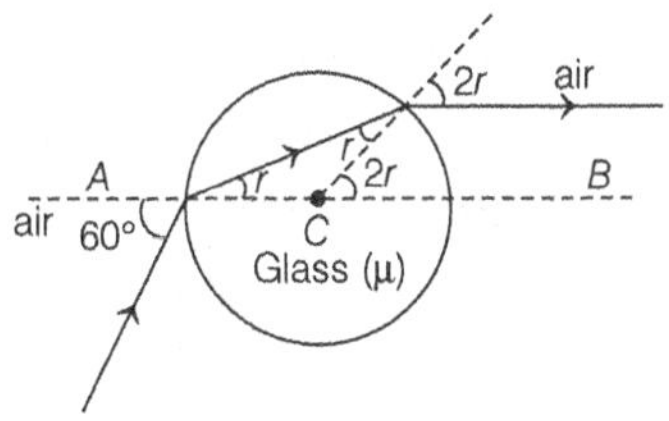

Using Snell's law for second refraction,

$$\mu \sin r = 1 \times \sin 2r$$

$$\Rightarrow \quad \mu \sin r = 2 \sin r \cos r$$

$$\Rightarrow \quad \mu = 2 \cos r$$

Using Snell's law for first refraction,

$$1 \times \sin 60° = \mu \sin r$$

$$\Rightarrow \quad \frac{\sqrt{3}}{2} = \mu \sqrt{1 - \left(\frac{\mu}{2}\right)^2} \qquad (\because \sin r = \sqrt{1 - \cos^2 r})$$

$$\Rightarrow \quad \mu^4 - 4\mu^2 + 3 = 0$$

$$\Rightarrow \quad \mu = \sqrt{3}$$

6.

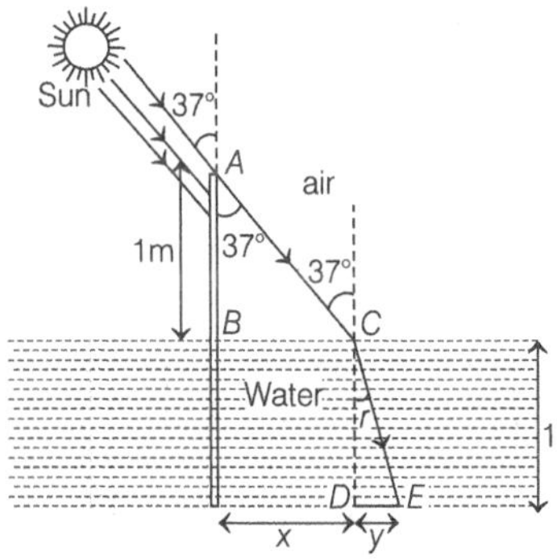

In ΔABC, $\tan 37° = \dfrac{x}{1}$

$$\Rightarrow \quad x = \frac{3}{4} \text{ m} = 0.75 \text{ m}$$

Using Snell's law,

$$1 \times \sin 37° = \frac{4}{3} \times \sin r$$

$$\Rightarrow \quad r = \sin^{-1}(0.45) = 26.8°$$

In ΔCDE,

$$\tan r = \frac{y}{1} \Rightarrow \tan(26.8°) = y$$

$$\Rightarrow \quad y = 0.5 \text{ m}$$

Length of shadow $= x + y = 0.75 + 0.5 = 1.25$ m

7. Let height of water in vessel be h.

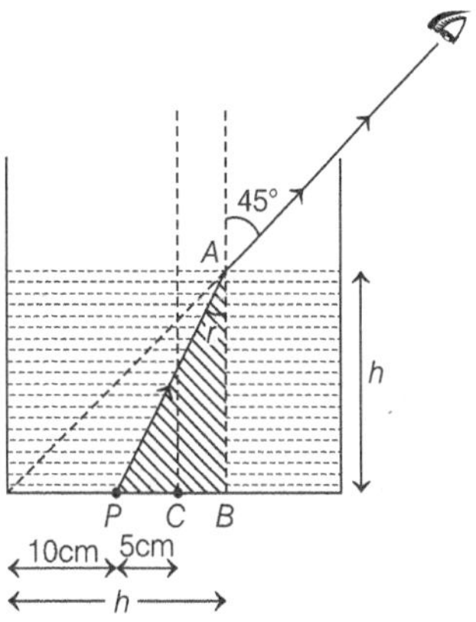

Using Snell's law,

$$1 \times \sin 45° = \frac{4}{3} \sin r$$

$$\Rightarrow \quad \sin r = \frac{3}{4\sqrt{2}}$$

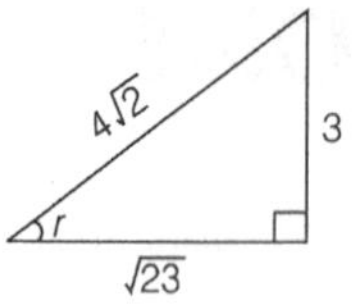

In ΔABP,

$$\tan r = \frac{h-10}{h}$$

$$\Rightarrow \quad \frac{3}{\sqrt{23}} = \frac{h-10}{h}$$

$$\Rightarrow \quad h = \left(\frac{10\sqrt{23}}{\sqrt{23}-3}\right) \text{cm}$$

8.

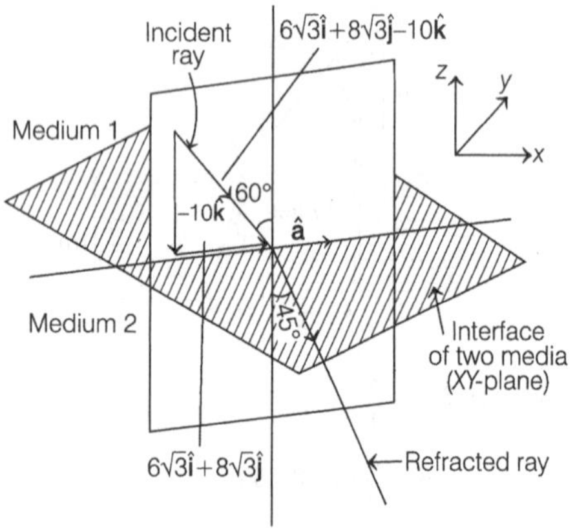

The angle made by the incident ray with Z-axis,

$$\cos \gamma = \frac{A_z}{A} = \frac{-10}{\sqrt{(6\sqrt{3})^2 + (8\sqrt{3})^2 + 10^2}} = -\frac{1}{2}$$

$$\Rightarrow \quad \gamma = 120°$$

i = Angle of incidence

$= 180° - 120° = 60°$

Applying Snell's law of refraction at the interface of two media,

$$\mu_1 \sin i = \mu_2 \sin r$$

$$\Rightarrow \quad \sqrt{2} \sin 60° = \sqrt{3} \sin r$$

$$\Rightarrow \quad r = 45°$$

x and y components remain unchanged during refraction

$$\hat{\mathbf{a}} = \frac{6\sqrt{3}\hat{\mathbf{i}} + 8\sqrt{3}\hat{\mathbf{j}}}{\sqrt{(6\sqrt{3})^2 + (8\sqrt{3})^2}} = \frac{3}{5}\hat{\mathbf{i}} + \frac{4}{5}\hat{\mathbf{j}}$$

So, unit vector along the direction of refracted ray,

$$\hat{\mathbf{r}} = (1 \sin 45°)\,\hat{\mathbf{a}} + (1 \cos 45°)(-\hat{\mathbf{k}})$$

$$= \frac{1}{\sqrt{2}}\left(\frac{3}{5}\hat{\mathbf{i}} + \frac{4}{5}\hat{\mathbf{j}}\right) + \frac{1}{\sqrt{2}}(-\hat{\mathbf{k}})$$

$$= \frac{3}{5\sqrt{2}}\hat{\mathbf{i}} + \frac{2\sqrt{2}}{5}\hat{\mathbf{j}} - \frac{1}{\sqrt{2}}\hat{\mathbf{k}}$$

2.2 Lateral Shift due to Parallel Glass Slab

1.

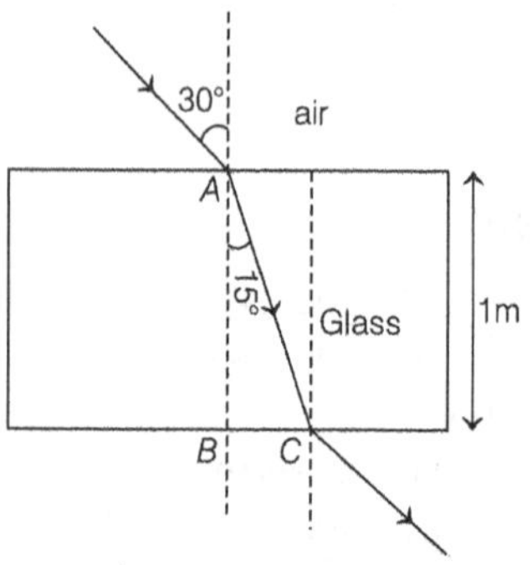

Applying Snell's law of refraction,

$$1 \times \sin 30° = \mu \times \sin 15°$$

$$\Rightarrow \quad \mu = \frac{1}{2 \sin 15°}$$

Speed of light in glass slab $= \dfrac{c}{\mu} = 2c \sin 15°$

Distance travelled by light in glass $= \dfrac{1}{\cos 15°}$

$$\text{Time taken} = \frac{\text{Distance}}{\text{Speed}} = \frac{1}{\cos 15° \, (2c \sin 15°)}$$

$$= \frac{1}{c \sin 30°} = \frac{2}{3} \times 10^{-8} \text{ s}$$

2. Using Snell's law of refraction,

$$\mu_1 \sin i = \mu_2 \sin r$$

$$\Rightarrow \quad 1 \times \sin 45° = \frac{3}{2} \times \sin r$$

$$\Rightarrow \quad \sin r = \frac{\sqrt{2}}{3}$$

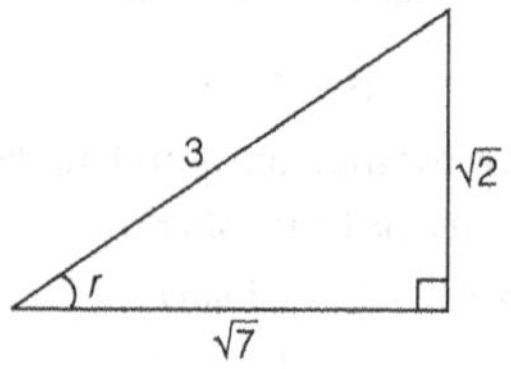

$$\text{Lateral displacement} = \frac{t \sin (i - r)}{\cos r}$$

$$= t\left(\frac{\sin i \cos r - \cos i \sin r}{\cos r}\right)$$

$$= t(\sin i - \cos i \tan r)$$

$$= 3\left[\frac{1}{\sqrt{2}} - \frac{1}{\sqrt{2}}\left(\frac{\sqrt{2}}{\sqrt{7}}\right)\right]$$

$$= 3\left(\frac{1}{\sqrt{2}} - \frac{1}{\sqrt{7}}\right) \text{cm}$$

$= 9.9$ mm

The ray will emerge at an angle of 45°.

2.3 Apparent Depth and Height

1. $H_{app} = \dfrac{H}{\mu_{12}} = \dfrac{40}{((4/3)/1)} = 30\text{ cm}$

2. (a) Apparent Height $= \dfrac{\text{Actual height}}{\mu_{12}}$

$$= \frac{36}{(1/(4/3))} = 48\text{ cm}$$

(b) Apparent depth $= \dfrac{\text{Actual depth}}{\mu_{12}} = \dfrac{36}{((4/3)/1)} = 27\text{ cm}$

(c) Distance between them as seen by fish

$$= 48 + 36 = 84\text{ cm}$$

(d) Distance between them as seen by bird

$$= 36 + 27 = 63\text{ cm}$$

3. $\dfrac{H_{app}}{\mu} = \dfrac{H_1}{\mu_1} + \dfrac{H_2}{\mu_2} + \dfrac{H_3}{\mu_3}$

$$\Rightarrow \quad \frac{H_{app}}{2} = \frac{18}{1.5} + \frac{15}{2.5} + \frac{8}{1.6}$$

$$\Rightarrow \quad H_{app} = 46\text{ cm}$$

4. (a) Distance of the observer as seen by fish,

$$\frac{H_{app}}{\mu} = \frac{H_1}{\mu_1} + \frac{H_2}{\mu_2} + \frac{H_3}{\mu_3}$$

$$\Rightarrow \quad \frac{H_{app}}{(4/3)} = \frac{8}{1} + \frac{3}{(8/5)} + \frac{10}{(4/3)}$$

$$\Rightarrow \quad H_{app} = \frac{139}{6}\text{ cm}$$

(b) Distance of the fish as seen by observer,

$$\frac{H_{app}}{\mu} = \frac{H_1}{\mu_1} + \frac{H_2}{\mu_2} + \frac{H_3}{\mu_3}$$

$$\Rightarrow \quad \frac{H_{app}}{1} = \frac{10}{4/3} + \frac{3}{8/5} + \frac{8}{1}$$

$$\Rightarrow \quad H_{app} = \frac{139}{8}\text{ cm}$$

5.

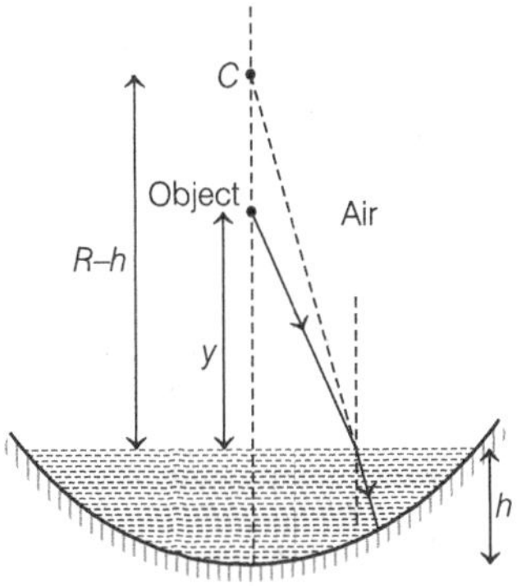

For the final image to be formed on the object itself, the rays should hit the mirror normally i.e., the rays incident on the mirror should appear to be coming from the centre of curvature (C) of the mirror.

For refraction,

$$H_{app} = \frac{H}{\mu_{12}} \Rightarrow R - h = \frac{y}{(1/\mu)}$$

$$\Rightarrow \quad y = \frac{R-h}{\mu}$$

6.

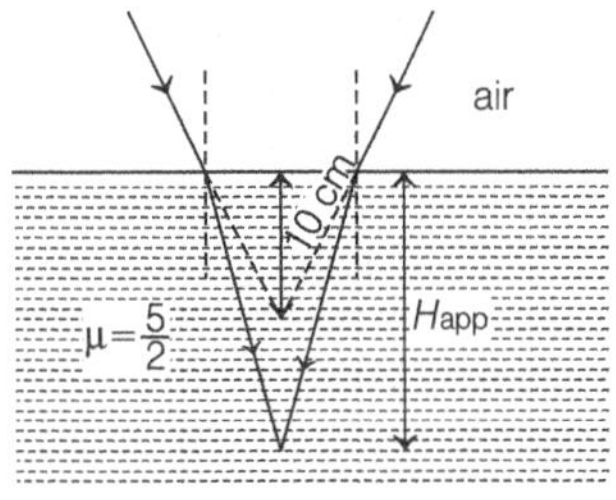

$$H_{app} = \frac{H}{\mu_{12}} \Rightarrow H_{app} = \frac{10}{(1/(5/2))} = 25\text{ cm}$$

7.

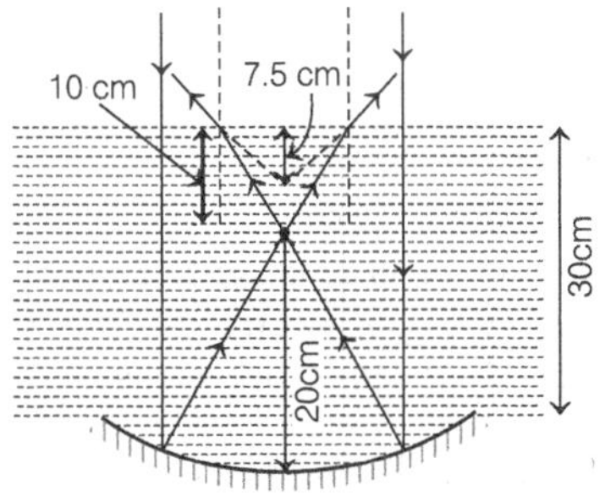

After reflection from mirror, rays will meet at the focus of the mirror i.e., 20 cm from the mirror.

For refraction of light from water to air,

Actual depth $= 30 - 20 = 10$ cm

Apparent depth $= \dfrac{\text{Actual Depth}}{\mu_{12}} = \dfrac{10}{(4/3)/1} = 7.5\text{ cm}$

So, the final image will be formed 7.5 cm below water surface.

8. Let the real velocity of bird be v.

Apparent velocity $= \dfrac{\text{Real velocity}}{\mu_{12}} = \dfrac{v}{1/(4/3)} = \dfrac{4v}{3}$

Velocity of bird w.r.t. fish = 16 cm/s

$$\Rightarrow \quad \frac{4v}{3} - (-4) = 16 \Rightarrow v = 9\text{ cm/s}$$

2.4 Longitudinal Shift due to Parallel Glass Slab

1. Shift due to glass slab $= t\left(1 - \dfrac{1}{\mu_{rel}}\right) = 6\left[1 - \dfrac{1}{(1.5/1)}\right] = 2\text{ cm}$

For reflection from mirror,

$$u = -(27 - 2) = -25\text{ cm}, f = -20\text{ cm}$$

$$\frac{1}{v} + \frac{1}{u} = \frac{1}{f}$$

$$\Rightarrow \quad \frac{1}{v} + \frac{1}{(-25)} = \frac{1}{(-20)} \quad \Rightarrow \quad v = -100\text{ cm}$$

Reflected rays from mirror will again pass through the glass slab.

So, the final image distance from mirror $= 100 + 2 = 102$ cm

2. The given system can be taken as a combination of a glass slab and a plane mirror. So, the rays first pass through the glass slab, get reflected from the plane mirror and finally again pass through the glass slab.

Shift due to slab $= t\left(1 - \frac{1}{\mu_{rel}}\right) = 6\left[1 - \frac{1}{(1.5/1)}\right] = 2$ cm

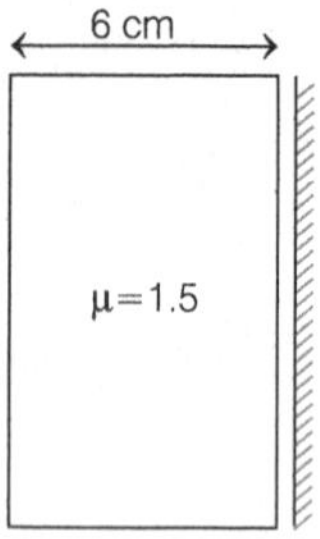

For plane mirror,
Object distance $= -(8 + 6 - 2) = -12$ cm
$\Rightarrow$ Image distance = +12 cm
So, the plane mirror forms image 12 cm behind the mirror.
The reflected rays again pass the glass slab. So, the final image will be $12 - 2 = 10$ cm behind the mirror.

2.5 Total Internal Reflection

1. $i_c = \sin^{-1}\left(\frac{1}{\mu}\right) = \sin^{-1}\left(\frac{1}{1.5}\right) = \sin^{-1}\left(\frac{2}{3}\right)$

2. Critical angle, $i_c = \sin^{-1}\left(\frac{1}{\mu}\right) = \sin^{-1}\left(\frac{1}{2}\right) = 30°$

Angle of incidence, $i = 2i_c = 60°$

Using Snell's law of refraction,

$$\mu_1 \sin i = \mu_2 \sin r$$

$$\Rightarrow \quad 1 \sin 60° = 2 \sin r$$

$$\Rightarrow \quad \sin r = \frac{\sqrt{3}}{4}$$

$$\Rightarrow \quad r = \sin^{-1}\left(\frac{\sqrt{3}}{4}\right)$$

3. For refraction, angle of deviation $= r - i$ which is less than 90°.

For angle of deviation to be 90°, total internal reflection must take place.

For reflection, $\delta = 180° - 2i$

$$\Rightarrow \quad 90° = 180° - 2i \Rightarrow i = 45°$$

4. Radius of circle, $r = \frac{h}{\sqrt{\mu^2 - 1}} = \frac{12}{\sqrt{\left(\frac{4}{3}\right)^2 - 1}} = \frac{36}{\sqrt{7}}$ cm

5. Radius of circle, $r = \frac{h}{\sqrt{\mu^2 - 1}}$

Area of circle of illuminance $= \pi r^2 = \frac{\pi h^2}{\mu^2 - 1}$

6.

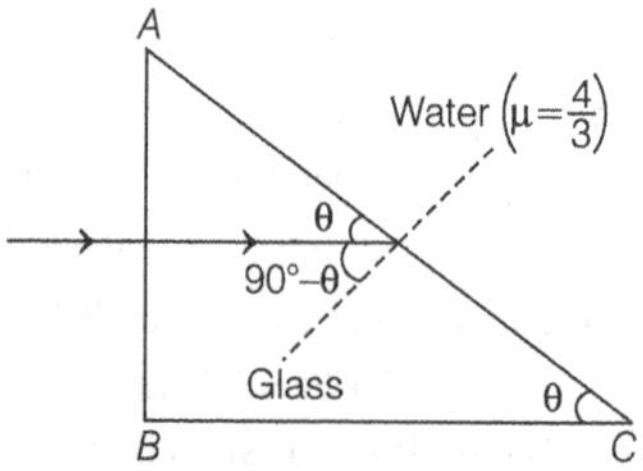

Critical angle, $i_c = \sin^{-1}\left(\frac{4/3}{3/2}\right) = \sin^{-1}\left(\frac{8}{9}\right)$

For TIR to happen at face AC,

$$i > i_c$$

$$\Rightarrow \quad 90° - \theta > \sin^{-1}\left(\frac{8}{9}\right)$$

$$\Rightarrow \quad \theta < 90° - \sin^{-1}\left(\frac{8}{9}\right)$$

$$\Rightarrow \quad \theta < \cos^{-1}\left(\frac{8}{9}\right) \Rightarrow \theta_{max} = \cos^{-1}\left(\frac{8}{9}\right)$$

7.

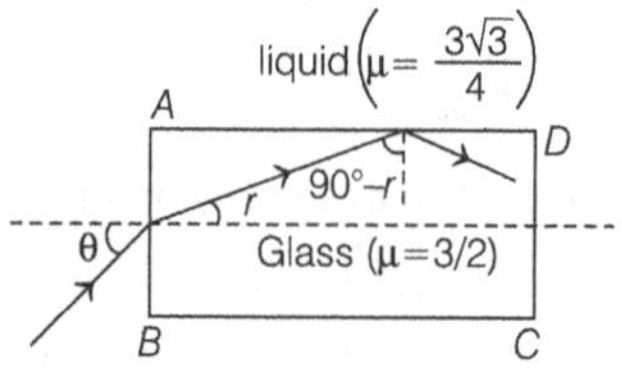

For refraction at AB,

$$\mu_1 \sin i = \mu_2 \sin r$$

$$\Rightarrow \quad \frac{3\sqrt{3}}{4} \sin\theta = \frac{3}{2} \sin r$$

$$\Rightarrow \quad \sin r = \frac{\sqrt{3}}{2} \sin\theta$$

For TIR to take place at face AD,

$$i \geq i_c \Rightarrow 90° - r \geq i_c$$

$$\Rightarrow \quad \sin(90° - r) \geq \sin i_c$$

$$\Rightarrow \quad \cos r \geq \frac{3\sqrt{3}/4}{3/2}$$

$$\Rightarrow \quad \sqrt{1 - \left(\frac{\sqrt{3}}{2}\sin\theta\right)^2} \geq \frac{\sqrt{3}}{2} \quad (\because \cos r = \sqrt{1 - \sin^2 r})$$

$$\Rightarrow \quad \sin\theta \leq \frac{1}{\sqrt{3}}$$

$$\Rightarrow \quad \theta_{max} = \sin^{-1}\left(\frac{1}{\sqrt{3}}\right)$$

2.6 Variable Refractive Index

1. (i) Slope of tangent $= \tan(90° - \phi) = \dfrac{dy}{dx}$

$$\Rightarrow \quad \cot\phi = 4x$$

$$y = 2x^2, \text{ At } y = 1, x = \frac{1}{\sqrt{2}}$$

$$\therefore \quad \cot\phi = 4\left(\frac{1}{\sqrt{2}}\right)$$

$$\Rightarrow \quad \sin\phi = \frac{1}{3}$$

Applying Snell's law of refraction,

$$\mu_1 \sin i = \mu_2 \sin r$$

$$\Rightarrow \quad 1 \times \sin 90° = \mu_2\left(\frac{1}{3}\right)$$

$$\Rightarrow \quad \mu_2 = 3$$

(ii) Angle of incidence, $\phi = \sin^{-1}\left(\dfrac{1}{3}\right)$

2. Applying Snell's law at A and B,

$$\mu_1 \sin i = \mu_2 \sin r$$

$$\Rightarrow \quad 1 \times \sin 90° = (ky^{3/2} + 1)^{1/2} \sin r$$

$$\Rightarrow \quad \sin r = \frac{1}{(ky^{3/2} + 1)^{1/2}}$$

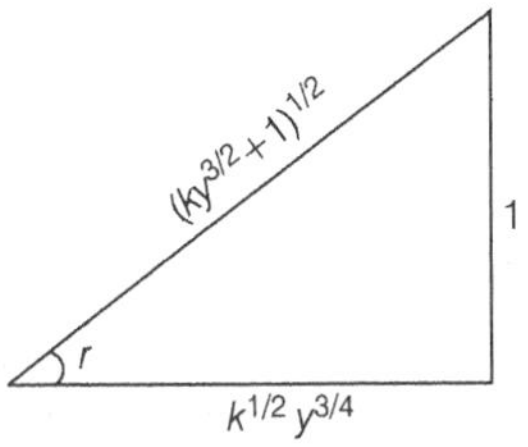

Slope of tangent at $B = \tan(90° - r) = \cot r = k^{1/2}y^{3/4}$

Also, slope of tangent $= \dfrac{dy}{dx} = k^{1/2}y^{3/4}$

$$\Rightarrow \quad \int_0^y y^{-3/4} dy = k^{1/2}\int_0^x dx$$

$$\Rightarrow \quad y^{1/4} = k^{1/2}\left(\frac{x}{4}\right)$$

$$\Rightarrow \quad y = k^2\left(\frac{x}{4}\right)^4$$

(ii) $y = k^2\left(\dfrac{x}{4}\right)^4$

At P, $y = 1 \quad \Rightarrow \quad 1 = (1)^2\left(\dfrac{x}{4}\right)^4$

$$\Rightarrow \quad x = 4$$

So, coordinates of P are (4.0, 1)

2.7 Prism

1.

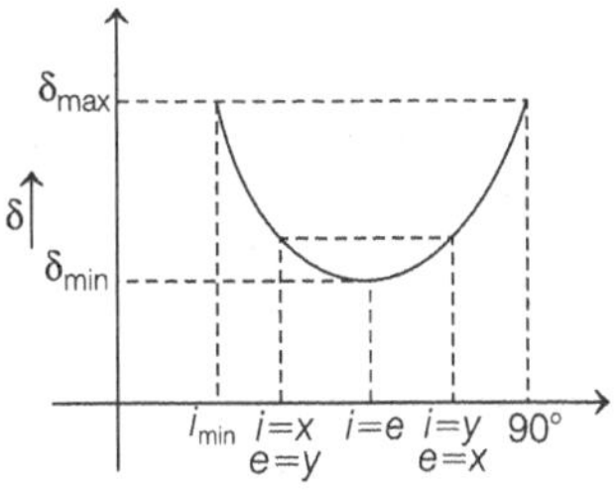

Deviation is minimum, when $i = e$ and $r_1 = r_2$

$$\delta = i + e - A$$

$$\delta_{min} = 2i - A \qquad \because (i = e)$$

$$\Rightarrow \quad i = \left(\frac{A + \delta_{min}}{2}\right)$$

Applying Snell's law,

$$\mu_1 \sin i = \mu_2 \sin r$$

$$\Rightarrow \quad 1 \times \sin\left(\frac{A + \delta_{min}}{2}\right) = \mu \sin\left(\frac{A}{2}\right)$$

$$\Rightarrow \quad \mu = \frac{\sin\left(\dfrac{A + \delta_{min}}{2}\right)}{\sin\left(\dfrac{A}{2}\right)}$$

2. Let $A = \delta = e = x$

$$\delta = i + e - A \quad \Rightarrow \quad x = 60° + x - x \quad \Rightarrow \quad x = 60°$$

Using Snell's law,

$$\mu_1 \sin i = \mu_2 \sin r_1$$

$$\Rightarrow \quad 1 \times \sin 60° = \mu \sin 30° \qquad \because \left\{r_1 = r_2 = \frac{A}{2} = 30°\right\}$$

$$\Rightarrow \quad \mu = \sqrt{3}$$

3. For minimum deviation,

$$r_1 = r_2 = \frac{A}{2} = \frac{60°}{2} = 30°$$

Applying Snell's law,

$$\mu_1 \sin i = \mu_2 \sin r_1$$

$$\Rightarrow \quad 1 \times \sin i = \sqrt{2} \sin 30°$$

$$\Rightarrow \quad i = 45°$$

4. Applying Snell's law for first refraction,

$$\mu_1 \sin i = \mu_2 \sin r_1 \quad \Rightarrow \quad 1 \times \sin 90° = 2 \sin r_1$$

$$\Rightarrow \quad \sin r_1 = \frac{1}{2} \quad \Rightarrow \quad r_1 = 30°$$

$$r_2 = A - r_1 = 60° - 30° = 30°$$

Applying Snell's law for second refraction,

$$\mu_2 \sin r_2 = \mu_1 \sin e$$

$$\Rightarrow \quad 2 \sin 30° = 1 \times \sin e$$

$$\Rightarrow \quad \sin e = 1$$

$$\Rightarrow \quad e = 90°$$

$$\delta = i + e - A = 90° + 90° - 60° = 120°$$

5. The emergent ray makes an angle of 30° with the incident ray i.e., deviation is 30°.

$$\delta = i + e - A$$

$\Rightarrow$ $30° = 60° + e - 30° \Rightarrow e = 0$

So, the emergent ray is perpendicular to the face through which it emerges.

$$e = 0 \Rightarrow r_2 = 0$$

$\therefore$ $r_1 = A - r_2 = 30° - 0 = 30°$

Applying Snell's law at first face,

$$\mu_1 \sin i = \mu_2 \sin r_1$$

$\Rightarrow$ $1 \times \sin 60° = \mu \sin 30° \Rightarrow \mu = \sqrt{3}$

6. For the ray to retrace its path, it should hit the silvered face perpendicularly.

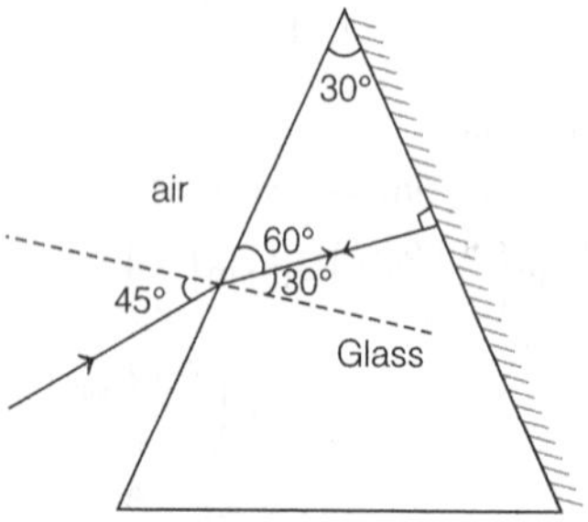

Applying Snell's law at first face,

$$\mu_1 \sin i = \mu_2 \sin r_1$$

$\Rightarrow$ $1 \times \sin 45° = \mu \sin 30°$

$\Rightarrow$ $\mu = \sqrt{2}$

7. Deviation produced by a thin prism,

$$\delta = (\mu_{real} - 1) A = \left(\frac{3/2}{1} - 1\right) 4° = 2°$$

2.8 Dispersion

1. $\theta = (\mu_V - \mu_R) A = (1.632 - 1.613) 5 = 0.095°$

2. Dispersive power, $\omega = \dfrac{\mu_V - \mu_R}{\mu_Y - 1}$

Refractive index for yellow light,

$$\mu_Y = \frac{\mu_V + \mu_R}{2} = 1.519$$

$\therefore$ $\omega = \dfrac{\mu_V - \mu_R}{\mu_Y - 1} = \dfrac{1.523 - 1.515}{1.519 - 1} = 0.0154$

3. $\theta = \theta_1 + \theta_2 = (\mu_V - \mu_R) A_1 + (\mu'_V - \mu'_R) A_2$

$= (1.5 - 1.4)(4°) + (1.7 - 1.5)(2°) = 0.8°$

$\delta = \delta_1 + \delta_2 = (\mu_Y - 1) A_1 + (\mu'_Y - 1) A_2$

$= \left(\dfrac{\mu_V + \mu_R}{2} - 1\right) A_1 + \left(\dfrac{\mu'_V + \mu'_R}{2} - 1\right) A_2$

$= (1.45 - 1)\, 4° + (1.6 - 1)\, 2° = 3°$

4. For achromatic combination, net angular dispersion is zero.

$\therefore$ $\theta = \theta_1 - \theta_2 = (\mu_V - \mu_R) A - (\mu'_V - \mu'_R) A' = 0$

$\Rightarrow$ $(1.42 - 1.35)\, 4° - (1.9 - 1.7) A' = 0$

$\Rightarrow$ $A' = 1.4°$

Net mean deviation, $\delta = \delta_1 - \delta_2$

$= (\mu_Y - 1) A - (\mu'_Y - 1) A'$

$= (1.40 - 1)\, 4° - (1.8 - 1)(1.4°) = 0.48°$

5. (i) $\delta = \delta_1 - \delta_2$

$= (\mu_Y - 1) A - (\mu'_Y - 1) A' = 0$

$\Rightarrow$ $\left(\dfrac{\mu_V + \mu_R}{2} - 1\right) A - \left(\dfrac{\mu'_V + \mu'_R}{2} - 1\right) A' = 0$

$\Rightarrow$ $(1.50 - 1)\, 6° - (1.75 - 1) A' = 0$

$\Rightarrow$ $A' = 4°$

(ii) $\theta = \theta_1 - \theta_2 = (\mu_V - \mu_R) A - (\mu'_V - \mu'_R) A'$

$= (1.51 - 1.49)\, 6° - (1.77 - 1.73)\, 4° = -0.04°$

Level 2

Single Choice Correct Questions

1. $i = 2r \Rightarrow r = \dfrac{i}{2}$

Applying Snell's law of refraction,

$$\mu_1 \sin i = \mu_2 \sin r$$

$\Rightarrow$ $1 \times \sin i = n \sin\left(\dfrac{i}{2}\right)$

$\Rightarrow$ $2 \sin\left(\dfrac{i}{2}\right) \cos\left(\dfrac{i}{2}\right) = n \sin\left(\dfrac{i}{2}\right)$

$\Rightarrow$ $\cos\left(\dfrac{i}{2}\right) = \dfrac{n}{2} \Rightarrow i = 2\cos^{-1}\left(\dfrac{n}{2}\right)$

2. Applying Snell's law,

$$\mu_1 \sin i = \mu_2 \sin r$$

$\Rightarrow$ $1 \times \sin\theta = n \sin r$

$\Rightarrow$ $\theta = nr$ $\quad\because$ {For small angle, $\sin x = x$}

$\Rightarrow$ $r = \dfrac{\theta}{n}$

Lateral shift $= \dfrac{t \sin(i - r)}{\cos r} = \dfrac{t(i - r)}{1} = t\left(\theta - \dfrac{\theta}{n}\right) = \dfrac{t\theta(n - 1)}{n}$

3.

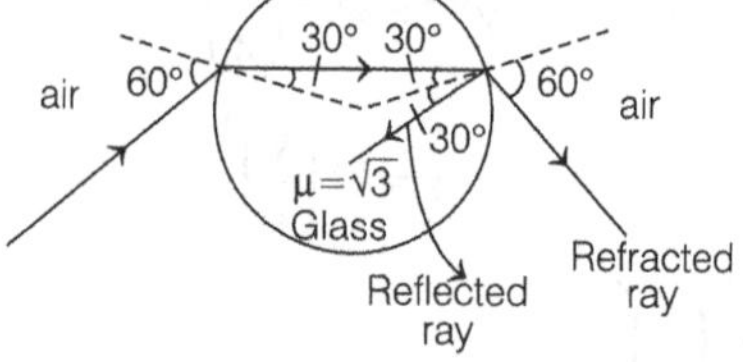

Applying Snell's law,

$\mu_1 \sin i = \mu_2 \sin r \Rightarrow 1 \times \sin 60° = \sqrt{3} \sin r$

$\Rightarrow$ $r = 30°$

Angle between the reflected and refracted rays

$= 180° - 60° - 30° = 90°$

4. Since AB and CD are parallel, both will make same angle with the normal.

Applying Snell's law for medium 1 and medium 4,

$$\mu_1 \sin i = \mu_4 \sin r$$

$$\Rightarrow \quad \mu_1 \sin\theta = \mu_4 \sin\theta \qquad \{\because i = r\}$$

$$\Rightarrow \quad \mu_1 = \mu_4$$

5. Applying Snell's law for glass and air mediums,

$$\mu_1 \sin i = \mu_2 \sin r \quad \Rightarrow \quad \mu_g \sin i = 1 \times \sin 90°$$

$$\Rightarrow \quad \mu_g = \frac{1}{\sin i}$$

6.

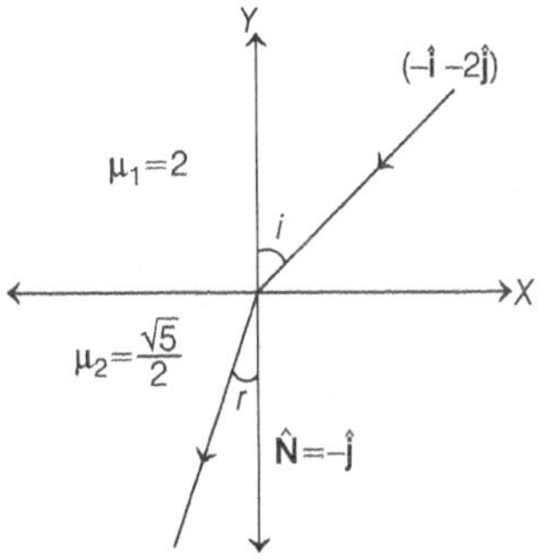

$$\cos\theta = \frac{\mathbf{A}\cdot\mathbf{B}}{AB} \Rightarrow \cos i = \frac{(-\hat{\mathbf{i}} - 2\hat{\mathbf{j}})\cdot(-\hat{\mathbf{j}})}{\sqrt{5}\,(1)} = \frac{2}{\sqrt{5}}$$

$$\cos i = \frac{2}{\sqrt{5}} \quad \text{or} \quad \sin i = \frac{1}{\sqrt{5}}$$

Applying Snell's law,

$$\mu_1 \sin i = \mu_2 \sin r$$

$$\Rightarrow \quad 2\left(\frac{1}{\sqrt{5}}\right) = \left(\frac{\sqrt{5}}{2}\right)\sin r$$

$$\Rightarrow \quad \sin r = \frac{4}{5} \text{ or } \cos r = \frac{3}{5}$$

x-component remains unchanged during refraction.

Unit vector along refracted ray

$$= (1 \sin r)(-\hat{\mathbf{i}}) + (1 \cos r)(-\hat{\mathbf{j}})$$

$$= \frac{4}{5}(-\hat{\mathbf{i}}) + \frac{3}{5}(-\hat{\mathbf{j}}) = \frac{-4\hat{\mathbf{i}} - 3\hat{\mathbf{j}}}{5}$$

7. Let height of water filled be h.

$$\text{Apparent depth} = \frac{\text{Actual depth}}{\mu_{12}} = \frac{h}{((4/3)/1)} = \frac{3h}{4}$$

For container to appear half filled,

Apparent depth = Height of empty space

$$\Rightarrow \quad \frac{3h}{4} = 21 - h$$

$$\Rightarrow \quad h = 12 \text{ cm}$$

8. Let thickness of glass slab be t and distance of bubble from one side to be x.

So, distance of bubble from the other side $= t - x$

$$\text{Apparent depth} = \frac{\text{Actual depth}}{\mu_{12}}$$

$$\Rightarrow \quad 6 = \frac{x}{(1.5/1)} \qquad \text{...(i)}$$

$$\text{and} \quad 4 = \frac{t - x}{(1.5/1)} \qquad \text{...(ii)}$$

Adding the two Eqs. we get

$$t = 15 \text{ cm}$$

9. Apparent depth

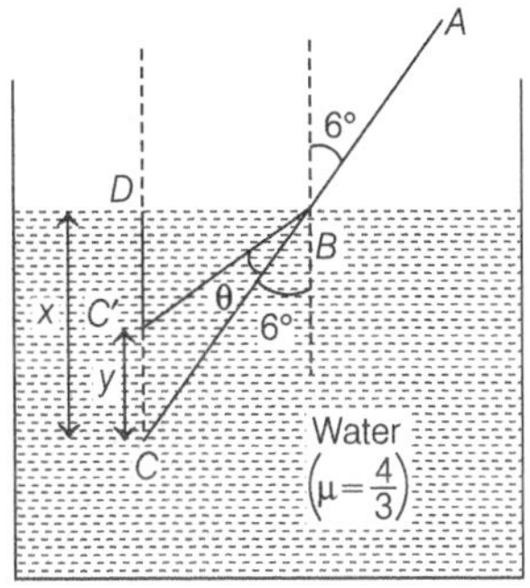

$$= \frac{\text{Actual Depth}}{\mu_{12}}$$

$$\Rightarrow \quad y = \frac{x}{((4/3)/1)}$$

$$\Rightarrow \quad y = \frac{3x}{4}$$

$$\text{In } \Delta BCD,\ \tan 6° = \frac{BD}{x}$$

$$\text{In } \Delta BC'D,\ \tan(6° + \theta) = \frac{BD}{y}$$

$$\therefore \quad \frac{\tan 6°}{\tan(6° + \theta)} = \frac{y}{x}$$

$$\Rightarrow \quad \frac{6°}{6° + \theta} = \frac{3x/4}{x} \qquad \{\because \tan\theta = \theta \text{ for small } \theta\}$$

$$\Rightarrow \quad \theta = 2°$$

10. The image of lower end of the rod will be formed L distance behind the mirror. The distance of the upper end w.r.t. mirror is $2L + \mu L$. So, its image will be formed the same distance behind the mirror.

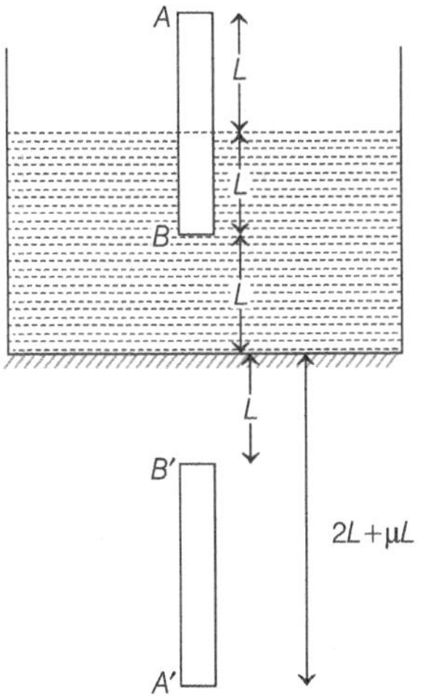

Length of image of rod as seen from water

$$= (2L + \mu L) - L$$

$$= \mu L + L$$

Length of image of rod as seen from air

$$= \frac{\mu L + L}{\mu} = L + \frac{L}{\mu}$$

11. Let actual velocity of bird be v.

Apparent velocity $= \dfrac{\text{Actual velocity}}{\mu_{12}} = \dfrac{v}{1/(4/3)} = \dfrac{4v}{3}$

$$v_{\text{bird, fish}} = v_{\text{bird}} - v_{\text{fish}}$$

$$\Rightarrow \quad 9 = \frac{4v}{3} - (-3)$$

$$\Rightarrow \quad v = 4.5 \text{ m/s}$$

12. $\dfrac{H_{app}}{\mu} = \dfrac{H_1}{\mu_1} + \dfrac{H_2}{\mu_2} + \dfrac{H_3}{\mu_3} + \dfrac{H_4}{\mu_4}$

$$\Rightarrow \quad \frac{H_{app}}{1} = \frac{2}{1} + \frac{1.5}{1.5} + \frac{1.5}{1} + \frac{1.5}{1.5}$$

$$\Rightarrow \quad H_{app} = 5.5 \text{ cm}$$

Actual depth of $P = 2 + 1.5 + 1.5 + 1.5 = 6.5$ cm

Shift $= 6.5 - 5.5 = 1$ cm

So, the image of point P will be 1 cm above P.

13. $H_{app} = \displaystyle\int_0^H \frac{dy}{1 + \frac{y}{H}} = H\left[\ln\left(1 + \frac{y}{H}\right)\right]_0^H = (\ln 2) H = 0.693H$

14. Distance of object from mirror

$$= \frac{33.25}{1.33} + 15 = 40 \text{ cm}$$

Distance of final image from mirror

$$= \frac{25}{1.33} + 15 = \frac{135}{4} \text{ cm}$$

For mirror, $\dfrac{1}{v} + \dfrac{1}{u} = \dfrac{1}{f}$

$$\Rightarrow \quad \frac{1}{-\left(\frac{135}{4}\right)} + \frac{1}{(-40)} = \frac{1}{f} \quad \Rightarrow f = -18.3 \text{ cm}$$

15. Angle of incidence in air is 90°. So, the angle of refraction in air while coming out of slab will also be 90°. Hence, total deviation produced by the slab is zero.

16.

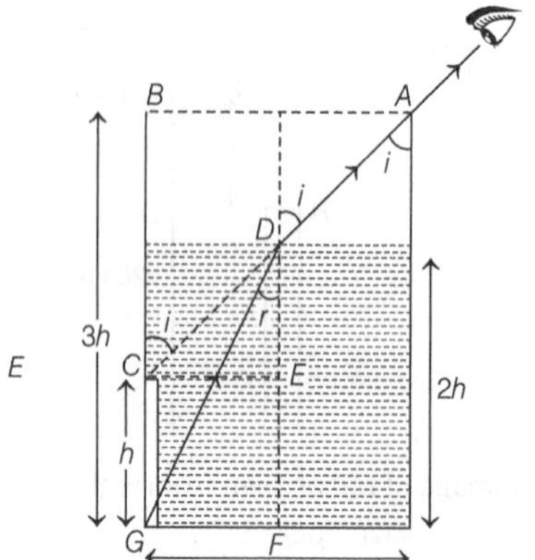

In ΔABC, $\tan i = \dfrac{AB}{BC} = \dfrac{2h}{2h} = 1$

$$\Rightarrow \quad i = 45°$$

In ΔCDE, $\tan i = \dfrac{CE}{DE}$

$$\Rightarrow \quad \tan 45° = \frac{CE}{(2h - h)}$$

$$\Rightarrow \quad CE = h$$

In ΔDFG, $\tan r = \dfrac{GF}{DF} = \dfrac{CE}{DF} \quad \Rightarrow \tan r = \dfrac{h}{2h} = \dfrac{1}{2}$

Applying Snell's law,

$$\mu_1 \sin i = \mu_2 \sin r$$

$$\Rightarrow 1 \times \sin 45° = \mu \times \frac{1}{\sqrt{5}} \quad \Rightarrow \mu = \sqrt{\frac{5}{2}}$$

17.

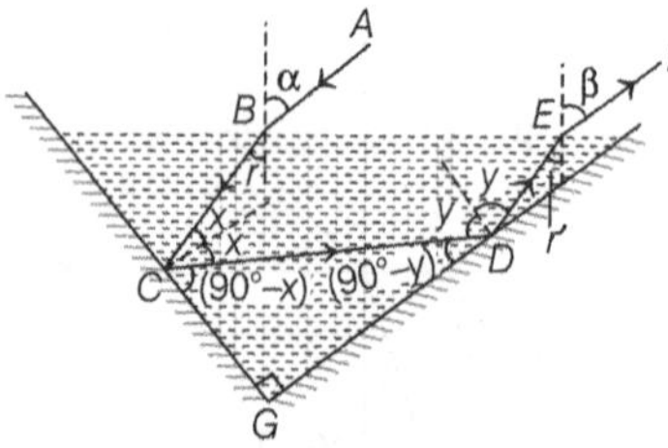

In ΔCGD,

$$90° + (90° - x) + (90° - y) = 180°$$

$$\Rightarrow \quad x + y = 90°$$

For BC and DE,

Sum of interior angles $= 2x + 2y = 2(x + y) = 180°$

So, BC and DE are parallel to each other.

So, $r = r'$ which implies $\alpha = \beta$

18.

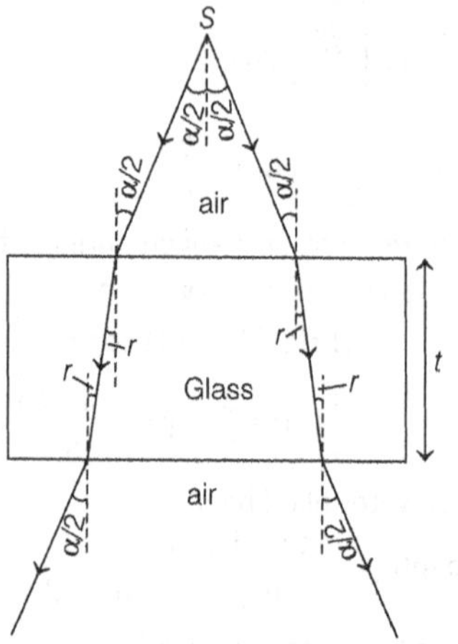

From figure we can see that the emergent ray is parallel to the incident ray. So, the divergence angle of the emergent beam will be also α.

19. Shift due to glass slab $= t\left(1 - \dfrac{1}{\mu}\right) = 10\left(1 - \dfrac{1}{\mu}\right)$

So, object distance from mirror $= 30 - 10\left(1 - \dfrac{1}{\mu}\right)$

For plane mirror,

Image distance from mirror = Object distance from mirror

$$= 30 - 10\left(1 - \frac{1}{\mu}\right)$$

The reflected rays will again pass through the glass slab. So, the distance of final image from mirror,

$$\left[30 - 10\left(1 - \frac{1}{\mu}\right)\right] - 10\left(1 - \frac{1}{\mu}\right) = 23.2 \Rightarrow \mu = \frac{200}{132}$$

20.

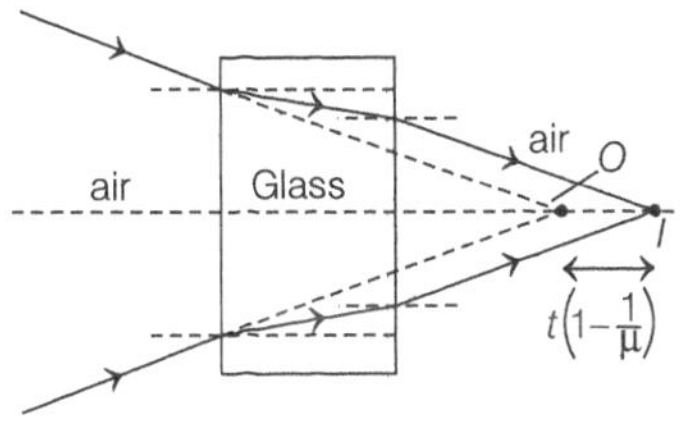

21. Shift $= t\left(1 - \frac{1}{\mu}\right) = (6-2)\left(1 - \frac{1}{3/2}\right) = \frac{4}{3}$ cm

22.

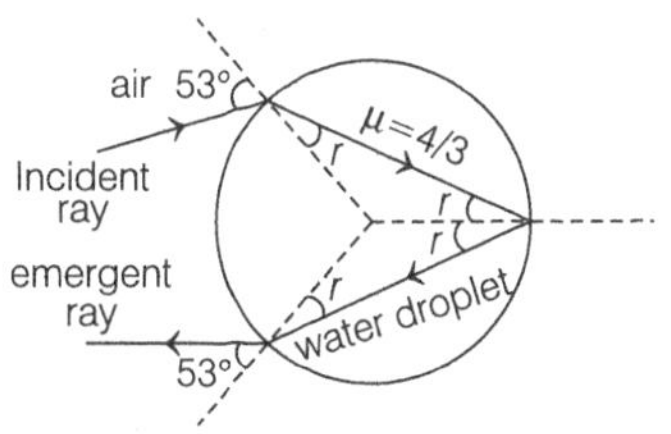

Using Snell's law for first refraction,

$$\mu_1 \sin i = \mu_2 \sin r$$

$\Rightarrow$ $1 \times \sin 53° = \frac{4}{3}\sin r \Rightarrow \sin r = \frac{3}{5}$

$\Rightarrow$ $r = 37°$

Total deviation, $\delta = \delta_1 + \delta_2 + \delta_3$

$= (53° - 37°) + [180° - 2(37°)] + (53° - 37°)$

$= 138°$

23. $i_c = \sin^{-1}\left(\frac{\mu_2}{\mu_1}\right) = \theta \Rightarrow \frac{\mu_2}{\mu_1} = \sin\theta$

$$\frac{\mu_2}{\mu_1} = \frac{v_1}{v_2} \Rightarrow \sin\theta = \frac{v}{v_2} \Rightarrow v_2 = \frac{v}{\sin\theta}$$

24. Radius $= \frac{h}{\sqrt{\mu^2 - 1}} = \frac{4}{\sqrt{\left(\frac{5}{3}\right)^2 - 1}} = 3$ m

$\therefore$ Diameter of the disc $= 2r = 6$ m

25. Radius $= \frac{h}{\sqrt{\mu^2 - 1}} = \frac{12}{\sqrt{\left(\frac{4}{3}\right)^2 - 1}} = \frac{36}{\sqrt{7}}$ cm

26. From figure, $r + 90° + r' = 180°$

$\Rightarrow$ $i + 90° + r' = 180°$ $\{\because i = r$ for reflection$\}$

$\Rightarrow$ $r' = 90° - i$

Using Snell's law,

$$\mu_1 \sin i = \mu_2 \sin r' \Rightarrow \mu_1 \sin i = \mu_2 \sin(90° - i)$$

$\Rightarrow$ $\tan i = \frac{\mu_2}{\mu_1}$

Critical angle, $i_c = \sin^{-1}\left(\frac{\mu_2}{\mu_1}\right) = \sin^{-1}(\tan i)$

27. Since angle of incidence is less than the critical angle, there will be partial reflection and refraction.

Angle between the reflected and refracted rays

$= 180° - r - \theta$

which is less than $180° - 2\theta$ as $r > \theta$.

In total internal reflection, there is 100% reflection and no refraction.

28. Critical angle for glass air interface,

$$i_c = \sin^{-1}\left(\frac{1}{\mu}\right) = \sin^{-1}\left(\frac{2}{3}\right)$$

Applying Snell's law at all boundaries,

$$\mu_1 \sin i = \mu_2 \sin r = \mu_3 \sin e$$

$\Rightarrow$ $\mu_1 \sin i = \mu_3 \sin e$

$\Rightarrow$ $\left(\frac{3}{2}\right) \times \sin i_c = 1 \times \sin e$

$\Rightarrow$ $\frac{3}{2} \times \frac{2}{3} = \sin e \Rightarrow e = 90°$

29. Deviation, $\delta = r - i$

Deviation is maximum, when $i = C$ and $r = \frac{\pi}{2}$

$\therefore$ $\delta_{max} = \frac{\pi}{2} - C$

30. Applying Snell's law at surface AB,

$$n_2 \sin\alpha = n_1 \sin r \Rightarrow \sin r = \frac{n_2}{n_1}\sin\alpha$$

For TIR to happen at surface AD,

$$i > i_c \Rightarrow \frac{\pi}{2} - r > \sin^{-1}\left(\frac{n_2}{n_1}\right)$$

$\Rightarrow$ $\cos\left(\frac{\pi}{2} - r\right) < \cos\left[\sin^{-1}\left(\frac{n_2}{n_1}\right)\right]$

$\Rightarrow$ $\sin r < \cos\left[\sin^{-1}\left(\frac{n_2}{n_1}\right)\right]$

$\Rightarrow$ $\frac{n_2}{n_1}\sin\alpha < \cos\left[\sin^{-1}\left(\frac{n_2}{n_1}\right)\right]$

$\Rightarrow$ $\alpha < \sin^{-1}\left[\frac{n_1}{n_2}\cos\left[\sin^{-1}\left(\frac{n_2}{n_1}\right)\right]\right]$

$\Rightarrow$ $\alpha_{max} = \sin^{-1}\left[\frac{n_1}{n_2}\cos\left[\sin^{-1}\left(\frac{n_2}{n_1}\right)\right]\right]$

31. Critical angle for glass air system $= \sin^{-1}\left(\frac{1}{\sqrt{2}}\right) = 45°$

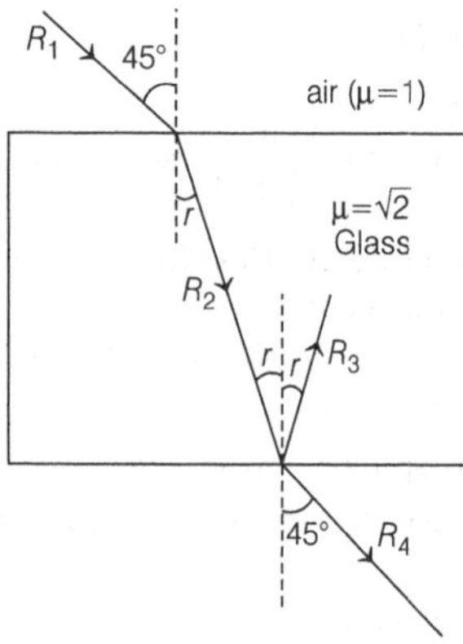

Applying Snell's law for first refraction,

$$1 \times \sin 45° = \sqrt{2}\sin r \Rightarrow \sin r = \frac{1}{2} \Rightarrow r = 30°$$

Angle between R_3 and $R_4 = 180° - 45° - 30° = 105°$

32.

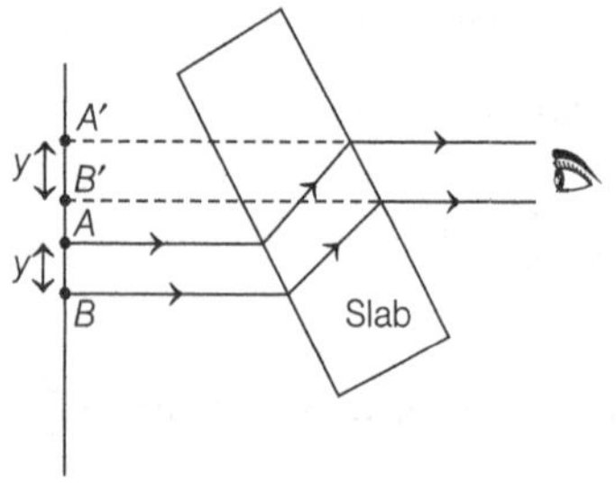

Emergent ray is parallel to incident ray. So, both dots will appear to the shifted upward by same distance.

Hence, distance between them remains same.

33. Lateral shift $= \frac{t\sin(i-r)}{\cos r} = \frac{t(\sin i\cos r - \cos i\sin r)}{\cos r}$

$$= t(\sin i - \cos i\tan r)$$

Lateral shift $= 5\sqrt{3}$

$$\Rightarrow \quad t(\sin i - \cos i\tan r) = 5\sqrt{3}$$

$$\Rightarrow \quad 15(\sin 60° - \cos 60°\tan r) = 5\sqrt{3}$$

$$\Rightarrow \quad \tan r = \frac{1}{\sqrt{3}} \Rightarrow r = 30°$$

Applying Snell's law,

$$1 \times \sin 60° = \mu \sin 30° \Rightarrow \mu = \sqrt{3} = 1.732$$

34.

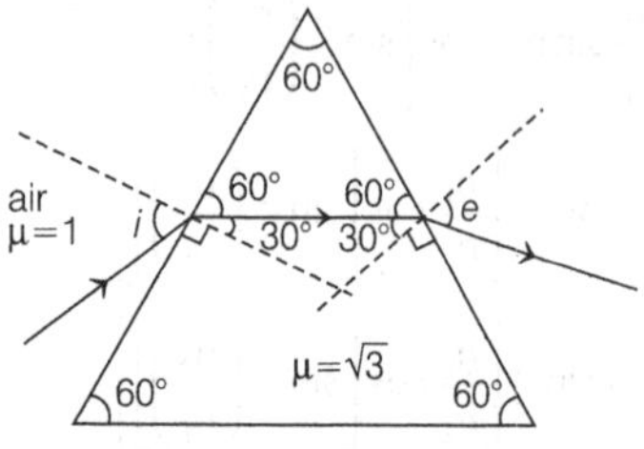

Applying Snell's law for first refraction,

$$1 \times \sin i = \sqrt{3} \times \sin 30°$$

$$\Rightarrow \quad \sin i = \frac{\sqrt{3}}{2}$$

$$\Rightarrow \quad i = 60°$$

35.

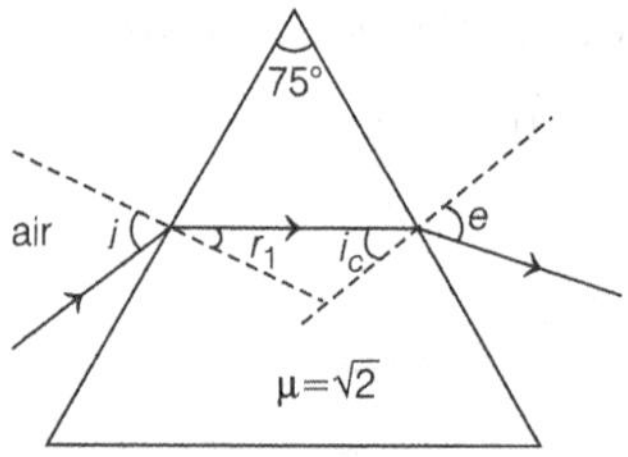

Critical angle, $i_c = \sin^{-1}\left(\frac{1}{\mu}\right) = \sin^{-1}\left(\frac{1}{\sqrt{2}}\right) = 45°$

$$r_1 + r_2 = A \Rightarrow r_1 + i_c = 75°$$

$$\Rightarrow \quad r_1 + 45° = 75° \Rightarrow r_1 = 30°$$

Applying Snell's law for first refraction,

$$1 \times \sin i = \mu \sin r_1$$

$$\Rightarrow \quad 1 \times \sin i = \sqrt{2}\sin 30°$$

$$\Rightarrow \quad \sin i = \frac{1}{\sqrt{2}} \Rightarrow i = 45°$$

36. $\delta = i + e - A \Rightarrow 44° = 42° + 62° - A \Rightarrow A = 60°$

$$\delta_{min} = 2i - A \Rightarrow 38° = 2i - 60° \Rightarrow i = 49°$$

37.

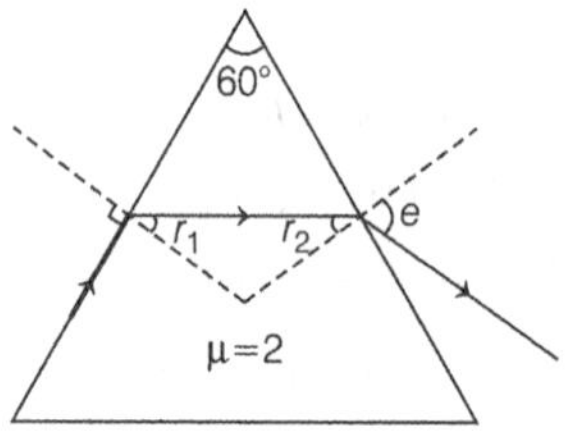

Applying Snell's law for first refraction,

$$1 \times \sin 90° = 2 \times \sin r_1$$

$$\Rightarrow \quad \sin r_1 = \frac{1}{2} \Rightarrow r_1 = 30°$$

$$r_1 + r_2 = A \Rightarrow 30° + r_2 = 60° \Rightarrow r_2 = 30°$$

Applying Snell's law for second refraction,

$$2 \times \sin r_2 = 1 \times \sin e$$

$$\Rightarrow \quad 2 \times \sin 30° = 1 \times \sin e$$

$$\Rightarrow \quad e = 90°$$

$$\delta = i + e - A = 90° + 90° - 60° = 120°$$

38. Applying Snell's law for first refraction,

$$1 \times \sin 90° = \mu \sin r_1 \Rightarrow \sin r_1 = \frac{1}{\mu}$$

Applying Snell's law for second refraction,

$$\mu \times \sin r_2 = 1 \times \sin 45° \Rightarrow \sin r_2 = \frac{1}{\sqrt{2}\mu}$$

$$A = r_1 + r_2 \Rightarrow r_1 = A - r_2$$

$\Rightarrow \sin r_1 = \sin(45° - r_2)$

$\Rightarrow \sin r_1 = \sin 45° \cos r_2 - \cos 45° \sin r_2$

$$\Rightarrow \quad \frac{1}{\mu} = \frac{1}{\sqrt{2}}\sqrt{1 - \frac{1}{2\mu^2}} - \frac{1}{\sqrt{2}}\left(\frac{1}{\sqrt{2}\mu}\right)$$

$\Rightarrow \quad \mu = \sqrt{5}$

39. For minimum deviation,

$$r_1 = r_2 = \frac{A}{2} = 45°$$

Applying Snell's law for first refraction,

$$1 \times \sin i = \sqrt{\frac{3}{2}} \sin r_1$$

$$\Rightarrow \quad \sin i = \sqrt{\frac{3}{2}} \sin 45°$$

$$\Rightarrow \quad i = 60°$$

$$\delta_{min} = 2i - A$$

$$\Rightarrow \quad \delta_{min} = 2(60°) - 90° = 30°$$

40. In ΔBDE,

$$60° + (90° - \theta_c) + (90° - r) = 180°$$

$$\Rightarrow \quad r + \theta_c = 60°$$

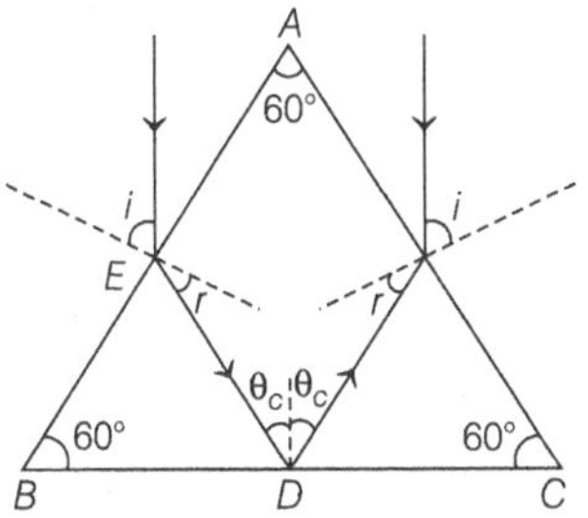

$$\delta = \delta_1 + \delta_2 + \delta_3$$

$$112° = (i - r) + (180° - 2\theta_c) + (i - r)$$

$$\Rightarrow \quad 112° = 2i - 2(r + \theta_c) + 180°$$

$$\Rightarrow \quad 112° = 2i - 2(60°) + 180° \Rightarrow i = 26°$$

41.

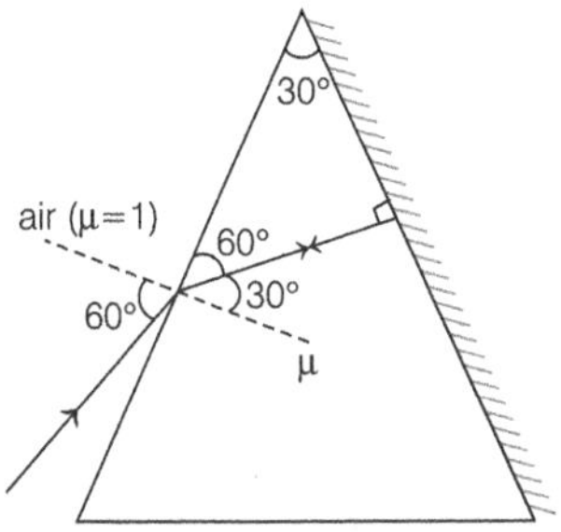

For ray to retrace its path, it should hit the reflecting surface perpendicularly.

Applying Snell's law for refraction,

$$1 \times \sin 60° = \mu \sin 30° \Rightarrow \mu = \sqrt{3}$$

42.

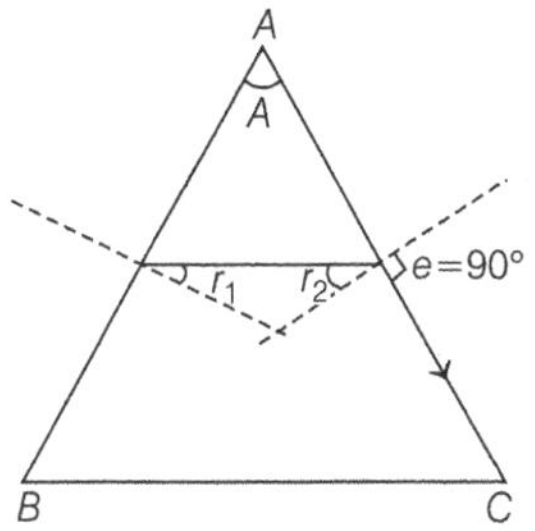

If the ray just emerges from face AC,

$$e = 90° \text{ and } r_2 = C \qquad \text{...(i)}$$

From Smell's law at face AB, we have

$$1 \times \sin i = \mu \sin r_1 \qquad \text{...(ii)}$$

From Eq. (ii), μ is minimum, when r_1 is maximum.

i.e., $r_1 = C$. In this case, $i = 90°$

$$A = r_1 + r_2 \Rightarrow A = C + C \Rightarrow C = \frac{A}{2}$$

As $\sin C = \frac{1}{\mu} \Rightarrow \sin\left(\frac{A}{2}\right) = \frac{1}{\mu}$

$$\Rightarrow \quad \mu = \text{cosec}\left(\frac{A}{2}\right)$$

43.

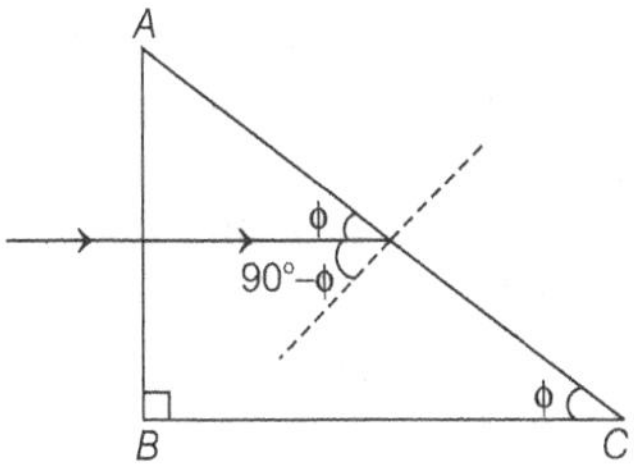

For TIR to happen at AC,

$$i > i_c$$

$$\Rightarrow \quad 90° - \phi > i_c$$

$$\Rightarrow \quad \sin(90° - \phi) > \sin i_c$$

$$\Rightarrow \quad \cos\phi > \frac{4/3}{3/2}$$

$$\Rightarrow \quad \phi < \cos^{-1}\left(\frac{8}{9}\right)$$

$$\Rightarrow \quad \phi_{max} = \cos^{-1}\left(\frac{8}{9}\right)$$

44.

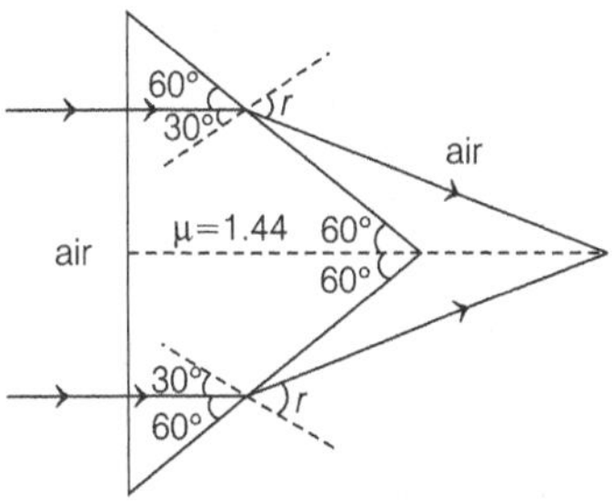

Applying Snell's law,

$$1.44 \times \sin 30° = 1 \times \sin r \quad \Rightarrow \quad r = \sin^{-1}(0.72)$$

Deviation of a ray $= r - i = \sin^{-1}(0.72) - 30°$

Angle between the emergent rays $= 2(r - i)$

$$= 2[\sin^{-1}(0.72) - 30°]$$

45. $\sin i_c = \dfrac{1}{\mu} \quad \Rightarrow \quad \sin 45° = \dfrac{1}{\mu}$

$\Rightarrow \qquad \mu = \sqrt{2} = 1.414$

Since refractive indices of green and blue are greater than 1.414, so they will suffer total internal reflection. Only red colour does not suffer total internal reflection.

46. Minimum deviation produced by a thin prism

$$\delta_{\min} = (\mu_{\text{rel}} - 1)A$$

In air, $\delta_1 = \left(\dfrac{3/2}{1} - 1\right)A = \dfrac{A}{2}$

In water, $\delta_2 = \left(\dfrac{3/2}{4/3} - 1\right)A = \dfrac{A}{8}$

$\therefore \qquad \dfrac{\delta_2}{\delta_1} = \dfrac{A/2}{A/8} = 4$

47. The deviation produced by small angled prism,

$$\delta = (\mu - 1)\alpha = (1.5 - 1)4° = 2° \text{ (clockwise)}$$

Let the mirror be rotated by angle β (clockwise)

So, angle of incidence for mirror $= 45° - \beta$

$$\delta = \delta_1 + \delta_2$$

$\Rightarrow \qquad 90° = [180° - 2(45° - \beta)] + 2°$

$\Rightarrow \qquad \beta = -1°$

So, the mirror should be rotated by an angle of 1° (anti-clockwise).

48. $\mu_V > \mu_R$. So, violet light will bend more towards normal than red light.

49. $\delta_Y = (\mu_Y - 1)A = (1.62 - 1)5° = 3.1°$

$$\omega = \frac{\mu_V - \mu_R}{\mu_Y - 1} \quad \Rightarrow \quad \omega = \frac{(\mu_V - \mu_R)A}{(\mu_Y - 1)A} \quad \Rightarrow \quad \omega = \frac{\theta}{\delta_Y}$$

$\Rightarrow \qquad \theta = \omega\delta_Y = 0.03 \times 3.1° = 0.093°$

50. $\delta = \delta_1 - \delta_2 = (\mu_Y - 1)A_1 - (\mu'_Y - 1)A' = 0$

$\Rightarrow \qquad (1.54 - 1)4° - (1.72 - 1)A' = 0$

$\Rightarrow \qquad A' = 3°$

51. $\theta = \omega\delta_Y$

$\Rightarrow \qquad \theta_C = \omega_C\delta_{CY}$ and $\theta_F = \omega_F\delta_{FY}$

Net angle of dispersion, $\theta = \theta_C - \theta_F$

$\Rightarrow \qquad 0 = \omega_C\delta_{CY} - \omega_F\delta_{FY}$

$\Rightarrow \qquad \dfrac{\omega_C}{\omega_F} = \dfrac{\delta_{FY}}{\delta_{CY}}$

52. $\theta = \theta_1 + \theta_2 + \theta_3$

$\Rightarrow \; 0 = (\mu_V - \mu_R)A - (\mu'_V - \mu'_R)A' + (\mu_V - \mu_R)A$

$\Rightarrow \qquad \dfrac{A'}{A} = \dfrac{2(\mu_V - \mu_R)}{(\mu'_V - \mu'_R)}$

Numerical Value Questions

1.

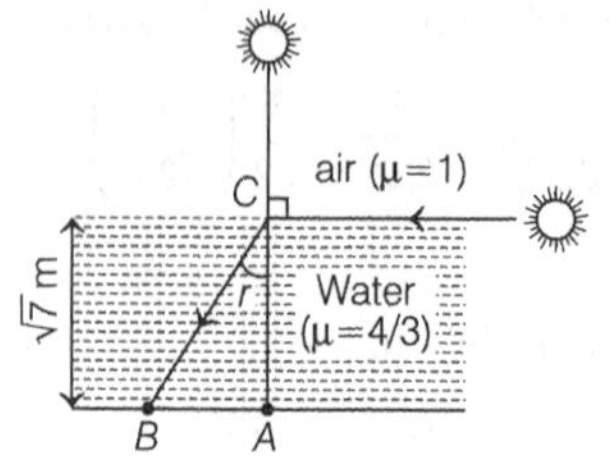

Using Snell's law,

$$1 \times \sin 90° = \frac{4}{3}\sin r$$

$\Rightarrow \qquad \sin r = \dfrac{3}{4}$ or $\tan r = \dfrac{3}{\sqrt{7}}$

In ΔABC, $\tan r = \dfrac{AB}{AC}$

$\Rightarrow \qquad \dfrac{3}{\sqrt{7}} = \dfrac{AB}{\sqrt{7}} \Rightarrow AB = 3 \text{ m}$

2. Object distance form mirror

$$= \frac{90}{((4/3)/1.2)} + 69 = 150 \text{ cm}$$

For plane mirror,

Image distance = Object distance = 150 cm

3. Object distance for mirror $= 12 + \dfrac{13.5}{(1/4/3)} = 30$ cm

$\therefore \; u = -30$ cm, $f = -20$ cm

$$\frac{1}{v} + \frac{1}{u} = \frac{1}{f} \quad \Rightarrow \quad \frac{1}{v} = \frac{1}{-30} = \frac{1}{-20} \quad \Rightarrow \quad v = -60 \text{ cm}$$

Now the reflected rays from mirror will again get refracted.

Apparent height $= \dfrac{\text{Actual height}}{\mu_{12}} = \dfrac{(60 - 12)}{((4/3)/1)} = 36$ cm

4.

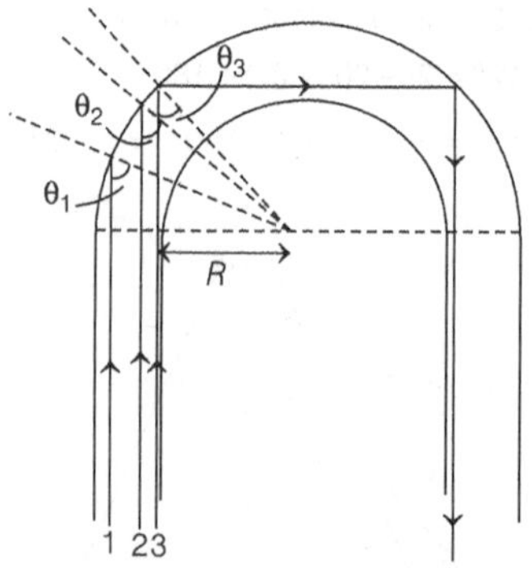

Figure shows three rays 1, 2 and 3 incident on flat surface A. We can see that angle of incidence at curved surface is least for ray 3. If ray 3 reflects at the curved suface, then all the rays will reflect as their angle of incidence is greater than θ_3.

For ray 3 to reflect, $\theta_3 \geq \theta_c$

$\Rightarrow \qquad \sin\theta_3 \geq \sin\theta_c$

$$\Rightarrow \qquad \frac{R}{d+R} \geq \frac{1}{\mu} \quad \Rightarrow \quad \frac{R}{d+R} \geq \frac{2}{3}$$

$$\Rightarrow \qquad \frac{R}{d} \geq 2 \quad \Rightarrow \quad \left(\frac{R}{d}\right)_{min} = 2$$

5. Radius of circle of illuminance

$$= \frac{h}{\sqrt{\mu^2 - 1}} = \frac{a/2}{\sqrt{\left(\frac{3}{2}\right)^2 - 1}} = \frac{a}{\sqrt{5}}$$

Area to be painted black $= 6\left[\pi\left(\frac{a}{\sqrt{5}}\right)^2\right] = 1.2\pi a^2$

6.

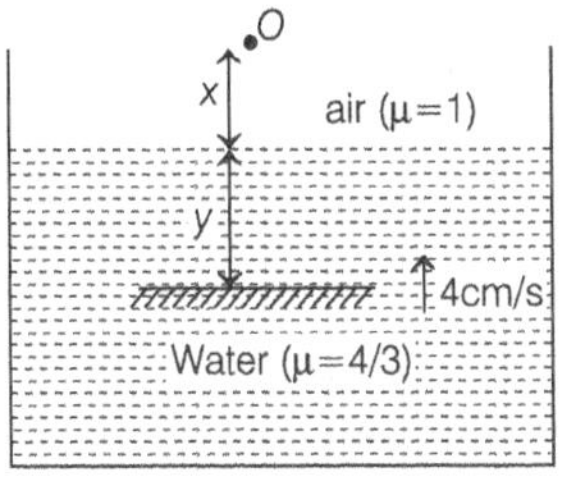

Apparent distance of mirror from O $= x + \frac{y}{\mu}$

Distance of final image from O $= 2\left(x + \frac{y}{\mu}\right)$

Velocity of final image $= 2\left(\frac{dx}{dt} + \frac{1}{\mu}\frac{dy}{dt}\right)$

$$= 2\left[0 + \left(\frac{1}{(4/3)}(4)\right)\right] = 6 \text{ cm/s}$$

7. Critical angle for $AB = \sin^{-1}\left(\frac{\sqrt{2}}{2}\right) = 45°$

Critical angle for $CD = \sin^{-1}\left(\frac{\sqrt{3}}{2}\right) = 60°$

Angle of incidence at AB and CD are equal. So, the minimum angle of incidence at Q will be 60°, so that the ray gets totally reflected by both the slabs.

8. Shift due to slabs

$$= t_1\left(1 - \frac{1}{\mu_1}\right) + t_2\left(1 - \frac{1}{\mu_2}\right) + t_3\left(1 - \frac{1}{\mu_3}\right)$$

$$= 45\left[1 - \frac{1}{(1.5/(4/3))}\right] + 24\left[1 - \frac{1}{(1/(4/3))}\right] + 54\left[1 - \frac{1}{(1.5/(4/3))}\right]$$

$$= 5 + (-8) + 6 = 3 \text{ cm}$$

∴ Object distance from mirror

$$= (20 + 45 + 24 + 54 + 10) - 3 = 150 \text{ cm}$$

The radius of curvature of mirror is also 150 cm. Since the object is at the centre of curvature, the rays incident on the mirror hit it perpendicularly and retrace their path. So, the final image will be formed on the object itself.

9. For bird,

Apparent velocity w.r.t. surface

$$= \frac{\text{Actual velocity w.r.t. surface}}{\mu_{12}}$$

$$\Rightarrow \qquad v - 2 = \frac{8 - 2}{1/(4/3)} \quad \Rightarrow \quad v = 10 \text{ m/s}$$

Velocity of bird w.r.t. fish $= 10 - 4 = 6$ m/s

10.

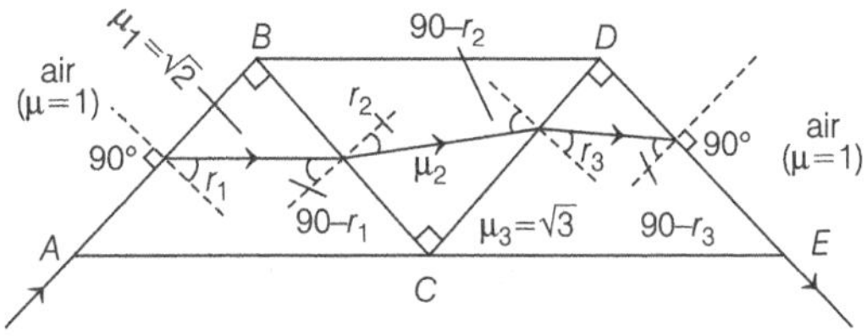

Apply Snell's law on various surfaces one by one,

At AB, $1 \times \sin 90° = \sqrt{2} \sin r_1$

$$\Rightarrow \qquad r_1 = 45°$$

At BC, $\sqrt{2}\sin(90° - 45°) = \mu_2 \sin r_2$

$$\Rightarrow \qquad \sin r_2 = \frac{1}{\mu_2}$$

At CD, $\mu_2 \sin(90° - r_2) = \sqrt{3}\sin r_3$

$$\Rightarrow \qquad \sin r_3 = \left(\frac{\mu_2\sqrt{1 - \sin^2 r_2}}{\sqrt{3}}\right)$$

At DE, $\sqrt{3}\sin(90° - r_3) = 1 \times \sin 90°$

$$\Rightarrow \qquad \cos r_3 = \frac{1}{\sqrt{3}}$$

$$\sin^2 r_3 + \cos^2 r_3 = 1$$

$$\Rightarrow \qquad \frac{\mu_2^2\left[1 - \left(\frac{1}{\mu_2}\right)^2\right]}{3} + \frac{1}{3} = 1 \quad \Rightarrow \quad \mu_2 = \sqrt{3}$$

Level 3

Single Choice Correct Questions

1.

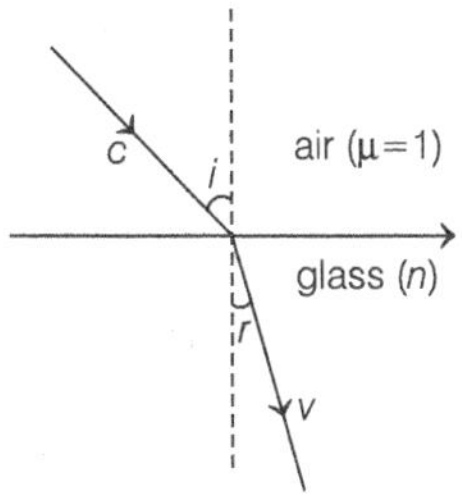

Component of velocity perpendicular to interface,

$$c \cos i = v \cos r$$

$$\Rightarrow \qquad c \cos i = \frac{c}{n}\cos r$$

$$\Rightarrow \qquad n = \frac{\cos r}{\cos i} \qquad \text{...(i)}$$

From Snell's law,

$$1 \times \sin i = n \times \sin r$$

$$n = \frac{\sin i}{\sin r} \qquad \text{...(ii)}$$

From Eqs. (i) and (ii), we get

$$\frac{\cos r}{\cos i} = \frac{\sin i}{\sin r}$$

$$\Rightarrow \qquad \sin r \cos r = \sin i \cos i$$

$$\Rightarrow \qquad \sin 2r = \sin 2i$$

$$\Rightarrow \qquad 2r = \pi - 2i \quad \Rightarrow \quad r = \frac{\pi}{2} - i$$

From Eq. (ii), $n = \dfrac{\sin i}{\sin\left(\dfrac{\pi}{2} - i\right)}$

$$\Rightarrow \qquad i = \tan^{-1}(n)$$

2.

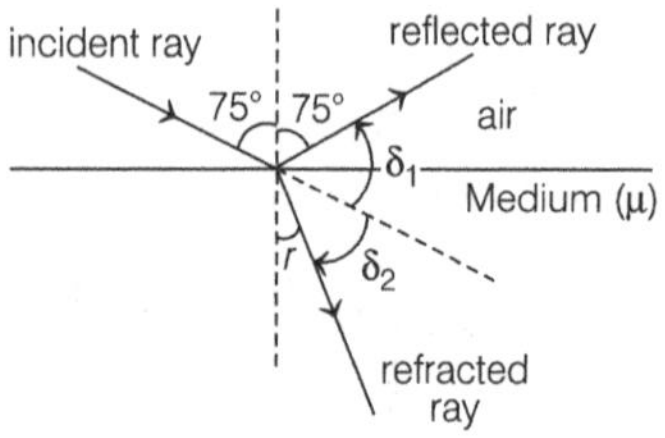

$$\delta_1 = \delta_2 \Rightarrow 180° - 2(75°) = 75° - r \Rightarrow r = 45°$$

From Snell's law,

$$1 \times \sin 75° = \mu \sin 45°$$

$$\mu = \frac{\sin(45° + 30°)}{\sin 45°} = \frac{\sqrt{3}+1}{2}$$

3.

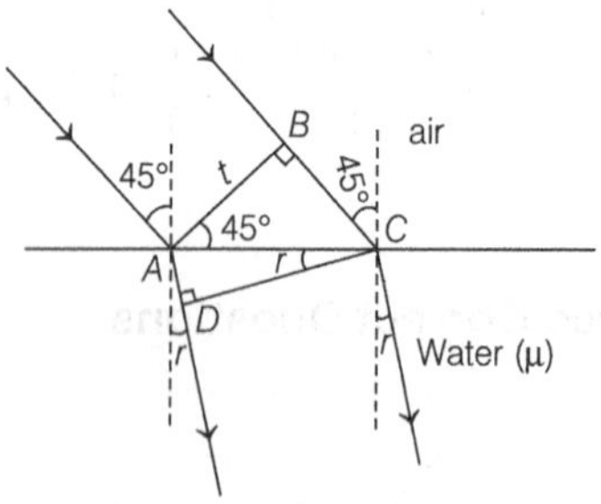

In ΔABC, $\cos 45° = \dfrac{t}{AC} \Rightarrow AC = \dfrac{t}{\cos 45°}$

In ΔADC, $\cos r = \dfrac{CD}{AC} \Rightarrow CD = AC \cos r = \dfrac{t \cos r}{\cos 45°}$

From Snell's law, $1 \times \sin 45° = \mu \sin r$

$$\Rightarrow \qquad \sin r = \frac{1}{\sqrt{2}\,\mu} \text{ or } \cos r = \sqrt{1 - \frac{1}{2\mu^2}}$$

$$\therefore \qquad CD = \frac{t \cos r}{\cos 45°} = \left(\frac{\sqrt{2\mu^2 - 1}}{\mu}\right)t$$

4.

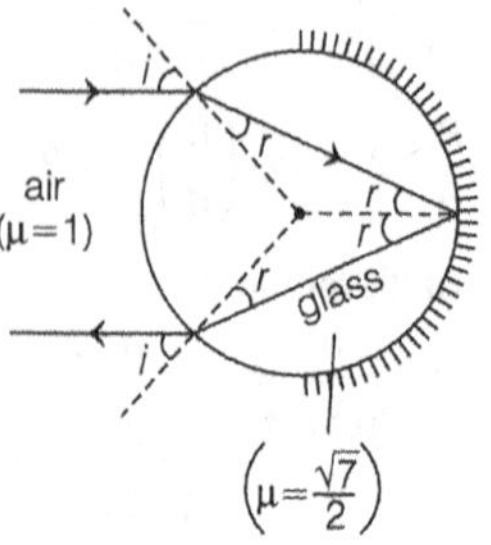

Total deviation,

$$\delta = (i - r) + (180° - 2r) + (i - r)$$

$$\Rightarrow \qquad \delta = 180° + 2i - 4r$$

For δ to be minimum, $\dfrac{d\delta}{di} = 0$

$$\Rightarrow \qquad 0 + 2 - 4\frac{dr}{di} = 0 \quad \Rightarrow \quad \frac{dr}{di} = \frac{1}{2}$$

From Snell's law,

$$1 \sin i = \mu \sin r$$

Differentiating both sides w.r.t. i,

$$\cos i = \mu \cos r \frac{dr}{di}$$

$$\Rightarrow \qquad \cos i = \mu \cos r \left(\frac{1}{2}\right) \qquad \left(\because \frac{dr}{di} = \frac{1}{2}\right)$$

$$\Rightarrow \qquad \cos i = \mu\left[\sqrt{1 - \left(\frac{\sin i}{\mu}\right)^2}\,\right]\left(\frac{1}{2}\right) \qquad (\because \cos r = \sqrt{1 - \sin^2 r})$$

$$\Rightarrow \qquad \cos i = \sqrt{\frac{\mu^2 - 1}{3}} = \frac{1}{2} \quad \Rightarrow \quad i = 60°$$

$$\therefore \qquad \sin 60° = \frac{\sqrt{7}}{2} \sin r \quad \Rightarrow \quad \sin r = \sqrt{\frac{3}{7}} \Rightarrow r = 41°$$

$$\delta = 180° + 2i - 4r = 180° + 2(60°) - 4(41°)$$

$$= 136°$$

5.

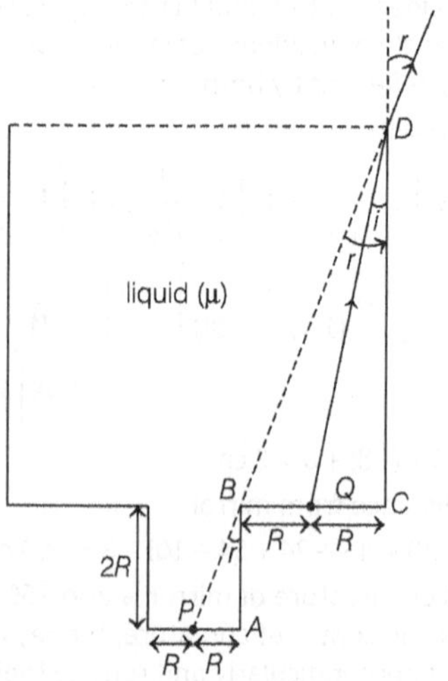

In ΔABP and ΔBCD,

$$\tan r = \frac{R}{2R} = \frac{2R}{CD} \Rightarrow CD = 4R$$

In ΔCDQ,

$$\tan i = \frac{R}{4R} = \frac{1}{4}$$

or $$\sin i = \frac{1}{\sqrt{17}}$$

From Snell's law,

$$1 \times \sin r = \mu \sin i$$

$$\Rightarrow \quad 1 \times \frac{1}{\sqrt{5}} = \mu\left(\frac{1}{\sqrt{17}}\right)$$

$$\Rightarrow \quad \mu = \frac{\sqrt{85}}{5}$$

6.

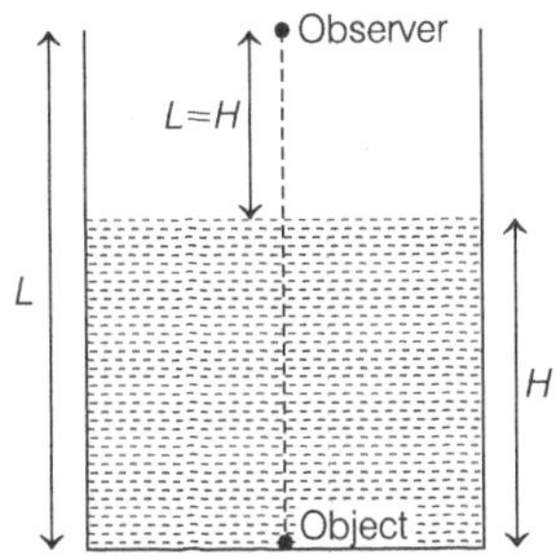

$$V = \pi r^2 H$$

$$\frac{dV}{dt} = \pi r^2 \frac{dH}{dt} + \pi H\, 2r\frac{dr}{dt}$$

$$\Rightarrow \quad 0 = \pi r^2 \frac{dH}{dt} + 2\pi r H(-K)$$

$$\Rightarrow \quad \frac{dH}{dt} = \frac{2KH}{r}$$

$$\Rightarrow \quad \frac{dH}{dt} = \frac{2K}{r}\left(\frac{V}{\pi r^2}\right) = \frac{2KV}{\pi r^3}$$

$$X_{app} = (L - H) + \frac{H}{\mu}$$

$$\Rightarrow \quad \frac{dX_{app}}{dt} = \left(\frac{1-\mu}{\mu}\right)\frac{dH}{dt} = \left(\frac{1-\mu}{\mu}\right)\left(\frac{2KV}{\pi r^3}\right)$$

7. Object distance for mirror $= \dfrac{7}{(1.4/1.2)} + 3 = 9$ cm

So, the plane mirror will form image 9 cm behind the mirror. Now the reflected rays will go from medium *A* to medium *B*.

$$\text{Apparent height} = \frac{\text{Actual height}}{\mu_{12}}$$

$$= \frac{(9+3)}{(1.2/1.4)} = 14 \text{ cm}$$

So, the final image as seen from medium *B* is 14 cm above interface or 11 cm behind the mirror.

8.

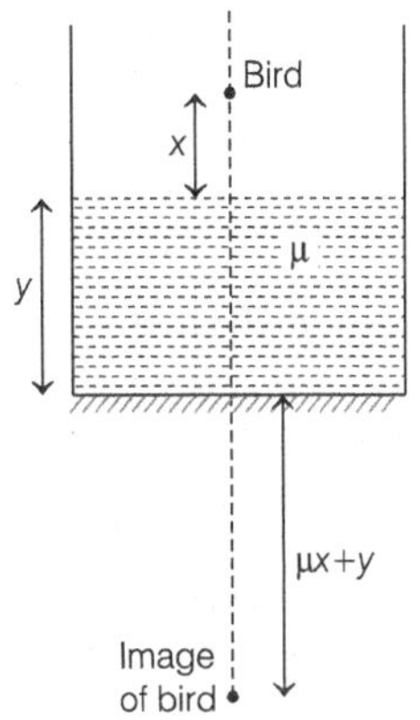

Object distance for mirror

$$= \frac{x}{(1/\mu)} + y = \mu x + y$$

So, the mirror will form image of the bird same distance behind the mirror. Now the reflected rays will go from water to air.

$$\text{Apparent depth} = \frac{\text{Actual depth}}{\mu_{12}}$$

$$\Rightarrow \quad h_{app} = \frac{(\mu x + y) + y}{\mu/1} \Rightarrow h_{app} = x + \left(\frac{2}{\mu}\right)y$$

Separation between bird and its final image $= z$

$$= x + \left(x + \frac{2y}{\mu}\right)$$

$$\Rightarrow \quad \frac{dz}{dt} = 2\left(\frac{dx}{dt}\right) + \left(\frac{2}{\mu}\right)\frac{dy}{dt}$$

$$\frac{dz}{dt} = 2(+1) + \frac{2}{(4/3)}(-1) = 0.5 \text{ cm/s}$$

So, velocity of image as seen by bird = 0.5 cm/s, downward.

9. First image will be formed by refraction from water surface.

$$H_{app} = \frac{H}{\mu_{12}} = \frac{40}{((4/3)/1)} = 30 \text{ cm}$$

So, the first image is 30 cm below water surface.

Second image will be formed by reflection and the refraction.

$$\frac{1}{v} + \frac{1}{u} = \frac{1}{f} \Rightarrow \frac{1}{v} + \frac{1}{(-80)} = \frac{1}{(-60)}$$

$$\Rightarrow \quad v = -240 \text{ cm}$$

$$\text{Apparent height} = \frac{\text{Actual height}}{\mu_{12}}$$

$$= \frac{240 - 120}{((4/3)/1)} = 90 \text{ cm}$$

So, the second image is 90 cm above water surface.

$\therefore$ Distance between the two images

$$= 90 + 30 = 120 \text{ cm}$$

10. Shift due to slab $= t\left(1-\frac{1}{\mu}\right) = 3\left(1-\frac{1}{1.5}\right) = 1$ cm

Object distance from mirror $= 16 - 1 = 15$ cm

$$\frac{1}{v}+\frac{1}{u}=\frac{1}{f} \Rightarrow \frac{1}{v}+\frac{1}{-15}+\frac{1}{10} \Rightarrow v = 6 \text{ cm}$$

The reflected rays from the mirror will again pass through the glass slab.

So, final image distance from mirror $= 6 - 1 = 5$ cm

Let the separation between the front face of slab and the object be x.

Due to partial reflection from the front face of the slab, image will be formed x distance behind the front face.

Since the two images coincide,

$$2x = 16 + 5 \Rightarrow x = 10.5 \text{ cm}$$

11. Object distance from mirror

$$= \frac{4}{(1/(4/3))} + 40 = \frac{136}{3} \text{ cm}$$

Since, image and object coincide, the object should be kept at the centre of curvature.

Therefore, radius of curvature $= \frac{136}{3}$ cm.

When the water level is reduced to zero, let the height of the object be H. For the image and object to coincide.

Apparent height = Radius of curvature

$$\Rightarrow \quad \frac{\text{Actual height}}{\mu_{12}} = \text{Radius of curvature}$$

$$\Rightarrow \quad \frac{H}{(1/(4/3))} = \frac{136}{3} \text{ cm} \Rightarrow H = 34 \text{ cm}$$

12. Shift $= m\left(1-\frac{1}{n_2}\right) + (l-m)\left(1-\frac{1}{n_1}\right) = 0$

$$\Rightarrow \quad \frac{l}{m} = \frac{n_1 - n_2}{n_2(n_1 - 1)}$$

13. In absence of water, $\Delta\theta = \frac{l}{4}$

In presence of water,

$$\Delta\theta' = \frac{l}{2 + \frac{2}{4/3}} = \frac{2l}{7}$$

$$\frac{\Delta\theta'}{\Delta\theta} = \frac{2l/7}{l/4} = \frac{8}{7}$$

14. Horizontal component of velocity remains unchanged.

$$v_x = v\cos\theta = \frac{4v}{5}$$

For vertical component of velocity,

$$\text{Apparent velocity} = \frac{\text{Actual velocity}}{\mu_{12}}$$

$$\Rightarrow \quad v_y = \frac{v\sin\theta}{1/(4/3)} = \frac{4}{3}v\left(\frac{3}{5}\right) = \frac{4v}{5}$$

$$\therefore \quad \mathbf{v}_{\text{bird}} = v_x\hat{\mathbf{i}} + v_y\hat{\mathbf{j}} = \frac{4v}{5}\hat{\mathbf{i}} + \frac{4v}{5}\hat{\mathbf{j}}$$

$$\tan\phi = \frac{v_y}{v_x} = 1 \Rightarrow \phi = 45^\circ$$

15. Applying Snell's law for first refraction,

$$1 \times \sin 45^\circ = 2\sin r$$

$$\Rightarrow \quad \sin r = \frac{1}{2\sqrt{2}}$$

Critical angle, $i_c = \sin^{-1}\left(\frac{1}{2}\right) = 30^\circ$

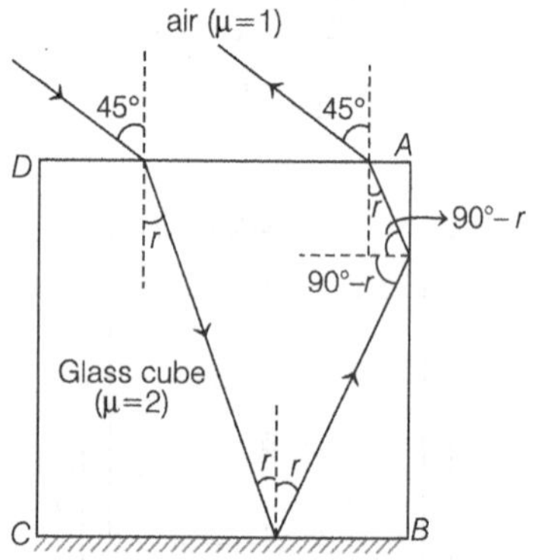

Since $90^\circ - r > i_c$, ray will be totally internally reflected at face AB. So, the incident ray and emergent ray are parallel to each other. Hence, the deviation of the ray will be 180°.

16. For parallel composite slab,

$\mu \sin\theta =$ constant

$$\therefore \quad \mu_0 \sin 30^\circ = \left(\mu_0 + \frac{\mu_0}{4n-18}\right)\sin 90^\circ$$

$$\Rightarrow \quad \frac{1}{2} = 1 + \frac{1}{4n-18}$$

$$\Rightarrow \quad n = 4$$

So, it will be upper layer of $n = 3$

17. If TIR takes place at the interface of Region III and Region IV, the beam will not enter region IV.

Applying Snell's law for Region I and Region III

$$n_0 \sin\theta = \frac{n_0}{6}\sin i$$

$$\Rightarrow \quad \sin i = 6\sin\theta$$

Critical angle for Region III,

$$i_c = \sin^{-1}\left(\frac{n_0/8}{n_0/6}\right) = \sin^{-1}\left(\frac{3}{4}\right)$$

For TIR to just happen,

$$i = i_c$$

$$\Rightarrow \quad \sin i = \sin i_c$$

$$\Rightarrow \quad 6\sin\theta = \frac{3}{4}$$

$$\Rightarrow \quad \theta = \sin^{-1}\left(\frac{1}{8}\right)$$

18.

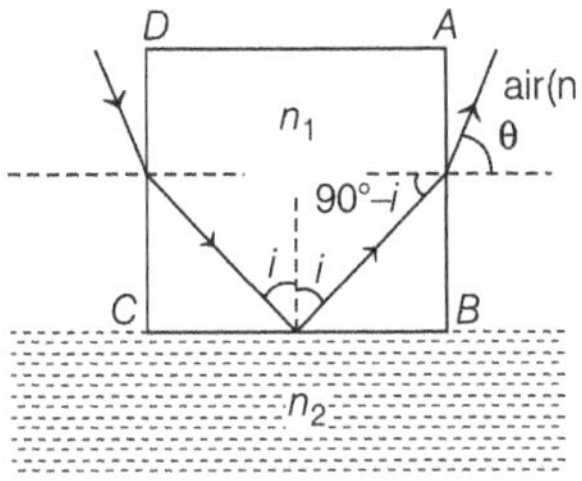

From Snell's law at face *AB*,

$$n_1 \sin(90° - i) = 1 \sin\theta$$

$$n_1 \cos i = \sin\theta$$

$$\Rightarrow \quad \cos i = \frac{\sin\theta}{n_1}$$

Critical angle for face *BC*,

$$i_c = \sin^{-1}\left(\frac{n_2}{n_1}\right)$$

$$\Rightarrow \quad \sin i_c = \frac{n_2}{n_1}$$

For TIR to happen at face *BC*,

$$i > i_c$$

$$\Rightarrow \quad \cos i < \cos i_c$$

$$\Rightarrow \quad \frac{\sin\theta}{n_1} < \sqrt{1 - \left(\frac{n_2}{n_1}\right)^2}$$

$$\Rightarrow \quad \sin\theta < \sqrt{n_1^2 - n_2^2}$$

19.

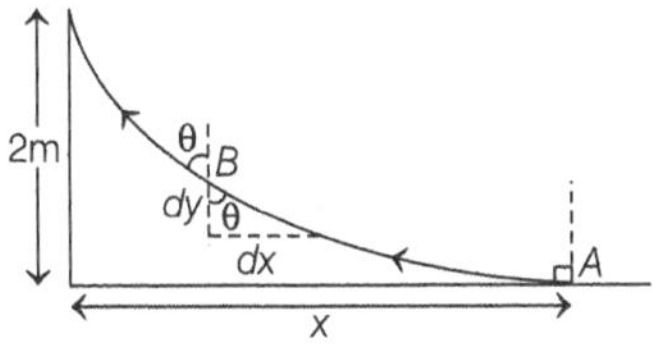

Applying Snell's law at *A* and *B*,

$$\mu_0 \sin 90° = \mu \sin\theta$$

$$\Rightarrow \quad \mu_0 = (\mu_0\sqrt{1 + ay})\sin\theta$$

$$\Rightarrow \quad \sin\theta = \frac{1}{\sqrt{1 + ay}}$$

$$\text{or} \quad \tan\theta = \frac{1}{\sqrt{ay}}$$

At *B*, $\tan\theta = \dfrac{dx}{dy}$

$$\Rightarrow \quad \frac{1}{\sqrt{ay}} = \frac{dx}{dy}$$

$$\Rightarrow \quad \int_0^x dx = \int_0^2 \frac{dy}{\sqrt{ay}}$$

$$\Rightarrow \quad x = \left[2\sqrt{\frac{y}{a}}\right]_0^2 = 2000 \text{ m}$$

20.

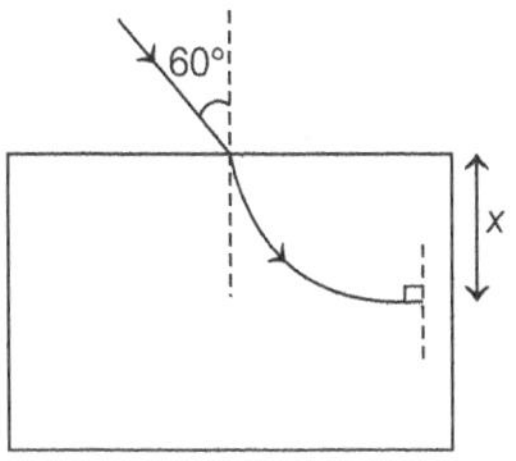

Applying Snell's law,

$$1 \times \sin 60° = \left(\sqrt{3} - \frac{1}{\sqrt{3}}x\right)\sin 90°$$

$$\Rightarrow \quad x = 1.5 \text{ m}$$

21. Applying Snell's law,

$$1 \times \sin 90° = \sqrt{1 + x^{2/3}}\,\sin\theta$$

$$\Rightarrow \quad \sin\theta = \frac{1}{\sqrt{1 + x^{2/3}}}$$

$$\text{or} \quad \tan\theta = \frac{1}{x^{1/3}}$$

$$\frac{dy}{dx} = \tan\theta \quad \Rightarrow \quad \frac{dy}{dx} = \frac{1}{x^{1/3}}$$

$$\Rightarrow \quad \int dy = \int x^{-1/3} dx$$

$$\Rightarrow \quad y = \frac{3}{2}x^{2/3} \qquad \text{...(i)}$$

Equation of line *BC*,

$$y = -\frac{1}{\sqrt{3}}x + \frac{15}{2} \qquad \text{...(ii)}$$

From Eqs. (i) and (ii), we get

$$x = 3\sqrt{3} \text{ and } y = \frac{9}{2}$$

22. Applying Snell's law,

$$1 \times \sin 90° = \left(\frac{\mu_0}{1 - \frac{x}{r}}\right)\sin\theta \quad \Rightarrow \quad \sin\theta = \frac{r - x}{\mu_0 r}$$

Let $r - x = X$

$$\therefore \quad \sin\theta = \frac{X}{\mu_0 r} \text{ or } \tan\theta = \frac{X}{\sqrt{\mu_0^2 r^2 - X^2}}$$

$$\tan\theta = \frac{dy}{dX} \quad \Rightarrow \quad \frac{dy}{dX} = \frac{X}{\sqrt{\mu_0^2 r^2 - X^2}}$$

$$\Rightarrow \quad \int dy = \int \frac{X\,dX}{\sqrt{\mu_0^2 r^2 - X^2}}$$

$$\Rightarrow \quad y = -\sqrt{\mu_0^2 r^2 - X^2}$$

$$\Rightarrow \quad y^2 + X^2 = \mu_0^2 r^2$$

$$\Rightarrow \quad (x - r)^2 + y^2 = \mu_0^2 r^2$$

which is equation of circle.

23. In minimum incidence case, the angles will be as shown in figure.

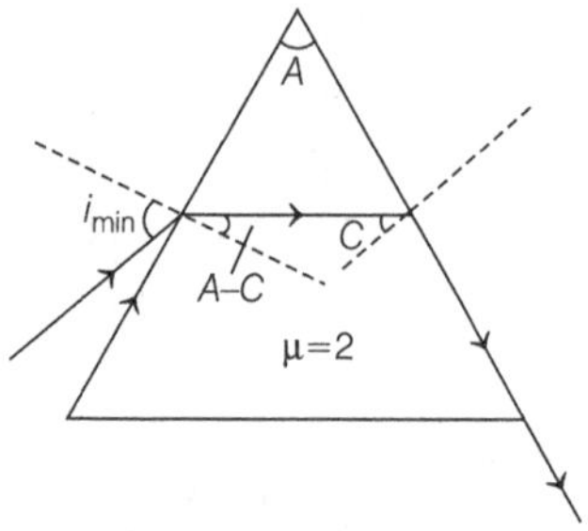

Applying Snell's law, we get

$$1 \times \sin i_{min} = \sqrt{\frac{7}{3}} \sin (A - C)$$

$$= \sqrt{\frac{7}{3}} (\sin A \cos C - \cos A \sin C)$$

$$= \sqrt{\frac{7}{3}} \left(\sin 60° \sqrt{1 - \frac{3}{7}} - \cos 60° \sqrt{\frac{3}{7}} \right) = \frac{1}{2}$$

$$\therefore \quad i_{min} = 30°$$

24. For minimum deviation,

$$\delta_{min} = 2i - A$$

$$\Rightarrow \quad 60° = 2(60°) - A \quad \Rightarrow \quad A = 60°$$

$$r_1 = r_2 = \frac{A}{2} = 30°$$

From Snell's law,

$$1 \times \sin i = \mu \sin r_1$$

$$\Rightarrow \quad 1 \times \sin 60° = \mu \sin 30° \quad \Rightarrow \quad \mu = \sqrt{3}$$

25. $\delta = i + e - A$

$$\Rightarrow \quad 70° = 40° + i_1 - 60° \quad \Rightarrow \quad i_1 = 90°$$

26. $\delta = i + e - A$

$$\Rightarrow \quad 2\alpha = 2\alpha + e - \alpha \quad \Rightarrow \quad e = \alpha$$

Applying Snell's law for first refraction,

$$1 \times \sin 2\alpha = \mu \sin r_1$$

$$\Rightarrow \quad \sin r_1 = \frac{\sin 2\alpha}{\mu}$$

and $\quad \cos r_1 = \sqrt{1 - \frac{\sin^2 2\alpha}{\mu^2}}$

Applying Snell's law for second refraction,

$$\mu \sin r_2 = 1 \times \sin e$$

$$\Rightarrow \quad \mu \sin (\alpha - r_1) = \sin \alpha \quad (\because r_2 = A - r_1 = \alpha - r_1)$$

$$\Rightarrow \quad \mu (\sin \alpha \cos r_1 - \cos \alpha \sin r_1) = \sin \alpha$$

$$\Rightarrow \quad \mu \left[\sin \alpha \sqrt{1 - \frac{\sin^2 2\alpha}{\mu^2}} - \cos \alpha \left(\frac{\sin 2\alpha}{\mu} \right) \right] = \sin \alpha$$

$$\Rightarrow \quad \sqrt{\mu^2 - \sin^2 2\alpha} - 2\cos^2 \alpha = 1$$

$$\Rightarrow \quad \mu^2 - \sin^2 2\alpha = 1 + 4\cos^4 \alpha + 4\cos^2 \alpha$$

$$\Rightarrow \quad \mu^2 - 4\sin^2 \alpha \cos^2 \alpha = 1 + 4\cos^4 \alpha + 4\cos^2 \alpha$$

$$\Rightarrow \quad \mu^2 = 1 + 4\cos^2 \alpha (\cos^2 \alpha + \sin^2 \alpha) + 4\cos^2 \alpha$$

$$\Rightarrow \quad \cos \alpha = \sqrt{\frac{\mu^2 - 1}{8}}$$

27.

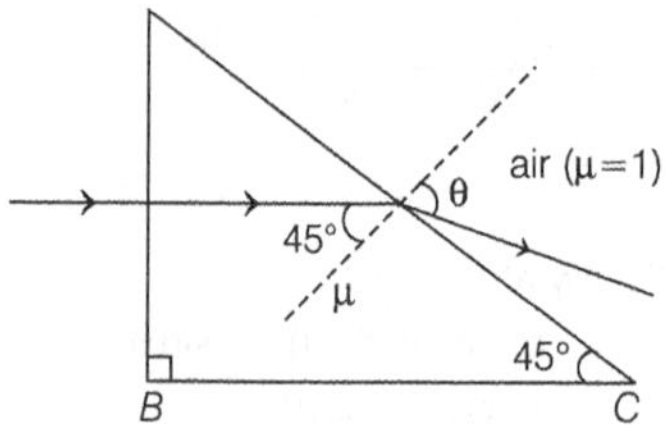

From Snell's law,

$$\mu \sin 45° = 1 \sin \theta$$

Differentiating both sides w.r.t. t

$$\Rightarrow \quad \frac{d\mu}{dt} \left(\frac{1}{\sqrt{2}} \right) = \cos \theta \frac{d\theta}{dt}$$

$$\Rightarrow \quad (0.4) \left(\frac{1}{\sqrt{2}} \right) = \cos \theta \frac{d\theta}{dt} \quad \text{...(i)}$$

$$(1 + 0.4t) \sin 45° = 1 \sin \theta$$

At $t = 1$, $\quad [1 + 0.4(1)] \left(\frac{1}{\sqrt{2}} \right) = \sin \theta$

$$\Rightarrow \quad \sin \theta = \frac{1.4}{\sqrt{2}}$$

or $\quad \cos \theta = \sqrt{1 - \left(\frac{1.4}{\sqrt{2}} \right)^2} = \frac{0.2}{\sqrt{2}}$

Substituting value of $\cos \theta$ in Eq. (i),

$$\frac{0.4}{\sqrt{2}} = \left(\frac{0.2}{\sqrt{2}} \right) \frac{d\theta}{dt} \quad \Rightarrow \quad \omega = \frac{d\theta}{dt} = 2 \text{ rad/s}$$

28.

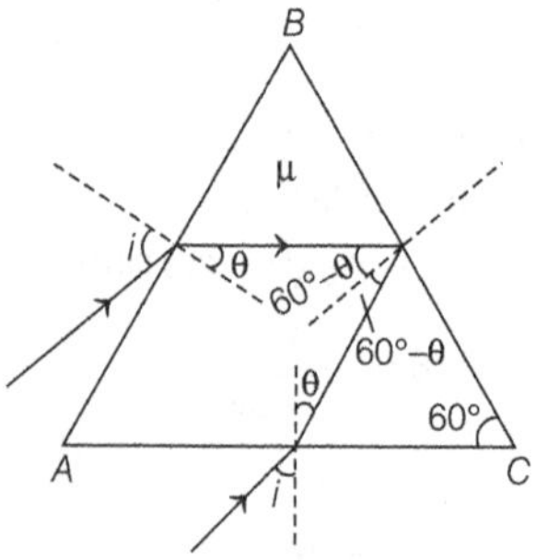

Total deviation $= (i - \theta) + [180° - 2(60° - \theta)] + (i - \theta) = 120°$

$$\Rightarrow \quad i = 30°$$

From Snell's law,

$$1 \times \sin i = \mu \sin \theta \quad \Rightarrow \quad \sin 30° = \mu \sin \theta$$

$$\Rightarrow \quad \sin \theta = \frac{1}{2\mu}$$

For TIR to happen at face BC,

$$60° - \theta > i_c$$

$$\Rightarrow \quad \sin (60° - \theta) > \sin i_c$$

$$\Rightarrow \quad \sin 60° \cos\theta - \cos 60° \sin\theta > \frac{1}{\mu}$$

$$\Rightarrow \quad \frac{\sqrt{3}}{2}\sqrt{1-\left(\frac{1}{2\mu}\right)^2} - \frac{1}{2}\left(\frac{1}{2\mu}\right) > \frac{1}{\mu}$$

$$\Rightarrow \quad \mu \geq \sqrt{\frac{7}{3}} \Rightarrow \mu_{min} = \sqrt{\frac{7}{3}}$$

29.

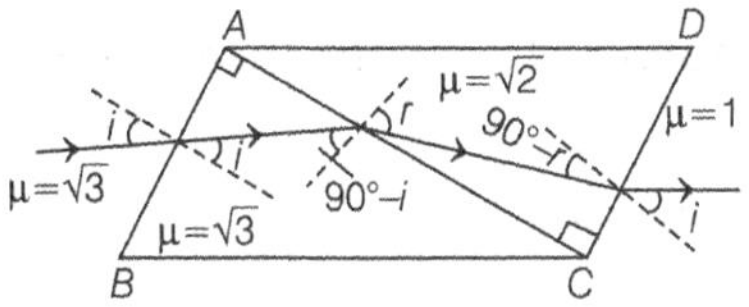

There is no refraction at face *AB* since refractive index of liquid and prism *ABC* are same.

Applying Snell's law at face *AC*,

$$\sqrt{3}\sin(90° - i) = \sqrt{2}\sin r$$

$$\Rightarrow \quad \sin r = \frac{\sqrt{3}}{\sqrt{2}}\cos i \quad \text{...(i)}$$

Applying Snell's law at face *CD*

$$\sqrt{2}\sin(90° - r) = 1 \sin i$$

$$\Rightarrow \quad \cos r = \frac{\sin i}{\sqrt{2}} \quad \text{...(ii)}$$

Squaring and adding Eqs. (i) and (ii)

$$\sin^2 r + \cos^2 r = \frac{3}{2}\cos^2 i + \frac{\sin^2 i}{2}$$

$$\Rightarrow \quad 1 = \frac{3\cos^2 i + 1 - \cos^2 i}{2}$$

$$\Rightarrow \quad \cos i = \frac{1}{\sqrt{2}} \Rightarrow i = 45°$$

30.

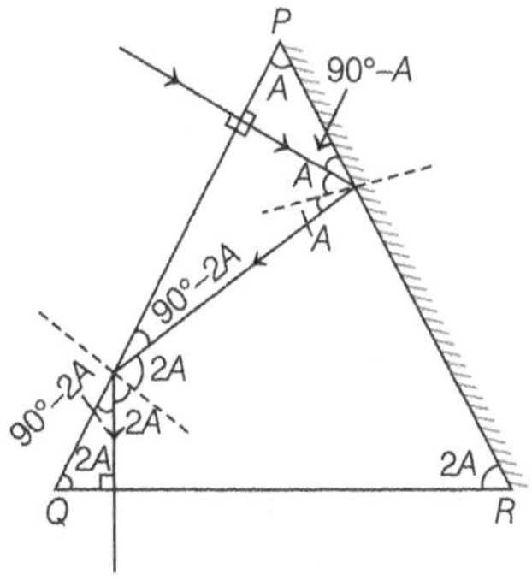

In ΔPQR, $A + 2A + 2A = 180°$

$$\Rightarrow \quad 5A = 180° \Rightarrow A = 36°$$

So, the angles of prism are 36°, 72° and 72°.

31. At face *BC*, $i_c = \sin^{-1}\left(\frac{1}{\sqrt{3}}\right)$

$$\Rightarrow \sin i_c = \frac{1}{\sqrt{3}} \text{ or } \cos i_c = \frac{\sqrt{2}}{\sqrt{3}}$$

Applying Snell's law at face *AB*,

$$\mu \sin(90° - r) = \sqrt{3}\sin(90° - i_c)$$

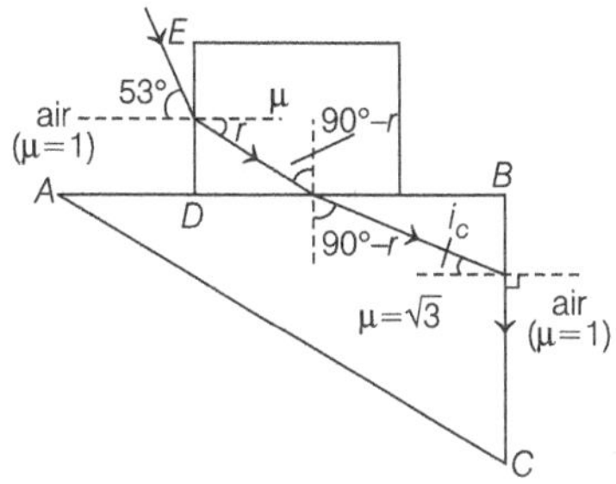

$$\Rightarrow \quad \mu \cos r = \sqrt{3}\cos i_c$$

$$\Rightarrow \quad \mu \cos r = \sqrt{3}\left(\frac{\sqrt{2}}{\sqrt{3}}\right)$$

$$\Rightarrow \quad \mu \cos r = \sqrt{2} \quad \text{...(i)}$$

Applying Snell's law at face *DE*,

$$1 \times \sin 53° = \mu \sin r$$

$$\Rightarrow \quad \mu \sin r = \frac{4}{5} \quad \text{...(ii)}$$

Squaring and adding Eqs. (i) and (ii), we get

$$\mu^2(\sin^2 r + \cos^2 r) = \frac{16}{25} + 2$$

$$\Rightarrow \quad \mu = \frac{\sqrt{66}}{5}$$

32.

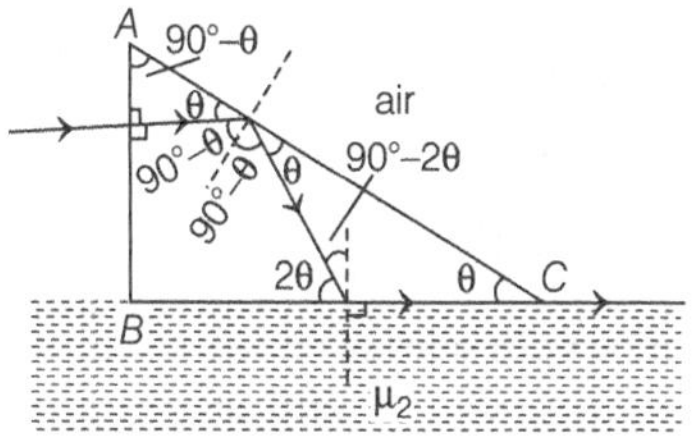

At face *AC*, $i_c = \sin^{-1}\left(\frac{1}{\mu_1}\right)$

$$\Rightarrow \quad 90° - \theta = \sin^{-1}\left(\frac{1}{\mu_1}\right)$$

$$\Rightarrow \quad \sin(90° - \theta) = \frac{1}{\mu_1}$$

$$\Rightarrow \quad \cos\theta = \frac{1}{\mu_1} \quad \text{...(i)}$$

At face *BC*,

$$\mu_1 \sin(90° - 2\theta) = \mu_2 \sin 90°$$

$$\Rightarrow \quad \cos 2\theta = \frac{\mu_2}{\mu_1} \quad \text{...(ii)}$$

From Eqs. (i) and (ii), we get

$$\frac{\cos 2\theta}{\cos\theta} = \mu_2$$

33. For complete prism,

$$\mu \sin A = 1 \sin 90^\circ \Rightarrow \mu = \frac{1}{\sin A}$$

For half prism,

$$\mu \sin\left(\frac{A}{2}\right) = 1 \sin e$$

$$\Rightarrow \left(\frac{1}{\sin A}\right) \sin\frac{A}{2} = \sin e$$

$$\Rightarrow \frac{\sin(A/2)}{2\sin(A/2)\cos(A/2)} = \sin e$$

$$\Rightarrow e = \sin^{-1}\left[\frac{1}{2}\sec\left(\frac{A}{2}\right)\right]$$

34. Deviation produced by the prism $= (\mu - 1)A$

$$= (1.5 - 1)\, 4^\circ = 2^\circ$$

So, angle of incidence on miror is 2°.

For deviation to be 180°, the ray should hit the mirror perpendicularity. So, the mirror should be rotated by 2° (clockwise).

35. $\delta = (\mu - 1)A = (1.5 - 1)(1.8^\circ) = 0.9^\circ$

$$y = f\theta = 10 \times \left(0.9^\circ \frac{\pi}{180^\circ}\right) = 0.157 \text{ cm}$$

36. Deviation, $\delta = (\mu - 1)A$

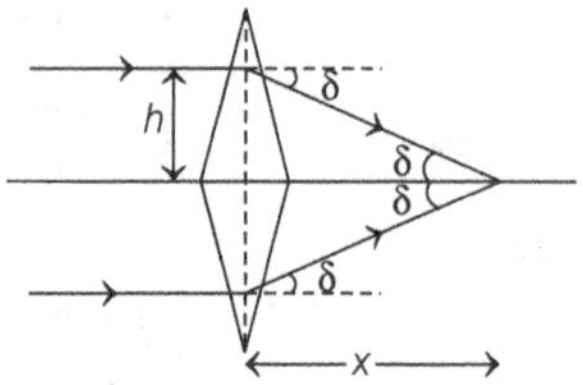

$$\tan\delta \simeq \delta = \frac{h}{x}$$

$$\Rightarrow x = \frac{h}{(\mu - 1)A}$$

37. Applying Snell's law,

$$1 \sin\theta = n \sin\theta'$$

$$\Rightarrow \sin\theta' = \frac{\sin\theta}{n}$$

Differentiating both sides w.r.t. λ,

$$\cos\theta' \frac{d\theta'}{d\lambda} = -\frac{\sin\theta}{n^2}\frac{dn}{d\lambda}$$

$$\Rightarrow \frac{d\theta'}{d\lambda} = -\frac{\tan\theta'}{n}\frac{dn}{d\lambda} \quad \left(\because \frac{\sin\theta}{n} = \sin\theta'\right)$$

$$\delta\theta' = \left|\frac{\tan\theta'}{n}\frac{dn(\lambda)}{d\lambda}\delta\lambda\right|$$

38.

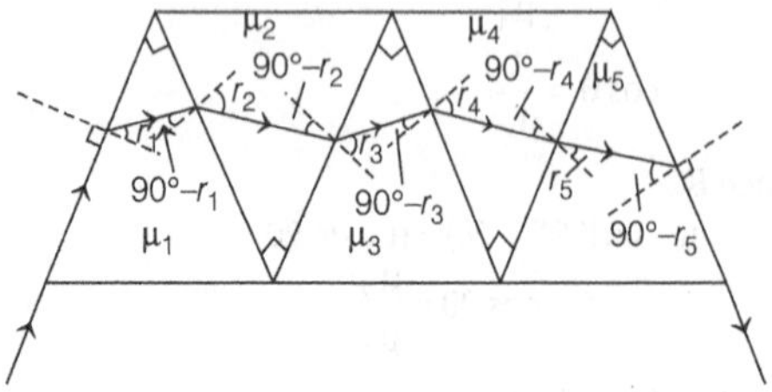

Applying Snell's law at various surfaces,

$$1 \sin 90^\circ = \mu_1 \sin r_1 \quad \text{...(i)}$$

$$\mu_1 \cos r_1 = \mu_2 \sin r_2 \quad \text{...(ii)}$$

$$\mu_2 \cos r_2 = \mu_3 \sin r_3 \quad \text{...(iii)}$$

$$\mu_3 \cos r_3 = \mu_4 \sin r_4 \quad \text{...(iv)}$$

$$\mu_4 \cos r_4 = \mu_5 \sin r_5 \quad \text{...(v)}$$

$$\mu_5 \cos r_5 = 1 \sin 90^\circ \quad \text{...(vi)}$$

Squaring and adding,

Eqs. (i), (ii), (iii), (iv), (v) and (vi), we get

$$\mu_1^2 + \mu_3^2 + \mu_5^2 = 1 + \mu_2^2 + \mu_4^2$$

Multiple Choice(s) Correct Questions

1. (a, c, d)

2. (b) $\frac{\sin r}{\sin i} = \tan 30^\circ = \frac{1}{\sqrt{3}}$

Also, $\frac{\sin r}{\sin i} = \frac{v_2}{v_1} = \frac{1}{\sqrt{3}}$

$\therefore \quad v_2 = \frac{1}{\sqrt{3}} v_1$

(d) $\frac{\sin r}{\sin i} = \frac{\mu_1}{\mu_2} = \frac{1}{\sqrt{3}}$

$\therefore \quad \mu_2 > \mu_1$

Total internal reflection can take place, when light travels from denser to rarer medium i.e., incidence is in y.

3. Apparent depth $= \frac{\text{Actual depth}}{\mu_{12}}$

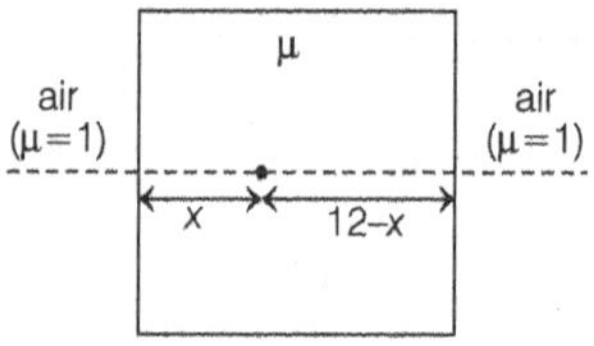

When viewed from the first face,

$$5 = \frac{x}{\mu} \quad \text{...(i)}$$

When viewed from the opposite face,

$$3 = \frac{12 - x}{\mu} \quad \text{...(ii)}$$

From Eqs. (i) and (ii), we get

$$\mu = 1.5 \text{ and } x = 7.5 \text{ cm}$$

4. (a) Depth of F, observed by B

$$= 6 + \frac{0.8}{((4/3)/1)} = 6.60 \text{ cm}$$

(b) Height of B, observed by

$$F = 0.8 + \frac{6}{(1/(4/3))} = 8.80 \text{ m}$$

(c) Apparent velocity of $B = \frac{3}{1/(4/3)} = 4$ m/s

Velocity of B w.r.t. $F = 4 - (-2) = 6$ m/s

(d) Apparent velocity of $F = \frac{2}{(4/3)/1} = 1.50$ m/s

Velocity of F w.r.t. $B = 1.50 - (-3) = 4.50$ m/s

5. For TIR to happen, $i > i_c$

$$\Rightarrow \quad 45° > \sin^{-1}\left(\frac{1}{n}\right) \Rightarrow \sin 45° > \frac{1}{n}$$

$$\Rightarrow \quad n > \sqrt{2}$$

$$\Rightarrow \quad n > 1.414$$

So, n can be 1.5 or 1.6.

6. (a) $n_3 < n_1$, so critical angle decreases. Therefore, TIR will take place at AB.
   (b) $n_3 > n_1$, so critical angle increases. Therefore, TIR will not take place.
   (c) If $n_3 > n_2$, then TIR will take place at CD and if $n_3 > n_1$, then TIR will take place at AB.
   (b) TIR will not take place at CD for $n_3 < n_1$ because ray is going from rarer to denser medium.

7. Critical angle at $A = \sin^{-1}\left(\frac{\mu_2}{4}\right)$
   (a) If $\mu_2 > 2$, critical angle will be more than 30°. So, TIR will not take place at A.
   Applying Snell's law,

$$4 \times \sin 30° = 2 \times \sin e$$

$$\Rightarrow \quad e = 90°$$

   So, deviation $= 90° - 30° = 60°$
   (d) If $\mu_2 < 2$, critical angle will be less than 30°. So, TIR will take place at A.
   So, deviation $= 180° - 2i = 180° - 2(30°) = 120°$

8. Lateral shift $= \dfrac{t \sin(i - r)}{\cos r}$

If $i = \theta = 45°$, then angle of incidence will be same for both the slabs. Since both slabs have same refractive indices, angle of refraction (r) will also be same.

If $t_1 = t_2$, both slabs produce same lateral shift but in opposite sense. So, the emergent ray passes from Q.

If $t_2 > t_1$, shift produced by slab 2 will be more than the shift produced by slab 1. So, the emergent ray passes above Q.

If $t_2 < t_1$, emergent ray passes below Q as explained before.

9.

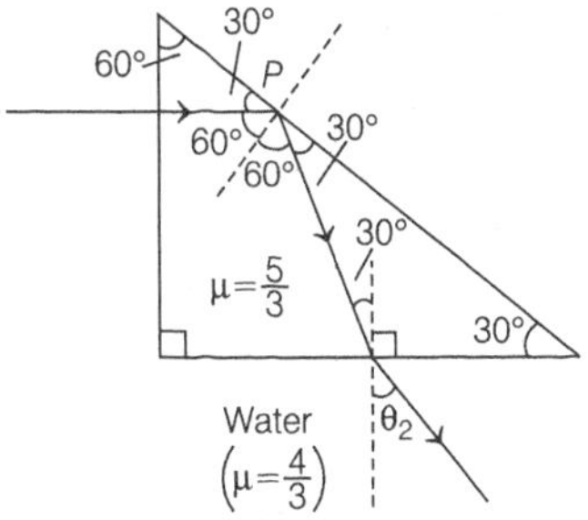

(a) Applying Snell's law,

$$\frac{5}{3}\sin 30° = \frac{4}{3} \times \sin\theta_2$$

$$\Rightarrow \quad \theta_2 = \sin^{-1}\left(\frac{5}{8}\right)$$

(c) Critical angle at $P = \sin^{-1}\left(\dfrac{5/2\sqrt{3}}{5/3}\right) = 60°$

For TIR to take place, angle of incidence should be greater than the critical angle. Since angle of incidence at P is 60°, TIR will cease.

10. Applying condition of minimum deviation,

$$\mu = \frac{\sin\left(\frac{A+\gamma}{2}\right)}{\sin\left(\frac{A}{2}\right)}$$

$$\Rightarrow \quad \mu = \frac{\sin\left(45° + \frac{\gamma}{2}\right)}{\sin 45°} \qquad (\because A = 90°)$$

$$\Rightarrow \quad \mu = \sin\left(\frac{\gamma}{2}\right) + \cos\left(\frac{\gamma}{2}\right)$$

Squaring both sides,

$$\mu^2 = \sin^2\left(\frac{\gamma}{2}\right) + \cos^2\left(\frac{\gamma}{2}\right) + 2\sin\left(\frac{\gamma}{2}\right)\cos\left(\frac{\gamma}{2}\right)$$

$$\Rightarrow \quad \mu^2 = 1 + \sin\gamma$$

$$\Rightarrow \quad \sin\gamma = \mu^2 - 1$$

Deviation at grazing incidence,

$$\delta = i + e - A$$

$$\Rightarrow \quad \beta = 90° + e - 90°$$

$$\Rightarrow \quad e = \beta$$

Applying Snell's law,

$$\mu \sin r_2 = 1 \times \sin e$$

$$\Rightarrow \quad \mu \sin\left(\frac{\pi}{2} - C\right) = \sin\beta \qquad \left(\because r_2 = A - r_1 = \frac{\pi}{2} - C\right)$$

$$\Rightarrow \quad \mu \cos C = \sin\beta$$

$$\Rightarrow \quad \mu\sqrt{1 - \frac{1}{\mu^2}} = \sin\beta \qquad (\because \cos C = \sqrt{1 - \sin^2 C})$$

$$\Rightarrow \quad \sin\beta = \sqrt{\mu^2 - 1}$$

$$\therefore \quad \sin\gamma = \sin^2\beta$$

11. For two different values of incidence, we have a single amount of deviation (other than minimum deviation). If we take i_1 as incidence, then i_2 will act as emergence and *vice-versa*.

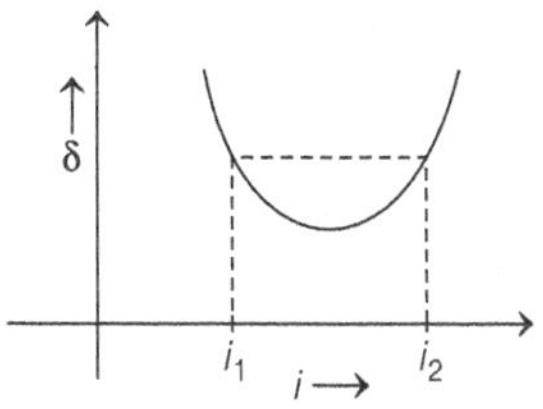

12. (a) For λ_{yellow}, the refractive index of liquid and glass are same, so there will be no deviation.

(b) The refractive index of blue light is higher in liquid i.e., blue ray enters from denser to rarer medium, so bends away from normal (towards the vertex).

(c) For red light, $\mu_{glass} > \mu_{liquid}$.

13. (a) $\mu_{Y_1} = \dfrac{\mu_{V_1} + \mu_{R_1}}{2} = 1.55$

$$\mu_{Y_2} = \frac{\mu_{V_2} + \mu_{R_2}}{2} = 1.45$$

$$\delta = (\mu_{Y_1} - 1) A_1 - (\mu_{Y_2} - 1) A_2 = 0$$

$$\Rightarrow \quad (1.55 - 1) 9° - (1.45 - 1) A_2 = 0$$

$$\Rightarrow \quad A_2 = 11°$$

(b) $\theta = (\mu_{V_1} - \mu_{R_1}) A_1 - (\mu_{V_2} - \mu_{R_2}) A_2 = 0$

$$\Rightarrow \quad (1.58 - 1.52) 9° - (1.48 - 1.42) A_2 = 0$$

$$\Rightarrow \quad A_2 = 9°$$

Comprehension Based Questions

1. $\mu_2 \sin i = \mu_1 \sin r$

$$\Rightarrow \quad K = \frac{\mu_1}{\mu_2} = \frac{\sin(\pi/3)}{\sin r}$$

K will be minimum, when r is maximum i.e., $r = \dfrac{\pi}{2}$

$$K_{min} = K_1 = \frac{\sin(\pi/3)}{\sin(\pi/2)} = \frac{\sqrt{3}}{2}$$

2. $\delta = |r - i|$

When $K = K_1, r = \dfrac{\pi}{2}, \ \theta = \left|\dfrac{\pi}{2} - \dfrac{\pi}{3}\right| = \dfrac{\pi}{6}$

3. Deviation is zero, when $\mu_1 = \mu_2$

So, $\quad K_2 = \dfrac{\mu_1}{\mu_2} = 1$

4. Shift due to slab $= t\left(1 - \dfrac{1}{\mu}\right) = 3\left(1 - \dfrac{1}{1.5}\right) = 1$ cm

So, object distance from mirror $= 61 - 1 = 60$ cm

$$\frac{1}{v} + \frac{1}{u} = \frac{1}{f} \Rightarrow \frac{1}{v} + \frac{1}{(-60)} = \frac{1}{-15} \Rightarrow v = -20 \text{ cm}$$

The reflected rays from mirror will again pass through the glass slab.

So, final image distance $= 20 + 1 = 21$ cm

5. Shifting a glass slab doesn't affect the final image.

6. The slab only causes apparent shift, but does not cause any change to velocity of image. Hence, the velocity of image is only due to mirror.

$$v_i = \left(-\frac{v^2}{u^2}\right) v_0 = -\left(\frac{-20}{-60}\right)^2 (18) = -2 \text{ m/s}$$

$$= 2 \text{ m/s towards right}$$

7. Given, $\sqrt{3}\, z + x = 10 \Rightarrow z = -\dfrac{1}{\sqrt{3}} x - 10$

$$\therefore \quad \tan\theta = -\frac{1}{\sqrt{3}} \Rightarrow \theta = 150°$$

Therefore, the ray is incident normally on the face AB. Thus, the angle of incidence on face AC is 60°.

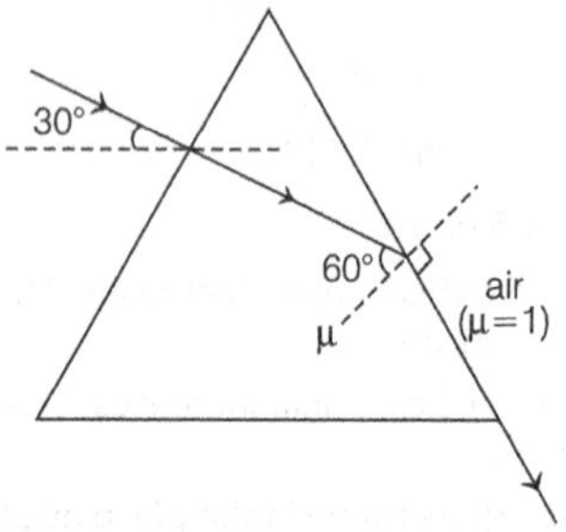

From Snell's law,

$$\mu \sin 60° = 1 \times \sin 90°$$

$$\Rightarrow \quad \mu = \frac{2}{\sqrt{3}}$$

8. $\sin i_c = \dfrac{1}{\mu} = \dfrac{2}{3}$ and $\sin i = \sin 60° = \dfrac{\sqrt{3}}{2}$

Since, $\sin i > \sin i_c$, TIR will take place at face AC.

The reflected ray from AC is incident normally on face BC. So, it will emerge normally from face BC.

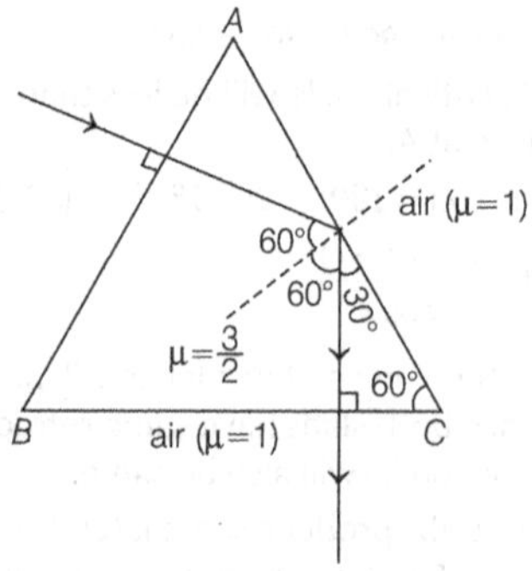

Hence, the emergent ray is parallel to Z-axis.

9. If bottom BC is silvered, the ray will retrace its path. So, its equation will be same as that of the incident ray.

10. $n_1 = n_2$

$$\Rightarrow \quad 1.20 + \frac{10.8 \times 10^4}{\lambda_0^2} = 1.45 + \frac{1.80 \times 10^4}{\lambda_0^2}$$

$$\Rightarrow \quad \lambda_0 = 600 \text{ nm}$$

11. For, $\lambda_0 = 600$ nm,

$$n_1 = n_2 = 1.20 + \frac{10.8 \times 10^4}{(600)^2} = 1.50$$

For minimum deviation,

$$r_1 = r_2 = \frac{A}{2} = \frac{60°}{2} = 30°$$

Applying Snell's law,

$$1 \times \sin i = (1.50) \sin 30°$$

$$\Rightarrow \quad i = \sin^{-1}\left(\frac{3}{4}\right)$$

Match the Columns Questions

1. (A) $v_{apparent} = \dfrac{v_{actual}}{\mu_{12}}$

$\Rightarrow \quad v-(-2) = \dfrac{2-(-2)}{4/3}$

$\Rightarrow \quad v = 1\text{ cm/s}$

$\therefore$ Velocity of fish as seen by bird $= 1-(-5) = 6\text{ cm/s}$

(B) Velocity of image of fish in mirror will be 2 cm/s (downward).

$v_{apparent} = \dfrac{v_{actual}}{\mu_{12}}$

$\Rightarrow \quad v-2 = \dfrac{2-2}{4/3}$

$\Rightarrow \quad v = 2\text{ cm/s (downward)}$

$\therefore$ Velocity of image of fish in mirror as seen by bird

$= 2-5 = -3\text{ cm/s} = 3\text{ cm/s, upward}$

(C) $v_{apparent} = \dfrac{v_{actual}}{\mu_{12}}$

$\Rightarrow \quad v-2 = \dfrac{5-2}{1/4/3}$

$\Rightarrow \quad v = 6\text{ cm/s}$

$\therefore$ Velocity of image of bird relative to fish

$= 6-(-2) = 8\text{ cm/s}$

(D) $v_{apparent} = \dfrac{v_{actual}}{\mu_{12}}$

$\Rightarrow \quad v-2 = \dfrac{5-2}{1/(4/3)}$

$\Rightarrow \quad v = 6\text{ cm/s (downward)}$

So, the velocity of image of bird in the mirror will be 6 cm/s (upward).

$\therefore$ Velocity of image of bird in the mirror as seen by fish

$= 6-2 = 4\text{ cm/s (upward)}$

2. $\mu_{Blue} > \mu_{Green} > \mu_{Yellow} > \mu_{Red}$

Critical angle, $i_c = \sin^{-1}\left(\dfrac{1}{\mu}\right)$

Critical angle is more for yellow and red as they have lesser refractive indices. So, yellow and red will get refracted. Yellow will bend more away from normal than red.

So, $\quad A \rightarrow \text{Red}, B \rightarrow \text{Yellow}$

1 will comprise of blue and green rays. Green will get refracted and blue will get totally internally reflected as critical angle is more for green than blue.

So, $\quad C \rightarrow \text{Green}, D \rightarrow \text{Blue}$

3. (A) Applying Snell's law at PQ,

$1 \times \sin 45° = \sqrt{2} \times \sin r$

$\Rightarrow \quad \sin r = \dfrac{1}{2}$

$\Rightarrow \quad r = 30°$

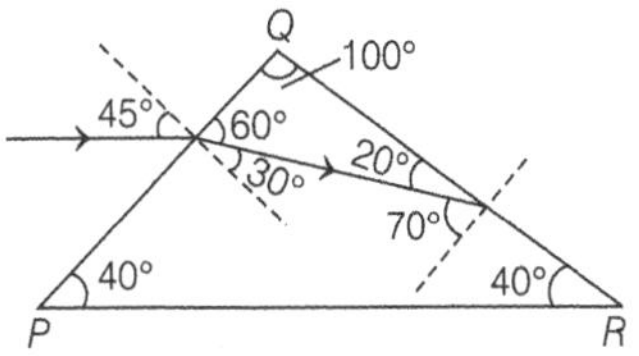

Critical angle for $QR = \sin^{-1}\left(\dfrac{1}{\sqrt{2}}\right) = 45°$

Since, angle of incidence is greater than the critical angle, TIR takes place at surface QR.

(B)

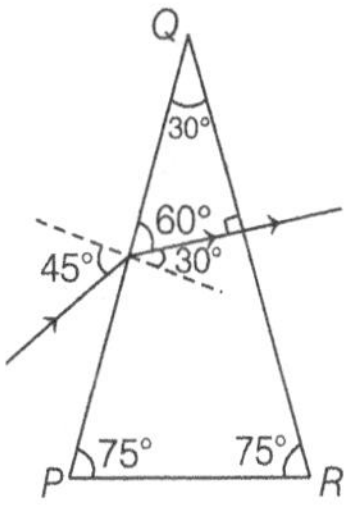

As the ray is incident normally on QR, it will emerge normally from the surface QR.

(C) Applying Snell's law at PQ,

$1 \times \sin 90° = \sqrt{2} \sin r_1$

$\Rightarrow \quad \sin r_1 = \dfrac{1}{\sqrt{2}} \Rightarrow r_1 = 45°$

$r_2 = A - r_1 = 90° - 45° = 45°$

Applying Snell's law at QR,

$\sqrt{2} \sin 45° = 1 \times \sin e$

$\Rightarrow \quad \sin e = 1 \Rightarrow e = 90°$

So, light emerges parallel to surface QR. When light ray passes through the prism, it is parallel to the base PR.

Numerical Value Questions

1.

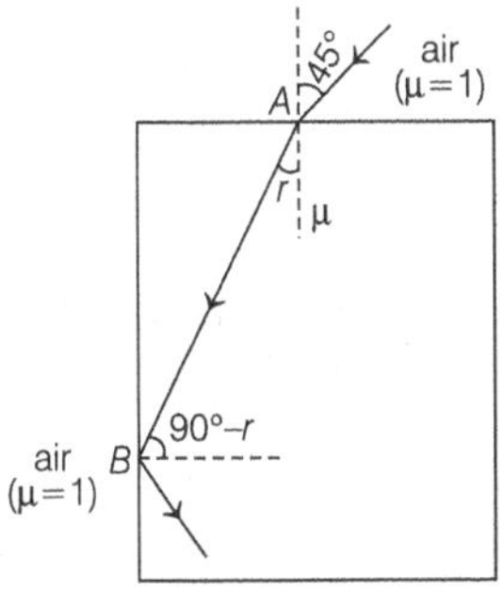

At A, $\quad 1 \times \sin 45° = \mu \sin r$

$\Rightarrow \quad \sin r = \dfrac{1}{\sqrt{2}\mu}$ or $\cos r = \sqrt{1 - \dfrac{1}{2\mu^2}}$

For TIR to happen at B,

$i > i_c \Rightarrow 90° - r > i_c \Rightarrow \sin(90° - r) > \sin i_c$

$\Rightarrow \cos r > \sin i_c \Rightarrow \sqrt{1 - \dfrac{1}{2\mu^2}} > \dfrac{1}{\mu} \Rightarrow \mu_{min} = \sqrt{\dfrac{3}{2}}$

2. From Snell's law,

$$1 \times \sin 90° = \sqrt{2} \sin r \Rightarrow \sin r = \frac{1}{\sqrt{2}}$$

$$\Rightarrow \quad r = 45°$$

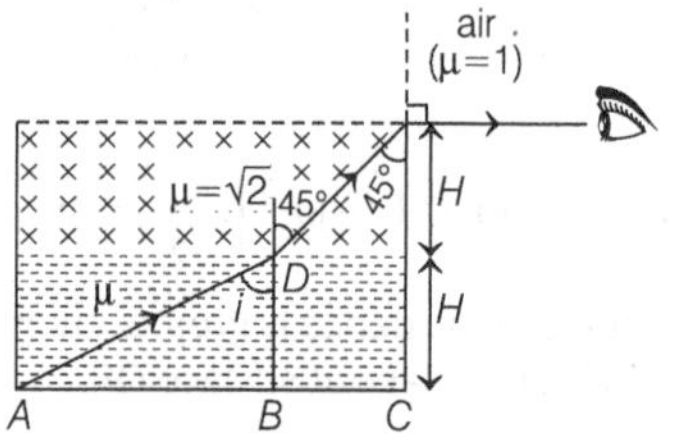

$$\tan 45° = \frac{BC}{H} \Rightarrow BC = H$$

$$\therefore \quad AB = 3H - H = 2H$$

$$\sin i = \frac{AB}{AD} = \frac{2H}{\sqrt{5}H} = \frac{2}{\sqrt{5}}$$

From Snell's law at the interface of two liquids,

$$\sqrt{2} \times \sin 45° = \mu \sin i$$

$$\Rightarrow \quad \sqrt{2} \times \frac{1}{\sqrt{2}} = \mu \left(\frac{2}{\sqrt{5}}\right)$$

$$\Rightarrow \quad \mu = \frac{\sqrt{5}}{2} = \sqrt{\frac{5}{4}} = \sqrt{1.25}$$

3. Image formed due to direction reflection from water surface will be formed 12 cm below water surface.

For the second image,

Object distance from mirror

$$= 24 + \frac{12}{1/(4/3)} = 40 \text{ cm}$$

$$\frac{1}{v} + \frac{1}{u} = \frac{1}{f} \Rightarrow \frac{1}{v} + \frac{1}{-40} = \frac{1}{60} \Rightarrow v = 24 \text{ cm}$$

The reflected rays from mirror will now go from water to air.

$$\text{Apparent depth} = \frac{\text{Actual depth}}{\mu_{12}} = \frac{24 + 24}{4/3} = 36 \text{ cm}$$

So, the second image is formed 36 cm below water surface.

Separation between the two images $= 36 - 12 = 24$ cm

4. $H_{app} = H_{\mu_{12}} = \frac{45}{(3/2)/(4/3)} = 40$ cm

$\therefore$ Object distance from mirror $= 40 + 20 = 60$ cm

Applying mirror formula,

$$\frac{1}{v} + \frac{1}{u} = \frac{1}{f} \Rightarrow \frac{1}{v} + \frac{1}{-60} = \frac{1}{-20} \Rightarrow v = -30 \text{ cm}$$

Now the reflected rays will first go from water to glass.

$$H_{app} = \frac{H}{\mu_{12}} = \frac{30 - 20}{(4/3)/(3/2)} = \frac{45}{4} \text{ cm}$$

Now the rays will go from glass to air

$$H_{app} = \frac{H}{\mu_{12}} = \frac{45 - \frac{45}{4}}{(3/2)/1} = \frac{45}{2} \text{ cm} = 22.5 \text{ cm}$$

So, the final image is 22.5 cm below the upper surface of the glass slab.

5.

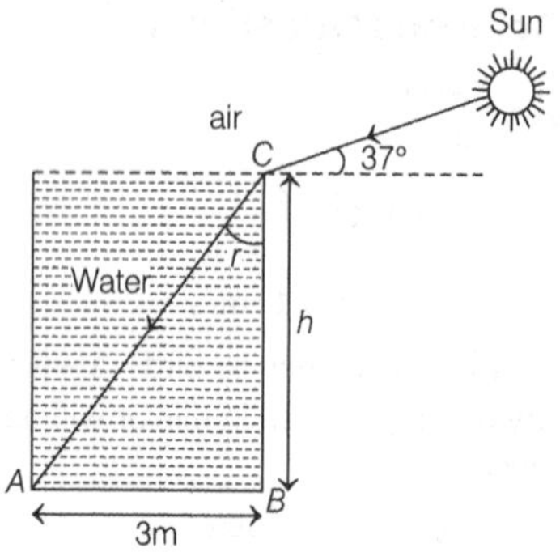

From Snell's law,

$$1 \times \sin(90° - 37°) = \frac{4}{3} \sin r$$

$$\Rightarrow \quad \sin r = \frac{3}{5} \text{ or } \tan r = \frac{3}{4}$$

$$\text{In } \Delta ABC, \tan r = \frac{3}{h} = \frac{3}{4}$$

$$\Rightarrow \quad h = 4 \text{ m}$$

6. $\sin C = \frac{1}{\mu}$ and $\cos C = \sqrt{1 - \frac{1}{\mu^2}}$

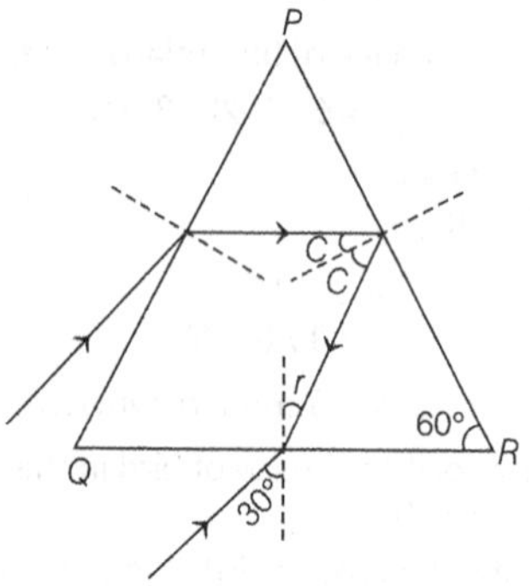

$$C + r = 60°$$

$$\Rightarrow \quad r = 60° - C$$

Applying Snell's law at face QR,

$$\mu \sin(60° - C) = 1 \times \sin 30°$$

$$\Rightarrow \mu (\sin 60° \cos C - \cos 60° \sin C) = 1 \times \sin 30°$$

$$\Rightarrow \quad \mu \left[\frac{\sqrt{3}}{2}\sqrt{1 - \frac{1}{\mu^2}} - \frac{1}{2}\left(\frac{1}{\mu}\right)\right] = \frac{1}{2}$$

$$\Rightarrow \quad \mu = \sqrt{\frac{7}{3}}$$

7. $i - e = 23°$ ...(i)

$$\delta = i + e - A$$

$$\Rightarrow \quad 23° = i + e - 60°$$

$$\Rightarrow \quad i + e = 83° \quad \text{...(ii)}$$

From Eqs. (i) and (ii), we get

$$i = 53° \text{ and } e = 30°$$

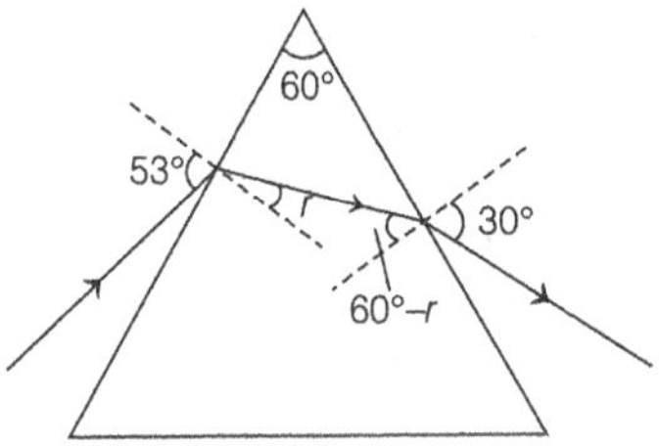

Applying Snell's law,

$$1 \times \sin 53° = \mu \sin r$$

$$\Rightarrow \quad \mu \sin r = \frac{4}{5} \quad \text{...(iii)}$$

$$\mu \sin(60° - r) = 1 \times \sin 30°$$

$$\Rightarrow \quad \mu \sin 60° \cos r - \mu \sin r \cos 60° = 1 \times \sin 30°$$

$$\Rightarrow \quad \mu\left(\frac{\sqrt{3}}{2}\right)\cos r - \left(\frac{4}{5}\right)\left(\frac{1}{2}\right) = \frac{1}{2}$$

$$\Rightarrow \quad \mu \cos r = \frac{9}{5\sqrt{3}} \quad \text{...(iv)}$$

Squaring and adding Eqs. (iii) and (iv)

$$\mu^2 \sin^2 r + \mu^2 \cos^2 r = \left(\frac{4}{5}\right)^2 + \left(\frac{9}{5\sqrt{3}}\right)^2$$

$$\Rightarrow \quad \mu = \frac{\sqrt{43}}{5}$$

8. $\phi = C, \delta_1 = \frac{\pi}{2} - C, \delta_2 = \pi - 2C$

$C = \text{critical angle} = \sin^{-1}\left(\frac{1}{\mu}\right) = 30°$

$$\therefore \quad \left[\frac{\sin(\delta_2 - \delta_1)}{\sin \phi}\right]^2 = \left[\frac{\sin\left(\frac{\pi}{2} - C\right)}{\sin C}\right]^2 = \cot^2 C = \cot^2 30° = 3$$

9.

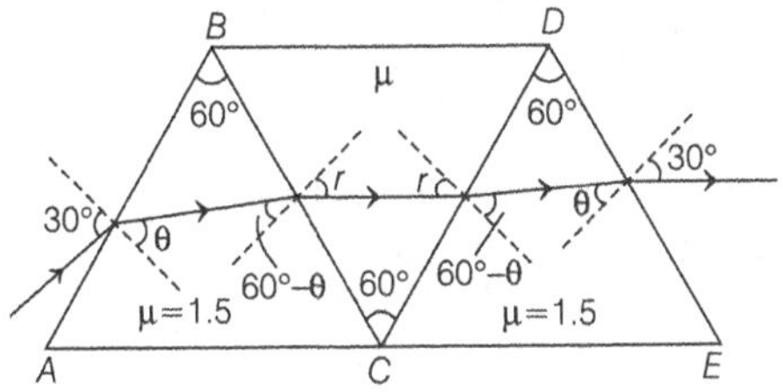

For middle prism,

$$r + r = 60° \Rightarrow r = 30°$$

Applying Snell's law at AB,

$$1 \times \sin 30° = 1.5 \sin\theta$$

$$\Rightarrow \quad \sin\theta = \frac{1}{3} \text{ or } \cos\theta = \frac{\sqrt{8}}{3}$$

Applying Snell's law at BC,

$$1.5 \sin(60° - \theta) = \mu \sin 30°$$

$$\Rightarrow \quad 1.5[\sin 60° \cos\theta - \cos 60° \sin\theta] = \mu \sin 30°$$

$$\Rightarrow \quad 1.5\left[\frac{\sqrt{3}}{2}\left(\frac{\sqrt{8}}{3}\right) - \frac{1}{2}\left(\frac{1}{3}\right)\right] = \mu\left[\frac{1}{2}\right]$$

$$\Rightarrow \quad \mu = \sqrt{6} - \frac{1}{2} = 1.95$$

10.

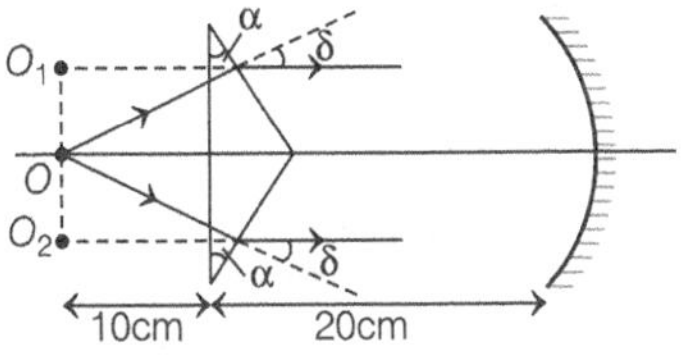

For the prism, $\delta = (\mu - 1)\alpha$

$$= (1.5 - 1)\left(1.8° \times \frac{\pi}{180°}\right) = \frac{\pi}{200} \text{ rad}$$

$$OO_1 = OO_2 = 10 \times \frac{\pi}{200} = \frac{\pi}{20} \text{ cm}$$

Therefore, $O_1O_2 = \frac{\pi}{10}$ cm

For the mirror, O_1 and O_2 are two points objects at a distance of 30 cm from mirror.

$$\frac{1}{v} + \frac{1}{u} = \frac{1}{f} \Rightarrow \frac{1}{v} + \frac{1}{-30} = \frac{1}{-10} \Rightarrow v = -15 \text{ cm}$$

$$m = -\frac{v}{u} = -\frac{(-15)}{(-30)} = -\frac{1}{2}$$

Therefore, if I_1 and I_2 are the images formed, then distance between them,

$$I_1I_2 = \frac{1}{2}(O_1O_2) = \frac{1}{2} \times \frac{\pi}{10} = \frac{\pi}{20} \text{ cm} = 1.57 \text{ mm}$$

Previous Year's Questions

JEE Main

1. By Snell's law

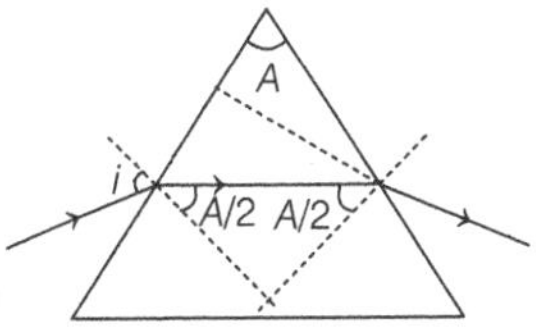

$$1 \sin i = \mu \sin\frac{A}{2}$$

$$\sin i = \mu \sin\left(\frac{A}{2}\right)$$

and $\quad \mu = \cot\frac{A}{2}$

$$\sin i = \cot\left(\frac{A}{2}\right) \cdot \sin\left(\frac{A}{2}\right)$$

$$\sin i = \frac{\cos\left(\frac{A}{2}\right)}{\sin\left(\frac{A}{2}\right)} \cdot \sin\left(\frac{A}{2}\right)$$

$$\sin i = \cos\left(\frac{A}{2}\right)$$

$$\sin i = \sin\left(\frac{\pi}{2} - \frac{A}{2}\right)$$

$$i = \frac{\pi}{2} - \frac{A}{2}$$

$$2i = \pi - A$$

$$\delta_{min} = 2i - A = \pi - A - A = \pi - 2A$$

2.

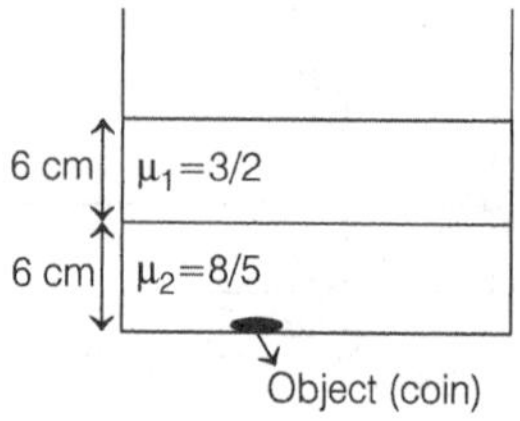

$$\text{Apparent depth} = \frac{h_1}{\mu_{rel\,1}} + \frac{h_2}{\mu_{rel\,2}} = \frac{6}{3/2} + \frac{6}{8/5} = 4 + \frac{15}{4}$$

$$= \frac{31}{4}\text{ cm} = \frac{\alpha}{4}\text{ cm} \qquad \text{(given)}$$

$$\alpha = 31$$

3. Given, $\mu = \cot\frac{A}{2}$

So, $$\cot\frac{A}{2} = \frac{\sin\left(\frac{A+\delta_m}{2}\right)}{\sin\left(\frac{A}{2}\right)}$$

$$\Rightarrow \quad \cos\frac{A}{2} = \sin\left(\frac{A+\delta_m}{2}\right)$$

$$\Rightarrow \sin\left(90° - \frac{A}{2}\right) = \sin\left(\frac{A+\delta_m}{2}\right)$$

or $$90° - \frac{A}{2} = \frac{A+\delta_m}{2}$$

$$\Rightarrow \quad 180° = 2A + \delta_m \quad \Rightarrow \quad \delta_m = 180° - 2A$$

4. Given, $\Delta x = \left(1 - \frac{1}{\mu}\right)d$

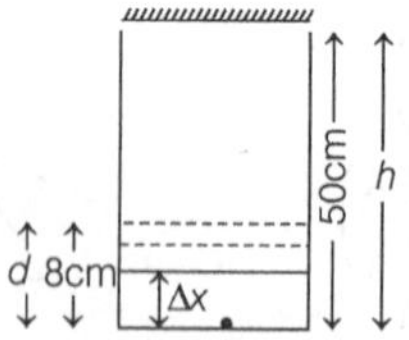

Image distance formed in plane mirror

$$= h - \Delta x = h - \left(1 - \frac{1}{\mu}\right)d = h - d + \frac{d}{\mu}$$

$$= 50 - 8 + \frac{8}{4/3} = 50 - 8 + \frac{8}{4} \times 3 = 56 - 8 = 48$$

5. $1\sin 45° = \mu \sin 30°$

$$\frac{1}{\sqrt{2}} = \mu \times \frac{1}{2}$$

$$\mu = \sqrt{2} \qquad \text{...(i)}$$

Now, $$\frac{\mu_1}{\mu_2} = \frac{v_2}{v_1} = \frac{\lambda_2}{\lambda_1} \qquad \text{...(ii)}$$

Using Eqs. (i) and (ii)

$$\lambda_2 = \frac{1}{\sqrt{2}}\lambda_1$$

Now, for relation between frequencies

Frequency, $(\nu) = \frac{v}{\lambda}$

$$\frac{\nu_1}{\nu_2} = \frac{v_1}{v_2} \times \frac{\lambda_2}{\lambda_1} = 1$$

$$\nu_1 = \nu_2$$

6. $$\sin i_c = \frac{\mu_r}{\mu_d}$$

$$i_c = 45 \qquad \text{[given]}$$

$$\sin 45° = \frac{\mu_r}{\mu_d} \quad \Rightarrow \quad \frac{\mu_r}{\mu_d} = \frac{1}{\sqrt{2}}$$

We know,

$$v \propto \frac{1}{\mu} \quad \Rightarrow \quad \frac{v_d}{v_r} = \frac{\mu_r}{\mu_d}$$

$$\frac{v_d}{3 \times 10^8} = \frac{1}{\sqrt{2}} \quad \Rightarrow \quad v_d = \frac{3 \times 10^8}{\sqrt{2}}$$

$$v_d = 3 \times 0.7 \times 10^8$$

$$v_d = 2.12 \times 10^8 \text{ m/s}$$

7. Let height of liquid filled in bucket be h.

To see image, a microscope should be focussed at that point where image is formed.

Apparent depth, $d_{app} = \frac{d}{\mu} = \frac{h}{\frac{5}{3}} = \frac{3h}{5}$

Shift in position of image = Original position – Apparent depth

$$\text{Shift} = h - \frac{3h}{5} = \frac{2h}{5}$$

Given that Shift = 30 cm

$$\therefore \quad 30 = \frac{2}{5}h \quad \Rightarrow \quad h = \frac{30 \times 5}{2} = 75 \text{ cm}$$

8. We know that for small angle prism,

$$\delta = (\mu - 1)A,$$

According to given situation, net deviation

$$A_1(\mu_1 - 1) - A_2(\mu_2 - 1) = 0$$

$$\Rightarrow \quad A_2 = \frac{A_1(\mu_1 - 1)}{\mu_2 - 1} = \frac{6(1.54 - 1)}{1.72 - 1} = 6 \times \frac{0.54}{0.72} = 4.5°$$

9. According to Snell's law,

$$\sin 60° = \frac{4}{3}\sin r$$

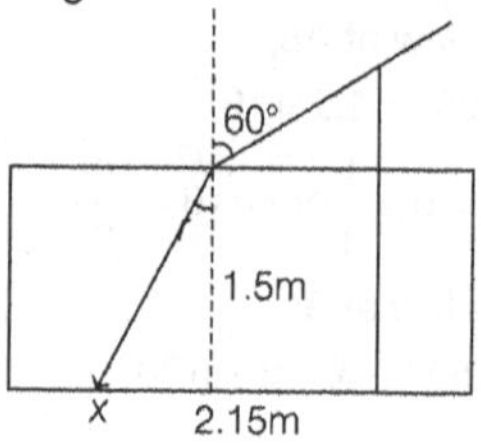

$$\sin r = \frac{3}{4} \times \frac{\sqrt{3}}{2} = \frac{3\sqrt{3}}{8} \quad ...(i)$$

$$\cos r = \sqrt{1 - \frac{27}{64}} = \frac{\sqrt{37}}{8} = 0.75$$

$$\tan r = \sqrt{\frac{27}{37}} \Rightarrow \frac{x}{1.5} = 0.85$$

$$x = 0.85 \times 1.5 = 1.275 \text{ m}$$

$$\tan 30^\circ = \frac{y}{2.15 - 1.275} = \frac{y}{0.875}$$

$$y = \frac{0.875}{1.732} = 0.50$$

So length of pole above water surface

$$= 0.50 \text{ m} = 50 \text{ cm}$$

10. Given, for equilateral prism,

$$A = 60^\circ, \mu = \sqrt{2}$$

We know that, $\mu = \dfrac{\sin\left(\dfrac{A+\delta_m}{2}\right)}{\sin\dfrac{A}{2}}$

$$\Rightarrow \sqrt{2} = \frac{\sin\left(\dfrac{60^\circ+\delta_m}{2}\right)}{\sin 30^\circ}$$

$$\Rightarrow \sin\left(\frac{A+\delta_m}{2}\right) = \frac{1}{\sqrt{2}} = \sin 45^\circ \Rightarrow \frac{A+\delta_m}{2} = 45^\circ$$

$$\Rightarrow \delta_m = 90^\circ - A = 90 - 60^\circ = 30^\circ$$

11. Here, $v_A - v_B = 2.6 \times 10^7$ m/s, $\mu_B = 1.47$, $c = 3 \times 10^8$ m / s

We know that

$$v_A = \frac{c}{\mu_A}, v_B = \frac{c}{\mu_B};$$

$$\because \quad v_A - v_B = c\left(\frac{1}{\mu_A} - \frac{1}{\mu_B}\right)$$

$$\Rightarrow 2.6 \times 10^7 = 3 \times 10^8\left(\frac{1}{\mu_A} - \frac{1}{\mu_B}\right);$$

$$\Rightarrow \frac{0.26}{3} = \frac{1}{1.47} - \frac{1}{\mu_B}$$

$$\Rightarrow \mu_B = 1.67;$$

So, $\dfrac{\mu_B}{\mu_A} = \dfrac{1.67}{1.47} = 1.13$

12. When a wave gets refracted into a denser medium, frequency of the light wave remains unchanged because it depends on the source of light.

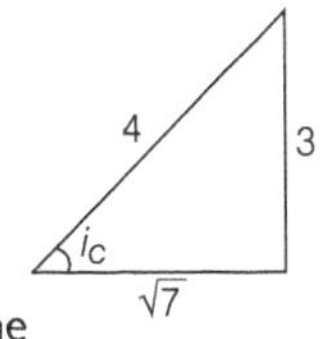

For any wave, velocity $v = f\lambda$, where f is the frequency and λ is wavelength. Since f is constant, therefore $v \propto \lambda$ *i.e.*, when light travels into a denser medium its speed decreases and hence its wavelength also decreases.

13. Angle of incidence, $i = 2r$

According to snell's law,

As, $\mu = \dfrac{\sin i}{\sin r} \Rightarrow \sqrt{2n} = \dfrac{\sin 2r}{\sin r} = \dfrac{2\sin r\cos r}{\sin r} = 2\cos r$

or $\cos r = \dfrac{\sqrt{2n}}{2} = \sqrt{\dfrac{n}{2}}$ or $r = \cos^{-1}\left(\sqrt{\dfrac{n}{2}}\right)$

Since, angle of incidence $i = 2r$.

Hence, $i = 2\cos^{-1}\left(\sqrt{\dfrac{n}{2}}\right)$

14. Angle of deviation, $\delta = 15^\circ$

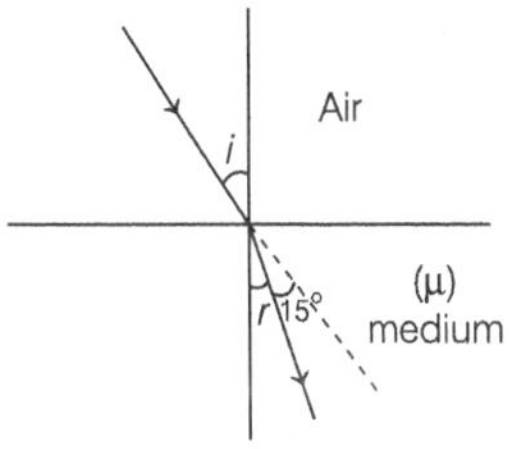

$\therefore$ Angle of refraction, $r = i - \delta = 45^\circ - 15^\circ = 30^\circ$

According to Snell's law,

$$\mu = \frac{\sin i}{\sin r} = \frac{\sin 45^\circ}{\sin 30^\circ} = \frac{\frac{1}{\sqrt{2}}}{\frac{1}{2}} = \frac{2}{\sqrt{2}} = \sqrt{2} = 1.414$$

15. Speed of light in medium m_1 and m_2 are given as $v_1 = 1.5 \times 10^8$ m/s, $v_2 = 2 \times 10^8$ m/s If i_c be the critical angle for incident light in medium m_1, then

$$\sin i_c = \frac{1}{{}^2\mu_1} \quad ...(i)$$

But $\;{}^2\mu_1 = \dfrac{v_2}{v_1} = \dfrac{2 \times 10^8}{1.5 \times 10^8} = \dfrac{4}{3}$

From Eq. (i), we get

$$\sin i_c = \frac{1}{4/3} \Rightarrow \sin i_c = \frac{3}{4}$$

$$\therefore \quad \tan i_c = \frac{3}{\sqrt{7}} \Rightarrow i_c = \tan^{-1}\left(\frac{3}{\sqrt{7}}\right)$$

16. The given situation is shown below

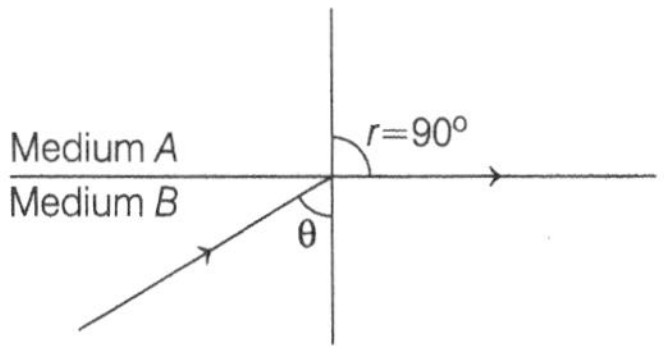

As total internal reflection occurs, so θ_{min} = critical incidence angle

$$\Rightarrow \frac{\sin\theta_{min}}{\sin r} = n_{AB} = \frac{v_B}{v_A}$$

$$\Rightarrow \sin\theta_{min} = \sin r \times \frac{v_B}{v_A}$$

Here, $r = 90^\circ$, $v_B = 1.5 \times 10^{10}$ cm/s

and $v_A = 2\times10^{10}$ cm/s

So, $\sin\theta_{min} = \dfrac{\sin 90°\times 1.5\times10^{10}}{2\times10^{10}}$

$\Rightarrow \sin\theta_{min} = \dfrac{3}{4}$ or $\theta_{min} = \sin^{-1}\dfrac{3}{4}$

$\Rightarrow \theta \geq \sin^{-1}\dfrac{3}{4}$ for TIR

17. By refraction formula through prism, we get

$$n = \frac{\sin\left(\frac{A+\delta_m}{2}\right)}{\sin\left(\frac{A}{2}\right)} = \cot\left(\frac{A}{2}\right) \text{ [Given]}$$

$$\Rightarrow \sin\left(\frac{A+\delta_m}{2}\right) = \frac{\cos\left(\frac{A}{2}\right)}{\sin\left(\frac{A}{2}\right)} \times \sin\left(\frac{A}{2}\right)$$

or $\sin\left(\dfrac{A+\delta_m}{2}\right) = \cos\left(\dfrac{A}{2}\right)$

$\Rightarrow \sin\left(\dfrac{A+\delta_m}{2}\right) = \sin\left(\dfrac{\pi}{2} - \dfrac{A}{2}\right)$

$\Rightarrow \dfrac{A+\delta_m}{2} = \dfrac{\pi}{2} - \dfrac{A}{2}$

or $\delta_m = 180° - 2A$

18. We know that for total internal reflection, $i > i_c$

$\therefore \sin i > \sin i_c$ ...(i)

But $\sin i_c = \dfrac{\mu_{rarer}}{\mu_{denser}}$ ...(ii)

From Eqs. (i) and (ii), we get

$\sin i > \dfrac{\mu_{rarer}}{\mu_{denser}}$ ...(iii)

Since, $\mu = \sqrt{\mu_r \cdot \varepsilon_r} = \sqrt{1\cdot\varepsilon_r} = \sqrt{\varepsilon_r}$

$\therefore \dfrac{\mu_{rarer}}{\mu_{denser}} = \sqrt{\dfrac{(\varepsilon_r)_{rarer}}{(\varepsilon_r)_{medium}}} = \sqrt{\dfrac{1}{4}} = \dfrac{1}{2}$

$\therefore$ From Eq. (iii), $\sin i > \dfrac{1}{2}$

$\Rightarrow \sin i > \sin 30° \Rightarrow i > 30°$

$\therefore i = 60°$ [From the given options]

19. If t is the thickness of the glass slab, then

$$l = t\sin i\left[1 - \frac{\cos i}{\sqrt{\mu^2 - \sin^2 i}}\right]$$

$$\Rightarrow 4\sqrt{3} = t\sin 60°\left[1 - \frac{\cos 60°}{\sqrt{(\sqrt{3})^2 - \sin^2 60°}}\right]$$

$$= \frac{\sqrt{3}}{2}t\left[1 - \frac{\frac{1}{2}}{\sqrt{3-\frac{3}{4}}}\right] = \frac{\sqrt{3}}{2}t\left[1 - \frac{\frac{1}{2}}{3/2}\right] = \frac{\sqrt{3}}{2}t\left[\frac{2}{3}\right]$$

$\Rightarrow 4\sqrt{3} = \dfrac{t}{\sqrt{3}} \Rightarrow t = 12$ cm

20. Let us draw the diagram of glass tumbler.

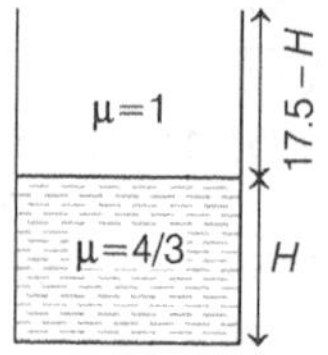

As we know that

$\mu_{water} = \dfrac{H_{real}}{H_{appearent}} \Rightarrow \dfrac{4}{3} = \dfrac{H}{H_{appearent}}$

$\Rightarrow H_{appearent} = 3H/4$

The height of air observed by observer $= 17.5 - H$

According to the above figure,

$\dfrac{3H}{4} = 17.5 - H \Rightarrow H = 10.11 \text{ cm} \approx 10$ cm

21. According to given situation

$r + r' = 90°$

$\Rightarrow r' = 90° - r = 90° - i$ ...(i)

By using Snell's law

$n_1 \sin i = n_2 \sin r'$,

From Eq. (i), we have

$n_1 \sin i = n_2 \sin(90° - i)$

$n_1 \sin i = n_2 \sin(90° - i)$

$n_1 \sin i = n_2 \cos i$

$\Rightarrow \tan i = \dfrac{n_2}{n_1}$ ...(ii)

Also $\sin C = \dfrac{n_2}{n_1}$ where, C is critical angle.

From Eq. (ii), we get

$\sin C = \tan i$

$C = \sin^{-1}(\tan i) = \sin^{-1}(\tan r)$

22. If the angle of incidence is increased gradually, then the angle of deviation first decreases, attains a minimum value (δ_m), and then again starts increasing.

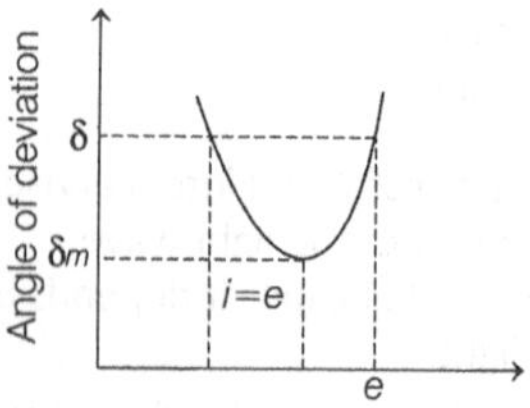

23.

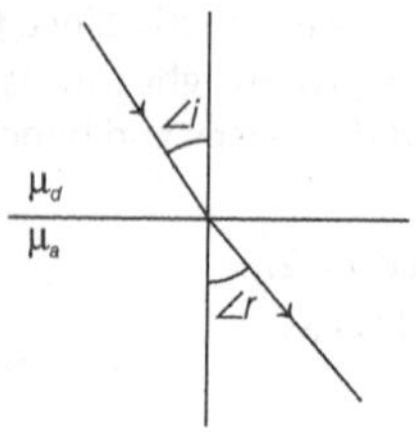

By using Snell's law,

$$\frac{\mu_a}{\mu_d} = \frac{\sin i}{\sin r}$$

$$\Rightarrow \quad \sin r = \frac{\mu_d}{\mu_a} \sin i$$

$$= 2.42 \times \sin 30^\circ$$

$$= 2.42 \times \frac{1}{2} = 1.21 > 1$$

But the maximum value of $\sin\theta$ is 1.

$\therefore$ In above case, refraction is not possible.

24. From the given figure,

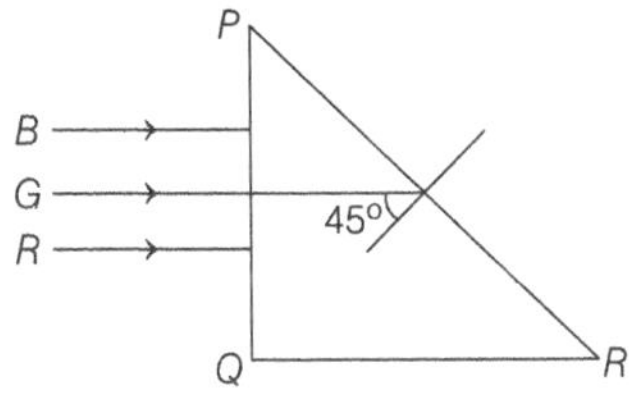

We know that,

$$\mu = \frac{1}{\sin i_C}$$

$$\Rightarrow \quad \mu = \frac{1}{\sin 45^\circ}$$

$$\Rightarrow \quad \mu = 1.414$$

As $\mu_R < \mu$ while μ_G and $\mu_B > \mu$, so only red colour will be transmitted through face PR while green and blue rays will suffer total internal reflection.

25. The propagation of light ray from a prism is shown below

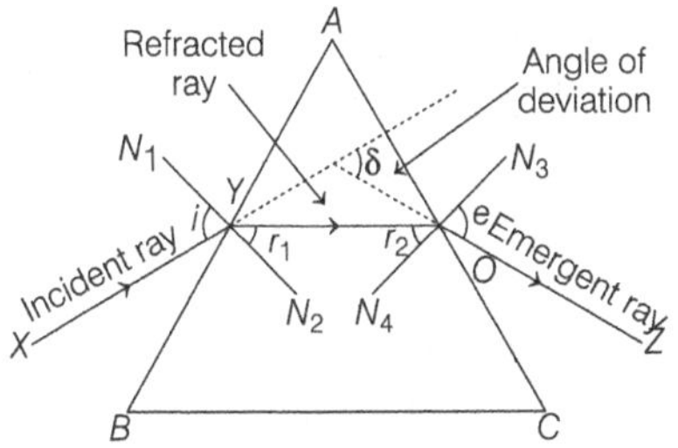

From the above figure, we can say that minimum value of angle of deviation can only be achieved when

A. incident ray and emergent ray are symmetric to the prism.

B. the refracted ray inside the prism becomes parallel to its base.

C. angle of incidence is equal to angle of emergence.

$\therefore$ Statement (A), (B) and (C) are true.

26. Since, $\lambda\nu = c =$ constant

Red light and blue light have different wavelengths and different frequencies but same speed.

JEE Advanced

1. For Fig. I (Blue light)

$$\mu = \tan i_p$$

$$i_p = \tan^{-1}\sqrt{3} = 60^\circ$$

$$\delta = i + e - A$$

$$\Rightarrow \quad 60^\circ = 60^\circ + e - A$$

$$\Rightarrow \quad e = A \quad \text{...(i)}$$

At incident surface, $\sin 60^\circ = \sqrt{3}\sin r_1$

$$\Rightarrow \quad r_1 = 30^\circ$$

$$\therefore \quad r_1 + r_2 = A$$

$$\Rightarrow \quad r_2 = A - 30^\circ$$

At emergent surface,

$$\sqrt{3}\sin r_2 = \sin e$$

$$\sqrt{3}\sin(A - 30^\circ) = \sin A$$

$$\Rightarrow \quad \frac{3}{2}\sin A - \frac{\sqrt{3}}{2}\cos A = \sin A$$

$$\Rightarrow \quad \tan A = \sqrt{3}$$

$$A = 60^\circ$$

Thus, $e = 60^\circ$

For Fig. II (Red light)

For minimum deviation,

$$\frac{\sin\left(\frac{A + \delta_m}{2}\right)}{\sin\frac{A}{2}} = \mu_R$$

$$\Rightarrow \quad \frac{\sin 45^\circ}{\sin 30^\circ} = \mu_R$$

or, $\mu_R = \sqrt{2}$

2.

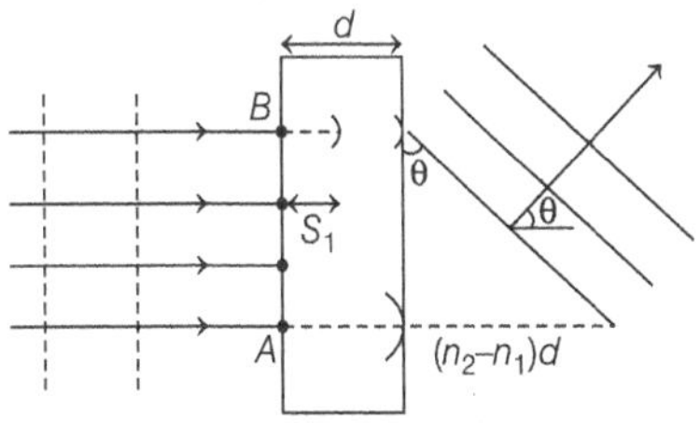

At A was wave front reach at the end of slab in time t.

$$t = \frac{d}{\frac{c}{n_1}} = \frac{n_1 d}{c}$$

in time t wave front at B travel S_1 ;

$$S_1 = \frac{c}{n_2} \times \frac{n_1 d}{c} \Rightarrow \frac{dn_1}{n_2}$$

when wave front of B reaches at end of slab, then further t_1 time take place

$$t_1 = \left(\frac{d - S_1}{c}\right) n_2 = \left[d - \frac{dn_1}{n_2}\right]\frac{n_2}{c}$$

$$\Rightarrow \qquad \frac{d(n_2 - n_1)}{c}$$

in t_1 time wave front at A travel $\Rightarrow S_2$

$$S_2 = ct_1 = d\,[n_2 - n_1]$$

$$\tan\theta = \frac{(n_2 - n_1)\,d}{n} \quad \Rightarrow \quad \theta = \tan^{-1}\frac{(n_2 - n_1)\,d}{h}$$

3.

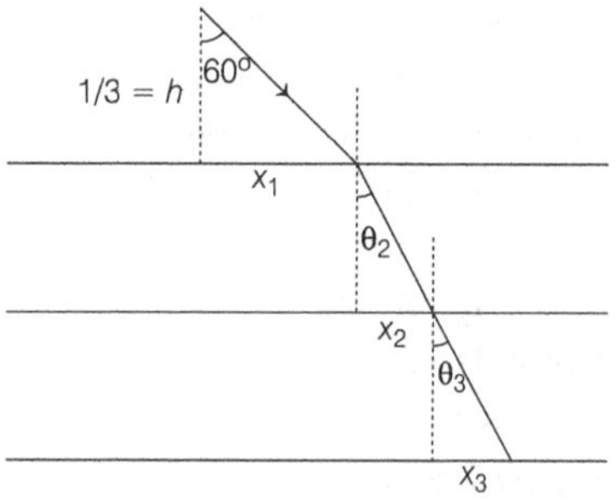

$$x_1 = \frac{1}{3} \times \tan 60° = \frac{1}{\sqrt{3}}\text{ cm}$$

and $$1 \times \frac{\sqrt{3}}{2} = \sqrt{\frac{3}{2}} \times \sin\theta_2$$

$$\Rightarrow \qquad \theta_2 = 45° \quad \Rightarrow \quad x_2 = d$$

and $$1 \times \frac{\sqrt{3}}{2} = \frac{\sqrt{3}}{2} \times \sin\theta_2$$

$$\Rightarrow \qquad \theta_3 = 30° \quad \Rightarrow \quad x_3 = \frac{d}{\sqrt{3}}$$

$$\therefore \; x_1 + x_2 + x_3 = \frac{1}{\sqrt{3}} + \frac{(\sqrt{3}-1)}{2}\left(1 + \frac{1}{\sqrt{3}}\right) = \frac{2}{\sqrt{3}}\text{ cm}$$

$$\therefore \qquad n = \frac{l}{x_1 + x_2 + x_3} = \frac{\frac{8}{\sqrt{3}}}{\frac{2}{\sqrt{3}}} = 4$$

4.

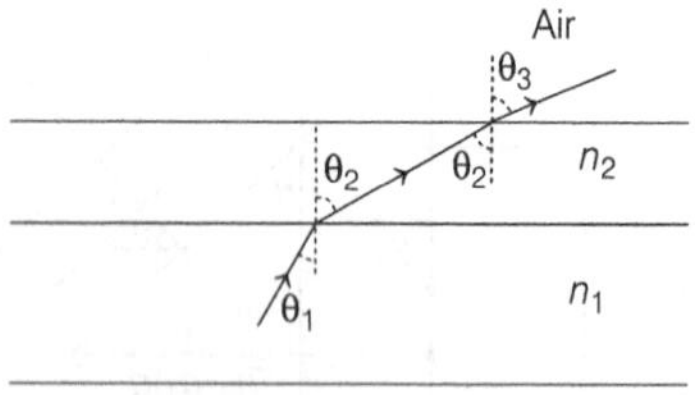

$$\sin\theta > \frac{1}{n_1} \qquad \text{(Given)}$$

i.e., $$\sin\theta_1 > \frac{1}{n_1}$$

$$n_1 \sin\theta_1 = n_2 \sin\theta_2 \quad \Rightarrow \quad \sin\theta_2 = \frac{n_1 \sin\theta_1}{n_2}$$

If $$n_1 = n_2,\text{ then } \theta_2 = \theta_1$$

$$n_2 \sin\theta_2 = (1)\sin\theta_3$$

$$\sin\theta_3 = n_2 \sin\theta_2$$

$$\sin\theta_3 = n_1 \sin\theta_1$$

$$\sin\theta_1 = \frac{\sin\theta_3}{n_1} > \frac{1}{n_1}$$

$$\sin\theta_3 > 1$$

$$\theta_3 > 90°$$

This means ray cannot enter air.

For $n_1 > n_2$; $\sin\theta_1 = \frac{n_2}{n_1}\sin\theta_2 > \frac{1}{n_1}$

$$\sin\theta_2 > \frac{1}{n_2}$$

For surface 2 – air interface

$$n_2 \sin\theta_2 = \sin\theta_3$$

$$\sin\theta_2 = \frac{\sin\theta_3}{n_2} > \frac{1}{n_2}$$

$$\theta_2 > 90°$$

It means ray is reflected back in medium-2

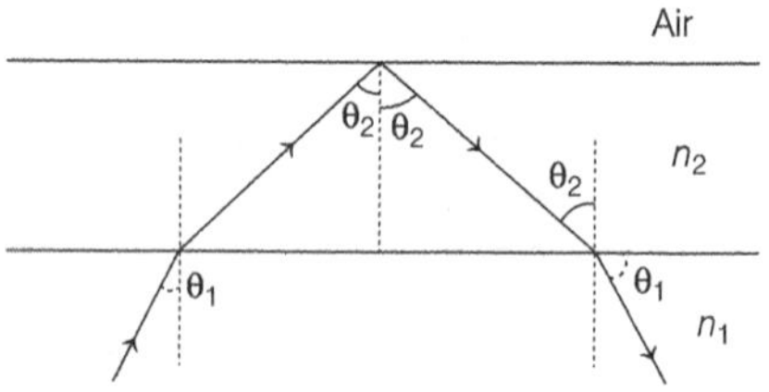

For surface 1 and surface 2 interface

$$n_2 \sin\theta_2 = n_1 \sin\theta_1$$

$$\sin\theta_{2C} = \frac{n_1}{n_2}$$

θ_{2C} : critical angle

For ray to enter medium-1

$$\theta_2 < \theta_{2C}$$

$$\sin\theta_2 < \sin 2\theta_C$$

$$\frac{n_1}{n_2}\sin\theta_1 < \frac{n_1}{n_2}$$

$$\sin\theta_1 < 1$$

$\theta_1 < 90°$, which is true.

Hence, ray enters medium-1

For $n_2 > n_1$

$$\frac{n_2}{n_1}\sin\theta_2 > \frac{n_2}{n_1} \quad \Rightarrow \quad \sin\theta_2 > \frac{1}{n_2}$$

For surface 2 – air interface

$$n_2 \sin\theta_2 = \sin\theta_3$$

$$\sin\theta_2 = \frac{\sin\theta_3}{n_2} > \frac{1}{n_2}$$

$$\theta_2 > 90$$

It means ray is reflected back in medium-2

$$n_2 \sin\theta_2 = n_1 \sin\theta_1$$

$$\sin\theta_1 = \frac{n_2}{n_1}\sin\theta_2$$

$$\sin\theta_{2C} = \frac{n_1}{n_2};\ \theta_{2C} \rightarrow \text{critical angle}$$

For ray to enter medium-1

$$\theta_2 < \theta_{2C}$$

$$\sin\theta_2 < \sin\theta_{2C}$$

$$\frac{n_1}{n_2}\sin\theta_1 < \frac{n_1}{n_2}$$

$$\sin\theta_1 < 1$$

$\theta_1 < 90°$, which is true.

Hence, ray enters medium-1

Let, $n_2 = 1$

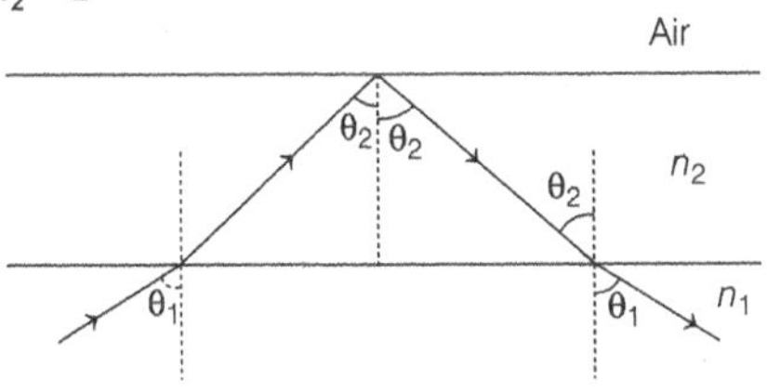

$$n_1 \sin\theta_1 = n_2 \sin\theta_2 \quad \Rightarrow \quad n_2 = 1$$

$$n_1 \sin\theta_1 = \sin\theta_2$$

$$\sin\theta_1 = \frac{\sin\theta_2}{n_1} > \frac{1}{n_1}$$

$$\sin\theta_2 > 1 \quad \Rightarrow \quad \theta_2 = 90°$$

$\therefore$ ray is reflected back in medium.

5.

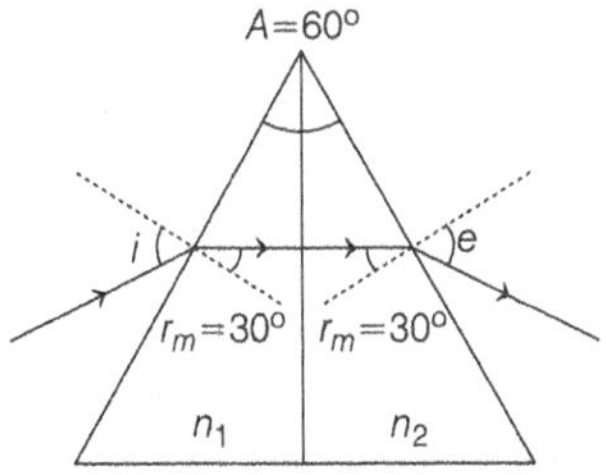

$$n_1 = n_2 = n = \frac{3}{2} \text{ for minimum deviation,}$$

$$r_m = \frac{A}{2} = \frac{60}{2} = 30° \quad \text{and } i = e = \theta$$

$$n = \frac{\sin\left(\frac{\delta_{min} + A}{2}\right)}{\sin\left(\frac{A}{2}\right)}$$

$$\Rightarrow \quad \frac{3}{2} = \frac{\sin\theta}{\sin\left(\frac{60}{2}\right)}$$

$$\Rightarrow \quad \sin\theta = \frac{3}{4} \quad \Rightarrow \quad \cos\theta = \frac{\sqrt{7}}{4}$$

If $n_1 = n = \frac{3}{2}$ and $n_2 = n + \Delta n$

$$e = \theta + \Delta\theta$$

$$(1)\sin\theta = n\sin 30°$$

$$(n + \Delta n)\sin 30° = (1)\sin(\theta + \Delta\theta)$$

Solving $\frac{1}{2}(\Delta n) = \sin(\theta + \Delta\theta) - \sin\theta$

$$\frac{\Delta n}{2} = \frac{\sin(\theta + \Delta\theta) - \sin\theta}{\Delta\theta} \times \Delta\theta$$

$$\frac{d(\sin\theta)}{d\theta} = \cos\theta$$

$$\frac{\Delta n}{2} = (\cos\theta)(\Delta\theta) \quad \Rightarrow \quad \frac{\Delta n}{2} = \frac{\sqrt{7}}{4}(\Delta\theta)$$

$$\Rightarrow \quad \frac{\Delta n}{\Delta\theta} = \frac{\sqrt{7}}{2} = \frac{2.64}{2}$$

$$\frac{\Delta n}{\Delta\theta} = 1.34 > 1$$

$\Rightarrow \Delta n > \Delta\theta$, so option (a) is incorrect.

$$\Delta n = (1.34)\Delta\theta$$

$\Rightarrow \quad \Delta\theta \propto \Delta n \quad \Rightarrow \quad$ option (b) is correct.

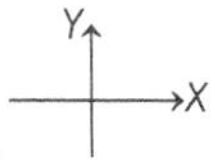

$$\frac{\Delta n}{\Delta\theta} = \frac{\sqrt{7}}{2} \quad \Rightarrow \quad \frac{2.8 \times 10^{-3}}{\Delta\theta} = \frac{\sqrt{7}}{2}$$

$$\Delta\theta = \frac{5.6 \times 10^{-3}}{\sqrt{7}} = \sqrt{7} \times 0.8 \times 10^{-3}$$

$$\Delta\theta = (2.64 \times 0.8) \times 10^{-3} = 2.11 \times 10^{-3} \text{ rad}$$

So, option (c) is correct.

6.

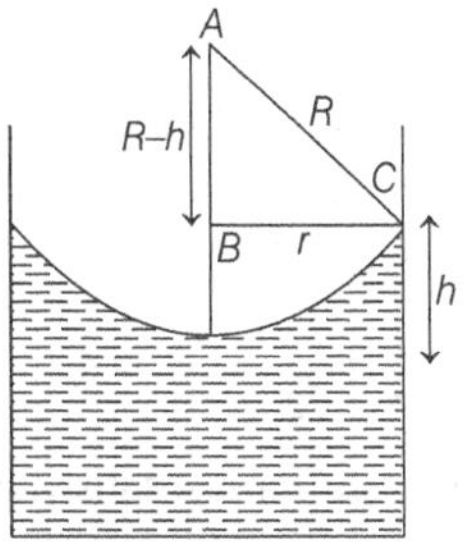

$$(R - h)^2 + r^2 = R^2$$

$$R^2 + h^2 - 2Rh + r^2 = R^2 \quad \Rightarrow \quad h^2 + r^2 = 2Rh$$

$$\frac{h^2 + r^2}{2h} = R \qquad \text{... (i)}$$

When $r >>> h$, then

$$R = \frac{r^2}{2h}$$

$$\because \quad h = \frac{\omega^2 r^2}{2g}$$

$$\Rightarrow \quad R = \frac{r^2 2g}{2\omega^2 r^2}$$

$$R = \frac{g}{\omega^2} \qquad \text{... (ii)}$$

$$\frac{\mu_1}{v} - \frac{\mu_2}{u} = \frac{\mu_1 - \mu_2}{R}$$

$$\Rightarrow \quad \frac{1}{v} + \frac{4}{3u} = \frac{1 - \frac{4}{3}}{R}$$

$$\frac{1}{v} = -\left(\frac{1}{3R} + \frac{4}{3(H - h)}\right)$$

$$\frac{1}{v} = -\left(\frac{1}{3R} + \frac{4}{3H}\right)$$

Putting the value of Eq. (ii) $h << H$

$$\frac{1}{v} = -\left[\frac{4}{3H}\left(1 + \frac{3H\,\omega^2}{4\ 39}\right)\right]$$

$$v = -\left[\frac{3H}{4}\left(1 + \frac{\omega^2 H}{4}\right)\right]^{-1}$$

7. Question was wrong. According to official website of IIT-JEE, marks were given to all students in this question.

8.

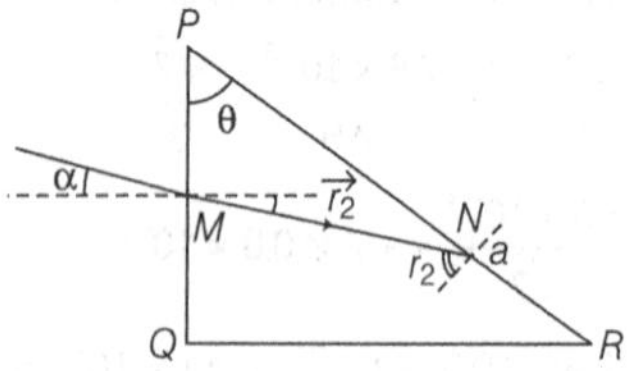

Applying Snell's law at M,

$$n = \frac{\sin\alpha}{\sin r_1} \quad \Rightarrow \quad \sqrt{2} = \frac{\sin 45^\circ}{\sin r_1}$$

$$\Rightarrow \quad \sin r_1 = \frac{\sin 45^\circ}{\sqrt{2}} = \frac{1/\sqrt{2}}{\sqrt{2}} = \frac{1}{2}$$

$$r_1 = 30^\circ$$

$$\sin\theta_c = \frac{1}{n} = \frac{1}{\sqrt{2}} \Rightarrow \theta_c = 45^\circ$$

Let us take $r_2 = \theta_c = 45^\circ$ for just satisfying the condition of TIR.

In ΔPNM, $\theta + 90 + r_1 + 90 - r_2 = 180^\circ$

or $\theta = r_2 - r_1 = 45^\circ - 30^\circ = 15^\circ$

NOTE

$\therefore$ $r_2 - r_1 = \theta$ or $r_2 = \theta + r_1$

For $r_1 = 30^\circ$ and $\theta = 15^\circ$, $r_2 = 45^\circ$

If $\alpha > 45^\circ$, then $r_1 > 30^\circ$ and $r_2 > 45^\circ$ or θ_c.

or TIR will take place. So, for taking TIR under all conditions α should be greater than 45° or this is the minimum value of α.

9. $\frac{4}{3}\sin i = \frac{\sqrt{45}}{4}\sin(90 - \theta\,) = \frac{\sqrt{45}}{4}\cos\theta_c$

$$\sin\theta_c = \frac{n_2}{n_1}$$

$$\therefore \quad \cos\theta_c = \sqrt{1 - \left(\frac{n_2}{n_1}\right)^2}$$

$$\Rightarrow \quad \frac{4}{3}\sin i = \frac{\sqrt{45}}{4}\frac{3}{\sqrt{45}} \Rightarrow \sin i = \frac{9}{16}$$

In second case,

$$\sin\theta = \frac{n_2}{n_1} = \frac{7}{8} \quad \Rightarrow \quad \cos\theta_c = \frac{\sqrt{15}}{8}$$

$$\frac{16}{3\sqrt{15}}\sin i = \frac{8}{5}\sin(90 - \theta_c)$$

Simplifying we get,

$$\sin i = 9/16$$

Same approach can be adopted for other options. Correct answers are (a) and (c).

10. $\sin i_m = n_1 \sin(90^\circ - \theta_c)$

$$\Rightarrow \quad \sin i_m = n_1 \cos\theta_c$$

$$\Rightarrow \quad NA = n_1\sqrt{1 - \sin^2\theta_c} = n_1\sqrt{1 - \frac{n_2^2}{n_1^2}} = \sqrt{n_1^2 - n_2^2}$$

Substituting the values we get,

$$NA_1 = \frac{3}{4} \quad \text{and} \quad NA_2 = \frac{\sqrt{15}}{5} = \sqrt{\frac{3}{4}}$$

$$NA_2 < NA_1$$

Therefore, the numerical aperture of combined structure is equal to the lesser of the two numerical aperture, which is NA_2.

CHAPTER~03

REFRACTION AT A SPHERICAL SURFACE

LEVEL 01 Starter Level

3.1 Refraction at a Spherical Boundary

1 A convex refracting surface of radius of curvature 15 cm separates two media of refractive indices 4/3 and 3/2. An object is kept in the first medium at a distance of 240 cm from the surface. Find the position of the image.

2 A small coin is kept 5 cm from centre inside a solid glass sphere ($\mu = 1.5$) of radius 10 cm as shown in figure. Locate the image of the coin as seen by

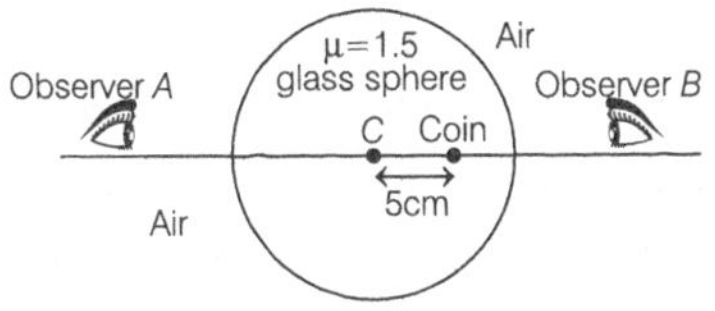

(i) observer A (ii) observer B

3 A parallel beam of light is incident on a solid glass sphere kept in air as shown in figure. Find out the position, where parallel rays will meet after coming out of the sphere and draw the appropriate ray diagram.

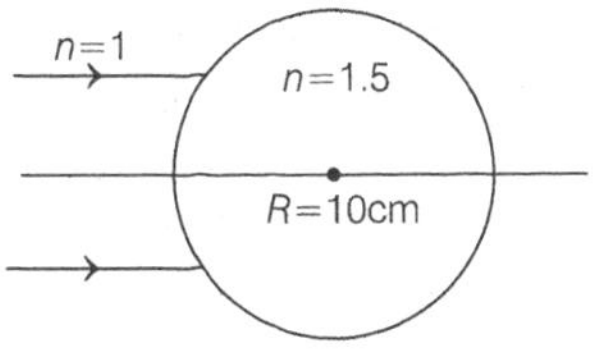

4 An object is placed 10 cm away from a glass piece ($n = 1.5$) of length 20 cm bound by spherical surfaces of radii of curvature 10 cm. Find the position of final image formed after twice refractions.

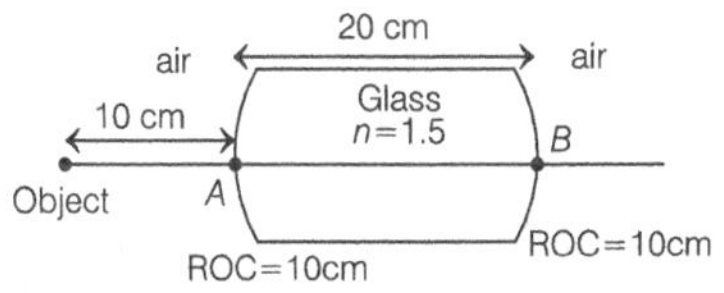

5 An extended object of size 2 cm is placed at a distance of 10 cm in air ($n = 1$) from pole, on the principal axis of a spherical curved surface. The medium on the other side of refracting surface has refractive index $n = 2$. Find the position, nature and size of image formed after single refraction through the curved surface.

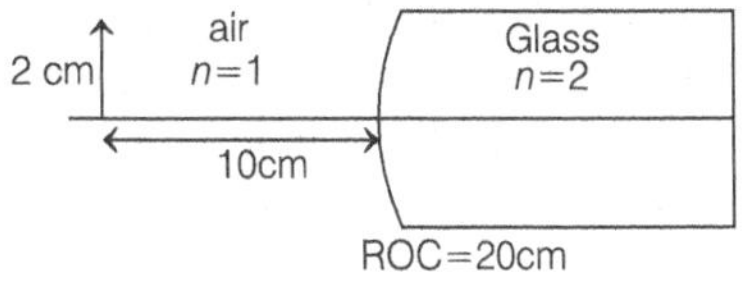

6 A paperweight of refractive index $n = \frac{3}{2}$ in the form of a hemisphere of radius 30 cm is used to hold down a printed page. An observer looks at the page vertically through the paperweight. At what height above the page will the printed letters near the centre appear to the observer?

7 Solve the previous problem if the paperweight is inverted at its place, so that the spherical surface touches the paper.

8 A point object O is moving with velocity 2 m/s in air as shown in figure. Find the velocity of image.

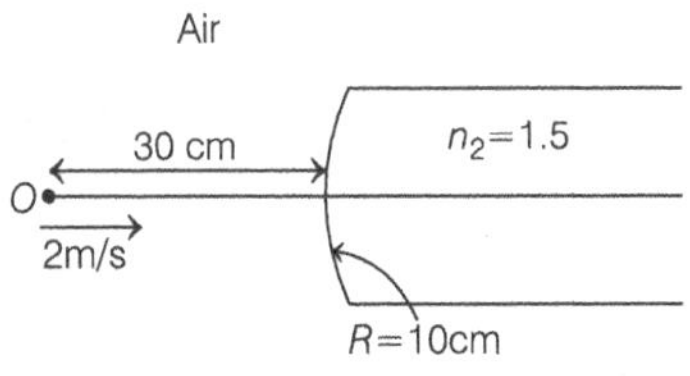

3.2 Lens Maker Formula

1 Find focal length of glass lens in each of the following cases.

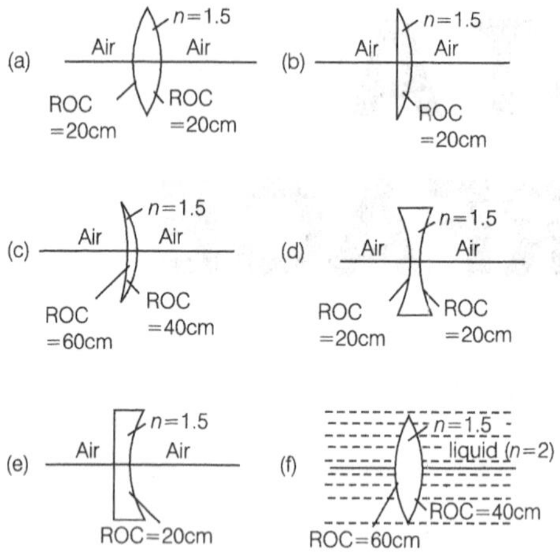

2 Lenses are constructed by a material of refractive index 1.50. The magnitude of the radii of curvature are 20 cm and 30 cm. Find the focal lengths of the possible lenses with the above specifications.

3 A lens has focal length +20 cm, when in air and its material has refractive index 1.50. If the lens is immersed completely in a liquid of refractive index 1.60, find the focal length of the lens in liquid.

4 A meniscus lens is made of a material of refractive index μ_2. Both its surfaces have radii of curvature R. It has two different media of refractive indices μ_1 and μ_3 respectively, on its two sides (shown in the figure). Calculate its focal length for $\mu_1 < \mu_2 < \mu_3$, when light is incident on it as shown.

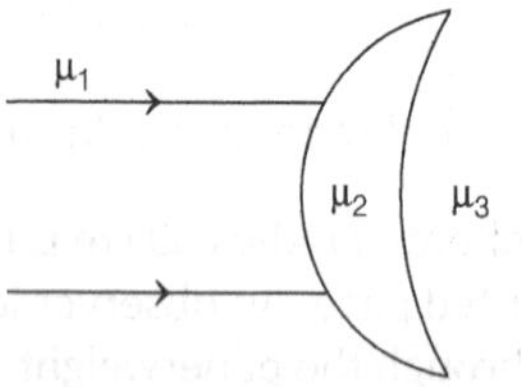

5 An equiconvex lens of focal length f is to be cut into two equal halves. Find the focal length of each half if it is cut along

(i) XOX' (ii) YOY'

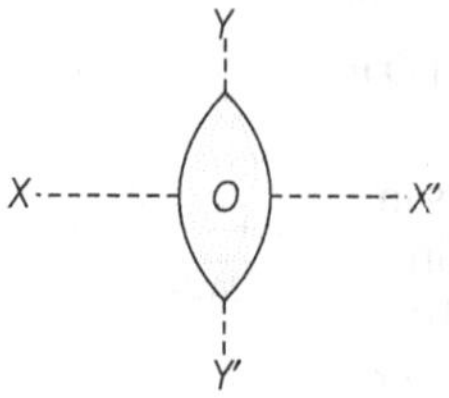

3.3 Ray Diagrams

1 What will the paths of the rays be after refraction in the lenses? [F_1 – First focus, F_2 – Second focus]

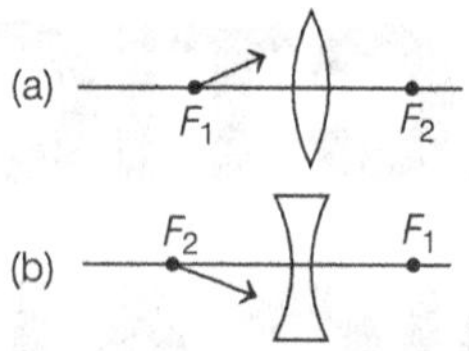

2 An image I is formed of a point object O by a lens whose optical axis is MN as shown in cases (a), (b) and (c). Draw a ray diagram to locate the lens and its focus. What type of lens is it?

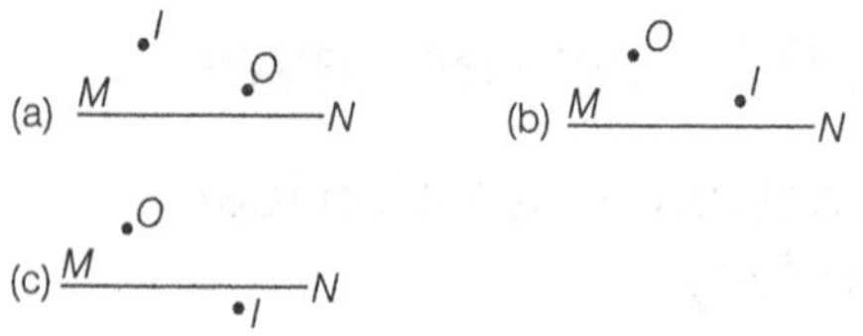

3.4 Lens Formula

1 An object of height 5 mm is set at right angles to the optical axis of a double convex lens of focal length 20 cm and 25 cm away from the lens. Determine the position of the image and the height of the image formed by it.

2 An object is placed in front of a converging lens of focal length 10 cm and image formed is double the size of object. Find out the position(s) of object.

3 A beam of light is incident on a converging lens of focal length as shown in figure. Find out the position of the image formed.

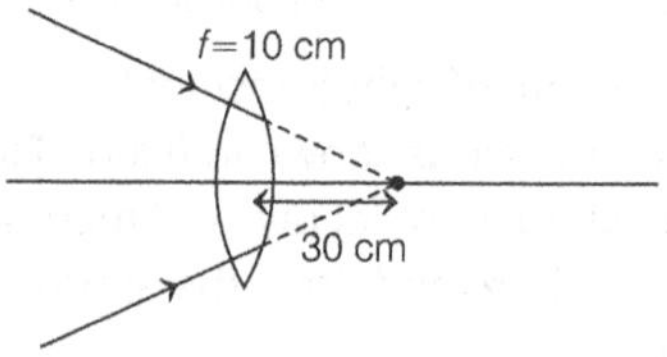

4 An object is placed 60 cm from a lens and a real image is formed. When the object is moved closer to the lens to a distance of 40 cm, the image moves 10 cm further away from the lens. What is the focal length of the lens?

5 The diameter of the sun is 1.4×10^9 m and its distance from the earth is 1.5×10^{11} m. Find the diameter of the image of the sun formed by a lens of focal length 40 cm.

6 Find out the linear length of the image of the object *AB* shown in figure.

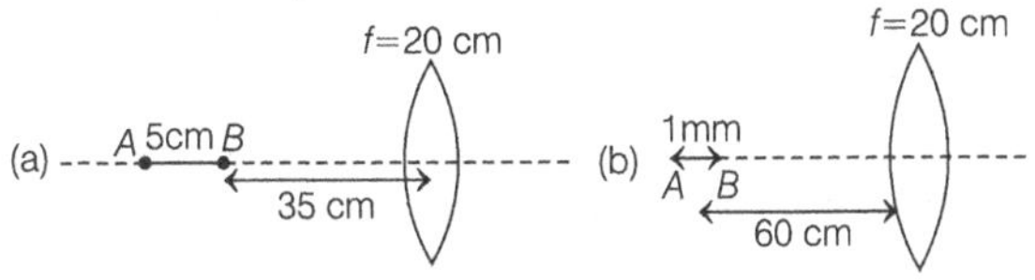

7 A point object is placed on the principal axis of a convex lens ($f = 15$ cm) at a distance of 30 cm from it. A glass plate ($\mu = 1.50$) of thickness 1 cm is placed on the other side of the lens perpendicular to the axis. Locate the image of the point object.

8 A convex lens is made up of three different materials as shown in the figure. For a point object placed on its axis, how many images will be formed?

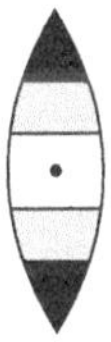

9 A point source of light is kept at a distance of 150 cm from a converging lens, on its optical axis. The focal length of the lens is 100 cm and its diameter is 3 cm. A screen is placed on the other side of the lens, perpendicular to the axis of lens, at a distance 200 cm from it. Then, find the area of the illuminated part of the screen (Assume all rays incident on lens as paraxial)

3.5 Displacement Method to Find Focal Length

1 A convex lens is placed between a fixed object and a fixed screen. The distance between the object and screen is 1 m. The real images of the object are formed on the screen for two successive positions separated by a distance of 60 cm. Find the focal length of the lens.

2 A convex lens makes a real image 4 cm long on a screen. When, the lens is shifted to a new position without disturbing the object or the screen, we again get real image on the screen which is 9 cm long. What is the length of the object?

3 The distance between an object and a screen is 270 cm. A lens is moved between the object and screen to find position of lens such that a real image is formed on the screen. The distance between two such positions (*P* and *Q*) of lens is found to be *x*. On changing distance between object and screen to 375 cm, distance *PQ* changes to $5x/2$. Find the value of focal length of the lens.

3.6 Velocity of Images

1 An object is placed at a distance of 0.4 m from a lens having focal length 0.3 m. The object is moving towards the lens at a speed of 0.01 m/s. Find the rates of change of position of image and lateral magnification of image.

2 A point object *O* is moving with velocity 1 cm/s and lens is moving with velocity 2 cm/s as shown in figure. Find the velocity of the image, when the object is 15 cm away from lens.

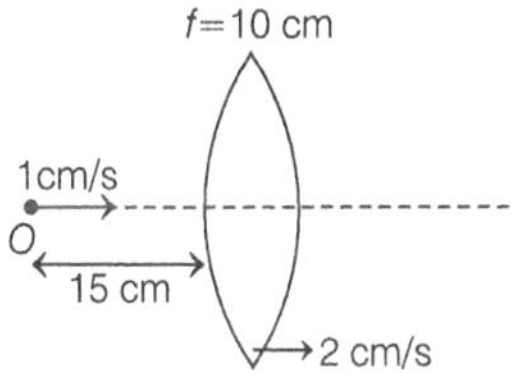

3 A point object *O* is moving with velocity 1 cm/s perpendicular to the principal axis as shown in figure. Find the velocity of the image, when the object is 15 cm away from lens.

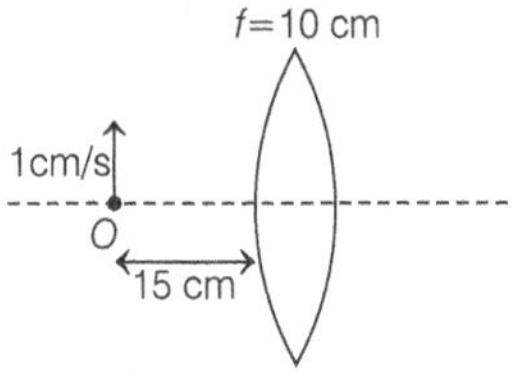

3.7 Combination of Lenses

1 A converging and diverging lens are separated by 25 cm. Find the position of final image formed of point object *O*.

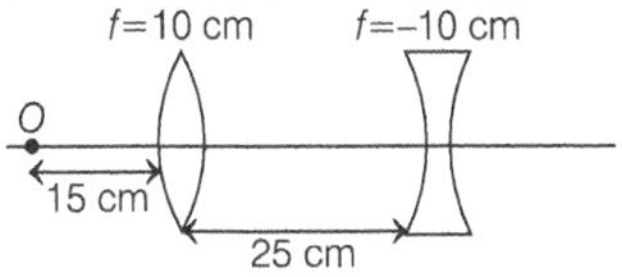

2 An object is placed 15 cm in a front of a converging lens of focal length 10 cm. It is required to produce an image on a screen 40 cm from the lens on the opposite side to the object. This is to be achieved by placing a second lens mid-way between the first lens and the screen. What type of lens and of what focal length should be used for this purpose?

3 A converging lens of 20 cm focal length is arranged coaxially with a diverging lens of focal length 8 cm. A point object lies on the same side as the converging lens and very far away on the axis.

(a) What is the smallest possible distance between the lenses if the combination is to form a real image?
(b) If the lens are placed 6 cm apart, what is the position and value of the final image of the distant object?

4 Consider a beam expander which consists of two converging lenses of focal lengths 40 cm and 100 cm having a common optical axis. A laser beam of diameter 4 mm is incident on the 40 cm focal length lens. Find the diameter of the final beam. (see figure)

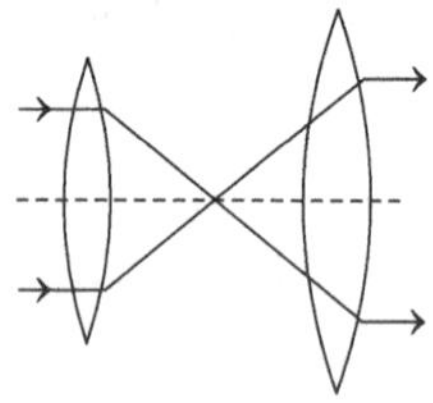

5 In the figure shown a converging lens and a diverging lens of focal lengths 20 cm and –5 cm respectively are separated by a distance such that a parallel beam of light of intensity 100 W/m^2 incident on the converging lens comes out as parallel beam from the diverging lens. What should be the separation between the lens? Also find the intensity of the outgoing beam.

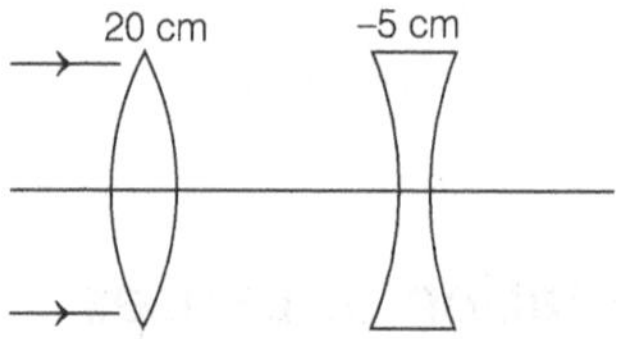

6 Space between two identical equiconcave lenses ($\mu = 1.5$) of radius of curvature 10 cm is filled with water $\left(\mu = \frac{4}{3}\right)$. Find out the equivalent focal length of the combination shown in the figure. Surrounding medium is air.

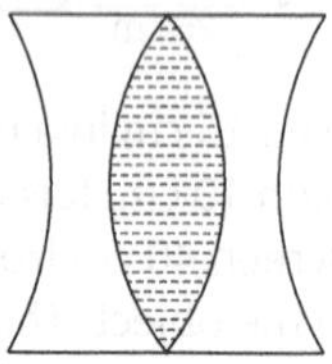

7 A point object is placed at a distance of 15 cm from a convex lens. The image is formed on the other side at a distance of 30 cm from the lens. When a concave lens is placed in contact with the convex lens, the image shifts away further by 30 cm. Calculate the focal lengths of the two lenses.

8 Two thin lenses, when in contact, produce a combination of power +10 D. When they are 0.25 m apart, the power reduces to +6 D. Find the focal length of the lenses.

9 A convex lens of focal length 25 cm and a concave lens of focal length 20 cm are mounted coaxially separated by a distance *d*. For what value of *d* will the power of the combination be zero?

3.8 Combination of Lens and Mirror

1 See the figure. Find the position of final image formed.

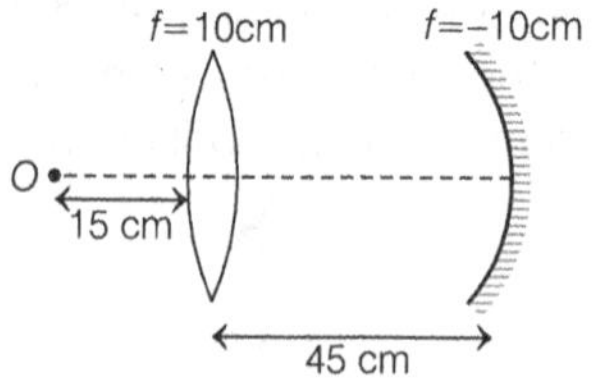

2 What should be the value of *d*, so that image is formed on the object itself?

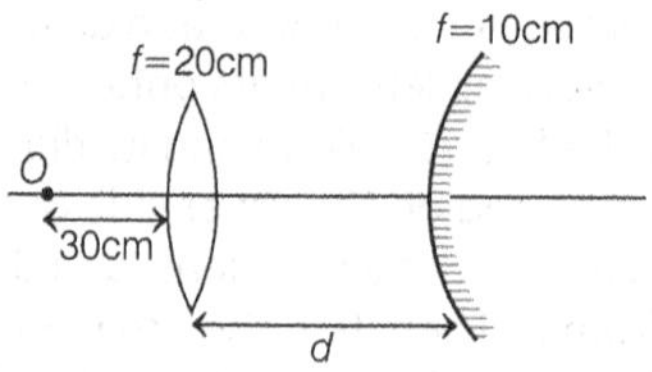

3 A diverging lens of focal length 20 cm is placed coaxially 5 cm towards left of a converging mirror of focal length 10 cm .Where should an object be placed towards left of the lens, so that a real image is formed at the object itself?

4 A converging lens and a diverging mirror are placed at a separation of 15 cm. The focal length of the lens is 25 cm and that of the mirror is 40 cm. Where should a point source be placed between the lens and the mirror, so that the light, after getting reflected by the mirror and then getting refracted by the lens, comes out parallel to the principal axis?

5 A converging lens and a converging mirror are placed with their principal axis coinciding. Their separation equals 40 cm. A point source *S* is placed on the principal axis at a distance of 12 cm from the lens as shown in the figure. It is found that the final beam comes out parallel to the principal axis. Focal length of the lens equals 15 cm. Find the focal length of the mirror.

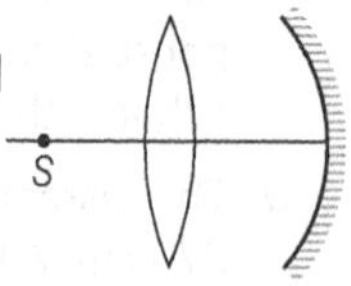

3.9 Silvered Lens

1 A pin is placed 10 cm infront of convex lens of focal length 20 cm made of material of refractive index 1.5 . The surface of the lens farther away from the pin is silvered and has a radius of curvature 22 cm. Determine the position of the final image.

2 A planoconvex lens, when silvered on the plane side, behaves like a concave mirror of focal length 30 cm. When it is silvered on the convex side, it behaves like a concave mirror of focal length 10 cm. Find the refractive index of the material of the lens.

3 The convex surface of a thin concavo-convex lens of glass of refractive index 1.5 has a radius of curvature 20 cm. The concave surface has a radius of curvature 60 cm. The convex side is silvered and placed on a horizontal surface as shown in figure.

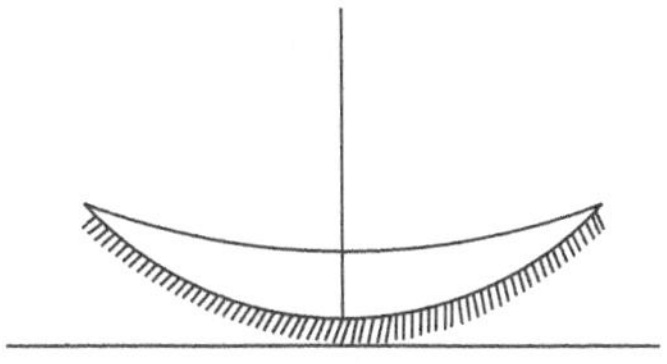

(a) Where should a pin be placed on the axis, so that its image is formed at the same place?

(b) If the concave part is filled with water $\left(\mu = \frac{4}{3}\right)$, find the distance through which the pin should be moved, so that the image of the pin again coincides with the pin.

LEVEL 02 JEE Main Level

Single Choice Correct Questions

1 A spherical surface of radius R separates two medium of refractive indices μ_1 and μ_2, as shown in Fig. Where should an object be placed in the medium 1, so that a real image is formed in medium 2 at the same distance?

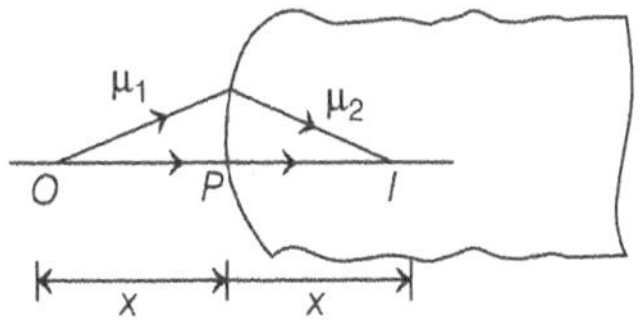

(a) $\left(\frac{\mu_2 - \mu_1}{\mu_2 + \mu_1}\right)R$ (b) $\left(\frac{\mu_2 + \mu_1}{\mu_2 - \mu_1}\right)R$

(c) $\left(\frac{\mu_2 + \mu_1}{\mu_2}\right)R$ (d) $\left(\frac{\mu_2}{\mu_2 + \mu_1}\right)R$

2 The image for the converging beam after refraction through the curved surface is formed at

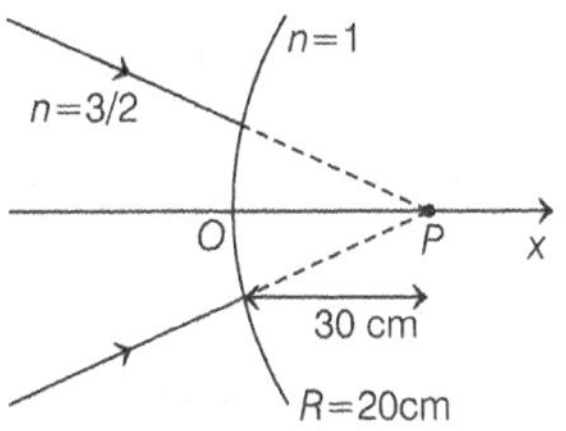

(a) $x = 40$ cm (b) $x = \frac{40}{3}$ cm

(c) $x = -\frac{40}{3}$ cm (d) $x = \frac{180}{7}$ cm

3 There is a small black dot at the centre C of a solid glass sphere of refractive index μ. When seen from outside, the dot will appear to be located

(a) away from C for all values of μ

(b) at C for all values of μ

(c) at C for $\mu = 1.5$, but away from C for $\mu \neq 1.5$

(d) at C only for $\sqrt{2} \leq \mu \leq 1.5$

4 In the figure shown a point object O is placed in air. A spherical boundary of radius of curvature 1.0 m separates two media. AB is principal axis. The refractive index above AB is 1.6 and below AB is 2.0. The separation between the images formed due to refraction at spherical surface is

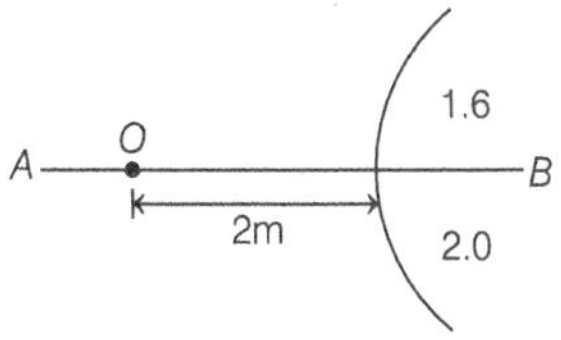

(a) 12 m (b) 20 m (c) 14 m (d) 10 m

5 A paraxial beam is incident on a glass ($\mu = 1.5$) hemisphere of radius $R = 6$ cm in air as shown. The distance of point of convergence F from the plane surface of hemisphere is

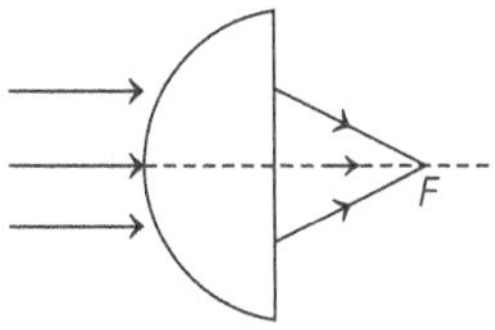

(a) 12 cm (b) 5.4 cm (c) 18 cm (d) 8 cm

6 A small object of height 0.5 cm is placed in front of a convex surface of glass ($\mu = 1.5$) of radius of curvature 10 cm. Find the height of the image formed in glass.

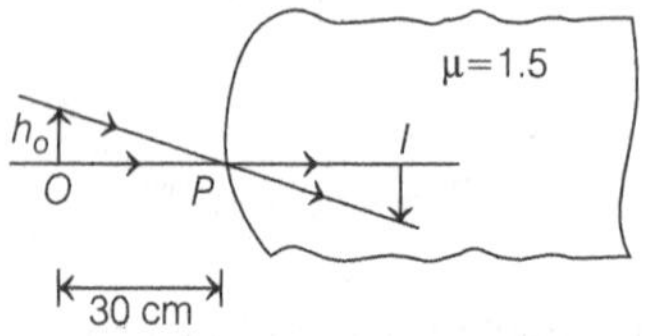

(a) 2 cm (b) 1 cm (c) 3 cm (d) 4 cm

7 A plastic hemisphere has a radius of curvature of 8 cm and an index of refraction of 1.6. On the axis half-way between the plane surface and the spherical one (4 cm from each) is a small object *O*. The distance between the two images, when viewed along the axis from the two sides of the hemisphere is approximately.

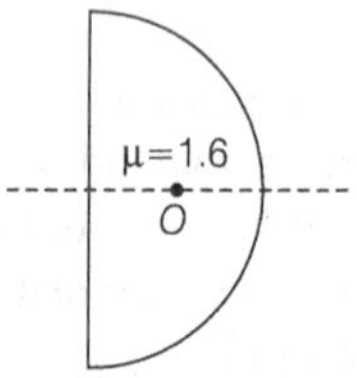

(a) 1.0 cm (b) 1.5 cm (c) 3.75 cm (d) 2.5 cm

8 A planoconcave lens is placed on paper on which a flower is drawn. How far above its actual position does the flower appear to an observer looking down from top?

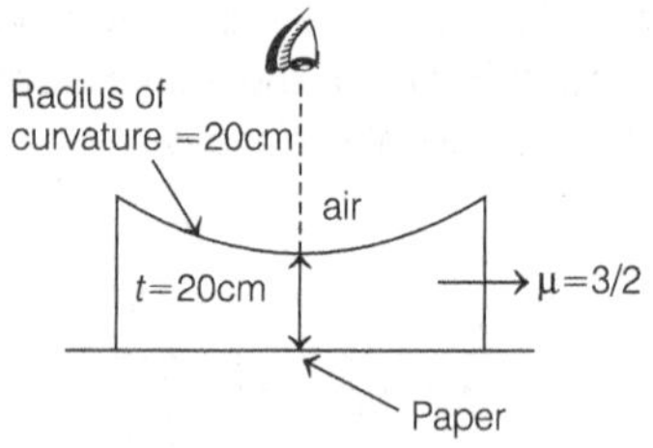

(a) 15 cm (b) 10 cm
(c) 50 cm (d) None of these

9 A convexo-concave diverging lens is made of glass of refractive index 1.5 and focal length 24 cm. Radius of curvature for one surface is double that of the other. Then, radii of curvature for the two surfaces are (in cm)

(a) 6, 12 (b) 12, 24 (c) 3, 6 (d) 18, 36

10 The focal length of a lens of refractive index 3/2 is 10 cm in air. The focal length of that lens in a medium of refractive index 7/5 is

(a) –70 cm (b) 10/7 cm
(c) 70 cm (d) None of these

11 A concave lens of glass, refractive index 1.5, has both surfaces of same radius of curvature *R*. On immersion in a medium of refractive index 1.75, it will behave as a

(a) convergent lens of focal length 3.5 *R*
(b) convergent lens of focal length 3.0 *R*
(c) divergent lens of focal length 3.5 *R*
(d) divergent lens of focal length 3.0 *R*

12 The diagram shows an equiconvex lens. What should be the condition on the refractive indices, so that the lens become diverging?

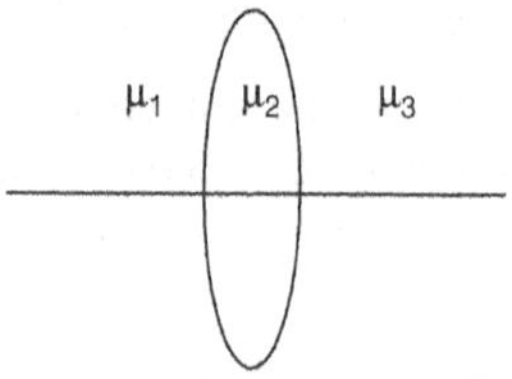

(a) $2\mu_2 > \mu_1 - \mu_3$ (b) $2\mu_2 < \mu_1 + \mu_3$
(c) $2\mu_2 > 2\mu_1 - \mu_3$ (d) $2\mu_2 > \mu_1 + \mu_3$

13. An equiconcave lens has focal length 10 cm in air. The refractive index of the material of the lens is 1.5. What should be the refractive index of the medium on the other side of the lens, so that the image of a real object placed at a distance 10 cm from the lens is formed at infinity?

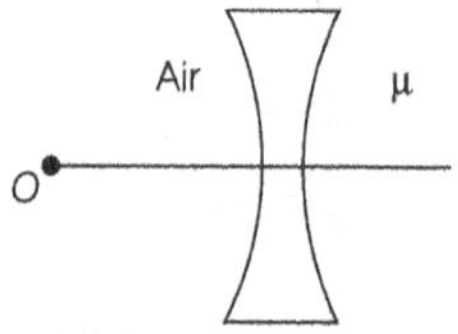

(a) 1.8 (b) 2.5
(c) 2 (d) 3

14. For a diverging lens that has focal length of magnitude *f*, the image size was identical to that of the object. How is this possible?

(a) The object was virtual and located a distance 2*f* from the lens.
(b) The object was virtual and located a distance *f* from the lens.
(c) The object was real and located a distance 2*f* from the lens.
(d) It is not possible.

15 The diameter of the sun subtends an angle of 0.5° at the surface of the earth. A converging lens of focal length 100 cm is used to provide an image of the sun on to a screen. The diameter of the image formed is nearly

(a) 1 mm (b) 3 mm
(c) 5 mm (d) 9 mm

16 When the object is at distances u_1 and u_2 the images formed by the same lens are real and virtual respectively and of the same size. Then, focal length of the lens is

(a) $\frac{1}{2}\sqrt{u_1 u_2}$ (b) $\frac{u_1 + u_2}{2}$ (c) $\sqrt{u_1 u_2}$ (d) $2(u_1 + u_2)$

17 A point object O is placed on the principal axis of a convex lens of focal length $f = 20$ cm at a distance of 40 cm to the left of it. The diameter of the lens is 10 cm. An eye is placed 60 cm to right of the lens and a distance h below the principal axis. The maximum value of h to see the image is

(a) 0 (b) 2.5 cm (c) 5 cm (d) 10 cm

18 A thin linear object of size 1 mm is kept along the principal axis of a convex lens of focal length 10 cm. The object is at 15 cm from the lens. The length of the image is

(a) 1 mm (b) 4 mm (c) 2 mm (d) 8 mm

19 The image of an illuminated square is obtained on a screen with the help of a converging lens. The distance of the square from the lens is 40 cm. The area of the image is 9 times that of the square. The focal length of the lens is

(a) 30 cm (b) 36 cm
(c) 27 cm (d) None of these

20 A real image of number 19 written on a card board placed normal to the optical axis of a converging lens is obtained on a screen. The image will look like

(a) 16 (b) 1∂ (c) 61 (d) ∂1

21 A thin lens of focal length f and its aperture diameter d, forms a real image of intensity I. Now the central part of the aperture upto diameter $(d/2)$ is blocked by an opaque paper. The focal length and image intensity would change to

(a) $\frac{f}{2}, \frac{I}{2}$ (b) $f, \frac{I}{4}$ (c) $\frac{3f}{4}, \frac{I}{2}$ (d) $f, \frac{3I}{4}$

22 A virtual erect image by a diverging lens is represented by (u, v, f are coordinates)

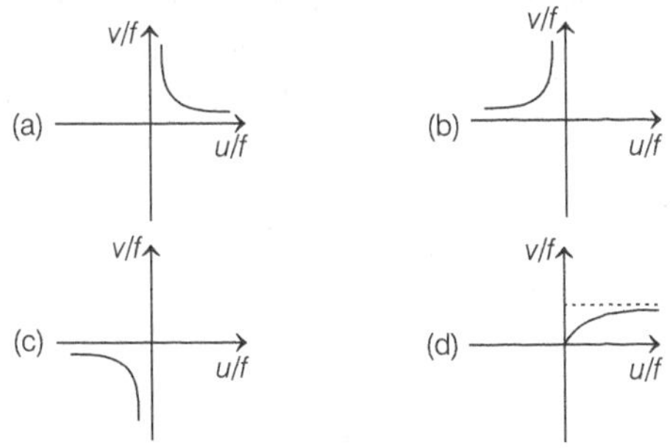

23 The graph between object coordinate u and image coordinate v for a lens is given below. The focal length of the lens is

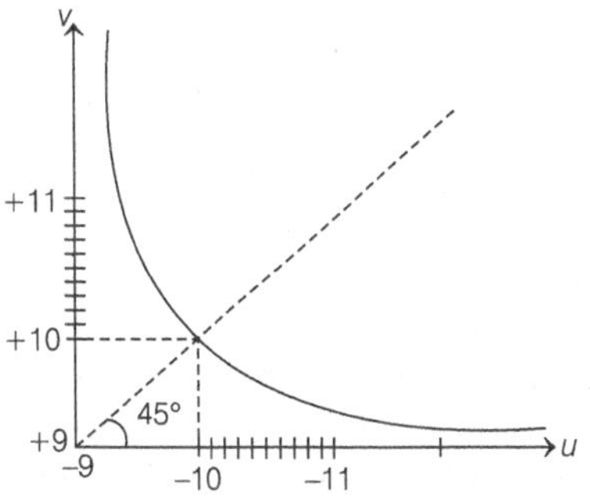

(a) 5 ± 0.1 (b) 5 ± 0.05 (c) 0.5 ± 0.1 (d) 0.5 ± 0.05

24 The image of an object, formed by a planoconvex lens at a distance of 8 m behind the lens, is real and is one-third the size of the object. The wavelength of light inside the lens is 2/3 times the wavelength in free space. The radius of the curved surface of the lens is

(a) 1 m (b) 2 m (c) 3 m (d) 6 m

25 The image of the sun is obtained on a screen with a convex lens of diameter 3π cm and focal length 45 cm. How many times will the intensity produced by sun's image be greater than that coming directly from the sun if the angular diameter of the sun is 30 min?

(a) 450 (b) 288
(c) 576 (d) None of these

26 A convex lens focuses a distant object 40 cm from it on a screen placed 10 cm away from it. A glass plate ($\mu = 1.5$) and of thickness 3 cm is inserted between the lens and the screen. Where should the object be placed, so that its image is again focused on the screen?

(a) 62 cm (b) 72 cm (c) 52 cm (d) 42 cm

27 Distance of an object from the first focus of an equiconvex lens is 10 cm and the distance of its real image from second focus is 40 cm. The focal length of the lens is

(a) 25 cm (b) 10 cm
(c) 20 cm (d) 40 cm

28 The distance between an object and the screen is 100 cm. A lens produces an image on the screen when the lens is placed at either of the positions 40 cm apart. The power of the lens is nearly

(a) 3 D (b) 5 D
(c) 2 D (d) 9 D

29 If m_1 and m_2 be the magnifications for two positions of the lens between the object and the screen and d the distance between the two positions of the lens, the focal length of the lens is

(a) $\left(\frac{m_1 - m_2}{d}\right)$ (b) $\frac{d}{(m_1 - m_2)}$

(c) $(m_1 - m_2)\,d$ (d) $\frac{m_1 m_2}{d^2}$

30 An object O is kept in air in front of a thin plano convex lens of radius of curvature 10 cm. Its refractive index is 3/2 and the medium towards right of plane surface is water of refractive index 4/3. What should be the distance x of the object, so that the rays become parallel finally?

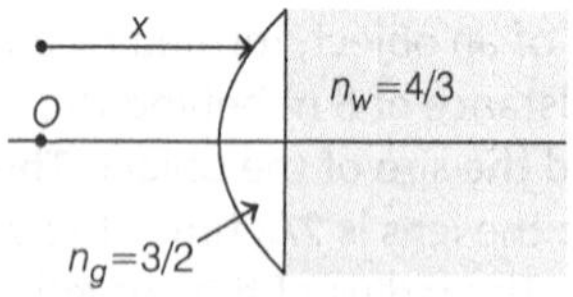

(a) 5 cm (b) 10 cm (c) 20 cm (d) None of these

31 Focal length of a thin convex lens is 30 cm, At a distance of 10 cm from the lens, there is a plane refracting surface beyond which the refractive index is 3/2. Where will the parallel rays incident on lens converge?

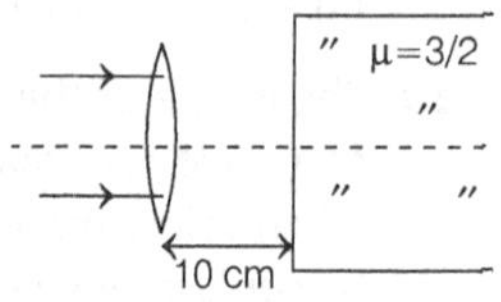

(a) At a distance of 60 cm from the lens
(b) At a distance of 50 cm from the lens
(c) At a distance of 70/3 cm from the lens
(d) At a distance of 40 cm from the lens

32 A real object is placed 1 cm above the optical axis of a convex lens of focal length 40 cm. The object distance is 60 cm. If the object now starts moving perpendicularly away from the optical axis with a speed = 10 cm/s, the speed of the image is

(a) 5 cm/s (b) 10 cm/s (c) 20 cm/s (d) 40 cm/s

33 In the diagram shown, the lens is moving towards the object with a velocity v and the object is also moving towards the lens with the same speed. What is the speed of the image with respect to earth, when the object is at a distance $2f$ from the lens? (f is the focal length.)

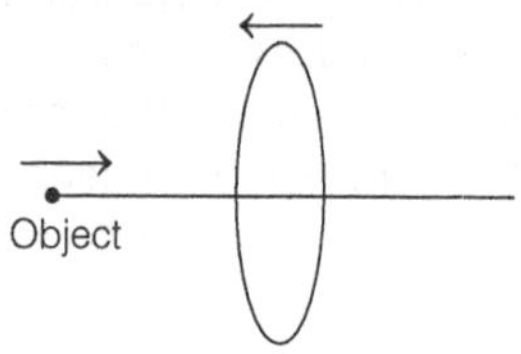

(a) $2v$ (b) $4v$ (c) $3v$ (d) v

34 An object starts moving at an angle of 45° with the principal axis as shown in the figure in front of a biconvex lens of focal length +10 cm. If θ denotes the angle at which image starts to move with principal axis then

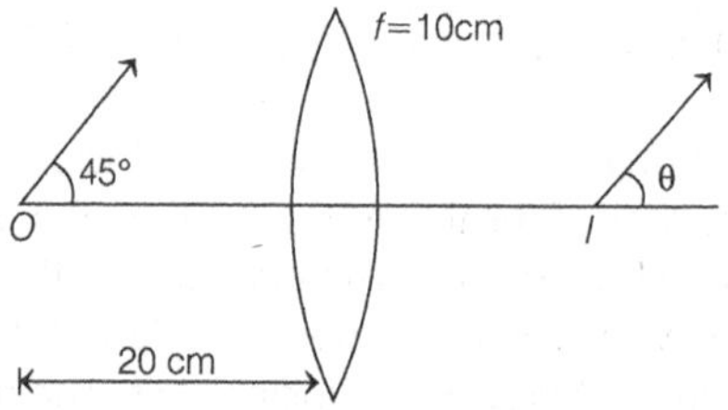

(a) $\theta = \frac{3\pi}{4}$ (b) $\theta = \frac{\pi}{2}$ (c) $\theta = \frac{\pi}{4}$ (d) $\theta = -\frac{\pi}{4}$

35 An object approaches a fixed diverging lens with a constant velocity from infinity along the principal axis. The relative velocity between object and its image will be

(a) increasing (b) decreasing
(c) first increases then decreases
(d) first decreases then increases.

36 Two convex lenses of focal length f and $2f$ are arranged to have their foci at the same point as shown in the figure. A beam of parallel light of diameter 1 cm is incident into the first lens. The beam emerging from the second lens is

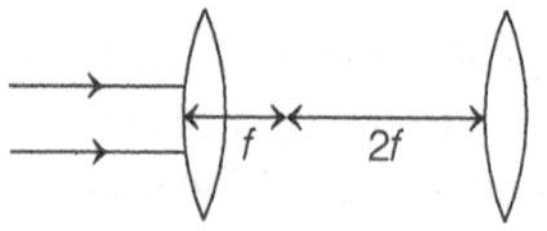

(a) diverging (b) converging
(c) parallel of diameter 0.5 cm
(d) parallel of diameter 2 cm

37 A thin convex lens of focal length 30 cm forms an image 2 cm high, of an object at infinity. A thin concave lens of focal length 20 cm is placed 26 cm from the convex lens on the side of the image. The height of the image now is

(a) 1.0 cm (b) 1.25 cm (c) 2 cm (d) 2.5 cm

38 What should be the value of distance d, so that final image is formed on the object itself? (focal lengths of the lenses are written on the lenses).

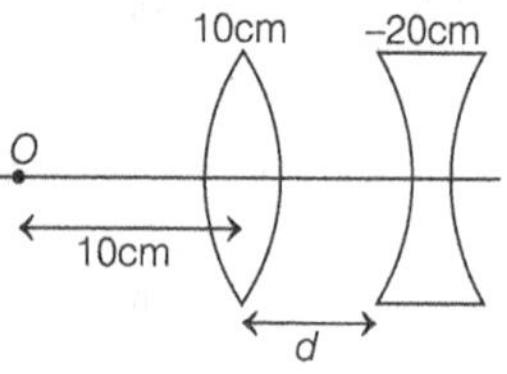

(a) 10 cm (b) 20 cm
(c) 5 cm (d) None of these

39 A plano convex glass lens ($\mu_g = 3/2$) of radius of curvature $R = 10$ cm is placed at a distance of b from a concave lens of focal length 20 cm. What should be the distance a of a point object O from the plano convex lens, so that the position of final image is independent of b ?

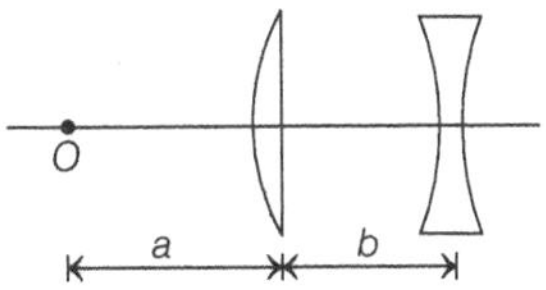

(a) 40 cm (b) 60 cm (c) 30 cm (d) 20 cm

40 Two diverging lenses are kept as shown in figure. The final image formed will be

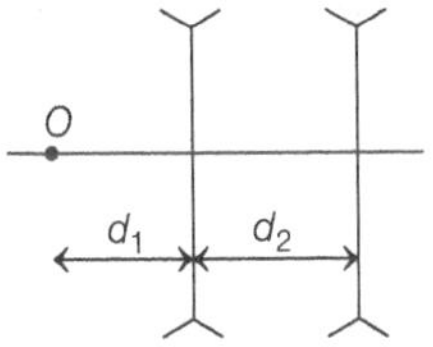

(a) virtual for any value of d_1 and d_2
(b) real for any value of d_1 and d_2
(c) virtual or real depends on d_1 and d_2 only
(d) virtual or real depends on d_1 and d_2 and also on the focal lengths of the lens

41 Consider a system of two thin lenses as shown in figure. An object of height 1 cm is placed at 40 cm from convex lens. Mark the correct option related to final image formed by the two lens system

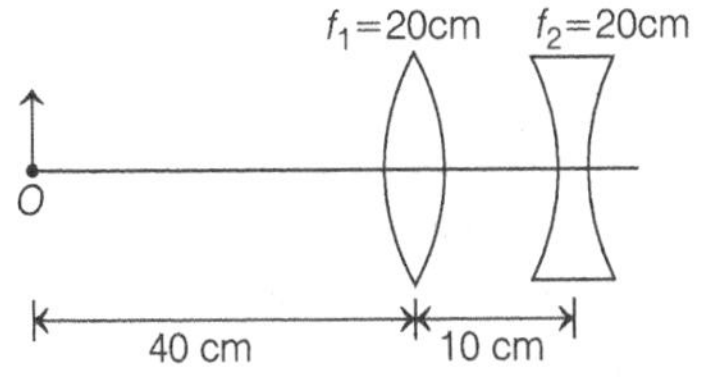

(a) Final image is formed at 60 cm on right of concave lens and is 2 cm in size.
(b) Final image is formed at 60 cm on left side of concave lens and is 2 cm in size.
(c) Final image is formed at 12 cm on the right of concave lens and is 0.4 cm in size.
(d) Final image is formed at 12 cm on the left of concave lens and is 0.4 cm in size.

42 A thin symmetric doubleconvex lens of power P is cut into three parts A, B and C as shown. The power of

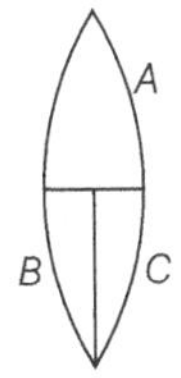

(a) A is P (b) A is $2P$ (c) B is P (d) B is $\frac{P}{4}$

43 An equiconcave diverging lens of focal length F is cut into two equal halves. The two halves are turned around and joined with some liquid between them. The lens obtained is converging with focal length F. If the refractive index of the liquid is 3, then what is the refractive index of the lens?

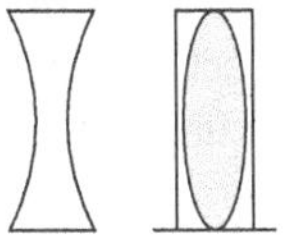

(a) 4 (b) 2 (c) 5 (d) 1.5

44 Two thin lenses have a combined power of +10 D. When separated by 20 cm, their equivalent power is + 6.25 D. Their individual powers, in D, are
(a) 3.5 and 6.5 (b) 5.0 and 5.0
(c) 7.5 and 2.5 (d) 9.0 and 1.0

45 A symmetrical converging convex lens of focal length 10 cm and diverging concave symmetrical lens of focal length −20 cm are cut from the middle and perpendicularly and symmetrically to their principal axis. The parts thus obtained are arranged as shown in the figure. The focal length of this arrangement will be

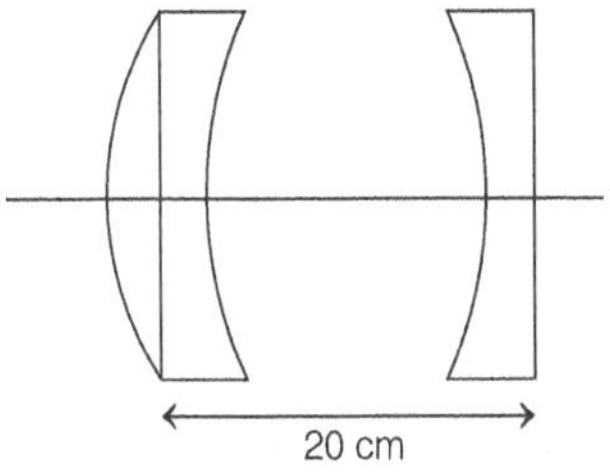

(a) ∞ (b) 20 cm (c) 40 cm (d) 80 cm

46 A concave convex lens has an index of refraction 1.5 and the radii of curvature of its surfaces are 10 cm and 20 cm. The concave surface is upwards and it is filled with oil $\mu = 1.6$. Find the focal length of oil glass combination.
(a) 18.18 cm (b) 15 cm (c) 22 cm (d) 17.5 cm

47 A point object O is placed at a distance of 20 cm from a convex lens of focal length 10 cm as shown in figure. At what distance x from the lens should a convex mirror of focal length 5 cm, be placed, so that final image coincides with the object?

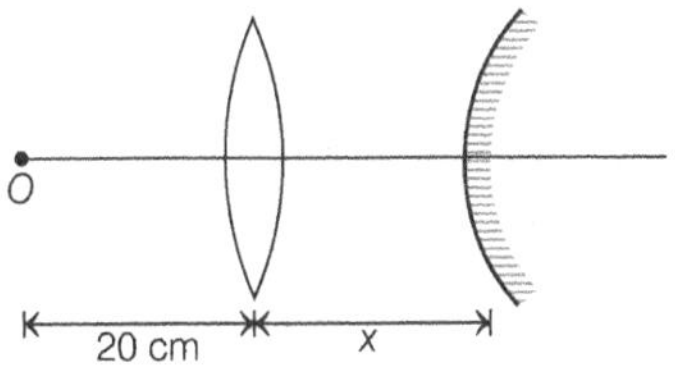

(a) 10 cm
(b) 15 cm
(c) 40 cm
(d) Final image can never coincide with the object in the given conditions.

48 A convex lens of focal length 40 cm is held coaxially above a concave mirror of focal length 18 cm. A luminous point object placed *d* cm above the lens on its axis gives rise to final image coincident with itself. Then, *d* is equal to

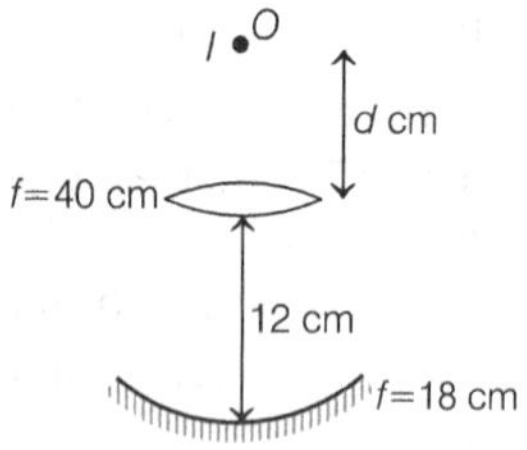

(a) 15 (b) 18 (c) 24 (d) 30

49 A diverging lens of focal length 10 cm is placed 10 cm in front of a plane mirror as shown in the figure. Light from a very far away source falls on the lens. The final image is at a distance

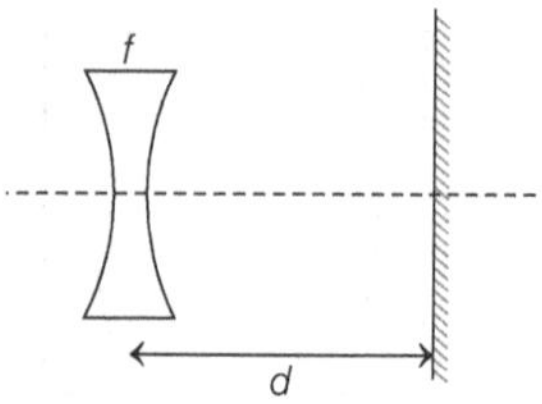

(a) 20 cm behind the mirror
(b) 7.5 cm infront of the mirror
(c) 7.5 cm behind the mirror
(d) 2.5 cm infront of the mirror

50 A point object is placed at distance of 20 cm from a thin planoconvex lens of focal length 15 cm. The plane surface of the lens is now silvered. The image created by the system is at

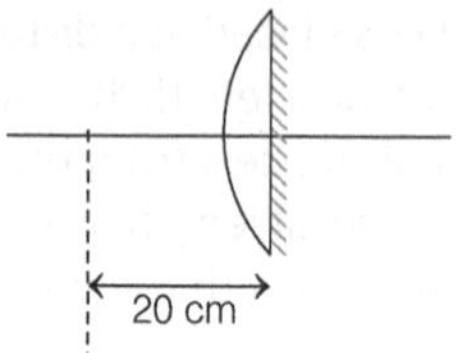

(a) 60 cm to the left of the system.
(b) 60 cm to the right of the system.
(c) 12 cm to the left of the system.
(d) 12 cm to the right of the system.

51 A planoconvex lens, when silvered at its plane surface is equivalent to a concave mirror of focal length 28 cm. When its curved surface is silvered and the plane surface not silvered, it is equivalent to a concave mirror of focal length 10 cm, then the refractive index of the material of the lens is

(a) $\frac{9}{8}$ (b) $\frac{14}{9}$
(c) $\frac{17}{9}$ (d) None of these

52 A thin hollow equiconvex lens, silvered at the back, converges a parallel beam of light at a distance of 0.2 m in front of it. Where, will it converge the same light if filled with water having $\mu = \frac{4}{3}$?

(a) 10 cm (b) 22 cm (c) 12 cm (d) 14 cm

Numerical Value Questions

1 The aperture of a planoconvex lens has its diameter 8 cm and its maximum thickness is 4 mm. If the speed of light in the material of the lens is 2×10^8 m/s, determine the focal length (in cm) of the lens.

2 Two objects are placed on the principal axis of a thin converging lens. One is 10 cm from the lens and the other is on the other side of the lens at a distance of 40 cm from the lens. The images of both objects are in the same plane. What is the focal length of the lens (in cm)?

3 A lens forms the image of sun on a screen 30 cm away. How far (in cm) from the lens should a second lens of focal length 30 cm be placed, so that the screen has to be moved 8 cm towards the first lens for the new image to be in focus?

4 Along the main optical axis of a converging lens with focal length $f = 5$ cm, two fireflies are moving towards each other. They are on opposite sides of the lens. The speed of the fireflies is the same $v = 2$ cm/s. After what minimum time (in second) does the first firefly meet the image of the second, if at the initial time they were at distances 20 cm and 30 cm from the lens respectively? Round off to nearest integer.

5 A lens is held directly above a coin lying on a table and forms an image of it. After the lens has been moved vertically a distance equal to its focal length, it forms another image of the coin equal in size to the previous image. If the diameter of the coin is 4.0 cm, what is the diameter (in cm) of the image?

6 Find distance l (in cm) of source from lens, so that final beam of light is parallel to the principal axis. Distance between lens and plane mirror is 10 cm. Focal length of the lens is 30 cm.

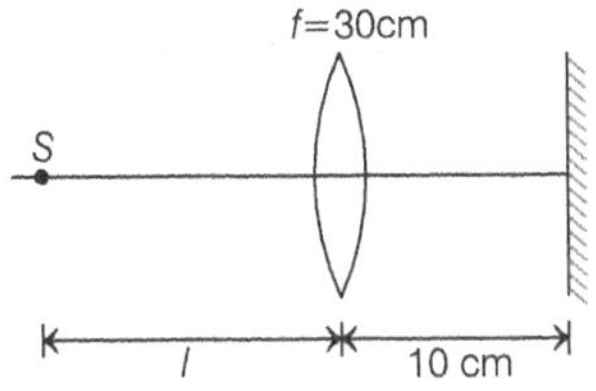

7 A point object is approaching a converging lens ($f = 100$ cm) along its optical axis, with a constant acceleration $= 10\ \text{cm/s}^2$. What is the magnitude of acceleration (in cm/s^2) of the image at the moment the speed of the object is 20 cm/s and its distance from the lens is 75 cm?

8 A double convex lens forms a real image of an object on a screen which is fixed. Now the lens is given a constant velocity $v = 1$ m/s along its axis and away from the screen. For the purpose of forming the image always on the screen, the object is also required to be given an appropriate velocity. Find the velocity of object (in m/s) at the instant its size is double the size of image.

9 A beam of light parallel to the principal axis is focused on a screen with the help of lens, forming a circular spot with a diameter of 1 cm. If we put a plane parallel glass plate of thickness 3 cm and refractive index 1.5 between the lens and the screen, the diameter of the bright spot on the screen increases. The diameter of the lens is 2 cm and focal length 10 cm. Find the new diameter (in mm).

10 An intense beam parallel to the principal axis is incident on a convex lens. Multiple extra images $F_1, F_2, F_3, \ldots\ldots$ are formed due to feeble internal reflections called flare spots as shown in the figure. The radii of curvature of the lens are 30 cm and 60 cm and the refraction index is 1.5. Find the distance (in cm) of the first flare spot from the lens.

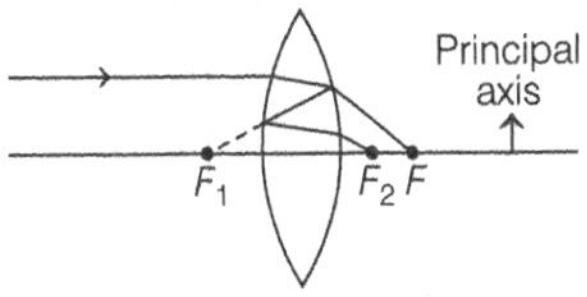

11 Figure A shows two identical planoconvex lenses in contact as shown. The combination has focal length 24 cm. Figure B shows the same with a liquid introduced between them. The refractive index of glass of the lenses is 1.50 and that of the liquid is 1.60.

If focal length of the system figure B is $-f$ cm, then find f.

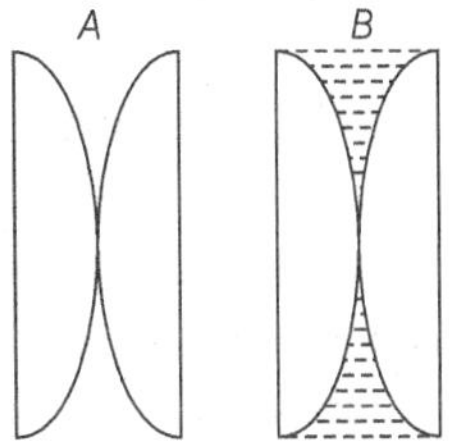

12 A parallel paraxial beam of light is incident on the arrangement as shown. $\mu_A = 3/2, \mu_B = 4/3$, the two spherical surfaces are very close and each has a radius of curvature 10 cm. Find the distance (in cm) from the lens, where the rays are focussed.

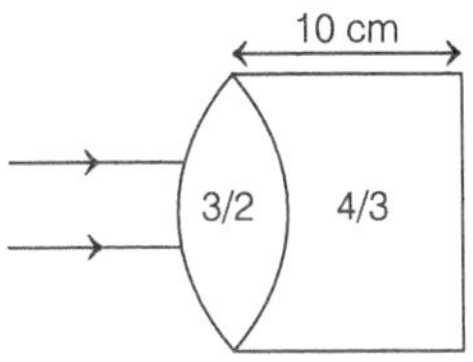

13 A person is standing at a point P, at a distance of 250 cm from a flat mirror, at the instant shown in the figure. A converging lens of focal length 50 cm is stationary and placed between the mirror and P as shown in figure. The flat mirror now starts moving towards the right with a constant velocity = 9 m/s. What will be the magnitude of velocity (in m/s) of his image as seen by the person, at the moment when the mirror just starts moving?

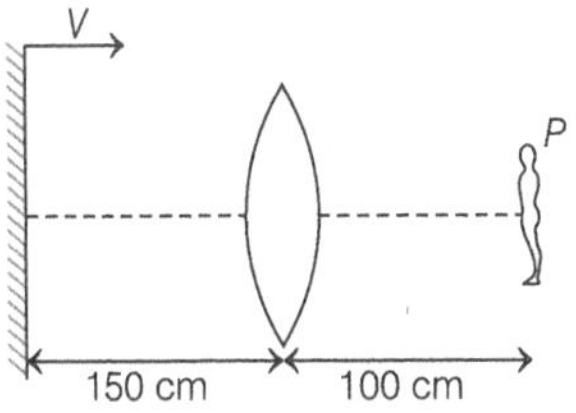

14 A thin concavo-concave lens is surrounded by two different liquids A and B as shown in figure. The system is supported by a plane mirror at the bottom. Refractive index of A, lens and B are 9/5, 3/2 and 4/3 respectively. The radius of curvature of the surfaces of the lens are same and equal to 10 cm. At what distance (in cm) should an object be placed in front of this system, so that final image is formed on the object itself?

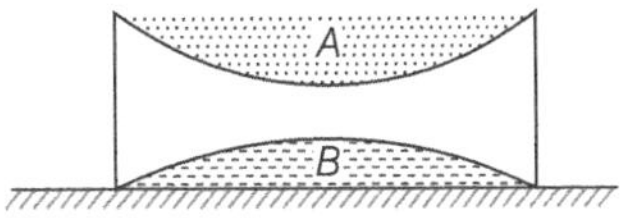

15 One side of radius of curvature $r_1 = 120$ cm of a convex lens of focal length $f_1 = 40$ cm is silvered. It is placed on a horizontal surface with silvered surface in contact with it. Another convex lens of focal length $f_2 = 20$ cm is fixed coaxially $d = 10$ cm above. A luminous point object O on the axis gives rise to an image coincident on it. Find its height (in cm) above the upper lens.

LEVEL 03 JEE Advanced Level

Single Choice Correct Questions

1 In the given situation, a spherical transparent surface of radius R is placed. The refractive index of sphere is such that image for an object kept at distance R is formed at the same distance of the opposite side. What is refractive index of sphere?

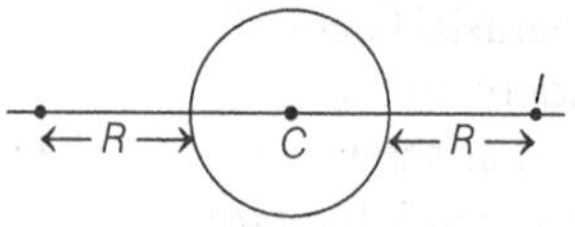

(a) 1.5 (b) 1.75 (c) 1.25 (d) 2

2 A beam of diameter d is incident on a glass hemisphere as shown. If the radius of curvature of the hemisphere is very large in comparison to d, then the diameter of the beam at the base of the hemisphere will be

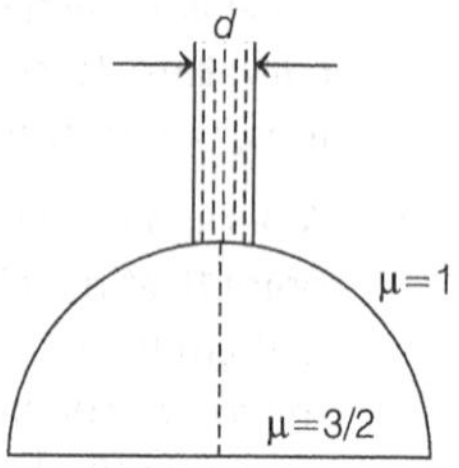

(a) $\frac{3}{4}d$ (d) d (c) $\frac{d}{3}$ (d) $\frac{2}{3}d$

3. A hollow sphere of glass of refractive index n has a small mark M on its interior surface which is observed by an observer O from a point outside the sphere. C is centre of the sphere. The inner cavity (air) is concentric with the external surface and thickness of the glass is everywhere equal to the radius of the inner surface. Find the distance by which the mark will appear nearer than it really is, in terms of n and R assuming paraxial rays.

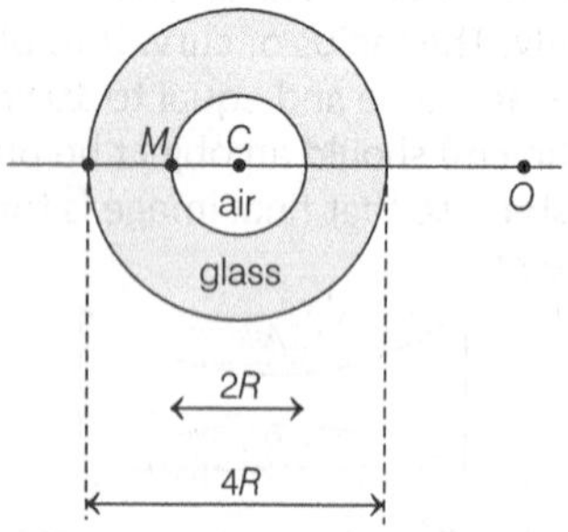

(a) $\frac{(n-1)R}{3n-1}$ (b) $\frac{(2n-1)R}{3n-1}$

(c) $\frac{(n-1)R}{3n-2}$ (d) $\frac{(2n-1)R}{3n-2}$

4 A quarter cylinder of radius R and refractive index 1.5 is placed on a table. A point object P is kept at a distance of mR from it.

Find the value of m for which a ray from P will emerge parallel to the table as shown in the figure.

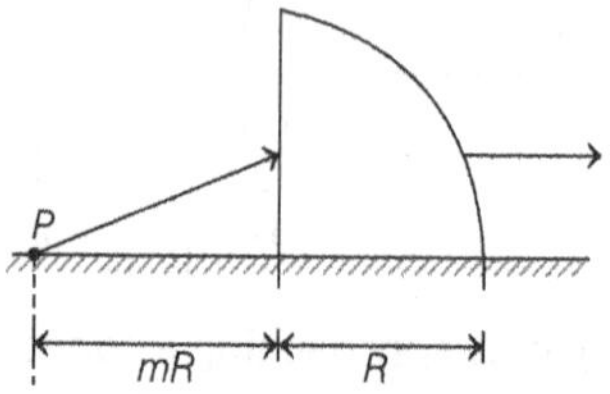

(a) $\frac{3}{4}$ (b) $\frac{4}{9}$ (c) $\frac{9}{4}$ (d) $\frac{4}{3}$

5 A glass hemisphere of refractive index $\frac{4}{3}$ and of radius 4 cm is placed on a plane mirror. A point object is placed on axis of this sphere at a distance d from O as shown. If the final image is formed at infinity, then find the value of d.

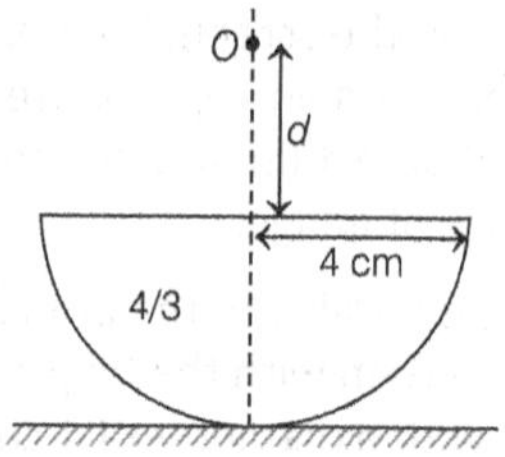

(a) 3 cm (b) 4 cm (c) 5 cm (d) 6 cm

6 The observer O sees the distance AB as infinitely large. If refractive index of liquid is μ_1 and that of glass is μ_2, then $\frac{\mu_1}{\mu_2}$ is

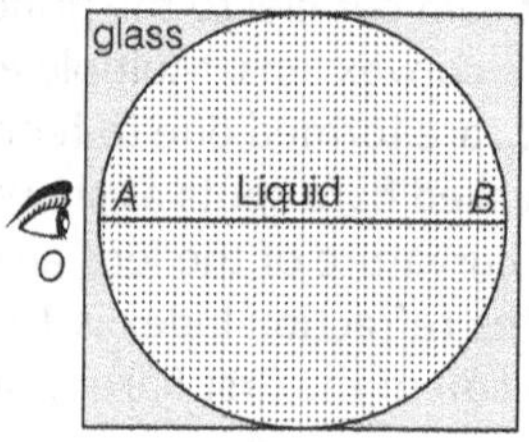

(a) 2 (b) $\frac{1}{2}$

(c) 4 (d) None of these

7 A spherical aquarium of radius 10 cm filled with water of refractive index $\frac{4}{3}$ is kept as shown. One half of aquarium is silvered and other half is smooth. The thickness of aquarium is negligible. A fish is moving towards left with a velocity 6 m/s.

An observer detects two images of the fish. Find the relative velocity between the two images of the fish as seen by the observer.

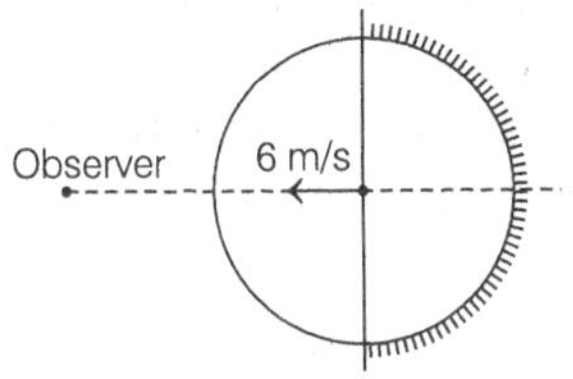

(a) 12 m/s (b) 8 m/s (c) 16 m/s (d) 0

8 In the figure shown for a equiconvex lens, if $f_1 = 30$ cm, then f_2 is equal to (here refractive indices of different mediums (μ) are shown in figure)

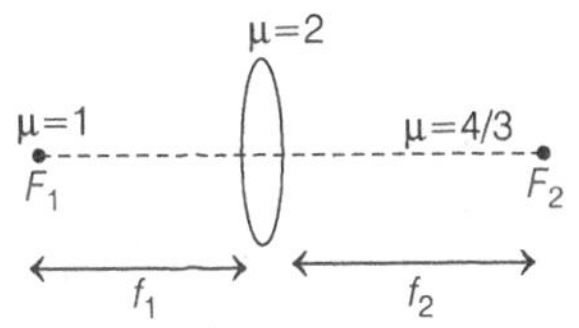

(a) 30 cm (b) 40 cm (c) 34 cm (d) 60 cm

9 The image of small electric bulb fixed on the wall of a room is to be obtained on the opposite wall 3 m away by means of large convex lens. What is the maximum possible focal length of the lens required for the purpose?

(a) 0.5 m (b) 0.75 m (c) 1.25 m (d) 1.5 m

10 The graph shows how the reciprocal of magnification $\left(\left|\frac{1}{m}\right|\right)$ produced by a converging thin lens varied with object distance u in displacement method. What was the focal length of the lens used?

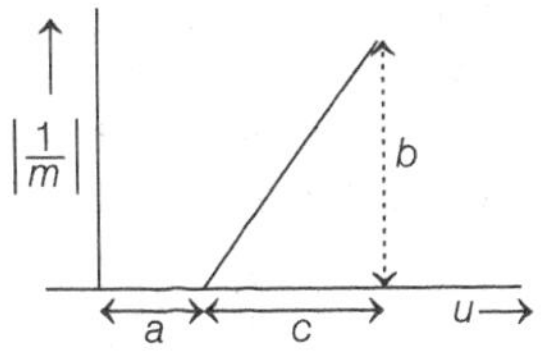

(a) $\frac{a}{b}$ (b) $\frac{bc}{a}$ (c) $\frac{c}{b}$ (d) $\frac{ab}{c}$

11 A convex lens of focal length f is placed somewhere in between an object and a screen. The distance between the object and the screen is x. If the numerical value of the magnification produced by the lens is m, the focal length of the lens is

(a) $\frac{mx}{(m+1)^2}$ (b) $\frac{mx}{(m-1)^2}$

(c) $\frac{(m+1)^2}{m}$ (d) $\frac{(m-1)^2}{m}$

12 A convex lens of focal length 15 cm is placed at the origin with its optical axis coinciding with the X-axis. A ray of light given by $y = -x/3 + 1$ is incident on the lens (x and y are in cm). The equation of refracted ray is

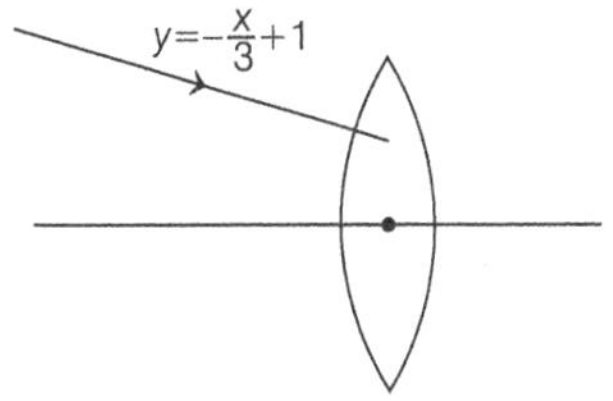

(a) $y = -0.2x + 1$ (b) $y = -0.3x + 1$
(c) $y = -0.4x + 1$ (d) $y = -0.5x + 1$

13 An object O is kept in air and a lens of focal length 10 cm (in air) is kept at the bottom of a container which is filled upto a height 44 cm by water. The refractive index of water is 4/3 and that of glass is 3/2. The bottom of the container is closed by a thin glass slab of refractive index 3/2. The distance of the final image formed by the system from the lens is

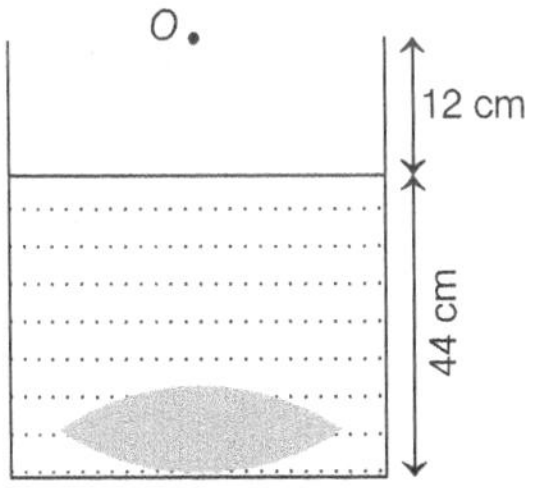

(a) 80 cm (b) 90 cm (c) 120 cm (d) 150 cm

14 A stationary observer O looking at a fish F (in water of, $\mu = 4/3$) through a converging lens of focal length 90 cm. The lens is allowed to fall freely from a height 62.0 cm with its axis vertical. The fish and the observer are on the principal axis of the lens. The fish moves up with constant velocity 100 cm/s. Initially it was at a depth of 44.0 cm. Find the velocity with which the fish appears to move to the observer at $t = 0.2$ s. ($g = 10$ m/s^2)

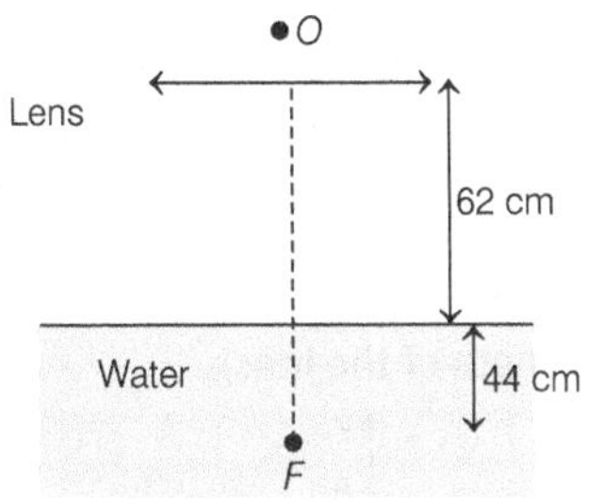

(a) 22.75 m/s (b) 45.5 m/s (c) 91 m/s (d) 15.25 m/s

15 Figure shows an object O placed in front of an equiconvex lens ($\mu = 1.5$) behind which there is water ($\mu = 4/3$) and a plane mirror at a distance of 20 m.

A point object O is placed at a distance of 45 cm from the lens as shown in the figure. The position of the image of the object coincides with the object itself, then radius of curvature of the lens is.

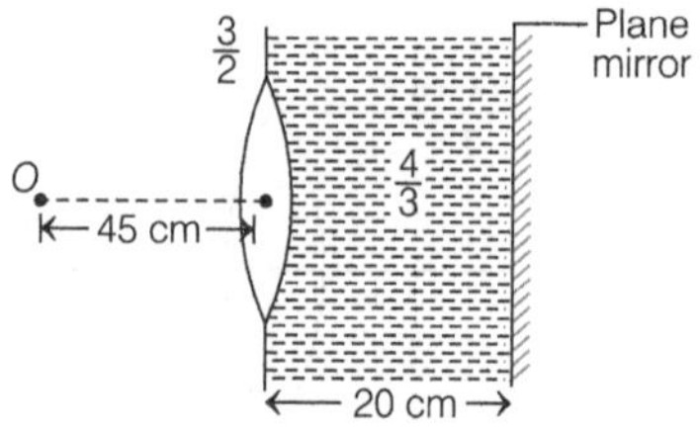

(a) 20 cm (b) 45 cm (c) 60 cm (d) 30 cm

16 A light ray hits the pole of a thin biconvex lens as shown in figure. The angle made by the emergent ray with the optic axis will be

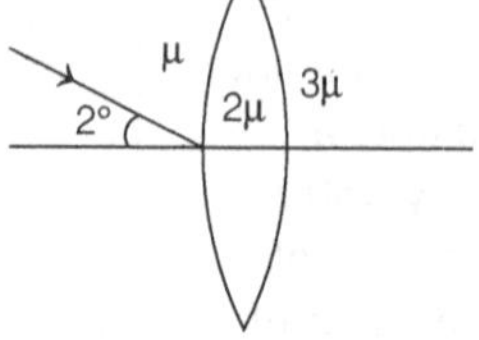

(a) 0° (b) (1/3)° (c) (2/3)° (d) 2°

17 Figures shows a convex lens cut symmetrically into two equal halves and separated laterally by a distance h. A point object placed at a distance 30 cm, from the lens halves, forms two real images separated by a distance d. A plot of d *versus* h is shown in figure. The focal length of the lens is

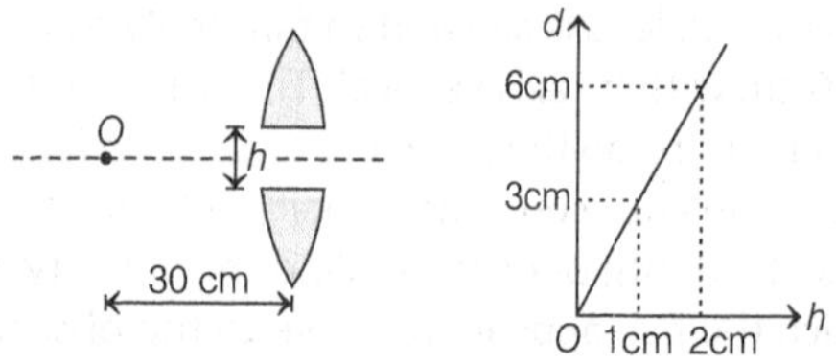

(a) 35 cm (b) 40 cm (c) 45 cm (d) 60 cm

18 Monochromatic light rays parallel to X-axis strike a convex lens AB. If the lens oscillates such that AB tilts upto a small angle θ (in radian) on either side of Y-axis, then find the distance between the extreme positions of the oscillating image
(f = focal length of the lens)

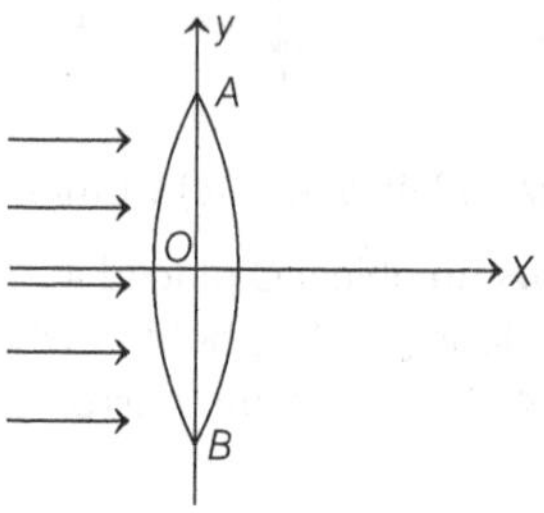

(a) $f \sec\theta$ (b) $f \sec^2\theta$
(c) $f(\sec\theta - 1)$ (d) $2f(\sec\theta - 1)$

19 The figure shows the initial position of a point source of light S, a detector D and lens L. Now at $t = 0$, all the three start moving towards right with different velocities as shown in figure. The time(s) at which detector receives the maximum light.

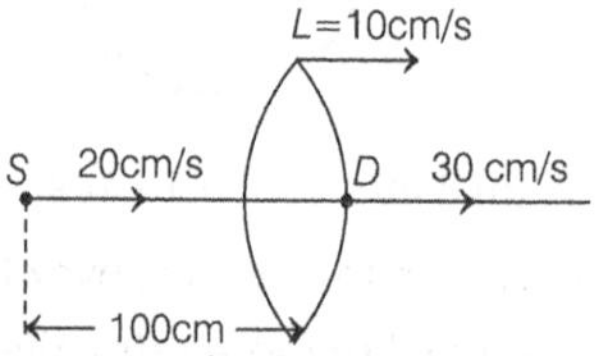

(a) 0.56 s and 8.94 s (b) 3.8 s
(c) 8.94 s and 19.62 s (d) 0.56 s

20 In the figure shown, find the relative speed of approach/separation of the two final images formed after the light rays pass through the lens, at the moment, when $u = 30$ cm. The speed of the object is 4 cm/s. The two lens halves are placed symmetrically w.r.t. the moving object.

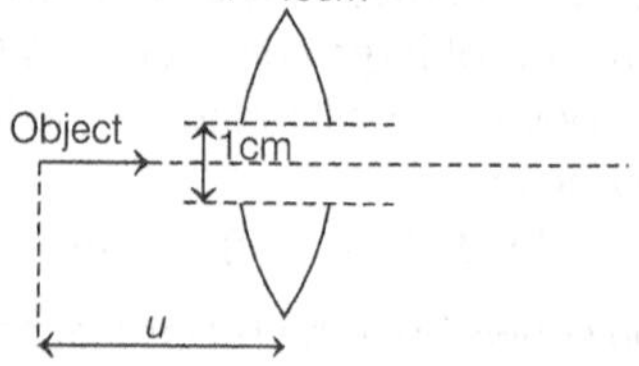

(a) $\frac{8}{5}$ cm/s (b) $\frac{4}{5}$ cm/s (c) 64 cm/s (d) 128 cm/s

21 A parallel beam of light passes parallel to the axis and falls on one face of a thin convex lens of focal length f and after two internal reflections emerges from the second face and forms a real image. Find the distance of the image from the lens if μ is the refractive index of the lens.

(a) $\left(\frac{\mu - 1}{3\mu - 1}\right)f$ (b) $\left(\frac{2\mu - 1}{3\mu - 1}\right)f$ (c) $\left(\frac{\mu - 1}{2\mu - 1}\right)f$ (d) $\left(\frac{3\mu - 1}{2\mu - 1}\right)f$

22 A thin biconvex lens of refractive index 3/2 is placed on a horizontal plane mirror as shown in the figure. The space between the lens and the mirror is, then filled with water of refractive index 4/3. It is found that, when a point object is placed 15 cm above the lens on its principal axis, the object coincides with its own image. On repeating with another liquid, the object and the image again coincide at a distance 25 cm from the lens. The refractive index of the liquid is

(a) 1.3 (b) 1.4 (c) 1.5 (d) 1.6

23 A parallel beam of light is incident on a thin prism of prism angle of $\left(\frac{4}{\pi}\right)^\circ$. The refractive index of the prism is 1.5. The focal length of the lens is 60 cm. The coordinates of converging point of the beam is

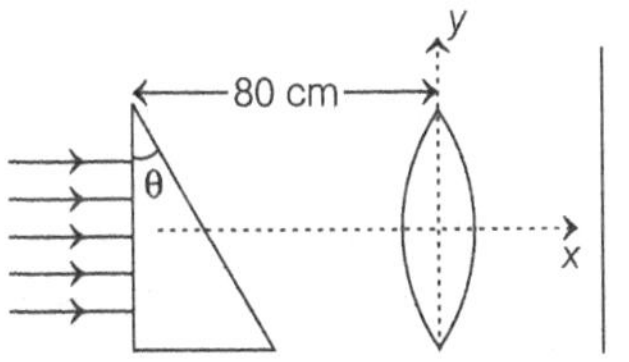

(a) (60 cm, 2/3 cm) (b) (60 cm, 1/3 cm)
(c) (60 cm, −1/3 cm) (d) (60 cm, −2/3 cm)

24 A thin converging lens L_1 forms a real image of an object located far away from the lens as shown in the figure. The image is located at a distance $4l$ and has height h. A diverging lens of focal length l is placed $2l$ from lens L_1. Another converging lens of focal length $2l$ is placed $3l$ from lens L_1. The height of final image thus formed is

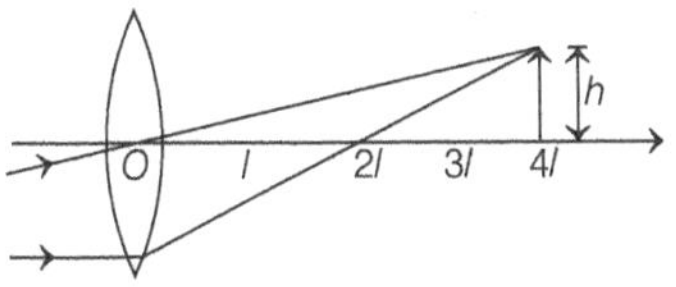

(a) h (b) $h/2$
(c) $4h$ (d) $2h$

25 A thin planoconvex lens of focal length f is split into two halves : one of the halves is shifted along the optical axis (figure). The separation between object and image planes is 1.8 m. The magnification of the image formed by one of the half-lenses is 2. Find the focal length of the lens and separation between the two halves.

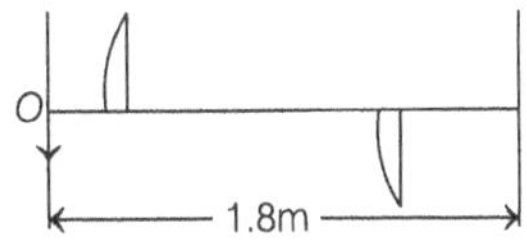

(a) $f = 0.4$ m, $d = 0.6$ m (b) $f = 0.8$ m, $d = 0.6$ m
(c) $f = 0.4$ m, $d = 0.3$ m (d) $f = 0.4$ m, $d = 0.8$ m

26 A convex lens of focal length 20 cm and another plano convex lens of focal length 40 cm are placed coaxially (see fig.). The plano convex lens is silvered on plane surface. What should be the distance d, so that final image of the object O is formed on O itself?

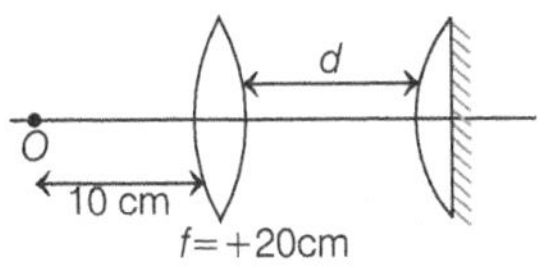

(a) 10 cm (b) 20 cm
(c) 30 cm (d) 40 cm

27 In the figure shown, the focal length of the two thin convex lenses is the same f. They are separated by a horizontal distance $3f$ and the optical axis of second lens is displaced by a vertical separation d ($d << f$), as shown. Taking the origin of coordinates O at the centre of the first lens, the x and y-coordinates of the point, where a parallel beam of rays coming from the left finally get focused, are given by

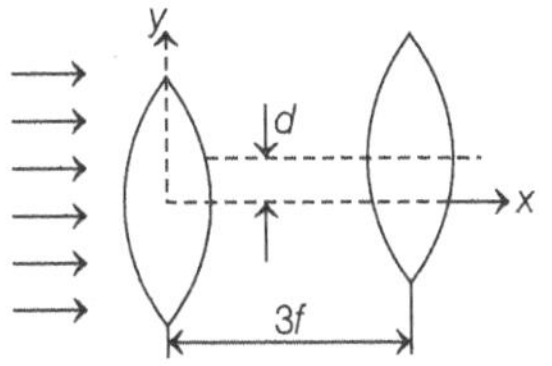

(a) $(5f, 2d)$ (b) $\left(6f, \frac{d}{2}\right)$ (c) $(4f, 2d)$ (d) $(2f, 4d)$

28 An observer to the right of the mirror lens combination shown in figure sees two real images that are of the same size and in the same location. One image is upright and the other is inverted. Both images are 1.50 times larger than the object. The lens has a focal length of 10.0 cm. The lens and mirror are separated by 40.0 cm. Determine the focal length of the mirror. Do not assume that the figure is drawn to scale.

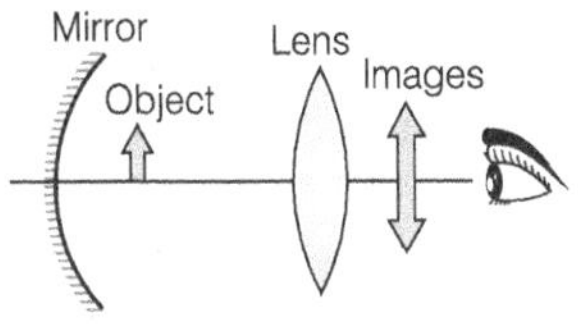

(a) $\frac{35}{6}$ cm (b) $\frac{35}{3}$ cm (c) 20 cm (d) 10 cm

Multiple Choice(s) Correct Questions

1 Two refracting media are separated by a spherical interface as shown in the figure. PP' is the principal axis, μ_1 and μ_2 are the refractive indices of medium of incidence and medium of refraction respectively. Then

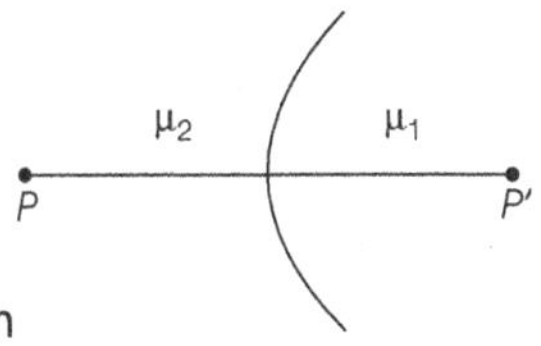

(a) if $\mu_2 > \mu_1$, then there cannot be a real image of real object.
(b) if $\mu_2 > \mu_1$, then there cannot be a real image of virtual object.
(c) if $\mu_1 > \mu_2$, then there cannot be a virtual image of virtual object.
(d) if $\mu_1 > \mu_2$, then there cannot be a real image of real object.

2 In the figure shown a point object O is placed in air on the principal axis. The radius of curvature of the spherical surface is 60 cm. I_f is the final image formed after all the refractions and reflections.

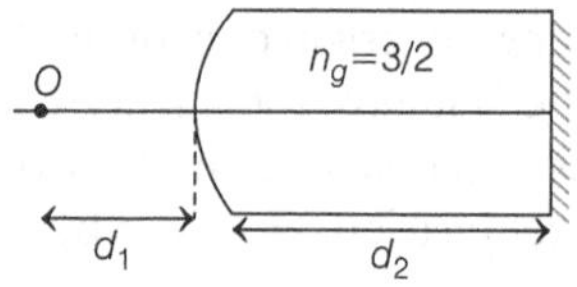

(a) If $d_1 = 120$ cm, then the I_f is formed on O for any value of d_2.

(b) If $d_1 = 240$ cm, then the I_f is formed on O only if $d_2 = 360$ cm.

(c) If $d_1 = 240$ cm, then the I_f is formed on O for all values of d_2.

(d) If $d_1 = 240$ cm, then the I_f cannot be formed on O.

3 A parallel beam of light is incident normally on the flat surface of a hemisphere of radius 6 cm and refractive index 1.5, placed in air as shown in figure (i). Assume paraxial ray approximation.

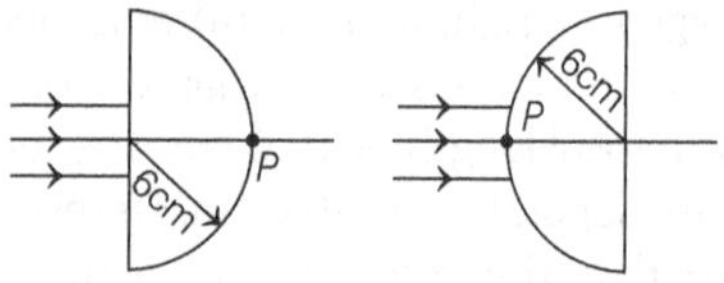

Figure (i) Figure (ii)

(a) The rays are focussed at 12 cm from the point P to the right, in the situation as shown in figure (i).

(b) The rays are focussed at 16 cm from the point P to the right, in the situation as shown in figure (i).

(c) If the rays are incident at the curved surface (figure (ii)), then these are focused at distance 18 cm from point P to the right.

(d) If the rays are incident at the curved surface (figure (ii)), then these are focused at distance 14 cm from point P to the right.

4 A thin lens of material of refractive index = 1.4 is formed with radii of curvatures of bounding surfaces 16 cm and 24 cm. Then

(a) the focal length of the lens is 24 cm, if it is biconvex lens.

(b) the power of the lens is 5/6 D, if it is a concave-convex converging lens.

(c) the focal length of the lens is 3 m, if it is a biconvex converging lens.

(d) the focal length of the lens is –76.8 cm, if it is biconvex lens and surrounded by a medium of refractive index = 1.6

5 An object and a screen are kept at a distance of 120 cm. A lens of focal length 22.5 cm is kept between them, so that a real image is formed on the screen.

Find the possible location(s) of the lens.

(a) 90 cm from object (b) 30 cm from object

(c) 40 cm from object (d) 80 cm from object

6 Optical axis of a thin equiconvex lens is the X-axis. The coordinates of a point object and its image are (–20 cm, 1 cm) and (25 cm, –2 cm) respectively

(a) the lens is located at $x = 5$ cm

(b) the lens is located at $x = -5$ cm

(c) the focal length of the lens is 10 cm

(d) the focal length of the lens is 15 cm

7 A lens of focal length f is placed in between an object and screen at a distance D. The lens forms two real images of object on the screen for two of its different positions, a distance x apart. The two real images have magnifications m_1 and m_2, respectively $(m_1 > m_2)$. Then

(a) $f = \dfrac{x}{m_1 - m_2}$ (b) $f = \dfrac{D^2 - x^2}{4D}$

(c) $m_1 m_2 = 1$ (d) $D \geq 4f$

8 In displacement method, the distance between object and screen is 96 cm. The ratio of length of two images formed by a convex lens placed between them is 4.84.

(a) Ratio of the length of object to the length of shorter image is 11/5.

(b) Distance between the two positions of the lens is 36 cm.

(c) Focal length of the lens is 22.5 cm.

(d) Distance of the lens from the shorter image is 30 cm.

9 If a symmetrical biconcave thin lens is cut into two identical halves. They are placed in different ways as shown

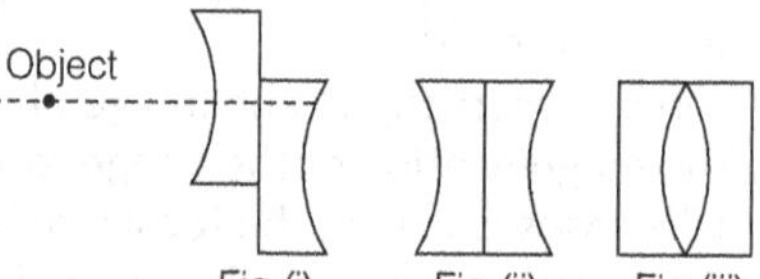

Fig (i) Fig (ii) Fig (iii)

(a) three images will be formed in case (i)

(b) two images will be formed in the case (i)

(c) the ratio of focal lengths in (ii) and (iii) is 1

(d) the ratio of focal lengths in (ii) and (iii) is 2

10 A luminous point object is placed at O, whose image is formed at I as shown in figure. Line AB is the optical axis. Which of the following statement is/are correct?

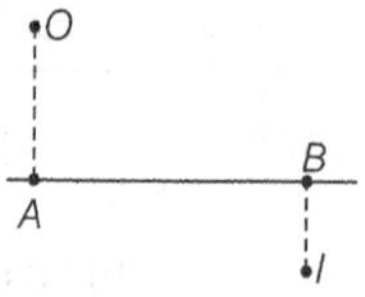

(a) If a lens is used to obtain the image, then it must be a diverging lens and its optical centre will be the intersection point of line AB and OI.

(b) If a lens is used to obtain the image, then it must be a converging lens and its optical centre will be the intersection point of line AB and OI.

(c) If a mirror is used to obtain the image, then the mirror must be concave and object and image subtend equal angles at the pole of the mirror.

(d) I is a real image.

11 Consider the ray shown in the diagram as paraxial. The image of the virtual point object O formed by the lens LL' is

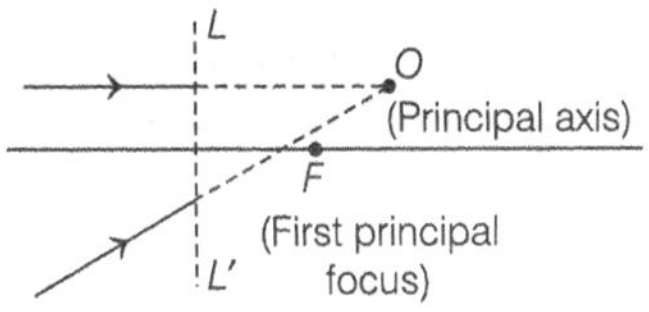

(a) virtual
(b) real
(c) located below the principal axis
(d) located left of the lens

12 A point source of light S is placed on the axis of a lens of focal length 20 cm as shown. A screen is placed normal to the axis of lens at a distance x from it. Treat all rays as paraxial.

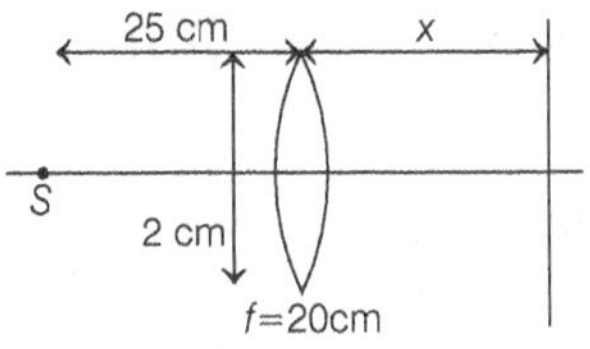

(a) As x is increased from zero, intensity continuously decreases

(b) As x is increased from zero, intensity first increases then decreases

(c) Intensity at centre of screen for $x = 90$ cm and $x = 110$ cm is same

(d) Radius of bright circle obtained on screen is equal to 1 cm for $x = 200$ cm

13 A thin convex lens of focal length f is having small rod at its optical axis at $3f$ distance in front of it. [angular velocity given is about axis perpendicular to plane of paper]

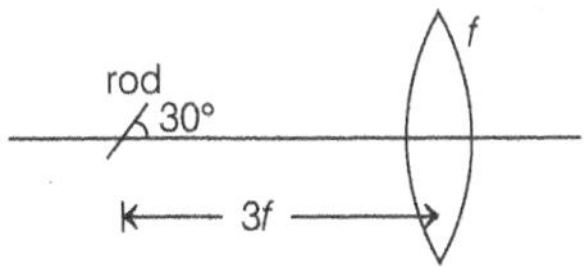

(a) Image of rod is inclined at angle $\tan^{-1}\left(\frac{2}{\sqrt{3}}\right)$ with optical axis.

(b) If rod is rotated with angular velocity 7 rad/s its image will start to rotate with angular velocity 8 rad/s.

(c) If lens is rotated with angular velocity 2 rad/s then image of rod will rotate with angular velocity 15 rad/s.

(d) length of image of rod is smaller than length of the rod.

14 The dashed part of the lens is cut and kept on the X-axis as shown in the diagram. If parallel paraxial rays are falling on this system, then the coordinates of image formed after refraction from both the lenses is (30, −1). If $x = 2.5$, then (all the distances are in cm) (Assume lens has no spherical aberration)

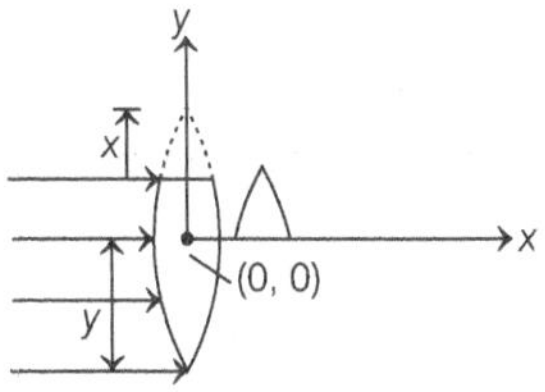

(a) $f = 30$ cm (b) $f = 60$ cm (c) $y = 3$ cm (d) $y = 4.5$ cm

15 The values of d_1 and d_2 for final rays to be parallel to the principal axis are (focal lengths of the lenses are written on the lenses)

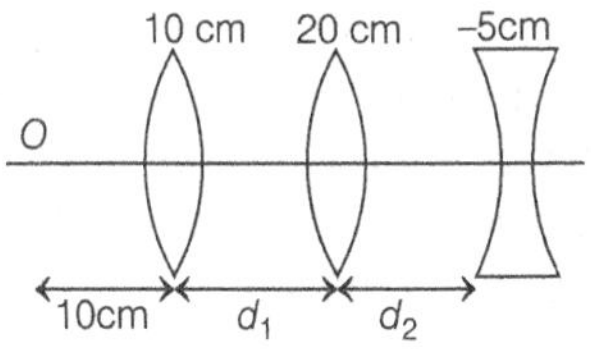

(a) $d_1 = 10$ cm, $d_2 = 15$ cm (b) $d_1 = 20$ cm, $d_2 = 15$ cm
(c) $d_1 = 30$ cm, $d_2 = 15$ cm (d) None of these

16 Two converging lenses have focal length f_1 and f_2 ($f_1 > f_2$). The optical axis of the two lenses coincide. This lens system is used to form an image of real object. It is observed that final magnification of the image does not depend on the distance x. Whole arrangement is shown in figure. Choose the correct options.

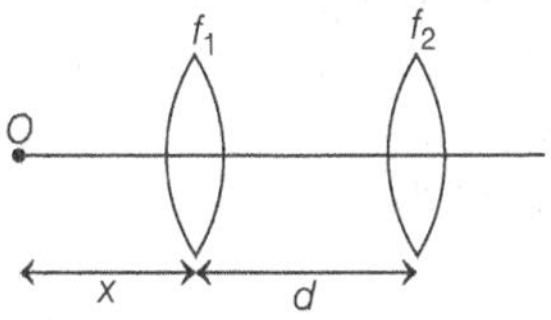

(a) Final magnification is $-\frac{f_1}{f_2}$

(b) Final magnification is $-\frac{f_2}{f_1}$

(c) Distance between the lenses is $\frac{f_1 f_2}{f_1+f_2}$

(d) Distance between the lenses is f_1+f_2

17 An object O is kept in front of a converging lens of focal length 30 cm behind which there is a plane mirror at 15 cm from the lens.

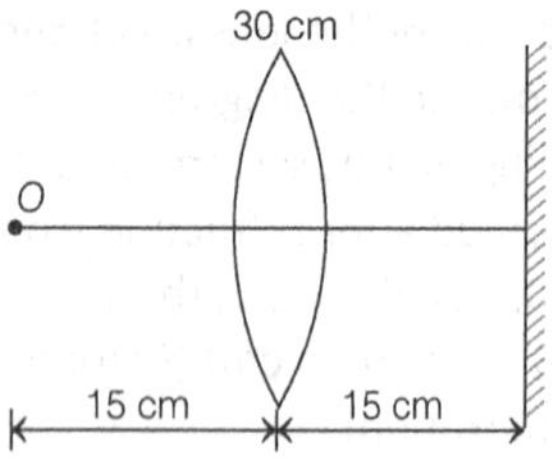

(a) The final image is formed at 60 cm from the lens towards right of it.

(b) The final image is at 60 cm from lens towards left of it.

(c) The final image is real.

(d) The final image is virtual.

18 A biconvex lens $f_1 = 20$ cm, is placed 5 cm in front of a convex mirror, $f_2 = 15$ cm. An object of length 2 cm is placed perpendicular to the principal axis at a distance 10 cm from the lens. Choose the correct statement(s) about the location and nature of the final image after the leftward travelling rays once again pass through the lens.

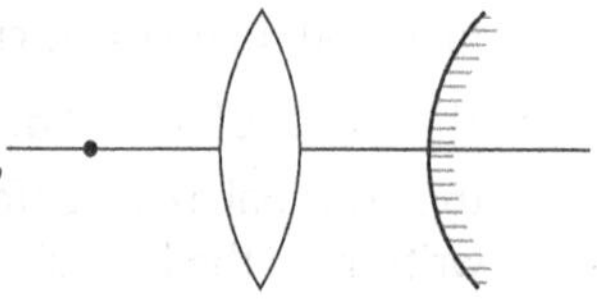

(a) 51.1 cm right of lens, real, erect and magnified

(b) Overall magnification = 8/3

(c) 62.7 cm from lens. real, inverted and magnified

(d) Overall magnification = 3

19 A linear object *AB* is at a distance of 36 cm from an equiconvex lens of focal length 30 cm. In front of lens, there is a plane mirror which is inclined at an angle 45° with the principal axis of the lens at a distance $l = 1$ m from the mirror as shown in figure.

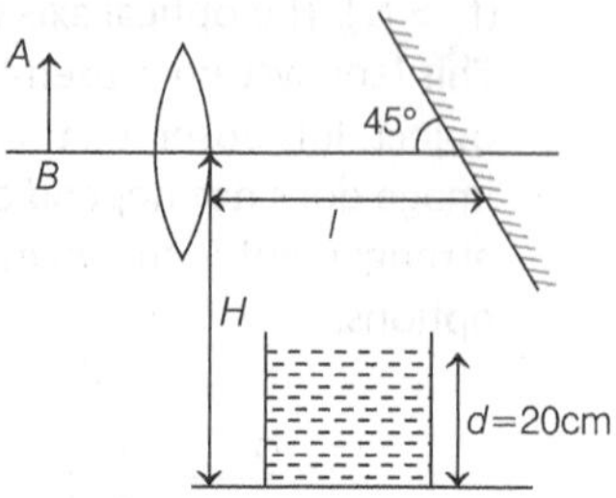

A container with water layer $d = 20$ cm is placed as shown in the figure. Then, choose the **CORRECT** statement(s). Take the refractive index of water as 4/3

(a) After reflection from the mirror, the image of *AB* will be parallel to principal axis of the lens.

(b) After reflection from the mirror, the image of *AB* will be perpendicular to principal axis of the lens.

(c) The value of *H* for which the sharp image of *AB* can be obtained at the bottom of the container is 80 cm.

(d) The value of *H* for which the sharp image of *AB* can be obtained at the bottom of the container is 85 cm.

20 The radius of curvature of the left and right surface of the concave lens are 10 cm and 15 cm respectively. The radius of curvature of the mirror is 15 cm.

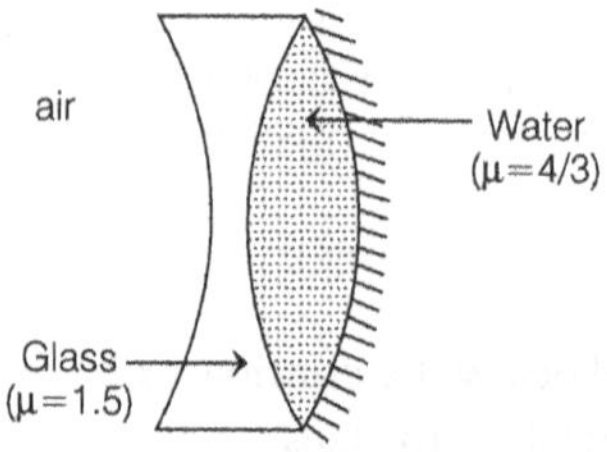

(a) Equivalent focal length of the combination is -18 cm.

(b) Equivalent focal length of the combination is +36 cm.

(c) The system behaves like a concave mirror.

(d) The system behaves like a convex mirror.

Comprehension Based Questions

Comprehension-I

A candle of height *h* is being moved along the axis from $u_1 = 3f$ towards a thin converging lens of focal length *f*. The adjacent graph represents the height of image as a function of the position of image with respect to lens as shown in figure. v_1 is the image position corresponding to the object position u_1.

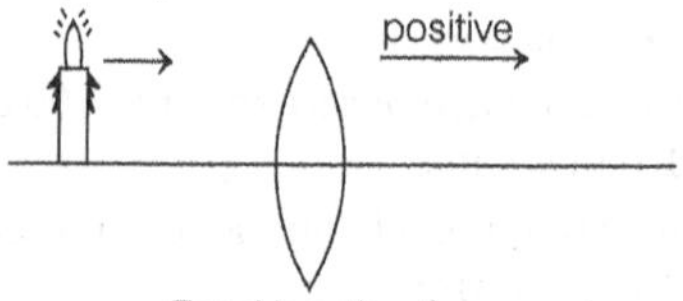

Focal length $= f$

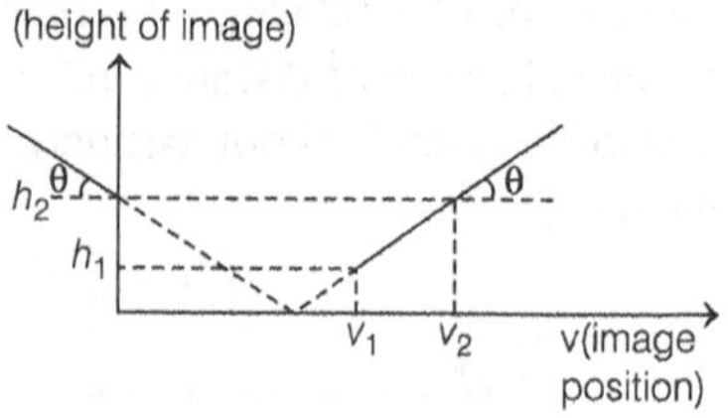

1 The value of h_2 is

(a) h (b) $\frac{h}{2}$ (c) $\frac{3h}{2}$ (d) None of these

2 The value of h_1 is

(a) h (b) $\frac{h}{2}$ (c) $\frac{3h}{2}$ (d) None of these

3 The value of ratio $\frac{V_1}{V_2}$ is

(a) $\frac{3}{2}$ (b) $\frac{3}{4}$ (c) $\frac{2}{3}$ (d) None of these

Comprehension-2

A planoconvex lens has a thickness of 4 cm. When placed on a horizontal table, with the curved surface in contact with it, the apparent depth of the bottom most point of the lens is found to be 3 cm. If the lens is inverted such that the plane face is in contact with the table, the apparent depth of the centre of the plane face is found to be $\frac{25}{8}$ cm.

4 Refractive index of the lens is

(a) $\frac{4}{3}$ (b) $\frac{8}{5}$ (c) $\frac{5}{3}$ (d) $\frac{8}{7}$

5 Radius of curvature of the curved surface is

(a) 25 cm (b) 50 cm (c) 75 cm (d) 100 cm

6 Focal length of the planoconvex lens is

(a) 25 cm (b) 50 cm (c) 75 cm (d) 100 cm

Comprehension-3

In the figure one converging lens and a concave mirror of focal length f each are arranged coaxially at a separation of $f/2$. An object of height 3.5 mm is placed at a distance $f/2$ from lens away from mirror. Consider refraction with lens, reflection from mirror and then refraction from lens again and corresponding images as I_1, I_2 and I_3 respectively. Answer the following questions.

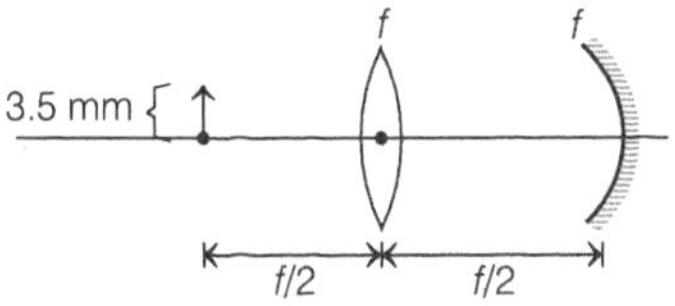

7 Which of the following is correct regarding nature of images?

(a) I_1 : Real, I_2 : Real, I_3 : Real
(b) I_1 : Virtual, I_2 : Real, I_3 : Real
(c) I_1 : Virtual, I_2 : Virtual, I_3 : Real
(d) None of the above

8 Net magnification in three consecutive optical events is

(a) $-\frac{8}{7}$ (b) $+\frac{2}{7}$

(c) $+\frac{8}{7}$ (d) None of these

9 Find the distance of tip of final image from optical centre of lens (if $f = 7$ cm) is

(a) 5 cm (b) $\sqrt{29}$ cm
(c) $\sqrt{2516}$ mm (d) None of these

Comprehension-4

In an experiment, a parallel beam of light falls successively on a thin convex lens L_1 of focal length 40 cm and then on a second thin convex lens L_2 of focal length 10 cm as shown in figure. Area illuminated by the beam of light on the screen is observed as A_1. Now lens L_2 is replaced by an equiconcave lens L_3 ($\mu = 1.5$) of focal length 10 cm and area illuminated on screen is observed as A_2. All the lenses have equal radius aperture of 1 cm.

When a liquid of refractive index μ' is filled between the second lens L_3 and screen, areas illuminated on the screen are found to be equal, then

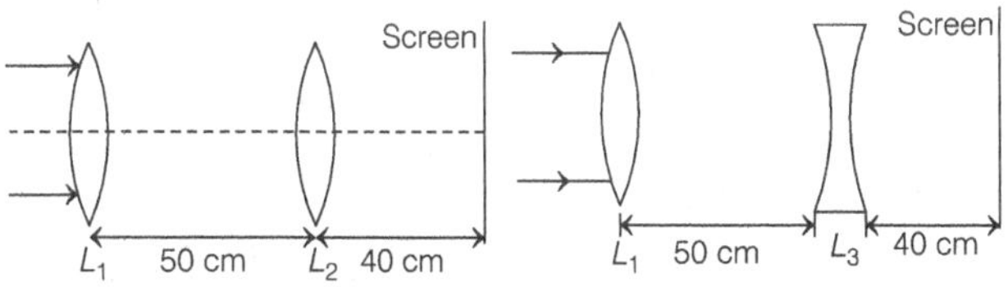

10 Area illuminated on screen A_1 (in cm^2) is

(a) $\frac{\pi}{4}$ (b) $\frac{\pi}{16}$ (c) $\frac{\pi}{2}$ (d) 4π

11 Area illuminated on screen A_2 (in cm^2) is

(a) $\frac{3\pi}{2}$ (b) $\frac{15\pi}{4}$ (c) $\frac{81\pi}{16}$ (d) $\frac{15\pi}{2}$

12 Value of refractive index μ' should be

(a) 1.5 (b) 3 (c) $\sqrt{3}$ (d) 2

Comprehension-5

A tank of depth 150 cm has silvered concave bottom of radius of curvature $R = 10$ cm. At the top of tank a thin small equiconvex lens made up of glass of refractive index 1.5 and focal length 40 cm is mounted. There is provision to fill water ($\mu = 4/3$) in the tank to desired heights. A point object is placed at a distance 60 cm above lens.

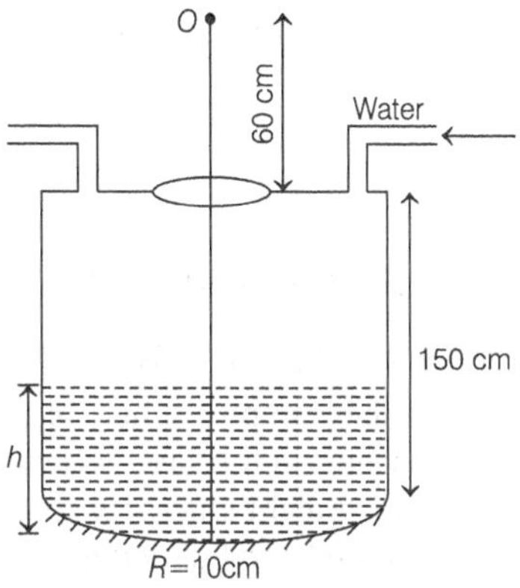

13 If height of water in tank is $h = 90$ cm, final image formed is

(a) 30 cm above lens (b) 40 cm above lens
(c) at object itself (d) at infinity

14 If height of water in tank is $h = 120$ cm, final image formed is

(a) 30 cm above lens (b) 40 cm above lens
(c) at object itself (d) at infinity

15 If tank is completely filled with water, position of image formed by bottom mirror from vertex of mirror is

(a) 5 cm above mirror (b) 10 cm above mirror
(c) 20 cm above mirror (d) at infinity

Comprehension-6

A cylindrical tube filled with water $\left(\mu_w = \frac{4}{3}\right)$ is closed at its both ends by two thin silvered planoconvex lenses as shown in the figure. Refractive index of lenses L_1 and L_2 are 2.0 and 1.5 while their radii of curvature are 5 cm and 9 cm respectively. A point object is placed some, where at a point O on the axis of cylindrical tube. It is found that the object and image coincide each other.

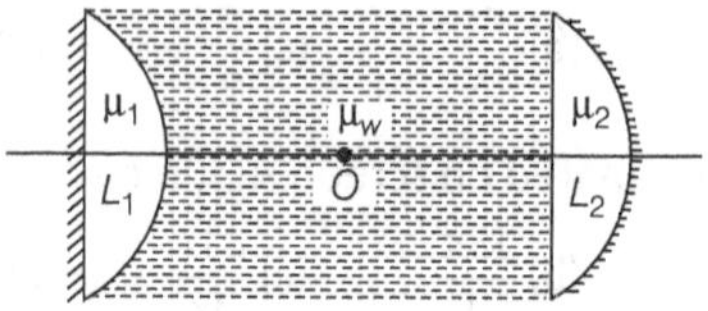

16 The distance of object O from lens L_1 is

(a) 5 cm (b) 6 cm
(c) 8 cm (d) 10 cm

17 The distance of object O from lens L_2 is

(a) 5 cm (b) 6 cm
(c) 8 cm (d) 10 cm

18 If $\mu_1 = \mu_2 = \mu_w$, then image after two reflections (once from each) will coincide with object if distance of O from (distance between two lenses remains same)

(a) L_1 is $9\sqrt{2}$ cm (b) L_2 is $9\sqrt{2}$ cm
(c) L_1 is 9 cm (d) L_2 is 9 cm

Match the Columns Questions

1 Column shows O_1-object and O_2-image. The optical system responsible can be a spherical mirror, plane mirror or a thin lens. In the case of the lens and spherical mirror, straight line shows the principal axis. Match Column I and Column II.

	Column I	Column II
A.	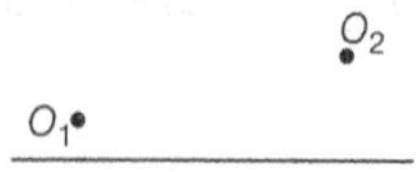	1. Concave mirror between O_1 and O_2
B.	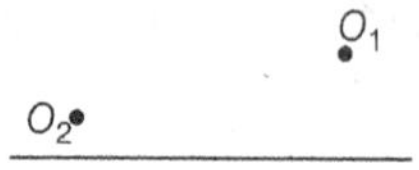	2. Diverging lens between O_1 and O_2
C.	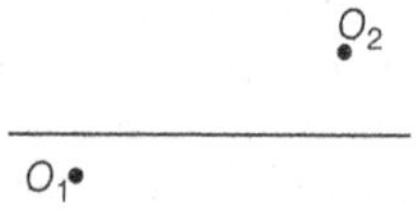	3. Convex mirror between O_1 and O_2
D.	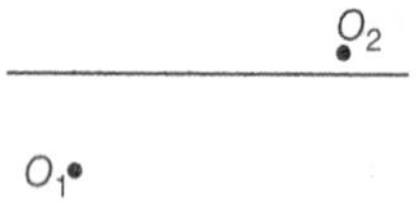	4. Converging lens between O_1 and O_2
		5. Inclined plane mirror somewhere between O_1 and O_2

2 In Column I certain combinations of small object and image are marked. Match them with possible refracting/reflecting body in Column II. In all cases, object is perpendicular to X-axis. Object can't be at zero distance from the interface.

Column I	Column II
A. Virtual image of virtual object	1. Converging lens
B. Real image of real object	2. 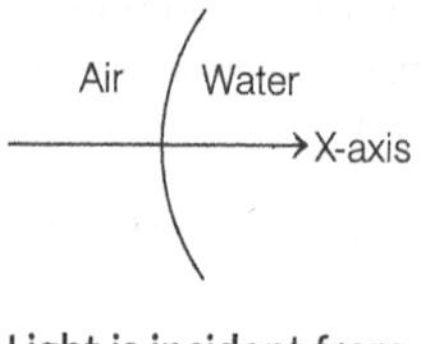 Light is incident from air on the spherical surface
C. Erect real image of same size as object	3. Convex mirror
D. Erect and virtual image of larger size than the object.	4. 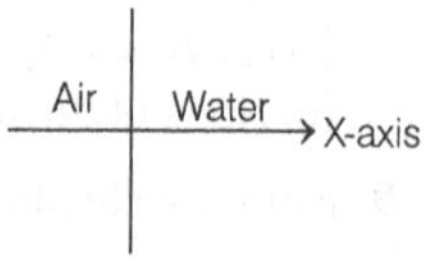 Light is incident from right to left.
	5. Diverging lens

3 Instruments are given in Column I. In Column II, there are results corresponding to a given situation. Match the optical instrument of Column I with the results in Column II.

	Column I		Column II
A.	Concave mirror	1.	Parallel rays can be obtained by using point source.
B.	Convex mirror	2.	Real image can be obtained for real object.
C.	Concave lens	3.	Virtual and diminished image can be obtained for real object.
D.	Convex lens	4.	Real and magnified image can be obtained for real object.
		5.	For a point object moving along optical axis, the image also moves in the same direction of motion of the object.

4 Consider the situation shown in Column I. A real object is moving towards a fixed optical component or an optical component is moving towards a fixed object.

Match the possible direction and magnitude of velocity of image as shown in Column II.(All velocities in Column I are equal to v_0)

	Column I		Column II
A.	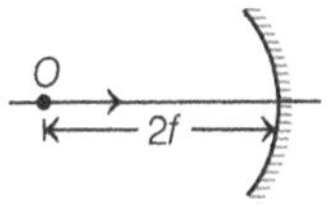	1.	⟵
B.	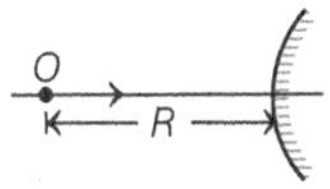	2.	⟶
C.	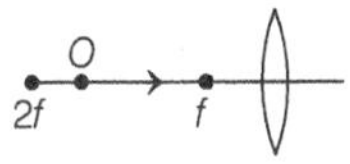	3.	More than v_0
D.	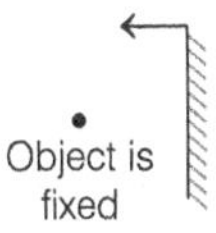	4.	Less than v_0
		5.	Equal to v_0

5 Column II shows few lenses with given refractive index and Column I shows their nature with variation in surrounding medium.

	Column I		Column II
A.	If $\mu_1 > \mu_2$, it will behave as converging lens	1.	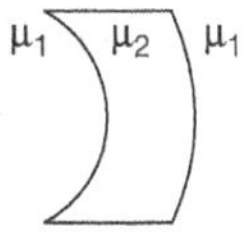
B.	If $\mu_1 > \mu_2$, it will behave as diverging lens	2.	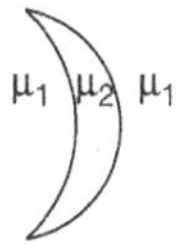
C.	If $\mu_1 < \mu_2$, it will behave as converging lens	3.	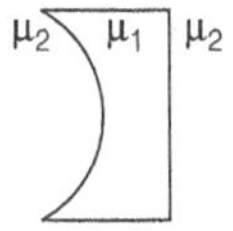
D.	If $\mu_1 < \mu_2$, it will behave as diverging lens	4.	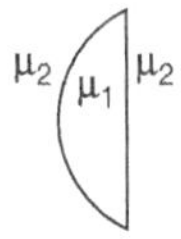
		5.	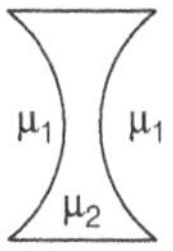

6 A glass disk whose plane surfaces are parallel is cut as shown in figure, then the lenses so obtained are moved apart. What will happen to a beam of parallel rays falling on to the system? (f is the focal length of converging lens).

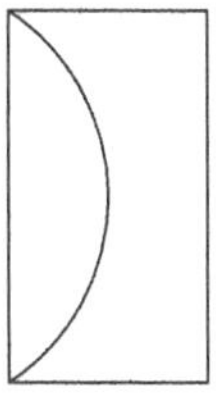

	Column I		Column II
A.	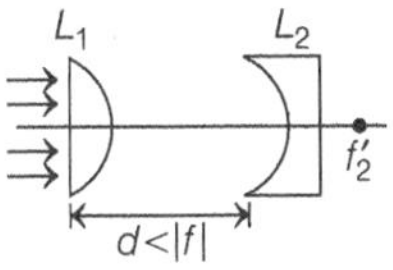	1.	Emerging rays are converging and image distance from $L_2 < f$
B.	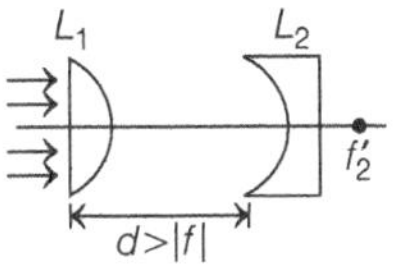	2.	Emerging rays are diverging and image distance from $L_2 < f$
C.	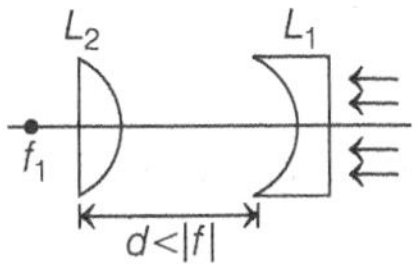	3.	Emerging rays are converging and image distance from $L_2 > f$
D.	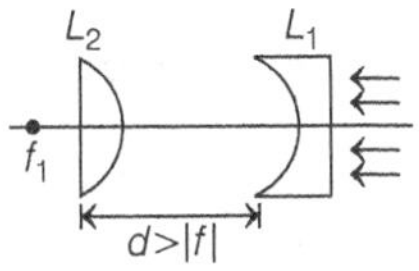	4.	Emerging rays are diverging and image distance from $L_2 > f$

7 An object O (real) is placed at focus of an equibiconvex lens as shown in figure. The refractive index of lens is $\mu = 1.5$ and the radius of curvature of either surface of lens is R. The lens is surrounded by air. In each statement of Column I some changes are made to situation given above and information regarding final image formed as a result is given in Column II. The distance between lens and object is unchanged in all statements of Column I. Match the statements in Column I with resulting image in Column II.

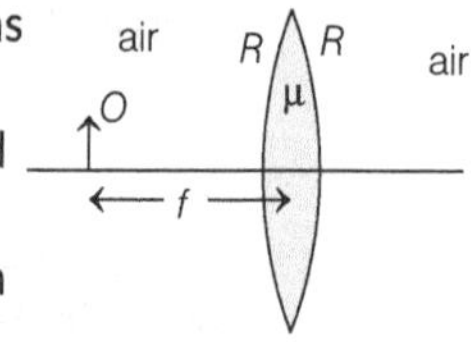

	Column I		Column II
A.	If the refractive index of the lens is doubled (that is, made 2μ) then	1.	final image is real
B.	If the radius of curvature is doubled (that is, made $2R$) then	2.	final image is virtual
C.	If a glass slab of refractive index $\mu = 1.5$ is introduced between the object and lens as shown, then 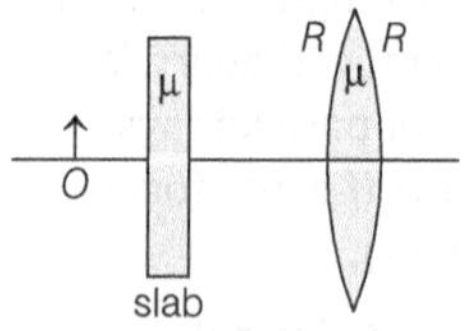	3.	final image becomes smaller in size in comparison to size of image before the change was made
D.	If the left side of lens is filled with a medium of refractive index $\mu = 1.5$ as shown, then 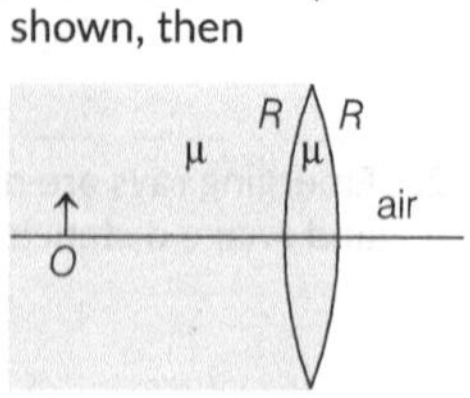	4.	final image is of same size of object.

Numerical Value Questions

1 There is a small air bubble inside a glass sphere ($\mu = 1.5$) of radius 5 cm. The bubble is at O at 2.5 cm below the centre of the glass sphere. The sphere is placed inside water $\left(\mu = \frac{4}{3}\right)$ such that the top surface of glass is 10 cm below the surface of water. The bubble is viewed normally from air. Find the apparent depth (in cm) of the bubble measured from the surface of water.

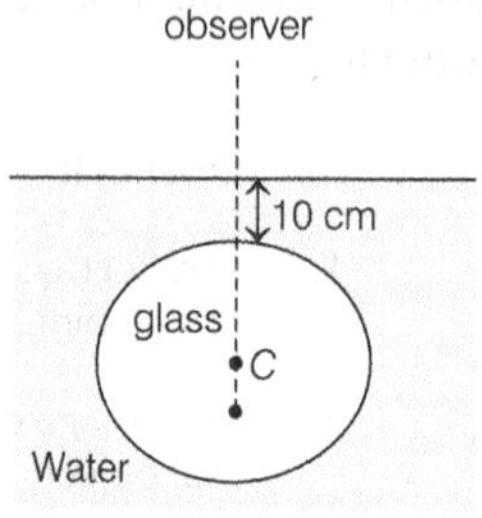

2 A ray of light in air is incident on face AB of an irregular block made of material with refractive index $\sqrt{2}$, as shown in figure. The face CD opposite to AB is a spherical surface of radius of curvature 0.4 m. From this face the refracted ray enters a medium of refractive index 1.514 and meets the axis PQ at point E. Determine the distance OE (in m) correct to two decimal places.

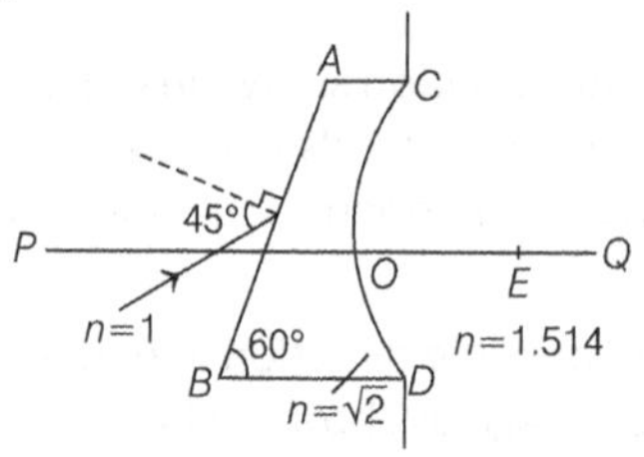

3 A point object is kept at a distance of 2 m from origin on X-axis. A quarter cylinder of radius $R = 30$ cm and refractive index $\mu = 1.5$ having its axis perpendicular to plane of paper is placed between the object and the parabolic reflector at a distance of 130 cm from origin as shown in figure. Find the distance (in cm) of the image from origin after reflection from the parabolic reflector $y^2 = 2x$.

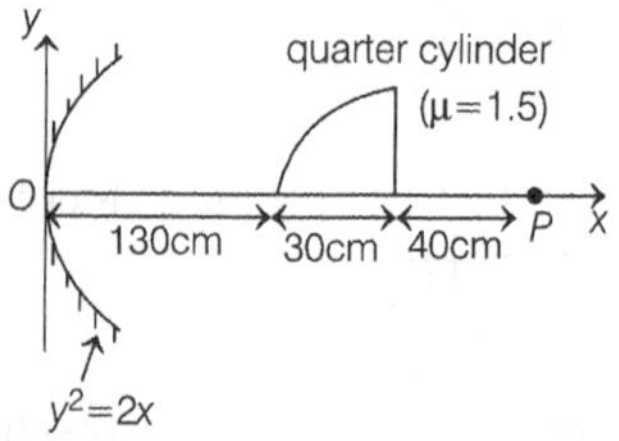

4 A light ray parallel to the principal axis is incident (as shown in the figure) on a thin planoconvex lens with radius of curvature of its curved part equal to 10 cm. Assuming that the refractive index of the material of the lens is 4/3 and medium on both sides of the lens is air, find the distance of the point from the right surface of lens where, this ray meets the principal axis.

Find your answer in the form $\frac{X}{7}$ cm and fill value of X.

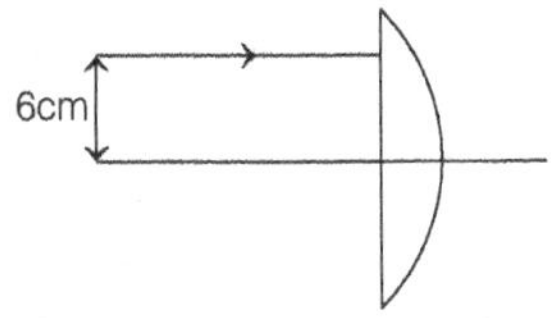

5 A concavo-convex lens made of glass of refractive index 1.5 has surfaces of radii 20 cm and 60 cm. A concave mirror of radius of curvature 20 cm is placed coaxially to the lens. A glass slab of thickness 3 cm and refractive index 1.5 is placed closer to the mirror in the space between the mirror and lens as shown in figure.

The distance of the nearest surface of the slab from lens is 248 cm. An object is placed 80 cm to the left of the lens. If final position of the image formed after refraction from lens, refraction from slab, reflection from mirror, refraction from the slab and lens is at the object O, find the distance x (in cm) of the mirror from nearer surface of slab.

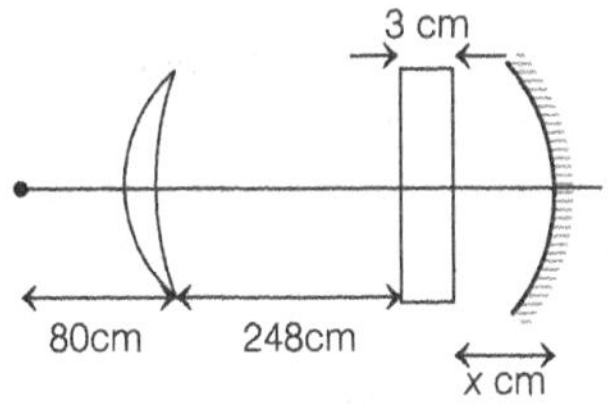

6 A point object O is placed in front of a plane mirror and planoconvex lens (whose convex side is silvered) assembly, as shown. Find the distance d (in cm) of the object from the plane mirror, so that the final image is created at the itself. Radius of curvature of the convex side of planoconvex lens is 42 cm and its refractive index is $\frac{3}{2}$.

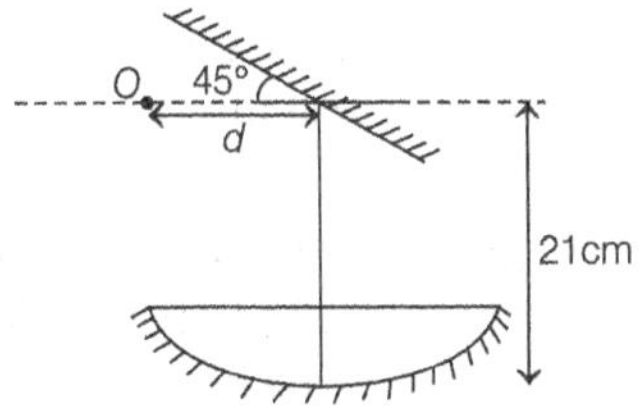

7 In the figure shown, L is a converging lens of focal length 10 cm and M is a concave mirror of radius of curvature 20 cm. A point object O is placed in front of the lens at a distance 15 cm. AB and CD are optical axes of the lens and mirror respectively. The distance between CD and AB is 1 cm. If the distance of the final image formed by this system from the optical centre of the lens is $6\sqrt{n}$ cm, then find n.

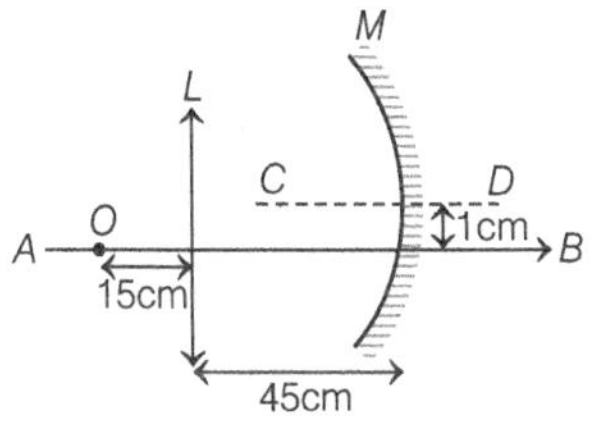

8 A convex lens of focal length 15 cm is split into two halves and the two halves are placed at a separation of 120 cm. Between the two halves of convex lens, a plane mirror is placed horizontally and at a distance of 4 mm below the principal axis of the lens halves. An object AB of length 2 mm is placed at a distance of 20 cm from one half lens as shown in figure. The final image of the point A is formed at a distance of $n/3$ mm from the principal axis. Determine the value of n.

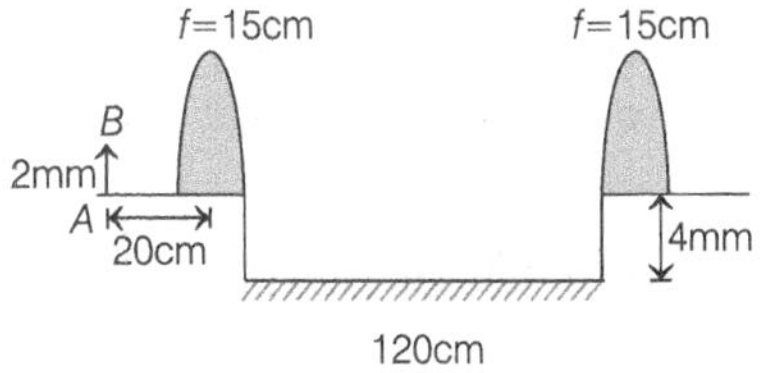

9 A transparent sphere of radius R has a cavity of radius $R/2$ as shown in figure. Find the refractive index of the sphere if a parallel beam of light falling on left surface focuses at point P. ($\sqrt{5} = 2.2$)

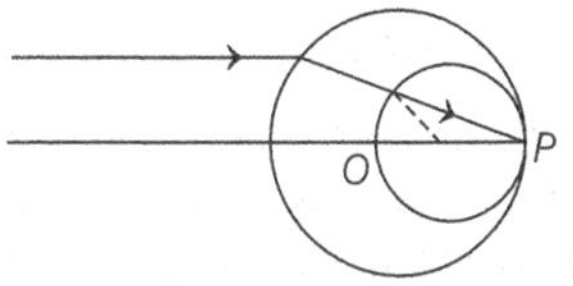

10 A thin converging lens is arranged between a small illuminated object and a screen, so that an image of the object of linear magnification 3 is formed on a screen. The object and the screen are then 64 cm apart. A thin biconcave lens is then placed between the converging lens and the screen, so that the lenses are coaxial and 6 cm apart. To restore a sharply focussed image on the image screen, the object was moved away from the converging lens through a distance of 14 cm. The biconcave lens has a surface of radii of curvature 14 cm and 21 cm. Find the refractive index of the biconcave lens.

11 An equiconvex lens of refractive index 3/2 and of radius of curvature 16 cm is placed coaxially at a distance of 90 cm in front of a concave mirror of radius of curvature 60 cm. The surrounding medium is air. A point object O is placed on the common axis of the lens and the mirror at a distance 90 cm left of the lens. At an instant ($t = 0$), the object, the lens and the mirror start moving with speed 2 cm/s, 3 cm/s and 8 cm/s respectively in the directions shown in the figure. Find the time (in second) after which the object and final image coincide for the first time.

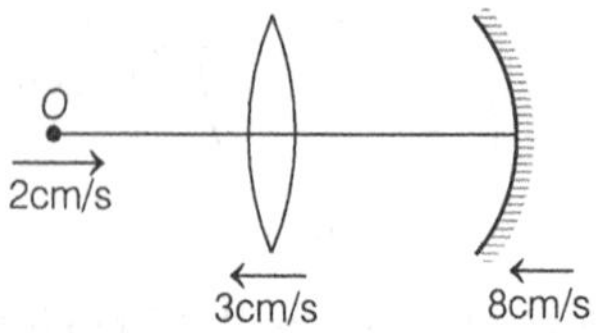

12. A thin convex lens of focal length 25 cm is inserted between a luminous point object and a screen separated by 100 cm. The lens forms a sharp image of the object on the screen. When a thin glass plate is introduced between the object and the lens, the screen has to be shifted away by $2\frac{4}{23}$ cm to form a sharp image on the screen. If instead of this, we put the same glass plate between the lens and the screen, by what distance (in cm) should the screen be shifted to form a sharp image of the object on the screen?

Previous Year's Questions

JEE Main

1 A biconvex lens of refractive index 1.5 has a focal length of 20 cm in air. Its focal length when immersed in a liquid of refractive index 1.6 will be **[2024, 29 Jan Shift-I]**

(a) −16 cm (b) +160 cm (c) −160 cm (d) +16 cm

2 The distance between object and its two times magnified real image as produced by a convex lens is 45 cm. The focal length of the lens used is ...... cm. **[2024, 30 Jan Shift-I]**

3 In an experiment to measure the focal length (f) of a convex lens, the magnitude of object distance (x) and the image distance (y) are measured with reference to the focal point of the lens. The y - x plot is shown in figure. The focal length of the lens is .... cm. **[2024, 30 Jan Shift-II]**

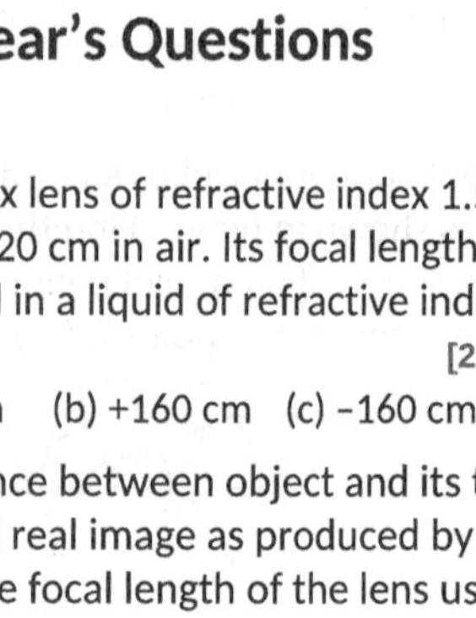

4 Two transparent media having refractive indices 1.0 and 1.5 are separated by a spherical refracting surface of radius of curvature 30 cm., The centre of curvature of surface is towards denser medium and a point object is placed on the principle axis in rarer medium at a distance of 15 cm from the pole of the surface. The distance of image from the pole of the surface is .... cm. **[2023, 8 April Shift-II]**

5 A point object, O is placed infront of two thin symmetrical coaxial convex lenses L_1 and L_2 with focal length 24 cm and 9 cm respectively. The distance between two lenses is 10 cm and the object is placed 6 cm away from lens L_1 as shown in the figure. The distance between the object and the image formed by the system of two lenses is .... cm. **[2023, 10 April Shift-II]**

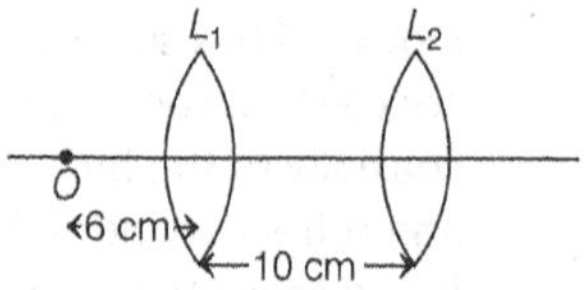

6 The radius of curvature of each surface of a convex lens having refractive index 1.8 is 20 cm. The lens is now immersed in a liquid of refractive index 1.5. The ratio of power of lens in air to its power in the liquid will be $x : 1$. The value of x is .... **[2023, 11 April Shift-I]**

7 Two convex lenses of focal length 20 cm each are placed coaxially with a separation of 60 cm between them. The image of distant object formed by the combination is at .... cm from the first lens. **[2023, 12 April Shift-I]**

8 A biconvex lens of focal length 10 cm is cut in two identical parts along a plane perpendicular to the principal axis. The power of each lens after cut is .... D. **[2023, 13 April Shift-II]**

9 An object is placed on the principal axis of convex lens of focal length 10 cm as shown. A plane mirror is placed on the other side of lens at a distance of 20 cm, The image produced by the plane mirror is 5 cm inside the mirror. The distance of the object from the lens is .... cm. **[2023, 25 Jan Shift-II]**

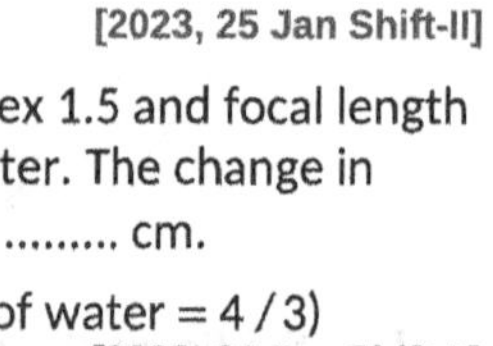

10 A convex lens of refractive index 1.5 and focal length 18 cm in air is immersed in water. The change in focal length of the lens will be .... cm.

(Given, refractive index index of water = 4 / 3) **[2023, 24 Jan Shift-II]**

11 The graph between $1/u$ and $1/v$ for a thin convex lens in order to determine its focal length is plotted as shown in the figure. The refractive index of lens is 1.5 and its both the surfaces have same radius of curvature R. The value of R will be .... cm.

(where, u = object distance and v = image distance)
[2022, 26 July Shift-I]

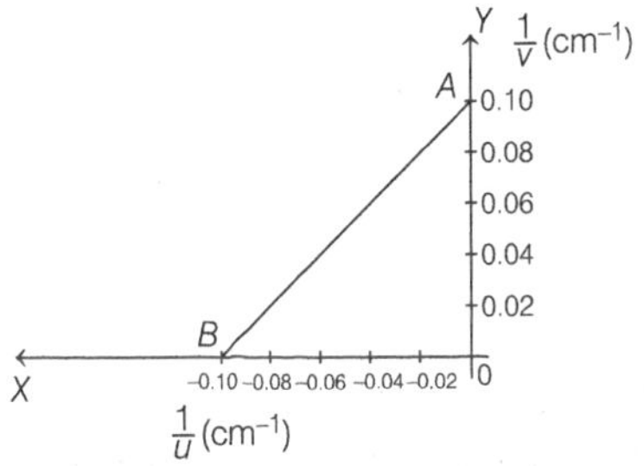

12 The power of a lens (biconvex) is 1.25 m^{-1} in particular medium. Refractive index of the lens is 1.5 and radii of curvature are 20 cm and 40 cm, respectively. The refractive index of surrounding medium **[2022, 28 July Shift-II]**

(a) 1.0 (b) 9/7 (c) 3/2 (d) 4/3

13 The image of an object placed in air formed by a convex refracting surface is at a distance of 10 m behind the surface. The image is real and is at 2/3 of the distance of the object from the surface .The wavelength of light inside the surface is 2/3 times the wavelength in air. The radius of the curved surface is $x/13$ m. The value of x is ………… .
[2021, 17 March Shift-II]

14 An object is placed at the focus of concave lens having focal length f. What is the magnification and distance of the image from the optical centre of the lens? **[2021, 31 Aug Shift-I]**

(a) 1, ∞ (b) Very high, ∞ (c) $\frac{1}{2}, \frac{f}{2}$ (d) $\frac{1}{4}, \frac{f}{4}$

15 Curved surfaces of a plano-convex lens of refractive index μ_1 and a plano-concave lens of refractive index μ_2 have equal radius of curvature as shown in figure. Find the ratio of radius of curvature to the focal length of the combined lenses.

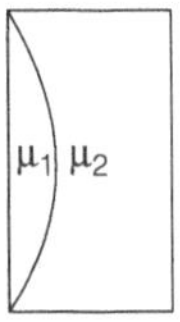

[2021, 27 Aug Shift-I]

(a) $\frac{1}{\mu_2 - \mu_1}$ (b) $\mu_1 - \mu_2$ (c) $\frac{1}{\mu_1 - \mu_2}$ (d) $\mu_2 - \mu_1$

16 Find the distance of the image from object O, formed by the combination of lenses in the figure.
[2021, 27 Aug Shift-II]

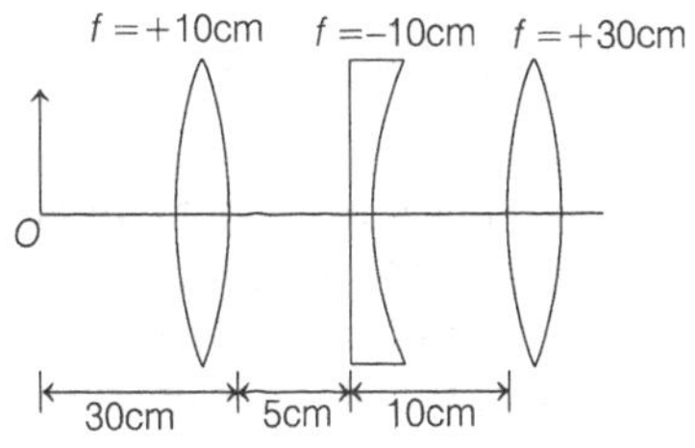

(a) 75 cm (b) 10 cm
(c) 20 cm (d) infinity

17 The thickness at the centre of a plano convex lens is 3 mm and the diameter is 6 cm. If the speed of light in the material of the lens is 2×10^8 ms^{-1}, then the focal length of the lens is **[2021, 17 March Shift-I]**

(a) 0.30 cm (b) 15 cm (c) 1.5 cm (d) 30 cm

18 The refractive index of a converging lens is 1.4. What will be the focal length of this lens if it is placed in a medium of same refractive index ? (Assume the radii of curvature of the faces of lens are R_1 and R_2 respectively) **[2021, 16 March Shift-II]**

(a) 1 (b) Infinite (c) $\frac{R_1 R_2}{R_1 - R_2}$ (d) Zero

19 An object is placed at a distance of 12 cm from a convex lens. A convex mirror of focal length 15 cm is placed on other side of lens at 8 cm as shown in the figure. Image of object coincides with the object.

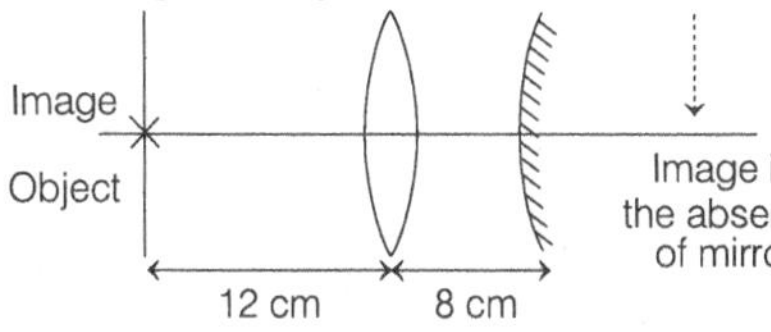

When the convex mirror is removed, a real and inverted image is formed at a position. The distance of the image from the object will be …….. cm.
[2021, 26 Aug Shift-II]

JEE Advanced

1. An optical arrangement consists of two concave mirrors M_1 and M_2 and a convex lens l, with a common principal axis, as shown in the figure. The focal length of L is 10 cm. The radii of curvature of M_1 and M_2 are 20 cm and 24 cm, respectively. The distance between L and M_2 is 20 cm. A point object S is placed at the mid-point between L and M_2 on the axis. When the distance between L and M_1 is $n/7$ cm, one of the images coincide with S. The value of n is …… **(2023 Adv.)**

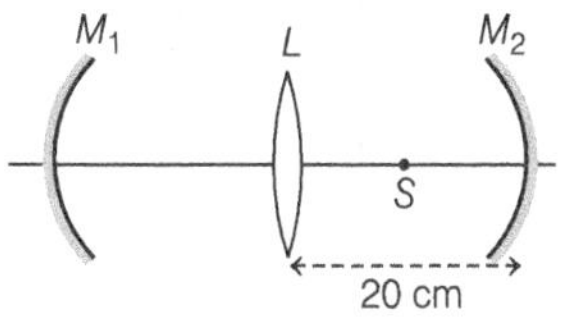

2. In an experiment for determination of the focal length of a thin convex lens, the distance of the object from the lens is 10 ± 0.1 cm and the distance of its real image from the lens is 20 ± 0.2 cm. The error in the determinantion of focal length of the lens is n%. The value of n is ……… . **(2023 Adv.)**

3. Column-I contains four combinations of two lenses (1 and 2) whose focal lengths (in cm) are indicated in the figures. In all cases, the object is placed 20 cm from the first lens on the left, and the distance between the two lenses is 5 cm. Column-II contains the positions of the final images.

	Column-I		Column-II
I.	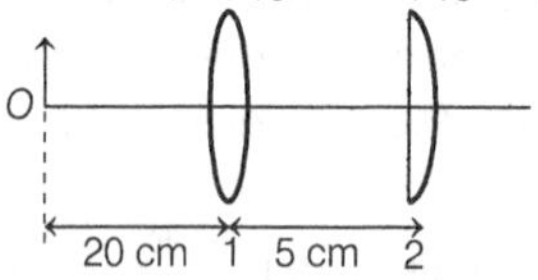	P.	Final image is formed at 7.5 cm on the right side of lens 2.
II.	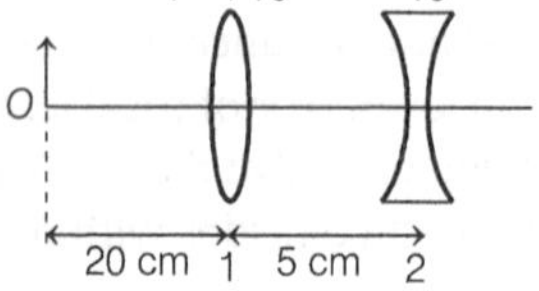	Q.	Final image is formed at 60.0 cm on the right side of lens 2.
III.	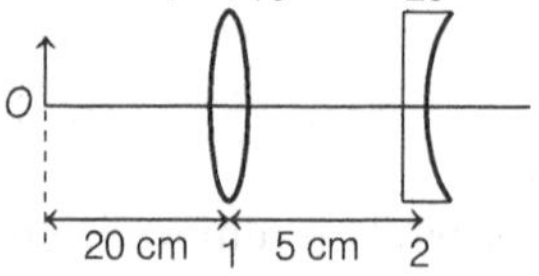	R.	Final image is formed at 30.0 cm on the left side of lens 2.
IV.	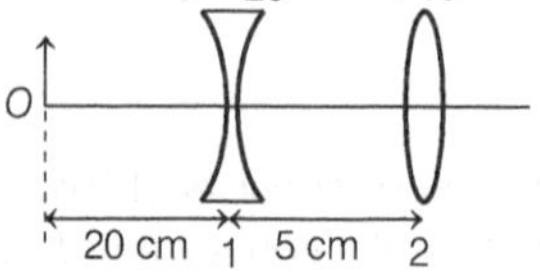	S.	Final image is formed at 6.0 cm on the right side of lens 2.
		T.	Final image is formed at 30.0 cm on the right side of lens 2.

Which one of the following options is correct? **(2022 Adv.)**

	I	II	III	IV
(a)	P	R	Q	T
(b)	Q	P	T	S
(c)	P	T	R	Q
(d)	T	S	Q	R

4. A rod of length 2 cm makes an angle $2\pi/3$ rad with the principal axis of a thin convex lens. The lens has a focal length of 10 cm and is placed at a distance of 40/3 cm from the object as shown in the figure. The height of the image is $\frac{30\sqrt{3}}{13}$ cm and the angle made by it with respect to the principal axis is α rad. The value of α is π/n rad, where n is .... **(2022 Adv.)**

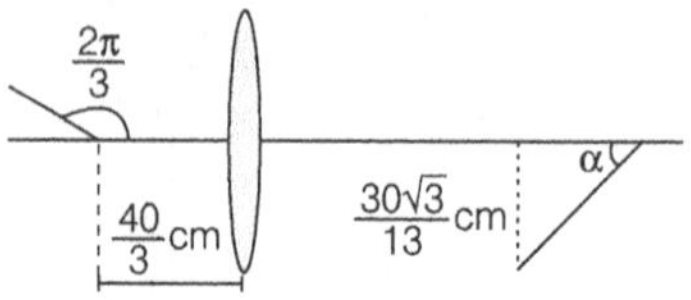

5. An extended object is placed at point O, 10 cm in front of a convex lens L_1 and a concave lens L_2 is placed 10 cm behind it, as shown in the figure. The radii of curvature of all the curved surfaces in both the lenses are 20 cm. The refractive index of both the lenses is 1.5. The total magnification of this lens system is **(2021 Adv.)**

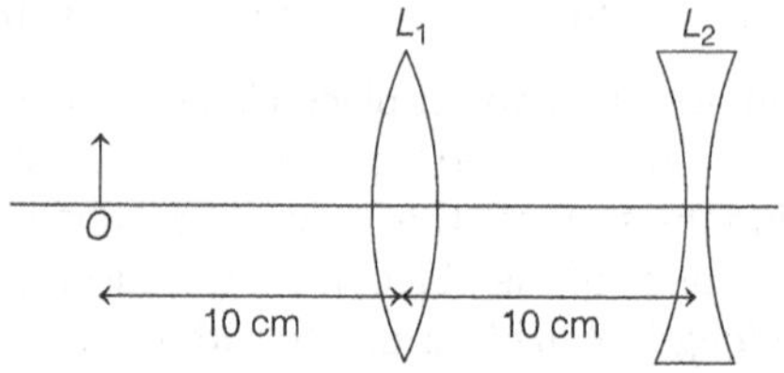

(a) 0.4 (b) 0.8 (c) 1.3 (d) 1.6

6. A parallel beam of light strikes a piece of transparent glass having cross section as shown in the figure below. Correct shape of the emergent wavefront will be (figures are schematic and not drawn to scale) **(2020 Adv.)**

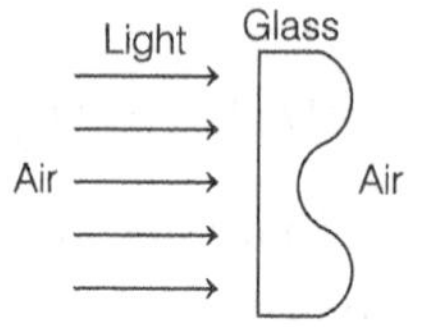

(a) 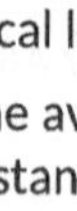 (b)  (c) 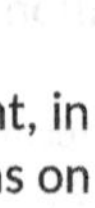 (d) 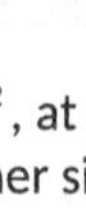

7. Sunlight of intensity 1.3 kWm^{-2} is incident normally on a thin convex lens of focal length 20 cm. Ignore the energy loss of light due to the lens and assume that the lens aperture size is much smaller than its focal length.

The average intensity of light, in $kW\,m^{-2}$, at a distance 22 cm from the lens on the other side is .... **(2018 Adv.)**

8. A plano-convex lens is made of material of refractive index n. When a small object is placed 30 cm away in front of the curved surface of the lens, an image of double the size of the object is produced.

Due to reflection from the convex surface of the lens, another faint image is observed at a distance of 10 cm away from the lens. Which of the following statement(s) is (are) true? **(2016 Adv.)**

(a) The refractive index of the lens is 2.5
(b) The radius of curvature of the convex surface is 45 cm
(c) The faint image is erect and real
(d) The focal length of the lens is 20 cm

9. Consider a concave mirror and a convex lens (refractive index = 1.5) of focal length 10 cm each, separated by a distance of 50 cm in air (refractive index = 1) as shown in the figure. An object is placed at a distance of 15 cm from the mirror. Its erect image formed by this combination has magnification M_1. When the set-up is kept in a medium of refractive index $\frac{7}{6}$, the magnification becomes M_2.

The magnitude $\left|\frac{M_2}{M_1}\right|$ is **(2015 Adv.)**

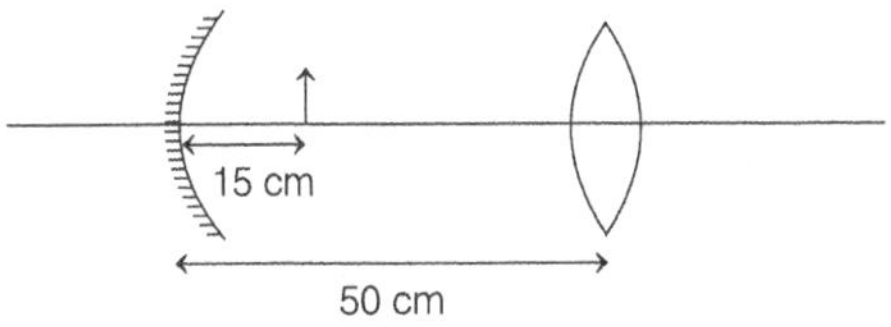

10. Two identical glass rods S_1 and S_2 (refractive index = 1.5) have one convex end of radius of curvature 10 cm. They are placed with the curved surfaces at a distance d as shown in the figure, with their axes (shown by the dashed line) aligned. When a point source of light P is placed inside rod S_1 on its axis at a distance of 50 cm from the curved face, the light rays emanating from it are found to be parallel to the axis inside S_2.

The distance d is **(2015 Adv.)**

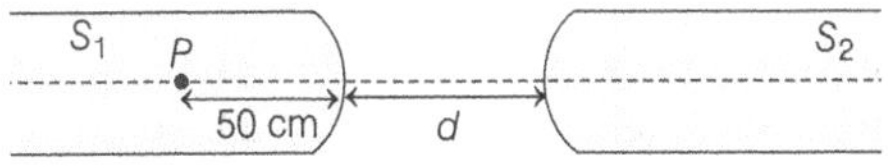

(a) 60 cm (b) 70 cm (c) 80 cm (d) 90 cm

Answer Key

Level 1

3.1 Refraction at a Spherical Boundary

1. 270 cm 2. (i) 10 cm right of C (ii) 6 cm right of C
3. 15 cm right of centre 4. 50 cm
5. 40 cm from pole in air, virtual errct and 4 cm in size.
6. No shift is observed 7. 1 cm
8. + 12 m/s

3.2 Lens-Maker Formula

1. (a) 20 cm (b) 40 cm (c) 240 cm (d) – 20 cm (e) – 40 cm (f) – 96 cm
2. ± 24 cm, ± 120 cm 3. – 160 cm
4. $f = \frac{\mu_3 R}{(\mu_3 - \mu_1)}$ 5. (i) f (ii) $2f$

3.3 Ray Diagrams

1. (a)
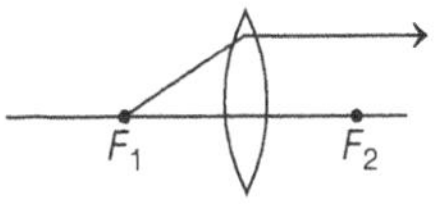

(b)
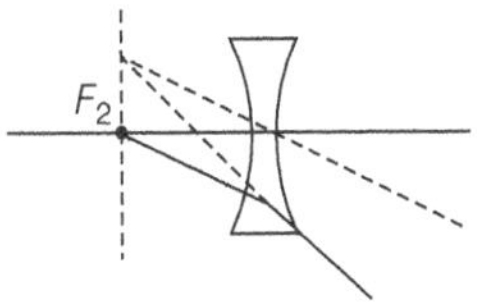

2. (a)
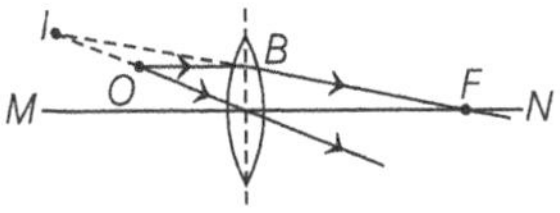

(b)
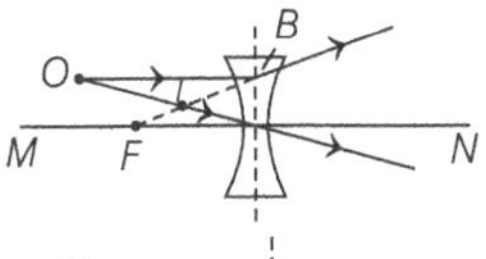

(c)
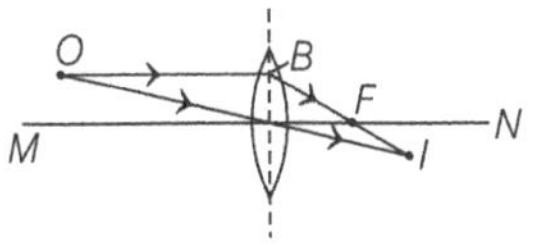

3.4 Lens Formula

1. 100 cm, 20 mm 2. $u = -15$ cm and $u = -5$ cm
3. v = 7.5 cm 4. 20 cm
5. 28/75 = 0.37 cm 6. (i) 20/3 cm (ii) 0.25 mm
7. 31 cm from the lens 8. 3 9. $(\pi/4)$ cm^2

3.5 Displacement Method to Find Focal Length

1. 16 cm 2. 6 cm 3. 58.33

3.6 Velocity of Image

1. $\frac{dv}{dt} = 0.09$ m/s; $\frac{dm}{dt} = -0.3\ s^{-1}$ 2. 2 cm/s, left
3. 2 cm/s (downward)

3.7 Combination of Lenses

1. 10 cm right of concave lens 2. – 20 cm, concave
3. (a) 12 cm b) 56/3 cm from concave lens, virtual
4. 1 cm 5. 15 cm, 1600 W/m^2

6. $f_{eq} = -7.5$ cm
7. 10 cm for convex lens and 60 cm for concave lens
8. 12.5 cm, 50 cm 9. 5 cm

3.8 Combination of Lens and Mirror

1. 30 cm left of the lens 2. 40 cm and 60 cm
3. 60 cm from the lens further away from the mirror
4. 1.67 cm from the lens 5. - 20 cm

3.9 Silvered Lens

1. 11 cm 2. 1.5
3. (a) 15 cm from the lens on the axis
   (b) 1.15 cm towards the lens

Level 2

Single Choice Correct Questions

1. (b)	2. (a)	3. (b)	4. (a)	5. (d)
6. (b)	7. (d)	8. (b)	9. (a)	10. (c)
11. (a)	12. (b)	13. (d)	14. (a)	15. (d)
16. (b)	17. (b)	18. (b)	19. (a)	20. (d)
21. (d)	22. (d)	23. (b)	24. (c)	25. (c)
26. (b)	27. (c)	28. (b)	29. (b)	30. (c)
31. (d)	32. (c)	33. (d)	34. (d)	35. (b)
36. (d)	37. (d)	38. (a)	39. (d)	40. (a)
41. (b)	42. (a)	43. (b)	44. (c)	45. (d)
46. (a)	47. (a)	48. (a)	49. (d)	50. (c)
51. (b)	52. (c)			

Numerical Value Questions

1. 40.4	2. 16	3. 10	4. 6
5. 8	6. 7.5	7. 352	8. 3
9. 12	10. 12	11. 120	12. 17.5
13. 2	14. 75	15. 10	

Level 3

Single Choice Correct Questions

1. (d)	2. (d)	3. (a)	4. (d)	5. (a)
6. (a)	7. (c)	8. (b)	9. (b)	10. (c)
11. (a)	12. (c)	13. (b)	14. (a)	15. (d)
16. (c)	17. (d)	18. (c)	19. (a)	20. (a)
21. (a)	22. (d)	23. (d)	24. (d)	25. (a)
26. (b)	27. (a)	28. (b)		

Multiple Choice(s) Correct Questions

1. (a, c)	2. (a, b)	3. (a, d)
4. (a, b, d)	5. (a, b)	6. (b, c)
7. (a, b, c, d)	8. (a, b, d)	9. (a, c)
10. (b, c, d)	11. (a, c, d)	12. (b, c, d)
13. (a, b, d)	14. (b, d)	15. (a, b, c)
16. (b, d)	17. (b, c)	18. (a, b)
19. (a, d)	20. (a, c)	

Comprehension Based Questions

1. (a)	2. (b)	3. (b)	4. (a)	5. (a)
6. (c)	7. (b)	8. (a)	9. (c)	10. (b)
11. (c)	12. (b)	13. (c)	14. (c)	15. (a)
16. (d)	17. (c)	18. (a)		

Match the Columns Questions

1. A $\rightarrow$ 1,5, B $\rightarrow$ 3,5, C $\rightarrow$ 4,5, D $\rightarrow$ 4,5
2. A $\rightarrow$ 3,5, B $\rightarrow$ 1,2, C $\rightarrow$ 4, D $\rightarrow$ 1,2
3. A $\rightarrow$ 1,2,4, B $\rightarrow$ 3, C $\rightarrow$ 3,5, D $\rightarrow$ 1,2,4,5
4. A $\rightarrow$ 1,5, B $\rightarrow$ 1,4, C $\rightarrow$ 2,3, D $\rightarrow$ 1,3
5. A $\rightarrow$ 1,4,5, B $\rightarrow$ 2,3, C $\rightarrow$ 2,3, D $\rightarrow$ 1,4,5
6. A $\rightarrow$ 1,3, B $\rightarrow$ 2, C $\rightarrow$ 3, D $\rightarrow$ 3
7. A $\rightarrow$ 1,3, B $\rightarrow$ 2,3, C $\rightarrow$ 2,3, D $\rightarrow$ 2,3

Numerical Value Questions

1. 13.5	2. 6.06	3. 50	4. 130
5. 10	6. 7	7. 26	
8. 8	9. 2.6	10. 1.4	
11. 2	12. 2		

Previous Year's Questions

JEE Main

1. (c)	2. (10)	3. (20)	4. (30)	5. (34)
6. (4)	7. (100)	8. (5)	9. (30)	10. (54)
11. (10)	12. (b)	13. (30)	14. (c)	15. (b)
16. (a)	17. (d)	18. (b)	19. (50)	

JEE Advanced

1. (150 or 180 or 220)		2. (1)	3. (a)
4. (6)	5. (b)	6. (a)	7. (130)
8. (a, d)	9. (7)	10. (b)	

SOLUTIONS

Level 1

3.1 Refraction at a Spherical Boundary

1. $$\frac{\mu_2}{v}-\frac{\mu_1}{u}=\frac{\mu_2-\mu_1}{R}$$

$$\Rightarrow \quad \frac{3/2}{v}-\frac{4/3}{(-240)}=\frac{3/2-4/3}{+15}$$

$$\Rightarrow \quad v = 270 \text{ cm}$$

2. (i) For observer A,

$$\frac{\mu_2}{v}-\frac{\mu_1}{u}=\frac{\mu_2-\mu_1}{R}$$

$$\Rightarrow \quad \frac{1}{v}-\frac{1.5}{-15}=\frac{1-1.5}{-10}$$

$$\Rightarrow \quad v=-20 \text{ cm} \quad \text{or} \quad 10 \text{ cm right of } C.$$

(ii) For observer B,

$$\frac{\mu_2}{v}-\frac{\mu_1}{u}=\frac{\mu_2-\mu_1}{R}$$

$$\Rightarrow \quad \frac{1}{v}-\frac{1.5}{-5}=\frac{1-1.5}{-10}$$

$$\Rightarrow \quad v=-4 \text{ cm} \quad \text{or} \quad 6 \text{ cm right of } C.$$

3. For first refraction (air to glass)

$$\frac{\mu_2}{v}-\frac{\mu_1}{u}==\frac{\mu_2-\mu_1}{R}$$

$$\Rightarrow \quad \frac{1.5}{v}-\frac{1}{-\infty}=\frac{1.5-1}{+10}$$

$$\Rightarrow \quad v = 30 \text{ cm}$$

For second refraction (glass to air)

$u=(30-20)=10 \text{ cm}, R=-10 \text{ cm}$

$$\frac{\mu_2}{v}-\frac{\mu_1}{u}=\frac{\mu_2-\mu_1}{R} \Rightarrow \frac{1}{v}-\frac{1.5}{+10}=\frac{1-1.5}{-10}$$

$\Rightarrow v = 5$ cm or 15 cm right of centre.

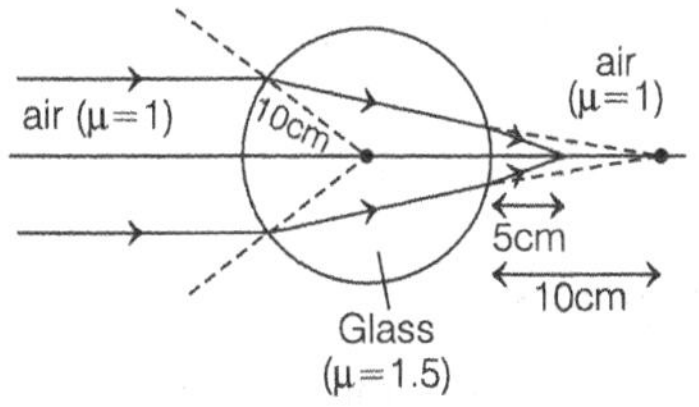

4. For first refraction (air to glass)

$$\frac{\mu_2}{v}-\frac{\mu_1}{u}=\frac{\mu_2-\mu_1}{R}$$

$$\Rightarrow \quad \frac{1.5}{v}-\frac{1}{-10}=\frac{1.5-1}{+10} \Rightarrow v=-30 \text{ cm}$$

For second refraction (glass to air)

$u=-(30+20)=-50 \text{ cm}, R=-10 \text{ cm}$

$$\frac{\mu_2}{v}-\frac{\mu_1}{u}=\frac{\mu_2-\mu_1}{R}$$

$$\Rightarrow \quad \frac{1}{v}-\frac{1.5}{-50}==\frac{1-1.5}{-10}$$

$$\Rightarrow \quad v = 50 \text{ cm}$$

5. $$\frac{\mu_2}{v}-\frac{\mu_1}{u}=\frac{\mu_2-\mu_1}{R} \Rightarrow \frac{2}{v}-\frac{1}{-10}=\frac{2-1}{+20}$$

$$\Rightarrow \quad v=-40 \text{ cm}$$

$$m=\frac{h_i}{h_0}=\frac{\mu_1 v}{\mu_2 u}$$

$$\Rightarrow \quad \frac{h_i}{2}=\frac{1(-40)}{2(-10)} \Rightarrow h_i = 4 \text{ cm}$$

So, the image is 40 cm from pole in air, virtual, erect and 4 cm in size.

6. $$\frac{\mu_2}{v}-\frac{\mu_1}{u}=\frac{\mu_2-\mu_1}{R}$$

$$\Rightarrow \quad \frac{1}{v}-\frac{1.5}{(-3)}=\frac{1-1.5}{(-3)} \Rightarrow v=-3 \text{ cm}$$

So, the printed letters will also appear near the centre.

7. $$\frac{\mu_2}{v}-\frac{\mu_1}{u}=\frac{\mu_2-\mu_1}{R}$$

$$\Rightarrow \quad \frac{1}{v}-\frac{1.5}{(-3)}=\frac{1-1.5}{\infty} \Rightarrow v=-2 \text{ cm}$$

So, the printed letters will appear 1 cm above the page.

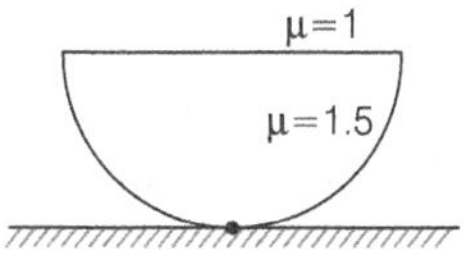

8. $$\frac{\mu_2}{v}-\frac{\mu_1}{u}=\frac{\mu_2-\mu_1}{R}$$

Differentiating both sides w.r.t. time,

$$-\frac{\mu_2}{v^2}\frac{dv}{dt}+\frac{\mu_1}{u^2}\frac{du}{dt}=0$$

$$\Rightarrow \quad \frac{dv}{dt}=\left(\frac{\mu_1}{\mu_2}\right)\left(\frac{v}{u}\right)^2\frac{du}{dt}$$

$$\Rightarrow \quad v_i=\left(\frac{\mu_1}{\mu_2}\right)\left(\frac{v}{u}\right)^2 v_0$$

$$\frac{\mu_2}{v}-\frac{\mu_1}{u}=\frac{\mu_2-\mu_1}{R}$$

$$\Rightarrow \quad \frac{1.5}{v}-\frac{1}{-30}=\frac{1.5-1}{+10}$$

$$\Rightarrow \quad v = 90 \text{ cm}$$

$$\therefore \quad v_i=\left(\frac{\mu_1}{\mu_2}\right)\left(\frac{v}{u}\right)^2 v_0$$

$$=\left(\frac{1}{1.5}\right)\left(\frac{90}{-30}\right)^2(2)=12 \text{ m/s}$$

3.2 Lens Maker Formula

1. (a) $$\frac{1}{f}=\left(\frac{\mu_1}{\mu_2}-1\right)\left(\frac{1}{R_1}-\frac{1}{R_2}\right)$$

$$\Rightarrow \quad \frac{1}{f}=\left(\frac{1.5}{1}-1\right)\left(\frac{1}{20}-\frac{1}{-20}\right)$$

$$\Rightarrow \quad f=20\text{ cm}$$

(b) $$\frac{1}{f}=\left(\frac{\mu_1}{\mu_2}-1\right)\left(\frac{1}{R_1}-\frac{1}{R_2}\right)$$

$$\Rightarrow \quad \frac{1}{f}=\left(\frac{1.5}{1}-1\right)\left(\frac{1}{\infty}-\frac{1}{-20}\right)$$

$$\Rightarrow \quad f=40\text{ cm}$$

(c) $$\frac{1}{f}=\left(\frac{\mu_1}{\mu_2}-1\right)\left(\frac{1}{R_1}-\frac{1}{R_2}\right)$$

$$\Rightarrow \quad \frac{1}{f}=\left(\frac{1.5}{1}-1\right)\left(\frac{1}{-60}-\frac{1}{-40}\right)$$

$$\Rightarrow \quad f=240\text{ cm}$$

(d) $$\frac{1}{f}=\left(\frac{\mu_1}{\mu_2}-1\right)\left(\frac{1}{R_1}-\frac{1}{R_2}\right)$$

$$\Rightarrow \quad \frac{1}{f}=\left(\frac{1.5}{1}-1\right)\left(\frac{1}{-20}-\frac{1}{20}\right)$$

$$\Rightarrow \quad f=-20\text{ cm}$$

(e) $$\frac{1}{f}=\left(\frac{\mu_1}{\mu_2}-1\right)\left(\frac{1}{R_1}-\frac{1}{R_2}\right)$$

$$\Rightarrow \quad \frac{1}{f}=\left(\frac{1.5}{1}-1\right)\left(\frac{1}{\infty}-\frac{1}{20}\right)$$

$$\Rightarrow \quad f=-40\text{ cm}$$

(f) $$\frac{1}{f}=\left(\frac{\mu_1}{\mu_2}-1\right)\left(\frac{1}{R_1}-\frac{1}{R_2}\right)$$

$$\Rightarrow \quad \frac{1}{f}=\left(\frac{1.5}{2}-1\right)\left(\frac{1}{60}-\frac{1}{-40}\right)$$

$$\Rightarrow \quad f=-96\text{ cm}$$

2. $$\frac{1}{f}=(\mu-1)\left(\frac{1}{R_1}-\frac{1}{R_2}\right)$$

$$\Rightarrow \quad \frac{1}{f}=(1.5-1)\left(\frac{1}{\pm 20}-\frac{1}{\pm 30}\right)$$

$$\Rightarrow \quad f=\pm 24\text{ cm}, \pm 120\text{cm}$$

3. When lens is in air,

$$\frac{1}{f}=\left(\frac{\mu_1}{\mu_2}-1\right)\left(\frac{1}{R_1}-\frac{1}{R_2}\right)$$

$$\Rightarrow \quad \frac{1}{20}=\left(\frac{1.5}{1}-1\right)\left(\frac{1}{R_1}-\frac{1}{R_2}\right) \quad \text{...(i)}$$

When lens is immersed in liquid,

$$\frac{1}{f}=\left(\frac{\mu_1}{\mu_2}-1\right)\left(\frac{1}{R_1}-\frac{1}{R_2}\right)$$

$$\Rightarrow \quad \frac{1}{f}=\left(\frac{1.5}{1.6}-1\right)\left(\frac{1}{R_1}-\frac{1}{R_2}\right) \quad \text{...(ii)}$$

Dividing Eq. (i) by (ii),

$$f=-160\text{ cm}$$

4. For refraction at first spherical surface,

$$\frac{\mu_2}{v}-\frac{\mu_1}{u}=\frac{\mu_2-\mu_1}{R}$$

$$\Rightarrow \quad \frac{\mu_2}{v_1}-\frac{\mu_1}{u}=\frac{\mu_2-\mu_1}{+R} \quad \text{...(i)}$$

For refraction at second spherical surface,

$$\frac{\mu_2}{v}-\frac{\mu_1}{u}=\frac{\mu_2-\mu_1}{R}$$

$$\Rightarrow \quad \frac{\mu_3}{v}-\frac{\mu_2}{v_1}=\frac{\mu_3-\mu_2}{+R} \quad \text{...(ii)}$$

Adding Eqs. (i) and (ii), we get,

$$\frac{\mu_3}{v}-\frac{\mu_1}{u}=\frac{\mu_3-\mu_1}{R}$$

Substituting $u=-\infty, v=f$

$$\Rightarrow \quad \frac{\mu_3}{f}-\frac{\mu_1}{-\infty}=\frac{\mu_3-\mu_1}{R} \quad \Rightarrow \quad f=\frac{\mu_3 R}{\mu_3-\mu_1}$$

5. $$\frac{1}{f}=(\mu-1)\left(\frac{1}{R_1}-\frac{1}{R_2}\right)$$

$$\Rightarrow \quad \frac{1}{f}=(\mu-1)\left(\frac{1}{R}-\frac{1}{-R}\right)$$

$$\Rightarrow \quad \frac{R}{\mu-1}=2f$$

(i) When it is cut along XOX', R_1 and R_2 are unaffected. So, focal length of each half will be f.

(ii) When it is cut along YOY',

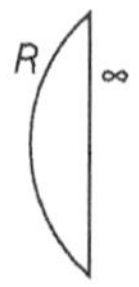

$$\frac{1}{f'}=(\mu-1)\left(\frac{1}{R}-\frac{1}{\infty}\right)$$

$$\Rightarrow \quad f'=\frac{R}{(\mu-1)}=2f$$

3.3 Ray Diagrams

1. (a) Incident ray passing through the first focus emerges parallel to the principal axis after passing through a convex lens.

(b) A parallel beam of light incident on a concave lens appears to be coming from focal plane after passing through the lens.

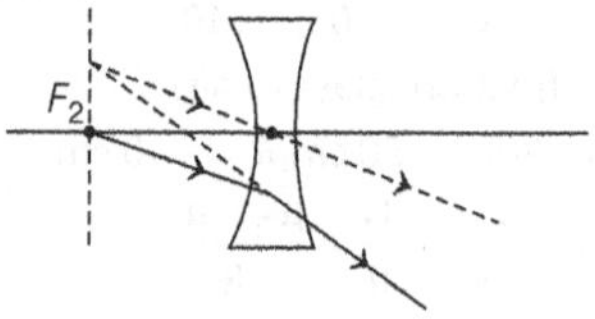

2. For finding position of lens and focus we follow two steps

Step-1 The ray passing through optical centre of the lens goes undeviated. It means, to obtain the position of optical centre join O and I by a straight line. The point of intersection of this line and optical axis should be the position of the optical centre of the lens.

Step-2 The ray travelling parallel to optical axis after refraction from lens passes through focus of the lens. For getting the position of focus, draw a line passing through O and parallel to optical axis. It will cut lens at position B. Join I and B and extend this line, it will intersect optical axis at focus.

Case-(a) Here rays are converging after refraction which means the lens should be convex. Also the virtual image is enlarged, hence the lens should be convex.

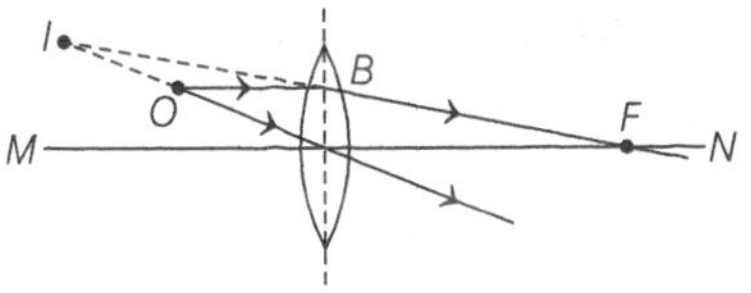

Case-(b) Here the rays are diverging after refraction which means lens should be concave. Also the virtual image is diminished, hence the lens must be concave.

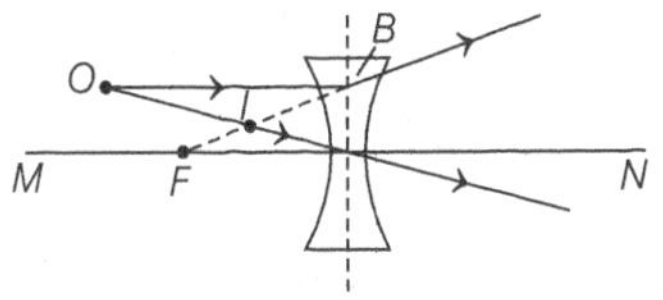

Case-(c) Since the image is real and on the other side of lens, the lens must be convex. Also the converging nature of rays after refraction means the lens is convex.

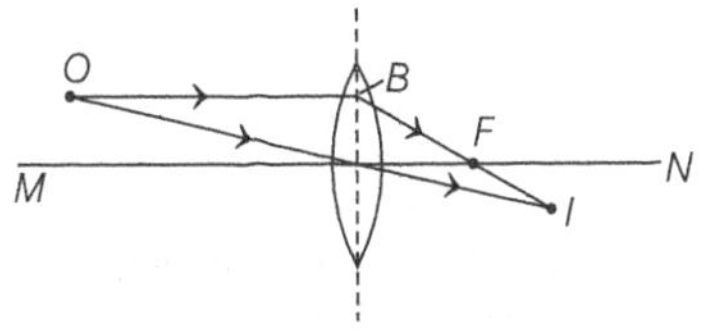

3.4 Lens Formula

1. $\frac{1}{v}-\frac{1}{u}=\frac{1}{f} \Rightarrow \frac{1}{v}-\frac{1}{-25}=\frac{1}{20}$

$\Rightarrow \quad v=100\text{ cm}$

$m=\frac{h_i}{h_0}=-\frac{v}{u}$

$\Rightarrow \quad \frac{h_i}{5}=-\frac{(100)}{(-25)}$

$\Rightarrow \quad h_i=20\text{ mm}$

2. $m=\frac{f}{f+u} \Rightarrow \pm 2=\frac{10}{10+u}$

$\Rightarrow \quad u=-50\text{ cm}$ and $u=-15\text{ cm}$

3. $\frac{1}{v}-\frac{1}{u}=\frac{1}{f}$

$\Rightarrow \frac{1}{v}-\frac{1}{(+30)}=\frac{1}{10} \Rightarrow v=7.5\text{ cm}$

4. $\frac{1}{v}-\frac{1}{-60}=\frac{1}{f}$ ...(i)

$\frac{1}{v+10}-\frac{1}{-40}=\frac{1}{f}$ ...(ii)

Solving Eqs. (i) and (ii), we get

$f=20\text{ cm}$

5. Angle subtended by object at the lens,

$\theta=\frac{1.4\times 10^9}{1.5\times 10^{11}}$

Diameter of image of sun $=f\theta=40\left(\frac{1.4\times 10^9}{1.5\times 10^{11}}\right)$

$=\frac{28}{75}\text{ cm}=0.37\text{ cm}$

6. (a) For end A, $u=-40$ cm

$\frac{1}{v}-\frac{1}{u}=\frac{1}{f}$

$\Rightarrow \frac{1}{v_A}-\frac{1}{-40}=\frac{1}{20} \Rightarrow v_A=-40\text{ cm}$

For end B, $u=-35$ cm

$\frac{1}{v}-\frac{1}{u}=\frac{1}{f}$

$\Rightarrow \frac{1}{v_B}-\frac{1}{-35}=\frac{1}{20}$

$\Rightarrow \quad v_B=-\frac{140}{3}\text{ cm}$

Length of image $=|v_A-v_B|=\frac{20}{3}$ cm

(b) $dv=-\frac{v^2}{u^2}du$

$\Rightarrow \quad dv=-\left(\frac{f}{f+u}\right)^2 du$

$\Rightarrow \quad dv=-\left[\frac{20}{20+(-60)}\right]^2 (1\text{ mm})$

$\Rightarrow \quad dv=-0.25\text{ mm}$

So, length of image $=0.25$ mm

7. $\frac{1}{v}-\frac{1}{u}=\frac{1}{f}$

$\Rightarrow \frac{1}{v}-\frac{1}{-30}=\frac{1}{15} \Rightarrow v=30\text{ cm}$

Shift due to slab $=t\left(1-\frac{1}{\mu}\right)=3\left(1-\frac{1}{1.5}\right)=1\text{ cm}$

So, final image will be 30 + 1 = 31 cm from lens.

8. $\frac{1}{f}=(\mu-1)\left(\frac{1}{R_1}-\frac{1}{R_2}\right)$

R_1 and R_2 are same for all the three parts but refractive indices are different. So, each part has different focal length. Therefore, 3 distinct images will be formed of a point object.

9.

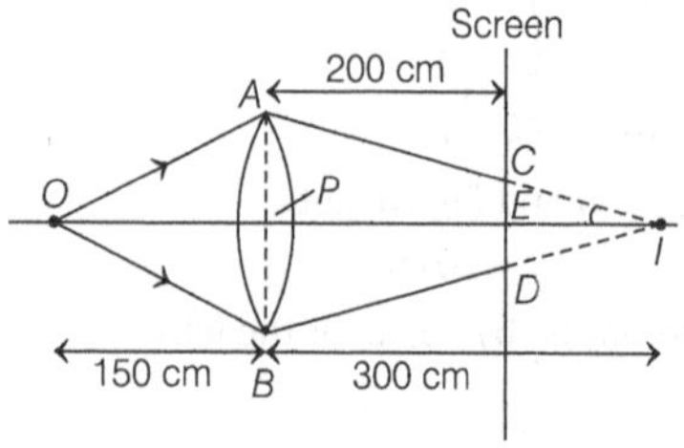

$$\frac{1}{v}-\frac{1}{u}=\frac{1}{f} \Rightarrow \frac{1}{v}-\frac{1}{-150}=\frac{1}{100} \Rightarrow v=300\text{ cm}$$

From similar triangles, $\frac{CD}{AB}=\frac{EI}{PI}$

$$\Rightarrow \frac{CD}{3}=\frac{100}{300} \Rightarrow CD=1\text{ cm}$$

Area of illuminated part on the screen $=\pi r^2$

$$=\pi\left(\frac{1}{2}\right)^2=\frac{\pi}{4}\text{ cm}^2$$

3.5 Displacement Method to Find Focal Length

1. $f=\frac{D^2-d^2}{4D}=\frac{(100)^2-(60)^2}{4(100)}=16\text{ cm}$
2. $h=\sqrt{h_1h_2}=\sqrt{4\times 9}=6\text{ cm}$
3. $f=\frac{D^2-d^2}{4D}$

   When, $D=270$ cm, $d=x$

   $$f=\frac{(270)^2-x^2}{4(270)} \quad \text{...(i)}$$

   When, $D=375$ cm, $d=\frac{5x}{2}$

   $$f=\frac{(375)^2-(5x/2)^2}{4(375)} \quad \text{...(ii)}$$

   From Eqs. (i) and (ii), we get

   $$f=58.33\text{ cm}$$

3.6 Velocity of Images

1. $\frac{dv}{dt}=\left(\frac{f}{f+u}\right)^2\frac{du}{dt}=\left[\frac{0.3}{0.3+(-0.4)}\right]^2(0.01)=0.09\text{ m/s}$

   $$m=\frac{f}{f+u} \Rightarrow \frac{dm}{dt}=-\frac{f}{(f+u)^2}\frac{du}{dt}$$

   $$=-\frac{0.3}{[0.3+(-0.4)]^2}(0.01)$$

   $$=-0.3\text{ s}^{-1}$$

2. $\frac{1}{v}-\frac{1}{u}=\frac{1}{f} \Rightarrow \frac{1}{v}-\frac{1}{-15}=\frac{1}{10} \Rightarrow v=30\text{ cm}$

   Along the principal axis,

   $$(v_{iL})_x=\frac{v^2}{u^2}(v_{oL})_x$$

   $$\Rightarrow v_i-2=\left(\frac{30}{-15}\right)^2(1-2)$$

   $$\Rightarrow v_i=-2\text{ cm/s}=2\text{ cm/s, left}$$

3. $\frac{1}{v}-\frac{1}{u}=\frac{1}{f} \Rightarrow \frac{1}{v}-\frac{1}{-15}=\frac{1}{10} \Rightarrow v=30\text{ cm}$

   Perpendicular to the principal axis,

   $$(v_i)_y=\frac{v}{u}(v_o)_y$$

   $$\Rightarrow v_i=\left(\frac{30}{-15}\right)(1)=-2\text{ cm/s}$$

   $$=2\text{ cm/s (downward)}$$

3.7 Combinaton of Lenses

1. For convex lens,

   $$\frac{1}{v}-\frac{1}{u}=\frac{1}{f}$$

   $$\Rightarrow \frac{1}{v}-\frac{1}{-15}=\frac{1}{10} \Rightarrow v=30\text{ cm}$$

   For concave lens,

   $$u=+(30-25)=+5\text{ cm}$$

   $$\frac{1}{v}-\frac{1}{u}=\frac{1}{f}$$

   $$\Rightarrow \frac{1}{v}-\frac{1}{5}=\frac{1}{(-10)} \Rightarrow v=10\text{ cm}$$

   So, the final image will be 10 cm right of the concave lens.

2. For converging lens,

   $$\frac{1}{v}-\frac{1}{u}=\frac{1}{f}$$

   $$\Rightarrow \frac{1}{v}-\frac{1}{-15}=\frac{1}{10} \Rightarrow v=30\text{ cm}$$

   Second lens is placed mid-way between the first lens and the screen. So, for second lens,

   $u=+(30-20)=+10$ cm, $v=+20$ cm

   $$\frac{1}{v}-\frac{1}{u}=\frac{1}{f} \Rightarrow \frac{1}{20}-\frac{1}{10}=\frac{1}{f}$$

   $$\Rightarrow f=-20\text{ cm}$$

   Hence, the second lens will be concave of focal length 20 cm.

3. (i)

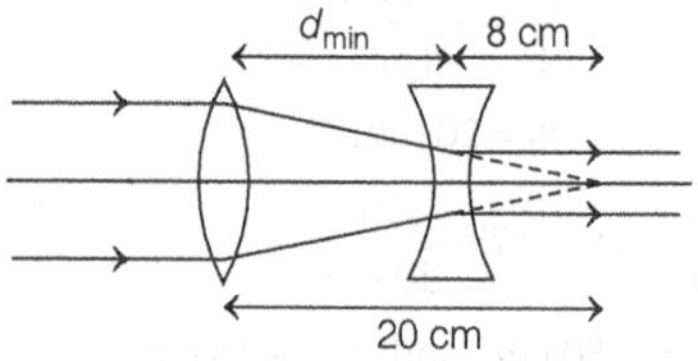

   $$d_{min}=20-8=12\text{ cm}$$

   (ii) For converging lens,

   $$\frac{1}{v}-\frac{1}{u}=\frac{1}{f}$$

$$\Rightarrow \quad \frac{1}{v} - \frac{1}{-\infty} = \frac{1}{20}$$

$$\Rightarrow \quad v = 20 \text{ cm}$$

For diverging lens,

$$u = +(20 - 6) = +14 \text{ cm}$$

$$\frac{1}{v} - \frac{1}{u} = \frac{1}{f}$$

$$\Rightarrow \quad \frac{1}{v} - \frac{1}{14} = \frac{1}{-8}$$

$$\Rightarrow \quad v = -\frac{56}{3} \text{ cm}$$

So, the final image is $\frac{56}{3}$ cm left of concave lens and virtual in nature.

4.

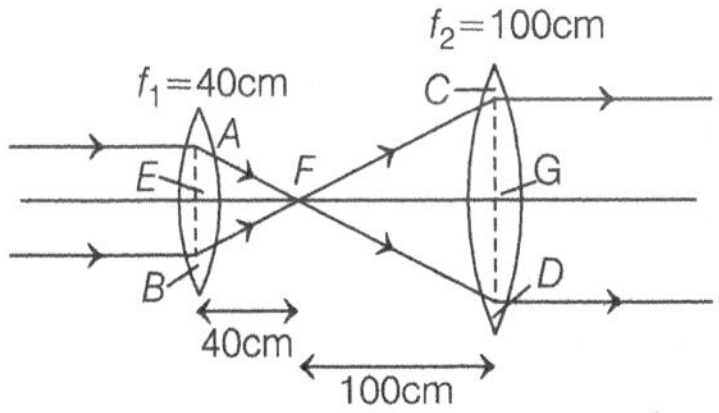

ΔABF and ΔCDF are similar triangles.

$$\therefore \quad \frac{CD}{AB} = \frac{GF}{EF}$$

$$\Rightarrow \quad \frac{CD}{4} = \frac{100}{40}$$

$$\Rightarrow \quad CD = 10 \text{ mm} = 1 \text{ cm}$$

5.

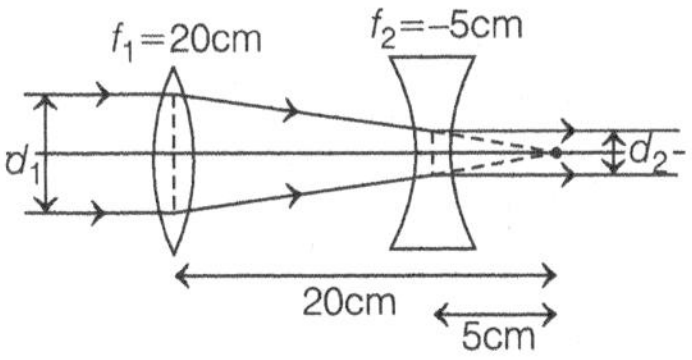

Separation between the lenses = 20 − 5 = 15 cm

Let diameters of the incident and emergent beams by d_1 and d_2 respectively.

$$\therefore \quad \frac{d_1}{d_2} = \frac{20}{5}$$

$$\Rightarrow \quad \frac{d_2}{d_1} = \frac{1}{4}$$

Intensity, $I = \frac{\text{Power}}{\text{Area}} = \frac{P}{A} = \frac{4P}{\pi d^2}$

$$\therefore \quad \frac{I_1}{I_2} = \frac{d_2^2}{d_1^2}$$

$$\Rightarrow \quad \frac{100}{I_2} = \left(\frac{1}{4}\right)^2$$

$$\Rightarrow \quad I_1 = 1600 \text{ W/m}^2$$

6.

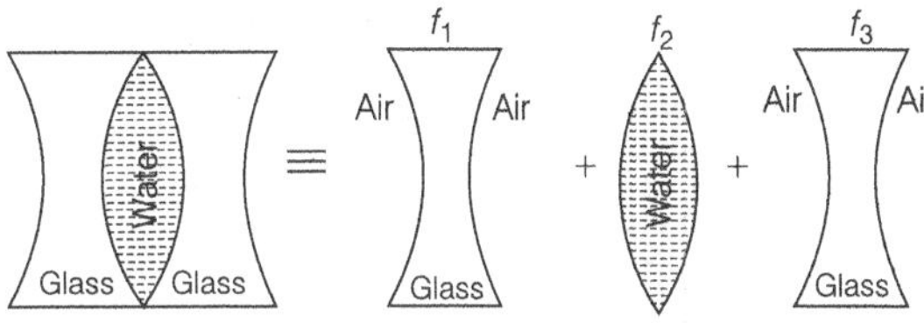

$$\frac{1}{f_1} = (1.5 - 1)\left(\frac{1}{-10} - \frac{1}{10}\right)$$

$$\Rightarrow \quad f_1 = -10 \text{ cm}$$

$$\frac{1}{f_2} = \left(\frac{4}{3} - 1\right)\left(\frac{1}{10} - \frac{1}{-10}\right)$$

$$\Rightarrow \quad f_2 = 15 \text{ cm}$$

$$\frac{1}{f_3} = (1.5 - 1)\left(\frac{1}{-10} - \frac{1}{10}\right)$$

$$\Rightarrow \quad f_3 = -10 \text{ cm}$$

$$\frac{1}{f_{eq}} = \frac{1}{f_1} + \frac{1}{f_2} + \frac{1}{f_3}$$

$$\Rightarrow \quad \frac{1}{f_{eq}} = \frac{1}{(-10)} + \frac{1}{15} + \frac{1}{(-10)}$$

$$\Rightarrow \quad f_{eq} = -7.5 \text{ cm}$$

7. For convex lens,

$$\frac{1}{v} - \frac{1}{u} = \frac{1}{f} \quad \Rightarrow \quad \frac{1}{30} - \frac{1}{-15} = \frac{1}{f_1}$$

$$\Rightarrow \quad f_1 = 10 \text{ cm}$$

For the combination,

$$\frac{1}{v} - \frac{1}{u} = \frac{1}{f} \quad \Rightarrow \quad \frac{1}{60} - \frac{1}{-15} = \frac{1}{f_{eq}}$$

$$\Rightarrow \quad f_{eq} = 12 \text{ cm}$$

$$\frac{1}{f_{eq}} = \frac{1}{f_1} + \frac{1}{f_2} \quad \Rightarrow \quad \frac{1}{12} = \frac{1}{10} + \frac{1}{f_2}$$

$$\Rightarrow \quad f_2 = -60 \text{ cm}$$

8. Lens in contact,

$$P_{eq} = P_1 + P_2 \Rightarrow 10 = P_1 + P_2 \quad \text{...(i)}$$

Lens held 0.25 m apart,

$$P_{eq} = P_1 + P_2 - dP_1P_2$$

$$\Rightarrow \quad 6 = P_1 + P_2 - 0.25P_1P_2 \quad \text{...(ii)}$$

Solving Eqs. (i) and (ii), we get

$$P_1 = 8 \text{ D} \quad \text{and} \quad P_2 = 2 \text{ D}$$

$$\therefore \quad f_1 = \frac{1}{P_1} = 12.5 \text{ cm}$$

$$\text{and} \quad f_2 = \frac{1}{P_2} = 50 \text{ cm}$$

9. $P_{eq} = \frac{1}{f_1} + \frac{1}{f_2} - \frac{d}{f_1 f_2} \Rightarrow 0 = \frac{1}{25} + \frac{1}{(-20)} - \frac{d}{(25)(-20)}$

$$\Rightarrow \quad d = 5 \text{ cm}$$

3.8 Combination of Lens and Mirror

1. For the first refraction through lens,

$$\frac{1}{v}-\frac{1}{u}=\frac{1}{f}$$

$$\Rightarrow \quad \frac{1}{v}-\frac{1}{-15}=\frac{1}{10}$$

$$\Rightarrow \quad v=30\text{ cm}$$

For reflection from mirror,

$$u=-(45-30)=-15\text{ cm}$$

$$\frac{1}{v}+\frac{1}{u}=\frac{1}{f}$$

$$\Rightarrow \quad \frac{1}{v}+\frac{1}{-15}=\frac{1}{-10} \quad \Rightarrow \quad v=-30\text{ cm}$$

For the final refraction through lens,

$$u=-(45-30)=-15\text{ cm}$$

$$\frac{1}{v}-\frac{1}{u}=\frac{1}{f}$$

$$\Rightarrow \quad \frac{1}{v}-\frac{1}{-15}=\frac{1}{10}$$

$$\Rightarrow \quad v=30\text{ cm}$$

So, the final image will be 30 cm left of lens.

2. For the first refraction through lens,

$$\frac{1}{v}-\frac{1}{u}=\frac{1}{f} \quad \Rightarrow \quad \frac{1}{v}-\frac{1}{-30}=\frac{1}{20}$$

$$\Rightarrow \quad v=60\text{ cm}$$

For the final image to be formed on the object itself,

Case-I The rays refracted from lens should be incident on the mirror normally, so that after reflection they retrace their path. Therefore, the rays incident on the mirror should be headed for the centre of curvature of the mirror.

$$\therefore \quad d+20=60$$

$$\Rightarrow \quad d=40\text{ cm}$$

Case-II The rays refracted from the lens should converge at the pole of the mirror.

$$\therefore \quad d=60\text{ cm}$$

3. For the final image to be on the object itself, the rays incident on the mirror should appear to be coming from the centre of curvature of the mirror.

For the first refraction through lens,

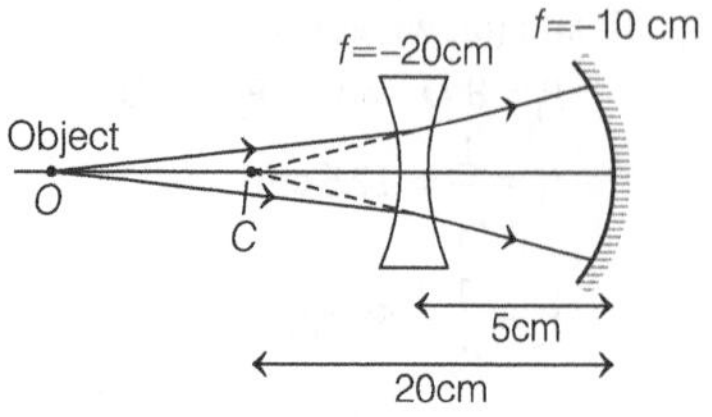

$$\frac{1}{v}-\frac{1}{u}=\frac{1}{f} \quad \Rightarrow \quad \frac{1}{-15}-\frac{1}{u}=\frac{1}{-20} \quad \Rightarrow \quad u=-60\text{ cm}$$

So, the object should be placed 60 cm left of the lens.

4. Let distance of the object from the lens be x.

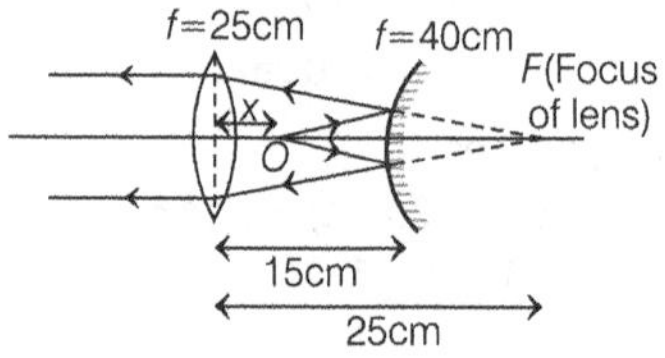

For the emergent beam to be parallel, the reflected rays from the mirror should appear to be coming from the focus of the lens.

So, for the mirror, $u=-(15-x)$,

$$v=+(25-15)=+10\text{ cm}$$

$$\frac{1}{v}+\frac{1}{u}=\frac{1}{f}$$

$$\Rightarrow \quad \frac{1}{10}+\frac{1}{-(15-x)}=\frac{1}{40} \quad \Rightarrow \quad x=\frac{5}{3}\text{ cm}=1.67\text{ cm}$$

5. For the first refraction through lens,

$$\frac{1}{v}-\frac{1}{u}=\frac{1}{f} \quad \Rightarrow \quad \frac{1}{v}-\frac{1}{-12}=\frac{1}{15} \quad \Rightarrow \quad v=-60\text{ cm}$$

For the emergent beam to be parallel, the mirror should form image at the second focus of the lens. So, for the mirror,

$$u=-(60+40)=-100\text{ cm},$$

$$v=-(40-15)=-25\text{ cm}$$

$$\frac{1}{v}+\frac{1}{u}=\frac{1}{f} \quad \Rightarrow \quad \frac{1}{(-25)}+\frac{1}{(-100)}=\frac{1}{f} \quad \Rightarrow \quad f=-20\text{ cm}$$

3.9 Silvered Lens

1.

$$P=2P_L+P_M$$

$$\Rightarrow \quad -\frac{1}{f}=2\left(\frac{1}{f_L}\right)+\left(-\frac{1}{f_M}\right)$$

$$\Rightarrow \quad -\frac{1}{f}=2\left(\frac{1}{20}\right)+\left[-\frac{1}{(-11)}\right]$$

$$\Rightarrow \quad f=-\frac{110}{21}\text{ cm}$$

So, the combination will act as a concave mirror of focal length $\frac{110}{21}$ cm.

$$\frac{1}{v}+\frac{1}{u}=\frac{1}{f} \quad \Rightarrow \quad \frac{1}{v}+\frac{1}{(-10)}=\frac{1}{-(110/21)}$$

$$\Rightarrow \quad v=-11\text{ cm}$$

So, the final image will be infront of the combination.

2. When silvered on the plane side,

$$P=2P_L+P_M$$

$$\Rightarrow \quad -\frac{1}{f}=\frac{2}{f_L}-\frac{1}{f_M} \quad \Rightarrow \quad -\frac{1}{-30}=\frac{2}{f_L}-\frac{1}{\infty}$$

$$\Rightarrow \quad f_L=60\text{ cm}$$

When silvered on the convex side,

$$P=2P_L+P_M$$

$\Rightarrow \quad -\frac{1}{f} = \frac{2}{f_L} - \frac{1}{f_M} \quad \Rightarrow \quad -\frac{1}{-10} = \frac{2}{60} - \frac{1}{(-R/2)}$

$\Rightarrow \quad R = 30$ cm

For lens,

$$\frac{1}{f_L} = (\mu - 1)\left(\frac{1}{R_1} - \frac{1}{R_2}\right)$$

$$\Rightarrow \quad \frac{1}{60} = (\mu - 1)\left(\frac{1}{30} - \frac{1}{\infty}\right) \quad \Rightarrow \quad \mu = 1.5$$

3. (a) For lens, $\frac{1}{f_L} = (\mu - 1)\left(\frac{1}{R_1} - \frac{1}{R_2}\right)$

$$\Rightarrow \quad \frac{1}{f_L} = (1.5 - 1)\left[\frac{1}{(-60)} - \frac{1}{(-20)}\right]$$

$\Rightarrow \quad f_L = 60$ cm

For combination,

$$P = 2P_L + P_M$$

$$\Rightarrow \quad -\frac{1}{f} = \frac{2}{f_L} - \frac{1}{f_M} \quad \Rightarrow \quad -\frac{1}{f} = \frac{2}{60} - \frac{1}{(-10)}$$

$\Rightarrow \quad f = -7.5$ cm

For image to coincide with the object, the object should be kept at the centre of curvature of the equivalent mirror.

$\therefore$ Object distance $= 2f = 15$ cm

(b) For water lens,

$$\frac{1}{f_W} = (\mu - 1)\left[\frac{1}{R_1} - \frac{1}{R_2}\right]$$

$$\Rightarrow \quad \frac{1}{f_W} = \left(\frac{4}{3} - 1\right)\left(\frac{1}{\infty} - \frac{1}{-60}\right)$$

$\Rightarrow \quad f_W = 180$ cm

For the combination of glass lens, water lens and concave mirror,

$$P = 2P_L + 2P_W + P_M$$

$$\Rightarrow \quad -\frac{1}{f} = \frac{2}{60} + \frac{2}{180} - \frac{1}{(-10)} \quad \Rightarrow \quad f = -\frac{90}{13} \text{ cm}$$

$\therefore$ New radius of curvature $= 2f = \frac{180}{13}$ cm

Displacement of object $= 15 - \frac{180}{13} = \frac{15}{13} = 1.15$ cm

Level 2

Single Choice Correct Questions

1. $u = -x, v = +x$

$$\frac{\mu_2}{v} - \frac{\mu_1}{v} = \frac{\mu_2 - \mu_1}{R}$$

$$\Rightarrow \quad \frac{\mu_2}{x} - \frac{\mu_1}{(-x)} = \frac{\mu_2 - \mu_1}{+R}$$

$$\Rightarrow \quad x = \left(\frac{\mu_2 + \mu_1}{\mu_2 - \mu_1}\right)R$$

2. $$\frac{\mu_2}{v} - \frac{\mu_1}{u} = \frac{\mu_2 - \mu_1}{R}$$

$$\Rightarrow \quad \frac{1}{v} - \frac{3/2}{+30} = \frac{1 - (3/2)}{+20}$$

$\Rightarrow \quad v = 40$ cm

3. $u = -R$, $\frac{\mu_2}{v} - \frac{\mu_1}{u} = \frac{\mu_2 - \mu_1}{R}$

$$\Rightarrow \quad \frac{1}{v} - \frac{\mu}{(-R)} = \frac{1 - \mu}{(-R)}$$

$\Rightarrow \quad v = -R$

So, the dot will appear at C for all values of μ.

4. Case-I $\mu_1 = 1, \mu_2 = 1.6$

$$\frac{\mu_2}{v} - \frac{\mu_1}{u} = \frac{\mu_2 - \mu_1}{R}$$

$$\Rightarrow \quad \frac{1.6}{v_1} - \frac{1}{(-2)} = \frac{1.6 - 1}{(+1)}$$

$\Rightarrow \quad v_1 = 16$ m

Case-II $\mu_1 = 1, \mu_2 = 2$

$$\frac{\mu_2}{v} - \frac{\mu_1}{u} = \frac{\mu_2 - \mu_1}{R}$$

$$\Rightarrow \quad \frac{2}{v_2} - \frac{1}{(-2)} = \frac{2 - 1}{(+1)}$$

$\Rightarrow \quad v_2 = 4$ m

$\therefore$ Separation between the two images $= v_1 - v_2$
$= 16 - 4 = 12$ m

5. For first refraction at spherical surface (air to glass),

$$\frac{\mu_2}{v} - \frac{\mu_1}{u} = \frac{\mu_2 - \mu_1}{R}$$

$$\Rightarrow \quad \frac{1.5}{v} - \frac{1}{(-\infty)} = \frac{1.5 - 1}{(+6)}$$

$\Rightarrow \quad v = 18$ cm

For second refraction at plane surface (glass to air)

$u = +(18 - 6) = 12$ cm

$$\frac{\mu_2}{v} - \frac{\mu_1}{u} = \frac{\mu_2 - \mu_1}{R}$$

$$\Rightarrow \quad \frac{1}{v} - \frac{1.5}{(+12)} = \frac{1 - 1.5}{\infty} \quad \Rightarrow \quad v = 8 \text{ cm}$$

So, the beam will converge 8 cm from the plane surface.

6. $$\frac{\mu_2}{v} - \frac{\mu_1}{u} = \frac{\mu_2 - \mu_1}{R}$$

$$\Rightarrow \quad \frac{1.5}{v} - \frac{1}{(-30)} = \frac{1.5 - 1}{+10}$$

$\Rightarrow \quad v = 90$ cm

Magnification, $m = \frac{h_i}{h_o} = \frac{\mu_1 v}{\mu_2 u}$

$$\Rightarrow \quad \frac{h_i}{0.5} = \frac{1(90)}{1.5(-30)}$$

$\Rightarrow \quad h_i = -1$ cm

7. When viewed from left,

$$\frac{\mu_2}{v}-\frac{\mu_1}{u}=\frac{\mu_2-\mu_1}{R} \Rightarrow \frac{1}{v_1}-\frac{1.6}{(-4)}=\frac{1-1.6}{\infty}$$

$$\Rightarrow \quad v_1=-2.5 \text{ cm}$$

So, the image is formed 2.5 cm from the plane surface inside the hemisphere.

When viewed from right,

$$\frac{\mu_2}{v}-\frac{\mu_1}{u}=\frac{\mu_2-\mu_1}{R}$$

$$\Rightarrow \quad \frac{1}{v_2}-\frac{1.6}{-4}=\frac{1-1.6}{(-8)}$$

$$\Rightarrow \quad v_2=-\frac{40}{13} \text{ cm} \approx -3 \text{ cm}$$

So, the image is formed 3 cm from the curved surface inside the hemisphere.

Separation between the two images

$$=8-2.5-3$$

$$=2.5 \text{ cm}$$

8. $$\frac{\mu_2}{v}-\frac{\mu_1}{u}=\frac{\mu_2-\mu_1}{R} \Rightarrow \frac{1}{v}-\frac{3/2}{-20}=\frac{1-(3/2)}{+20}$$

$$\Rightarrow \quad v=-10 \text{ cm}$$

So, the flowers will appear 10 cm below the curved surface or $(20-10)=10$ cm above its actual position.

9.

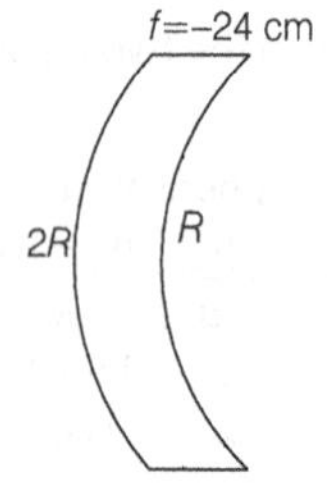

$$\frac{1}{f}=(\mu-1)\left(\frac{1}{R_1}-\frac{1}{R_2}\right)$$

$$\Rightarrow \quad \frac{1}{-24}=(1.5-1)\left(\frac{1}{2R}-\frac{1}{R}\right)$$

$$\Rightarrow \quad R=6 \text{ cm}$$

So, radii of curvature for the two surfaces are 6 cm and 12 cm.

10. When lens in air,

$$\frac{1}{f}=(\mu-1)\left(\frac{1}{R_1}-\frac{1}{R_2}\right)$$

$$\Rightarrow \quad \frac{1}{10}=\left(\frac{3}{2}-1\right)\left(\frac{1}{R_1}-\frac{1}{R_2}\right)$$

$$\Rightarrow \quad \frac{1}{R_1}-\frac{1}{R_2}=\frac{1}{5}$$

When lens in medium of refractive index 7/5,

$$\frac{1}{f}=\left(\frac{\mu_1}{\mu_2}-1\right)\left(\frac{1}{R_1}-\frac{1}{R_2}\right)$$

$$\Rightarrow \quad \frac{1}{f}=\left(\frac{3/2}{7/5}-1\right)\left(\frac{1}{5}\right)$$

$$\Rightarrow \quad f=70 \text{ cm}$$

11. $$\frac{1}{f}=\left(\frac{\mu_1}{\mu_2}-1\right)\left(\frac{1}{R_1}-\frac{1}{R_2}\right)$$

$$\Rightarrow \quad \frac{1}{f}=\left(\frac{1.5}{1.75}-1\right)\left[\frac{1}{(-R)}-\frac{1}{R}\right]$$

$$\Rightarrow \quad f=3.5R$$

So, it will behave as a convergent lens of focal lens $3.5R$.

12. For refraction at first surface,

$$\frac{\mu_2}{v_1}-\frac{\mu_1}{u}=\frac{\mu_2-\mu_1}{(+R)} \quad \text{...(i)}$$

For refraction at second surface,

$$\frac{\mu_3}{v}-\frac{\mu_2}{v_1}=\frac{\mu_3-\mu_2}{(-R)} \quad \text{...(ii)}$$

Adding Eqs. (i) and (ii), we get

$$\frac{\mu_3}{v}-\frac{\mu_1}{u}=\frac{2\mu_2-\mu_1-\mu_3}{R}$$

Substituting $u=-\infty, v=f$

$$\Rightarrow \quad \frac{\mu_3}{f}-\frac{\mu_1}{(-\infty)}=\frac{2\mu_2-\mu_1-\mu_3}{R}$$

For lens to be diverging, f should be negative

$$\therefore \quad \frac{\mu_3 R}{2\mu_2-\mu_1-\mu_3}<0 \Rightarrow 2\mu_2<\mu_1+\mu_3$$

13. $$\frac{1}{f}=(\mu-1)\left(\frac{1}{R_1}-\frac{1}{R_2}\right)$$

$$\Rightarrow \quad \frac{1}{10}=(1.5-1)\left(\frac{1}{-R}-\frac{1}{R}\right) \Rightarrow R=10 \text{ cm}$$

For refraction at first spherical surface,

$$\frac{\mu_2}{v}-\frac{\mu_1}{u}=\frac{\mu_2-\mu_1}{R}$$

$$\Rightarrow \quad \frac{1.5}{v_1}-\frac{1}{(-10)}=\frac{1.5-1}{-10} \quad \text{...(i)}$$

For refraction at second spherical surface,

$$\frac{\mu_2}{v}-\frac{\mu_1}{u}=\frac{\mu_2-\mu_1}{R} \Rightarrow \frac{\mu}{\infty}-\frac{1.5}{v_1}=\frac{\mu-1.5}{10} \quad \text{...(ii)}$$

Adding Eqs. (i) and (ii), we get

$$\mu=3$$

14. $m=\dfrac{f}{f+u} \Rightarrow -1=\dfrac{-f}{-f+u} \Rightarrow u=2f$

So, the object is virtual and located at a distance $2f$ from the lens.

15. Diameter of image $=f\theta=100\times 0.5\dfrac{\pi}{180}=0.9$ cm = 9 mm

16. $$m_1=-m_2$$

$$\Rightarrow \quad \frac{f}{f+(-u_1)}=-\frac{f}{f+(-u_2)} \Rightarrow f=\frac{u_1+u_2}{2}$$

17.

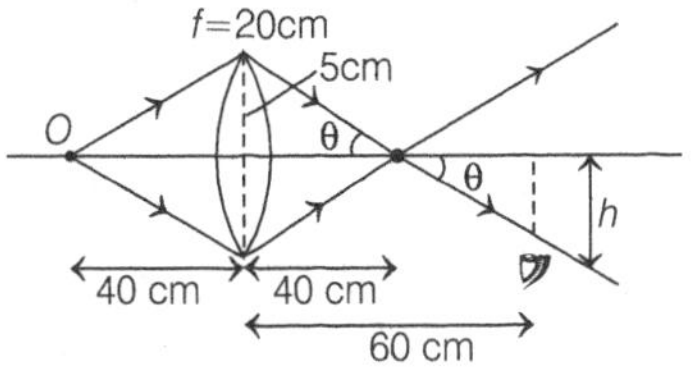

$$\tan\theta = \frac{5}{40} = \frac{h}{20} \Rightarrow h = 2.5 \text{ cm}$$

18. $\frac{1}{v} - \frac{1}{u} = \frac{1}{f} \Rightarrow \frac{1}{v} - \frac{1}{-15} = \frac{1}{10} \Rightarrow v = 30 \text{ cm}$

$$dv = \frac{v^2}{u^2} du = \frac{(30)^2}{(-15)^2}(1) = 4 \text{ mm}$$

19. Areal magnification = (linear magnification)^2

$\Rightarrow \quad 9 = m^2 \Rightarrow m = \pm 3$

Magnification, $m = \frac{f}{f+u}$

$\Rightarrow \quad -3 = \frac{f}{f+(-40)} \Rightarrow f = = 30 \text{ cm}$

20. (d)

21. Focal length will be same but amount of light getting refracted will decrease.

$$\frac{I_1}{I_2} = \frac{A_1}{A_2}$$

$\Rightarrow \quad \frac{I}{I_2} = \frac{\pi d^2/4}{\frac{\pi d^2}{4} - \frac{\pi(d/2)^2}{4}} \Rightarrow I_2 = \frac{3I}{4}$

22. $\frac{1}{v} - \frac{1}{u} = \frac{1}{f} \Rightarrow \frac{1}{v/f} - \frac{1}{u/f} = 1$

$\Rightarrow \quad \frac{1}{y} - \frac{1}{x} = 1 \Rightarrow y = \frac{x}{x+1}$

23. $\frac{1}{v} - \frac{1}{u} = \frac{1}{f} \Rightarrow \frac{1}{10} - \frac{1}{(-10)} = \frac{1}{f} \Rightarrow f = 5 \text{ cm}$

$$\frac{\Delta v}{v^2} + \frac{\Delta u}{u^2} = \frac{\Delta f}{f^2}$$

$\Rightarrow \quad \frac{0.1}{(10)^2} + \frac{0.1}{(10)^2} = \frac{\Delta f}{(5)^2}$

$\Rightarrow \quad \Delta f = 0.05$

So, focal length $= 5 \pm 0.05$

24. $m = \frac{v}{u} \Rightarrow -\frac{1}{3} = \frac{8}{u} \Rightarrow u = -24 \text{ cm}$

$$\frac{1}{v} - \frac{1}{u} = \frac{1}{f} \Rightarrow \frac{1}{8} - \frac{1}{(-24)} = \frac{1}{f} \Rightarrow f = 6 \text{ m}$$

Wavelength of light inside lens, $\lambda' = \frac{\lambda}{\mu}$

$\Rightarrow \quad \frac{2}{3}\lambda = \frac{\lambda}{\mu} \Rightarrow \mu = 1.5$

$$\frac{1}{f} = (\mu - 1)\left(\frac{1}{R_1} - \frac{1}{R_2}\right)$$

$\Rightarrow \quad \frac{1}{6} = (1.5 - 1)\left(\frac{1}{R} - \frac{1}{\infty}\right)$

$\Rightarrow \quad R = 3 \text{ m}$

25. Diameter of image of sun $= f\theta = 45 \times \left(\frac{30}{60} \times \frac{\pi}{180}\right)$ cm

$$= \frac{\pi}{8} \text{ cm}$$

$$\frac{I_1}{I_2} = \frac{A_2}{A_1} = \frac{\pi d_2^2/4}{\pi d_1^2/4} = \frac{d_2^2}{d_1^2}$$

$\Rightarrow \quad \frac{I_1}{I_2} = \left(\frac{3\pi}{\pi/8}\right)^2 \Rightarrow \frac{I_1}{I_2} = 576$

26. $\frac{1}{v} - \frac{1}{u} = \frac{1}{f} \Rightarrow \frac{1}{10} - \frac{1}{(-40)} = \frac{1}{f} \Rightarrow f = 8 \text{ cm}$

Shift due to glass slab $= t\left(1 - \frac{1}{\mu}\right) = 3\left(1 - \frac{1}{1.5}\right) = 1 \text{ cm}$

After insertion of slab,

$$v = (10 - 1) = 9 \text{ cm}, u = ?, f = 8 \text{ cm}$$

$$\frac{1}{v} - \frac{1}{u} = \frac{1}{f}$$

$\Rightarrow \quad \frac{1}{9} - \frac{1}{u} = \frac{1}{8} \Rightarrow u = -72 \text{ cm}$

So, the object should be placed 72 cm from the lens.

27. Let focal length be f

$\therefore \quad u = -(10 + f), v = 40 + f$

$$\frac{1}{v} - \frac{1}{u} = \frac{1}{f}$$

$\Rightarrow \quad \frac{1}{40+f} - \frac{1}{-(10+f)} = \frac{1}{f}$

$\Rightarrow \quad f = 20 \text{ cm}$

28. $f = \frac{D^2 - d^2}{4D} = \frac{(100)^2 - (40)^2}{4(100)} = 21 \text{ cm}$

Power of lens, $P = \frac{1}{f} = \frac{1}{0.21} \simeq 5 \text{ D}$

29.

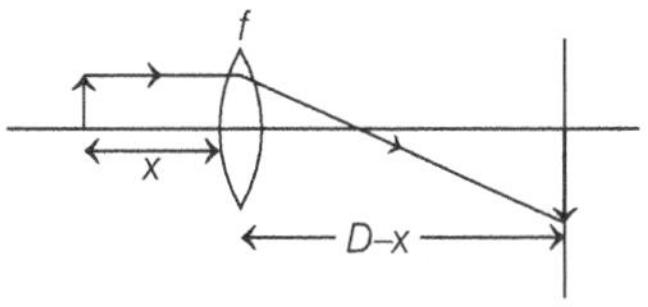

$$\frac{1}{v} - \frac{1}{u} = \frac{1}{f}$$

$\Rightarrow \quad \frac{1}{D-x} - \frac{1}{(-x)} = \frac{1}{f}$

$\Rightarrow \quad x^2 - Dx + Df = 0$

$\therefore \quad x_1 x_2 = Df \text{ and } x_1 - x_2 = d$

$$m_1 = \frac{D - x_1}{(-x_1)} \text{ and } m_2 = \frac{D - x_2}{(-x_2)}$$

$$\therefore \quad m_1 - m_2 = -\frac{D - x_1}{x_1} + \frac{D - x_2}{x_2} = \frac{D(x_1 - x_2)}{x_1 x_2} = \frac{Dd}{Df}$$

$$\Rightarrow \quad f = \frac{d}{m_1 - m_2}$$

30. $\frac{\mu_2}{v} - \frac{\mu_1}{u} = \frac{\mu_2 - \mu_1}{R}$

For refraction from air to glass,

$$\frac{3/2}{v_1} - \frac{1}{(-x)} = \frac{3/2 - 1}{+10} \quad \text{...(i)}$$

For refraction from glass to water,

$$\frac{4/3}{\infty} - \frac{3/2}{v_1} = \frac{4/3 - 3/2}{\infty} \quad \text{...(ii)}$$

Adding Eqs. (i) and (ii), we get

$$x = 20 \text{ cm}$$

31. For lens, $\frac{1}{v} - \frac{1}{u} = \frac{1}{f} \Rightarrow \frac{1}{v} - \frac{1}{\infty} = \frac{1}{30} \Rightarrow v = 30 \text{ cm}$

For refraction at plane refracting surface,

$$\frac{\mu_2}{v} - \frac{\mu_1}{u} = \frac{\mu_2 - \mu_1}{R}$$

$$\Rightarrow \frac{3/2}{v} - \frac{1}{+(30-10)} = \frac{3/2 - 1}{\infty}$$

$$\Rightarrow \quad v = 30 \text{ cm}$$

So, the rays will converge 30 cm from plane refracting surface or 40 cm from the lens.

32. $\frac{1}{v} - \frac{1}{u} = \frac{1}{f} \Rightarrow \frac{1}{v} - \frac{1}{-60} = \frac{1}{40} \Rightarrow v = 120 \text{ cm}$

$$(v_i)_y = \frac{v}{u}(v_O)_y$$

$$\Rightarrow \quad (v_i)_y = \left(\frac{120}{-60}\right)(10) = -20 \text{ cm/s}$$

33. $\frac{1}{v} - \frac{1}{u} = \frac{1}{f} \Rightarrow \frac{1}{v} - \frac{1}{(-2f)} = \frac{1}{f} \Rightarrow v = 2f$

Along the principal axis,

$$v_{iL} = \frac{v^2}{u^2} v_{OL}$$

$$\Rightarrow \quad (v_i - v_L) = \frac{v^2}{u^2}(v_O - v_L)$$

$$\Rightarrow \quad v_i - (-v) = \left(\frac{2f}{-2f}\right)^2 [v - (-v)]$$

$$\Rightarrow \quad v_i = v$$

34.

$$(v_i)_x = \frac{v^2}{u^2}(v_O)_x$$

$$\Rightarrow \quad (v_i)_x = \left(\frac{2f}{-2f}\right)^2 (v \cos 45°)$$

$$\Rightarrow \quad (v_i)_x = v \cos 45°$$

$$(v_i)_y = \frac{v}{u}(v_O)_y$$

$$\Rightarrow \quad (v_i)_y = \left(\frac{2f}{-2f}\right)(v \sin 45°)$$

$$\Rightarrow \quad (v_i)_y = -v \sin 45°$$

$$\therefore \quad \mathbf{v}_i = v \cos 45° \,\hat{\mathbf{i}} - v \sin 45° \,\hat{\mathbf{j}}$$

$$\tan\theta = \frac{v_y}{v_x} = -\frac{v \sin 45°}{v \cos 45°} = -1$$

$$\Rightarrow \quad \theta = -\frac{\pi}{4}$$

35. $v_i = \frac{v^2}{u^2} v_O = \left(\frac{f}{f+u}\right)^2 v_O$

$$v_{rel} = v_i - v_O = \left[1 - \left(\frac{f}{f+u}\right)^2\right] v_O$$

$\therefore$ As u increases, v_{rel} decreases.

36.

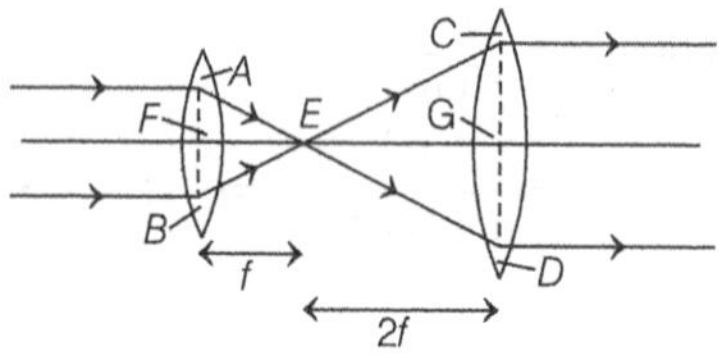

From similar triangles,

$$\frac{CD}{AB} = \frac{EG}{EF} \Rightarrow \frac{CD}{1} = \frac{2f}{f} \Rightarrow CD = 2 \text{ cm}$$

37. For concave lens, $u = +(30 - 26) = +4$ cm

$$\frac{1}{v} - \frac{1}{u} = \frac{1}{f}$$

$$\Rightarrow \quad \frac{1}{v} - \frac{1}{4} = \frac{1}{-20} \Rightarrow v = 5 \text{ cm}$$

$$m = \frac{h_i}{h_O} = \frac{v}{u} \Rightarrow \frac{h_i}{2} = \frac{5}{4} \Rightarrow h_i = 2.5 \text{ cm}$$

38. Object is kept at the focus of the convex lens. So, the refracted rays from the convex lens will be parallel to the principal axis. A parallel beam of light incident on a concave lens appears to be coming from its second focus after refraction. So, for the final image to be on the object itself,

$$d + 10 = 20 \Rightarrow d = 10 \text{ cm}$$

39. $\frac{1}{f} = (\mu - 1)\left(\frac{1}{R_1} - \frac{1}{R_2}\right) \Rightarrow \frac{1}{f} = \left(\frac{3}{2} - 1\right)\left(\frac{1}{10} - \frac{1}{\infty}\right)$

$$\Rightarrow \quad f = 20 \text{ cm}$$

For the final image to be independent of b, the rays refracted from the planoconvex lens should be parallel to the principal axis. So, the object should be kept at the focus of the planoconvex lens.

$$\therefore \quad a = f = 20 \text{ cm}$$

40. A diverging lens always forms a virtual, erect and diminished image for all object distances. Thus, the image formed by first lens will be virtual and erect and will act as object for second diverging lens. Second lens will again form a virtual and erect image.

41. For convex lens,

$$\frac{1}{v}-\frac{1}{u}=\frac{1}{f} \Rightarrow \frac{1}{v}-\frac{1}{(-40)}=\frac{1}{20} \Rightarrow v=40\text{ cm}$$

$$m_1=\frac{v}{u}=\frac{40}{(-40)}=-1$$

For concave lens,

$$u=+(40-10)=+30\text{ cm}$$

$$\frac{1}{v}-\frac{1}{u}=\frac{1}{f} \Rightarrow \frac{1}{v}-\frac{1}{30}=\frac{1}{-20} \Rightarrow v=-60\text{ cm}$$

$$m_2=\frac{v}{u}=\frac{-60}{+30}=-2$$

Overall magnification, $m=m_1m_2$

$$\Rightarrow \frac{h_i}{h_0}=(-1)(-2)$$

$$\Rightarrow \frac{h_i}{1}=2 \Rightarrow h_i=2\text{ cm}$$

So, the final image is 60 cm on left side of concave lens and is 2 cm in size.

42. On cutting a lens parallel to the principal axis, focal length does not change. So, power of A will be P. For B and C focal lengths gets doubled. So power of B and C each will be $P/2$.

43. For equiconcave diverging lens,

$$\frac{1}{f}=(\mu-1)\left(\frac{1}{R_1}-\frac{1}{R_2}\right)$$

$$\Rightarrow \frac{1}{-F}=(\mu-1)\left(\frac{1}{-R}-\frac{1}{R}\right)$$

$$\Rightarrow \frac{1}{F}=\frac{2(\mu-1)}{R}$$

For liquid lens in air,

$$\frac{1}{f}=(\mu-1)\left(\frac{1}{R_1}-\frac{1}{R_2}\right) \Rightarrow \frac{1}{f_2}=(3-1)\left(\frac{1}{R}-\frac{1}{-R}\right)$$

$$\Rightarrow f_2=\frac{R}{4}$$

For combination of lenses,

$$\frac{1}{f}=\frac{1}{f_1}+\frac{1}{f_2}+\frac{1}{f_3}$$

$$\Rightarrow \frac{1}{F}=\frac{1}{(-2F)}+\frac{1}{R/4}+\frac{1}{(-2F)}$$

$$\Rightarrow \frac{1}{F}=\frac{2}{R} \Rightarrow \frac{2(\mu-1)}{R}=\frac{2}{R}$$

$$\Rightarrow \mu=2$$

44. $P_1+P_2=+10$ ...(i)

When separated by 20 cm,

$$P_{eq}=P_1+P_2-dP_1P_2$$

$$\Rightarrow 6.25=10-(0.2)P_1P_2$$

$$\Rightarrow P_1P_2=18.75 \quad \text{...(ii)}$$

From Eqs. (i) and (ii), we get

$$P_1=7.5\text{ D and } P_2=2.5\text{ D}$$

45. When a lens is cut from the middle and perpendicular to the principal axis into two equal halves, focal length of each half is double of the focal length of the original lens.

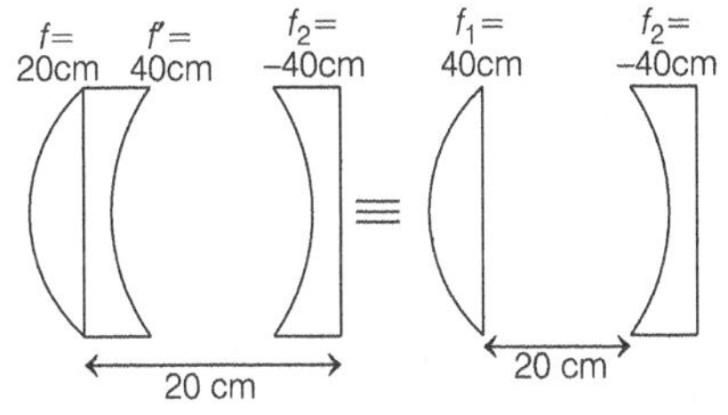

$$\frac{1}{f_1}=\frac{1}{f}+\frac{1}{f'}$$

$$\Rightarrow \frac{1}{f_1}=\frac{1}{20}+\frac{1}{(-40)}$$

$$\Rightarrow f_1=40\text{ cm}$$

$$\frac{1}{f_{eq}}=\frac{1}{f_1}+\frac{1}{f_2}-\frac{d}{f_1f_2}$$

$$\Rightarrow \frac{1}{f_{eq}}=\frac{1}{40}+\frac{1}{(-40)}-\frac{20}{(40)(-40)}$$

$$\Rightarrow f_{eq}=80\text{ cm}$$

46. $\frac{1}{f_{eq}}=\frac{1}{f_1}+\frac{1}{f_2}$

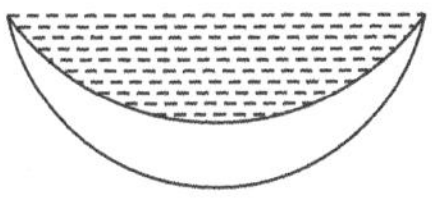

$$\Rightarrow \frac{1}{f_{eq}}=(\mu_g-1)\left(\frac{1}{R_1}-\frac{1}{R_2}\right)+(\mu_{oil}-1)\left(\frac{1}{R'_1}-\frac{1}{R'_2}\right)$$

$$\Rightarrow \frac{1}{f_{eq}}=(1.5-1)\left(\frac{1}{10}-\frac{1}{20}\right)+(1.6-1)\left(\frac{1}{20}-\frac{1}{\infty}\right)$$

$$\Rightarrow f_{eq}=18.18\text{ cm}$$

47. For final image to coincide with the object, the rays refracted from lens should be incident normally on the mirror, so that they retrace their path.

For lens, $\frac{1}{v}-\frac{1}{u}=\frac{1}{f} \Rightarrow \frac{1}{v}-\frac{1}{-20}=\frac{1}{10} \Rightarrow v=20\text{ cm}$

For convex mirror, the rays refracted by the lens should be converging at the centre of curvature of the mirror.

$$\therefore \quad x+10=20 \Rightarrow x=10\text{ cm}$$

48. The rays refracted by lens should be incident normally on the mirror i.e., the image formed by lens should coincide with the centre of curvature of mirror.

$\therefore$ For lens, $v=-[2(18)-12]=-24\text{ cm}$

$$\frac{1}{v}-\frac{1}{u}=\frac{1}{f} \Rightarrow \frac{1}{-24}-\frac{1}{-d}=\frac{1}{40} \Rightarrow d=15\text{ cm}$$

49. For lens, $\frac{1}{v}-\frac{1}{u}=\frac{1}{f}$

$$\Rightarrow \frac{1}{v}-\frac{1}{(-\infty)}=\frac{1}{-10} \Rightarrow v=-10\text{ cm}$$

For plane mirror,

Object distance = – (10 + 10) = – 20 cm

∴ Image distance = 20 cm

For lens again,

$$u = -(20+10) = -30 \text{ cm}$$

$$\frac{1}{v} - \frac{1}{u} = \frac{1}{f}$$

$$\Rightarrow \quad \frac{1}{v} - \frac{1}{-30} = \frac{1}{-10} \quad \Rightarrow \quad v = -7.5 \text{ cm}$$

So, the final image is 7.5 cm right of lens or 2.5 cm infront of the mirror.

50. $$P = 2P_L + P_M$$

$$\Rightarrow \quad -\frac{1}{f} = 2\left(\frac{1}{f_L}\right) - \frac{1}{f_M}$$

$$\Rightarrow \quad -\frac{1}{f} = \frac{2}{15} - \frac{1}{\infty}$$

$$\Rightarrow \quad f = -7.5 \text{ cm}$$

So, the combination will act as a concave mirror of focal length 7.5 cm.

$$\frac{1}{v} + \frac{1}{u} = \frac{1}{f} \Rightarrow \frac{1}{v} + \frac{1}{-20} = \frac{1}{-7.5} \quad \Rightarrow \quad v = -12 \text{ cm}$$

So, the final image will be 12 cm to the left of the system.

51. When plane surface is silvered,

$$P = 2P_L + P_M \quad \Rightarrow \quad -\frac{1}{f} = \frac{2}{f_L} - \frac{1}{f_M}$$

$$\Rightarrow \quad -\frac{1}{-28} = \frac{2}{f_L} - \frac{1}{\infty} \quad \Rightarrow \quad f_L = 56 \text{ cm}$$

When curved surface is silvered,

$$P = 2P_L + P_M$$

$$\Rightarrow \quad -\frac{1}{f} = \frac{2}{f_L} - \frac{1}{f_M}$$

$$\Rightarrow \quad -\frac{1}{-10} = \frac{2}{56} - \frac{1}{(-R/2)} \quad \Rightarrow \quad R = \frac{280}{9} \text{ cm}$$

For lens, $$\frac{1}{f} = (\mu - 1)\left(\frac{1}{R_1} - \frac{1}{R_2}\right)$$

$$\Rightarrow \quad \frac{1}{56} = (\mu - 1)\left(\frac{1}{280/9} - \frac{1}{\infty}\right)$$

$$\Rightarrow \quad \mu = \frac{14}{9}$$

52. Radius of curvature of curved surface =2(0.2) = 0.4 m

When filled with water,

$$P = 2P_L + P_m$$

$$\Rightarrow \quad -\frac{1}{f} = \frac{2}{f_L} - \frac{1}{f_M}$$

$$\Rightarrow \quad -\frac{1}{f} = 2\left(\frac{4}{3} - 1\right)\left[\frac{1}{0.4} - \frac{1}{(-0.4)}\right] - \frac{1}{(-0.2)}$$

$$\Rightarrow \quad f = -\frac{3}{25} \text{ m} = -12 \text{ cm}$$

Numerical Value Questions

1. Refractive index, $\mu = \frac{c}{v} = \frac{3 \times 10^8}{2 \times 10^8} = 1.5$

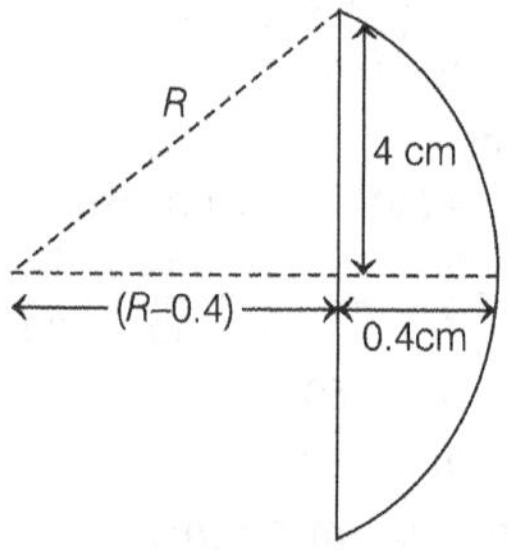

From Pythagoras Theorem,

$$(R - 0.4)^2 + 4^2 = R^2$$

$$\Rightarrow \quad R^2 + 0.16 - 0.8R + 16 = R^2$$

$$\Rightarrow \quad R = 20.0 \text{ cm}$$

$$\frac{1}{f} = (\mu - 1)\left(\frac{1}{R_1} - \frac{1}{R_2}\right)$$

$$\Rightarrow \quad \frac{1}{f} = (1.5 - 1)\left(\frac{1}{20.2} - \frac{1}{\infty}\right)$$

$$\Rightarrow \quad f = 40.4 \text{ cm}$$

2. $\frac{1}{v} - \frac{1}{u} = \frac{1}{f} \quad \Rightarrow \quad v = \frac{fu}{f+u}$

$$|v_1| = |v_2|$$

$$\Rightarrow \quad \left|\frac{fu_1}{f+u_1}\right| = \left|\frac{fu_2}{f+u_2}\right|$$

$$\Rightarrow \quad \left|\frac{f(-10)}{f+(-10)}\right| = \left|\frac{f(-40)}{f+(-40)}\right|$$

$$\Rightarrow \quad f - 40 = \pm 4(f - 10)$$

$$\Rightarrow \quad f = 16 \text{ cm}$$

3. Let separation between the lenses be d.

For second lens, $u = +(30 - d), v = +(22 - d), f = 30$ cm

$$\frac{1}{v} - \frac{1}{u} = \frac{1}{f}$$

$$\Rightarrow \frac{1}{22-d} - \frac{1}{30-d} = \frac{1}{30} \quad \Rightarrow \quad d = 10 \text{ cm}$$

4. At time t,

Distance of first firefly from lens = $20 - 2t$

Distance of second firefly from lens = $30 - 2t$

For second firefly, $\frac{1}{v} - \frac{1}{u} = \frac{1}{f}$

$$\Rightarrow \quad \frac{1}{20-2t} - \frac{1}{-(30-2t)} = \frac{1}{5}$$

$$\Rightarrow \quad 2t^2 - 40t + 175 = 0 \quad \Rightarrow \quad t = \frac{20 \pm 5\sqrt{2}}{2}$$

$$\Rightarrow \quad t = 6 \text{ (nearest integer)}$$

5. Magnification, $m = \frac{f}{f+u}$

$$|m_1| = |m_2|$$

$$\Rightarrow \quad \left|\frac{f}{f+u_1}\right| = \left|\frac{f}{f+u_2}\right|$$

$$\Rightarrow \quad u_1 + u_2 = -2f \quad \text{...(i)}$$

$$u_1 - u_2 = f \quad \text{...(ii)}$$

From Eqs. (i) and (ii), we get

$$u_1 = -\frac{f}{2}$$

$$\therefore \quad m_1 = \frac{f}{f - \frac{f}{2}} = 2$$

Also, $m_1 = \frac{h_i}{h_O} = 2 \Rightarrow h_i = 2(4) = 8$ cm

6. For the final beam of light to be parallel to the principal axis, image formed by the plane mirror should coincide with the focus of the lens i.e., image formed by the plane mirror is 20 cm behind the mirror. So, the object distance for plane mirror will be 20 cm infront of mirror.

For first refraction through lens,

$u = -l, v = -(20-10) = -10$ cm, $f = 30$ cm

$$\frac{1}{v} - \frac{1}{u} = \frac{1}{f}$$

$$\Rightarrow \quad \frac{1}{-10} - \frac{1}{(-l)} = \frac{1}{30}$$

$$\Rightarrow \quad l = 7.5 \text{ cm}$$

7.
$$v_i = \left(\frac{f}{f+u}\right)^2 v_O$$

$$\Rightarrow \quad \frac{dv_i}{dt} = \left(\frac{f}{f+u}\right)^2 \frac{dv_O}{dt} + \frac{v_O f^2}{(f+u)^3}(-2)\frac{du}{dt}$$

$$\Rightarrow \quad a_i = \left(\frac{f}{f+u}\right)^2 a_O - \frac{2v_O f^2}{(f+u)^3} v_O$$

Substituting $a_O = 10 \text{ cm/s}^2, u = -75$ cm, $v_O = 20$ cm/s

$$a_i = \left(\frac{100}{100-75}\right)^2 (10) - \frac{2(20)(100)^2}{(100-75)^3}(20)$$

$$= -352 \text{ cm/s}^2$$

8. Since the screen is fixed, velocity of image is zero.

$$v_{iL} = \frac{v^2}{u^2} v_{OL}$$

$$\Rightarrow \quad v_i - v_L = \left(\frac{v}{u}\right)^2 (v_O - v_L)$$

$$\Rightarrow \quad 0 - (-1) = \left(\frac{1}{2}\right)^2 [v_O - (-1)]$$

$$\Rightarrow \quad v_O = 3 \text{ m/s}$$

9.

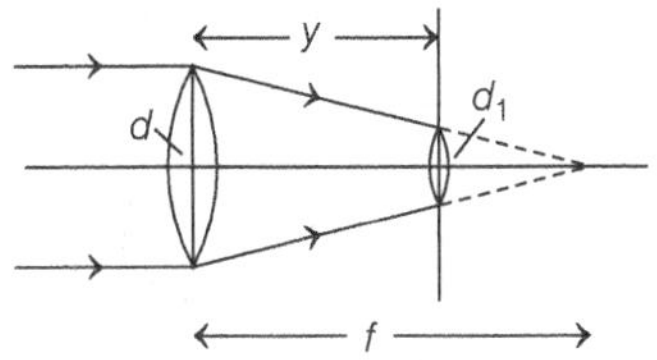

$$\frac{f-y}{f} = \frac{d_1}{d} \Rightarrow \frac{10-y}{10} = \frac{1}{2}$$

$$\Rightarrow \quad y = 5 \text{ cm}$$

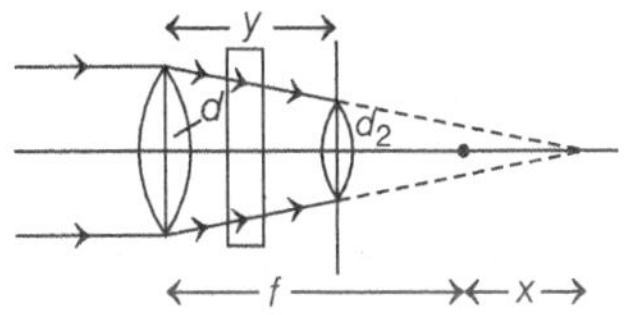

$$\text{Normal shift} = x = t\left(1 - \frac{1}{\mu}\right) = 3\left(1 - \frac{1}{1.5}\right) = 1 \text{ cm}$$

$$\frac{(f+x)-y}{f} = \frac{d_2}{d}$$

$$\Rightarrow \quad \frac{10+1-5}{10} = \frac{d_2}{2}$$

$$\Rightarrow \quad d_2 = 1.2 \text{ cm = 12 mm}$$

10. First flare spot is formed due to refraction at first spherical surface, reflection at second spherical surface and refraction again at first spherical surface.

Refraction at first spherical surface,

$$\frac{\mu_2}{v} - \frac{\mu_1}{u} = \frac{\mu_2 - \mu_1}{R}$$

$$\Rightarrow \quad \frac{1.5}{v_1} - \frac{1}{(-\infty)} = \frac{1.5-1}{+30} \Rightarrow v_1 = 90 \text{ cm}$$

Reflection at second spherical surface,

$$\frac{1}{v} + \frac{1}{u} = \frac{1}{f} \Rightarrow \frac{1}{v_2} + \frac{1}{(+90)} = \frac{1}{-(60/2)}$$

$$\Rightarrow \quad v_2 = -\frac{45}{2} \text{ cm}$$

Reflection again at first spherical surface,

$$\frac{\mu_2}{v} - \frac{\mu_1}{u} = \frac{\mu_2 - \mu_1}{R}$$

$$\Rightarrow \quad \frac{1}{v} - \frac{1.5}{(45/2)} = \frac{1-1.5}{-30}$$

$$\Rightarrow \quad v = 12 \text{ cm}$$

11. Focal length of each planoconvex lens $= 2(24) = 48$ cm

$$\frac{1}{f} = (\mu - 1)\left(\frac{1}{R_1} - \frac{1}{R_2}\right)$$

$$\Rightarrow \quad \frac{1}{48} = (1.5-1)\left(\frac{1}{R} - \frac{1}{\infty}\right)$$

$$\Rightarrow \quad R = 24 \text{ cm}$$

Focal length of liquid lens in air,

$$\frac{1}{f}=(\mu-1)\left(\frac{1}{R_1}-\frac{1}{R_2}\right)$$

$$\Rightarrow \quad \frac{1}{f_L}=(1.6-1)\left(\frac{1}{-24}-\frac{1}{24}\right)$$

$$\Rightarrow \quad f_L=-20\text{ cm}$$

For combination in figure *B*,

$$\frac{1}{f}=\frac{1}{f_1}+\frac{1}{f_2}+\frac{1}{f_3}$$

$$\Rightarrow \quad \frac{1}{f}=\frac{1}{48}+\frac{1}{(-20)}+\frac{1}{48}$$

$$\Rightarrow \quad f=-120\text{ cm}$$

12. For refraction at first spherical surface,

$$\frac{\mu_2}{v}-\frac{\mu_1}{u}=\frac{\mu_2-\mu_1}{R}$$

$$\Rightarrow \quad \frac{3/2}{v_1}-\frac{1}{\infty}=\frac{3/2-1}{+10}$$

$$\Rightarrow \quad v_1=30\text{ cm}$$

For refraction at second spherical surface,

$$\frac{\mu_2}{v}-\frac{\mu_1}{u}=\frac{\mu_2-\mu_1}{R}$$

$$\Rightarrow \quad \frac{4/3}{v_2}-\frac{3/2}{+30}=\frac{4/3-3/2}{-10}$$

$$\Rightarrow \quad v_2=20\text{ cm}$$

For refraction at plane surface,

$$\frac{\mu_2}{v}-\frac{\mu_1}{u}=\frac{\mu_2-\mu_1}{R}$$

$$\Rightarrow \quad \frac{1}{v}-\frac{4/3}{+(20-10)}=\frac{1-4/3}{\infty}$$

$$\Rightarrow \quad v=7.5\text{ cm}$$

Distance from lens = 10 + 7.5 = 17.5 cm

13. For lens, $\frac{1}{v}-\frac{1}{u}=\frac{1}{f}$

$$\Rightarrow \quad \frac{1}{v}-\frac{1}{-100}=\frac{1}{50} \quad \Rightarrow \quad v=100\text{ cm}$$

So, the lens forms image 100 cm from lens i.e., 50cm from the mirror. The mirror will form image 50 cm behind the mirror.

For mirror, $v_{im}=-v_{Om}$

$$\Rightarrow \quad v_i-v_m=-(v_O-v_m)$$

$$\Rightarrow \quad v_i-9=-(0-9)$$

$$\Rightarrow \quad v_i=18\text{ m/s}$$

For final refraction through lens,

$$u=-200\text{ cm}$$

$$\frac{1}{v}-\frac{1}{u}=\frac{1}{f}$$

$$\Rightarrow \quad \frac{1}{v}-\frac{1}{-200}=\frac{1}{50}$$

$$\Rightarrow \quad v=\frac{200}{3}\text{ cm}$$

$$v_i=-\frac{v^2}{u^2}v_O$$

$$\Rightarrow \quad v_i=-\left(\frac{200/3}{200}\right)^2(18)=-2\text{ m/s}$$

14. $\frac{1}{f}=(\mu-1)\left(\frac{1}{R_1}-\frac{1}{R_2}\right)$

For lens of liquid *A*,

$$\frac{1}{f_1}=\left(\frac{9}{5}-1\right)\left(\frac{1}{\infty}-\frac{1}{-10}\right)=\frac{2}{25}$$

For lens of glass,

$$\frac{1}{f_2}=\left(\frac{3}{2}-1\right)\left(\frac{1}{-10}-\frac{1}{10}\right)=-\frac{1}{10}$$

For lens of liquid *B*,

$$\frac{1}{f_3}=\left(\frac{4}{3}-1\right)\left(\frac{1}{10}-\frac{1}{\infty}\right)=\frac{1}{30}$$

For the combination,

$$P=2P_1+2P_2+2P_3+P_M$$

$$\Rightarrow \quad -\frac{1}{f}=2\left(\frac{1}{f_1}\right)+2\left(\frac{1}{f_2}\right)+2\left(\frac{1}{f_3}\right)-\frac{1}{f_M}$$

$$\Rightarrow \quad -\frac{1}{f}=2\left(\frac{2}{25}\right)+2\left(-\frac{1}{10}\right)+2\left(\frac{1}{30}\right)-\frac{1}{\infty}$$

$$\Rightarrow \quad f=-37.5\text{ cm}$$

For the final image to coincide with the object, object should be kept at the centre of curvature of the equivalent mirror.

∴ Object distance $=2f=2(37.5)=75$ cm

15. For silvered lens,

$$P=2P_L+P_M \quad \Rightarrow \quad -\frac{1}{f}=2\left(\frac{1}{f_L}\right)-\frac{1}{f_M}$$

$$\Rightarrow \quad -\frac{1}{f}=\frac{2}{40}-\frac{1}{(-60)} \quad \Rightarrow \quad f=-15\text{ cm}$$

So, the silvered lens will behave as a concave mirror of focal length 15 cm.

For the final image to coincide with the object, the rays refracted from the lens should be incident normally on the equivalent concave mirror i.e., the lens should form image at the centre of curvature of the concave mirror.

For first refraction through lens,

$u=-x, v==-(30-10)=-20\text{ cm}, f=20\text{ cm}$

$$\frac{1}{v}-\frac{1}{u}=\frac{1}{f}$$

$$\Rightarrow \quad \frac{1}{-20}-\frac{1}{(-x)}=\frac{1}{20}$$

$$\Rightarrow \quad x=10\text{ cm}$$

Level 3

Single Choice Correct Questions

1. From symmetry, ray inside the sphere will be parallel to the principal axis.

For refraction at first spherical surface,

$$\frac{\mu_2}{v} - \frac{\mu_1}{u} = \frac{\mu_2 - \mu_1}{R}$$

$$\Rightarrow \quad \frac{\mu}{\infty} - \frac{1}{(-R)} = \frac{\mu - 1}{+R}$$

$$\Rightarrow \quad \mu = 2$$

2. For refraction at spherical surface,

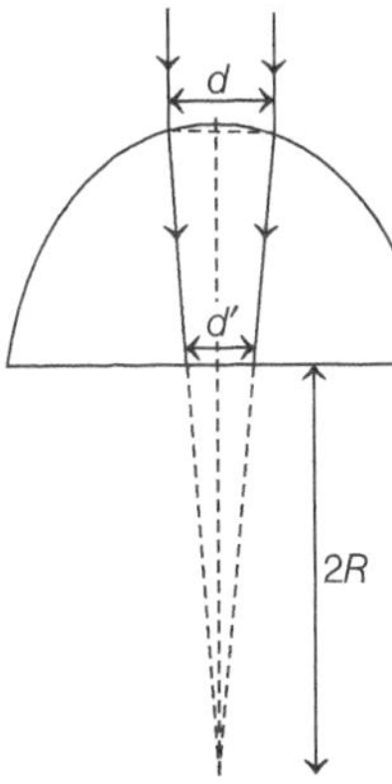

$$\frac{\mu_2}{v} - \frac{\mu_1}{u} = \frac{\mu_2 - \mu_1}{R}$$

$$\Rightarrow \quad \frac{3/2}{v} - \frac{1}{\infty} = \frac{3/2 - 1}{+R}$$

$$\Rightarrow \quad v = 3R$$

From similar triangles,

$$\frac{d}{3R} = \frac{d'}{2R}$$

$$\Rightarrow \quad d' = \frac{2d}{3}$$

3. For first refraction at inner surface (air to glass)

$$\frac{\mu_2}{v} - \frac{\mu_1}{u} = \frac{\mu_2 - \mu_1}{R}$$

$$\Rightarrow \quad \frac{n}{v_1} - \frac{1}{(-2R)} = \frac{n-1}{-R} \Rightarrow v_1 = \frac{2nR}{1-2n}$$

For second refraction at outer surface (glass to air)

$$u = v_1 - R = \frac{2nR}{1-2n} - R = \left(\frac{4n-1}{1-2n}\right)R$$

$$\frac{\mu_2}{v} - \frac{\mu_1}{u} = \frac{\mu_2 - \mu_1}{R}$$

$$\Rightarrow \frac{1}{v} - \frac{n}{\left(\frac{4n-1}{1-2n}\right)R} = \frac{1-n}{-2R}$$

$$\Rightarrow \quad v = -\frac{2R(4n-1)}{3n-1}$$

$$\text{Shift} = 3R - \frac{2R(4n-1)}{3n-1} = \frac{R(n-1)}{3n-1}$$

4. For refraction at plane surface,

$$\frac{1.5}{v_1} - \frac{1}{(-mR)} = \frac{1.5 - 1}{\infty} \quad \Rightarrow \quad v_1 = -1.5mR$$

For refraction at curved surface,

$$u = -(R + 1.5mR)$$

$$\frac{1}{\infty} - \frac{1.5}{-(R + 1.5mR)} = \frac{1 - 1.5}{-R}$$

$$\Rightarrow \quad m = \frac{4}{3}$$

5. For refraction at plane surface,

$$\frac{4/3}{v} - \frac{1}{(-d)} = \frac{4/3 - 1}{\infty}$$

$$\Rightarrow \quad v = -\frac{4d}{3}$$

For refraction at spherical surface,

$$u = -\left(\frac{4d}{3} + 4\right)$$

$$\frac{1}{v} - \frac{4/3}{-\left(\frac{4d}{3} + 4\right)} = \frac{1 - 4/3}{-4}$$

$$\Rightarrow \quad v = \frac{12(d+3)}{d-9}$$

For reflection at plane mirror,

$$v = -u = -\frac{12(d+3)}{d-9}$$

For refraction again at spherical surface,

$$\frac{4/3}{\infty} - \frac{1}{\frac{12(d+3)}{d-9}} = \frac{4/3 - 1}{+4}$$

$$\Rightarrow \quad d = 3 \text{ cm}$$

6. Image of end B should be formed at infinity as seen by the observer.

$$\frac{\mu_2}{\infty} - \frac{\mu_1}{(-2R)} = \frac{\mu_2 - \mu_1}{-R}$$

$$\Rightarrow \quad \frac{\mu_1}{\mu_2} = 2$$

7. First image will be due to direct refraction from water to air

$$\frac{\mu_2}{v} - \frac{\mu_1}{u} = \frac{\mu_2 - \mu_1}{R}$$

$$\Rightarrow \quad -\frac{\mu_2}{v^2}\frac{dv}{dt} + \frac{\mu_1}{u^2}\frac{du}{dt} = 0$$

$$\Rightarrow \quad \frac{dv}{dt} = \left(\frac{\mu_1}{\mu_2}\right)\left(\frac{v}{u}\right)^2 \frac{du}{dt}$$

$$\Rightarrow \quad v_i = \left(\frac{4/3}{1}\right)\left(\frac{-10}{-10}\right)^2 (-6) = -8 \text{ m/s}$$

Second image will be formed due to reflection and then refraction.

For concave mirror,

$$v_i = -\frac{v^2}{u^2} v_O = -\left(\frac{-10}{-10}\right)^2 (-6) = 6 \text{ m/s}$$

For refraction,

$$v_i = \left(\frac{\mu_1}{\mu_2}\right)\left(\frac{v}{u}\right)^2 v_O = \left(\frac{4/3}{1}\right)\left(\frac{-10}{-10}\right)^2 (6) = 8 \text{ m/s}$$

Relative velocity between the two images

$$= 8 - (-8) = 16 \text{ m/s}$$

8. $f_2 = \dfrac{\mu_3 R}{2\mu_2 - \mu_1 - \mu_3}$, $f_1 = \dfrac{\mu_1 R}{2\mu_2 - \mu_1 - \mu_3}$

$\therefore \quad \dfrac{f_2}{f_1} = \dfrac{\mu_3}{\mu_1} \Rightarrow \dfrac{f_2}{30} = \dfrac{4/3}{1} \Rightarrow f_2 = 40 \text{ cm}$

9. Let distance of bulb from lens be x.

$\therefore \quad u = -x, v = 3 - x$

$$\frac{1}{v} - \frac{1}{u} = \frac{1}{f}$$

$$\Rightarrow \frac{1}{3-x} - \frac{1}{-x} = \frac{1}{f}$$

$$\Rightarrow \quad f = \frac{x(3-x)}{3}$$

For focal length to be maximum,

$$\frac{df}{dx} = 0 \Rightarrow \frac{3-2x}{3} = 0$$

$$\Rightarrow \quad x = 1.5 \text{ m}$$

$$\therefore \quad f = \frac{1.5(3-1.5)}{3} = 0.75 \text{ m}$$

10. $m = \dfrac{v}{u} = \dfrac{f}{f+u}$

$$\therefore \quad \frac{1}{m} = \frac{f+u}{f} \Rightarrow \frac{1}{m} = \left(\frac{1}{f}\right)u + 1$$

So, slope of graph $= \dfrac{1}{f} = \dfrac{b}{c} \Rightarrow f = \dfrac{c}{b}$

11. $v + u = x$ and $m = \dfrac{v}{u}$

$\therefore \quad x = mu + u = u(m+1)$

$$\Rightarrow u = \frac{x}{m+1} \text{ and } v = \frac{mx}{m+1}$$

$$\frac{1}{v} - \frac{1}{u} = \frac{1}{f}$$

$$\Rightarrow \frac{1}{\frac{mx}{m+1}} - \frac{1}{\left(-\frac{x}{m+1}\right)} = \frac{1}{f}$$

$$\Rightarrow \quad f = \frac{mx}{(m+1)^2}$$

12.

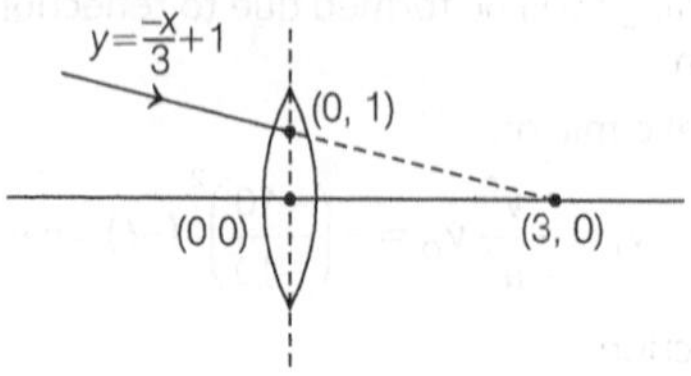

$$y = -\frac{x}{3} + 1 = 0 \Rightarrow x = 3$$

$$\frac{1}{v} - \frac{1}{u} = \frac{1}{f} \Rightarrow \frac{1}{v} - \frac{1}{+3} = \frac{1}{15}$$

$$\Rightarrow \quad v = \frac{5}{2}$$

So, the refracted ray passes through (0, 1) and $\left(\dfrac{5}{2}, 0\right)$.

$$\text{Slope} = \frac{1-0}{0-\frac{5}{2}} = -0.4$$

$\therefore \quad y = -0.4x + 1$

13. Apparent height $= \dfrac{\text{Actual height}}{\mu_{12}}$

$$\Rightarrow \quad H_{app} = \frac{12}{1/(4/3)} = 16 \text{ cm}$$

For lens,

In air, $\dfrac{1}{10} = \left(\dfrac{3}{2} - 1\right)\left(\dfrac{1}{R_1} - \dfrac{1}{R_2}\right)$ ...(i)

In water,

$$\frac{1}{f_L} = \left(\frac{(3/2)}{(4/3)} - 1\right)\left(\frac{1}{R_1} - \frac{1}{R_2}\right) \quad \text{...(ii)}$$

For Eqs. (i) and (ii), we get

$$f_L = 40 \text{ cm}$$

$$\frac{1}{v} - \frac{1}{u} = \frac{1}{f} \Rightarrow \frac{1}{v} - \frac{1}{-(44+16)} = \frac{1}{40}$$

$$\Rightarrow \quad v = 120 \text{ cm}$$

For refraction from water to air,

$$H_{app} = \frac{H}{\mu_{12}} = \frac{120}{(4/3)/1} = 90 \text{ cm}$$

Since the thickness of glass slab at the bottom is zero, it will not affect the image formation.

14. Apparent velocity $= \dfrac{\text{Actual velocity}}{\mu_{12}}$

$$\Rightarrow \quad v_{app} = \frac{100}{(4/3)/1} = 75 \text{ cm/s}$$

Distance fallen by lens in 0.2s $= \dfrac{1}{2}gt^2 = \dfrac{1}{2} \times 10 \times (0.2)^2$

$= 0.2$ m = 20 cm

Distance moved by fish in 0.2 s $= 100 \times 0.2 = 20$ cm

Object distance for lens $= \left(\dfrac{44-20}{4/3}\right) + (62-20) = 60$ cm

$$\frac{1}{v} - \frac{1}{u} = \frac{1}{f}$$

$$\Rightarrow \quad \frac{1}{v} - \frac{1}{-60} = \frac{1}{90}$$

$$\Rightarrow \quad v = -180 \text{ cm}$$

Velocity of lens at 0.2 s $= gt = 10(0.2) = 2$ m/s = 200 cm/s

Velocity of image, $v_{iL} = \dfrac{v^2}{u^2} v_{OL}$

$$\Rightarrow \quad v_i - (-200) = \left(\frac{-180}{-60}\right)^2 [75 - (-200)]$$

$$\Rightarrow \quad v_i = 2275 \text{ cm/s} = 22.75 \text{ m/s}$$

15. For the final image to coincide with the object, the rays should hit the plane mirror perpendicularly. So, the rays inside water will be parallel to the principal axis.

For refraction at first spherical surface,

$$\frac{3/2}{v_1} - \frac{1}{(-45)} = \frac{3/2-1}{+R} \quad \text{...(i)}$$

For refraction at second spherical surface,

$$\frac{4/3}{\infty} - \frac{3/2}{v_1} = \frac{4/3-3/2}{-R} \quad \text{...(ii)}$$

Adding Eqs. (i) and (ii), we get

$$R = 30 \text{ cm}$$

16. Applying Snell's law,

$$\mu \sin 2^\circ = 2\mu \sin r = 3\mu \sin e$$

$$\Rightarrow \quad \mu\,(2^\circ) = 2\mu r = 3\mu e$$

$$\Rightarrow \quad e = \left(\frac{2}{3}\right)^\circ$$

17. Magnification, $m = \frac{f}{f+u}$

Distance of each image from corresponding principal axis

$$= m\frac{h}{2}$$

Distance of each image from dotted line $= m\frac{h}{2} + \frac{h}{2}$

d = Separation between the images

$$= 2\left(\frac{mh}{2} + \frac{h}{2}\right) = (m+1)\,h$$

Slope of graph $= m + 1 = 3$

$$\Rightarrow \quad \frac{f}{f+u} + 1 = 3$$

$$\Rightarrow \quad f = -2u = -2(-30) = 60 \text{ cm}$$

18.

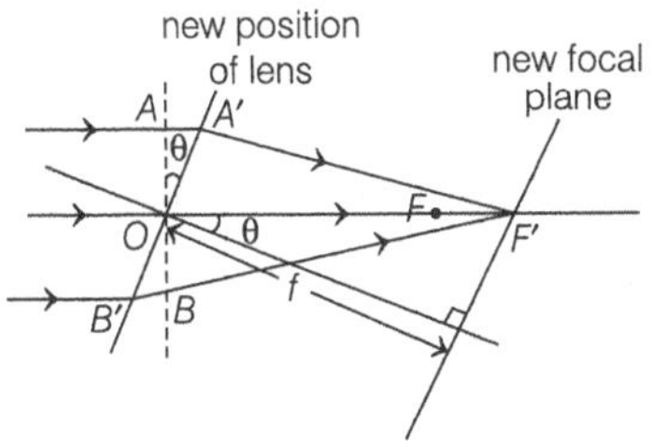

$$OF = f, OF' = f \sec\theta$$

Distance between extreme positions $= OF' - OF$

$$= f \sec\theta - f$$

$$= f(\sec\theta - 1)$$

19. $u = 100 - (20 - 10)\,t = 100 - 10t$

$v = 0 + (30 - 10)\,t = 20t$

$$\frac{1}{v} - \frac{1}{u} = \frac{1}{f}$$

$$\Rightarrow \quad \frac{1}{20t} - \frac{1}{-(100-10t)} = \frac{1}{10}$$

$$\Rightarrow \quad 2t^2 - 19t + 10 = 0$$

$$\Rightarrow \quad t = \frac{19 \pm \sqrt{281}}{4}$$

$$\Rightarrow \quad t = 0.56 \text{ s} \quad \text{and} \quad t = 8.94 \text{ s}$$

20. $$m = \frac{h_i}{h_O} = \frac{f}{f+u}$$

$$\Rightarrow \quad h_i = \frac{h_O f}{f+u}$$

Velocity of image in y-direction

$$\frac{dh_i}{dt} = \frac{h_O f}{(f+u)^2}(-1)\frac{du}{dt}$$

$$\Rightarrow \quad (v_i)_y = \frac{0.5(40)}{[40+(-30)]^2}(-1)\,(4) = -\frac{4}{5} \text{ cm/s}$$

Relative velocity of the images $= 2(v_i)_y = 2\left(\frac{4}{5}\right) = \frac{8}{5}$ cm/s

21.

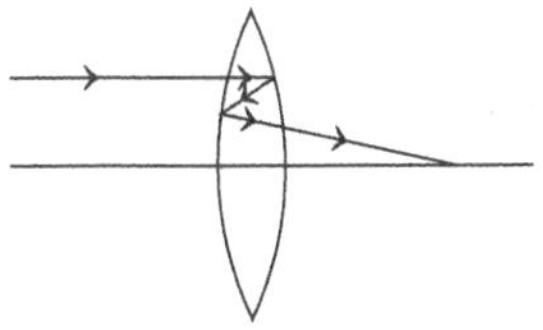

For refraction at first surface,

$$\frac{\mu}{v_1} - \frac{1}{\infty} = \frac{\mu - 1}{R} \quad \text{...(i)}$$

For reflection at second surface,

$$\frac{1}{v_2} + \frac{1}{v_1} = \frac{1}{(-R/2)} \quad \text{...(ii)}$$

For reflection at first surface,

$$\frac{1}{v_3} + \frac{1}{(-v_2)} = \frac{1}{(-R/2)} \quad \text{...(iii)}$$

For refraction at second surface,

$$\frac{1}{v} - \frac{\mu}{(-v_3)} = \frac{1-\mu}{-R} \quad \text{...(iv)}$$

From Eqs. (i), (ii), (iii) and (iv), we get

$$v = \frac{R}{2(3\mu - 1)}$$

For lens, $\frac{1}{f} = (\mu - 1)\left[\frac{1}{R} - \frac{1}{(-R)}\right]$

$$\Rightarrow \quad R = 2(\mu - 1)\,f$$

$$\therefore \quad v = \frac{2(\mu-1)\,f}{2(3\mu-1)} = \frac{(\mu-1)\,f}{(3\mu-1)}$$

22. Let f_1 be focal length of convex lens in air,

$$\therefore \quad \frac{1}{f_1} = \left(\frac{3}{2} - 1\right)\left(\frac{1}{R} - \frac{1}{-R}\right) \Rightarrow f_1 = R$$

Let f_2 be focal length of water lens in air,

$$\therefore \quad \frac{1}{f_2} = \left(\frac{4}{3} - 1\right)\left(\frac{1}{-R} - \frac{1}{\infty}\right) \Rightarrow f_2 = -3R$$

For combination,

$$P = 2P_1 + 2P_2 + P_M$$

$$\Rightarrow \quad -\frac{1}{f} = 2\left(\frac{1}{f_1}\right) + 2\left(\frac{1}{f_2}\right) - \frac{1}{f_M}$$

$$\Rightarrow \quad -\frac{1}{f} = \frac{2}{R} + \frac{2}{(-3R)} - \frac{1}{\infty}$$

$$\Rightarrow \quad f = -\frac{3R}{4}$$

So, radius of curvature of equivalent mirror

$$= 2\left(\frac{3R}{4}\right) = \frac{3R}{2}$$

For object and image to coincide,

$$\frac{3R}{2} = 15 \quad \Rightarrow \quad R = 10 \text{ cm}$$

On repeating with another liquid,

Radius of curvature of equivalent mirror = 25 cm

$$\Rightarrow \quad 2f = -25 \quad \Rightarrow \quad f = -\frac{25}{2} \text{ cm}$$

For combination,

$$P = 2P_1 + 2P_2 + P_M$$

$$\Rightarrow \quad -\frac{1}{f} = \frac{2}{f_1} + \frac{2}{f_2} - \frac{1}{f_M}$$

$$\Rightarrow \quad -\frac{1}{(-25/2)} = \frac{2}{10} + 2(\mu - 1)\left(-\frac{1}{R}\right) - \frac{1}{\infty}$$

$$\Rightarrow \quad \mu = 1.6$$

23. Deviation produced by prism

$$= (\mu - 1)A = (1.5 - 1)\left(\frac{4}{\pi}\frac{\pi^\circ}{180}\right) = \frac{1}{90} \text{ rad}$$

y-coordinate of converging beam $= -f\theta$

$$= -60\left(\frac{1}{90}\right) = -\frac{2}{3} \text{ cm}$$

$\therefore$ Coordinates will be $\left(60 \text{ cm}, -\frac{2}{3} \text{ cm}\right)$

24. $m = \frac{f}{f + u}$

For diverging lens,

$$m_2 = \frac{-l}{-l + 2l} = -1$$

$$\frac{1}{v} - \frac{1}{u} = \frac{1}{f}$$

$$\Rightarrow \quad \frac{1}{v_2} - \frac{1}{2l} = \frac{1}{(-l)} \quad \Rightarrow \quad v_2 = -2l$$

For another converging lens, $u = -3l$

$$m_3 = \frac{2l}{2l + (-3l)} = -2$$

$$\therefore \quad \frac{h_i}{h_0} = m_2 m_3$$

$$\Rightarrow \quad \frac{h_i}{h} = (-1)(-2) \quad \Rightarrow \quad h_i = 2h$$

25. $m = \frac{v}{u} = -2 \Rightarrow v = -2u$ ...(i)

$v - u = 1.8$ ...(ii)

For Eqs. (i) and (ii), we get

$$u = -0.6 \text{ m and } v = 1.2 \text{ m}$$

$$\frac{1}{v} - \frac{1}{u} = \frac{1}{f}$$

$$\Rightarrow \quad \frac{1}{1.2} - \frac{1}{(-0.6)} = \frac{1}{f} \Rightarrow f = 0.4 \text{ m}$$

Let the separation between the two halves be d.

For second half, $u = -(0.6 + d), v = (1.2 - d)$

$$\frac{1}{v} - \frac{1}{u} = \frac{1}{f}$$

$$\Rightarrow \quad \frac{1}{1.2 - d} - \frac{1}{-(0.6 + d)} = \frac{1}{0.4}$$

$$\Rightarrow \quad d = 0.6 \text{ m}$$

26. For silvered lens, $P = 2P_L + P_M$

$$\Rightarrow \quad -\frac{1}{f} = 2\left(\frac{1}{f}\right) - \frac{1}{f_M}$$

$$\Rightarrow \quad -\frac{1}{f} = \frac{2}{40} - \frac{1}{\infty} \quad \Rightarrow \quad f = -20 \text{ cm}$$

So, the silvered planoconvex lens acts as a concave mirror of radius of curvature 40 cm.

For final image to coincide with the object, the rays refracted from convex lens should be incident normally on the equivalent concave mirror i.e., the convex lens should form image at the centre of curvature of the equivalent concave mirror.

For convex lens,

$$\frac{1}{v} - \frac{1}{u} = \frac{1}{f}$$

$$\Rightarrow \quad \frac{1}{v} - \frac{1}{(-10)} = \frac{1}{20} \quad \Rightarrow \quad v = -20 \text{ cm}$$

For convex lens to form image at centre of curvature of equivalent concave mirror,

$$20 + d = 40 \quad \Rightarrow \quad d = 20 \text{ cm}$$

27. For the first lens, $\frac{1}{v} - \frac{1}{u} = \frac{1}{f}$

$$\Rightarrow \quad \frac{1}{v_1} - \frac{1}{\infty} = \frac{1}{f}$$

$$\Rightarrow \quad v_1 = f$$

For the second lens,

$$u = -(3f - f) = -2f$$

$$\frac{1}{v} - \frac{1}{u} = \frac{1}{f} \quad \Rightarrow \quad \frac{1}{v} - \frac{1}{(-2f)} = \frac{1}{f} \quad \Rightarrow \quad v = 2f$$

$$m = \frac{h_i}{h_o} = \frac{v}{u} \quad \Rightarrow \quad \frac{h_i}{(-d)} = \frac{2f}{-2f} \quad \Rightarrow \quad h_i = d$$

x-coordinate of final image $= 3f + 2f = 5f$

y-coordinate of final image $= d + d = 2d$

28. For direct refraction from lens,

$$m=\frac{f}{f+u} \Rightarrow -1.5=\frac{10}{10+u}$$

$$\Rightarrow \quad u=-\frac{50}{3}\text{ cm}$$

$\therefore$ Distance of object from mirror $=40-\frac{50}{3}=\frac{70}{3}$ cm

For first reflection from mirror and then refraction from lens,

$$m=m_1m_2=1.5 \Rightarrow m_1(-1.5)=1.5 \Rightarrow m_1=-1$$

So, magnification produced by the mirror is -1

$$\therefore \quad m=\frac{f}{f-u} \Rightarrow -1=\frac{f}{f-\left(-\frac{70}{3}\right)}$$

$$\Rightarrow \quad f=-\frac{35}{3}\text{ cm}$$

Multiple Choice(s) Correct Questions

1. $\frac{\mu_2}{v}-\frac{\mu_1}{u}=\frac{\mu_2-\mu_1}{R}$

Now, R is always negative.

Case-1 $\mu_2>\mu_1$ and $u<0$ (Real object)

$$\frac{\mu_2}{v}=\frac{\mu_2-\mu_1}{R}+\frac{\mu_1}{u}<0$$

$$\Rightarrow \quad v<0$$

So, the image can never be real.

Case-2 $\mu_2<\mu_1$ and $u>0$ (Virtual object)

$$\frac{\mu_2}{v}=\frac{\mu_2-\mu_1}{R}+\frac{\mu_1}{u}>0$$

$$\Rightarrow \quad v>0$$

So, the image can never be virtual.

2. **Case-1** $d_1=120$ cm

For refraction at spherical surface,

$$\frac{\mu_2}{v}-\frac{\mu_1}{u}=\frac{\mu_2-\mu_1}{R} \Rightarrow \frac{3/2}{v}-\frac{1}{(-120)}=\frac{3/2-1}{+60}$$

$$\Rightarrow \quad v=\infty$$

So, the rays after refraction are parallel and after striking the plane mirror they will retrace their path and final image will be formed on the object O for any value of d_2.

Case-2 $d_1=240$ cm

$$\frac{3/2}{v}-\frac{1}{(-240)}=\frac{3/2-1}{+60} \Rightarrow v=360\text{ cm}$$

If $d_2=360$ cm, then the first image is formed on the mirror and the rays will retrace their path to form final image at O.

3. In figure (i), for refraction at curved surface,

$$\frac{\mu_2}{v}-\frac{\mu_1}{u}=\frac{\mu_2-\mu_1}{R}$$

$$\Rightarrow \quad \frac{1}{v}-\frac{1.5}{(-\infty)}=\frac{1-1.5}{(-6)}$$

$$\Rightarrow \quad v=12\text{ cm}$$

In figue (ii), for refraction at curved surface,

$$\frac{\mu_2}{v}-\frac{\mu_1}{u}=\frac{\mu_2-\mu_1}{R}$$

$$\Rightarrow \quad \frac{1.5}{v}-\frac{1}{(-\infty)}=\frac{1.5-1}{(+6)}$$

$$\Rightarrow \quad v=18\text{ cm}$$

For refraction at flat surface,

$$\frac{\mu_2}{v}-\frac{\mu_1}{u}=\frac{\mu_2-\mu_1}{R}$$

$$\Rightarrow \quad \frac{1}{v}-\frac{1.5}{(18-6)}=\frac{1-1.5}{\infty} \Rightarrow v=8\text{ cm}$$

So, the distance from point $P=8+6=14$ cm

4. (a) $\frac{1}{f}=(\mu-1)\left(\frac{1}{R_1}-\frac{1}{R_2}\right)$

$$\Rightarrow \quad \frac{1}{f}=(1.4-1)\left[\frac{1}{16}-\frac{1}{(-24)}\right]$$

$$\Rightarrow \quad f=24\text{ cm}$$

(b) $\frac{1}{f}=(\mu-1)\left(\frac{1}{R_1}-\frac{1}{R_2}\right)$

$$\Rightarrow \quad \frac{1}{f}=(1.4-1)\left[\frac{1}{(-16)}-\frac{1}{(-24)}\right]$$

$$\Rightarrow \quad f=120\text{ cm}=1.2\text{ m}$$

$$\therefore \quad P=\frac{1}{f}=\frac{1}{1.2}=\frac{5}{6}\text{D}$$

(d) $\frac{1}{f}=(\mu_{rel}-1)\left(\frac{1}{R_1}-\frac{1}{R_2}\right)$

$$\Rightarrow \quad \frac{1}{f}=\left(\frac{1.4}{1.6}-1\right)\left[\frac{1}{16}-\frac{1}{(-24)}\right]$$

$$\Rightarrow \quad f=-76.8\text{ cm}$$

5. Let object distance be x

$$\frac{1}{v}-\frac{1}{u}=\frac{1}{f} \Rightarrow \frac{1}{120-x}-\frac{1}{(-x)}=\frac{1}{22.5}$$

$$\Rightarrow \quad x^2-120x+2700=0$$

$$\Rightarrow \quad x=30\text{ cm} \quad \text{and} \quad x=90\text{ cm}$$

6.

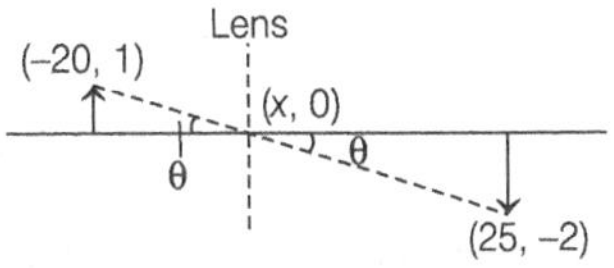

$$\tan\theta=\frac{1}{x-(-20)}=\frac{2}{25-x}$$

$$\Rightarrow \quad x=-5\text{ cm}$$

$$\frac{1}{v}-\frac{1}{u}=\frac{1}{f}$$

$$\Rightarrow \quad \frac{1}{30}-\frac{1}{-15}=\frac{1}{f}$$

$$\Rightarrow \quad f=10\text{ cm}$$

7. $v+u=D$ and $v-u=x$

$$\Rightarrow \quad v=\frac{D+x}{2},\ u=\frac{D-x}{2} \text{ and } f=\frac{D^2-x^2}{4D}$$

$$m_1=\frac{D+x}{D-x} \text{ and } m_2=\frac{D-x}{D+x}$$

$$\therefore \quad m_1m_2=1 \text{ and } f=\frac{x}{m_1-m_2}$$

8. (a) $\frac{h_2}{h_1}=4.84$

Let $h_2=4.84a$ and $h_1=a$

$$\therefore \quad h=\sqrt{h_1h_2}=2.2a$$

$$\text{Required ratio}=\frac{2.2a}{a}=\frac{11}{5}$$

(b)
$$\frac{v}{u}=\frac{11}{5} \quad \text{...(i)}$$

$$v+u=96 \quad \text{...(ii)}$$

Solving Eqs. (i) and (ii), we get

$$v=66 \text{ cm} \quad \text{and} \quad u=30 \text{ cm}$$

Distance between the two positions of lens

$$=v-u=36 \text{ cm}$$

(c) $f=\frac{D^2-d^2}{4D}=\frac{(96)^2-(36)^2}{4(96)}=20.625$ cm

(d) $v=30$ cm for the shorter image.

9. (a, c)

10. Since image is inverted, it is a real image. Real image of a real object can be obtained either by convex/converging lens or concave mirror. Optical centre is the intersection point of line AB and OI.

For mirror, object and image subtend equal angles at the pole.

11. Since the first principal focus is on the right side, it must be a diverging lens.

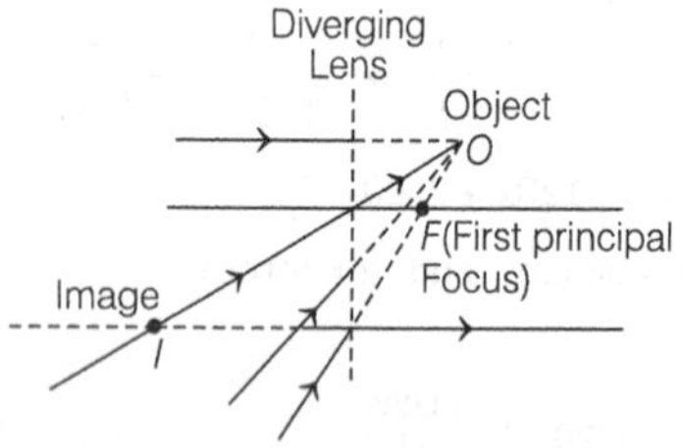

12. $\frac{1}{v}-\frac{1}{u}=\frac{1}{f} \Rightarrow \frac{1}{v}-\frac{1}{(-25)}=\frac{1}{20} \Rightarrow v=100$ cm

The intensity of light will be maximum at image position i.e., at $x=100$ cm. The intensity of light increases from $x=0$ and becomes maximum at $x=100$ cm, then decreases.

The intensity of light is same at equal distance from $x=100$ cm, (image position) in both directions.

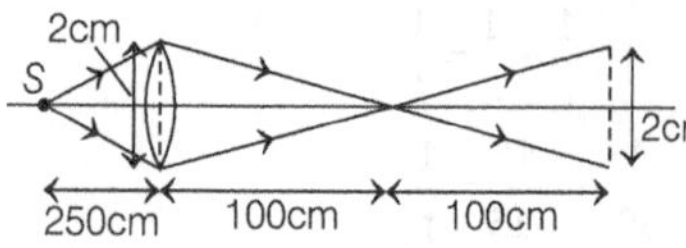

As shown in figure at $x=200$ cm, diameter of bright circle is 2 cm. So, radius is 1 cm.

13. (a) $m_\perp=\frac{h'}{h}=\frac{f}{f+u}$

$$\Rightarrow \quad \frac{h'}{h}=\frac{f}{f-3f} \Rightarrow h'=-\frac{h}{2}$$

$$m_{||}=\frac{x'}{x}=\left(\frac{f}{f+u}\right)^2 \Rightarrow \frac{x'}{x}=\frac{1}{4} \Rightarrow x'=\frac{x}{4}$$

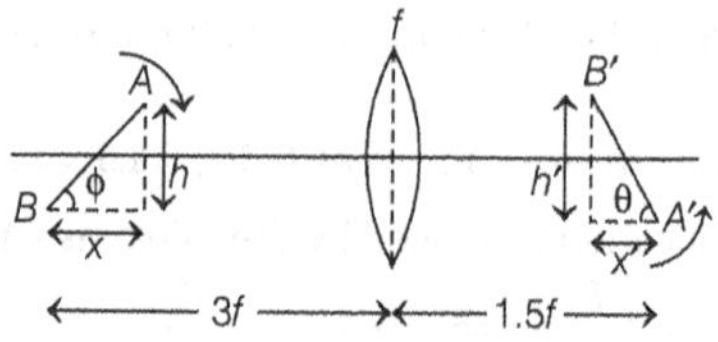

$$\tan\phi=\frac{h}{x},\ \tan\theta=\frac{h'}{x'}=\frac{h/2}{x/4}=2\tan\phi$$

$$\therefore \quad \text{If } \phi=30°, \theta=\tan^{-1}\left(\frac{2}{\sqrt{3}}\right)$$

(b) $\tan\theta=2\tan\phi$

$$\Rightarrow \quad \sec^2\theta\frac{d\theta}{dt}=2\sec^2\phi\frac{d\phi}{dt}$$

$$\Rightarrow \quad \frac{d\theta}{dt}=\frac{2\sec^2\phi}{\sec\theta}\frac{d\phi}{dt}$$

$$\Rightarrow \quad \omega_{\text{image}}=2\left(\frac{4/3}{7/3}\right)7=8 \text{ rad/s}$$

14. Final image distance is 30 cm i.e., focal length of set up is 30 cm.

At this lenses are kept near to each other, effective focal length is,

$$\frac{1}{F}=\frac{1}{f}+\frac{1}{f}$$

$$\Rightarrow \quad \frac{1}{30}=\frac{2}{f} \Rightarrow f=60 \text{ cm}$$

After refraction from first lens, image is formed at 60 cm, while final image is formed at 30 cm.

As optical axis shifts down by $(y-x)$ for second lens,

$$m=\frac{y-x-1}{y-x}=\frac{v}{u}=\frac{30}{60}=\frac{1}{2}$$

$$\Rightarrow \quad y=x+2$$

$$\Rightarrow \quad y=2.5+2=4.5 \text{ cm}$$

15.

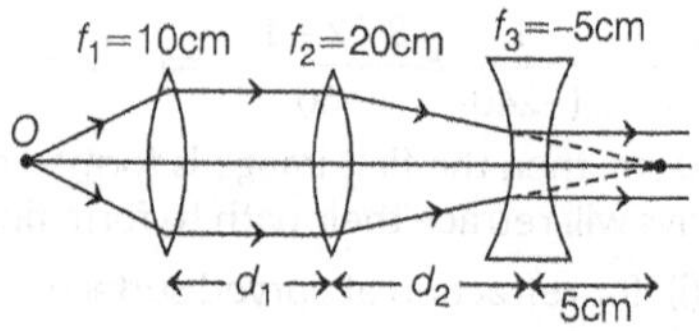

From figure we can see that d_1 can have any value.

Second focus of second lens should coincide with the first focus of the third lens.

So, $d_2+5=20$

$$\Rightarrow \quad d_2=15 \text{ cm}$$

16. Magnification, $m = \dfrac{f}{f+u}$

For the first lens, $m_1 = \dfrac{f_1}{f_1 + (-x)} = \dfrac{f_1}{f_1 - x}$

Also, $m_1 = \dfrac{v_1}{u_1} \Rightarrow \dfrac{f_1}{f_1 - x} = \dfrac{v_1}{(-x)} \Rightarrow v_1 = \dfrac{xf_1}{x - f_1}$

For the second lens, $u_2 = -(d - v_1)$

$$m_2 = \frac{f_2}{f_2 - (d - v_1)}$$

$$m = m_1 m_2 = \left(\frac{f_1}{f_1 - x}\right)\left[\frac{f_2}{f_2 - \left(d - \dfrac{xf_1}{x - f_1}\right)}\right]$$

$$= \frac{f_1 f_2}{x(d - f_1 - f_2) - df_1 + f_1 f_2}$$

As m is independent of x,

$\Rightarrow \quad d - f_1 - f_2 = 0$

$\Rightarrow \quad d = f_1 + f_2$

$\therefore \quad m = -\dfrac{f_2}{f_1}$

17. For first refraction through lens,

$$\frac{1}{v} - \frac{1}{u} = \frac{1}{f} \Rightarrow \frac{1}{v} - \frac{1}{(-15)} = \frac{1}{30} \Rightarrow v = -30 \text{ cm}$$

For reflection from plane mirror,

Object distance $= 30 + 15 = 45$ cm

$\therefore$ Image distance = 45 cm

So, the image formed by plane mirror is 45 cm behind the mirror.

For final refraction through lens,

$$\frac{1}{v} - \frac{1}{u} = \frac{1}{f} \Rightarrow \frac{1}{v} - \frac{1}{[-(15+45)]} = \frac{1}{30}$$

$\Rightarrow \quad v = 60$ cm

So, the final image is real and 60 cm from lens towards left of it.

18. For first refraction through lens,

$$\frac{1}{v} - \frac{1}{u} = \frac{1}{f} \Rightarrow \frac{1}{v} - \frac{1}{(-10)} = \frac{1}{20} \Rightarrow v = -20 \text{ cm}$$

For reflection from convex mirror,

$$u = -(20 + 5) = -25 \text{ cm}$$

$$\frac{1}{v} + \frac{1}{u} = \frac{1}{f}$$

$$\Rightarrow \frac{1}{v} + \frac{1}{(-25)} = \frac{1}{15} \Rightarrow v = \frac{75}{8} \text{ cm}$$

For final refraction through lens,

Object distance,

$$u = -\left(\frac{75}{8} + 5\right) = -\frac{115}{8} \text{ cm}$$

$$\frac{1}{v} - \frac{1}{u} = \frac{1}{f} \Rightarrow \frac{1}{v} - \frac{1}{\left(-\dfrac{115}{8}\right)} = \frac{1}{20}$$

$\Rightarrow \quad v = -\dfrac{460}{9}$ cm $= -51.1$ cm

Overall magnification,

$$m = m_1 \times m_2 \times m_3$$

$$= \left(\frac{-20}{-10}\right) \times \left(\frac{-75/8}{-25}\right) \times \left(\frac{-460/9}{-115/8}\right) = \frac{8}{3}$$

19. For lens, $\dfrac{1}{v} - \dfrac{1}{u} = \dfrac{1}{f}$

$$\Rightarrow \frac{1}{v} - \frac{1}{(-36)} = \frac{1}{30} \Rightarrow v = 180 \text{ cm}$$

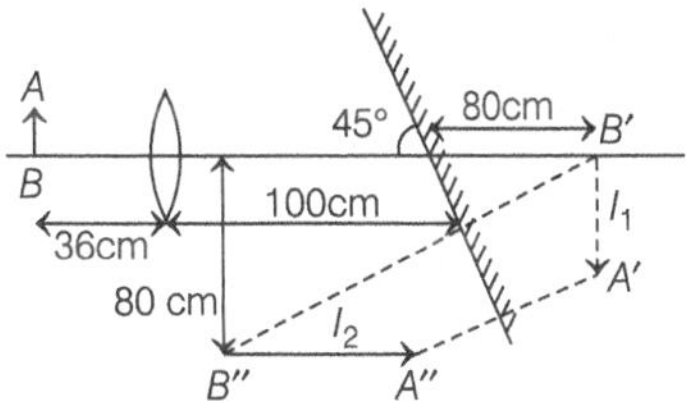

So, after reflection from the mirror, the image of AB is parallel to the principal axis of the lens.

For refraction from liquid,

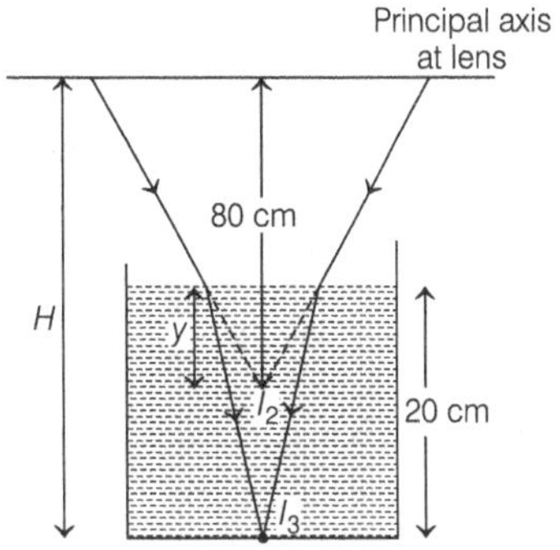

$$\text{Apparent depth} = \frac{\text{Actual depth}}{\mu_{12}}$$

$\Rightarrow \quad y = \dfrac{20}{(4/3)/1} = 15$ cm

$\therefore \quad H = (80 - y) + 20 = 85$ cm

20. For glass lens in air,

$$\frac{1}{f_g} = (1.5 - 1)\left(\frac{1}{-10} - \frac{1}{15}\right) = -\frac{1}{12}$$

For water lens in air,

$$\frac{1}{f_w} = \left(\frac{4}{3} - 1\right)\left[\frac{1}{15} - \frac{1}{(-15)}\right] = \frac{2}{45}$$

For combination,

$$P = 2P_g + 2P_w + P_M$$

$$\Rightarrow -\frac{1}{f} = 2\left(\frac{1}{f_g}\right) + 2\left(\frac{1}{f_w}\right) - \frac{1}{f_M}$$

$$\Rightarrow \quad -\frac{1}{f}=2\left(-\frac{1}{12}\right)+2\left(\frac{2}{45}\right)-\frac{1}{(-15/2)}$$

$$\Rightarrow \quad f=-18 \text{ cm}$$

Since, focal length is negative, the system behaves like a concave mirror.

Comprehension Based Questions

1. $\frac{1}{v}-\frac{1}{u}=\frac{1}{f} \Rightarrow \frac{v}{u}=\frac{f-v}{f}$

$$m=\frac{h_i}{h_o} \Rightarrow \frac{f-v}{f}=\frac{h_i}{h} \Rightarrow |h_i|=h\left|1-\frac{v}{f}\right|$$

For $v=0, |h_i|=h_2 \Rightarrow h_2=h$

2. $$\frac{1}{v}-\frac{1}{u}=\frac{1}{f}$$

$$\Rightarrow \quad \frac{1}{v}-\frac{1}{(-3f)}=\frac{1}{f} \Rightarrow v=\frac{3f}{2}$$

$$\therefore \quad h_1=h\left|1-\frac{3f/2}{f}\right|==\frac{h}{2}$$

3. When $v=v_2, h_i=h$

$$\therefore \quad h=h\left|1-\frac{v_2}{f}\right|$$

$$\Rightarrow \quad v_2=0 \text{ and } v_2=2f$$

$$\frac{v_1}{v_2}=\frac{3f/2}{2f}=\frac{3}{4}$$

4. When curved surface is in contact with the table,

$$\text{Apparent depth}=\frac{\text{Actual Depth}}{\mu}$$

$$\Rightarrow \quad 3=\frac{4}{\mu} \Rightarrow \mu=\frac{4}{3}$$

5. When the plane face is in contact with the table,

$$\frac{\mu_2}{v}-\frac{\mu_1}{u}=\frac{\mu_2-\mu_1}{R}$$

$$\Rightarrow \quad \frac{1}{(-25/8)}-\frac{4/3}{(-4)}=\frac{1-4/3}{(-R)}$$

$$\Rightarrow \quad R=25 \text{ cm}$$

6. $$\frac{1}{f}=(\mu-1)\left(\frac{1}{R_1}-\frac{1}{R_2}\right)$$

$$\Rightarrow \quad \frac{1}{f}=\left(\frac{4}{3}-1\right)\left(\frac{1}{25}-\frac{1}{\infty}\right)$$

$$\Rightarrow \quad f=75 \text{ cm}$$

7. For first refraction from lens,

$$\frac{1}{v}-\frac{1}{u}=\frac{1}{f} \Rightarrow \frac{1}{v}-\frac{1}{(-f/2)}=\frac{1}{f}$$

$$\Rightarrow \quad v=-f$$

Since I_1 is formed left of lens, it will be virtual image.

$$m_1=\frac{v}{u}=\frac{-f}{(-f/2)}=2$$

For reflection from mirror,

$$u=-\left(f+\frac{f}{2}\right)=-\frac{3f}{2}$$

$$\frac{1}{v}+\frac{1}{u}=\frac{1}{f} \Rightarrow \frac{1}{v}+\frac{1}{(-3f/2)}=\frac{1}{(-f)}$$

$$\Rightarrow \quad v=-3f$$

Since image I_2 is formed in front of the mirror, it will be a real image.

$$m_2=-\frac{(-3f)}{(-3f/2)}=-2$$

For final refraction from lens,

$$u=+\left(3f-\frac{f}{2}\right)=+\frac{5f}{2}$$

$$\frac{1}{v}-\frac{1}{u}=\frac{1}{f} \Rightarrow \frac{1}{v}-\frac{1}{(5f/2)}=\frac{1}{f}$$

$$\Rightarrow \quad v=\frac{5f}{7}$$

Since I_3 is formed left of lens, it will be real image.

$$m_3=\frac{5f/7}{5f/2}=\frac{2}{7}$$

8. $m=m_1\times m_2\times m_3=2\times(-2)\times\left(\frac{2}{7}\right)=-\frac{8}{7}$

9. $$m=\frac{h_i}{h}=-\frac{8}{7}$$

$$\Rightarrow \quad \frac{h_i}{3.5}=-\frac{8}{7} \Rightarrow h_i=-4 \text{ mm}$$

$$v=\frac{5f}{7}=\frac{5}{7}\times 7=5 \text{ cm}=50 \text{ mm}$$

$$\text{Required distance}=\sqrt{(50)^2+(4)^2}=\sqrt{2516} \text{ mm}$$

10.

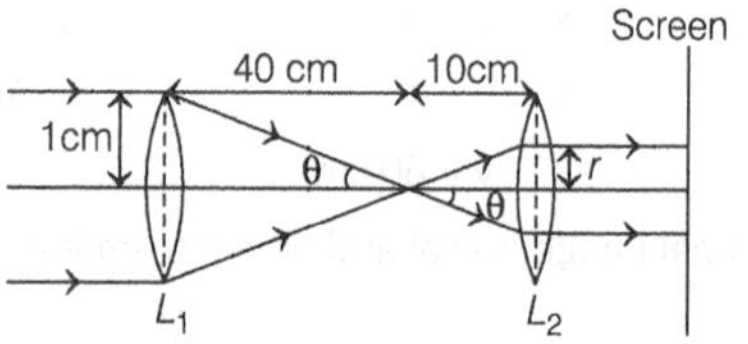

$$\tan\theta=\frac{1}{40}=\frac{r}{10} \Rightarrow r=\frac{1}{4} \text{ cm}$$

$$A_1=\pi r^2=\pi\left(\frac{1}{4}\right)^2=\frac{\pi}{16} \text{ cm}^2$$

11.

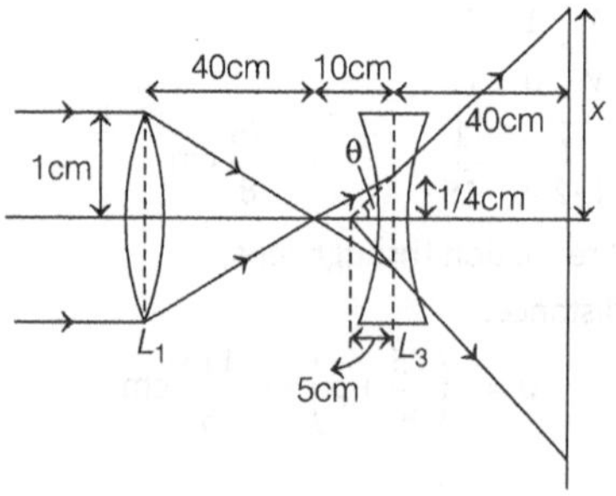

For L_3, $\frac{1}{v}-\frac{1}{u}=\frac{1}{f} \Rightarrow \frac{1}{v}-\frac{1}{-10}=\frac{1}{-10}$

$\Rightarrow \quad v=-5\text{ cm}$

$\tan\theta=\frac{1/4}{5}=\frac{x}{45} \Rightarrow x=\frac{9}{4}\text{ cm}$

$\therefore \quad A_2=\pi\left(\frac{9}{4}\right)^2=\frac{81\pi}{16}\text{ cm}^2$

12. For L_2, $\frac{1}{f}=(\mu-1)\left(\frac{1}{R_1}-\frac{1}{R_2}\right)$

$\Rightarrow \quad \frac{1}{-10}=(1.5-1)\left(\frac{1}{-R}-\frac{1}{R}\right)$

$\Rightarrow \quad R=10\text{ cm}$

When, liquid of refractive index μ is filled to the right of L_3, the first surface of lens (radius of curvature = 10 cm) forms the image at the object itself.

Considering the refraction at the second surface,

$$\frac{\mu_2}{v}-\frac{\mu_1}{u}=\frac{\mu_2-\mu_1}{R}$$

$\Rightarrow \quad \frac{\mu'}{\infty}-\frac{1.5}{(-10)}=\frac{\mu'-1.5}{10} \qquad \{\because \text{Same area} \Rightarrow v=\infty\}$

$\Rightarrow \quad \mu'=3$

13. For lens, $\frac{1}{v}-\frac{1}{u}=\frac{1}{f}$

$\Rightarrow \quad \frac{1}{v}-\frac{1}{(-60)}=\frac{1}{40} \Rightarrow v=120\text{ cm}$

So, the image is formed 30 cm above the mirror or 60 cm below water surface.

$$H_{app}=\frac{H}{\mu_{12}} \Rightarrow H_{app}=\frac{60}{(1/4/3)}=80\text{ cm}$$

So, after refraction image is formed 80 cm below water surface i.e., at centre of curvature of the concave mirror. Therefore, the rays will retrace their path and the final image will be formed on the object itself.

14. $H_{app}=\frac{H}{\mu_{12}}=\frac{120-30}{1/(4/3)}=120\text{ cm}$

So, the image is formed at the pole of the concave mirror. Therefore, the final image will be formed on the object itself.

15. $$\frac{\mu_3}{v}-\frac{\mu_1}{u}=\frac{\mu_2-\mu_1}{R_1}+\frac{\mu_3-\mu_2}{R_2}$$

$\Rightarrow \quad \frac{4/3}{v}-\frac{1}{(-60)}=\frac{1.5-1}{40}+\frac{(4/3)-(3/2)}{-40}$

$\Rightarrow \quad v=\infty$

$\therefore$ Image formed by bottom mirror is at its focus 5 cm above itself.

16. For image and object to coincide, rays should strike the plane silvered surface perpendicularly i.e., the refracted light from the curved surface of L_1 should be parallel to the principal axis.

For refraction at curved surface of L_1,

$\frac{\mu_2}{v}-\frac{\mu_1}{u}=\frac{\mu_2-\mu_1}{R} \Rightarrow \frac{2}{\infty}-\frac{4/3}{(-x_1)}=\frac{2-(4/3)}{5}$

$\Rightarrow \quad x_1=10\text{ cm}$

17. For refraction at plane surface of L_2,

$\frac{\mu_2}{v}-\frac{\mu_1}{u}=\frac{\mu_2-\mu_1}{R} \Rightarrow \frac{1.5}{v}-\frac{4/3}{(-x_2)}=\frac{1.5-(4/3)}{\infty}$

$\Rightarrow \quad v=-\frac{9}{8}x_2$

For rays to retrace their path, the image formed should coincide with the centre of curvature of the silvered curved surface.

$\Rightarrow \quad \frac{9}{8}x_2=9 \Rightarrow x_2=8\text{ cm}$

18.

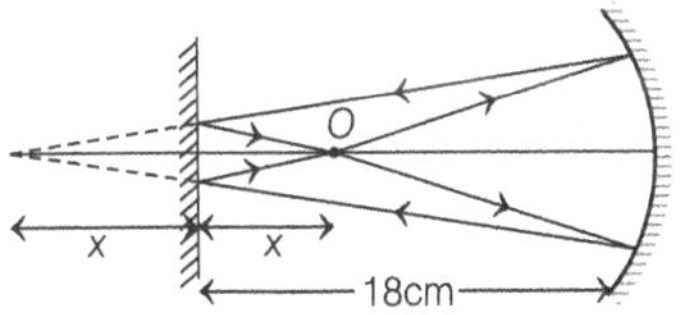

For concave mirror, $\frac{1}{v}+\frac{1}{u}=\frac{1}{f}$

$\Rightarrow \quad \frac{1}{-(18+x)}+\frac{1}{-(18-x)}=\frac{1}{-9/2}$

$\Rightarrow \quad x=9\sqrt{2}\text{ cm}$

Match the Columns Questions

1. (A)

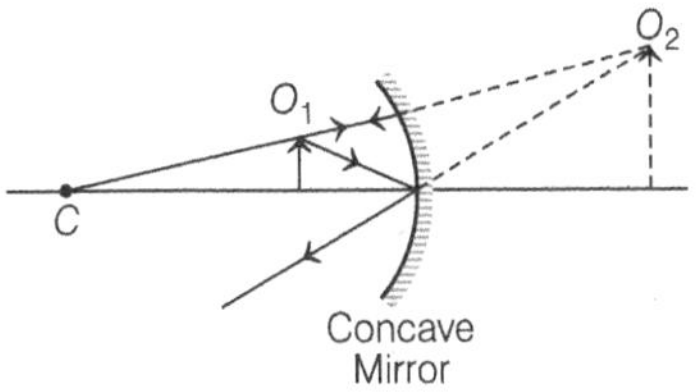

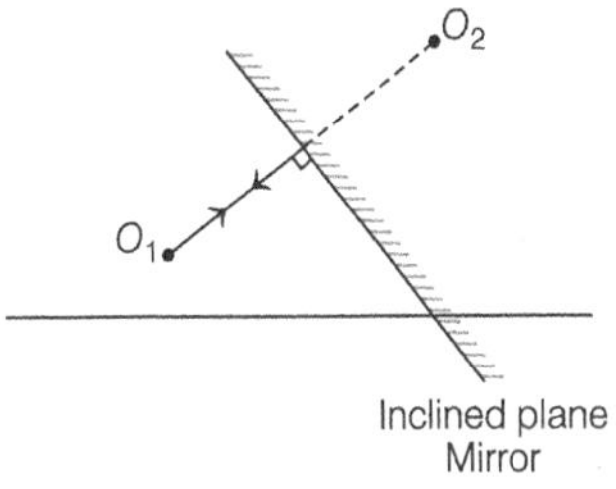

(B)

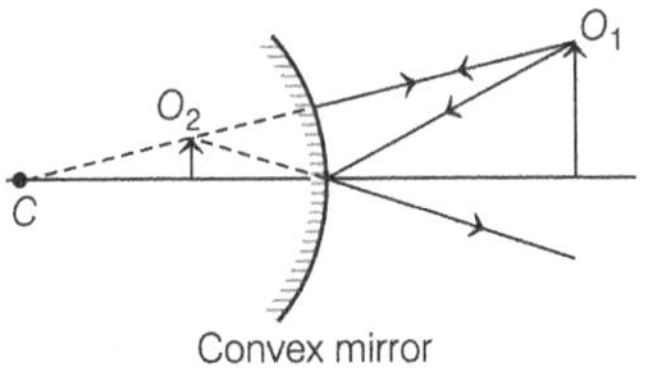

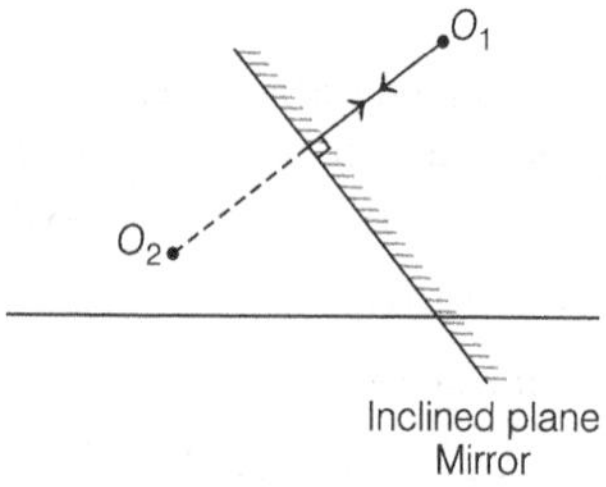

(C)

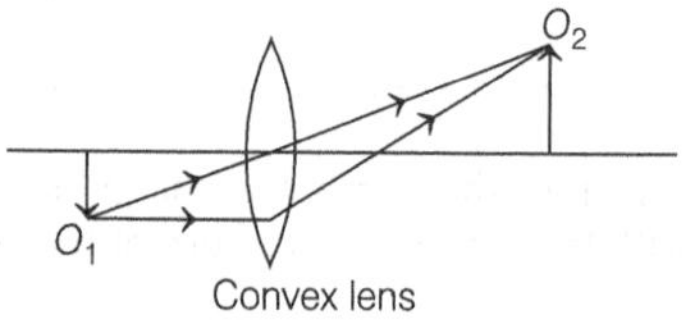

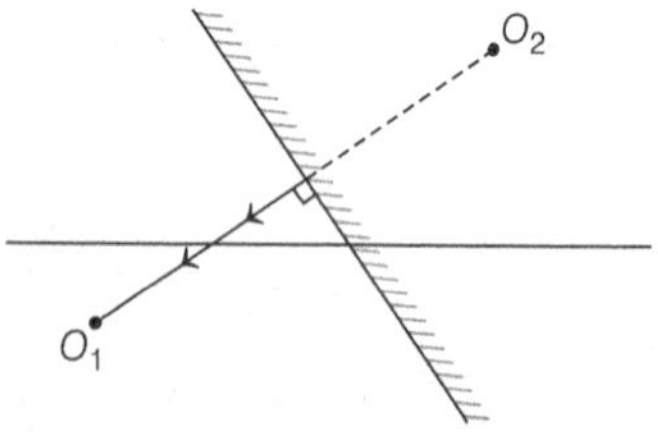

(D) Same as C.

2. (A) For mirror, $\frac{1}{v}=\frac{1}{f}-\frac{1}{u}$

For virtual object, $u>0$

For convex mirror, $f>0$

$\therefore$ If $u<f \Rightarrow v<0$

So, convex mirror can form virtual image of virtual object. Similarly for diverging lens, $u<0, f<0$.

2. (A) For virtual object ($u>0$)

Case-I Convex mirror ($f>0$)

$$\frac{1}{v}=\frac{1}{f}-\frac{1}{u}$$

If $u<f \quad \Rightarrow \quad v<0$ (virtual image)

Case-II Diverging lens ($f<0$)

$$\frac{1}{v}=\frac{1}{f}+\frac{1}{u}$$

If $u>|f| \quad \Rightarrow \quad v<0$ (virtual image)

(B) For real object ($u<0$)

Case-I Converging lens ($f>0$)

$$\frac{1}{v}=\frac{1}{f}+\frac{1}{u}$$

If $|u|>f \quad \Rightarrow \quad v>0$ (Real image)

Case-II $\frac{\mu_w}{v}=\frac{\mu_{air}}{u}+\frac{\mu_w-\mu_{air}}{R}$

If $\frac{\mu_{air}}{|u|}<\frac{\mu_w-\mu_{air}}{R} \quad \Rightarrow \quad v>0$ (Real image)

(C) $\frac{\mu_{air}}{v}-\frac{\mu_w}{u}=0$

For a virtual object, erect real image of same size as object will be formed.

(D) For converging lens,

$$m=\frac{v}{u}=\frac{f}{f+u}$$

If $|u|<f \quad \Rightarrow \quad m>1$

For spherical surface,

$$m=\left(\frac{\mu_{air}}{\mu_w}\right)\frac{v}{u}$$

Using $\frac{\mu_w}{v}-\frac{\mu_{air}}{u}=\frac{\mu_w-\mu_{air}}{R}$, we get

$$m=1-\left(\frac{\mu_w-\mu_{air}}{\mu_w R}\right)v$$

$\because v<0$ (virtual image) $\Rightarrow m>1$

3. (P) Parallel rays can be obtained in case of concave mirror and convex lens if point source is placed at their focus.
(Q) Real image of real object can be obtained for concave mirror and convex lens.
(R) Convex mirror and concave lens form virtual and diminished image for real object.
(S) Concave mirror and convex lens can form real and magnified image for real object.
(T) For lens, $v_i=\left(\frac{v^2}{u^2}\right)v_O$

So, velocity of object and image are in same direction.

4. For spherical mirror, $v_i=-\frac{v^2}{u^2}v_O$

For lens, $v_i=\frac{v^2}{u^2}v_O$

For plane mirror, $v_i=2v_m$

5. If surroundings are rarer then convex lens is converging and concave lens is diverging.

If surroundings are denser then convex lens is diverging and concave lens is converging.

6. (A) Object for diverging lens will be virtual. From $v=\frac{uf}{u+f}$, v may be less than, equal to or more than f.
(B) Object for diverging lens will be a real object (diverging rays fall on diverging lens).
Hence, $v<f$
(C) For converging lens, object distance will be between f and $2f$. So, image formed by the converging lens will be beyond $2f$.
Hence, $L_2>f$
(D) For converging lens, object distance will be greater than $2f$. So, image formed by it will be between F and $2F$.
Hence, $L_2>f$

7. Initially, the image is formed at infinity.
(i) As μ is increased, the focal length decreases. Hence, the object is at a distance larger than the focal length. Therefore, final image is real. Also, final image becomes smaller in size in comparison to the size of image before the change was made.

(ii) If the radius of curvature is doubled, the focal length decreases. Hence, the object is at a distance lesser than the focal length. Therefore, final image is virtual. Also, final image becomes smaller in size in comparison to the size of image before the change was made.

(iii) Due to insertion of slab, the effective object for lens shifts rightward. Hence, final image is virtual. Also, final image becomes smaller in size in comparison to the size of image before the change was made.

(iv) The object comes to centre of curvature of right spherical surface. Hence, the final image is virtual. Also, final image becomes smaller in size in comparison to the size of image before the change was made.

Numerical Value Questions

1. For refraction from glass to water,

$$\frac{\mu_2}{v}-\frac{\mu_1}{u}=\frac{\mu_2-\mu_1}{R}$$

$$\Rightarrow \quad \frac{4/3}{v}-\frac{3/2}{(-7.5)}=\frac{4/3-3/2}{-5}$$

$$\Rightarrow \quad v=-8\text{ cm}$$

For refraction from water to air,

Object distance, $u=-(10+8)=-18$ cm

$$\frac{\mu_2}{v}-\frac{\mu_1}{u}=\frac{\mu_2-\mu_1}{R} \Rightarrow \frac{1}{v}-\frac{4/3}{(-18)}=\frac{1-(4/3)}{\infty}$$

$\Rightarrow$ $v=-13.5$ cm i.e., 13.5 cm below the surface of water.

2. For refraction at AB,

$$\mu_1 \sin i=\mu_2 \sin r$$

$$\Rightarrow \quad 1\times \sin 45^\circ=\sqrt{2}\times \sin r$$

$$\Rightarrow \quad \sin r=\frac{1}{2}$$

$$\Rightarrow \quad r=30^\circ$$

So, the refracted ray is parallel to PQ.

For refraction at CD,

$$\frac{\mu_2}{v}-\frac{\mu_1}{u}=\frac{\mu_2-\mu_1}{R}$$

$$\Rightarrow \quad \frac{1.514}{v}-\frac{\sqrt{2}}{\infty}=\frac{1.514-1.414}{0.4}$$

$$\Rightarrow \quad v=6.056\text{ m}=6.06\text{ m}$$

3. For refraction at plane surface,

$$\frac{\mu_2}{v}-\frac{\mu_1}{u}=\frac{\mu_2-\mu_1}{R}$$

$$\Rightarrow \quad \frac{1.5}{v}-\frac{1}{(-40)}=\frac{1.5-1}{\infty}$$

$$\Rightarrow \quad v=-60\text{ cm}$$

For refraction at curved surface,

$$u=-(60+30)=-90\text{ cm}$$

$$\frac{\mu_2}{v}-\frac{\mu_1}{u}=\frac{\mu_2-\mu_1}{R} \Rightarrow \frac{1}{v}-\frac{1.5}{(-90)}=\frac{1-1.5}{(-30)}$$

$$\Rightarrow \quad v=\infty$$

So, the light incident on the parabolic reflector is parallel to the X-axis. Reflected ray will pass through the focus of the parabolic reflector.

Comparing with $y^2=4ax$, $a=0.5$ m $=50$ cm

Coordinates of focus of a parabola $=(a, 0)$

4. The given ray is not a paraxial ray

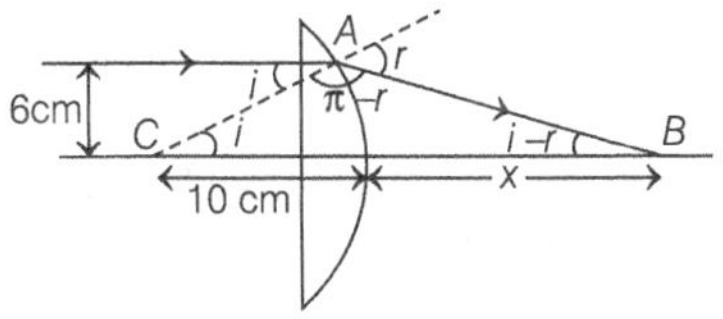

$$\sin i=\frac{6}{10}=\frac{3}{5}$$

Using Snell's law,

$$\mu_1 \sin i=\mu_2 \sin r \quad \Rightarrow \quad \frac{4}{3}\times\frac{3}{5}=1\times \sin r$$

$$\Rightarrow \quad \sin r=\frac{4}{5}$$

$$\sin(i-r)=\sin i\cos r-\cos i\sin r$$

$$=\left(\frac{4}{5}\right)\left(\frac{4}{5}\right)-\left(\frac{3}{5}\right)\left(\frac{3}{5}\right)=\frac{7}{25}$$

By sine law in ΔABC,

$$\frac{\sin(\pi-r)}{10+x}=\frac{\sin(i-r)}{10} \quad \Rightarrow \quad x=\frac{130}{7}\text{ cm}$$

5. For lens, $\frac{1}{f}=(\mu-1)\left(\frac{1}{R_1}-\frac{1}{R_2}\right)$

$$\Rightarrow \quad \frac{1}{f}=(1.5-1)\left(\frac{1}{20}-\frac{1}{60}\right)$$

$$\Rightarrow \quad f=60\text{ cm}$$

$$\frac{1}{v}-\frac{1}{u}=\frac{1}{f} \quad \Rightarrow \quad \frac{1}{v}-\frac{1}{(-80)}=\frac{1}{60}$$

$$\Rightarrow \quad v=240\text{ cm}$$

Shift due to glass slab $=t\left(1-\frac{1}{\mu}\right)=3\left(1-\frac{1}{1.5}\right)=1$ cm

So, after refraction through glass slab, image is formed $(248-240-1)=7$ cm from left surface of glass slab.

For final image to be on the object itself, the rays should hit the mirror normally i.e., image formed from glass slab should coincide with the centre of curvature of the concave mirror.

$$\Rightarrow \quad 7+3+x=20 \quad \Rightarrow \quad x=10\text{ cm}$$

6. For silvered lens, $P=2P_L+P_M$

$$\Rightarrow \quad -\frac{1}{f}=2\left(\frac{1}{f}\right)-\frac{1}{f_M}$$

$$\Rightarrow \quad -\frac{1}{f}=2\left(\frac{3}{2}-1\right)\left(\frac{1}{42}-\frac{1}{\infty}\right)-\frac{1}{(-21)}$$

$$\Rightarrow \quad f=-14\text{ cm}$$

Radius of curvature of the equivalent concave mirror

$$= 2(14) = 28 \text{ cm}$$

For final image to be at the object itself,

$$21 + d = 28 \quad \Rightarrow \quad d = 7 \text{ cm}$$

7. For lens, $\frac{1}{v} - \frac{1}{u} = \frac{1}{f}$

$$\Rightarrow \quad \frac{1}{v} - \frac{1}{(-15)} = \frac{1}{10} \quad \Rightarrow \quad v = 30 \text{ cm}$$

So, the image is formed 30 cm from lens or $45 - 30 = 15$ cm from the mirror on axis AB.

For concave mirror, $\frac{1}{v} + \frac{1}{u} = \frac{1}{f}$

$$\Rightarrow \quad \frac{1}{v} + \frac{1}{(-15)} = \frac{1}{(-10)} \quad \Rightarrow \quad v = -30 \text{ cm}$$

$$m = -\frac{v}{u} \quad \Rightarrow \quad \frac{h_i}{1} = -\frac{(-30)}{(-15)}$$

$$\Rightarrow \quad h_i = -2 \text{ cm}$$

So, the image formed by mirror is 2 cm above CD or 3 cm above AB.

For final refraction through lens,

$$\frac{1}{v} - \frac{1}{u} = \frac{1}{f}$$

$$\Rightarrow \quad \frac{1}{v} - \frac{1}{(-15)} = \frac{1}{10} \quad \Rightarrow \quad v = 30 \text{ cm}$$

$$m = \frac{v}{u} \quad \Rightarrow \quad \frac{h_i}{3} = \frac{30}{(-15)} \quad \Rightarrow \quad h_i = -6 \text{ cm}$$

Required distance $= \sqrt{(30)^2 + 6^2} = 6\sqrt{26}$ cm

8.

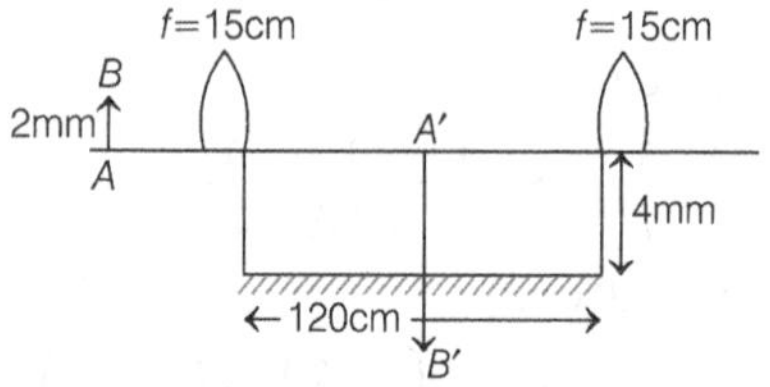

For first lens, $\frac{1}{v} - \frac{1}{u} = \frac{1}{f}$

$$\Rightarrow \quad \frac{1}{v} - \frac{1}{(-20)} = \frac{1}{15} \quad \Rightarrow \quad v = 60 \text{ cm}$$

$$m = \frac{v}{u} \quad \Rightarrow \quad \frac{h_i}{2} = \frac{60}{(-20)}$$

$$\Rightarrow \quad h_i = -6 \text{ mm}$$

A' is 4 mm above plane mirror. Image of A' in plane mirror will be 4 mm below the mirror i.e., 8 mm below the principal axis of second half lens.

For second half lens,

$$u = -(120 - 60) = -60 \text{ cm}$$

$$\frac{1}{v} - \frac{1}{u} = \frac{1}{f} \Rightarrow \frac{1}{v} - \frac{1}{(-60)} = \frac{1}{15}$$

$$\Rightarrow \quad v = 20 \text{ cm}$$

$$m = \frac{h_i}{h_o} = \frac{v}{u} \quad \Rightarrow \quad \frac{h_i}{8} = \frac{20}{(-60)} \quad \Rightarrow \quad h_i = -\frac{8}{3} \text{ mm}$$

So, final image of A will be 8/3 mm above the principal axis.

9. For refraction from air to glass,

$$\frac{\mu_2}{v} - \frac{\mu_1}{u} = \frac{\mu_2 - \mu_1}{R} \quad \Rightarrow \quad \frac{\mu}{v_1} - \frac{1}{\infty} = \frac{\mu - 1}{R} \quad \Rightarrow v_1 = \frac{\mu R}{\mu - 1}$$

For refraction from glass to air,

$$u = \frac{\mu R}{\mu - 1} - R = \frac{R}{\mu - 1}$$

$$\frac{\mu_2}{v} - \frac{\mu_1}{u} = \frac{\mu_2 - \mu_1}{R} \Rightarrow \frac{1}{R} - \frac{\mu}{(R/(\mu - 1))} = \frac{1 - \mu}{R/2}$$

$$\Rightarrow \quad \mu^2 - 3\mu + 1 = 0 \quad \Rightarrow \quad \mu = \frac{3 + \sqrt{5}}{2} = 2.6$$

10. For converging lens,

$$v - u = 64 \text{ and } \frac{v}{u} = -3$$

$$\Rightarrow \quad v = 48 \text{ cm}, \quad u = -16 \text{ cm} \quad \text{and} \quad f = 12 \text{ cm}$$

After shifting of object,

$$u = -(16 + 14) = -30 \text{ cm}$$

$$\frac{1}{v} - \frac{1}{u} = \frac{1}{f} \quad \Rightarrow \quad \frac{1}{v} - \frac{1}{-30} = \frac{1}{12} \quad \Rightarrow v = 20 \text{ cm}$$

For diverging lens,

$$u = 20 - 6 = 14 \text{ cm}, \; v = 48 - 6 = 42 \text{ cm}$$

$$\frac{1}{v} - \frac{1}{u} = \frac{1}{f} \quad \Rightarrow \quad \frac{1}{42} - \frac{1}{14} = \frac{1}{f} \quad \Rightarrow \quad f = -21 \text{ cm}$$

$$\frac{1}{f} = (\mu - 1)\left(\frac{1}{R_1} - \frac{1}{R_2}\right)$$

$$\Rightarrow \quad \frac{1}{(-21)} = (\mu - 1)\left(\frac{1}{-14} - \frac{1}{21}\right) \quad \Rightarrow \mu = 1.4$$

11.

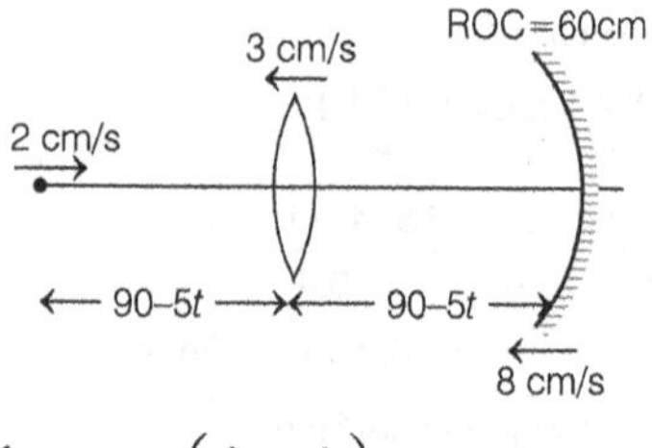

For lens, $\frac{1}{f} = (\mu - 1)\left(\frac{1}{R_1} - \frac{1}{R_2}\right)$

$$\frac{1}{f} = \left(\frac{3}{2} - 1\right)\left[\frac{1}{16} - \frac{1}{(-16)}\right] \quad \Rightarrow f = 16 \text{ cm}$$

For the final image and object to coincide, image formed by the lens should coincide with the centre of curvature of the concave mirror.

For lens, $v = (90 - 5t) - 60 = 30 - 5t$

$$\frac{1}{v} - \frac{1}{u} = \frac{1}{f} \quad \Rightarrow \quad \frac{1}{30 - 5t} - \frac{1}{-(90 - 5t)} = \frac{1}{16}$$

$$\Rightarrow \quad t = 2 \text{ s}$$

12. Let object distance be x and image distance $100 - x$.

$$\frac{1}{v} - \frac{1}{u} = \frac{1}{f} \Rightarrow \frac{1}{100 - x} - \frac{1}{(-x)} = \frac{1}{25} \Rightarrow x = 50 \text{ cm}$$

Let shift due to glass slab be y.

When glass slab is introduced between the object and the lens,

$$u = 50 - y, \quad v = 50 + \frac{50}{23} = \frac{1200}{23} \text{ cm}$$

$$\frac{1}{v} - \frac{1}{u} = \frac{1}{f} \Rightarrow \frac{1}{\left(\frac{1200}{23}\right)} - \frac{1}{-(50 - y)} = \frac{1}{25} \Rightarrow y = 2 \text{ cm}$$

When glass slab is introduced between the lens and screen, shift of the screen $= y = 2$ cm.

Previous Year's Questions

JEE Main

1. Given, $\mu_a = 1.5$

$$\mu_m = 1.6 \Rightarrow f_a = 20 \text{ cm}$$

Ratio of focal lengths in air and in medium using lens Maker's formula is,

As $$\frac{f_m}{f_a} = \frac{(\mu_a - 1)\mu_m}{(\mu_a - \mu_m)} \Rightarrow \frac{f_m}{20} = \frac{(1.5 - 1)1.6}{(1.5 - 1.6)}$$

$$\frac{f_m}{20} = -\frac{0.5 \times 1.6}{0.1} \Rightarrow f_m = -\frac{20 \times 0.5 \times 1.6}{0.1}$$

$$f_m = -\frac{32 \times 5}{1} = -160 \text{ cm}$$

2. Given,

Distance between object and image = 45 cm

Magnification = 2 (real image)

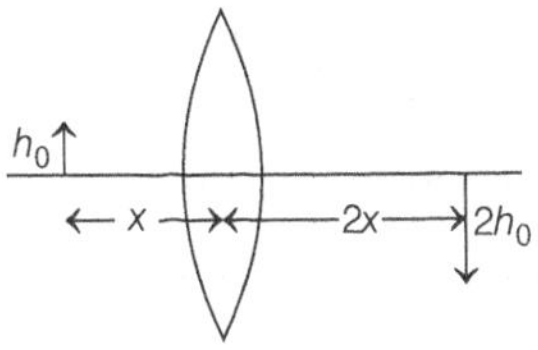

Let object height $= h_0$

then, magnification $= \dfrac{\text{Image height}}{\text{Object height}}$

Image height $= 2h_0$

Also, magnification $= \dfrac{\text{Image distance}}{\text{Object distance}}$

Let object distance $= x$

Image distance $= 2x$

$$x + 2x = 45 \qquad \text{(given)}$$

$x = 15$ cm, (object distance) $= u$

Image distance, $2x = 30$ cm $= v$

Using lens formula,

$$\frac{1}{v} - \frac{1}{u} = \frac{1}{f} \Rightarrow \frac{1}{30} - \frac{1}{-15} = \frac{1}{f}$$

$$\Rightarrow \frac{1+2}{30} = \frac{1}{f} \Rightarrow f = 10 \text{ cm}$$

3. If we draw $y = x$ line on graph, then it cuts the curve at point (20 cm, 20 cm).

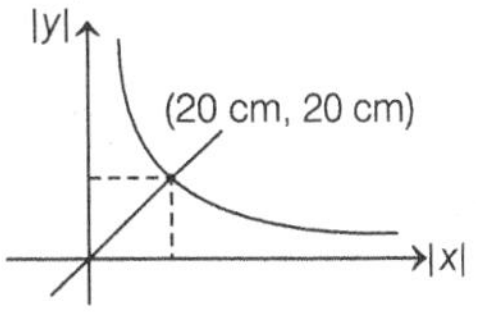

From the Newton's formula

$$xy = f^2 \Rightarrow 20 \times 20 = f^2 \Rightarrow f = 20 \text{ cm}$$

4. Given, $n_1 = 1$

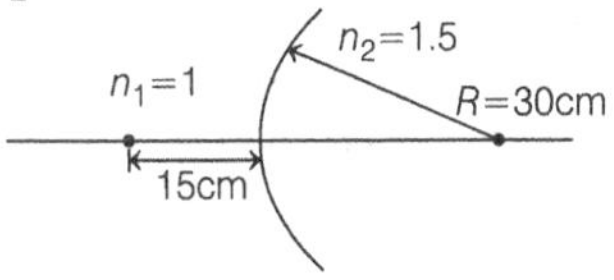

Using refraction formula, $\dfrac{n_2}{v} - \dfrac{n_1}{u} = \dfrac{n_2 - n_1}{R}$

We get, $$\frac{1.5}{v} - \frac{1}{(-15)} = \frac{1.5 - 1}{30} \Rightarrow v = -30 \text{ cm}$$

(Negative sign shows image is formed on same side as that of object)

5. Given focal length of $L_1 = 24$ m

Focal length of $L_2 = 9$ cm, distance b/w two lenses = 10 cm

According to question, for L_1

$$\frac{1}{v} + \frac{1}{6} = \frac{1}{24} \Rightarrow v = -8 \text{ cm}$$

For L_2

$$\frac{1}{v} + \frac{1}{18} = \frac{1}{9} \Rightarrow \frac{1}{v} = \frac{1}{18} \Rightarrow v = 18 \text{ cm}$$

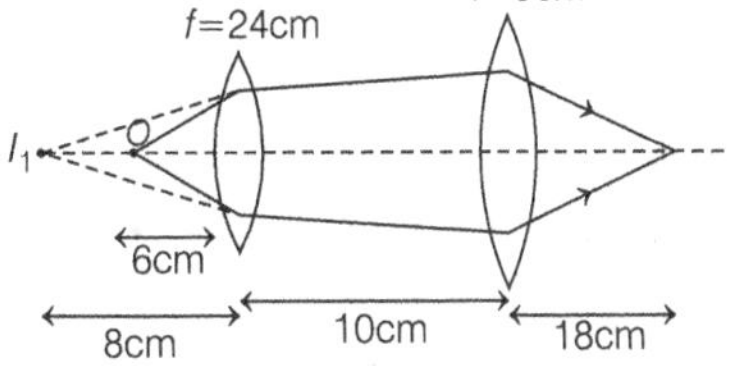

6. $$\frac{1}{f} = \left(\frac{\mu_l}{\mu_m} - 1\right)\left(\frac{1}{R} - \frac{1}{-R}\right)$$

$$P_l = \frac{2}{R}\left[\frac{1 \cdot 8}{1} - 1\right]$$

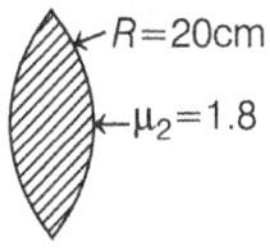

$$P_l = \frac{2}{R} \times 0 \cdot 8$$

$$P_l = \frac{1 \cdot 6}{R} \qquad \text{...(i)}$$

Now, $$P_2 = \frac{2}{R}\left[\frac{1 \cdot 8}{1 \cdot 5} - 1\right]$$

$$P_2 = \frac{2}{R}\left[\frac{0 \cdot 3}{1 \cdot 5}\right] = \frac{2}{R} \times \frac{3}{15} = \frac{2}{5R}$$

$$\frac{P_{air}}{P_{liquid}} = \frac{P_1}{P_2} = \frac{\left(\frac{1 \cdot 6}{R}\right)}{\left(\frac{0 \cdot 4}{R}\right)} = \frac{4}{1} = \frac{x}{1}$$

7. According to question, the situation described is given below

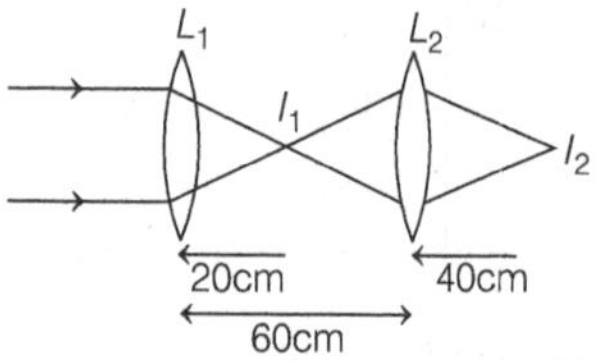

For L_1; $\frac{1}{v}-\frac{1}{u}=\frac{1}{f} \Rightarrow \frac{1}{v}-\frac{1}{\infty}=\frac{1}{f}$ $(\because f = 20\text{ cm})$

$\therefore \quad v = f$

For L_2; $I_1 \rightarrow$ object and $I_2 \rightarrow$ image

$\Rightarrow \quad u = -40$ cm and $f = 20$ cm

$$\frac{1}{v}-\frac{1}{u}=\frac{1}{f} \Rightarrow \frac{1}{v}-\frac{1}{(-40)}=\frac{1}{20}$$

$$\Rightarrow \frac{1}{v}=\frac{1}{20}-\frac{1}{40}=\frac{6-3}{120} \Rightarrow \frac{1}{v}=\frac{3}{120}=\frac{1}{40}$$

$\therefore \quad v = 40$ cm

Hence, the distance from $L_1 = 60 + 40 = 100$ cm

8. Given $f = 10\text{ cm} = 0.1\text{ m}$

$$P_1 + P_2 = P = \frac{1}{f}$$

$$2P_1 = \frac{1}{0.1}$$

$$P_1 = \frac{1}{0.2} \Rightarrow P_1 = \frac{10}{2}$$

$\Rightarrow \quad P_1 = 5\text{D}$

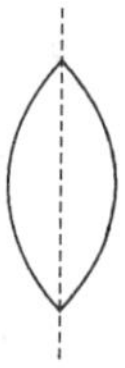

9. Focal length of convex lens, $f = 10$ cm

Since, image produced by the plane mirror is 5 cm inside the mirror.

Hence, distance image formed by the convex mirror,

$$v = 20 - 5 = 15\text{ cm}$$

$\therefore$ By lens formula, $\frac{1}{v}-\frac{1}{u}=\frac{1}{f}$

$$\Rightarrow \frac{1}{u}=\frac{1}{v}-\frac{1}{f}=\frac{1}{15}-\frac{1}{10}=-\frac{1}{30} \Rightarrow u = -30\text{ cm}$$

Thus, distance of the object from the lens is 30 cm.

10. Focal length of a lens in a liquid f_l can be determined by

$$\frac{f_l}{f_a}=\frac{{}_a\mu_g - 1}{{}_l\mu_g - 1}=\frac{\frac{\mu_g}{\mu_a}-1}{\frac{\mu_g}{\mu_l}-1}$$

Here, f_a = focal length of lens in air = 18 cm

$$\mu_g = 1.5;\ \mu_l = \frac{4}{3} = \frac{3}{2}$$

$$\text{So,}\quad f_l = \frac{f_a\left(\frac{\mu_g}{\mu_a}-1\right)}{\left(\frac{\mu_g}{\mu_l}-1\right)} = \frac{18\times\left(\frac{3}{2}-1\right)}{\left(\frac{3/2}{4/3}-1\right)} = 72\text{ cm}$$

$\therefore$ Change in focal length $= 72 - 18 = 54$ cm

11. Given, refractive index, $\mu = 1.5$

For convex lens, $R_1 = R$ and $R_2 = -R$

From the given graph, at point A,

$$\frac{1}{v} = 0.10\text{ cm}^{-1} \text{ and } \frac{1}{u} = 0$$

$$\frac{1}{f}=\frac{1}{v}-\frac{1}{u}=0.10-0=0.10$$

$$\Rightarrow f = \frac{1}{0.10}\text{ cm} = 10\text{ cm}$$

By using lens maker's formula,

$$\Rightarrow \frac{1}{f}=(\mu-1)\left(\frac{1}{R_1}-\frac{1}{R_2}\right) \Rightarrow \frac{1}{10}=(1.5-1)\left(\frac{1}{R}-\frac{1}{-R}\right)$$

$$\Rightarrow \frac{1}{10}=(0.5)\left(\frac{1}{R}+\frac{1}{R}\right) \Rightarrow \frac{1}{10}=0.5\times\frac{2}{R}$$

$$\Rightarrow \frac{1}{10}=\frac{1}{R} \Rightarrow R = 10\text{ cm}$$

12. Given, power $P = 1.25\text{ m}^{-1}$

Refractive index of lens, $\mu_l = 1.5$

Radii of curvature of lens are

$$R_1 = 20\text{ cm}, R_2 = -40\text{ cm}$$

Using Lens makers formula,

$$\frac{1}{f}=\left(\frac{\mu_l}{\mu_s}-1\right)\left(\frac{1}{R_1}-\frac{1}{R_2}\right)$$

Where, μ_s = Refractive index of surrounding medium

$$\Rightarrow \frac{1.25}{100}=\left(\frac{1.5}{\mu_s}-1\right)\left(\frac{1}{20}+\frac{1}{40}\right) \quad \left(\because f = \frac{1}{P}\right)$$

$$\Rightarrow \frac{1}{80}=\left(\frac{1.5}{\mu_s}-1\right)\frac{6}{80} \Rightarrow \frac{1.5}{\mu_s}-1=\frac{1}{6}$$

$$\text{or}\quad \mu_s = \frac{6}{7}\times 1.5 = \frac{9}{7}$$

13. Given, Image distance, $v = 10$ m

Object distance, $u = \left(\frac{3}{2}\right)\times 10 - 15$ m

$$\text{and}\quad n_2 = \frac{3}{2}n_1 \quad \left(\because n \propto \frac{1}{\lambda}\right)$$

Using the refraction through spherical surface,

$$\frac{n_2}{v}-\frac{n_1}{u}=\left(\frac{n_2-n_1}{R}\right)$$

On substituting the values in the above equation, we get

$$\frac{\frac{3}{2}n_1}{10}-\frac{n_1}{-15}=\left(\frac{\frac{3}{2}n_1-n_1}{R}\right)$$

$$\Rightarrow R = \frac{30}{13}\text{ m} = \frac{x}{13}\text{ m} \quad \text{[given]}$$

$\therefore \quad x = 30$

14. Given, focal length of concave lens, $f' = -f$

By using lens formula,

$$\frac{1}{f'}=\frac{1}{v}-\frac{1}{u}$$

$\Rightarrow \quad \frac{1}{v}=\frac{1}{f'}+\frac{1}{u}=-\frac{1}{f}-\frac{1}{f}=-2/f$

$\Rightarrow \quad v=-f/2$

$\therefore \quad |v|=\frac{f}{2}$

$\therefore \quad m=\frac{v}{u}=\frac{-f/2}{-f}=\frac{1}{2}$

15. According to given diagram,

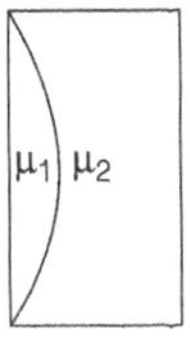

Refractive indices are μ_1 and μ_2.

Radius of two lenses are

$R_1=R_2=R$

By using lens Maker's formula,

$$\frac{1}{f}=(\mu-1)\left(\frac{1}{R_1}-\frac{1}{R_2}\right)$$

Where, f = focal length.

Now, for plano-convex lens $R_1=\infty$ and $R_2=-R$

$$\frac{1}{f_1}=(\mu_1-1)\left(\frac{1}{\infty}-\frac{1}{-R}\right)$$

$$\Rightarrow \quad \frac{1}{f_1}=(\mu_1-1)\left(\frac{1}{R}\right) \quad ...(i)$$

For plano-concave lens, $R_1=-R$ and $R_2=\infty$

$$\frac{1}{f_2}=(\mu_2-1)\left(\frac{1}{-R}-\frac{1}{\infty}\right)$$

$$\frac{1}{f_2}=(\mu_2-1)\left(-\frac{1}{R}\right) \quad ...(ii)$$

Therefore, combined focal length

$$\frac{1}{f}=\frac{1}{f_1}+\frac{1}{f_2}=(\mu_1-1)\left(\frac{1}{R}\right)+(\mu_2-1)\left(-\frac{1}{R}\right)$$

$$=\frac{\mu_1}{R}-\frac{1}{R}-\frac{\mu_2}{R}+\frac{1}{R}$$

$$\frac{1}{f}=\frac{\mu_1-\mu_2}{R}$$

$$\therefore \quad \frac{R}{f}=\mu_1-\mu_2$$

16. Given, focal length of first lens, $f_1=+10$ cm

Focal length of second lens, $f_2=-10$ cm

Focal length of third lens, $f_3=+30$ cm

Object distance from first lens, $u_1=-30$ cm

Using lens formula for first lens, we get

$$\frac{1}{f_1}=\frac{1}{v_1}-\frac{1}{u_1} \Rightarrow \frac{1}{-10}=\frac{1}{v_1}-\frac{1}{-30}$$

$$\Rightarrow \quad \frac{1}{v_1}=\frac{1}{10}-\frac{1}{30}=\frac{2}{30} \Rightarrow v_1=15 \text{ cm}$$

Thus, the image formed by first lens is 15 cm to the right of first lens.

The object distance for second lens will be $u_2=15$ cm -5 cm $=10$ cm

Using lens formula for first lens, we get

$$\frac{1}{f_2}=\frac{1}{v_2}-\frac{1}{u_2} \Rightarrow \frac{1}{-10}=\frac{1}{v_2}-\frac{1}{10} \Rightarrow v_2=\infty$$

Thus, the object distance for third lens, $u_3=\infty$.

Using lens formula for third lens, we get

$$\frac{1}{f_3}=\frac{1}{v_3}-\frac{1}{u_3} \Rightarrow \frac{1}{30}=\frac{1}{v_3}-\frac{1}{\infty} \Rightarrow \frac{1}{v_3}=\frac{1}{30}$$

$v_3=30$ cm

The final image will form 30 cm from the third lens.

The distance of final image from object will be $30+10+5+30=75$ cm.

Thus, the distance of final image formed from object O is 75 cm.

17. Given, thickness

$t=3 \text{ mm}=3\times10^{-3}$ m

$d=6$ cm

$\therefore$ Radius of plano-convex lens,

$r=3 \text{ cm}=3\times10^{-2}$ m

$$\text{Refractive index}=\frac{\text{Speed of light in air}}{\text{Speed of light in medium}}$$

$$\mu=\frac{3\times10^8}{2\times10^8}=\frac{3}{2}=1.5 \Rightarrow \mu=1.5$$

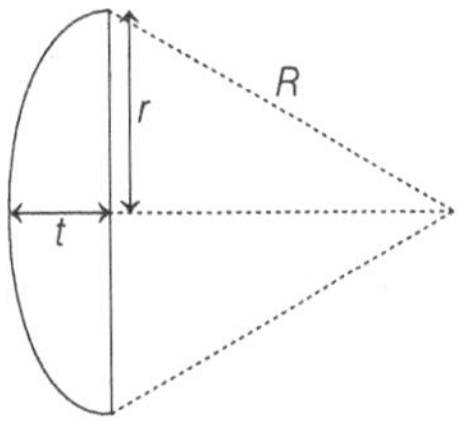

We know that $R^2=(R-t)^2+r^2$

where, R is the radius of curvature of plano convex lens.

$$\Rightarrow \quad R^2=R^2+t^2-2Rt+r^2 \Rightarrow 2Rt=r^2+t^2$$

As, t is small, then t^2 will be very very small, so it can be neglected.

$$\Rightarrow \quad 2Rt=r^2 \Rightarrow R=r^2/2t \quad ...(i)$$

From lens Maker's formula, we have

$$\frac{1}{f}=(\mu-1)\left(\frac{1}{R_1}-\frac{1}{R_2}\right)$$

Here, $R_1=R$ and $R_2=\infty$

$$\Rightarrow \quad \frac{1}{f}=(\mu-1)\left(\frac{1}{R}-\frac{1}{\infty}\right) \Rightarrow \frac{1}{f}=\frac{\mu-1}{R} \quad ...(ii)$$

From Eqs. (i) and (ii), we get

$$\frac{1}{f}=\frac{\mu-1(2t)}{r^2} \Rightarrow f=\frac{r^2}{(\mu-1)2t}$$

On putting the given values in above equation, we get

$$\frac{1}{f}=\frac{(3\times10^{-2})^2}{(1.5-1)2\times3\times10^{-3}} \Rightarrow f=0.3 \text{ m} \Rightarrow f=30 \text{ cm}$$

18. Consider a convex lens of refractive index μ_2 and μ_1 is the refractive index of the medium in which it is placed.

i.e., $\quad \mu_2=\mu_1 \quad ...(i)$

According to the lens Maker's formula,

$$\frac{1}{f}=\left[\frac{\mu_1}{\mu_2}-1\right]\left[\frac{1}{R_1}-\frac{1}{R_2}\right] \quad ...(ii)$$

$$\frac{1}{f}=[1-1]\left[\frac{1}{R_1}-\frac{1}{R_2}\right]=0$$

$$\Rightarrow \quad \frac{1}{f}=0 \quad \Rightarrow f=\text{Infinite}$$

19. When the ray on mirror falls directly perpendicular on the surface of it.

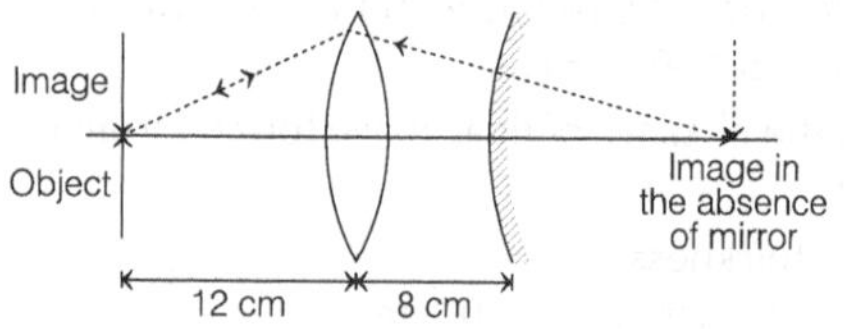

The light will converge at centre of curvature of mirror and due to that after removing the mirror the light will converge at same position.

The focal length of mirror, $f = 15$ cm. So, radius of curvature of mirror, $2f = 30$ cm

The image distance from the object after convex mirror is removed will be calculated as,

12 cm + 8 cm + 30 cm = 50 cm.

Thus, the image will formed at a distance of 50 cm from object.

JEE Advanced

1. Case 1 : Ist refraction from lens

Since, object is at focus $\Rightarrow$ light will become parallel.

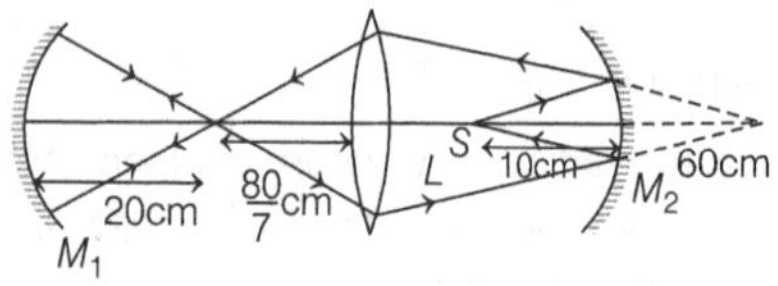

Ist reflection at M_1,

Light is parallel $\Rightarrow$ Image will be at focus.

IInd refraction from L,

$$u=-(d-10)$$

$$f=10\text{ cm}$$

$$\frac{1}{v}-\frac{1}{u}=\frac{1}{f} \Rightarrow \frac{1}{v}+\frac{1}{d-10}=\frac{1}{10}$$

$$\frac{1}{v}=\frac{1}{10}-\frac{1}{(d-10)} \quad ...(i)$$

This v will be object distance for mirror M_2, and image should be at 10 cm

$$\therefore \quad \frac{1}{u}+\frac{1}{v_1}=\frac{1}{f} \quad -\frac{1}{(20-v)}-\frac{1}{10}=-\frac{1}{12}$$

$$\Rightarrow \quad \frac{1}{12}-\frac{1}{10}=\frac{1}{20-v} \quad -\frac{2}{120}=\frac{1}{20-v}$$

$$\Rightarrow \quad 20-v=-60 \Rightarrow v=80\text{ cm}$$

From Eq. (i)

$$\frac{1}{80}=\frac{1}{10}-\frac{1}{d-10} \Rightarrow \frac{1}{d-10}=\frac{1}{10}-\frac{1}{80}$$

$$\Rightarrow \quad \frac{1}{d-10}=\frac{80-10}{800}=\frac{70}{800}$$

$$\Rightarrow \quad d-10=\frac{80}{7} \Rightarrow d=10+\frac{80}{7}=\frac{150}{7}$$

$$n=150$$

Case II : Ist reflection from mirror M_2,

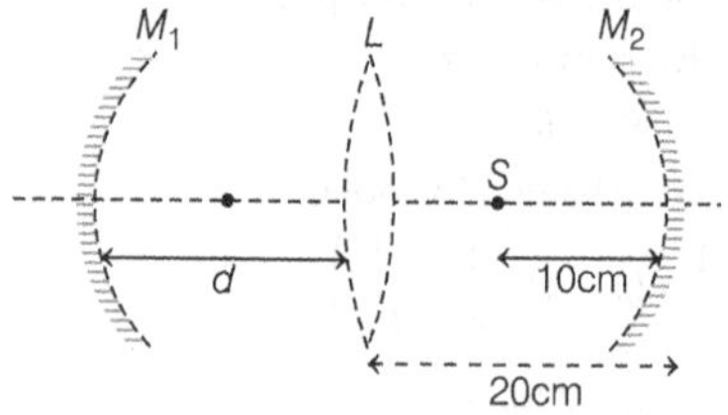

For M_2,

$$\frac{1}{v_1}+\frac{1}{-10}=\frac{1}{-12}$$

$$v_1=60\text{ cm}$$

Then, refraction on lens L,

$$v_2=-80\text{ cm}$$

$$\frac{1}{v_2}-\frac{1}{-60}=\frac{1}{10}$$

$$v_2=\frac{80}{7}$$

Then, reflection on M_2

Either v_2 is at centre (normal incidence)

$$d-\frac{80}{7}=20$$

$$d=\frac{220}{7} \Rightarrow \frac{n}{7}=\frac{220}{7}$$

$$n=220$$

v_2 is at pole of M_2

$$d-\frac{80}{7}=0$$

$$d=\frac{80}{7} \Rightarrow \frac{n}{7}=\frac{80}{7}$$

$$n=80$$

2. Object distance $=10 \pm 0.1$ cm

Image distance $=20 \pm 0.2$ cm

Applying lens formula,

$$\frac{1}{v}-\frac{1}{u}=\frac{1}{f} \quad ...(i)$$

$$\Rightarrow \quad \frac{1}{20}-\frac{1}{(-10)}=\frac{1}{f} \Rightarrow f=\frac{20}{3}\text{ cm}$$

Differentiate Eq. (i)

$$-\frac{1}{v^2}dv+\frac{1}{u^2}du=\frac{-1}{f^2}df$$

For calculating error

$$\frac{1}{f^2}\Delta f=+\frac{1}{v^2}\Delta v+\frac{1}{u^2}\Delta u$$

$$\frac{\Delta f}{f}\times 100=\left(\frac{0.2}{20^2}+\frac{0.1}{10^2}\right)\frac{20}{3}\times 100$$

$$\left(\frac{0.2}{4}+\frac{0.1}{1}\right)\frac{20}{3}=1$$

$\therefore$ $$\frac{\Delta f}{f}\times 100=1\%$$

3. (I) $\frac{1}{v}-\frac{1}{u}=\frac{1}{f}\Rightarrow v=\frac{uf}{u+f}$

$\therefore$ $$v_1=\frac{(-20)(10)}{(-20)+(10)}=+20\text{ cm}$$

$$u_2=+15\text{ cm}$$

$$v_2=\frac{(15)(15)}{(15)+(15)}=+7.5\text{ cm}$$

(II) $v_1=+20$ cm

$$u_2=+15\text{ cm}$$

$$v_2=\frac{(15)(-10)}{(15)+(-10)}=-30\text{ cm}$$

(III) $v_1=+20$ cm

$$u_2=+15\text{ cm}$$

$$v_2=\frac{(15)(-20)}{(15)+(-20)}=60\text{ cm}$$

(IV) $v_1=\frac{(-20)(-20)}{(-20)+(-20)}=-10$ cm

$$u_2=-15\text{ cm}$$

$$v_2=\frac{(-15)(10)}{(-15)+(10)}=30\text{ cm}$$

4.

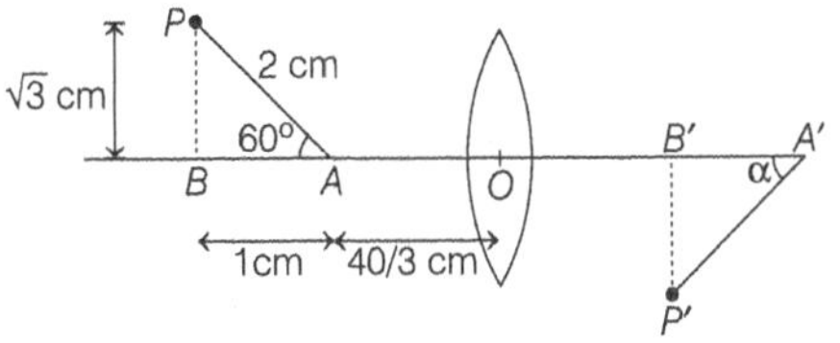

Using lens formula for point A,

$$\frac{1}{v}-\frac{1}{u}=\frac{1}{f}\Rightarrow\quad \frac{1}{v}-\frac{1}{\left(-\frac{40}{3}\right)}=\frac{1}{10}$$

$\therefore$ $$v=OA'=40\text{ cm}$$

For B, $$\frac{1}{v}-\frac{1}{-\left(\frac{40}{3}+1\right)}=\frac{1}{10}$$

$\therefore$ $$v=OB'=\frac{430}{13}\text{ cm}$$

$\therefore$ $$A'B'=OA'-OB'=40-\frac{430}{13}=\frac{90}{13}\text{ cm}$$

Linear magnification for B,

$$m_B=\left(\frac{v}{u}\right)_{\text{For }B}=\frac{\left(\frac{430}{13}\right)}{-\left(\frac{43}{3}\right)}=-\frac{30}{13}$$

$\therefore$ $$P'B'=(PB)(|m_B|)=\frac{30\sqrt{3}}{13}$$

Now, $$\tan\alpha=\frac{P'B'}{A'B'}=\frac{\left(\frac{30\sqrt{3}}{13}\right)}{\left(\frac{90}{13}\right)}=\frac{1}{\sqrt{3}}$$

$\therefore$ $$\alpha=30^\circ\text{ or }\frac{\pi}{6}\text{ rad}$$

or, $n=6$

5. Focal length of convex lens f_1,

$$\therefore\quad \frac{1}{f_1}=(\mu-1)\left[\frac{1}{R_1}-\frac{1}{R_2}\right]=(1.5-1)\left[\frac{1}{20}-\left(\frac{1}{-20}\right)\right]$$

$\Rightarrow f_1=+20$ cm

Focal length of concave lens f_2,

$$\therefore\quad \frac{1}{f_2}=(\mu-1)\left[\frac{1}{R_1}-\frac{1}{R_2}\right]$$

$$\frac{1}{f_2}=(1.5-1)\left[-\frac{1}{20}-\frac{1}{20}\right]=\frac{1}{-20}$$

$\Rightarrow f_2=-20$ cm

For lens 1

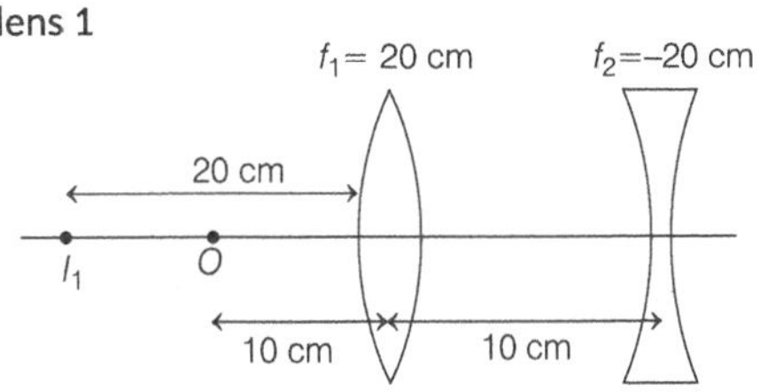

$$\frac{1}{v}-\frac{1}{u}=\frac{1}{f}\quad\Rightarrow\quad v=-20\text{ cm}$$

$$m_1=\frac{v}{u}=\frac{-20}{-10}=2$$

For lens 2

$$u=-30\text{ cm},\ f=-20\text{ cm},$$

$$\frac{1}{v}-\frac{1}{u}=\frac{1}{f}\Rightarrow v=-12\text{ cm}$$

$$m_2=\frac{v}{u}=\frac{-12}{-30}=\frac{2}{5}$$

Net magnification,

$$m=m_1m_2=2\times\frac{2}{5}=\frac{4}{5}=0.8$$

6.

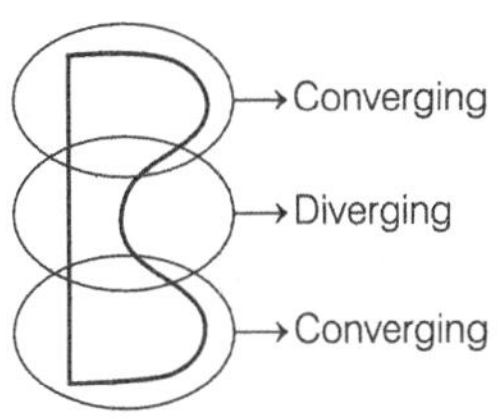

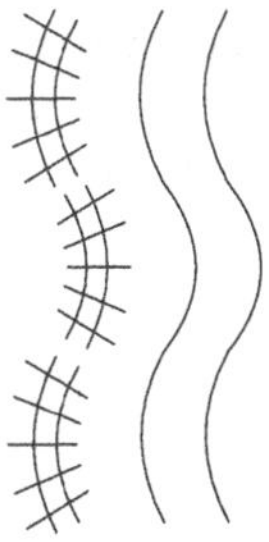

7.

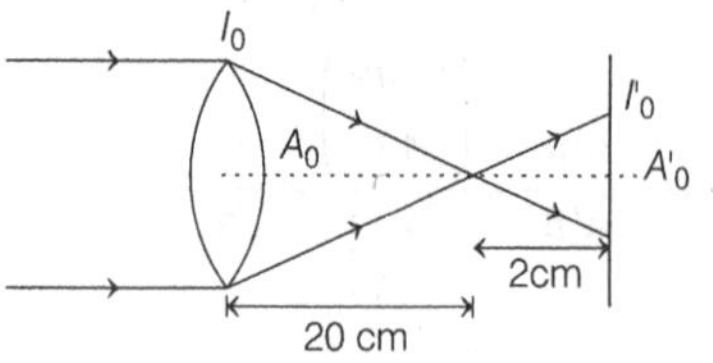

$$\frac{A_0'}{A_0} = \left(\frac{2}{20}\right)^2 = \frac{1}{100} \Rightarrow A_0' = \frac{A_0}{100}$$

$$P = I_0 A_0 = I_0' A_0'$$

$$\Rightarrow \quad I_0' = \frac{I_0 A_0}{\frac{A_0}{100}} = 100 I_0 = 130 \text{ kW/m}^2$$

8. Case 1

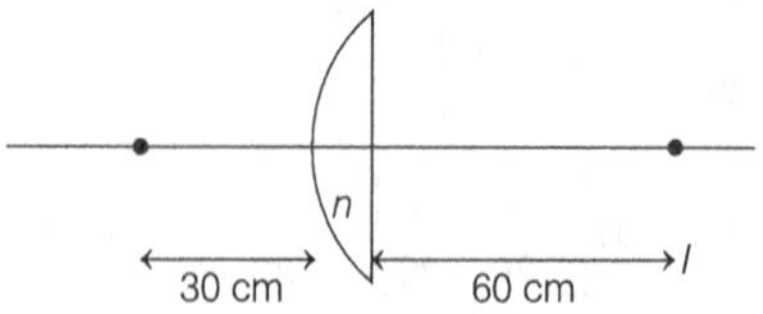

Using lens formula,

$$\frac{1}{60} + \frac{1}{30} = \frac{1}{f} \Rightarrow \frac{1}{f} = \frac{1}{60} + \frac{2}{60}$$

$$\Rightarrow \quad f = 20 \text{ cm}$$

Further, $\frac{1}{f} = (n-1)\left(\frac{1}{R} - \frac{1}{\infty}\right) \Rightarrow f = \frac{R}{n-1} = +20 \text{ cm}$

Case 2

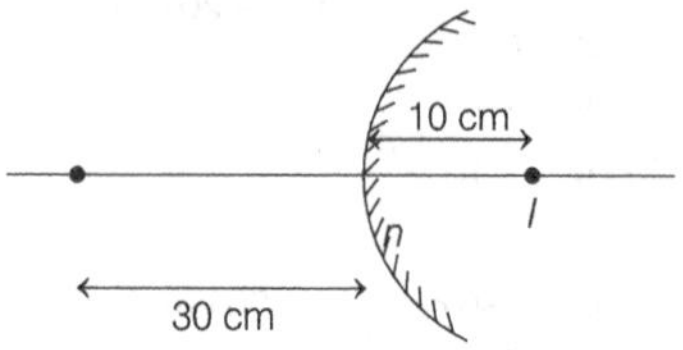

Using mirror formula

$$\frac{1}{10} - \frac{1}{30} = \frac{1}{f} \Rightarrow f_2 = 15 = \frac{R}{2} \Rightarrow R = 30$$

$$\therefore \quad R = 30 \text{ cm} \Rightarrow \frac{R}{n-1} = 20 \text{ cm}$$

Solving this equation with $R = 30$ cm, we get $n = 2.5$.

9. Case I

Reflection from mirror

$$\frac{1}{f} = \frac{1}{v} + \frac{1}{u} \Rightarrow \frac{1}{-10} = \frac{1}{v} + \frac{1}{-15} \Rightarrow v = -30$$

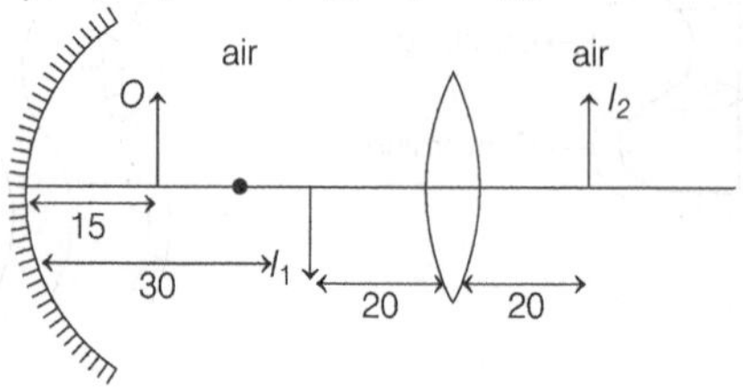

For lens $\frac{1}{f} = \frac{1}{v} - \frac{1}{u}$

$$\frac{1}{10} = \frac{1}{v} - \frac{1}{-20}$$

$$v = 20$$

$$|M_1| = \left|\frac{v_1}{u_1}\right|\left|\frac{v_2}{u_2}\right| = \left(\frac{30}{15}\right)\left(\frac{20}{20}\right) = 2 \times 1 = 2 \quad \text{(in air)}$$

Case II For mirror, there is no change.

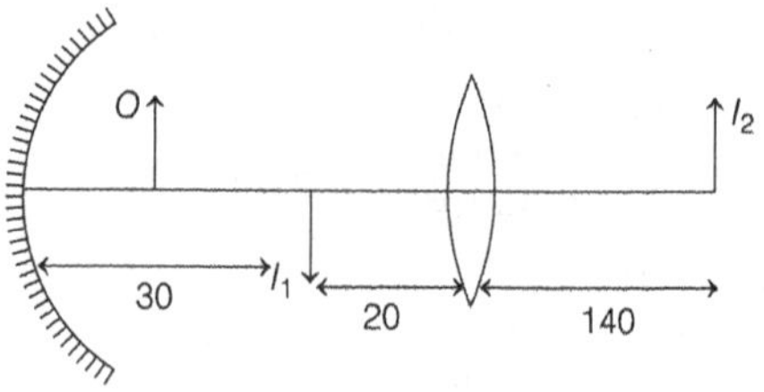

For lens, $\frac{1}{f_{air}} = \left(\frac{3/2}{1} - 1\right)\left(\frac{1}{R_1} - \frac{1}{R_2}\right)$

$$\frac{1}{f_{medium}} = \left(\frac{3/2}{7/6} - 1\right)\left(\frac{1}{R_1} - \frac{1}{R_2}\right)$$

with $f_{air} = 10$ cm

We get $\frac{1}{f_{medium}} = \frac{4}{70} \text{ cm}^{-1}$

$$\frac{1}{v} - \frac{1}{(-20)} = \frac{4}{70}$$

$$\Rightarrow \quad \frac{1}{v} = \frac{4}{70} - \frac{1}{20}$$

$$\Rightarrow \quad v = 140 \quad ,$$

$$|M_2| = \left|\frac{v_1}{u_1}\right|\left|\frac{v_2}{u_2}\right| = \left(\frac{30}{15}\right)\left(\frac{140}{20}\right) = 14$$

$$\Rightarrow \quad \left|\frac{M_2}{M_1}\right| = \frac{14}{2} = 7$$

10. $R = 10$ cm

Applying $\frac{\mu_2}{v} - \frac{\mu_1}{u} = \frac{\mu_2 - \mu_1}{R}$ two times

$$\frac{1}{v} - \frac{1.5}{-50} = \frac{1 - 1.5}{-10} \quad \text{or} \quad v = 50$$

$$MN = d, MI_1 = 50 \text{ cm},$$

$$NI_1 = (d - 50) \text{ cm}$$

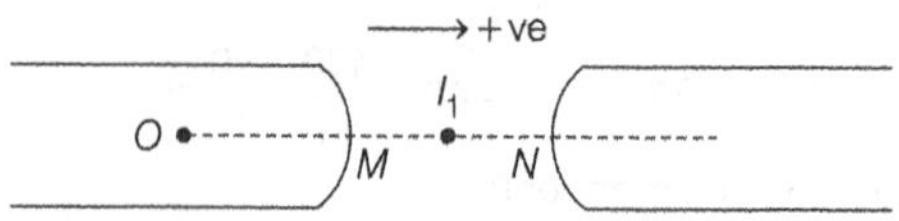

Again, $\frac{1.5}{\infty} - \frac{1}{-(d-50)} = \frac{1.5 - 1}{10}$

$$\therefore \quad d = 70 \text{ cm}$$

CHAPTER~04

OPTICAL INSTRUMENTS

LEVEL 01 Starter Level

4.1 Human Eye Defects

1 A person wears glasses of power –2.5 D. Is the person far-sighted or near-sighted? What is the far point of the person without glasses?

2 The far point of a myopic person is 150 cm in front of the eye. Calculate the focal length and the power of the lens required to enable him to see distant objects clearly.

3 A short-sighted person can see most clearly at a distance of 15 cm acquires spectacles enabling him to see clearly objects at a distance of 60 cm. Calculate the focal length of the lens and power of the lens.

4 The near point of hypermetropic person is 50 cm from the eye. What is the power of the lens required to enable the person to read clearly a book held at 25 cm from the eye?

4.2 Simple Microscope

1 A thin convex lens of focal length 5 cm is used as a simple microscope by a person with normal near point (25 cm). Find the magnifying power of the microscope, if the image is formed at
(i) the least distance of distinct vision
(ii) infinity

2 An object is to be seen through a simple microscope of power 10 D. Where should the object be placed, so as to produce maximum angular magnification? The least distance of distinct vision is 25 cm.

3 A simple microscope is rated 5X for a normal relaxed eye. What will be its magnifying power for a relaxed far-sighted eye whose near point is 40 cm?

4 A man with normal near point (25 cm) reads a book with small print using a magnifying glass : A thin convex lens of focal length 5 cm. What is the closest and the farthest distance at which he can read the book, when viewing through the magnifying glass?

5 The magnifying glass is made of combination of lenses of power + 20 D and – 4 D. If the distance of distinct vision is 25 cm, calculate the size of an object 2 cm high seen through the magnifying glass.

6 A magnifying glass is a combination of a convex lens of focal length 5 cm and a concave lens of power – 5 D. If the distance of distinct vision is 20 cm, calculate the magnifying power of the magnifying glass.

4.3 Compound Microscope

1 A compound microscope has a magnification of 30. The focal length of its eyepiece is 5 cm. Assuming the final image to formed at least distance of distinct vision (25 cm), calculate the magnification produced by the objective.

2 A compound microscope with an objective of 1.0 cm focal length and an eyepiece of 2.0 cm focal length has a tube length of 20 cm. Calculate the magnifying power of the microscope, if the final image is formed at the near point of the eye.

3 The focal lengths of the eyepiece and the objective of a compound microscope are 5 cm and 1 cm, respectively and the length of the tube is 20 cm. Calculate the magnifying power of the microscope, if the final image is formed at infinity. The value of least distance of distinct vision is 25 cm.

4 The focal lengths of the objective and eyepiece of compound microscope are 4 cm and 6 cm, respectively. If any object is placed at a distance of 6 cm from the objective, what is the magnification produced by the microscope? Least distance of the distinct vision is 25 cm.

5 The focal lengths of the objective and the eyepiece of a microscope are 2 cm and 5 cm, respectively and the distance between them is 20 cm. Find the distance of the object from the objective, when the final image seen by the eye is 25 cm from the eyepiece. Also, find the magnifying power.

6 A compound microscope is made using a lens of focal length 10 mm as objective and another lens of focal length 15 mm as eyepiece. An object is held at 1.1 cm from the objective and final image is formed at infinity. Calculate distance between objective and eyepiece.

7 The total magnification produced by a compound microscope is 20, while that produced by the eyepiece alone is 5. When the microscope is focussed on a certain object, the distance between objective and eyepiece is 14 cm, Find the focal length of objective and eyepiece, if distance of distinct vision is 20 cm.

4.4 Telescope

1 A telescope has an objective of focal length 200 cm and eyepiece of focal length 5 cm. Calculate its magnifying power when the final image is formed (a) at infinity and (b) at least distance of distinct vision.

2 An astronomical telescope when in normal adjustment has magnifying power 5. If the distance between two lenses is 24 cm, find the focal lengths of both the lenses.

3 The focal lengths of the objective and the eyepiece of an astronomical telescope are 60 cm and 5 cm respectively. Calculate the length of the telescope when the final image is formed at

(i) infinity, (ii) least distance of distinct vision (25 cm).

4 A telescope has an objective of focal length 50 cm and an eyepiece of focal length 5 cm. The least distance of distinct vision is 25 cm. The telescope is focussed for distinct vision on a scale distant 200 cm away from the object. Calculate

(a) the separation between the objective and the eyepiece

(b) the magnification produced.

5 The diameter of the moon is 3.5×10^3 km and its distance from the earth is 3.8×10^5 km. It is viewed by a telescope which consists of two lenses of focal lengths 4 m and 10 cm. Find the angle subtended at eye by the final image.

6 A small telescope has an objective lens of focal length 150 cm and an eyepiece of focal length 5 cm. If this telescope is used to view a 100 m high tower 3 km away, find the height of the final image when it is formed 25 cm away from the eyepiece.

7 An amateur astronomer wishes to estimate roughly the size of the sun using his crude telescope consisting of an objective lens of focal length 200 cm and an eyepiece of focal length 10 cm. By adjusting the distance of the eyepiece from the objective, he obtains an image of the sun on a screen 40 cm behind the eyepiece. The diameter of the sun's image is measured to be 6.0 cm. What is the estimate of the sun's size, given that the average earth-sun distance is 1.5×10^{11} m?

8 A terrestrial telescope has an objective of focal length 180 cm and an eyepiece of focal length 5 cm. The erecting lens has a focal length of 3.5 cm. What is the separation between the objective and the eyepiece? What is the magnifying power of the telescope? Can we use the telescope for viewing astronomical objects?

9 A reflecting type telescope has a concave reflector of radius of curvature 120 cm. Calculate focal length of eyepiece to secure a magnification of 20.

LEVEL 02 JEE Main Level

Single Choice Correct Questions

1 Near and far points of a human eye are

(a) 0 and 25 cm (b) 0 and ∞

(c) 25 cm and 100 cm (d) 25 cm and ∞

2 A person wears glasses of power −2.0 D. The defect of the eye and the far point of the person without the glasses will be

(a) nearsighted, 50 cm (b) farsighted, 50 cm

(c) nearsighted, 250 cm (d) astigmatism, 50 cm

3 A person's near point is 50 cm and his far point is 3 m. Power of the lenses he requires for

(i) reading and (ii) seeing distant stars are

(a) −2 D and 0.33 D (b) 2 D and − 0.33 D

(c) −2 D and 3 D (d) 2 D and −3 D

4 A person is suffering from myopic defect. He is able to see clear objects placed at 15 cm. What type and of what focal length of lens, he should use to see clearly the object placed 60 cm away?

(a) Concave lens of 20 cm focal length
(b) Convex lens of 20 cm focal length
(c) Concave lens of 12 cm focal length
(d) Convex lens of 12 cm focal length

5 A person can see clearly objects at 100 cm distance. If he wants to see objects at 40 cm distance, then the power of the lens he shall require is
(a) +1.5 D (b) – 1.5 D (c) +3.0 D (d) – 3.0 D

6 A man, wearing glasses of power +2 D can read clearly a book placed at a distance of 40 cm from the eye. The power of the lens required, so that he can read at 25 cm from the eye is
(a) +4.5 D (b) +4.0 D (c) +3.5 D (d) +3.0 D

7 A man can see the object between 15 cm and 30 cm. He uses the lens to see the far objects, then due to the lens used, the near point will be at
(a) $\frac{10}{3}$ cm (b) 30 cm (c) 15 cm (d) $\frac{100}{3}$ cm

8 Microscope is an optical instrument which
(a) enlarges the object
(b) increases the visual angle formed by the object at the eye
(c) decreases the visual angle formed by the object at the eye
(d) brings the object nearer

9 Least distance of distinct vision is 25 cm. Magnifying power of simple microscope of focal length 5 cm is [for distinct vision]
(a) $\frac{1}{5}$ (b) 5 (c) $\frac{1}{6}$ (d) 6

10 The focal length of a simple convex lens used as a magnifier is 10 cm. For the image to be formed at a distance of distinct vision $D = 25$ cm, the object must be placed away from the lens nearly at a distance of
(a) 5 cm (b) 7 cm
(c) 8 cm (d) 16 cm

11 Magnifying power of a simple microscope A is 1.25 less than that of a simple microscope B. If the power of the lens used in B is 25 D, find the power of lens used in A. Given that, distance of distinct vision is 25 cm.
(a) 10 D (b) 15 D (c) 20 D (d) 30 D

12 In a compound microscope, if the objective produces an image I_o and eyepiece produces an image I_e, then
(a) I_o virtual but I_e is real.
(b) I_o is real but I_e is virtual.
(c) I_o and I_e are both real.
(d) I_o and I_e are both virtual.

13 A compound microscope has magnifying power as 32 and magnifying power of eyepiece is 4, then the magnifying power of objective is
(a) 8 (b) 10
(c) 6 (d) 12

14 Magnification of a compound microscope is 30. Focal length of eyepiece is 5 cm and image is formed at a distance of 25 cm from eyepiece. The magnification of objective lens is
(a) 6 (b) 5
(c) 7.5 (d) 10

15 The focal lengths of the objective and eyepiece of a compound microscope are 1 cm and 5 cm, respectively. An object is placed at a distance of 1.1 cm from objective. If final image is formed at least distance of distinct vision, the magnifying power is
(a) 60 (b) 50
(c) 40 (d) None of these

16 In a compound microscope, the focal lengths of objective and eyelenses are 1.2 cm and 3 cm, respectively. If the object is put 1.25 cm away from the objective lens and the final image is formed at infinity, the magnifying power of the microscope is
(a) 150 (b) 200 (c) 250 (d) 400

17 In a microscope, the focal lengths of two lenses are 1.5 cm and 6.25 cm. If an object is placed at 2 cm from objective and final image is formed at 25 cm from eye lens, the distance between two lenses is
(a) 6 cm (b) 7.75 cm
(c) 9.25 cm (d) 11 cm

18 The focal lengths of the objective and the eyepiece of a compound microscope are 2.0 cm and 3.0 cm, respectively. The distance between the objective and the eyepiece is 15.0 cm. The final image formed by the eyepiece is at infinity. The two lenses are thin. The distances (in cm) of the object and the image produced by the objective measured from the objective lens are respectively
(a) 2.4 and 12.0 (b) 2.4 and 15.0
(c) 2.3 and 12.0 (d) 2.3 and 3.0

19 A compound microscope has a magnifying power of 100, when the image is formed at infinity. The objective has a focal length of 0.5 cm and the tube length is 6.5 cm, then the focal length of the eyepiece is
(a) 0.2 cm (b) 2.5 cm
(c) 2 cm (d) 4.0 cm

20 The focal length of objective and eyepiece of a microscope are 1 cm and 5 cm, respectively. If the magnifying power for relaxed eye is 45, then length of the tube is

(a) 6 cm (b) 9 cm (c) 12 cm (d) 15 cm

21 The focal length of the objective and the eyepiece of a microscope are 2 cm and 5 cm, respectively and the distance between them is 30 cm. If the image seen by the eye is 25 cm from the eyepiece, the distance of the object from the objective is

(a) 1.75 cm (b) 2.17 cm
(c) 3.24 cm (d) 4.67 cm

22 The focal lengths of the objective and eyepiece of a microscope are 1.25 cm and 5 cm, respectively. Find the position of object relative the objective in order to obtain an angular magnification of 30 in normal adjustment.

(a) 1.46 cm (b) 2.36 cm
(c) 3.76 cm (d) 4.55 cm

23 A telescope has focal length of objective and eyepiece as 200 cm and 5 cm, respectively. What is the value of magnifying power?

(a) 40 (b) 80 (c) 50 (d) 10

24 The magnifying power of an astronomical telescope is 8 and the distance between the two lenses is 54 cm. The focal length of eye lens and objective lens will be respectively

(a) 6 cm and 48 cm (b) 48 cm and 6 cm
(c) 8 cm and 64 cm (d) 64 cm and 8 cm

25 An astronomical telescope has an eye lens of focal length 20 mm. In normal adjustment, when the final image of a distant object is at infinity, the separation of the lenses is 500 mm. The angular magnification of the telescope under these conditions is

(a) 22 (b) 23 (c) 24 (d) 25

26 An astronomical telescope has a converging eyepiece of focal length 5 cm and objective of focal length 80 cm. When the final image is formed at the least distance of distinct vision (25 cm), the separation between the two lenses is

(a) 75.0 cm (b) 80.0 cm
(c) 84.2 cm (d) 85.0 cm

27 The magnifying power of a telescope is 10 and length of telescope is 1.1 m for normal adjustment. The magnification when image is formed at least distance of distinct vision is

(a) 14 (b) 6
(c) 16 (d) 18

28 A simple telescope, consisting of an objective of focal length 60 cm and a single eye lens of focal length 5 cm is focussed on a distant object is such a way that parallel ray comes out from the eye lens. If the object subtends an angle 2° at the objective, the angular width of the image

(a) 10° (b) 24° (c) 50° (d) 1/6°

29 A simple telescope consisting of an objective lens of focal length 30 cm and that of its eyelens is 3 cm. It is focused on a scale 2 m distant from it. The distance of objective lens from eye lens to see with relaxed eye is

(a) 33 cm (b) 65.3 cm (c) 38.3 cm (d) 40.3 cm

30 A telescope has an objective of focal length 50 cm and an eyepiece of focal length 5 cm. The least distance of distinct vision is 25 cm. The telescope is focussed for distinct vision on a scale 200 cm away. The separation between the objective and the eyepiece is (nearly)

(a) 75 cm (b) 60 cm (c) 71 cm (d) 74 cm

31 The objective of a telescope has a focal length of 1.2 m. It is used to view a 10.0 m tall tower 2 km away. What is the height of the image of the tower formed by the objective?

(a) 2 mm (b) 4 mm (c) 6 mm (d) 8 mm

32 A giant telescope in an observatory has an objective of focal length 19 m and an eyepiece of focal length 1.0 cm. In normal adjustment, the telescope is used to view the moon. What is the diameter of the image of the moon formed by the objective? The diameter of the moon is 3.5×10^6 m and the radius of the lunar orbit round the earth is 3.8×10^8 m

(a) 10 cm (b) 12.5 cm (c) 15 cm (d) 17.5 cm

33 A simple two lens telescope has an objective of focal length 50 cm and an eyepiece of 2.5 cm. The telescope is pointed at an object at a very large distance which subtends at an angle of 1 milliradian on the naked eye. The eyepiece is adjusted so that the final virtual image is formed at infinity. The size of the real image formed by the objective is

(a) 5 mm (b) 1 mm (c) 0.5 mm (d) 0.1 mm

34 An astronomical telescope in normal adjustment receives light from a distant source *S*. The tube length is now decreased slightly,

(a) a virtual image of *S* will be formed at a finite distance.
(b) no image will be formed.
(c) a small, real image of *S* will be formed behind the eyepiece, close to it.
(d) a large, real image of *S* will be formed behind the eyepiece, far away from it.

Previous Year's Questions

JEE Main

1 A person has been using spectacles of power −1.0 dioptre for distant vision and a separate reading glass of power 2.0 dioptres. What is the least distance of distinct vision for this person **[2023, 30 Jan Shift-I]**

(a) 50 cm (b) 30 cm (c) 10 cm (d) 40 cm

2 In a reflecting telescope, a secondary mirror is used to **[2023, 8 April Shift-I]**

(a) remove spherical aberration
(b) reduce the problem of mechanical support
(c) make chromatic aberration zero
(d) move the eyepiece outside the telescopic tube

3 Your friend is having eye sight problem. She is not able to see clearly a distant uniform window mesh and it appears to her as non-uniform and distorted. The doctor diagnosed the problem as **[2021, 18 March Shift-I]**

(a) astigmatism (b) myopia with astigmatism
(c) presbyopia with astigmatism
(d) myopia and hypermetropia

4 Given below are two statements: one is labelled as Assertion (A) and the other is labelled as Reason (R).

Assertion (A) For a simple microscope, the angular size of the object equals the angular size of the image.

Reason (R) Magnification is achieved as the small object can be kept much closer to the eye than 25 cm and hence, it subtends a large angle. In the light of the above statements, choose the most appropriate answer from the options given below. **[2021, 26 Feb Shift-II]**

(a) A is true but R is false.
(b) Both A and R are true but R is not the correct explanation of A.
(c) Both A and R are true and R is the correct explanation of A.
(d) A is false but R is true.

5 An object viewed from a near point distance of 25 cm, using a microscopic lens with magnification 6, gives an unresolved image. A resolved image is observed at infinite distance with a total magnification double the earlier using an eyepiece along with the given lens and a tube of length 0.6 m, if the focal length of the eyepiece is equal to ……… cm. **[2021, 20 July Shift-I]**

6 The magnifying power of a telescope with tube length 60 cm is 5. What is the focal length of its eyepiece? **[2020, 8 Jan Shift-I]**

(a) 10 cm (b) 20 cm (c) 30 cm (d) 40 cm

7 In a compound microscope, the magnified virtual image is formed at a distance of 25 cm from the eye-piece. The focal length of its objective lens is 1 cm. If the magnification is 100 and the tube length of the microscope is 20 cm, then the focal length of the eye-piece lens (in cm) is ……… . **[2020, 4 Sep Shift-I]**

8 A compound microscope consists of an objective lens of focal length 1 cm and an eye piece of focal length 5 cm with a separation of 10 cm. The distance between an object and the objective lens, at which the strain on the eye is minimum is $n/40$ cm. The value of n is …… . **[2020, 5 Sep Shift-I]**

Answer Key

Level 1

4.1 Human Eye Defects

1. Near-sighted, 40 cm **2.** - 150 cm, - 0.67 D
3. - 20 cm, - 5 D **4.** + 2 D

4.2 Simple Microscope

1. (i) 6 (ii) 5 **2.** – 50/7 cm **3.** 8
4. 4.2 cm, 5 cm **5.** 10 cm **6.** 4

4.3 Compound Microscope

1. 5 **2.** 270 **3.** 70 **4.** 10.33
5. $u_0 = -2.3$ cm, $m = 41.5$ **6.** 12.5 cm
7. $f_e = 5$ cm, $f_0 = 2$ cm

4.4 Telescope

1. (a) 40 (b) 48 **2.** 20 cm, 4 cm **3.** (i) 65 cm (ii) 64.17 cm
4. (a) 70.83 cm (b) – 2 **5.** 21.1°
6. 30 cm **7.** 1.5×10^9 m **8.** 199 cm, 36, yes but final image will be less brighter **9.** 3 cm

Level 2

Single Choice Correct Questions

1. (d)	2. (a)	3. (b)	4. (a)	5. (a)
6. (c)	7. (b)	8. (b)	9. (d)	10. (b)
11. (c)	12. (b)	13. (a)	14. (b)	15. (a)
16. (b)	17. (d)	18. (a)	19. (c)	20. (d)
21. (b)	22. (a)	23. (a)	24. (b)	25. (c)
26. (c)	27. (a)	28. (b)	29. (c)	30. (c)
31. (c)	32. (d)	33. (c)	34. (a)	

Previous Year's Questions

JEE Main

1. (b) **2.** (d) **3.** (b) **4.** (c) **5.** (25) **6.** (a) **7.** (6) **8.** (50)

SOLUTIONS

Level 1

4.1 Human Eye Defects

1. Let, the far point of the near-sighted person be x.

$$P = -\frac{1}{x} \Rightarrow -2.5 = -\frac{1}{x}$$

$$\Rightarrow \quad x = 0.4\,\text{m} = 40\text{ cm}$$

2. $x = 150\text{ cm}, f = -x = -150\text{ cm}$

$$P = -\frac{1}{x} = -0.67\text{ D}$$

3. $$\frac{1}{v} - \frac{1}{u} = \frac{1}{f} \Rightarrow \frac{1}{(-15)} - \frac{1}{(-60)} = \frac{1}{f}$$

$$\Rightarrow \quad f = -20\text{ cm}$$

$$P = \frac{1}{f} = \frac{1}{(-0.2)} = -5\text{ D}$$

4. Near point, $y = 50$ cm

Least distance of distinct vision, $D = 25$ cm

$$f = \frac{Dy}{y-D} = \frac{(25)(50)}{50-25} = 50\text{cm} = 0.5\text{ m}$$

$$P = \frac{1}{f} = \frac{1}{0.5} = +2\text{ D}$$

4.2 Simple Microscope

1. (i) $m = 1 + \frac{D}{f} = 1 + \frac{25}{5} = 6$ (ii) $m = \frac{D}{f} = \frac{25}{5} = 5$

2. Angular magnification is maximum, when the final image is formed at the near point.

$$\therefore \quad v = -25\text{ cm},\ f = \frac{1}{P} = \frac{1}{10}\text{m} = 10\text{ cm}$$

Now, $$\frac{1}{v} - \frac{1}{u} = \frac{1}{f} \Rightarrow \frac{1}{(-25)} - \frac{1}{u} = \frac{1}{10}$$

$$\Rightarrow \quad u = -\frac{50}{7}\text{ cm}$$

3. For normal eye, $D = 25\text{ cm}, m = 5$

As, $m = \frac{D}{f} \Rightarrow 5 = \frac{25}{f} \Rightarrow f = 5\text{ cm}$

For relaxed far sighted eye,

$D' = 40\text{ cm}, f = 5\text{ cm}$

$$\therefore \quad m = \frac{D'}{f} = \frac{40}{5} = 8$$

4. For the closest distance,

$$v = -25\text{ cm},\quad f = 5\text{ cm},\quad u = ?$$

$$\frac{1}{v} - \frac{1}{u} = \frac{1}{f} \Rightarrow \frac{1}{-25} - \frac{1}{u} = \frac{1}{5} \Rightarrow u = -4.2\text{ cm}$$

For the farthest distance,

$$v = \infty, f = 5\text{ cm}, u = ?$$

$$\frac{1}{v} - \frac{1}{u} = \frac{1}{f} \Rightarrow \frac{1}{\infty} - \frac{1}{u} = \frac{1}{5} \Rightarrow u = -5\text{ cm}$$

5. $P = P_1 + P_2 = +20 - 4 = 16$ D

$$f = \frac{1}{P} = \frac{1}{16}\text{m} = \frac{25}{4}\text{ cm}$$

$$m = 1 + \frac{D}{f} = 1 + \frac{25}{\left(\frac{25}{4}\right)} = 5$$

$$m = \frac{h_i}{h_o} \Rightarrow 5 = \frac{h_i}{2} \Rightarrow h_i = 10\text{ cm}$$

6. $P = P_1 + P_2 \Rightarrow P = \frac{1}{\left(\frac{5}{100}\right)} - 5 = 15\text{ D}$

$$f = \frac{1}{P} = \frac{1}{15}\text{m} = \frac{20}{3}\text{ cm}$$

$$m = 1 + \frac{D}{f} = 1 + \frac{20}{\left(\frac{20}{3}\right)} = 4$$

4.3 Compound Microscope

1. $m_e = 1 + \frac{D}{f_e} = 1 + \frac{25}{5} = 6$

$$m = m_o m_e \Rightarrow 30 = m_o(6) \Rightarrow m_o = 5$$

2. $f_o = 1\text{ cm},\ f_e = 2\text{ cm}$

$$L = 20\text{ cm},\ D = 25\text{ cm}$$

When, the final image is formed at the near point of the eye, the magnifying power is

$$m = \frac{L}{f_o}\left(1 + \frac{D}{f_e}\right) = \frac{20}{1}\left(1 + \frac{25}{2}\right) = 270$$

3. As the final image is being formed at infinity, the image formed by the objective must lie at the focus of the eyepiece i.e. at a distance of 5 cm from eyepiece.

$$\Rightarrow \quad L = v_o + f_e \Rightarrow 20 = v_o + 5$$

$$\Rightarrow \quad v_o = 15\text{ cm}$$

$$\frac{1}{v} - \frac{1}{u} = \frac{1}{f} \Rightarrow \frac{1}{v_o} - \frac{1}{u_o} = \frac{1}{f_o}$$

$$\frac{1}{15} - \frac{1}{u_0} = \frac{1}{1} \Rightarrow u = -\frac{15}{14}\text{ cm}$$

When the final image is formed at infinity,

$$m = \frac{v_o}{u_o} \times \frac{D}{f_e} = \frac{15}{\frac{15}{14}} \times \frac{25}{5} = 70$$

4. $\frac{1}{v_o}-\frac{1}{u_o}=\frac{1}{f_o} \Rightarrow \frac{1}{v_o}-\frac{1}{-6}=\frac{1}{4}$

$\Rightarrow v_o = 12$ cm

$$m = m_o m_e = \frac{v_o}{u_o}\left(1+\frac{D}{f_e}\right)$$

$$= \frac{12}{6}\left(1+\frac{25}{6}\right) = 10.33$$

5. For eyepiece, $\frac{1}{v_e}-\frac{1}{u_e}=\frac{1}{f_e}$

$\Rightarrow \frac{1}{(-25)}-\frac{1}{u_e}=\frac{1}{5} \Rightarrow u_e = -\frac{25}{6}$ cm

Length of tube, $L = v_o + u_e$

$\Rightarrow 20 = v_o + \frac{25}{6} \Rightarrow v_o = \frac{95}{6}$ cm

For objective, $\frac{1}{v_o}-\frac{1}{u_o}=\frac{1}{f_o}$

$\Rightarrow \frac{1}{\left(\frac{95}{6}\right)}-\frac{1}{u_o}=\frac{1}{2} \Rightarrow u_o = -\frac{190}{83}$ cm $= -2.3$ cm

Magnifying power,

$$m = m_o m_e = \frac{v_o}{u_o}\left(1+\frac{D}{f_e}\right) = \left(\frac{\frac{95}{6}}{\frac{190}{83}}\right)\left(1+\frac{25}{5}\right) = 41.5$$

6. For objective, $\frac{1}{v_o}-\frac{1}{u_o}=\frac{1}{f_o}$

$\Rightarrow \frac{1}{v_o}-\frac{1}{-(1.1)}=\frac{1}{1} \Rightarrow v_o = 11$ cm

Distance between objective and eyepiece,

$L = v_o + f_e \Rightarrow L = 11 + 1.5 = 12.5$ cm

7. $m_e = 1 + \frac{D}{f_e}$

$\Rightarrow 5 = 1 + \frac{20}{f_e} \Rightarrow f_e = 5$ cm

$m_e = \frac{v_e}{u_e} \Rightarrow 5 = \frac{20}{u_e}$

$\Rightarrow u_e = 4$ cm

$L = v_o + u_e$

$\Rightarrow 14 = v_o + 4 \Rightarrow v_o = 10$ cm

$m = m_o m_e \Rightarrow 20 = m_o(5)$

$\Rightarrow m_o = 4$

$m_o = \frac{v_o}{u_o} \Rightarrow 4 = \frac{10}{u_o}$

$\Rightarrow u_o = 2.5$ cm

$\frac{1}{v_o}-\frac{1}{u_o}=\frac{1}{f_o} \Rightarrow \frac{1}{10}-\frac{1}{-2.5}=\frac{1}{f_o}$

$f_o = 2$ cm

4.4 Telescope

1. (i) $m = \frac{f_o}{f_e} = \frac{200}{5} = 40$

(ii) $m = \frac{f_o}{f_e}\left(1+\frac{f_e}{D}\right) = \frac{200}{5}\left(1+\frac{5}{25}\right) = 48$

2. $L = f_o + f_e = 24$ cm ... (i)

$m = \frac{f_o}{f_e} = 5$ ...(ii)

Solving Eqs. (i) and (ii), we get

$f_o = 20$ cm, $f_e = 4$ cm

3. (i) $L = f_o + f_e = 60 + 5 = 65$ cm

(ii) For eyepiece, $\frac{1}{v_e}-\frac{1}{u_e}=\frac{1}{f_e}$

$\Rightarrow \frac{1}{(-25)}-\frac{1}{u_e}=\frac{1}{5} \Rightarrow u_e = -\frac{25}{6}$ cm

$L = f_o + u_e = 60 + \frac{25}{6} = 64.17$ cm

4. For objective, $\frac{1}{v_o}-\frac{1}{u_o}=\frac{1}{f_o}$

$\Rightarrow \frac{1}{v_o}-\frac{1}{(-200)}=\frac{1}{50} \Rightarrow v_o = \frac{200}{3}$ cm

$$m_o = \frac{v_o}{u_o} = \frac{\frac{200}{3}}{(-200)} = -\frac{1}{3}$$

For eyepiece, $\frac{1}{v_e}-\frac{1}{u_e}=\frac{1}{f_e}$

$\Rightarrow \frac{1}{(-25)}-\frac{1}{u_e}=\frac{1}{5} \Rightarrow u_e = -\frac{25}{6}$ cm

$$m_e = \frac{v_e}{u_e} = \frac{-25}{\left(\frac{-25}{6}\right)} = 6$$

(i) $L = v_o + u_e = \frac{200}{3} + \frac{25}{6} = \frac{425}{6}$ cm $= 70.83$ cm

(ii) $m = m_o m_e = \left(-\frac{1}{3}\right)(6) = -2$

5. $m = \frac{f_o}{f_e} = \frac{400}{10} = 40$

Also, $m = \frac{\beta}{\alpha} \Rightarrow \beta = m\alpha$

$\Rightarrow \beta = 40 \times \frac{\text{Diameter of moon}}{\text{Distance from earth}}$

$= 40 \times \frac{3.5 \times 10^3}{3.8 \times 10^5}$

$= 36.84 \times 10^{-2}$ rad $= 21.1°$

6. Angle subtended by the 100 m tall tower at 3 km away,

$\alpha \approx \tan\alpha = \frac{100}{3 \times 10^3} = \frac{1}{30}$ rad

$$m = \frac{f_o}{f_e}\left(1+\frac{f_e}{D}\right) = \frac{150}{5}\left(1+\frac{5}{25}\right) = 36$$

Also, $m = \frac{\beta}{\alpha} \Rightarrow \beta = m\alpha = 36\left(\frac{1}{30}\right) = 1.2$ rad

$$\beta \simeq \tan\beta = \frac{h}{25} \Rightarrow h = 25\beta = 25 \times 1.2 = 30 \text{ cm}$$

7. $\frac{1}{v_e} - \frac{1}{u_e} = \frac{1}{f_e} \Rightarrow \frac{1}{40} - \frac{1}{u_e} = \frac{1}{10}$

$$\Rightarrow \quad u_e = -\frac{40}{3} \text{ cm}$$

$$m_e = \frac{v_e}{u_e} = \frac{40}{\frac{40}{3}} = 3$$

Diameter of image formed by the objective,

$$d = \frac{6}{3} = 2 \text{ cm}$$

If D is the diameter of the sun, then the angle subtended by it on the objective will be

$$\alpha = \frac{D}{1.5 \times 10^{11}} \text{ rad}$$

Angle subtended by the image at the objective will be equal to this angle and is given by

$$\alpha = \frac{\text{size of image}}{f_o} = \frac{2}{200} = \frac{1}{100} \text{ rad}$$

$$\therefore \quad \frac{D}{1.5 \times 10^{11}} = \frac{1}{100} \Rightarrow D = 1.5 \times 10^{9} \text{ m}$$

8. In a terrestrial telescope, the inverted image formed by the objective is made erect by positioning it at the $2f$ point of an erecting lens of focal length f.

In normal adjustment, the separation between the objective and the eyepiece is

$$L = f_o + 4f + f_e = 180 + 4(3.5) + 5 = 199 \text{ cm}$$

Magnifying power, $m = \frac{f_o}{f_e} = \frac{180}{5} = 36$

Yes, the telescope can be used to view astronomical objects though there is no need to make the inverted image of a star upright. But the final image is less bright than in an equivalent astronomical telescope because of the extra loss of some light due to reflection and absorption by the erecting lens.

9. $f_o = \frac{R}{2} = \frac{120}{2} = 60$ cm

$$m = \frac{f_o}{f_e} \Rightarrow 20 = \frac{60}{f_e} \Rightarrow f_e = 3 \text{ cm}$$

Level 2

Single Choice Correct Questions

1. Near point = 25 cm, Far point = ∞

2. $P = -\frac{1}{x} \Rightarrow -2 = \frac{1}{x}$

$$\Rightarrow \quad x = 0.5 \text{ m} = 50 \text{ cm}$$

The person is near sighted.

3. For reading,

$$f = \frac{yD}{y-D} = \frac{(50)(25)}{50-25} = 50 \text{ cm}$$

$$P = \frac{1}{f} = \frac{1}{0.5} = 2 \text{ D}$$

For seeing distant starts,

$$P = \frac{1}{f} = -\frac{1}{x} = -\frac{1}{3} = -0.33 \text{ D}$$

4. $\frac{1}{v} - \frac{1}{u} = \frac{1}{f} \Rightarrow \frac{1}{-15} - \frac{1}{-60} = \frac{1}{f} \Rightarrow f = -20$ cm

So, he should use concave lens of focal length 20 cm.

5. $\frac{1}{v} - \frac{1}{u} = \frac{1}{f} \Rightarrow \frac{1}{-100} - \frac{1}{-40} = \frac{1}{f}$

$$f = \frac{200}{3} \text{ cm} = \frac{2}{3} \text{ m}$$

$$P = \frac{1}{f} = \frac{3}{2} = 1.5 \text{ D}$$

6. Let his near point be y.

$$\frac{1}{v} - \frac{1}{u} = \frac{1}{f}$$

$$\Rightarrow \quad \frac{1}{-y} - \frac{1}{(-40)} = \frac{1}{\left(\frac{100}{2}\right)}$$

$$\Rightarrow \quad y = 200 \text{ cm}$$

$$\frac{1}{v} - \frac{1}{u} = \frac{1}{f} \Rightarrow \frac{1}{(-200)} - \frac{1}{(-25)} = \frac{1}{f}$$

$$\Rightarrow \quad f = \frac{200}{7} \text{ cm} = \frac{2}{7} \text{ m}$$

$$\therefore \quad P = \frac{1}{f} = \frac{7}{2} = +3.5 \text{ D}$$

7. The man can see far away objects i.e. objects at infinity only, when the lens forms the image of these objects at his far point i.e. 30 cm.

So, $\frac{1}{v} - \frac{1}{u} = \frac{1}{f} \Rightarrow \frac{1}{(-30)} - \frac{1}{(-\infty)} = \frac{1}{f}$

$$\Rightarrow \quad f = -30 \text{ cm}$$

Let his near point be y after using the lens.

$$\frac{1}{v} - \frac{1}{u} = \frac{1}{f} \Rightarrow \frac{1}{(-15)} - \frac{1}{(-y)} = \frac{1}{(-30)}$$

$$\Rightarrow \quad y = 30 \text{ cm}$$

8. Microscope increases the visual angle formed by the object at the eye.

9. $m = 1 + \frac{D}{f} = 1 + \frac{25}{5} = 6$

10. $\frac{1}{v} - \frac{1}{u} = \frac{1}{f} \Rightarrow \frac{1}{(-25)} - \frac{1}{u} = \frac{1}{10}$

$$\Rightarrow u = -\frac{50}{7} \text{ cm} \simeq -7 \text{ cm}$$

11. For $B, P = 25 \Rightarrow \frac{1}{f} = 25 \Rightarrow f = \frac{1}{25}\text{ m} = 4\text{ cm}$

$$m = 1 + \frac{D}{f}$$

$$\Rightarrow \quad m_B = 1 + \frac{25}{4} = \frac{29}{4}$$

$$\therefore \quad m_A = m_B - 1.25 = \frac{29}{4} - \frac{5}{4} = 6$$

Also, $m_A = 1 + \frac{D}{f_A} \Rightarrow 6 = 1 + \frac{25}{f_A}$

$$\Rightarrow \quad f_A = 5\text{ cm} = 0.05\text{ cm}$$

$$\therefore \quad P_A = \frac{1}{f_A} = \frac{1}{0.05} = 20\text{ D}$$

12. I_0 is real and I_e is virtual.

13. $m = m_o m_e \Rightarrow 32 = m_o(4) \Rightarrow m_o = 8$

14. $m_e = 1 + \frac{D}{f} = 1 + \frac{25}{5} = 6$

$$m = m_o m_e \Rightarrow 30 = m_o(6) \Rightarrow m_o = 5$$

15. $\frac{1}{v_o} - \frac{1}{u_o} = \frac{1}{f_o} \Rightarrow \frac{1}{v_o} - \frac{1}{(-1.1)} = \frac{1}{1}$

$$\Rightarrow \quad v_o = 11\text{ cm}$$

$$m_o = \frac{v_o}{u_o} = \frac{11}{1.1} = 10,\ m_e = 1 + \frac{D}{f} = 1 + \frac{25}{5} = 6$$

$$\therefore \quad m = m_o m_e = 10 \times 6 = 60$$

16. $\frac{1}{v_o} - \frac{1}{u_0} = \frac{1}{f_o} \Rightarrow \frac{1}{v_o} - \frac{1}{(-1.25)} = \frac{1}{1.2}$

$$\Rightarrow v_o = 30\text{ cm}$$

$$m_o = \frac{v_o}{u_o} = \frac{30}{1.25} = 24,\ m_e = \frac{D}{f} = \frac{25}{3}$$

$$\therefore \quad m = m_o m_e = 24 \times \frac{25}{3} = 200$$

17. $\frac{1}{v_o} - \frac{1}{u_o} = \frac{1}{f_o} \Rightarrow \frac{1}{v_o} - \frac{1}{(-2)} = \frac{1}{1.5} \Rightarrow v_o = 6\text{ cm}$

$$\frac{1}{v_e} - \frac{1}{u_e} = \frac{1}{f_e} \Rightarrow \frac{1}{(-25)} - \frac{1}{u_e} = \frac{1}{6.25}$$

$$\Rightarrow \quad u_e = -5\text{ cm}$$

Distance between two lenses

$$= v_o + |u_e| = 6 + 5 = 11\text{ cm}$$

18. $L = v_o + f_e$

$$\Rightarrow \quad 15 = v_o + 3$$

$$\Rightarrow \quad v_o = 12\text{ cm}$$

$$\frac{1}{v_o} - \frac{1}{u_o} = \frac{1}{f_o} \Rightarrow \frac{1}{12} - \frac{1}{u_o} = \frac{1}{2}$$

$$\Rightarrow \quad u_o = -2.4\text{ cm}$$

19. $L = v_o + u_e$

$$\Rightarrow \quad 6.5 = v_o + f_e$$

$$\Rightarrow \quad v_0 = 6.5 - f_e$$

$$\frac{1}{v_o} - \frac{1}{u_o} = \frac{1}{f_o}$$

$$\Rightarrow \quad \frac{v_o}{u_o} = 1 - \frac{v_o}{f_o} = 1 - \frac{6.5 - f_e}{f_o}$$

$$m = -\frac{v_o D}{u_o f_e}$$

$$\Rightarrow \quad 100 = -\left(1 - \frac{6.5 - f_e}{0.5}\right)\frac{25}{f_e}$$

$$\Rightarrow \quad f_e = 2\text{ cm}$$

20. $m = -\frac{v_o D}{u_o f_e}$

$$\Rightarrow \quad 45 = -\left(1 - \frac{v_o}{f_o}\right)\frac{D}{f_e}$$

$$\Rightarrow \quad 45 = -\left(1 - \frac{v_o}{1}\right)\left(\frac{25}{5}\right)$$

$$\Rightarrow \quad v_o = 10\text{ cm}$$

$$L = v_o + f_e = 10 + 5 = 15\text{ cm}$$

21. $\frac{1}{v_e} - \frac{1}{u_e} = \frac{1}{f_e} \Rightarrow \frac{1}{(-25)} - \frac{1}{u_e} = \frac{1}{5}$

$$\Rightarrow \quad u_e = -\frac{25}{6}\text{ cm}$$

$$L = v_o + |u_e| \Rightarrow 30 = v_o + \frac{25}{6}$$

$$\Rightarrow \quad v_o = \frac{155}{6}\text{ cm}$$

$$\frac{1}{v_o} - \frac{1}{u_o} = \frac{1}{f_o} \Rightarrow \frac{1}{\frac{155}{6}} - \frac{1}{u_o} = \frac{1}{2}$$

$$\Rightarrow \quad u_o = -\frac{310}{143} = -2.17\text{ cm}$$

22. $m = m_o m_e \Rightarrow m = m_o\left(\frac{D}{f_e}\right) \Rightarrow 30 = m_o\left(\frac{25}{5}\right)$

$$\Rightarrow \quad m_o = 6$$

Also, $m_o = -\frac{v_o}{u_o} = -\left(\frac{f_o}{f_o + u_o}\right)$

$$\Rightarrow \quad 6 = -\frac{1.25}{1.25 + u_o}$$

$$\Rightarrow \quad u_o = -\frac{35}{24}\text{ cm} = -1.46\text{ cm}$$

23. $m = \frac{f_o}{f_e} = \frac{200}{5} = 40$

24. $m = \frac{f_o}{f_e} = 8 \Rightarrow f_o = 8f_e$

$$f_o + f_e = 54 \Rightarrow 8f_e + f_e = 54$$

$$\Rightarrow \quad f_e = 6\text{ cm}$$

$$\therefore \quad f_o = 8(6) = 48\text{ cm}$$

25. $f_o + f_e = 500 \Rightarrow f_o + 20 = 500$

$\Rightarrow f_o = 480$ mm

$$m = \frac{f_o}{f_e} = \frac{480}{20} = 24$$

26. $\frac{1}{v_e} - \frac{1}{u_e} = \frac{1}{f_e} \Rightarrow \frac{1}{(-25)} - \frac{1}{u_e} = \frac{1}{5} \Rightarrow u_e = -\frac{25}{6}$ cm

$$L = f_o + |u_e| = 80 + \frac{25}{6} = 84.2 \text{ cm}$$

27. For normal adjustment, $m = \frac{f_o}{f_e} = 10$

$\Rightarrow f_o = 10f_e$

$L = f_o + f_e = 1.1 \text{ m} = 110$ cm

$\Rightarrow 10f_e + f_e = 110$

$\Rightarrow f_e = 10$ cm

$\therefore f_o = 10(10) = 100$ cm

When image is formed at least distance of distinct vision,

$$m = \frac{f_o}{f_e}\left(1 + \frac{f_e}{D}\right) = \frac{100}{10}\left(1 + \frac{10}{25}\right) = 14$$

28. $m = \frac{f_o}{f_e} = \frac{60}{5} = 12$

Also, $m = \frac{\beta}{\alpha} \Rightarrow \beta = m\alpha = 12(2°) = 24°$

29. $\frac{1}{v_o} - \frac{1}{u_o} = \frac{1}{f_o}$

$\Rightarrow \frac{1}{v_o} - \frac{1}{(-200)} = \frac{1}{30}$

$\Rightarrow v_o = \frac{600}{17}$ cm

$$L = v_o + f_e = \frac{600}{17} + 3 = \frac{651}{17} \text{ cm} = 38.3 \text{ cm}$$

30. $\frac{1}{v_o} - \frac{1}{u_o} = \frac{1}{f_o} \Rightarrow \frac{1}{v_o} - \frac{1}{(-200)} = \frac{1}{50}$

$\Rightarrow v_o = \frac{200}{3}$ cm

$\frac{1}{v_e} - \frac{1}{u_e} = \frac{1}{f_e} \Rightarrow \frac{1}{(-25)} - \frac{1}{u_e} = \frac{1}{5}$

$\Rightarrow u_e = \frac{-25}{6}$ cm

$$L = v_o + |u_e| = \frac{200}{3} + \frac{25}{6} = \frac{425}{6} \text{ cm} \simeq 71 \text{ cm}$$

31. $\alpha \simeq \tan\alpha = \frac{10}{2 \times 10^3} = 5 \times 10^{-3}$ rad

Also, $\alpha = \frac{h_i}{f_o}$

$\Rightarrow h_i = f_o\alpha = 1.2 \times 5 \times 10^{-3}$

$= 6 \times 10^{-3}\text{m} = 6$ mm

32. $m = \frac{f_o}{f_e} = \frac{19}{1 \times 10^{-2}} = 1900$

Angle subtended by the moon at objective.

$$\alpha = \frac{\text{Diameter of moon}}{\text{Radius of lunar orbit}} = \frac{3.5 \times 10^6}{3.8 \times 10^8}$$

Angle subtended by the image of the moon formed by objective,

$$\beta = \frac{\text{Diameter of image of moon}}{\text{Focal length of eyepiece}} = \frac{D}{1 \times 10^{-2}}$$

Also, $m = \frac{\beta}{\alpha} \Rightarrow \beta = m\alpha$

$\Rightarrow \frac{D}{1 \times 10^{-2}} = 1900 \times \frac{3.5 \times 10^6}{3.8 \times 10^8}$

$\Rightarrow D = 17.5 \times 10^{-2}$ m $= 17.5$ cm

33. $m = \frac{f_o}{f_e} = \frac{50}{2.5} = 20$

Also, $m = \frac{\beta}{\alpha} \Rightarrow \beta = m\alpha = 20 \times 1 \times 10^{-3}$

$\beta = \frac{h}{f_e} \Rightarrow 20 \times 1 \times 10^{-3} = \frac{h}{2.5}$

$\Rightarrow h = 0.05$ cm $= 0.5$ mm

34. In normal adjustment, $L = f_o + f_e$

When L is decreased, object distance (u_e) for eyepiece will become less than focal length of eyepiece (f_e). So, eyepiece will form virtual image of S at a finite distance.

Previous year's Questions

JEE Main

1. Given, power of lens used for distant ($u = \infty$) vision is,

$P_1 = -1.0$ D

$\Rightarrow$ Focal length of lens used $f_1 = -100$ cm

$$\left(\because f\,(\text{cm}) = \frac{100}{P(\text{in D})}\right)$$

So, image of distant object must be formed with in the far point (point upto which person can see).

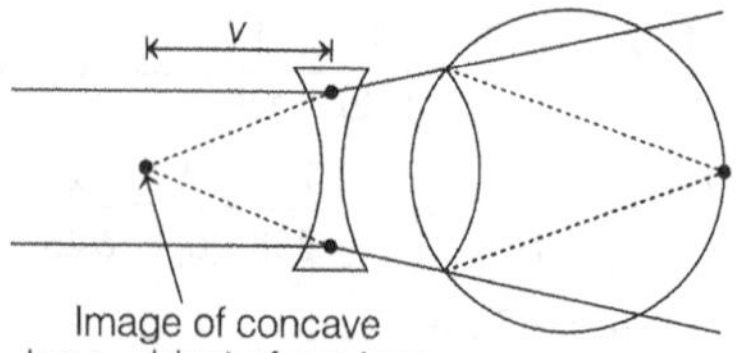

For concave lens;

$$\frac{1}{v} - \frac{1}{u} = \frac{1}{f_1}$$

$u = \infty$, $v = ?$, $f_1 = -100$ cm

$\Rightarrow \frac{1}{v} = -\frac{1}{100}$ or $v = -100$ cm.

Now, person is using a lens of power +2D for reading.

Focal length of convex lens used

$$= f_2 = \frac{100}{P(\text{in D})} = +50 \text{ cm}$$

Now, if distance of distinct vision is x, then image of x must be formed at 100 cm from eye.

$$u = -x, v = -100 \text{ cm}$$
$$f = 50 \text{ cm}$$
$$\frac{1}{-100} - \frac{1}{-x} = \frac{1}{50}$$
$$\Rightarrow \quad \frac{1}{x} = \frac{1}{50} + \frac{1}{100} = \frac{3}{100}$$
$$x = \frac{100}{3} = 33.33 \text{ cm.}$$

Nearest answer is 30 cm.

2.

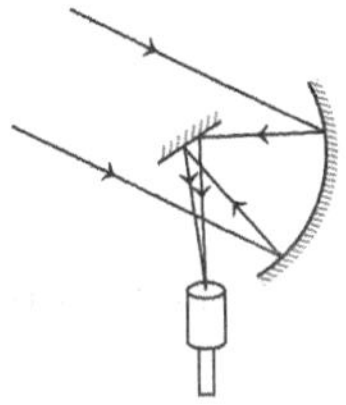

In a reflecting telescope secondary mirror turns light towards eyepiece which is outside the telescope tube.

3. A friend is not seen clearly the distant object, then its diagnosis is myopia because in myopia the distant object is blurry and it also appear non-uniform and distorted images of the object, then its diagnosis is astigmatism also.

4. The formation of image with simple microscope is shown below.

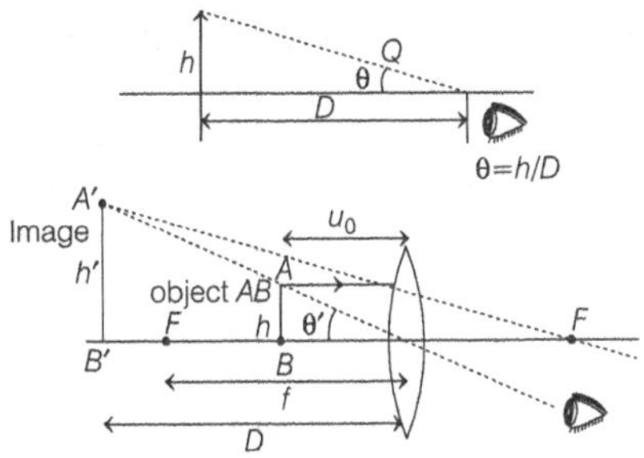

Here, $\theta' = \frac{h}{u_0} = \frac{h'}{D} = \frac{h'}{25}$

Where, $D = 25$ cm (least distance of distinct vision)

Here, θ' is same for both object and image, hence Assertion is true.

Magnification, $m = \frac{\theta'}{\theta} = \frac{D}{u_0}$

Hence, if $u_0 < D$ (25 cm), hence the value of θ' will obtain large.

So, option (c) is the correct.

5. Given, magnification, $M = 6$

Since, we know that

$$M = 1 + \frac{D}{f_0}$$

Where, D = least distance of distinct vision = 25 cm

and $\quad f_0$ = focal length of objective lens.

$$\Rightarrow \quad 6 = 1 + \frac{D}{f_0} \quad \Rightarrow \quad 6 = 1 + \frac{25}{f_0}$$
$$\Rightarrow \quad 5 = \frac{25}{f_0} \quad \Rightarrow \quad f_0 = 5 \text{ cm}$$

For compound microscope, magnifying power is given by

$$M = \frac{l \cdot D}{f_0 f_e} = 2M_{\text{simple microscope}}$$

and $\quad l$ = length of the given tube = 0.6 m

$$\Rightarrow \quad 12 = \frac{60 \times 25}{5 \cdot f_e} \qquad [\because \text{Magnification is doubled}]$$
$$\Rightarrow \quad f_e = 25 \text{ cm}$$

6. For a telescope in normal setting,

$$f_o + f_e = L$$

(length of the tube of telescope)

and $\quad \frac{f_o}{f_e} = m \qquad$ (magnification)

According to the given values in the question, we have

$$f_o + f_e = 60 \text{ cm} \quad \text{and} \quad \frac{f_o}{f_e} = 5$$
$$\Rightarrow \quad f_o = 5 f_e$$

On solving the above equations, we have

$$f_e = 10 \text{ cm}$$

7. When the final image is formed at least distance of distinct vision (i.e., at 25 cm) from eye-piece of a compound microscope, then the magnification is given by

$$m = -\frac{v_0}{u_0}\left(1 + \frac{D}{f_e}\right)$$
$$\Rightarrow \quad m = \frac{-L}{f_0}\left(1 + \frac{D}{f_e}\right)$$
$$\Rightarrow \quad -100 = -\frac{20}{1}\left(1 + \frac{25}{f_e}\right)$$
$$\Rightarrow \quad 5 = 1 + \frac{25}{f_e} \quad \Rightarrow \quad 4 = \frac{25}{f_e}$$
$$\Rightarrow \quad f_e = \frac{25}{4} = 6.25 \simeq 6 \text{ cm}$$

8. Strain on the eye is minimum so the intermediate image is formed at focal length of eye-piece.

For objective, $\quad v = 5$ cm, $f = 1$ cm

$\therefore$ Using lens formula,

$$\frac{1}{v} - \frac{1}{u} = \frac{1}{f}$$
$$\Rightarrow \quad \frac{1}{5} - \frac{1}{u} = \frac{1}{1} \quad \Rightarrow \quad u = \frac{-5}{4} \text{ cm}$$
$$\Rightarrow \quad |u| = \frac{5}{4} \text{ cm} \quad \Rightarrow \quad \frac{n}{40} = \frac{5}{4}$$
$$\Rightarrow \quad n = \frac{5}{4} \times 40 \quad \Rightarrow \quad n = 50$$

CHAPTER~05

WAVE OPTICS

LEVEL 01 Starter Level

5.1 Interference

1 If two waves represented by $y_1 = 4 \sin \omega t$ and $y_2 = 3 \sin\left(\omega t + \frac{\pi}{3}\right)$ interfere at a point. Find out the amplitude of the resulting wave.

2 S_1 and S_2 are two sources of light which produce individually disturbance at point P given by $E_1 = 3 \sin \omega t$, $E_2 = 4 \cos \omega t$. Assuming $\mathbf{E}$ and $\mathbf{E}_2$ to be along the same line, find the resultant after their superposition.

3 Two sources of intensity I and $4I$ are used in an interference experiment. Find the intensity at points where the waves from the two sources superimpose with a phase difference of

(a) zero (b) $\pi/2$ (c) π

4 Waves emitted by two identical sources produce intensity of K unit at a point on screen where path difference between these waves is λ, calculate the intensity at that point on screen at which path difference is $\lambda/4$.

5 S_1 and S_2 are two coherent sources of frequency f each having no initial phase difference. Find f, so that

(a) constructive interference at P

(b) destructive interference at P

Velocity of sound = 330 m/s

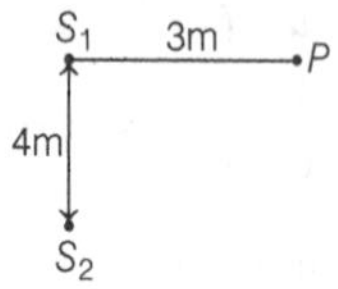

6 Two coherent monochromatic sources S_1 and S_2 emit light of wavelength λ. The distance between S_1 and S_2 is 3λ. If the detector is moved along a line perpendicular to S_1S_2 and starting from S_2, as shown in figure,

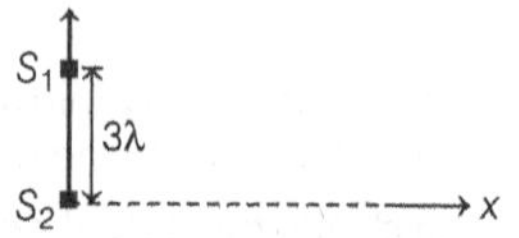

(a) what is the total number of maxima and minima observed?

(b) Find the position of farthest minima.

7 Two coherent sources S_1 and S_2 separated by distance 2λ emit light of wavelength λ in phase as shown in figure. A circular wire of radius 100λ is placed in such a way that S_1S_2 lies in its plane and the mid-point of S_1S_2, is at the centre of wire. Find total number of maxima and minima on the wire.

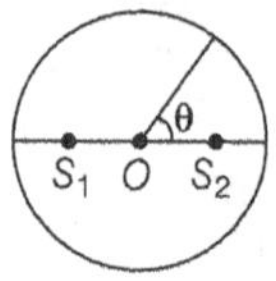

8 In fig. shown, a screen is placed normal to the line joining the two point coherent sources S_1 and S_2. The interference pattern consists of concentric circles. Given $D >> d$.

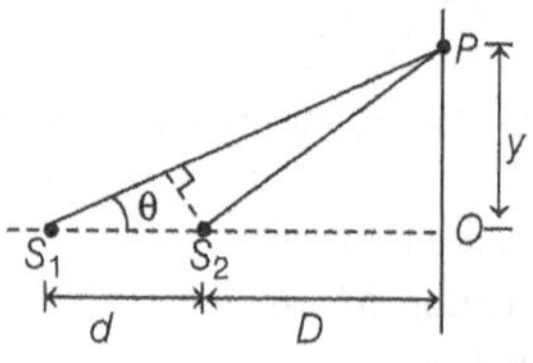

(a) Find the condition of maxima at P

(b) If $d = 0.5$ mm, $\lambda = 5000$ Å and $D = 100$ cm, find the order of the central bright fringe and

(c) also find the radius of the closest second bright ring.

5.2 YDSE Pattern on the Screen

1 What is the effect on the the fringe width of interference fringes in a Young's double slit experiment due to each of the following operations?
 (a) The screen is moved away from the plane of the slits.
 (b) the (monochromatic) source is replaced by another (monochromatic) source of shorter wavelength.
 (c) The separation between the two slits is increased.
 (d) The width of two slits are slightly increased.

 [In each operation, take all parameters, other than the one specified to remain unchanged]

2 Monochromatic light of wavelength 5000 Å is used in YDSE, with slit separation, $d = 1$ mm, distance between screen and slits, $D = 1$ m. Find
 (a) fringe width β
 (b) distance of 4th maxima from the central maxima on the screen
 (c) distance of 5th minima from the central maxima on the screen
 (d) distance of the 1000th maxima from the central maxima on the screen.
 (e) total number of maxima and minima on the screen.

3 In a YDSE, $D = 1$ m, $d = 1$ mm and $\lambda = 0.5$ mm
 (a) Find the distance between the first and central maxima on the screen.
 (b) Find the number of maxima and minima obtained on the screen.

4 In a Young's double slit experiment, the fringe width is found to be 0.4 mm. If the whole apparatus is immersed in water of refractive index (4/3), without disturbing the geometrical arrangement, what is the new fringe width?

5 Find the angular fringe width in a Young's double slits experiment with blue-green light of wavelength 6000 Å. The separation between the slits is 3.0×10^{-3} m.

5.3 Intensity Distribution on the Screen

1 Two coherent monochromatic light beams of intensities I and $4I$ are superposed. Find the maximum and minimum possible intensities in the resulting beam.

2 In Young's double slit experiment the two slits act as coherent sources of equal amplitude A and of wavelength λ.

 In another experiment with the same set up the two slits are sources of equal amplitude A and wavelength λ, but are incoherent. The ratio of the intensity of light at the mid-point of the screen in the first case to that in the second case is ....

3 In a YDSE with identical slits, the intensity of the central bright fringe is I_0. If one of the slits is covered, what will be the intensity at the same point?

4 Monochromatic light of wavelength 5000 Å is used in YDSE, with slit separation, $d = 1$ mm, distance between screen and slits, $D = 1$ m. If intensity at the two slits are, $I_1 = 4I_0, I_2 = I_0$, find intensity at $y = 1/3$ mm

5 In a Young's double-slit interference experiment the fringe pattern is observed on a screen placed at a distance D. The slits are separated by d and are illuminated by light of wavelength λ. Find the least distance from the central point where the intensity falls to half the maximum.

6 If one of the two slits of a Young's double slit experiment is painted over so that it transmits half the light intensity of the other, then what will happen to the brightness of dark and bright fringes?

5.4 YDSE with Polychromatic Light

1 White coherent light (400-700 nm) is sent through the slits of a YDSE. The separation between the slits is 0.5 mm and screen is 50 cm away from the slits. There is a hole in the screen at a point 1.0 mm away (along the width of the fringe) from the central line. Which wavelength(s) will be absent in the light coming from the hole?

2 A beam of light consisting of wavelengths 6000 Å and 4500 Å is used in a YDSE with $D = 1$ m and $d = 1$ mm. Find the least distance from the central maxima, where bright fringes due to the two wavelengths coincide.

3 In a Young's double slit experiment a parallel light beam containing wavelength $\lambda_1 = 4000$ Å and $\lambda_2 = 5600$ Å is incident on a diaphragm having two narrow slits. Separation between the slits is $d = 2$ mm. If distance between diaphragm and screen is $D = 40$ cm, calculate
 (i) distance of first black line from central bright fringe,
 (ii) distance between the consecutive black lines.

5.5 Oblique Incidence

1 In YDSE with $D = 1$ m, $d = 1$ mm, light of wavelength 500 nm is incident at an angle of 0.57° w.r.t. the axis of symmetry of the experimental set up. If centre of symmetry of screen is O as shown,

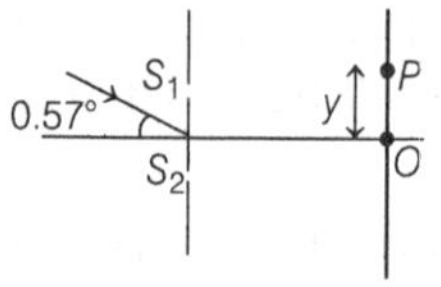

(a) find the position of central maxima

(b) Intensity at point O in terms of intensity of central maxima I_0.

(c) Number of maxima lying between O and the central maxima.

2 In a Young's double slit experiment, a parallel beam of light of wavelength 0.5 mm is incident on the slits at an angle of 30° as shown in the figure.

(a) Find the position of central maxima.

(b) Find the position of first order minima on either side of central maxima.

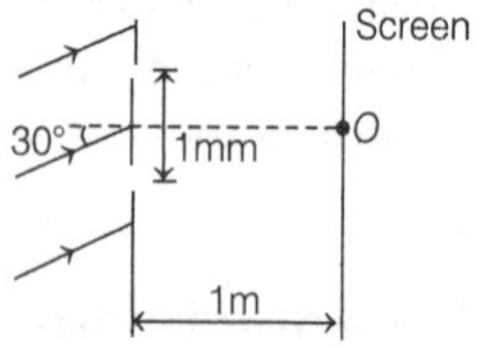

5.6 Source Placed Beyond the Central Line

1 In Young's double-slit experiment, the point source is placed slightly off the central axis shown in fig. If $\lambda = 500$ nm. find the nature and order of the interference.

(a) at point P (b) at point O

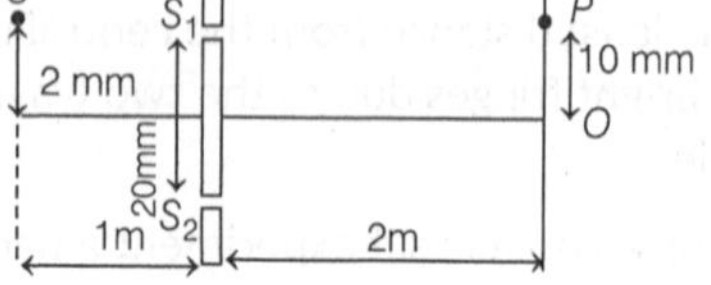

2 In a Young's double slit experiment the light source is at distance $l_1 = 20\ \mu m$ and $l_2 = 40\ \mu m$ from the slits. The light of wavelength $\lambda = 500$ nm is incident on slits separated by a distance $d = 10\ \mu m$.
A screen is placed at a distance $D = 2$ m away from the slits as shown in the figure.

(a) Find the values of θ relative to the central line where maxima appear on the screen.

(b) How many maxima will appear on the screen?

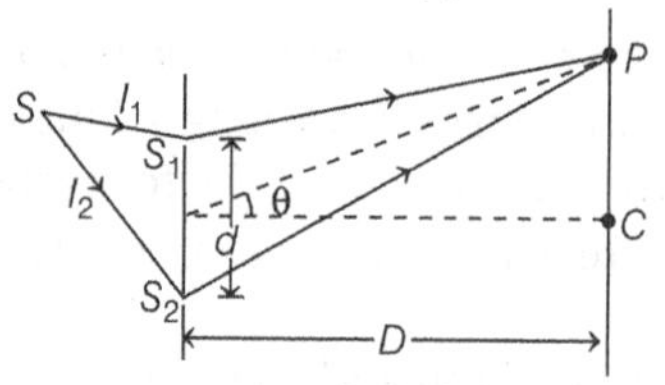

5.7 Introduction of Glass Slab

1 The central fringe of the interference pattern produced by the light of wavelength 6000 Å is found to shift to the position of 4th bright fringe after a glass sheet of refractive index 1.5 is introduced. Find the thickness of glass sheet.

2 A two slit Young's interference experiment is done with monochromatic light of wavelength 6000 Å. This slits are 2 mm apart. The fringes are observed on a screen placed 10 cm away from the slits. A transparent plate of thickncss 0.5 mm is placed in front of one of the slits. It is found that the interference pattern shifts by 5 mm. What is the refractive index of the transparent plate?

3 A double-slit apparatus is immersed in a liquid of refractive index 1.33. It has slit separation of 1 mm and distance between the plane of the slits and screen is 1.33 m. The slits are illuminated by a parallel beam of light whose wavelength in air is 6300 Å.

(a) Calculate the fringe width

(b) One of the slits of the apparatus is covered by a thin glass sheet of refractive index 1.53. Find the smallest thickness of the sheet to bring the adjacent minima on the axis.

4 In Young's double slit experiment, the upper slit is covered by a thin glass plate of refractive index 1.4 and thickness 2 micron. While the other slit is covered by another glass plate of thickness 4 micron and refractive index 1.6. Interference pattern is observed using light of wavelength 4800 Å. The intensity of the central maximum point P is I_0 without the plates in the experiment. Find the intensity of the point P after the insertion of plates in the path of the wavefronts.

5 A Young's double slit apparatus is immersed in a liquid of refractive index μ_1. The slit plane touches the liquid surface. A parallel beam of monochromatic light of wavelenght λ (in air) is incident normally on the slits.

(a) If one of the slits (say S_2) is covered by a transparent slab of refractive index μ_2, and thickness t as shown, find the new position of central maxima.

(b) Now, the other slit S_1 is also covered by a slab of same thickness and refractive index μ_3 as shown in figure due to which the central maxima recovers its position. Find the value of μ_3.

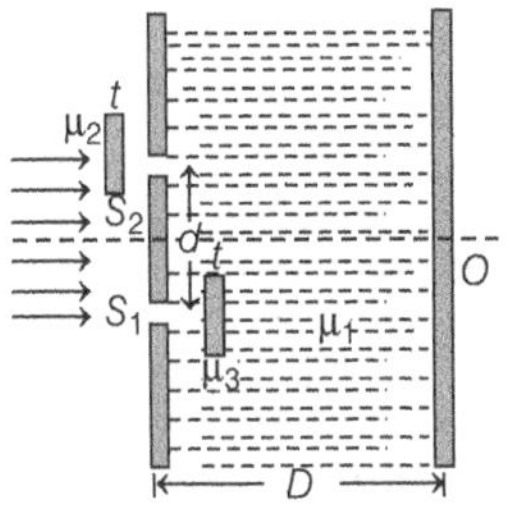

5.8 Fresnel Biprism and Llyod Mirror

1 Two small angled transparent prisms (each of refracting angle $A = 1°$) are so placed that their bases coincide, so that common base is BC. This device is called Frcsnel's biprism and is used to obtain coherent sources of a point source S illuminated by monochromatic light of wavelength 6000 Å placed at a distance $a = 20$ cm.

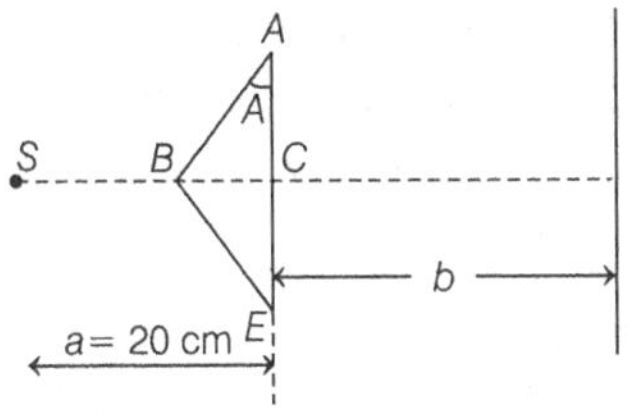

Calculate

(a) the separation between coherent sources.

(b) If a screen is placed at a distance $b = 80$ cm from the device, what is the fringe width?
(Refractive index of material of each prism = 1.5).

2 A whole biprism experiment is immersed in water. If the fringe width in air is 1 mm and refractive index of biprism material and water are 1.5 and 1.33. respectively. Find the value of new fringe width.

3 A source of light of wavelength 5000 Å is placed as shown in figure. Considering interference of direct and reflected rays, determine the position of the region where the fringes will be visible and calculate the number of fringes.

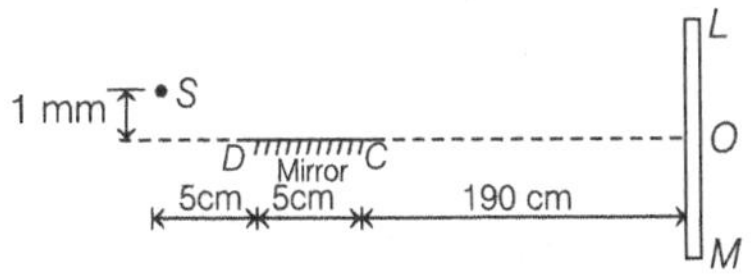

4 Two plane mirrors, a source S of light, emitting monochromatic rays of wavelength λ and a screen are arranged as shown in figure. If angle θ is very small, calculate fringe width of interference pattern formed on screen by reflected rays.

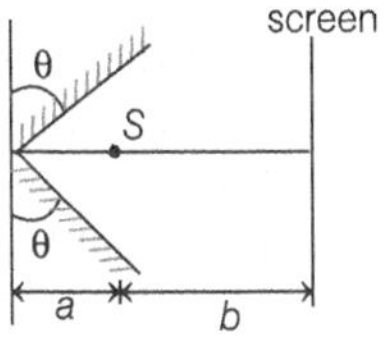

5.9 Thin Film Interference

1 What is the minimum thickness of a thin film of index 1.40 such that the violet colour is absent in the reflected white light, which was incident normally on the film? [Use $\lambda_v = 400$ nm]

2 White light is incident normally on a glass plate of thickness 0.50×10^{-6} m and index of refraction 1.50. Which wavelengths in the visible region (400 nm – 700 nm) are strongly reflected by the plate?

3 A lens ($\mu = 1.5$) is coated with a thin film of refractive index 1.25 in order to reduce the reflection from its surface at $\lambda = 5000$ Å. What should be the minimum thickness of the film which will minimize the intensity of the reflected light?

4 A parallel beam of light is incident at an angle 53° ($\sin 53° \approx 4/5$) on a 0.25 μm thick film of water ($\mu = 4/3$) formed on glass ($\mu_g = 3/2$). If the light is strongly reflected find maximum possible value of the wavelength of light.

5 Light is incident on a glass plate ($\mu = 1.5$) such that angle of refraction is 60°. Dark band is observed corresponding to the wavelength of 6000Å. If the thickness of glass plate is 1.2×10^{-3} mm, calculate the order of the interference band.

6 Two smooth glass plates of length 10 cm each are placed face-to-face with a 2 micron spacer between them at one end, to create a thin air wedge. How many bright lines are seen by reflection when light of wavelength 400 nm is incident normally on the plates?

7 A beam of monochromatic light of wavelength 5.82×10^{-7} m falls normally on a glass wedge with the wedge angle of 20 second of an arc. If the refractive index of glass is 1.5, find the number of dark interference fringes per cm of the wedge length.

LEVEL 02 JEE Main Level

Single Choice Correct Questions

1 In a two slit experiment with monochromatic light, fringes are obtained on a screen placed at some distance from the slits. If the screen is moved by 5×10^{-2} m towards the slits, the change in fringe width is 3×10^{-5} m. If separation between the slits is 10^{-3} m, the wavelength of light used is

(a) 6000 Å (b) 5000 Å (c) 3000 Å (d) 4500 Å

2 In a Young's double slit experiment, 60 fringes were seen in the field view for light of wavelength 7200 Å. The number of fringes observed when light of wavelength 5400 Å. is used are

(a) 64 (b) 80 (c) 45 (d) 54

3 In Young's double slit experiment, the slits are 0.5 mm apart and the interference is observed on a screen at a distance of 100 cm from the slit. It is found that the 9th bright fringe is at a distance of 7.5 mm from the second dark fringe from the centre of the fringe pattern. The wavelength of the light used is

(a) 2500/7 Å (b) 2500 Å (c) 5000 Å (d) 5000/7 Å

4 In a double slit interference experiment, the angular spacing between the second and third maxima on same side is observed to be 2°. The ratio of wavelength to slit spacing is

(a) 2 (b) 0.5 (c) 0.011 (d) 0.035

5 In a YDSE $D = 1$ m, $d = 1$ mm and $\lambda = 500$ nm. The distance of 1000th maxima from the central maxima is

(a) 0.5 m (b) 0.577 m
(c) 0.495 m (d) does not exist

6 Young's double slit experiment is made in a liquid. The 10th bright fringe in liquid lies where 6th dark fringe lies in vacuum. The refractive index of the liquid is approximately

(a) 1.8 (b) 1.54
(c)1.67 (d) 1.2

7 In Young's double slit experiment a coordinate axis is printed on the screen. The y-coordinates of central maxima and 10th maxima are 2 cm and 5 cm, respectively. When the YDSE apparatus is immersed in a liquid of refractive index 1.5, the corresponding y-coordinates will be

(a) 2 cm, 7.5 cm (b) 3 cm, 6 cm
(c) 4/3 cm, 10/3 cm (d) 2 cm, 4 cm

8 In the figure shown if a parallel beam of white light is incident on the plane of the slits, then the distance of the nearest white spot on the screen from O is [assume $d << D$, $\lambda << d$]

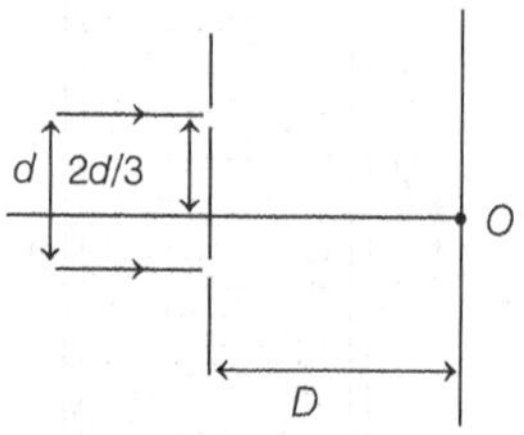

(a) 0 (b) d/2 (c) d/3 (d) d/6

9 Plane microwaves from a transmitter are directed normally towards a plane reflector. A detector moves along the normal to the reflector. Between positions of 14 successive maxima, the detector travels a distance 0.13 m. If the velocity of light is 3×10^8 m/s, find the frequency of the transmitter.

(a) 1.5×10^{10} Hz (b) 10^{10} Hz
(c) 3×10^{10} Hz (d) 6×10^{10} Hz

10 In a Young's double slit experiment, the separation between the slits is d, distance between the slit and screen is D (D >> d). In the interference pattern, there is a maxima exactly in front for each slit. Then, the possible wavelcngth(s) used in the experiment are

(a) $\frac{d^2}{D}, \frac{d^2}{2D}, \frac{d^2}{3D}$ (b) $\frac{d^2}{D}, \frac{d^2}{3D}, \frac{d^2}{5D}$
(c) $\frac{d^2}{2D}, \frac{d^2}{4D}, \frac{d^2}{6D}$ (d) None of these

11 Two closely located, monochromatic coherent sources create a fixed interference pattern on a screen. The frequency of one of the sources is then decreased. What will happen to the interference pattern as a result?

(a) The pattern will completely disappear
(b) The fringe spacing will increase
(c) The fringes will shift up or down, but the spacing will remain constant
(d) The fringe spacing will decrease

12 A student is asked to measure the wavelength of monochromatic light. He sets up the apparatus sketched below. S_1, S_2, S_3 are narrow parallel slits, L is a sodium lamp and M

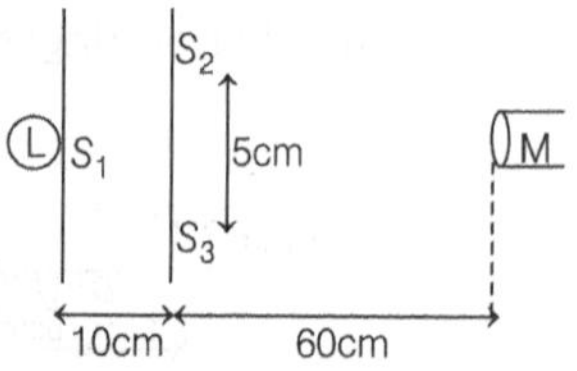

is a microscope eyepiece. The student fails to observe interference fringes. Your first advice to him will be.

(a) increase the width of S_1
(b) decrease the distance between S_2 and S_3
(c) replace L with a white light source
(d) make S_2 and S_3 wider

13 In a double slit experiment, instead of taking slits of equal widths, one slit is made twice as wide as the other. Then, in the interference pattern

(a) the intensities of both the maxima and minima increase.
(b) the intensity of the maxima increases and the minima has zero intensity.
(c) the intensity of the maxima decreases and that of minima increases.
(d) the intensity of the maxima decreases and the minima has zero intensity.

14 In a Young's Double slit experiment, first maxima is observed at a fixed point P on the screen. Now, the screen is continuously moved away from the plane of slits. The ratio of intensity at point P to the intensity at point O (centre of the screcn)

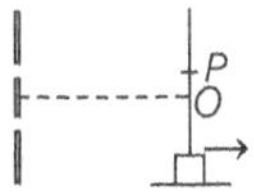

(a) remains constant (b) keeps on decreasing
(c) first decreases and then increases
(d) first decreases and then becomes constant

15 Two coherent sources of intensity ratio β interfere. Find the ratio $\dfrac{I_{max} - I_{min}}{I_{max} + I_{min}}$ in the interference pattern

(a) $\dfrac{2\sqrt{\beta}}{1+\beta}$ (b) $\dfrac{2\beta}{1+\beta}$ (c) $\dfrac{\sqrt{\beta}+1}{\sqrt{\beta}-1}$ (d) $\dfrac{\sqrt{\beta}}{1+\sqrt{\beta}}$

16 At a certain point on a screen in a YDSE apparatus, the path difference for the two interfering rays is (1/3)rd of the wavelength. Find the ratio of the intensity at this point to that at the centre of a bright fringe.

(a) $\dfrac{1}{2}$ (b) $\dfrac{1}{4}$ (c) $\dfrac{1}{3}$ (d) $\dfrac{3}{4}$

17 In YDSE, if the intensity of central maxima is I_0, then the y-coordinate of point where the intensity is $I_0/2$, $d = 0.1$ mm, $D = 1$ m, $\lambda = 5000$ Å

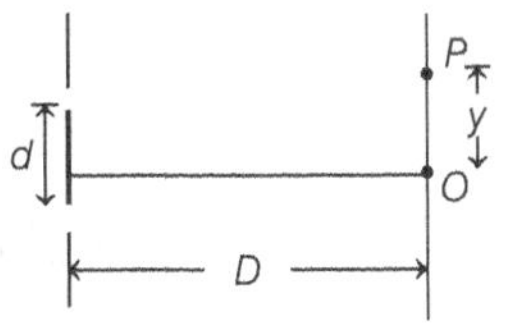

(a) 1.5 mm (b) 2 mm (c) 1.75 mm (d) 1.25 mm

18 In a YDSE experiment, I_0 is given to be the intensity of the central bright fringe and β is the fringe width. Then, at a distance y from the central bright fringe, the intensity will be

(a) $I_0 \cos(\pi y/\beta)$ (b) $I_0 \cos^2(\pi y/\beta)$
(c) $I_0 \cos(2\pi y/\beta)$ (d) $I_0 \cos^2(\pi y/2\beta)$

19 Intensities of light due to the two slits of YDSE are I and $4I$. How far from the central maxima will the intensity be equal to the average intensity on the screen? (β is the fringe width).

(a) $\beta/2$ (b) $\beta/3$ (c) $\beta/6$ (d) $\beta/4$

20 In a Young's double slit interference pattern, the intensity of the central fringe at P is I_0 .When one slit width is reduced to one fourth, the intensity at P will be

(a) $\dfrac{I_0}{2}$ (b) $\dfrac{I_0}{4}$ (c) $\dfrac{9}{16}I_0$ (d) $\dfrac{3}{4}I_0$

21 In Young's double slit experiment, the wavelength of red light is 7800 Å and that of blue light is 5200 Å. The value of n for which nth bright band due to red light coincides with $(n+1)$th bright band due to blue light is

(a) 1 (b) 2 (c) 3 (d) 4

22 A beam of light consisting of two wavelength 6300 Å and λ Å is used to obtain interference fringes in a Young's double slit experiment. If 4th bright fringe of 6300 Å coincides with 5th dark fringe of λ Å, the value of λ is

(a) 5200 (b) 4800 (c) 6200 (d) 5600

23 A beam of light consisting of two wavelengths 6500 Å and 5200 Å is used to obtain interference fringes in Young's double slit experiment. The distance between slits is 2 mm and the distance of screen from slits is 120 cm. What is the least distance from central maximum where the bright fringes due to both wavelengths coincide?

(a) 0.156 cm (b) 0.312 cm (c) 0.078 cm (d) 0.468 cm

24 If the Young's double slit experiment is performed with white light, then which of the following is not true?

(a) the central maximum will be white
(b) there will not be a completely dark fringe
(c) the bright fringe next to the central will be red
(d) the bright fringe next to the central will be violet

25 Two ideal slits S_1 and S_2 are at a distance d apart, and illuminated by light of wavelength λ passing through an ideal source slit S placed on the line through S_2, as shown.

The distance between the planes of slits and the source slit is D. A screen is held at a distance D from the plane of the slits. The minimum value of d for which there is darkness at O is

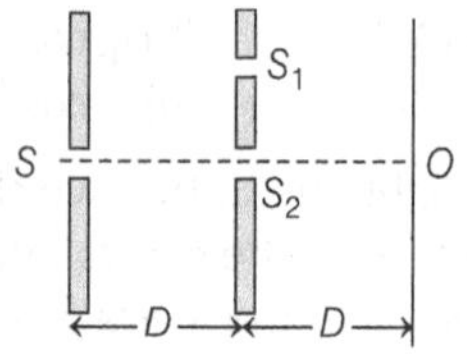

(a) $\sqrt{\frac{3\lambda D}{2}}$ (b) $\sqrt{\lambda D}$ (d) $\sqrt{\frac{\lambda D}{2}}$ (d) $\sqrt{3\lambda D}$

26 Air has refractive index 1.0003. The thickness of air column which will have one more wavelength of yellow light (6000 Å) than in the same thickness of vacuum is

(a) 2 mm (b) 2 cm (c) 2m (d) 2 km

27 The figure shows a transparent slab of length 1 m placed in air whose refractive index in x-direction varies as $\mu = 1 + x^2$ $(0 \le x \le 1)$. The optical path length of ray R will be

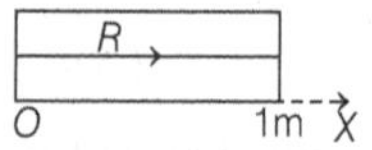

(a) 1 m (b) 2/3 m (c) 4/3 m (d) $\sqrt{2}$ m

28 Two waves of light in air have the same wavelength and are initially in phase. They then travel through plastic layers with thickness of $L_1 = 3.5$ mm and $L_2 = 5.0$ mm and indices of refraction $n_1 = 1.7$ and $n_2 = 1.25$ as shown in figure. The rays later arrive at a common point. The longest wavelength of light for which constructive interference occurs at the point is

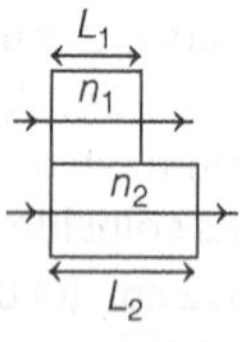

(a) 0.6 mm (b) 1.2 mm (c) 2.4 mm (d) 0.3 mm

29 Interference fringes were produced by white light by a double slit arrangement. When a mica sheet of uniform thickness of refractive index 1.6 (relative to air) is placed in the path of light from one of the slits, the central fringe moves through a distance. This distance is equal to the width of 30 interference bands if light of wavelength 4800 Å is used. The thickness (in 10^{-5} m) of mica is

(a) 9 (b) 1.2 (c) 1.4 (d) 2.4

30 Fringes are produced by light of $\lambda = 5450$ Å when a thin plate of $\mu = 1.5$ is placed normally in the path of one of the interfering beams, the central bright fringe moves to the position previously occupied by third bright fringe. The thickness of glass plate is

(a) 3.27×10^{-6} m (b) 1.6×10^{-6} m
(c) 0.82×10^{-6} m (d) 2.5×10^{-6} m

31 In the figure shown in a YDSE, a parallel beam of light is incident on the slits from a medium of refractive index n_1. The wavelength of light in this medium is λ_1. A transparent slab of thickness t and refractive index n_3 is put in front of one slit. The medium between the screen and the plane of the slits is n_2. The phase difference between the light waves reaching point O (symmetrical, relative to the slits) is

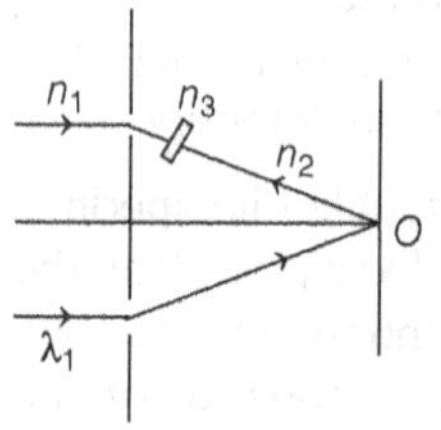

(a) $\frac{2\pi}{n_1\lambda_1}(n_3 - n_2)t$ (b) $\frac{2\pi}{\lambda_1}(n_3 - n_2)t$
(c) $\frac{2\pi n_1}{n_2\lambda_1}\left(\frac{n_3}{n_2} - 1\right)t$ (d) $\frac{2\pi n_1}{\lambda_1}(n_3 - n_2)t$

32 Interference fringes are obtained in Young's double slit experiment on a screen. Which of the following statements will be incorrect about the effect of introducing a thin transparent plate in the path of one of the two interfering beams?

(a) The separation between fringes remain unaffected.
(b) The entire fringe system shifts towards the side on which plate is placed
(c) The conditions for maxima and minima are reversed *i.e.*, maxima for odd multiple of $\lambda/2$ and minima for even multiple of $\lambda/2$.
(d) Shape of the fringe also remains unaffected.

33 A thin perfectly transparent glass sheet of thickness t and refractive index μ is pasted on one of the two identical slits. If the intensity of light at the centre of the screen is I_0 in the absence of glass sheet, the intensity at O as a function of thickness t of the glass plate is

(a) $I_0 \cos\left(\frac{\mu t}{\lambda}\right)$ (b) $I_0 \cos^2\left(\frac{\mu t}{\lambda}\right)$
(c) $I_0 \cos^2\left(\frac{\pi(\mu - 1)t}{\lambda}\right)$ (d) $I_0 \cos\left(\frac{\pi(\mu - 1)t}{\lambda}\right)$

34 In a YDSE both slits produce equal intensities on the screen. A 100% transparent thin film is placed in front of one of the slits. Now, the intensity of the geometrical centre of system on the screen becomes 75% of the previous intensity. The wavelength of the light is 6000 Å and $\mu_{glass} = 1.5$. The thickness of the film cannot be

(a) 0.2 μm (b) 1.0 μm (c) 1.4 μm (d) 1.6 μm

35 A light of wavelength 6000 Å shines on a two narrow slits separated by a distance 1.0 mm and illuminates a screen at a distance 1.5 m away. When one slit is covered by a thin glass plate of refractive index 1.8 and other slit by a thin glass plate of refractive index μ, the central maxima shifts by 0.1 rad. Both plates have the same thickness of 0.5 mm.

The value of refractive index μ of the glass is

(a) 1.4 (b) 1.5
(c) 1.6 (d) None of these

36 In a Young's Double slit experiment, the slits are illuminated by monochromatic light. The entire set up is immersed in pure water. Which one of the following act can't restore the original fringe width?

(a) briging the slits close together
(b) moving the screen away from the slit plane
(c) replacing the incident light by that of a longer wavelength
(d) introducing a thin transparent slab in front of one of the slits.

37 Young's double slit experiment is carried with two thin sheets of thickness 10.4 μm each and refractive index $\mu_1 = 1.52$ and $\mu_2 = 1.40$ covering the slits S_1 and S_2, respectively. If white light of range 400 nm to 780 nm is used, then which wavelength will form maxima exactly at point O, the centre of the screen?

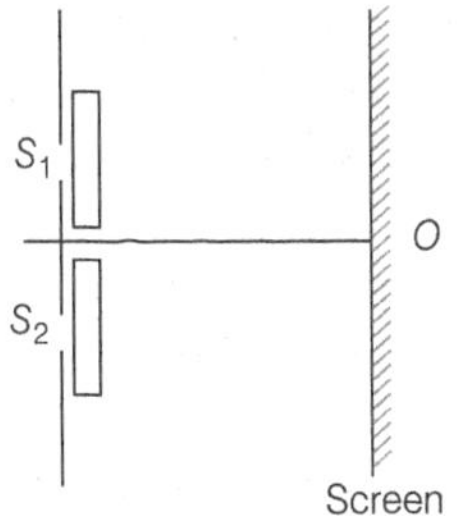

(a) 416 nm only (b) 624 nm only
(c) 416 nm and 624 nm only (d) None of these

38 Two monochromatic (wavelength $= a/5$) and coherent sources of electromagnetic waves are placed on the X-axis at the points $(2a, 0)$ and $(-a, 0)$. A detector moves in a circle of radius $R(>> 2a)$ whose centre is at the origin.

The number of maximas detected during one circular revolution by the detector are

(a) 60 (b) 15
(c) 64 (d) None of these

39 Two coherent light sources P and Q each of wavelength λ are separated by a distance 3λ as shown. The maximum number of minima formed on line AB which runs from $-\infty$ to $+\infty$ is

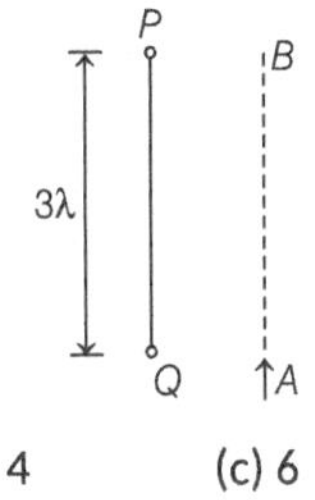

(a) 2 (b) 4 (c) 6 (d) 8

40 Figure, shows wavefronts in still water, moving in the direction of the arrow towards the interface PQ between a shallow region and a deep(denser) region. Which of the lines shown may represent one of the wavefronts in the deep region?

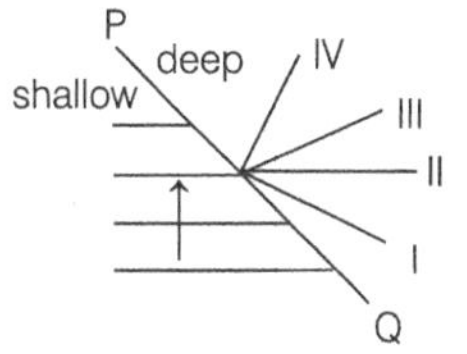

(a) I (b) II (c) III (d) IV

41 The wavefront of a light beam is given by the equation $x + 2y + 3z = c$, (where c is arbitary constant), then the angle made by the direction of light with the Y-axis is

(a) $\cos^{-1}\frac{1}{\sqrt{14}}$ (b) $\sin^{-1}\frac{2}{\sqrt{14}}$

(c) $\cos^{-1}\frac{2}{\sqrt{14}}$ (d) $\sin^{-1}\frac{3}{\sqrt{14}}$

42 In a biprism experiment the distance of source from biprism is 1 m and the distance of screen from biprism is 4 m. The angle of refraction of biprism is 2×10^{-3} radians. μ of biprism is 1.5 and the wavelength of light used is 6000 Å. How many fringes will be seen on the screen?

(a) 4 (b) 5 (c) 3 (d) 6

43 If the whole bi-prism experiment is immersed in water, then the fringe width becomes, if the refractive indices of bi-prism material and water are 1.5 and 1.33, respectively

(a) 3 times (b) 3/4 times
(c) 4/3 limes (d) 1/3 limes

44 A long narrow horizontal slit lies 1 mm above a plane mirror. The interference pattern produced by the slit and its image is viewed on a screen S distant 1m from the slit. The wavelength of light is 600 nm. Then, the distance of the first maxima above the mirror is equal to ($d << D$)

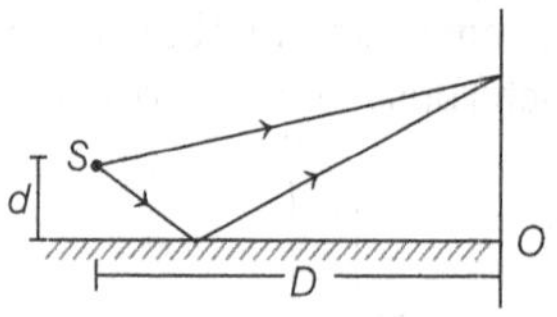

(a) 0.30 mm (b) 0.15 mm
(c) 60mm (d) 7.5 mm

45 Consider the optical system shown in figure. The point source of light S is having wavelength equals to λ. The light is reaching screen only after reflection. For point P to be 2nd maxima, the value of λ would be ($D >> d$ and $d >> \lambda$)

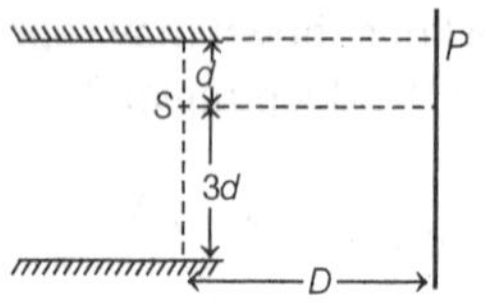

(a) $\frac{12d^2}{D}$ (b) $\frac{6d^2}{D}$ (c) $\frac{3d^2}{D}$ (d) $\frac{24d^2}{D}$

46 While light is incident normal to a thin layer of soap. Given the figure, what is the minimum thickness of the soap film that gives the soap a bluish color ($\lambda_{blue} = 500$ nm)?

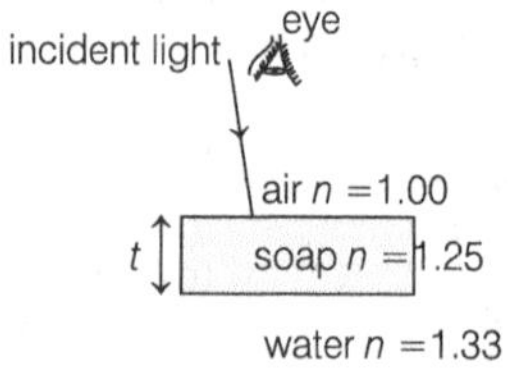

(a) 100nm (b)200nm (c) 250nm (d) 400nm

47 While light (400-700nm) is normally incident on a 0.5 micron thick soap film having refractive index 1.61. How many wavelengths will be absent in the reflected light?

(a) 1 (b) 2 (c) 3 (d) 4

48 A thin film of oil ($\mu = 1.25$) covers a smooth wet pavement. When viewed perpendicular to them pavement, the film appears to be predominantly red ($\lambda_{red} = 640$) and has no blue ($\lambda_{blue} = 512$). How thick the film is?

(a) 256 nm (b) 640 nm
(c) 512 nm (d) 320 nm

49 A hair is placed at one edge between two flat glass plates. When this arrangement is illuminated with yellow light of wavelength $\lambda = 600$ nm, a total of 121 dark bands are counted starting at the contact point between the plates, and ending at the hair. How thick is the hair?

(a) 3.6×10^{-5} m (b) 1.8×10^{-5} m
(c) 3.6×10^{-4} m (d) 1.8×10^{-4} m

50 Two glass plates are touching at one end and separated by a thin wire at the other end. When a monochromatic parallel beam of wavelength 4200 Å incident normally on the glass plates is reflected, an interference pattern of 30 fringes are observed. If the wavelength of light used is taken 7000 Å instead of 4200 Å, the number of fringes observed will be

(a) 50 (b) 40
(c) 30 (d) 18

Numerical Value Questions

1 Light of wavelength 627 nm illuminates two slits. What is the minimum path difference (in nm) between the waves from the slits for the resultant intensity to fall to 25% of the central maximum?

2 In a YDSE setup, one of the slit width is four times that of the other. The separation between the slits is $d = 1$ mm and the distance between slits and screen is $D = 5$ m. A monochromatic light of wavelength $\lambda = 6000$ Å incidents on slits normally. The intensity of light only due to narrow slit on screen is I_0. If the intensity of light on screen at a point infront of the narrow slit is nI_0, fill n in the OMR sheet.

3 A parallel beam of light of all wavelengths greater than 3000 Å falls on a double slit in a Young's double slit experiment. It is observed that the wavelengths 3600 Å and 6000 Å are absent at a distance of 31.5 mm from the position of the central maximum, and the orders of the interference at this point for the two wavelengths differ by 7. If the distance between the slit and the screen is 1 m, find the separation (in μm) between the two slits.

4 In the ideal double slit experiment, when a glass plate (refractive index 1.5) of thickness t is introduced in the path of one of the interfering beams of wavelength 140 nm. the intensity at the position where the central maximum occurred previously remains unchanged. Find the minimum thickness (in nm) of the glass plate.

5 In a YDSE experiment, one of the slits is covered with a glass plate of thickness 2.4×10^{-4} m, refractive index of which varies with time as $\mu_s = t^2 + 12t + 8$. The separation between the slits is 2 mm and the distance between the plane of slits and the screen is 2 m. Find the velocity (in m/s) of the central maxima at $t = 4$ s. (Take refractive index of air = 1)

6 In the Young's experiment using monochromatic light, the fringe pattern shifts by a certain distance on the screen when a micasheet of $\mu = 1.6$ and thickness $t = 1.964$ micron is introduced in the path of one of the slits. The mica sheet is now removed and the distance between the slits and screen is doubled. It is found that the distance between successive maxima (or minima) is the same as the observed fringe shift upon the introduction of mica. Calculate λ (in Å).

7 Young's double slit experiment is conducted with white light (4000Å – 7000Å). As shown in the diagram, the slit separation $d = 0.5$ mm, and the screen slit distance, $D = 1$ m. The upper slit is covered with a film of thickness, $t = 1\ \mu$m having a refractive index, $\mu = 3/2$. Find the number of wavelengths which will form a maxima at $y = 3$ mm

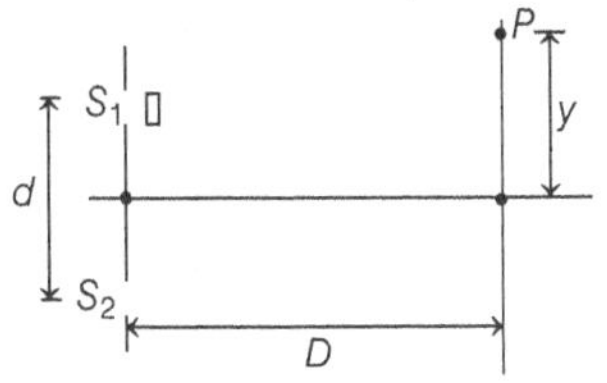

8 Find the minimum height (in μm) above the mirror where a maximum is formed on screen in the Lloyd's mirror arrangement shown.

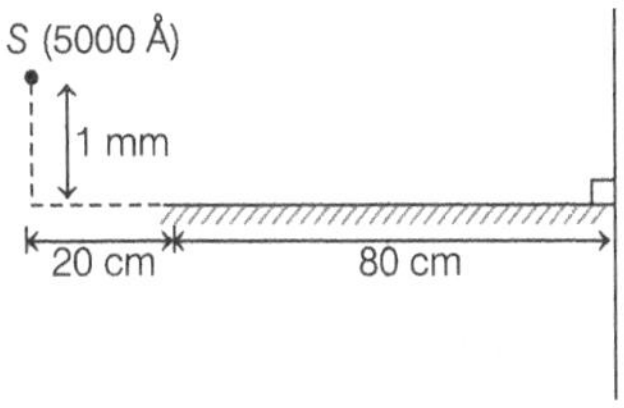

9 A certain crude oil has an index of refraction of 1.25. A ship dumps 1 m^3 of this oil into the ocean and oil spreads into a thin uniform film on water surface ($\mu = 4/3$). When light of wavelength 500 nm is incident on it, the reflected light shows maxima. What is the area (in km^2) covered by the spilled oil? Assume that the thickness of film is minimum required to satisfy this criterion.

10 A thin film of plastic ($n = 1.56$) is 0.25 μm thick. It is sandwiched between two glass slabs with refractive indice of 1.58 and 1.52, respectively. White light (400 – 700 nm) is first incident normally on the slab for which $n = 1.58$. Which visible wavelength (in nm) is missing in the reflected light?

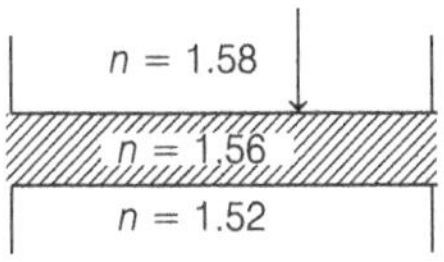

LEVEL 03 JEE Advanced Level

Single Choice Correct Questions

1 In a standard YDSE setup if the screen is kept titled as shown find the distance OA if first maximum is formed at A. Wavelength of light emitted by source is λ.

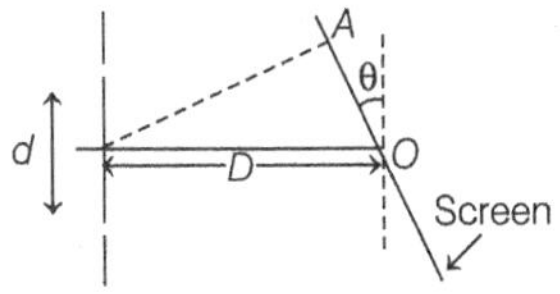

(a) $\dfrac{D\lambda\sec\theta}{d + \lambda\tan\theta}$ (b) $\dfrac{D\lambda\sec\theta}{d + \lambda\sin\theta}$

(c) $\dfrac{D\lambda\cos\theta}{d + \lambda\tan\theta}$ (d) $\dfrac{D\lambda\sec\theta\tan\theta}{d + \lambda\tan\theta}$

2 Figure shows two coherent sources S_1 and S_2 vibrating in same phase. AB is an irregular wire lying at a far distance from the sources S_1 and S_2. Let $\dfrac{\lambda}{d} = 10^{-3}$, $\angle BOA = 0.12°$. How many bright spots will be seen on the wire, including points A and B?

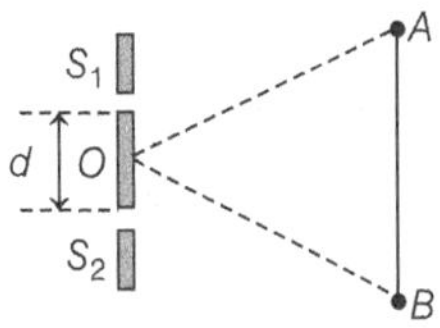

(a) 2 (b) 3

(c) 4 (d) More than 4

3 Two slits are separated by 0.3 mm. A beam of 500nm light strikes the slits producing an interference pattern. The number of maxima observed in the angular range $-30° < \theta < 30°$

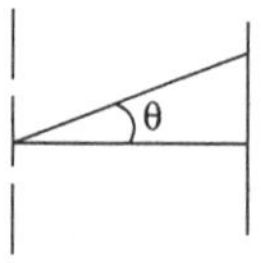

(a) 300 (b) 150 (c) 599 (d) 601

4 Two thin parallel slits are made in an opaque sheet of film when a monochromatic beam of light is shone throught them at normal incidence. The first bright fringes in the transmitted light occur at $\pm 45°$ with the original direction of the light beam on a distant screen when the apparatus is in air. When the apparatus is immersed in a liquid, the same bright fringes now occurs at $\pm 30°$. The index of refraction of the liquid is

(a) $\sqrt{2}$ (b) $\sqrt{3}$ (c) $4/3$ (d) $3/2$

5 Light of wavelenght 520 nm passing through a double slit, produces interference pattern of relative intensity *versus* deflection angle θ as shown in the figure. The separation d between the slits is

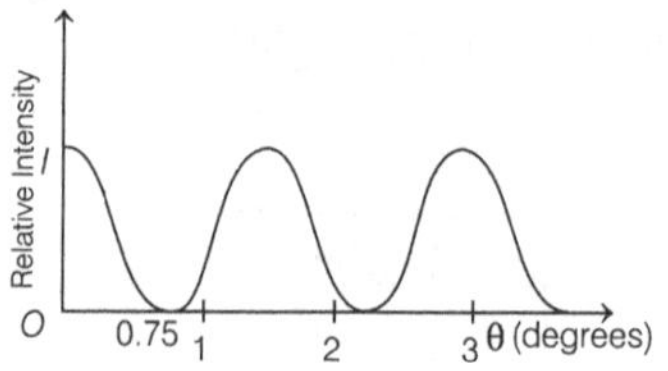

(a) 2×10^{-2} mm
(b) 5×10^{-2} mm
(c) 4.5×10^{-2} mm (d) 1.1×10^{-2} mm

6 In a Young's double slit experiment, $d = 1$ mm $\lambda = 6000$ Å and $D = 1$ m. The slits produce same intensity on the screen. The minimum distance between two points on the screen having 75% intensity of the maximum intensity is

(a) 0.45 mm (b) 0.40 mm (c) 0.30 mm (d) 0.20 mm

7 In a Young's double slit experiment, the intensity of the central maximum is I_0. The width of one slit is now doubled. The intensity at the point where the intensity was originally $0.5 I_0$ will now be

(a) $0.75 I_0$ (b) I_0
(c) $1.5 I_0$ (d) None of these

8 The maximum intensity in Young's double slit experiment is I_0. Distance between the slits is $d = 5\lambda$, where λ is the wavelength of monochromatic light used in the experiment. What will be the intensity of light in front of one of the slits on a screen at a distance $D = 10\,d$?

(a) $\frac{I_0}{2}$ (b) $\frac{3}{4} I_0$
(c) I_0 (d) $\frac{I_0}{4}$

9 Figure shows a wavefront P passing through two systems A and B, and emerging as Q and then as R. The systems A and B could, respectively be

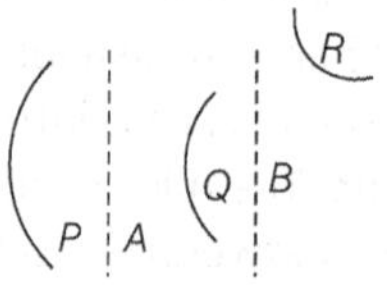

(a) A prism and a convergent lens
(b) A convergent lens and a prism
(c) A divergent lens and a prism
(d) A convergent lens and a divergent lens

10 Three coherent point sources S_1, S_2 and S_3 are placed on a line perpendicular to the screen as shown in the figure. The wavelength of the light emitted by the sources is λ. The distance between adjacent sources is $d = 3\lambda$. The distance of S_2 from the screen is D ($>> \lambda$). Find the minimum (non-zero) distance x of a point P on the screen at which complete darkness is obtained.

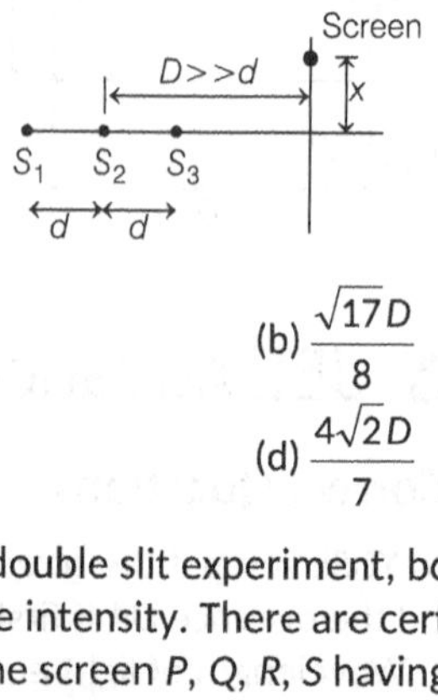

(a) $\frac{2\sqrt{2}D}{7}$ (b) $\frac{\sqrt{17}D}{8}$
(c) $4\sqrt{5}D$ (d) $\frac{4\sqrt{2}D}{7}$

11 In Young's double slit experiment, both slits are having same intensity. There are certain consecutive points on the screen P, Q, R, S having equal intensity (they are not maxima or minima), such that $PQ = QR = RS$. Then, choose the correct option (Let I_0 be the maximum intensity). Assume ($D >> d >> \lambda, D >> y$)

(a) Intensity at these points must be $\frac{I_0}{\sqrt{2}}$
(b) Intensity at these points must be $\frac{I_0}{2}$
(c) Intensity at these points is $3I_0/4$
(d) Intensity at these points may have any value

12 Four monochromatic and coherent sources of light, emitting waves in phase of wavelength λ, are placed at the points $\rightarrow x = 0, d, 2d$ and $3d$ on the X-axis. Then,

(a) points having $|x| >> d$ appear dark if $d = \lambda/4$

(b) points having $|x| >> d$ appear dark if $d = \lambda/8$

(c) points having $|x| >> d$ appear maximum bright if $d = \lambda/4$

(d) points having $|x| >> d$ appear maximum bright if $d = \lambda/8$

13 In the above question, the intensity of the waves reaching a point P far away on the $+X$-axis from each of the four sources is almost the same, and equal to I_0. Then,

(a) If $d = \lambda/4$, the intensity at P is $4I_0$

(b) If $d = \lambda/6$, the intensity at P is $3I_0$.

(c) If $d = \lambda/2$, the intensity at P is $3I_0$

(d) None of these is true

14 In the adjacent diagram, CP represents a wavefront and AO and BP, the corres- ponding two rays. Find the condition on θ for constructive interference at P between the ray BP and reflected rays OP

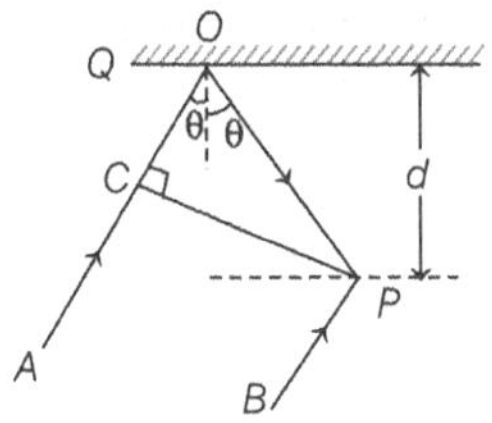

(a) $\cos\theta = \dfrac{3\lambda}{2d}$ (b) $\cos\theta = \dfrac{\lambda}{4d}$

(c) $\sec\theta - \cos\theta = \dfrac{\lambda}{d}$ (d) $\sec\theta - \cos\theta = \dfrac{4\lambda}{d}$

15 In standard YDSE slits were moved apart symmetrically with relative velocity v, calculate the rate at which fringes pass a point at a distance x from the centre of the fringe system formed on a screen at y distance away from the double slits if wavelength of light is λ and distance between the slits is b. Assuming, $y >> b$ and $b >> \lambda$

(a) $\dfrac{2xv}{\lambda y}$ (b) $\dfrac{xv}{2\lambda y}$ (c) $\dfrac{xv}{\lambda y}$ (d) Zero

16 At a point on the screen at a distance D from the slits in standard YDSE experiment, 3rd maxima is observed at $t = 0$. Now, screen is slowly moved with constant speed away from the slits in such a way that the centre of slits and centre of screen always lie on the same line and at $t = 1$ s the intensity at that point is observed to be 3/4th of maximum intensity in between 2nd and 3rd maxima.

The speed of screen is

(a) 5D/13 (b) 13D/5

(c) 17D/5 (d) 7D/17

17 In the given YDSE apparatus as shown in figure, wavelength of light used is λ. The initial distance between screen and plane of slits is D Point A is point on screen where 4th order maxima lies. Now, screen is moved from rest with constant acceleration a_0 towards right. Then, find the time after which second order maxima is formed at point A.

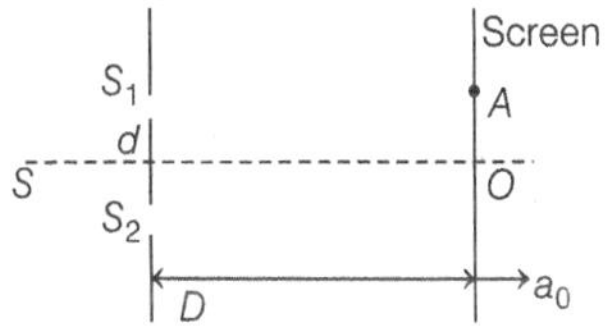

(a) $\sqrt{\dfrac{2D}{a_0}}$ (b) $\sqrt{\dfrac{D}{a_0}}$ (c) $2\sqrt{\dfrac{D}{a_0}}$ (d) $\sqrt{\dfrac{D}{2a_0}}$

18 Suppose a monochromatic coherent, parallel beam of light, of wavelength λ passes three parallel slits each separated by a distance d from its neighbour. The distance of a point on the screen from the centre point O at which a minima is formed ($L >> d$)

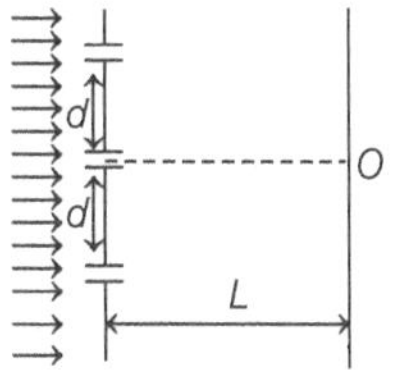

(a) $\dfrac{\lambda L}{3d}$ (b) $\dfrac{2\lambda L}{3d}$ (c) $\dfrac{4\lambda L}{3d}$ (d) $\dfrac{\lambda L}{d}$

19 The slits in a double slit interference experiment are illuminated by orange light ($\lambda = 600$ nm). A thin transparent plastic of thickness t is placed in front of one of the slits. The number of fringes shifting on screen is plotted *versus* the refractive index μ of the plastic in graph. The value of t is

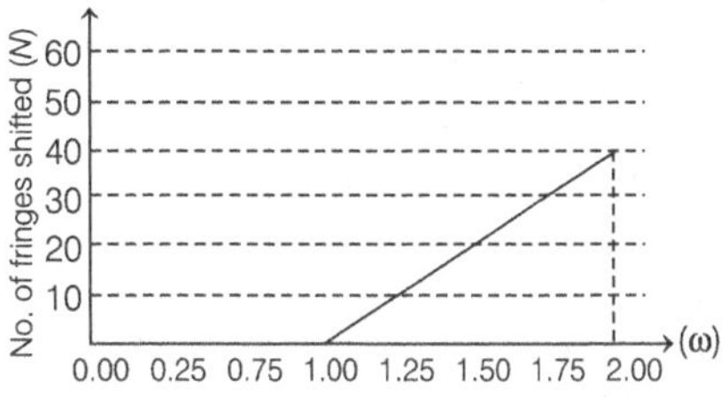

(a) 4.8 mm

(b) 640 μm

(c) 24 μm

(d) None of the above

20 The figure shows the Young's double slit experiment with a mica sheet of thickness t and refractive index μ, introduced in front of S_1. If the mica sheet is removed from earlier position and placed in front of S_2, find the number of fringes crossing O.

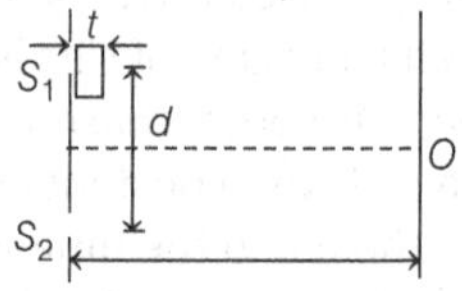

(a) $\frac{(\mu-1)t}{2\lambda}$ (b) $\frac{(\mu-1)t}{\lambda}$ (c) $\frac{2(\mu-1)t}{\lambda}$ (d) $\frac{4(\mu-1)t}{\lambda}$

21 Minimum thickness of a mica sheet having $\mu = 3/2$ which should be placed in front of one of the slits in YDSE is required to reduce the intensity at the centre of screen to half of maximum intensity is

(a) $\lambda/4$ (b) $\lambda/8$ (c) $\lambda/2$ (d) $\lambda/3$

22 In a YDSE experiment if a slab whose refractive index can be varied is placed in front of one of the slits, then the variation of resultant intensity at mid-point of screen with μ will be best represented by ($\mu \geq 1$). [Assume slits of equal width and there is no absorption by slab]

(a)

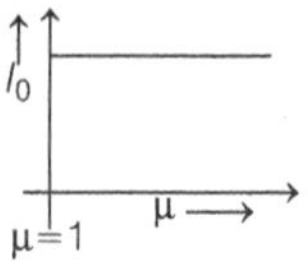

(b)

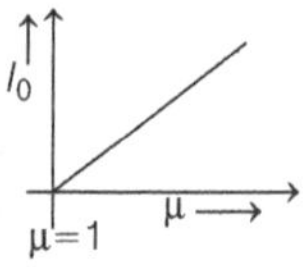

(c)

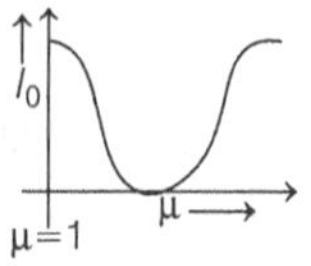

(d)

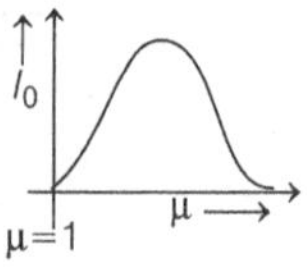

23 In a Young's double slit experiment, the slits are illuminated by a parallel beam of light from the medium of refractive index $n_1 = 1.2$. A thin transparent film of thickness 1.2 μm and refractive index $n = 1.5$ is placed infront of S_1 perpendicular to path of light.

Wavelength of light measured in medium n_1 is 400 nm. The refractive index of medium between plane of slits and screen is $n_2 = 1.4$. If the light coming from the film and S_2 have equal intensities I_0, then intensity at geometrical centre of the screen is

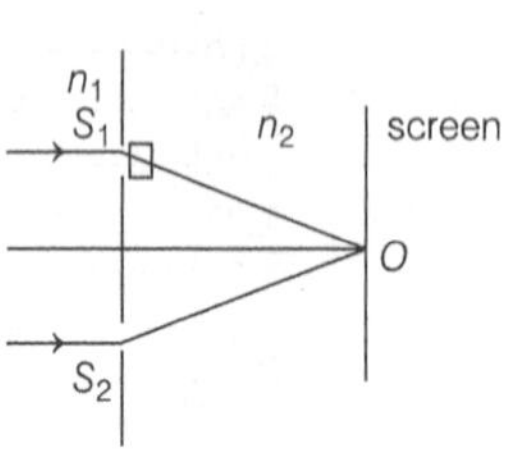

(a) 0 (b) $2I_0$
(c) $4I_0$ (d) None of these

24 As shown in arrangement, waves with identical wavelengths and amplitudes and that are initially in phase travel through different media, Ray 1 travels through air and Ray 2 through a transparent medium for equal length L, in four different situations. In each situation the two rays reach a common point on the screen. The number of wavelengths in length L is N_2 for Ray 2 and N_1 for Ray 1. In the following table, values of N_1 and N_2 are given for all four situations, The order of the situations according to the intensity of the light at the common point in descending order is

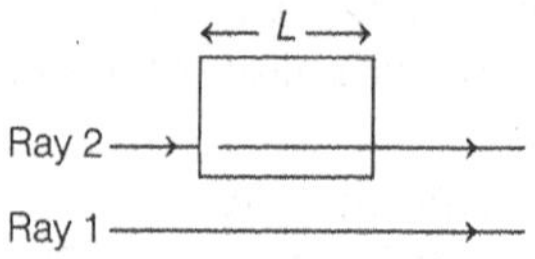

Situations	1	2	3	4
N_1	2.25	1.80	3.00	3.25
N_2	2.75	2.80	3.25	4.00

(a) $I_3 = I_4 > I_2 > I_1$ (b) $I_1 > I_3 = I_4 > I_2$
(c) $I_1 > I_2 > I_3 > I_4$ (d) $I_2 > I_3 = I_4 > I_1$

25 In a YDSE set up, a thin sheet is placed in front of one of the slits as shown.

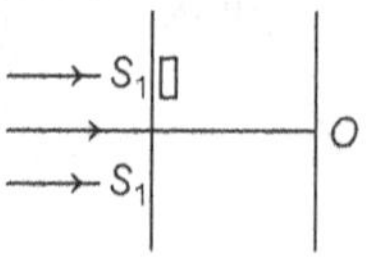

Refractive index of material of slit varies as $\mu = \mu_0\left(1+\frac{x}{l}\right)$ where $\mu_0 = 1$, x is distance from left edge of sheet and l is thickness of sheet. If wavelength of light used is 6000 Å, find minimum thickness of sheet for which point O, which is symmetrically located, records a maxima.

(a) 3000 Å (b) 6000 Å
(c) 9000 Å (d) 12000 Å

26 In a regular YDSE, when thin film of refractive index μ is placed in front of the upper slit, then it is observed that the intensity at the central point becomes half of the original intensity. It is also observed that the initial 3rd maxima is now below the central point and the initial 4th minima is above the central point. Now, a film of refractive index μ_1 and thickness same as the above film, is put in the front of the lower slit also. It is observed that whole fringe pattern shifts by one fringe width. What is the value of μ_1?

(a) $(4\mu+9)/12$ (b) $(4\mu+9)/13$
(c) $(4\mu+9)/11$ (d) None of these

27 In a standard YDSE, the region between screen and slits is immersed in a liquid whose refractive index varies with time as $\mu_1 = \frac{5}{2} - \frac{T}{4}$ until it reaches a steady state value of 5/4. A glass plate of thickness 36 μm and refractive index 3/2 is introduced in front of one of the slits. Find the velocity of central maximum when it is at the centre of the screen? (take $d = 2$ mm and $D = 1$ m)

(a) 2×10^{-3} ms^{-1} (b) 3×10^{-3} ms^{-1}
(c) 4×10^{-3} ms^{-1} (d) 5×10^{-3} ms^{-1}

28 In a Young's experiment, the upper slit is covered by a thin glass plate of refractive index 1.4, while the lower slit is covered by another glass plate, having the same thickness as the first one but having refractive index 1.7.

Interference pattern is observed using light of wavelength 5400 Å. It is found that the point P on the screen, where the central maximum ($n = 0$) fell before the glass plates were inserted, now has (3/4)th of the original intensity. It is further observed that what used to be the fifth maximum earlier lies below the point P while the sixth minima lies above P. Calculate the thickness of glass plate. (Absorption of light by glass plate may be neglected).

(a) 9.3 μm (b) 6.2 μm (c) 8.5 μm (d) 5.8 μm

29 Light of wavelength λ is incident normally on a plane having two slits separated by distance 2 mm. The interference is observed on a screen 6m away from slits. Space between plane and screen has a uniform refractive index 1.5. A thin vacuum film of thickness 0.2 μm is created in front of the slit S_1. What is the maximum wavelength (in vacuum) for which a maxima is observed at point P exactly in front of the slit S_1?

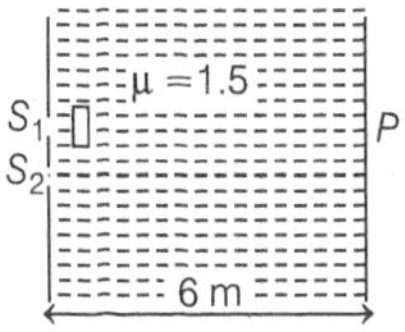

(a) 4000Å (b) 5500Å (c) 6000 Å (d) 6500 Å

30 A screen is at a distance $D = 80$ cm from a diaphragm having two narrow slits S_1 and S_2 which are $d = 2$ mm apart. Slit S_1 is covered by a transparent sheet of thinckness $t_1 = 2.5\,\mu$m and slit S_2 is covered by another sheet of thickness $t_2 = 1.25\,\mu$m as shown in figure. Both sheets are made of same material having refractive index $\mu = 1.4$. Water is filled in the space between the diaphragm and screen.

A monochromatic light beam of wavelenght $\lambda = 5000$ Å is incident normally on the diaphragm. Assuming intensity of beam to be uniform calculate ratio of intensity at C to the maximum intensity of interference pattern obtained on the screen ($\mu_w = 4/3$)

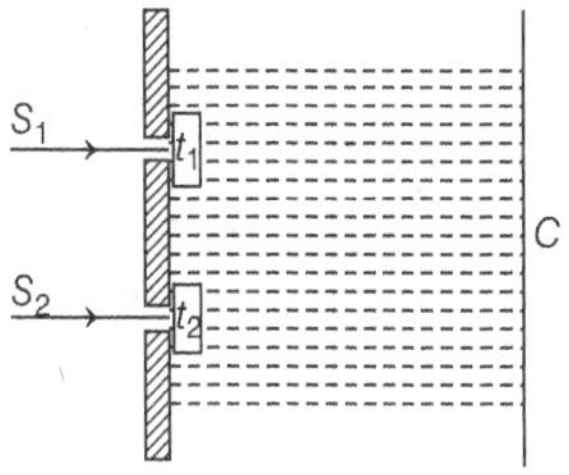

(a) 3/4 (b) 2/3 (c) 8/9 (d) 5/7

31 In a YDSE experiment, thin films of thickness t_1 and t_2 are placed infront of slits S_1 and S_2 as shown in figure 1 and figure 2. It is observed that first minima and second maxima are produced at point O in first and second experiment, respectively. Point O and S are symmetrical with respect to S_1 and S_2. Both the films have same refractive index. If $\frac{t_2}{t_1} = \frac{x}{25}$, then calculate x.

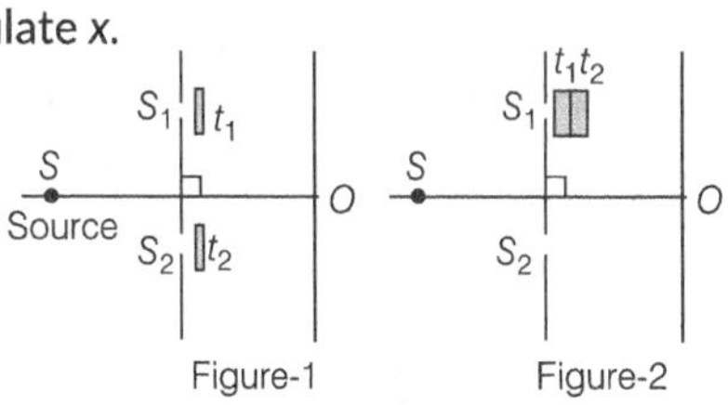

(a) 3 (b) 9 (c) 12 (d) 15

32 In Young's double slit experiment, distance between the slits is d and that between the slits and screen is D. Angle between principal axis of lens and perpendicular bisector of S_1 and S_2 is 45°. The point source S is placed at the focus of lens and aperture of lens is much larger than d. Assuming only the reflected light from plane mirror M is incident on slits, distance of central maxima from O will be

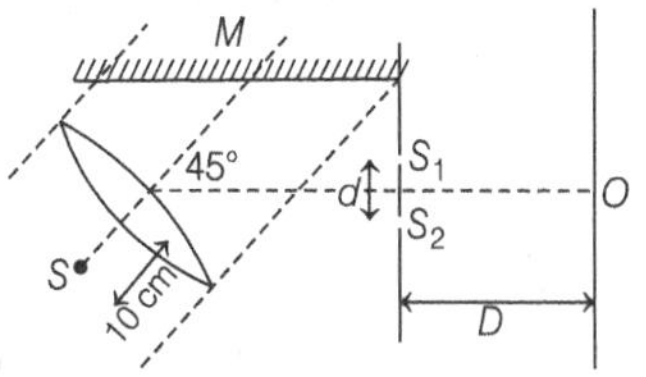

(a) D (b) $\frac{D}{\sqrt{3}}$

(c) $D\sqrt{3}$ (d) $\frac{D}{\sqrt{4}}$

33 In the given figure, S is a monochromatic point source emitting light of wavelength $\lambda = 500$ nm. A thin lens of circular shape and focal length 0.1 m is cut into two identical halves L_1 and L_2, by a plane passing through diameter. The two halves are symmetrically placed about the central axis SO with gap of 0.5 mm. The distance along the axis from S to L_1 and L_2 is 0.15 m, while that from L_1 and L_2 to O is 1.3 m. The screen at O is normal to SO. If the third maxima occurs at point A on the screen, then the distance OA is

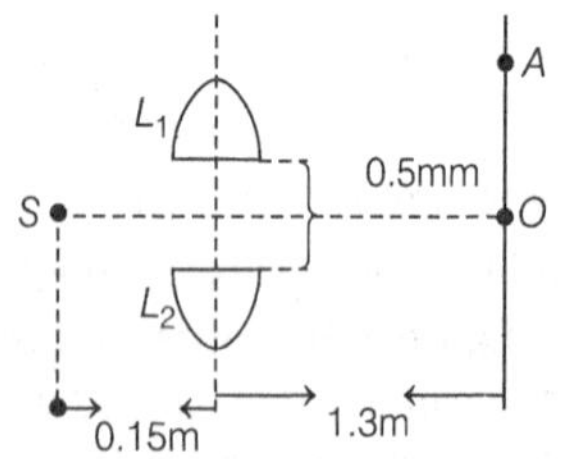

(a) 1 mm (b) 2 mm (c) 1.5mm (d) 2.5 mm

34 A monochromatic light source of wavelength λ is placed at S. Three slits S_1, S_2 and S_3 are equidistant from the source S and the point P on the screen. $S_1P - S_2P = \lambda/6$ and $S_1P - S_3P = 2\lambda/3$. If I be the intensity at P when only one slit is open, the intensity at P when all the three slits are open is

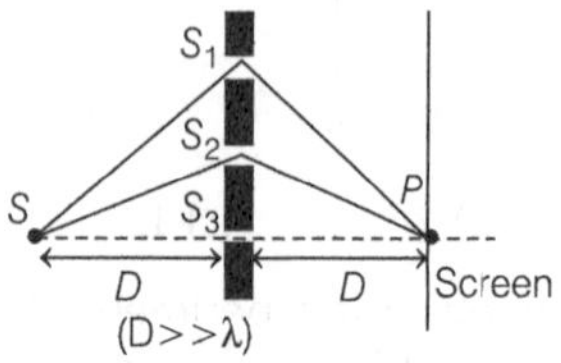

(a) $3I$ (b) $5I$ (c) $8I$ (d) Zero

35 ABC is a spherical wavefront centred at O symmetric about BE is incident on slits S_1 and S_2. $BS_1 = 3\lambda$, $S_1S_2 = 4\lambda$; $BO = 6\lambda$; $S_1E = 128\ \lambda$ and λ is the wavelength of incident light wave. A mica sheet of refractive index 1.5 is pasted on S_2. Find the minimum value of thickness of mica sheet for which central fringe forms at E

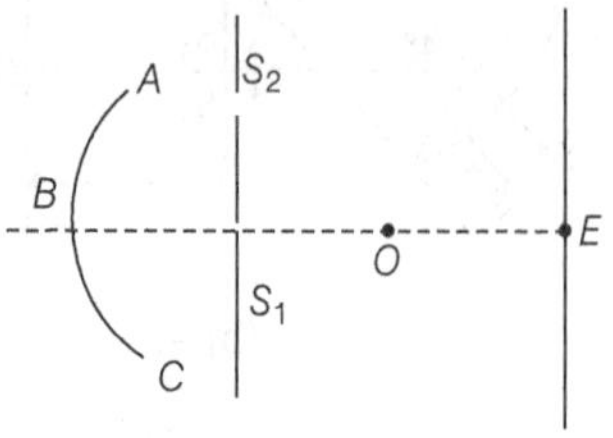

(a) $\frac{31\lambda}{8}$ (b) $\frac{15\lambda}{8}$ (c) $\frac{5\lambda}{8}$ (d) $\frac{7\lambda}{8}$

36 In a Llyod's mirror set up for interference of waves of frequency $6 \times 10^{14}\ s^{-1}$ emitted from point source S. Distance SO, OA and AC arc 1 mm, 50 cm, and 50 cm, respectively. Then, the number of dark and bright fringes obtained on the screen will be

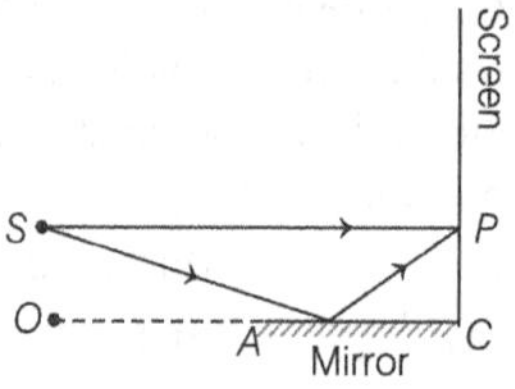

(a) Dark = 4, Bright = 4 (b) Dark = 4, Bright = 5
(c) Dark = 5, Bright = 4 (d) Dark = 5, Bright = 5

37 A glass plate of refractive index 1.5 is coated with a thin layer of thickness t and refractive index 1.8. Light of wavelength λ travelling in air is incident normally on the layer. It is partly reflected at the upper and lower surfaces of the layer and the two reflected rays interfere. If $\lambda = 648$ nm, then find the least value of t for which the rays interfere constructively

(a) 30 nm (b) 60 nm (c) 90 nm (d) 120 nm

38 Light of wavelength λ is incident normally on a thin film. The reflected light shows a minima for reflection. The thickness of film is minimum possible. Now, the same film is placed in front of upper slit of the YDSE apparatus. The fringe pattern shifts up by 7.5 mm. The refractive index of material is (Take $D = 5$ m, $d = 0.1$ mm, $\lambda = 500$ nm).

(a) 1.25 (b) 2.5 (c) 1.5 (d) 1.75

39 A ray of light of intensity I is incident on a parallel glass-slab at a point A as shown in fig. It undergoes partial reflection and refraction. At each reflection 25% of incident energy is reflected. The rays AB and $A'B'$ undergo interference. The ratio I_{max}/I_{min} is

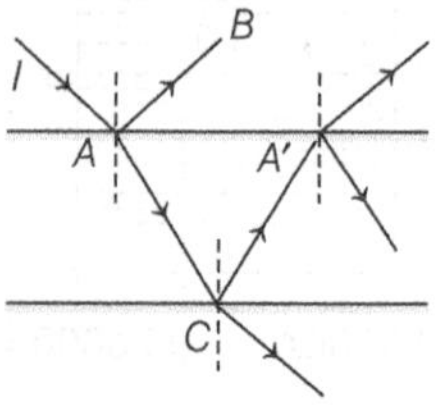

(a) 4 : 1 (b) 8 : 1 (c) 7 : 1 (d) 49 : 1

40 A plane wave of monochromatic light falls normally on a uniformly thin film of oil which covers a glass plate. The wavelength of source can be varied continuously. Complete constructive interference is observed for $\lambda_1 = 5000$ Å and $\lambda_2 = 10000$ Å and for no other wavelength in between.

If μ of oil is 1.25 and that of glass is 1.5, the thickness of film will be

(a) 0.2 μm (b) 0.4 μm
(c) 0.6 μm (d) 0.8 μm

Multiple Choice(s) Correct Questions

1 Mark the correct statemcnts(s) :

(a) Direction of wave propagation is along the normal to wavefront
(b) For a point source of light, the shape of wavefronts can be considered to be plane at very large distance from the source
(c) A point source of light is placed at the focus of a thin spherical lens, then the shape of the wavefront for emergent light can be plane
(d) If the shape of the wavefront for the light incident on a thin spherical lens is plane, then the shape of the wavefront corresponding to emergent light would be always spherical

2 To observe a stationary interference pattern formed by two light waves, it is NOT necessary that they must have

(a) the same frequency (b) the same amplitude
(c) a constant phase difference
(d) the same intensity

3 A Young's double slit experiment is performed with white light

(a) The maxima next to the central will be red
(b) The central maxima will be white
(c) The maxima next to the central will be violet
(d) There will not be a completely dark fringe

4 Consider the standard Young's double slit experiment setup. Let Δx represent the path difference between the waves reaching P. Mark the correct statement (s)

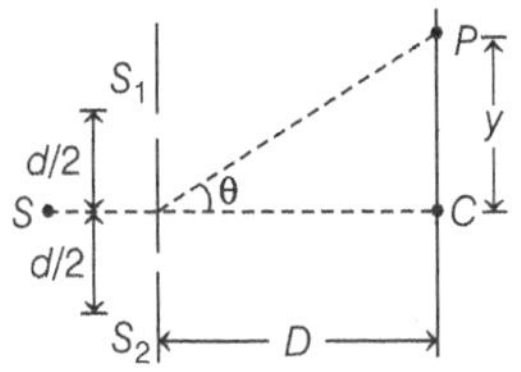

(a) Path difference $\Delta x = d \sin\theta$ is applicable only when $D >> d$
(b) Path difference $\Delta x = yd / D$ is applicable only when $D >> y$
(c) Almost equally spaced fringes near C only when $D>> y$
(d) Total number of minima on the screen is 6 when $d = 3\lambda$

5 White light is used to illuminate two slits in a YDSE. The separation between the slits is d and the screen is at a distance D ($D >> d$) from the slits. At a point on the screen directly in front of one of the slits, which of the following wavelengths are missing?

(a) $\frac{d^2}{D}$ (b) $\frac{2d^2}{D}$ (c) $\frac{d^2}{3D}$ (d) $\frac{2d^2}{3D}$

6 Coherent light consisting of two wavelengths $\lambda_1 = 4500$ Å and $\lambda_2 = 6000$ Å is sent through both slits of a Young's double slit apparatus

(a) Central maxima for both wavelengths will coincide
(b) The third order bright fringe of λ_1 will coincide with the fourth order bright fringe of λ_2,
(c) The third order bright fringe of λ_2 will coincide with fourth order bright fringe of λ_1
(d) The fringes of wavelength λ_1 will be wider than the fringes of wavelength λ_2

7 A thin paper of thickness 0.02 mm having refractive index 1.45 is pasted across one of the slit in a Young's double slit experiment. The paper transmits (4/9)th of light falling on it. ($\lambda_{light} = 600$ nm)

(a) Amplitude of light wave transmitted through the paper will be 2/3 times of incident wave.
(b) The ratio of maximum and minimum intensity in the fringe pattern will be 25.
(c) The total number of fringe crossing the centre if an identical paper is pasted on the other slit is 15.
(d) The ratio of maximum and minimum intensity in the fringe pattern will be 5.

8 In a YDSE with two identical slits, when the upper slit is covered with a thin, perfectly transparent sheet of mica, the intensity at the centre of the screen reduces to 75% of the initial value. Second minima is observed to be above this point and third maxima below it. Which of the following can not be a possible value of phase difference caused by the mica sheet?

(a) $\frac{\pi}{3}$ (b) $\frac{13\pi}{3}$ (c) $\frac{5\pi}{3}$ (d) $\frac{11\pi}{3}$

9 A parallel beam of light $\lambda = 5000$ Å is incident at an angle $\alpha = 30°$ with the normal to the slit plane in a Young's double slit experiment. Assume that the intensity due to each slit at any point on the screen is I_0. Point O is equidistant from S_1 and S_2. The distance between slits is 1 mm.

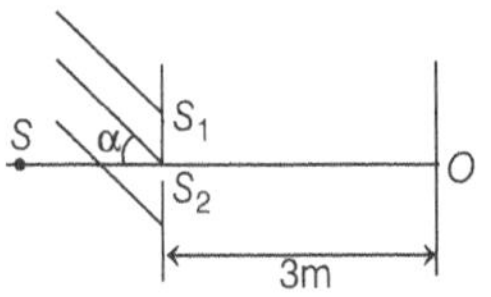

(a) the intensity at O is $4I_0$
(b) the intensity at O is zero
(c) the intensity at a point on the screen 4m below O is $4I_0$
(d) the intensity at a point on the screen 4m below O is zero

10 The minimum value of d, so that there is a dark fringe at O is d_{min}. For the value of d_{min} the distance at which the next bright fringe is formed is x. Then,

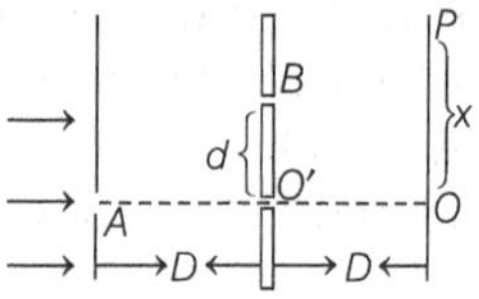

(a) $d_{min} = \sqrt{\lambda D}$ (b) $d_{min} = \sqrt{\frac{\lambda D}{2}}$

(c) $x = \frac{d_{min}}{2}$ (d) $x = d_{min}$

11 In an interfrcnce arrangement similar to Young's double slit experiment, the slits S_1 and S_2 are illuminated with coherent microwave sources, each of frequency 10^6 Hz. The sources are synchronized to have zero phase difference. The slits are separated by a distance $d = 150.0$ m and screen is at very large distance from slits. The intensity $I(\theta)$ is measured as a function of θ, where θ is defined as shown. If I_0 is the maximum intensity, then $I(\theta)$ for $0 \leq \theta \leq 90°$ is given by

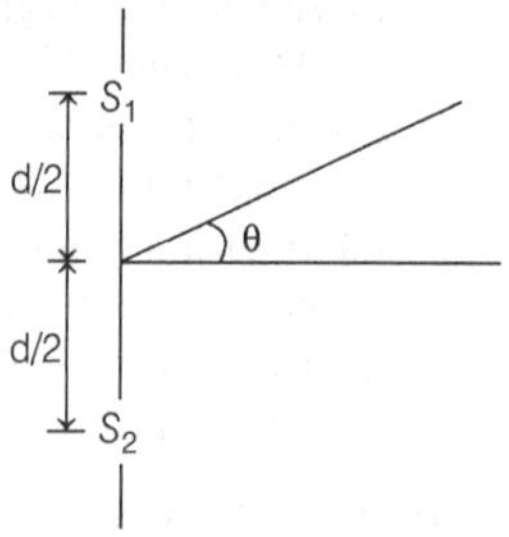

(a) $I(\theta) = \frac{I_0}{2}$ for $\theta = 30°$ (b) $I(\theta) = \frac{I_0}{4}$ for $\theta = 90°$

(c) $I(\theta) = I_0$ for $\theta = 0°$

(d) $I(\theta)$ is constant for all values of θ.

12 Space between slit and screen and sources and slits is filled with a liquid of refractive index μ_3. A plate of thickness t and refractive index μ_2 is placed in front of one of the slits. A source S is placed above OP at a distance d in front of slit.

(Given $D = 1$ m, $d = 2$ mm, $t = 6 \times 10^{-6}$ m, $\mu_2 = 1.2, \mu_3 = 1.8$)

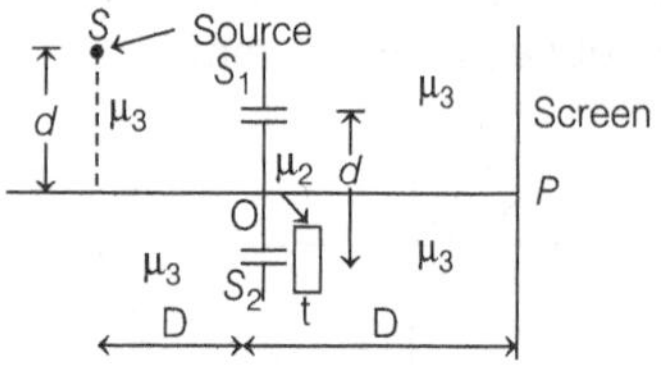

(a) position of central maxima from point P is 2 mm
(b) position of central maxima from point P is 1 mm
(c) If slab is removed, the central maxima shifts by a distance of 2 mm
(d) If slab is removed the central maxima shifts by a distance of 1 mm.

13 In Young's experiment, the upper slit is covered by a thin glass plate of refractive index 4/3 and of thickness 9λ, where λ is the wavelength of light used in the experiment. The lower slit is also covered by another glass plate of thickness 2λ and refractive index 3/2, as shown in figure.If I_0 is the intensity at point P due to slits S_1 and S_2 each, then

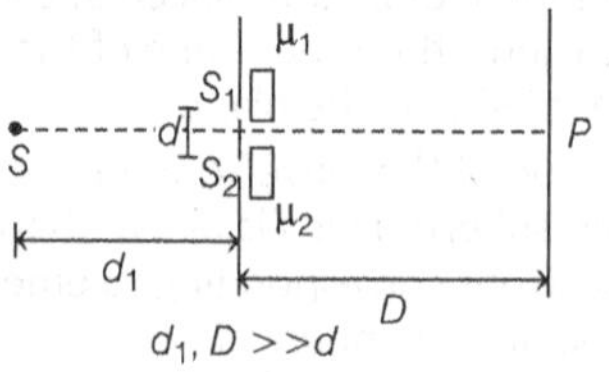

(a) Intensity at point P is $4I_0$
(b) Two fringes have been shifted in upward direction after insertion of both the glass plates together.
(c) Optical path difference between the waves from S_1 and S_2 at point P is 2λ.
(d) If the source S is shifted upwards by a small distance d_2, then the fringe originally at P after inserting the plates, shifts downward by $D\left(\frac{d_2}{d_1}\right)$

14 A narrow slit S transmitting light of wavelength λ is placed a distance d above a large plane mirror as shown in the figure. The light coming directly form the slit and that coming after reflection from the plane mirror interfere on a screen Σ placed at a distance D from the slit. Assume that the mirror is 100% reflecting.

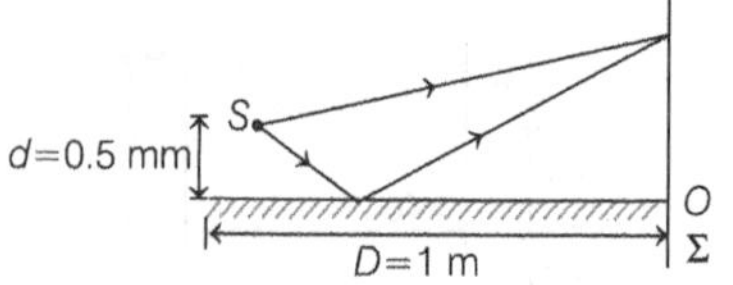

(Given $D = 1$ m, $d = 0.5$ mm and $\lambda = 500$ nm)

(a) Distance from O, where first interference maximum is formed on the screen is 1/4 mm.
(b) Distance from O, where closest interference minimum is formed on the screen is zero.
(c) Fringe width of the interference pattern formed on the screen is 1/2 mm.
(d) Closest point to O on the screen where waves interfere with a phase difference of $\pi/2$ is 1/8 mm.

15 A slab of transparent materials is made as shown in the figure. Monochromatic parallel beams of light are normally incident on the slabs. The thickness of *C* is twice the thickness of *B*. The number of waves in *A* = the number of waves in the combination of *B* and *C*. The refractive index of material *A* is $\mu_0 = 1.5$ and that of *C* is $\mu_2 = 1.4$

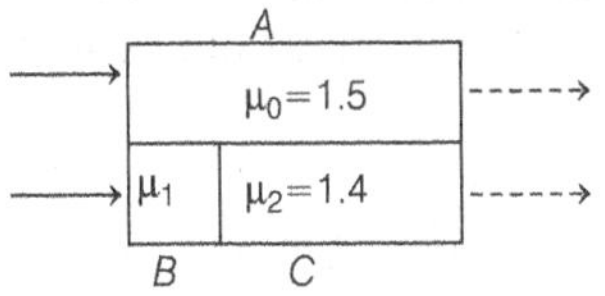

(a) The refractive index of *B* is 1.6
(b) The frequency of light in *B* is two times the frequency of light in *C*.
(c) The refractive index of *B* is 1.7
(d) The frequency of light in *B* is the same as the frequency of light in *C*.

16 For the biprism experiment shown in the figure, the fringe width increases when

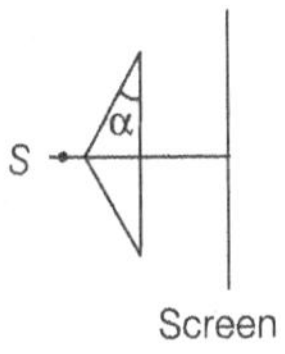

(a) biprism is moved towards the slit
(b) entire apparatus is submerged in a liquid having refractive index less than that of prism
(c) a biprism having smaller angle α is used
(d) the slit width is reduced

17 When monochromatic light is incident normally on a wedge-shaped thin air film, refer figure, an interference pattern may be seen by reflection. Which of the following is/are correct?

(a) Parallel fringes are observed
(b) If water is introduced into the region between the plates, the fringe separation decreases
(c) If the angle of the wedge is increased, the fringe separation decreases
(d) When white light is used there will not be a completely dark fringe

18 A thin film of magnesium fluoride ($n = 1.38$) is used to coat a camera lens ($n = 1.56$). Which of the following thickness of coating will not allow any strong reflection for the wavelength 552 nm?
(a) 1000 nm (b) 500 nm (c) 300 nm (d) 100 nm

19 Two point, monochromatic and coherent sources of light of wavelength λ each are placed as shown in figure. The initial phase difference between the sources is zero. ($D >> d$). Mark the correct statement(s)

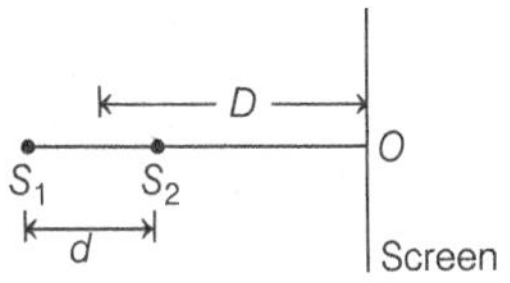

(a) If $d = 3.5\lambda$, *O* will be a minima
(b) If $d = \lambda$, only one maxima can be observed on the screen
(c) If $d = 4.8\lambda$, then total 10 minima would be there on the screen
(d) If $d = 2.5\lambda$, the intensity at *O* would be minimum

20 A thin slice is cut out of a glass cylinder along a plane parallel to its axis. The slice is placed on a flat glass plate as shown in figure. The observed interference fringes from this combination shall be

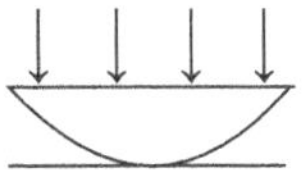

(a) straight (b) circular
(c) equally spaced
(d) having fringe spacing which increases as we go outwards

Comprehension Based Questions

Comprehension-1

A plane wave of monochromatic light of wavelength 6000Å is incident on the plane of two slits S_1 and S_2 at angle of incidence $\alpha = (1.8/\pi)°$. The widths of S_1 and S_2 are *w* and 2*w*, respectively. A thin transparent film of thickness 4μm and R.I. 3/2 is placed infront of S_1. It absorbs 50% light energy and transmits the remaining. The interference is observed on the screen. Point *O* is equidistant from S_1 and S_2. If the maximum intensity on the screen is *I*, then

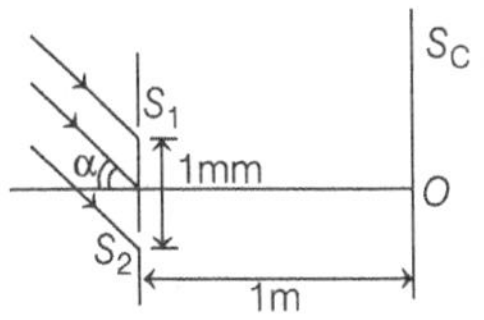

1 Intensity at O is
(a) I/2 (b) I/3 (c) I/4 (d) 3I/4

2 Distance of central maxima from O is
(a) 2 mm (b) 4 mm (c) 6 mm (d) 8 mm

3 Intensity at 4 mm from O upwards.
(a) I/3 (b) I/6 (c) I/9 (d) I

Comprehension-2

In the front of the upper slit of YDSE apparatus, a thin film of a liquid of refractive index 1.40 is placed. It is a hot day and the liquid starts evaporating from the surface. A beam of light at wavelength 560 nm is incident onto the YDSE apparatus and the intensity *I* at the centre of the screen is monitored.

Figure gives intensity I as a function of time t. The intensity changes because of evaporation from the two sides of the film. Assume that the film is flat and has parallel sides. Also assume that the film's thickness decreases at a constant rate.

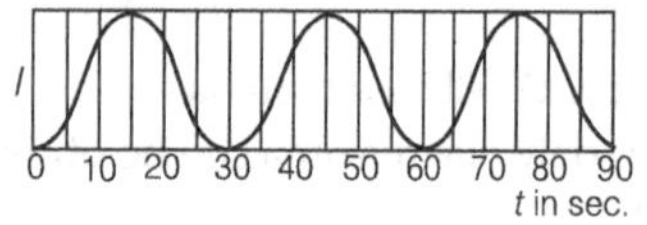

4 What can't be the initial thickness of the film ?

(a) 7 μm (b) 4.9 μm
(c) 7.7 μm (d) 9.1 μm

5 The rate of change of thickness can be

(a) $\frac{140}{3}$ nm/sec (b) 70 nm/sec
(c) $\frac{28}{3}$ nm/sec (d) $\frac{56}{3}$ nm/sec

6 If the maximum intensity is I_0, then

(a) Intensity at $t = 10$ s is $\frac{I_0}{\sqrt{2}}$
(b) Intensity at $t = 10$ s is $\frac{3I_0}{4}$
(c) Intensity at $t = 5$ s is $\frac{I_0}{2}$
(d) Intensity at $t = 5$ s is $\frac{I_0}{2\sqrt{2}}$

Comprehension-3

In a Young's double-slit experiment, a point source is placed on a solid slab of refractive index 6/5 at a distance of 2 mm from two slits placed 3 mm apart as shown and at equal distance from both slits. The screen is at a distance of 1 m from the slits. Wavelength of light used is 500 nm.

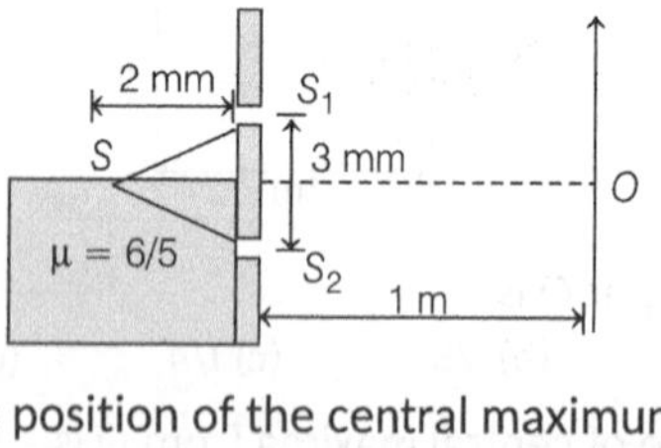

7 Find the position of the central maximum.

(a) 1/3 m above O (b) 1/3 m below O
(a) 1/6 m above O (d) 1/6 m below O

8 Find the order of fringe formed at O,

(a) 750 (b) 1000
(c) 1500 (d) 2000

9 A film of refractive index 1.8 is to be placed in front of S_1, so that central maxima is formed where 200th maxima was formed. Find the thickness of film.

(a) 125 μm (b) 250 μm
(c) 400 μm (d) 500 μm

Comprehension-4

In YDSE arrangement shown in figure, fringes are seen on screen using monochromatic source S having wavelength 3000Å (in air). S_1 and S_2 are two slits separated by $d = 1$ mm and $D = 1$ m. Left of slits S_1 and S_2, medium of refractive index $\mu_1 = 2$ is present and to the right of slits S_1 and S_2 medium of refractive index $\mu_2 = 3/2$ is present. A thin slab of thickness t is placed in front of S_1. The refractive index of slab μ_3 varies with distance from its starting face as shown in figure.

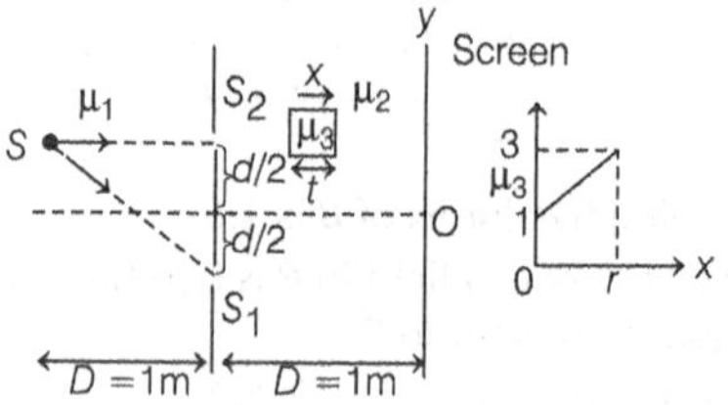

10 In order to get central maxima at the centre of the screen, the thickness of slab required is

(a) 1 μm (b) 2 μm (c) 0.5 μm (d) 1.5 μm

11 If the thickness of the slab is selected 1 μm, then the position of the central maxima will be (y-coordinate)

(a) $\frac{1}{3}$ mm (b) $-\frac{1}{3}$ mm (c) $\frac{1}{6}$ mm (d) $-\frac{1}{6}$ mm

12 Fringe width on the screen is

(a) 0.4 mm (b) 0.1 mm (c) 0.2 mm (d) 0.3 mm

Comprehension-5

In the figure, light of wavelength $\lambda = 5000$ Å is incident on the slits (in a horizontally fixed place). Here, $d = 1$ mm and $D = 1$ m. Take origin O and XY-plane as shown in figure. The screen is released from rest from the initial position as shown.

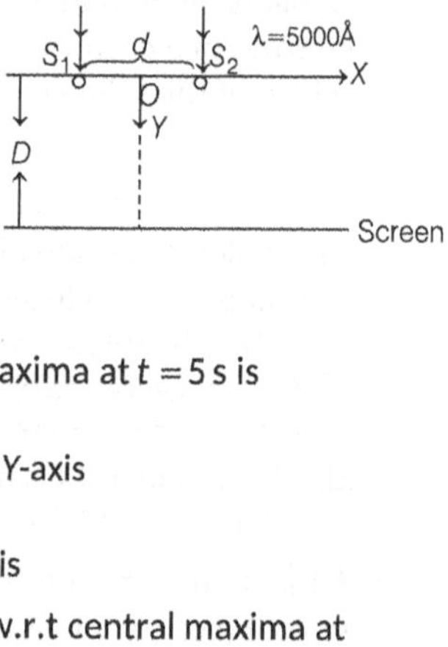

($g = 10$ ms^{-2})

13 The velocity of central maxima at $t = 5$ s is

(a) 50 m/s along Y-axis
(b) 50 m/s along negative Y-axis
(c) 25 m/s along Y-axis
(d) 3×10^8 m/s along Y-axis

14 Velocity of 2nd maxima w.r.t central maxima at $t = 2$ s is

(a) $8(\text{cms}^{-1})\hat{i} + 20(\text{ms}^{-1})\hat{j}$ (b) $8(\text{cms}^{-1})\hat{i}$
(c) $2(\text{cms}^{-1})\hat{i}$ (d) $86(\text{ms}^{-1})\hat{i}$

15 Acceleration of 3rd maxima w.r.t. 3rd maxima on the other side of central maxima at $t = 3$ s is

(a) 0.02 ms^{-2} $\hat{i}$ (b) 0.03ms^{-2} $\hat{i}$
(c) 10 ms$^{-2}\hat{i}$ (d) 0.6 ms$^{-2}\hat{i}$

Comprehension-6

In a YDSE experiment, the two slits are covered with transparent membranes of negligible thickness which allow light to pass through it but does not allow water. A glass slab of thickness $t = 0.41$ mm and refractive index $\mu_g = 1.5$ is placed in front of one of the slits as shown in figure. The separation between the slits $d = 0.30$ mm. The entire space to the left of the slits is filled with water of refractive index $\mu_w = 4/3$. A coherent light of intensity I and absolute wavelength $\lambda = 5000$Å is being incident on the slits making an angle of 30° with horizontal. Screen is placed at a distance $D = 1$ m from the slits.

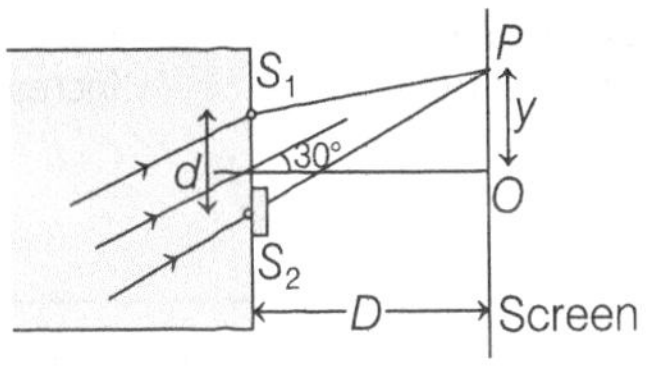

16 At point O, equidistant from slits we get
(a) 10th bright fringe (b) 11th bright fringe
(c) 9th dark fringe (d) 10th dark fringe

17 Location of central maxima is for $y =$
(a) $+\frac{5}{3}$ cm (b) $-\frac{5}{3}$ cm
(c) $+\frac{5}{6}$ cm (d) $-\frac{5}{6}$ cm

18 Ratio of intensity at $P(y = 1/8$ cm) and maximum intensity is
(a) 1 (b) $1/\sqrt{2}$ (c) 1/2 (d) 0

Comprehension 7

In YDSE set up (see fig.), the light source executes SHM between P and Q according to the equation $x = A\sin\omega t$, S being the mean position. Assume $d \to 0$ and $A << L$. ω is small enough to neglect Doppler effect. If the source were stationary at S, intensity at O would be I_0.

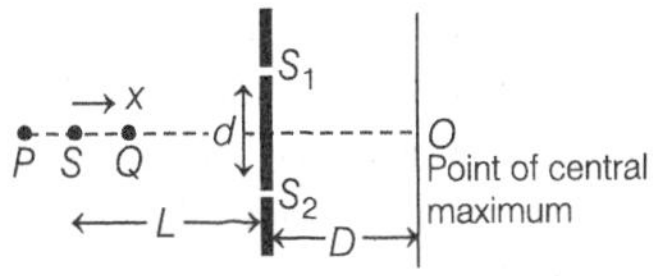

Read the paragraph carefully and answer the following questions.

19 The fractional change in intensity of the central maximum as function of time is
(a) $\frac{A\sin\omega t}{L}$ (b) $\frac{2A\sin\omega t}{L}$
(c) $\frac{3A\sin\omega t}{L}$ (d) $\frac{4A\sin\omega t}{L}$

20 When the source comes towards the point Q,
(a) The bright fringes will be less bright.
(b) The dark fringes will no longer remain dark.
(c) The fringe width will increase.
(d) None of the above

21 The fringe width β can be expressed as
(a) $\beta = \beta_0 \sin\omega t$ (b) $\beta = \beta_0 \cos\omega t$
(c) $\beta = \beta_0 \sin 2\omega t$ (d) None of these

Comprehension-8

In the arrangement shown in figure, slits S_3 and S_4 are having a variable separation Z. Point O on the screen is at the common perpendicular bisector of S_1S_2 and S_3S_4. (Assume $D >>> d$).

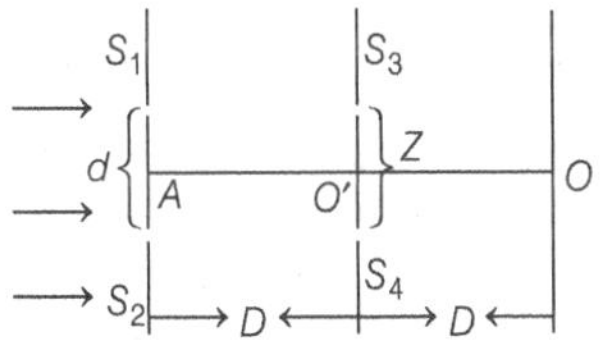

22 When $Z = \frac{\lambda D}{2d}$ the intensity meausred at O is I_0. The intensity at O when $Z = \frac{2\lambda D}{d}$ is
(a) I_0 (b) $2I_0$ (c) $3I_0$ (d) $4I_0$

23 The minimum value of Z for which the intensity at O is zero is
(a) $\frac{3\lambda D}{2d}$ (b) $\frac{\lambda D}{2d}$ (c) $\frac{\lambda D}{3d}$ (d) $\frac{\lambda D}{d}$

24 If a hole is made at O' on AO'O and the slit S_4 is closed, then the ratio of the maximum to the minimum observed on screen at O if $O'S_3$ is equal to $\frac{\lambda D}{4d}$ is
(a) 1 (b) Infinity (c) 34 (d) 4

Comprehension-9

In the figure shown, S is a point monochromatic light source of frequency 6×10^{14} Hz. M is a concave mirror of radius of curvature 20cm and L is a thin converging lens of focal length 3.75 cm. AB is the principal axis of M and L.

Light reflected from the mirror and refracted from the lens in succession reaches the screen. An interference pattern is obtained on the screen by this arrangement.

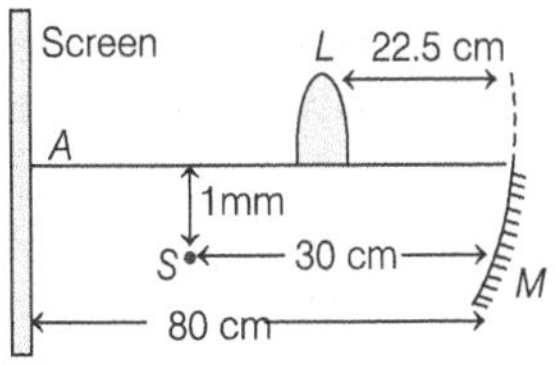

25 Distance between two coherent sources which make interference pattern on the screen is

(a) 1 mm (b) 0.5 mm (c) 1.5 mm (d) 0.25 mm

26 Fringe width is

(a) 1mm (b) 0.5 mm (c) 1.5 mm (d) 0.25 mm

27 If the lens is replaced by another converging lens of focal length 10/3 cm and the lens is shifted towards right by 2.5 cm, then

(a) Fringe width remains same
(b) Intensity of pattern will remain same
(c) Fringe width will change
(d) No interference pattern will form

Match The Columns Questions

1 In a standard Young's Double Slit Experiment, light of wavelength $\lambda = 6000Å$ is used, screen distance $D = 1$ m and slit separation $d = 0.5$ mm. Intensity of light on screen emerging from slits are individually I_0 and $4I_0$ Column I indicates distance of certain point P on screen from central maxima.

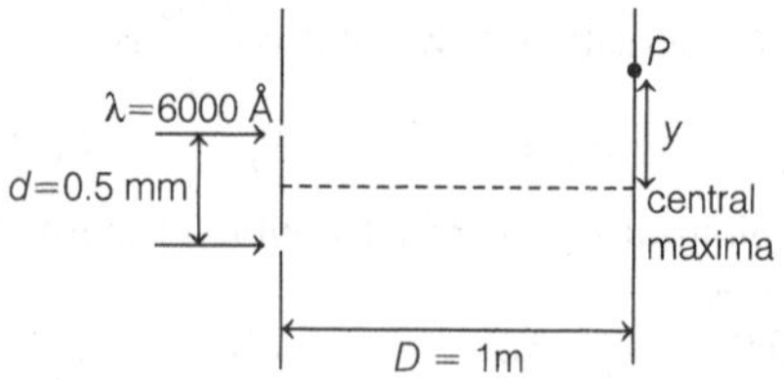

Column I	Column II
A. $y = 2$ mm	1. Inensity $= 7I_0$ at P
B. $y = 2.2$ mm	2. Intensity $= 3I_0$ at$P$
C. $y = 2.6$ mm	3. P lies between 2nd minima and 3rd maxima
D. $y = 2.8$ mm	4. P lies between 3rd minima and 2nd maxima

2 In a typical Young's double slit experiment, S_1 and S_2 are identical slits and equidistant from a point monochromatic source S of light having wavelength λ. The distance between slits is represented by d and that between slits and screen is represented by D. P is a fixed point on the screen at a distance $y = \frac{\lambda D_0}{2d_0}$ from central order bright on the screen where D_0, d_0 are initial values of D and d, respectively. In each statement of column I some changes are made to above mentioned situation. The distance between the slits and the source is very large.

The effect of corresponding changes is given in column II. Match the statements in column I with resulting changes in column II.

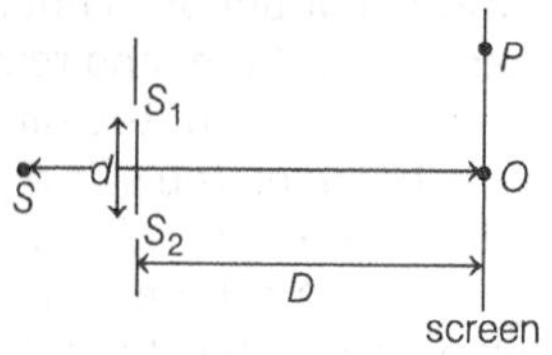

Column I	Column II
A. The distance d between the slits is doubled keeping distance between slits and screen fixed	1. fringe width increases
B. The distance D between slit and screen is doubled by shifting screen to right	2. Magnitude of optical path difference between interfering waves at P will decrease
C. The width of slit S_1, is decreased (such that intensity of light due to slit S_1 on screen decreases) and the distance D between slit and screen is doubled by shifting screen to right	3. Magnitude of optical path difference between interfering waves at P will increase.
D. The whole setup is submerged in water of refractive index 4/3. (neglecting absorption in medium)	4. The intensity at P will increase

3 A parallel beam of visible light consisting of wavelengths λ_1 and λ_2 is incident on a standard YDSE apparatus with $d = 1$ mm, $D = 1$ m. P is a point on the screen at a distance y from center of screen O, $y = y_1$ is the nearest point above O where the two maxima coincide. $y = y_2$ is the nearest point above O where the two minima coincide. β_1 and β_2 are fringe width corresponding to wave length λ_1 and λ_2.

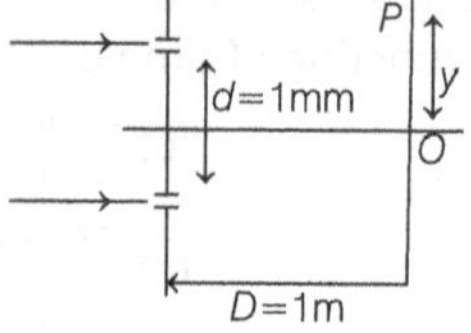

Column I	Column II
A. $\beta_1 = 0.3$ mm, $\beta_2 = 0.5$ mm	1. The 2nd nearest point above O where two maxima coincide is $y = 2y_1$
B. $\beta_1 = 0.3$ mm, $\beta_2 = 0.4$ mm	2. y_2 has no finite value
C. $\beta_1 = 0.2$ mm, $\beta_2 = 0.4$ mm	3. The 2nd nearest point above O where the two minima coincide is $y = 3y_2$
D. $\beta_1 = 0.2$ mm, $\beta_2 = 0.6$ mm	4. y_1 = LCM of β_1 and β_2
	5. The 2nd nearest point above O where two minima coincide is $y = 2y_2$

4 A monochromatic parallel beam of light of wavelength λ is incident normally on the plane containing slits S_1 and S_2.The slits are of unequal width such that intensity only due to one slit on screen is four times that only due to the other slit. The screen is placed perpendicular to X-axis as shown. The distance between slits is d and that between screen and slit is D. Match the statements in column I with results in column II. ($S_1S_2 << D$ and $\lambda << S_1S_2$)

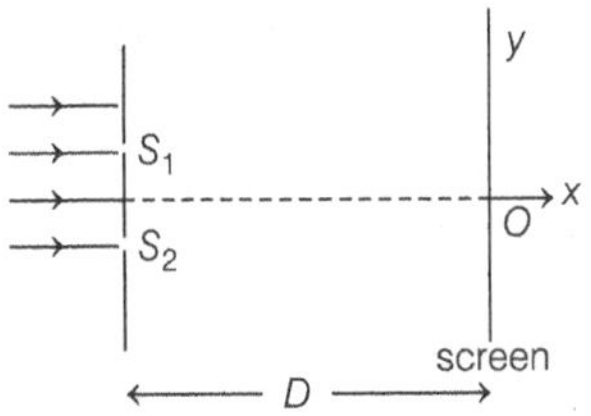

Column I	Column II
A. The distance between two points on screen having equal intensities, such that intensity at those points is (1/9)th of maximum intensity.	1. $\dfrac{D\lambda}{3d}$
B. The distance between two points on screen having equal intensities, such that intensity at those points is (3/9)th of maximum intensity.	2. $\dfrac{D\lambda}{d}$
C. The distance between two points on screen having equal intensities, such that intensity at those points is (5/9)th of maximum intensity.	3. $\dfrac{2D\lambda}{d}$
D. The distance between two points on screen having equal intensities, such that intensity at those points is (7/9)th of maximum intensity.	4. $\dfrac{3D\lambda}{d}$

5 In Young's double slit experiment, the point source S is placed slightly of the central axis as shown in figure. If $\lambda = 500$ nm, then match the following

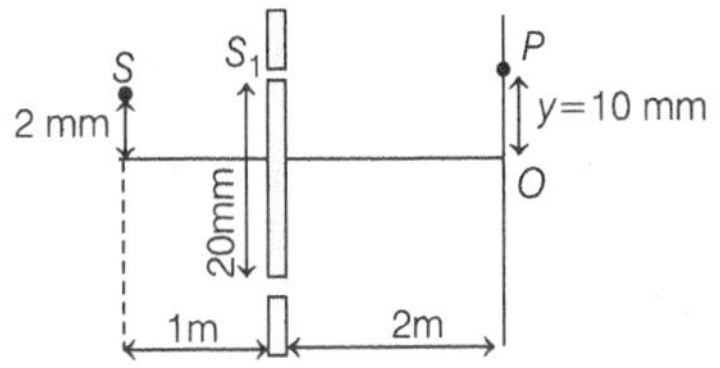

Column I	Column II
A. Nature and order of interference at the point P, $OP = 10$ mm	1. Bright fringe of order 80
B. Nature and order of interference at point O	2. Bright fringe of order 262
C. If a transparent paper (refractive index $\mu = 1.45$) of thickness $t = 0.02$ mm is pasted on S_1, *i.e.*, one of the slits, the nature and order of the interference at P	3. Bright fringe of order 62
D. After inserting the transparent paper in front of slit S_1,the nature and order of interference at O	4. Bright fringe of order 280

6 In a YDSE setup, light of wavelength 4000 Å is used. Distance of screen from the slits is 2 m and distance between slils is 1 mm. There are three slabs, slab 1 (thickness 2mm, $\mu = 2$) slab 2 (thickness 1mm, $\mu = 3$), slab 3 (thickness 4 mm $\mu = 3/2$)

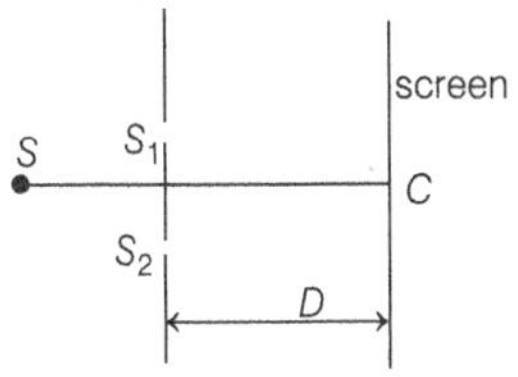

Column I	Column II
A. If slab 1 is placed in front of slit S_1 .	1. Central maxima at C
B. If slab 2 is placed in front of slit S_2 along with condition (A)	2. Central maxima above C
C. If slab 3 is placed in front of slab 1 along with condition (B)	3. Fringe width $= 0.8$ mm
	4. Number of fringes crossing central maxima as a result of slab placing is 5000.

Numerical Value Questions

1 In a modified YDSE the source S of wavelength 5000Å oscillates about axis of setup according to the equation, $y = 0.5\sin\left(\frac{\pi}{6}\right)t$, where y is in millimeter and t in second. At what time t will the intensity at P, a point exactly in front of slit S_1, be maximum for the first time?

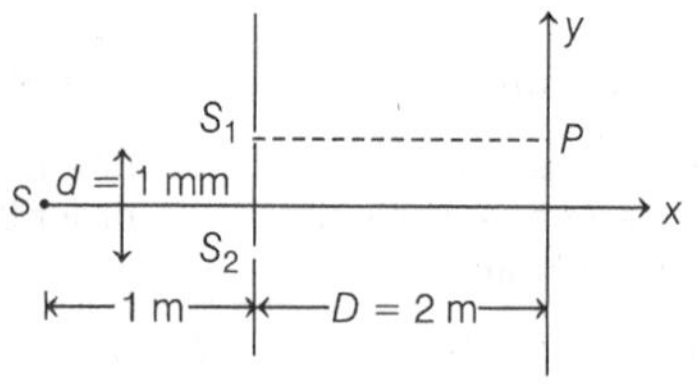

2 In a typical Young's double slit experiment a point source of monochromatic light is kept as shown in the figure. If the source is given an instantaneous velocity $v = 1$ mm per second towards the screen, then the instantaneous velocity of central maxima is given as $\alpha \times 10^{-\beta}$ cm/s in scientific notation. Find the value of $\alpha + \beta$.

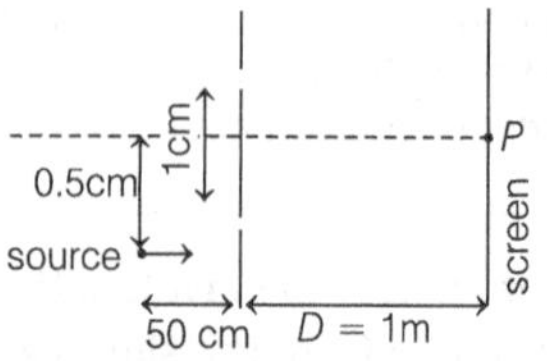

3 Figure shows two coherent microwave source S_1 and S_2 emitting waves of wavelength λ and separated by a distance 3λ. For $\lambda << D$ and $y \neq 0$, the minimum value of y for point P to be an intensity maximum is $\frac{\sqrt{mD}}{n}$. Determine the value of $m + n$, if m and n are coprime numbers.

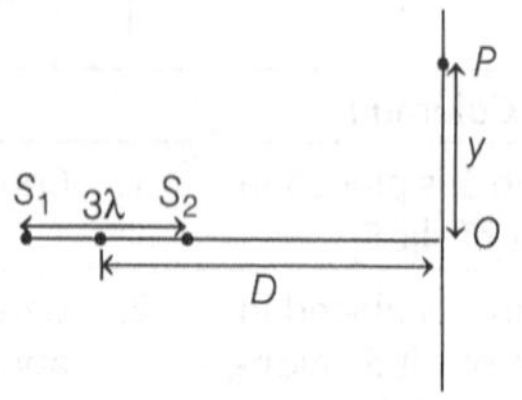

4 Three slabs A, B and C are placed in front of slits in YDSE as shown in figure. Refractive index of slabs A, B and C are 4/3, 5/3 and 8/3, respectively and thickness of A, B and C are 2 mm, 1 mm and 1.5 mm, respectively. A liquid of refractive index $2\mu/3$ is filled between slits and screen. A monochromatic light of wavelength 5000 Å is incident on the slits. If the central bright fringe is obtained at C, then find the value of μ

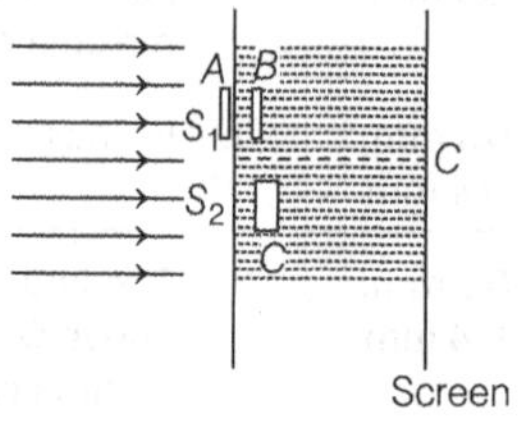

5 The YDSE apparatus is modified by placing an isotropic transparent plate of high melting point in front of one of the slits. The refractive index of the plate is $\mu_r = 1.5$ at room temperature and its thickness is $t = 2\ \mu$m. The refractive index of plate will increase when temperature increases and temperature coefficient of refractive index of the plate (i.e. the fractional change in refractive index per unit rise in temperature) is 3×10^{-3}/°C. The incident light is having wavelength $\lambda = 6000$Å. The separation between the slits is $d = 0.2$ cm, and separation between the slit and the screen is 2 m. If the plate is heated so that its temperature rises by 100°C, then how many fringes will cross a particular point? Give your answer in integer only. Neglect the thermal expansion of plate.

6 Two identical monochromatic light sources A and B intensity 10^{-15} W/m^2 produce wavelength of light $4000\sqrt{3}$Å. A glass of thickness 3mm is placed in the path of the ray as shown in fig. The glass has a variable refractive index $n = 1 + \sqrt{x}$ where x (in mm) is distance of plate from left to right. If total intensity at focal point F of the lens is $n \times 10^{-15}$ W, then find n.

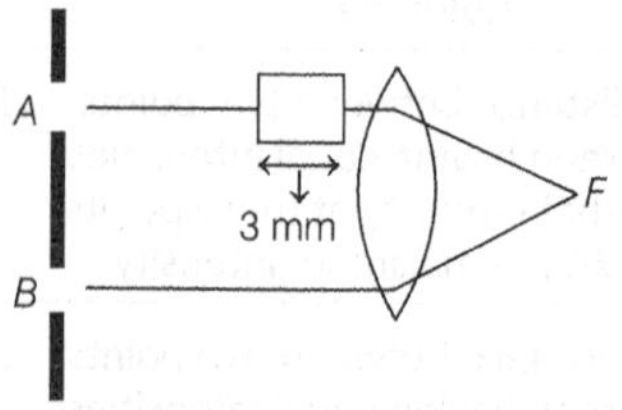

7 In Young's double slits experiment parallel monochromatic electromagnetic waves of wavelength 3×10^{-5}m fall on the slits at an angle of 30° with the normal to the plane of slits as shown in figure. A transparent sheet of thickness 5×10^{-5}m and refractive index 1.5 is introduced near the slits S_1.

The distance between the two slits is 0.5 mm and the distance between the plane of slits and the screen is

1 m. Find the y-coordinate (in cm) of the closest maxima to the origin on the positive Y-axis.

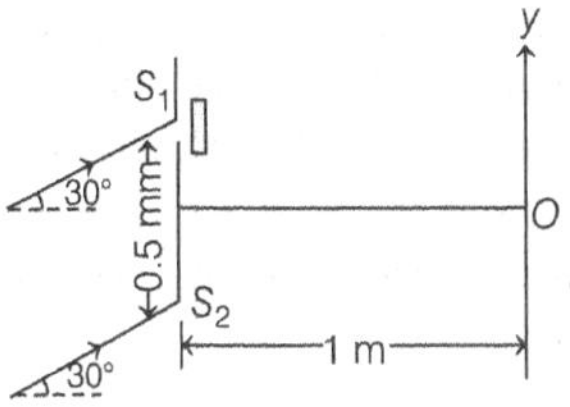

8 In Young's double slit experiment set-up with light of wavelength $\lambda = 6000Å$, distance between the two slits is 2 mm and distance between the plane of slits and the screen is 2 m. The slits are of equal width. When a sheet of glass of refractive index 1.5 (which permits only a fraction η of the incident light to pass through) and thickness 8000Å is placed in front of the lower slit, it is observed that the intensity at a point P, 0.15 mm above the initial central maxima does not change. If the value of η is $\frac{5-\sqrt{\beta}}{2}$, then find β.

9 Two coherent sources S_1 and S_2 separated by distance 2λ emit light of wavelength λ in phase as shown in figure. A circular wire of radius 100λ is placed in such a way that S_1S_2 lies in its plane and the mid-point of S_1S_2 is at the centre of wire. The angular positions θ on the wire for which intensity reduces to half of its maximum value for the first time is given as θ. Find the value of 32 $\cos\theta$

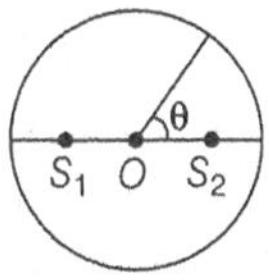

10 Light from a monochromatic point source S falls on the opaque wall having two slits. Intensity of interference pattern is observed at a point P on the screen. The light source S and point P are at same distance $L = 1$ m from the wall. By slowly moving only the upper slit and thereby increasing the distance d between the slits, from $200\sqrt{15}$ μm to $400\sqrt{5}$μm, the intensity at point P gradually changes from maxima to 25 % of maxima. The wavelength of light used is $\alpha \times 10^3$Å Find the value of α.

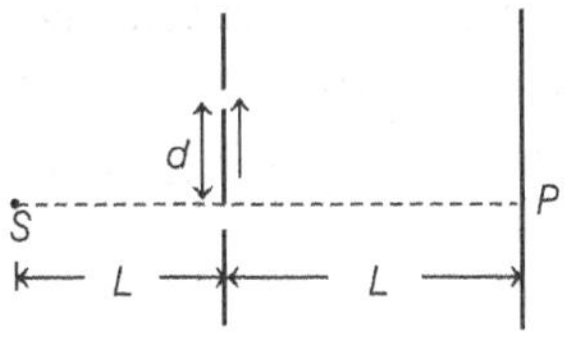

11 A very fine hair-like fiber is stuck between two microscope slides. As a result of this, there is a wedge of air between them. When the slides are illuminated normally (from above) with light of wavelength 550 nm, bright and dark interference bands are formed. The fiber is seen to lie at the position of fifth dark band counting from the common edge. What is the diameter (in nm) of the fiber?

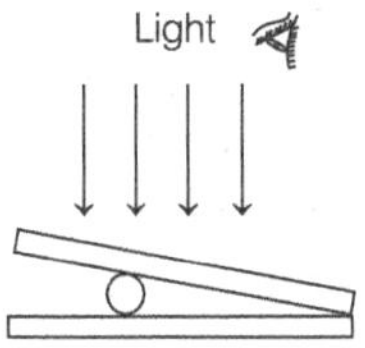

Previous Year's Questions

JEE Main

1 In a double slit experiment shown in figure, when light of wavelength 400 nm is used, dark fringe is observed at P. If $D = 0.2$ m, the minimum distance between the slits S_1 and S_2 is ...... mm. **[2024, 29 Jan Shift-I]**

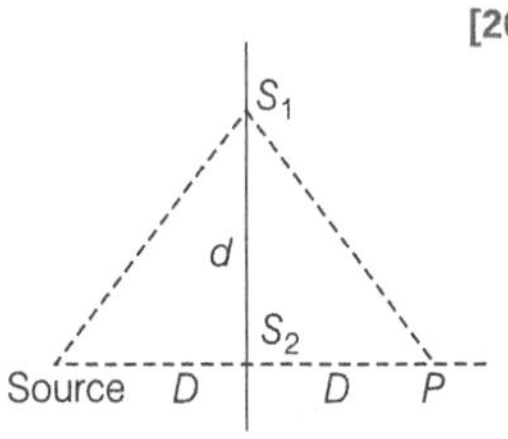

2 In Young's double slit experiment, light from two identical sources are superimposing on a screen. The path difference between the two lights reaching at a point on the screen is $\frac{7\lambda}{4}$. The ratio of intensity of fringe at this point with respect to the maximum intensity of the fringe is **[2024, 29 Jan Shift-II]**

(a) $\frac{3}{4}$ (b) $\frac{1}{3}$ (c) $\frac{1}{2}$ (d) $\frac{1}{4}$

3 Two waves of intensity ratio 1 : 9 cross each other at a point. The resultant intensities at that point, when (a) waves are incoherent is I_1 (b) waves are coherent is I_2 and differ in phase by 60°. If $\frac{I_1}{I_2} = \frac{10}{x}$, then x =....... . **[2024, 31 Jan Shift-I]**

4 The width of fringe is 2 mm on the screen in a double slits experiment for the light of wavelength of 400 nm. The width of the fringe for the light of wavelength 600 nm will be **[2023, 8 April Shift-II]**

(a) 1.33 mm (b) 2 mm (c) 4 mm (d) 3 mm

5 The ratio of intensities at two points P and Q on the screen in a Young's double slit experiment where phase difference between two waves of same amplitude are $\frac{\pi}{3}$ and $\frac{\pi}{2}$, respectively are [2023, 10 April Shift-II]

(a) 2 : 3 (b) 3 : 1
(c) 3 : 2 (d) 1 : 3

6 In Young's double slits experiment, the position of 5th bright fringe from the central maximum is 5 cm. The distance between slits and screen is 1 m and wavelength of used monochromatic light is 600 nm. The separation between the slits is [2023, 25 Jan Shift-I]

(a) 36 μm (b) 48 μm (c) 12 μm (d) 60 μm

7 In Young's double slit experiment, two slits are illuminated with a light of wavelength 800 nm. The line joining A_1P is perpendicular to A_1A_2 as shown in the figure. If the first minimum is detected at P, the value of slits separation a will be

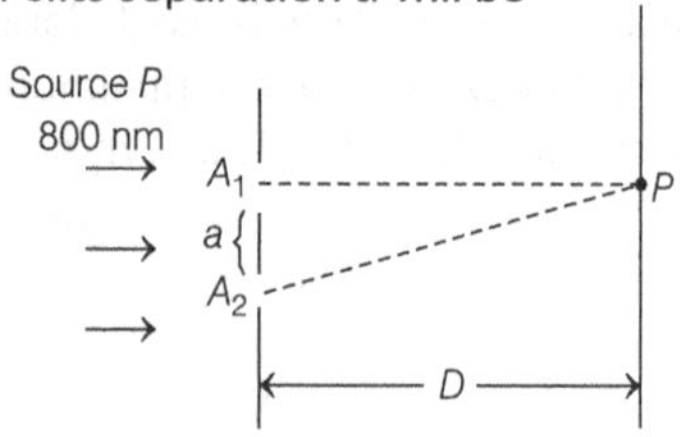

The distance of screen from slits, $D = 5$ cm [2023, 29 Jan Shift-I]

(a) 0.5 mm (b) 0.1 mm (c) 0.4 mm (d) 0.2 mm

8 A beam of light consisting of two wavelengths 7000 Å and 5500 Å is used to obtain interference pattern in Young's double slit experiment. The distance between the slits is 2.5 mm and the distance between the plane of slits and the screen is 150 cm. The least distance from the central fringe, where the bright fringes due to both the wavelengths coincide, is $n \times 10^{-5}$ m. The value of n is .... [2023, 6 April Shift-II]

9 In Young's double slit experiment, two slits S_1 and S_2 are d distance apart and the separation from slits to screen is D (as shown in figure). Now, if two transparent slabs of equal thickness 0.1 mm but refractive index 1.51 and 1.55 are introduced in the path of beam ($\lambda = 4000$ Å) from S_1 and S_2 respectively, the central bright fringe spot will shift by .... number of fringes. [2023, 30 Jan Shift-I]

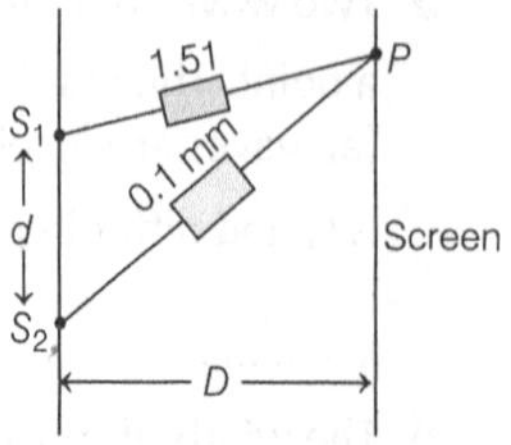

10 Two light waves of wavelengths 800 and 600 nm are used in Young's double slit experiment to obtain interference fringes on a screen placed 7 m away from plane of slits. If the two slits are separated by 0.35 mm, then shortest distance from the central bright maximum to the point where the bright fringes of the two wavelength coincide will be .... mm. [2023, 31 Jan Shift-II]

11 Two coherent sources of light interfere. The intensity ratio of two sources is 1 : 4. For this interference pattern if the value of $\frac{I_{max} + I_{min}}{I_{max} - I_{min}}$ is equal to $\frac{2\alpha + 1}{\beta + 3}$, then α/β will be [2022, 27 July Shift-II]

(a) 1.5 (b) 2
(c) 0.5 (d) 1

12 In Young's double slit experiment, the fringe width is 12 mm. If the entire arrangement is placed in water of refractive index 4/3, then the fringe width becomes (in mm) [2022, 26 July Shift-I]

(a) 16 (b) 9
(c) 48 (d) 12

13 Using Young's double slit experiment, a monochromatic light of wavelength 5000 Å produces fringes of fringe width 0.5 mm. If another monochromatic light of wavelength 6000 Å is used and the separation between the slits is doubled, then the new fringe width will be [2022, 29 June Shift-I]

(a) 0.5 mm (b) 1.0 mm
(c) 0.6 mm (d) 0.3 mm

14 In Young's double slit experiment performed using a monochromatic light of wavelength λ, when a glass plate ($\mu = 1.5$) of thickness $x\lambda$ is introduced in the path of one of the interfering beams, the intensity at the position where the central maxima occurred previously remains unchanged. The value of x will be [2022, 28 June Shift-II]

(a) 3 (b) 2 (c) 1.5 (d) 0.5

15 Two light beams of intensities in the ratio of 9 : 4 are allowed to interfere. The ratio of the intensity of maxima and minima will be [2022, 24 June Shift-II]

(a) 2 : 3 (b) 16 : 81 (c) 25 : 169 (d) 25 : 1

16 The interference pattern is obtained with two coherent light sources of intensity ratio 4 : 1 And the ratio $\frac{I_{max} + I_{min}}{I_{max} - I_{min}}$ is $\frac{5}{x}$. Then, the value of x will be equal to [2022, 25 June Shift-II]

(a) 3 (b) 4 (c) 2 (d) 1

17 The two light beams having intensities I and $9I$ interfere to produce a fringe pattern on a screen. The phase difference between the beams is $\pi/2$ at point P and π at point Q. Then the difference between the resultant intensities at P and Q will be **[2022, 25 June Shift-I]**

(a) $2I$ (b) $6I$ (c) $5I$ (d) $7I$

18 In a double slit experiment with monochromatic light, fringes are obtained on a screen placed at some distance from the plane of slits. If the screen is moved by 5×10^{-2} m towards the slits, the change in fringe width is 3×10^{-3} cm. If the distance between the slits is 1 mm, then the wavelength of the light will be .... nm **[2022, 29 June Shift-II]**

19 Two light beams of intensities $4I$ and $9I$ interfere on a screen. The phase difference between these beams on the screen at point A is zero and at point B is π. The difference of resultant intensities, at the point A and B, will be .... I. **[2022, 29 July Shift-I]**

20 In Young's double slit experiment, a laser light of 560 nm produces an interference pattern with consecutive bright fringes separation of 7.2 mm. Now, another light is used to produce an interference pattern with consecutive bright fringes separation of 81 mm. The wavelength of second light is .... nm. **[2022, 28 July Shift-I]**

21 The light waves from two coherent sources have same intensity $I_1 = I_2 = I_0$. In interference pattern the intensity of light at minima is zero. What will be the intensity of light at maxima? **[2021, 27 Aug Shift-II]**

(a) I_0 (b) $2I_0$ (c) $5I_0$ (d) $4I_0$

22 In Young's double slit experiment the two slits are separated by 2 mm and the screen is placed one meter away. When a light of wavelength 500 nm is used, the fringe separation will be **[2021, 26 Feb Shift-I]**

(a) 0.75 mm (b) 0.25 mm
(c) 1 mm (d) 0.50 mm

23 In Young's double slit experiment, if the source of light changes from orange to blue, then **[2021, 27 July Shift-I]**

(a) the central bright fringe will become a dark fringe
(b) the distance between consecutive fringes will decrease
(c) the distance between consecutive fringes will increase
(d) the intensity of the minima will increase

24 In Young's double slit experiment, the distance between the slits varies in time as $d(t) = d_0 + a_0 \sin \omega t$, where d_0, ω and a_0 are constants. The difference between the largest fringe width and the smallest fringe width obtained over time is given as **[2021, 25 July Shift-I]**

(a) $\frac{2\lambda D(d_0)}{(d_0^2 - a_0^2)}$ (b) $\frac{2\lambda D a_0}{(d_0^2 - a_0^2)}$ (c) $\frac{\lambda D}{d_0^2} a_0$ (d) $\frac{\lambda D}{d_0 + a_0}$

25 In Young's double slit arrangement, slits are separated by a gap of 0.5 mm, and the screen is placed at a distance of 0.5 m from them. The distance between the first and the third bright fringe formed when the slits are illuminated by a monochromatic light of 5890 Å is **[2021, 18 March Shift-I]**

(a) 1178×10^{-9} m (b) 1178×10^{-6} m
(c) 1178×10^{-12} m (d) 5890×10^{-7} m

26 In Young's double slit experiment, two slits are separated by 2 mm and the screen is placed one metre away. When a light of wavelength 500 nm is used, the fringe separation will be **[2021, 26 Feb Shift-I]**

(a) 0.25 mm (b) 0.50 mm (c) 0.75 mm (d) 1 mm

27 Two coherent light sources having intensity in the ratio $2x$ produce an interference pattern. The ratio $\frac{I_{max} - I_{min}}{I_{max} + I_{min}}$ will be **[2021, 25 Feb Shift-I]**

(a) $\frac{2\sqrt{2x}}{x+1}$ (b) $\frac{\sqrt{2x}}{2x+1}$ (c) $\frac{\sqrt{2x}}{x+1}$ (d) $\frac{2\sqrt{2x}}{2x+1}$

JEE Advanced

1. A double slit set up is shown in the figure. One of the slit is in medium-2 of refractive index n_2. The other slit is at the interface of this medium with another medium-1 of refractive index $n_1 (\neq n_2)$. The line joining the slits is perpendicular to the interface and the distance between the slits is d. The slit widths are much smaller than d. A monochromatic parallel beam of light is incident on the slits from medium-1. A detector is placed in medium-2 at a large distance from the slits and at an angle θ from the line joining them, so that θ equals the angle of refraction of the beam. Consider two approximately parallel rays from the slits received by the detector. **(2022 Adv.)**

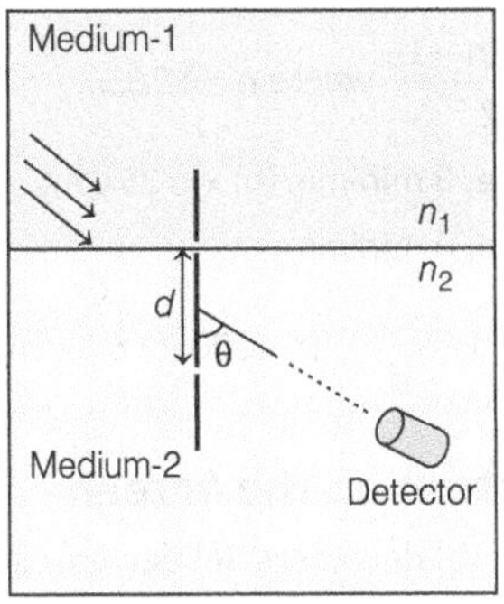

Which of the following statement(s) is(are) correct?

(a) The phase difference between the two rays is independent of d.

(b) The two rays interfere constructively at the detector.

(c) The phase difference between the two rays depends on n_1 but is independent of n_2.

(d) The phase difference between the two rays vanishes only for certain values of d and the angle of incidence of the beam, with θ being the corresponding angle of refraction.

2. Two coherent monochromatic point sources S_1 and S_2 of wavelength $\lambda = 600$ nm are placed symmetrically on either side of the centre of the circle as shown. The sources are separated by a distance $d = 1.8$ mm. This arrangement produces interference fringes visible as alternate bright and dark spots on the circumference of the circle. The angular separation between two consecutive bright spots is $\Delta\theta$. Which of the following options is/are correct? **(2017 Adv.)**

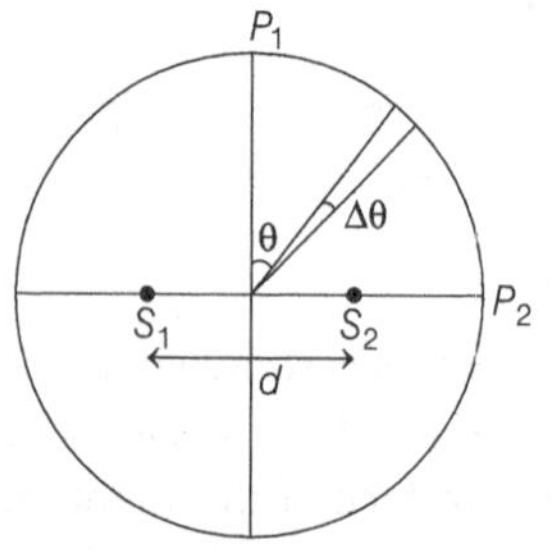

(a) The angular separation between two consecutive bright spots decreases as we move from P_1 to P_2 along the first quadrant

(b) A dark spot will be formed at the point P_2

(c) The total number of fringes produced between P_1 and P_2 in the first quadrant is close to 3000

(d) At P_2 the order of the fringe will be maximum

3. While conducting the Young's double slit experiment, a student replaced the two slits with a large opaque plate in the x-y plane containing two small holes that act as two coherent point sources (S_1, S_2) emitting light of wavelength 600 mm. The student mistakenly placed the screen parallel to the x-z plane (for $z > 0$) at a distance $D = 3$m from the mid-point of S_1S_2, as shown schematically in the figure. The distance between the source $d = 0.6003$ mm. The origin O is at the intersection of the screen and the line joining S_1S_2. **(2016 Adv.)**

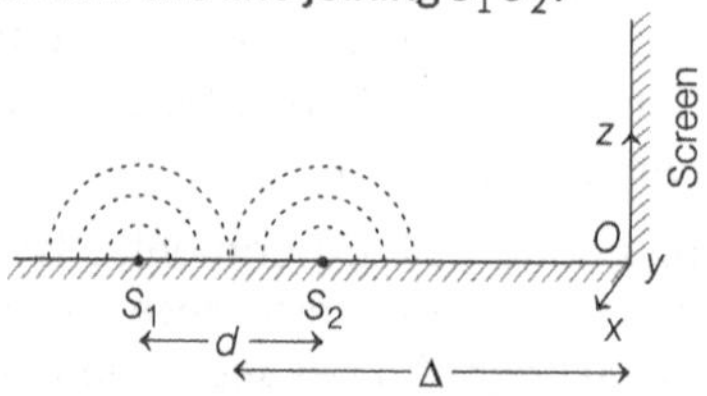

Which of the following is (are) true of the intensity pattern on the screen?

(a) Semi circular bright and dark bands centered at point O

(b) The region very close to the point O will be dark

(c) Straight bright and dark bands parallel to the X-axis

(d) Hyperbolic bright and dark bands with foci symmetrically placed about O in the x-direction

Answer Key

5.1 Interference

1. $\sqrt{37}$ **2.** $E = 5\sin[\omega t + 53°]$

3. (a) $9I$ (b) $5I$ (c) I **4.** $K/2$

5. (i) $f = 165\,n$ where $n = 1,2,3...$

(ii) $f = \dfrac{165(2n-1)}{2}$ where $n = 1,2,3....$

6. (a) 4 maxima, 3 minima (b) $x = 35\lambda/4$

7. (a) 8 maxima, 4 minima

8. (a) $y = D\sqrt{2\left(1 - \dfrac{n\lambda}{d}\right)}$ (b) 1000 (c) 6.32 cm

(d) $\dfrac{1}{\sqrt{3}}$ m (e) 4001 maxima, 4000 minima

5.2 YDSE Pattern on the Screen

1. (a) increase (b) decreases (c) decreases (d) no change

2. (a) 0.5 mm (b) 2 mm (c) 2.25 mm

3. (a) $\dfrac{1}{\sqrt{3}}$ m (b) 5 maxima, 4 minima **4.** 0.3 mm

5. 0.011°

5.3 Intensity Distribution on the Screen

1. $I_{max} = 9I, I_{min} = I$ **2.** 2 : 1 **3.** $I_0/4$

4. $3I_0$ **5.** $\dfrac{\lambda D}{4d}$

6. The dark fringes would be brighter and bright fringes would be darker

5.4 YDSE with Polychromatic Light

1. 400 nm, 667 nm **2.** 1.8 mm **3.** (i) 280 μm, (ii) 560 μm

5.5 Oblique Incidence

1. (a) $y = -1$ cm (b) I_0 (c) 19
2. (i) $\frac{1}{\sqrt{3}}$ m (ii) $\frac{1}{\sqrt{15}}$ m, $\frac{3}{\sqrt{7}}$ m

5.6 Source Placed Beyond the Central Line

1. (a) maxima of order 280 (b) maxima of order 80
2. (a) $\theta = \sin^{-1}\left[2\left(\frac{n}{40} - 1\right)\right]$ (b) 41

5.7 Introduction of Glass Slab

1. 4.8 μm
2. 1.2
3. 0.63 mm, 1.575 μm
4. $I_0 / 4$
5. (a) $\frac{(\mu_2 - 1)tD}{d}$ (b) $\mu_1\mu_2$

5.8 Fresnel Biprism and Llyod Mirror

1. (a) 0.349 cm (b) 0.1719 mm
2. 2.94 mm
3. (a) 2 cm (b) 40
4. $\frac{\lambda(b + 2a)}{4a\theta}$

5.9 Thin Film Interference

1. 143 mm
2. 429 nm and 600 nm
3. 10^{-7}m
4. $\frac{16}{3} \times 10^{-7}$m 5. 3
6. 10 7. 5 per cm

Level 2

Single Choice Correct Questions

1. (a)	2. (b)	3. (c)	4. (d)	5. (b)
6. (a)	7. (d)	8. (d)	9. (a)	10. (c)
11. (a)	12. (b)	13. (a)	14. (c)	15. (a)
16. (b)	17. (d)	18. (b)	19. (d)	20. (c)
21. (b)	22. (d)	23. (a)	24. (c)	25. (c)
26. (a)	27. (c)	28. (b)	29. (d)	30. (a)
31. (a)	32. (c)	33. (c)	34. (d)	35. (c)
36. (d)	37. (c)	38. (a)	39. (c)	40. (a)
41. (c)	42. (b)	43. (a)	44. (b)	45. (a)
46. (b)	47. (b)	48. (c)	49. (a)	50. (d)

Numerical Value Questions

1. 209	2. 7	3. 200	4. 280
5. 4.80	6. 5892	7. 1	8. 125
9. 5	10. 520		

Level 3

Single Choice Correct Questions

1. (a)	2. (b)	3. (c)	4. (a)	5. (a)
6. (d)	7. (a)	8. (a)	9. (b)	10. (b)
11. (b)	12. (a)	13. (b)	14. (b)	15. (c)
16. (a)	17. (a)	18. (a)	19. (c)	20. (c)
21. (c)	22. (c)	23. (b)	24. (d)	25. (d)
26. (b)	27. (b)	28. (a)	29. (c)	30. (a)
31. (d)	32. (a)	33. (a)	34. (a)	35. (a)
36. (c)	37. (c)	38. (b)	39. (d)	40. (b)

Multiple Choice(s) Correct Questions

1. (a, b, c)	2. (b, d)	3. (b, c, d)
4. (a,b,c,d)	5. (a, c)	6. (a, c)
7. (a, b, c)	8. (a, c)	9. (a, c)
10. (b, d)	11. (a, c)	12. (b, d)
13. (a,b,c,d)	14. (a, c, d)	15. (c, d)
16. (a, b, c)	17. (a, b, c)	18. (b, d)
19. (a,b,c,d)	20. (a)	

Comprehension Based Questions

1. (b)	2. (d)	3. (d)	4. (a)	5. (a)
6. (b)	7. (d)	8. (b)	9. (a)	10. (b)
11. (b)	12. (c)	13. (a)	14. (c)	15. (b)
16. (a)	17. (b)	18. (c)	19. (b)	20. (d)
21. (d)	22. (b)	23. (d)	24. (c)	25. (b)
26. (b)	27. (d)			

Match the Columns Questions

1. A $\rightarrow$ 2,3; B $\rightarrow$ 1, 3; C $\rightarrow$ 1, 3,4; D $\rightarrow$ 2,3,4
2. A $\rightarrow$ 3,4; B $\rightarrow$ 1,2,4; C $\rightarrow$ 1,2,4; D $\rightarrow$ 3,4
3. A $\rightarrow$ 1,3,4; B $\rightarrow$ 1,2,4; C $\rightarrow$ 1,2,4; D $\rightarrow$ 1,3,4
4. A $\rightarrow$ 2,3,4; B $\rightarrow$ 1,2,3,4; C $\rightarrow$ 2,3,4; D $\rightarrow$ 1,2,3,4
5. A $\rightarrow$ 4; B $\rightarrow$ 1; C $\rightarrow$ 2; D $\rightarrow$ 3
6. A $\rightarrow$ 2,3,4; B $\rightarrow$ 1,3; C $\rightarrow$ 1,3

Numerical Value Questions

1. 1	2. 5	3. 7	4. 5	5. 1
6. 4	7. 1	8. 21	9. 4	10. 6
11. 1100				

Previous Year's Questions

JEE Main

1. (0.2)	2. (c)	3. (13)	4. (d)	5. (c)
6. (d)	7. (d)	8. (462)	9. (10)	10. (48)
11. (b)	12. (b)	13. (d)	14. (b)	15. (d)
16. (b)	17. (b)	18. (600)	19. (24)	20. (630)
21. (d)	22. (b)	23. (b)	24. (b)	25. (b)
26. (a)	27. (d)			

JEE Advanced

1. (a, b)	2. (c, d)	3. (a, b)

SOLUTIONS

Level 1

5.1 Interference

1. $A = \sqrt{A_1^2 + A_2^2 + 2A_1A_2\cos\phi}$

$$= \sqrt{4^2 + 3^2 + 2\times4\times3\cos\left(\frac{\pi}{3}\right)} = \sqrt{37}$$

2. $E_1 = 3\sin\omega t,\ E_2 = 4\cos\omega t = 4\sin\left(\omega t + \frac{\pi}{2}\right)$

$$\mathbf{E} = \mathbf{E}_1 + \mathbf{E}_2$$

$$E = \sqrt{E_1^2 + E_2^2 + 2E_1E_2\cos\phi}$$

$$\Rightarrow \quad E = \sqrt{3^2 + 4^2 + 2\times3\times4\cos\left(\frac{\pi}{2}\right)} = 5$$

$$\tan\phi = \frac{E_2\sin\phi}{E_1 + E_2\cos\phi} = \frac{4\sin\left(\frac{\pi}{2}\right)}{3 + 4\cos\left(\frac{\pi}{2}\right)} = \frac{4}{3}$$

$$\Rightarrow \quad \phi = 53°$$

$\therefore\ E = 5\sin(\omega t + 53°)$

3. $I = I_1 + I_2 + 2\sqrt{I_1}\sqrt{I_2}\cos\phi$

(a) $I' = I + 4I + 2\sqrt{I}\sqrt{4I}\cos 0° = 9I$

(b) $I' = I + 4I + 2\sqrt{I}\sqrt{4I}\cos\left(\frac{\pi}{2}\right) = 5I$

(c) $I' = I + 4I + 2\sqrt{I}\sqrt{4I}\cos\pi = I$

4. $$\Delta\phi = \frac{2\pi}{\lambda}\Delta x = \frac{2\pi}{\lambda}(\lambda) = 2\pi$$

$$I = I_1 + I_2 + 2\sqrt{I_1}\sqrt{I_2}\cos\Delta\phi$$

$$\Rightarrow \quad K = I + I + 2\sqrt{I}\sqrt{I}\cos 2\pi$$

$$\Rightarrow \quad I = \frac{K}{4}$$

For path difference of $\frac{\lambda}{4}$,

$$\Delta\phi = \frac{2\pi}{\lambda}\Delta x = \frac{2\pi}{\lambda}\left(\frac{\lambda}{4}\right) = \frac{\pi}{2}$$

$$I = I_1 + I_2 + 2\sqrt{I_1}\sqrt{I_2}\cos\Delta\phi$$

$$\Rightarrow \quad I' = I + I + 2\sqrt{I}\sqrt{I}\cos\left(\frac{\pi}{2}\right)$$

$$\Rightarrow \quad I' = 2I = 2\left(\frac{K}{4}\right) = \frac{K}{2}$$

5 $\Delta x = S_2P - S_1P = \sqrt{3^2 + 4^2} - 3 = 2\text{ m}$

$$\lambda = \frac{v}{f} = \frac{330}{f}$$

(a) For constructive interference,

$$\Delta x = n\lambda \text{ where } n \in I$$

$$\Rightarrow \quad 2 = n\left(\frac{330}{f}\right)$$

$$\Rightarrow \quad f = 165n \text{ where } n \in I \ (1, 2, 3, \ldots\ldots)$$

(b) For destructive interference

$$\Delta x = (2n-1)\frac{\lambda}{2} \text{ where } n \in I$$

$$\Rightarrow \quad 2 = (2n-1)\frac{1}{2}\left(\frac{330}{f}\right)$$

$$\Rightarrow \quad f = \frac{(2n-1)165}{2} \text{ where } n \in I \ (1, 2, 3, \ldots\ldots)$$

6.

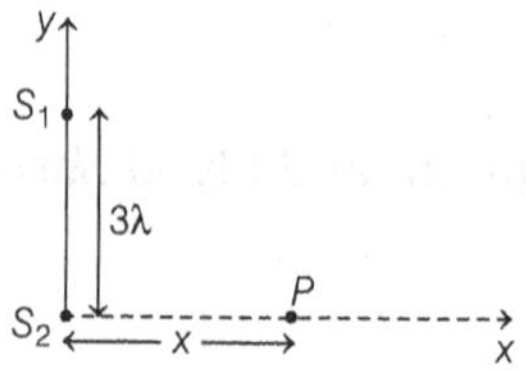

For $x = 0$, $\Delta x = S_1P - S_2P = 3\lambda$

For $x = \infty$, $\Delta x = S_1P - S_2P = 0$

So, the path difference on the X-axis varies from 3λ to 0 as we move from $x = 0$ to $x = \infty$

(a) For maxima, $\Delta x = n\lambda$

Possible values of n are 0, 1, 2, 3.

So, total no. of maxima = 4

For minima, $\Delta x = (2n-1)\frac{\lambda}{2}$

Possible values of n are 1, 2, 3.

So, total number of minima = 3

(b) For farthest minima, $n = 1$

$$\therefore \quad \Delta x = (2n-1)\frac{\lambda}{2} = \frac{\lambda}{2}$$

Also, $\quad \Delta x = S_1P - S_2P$

$$\Rightarrow \quad \frac{\lambda}{2} = \sqrt{(3\lambda)^2 + x^2} - x$$

$$\Rightarrow \quad x = \frac{35\lambda}{4}$$

7.

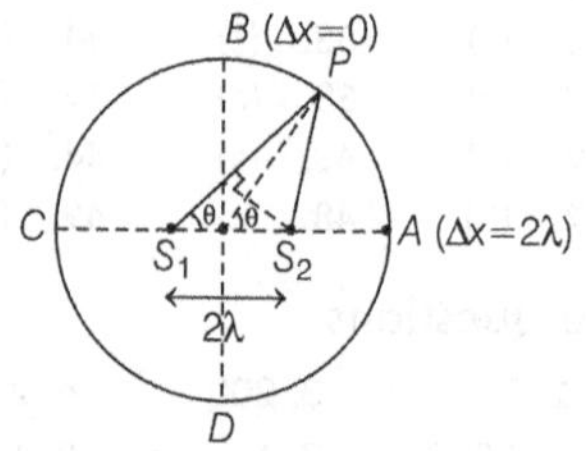

$$\Delta x = S_1P - S_2P = 2\lambda\cos\theta$$

Points A, B, C and D are maxima

As we move from A to B on the circle, somewhere path difference will be equal. Therefore, we will get one maxima in each quadrant.

So, total number of maxima $= 8$

In each quadrant, there will be 2 minima corresponding to $\Delta x = \frac{\lambda}{2}$ and $\Delta x = \frac{3\lambda}{2}$.

So, total number of minima $= 2 \times 4 = 8$

8. (a) $\Delta x = S_1P - S_2P = d\cos\theta$

$$\cos\theta = 1 - 2\sin^2\left(\frac{\theta}{2}\right) = 1 - \frac{\theta^2}{2} \quad \text{[As } \theta \text{ is small]}$$

$$= 1 - \frac{1}{2}\left(\frac{y}{D}\right)^2 \quad [\because \tan\theta \approx \theta = \frac{y}{D}]$$

$$\therefore \quad \Delta x = d\cos\theta = d\left(1 - \frac{y^2}{2D^2}\right)$$

For maxima at P,

$$\Delta x = n\lambda$$

$$\Rightarrow \quad d\left(1 - \frac{y^2}{2D^2}\right) = n\lambda \Rightarrow y = D\sqrt{2\left[1 - \frac{n\lambda}{d}\right]}$$

(b) For central maxima, $y = 0$

$$\Rightarrow \quad D\sqrt{2\left(1 - \frac{n\lambda}{d}\right)} = 0$$

$$\Rightarrow \quad n = \frac{d}{\lambda} = \frac{0.5 \times 10^{-3}}{5000 \times 10^{-10}} = 1000$$

(c) For central maxima, $n = 1000$

$$y = D\sqrt{2\left(1 - \frac{n\lambda}{d}\right)}$$

As y increase, n decreases. So, for the second maxima n will be 998.

$$y = D\sqrt{2\left(1 - \frac{n\lambda}{d}\right)} = 100\sqrt{2\left(1 - \frac{998 \times 5000 \times 10^{-10}}{0.5 \times 10^{-3}}\right)}$$

$$= 6.32 \text{ cm}$$

So, the radius of the closest second bright ring will be 6.32 cm.

(d) For maxima, $\Delta x = d\sin\theta = n\lambda$

$$\Rightarrow (1 \times 10^{-3})\sin\theta = 1000 \times (5000 \times 10^{-10})$$

$$\Rightarrow \quad \sin\theta = \frac{1}{2} \quad \Rightarrow \quad \theta = 30^\circ$$

$$y = D\tan\theta = 1(\tan 30^\circ) = \frac{1}{\sqrt{3}} \text{ m}$$

(e) $n_{max} = \left[\frac{d}{\lambda}\right] = \left[\frac{1 \times 10^{-3}}{5000 \times 10^{-10}}\right] = 2000$

So, total no. of maxima $= 2(2000) + 1 = 4001$

Total no. of minima $= 2(2000) = 4000$

5.2 YDSE Pattern on the Screen

1. Fringe width, $\beta = \frac{\lambda D}{d}$

(a) $\beta \propto D$ (b) $\beta \propto \lambda$

(c) $\beta \propto \frac{1}{d}$ (d) β is independent of slit width.

2. (a) $\beta = \frac{\lambda D}{d} = \frac{5000 \times 10^{-10} \times 1}{1 \times 10^{-3}} = 0.5 \times 10^{-3} \text{ m} = 0.5 \text{ mm}$

(b) $y = \frac{4\lambda D}{d} = 4\beta = 4(0.5) = 2 \text{ mm}$

(c) $y = (2n-1)\frac{\lambda D}{2d} = (2 \times 5 - 1)\frac{\lambda D}{2d} = 4.5\beta = 2.25 \text{ mm}$

3. $n_{max} = \left[\frac{d}{\lambda}\right] = \left[\frac{1 \times 10^{-3}}{0.5 \times 10^{-3}}\right] = 2$

(a) For first maxima, $d\sin\theta = n\lambda$

$$\Rightarrow \quad (1 \times 10^{-3})\sin\theta = 1 \times 0.5 \times 10^{-3}$$

$$\Rightarrow \quad \sin\theta = 0.5$$

$$\Rightarrow \quad \theta = 30^\circ$$

$$y = D\tan\theta = 1 \times \tan 30^\circ = \frac{1}{\sqrt{3}} \text{ m}$$

(b) Total no. of maxima $= 2n_{max} + 1 = 5$

Total no. of minima $= 2n_{max} = 4$

4. In water $\lambda' = \frac{\lambda}{\mu} = \frac{\lambda}{4/3} = \frac{3\lambda}{4}$

$$\beta' = \frac{\lambda' D}{d} = \frac{3}{4}\left(\frac{\lambda D}{d}\right) = \frac{3}{4}(0.4) = 0.3 \text{ mm}$$

5. Angular fringe width $= \frac{\lambda}{d} = \frac{6000 \times 10^{-10}}{3 \times 10^{-3}}$

$$= 2 \times 10^{-4} \text{ rad} = 2 \times 10^{-4} \times \frac{180^\circ}{\pi}$$

$$= 0.011^\circ$$

5.3 Intensity Distribution on the Screen

1. $I_{max} = (\sqrt{I_1} + \sqrt{I_2})^2 = (\sqrt{4I} + \sqrt{I})^2 = 9I$

$I_{min} = (\sqrt{I_1} - \sqrt{I_2})^2 = (\sqrt{4I} - \sqrt{I})^2 = I$

2. Let the intensity of each source be I_0.

For coherent sources,

$$I = I_1 + I_2 + 2\sqrt{I_1}\sqrt{I_2}\cos\Delta\phi$$

$$\Rightarrow \quad I = I_0 + I_0 + 2\sqrt{I_0}\sqrt{I_0}\cos 0^\circ$$

[At the mid-point $\Delta x = 0$, $\Delta\phi = 0$]

$$\Rightarrow \quad I = 4I_0$$

For incoherent source, average value of $\cos\Delta\phi$ is zero.

$$I' = I_1 + I_2 + 2\sqrt{I_1}\sqrt{I_2}\cos\Delta\phi$$

$$I' = I_0 + I_0 = 2I_0$$

$$\therefore \quad \frac{I}{I'} = \frac{4I_0}{2I_0} = 2:1$$

3. For central bright fringe,

$$I = I_1 + I_2 + 2\sqrt{I_1}\sqrt{I_2}\cos\Delta\phi$$

$$\Rightarrow \quad I_0 = I + I + 2\sqrt{I}\sqrt{I}\cos 0^\circ$$

$$\Rightarrow \quad I = \frac{I_0}{4}$$

It one of the slits is covered, then intensity at the centre of the screen will be only due to the light reaching from the other slit. So, new intesnity will be I or $\frac{I_0}{4}$.

4. $\Delta x = d\sin\theta = \frac{dy}{D} = \frac{1\times10^{-3}\times(1/3)\times10^{-3}}{1} = \frac{1}{3}\times10^{-6}$ m

$$\Delta\phi = \frac{2\pi}{\lambda}\Delta x = \frac{2\pi}{5000\times10^{-10}}\times\frac{1}{3}\times10^{-6} = \frac{4\pi}{3}$$

$$I = I_1 + I_2 + 2\sqrt{I_1}\sqrt{I_2}\cos\Delta\phi$$

$$= 4I_0 + I_0 + 2\sqrt{4I_0}\sqrt{I_0}\cos\left(\frac{4\pi}{3}\right) = 3I_0$$

5. $I = \frac{1}{2}I_{max} = \frac{1}{2}(4I_0) = 2I_0$

$$I = I_1 + I_2 + 2\sqrt{I_1}\sqrt{I_2}\cos\Delta\phi$$

$$\Rightarrow \quad 2I = I + I + 2\sqrt{I}\sqrt{I}\cos\Delta\phi$$

$$\Rightarrow \quad \cos\Delta\phi = 0 \quad \Rightarrow \quad \Delta\phi = (2n-1)\frac{\pi}{2}$$

For least distance, $n = 1$

$$\therefore \quad \Delta\phi = (2(1)-1)\frac{\pi}{2} = \frac{\pi}{2}$$

$$\Delta\phi = \frac{2\pi}{\lambda}\Delta x \quad \Rightarrow \quad \frac{\pi}{2} = \frac{2\pi}{\lambda}\Delta x$$

$$\Rightarrow \quad \Delta x = \frac{\lambda}{4}$$

Also, $\Delta x = d\sin\theta = \frac{dy}{D}$

$$\Rightarrow \quad \frac{\lambda}{4} = \frac{dy}{D} \quad \Rightarrow \quad y = \frac{\lambda D}{4d}$$

6. $I_{max} = (\sqrt{I_1} + \sqrt{I_2})^2, I_{min} = (\sqrt{I_1} - \sqrt{I_2})^2$

Initially, $I_1 = I_2 = I_0$

So, $I_{max} = (\sqrt{I_0} + \sqrt{I_0})^2 = 4I_0$

$$I_{min} = (\sqrt{I_0} - \sqrt{I_0})^2 = 0$$

Now, if intensity of one of the slits decreases I_{max} will decrease and I_{min} will be non-zero, so the dark fringes would be brighter and bright fringes would be darker.

5.4 YDSE with Polychromatic Light

1. $\Delta x = \frac{dy}{D} = \frac{0.5\times10^{-3}\times1\times10^{-3}}{50\times10^{-2}} = 10^{-6}$ m

For wavelengths to be absent (minima)

$$\Delta x = (2n-1)\frac{\lambda}{2} \quad \Rightarrow \quad 10^{-6} = (2n-1)\frac{\lambda}{2}$$

$$\Rightarrow \quad \lambda = \frac{2000}{2n-1}\text{ nm}$$

For $n = 1$, $\lambda = 2000$ nm

$n = 2$, $\lambda = \frac{2000}{3}$ nm $= 667$ nm

$n = 3$, $\lambda = \frac{2000}{5} = 400$ nm

$n = 4$, $\lambda = \frac{2000}{7}$ nm $= 285.71$ nm

So, for white light (400 – 700 nm), wavelengths which will be absent are 400 nm and 667 nm.

2. $y_1 = \frac{n_1\lambda_1 D}{d}$ and $y_2 = \frac{n_2\lambda_2 D}{d}$

For bright fringes to coincide,

$$y_1 = y_2 \quad \Rightarrow \quad \frac{n_1\lambda_1 D}{d} = \frac{n_2\lambda_2 D}{d}$$

$$\Rightarrow \quad n_1(6000) = n_2(4500)$$

$$\Rightarrow \quad 4n_1 = 3n_2$$

$$\Rightarrow \quad n_1 = 3 \text{ and } n_2 = 4 \text{ (For least distance)}$$

$$y_1 = \frac{n_1\lambda_1 D}{d} = \frac{3\times6000\times10^{-10}\times1}{1\times10^{-3}}$$

$$= 1.8\times10^{-3}\text{m} = 1.8 \text{ mm}$$

3. For dark fringes to coincide,

$$y_1 = y_2$$

$$\Rightarrow \quad (2n_1-1)\frac{\lambda_1 D}{2d} = (2n_2-1)\frac{\lambda_2 D}{2d}$$

$$\Rightarrow \quad (2n_1-1)(4000) = (2n_2-1)(5600)$$

$$\Rightarrow \quad 5(2n_1-1) = 7(2n_2-1)$$

$$\Rightarrow \quad n_1 = 4 \text{ and } n_2 = 3$$

$$n_1 = 11 \text{ and } n_2 = 8, \text{ So on,}$$

(a) For first black line,

$$n_1 = 4 \text{ and } n_2 = 3$$

$$y_1 = (2n_1-1)\frac{\lambda_1 D}{2d}$$

$$= (2\times4-1)\frac{4000\times10^{-10}\times40\times10^{-2}}{2\times2\times10^{-3}}$$

$$= 280\mu\text{m}$$

(b) For second black line,

$$n_1 = 11 \text{ and } n_2 = 8$$

$$y_1 = (2n_1-1)\frac{\lambda_1 D}{2d} = 840\,\mu\text{m}$$

Distance between two consecutive black lines

$$= 840 - 280 = 560\,\mu\text{m}$$

5.5 Oblique Incidence

1. (a) $\Delta x = d\sin\theta + d\sin\theta_0$

For central maxima, $\Delta x = 0$

$$\Rightarrow \quad d\sin\theta + d\sin\theta_0 = 0$$

$$\Rightarrow \quad \theta = -\theta_0 = -0.57°$$

$$\tan\theta = \frac{y}{D} \quad \Rightarrow \quad \theta = \frac{y}{D} \quad \Rightarrow \quad -0.57\frac{\pi}{180} = \frac{y}{100}$$

$$\Rightarrow \quad y = -1 \text{ cm}$$

(b) At point O, $\theta = 0$

So, $\Delta x = d\sin\theta_0$

$$= d\theta_0 = 1\times10^{-3}\times0.57\frac{\pi}{180} = 10^{-5}\text{m}$$

$$\Delta\phi = \frac{2\pi}{\lambda}\Delta x = \frac{2\pi}{5000\times10^{-9}}\times10^{-5} = 40\pi$$

Hence, point O corresponds to 20th maxima and intensity at O will be equal to I_0.

(c) 19 maxima will lie between O and the central maxima.

2. (a) For central maxima,

$$\Delta x = d\sin\theta - d\sin 30^\circ = 0 \Rightarrow \theta = 30^\circ$$

$$\tan\theta = \frac{y}{D} \Rightarrow \tan 30^\circ = \frac{y}{1} \Rightarrow y = \frac{1}{\sqrt{3}}\text{ m}$$

(b) For first order minima,

$$\Delta x = d\sin\theta - d\sin 30^\circ = \pm\frac{\lambda}{2}$$

$$\Rightarrow 1\sin\theta - 1(0.5) = \pm\frac{0.5}{2}$$

$$\Rightarrow \sin\theta = \frac{3}{4} \text{ and } \sin\theta = \frac{1}{4}$$

$$\Rightarrow \tan\theta = \frac{3}{\sqrt{7}} \text{ and } \tan\theta = \frac{1}{\sqrt{15}}$$

$$y = D\tan\theta = 1\left(\frac{3}{\sqrt{7}}\right) = \frac{3}{\sqrt{7}}\text{ m}$$

and $$y = D\tan\theta = 1\left(\frac{1}{\sqrt{15}}\right) = \frac{1}{\sqrt{15}}\text{ m}$$

5.6 Source Placed beyond the central Line

1. (a) Path difference at P,

$$\Delta x = (SS_2 + S_2P) - (SS_1 + S_1P) = (S_2P - S_1P) + (SS_2 - SS_1)$$

$$= d\sin\theta + d\sin\theta_0 = 20\left(\frac{10\times10^{-3}}{2}\right) + 20\left(\frac{2\times10^{-3}}{1}\right)$$

$$= 140\times10^{-3}\text{ mm}$$

For maxima, $\Delta x = n\lambda$

$$\Rightarrow 140\times10^{-3}\times10^{-3} = n(500\times10^{-9})$$

$$\Rightarrow n = 280$$

(b) Path difference at O,

$$\Delta x = d\sin\theta_0 = 20\left(\frac{2\times10^{-3}}{1}\right) = 40\times10^{-3}\text{ mm}$$

For maxima, $\Delta x = n\lambda$

$$\Rightarrow 40\times10^{-3} = n(500\times10^{-9}) \Rightarrow n = 80$$

2. (a) Path difference at P,

$$\Delta x = (l_2 - l_1) + d\sin\theta$$

For maxima, $\Delta x = n\lambda$

$$\Rightarrow (l_2 - l_1) + d\sin\theta = n\lambda$$

$$\Rightarrow (40-20)\times10^{-6} + 10\times10^{-6}\sin\theta = n(500\times10^{-9})$$

$$\Rightarrow \sin\theta = 2\left(\frac{n}{40} - 1\right)$$

$$\Rightarrow \theta = \sin^{-1}\left[2\left(\frac{n}{40} - 1\right)\right]$$

(b) $-1 \le \sin\theta \le 1$

$$\Rightarrow -1 \le 2\left(\frac{n}{40} - 1\right) \le 1 \Rightarrow 20 \le n \le 60$$

Hence, number of maxima = 41

5.7 Introduction of Glass Slab

1. $$\Delta x = (\mu - 1)t = 4\lambda$$

$$\Rightarrow (1.5 - 1)t = 4\times6000\times10^{-10}$$

$$\Rightarrow t = 4.8\,\mu\text{m}$$

2. $$\Delta x = \frac{dy}{D} = (\mu - 1)t$$

$$\Rightarrow \frac{(2\times10^{-3})(5\times10^{-3})}{10\times10^{-2}} = (\mu - 1)(0.5\times10^{-3})$$

$$\Rightarrow \mu = 1.2$$

3. (a) $$\lambda' = \frac{\lambda}{\mu}$$

$$\beta = \frac{\lambda' D}{d} = \frac{\lambda D}{\mu d} = \frac{6300\times10^{-10}\times1.33}{1.33\times1\times10^{-3}} = 0.63\text{ mm}$$

(b) $$\Delta x = (\mu_{rel} - 1)t = \frac{\lambda'}{2}$$

$$\Rightarrow \left(\frac{1.53}{1.33} - 1\right)t = \frac{6300\times10^{-10}}{1.33\times2}$$

$$\Rightarrow t = 1.575\,\mu\text{m}$$

4. $$\Delta x = |(\mu_1 - 1)t_1 - (\mu_2 - 1)t_2|$$

$$= |(1.4-1)(2\times10^{-6} - (1.6-1)(4\times10^{-6})|$$

$$= 1.6\times10^{-6}\text{ m}$$

$$\Delta\phi = \frac{2\pi}{\lambda}\Delta x = \frac{2\pi}{4800\times10^{-10}}\times1.6\times10^{-6} = \frac{20\pi}{3}$$

Intensity due to each slit $= I_0/4$

$$I = I_1 + I_2 + 2\sqrt{I_1}\sqrt{I_2}\cos\Delta\phi$$

$$= \frac{I_0}{4} + \frac{I_0}{4} + 2\sqrt{\frac{I_0}{4}}\sqrt{\frac{I_0}{4}}\cos\left(\frac{20\pi}{3}\right) = \frac{I_0}{4}$$

5. (a) $$\Delta x = d\sin\theta = (\mu_2 - i)t$$

$$\Rightarrow \frac{dy}{D} = (\mu_2 - 1)t \Rightarrow y = \frac{(\mu_2 - 1)tD}{d}$$

(b) $$\Delta x = (\mu_2 - 1)t - \left(\frac{\mu_3}{\mu_1} - 1\right)t = 0$$

$$\Rightarrow \mu_3 = \mu_1\mu_2$$

5.8 Fresnel Biprism and Llyod's Mirror

1. (a) $\delta = (\mu - 1)A$

Also, $\tan\delta = \delta = \frac{d/2}{a}$

$$\Rightarrow d = 2a\delta = 2a(\mu - 1)A$$

Here, $a = 20$ cm, $A = 1^\circ = \frac{\pi}{180}$ rad

$$\therefore d = 2\times20\times(1.5-1)\times\frac{\pi}{180^\circ} = 0.349\text{ cm}$$

(b) $\beta = \frac{\lambda D}{d}$, $D = a + b$

$$\therefore \beta = \frac{\lambda(a+b)}{d} = \frac{6000\times10^{-10}\times(20+80)\times10^{-2}}{0.349\times10^{-2}}$$

$$= 0.1719\times10^{-3} = 0.1719\text{ mm}$$

2. In air, $\beta = \dfrac{\lambda(a+b)}{2(\mu_g - 1)Aa}$

In water, $\beta' = \left(\dfrac{\lambda}{\mu_w}\right)\dfrac{(a+b)}{2\left(\dfrac{\mu_g}{\mu_w} - 1\right)Aa}$

$\therefore \quad \dfrac{\beta'}{\beta} = \dfrac{\mu_g - 1}{\mu_g - \mu_w}$

$\Rightarrow \quad \dfrac{\beta'}{1} = \dfrac{1.5 - 1}{1.5 - 1.33}$

$\Rightarrow \quad \beta' = 2.94 \text{ mm}$

3.

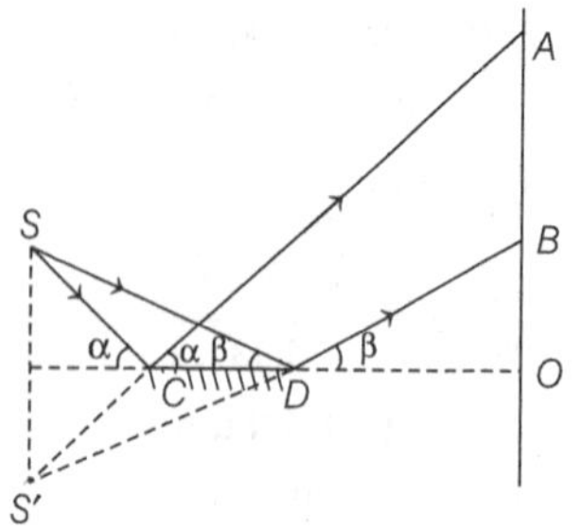

The reflected rays at the ends C and D of the plane mirror will hit the screen at the points A are B, respectively. The superposition of the reflected rays S and direct rays from S will take place between A and B.

$$AB = OA - OB = OC\tan\alpha - OD\tan\beta$$

$$= 195\left(\frac{0.1}{5}\right) - 190\left(\frac{0.1}{10}\right) = 2 \text{ cm}$$

Fringe width $= \dfrac{\lambda D}{d} = \dfrac{5000 \times 10^{-10} \times (190 + 5 + 5) \times 10^{-2}}{2 \times 10^{-3}}$

$= 0.5 \text{ mm}$

Number of fringes $= \dfrac{AB}{\text{Fringe width}}$

$= \dfrac{2 \times 10}{0.5} = 40$

4.

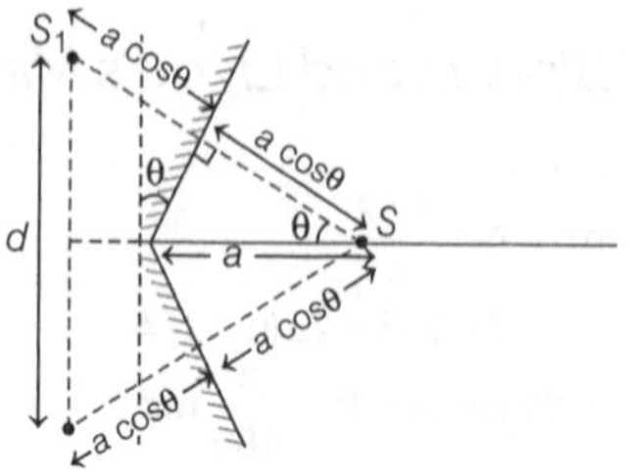

Distance between two source S_1 and S_2,

$$d = 2(2a\cos\theta\sin\theta) = 2a\sin 2\theta$$

Screen distance, $D = b + (2a\cos\theta)\cos\theta = b + 2a\cos^2\theta$

$$\beta = \frac{\lambda D}{d} = \frac{\lambda(b + 2a\cos^2\theta)}{2a\sin 2\theta} = \frac{\lambda(b + 2a)}{4a\theta}$$

[$\because \theta$ is very small]

5.9 Thin Film Interference

1. Condition for minima,

$$\Delta x = 2\mu t = n\lambda$$

$\Rightarrow 2 \times 1.40 \times t = 1 \times 400 \times 10^{-9}$

{$\because n = 1$ for minimum thickness}

$\Rightarrow \quad t = 143 \times 10^{-9}\text{m} = 143 \text{ nm}$

2. Condition for maxima,

$$\Delta x = 2\mu t = (2n - 1)\frac{\lambda}{2}$$

$\Rightarrow \quad \lambda = \dfrac{4\mu t}{2n - 1}$

$= \dfrac{4 \times 1.5 \times 0.5 \times 10^{-6}}{2n - 1} = \dfrac{3000}{2n - 1} \text{ nm}$

For $n = 1, \lambda = 3000$ nm
$n = 2, \lambda = 1000$ nm
$n = 3, \lambda = 600$ nm
$n = 4, \lambda = 429$ nm
$n = 5, \lambda = 333$ nm

So, in the visible region (400 – 700nm), wavelengths strongly reflected will be 429nm and 600 nm.

3. Since, glass is denser than the film, condition for minima will be $\Delta x = 2\mu t = (2n - 1)\dfrac{\lambda}{2}$

$\Rightarrow \quad 2 \times 1.25 \times t = (2n - 1)\dfrac{(5000 \times 10^{-10})}{2}$

$\Rightarrow \quad t = 10^{-7}$ m $\qquad \because [n = 1$ for minimum thickness]

4. For refraction from air to water,

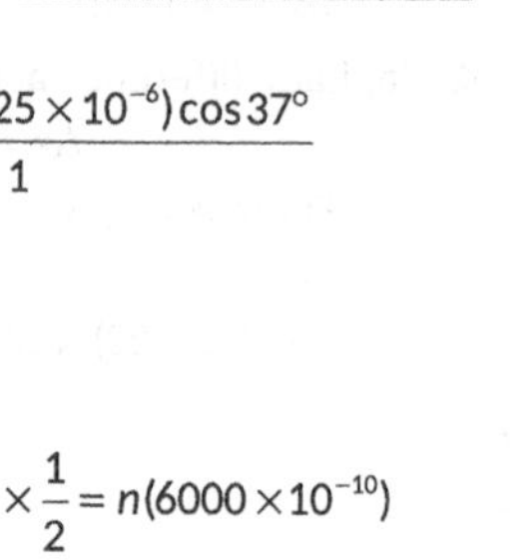

$1 \times \sin 53° = \dfrac{4}{3}\sin r$

$\Rightarrow \quad \sin r = \dfrac{3}{5}$

$\Rightarrow \quad r = 37°$

Condition for maxima,

$$\Delta x = 2\mu t\cos r = n\lambda$$

$\Rightarrow \quad \lambda = \dfrac{2\mu t\cos r}{n}$

$= \dfrac{2 \times (4/3) \times (0.25 \times 10^{-6})\cos 37°}{1}$

$= \dfrac{16}{3} \times 10^{-7}$ m

5. Condition for minima,

$$2\mu t\cos r = n\lambda$$

$\Rightarrow \quad 2 \times 1.5 \times 1.2 \times 10^{-3} \times 10^{-3} \times \dfrac{1}{2} = n(6000 \times 10^{-10})$

$\Rightarrow \quad n = 3$

6. $\dfrac{t}{x} = \dfrac{h}{l} \quad \Rightarrow \quad t = \dfrac{hx}{l}$

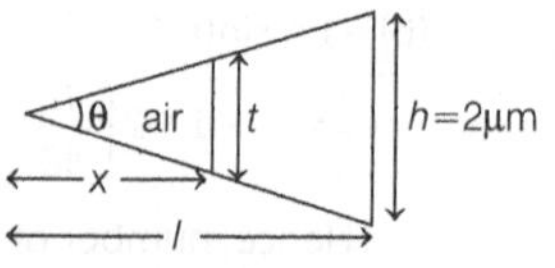

Condition for maxima, $2\mu t = n\lambda$

$\Rightarrow \quad 2\mu\left(\dfrac{hx_n}{l}\right) = n\lambda$

$\Rightarrow \quad x_n = \left(\frac{\lambda l}{2\mu h}\right) n$

Fringe width, $\beta = x_n - x_{n-1} = \frac{\lambda l}{2\mu h}$

Number of bright lines $= \frac{l}{\beta} = \frac{2\mu h}{\lambda} = \frac{2 \times 1 \times 2 \times 10^{-6}}{400 \times 10^{-9}} = 10$

7. $t = x \tan\theta = x\theta$

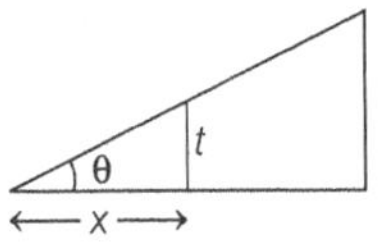

Condition for minima, $2\mu t = n\lambda$

$\Rightarrow \quad 2\mu(x_n\theta) = n\lambda$

$\Rightarrow \quad x_n = \frac{n\lambda}{2\mu\theta}$

Fringe width, $\beta = x_n - x_{n-1} = \frac{\lambda}{2\mu\theta}$

N = No. of fringes per cm of wedge length $= \frac{1}{\beta}$

$\Rightarrow \quad N = \frac{2\mu\theta}{\lambda} = \frac{2 \times 1.5 \times \left(\frac{20}{3600} \times \frac{\pi}{180}\right)}{5.82 \times 10^{-7}}$

$= 500$ per meter $= 5$ per cm

Level 2

Single Choice Correct Questions

1. Fringe width, $\beta = \frac{\lambda D}{d}$ ...(i)

After shifting the screen,

$\beta = 3 \times 10^{-5} = \frac{\lambda(D - 5 \times 10^{-2})}{d}$ ...(ii)

Subtracting Eq. (ii) from Eq. (i),

$3 \times 10^{-5} = \frac{\lambda(5 \times 10^{-2})}{10^{-3}} \quad \Rightarrow \quad \lambda = 6000$ Å

2. Width of field view $= n\beta = \frac{n\lambda D}{d}$

$\therefore \quad n_1\lambda_1 = n_2\lambda_2$

$\Rightarrow \quad 60 \times 7200 = n_2 \times 5400$

$\Rightarrow \quad n_2 = 80$

3. For 9th bright fringe, $y_1 = \frac{9\lambda D}{d}$

For 2nd dark fringe, $y_2 = \frac{3\lambda D}{2d}$

$y_1 - y_2 = 7.5 \times 10^{-3}$

$\Rightarrow \quad \frac{9\lambda D}{d} - \frac{3\lambda D}{2d} = 7.5 \times 10^{-3}$

$\Rightarrow \quad \frac{15}{2} \times \frac{\lambda \times 1}{0.5 \times 10^{-3}} = 7.5 \times 10^{-3}$

$\Rightarrow \quad \lambda = 5000$ Å

4. Angular fringe width $= \frac{\lambda}{d} = 2°$

$\Rightarrow \quad \frac{\lambda}{d} = 2\left(\frac{\pi}{180°}\right) = 0.035$

5. For maxima, $\Delta x = d \sin\theta = n\lambda$

$\Rightarrow \quad 1 \times 10^{-3} \sin\theta = 1000 \times 500 \times 10^{-9}$

$\Rightarrow \quad \sin\theta = \frac{1}{2} \quad \Rightarrow \quad \theta = 30°$

$\tan\theta = \frac{y}{D} \quad \Rightarrow \quad y = D\tan\theta$

$\Rightarrow \quad y = 1 \times \tan 30° = 0.577$ m

6. For 10th bright fringe in liquid,

$y_1 = \frac{10\lambda D}{\mu d}$

For 6th dark fringe in vacuum, $y_2 = \frac{11\lambda D}{2d}$

$y_1 = y_2 \quad \Rightarrow \quad \frac{10\lambda D}{\mu d} = \frac{11\lambda D}{2d}$

$\Rightarrow \quad \mu = 1.8$

7. Central maxima will be unaffected.

$\therefore$ y-coordinate of central maxima = 2 cm

Fringe width will decrese by a factor of $\mu = 1.5$

$\therefore$ y-coordinate of 10th maxima $= 2 + \frac{(5-2)}{1.5} = 4$ cm

8. Central maxima will be white

$\therefore$ Distance of central maxima from $O = \frac{2d}{3} - \frac{d}{2} = \frac{d}{6}$

9. Detector recieves direct and reflected waves.

Distance between 2 successive positions of maxima $= \frac{\lambda}{2}$

For 14th successive maxima, $\frac{13\lambda}{2} = 0.13$

$\Rightarrow \quad \lambda = 0.02$ m

$f = \frac{v}{\lambda} = \frac{3 \times 10^8}{0.02} = 1.5 \times 10^{10}$ Hz

10. For nth maxima, $y = \frac{n\lambda D}{d}$

For the maxima exectly infront of a slit,

$y = \frac{n\lambda D}{d} = \frac{d}{2}$

$\Rightarrow \quad \lambda = \frac{d^2}{2nD}$

where $n = 1, 2, 3, \ldots\ldots$

$\Rightarrow \quad \lambda = \frac{d^2}{2D}, \frac{d^2}{4D}, \frac{d^2}{6D} \ldots\ldots$

11. To obtain an interference pattern we need a monochromatic light with two sources of same frequency i.e., coherent sources.

12. To make the fringe pattern visible, the fringe width must be increased for which d should be decreased d is the distance between S_2 and S_3

13. When slits are of equal width, then intensity at maxima is $4I_0$ and intensity at minima is zero. When width of one slit is doubled, intensity at maxima will increase and intensity at minima is non-zero and hence will also increase.

14. For first maxima, $\Delta x = d\sin\theta = \lambda$

If the screen is moved away, path difference at P decreases. When path difference decreases to $\lambda/2$, first minima will be observed at P. Hence, point P will observe a decrease in intensity till the position of minima is reached and after that intensity will increase due to the central maxima.

15. $\frac{I_1}{I_2} = \beta \Rightarrow I_1 = \beta I_2$

$$I_{max} = (\sqrt{I_1} + \sqrt{I_2}) = I_2(\sqrt{\beta}+1)^2$$
$$I_{max} = (\sqrt{I_1} - \sqrt{I_2}) = I_2(\sqrt{\beta}-1)^2$$
$$\therefore \quad \frac{I_{max} - I_{min}}{I_{max} + I_{min}} = \frac{2\sqrt{\beta}}{1+\beta}$$

16. $\Delta\phi = \frac{2\pi}{\lambda}\Delta x = \frac{2\pi}{\lambda}\left(\frac{\lambda}{3}\right) = \frac{2\pi}{3}$

$$I = I_1 + I_2 + 2\sqrt{I_1}\sqrt{I_2}\cos\Delta\phi = I_0 + I_0 + 2\sqrt{I_0}\sqrt{I_0}\cos\left(\frac{2\pi}{3}\right) = I_0$$

For bright fringe, $I = 4I_0$

Required ratio $= \frac{I_0}{4I_0} = \frac{1}{4}$

17 Intensity due to each slit $= \frac{I_0}{4}$

$$I = I_1 + I_2 + 2\sqrt{I_1}\sqrt{I_2}\cos\Delta\phi$$
$$\Rightarrow \frac{I_0}{2} = \frac{I_0}{4} + \frac{I_0}{4} + 2\sqrt{\frac{I_0}{4}}\sqrt{\frac{I_0}{4}}\cos\Delta\phi$$
$$\Rightarrow \cos\Delta\phi = 0$$
$$\Rightarrow \Delta\phi = (2n-1)\frac{\pi}{2} \text{ where } n \in I$$

Also, $\Delta\phi = \frac{2\pi}{\lambda}\Delta x \Rightarrow (2n-1)\frac{\pi}{2} = \frac{2\pi}{\lambda}\Delta x$

$$\Rightarrow \Delta x = \frac{(2n-1)\lambda}{4}$$

Also, $\Delta x = d\sin\theta$

$$\Rightarrow (2n-1)\frac{\lambda}{4} = \frac{dy}{D} \Rightarrow y = \frac{(2n-1)D\lambda}{4d}$$

If $n = 1$, $y = 1.25$ mm

18. $\Delta x = d\sin\theta = \frac{dy}{D}$

$$\Delta\phi = \frac{2\pi}{\lambda}\Delta x \Rightarrow \Delta\phi = \frac{2\pi}{\lambda}\frac{dy}{D} = \frac{2\pi y}{\beta}$$

Intensity due to each slit $= \frac{I_0}{4}$

$$I = I_1 + I_2 = 2\sqrt{I_1}\sqrt{I_2}\cos\Delta\phi$$
$$= \frac{I_0}{4} + \frac{I_0}{4} + 2\sqrt{\frac{I_0}{4}}\sqrt{\frac{I_0}{4}}\cos\left(\frac{2\pi y}{\beta}\right)$$
$$= \frac{I_0}{2}\left(1 + \cos\left(\frac{2\pi y}{\beta}\right)\right)$$
$$= \frac{I_0}{2}2\cos^2\left(\frac{\pi y}{\beta}\right) = I_0\cos^2\left(\frac{\pi y}{\beta}\right)$$

19. $I_{max} = (\sqrt{I_1} + \sqrt{I_2})^2 = (\sqrt{I} + \sqrt{4I})^2 = 9I$

$$I_{min} = (\sqrt{I_1} - \sqrt{I_2})^2 = (\sqrt{I} - \sqrt{4I})^2 = I$$
$$I_{avg} = \frac{I_{max} + I_{min}}{2} = \frac{9I + I}{2} = 5I$$

Also, $I = I_1 + I_2 + 2\sqrt{I_1}\sqrt{I_2}\cos\Delta\phi$

$$\Rightarrow 5I = I + 4I + 2\sqrt{I}\sqrt{4I}\cos\Delta\phi$$
$$\Rightarrow \cos\Delta\phi = 0 \Rightarrow \Delta\phi = (2n-1)\frac{\pi}{2}$$

Also, $\Delta\phi = \frac{2\pi}{\lambda}\Delta x$

$$\Rightarrow (2n-1)\frac{\pi}{2} = \frac{2\pi}{\lambda}\Delta x$$
$$\Rightarrow \Delta x = \frac{(2n-1)\lambda}{4}$$

Also, $\Delta x = d\sin\theta$

$$\Rightarrow \frac{(2n-1)\lambda}{4} = \frac{dy}{D}$$
$$\Rightarrow y = \frac{(2n-1)\beta}{4}$$

For $n = 1$, $y = \frac{\beta}{4}$

20. Intensity due to each slit $= \frac{I_0}{4}$

When one slit is reduced to one fourth, its intensity will also become one fourth i.e. $\frac{I_0}{16}$

$$I_{max} = (\sqrt{I_1} + \sqrt{I_2})^2 = \left(\sqrt{\frac{I_0}{4}} + \sqrt{\frac{I_0}{16}}\right)^2 = \frac{9I_0}{16}$$

21.
$$y_1 = y_2$$
$$\Rightarrow \frac{n_1\lambda_1 D}{d} = \frac{n_2\lambda_2 D}{d}$$
$$\Rightarrow n(7800) = (n+1)(5200)$$
$$\Rightarrow 3n = 2(n+1)$$
$$\Rightarrow n = 2$$

22.
$$y_1 = y_2$$
$$\Rightarrow 4\frac{\lambda_1 D}{d} = \frac{9}{2}\frac{\lambda_2 D}{d}$$
$$\Rightarrow 4(6300) = \frac{9}{2}(\lambda)$$
$$\Rightarrow \lambda = 5600 \text{ Å}$$

23.
$$y_1 = y_2$$
$$\Rightarrow n_1\frac{\lambda_1 D}{d} = n_2\frac{\lambda_2 D}{d}$$
$$\Rightarrow n_1\lambda_1 = n_2\lambda_2$$
$$\Rightarrow n_1(6500) = n_2(5200) \Rightarrow 5n_1 = 4n_2$$

For the least distance, $n_1 = 4$ and $n_2 = 5$

$$\therefore \quad y_1 = \frac{n_1\lambda_1 D}{d} = \frac{4 \times 6500 \times 10^{-10} \times 1.2}{2 \times 10^{-3}}$$
$$= 0.156 \times 10^{-2}\text{m} = 0.156 \text{ cm}$$

24. Fringe width, $\beta = \frac{\lambda D}{d}$

Violet has the least wavelength. So, fringe width will be least for violet. Thus the bright fringe next to the central will be violet.

25. $\Delta x = (SS_1 + S_1O) - (SS_2 + S_2O) = 2(\sqrt{D^2 + d^2} - D)$

$$= 2\left[D\left[1 + \frac{d^2}{D^2}\right]^{1/2} - D\right]$$

$$= 2\left[D\left[1 + \frac{d^2}{2D^2}\right] - D\right] = \frac{d^2}{D}$$

For minima, $\Delta x = (2n-1)\frac{\lambda}{2}$

$\Rightarrow \quad \frac{d^2_{min}}{D} = \frac{\lambda}{2} \qquad \because \{n = 1\}$

$\Rightarrow \quad d_{min} = \sqrt{\frac{\lambda D}{2}}$

26. Let thickness be t,

No. of wavelengths of yellow light in air, $n_1 = \frac{t}{\lambda_1}$

No. of wavelengths of yellow light in vacuum, $n_2 = \frac{t}{\lambda_2}$

$\therefore \quad n_1 = n_2 + 1$

$\Rightarrow \quad \frac{t}{\left(\frac{6000 \times 10^{-10}}{1.0003}\right)} = \frac{t}{6000 \times 10^{-10}} + 1$

$\Rightarrow \quad t = 2 \times 10^{-3} \text{m} = 2 \text{ mm}$

27. Optical path length $= \int_0^1 \mu dx$

$$= \int_0^1 (1 + x^2)\, dx = \left[x + \frac{x^3}{3}\right]_0^1 = \frac{4}{3} \text{m}$$

28. For constructive interference,

$\Delta x = n\lambda$

$\Rightarrow \quad (n_1 - 1)L_1 - (n_2 - 1)L_2 = n\lambda$

$\Rightarrow \quad (1.7 - 1)3.5 - (1.25 - 1)5 = n\lambda$

$\Rightarrow \quad \lambda = 1.2 \text{ mm} \qquad \because$ {for longest wavelength, $n = 1$}

29. $\Delta x = (\mu - 1)t = 30\lambda$

$\Rightarrow \quad (1.6 - 1)t = 30 \times 4800 \times 10^{-10}$

$\Rightarrow \quad t = 2.4 \times 10^{-5}$ m

30. $\Delta x = (\mu - 1)t = 3\lambda$

$\Rightarrow \quad (1.5 - 1)t = 3 \times 5450 \times 10^{-10}$

$\Rightarrow \quad t = 3.27 \times 10^{-6}$ m

31. Optical path difference $= (\mu_{rel} - 1)t = \left(\frac{n_3}{n_2} - 1\right)t$

Wavelength of light in medium, $n_2 = \frac{\lambda_{vacuum}}{n_2} = \frac{n_1\lambda_1}{n_2}$

$$\Delta\phi = \frac{2\pi}{\lambda}\Delta x = \frac{2\pi}{\left(\frac{n_1\lambda_1}{\lambda_2}\right)} \times \left(\frac{n_3}{n_2} - 1\right)t = \frac{2\pi}{n_1\lambda_1}(n_3 - n_2)$$

32. (c)

33. $\Delta\phi = \frac{2\pi}{\lambda}\Delta x = \frac{2\pi}{\lambda}(\mu - 1)t$

Intensity due to each slit $= \frac{I_0}{4}$

$$I = I_1 + I_2 + 2\sqrt{I_1}\sqrt{I_2}\cos\Delta\phi$$

$$= \frac{I_0}{4} + \frac{I_0}{4} + 2\sqrt{\frac{I_0}{4}}\sqrt{\frac{I_0}{4}}\cos\Delta\phi$$

$$= I_0\cos^2\left(\frac{\Delta\phi}{2}\right) = I_0\cos^2\left(\frac{\pi(\mu - 1)t}{\lambda}\right)$$

34. New intensity of the geometrical centre $= \frac{75}{100}(4I_0) = 3I_0$

Also, $I = I_1 + I_2 + 2\sqrt{I_1}\sqrt{I_2}\cos\Delta\phi$

$\Rightarrow 3I_0 = I_0 + I_0 + 2\sqrt{I_0}\sqrt{I_0}\cos\Delta\phi$

$\Rightarrow \quad \cos\Delta\phi = \frac{1}{2} \Rightarrow \Delta\phi = 2n\pi \pm \frac{\pi}{3}$

where $n = 0, 1, 2, 3$ ......

$$\Delta x = (\mu - 1)t = (1.5 - 1)t = \frac{t}{2}$$

$$\Delta\phi = \frac{2\pi}{\lambda}\Delta x$$

$\Rightarrow \quad 2n\pi \pm \frac{\pi}{3} = \frac{2\pi}{6000 \times 10^{-10}} \times \frac{t}{2}$

$\Rightarrow \quad t = (1.2n \pm 0.2)\mu\text{m}$

For $n = 0, t = 0.2\,\mu\text{m}$

$n = 1, t = 1\mu\text{m}$ or $t = 1.4\ \mu\text{m}$

35. $\Delta x = |\mu_1 - \mu_2|t = d\sin\theta$

$\Rightarrow \quad |\mu_1 - \mu_2|t = d\theta$

$\Rightarrow \quad |1.8 - \mu|(0.5) = 1 \times 0.1$

$\Rightarrow \quad \mu = 1.6$ or $\mu = 2$

36. (d)

37. $\Delta x = |\mu_1 - \mu_2|t = n\lambda$

$\Rightarrow (1.52 - 1.40)(10.4 \times 10^{-6}) = n\lambda$

$\Rightarrow \quad \lambda = \frac{1248}{n}$ nm

For $n = 1, \lambda = 1248$ nm

$n = 2, \lambda = 624$ nm

$n = 3, \lambda = 416$ nm

$n = 4, \lambda = 312$ nm

So, in the range 400 nm to 780 nm, only 416 nm and 624 nm will form maxima at O.

38. $\Delta x = 3a\cos\theta = n\lambda$

$\Rightarrow \quad 3a\cos\theta = n\left(\frac{a}{5}\right) \Rightarrow \cos\theta = \frac{n}{15}$

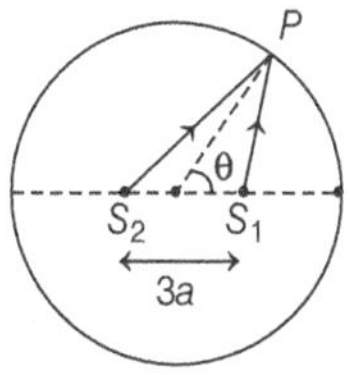

For $n = 0, 1, 2, 3, \ldots\ldots 15$, there will be 16 maxima in each quadrant and total no. of maxima will be $4 \times 16 - 4 = 60$. Since, 4 maxima conicide at the edges of quadrants.

39. $$\Delta x = d \sin\theta = (2n-1)\frac{\lambda}{2}$$

$$\Rightarrow \quad 3\lambda \sin\theta = (2n-1)\frac{\lambda}{2} \Rightarrow \sin\theta = \frac{2n-1}{6}$$

where $n = 1, 2, 3, \ldots\ldots$

Also, $\sin\theta \le 1$

$$\Rightarrow \quad \frac{2n-1}{6} \le 1 \quad \Rightarrow \quad n \le 3.5$$

So, we get 3 minima corresponding to values of $n = 1, 2$ and 3 from 0 to ∞. Similarly, we get another 3 minima from $-\infty$ to 0.

$\therefore$ Total no. of minima from $-\infty$ to $\infty = 6$

40. When a ray (here water wavefront) refracts from a rarer to denser medium, it bends towards the normal of the interface. Wavefront is perpendicular to wave motion.

The wavefront we got for the deep region is similar to the wavefront *I* in the question.

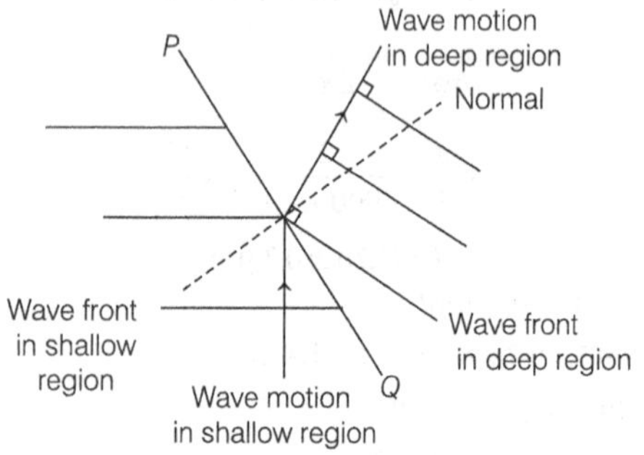

41. The wavefront equation must be of form

$$ax + by + cz = 1 \text{ where } a^2 + b^2 + c^2 = 1$$

(a, b, c are cosine of angles made with x, y, z axes, respectively)

Applying this to the given equation,

$$1^2 + 2^2 + 3^2 = c \quad \Rightarrow \quad c = \sqrt{14}$$

$$\therefore \text{ Angle made with } Y\text{-axis} = \cos^{-1}\left(\frac{2}{\sqrt{14}}\right)$$

42. Separation between the sources $= 2a(\mu_g - 1)A$

$$d = 2 \times 1(1.5 - 1)(2 \times 10^{-3}) = 2 \times 10^{-3} \text{ m}$$

$$\text{Fringe width, } \beta = \frac{\lambda D}{d} = \frac{(6000 \times 10^{-10})(1+4)}{2 \times 10^{-3}} = 1.5 \text{ mm}$$

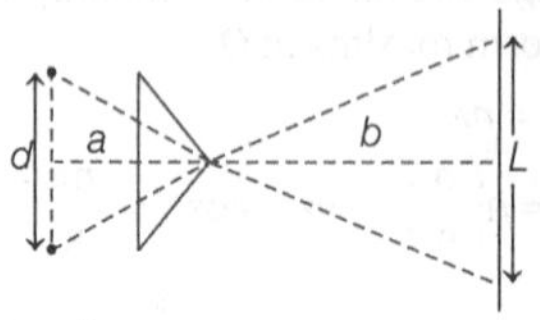

From figure, $\frac{L}{d} = \frac{b}{a}$

$$\Rightarrow \quad L = \frac{4}{1} \times 2 \times 10^{-3} = 8 \text{ mm}$$

$$\text{Number of fringes, } N = \frac{L}{\beta} = \frac{8}{1.5} = 5.3 \approx 5$$

43. Fringe width in air, $\beta_1 = \frac{\lambda_a(a+b)}{2a(\mu_g - 1)A}$

Fringe width in water, $\beta_2 = \frac{(\lambda_a/\mu_w)(a+b)}{2a\left(\frac{\mu_g}{\mu_w} - 1\right)A} = \frac{\lambda_a(a+b)}{2a(\mu_g - \mu_w)A}$

$$\therefore \quad \frac{\beta_2}{\beta_1} = \frac{\mu_g - 1}{\mu_g - \mu_w} = \frac{(3/2) - 1}{\frac{3}{2} - \frac{4}{3}} = 3$$

44. For first maxima, $\Delta x = \frac{\lambda}{2}$

$$\Rightarrow \quad d \sin\theta = \frac{\lambda}{2}$$

$$\Rightarrow \quad (2 \times 10^{-3})\left(\frac{y}{1}\right) = \frac{600 \times 10^{-9}}{2}$$

$$\Rightarrow \quad y = 0.15 \text{ mm}$$

45.

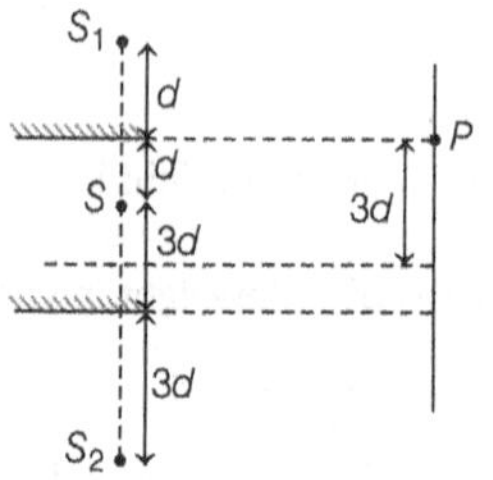

Distance between S_1 and $S_2 = 8d$

Due to phase reversal of reflected light at both the mirrors, condition for point *P* to be 2nd maxima,

$$\Delta x = S_2P - S_1P = (8d)\sin\theta = 2\lambda$$

$$\Rightarrow \quad (8d)\left(\frac{3d}{D}\right) = 2\lambda \quad \Rightarrow \quad \lambda = \frac{12d^2}{D}$$

46. Due to phase reversal at both the interfaces, condition for constructive interference,

$$2\mu t = n\lambda$$

$$\Rightarrow \quad 2 \times 1.25 \times t_{min} = 1 \times 500 \times 10^{-9}$$

$$\Rightarrow \quad t_{min} = 200 \times 10^{-9} \text{ m} = 200 \text{ nm}$$

47. Condition for destructive intefrence,

$$2\mu t = n\lambda \quad \Rightarrow \quad 2 \times 1.61 \times 0.5 \times 10^{-6} = n\lambda$$

$$\Rightarrow \quad \lambda = \left(\frac{1610}{n}\right) \text{nm}$$

For $n = 1, \lambda = 1610$ nm

$n = 2, \lambda = 805$ nm

$n = 3, \lambda = 537$ nm

$n = 4, \lambda = 402.5$ nm

$n = 5, \lambda = 322$ nm

So, wavelengths absent in the range (400 – 700 nm) are 537 nm and 402.5 nm.

48. The layers are air, oil and water. Because $1 < 1.25 < 1.33$, light reflected both from the top and from the bottom surface of the oil suffers phase reversal.

Condition for constructive interference,

$$2\mu t = n\lambda_{red}$$

Condition for destructive interference,

$$2\mu t = \left(n+\frac{1}{2}\right)\lambda_{\text{blue}}$$

$$\therefore \quad \frac{\lambda_{\text{red}}}{\lambda_{\text{blue}}} = 1+\frac{1}{2n} = \frac{640}{512}$$

$$\Rightarrow \quad n = 2$$

Therefore, $t = \dfrac{2(640)}{2(1.25)} = 512\text{ nm}$

49. No. of bright bands $= \dfrac{2\mu t}{\lambda} = 121 - 1$

$$\Rightarrow \quad \frac{2\times 1\times t}{600\times 10^{-9}} = 120 \quad \Rightarrow \quad t = 3.6\times 10^{-5}\text{m}$$

50. Number of fringes $= n = \dfrac{2\mu t}{\lambda}$

$$\Rightarrow \quad n \propto \frac{1}{\lambda} \quad \Rightarrow \quad \frac{n_1}{n_2} = \frac{\lambda_2}{\lambda_1}$$

$$\Rightarrow \quad \frac{30}{n_2} = \frac{7000}{4200} \quad \Rightarrow \quad n_2 = 18$$

Numerical Value Questions

1. Intensity of central maxima $= 4I_0$

$$I = I_1 + I_2 + 2\sqrt{I_1}\sqrt{I_2}\cos\Delta\phi$$

$$\Rightarrow \quad \frac{25}{100}\times 4I_0 = I_0 + I_0 + 2\sqrt{I_0}\sqrt{I_0}\cos\Delta\phi$$

$$\Rightarrow \quad \cos\Delta\phi = -\frac{1}{2} \quad \Rightarrow \quad \Delta\phi = \frac{2\pi}{3}$$

Also, $\quad \Delta\phi = \dfrac{2\pi}{\lambda}\Delta x \quad \Rightarrow \quad \dfrac{2\pi}{3} = \dfrac{2\pi}{627}\Delta x$

$$\Rightarrow \quad \Delta x = 209\text{ nm}$$

2. Intensity of light $\propto$ width of slit

$\therefore$ Intensity of light only due to wider slit $= 4I_0$

For a point on screen intfront of the narrow slit,

$$\Delta x = d\sin\theta = \frac{dy}{D} = \frac{d}{D}\left(\frac{d}{2}\right) = \frac{d^2}{2D}$$

$$\therefore \quad \Delta\phi = \frac{2\pi}{\lambda}\Delta x = \frac{2\pi}{\lambda}\left(\frac{d^2}{2D}\right) = \frac{2\pi}{6000\times 10^{-10}}\times\frac{(1\times 10^{-3})^2}{2\times 5}$$

$$= \frac{\pi}{3}$$

$$I = I_1 + I_2 + 2\sqrt{I_1}\sqrt{I_2}\cos\Delta\phi$$

$$I_0 + 4I_0 + 2\sqrt{I_0}\sqrt{4I_0}\cos\left(\frac{\pi}{3}\right) = 7I_0$$

3. $\quad \Delta x = \left(n+\dfrac{1}{2}\right)\lambda_1 = \left(n+\dfrac{1}{2}-7\right)\lambda_2$

$$\Rightarrow \quad \left(n+\frac{1}{2}\right)3600 = \left(n+\frac{1}{2}-7\right)6000$$

$$\Rightarrow \quad n = 17$$

$$\Delta x = d\sin\theta = \left(n+\frac{1}{2}\right)\lambda_1$$

$$\Rightarrow \quad \frac{dy}{D} = \left(n+\frac{1}{2}\right)\lambda_1$$

$$\Rightarrow \quad \frac{d\times 31.5\times 10^{-3}}{1} = \left(17+\frac{1}{2}\right)(3600\times 10^{-10})$$

$$\Rightarrow \quad d = 2\times 10^{-4}\text{m} = 200\mu\text{m}$$

4. $\quad \Delta x = (\mu - 1)t = n\lambda$

$$\Rightarrow \quad (1.5-1)t_{\min} = (1)\lambda$$

$$\Rightarrow \quad t_{\min} = 2\lambda$$

$$\Rightarrow \quad t_{\min} = 2(140) = 280\text{ nm}$$

5. Let the central maximum be shifted by y

$$\Delta x = d\sin\theta \quad \Rightarrow \quad (\mu-1)t = \frac{dy}{D}$$

$$\Rightarrow \quad y = \frac{(\mu-1)tD}{d} \quad \Rightarrow \quad \frac{dy}{dt} = \left(\frac{d\mu}{dt}\right)\frac{tD}{d}$$

$$\Rightarrow \quad v = (2t+12)\frac{2.4\times 10^{-4}\times 2}{2\times 10^{-3}} = 0.48(t+6)$$

At $t = 4$s, $v = 0.48(4+6) = 4.80$ m/s

6. Let shift of fringe pattern be y

$$\Delta x = d\sin\theta \quad \Rightarrow \quad (\mu-1)t = d\left(\frac{y}{D}\right)$$

$$\Rightarrow \quad y = \frac{(\mu-1)tD}{d}$$

New fringe width $= \dfrac{\lambda(2D)}{d}$

$$\therefore \quad \frac{(\mu-1)tD}{d} = \frac{\lambda(2D)}{d}$$

$$\Rightarrow \quad \lambda = \frac{(\mu-1)t}{2} = \frac{(1.6-1)(1.964\times 10^{-6})}{2} = 5892\text{ Å}$$

7. $\quad \Delta x = d\sin\theta - (\mu-1)t$

$$\Rightarrow \quad n\lambda = \frac{dy}{D} - (\mu-1)t$$

$$\Rightarrow \quad \lambda = \frac{1}{n}\left(\frac{0.5\times 10^{-3}\times 3\times 10^{-3}}{1} - \left(\frac{3}{2}-1\right)(1\times 10^{-6})\right)$$

$$\Rightarrow \quad \lambda = \left(\frac{10000}{n}\right)\text{Å}$$

So, wavelength in the range (4000 – 7000 Å) will be only 5000 Å corresponding to $n = 2$.

$\therefore$ No. of required wavelengths = 1

8. Due to phase reversal from mirror, condition for maximum is

$$\Delta x = d\sin\theta = (2n-1)\frac{\lambda}{2} \quad \Rightarrow \quad \frac{dy}{D} = (2n-1)\frac{\lambda}{2}$$

$$\Rightarrow \quad \frac{(2\times 10^{-3})y_{\min}}{(20+80)\times 10^{-2}} = (2(1)-1)\frac{(5000\times 10^{-10})}{2}$$

$$\Rightarrow \quad y_{\min} = 125\times 10^{-6}\text{m} = 125\,\mu\text{m}$$

9. Due to phase reversal at both the interfaces, condition for maxima is $2\mu t = n\lambda$

$$\Rightarrow \quad 2\times 1.25\times t = 1\times 500\times 10^{-9}$$

$$\Rightarrow \quad t = 2\times 10^{-7}\text{m}$$

Volume = Area × Thickness

$$\Rightarrow \quad 1 = A\times 2\times 10^{-7} \quad \Rightarrow \quad A = 5\times 10^{6}\text{ m}^2 = 5\text{ km}^2$$

10. Phase reversal doesn't take place at both the interfaces. So, condition for minima,

$$2\mu t = (2n-1)\frac{\lambda}{2}$$

$$\Rightarrow \quad 2 \times 1.56 \times 0.25 \times 10^{-6} = (2n-1)\frac{\lambda}{2}$$

$$\Rightarrow \quad \lambda = \left(\frac{1560}{2n-1}\right)\text{nm}$$

For $n = 2$, $\lambda = 520$ nm

Level 3

Single choice correct Questions.

1.

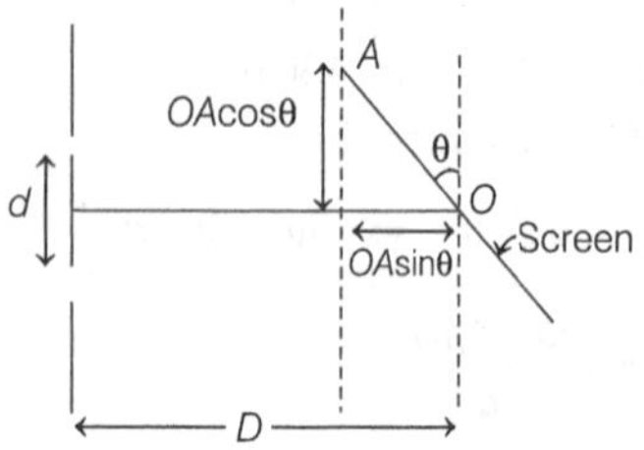

$$\text{Fringe width} = \frac{\lambda(D - OA\sin\theta)}{d} = OA\cos\theta$$

$$\Rightarrow \quad OA = \frac{D\lambda}{d\cos\theta + \lambda\sin\theta} = \frac{D\lambda\sec\theta}{d + \lambda\tan\theta}$$

2. Angular fringe width $= \dfrac{\lambda}{d} = 10^{-3}$rad

No. of fringes on wire AB

$$= \frac{\angle BOA}{\text{Angular fringe width}} = \frac{0.12 \times \frac{\pi}{180}}{10^{-3}} \simeq 2.09$$

$\therefore$ No. of bright spots will be 3.

3.
$$d\sin\theta = n\lambda$$

$$\Rightarrow \quad (0.3 \times 10^{-3})\sin 30° = n(500 \times 10^{-9}) \quad \Rightarrow \quad n = 300$$

Maxima of order 300 occurs at $\theta = \pm 30°$.

So, no of maxima in range $-30° < \theta < 30°$ including central maxima $= 2(299) + 1 = 599$

4. In air, $d\sin 45° = (1)\lambda$

In liquid, $d\sin 30° = (1)\dfrac{\lambda}{\mu}$

$$\therefore \quad \mu = \sqrt{2}$$

5. Angular position of first minimum $= 0.75°$

$$\Rightarrow \quad \frac{\lambda}{2d} = 0.75 \times \frac{\pi}{180}$$

$$\Rightarrow \quad \frac{520 \times 10^{-9}}{2d} = 0.75 \times \frac{\pi}{180}$$

$$\Rightarrow \quad d = 1.986 \times 10^{-5}\text{ m} = 2 \times 10^{-2}\text{ mm}$$

6.
$$I = \frac{75}{100}I_{max} = \frac{3}{4}(4I_0) = 3I_0$$

$$I = I_1 + I_2 + 2\sqrt{I_1}\sqrt{I_2}\cos\Delta\phi$$

$$\Rightarrow \quad 3I_0 = I_0 + I_0 + 2\sqrt{I_0}\sqrt{I_0}\cos\Delta\phi$$

$$\Rightarrow \cos\Delta\phi = \frac{1}{2} \quad \Rightarrow \quad \Delta\phi = \frac{\pi}{3}$$

$$\Delta\phi = \frac{2\pi}{\lambda}\Delta x \quad \Rightarrow \quad \frac{\pi}{3} = \frac{2\pi}{\lambda}\Delta x \quad \Rightarrow \quad \Delta x = \frac{\lambda}{6}$$

Also, $\Delta x = d\sin\theta = \dfrac{\lambda}{6} \quad \Rightarrow \quad \dfrac{dy}{D} = \dfrac{\lambda}{6} \quad \Rightarrow \quad y = \dfrac{\lambda D}{6d}$

$$\text{Required distance} = 2y = 2\left(\frac{\lambda D}{6d}\right) = \frac{\lambda D}{3d}$$

$$= \frac{6000 \times 10^{-10} \times 1}{3 \times 1 \times 10^{-3}} = 0.20\text{ mm}$$

7. Intensity due to each slit $= \dfrac{I_0}{4}$

$$I = I_1 + I_2 + 2\sqrt{I_1}\sqrt{I_2}\cos\Delta\phi$$

$$\Rightarrow \quad 0.5I_0 = \frac{I_0}{4} + \frac{I_0}{4} + 2\sqrt{\frac{I_0}{4}}\sqrt{\frac{I_0}{4}}\cos\Delta\phi$$

$$\Rightarrow \quad \cos\Delta\phi = 0$$

After doubling the width of one slit,

$$I = I_1 + I_2 + 2\sqrt{I_1}\sqrt{I_2}\cos\Delta\phi$$

$$= 2\left(\frac{I_0}{4}\right) + \frac{I_0}{4} + 0 = 0.75\,I_0$$

8.
$$\Delta x = d\sin\theta = \frac{dy}{D} = \frac{d(d/2)}{10d} = \frac{d}{20}$$

$$\Delta\phi = \frac{2\pi}{\lambda}\Delta x = \frac{2\pi}{d/5} \times \frac{d}{20} = \frac{\pi}{2}$$

Intensity due to each slit $= \dfrac{I_0}{4}$

$$I = I_1 + I_2 + 2\sqrt{I_1}\sqrt{I_2}\cos\Delta\phi = \frac{I_0}{4} + \frac{I_0}{4} + 0 = \frac{I_0}{2}$$

9. P to Q : Convergence is increasing

Q to R : Direction is changing

10.

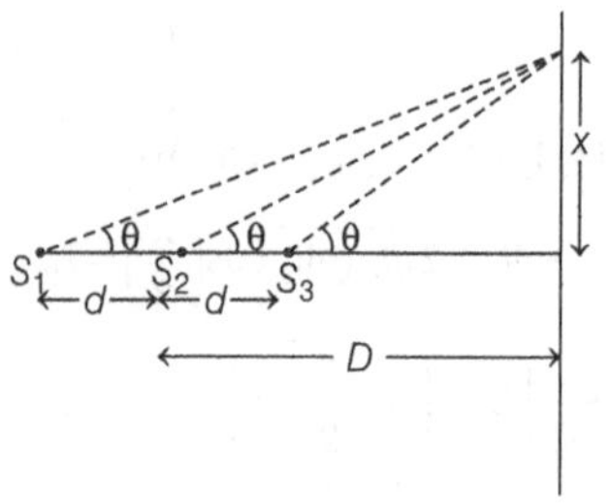

For nearest minima,

$$d\cos\theta = \frac{2\lambda}{3} + \lambda + \lambda \quad \Rightarrow \quad 3\lambda\cos\theta = \frac{8\lambda}{3}$$

$$\Rightarrow \quad \cos\theta = \frac{8}{9}$$

$$\tan\theta = \frac{x}{D} \quad \Rightarrow \quad \frac{\sqrt{17}}{8} = \frac{x}{D} \quad \Rightarrow \quad x = \frac{\sqrt{17}D}{8}$$

11. (b)

12. For $|x| >> d$,

$$\Delta x = \underbrace{d+2d+3d}_{\text{for } x=0} + \underbrace{d+2d}_{\text{for } x=d} + \underbrace{d}_{\text{for } x=2d} = 10d$$

For minima, $\Delta x = (2n-1)\frac{\lambda}{2} \Rightarrow 10d = (2n-1)\frac{\lambda}{2}$

For $n = 3$, $d = \frac{\lambda}{4}$

For maxima, $\Delta x = n\lambda$

$\Rightarrow \quad 10d = n\lambda \Rightarrow d = \frac{n\lambda}{10}$ where $n = 1, 2, 3, ...$

13. (b)

14. Reflected ray from mirror will undergo phase reversal of π.

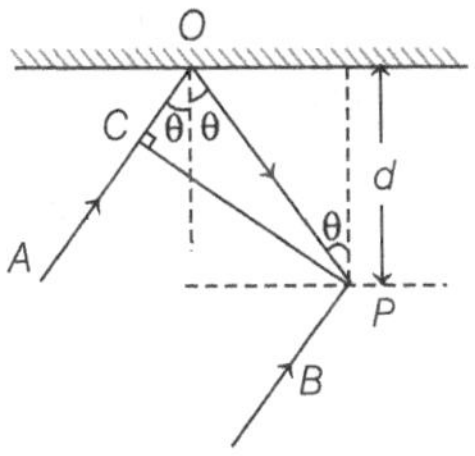

$OP = d\sec\theta, OC = OP\cos 2\theta = d\sec\theta\cos 2\theta$

$\Delta x = OC + OP$

$= d\sec\theta + d\sec\theta\cos 2\theta$

$= d\sec\theta(1+\cos 2\theta)$

$= d\sec\theta(2\cos^2\theta) = 2d\cos\theta$

Condition for constructive interference

$\Delta x = (2n-1)\frac{\lambda}{2}$

$\Rightarrow \quad 2d\cos\theta = \frac{\lambda}{2} \quad \because \{n = 1\}$

$\Rightarrow \quad \cos\theta = \frac{\lambda}{4d}$

15. $\Delta x = d\sin\theta = n\lambda$

$\Rightarrow \quad b\left(\frac{x}{y}\right) = n\lambda \Rightarrow n = \frac{bx}{\lambda y}$

$\frac{dn}{dt} = \frac{x}{\lambda y}\frac{db}{dt} = \frac{xv}{\lambda y}$

16. $I = I_1 + I_2 + 2\sqrt{I_1}\sqrt{I_2}\cos\Delta\phi$

$\Rightarrow \quad \frac{3}{4}(4I_0) = I_0 + I_0 + 2\sqrt{I_0}\sqrt{I_0}\cos\Delta\phi$

$\Rightarrow \quad \cos\Delta\phi = \frac{1}{2}$

$\Rightarrow \quad \Delta\phi = 4\pi + \frac{\pi}{3}$ or $6\pi - \frac{\pi}{3} = \frac{13\pi}{3}$ or $\frac{17\pi}{3}$

Also, $\quad \Delta\phi = \frac{2\pi}{\lambda}\Delta x \Rightarrow \frac{13\pi}{3}$ or $\frac{17\pi}{3} = \frac{2\pi}{\lambda}\Delta x$

$\Rightarrow \quad \Delta x = \frac{13\lambda}{6}$ or $\frac{17\lambda}{6}$

At $t = 0$, y-coordinate of the point $= \frac{3\lambda D}{d}$

At $t = 1$, $\Delta x = d\sin\theta = \frac{dy}{D}$

$\Rightarrow \quad \frac{13\lambda}{6}$ or $\frac{17\lambda}{6} = \frac{d\left(\frac{3\lambda D}{d}\right)}{D + v(1)}$

$\Rightarrow \quad v = \frac{5D}{13}$ or $\frac{D}{17}$

17. y = Distance of point A from $O = 4\left(\frac{\lambda D}{d}\right)$

At time t, $\quad \Delta x = d\sin\theta = n\lambda$

$\Rightarrow \quad d\left(\frac{y}{D'}\right) = 2\lambda \quad \because \{n = 2$ for 2nd order maxima$\}$

$\Rightarrow \quad d\frac{\left(\frac{4\lambda D}{d}\right)}{D'} = 2\lambda \Rightarrow D' = 2D$

Also, $\quad S = ut + \frac{1}{2}at^2$

$\Rightarrow \quad D' - D + 0 + \frac{1}{2}a_0t^2$

$\Rightarrow \quad t = \sqrt{\frac{2D}{a_0}}$

18. $\Delta x = d\sin\theta = \frac{dy}{L}$

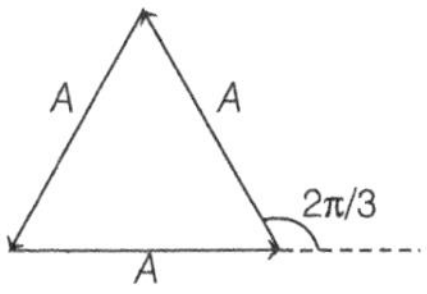

$\Delta\phi = \frac{2\pi}{\lambda}\Delta x$

$\Rightarrow \quad \frac{2\pi}{3} = \frac{2\pi}{\lambda}\left(\frac{dy}{L}\right)$

$\Rightarrow \quad y = \frac{\lambda L}{3d}$

19. $\Delta x = n\lambda$

$\Rightarrow \quad (\mu - 1)t = N\lambda$

$\Rightarrow \quad (2-1)t = 40 \times 600 \times 10^{-9}$

$\Rightarrow \quad t = 24 \times 10^{-6}$ m $= 24\,\mu$m

20. When mica sheet is shifted from S_1 to S_2,

$\Delta x = 2(\mu - 1)t = n\lambda \Rightarrow n = \frac{2(\mu-1)t}{\lambda}$

21. $I = I_1 + I_2 + 2\sqrt{I_1}\sqrt{I_2}\cos\Delta\phi$

$\Rightarrow \quad \frac{1}{2}(4I_0) = I_0 + I_0 + 2\sqrt{I_0}\sqrt{I_0}\cos\Delta\phi$

$\Rightarrow \quad \cos\Delta\phi = 0 \Rightarrow \Delta\phi = \frac{\pi}{2}$

Also, $\Delta\phi = \frac{2\pi}{\lambda}\Delta x \Rightarrow \frac{\pi}{2} = \frac{2\pi}{\lambda}\Delta x \Rightarrow \Delta x = \frac{\lambda}{4}$

$\Delta x = (\mu - 1)t \Rightarrow \frac{\lambda}{4} = \left(\frac{3}{2} - 1\right)t \Rightarrow t = \frac{\lambda}{2}$

22. $\Delta x = (\mu - 1)t, \quad \Delta\phi = \frac{2\pi}{\lambda}\Delta x = \frac{2\pi(\mu-1)t}{\lambda}$

$I = 4I_0\cos^2\left(\frac{\Delta\phi}{2}\right) = 4I_0\cos^2\left(\frac{\pi(\mu-1)t}{\lambda}\right)$

23. Wavelength of light in $n_2 = \frac{\lambda n_1}{n_2}$

$$\Delta x = \left(\frac{n}{n_2} - 1\right)t$$

$$\Delta\phi = \frac{2\pi}{\lambda'}\Delta x = \frac{2\pi}{\left(\frac{\lambda n_1}{n_2}\right)}\left(\frac{n}{n_2} - 1\right)t$$

$$= \frac{2\pi(n - n_2)t}{\lambda n_1} = \frac{2\pi(1.5 - 1.4)(1.2 \times 10^{-6})}{400 \times 10^{-9} \times 1.2} = \frac{\pi}{2}$$

$$I = I_1 + I_2 + 2\sqrt{I_1}\sqrt{I_2}\cos\Delta\phi = I_0 + I_0 + 0 = 2I_0$$

24.

$$\Delta\phi = (N_2 - N_1)2\pi$$

$\therefore$ $\Delta\phi_1 = (2.75 - 2.25)\,2\pi = \pi$

$$\Delta\phi_2 = (2.80 - 1.80)\,2\pi = 2\pi$$

$$\Delta\phi_3 = (3.25 - 3.00)\,2\pi = \frac{\pi}{2}$$

$$\Delta\phi_4 = (4.00 - 3.25)2\pi = \frac{3\pi}{2}$$

$$I = 4I_0\cos^2\left(\frac{\Delta\phi}{2}\right)$$

$\therefore$ $I_1 = 0, I_2 = 4I_0, I_3 = 2I_0, I_4 = 2I_0$

Hence, $I_2 > I_3 = I_4 > I_1$

25. $\Delta x = \int_0^l (\mu - \mu_0)dx = \int_0^l \frac{\mu_0 x}{l}dx = \frac{\mu_0 l}{2}$

For maxima at O,

$$\Delta x = n\lambda$$

$\Rightarrow$ $\frac{\mu_0 l_{min}}{2} = (1)(6000\ \text{Å})$

$\Rightarrow$ $l_{min} = 12000\ \text{Å}$

26.

$$I = I_1 + I_2 + 2\sqrt{I_1}\sqrt{I_2}\cos\Delta\phi$$

$\Rightarrow$ $\frac{1}{2}(4I_0) = I_0 + I_0 + 2\sqrt{I_0}\sqrt{I_0}\cos\Delta\phi$

$$\cos\Delta\phi = 0 \quad \Rightarrow \quad \Delta\phi = 2n\pi \pm \frac{\pi}{2}$$

Since, the point lies between 3rd maxima and 4th minima, $6\pi < \Delta\phi < 7\pi$

Therefore, $\Delta\phi = \frac{13\pi}{2}$ corresponding to $n = 3$

Also, $\Delta\phi = \frac{2\pi}{\lambda}\Delta x$

$\Rightarrow$ $\frac{13\pi}{2} = \frac{2\pi}{\lambda}(\mu - 1)t$

$\Rightarrow$ $(\mu - 1)t = \frac{13\lambda}{4}$ ...(i)

On introducing another film infront of lower slit, fringe pattern shifts by one fringe which means

$(\mu_1 - 1)t = 1(\lambda)$ ...(ii)

From Eqs. (i) and (ii), we get

$$\mu_1 = \frac{4\mu + 9}{13}$$

27. Path difference, $\Delta x = d\sin\theta - \left(\frac{\mu_g}{\mu_l} - 1\right)t$

For central maxima, $\Delta x = 0$

$\Rightarrow$ $\frac{dy}{D} - \left(\frac{\mu_g}{\mu_l} - 1\right)t = 0 \Rightarrow y = \frac{Dt}{d}\left(\frac{\mu_g}{\mu_l} - 1\right)$

$\Rightarrow$ $y = \frac{Dt}{d}\left(\frac{3/2}{\frac{5}{2} - \frac{T}{4}} - 1\right) \Rightarrow y = \frac{Dt}{d}\left(\frac{T - 4}{10 - T}\right)$

When central maxima is at the centre of the screen,

$$y = \frac{Dt}{d}\left(\frac{T - 4}{10 - T}\right) = 0 \quad \Rightarrow \quad T = 4\ \text{s}$$

Velocity of central maxima, $v = \frac{dy}{dT} = \frac{6Dt}{d(10 - T)^2}$

At $T = 4$ s, $v = \frac{6Dt}{d(10 - 4)^2} = \frac{Dt}{6d} = \frac{1 \times 36 \times 10^{-6}}{6 \times 2 \times 10^{-3}}$

$$= 3 \times 10^{-3}\ \text{m/s}$$

28. P is the centre of the screen,

$$I = I_1 + I_2 + 2\sqrt{I_1}\sqrt{I_2}\cos\Delta\phi$$

$\Rightarrow$ $\frac{3}{4}(4I_0) = I_0 + I_0 + 2\sqrt{I_0}\sqrt{I_0}\cos\Delta\phi$

$\Rightarrow$ $\cos\Delta\phi = \frac{1}{2} \Rightarrow \Delta\phi = 2n\pi \pm \frac{\pi}{3}$

Since, P lies between 5th bright and 6th dark fringe. $10\pi < \Delta\phi < 11\pi$

Therefore, $\Delta\phi = \frac{31\pi}{3}$ corresponding to $n = 5$.

Also, $\Delta\phi = \frac{2\pi}{\lambda}\Delta x \Rightarrow \frac{31\pi}{3} = \frac{2\pi}{\lambda}\Delta x \Rightarrow \Delta x = \frac{31\lambda}{6}$

Also, $\Delta x = (\mu_2 - \mu_1)t \Rightarrow \frac{31\lambda}{6} = (\mu_2 - \mu_1)t$

$\Rightarrow$ $t = \frac{31\lambda}{6(\mu_2 - \mu_1)} = \frac{31 \times 5400 \times 10^{-10}}{6(1.7 - 1.4)} = 9.3\ \mu\text{m}$

29.

$$\Delta x = d\sin\theta - \left(\frac{\mu_0}{\mu} - 1\right)t$$

$\Rightarrow$ $n\left(\frac{\lambda}{\mu}\right) = d\left(\frac{d/2}{D}\right) - \left(\frac{\mu_0}{\mu} - 1\right)t$

$\Rightarrow$ $\lambda = \frac{1}{n}\left(\frac{\mu d^2}{2D} - (\mu_0 - \mu)t\right)$

$\Rightarrow$ $\lambda_{max} = \frac{1}{(1)}\left(\frac{1.5 \times (2 \times 10^{-3})^2}{2 \times 6} - (1 - 1.5)(0.2 \times 10^{-6})\right)$

$$= 6 \times 10^{-7}\text{m} = 6000\ \text{Å}$$

30. At C, $\Delta x = \left(\frac{\mu}{\mu_w} - 1\right)t_1 - \left(\frac{\mu}{\mu_w} - 1\right)t_2 = \left(\frac{\mu}{\mu_w} - 1\right)(t_1 - t_2)$

$$= \left(\frac{1.4}{4/3} - 1\right)(2.5 \times 10^{-6} - 1.25 \times 10^{-6})$$

$$= 6.25 \times 10^{-8}\text{m}$$

$$\Delta\phi = \frac{2\pi}{\lambda}\Delta x = \frac{2\pi}{\left(\frac{5000\times10^{-10}}{4/3}\right)}\times 6.25\times10^{-8} = \frac{\pi}{3}$$

$$I = I_1 + I_2 + 2\sqrt{I_1}\sqrt{I_2}\cos\Delta\phi$$

$$= I_0 + I_0 + 2\sqrt{I_0}\sqrt{I_0}\cos\left(\frac{\pi}{3}\right) = 3I_0$$

$$\therefore \quad \frac{I}{I_{max}} = \frac{3I_0}{4I_0} = \frac{3}{4}$$

31. At O,

In figure 1, $\Delta x = (\mu - 1)(t_1 - t_2) = \frac{\lambda}{2}$ ...(i)

In figure 2, $\Delta x = (\mu - 1)(t_1 + t_2) = 2\lambda$ ...(ii)

Dividing equation (i) by (ii), we get

$$\frac{t_1 - t_2}{t_1 + t_2} = \frac{1}{4} \Rightarrow \frac{t_2}{t_1} = \frac{3}{5} = \frac{15}{25}$$

$$\therefore \quad x = 15$$

32. $\Delta x = d\sin\theta - d\sin\theta_0 = 0$

$\Rightarrow d\sin\theta - d\sin 45° = 0 \Rightarrow \theta = 45°$

$$\tan\theta = \frac{y}{D} \Rightarrow \tan 45° = \frac{y}{D} \Rightarrow y = D$$

33. $$\frac{1}{v} - \frac{1}{u} = \frac{1}{f}$$

$$\Rightarrow \frac{1}{v} - \frac{1}{-(0.15)} = \frac{1}{0.1} \Rightarrow v = 0.3\text{ m}$$

$$m = \frac{h_i}{h_0} = \frac{v}{u} \Rightarrow \frac{h_i}{0.25} = \frac{0.3}{-(0.15)} \Rightarrow h_i = -0.5\text{ mm}$$

Let, S_1 and S_2 be the images of S formed by L_1 and L_2, respectively

Distance between S_1 and $S_2 = d = 0.5 + 0.5 + 0.5 = 1.5$ mm

Distance between plane of S_1S_2 and the screen

$$= D = 1.3 - 0.3 = 1\text{ m}$$

$$OA = \frac{3\lambda D}{d} = \frac{3\times500\times10^{-9}\times1}{1.5\times10^{-3}} = 1\text{ mm}$$

34. For S_1 and S_2,

$$\Delta x = 2(S_1P - S_2P) = 2\left(\frac{\lambda}{6}\right) = \frac{\lambda}{3}$$

$$\Delta\phi = \frac{2\pi}{\lambda}\Delta x = \frac{2\pi}{\lambda}\left(\frac{\lambda}{3}\right) = \frac{2\pi}{3}$$

For S_1 and S_3,

$$\Delta x = 2(S_1P - S_3P) = 2\left(\frac{2\lambda}{3}\right) = \frac{4\lambda}{3}$$

$$\Delta\phi = \frac{2\pi}{\lambda}\left(\frac{4\lambda}{3}\right) = \frac{8\pi}{3}$$

$\therefore$ Phase difference of S_2 and $S_3 = \frac{8\pi}{3} - \frac{2\pi}{3} = 2\pi$

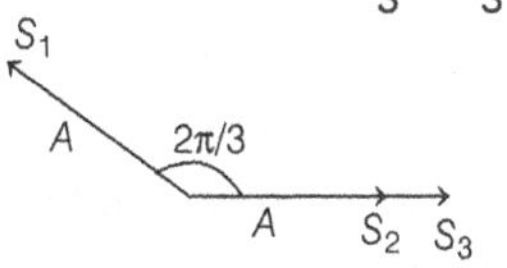

$$A_R = \sqrt{(2A)^2 + A^2 + 2(2A)(A)\cos\left(\frac{2\pi}{3}\right)} = \sqrt{3}A$$

$$I_R \propto A_R^2 \Rightarrow I_R \propto (\sqrt{3}A)^2 \Rightarrow I_R = 3I$$

35.

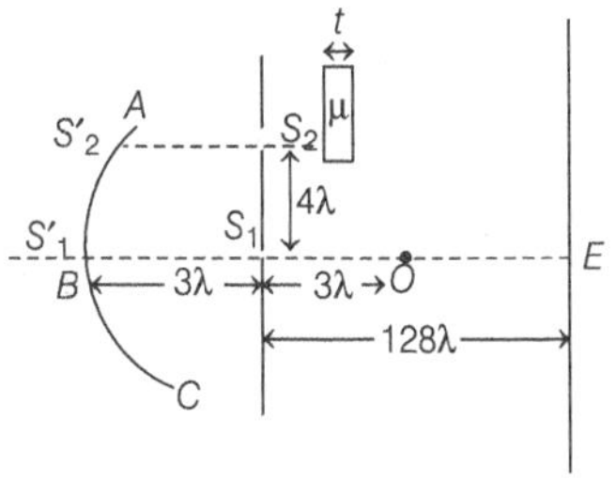

For central fringe to form at E,

$$\Delta x = (S_2S_2' + (\mu - 1)t + S_2E) - (S_1S_1' + S_1E) = 0)$$

$$\Rightarrow (OS_2' - OS_2) + (\mu - 1)t + \sqrt{D^2 + d^2} = (OS_1' - OS_1) + D$$

$$\Rightarrow (\mu - 1)t = (OS_2 - OS_1) - (\sqrt{D^2 + d^2} - D) \quad \because \{OS_1' = OS_2'\}$$

$$\Rightarrow (\mu - 1)t = (5\lambda - 3\lambda) - \left[D\left(1 + \frac{d^2}{D^2}\right)^{1/2} - D\right]$$

$$\Rightarrow (\mu - 1)t = 2\lambda - \frac{d^2}{2D} \Rightarrow \left(\frac{3}{2} - 1\right)t = 2\lambda - \frac{(4\lambda)^2}{2(128\lambda)}$$

$$\Rightarrow \lambda = \frac{31\lambda}{8}$$

36. $\lambda = \frac{c}{f} = \frac{3\times10^8}{6\times10^{14}} \times 0.5\times10^{-6}$ m

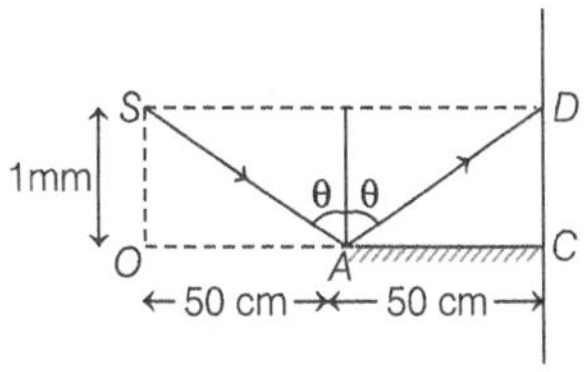

$$\tan\theta = \frac{OA}{OS} = \frac{AC}{CD} \Rightarrow CD = 1\text{ mm}$$

$$\text{Fringe width} = \frac{\lambda D}{d}$$

$$\Rightarrow \beta = \frac{0.5\times10^{-6}(50 + 50)\times10^{-2}}{2\times10^{-3}}$$

$$= 0.25\text{ mm}$$

$$\text{No. of bright fringes} = \frac{CD}{\beta} = \frac{1}{0.25} = 4$$

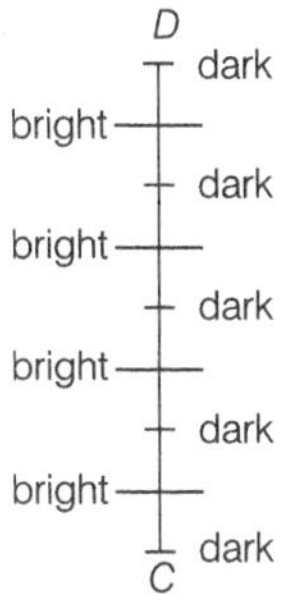

C and D correspond to dark fringes

$\therefore$ No. of dark fringes = 5

37. Phase reversal happens only at the upper interface.

So, condition of constructive interference,

$$\Delta x = 2\mu t = (2n - 1)\frac{\lambda}{2}$$

$$\Rightarrow 2\times1.8\times t_{min} = (2(1) - 1)\frac{(648)}{2}$$

$$\Rightarrow t_{min} = 90\text{ nm}$$

38. Condition for minima due to phase reversal at the top interface,

$$\Delta x = 2\mu t = n\lambda$$

$\Rightarrow$ $2\mu t = 1(\lambda)$ $\because [n = 1$ for minimum thickness$]$

$\Rightarrow$ $t = \dfrac{\lambda}{2\mu}$

Introducing the same film in YDSE,

$$\Delta x = d\sin\theta - (\mu - 1)t \quad \Rightarrow \quad 0 = \frac{dy}{D} - (\mu - 1)\left(\frac{\lambda}{2\mu}\right)$$

$\Rightarrow$ $\mu = \dfrac{D\lambda}{D\lambda - 2dy}$

$$= \frac{5 \times 500 \times 10^{-9}}{5 \times 500 \times 10^{-9} - 2 \times 0.1 \times 10^{-3} \times 7.5 \times 10^{-3}}$$

$= 2.5$

39.

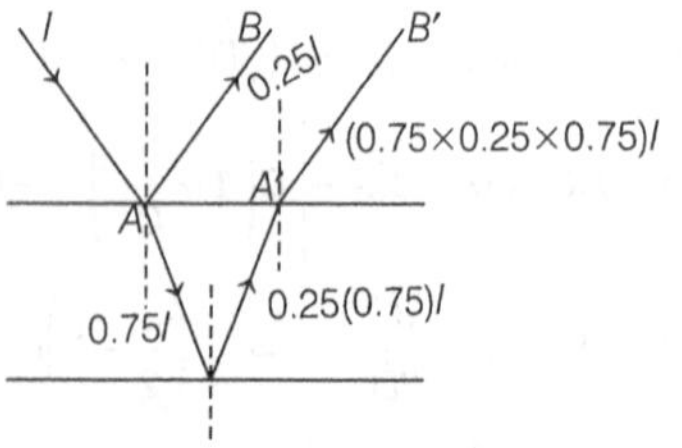

At each interface 25% of incident energy is reflected and 75% of indicent energy is transmitted

$$I_{AB} = 0.25I = \frac{I}{4}$$

$$I_{A'B'} = (0.75 \times 0.25 \times 0.75)I = \frac{9I}{64}$$

$$I_{max} = (\sqrt{I_{AB}} + \sqrt{I_{A'B'}})^2 = \frac{49}{64}$$

$$I_{min} = (\sqrt{I_{AB}} - \sqrt{I_{A'B'}})^2 = \frac{1}{64}$$

$\therefore$ $\dfrac{I_{max}}{I_{min}} = \dfrac{49}{1}$

40. Due to phase reversal at both the interface, condition for constructive interference is

$$2\mu t = n\lambda$$

For λ_1 and λ_2,

$$2\mu t = n_1\lambda_1 = n_2\lambda_2$$

$\Rightarrow$ $n_1(5000) = n_2(10000)$

$\Rightarrow$ $n_1 = 2n_2$

$\therefore$ $n_2 = 1$ and $n_1 = 2$

Hence, $t = \dfrac{n_1\lambda_1}{2\mu} = \dfrac{2 \times 5000 \times 10^{-10}}{2 \times 1.25} = 0.4\,\mu\text{m}$

Multiple Choice(s) Correct Questions

1. (a, b, c)
2. (b, d)
3. (b, c, d)
4. (a, b, c, d)
5. For destructive interference,

$$\Delta x = d\sin\theta = (2n - 1)\frac{\lambda}{2} \quad \Rightarrow \quad d\left(\frac{d/2}{D}\right) = (2n - 1)\frac{\lambda}{2}$$

$\Rightarrow$ $\lambda = \dfrac{d^2}{(2n - 1)D}$

(a) For $n = 1$, $\lambda = \dfrac{d^2}{D}$ (c) For $n = 2$, $\lambda = \dfrac{d^2}{3D}$

6. (c) $y = n_1\left(\dfrac{\lambda_1 D}{d}\right) = n_2\left(\dfrac{\lambda_2 D}{d}\right)$

$\Rightarrow$ $n_1\lambda_1 = n_2\lambda_2$

$\Rightarrow$ $n_1(4500) = n_2(6000)$

$\Rightarrow$ $3n_1 = 4n_2$

$\therefore$ $n_1 = 4$ and $n_2 = 3$

So, the third order bright fringe of λ_2 will coincide with fourth order bright fringe.

(d) $\beta_1 < \beta_2$ $\because \{\lambda_1 < \lambda_2\}$

7. (a) $I \propto A^2 \Rightarrow \dfrac{4I}{9} \propto A_t^2 \Rightarrow A_t = \dfrac{2A_I}{3}$

(b) $$\frac{I_{max}}{I_{min}} = \frac{(\sqrt{I_1} + \sqrt{I_2})^2}{(\sqrt{I_1} - \sqrt{I_2})^2} = \left(\frac{\sqrt{\frac{I_1}{I_2}} + 1}{\sqrt{\frac{I_1}{I_2}} - 1}\right)^2 = \left(\frac{\sqrt{\frac{9}{4}} + 1}{\sqrt{\frac{9}{4}} - 1}\right)$$

(c) $(\mu - 1)t = n\lambda$

$\Rightarrow$ $(1.45 - 1)(0.02 \times 10^{-3}) = n(600 \times 10^{-9})$

$\Rightarrow$ $n = 15$

8. $I = I_1 + I_2 + 2\sqrt{I_1}\sqrt{I_2}\cos\Delta\phi$

$\Rightarrow$ $\dfrac{3}{4}(4I_0) = I_0 + I_0 + 2\sqrt{I_0}\sqrt{I_0}\cos\Delta\phi$

$\Rightarrow$ $\cos\Delta\phi = \dfrac{1}{2} \Rightarrow \Delta\phi = 2n\pi \pm \dfrac{\pi}{3}$

Also, $3\pi < \Delta\phi < 6\pi$

$\because$ {The point lies between 2nd minima and 3rd maxima}

$\therefore$ Possible values of $\Delta\phi = \dfrac{11\pi}{3}, \dfrac{13\pi}{3}, \dfrac{17\pi}{3}$

9. (a) At O,

$$\Delta x = d\sin\alpha = (1 \times 10^{-3})\sin 30° = 5 \times 10^{-4}\text{ m}$$

$$\Delta\phi = \frac{2\pi}{\lambda}\Delta x = \frac{2\pi}{5000 \times 10^{-10}} \times 5 \times 10^{-4} = 2000\,\pi$$

So, O corresponds to maxima and intensity at O will be $4I_0$.

(c) 4 m below O,

$$\Delta x = d\sin\theta - d\sin\alpha$$

$$= d(\sin 53° - \sin 30°)$$

$$= 1 \times 10^{-3} \times \frac{3}{10}\text{ m} = 3 \times 10^{-4}\text{m}$$

$$\Delta\phi = \frac{2\pi}{\lambda}\Delta x = \frac{2\pi}{5000 \times 10^{-10}} \times 3 \times 10^{-4} = 1200\,\pi$$

So, this point also corresponds to a maxima and intensity will be $4I_0$.

10. (b) $\Delta x = ABO - AO'O = 2(\sqrt{D^2 + d^2} - D)$

$$= 2\left(D\left(1 + \frac{d^2}{D^2}\right)^{1/2} - D\right) = 2\left[D\left(1 + \frac{d^2}{2D^2}\right) - D\right] = \frac{d^2}{D}$$

For dark fringe to form at O,

$$\Delta x = (2n-1)\frac{\lambda}{2} \Rightarrow \frac{d^2_{min}}{D} = (2(1)-1)\frac{\lambda}{2}$$

$$\Rightarrow \quad d_{min} = \sqrt{\frac{\lambda D}{2}}$$

(d) The bright fringe is formed at P if the path difference,

$$\Delta x = AO'P - ABP = 0$$

$$\Rightarrow \quad D + \sqrt{D^2 + x^2} - \sqrt{D^2 + d^2} - \sqrt{D^2 + (x-d)^2} = 0$$

$$\Rightarrow \quad \frac{x^2}{2D} - \frac{d^2}{2D} - \frac{(x-d)^2}{2D} = 0$$

Given, $d = d_{min}$

On solving, $x = d_{min} = \sqrt{\frac{\lambda D}{2}}$

11. $\lambda = \frac{c}{f} = \frac{3 \times 10^8}{10^6} = 300$ m

$$\Delta\phi = \frac{2\pi}{\lambda}\Delta x = \frac{2\pi}{300}(150 \sin\theta) = \pi \sin\theta$$

$$I = I_0 \cos^2\left(\frac{\Delta\phi}{2}\right) = I_0 \cos^2\left(\frac{\pi \sin\theta}{2}\right)$$

For $\theta = 30°, I = I_0 \cos^2\left(\frac{\pi \sin 30°}{2}\right) = \frac{I_0}{2}$

$$\theta = 0°, I = I_0 \cos^2\left(\frac{\pi \sin 0°}{2}\right) = I_0$$

$$\theta = 90°, I = I_0 \cos^2\left(\frac{\pi \sin 90°}{2}\right) = 0$$

12. (b) For the central maxima, $\Delta x = 0$

$$\Rightarrow \quad d \sin\phi + d \sin\theta + \left(\frac{\mu_2}{\mu_3} - 1\right)t = 0$$

$$\Rightarrow \quad d\left(\frac{d}{D}\right) + d\left(\frac{y}{D}\right) + \left(\frac{\mu_2}{\mu_3} - 1\right)t = 0$$

$$\Rightarrow \quad y = -\left(\frac{D}{d}\left(\frac{\mu_2}{\mu_3} - 1\right)t + d\right)$$

$$= -\left(\frac{1}{2 \times 10^{-3}}\left(\frac{1.2}{1.8} - 1\right)(6 \times 10^{-6}) + 2 \times 10^{-3}\right)$$

$$= -1 \times 10^{-3} \text{ m} = -1 \text{ mm}$$

(d) When the slab is removed,

$$\left(\frac{\mu_2}{\mu_3} - 1\right)t = \frac{dy}{D} \quad \Rightarrow \quad y = -1 \text{ mm}$$

13. At P, $\Delta x = (\mu_1 - 1)t_1 - (\mu_2 - 1)t_2$

$$= \left(\frac{4}{3} - 1\right)(9\lambda) - \left(\frac{3}{2} - 1\right)(2\lambda) = 2\lambda$$

So, the point P corresponds to a maximum and intensity will be $4I_0$

(b) $\Delta x = 2\lambda$

Hence, two fringes have been shifted in upward direction.

(c) $\Delta x = 2\lambda$

(d) $\Delta x = d \sin\theta_0 + d \sin\theta = 0$

$$\Rightarrow \quad d\left(\frac{d_2}{d_1}\right) + d\left(\frac{y}{D}\right) = 0 \Rightarrow y = -D\left(\frac{d_2}{D_1}\right)$$

14. (a) There will be phase reversal of π due to reflection from mirror. So, condition for first maximum is

$$\Delta x = \frac{\lambda}{2} \quad \Rightarrow \quad d'\left(\frac{y}{D}\right) = \frac{\lambda}{2}$$

$$\Rightarrow \quad y = \frac{\lambda D}{2d'} = \frac{500 \times 10^{-9} \times 1}{2 \times (2 \times 0.5 \times 10^{-3})} = \frac{1}{4} \text{ mm}$$

(c) $\beta = \frac{\lambda D}{d'} = \frac{500 \times 10^{-9} \times 1}{2 \times 0.5 \times 10^{-3}} = \frac{1}{2}$ mm

(d) $\Delta\phi = \frac{2\pi}{\lambda}\Delta x \quad \Rightarrow \quad \pi - \frac{\pi}{2} = \frac{2\pi}{\lambda}\Delta x \quad \Rightarrow \quad \Delta x = \frac{\lambda}{4}$

Also, $\Delta x = \frac{d'y}{D} \quad \Rightarrow \quad \frac{\lambda}{4} = \frac{d'y}{D} \quad \Rightarrow \quad y = \frac{\lambda D}{4d'} = \frac{1}{8}$ mm

15. Let thickness of $B = t$ and thickness of $C = 2t$

No. of waves in A = No. of waves in B + No. of waves in C

$$\Rightarrow \quad \frac{3t}{\left(\frac{\lambda}{1.5}\right)} = \frac{t}{\left(\frac{\lambda}{\mu_1}\right)} + \frac{2t}{\left(\frac{\lambda}{1.4}\right)} \quad \Rightarrow \quad \mu_1 = 1.7$$

Frequency of light doesn't depend on the medium.

16. Fringe width in air $= \frac{\lambda(a+b)}{2(\mu_g - 1)\alpha\, a} = \frac{\lambda D}{2(\mu_g - 1)\alpha\, a}$

If a decreases, fringe width increases.

If α decreases, fringe width increases.

Fringe width in liquid $= \frac{\frac{\lambda}{\mu_l}(a+b)}{2\left(\frac{\mu_g}{\mu_l} - 1\right)\alpha\, a} = \frac{\lambda(a+b)}{2(\mu_g - \mu_l)\alpha}$

So, in liquid, fringe width will be more.

17. (a, b, c)

18. Due to phase reversal at both the interfaces, condition for constructive interference will be

$$2\mu t = n\lambda \quad \Rightarrow \quad 2 \times 1.38 \times t = n(552 \text{ nm})$$

$$\Rightarrow \quad t = (200\, n) \text{ nm where } n = 1, 2, 3, \ldots$$

So, possible values of t = 200 nm, 400 nm, 600 nm, 800 nm, 1000 nm, ...

19. At O, $\Delta x = d$ {Path difference is maxima at O}

(a) If $d = 3.5\lambda$, O will be minima.

(b) If $d = \lambda$, O will be maxima and there will not be any other maxima.

(c) If $d = 4.8\lambda$, then total 10 minima can be observed on the screen, 5 above O and 5 below O, which correspond to,

$$\Delta x = \pm\frac{\lambda}{2}, \pm\frac{3\lambda}{2}, \pm\frac{5\lambda}{2}, \pm\frac{7\lambda}{2}, \pm\frac{9\lambda}{2}$$

(d) If $d = 2.5\lambda$, O will be minima and intensity at O would be minimum.

20. Locus of equal path difference are lines running parallel to the axis of the cylinder. Hence, straight fringes will be observed.

Comprehension Based Questions

1. Intensity $\propto$ Width of slit

Let, intensites due to slits S_1 and S_2 be I_0 and $2I_0$, respectively.

Intensity of light coming out of film $= \frac{50}{100} \times I_0 = \frac{I_0}{2}$

Maxima intensity, $I = \left(\sqrt{\frac{I_0}{2}} + \sqrt{2I_0}\right)^2 = \frac{9I_0}{2}$

At O,

$$\Delta x = d\sin\alpha - (\mu - 1)t$$
$$= 1 \times 10^{-3}\left(\frac{1.8}{\pi} \times \frac{\pi}{180}\right) - \left(\frac{3}{2} - 1\right)(4 \times 10^{-6})$$
$$= 8 \times 10^{-6}\ \text{m}$$
$$\Delta\phi = \frac{2\pi}{\lambda}\Delta x = \frac{2\pi}{6000 \times 10^{-10}} \times 8 \times 10^{-6} = \frac{80\pi}{3}$$
$$I_R = I_1 + I_2 + 2\sqrt{I_1}\sqrt{I_2}\cos\Delta\phi$$
$$= \frac{I_0}{2} + 2I_0 + 2\sqrt{\frac{I_0}{2}}\sqrt{2I_0}\cos\frac{80\pi}{3}$$
$$= \frac{3I_0}{2} = \frac{I}{3}$$

2. $\Delta x = d\sin\theta + d\sin\alpha - (\mu - 1)t = 0$

$$\Rightarrow \quad \frac{dy}{D} = -(d\sin\alpha - (\mu - 1)t)$$
$$\Rightarrow \quad \frac{1 \times 10^{-3} y}{1} = -8 \times 10^{-6}$$
$$\Rightarrow \quad y = -8 \times 10^{-3}\ \text{m} = -8\ \text{mm}$$

3. $\Delta x = d\sin\theta + d\sin\alpha - (\mu - 1)t$

$$= \frac{dy}{D} + (d\sin\alpha - (\mu - 1)t)$$
$$= \frac{1 \times 10^{-3} \times 4 \times 10^{-3}}{1} + 8 \times 10^{-6}$$
$$= 12 \times 10^{-6}\ \text{m}$$
$$\Delta\phi = \frac{2\pi}{\lambda}\Delta x = \frac{2\pi}{6000 \times 10^{-10}} \times 12 \times 10^{-6} = 40\pi$$

So, the given point corresponds to a maxima and hence intensity will be I.

4. $(\mu - 1)t = \left(n + \frac{1}{2}\right)\lambda$

$$\Rightarrow \quad (1.40 - 1)t = \left(n + \frac{1}{2}\right)(560 \times 10^{-9})$$
$$\Rightarrow \quad t = (2n + 1)\,0.7\,\mu\text{m}$$

Since, we observe 3 maxima, $n \geq 3$

5. In 30 s, $(\mu - 1)t = \lambda$

$$\Rightarrow \quad (1.4 - 1)t = 560 \times 10^{-9}$$
$$\Rightarrow \quad t = 1400\ \text{nm}$$

Rate of change of thickness $= \frac{1400}{30}$ nm/s $= \frac{140}{3}$ nm/s

6. In 5 s, $\Delta\phi = \frac{2\pi}{30} \times 5 = \frac{\pi}{3}$

$$\phi = \pi + \frac{\pi}{3}$$
$$I = I_0\cos^2\left(\frac{\phi}{2}\right) = I_0\cos^2\left(\frac{\pi}{2} + \frac{\pi}{6}\right) = \frac{I_0}{4}$$

In 10s, $\Delta\phi = \frac{2\pi}{30} \times 10 = \frac{2\pi}{3}$

$$\phi = \pi + \frac{2\pi}{3}$$
$$I = I_0\cos^2\left(\frac{\phi}{2}\right)$$
$$= I_0\cos^2\left(\frac{\pi}{2} + \frac{\pi}{3}\right) = \frac{3I_0}{4}$$

7. $SS_1 = SS_2 = \sqrt{2^2 + \left(\frac{3}{2}\right)^2} = \frac{5}{2}$ mm

$$S_2P - S_1P = d\sin\theta = \frac{dy}{D}$$
$$\Delta x = (\mu SS_2 + S_2P) - (SS_1 + S_1P)$$
$$\Rightarrow \quad 0 = (\mu - 1)SS_1 + (S_2P - S_1P)$$
$$\Rightarrow \quad 0 = \left(\frac{6}{5} - 1\right)\left(\frac{5}{2} \times 10^{-3}\right) + (3 \times 10^{-3})\left(\frac{y}{1}\right)$$
$$\Rightarrow \quad y = -\frac{1}{6}\ \text{m} = \frac{1}{6}\ \text{m below } O$$

8. At O, $\Delta x = \mu SS_2 - SS_1$

$$\Rightarrow \quad n\lambda = (\mu - 1)SS_1$$
$$\Rightarrow \quad n(500 \times 10^{-9}) = \left(\frac{6}{5} - 1\right)\left(\frac{5}{2} \times 10^{-3}\right)$$
$$\Rightarrow \quad n = 1000$$

9. $(\mu - 1)t = 200\lambda$

$$\Rightarrow \quad (1.8 - 1)t = 200 \times 500 \times 10^{-9}$$
$$\Rightarrow \quad t = 125 \times 10^{-6}\ \text{m} = 125\,\mu\text{m}$$

10. Area under μ_3 vs x graph $= \int \mu_3 dx = \frac{(1+3)t}{2} = 2t$

$$\Delta x = [\mu_1 SS_2 + \mu_2 S_2P] - [\mu_1 SS_1 + \mu_2 S_1P + \int_0^t (\mu_3 - \mu_2)\,dx]$$
$$\Delta x = \mu_1(SS_2 - SS_1) + \mu_2(S_2P - S_1P) - \int_0^t \mu_3 dx + \int_0^t \mu_2 dx$$
$$\Delta x = \mu_1(d\sin\theta_0) + \mu_2(d\sin\theta) - \int_0^t \mu_3 dx + \mu_2\int_0^t dx$$
$$\Rightarrow \quad 0 = 2\left(1 \times 10^{-3} \times \left(\frac{0.5 \times 10^{-3}}{1}\right)\right) + 0 - 2t + \frac{3}{2}t$$
$$\Rightarrow \quad t = 2 \times 10^{-6}\ \text{m} = 2\,\mu\text{m}$$

11. $\Delta x = \mu_1(d\sin\theta_0) + \mu_2(d\sin\theta) - \int_0^t \mu_3 dx + \mu_2\int_0^t dx$

$$\Rightarrow \quad 0 = 2\left(1 \times 10^{-3}\left(\frac{0.5 \times 10^{-3}}{1}\right)\right) + \frac{3}{2}\left(1 \times 10^{-3}\left(\frac{y}{1}\right)\right) - 2(1 \times 10^{-6}) + \frac{3}{2}(1 \times 10^{-6})$$
$$\Rightarrow \quad y = -\frac{1}{3}\ \text{mm}$$

12. $\beta = \dfrac{\lambda D}{\mu_2 d} = \dfrac{3000 \times 10^{-10} \times 1}{(3/2) \times 1 \times 10^{-3}} = 0.2$ mm

13. Central maxima will be always at the centre of the screen and the screen is in free fall.

$\therefore \quad v + u + at \quad \Rightarrow \quad v = 0 + 10(5) = 50$ m/s

$\vec{v} = (50 \text{ m/s})\,\hat{\mathbf{j}} = 50$ m/s along Y-axis

14. For 2nd maxima, $d \sin\theta = 2\lambda$

$\Rightarrow \quad d\left(\dfrac{x}{y}\right) = 2\lambda \quad \Rightarrow \quad x = \dfrac{2\lambda y}{d}$

Velocity of 2nd mixima w.r.t. central maxima,

$$v = \frac{dx}{dt} = \frac{2\lambda}{d}\left(\frac{dy}{dt}\right) = \frac{2\lambda}{d}(gt)$$

$$= \frac{2 \times 5000 \times 10^{-10}}{1 \times 10^{-3}}(10 \times 2)$$

$$= 0.02 \text{ m/s}$$

$\therefore \quad \vec{v} = (2 \text{ cm/s})\,\hat{\mathbf{i}}$

15. x-coordinate of 3rd maxima $= \dfrac{3\lambda y}{d}$

Acceleration of 3rd maxima w.r.t. central maxima

$$= \frac{d^2x}{dt^2} = \frac{3\lambda}{d}\frac{d^2y}{dt^2} = \frac{3\lambda g}{d}$$

Relative acceleration of 3rd maxima w.r.t. 3rd maxima on the other side

$$= \frac{3\lambda g}{d} - \left(-\frac{3\lambda g}{d}\right)$$

$$= \frac{6\lambda g}{d} = \frac{6 \times 5000 \times 10^{-10} \times 10}{1 \times 10^{-3}} = 0.03 \text{ m/s}^2$$

16. At point O,

$$\Delta x = |\mu_w(d \sin 30°) - (\mu_g - 1)t|$$

$$= \left|\frac{4}{3} \times 0.30 \times 10^{-3} \times \frac{1}{2} - (1.5 - 1)(0.41 \times 10^{-3})\right|$$

$$= 5 \times 10^{-6} \text{ m}$$

$$\Delta\phi = \frac{2\pi}{\lambda}\Delta x = \frac{2\pi}{5000 \times 10^{-10}} \times 5 \times 10^{-6} = 20\pi$$

So, point O corresponds to 10th bright fringe.

17. For central maxima,

$$\Delta x = (\mu_w(d \sin 30°) - (\mu_g - 1)t) - d\sin\theta$$

$$\Rightarrow \quad 0 = -5 \times 10^{-6} - 0.30 \times 10^{-3}\left(\frac{y}{1}\right) \quad \Rightarrow \quad y = -\frac{5}{3} \text{ cm}$$

18. At $y = \dfrac{1}{8}$ cm

$$\Delta x = (\mu_w(d \sin 30°) - (\mu_g - 1)t) - d\left(\frac{y}{D}\right)$$

$$= -5 \times 10^{-6} - (0.30 \times 10^{-3})\left(\frac{1 \times 10^{-2}}{8 \times 1}\right)$$

$$= \frac{-43}{8} \times 10^{-6} \text{m}$$

$$\Delta\phi = \frac{2\pi}{\lambda}\Delta x = \frac{2\pi}{5000 \times 10^{-10}} \times \frac{43}{8} \times 10^{-6} = \frac{43\pi}{2}$$

$$I = I_0 \cos^2\left(\frac{\Delta\phi}{2}\right)$$

$$\Rightarrow \quad \frac{I}{I_0} = \cos^2\left(\frac{43\pi}{4}\right) = \frac{1}{2}$$

19. $I \propto \dfrac{1}{r^2}$

$$\therefore \quad \frac{\Delta I}{I_0} = \frac{L^2 - (L - x)^2}{L^2} = \frac{2A \sin\omega t}{L}$$

20. Intensity of the fringes will increase.

21. $\beta = \dfrac{\lambda D}{d}$ = constant

22. Intensity at O is proportional to intensity at S_3 and at S_4.

$I = K\cos^2\left(\dfrac{\Delta\phi}{2}\right)$, where K is a constant and

$\Delta\phi$ is the phase difference.

$\Delta\phi = \dfrac{2\pi}{\beta} \times \dfrac{Z}{2}$, where β is fringe width.

When $Z = \dfrac{\lambda D}{2d}$, $\Delta\phi = \dfrac{2\pi}{\left(\dfrac{\lambda D}{d}\right)} \times \dfrac{1}{2}\left(\dfrac{\lambda D}{2d}\right) = \dfrac{\pi}{2}$

$$I = I_0 = K\cos^2\left(\frac{\pi}{4}\right)$$

$$\Rightarrow \quad K = 2I_0$$

When, $Z = \dfrac{2\lambda D}{d}$, $\Delta\phi = \dfrac{2\pi}{\left(\dfrac{\lambda D}{d}\right)} \times \dfrac{2\lambda D}{2d} = 2\pi$

$$I' = K\cos^2\pi = 2I_0$$

23. Intensity at O is zero, if $\dfrac{\Delta\phi}{2} = \dfrac{\pi}{2}$. That is,

$$\Delta\phi = \frac{2\pi}{\beta}\left(\frac{Z}{2}\right) = \pi \quad \Rightarrow \quad Z = \beta = \frac{\lambda D}{d}$$

24. At S_3, $\Delta\phi = \dfrac{2\pi}{\beta}\left(\dfrac{\lambda D}{4d}\right) = \dfrac{2\pi d}{\lambda D}\left(\dfrac{\lambda D}{4d}\right) = \dfrac{\pi}{2}$

$$I_{S_3} = I + I + 2\sqrt{I}\sqrt{I}\cos\left(\frac{\pi}{2}\right) = 2I$$

$$I_{O'} = I + I + 2\sqrt{I}\sqrt{I}\cos 0° = 4I$$

At O', $I_{max} = (\sqrt{2I} + \sqrt{4I})^2$, $I_{min} = (\sqrt{4I} - \sqrt{2I})^2$

$$\frac{I_{max}}{I_{min}} = \left(\frac{2 + \sqrt{2}}{2 - \sqrt{2}}\right)^2 = (\sqrt{2} + 1)^4 \approx 34$$

25. $\lambda = \dfrac{C}{f} = \dfrac{3 \times 10^8}{6 \times 10^{14}} = 5 \times 10^{-7}$m

Image formed by M: $\dfrac{1}{v} + \dfrac{1}{-30} = \dfrac{1}{-10}$

$$\Rightarrow \quad v = -15 \text{ cm}$$

$$m = -\frac{v}{u} = -\frac{(-15)}{(-30)} = -\frac{1}{2}$$

This will be located at 15 cm left of M and 0.5 mm above the line AB.

This will act as an object for the lens L.

Now, for the lens, $u = -7.5$ cm and $m = \frac{v}{u} = \frac{7.5}{-7.5} = -1$

So, it will be at 7.5 cm to the left of L and 0.5 mm below line AB. See the ray diagram. Second image I_2 and source S will act as two slits (as in YDSE) to produce the interference pattern.

Distance between them = 0.5 mm (= d)

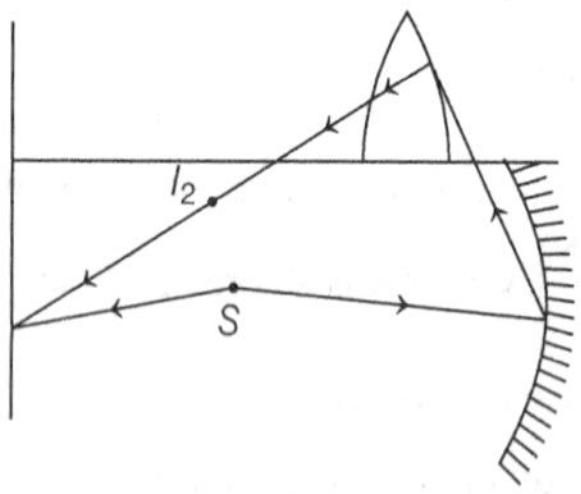

26. $\beta = \frac{\lambda D}{d} = \frac{5 \times 10^{-7} \times 50 \times 10^{-2}}{0.5 \times 10^{-3}} = 5 \times 10^{-4}$ m = 0.5 mm

27. Image formed by the combination is I_2 at

$$\frac{1}{v} - \frac{1}{-5} = \frac{3}{10} \Rightarrow v = 10 \text{ cm}$$

It will coincide with S. So, no interference pattern on the screen will be observed.

Match the Columns Questions

1. $\beta = \frac{\lambda D}{d} = \frac{6000 \times 10^{-10} \times 1}{0.5 \times 10^{-3}} = 1.2$ mm

$$\Delta\phi = \frac{2\pi}{\lambda}\Delta x = \frac{2\pi}{\lambda}\left(\frac{dy}{D}\right) = \frac{2\pi}{\beta}y$$

(A) $\Delta\phi = \frac{2\pi}{\beta}y = \frac{2\pi}{1.2} \times 2 = \frac{10\pi}{3}$

$$I = I_0 + 4I_0 + 2\sqrt{I_0}\sqrt{4I_0}\cos\left(\frac{10\pi}{3}\right) = 3I_0$$

Since, $3\pi < \Delta\phi < 6\pi$, P lies between 2nd minima and 3rd maxima.

(B) $\Delta\phi = \frac{2\pi}{1.2} \times 2.2 = \frac{11\pi}{3}$

$$I = I_0 + 4I_0 + 2\sqrt{I_0}\sqrt{4I_0}\cos\left(\frac{11\pi}{3}\right) = 7I_0$$

Again, $3\pi < \Delta\phi < 6\pi$

(C) $\Delta\phi = \frac{2\pi}{1.2} \times 2.6 = \frac{13\pi}{3}$

$$I = I_0 + 4I_0 + 2\sqrt{I_0}\sqrt{4I_0}\cos\left(\frac{13\pi}{3}\right) = 7I_0$$

$3\pi < \Delta\phi < 6\pi$ and also $4\pi < \Delta\phi < 5\pi$

(D) $\Delta\phi = \frac{2\pi}{1.2} \times 2.8 = \frac{14\pi}{3}$

$$I = 3I_0$$

$3\pi < \Delta\phi < 6\pi$ and also $4\pi < \Delta\phi < 5\pi$

2. (A) $\Delta x_0 = \frac{d_0 y}{D_0} = \frac{d_0}{D_0}\left(\frac{\lambda D_0}{2d_0}\right) = \frac{\lambda}{2}$

On doubling slit separation, optical path difference will also get doubled.

$\therefore$ $\Delta x = \lambda$ which corresponds to first order maxima. Hence, intensity at P will increase.

(B) $\beta = \frac{\lambda D}{d}$, $\Delta x = \frac{dy}{D}$

On doubling D, fringe width gets doubled and optical path difference gets halved.

$\Delta x_0 = \frac{\lambda}{2}$ (corresponds to minima)

$\Delta x = \frac{\lambda}{4}$

Hence, intensity also increases.

(C) Same as B. Intensity initially is zero and then becomes non-zero. So, intensity at P will increase.

(D) $\beta = \frac{\lambda D}{\mu d}$, $\Delta x = \mu\frac{dy}{D}$

So, fringe width decreases, optical path difference increases.

Intensity becomes non-zero. So, intensity at P will increase.

3. (A) For two maxima to coincide,

$$y = n_1\beta_1 = n_2\beta_2 \Rightarrow n_1(0.3) = n_2(0.5)$$

$\Rightarrow$ $3n_1 = 5n_2$

For $y = y_1$, $n_1 = 5$ and $n_2 = 3$

For 2nd nearest point above O where two maxima coincide, $n_1 = 10$ and $n_2 = 6$

$\Rightarrow$ $y = 2y_1$

For two minima to coincide,

$$y = \left(\frac{2n_1 - 1}{2}\right)\beta_1 = \left(\frac{2n_2 - 1}{2}\right)\beta_2$$

$\Rightarrow$ $(2n_1 - 1)(0.3) = (2n_2 - 1)(0.5)$

$\Rightarrow$ $3(2n_1 - 1) = 5(2n_2 - 1)$

For $y = y_2$, $n_1 = 3$ and $n_2 = 2$

For 2nd nearest point above O where two minima coincide,

$n_1 = 8$ and $n_2 = 5$

$\Rightarrow$ $y = 3y_2$

y_1 is LCM of β_1 and β_2

(B) For two minima to coincide,

$$y = \left(\frac{2n_1 - 1}{2}\right)\beta_1 = \left(\frac{2n_2 - 1}{2}\right)\beta_2$$

$\Rightarrow$ $(2n_1 - 1)(0.3) = (2n_2 - 1)(0.4)$

$\Rightarrow$ $3(2n_1 - 1) = 4(2n_2 - 1)$

For $y = y_2$, no solution exists.

4. Intensity at a distance y from central maxima on screen is

$$I = I_0 + 4I_0 + 2\sqrt{I_0}\sqrt{4I_0}\cos\left(\frac{2\pi y}{\beta}\right)$$

Where, $\beta = \frac{\lambda D}{d}$

$I_{max} = 9I_0$ and $I_{min} = I_0$

(A) At points where intensity is (1/9)th of maximum intensity, minima is formed. Therefore, distance between such points is $\beta, 2\beta, 3\beta$ ....

(B) At points where intensity is (3/9)th of maximum intensity,

$$\cos\left(\frac{2\pi y}{\beta}\right) = -\frac{1}{2} \Rightarrow y = \frac{\beta}{3}$$

Hence, distance between such points is

$$\frac{\beta}{3}, \frac{2\beta}{3}, \beta, \frac{4\beta}{3}, \frac{5\beta}{3}, 2\beta \ldots\ldots$$

(C) $I = \frac{5}{9}I_{max} \Rightarrow \cos\left(\frac{2\pi y}{\beta}\right) = 0 \Rightarrow y = \frac{\beta}{6}$

Hence, distance between such points is,

$$\frac{\beta}{2}, \beta, \frac{3\beta}{2}, 2\beta \ldots\ldots$$

(D) $I = \frac{7}{9}I_{max} \Rightarrow \cos\left(\frac{2\pi y}{\beta}\right) = \frac{1}{2} \Rightarrow y = \frac{\beta}{6}$

Hence, distance between such points is,

$$\frac{\beta}{3}, \frac{2\beta}{3}, \beta, \frac{4\beta}{3}, \frac{5\beta}{3}, 2\beta \ldots\ldots$$

5. (A) $\Delta x = d\sin\theta_0 + d\sin\theta = n\lambda$

$$\Rightarrow \frac{dy_0}{D_1} + \frac{dy}{D_2} = n\lambda$$

$$\Rightarrow \frac{20\times10^{-3}\times2\times10^{-3}}{1} + \frac{20\times10^{-3}\times10\times10^{-3}}{2} = n(500\times10^{-9})$$

$$\Rightarrow n = 280$$

(B) $\Delta x = d\sin\theta_0 = n\lambda$

$$\Rightarrow \frac{dy_0}{D_1} = n\lambda$$

$$\Rightarrow \frac{20\times10^{-3}\times2\times10^{-3}}{1} = n(500\times10^{-9})$$

$$\Rightarrow n = 80$$

(C) $\Delta x = d\sin\theta_0 + d\sin\theta - (\mu-1)t = n\lambda$

$$\Rightarrow \left(\frac{dy_0}{D_1} + \frac{dy}{D_2}\right) - (\mu-1)t = n\lambda$$

$$\Rightarrow 280\times500\times10^{-9} - (1.45-1)(0.02\times10^{-3}) = n(500\times10^{-9})$$

$$0.14\times10^{-3} - 0.009\times10^{-3} = n(500\times10^{-9})$$

$$\Rightarrow n = 262$$

(D) $\Delta x = \frac{dy_0}{D_1} - (\mu-1)t = n\lambda$

$$\Rightarrow 80\times500\times10^{-9} - (1.45-1)(0.02\times10^{-3}) = n(500\times10^{-9})$$

$$\Rightarrow n = 62$$

6. $\beta = \frac{\lambda D}{d} = \frac{4000\times10^{-10}\times2}{1\times10^{-3}} = 0.8$ mm

(A) Fringe width does not change and central maxima will be above C.

$$(\mu-1)t = n\lambda$$

$$\Rightarrow (2-1)(2\times10^{-3}) = n(4000\times10^{-10})$$

$$\Rightarrow n = 5000$$

(B) $\Delta x = (\mu_1-1)t_1 - (\mu_2-1)t_2$

$$= (2-1)(2\times10^{-3}) - (3-1)(1\times10^{-3})$$

$$= 0$$

So, central maxima doesn't shift

(C) $\Delta x = (\mu_3-1)t_3 - (\mu_2-1)t_2$

$$= (1.5-1)\,4\times10^{-3} - (3-1)\,(1\times10^{-3})$$

$$= 0$$

So, central maxima doesn't shift.

Numerical Value Questions

1. $\Delta x = (SS_2 - SS_1) + (S_2P - S_1P) = \frac{dy}{D_1} + \frac{d(d/2)}{D_2}$

For constructive interference,

$$\Delta x = \frac{dy}{D_1} + \frac{d^2}{2D_2} = n\lambda$$

$$\Rightarrow \frac{1\times10^{-3}\times0.5\sin\left(\frac{\pi}{6}t\right)\times10^{-3}}{1} + \frac{(1\times10^{-3})^2}{2(2)} = n(5000\times10^{-10})$$

$$\Rightarrow \sin\left(\frac{\pi}{6}t\right) = n - \frac{1}{2}$$

For the minimum value of t, $n = 1$

$$\Rightarrow \sin\left(\frac{\pi}{6}\right)t = \frac{1}{2} \Rightarrow \left(\frac{\pi}{6}\right)t = \frac{\pi}{6}$$

$$\Rightarrow t = 1\text{ s}$$

2. $\Delta x = d\sin\theta_0 - d\sin\theta = 0$

$$\Rightarrow d\left(\frac{0.5\times10^{-2}}{x}\right) - d\left(\frac{y}{1}\right) = 0$$

$$\Rightarrow y = \frac{0.5\times10^{-2}}{x}$$

Velocity of central maxima

$$= \frac{dy}{dt} = \frac{-0.5\times10^{-2}}{x^2}\times\frac{dx}{dt} = -\frac{0.5\times10^{-2}}{(0.5)^2}\times1\times10^{-3}$$

$$= -2\times10^{-3}\text{ cm/s}$$

$\therefore \alpha + \beta = 2 + 3 = 5$

3. At O, $\Delta x = 3\lambda$ which is the maximum path difference possible.

$$\Delta x = 3\lambda\cos\theta = n\lambda$$

$$\Rightarrow 3\lambda\cos\theta = 2\lambda \text{ \{For nearest maxima\}}$$

$$\Rightarrow \cos\theta = \frac{2}{3}$$

$$y = D\tan\theta = D\left(\frac{\sqrt{5}}{2}\right)$$

$\therefore m + n = 5 + 2 = 7$

4. $\Delta x = (\mu_A - 1)t_A + (\mu_B - \mu_L)t_B - (\mu_C - \mu_L)t_C = 0$

$$\Rightarrow \quad \left(\frac{4}{3} - 1\right)2 + \left(\frac{5}{3} - \mu_L\right)1 - \left(\frac{8}{3} - \mu_L\right)(1.5) = 0$$

$$\Rightarrow \quad \mu_L = \frac{10}{3}$$

$$\therefore \quad \frac{2\mu}{3} = \frac{10}{3} \quad \Rightarrow \quad \mu = 5$$

5. $\mu = 1 + \alpha\theta \quad \Rightarrow \quad d\mu = \alpha d\theta$

Path difference $= \Delta x = (\mu - 1)t$

$$\Rightarrow \quad d(\Delta x) = d\mu t = \alpha d\theta t$$

Also, $\quad d(\Delta x) = n\lambda \quad \Rightarrow \quad \alpha d\theta\, t = n\lambda$

$$\Rightarrow \quad n = \frac{\alpha d\theta t}{\lambda} = \frac{3 \times 10^{-3} \times 100 \times 2 \times 10^{-6}}{6000 \times 10^{-10}} = 1$$

6. $\Delta x = \int (\mu - 1)dx = \int_0^3 (1 + \sqrt{x} - 1)dx = \int_0^3 \sqrt{x}dx = 2\sqrt{3}$ mm

$$\Delta\phi = \frac{2\pi}{\lambda}\Delta x = \frac{2\pi}{4000\sqrt{3} \times 10^{-10}} \times 2\sqrt{3} \times 10^{-3} = 10000\pi$$

So, the point corresponds to a maxima.

$$I = I_0 + I_0 + 2\sqrt{I_0}\sqrt{I_0}\cos(10000\pi) = 4I_0 = 4 \times 10^{-15}\ \text{W/m}^2$$

7. At $x = 0$,

$$\Delta x = d\sin 30^\circ + (\mu - 1)t$$
$$= (0.5 \times 10^{-3})\frac{1}{2} + (1.5 - 1)(5 \times 10^{-5})$$
$$= 0.275 \times 10^{-3}\ \text{m}$$

$$\therefore \quad \Delta\phi = \frac{2\pi}{\lambda}\Delta x = \frac{2\pi}{3 \times 10^{-5}} \times 0.275 \times 10^{-3} = \frac{55\pi}{3}$$

$$\Delta\phi = \frac{55\pi}{3} = 18\pi + \frac{\pi}{3}$$

Minimum phase difference to be introduced $= -\dfrac{\pi}{3}$

$$\Delta\phi = \frac{2\pi}{\lambda}\Delta x \Rightarrow \frac{\pi}{3} = \frac{2\pi}{\lambda}\Delta x \quad \Rightarrow \quad \Delta x = \frac{\lambda}{6}$$

Also, $\Delta x = \dfrac{dy}{D} = \dfrac{\lambda}{6}$

$$\Rightarrow \quad y = \frac{\lambda D}{6d} = \frac{3 \times 10^{-5} \times 1}{6 \times 0.5 \times 10^{-3}} = 1 \times 10^{-2}\ \text{m} = 1\ \text{cm}$$

8. Without inserting the glass sheet, path difference at P,

$$\Delta x = \frac{dy}{D} = \frac{2 \times 10^{-3} \times 0.15 \times 10^{-3}}{2} = 1.5 \times 10^{-7}\ \text{m}$$

$$\Delta\phi = \frac{2\pi}{\lambda}\Delta x = \frac{2\pi}{6000 \times 10^{-10}} \times 1.5 \times 10^{-7} = \frac{\pi}{2}$$

$$I = 4I_0\cos^2\left(\frac{\Delta\phi}{2}\right) = 2I_0$$

Phase difference after placing the glass sheet,

$$\Delta\phi = \frac{\pi}{2} + \frac{2\pi}{\lambda}(\mu - 1)t$$
$$= \frac{\pi}{2} + \frac{2\pi}{6000 \times 10^{-10}}(1.5 - 1)(8000 \times 10^{-10})$$
$$= \frac{11\pi}{6}$$

The intensity at P now,

$$I' = I_0 + \eta I_0 + 2\sqrt{I_0}\sqrt{\eta I_0}\cos\left(\frac{11\pi}{6}\right) = 2I_0$$

$$\Rightarrow \quad \eta + \sqrt{3\eta} = 1 \quad \Rightarrow \quad \sqrt{3\eta} = 1 - \eta$$

$$\Rightarrow \quad \eta^2 - 5\eta + 1 = 0 \quad \Rightarrow \quad \eta = \frac{5 - \sqrt{21}}{2}$$

$$\therefore \quad \beta = 21$$

9. $I = I_1 + I_2 + 2\sqrt{I_1}\sqrt{I_2}\cos\Delta\phi$

$$\Rightarrow \quad \frac{1}{2}(4I_0) = I_0 + I_0 + 2\sqrt{I_0}\sqrt{I_0}\cos\Delta\phi$$

$$\Rightarrow \quad \Delta\phi = \frac{\pi}{2}$$

Path difference, $\Delta x = 2\lambda\cos\theta$

$$\Delta\phi = \frac{2\pi}{\lambda}\Delta x = \frac{2\pi}{\lambda}(2\lambda\cos\theta) = 4\pi\cos\theta$$

$$\therefore \quad 4\pi\cos\theta = \frac{\pi}{2} \quad \Rightarrow \quad \cos\theta = \frac{1}{8}$$

So, $32\cos\theta = 32\left(\dfrac{1}{8}\right) = 4$

10. $\Delta x = 2(\sqrt{L^2 + d^2} - L)$

$$= 2L\left(\left(1 + \frac{d^2}{L^2}\right)^{1/2} - 1\right)$$

$$= 2L\left[1 + \frac{d^2}{2L^2} - 1\right] = \frac{d^2}{L}$$

$$\Delta x_1 = \frac{d_1^2}{L} \quad \text{and} \quad \Delta x_2 = \frac{d_2^2}{L}$$

$$\Delta x_1 = \frac{d_1^2}{L} = n\lambda \quad \text{and} \quad \Delta x_2 = \frac{d_2^2}{L} = n\lambda + \frac{\lambda}{3}$$

$$\therefore \quad \frac{d_2^2 - d_1^2}{L} = \frac{\lambda}{3}$$

$$\Rightarrow \quad \lambda = \frac{3(d_2^2 - d_1^2)}{L}$$

$$= \frac{3((400\sqrt{5})^2 - (200\sqrt{15})^2 \times 10^{-12}}{1} = 6000\ \text{Å}$$

$$\therefore \quad \alpha = 6$$

11. $d = x\theta$

$2x\theta = n\lambda$ (condition of dark fringe)

$n = 0$ (First dark fringe at join of plates)

$n = 4$ (Fifth dark fringe at fiber)

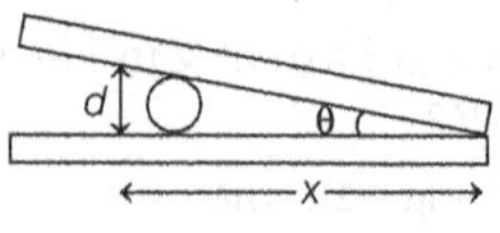

$$d = x\theta = \frac{4\lambda}{2} = 2\lambda$$

$$\therefore \quad d = 2 \times 550 = 1100\ \text{nm}$$

Previous Year's Questions

JEE Main

1. Path difference ΔL for minima at P is,

$(SS_1 + S_1P) - (SS_2 + S_2P)$

$$\Delta L = 2\sqrt{D^2 + d^2} - 2D = \frac{\lambda}{2}$$

(for minima)

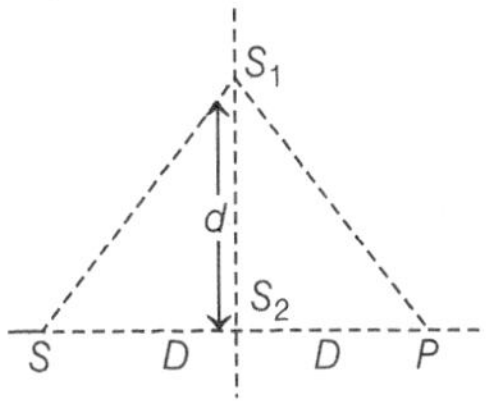

$$\sqrt{D^2 + d^2} - D = \lambda/4$$

$$\sqrt{D^2 + d^2} = \frac{\lambda}{4} + D$$

$$D^2 + d^2 = \left(\frac{\lambda}{4} + D\right)^2$$

So, $d^2 = \left(\frac{\lambda}{4} + D\right)^2 - D^2$

$$\lambda = 400 \times 10^{-9}\ \text{m} = 400 \times 10^{-9} \times 10^3\ \text{mm} = 4 \times 10^{-4}\ \text{mm}$$

$$D = 0.2\ \text{m} = 0.2 \times 10^3\ \text{mm} = 2 \times 10^2\ \text{mm}$$

So, $d^2 = (10^{-4} + 2 \times 10^2)^2 - (2 \times 10^2)^2$

$$= (10^{-4} + 2 \times 10^2 + 2 \times 10^2) \times (10^{-4})$$

Using, $= (A + B)(A - B) = A^2 - B^2$

$$\approx 4 \times 10^2 \times 10^{-4} = 4 \times 10^{-2}\ \text{mm}$$

$\therefore$ $d = \sqrt{4 \times 10^{-2}} = 2 \times 10^{-1}\ \text{mm} = 0.2\ \text{mm}$

2. Given,

Path difference, $\Delta x = \frac{7\lambda}{4}$

If I be the intensity of two identical source, then

$$I_{max} = I_1 + I_2 + 2\sqrt{I_1 I_2}\cos\phi = I + I + 2I\cos 0° = 4I$$

When, $\Delta x = \frac{7\lambda}{4}$

Then, $\Delta\phi' = \frac{2\pi}{\lambda} \times \Delta x = \frac{2\pi}{\lambda} \times \frac{7\lambda}{4} = \frac{7}{2}\pi$

$\therefore$ Intensity

$$I' = I_1 + I_2 + 2\sqrt{I_1 I_2}\cos\Delta\phi'$$

$$= I + I + 2\sqrt{I \cdot I}\cos\frac{7\pi}{2}$$

$$= 2I + 2I\cos\left(2\pi + \frac{3\pi}{2}\right)$$

$$= 2I + 2I\cos\left(\frac{3\pi}{2}\right)$$

$$= 2I + 2I\cos(\pi + \pi/2)$$

$$= 2I + 2I(-\cos\pi/2) = 2I$$

$\therefore$ $\frac{I'}{I_{max}} = \frac{2I}{4I} = \frac{1}{2}$

3. Given intensity ratio of waves A and B is,

$$\frac{I_A}{I_B} = \frac{1}{9}$$

So, if $I_A = x', I_B = 9x'$

Now, I_1 = resultant intensity due to incoherent addition

$$= x' + 9x' = 10x'.$$

and I_2 resultant intensity due to coherent addition $(\Delta\phi = 60°)$

$$= I_A + I_B + 2\sqrt{I_A}\sqrt{I_B}\cos\phi$$

$$= x' + 9x' + 2\sqrt{x'}\sqrt{9x'}\cos 60°$$

$$= x' + 9x' + 3x' = 13x'$$

Ratio, $\frac{I_1}{I_2} = \frac{10x'}{13x'} = \frac{10}{x}$ or $x = 13$

4. Fringe width in YDSE; $\beta = \frac{\lambda D}{d}$

So, (In same experimental set up)

$$\frac{\beta_2}{\beta_1} = \lambda_2/\lambda_1 \Rightarrow \beta_2 = \beta_1 \cdot \frac{\lambda_2}{\lambda_1}$$

Here $\beta_1 = 2$ mm

$\lambda_2 = 600$ nm, $\lambda_1 = 400$ nm.

$\therefore$ $\beta_2 = 2\text{mm} \times \frac{600\ \text{nm}}{400\ \text{nm}} = \frac{2 \times 6}{4}\ \text{mm} = 3\ \text{mm}$

5. For same amplitude,

$$I_1 = I_2 = Ka^2 = I_0$$

When, $\phi_1 = \pi/3$

$$I_{0_1} = I_1 + I_2 + 2\sqrt{I_1 I_2}\cos\phi$$

$$I_{0_1} = I_0 + I_0 + 2I_0\cos\frac{\pi}{3} = 3I_0$$

When, $\phi_2 = \pi/2$

$$I_{0_2} = I_1 + I_2 + 2\sqrt{I_1 I_2}\cos\phi = 2I_0 + 2I_0\cos\frac{\pi}{2} = 2I_0$$

Hence ratio, $\frac{I_{0_1}}{I_{0_2}} = \frac{3}{2}$

6. Given, $D = 1$ m

$\lambda = 600\ \text{nm} = 6 \times 10^{-7}$ m

$x_5 = 5\ \text{cm} = 5 \times 10^{-2}$ m

We know that position of nth bright fringe, $x_n = \frac{nD\lambda}{d}$

Here, $n = 5$,

$\therefore$ $x_5 = \frac{5D\lambda}{d} \Rightarrow d = \frac{5D\lambda}{x_5}$

$$= \frac{5 \times 1 \times 6 \times 10^{-7}}{5 \times 10^{-2}} = 60\ \mu\text{m}$$

7. In given YDSE, first minimum occurs at P. When wavelength of light used is

$\lambda = 800$ nm

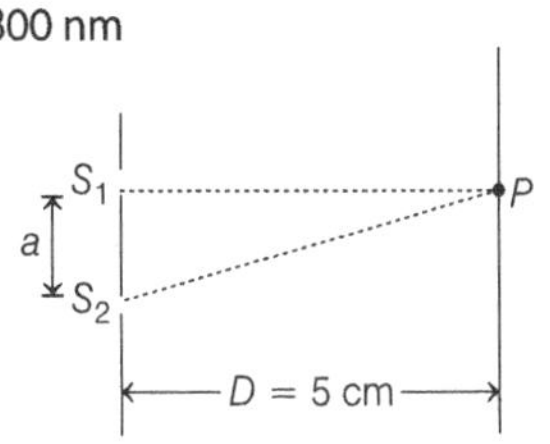

For 1st minima,

Path difference,

$$S_2P - S_1P = \sqrt{(5+a)^2} - 5 = \frac{\lambda}{2}$$

Taking cm unit for length

$$\Rightarrow \sqrt{(5+a)^2} - 5 = \frac{800 \times 10^{-9} \times 100}{2}$$

$$\Rightarrow \quad \sqrt{(5+a)^2} = 5 + 4 \times 10^{-5}$$

On squaring, we get

$$5^2 + a^2 + 10a = 5^2 + (4 \times 10^{-5})^2 + 40 \times 10^{-5}$$

Neglecting 10 a and $(4 \times 10^{-5})^2$ being too small, we get

$$a^2 = 400 \times 10^{-6}$$

$$\Rightarrow \quad a = 20 \times 10^{-3} \text{ cm}$$

$$= 20 \times 10^{-3} \times 10 \text{ mm} = 0.2 \text{ mm}$$

8. Let $n_1$maxima of 7000 Å coincide. with n_2 maxima of 5500 Å, therefore $n_1 = n_2$

$$\Rightarrow \quad n_1 \frac{D\lambda_1}{d} = n_2 \frac{D\lambda_2}{d}$$

$$\Rightarrow \quad \frac{n_1}{n_2} = \frac{\lambda_2}{\lambda_1} = \frac{5500}{7000} = \frac{11}{14}$$

Therefore, 11th maxima of 7000 Å will coincide with 14th maxima of 5500 A° Least distance from central bright fringe

$$y = n_1 \beta_1$$

$$y = \frac{n_1 \lambda_1 D}{d} = \frac{11 \times 7000 \times 10^{-10}}{2.5 \times 10^{-3}} \times 150 \times 10^{-2}$$

$$= \frac{11 \times 7 \times 5}{2.5} \times 10^{-5} \text{m}$$

$$y = 462 \times 10^{-5} \text{m}$$

Therefore, $n = 462$

9. Here, $\mu_1 = 1.51, t = 0.1$ mm

$$\mu_2 = 1.55, \lambda = 4000 \text{ Å}$$

Shifting central maxima

$$\Delta x = [S_1P + (\mu_1 - 1)t] - [S_2P + (\mu_2 - 1)t]$$

$$0 = (S_1P - S_2P) + (\mu_1 - 1)t - (\mu_2 - 1)t$$

$$0 = \frac{yd}{D} + (\mu_1 - \mu_2)t \quad \Rightarrow \quad (\mu_2 - \mu_1)t = \frac{yd}{D}$$

$$(1.55 - 1.51)\ (0.1 \text{ mm}) = y \times \frac{d}{D}$$

$$\frac{D}{d}(0.04 \times 0.1) \times 10^{-3} = y \quad \text{... (i)}$$

Now, Fringe width $\Rightarrow \beta = \frac{\lambda D}{d}$

Number of fringes shifted $= \frac{y}{\beta} = \frac{4 \times 10^{-6}}{4000\text{Å}} = 10$

10. Given that $d = 0.35$ mm,

$$D = 7 \text{ m}, \lambda_1 = 800 \text{ nm},$$

$$\lambda_2 = 600 \text{ nm}$$

If bright fringes of the two wavelength coincide, then their position on screen are same.

i.e., $y_1 = y_2$

$$n_1 \frac{\lambda_1 D}{d} = \frac{n_2 \lambda_2 D}{d} \quad \Rightarrow \quad n_1 \lambda_1 = n_2 \lambda_2$$

or $\dfrac{n_1}{n_2} = \dfrac{\lambda_2}{\lambda_1} = \dfrac{600}{800} = \dfrac{3}{4}$

3rd maxima of λ_1 and 4th maxima of λ_2 will coincide. Shortest distance from central point,

$$Y = \frac{n_1 \lambda_1 D}{d} = \frac{3 \times 800 \times 10^{-9} \times 7}{0.35 \times 10^{-3}}$$

$$Y = 48 \times 10^{-3}$$

$$Y = 48 \text{ mm}$$

11. Given, $I_1 : I_2 = 1:4$

$$\Rightarrow \quad I_1 = k \text{ and } I_2 = 4k$$

$$\therefore \quad I_{max} = I_1 + I_2 + 2\sqrt{I_1 I_2}$$

$$\Rightarrow \quad I_{max} = k + 4k + 2\sqrt{k4k}$$

$$\Rightarrow \quad I_{max} = 5k + 4k = 9k$$

Now, $I_{min} = I_1 + I_2 - 2\sqrt{I_1 I_2}$

$$I_{min} = k + 4k - 4k = k$$

$$\therefore \quad \frac{I_{max} + I_{min}}{I_{max} - I_{min}} = \frac{9k + k}{9k - k} = \frac{10k}{8k} = \frac{5}{4}$$

Now, since given that

$$\frac{I_{max} + I_{min}}{I_{max} - I_{min}} = \frac{5}{4} = \frac{2\alpha + 1}{\beta + 3}$$

$$\Rightarrow \quad 2\alpha + 1 = 5\,;\, \beta + 3 = 4$$

$$\Rightarrow \quad \alpha = \frac{4}{2} = 2; \text{ and } \beta = 1$$

$$\alpha / \beta = 2$$

12. In Young's double slit experiment, Fringe width, $\beta = 12 \text{ mm} = 1.2 \times 10^{-2}$ m

When entire arrangement of Young's double slit experiment is placed in water of refractive index, $\mu = \frac{4}{3}$, then fringe width, $\beta' = \frac{\beta}{\mu} = \frac{1.2 \times 10^{-2}}{4/3}$

$$= 0.9 \times 10^{-2} \text{ m} = 9 \times 10^{-3} \text{ m} = 9 \text{ mm}$$

13. Fringe width, $\beta = \frac{\lambda D}{d}$

$$\Rightarrow \quad \frac{\beta_2}{\beta_1} = \frac{\lambda_2}{\lambda_1} \times \frac{d_1}{d_2} \quad \text{...(i)}$$

Here, $d_2 = 2\,d_1$ and $\lambda_1 = 5000$ Å

$\lambda_2 = 6000$ Å, and $\beta_1 = 0.5$ mm

Hence, from Eq. (i), we get

$$\beta_2 = 0.5 \times \frac{6000}{5000} \times \frac{1}{2} \quad \Rightarrow \quad \beta_2 = 0.3 \text{ mm}$$

14. In YDSE, maximum occurs at same position. This means extra path difference due to glass plate is a multiple of wavelength λ.

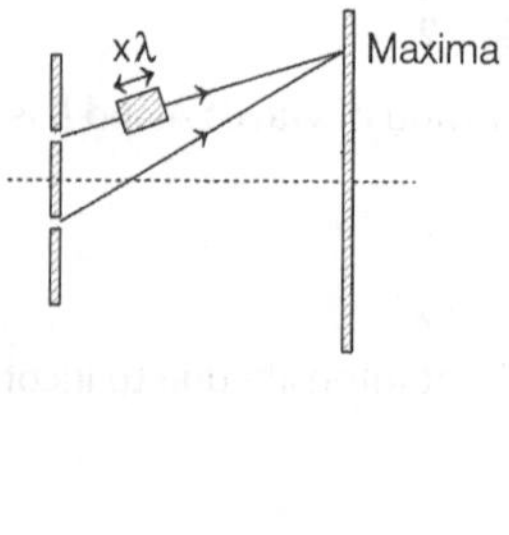

Now, extra path difference due to glass plate is

$$\Delta L = (\mu - 1)t \qquad (\because t = \text{thickness} = x\lambda)$$

$$\Rightarrow \quad \Delta L = (1.5 - 1)x\lambda \Rightarrow \Delta L = \frac{x\lambda}{2}$$

Now, for given case,

$$\Delta L = \frac{x\lambda}{2} = n\lambda$$

(As maxima stays at same place)

$$\Rightarrow \quad x = 2n$$

As, $n = 0, 1, 2, 3$ ......

So, value of x can be

$$x = 0, 2, 4, 6 \text{ ...... etc.}$$

15. Given, $I_1 : I_2 = 9 : 4$

$$\therefore \quad I \propto a^2 \qquad \text{[Where, } a = \text{amplitude of wave]}$$

$$\therefore \quad \frac{I_1}{I_2} = \left(\frac{a_1}{a_2}\right)^2 = \frac{9}{4}$$

$$\Rightarrow \quad \left(\frac{a_1}{a_2}\right)^2 = \left(\frac{3}{2}\right)^2$$

$$\Rightarrow \quad \frac{a_1}{a_2} = \frac{3}{2} \qquad \text{... (i)}$$

$$\therefore \quad \frac{I_{max}}{I_{min}} = \frac{(a_1 + a_2)^2}{(a_1 - a_2)^2}$$

$$= \frac{a_2^2\left(\frac{a_1}{a_2} + 1\right)^2}{a_2^2\left(\frac{a_1}{a_2} - 1\right)^2} = \frac{\left(\frac{a_1}{a_2} + 1\right)^2}{\left(\frac{a_1}{a_2} - 1\right)^2}$$

$$= \frac{\left(\frac{3}{2} + 1\right)^2}{\left(\frac{3}{2} - 1\right)^2} = \frac{25/4}{1/4} = \frac{25}{1}$$

$$I_{max} : I_{min} = 25 : 1$$

16. According to given situation,

$$\frac{I_1}{I_2} = \frac{4}{1}; \text{ So, } \frac{I_1}{I_2} = \left(\frac{A_1}{A_2}\right)^2$$

$$\left(\frac{A_1}{A_2}\right)^2 = \frac{4}{1} \Rightarrow \frac{A_1}{A_2} = \frac{2}{1};$$

$$\frac{A_{max}}{A_{min}} = \frac{2+1}{2-1} = \frac{3}{1}$$

$$\frac{I_{max}}{I_{min}} = \left(\frac{A_{max}}{A_{min}}\right)^2 = \frac{9}{1}$$

$$\Rightarrow \quad \frac{I_{max} + I_{min}}{I_{max} - I_{min}} = \frac{5}{4} = \frac{5}{x}$$

So, $\quad x = 4$

17. Given, $\quad I_1 = I, I_2 = 9I, \phi_P = \frac{\pi}{2}, \phi_Q = \pi$

$$I_P = I + 9I + 2\sqrt{I \times 9I}\cos\frac{\pi}{2} = 10I$$

$$I_Q = I_1 + I_2 + 2\sqrt{I_1 I_2}\cos\pi;$$

$$I_Q = I + 9I - 2\sqrt{I \times 9I} = 4I$$

Then, the difference between the resultant intensities at P and Q will be $10I - 4I = 6I$.

18. We know that

$$\beta = \frac{\lambda D}{d}$$

$$\Delta\beta = \lambda\frac{\Delta D}{d}$$

$$\lambda = \frac{\beta d}{\Delta d} = \frac{3 \times 10^{-5} \times 10^{-3}}{5 \times 10^{-2}}$$

$$= 0.6 \times 10^{-6} = 600 \times 10^{-9}\text{m}$$

$$= 600 \text{ nm}$$

19. Given, $I_1 = 4I \quad \Rightarrow \quad I_2 = 9I$

At point A, $\Delta\phi_A = 0$

At point B, $\Delta\phi_B = \pi$

To find, $(I_A)_{resultant} - (I_B)_{resultant}$

But we know that, in interference when $\Delta\phi = 0$, then resultant intensity in maximum i.e.

$$(I_A)_{resultant} = I_{max}$$

and when $\Delta\phi = \pi$ then resultant intensity is minimum i.e.

$$(I_B)_{resultant} = I_{min}$$

$\therefore$ We have to find,

$$(I_{max} - I_{min})$$

Now, $\quad I_{max} = (\sqrt{I_1} + \sqrt{I_2})^2 = (\sqrt{4I} + \sqrt{9I})^2$

$$= 4I + 9I + 12I$$

$$\Rightarrow \quad I_{max} = 25I$$

Also, $\quad I_{min} = (\sqrt{I_1} - \sqrt{I_2})^2 = (\sqrt{4I} - \sqrt{9I})^2$

$$= 4I + 9I - 12I = I$$

$$\Rightarrow \quad I_{min} = I$$

$$\therefore \quad I_{max} - I_{min} = 25I - I = 24I$$

20. In Young's double slit experiment, wavelength of laser light,

$$\lambda_1 = 560 \text{ nm} = 5.6 \times 10^{-7} \text{ m}$$

Seperation of consecutive bright fringes is equal to fringe width (β).

$$\therefore \quad \beta = \frac{D\lambda}{d}$$

$$\Rightarrow \quad \frac{\beta_1}{\beta_2} = \frac{\lambda_1}{\lambda_2} \qquad \text{...(i)}$$

$\Rightarrow$ Here, $\beta_1 = 7.2 \text{ nm} = 7.2 \times 10^{-3}$ m

and $\quad \beta_2 = 8.1 \text{ mm} = 8.1 \times 10^{-3}$ m

On putting these values in Eq. (i), we get

$$\frac{7.2 \times 10^{-3}}{8.1 \times 10^{-3}} = \frac{5.6 \times 10^{-7}}{\lambda_2}$$

$$\Rightarrow \quad \frac{8}{9} = \frac{5.6 \times 10^{-7}}{\lambda_2}$$

$$\Rightarrow \qquad \lambda_2 = \frac{9}{8} \times 5.6 \times 10^{-7}$$
$$= 6.3 \times 10^{-7} \text{ m}$$
$$= 630 \times 10^{-9} \text{ m} = 630 \text{ nm}$$

21. Given, intensity of two light waves

$$I_1 = I_2 = I_0$$
$$I_{min} = 0$$

Since, $$I_{min} = (\sqrt{I_1} - \sqrt{I_2})^2$$

and $$I_{max} = (\sqrt{I_1} + \sqrt{I_2})^2$$
$$= (\sqrt{I_0} + \sqrt{I_0})^2$$
$$= (2\sqrt{I_0})^2 = 4I_0$$

22. Fringe width,

$$\beta = \frac{D\lambda}{d} = \frac{1 \times 500 \times 10^{-9}}{2 \times 10^{-3}}$$
$$= 2.5 \times 10^{-4} \text{ m}$$
$$\Rightarrow \qquad \beta = 0.25 \text{ mm}$$

23. We know that in Young's double slit experiment, fringe width, $\beta = \frac{D\lambda}{d}$

$$\beta \propto \lambda$$

Since, $\lambda_{blue} < \lambda_{orange}$

Thus, $\beta_{blue} < \beta_{orange}$

$\therefore$ In Young's double slit experiment, if the source of light changes from orange to blue, then distance between the consecutive fringes will decrease.

24. Given, separation between slits,

$$d(t) = d_0 + a_0 \sin \omega t$$

As we know that,

Fringe width $(\beta) = \frac{\lambda D}{d}$

$$\Rightarrow \qquad \beta = \frac{\lambda D}{d_0 + a_0 \sin \omega t}$$

Now, maximum fringe width

$$(\beta_{max}) = \frac{\lambda D}{d_0 - a_0} \qquad (\text{for } \sin \omega t = -1)$$

and minimum fringe width

$$(\beta_{min}) = \frac{\lambda D}{d_0 + a_0} \qquad (\text{for } \sin \omega t = +1)$$

$$\therefore \qquad \beta_{max} - \beta_{min} = \lambda D \left[\frac{1}{d_0 - a_0} - \frac{1}{d_0 + a_0} \right]$$
$$= \lambda D \left[\frac{2a_0}{d_0^2 - a_0^2} \right]$$

25. Given, The distance of sources from the screen,

$$D = 0.5 \text{ m}$$

The distance between the slits,

$$d = 0.5 \text{ mm} = 0.0005 \text{ m}$$

The wavelength of the monochromatic light,

$$\lambda = 5890 \text{ Å} = 5890 \times 10^{-10} \text{m}$$

The distance between the first and the third bright fringe formed, $Y = 2\beta$

As we know, $\beta = \frac{\lambda D}{d}$

On substituting the values in the above equation, we get

$$Y = 2\left(\frac{\lambda D}{d}\right) = 2\left(\frac{5890 \times 10^{-10} \times 0.5}{0.0005}\right)$$
$$= 1178 \times 10^{-6} \text{ m}$$

26. Given, in YDSE, the separation between two slits,

$$d = 2 \text{ mm} = 2 \times 10^{-3} \text{ m}$$

Distance between slit and screen,

$$D = 1 \text{ m}$$

Wavelength of light, $\lambda = 500$ nm

$$= 500 \times 10^{-9} \text{ m}$$

Let β will be the fringe width

$$\therefore \qquad \beta = \frac{\lambda D}{d} = \frac{500 \times 10^{-9} \times 1}{2 \times 10^{-3}} = 250 \times 10^{-6}$$
$$= 0.25 \text{ mm}$$

27. Given, $\frac{I_1}{I_2} = 2x$

$$\Rightarrow \qquad I_1 = 2I_2 x$$

As we know,

$$I_{max} = (\sqrt{I_1} + \sqrt{I_2})^2$$

and $$I_{min} = (\sqrt{I_1} - \sqrt{I_2})^2$$

$$\therefore \qquad \frac{I_{max} - I_{min}}{I_{max} + I_{min}} = \frac{2\sqrt{I_1 I_2}}{I_1 + I_2} \qquad \text{(using dividendo rule)}$$
$$= \frac{2\sqrt{2I_2 x \cdot I_2}}{2I_2 x + I_2} = \frac{2\sqrt{2x}}{2x + 1}$$

JEE Advanced

1.

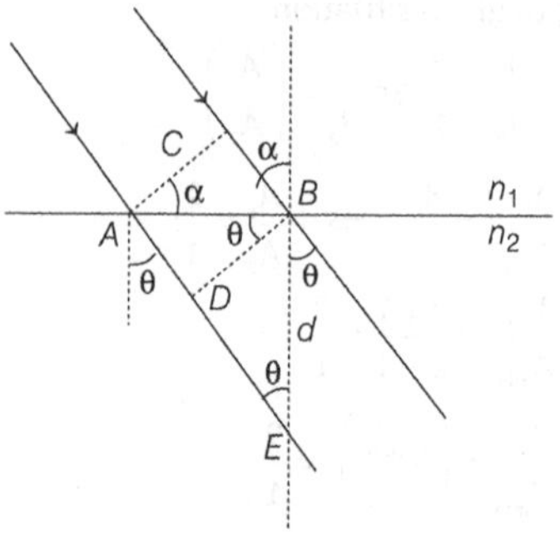

$AB = (d)(\tan\theta)$ and $BC = AB \sin\alpha = (d)(\tan\theta)(\sin\alpha)$

Also, $AD = AB \sin\theta$

Path difference (in vacuum) at detector,

$$\Delta x = n_1 BC - n_2 AD$$
$$= n_1 (AB) \sin\alpha - n_2 (AB \sin\theta)$$

$$= AB\,(n_1 \sin\alpha - n_2 \sin\theta)$$

From Snell's law, $n_1 \sin\alpha = n_2 \sin\theta$

$\therefore \quad \Delta x = 0$ or $\Delta\phi = 0$

Therefore, rays interfere constructively at detector.

$\Rightarrow$ (*a*), (*b*) are correct and (*c*), (*d*) are incorrect.

2.

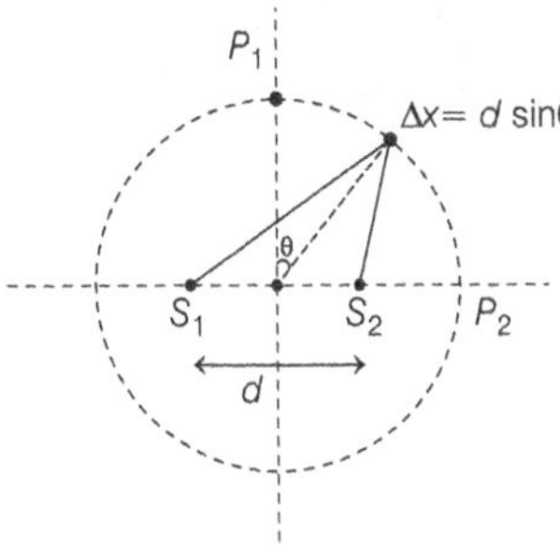

$$\lambda = 600\,\text{nm}$$

at P_1 $\quad \Delta x = 0$

at P_2 $\quad \Delta x = d = 1.8\text{ mm} = n\lambda$

Number of maximas will be $n = \dfrac{\Delta x}{\lambda} = \dfrac{1.8\text{ mm}}{600\,\text{nm}} = 3000$

at P_2 $\quad \Delta x = 3000\lambda$

Hence, bright fringe will be formed at P_2.

At P_2, 3000th maxima is formed.

For (a) option

At P_1, $\Delta X_1 = d\sin\theta_1 = 0$, the zero order maxima. For next maxima, $\Delta X_2 = d\sin\theta_2 = \lambda$ or $\sin\theta_2 = \lambda/d$. Similarly for next maxima $\sin\theta_3 = 2\lambda/d$ and so on.

Therefore betweeen two consecutive maximas,

$$\sin\theta_n - \sin\theta_{n-1} = \frac{(n+1)\lambda}{d} - \frac{n\lambda}{d} = \frac{\lambda}{d} = \text{constant.}$$

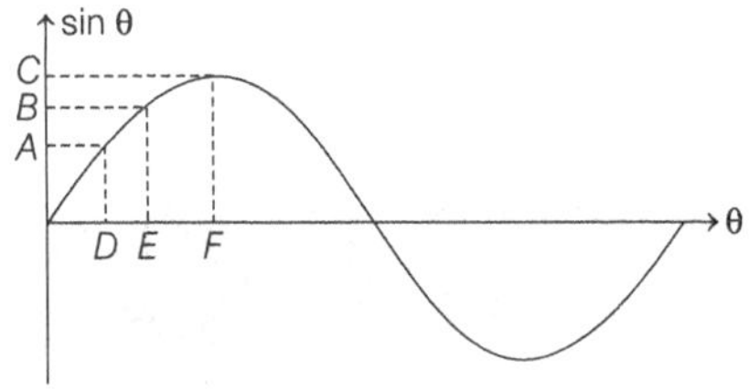

From the graph we can see that

$$AB = BC = \lambda/d \text{ but } EF > DE.$$

3.

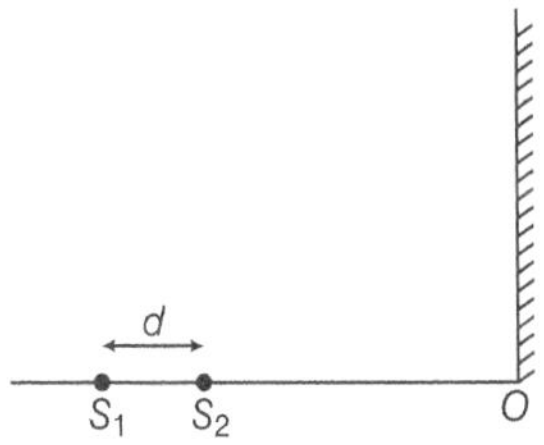

Path difference at point $O = d = 0.6003\text{ mm} = 600300\text{ nm}$.

This path difference is equal to $\left(1000\lambda + \dfrac{\lambda}{2}\right)$.

$\Rightarrow$ Minima is formed at point *O*.

Line S_1S_2 and screen are $\perp$ to each other so fringe pattern is circular (semi-circular because only half of screen is available)

CHAPTER~06

DIFFRACTION AND POLARISATION

LEVEL 01 Starter Level

6.1 Diffraction

1 Light of wavelength 5000 Å is incident on a slit of width 0.1 mm. Find out the width of the central bright line on a screen distance 2 m from the slit.

2 Light of wavelength 5000 Å is incident normally on a slit of width 1 μm. Calculate the half angular width of central maximum on a screen distance 9 m.

3 Light of wavelength 6000 Å is incident on a slit of width 0.30 mm. The screen is placed 2 m from the slit. Find the position of
(a) the first dark fringe and
(b) second bright fringe.

4 A slit of width *a* is illuminated by monochromatic light of wavelength 650 nm at normal incidence. Calculate the value of *a* when
(a) the first minimum falls at an angle of diffraction of 30°
(b) the first maximum falls at an angle of diffraction of 30°.

5 Light of wavelength 6000 Å is incident normally on a slit of width 24×10^{-5} cm. Find out the angular position of second minimum from central maximum.

6 The fraunhofer diffraction pattern of a single slit is formed at the focal plane of a lens of focal length 1 m. The width of the slit is 0.3 mm. If the third minimum is formed at a distance of 5 mm from the central maximum, then calculate the wavelength of light.

7 In the diffraction due to a single slit experiment, the aperture of the slit is 3 mm. If monochromatic light of wavelength 620 nm is incident normally on the slit, calculate the separation between the first order minima and the third order maxima on one side of the screen. The distance between the slit and the screen is 1.5 m.

8 In a single slit diffraction experiment first minimum for $\lambda_1 = 660$ nm coincides with first maxima for wavelength λ_2. Calculate λ_2.

9 For what distance is ray optics a good approximation, when the aperture is 3 mm wide and the wave length is 500 nm?

6.2 Polarisation

1 If the angle between the pass axis of polariser and the analyser is 45°, what is the ratio of the intensities of original light and the transmitted light after passing through the analyser?

2 A beam of unpolarised light of intensity 32 Wm^{-2} passes successively through two parallel polarising sheets sheet P_1 and P_2. If the angle between the pass axes of P_1 and P_2 is made 60°, find the intensity of light transmitted by P_2.

3 Two polaroids are crossed to each other. When one of them is rotated through 60°, then what percentage of the incident unpolarised light will be transmitted by the polaroids?

4 Four polaroids are so placed that the transmission axis of each is inclined at an angle of 30° from the axis of the previous polaroid in the same direction. If unpolarised light beam of intensity I_0 falls on the first polaroid, then what will be the intensity of the light emerging from the last polaroid?

5 At what angle of incidence will the light reflected from water ($\mu = 1.33$) be completely polarised ?

6 If light beam is incident at polarising angle (56.3°) on air-glass interface, then what is the angle of refraction in glass?

LEVEL 02 JEE Main/Advanced Level

1 Microwaves of frequency 24000 MHz are incident normally on a rectangular slit of width 5 cm. Calculate the angular spread of the central maximum of the diffraction pattern
(a) 0.5 rad (b) 0.5°
(c) 0.25 rad (d) 0.25°

2 Light of wavelength 5000 Å incidents over a slit of width 1 μm. The angular width of central maxima will be
(a) 30° (b) 60° (c) 90° (d) 120°

3 A slit of size 0.15 cm is placed at 2.1 m from a screen. On illuminated it by a light of wavelength 5×10^{-5} cm, the width of diffraction pattern will be
(a) 70 mm (b) 0.14 mm
(c) 1.4 mm (d) 14 mm

4 The first diffraction minima due to a single slit diffraction is at $\theta = 30°$ for a light of wavelength 5000 Å. The width of the slit is
(a) 5×10^{-5} cm (b) 1.0×10^{-4} cm
(c) 2.5×10^{-5} cm (d) 1.25×10^{-5} cm

5 Light of wavelength $\lambda = 5000$ Å falls normally on a narrow slit. A screen placed at a distance of 1 m from the slit and perpendicular to the direction of light. The first minima of the diffraction pattern is situated at 5 mm from the centre of central maximum. The width of the slit is
(a) 0.1 mm (b) 1.0 mm (c) 0.5 mm (d) 0.2 mm

6 If light of wavelength 4000 Å incidents on a slit of width 0.5 mm and diffraction pattern is obtained on a screen 2 m from slit, then distance of first bright fringe from central bright ring
(a) 1.2 mm (b) 0.8 mm
(c) 0.4 mm (d) None of these

7 A beam of light of wavelength 600 nm from a distant source falls on a single slit 1 mm wide and the resulting diffraction pattern is observed on a screen 2 m away. The distance between the first dark fringes on either side of central bright fringe is
(a) 1.2 cm (b) 1.2 mm (c) 2.4 cm (d) 2.4 mm

8 Direction of the first secondary maximum in the Fraunhofer diffraction pattern at a single slit is given by (a is the width of the slit)
(a) $a\sin\theta = \frac{\lambda}{2}$ (b) $a\cos\theta = \frac{3\lambda}{2}$
(c) $a\sin\theta = \lambda$ (d) $a\sin\theta = \frac{3\lambda}{2}$

9 In a Fraunhofer diffraction experiment at a single slit using light of wavelength 400 nm, the first minimum is formed at an angle 30°. Then, the direction θ of the first secondary maximum is
(a) $\tan^{-1}\left(\frac{4}{3}\right)$ (b) 60°
(c) $\sin^{-1}\left(\frac{3}{4}\right)$ (d) $\tan^{-1}\left(\frac{3}{4}\right)$

10 A light wave is incident normally over a slit of width 24×10^{-5} cm. The angular position of second dark fringe from the central maxima is 30°. What is the wavelength of light?
(a) 6000 Å (b) 5000 Å
(c) 3000 Å (d) 1500 Å

11 Light falls normally on a slit of width 0.3 mm. A convex lens of focal length 40 cm collects the rays at its focal plane. The distance of the first dark band from the centre of central bright fringe is 0.8 mm. The wavelength of light is
(a) 4800 Å (b) 5000 Å
(c) 6000 Å (d) 5896 Å

12 Light of wavelength 600 nm is incident upon a single slit with width 4×10^{-4} m. The figure shows the pattern observed on a screen positioned 2 m from the slits. Determine the distance s.

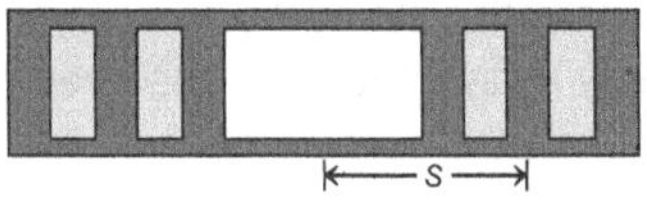

(a) 2 mm (b) 3 mm
(c) 4 mm (d) 6 mm

13 A beam of electrons with de-Broglie wavelength of 10^{-4} m pass through a slit 10^{-3} m wide. Calculate the angular spread introduced because of diffraction by slit.

(a) $\frac{9^\circ}{\pi}$ (b) $\frac{18^\circ}{\pi}$ (c) $\frac{36^\circ}{\pi}$ (d) $\frac{4.5^\circ}{\pi}$

14 In Young's double slit experiment the distance d between the slits S_1 and S_2 is 1 mm. What should be the width of each slit be so as to obtain 10 maxima of the two slit interference pattern with in the central maximum of the single slit diffraction pattern?

(a) 0.1 mm (b) 0.2 mm
(c) 0.3 mm (d) 0.4 mm

15 In the far field diffraction pattern of a single slit under polychromatic illumination, the first minimum with the wavelength λ_1 is found to be coincident with the third maximum at λ_2. So

(a) $\lambda_1 = 2.5\,\lambda_2$ (b) $3\lambda_1 = \lambda_2$
(c) $\lambda_1 = 3.5\lambda_2$ (d) $\lambda_1 = 6\lambda_2$

16 A parallel monochromatic beam of light is incident normally on a narrow slit. A diffraction pattern is formed on a screen placed perpendicular to the direction of incident beam. At the first maximum of the diffraction pattern, the phase difference between the rays coming from the edges of the slit is

(a) 0 (b) $\frac{\pi}{2}$ (c) π (d) 2π

17 A parallel monochromatic beam of light is incident at an angle θ to the normal of a slit of width a. The central point O of the screen will be dark if

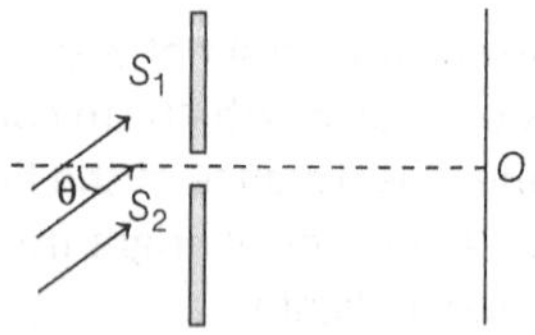

(a) $a \sin\theta = n\lambda$ where $n = 1, 3, 5 ...$
(b) $a \sin\theta = n\lambda$ where $n = 1, 2, 3 ...$
(c) $a \sin\theta = \frac{(2n-1)\,\lambda}{2}$ where $n = 1, 2, 3...$
(d) $a \cos\theta = n\lambda$ where $n = 1, 2, 3, 4 ...$

18 Yellow light is used in a single slit diffraction experiment with a slit of 0.6 mm. If yellow light is replaced by X-rays, than the observed pattern will reveal

(a) that the central maxima is narrower
(b) more number of fringes
(c) less number of fringes
(d) no diffraction pattern

19 In a single slit diffraction pattern, as the width of the slit is increased,

(a) the peak intensity of central maxima increases and its width also increases
(b) the peak intensity of central maxima increases and its width decreases.
(c) the peak intensity of central maxima decreases and its width increases
(d) the peak intensity of central maxima decreases and its width also decreases

20 To observe diffraction, the size of an obstacle

(a) should be of the same order as wavelength
(b) should be much larger than the wavelength
(c) have no relation to wavelength
(d) should be exactly $\frac{\lambda}{2}$

21 Diffraction effects are easier to notice in the case of sound waves than in the case of light waves because

(a) sound waves are longitudinal
(b) sound is perceived by the ear
(c) sound waves are mechanical waves
(d) sound waves are of longer wavelength

22 Plane polarised light is passed through a polaroid. On viewing through the polariod we find that, when the polaroid is given one complete rotation about the direction of the light, one of the following is observed.

(a) The intensity of light gradually decreases to zero and remains at zero
(b) The intensity of light gradually increases to a maximum and remains at maximum
(c) There is no change in intensity
(d) The intensity of light is twice maximum and twice zero

23. An unpolarised beam of intensity I_0 is incident on a pair of nicol prisms making an angle of 60° with each other. The intensity of light emerging from the pair is

(a) I_0 (b) $\frac{I_0}{2}$
(c) $\frac{I_0}{4}$ (d) $\frac{I_0}{8}$

24 Unpolarised light of intensity 32 Wm^{-2} passes through three polarisers such that transmission axes of the first and second polariser makes an angle of 30° with each other and the transmission axis of the last polariser is crossed with that of the first. The intensity of final emerging light will be

(a) 32 Wm^{-2} (b) 3 Wm^{-2}
(c) 8 Wm^{-2} (d) 4 Wm^{-2}

25 A beam of natural light falls on a system of 5 polaroids, which are arranged in succession such that the pass axis of each polaroid is turned through 60° with respect to the preceding one. The fraction of the incident light intensity that passes through the system

(a) $\frac{1}{64}$ (b) $\frac{1}{32}$ (c) $\frac{1}{512}$ (d) $\frac{1}{128}$

26 A beam of natural light falls on a system of 6 polaroids, which are arranged in succession such that each polaroid is turned through 30° with respect to the preceding one. The percentage of incident intensity that passes through the system will be

(a) 100% (b) 50% (c) 30% (d) 12 %

27 Two polaroids are present in the path of unpolarised beam of intensity I_0 such that no light is emitted from the second polaroid. If a third polaroid, whose transmission axis makes an angle θ with the transmission axis of the first polaroid, is placed between these polaroids. Then, the intensity of light emerging from the last polaroid will be,

(a) $\frac{I_0}{8}\sin^2 2\theta$ (b) $\frac{I_0}{4}\sin^2 2\theta$

(c) $\frac{I_0}{2}\cos^4\theta$ (d) $I_0\cos^4\theta$

28 A beam of plane polarised light falls normally on a polariser of cross-sectional area 3×10^{-4} m^2. Flux of energy of incident ray is 10^{-3} W. The polariser rotates with an angular frequency of 31.4 rad/s. The energy of light passing through the polariser per revolution will be

(a) 10^{-4} J (b) 10^{-3} J (c) 10^{-2} J (d) 10^{-1} J

29 The angle of polarisation for any medium is 60°, what will be critical angle for this?

(a) $\sin^{-1}\sqrt{3}$ (b) $\tan^{-1}\sqrt{3}$ (c) $\cos^{-1}\sqrt{3}$ (d) $\sin^{-1}\frac{1}{\sqrt{3}}$

30 A ray of light is incident on the surface of a glass plate at an angle of incidence equal to Brewster's angle ϕ. If μ represents the refractive index of glass with respect to air, then the angle between reflected and refracted rays is

(a) $90° + \phi$ (b) $\sin^{-1}(\mu\cos\phi)$

(c) 90° (d) $90° - \sin^{-1}(\sin\phi/\mu)$

31 The angle of incidence at which reflected light is totally polarised for reflection from air to glass (refraction index n) is

(a) $\sin^{-1}(n)$ (b) $\sin^{-1}\left(\frac{1}{n}\right)$

(c) $\tan^{-1}\left(\frac{1}{n}\right)$ (d) $\tan^{-1}(n)$

32 When the angle of incidence on a material is 60°, the reflected light is completely polarised. The velocity of the refracted ray inside the material is (in ms^{-1})

(a) 3×10^8 (b) $\left(\frac{3}{\sqrt{2}}\right)\times10^8$

(c) $\sqrt{3}\times10^8$ (d) 0.5×10^8

33 In the propagation of electromagnetic waves, the angle between the direction of propagation and plane of polarisation is

(a) 0° (b) 45° (c) 90° (d) 180°

34 Light waves can be polarised as they are

(a) transverse (b) of high frequency

(c) longitudinal (d) reflected

35 A beam of light AO is incident on a glass slab ($\mu = 1.732$) in a direction as shown in figure. The reflected ray OB is passed through a Nicol prism. On viewing through a Nicol prism, we find on rotating the prism that

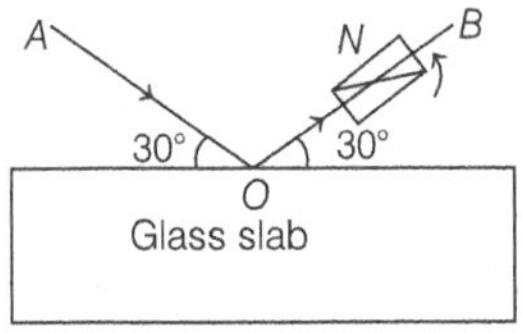

(a) the intensity is reduced down to zero and remains zero

(b) the intensity is reduces down some what and rises again

(c) there is no change in intensity

(d) the intensity gradually reduces to zero and then again increases

Previous Year's Questions

JEE Main

1 When a polaroid sheet is rotated between two crossed polaroids then the transmitted light intensity will be maximum for a rotation of **[2024, 27 Jan Shift-II]**

(a) 45° (b) 60°

(c) 90° (d) 30°

2 A parallel beam of monochromatic light of wavelength 5000 Å is incident normally on a narrow slit of width 0.001 mm. The light is focused by convex lens on screen, placed on its focal plane. The first minima will be formed for the angle of diffraction of .... (degree). **[2024, 27 Jan Shift-II]**

3 In a single slit diffraction pattern, a light of wavelength 6000 Å is used. The distance between the first and third minima in the diffraction pattern is found to be 3 mm, when the screen in placed 50 cm away from slits. The width of the slit is .... $\times 10^{-4}$ m. [2024, 29 Jan Shift-II]

4 A single slit of width a is illuminated by a monochromatic light of wavelength 600 nm. The value of a for which first minimum appears at $\theta = 30°$ on the screen will be [2023, 15 April Shift-I]

(a) 1.2 μm (b) 3 μm
(c) 0.6 μm (d) 1.8 μm

5 Given below are two statements.

Statement I If the Brewster's angle for the light propagating from air to glass is θ_B, then the Brewster's angle for the light propagating from glass to air is $\frac{\pi}{2} - \theta_B$.

Statement II The Brewster's angle for the light propagating from glass to air is $\tan^{-1}(\mu_g)$, where μ_g is the refractive index of glass.

In the light of the above statements, choose the correct answer from the options given below. [2023, 24 Jan shift-I]

(a) Statement I is false but Statement II is true.
(b) Statement I is true but Statement II is false.
(c) Both Statement I and Statement II are false.
(d) Both Statement I and Statement II is true.

6 n polarising sheets are arranged such that each makes an angle 45° with the preceeding sheet. An unpolarised light of intensity I is incident into this arrangement. The output intensity is found to be $I/64$. The value of n will be [2023, 1 Feb Shift-I]

(a) 3 (b) 6
(c) 4 (d) 5

7 Sodium light of wavelengths 650 nm and 655 nm is used to study diffraction at a single slit of aperture 0.5 mm. The distance between the slit and the screen is 2.0 m. The separation between the positions of the first maxima of diffraction pattern obtained in the two cases is ...... $\times 10^{-5}$ m. [2022, 24 June Shift-I]

8 Consider the diffraction pattern obtained from the sunlight incident on a pinhole of diameter 0.1μm. If the diameter of the pinhole is slightly increased, it will affect the diffraction pattern such that [2021, 25 Feb Shift-II]

(a) its size increases and intensity increases
(b) its size increases, but intensity decreases
(c) its size decreases, but intensity increases
(d) its size decreases and intensity decreases

9 Orange light of wavelength 6000×10^{-10} m illuminates a single slit of width 0.6×10^{-4} m. The maximum possible number of diffraction minima produced on both sides of the central maximum is .... [2020, 4 Sep Shift-II]

Answer Key

Level 1

6.1 Diffraction

1. 20 mm
2. 30°
3. (a) ± 4 mm (b) 10 mm
4. (a) 1.3×10^{-6} m (b) 1.95×10^{-6} m
5. $\theta = 30°$
6. 5000 Å
7. 7.75×10^{-4} m
8. 440 nm
9. 18 m

6.2 Polarisation

1. 4 : 1 **2.** 4 Wm^{-2} **3.** 37.5% **4.** 0.21 I_0
5. $\theta = \tan^{-1} 1.33 = 53°$ **6.** 33.7°

Level 2

Single Choice Correct Questions

1. (a)	2. (b)	3. (c)	4. (b)	5. (a)
6. (b)	7. (d)	8. (d)	9. (c)	10. (a)
11. (c)	12. (d)	13. (c)	14. (b)	15. (c)
16. (c)	17. (b)	18. (a)	19. (b)	20. (a)
21. (d)	22. (d)	23. (d)	24. (b)	25. (c)
26. (d)	27. (a)	28. (a)	29. (d)	30. (c)
31. (d)	32. (c)	33. (a)	34. (a)	35. (d)

Previous Year's Questions

JEE Main

1. (a)	2. (30)	3. (2)	4. (a)	5. (b)
6. (b)	7. (3)	8. (c)	9. (198)	

SOLUTIONS

Level 1

6.1. Diffraction

1. $\beta_0 = \frac{2\lambda D}{a} = \frac{2 \times 5000 \times 10^{-10} \times 2}{0.1 \times 10^{-3}} = 20 \times 10^{-3} \text{ m} = 20 \text{ mm}$

2. $\sin\theta = \frac{\lambda}{a}$

$\Rightarrow \quad \sin\theta = \frac{5000 \times 10^{-10}}{1 \times 10^{-6}} = \frac{1}{2} \quad \Rightarrow \quad \theta = 30°$

3. (a) For first dark fringe,

$$y = \frac{\lambda D}{a} = \frac{6000 \times 10^{-10} \times 2}{0.30 \times 10^{-3}} = 4 \times 10^{-3} \text{ m} = 4 \text{ mm}$$

(b) For second bright fringe,

$$y = \frac{5\lambda D}{2a} = \frac{5 \times 6000 \times 10^{-10} \times 2}{2 \times 0.30 \times 10^{-3}} = 10 \text{ mm}$$

4. (a) For first minima,

$$a\sin\theta = \lambda$$

$\Rightarrow \quad a\sin 30° = 650 \times 10^{-9}$

$\Rightarrow \quad a = 1.3 \times 10^{-6} \text{m}$

(b) For first maxima,

$$a\sin\theta = \frac{3\lambda}{2}$$

$\Rightarrow \quad a\sin 30° = \frac{3}{2} \times 650 \times 10^{-9}$

$\Rightarrow \quad a = 1.95 \times 10^{-6} \text{m}$

5. For second minima,

$$a\sin\theta = 2\lambda$$

$\Rightarrow \quad \sin\theta = \frac{2\lambda}{a}$

$\Rightarrow \quad \sin\theta = \frac{2 \times 6000 \times 10^{-10}}{24 \times 10^{-5} \times 10^{-2}} = \frac{1}{2}$

$\Rightarrow \quad \theta = 30°$

6. For the third minimum,

$$y = \frac{3\lambda D}{a} \quad \Rightarrow \quad 5 \times 10^{-3} = \frac{3 \times \lambda \times 1}{0.3 \times 10^{-3}}$$

$\Rightarrow \quad \lambda = 5 \times 10^{-7} \text{m} = 5000 \text{ Å}$

7. For first order minima, $y_1 = \frac{\lambda D}{a}$

For third order maxima, $y_2 = \frac{7\lambda D}{2a}$

$\therefore \quad y_2 - y_1 = \frac{7\lambda D}{2a} - \frac{\lambda D}{a} = \frac{5\lambda D}{2a} = \frac{5 \times 620 \times 10^{-9} \times 1.5}{2 \times 3 \times 10^{-3}}$

$$= 7.75 \times 10^{-4} \text{ m}$$

8. $y_1 = y_2$

$\Rightarrow \quad \frac{\lambda_1 D}{a} = \frac{3\lambda_2 D}{2a}$

$\Rightarrow \quad \lambda_2 = \frac{2\lambda_1}{3} = \frac{2(660)}{3} = 440\text{nm}$

9. Fresnel's distance,

$$D_F = \frac{a^2}{\lambda} = \frac{(3 \times 10^{-3})^2}{500 \times 10^{-9}} = 18 \text{ m}$$

6.2. Polarisation

1. $I_{\text{Transmitted}} = \frac{I_o}{2}\cos^2\theta$

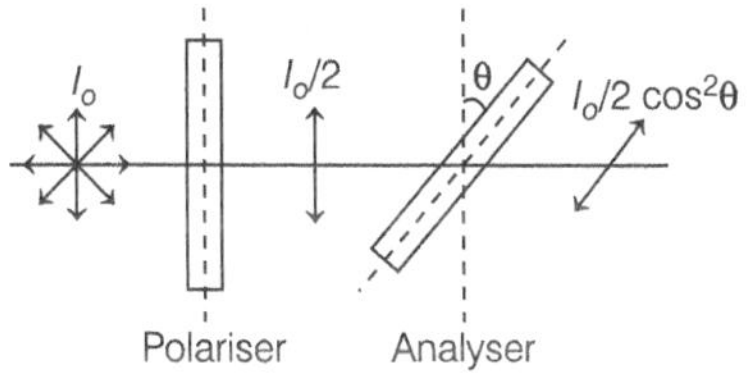

Here, $\theta = 45°$

$\therefore \quad \frac{I_{\text{Original}}}{I_{\text{Transmitted}}} = \frac{I_o}{\frac{I_o}{2}\cos^2 45°} = \frac{4}{1}$

2. $I_o = 32 \text{ Wm}^{-2}$

Intensity of light transmitted by P_1,

$$I_1 = \frac{I_o}{2} = 16 \text{Wm}^{-2}$$

Intensity of light transmitted by P_2,

$$I_2 = I_1\cos^2\theta = 16\cos^2 60° = 4\text{Wm}^{-2}$$

3. Let intensity of incident unpolarised light be I_o.

Intensity of light transmitted by first polaroid,

$$I_1 = \frac{I_0}{2}$$

Intensity of light transmitted by second polaroid,

$$I_2 = I_1\cos^2\theta = \frac{I_0}{2}\cos^2(90° - 60°) = \frac{3I_0}{8}$$

Percentage of light transmitted $= \frac{(3I_0/8)}{I_0} = \times 100 = 37.5\%$

4. Emerging out intensity from first polaroid,

$$I_1 = \frac{I_0}{2}$$

Emerging out intensity from second polaroid,

$$I_2 = I_1\cos^2 30° = \frac{I_0}{2}\left(\frac{\sqrt{3}}{2}\right)^2 = \frac{3I_0}{8}$$

In the same way,

$$I_3 = I_2\cos^2 30° = \frac{3I_0}{8} \times \frac{3}{4} = \frac{9I_0}{32}$$

$$I_4 = I_3\cos^2 30° = \frac{9I_0}{32} \times \frac{3}{4} = \frac{27I_0}{128} = 0.21I_0$$

5. Brewster's angle,

$$\theta_P = \tan^{-1}(\mu) = \tan^{-1}(1.33) = 53°$$

6. When light is incident at polarising angle, reflected ray and refracted rays are perpendicular to each other.

So, $r = 90° - i = 90° - 56.3° = 33.7°$

Level 2

Single Choice Correct Questions

1. $\lambda = \frac{c}{f} = \frac{3 \times 10^8}{24000 \times 10^6} = \frac{1}{80} \text{m}$

Angular spread of central maxima

$$= \frac{2\lambda}{a} = \frac{2 \times \left(\frac{1}{80}\right)}{5 \times 10^{-2}} = 0.5 \text{ rad}$$

2. For first minima, $a \sin\theta = \lambda$

$\Rightarrow \quad 1 \times 10^{-6} \sin\theta = 5000 \times 10^{-10}$

$\Rightarrow \quad \sin\theta = 0.5$

$\Rightarrow \quad \theta = 30°$

$\therefore$ Angular width of central maxima $= 2\theta = 60°$

3. Width of central maxima $= \frac{2\lambda D}{a} = \frac{2 \times 5 \times 10^{-5} \times 2.1}{0.15}$

$= 1.4 \times 10^{-3} \text{m} = 1.4 \text{ mm}$

4. $a \sin\theta = \lambda$

$\Rightarrow \quad a \sin 30° = 5000 \times 10^{-10}$

$\Rightarrow \quad a = 1.0 \times 10^{-6} \text{m} = 1.0 \times 10^{-4} \text{ cm}$

5. $y = \frac{\lambda D}{a}$

$\Rightarrow \quad 5 \times 10^{-3} = \frac{5000 \times 10^{-10} \times 1}{a}$

$\Rightarrow \quad a = 0.1 \times 10^{-3} \text{m} = 0.1 \text{mm}$

6. For first bright fringe,

$$y = \frac{3\lambda D}{2a} = \frac{3 \times 4000 \times 10^{-10} \times 2}{2 \times 0.5 \times 10^{-3}}$$

$= 2.4 \times 10^{-3} \text{m} = 2.4 \text{ mm}$

For central bright fringe, $y = \frac{\lambda D}{a} = 1.6 \text{ mm}$

$\therefore$ Distance of first bright fringe from central bright ring

$= 2.4 - 1.6 = 0.8 \text{ mm}$

7. For first dark fringe,

$$y = \frac{\lambda D}{a} = \frac{600 \times 10^{-9} \times 2}{1 \times 10^{-3}} = 1.2 \times 10^{-3} \text{m} = 1.2 \text{ mm}$$

Required distance $= 2(1.2) = 2.4 \text{ mm}$

8. For the first secondary maxima, $a \sin\theta = \frac{3\lambda}{2}$

9. For first minimum, $a \sin\theta = \lambda$

$\Rightarrow \quad a \sin 30° = \lambda \quad \Rightarrow \quad a = 2\lambda$

For First secondary maxima,

$$a \sin\theta = \frac{3\lambda}{2} \quad \Rightarrow \quad (2\lambda) \sin\theta = \frac{3\lambda}{2}$$

$$\Rightarrow \quad \sin\theta = \frac{3}{4} \quad \Rightarrow \quad \theta = \sin^{-1}\left(\frac{3}{4}\right)$$

10. For second dark fringe, $a \sin\theta = 2\lambda$

$\Rightarrow \quad (24 \times 10^{-5}) \sin 30° = 2\lambda$

$\Rightarrow \quad \lambda = 6 \times 10^{-5} \text{cm} = 6000 \text{ Å}$

11. $y = \frac{\lambda D}{a}$

$\Rightarrow \quad 0.8 \times 10^{-3} = \frac{\lambda(40 \times 10^{-2})}{0.3 \times 10^{-3}}$

$\Rightarrow \quad \lambda = 6 \times 10^{-7} \text{m} = 6000 \text{ Å}$

12. s is the distance of second dark fringe from the centre of the screen.

$$s = \frac{2\lambda D}{a} = \frac{2 \times 600 \times 10^{-9} \times 2}{4 \times 10^{-4}} = 6 \times 10^{-3} \text{m} = 6 \text{ mm}$$

13. $\theta = \frac{2\lambda}{a} = \frac{2 \times 10^{-4}}{10^{-3}} = 0.2 \text{ rad} = 0.2 \times \frac{180°}{\pi} = \frac{36°}{\pi}$

14. Width of central maxima of the single slit diffraction pattern, $\Delta y = \frac{2\lambda D}{a}$

For YDSE, fringe width $= \beta = \frac{\lambda D}{d}$

$\therefore \quad \Delta y = 10\beta$

$\Rightarrow \quad \frac{2\lambda D}{a} = 10\left(\frac{\lambda D}{d}\right)$

$\Rightarrow \quad a = \frac{d}{5} = 0.2 \text{ mm}$

15. For, the first minimum of λ_1,

$$y_1 = \frac{\lambda_1 D}{a}$$

For, the third maximum of λ_2, $y_2 = \frac{7\lambda_2 D}{a}$

$y_1 = y_2$

$\Rightarrow \quad \frac{\lambda_1 D}{a} = \frac{7\lambda_2 D}{a} \quad \Rightarrow \quad \lambda_1 = 3.5\lambda_2$

16. For the first maxima,

$$\Delta x = a \sin\theta = \frac{3\lambda}{2}$$

$$\therefore \quad \Delta\phi = \frac{2\pi}{\lambda} \Delta x = \frac{2\pi}{\lambda}\left(\frac{3\lambda}{2}\right) = 3\pi$$

So, the phase difference is 3π or π.

17. Path difference at $O = a \sin\theta$

For O to be dark,

$\Delta x = a \sin\theta = n\lambda$ where $n = 1, 2, 3, \ldots$

18. Width of central maxima $\propto \lambda$

As X- rays have lesser wavelength than yellow light, the central maxima will get narrower.

19. Width of central maxima $\propto \frac{1}{\text{Slit width}}$

20. (a) 21. (d)

22. $I = I_0 \cos^2\theta$

I is maximum when $\theta = 0°$ or $\theta = \pi$

I is zero when $\theta = \frac{\pi}{2}$ or $\theta = \frac{3\pi}{2}$

23. Intensity of light emerging out of first prism, $I_1 = \frac{I_0}{2}$

Intensity of light emerging out of second prism,

$$I_2 = I_1 \cos^2\theta = \left(\frac{I_0}{2}\right)\cos^2 60° = \frac{I_0}{8}$$

24. Angle between P_1 and $P_2 = 30°$ (given)

Angle between P_2 and $P_3 = 90° - 30° = 60°$

The intensity of light transmitted by P_1,

$$I_1 = \frac{I_0}{2} = \frac{32}{2} = 16 \text{Wm}^{-2}$$

The intensity of light transmitted by P_2,

$$I_2 = I_1 \cos^2 30° = 16\left(\frac{\sqrt{3}}{2}\right)^2 = 12 \text{ Wm}^{-2}$$

Similarly, $I_3 = I_2 \cos^2 60° = 12\left(\frac{1}{2}\right)^2 = 3 \text{ Wm}^{-2}$

25. Let intensity of incident unpolarised light be I_0

Intensity of light transmitted by the first polaroid, $I_1 = \frac{I_0}{2}$

Intensity of light transmitted by the second polaroid,

$$I_2 = I_1 \cos^2 60° = \left(\frac{I_0}{2}\right)\left(\frac{1}{2}\right)^2 = \frac{I_0}{8}$$

Similarly, $I_3 = I_2 \cos^2 60° = \left(\frac{I_0}{8}\right)\left(\frac{1}{4}\right) = \frac{I_0}{32}$

$$I_4 = I_3 \cos^2 60° = \frac{I_0}{128}$$

and $I_5 = I_4 \cos^2 60° = \frac{I_0}{512}$

$\therefore \quad \frac{I_5}{I_0} = \frac{1}{512}$

26. $I_1 = \frac{I_0}{2}, I_2 = I_1 \cos^2 30°, \quad I_3 = I_2 \cos^2 30°$

Similarly $I_6 = I_5 \cos^2 30° = \left(\frac{I_0}{2}\right)(\cos^2 30°)^5 = 0.12 I_0$

$\therefore \quad \frac{I_6}{I_0} \times 100 = \frac{0.12 I_0}{I_0} \times 100 = 12\%$

27. Since, no light is transmitted by second polaroid, angle between the first and the second polaroid is 90°.

Angle between first and third polaroid $= \theta$

Angle between third and second polaroid $= 90° - \theta$

Intensity of light transmitted by first polaroid,

$$I_1 = \frac{I_0}{2}$$

Intensity of light transmitted by third polaroid,

$$I_3 = I_1 \cos^2\theta = \frac{I_0}{2}\cos^2\theta$$

Intensity of light transmitted by second polaroid,

$$I_2 = I_3 \cos^2(90° - \theta) = \frac{I_0}{2}\cos^2\theta \sin^2\theta = \frac{I_0}{8}\sin^2 2\theta$$

28. $I = I_o \cos^2\theta$

$$I_{avg.} = I_0 < \cos^2\theta > = \frac{I_0}{2}$$

Where, $I_0 = \frac{\text{Power}}{\text{Area}} = \frac{10^{-3}}{3 \times 10^{-4}} = \frac{10}{3} \text{Wm}^{-2}$

$\Rightarrow \quad I_{avg.} = \frac{1}{2}\left(\frac{10}{3}\right) = \frac{5}{3} \text{Wm}^{-2}$

Time period, $T = \frac{2\pi}{\omega} = \frac{2(3.14)}{31.4} = \frac{1}{5}$ s

So, energy of light passing through the polariser per revolution,

$$E = I_{avg.} \times \text{Area} \times T = \frac{5}{3} \times 3 \times 10^{-4} \times \frac{1}{5} = 10^{-4} \text{J}$$

29. $i_p = 60° = \tan^{-1}\mu \quad \Rightarrow \quad \mu = \sqrt{3}$

Critical angle, $i_c = \sin^{-1}\left(\frac{1}{\mu}\right) = \sin^{-1}\left(\frac{1}{\sqrt{3}}\right)$

30. When angle of incidence equals to Brewster's angle, angle between reflected and refracted rays is 90°.

31. $i_p = \tan^{-1}(n)$

32. Refractive index, $\mu = \tan 60° = \sqrt{3}$

Velocity of light inside material $= \frac{c}{\mu} = \frac{3 \times 10^8}{\sqrt{3}} = \sqrt{3} \times 10^8$ m/s

33. Angle between the direction of propagation and plane of polarisation is always zero.

34. (a)

35. i = Angle of incidence $= 90° - 30° = 60°$

i_p = Polarising angle $= \tan^{-1}(\mu) = \tan^{-1}(1.732) = 60°$

Since $i = i_p$, the reflected ray OB will be plane polarised.

We know, when a plane polarised light is passed through a Nicol prism, the intensity of emergent light varies as

$$I = I_0 \cos^2\theta$$

So, the intensity of the emergent ray gradually reduces to zero and then again increases.

Previous Year's Questions

JEE Main

1. When a polaroid sheet is rotated through an angle ϕ between two crossed polaroids, then intensity of transmitted light.

$$I = I_0 \cos^2\phi \cdot \sin^2\phi$$

$\therefore \quad I_{max}$ at $\phi = 45° \quad \Rightarrow \quad \phi = 45°$

2. $a \sin\theta = n\lambda$

For 1st minima, $\sin\theta = \frac{1 \times 5000 \times 10^{-10}}{0.001 \times 10^{-3}}$

$\sin\theta = 5 \times 10^{-1} \quad \Rightarrow \quad \sin\theta = 0.5$

$\sin\theta = \frac{1}{2} \quad \Rightarrow \quad \theta = 30°$

3. Given, $D = 50\text{ cm} = 0.5\text{ m}$

$$\lambda = 6000\text{Å} = 6\times10^{-7}\text{m}$$

$$\Delta x = 3\text{ mm} = 3\times10^{-3}\text{m}$$

Position of n th minima, $x_n = \frac{nD\lambda}{d}$

Distance between 3rd order minima and Ist order minimum,

$$\Delta x = x_3 - x_1 = \frac{(3-1)\lambda D}{d}$$

$$\Delta x = \frac{2\lambda D}{d}$$

$$\Rightarrow \quad d = \frac{2\lambda D}{\Delta x} = \frac{2\times6\times10^{-7}\times0.5}{3\times10^{-3}} = 2\times10^{-4}\text{m}$$

4. Given, $\lambda = 600\text{ nm} = 6\times10^{-7}$ m

According to given situation,

$$\frac{x}{D} = \sin\theta = \frac{\lambda}{a} \Rightarrow \sin\theta = \frac{\lambda}{a}$$

$$a = \frac{\lambda}{\sin\theta} = \frac{6\times10^{-7}}{\sin30^\circ} = 12\times10^{-7}\text{ m}$$

$$= 1.2\times10^{-6}\text{ m} = 1.2\,\mu\text{m}$$

5.

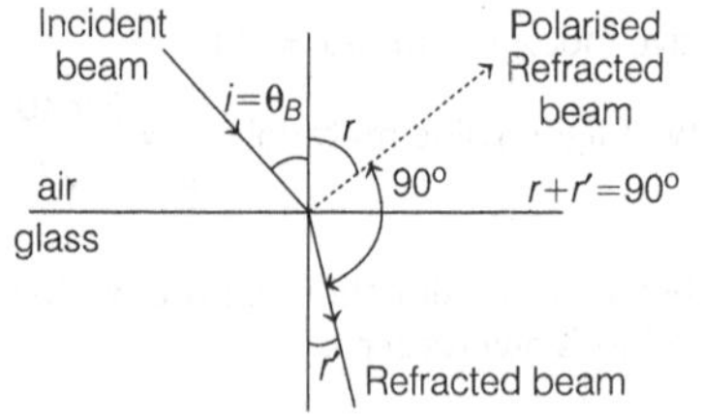

As, angle of incidence = angle of refraction

So, $\theta_B + r' = 90^\circ$ or $r' = 90 - \theta_B = \frac{\pi}{2} - \theta_B$

So, Statement I is correct

Also, For light propagating from air to glass,

$$\mu_g = \frac{\sin i}{\sin r} = \frac{\sin\theta_B}{\sin\left(\frac{\pi}{2}-\theta_B\right)} = \frac{\sin\theta_B}{\cos\theta_B} = \tan\theta_B$$

or $\theta_B(\text{air to glass}) = \tan^{-1}(\mu_g)$

So, $\theta_B(\text{glass to air}) = \tan^{-1}\left(\frac{1}{\mu_g}\right)$

Hence, Statement II is incorrect.

6. If an unpolarised light is converted into plane polarised light, then its intensity becomes half. $I = \frac{I_0}{2}$, where I_0 is intensity of unpolarised light.

According to Malus, $I = I_0\cos^2\theta$,

$$I = \frac{I_0}{2} \quad [\cos^2 45\times\cos^2 45\times\ldots\times(n-1)\text{ times}]$$

$$\Rightarrow \quad \frac{I_0}{64} = \frac{I_0}{2}\times\left(\frac{1}{2}\right)^{n-1}$$

$$\Rightarrow \quad \frac{1}{32} = \frac{1}{2^{n-1}} \Rightarrow \frac{1}{2^5} = \frac{1}{2^{n-1}}$$

$$\therefore \quad n-1 = 5 \text{ or } n = 6$$

7. Given, $\lambda_1 = 650\text{ nm} = 650\times10^{-9}$m

$$\lambda_2 = 655\text{ nm} = 655\times10^{-9}\text{ m}$$

Width of aperture,

$$a = 0.5\text{ mm} = 5\times10^{-4}\text{ m}$$

Distance between screen and source, $D = 2$ m

We know that position of first maxima, $a\sin\theta = 3\lambda/2$

Since, $\sin\theta \approx \theta = \frac{Y}{D}$

$$\therefore \quad a\cdot\frac{Y}{D} = \frac{3\lambda}{2} \Rightarrow y = \frac{3\lambda D}{2a}$$

$$\therefore \quad y_1 = \frac{3\lambda_1 D}{2a} \text{ and } y_2 = \frac{3\lambda_2 D}{2a}$$

$$\therefore \quad \Delta y = y_2 - y_1 = \frac{3\lambda_2 D}{2a} - \frac{3\lambda_1 D}{2a}$$

$$= \frac{3D}{2a}(\lambda_2 - \lambda_1)$$

$$= \frac{3\times2}{2\times5\times10^{-4}}(655\times10^{-9} - 650\times10^{-9})$$

$$= 3\times10^{-5}\text{ m}$$

8. Given, diameter of pinhole,

$$a = 0.1\,\mu\text{m} = 0.1\times10^{-6}\text{ m}$$

$\because$ Path difference

$$(\Delta x) = a\sin\phi = n\lambda \quad \text{...(i)}$$

Where, ϕ is the phase difference and λ be the wavelength.

As, $I = 4I_0\cos^2\phi$

and $\sin\phi = \frac{n\lambda}{a}$ [From Eq. (i)]

If a increases $\leftrightarrow$ $\sin\phi$ or ϕ decreases

As ϕ decreases $\leftrightarrow$ $\cos\phi$ increases

Hence, on decreasing diameter of pinhloe, the size of diffraction pattern decreases and intensity increases.

9. In single slit diffraction, if width of slit is a, wavelength of light is λ and angular position on screen is θ, then for nth minima, the condition is

$$a\sin(\theta) = n\lambda \Rightarrow \sin(\theta) = \frac{n\lambda}{a} \quad \text{...(i)}$$

$$\because \quad \sin(\theta) < 1 \Rightarrow \frac{n\lambda}{a} < 1$$

$$\Rightarrow \quad n < \frac{a}{\lambda} \Rightarrow n < \frac{0.6\times10^{-4}}{6000\times10^{-10}}$$

$$\Rightarrow \quad n < \frac{10^{-4}}{10^4\times10^{-10}} \Rightarrow n < 10^2$$

$$\Rightarrow \quad n < 100$$

So, maximum possible number of minima on one side of central maximum = 99.

Therefore, maximum possible number of minima on both sides of central maximum = 2 × 99 = 198

CHAPTER~07

PHOTOELECTRIC EFFECT

LEVEL 01 Starter Level

7.1 Radiation from Source

1 A sodium lamp of power 10 W is emitting photons of wavelength 590 nm. Assuming that 60% of the consumed energy is converted into light, find the number of photons emitted per second by the lamp.

2 663 mW of light from a 540 nm source is incident on the surface of a metal. If only 1 of each 5×10^9 incident photons is absorbed and causes an electron to be ejected from the surface, then find the total photocurrent in the circuit.

3 The power of light emitted by the sun is 3.9×10^{26} W. Assuming the mean wavelength of sunlight to be 6000 Å, calculate the photon flux arriving at earth perpendicular to light radiations. The average radius of earth's orbit around the sun is 1.49×10^{11} m.

7.2 Photoelectric Effect

1 Find the maximum kinetic energy of the photoelectrons ejected, when light of wavelength 350 nm is incident on a cesium surface. Work function of cesium = 1.9 eV.

2 The work function of a photoelectric material is 4.0 eV.
(a) What is the threshold wavelength?
(b) Find the wavelength of light for which the stopping potential is 2.5 V.

3 A photometer is illuminated by monochromatic light of unknown wavelength. It is known that no photoelectrons are emitted above a wavelength 5000 Å from the same metal. Find the unknown wavelength, if the stopping potential is found to be 3.1 V.

4 What will be the change in the stopping potential for photoelectrons emitted from a surface if the wavelength of the incident radiation is reduced from 4000 Å to 3600 Å?

5 When a metallic surface is illuminated with monochromatic light of wavelength λ, the stopping potential is $5V_0$. When the same surface is illuminated with light of wavelength 3λ, the stopping potential is V_0. Find the threshold wavelength of the metallic surface.

6 On illuminating the surface of a certain metal alternately with light of wavelengths $\lambda_1 = 0.35\ \mu m$ and $\lambda_2 = 0.54\ \mu m$ it is found that the corresponding maximum velocities of the photoelectrons differ by a factor $\eta = 2$. Find the work function of the metal.

7 When a surface is irradiated with light of wavelength 4950 Å, a photocurrent appears which vanishes if a retarding potential greater than 0.6 V is applied across the photo tube. When a different source of light is used, it is found that the critical retarding potential is changed to 1.1 V. Find the work function of the emitting surface and the wavelength of second source.

8 In a photoelectric experiment, the collector plate is at 2.0 V with respect to the emitter plate made of copper ($\phi = 4.5$ eV). The emitter is illuminated by a source of monochromatic light of wavelength 200 nm. Find the minimum and maximum kinetic energy of the photoelectrons reaching the collector.

9 A beam of light consists of four wavelength 4000 Å, 4800 Å, 6000 Å and 7000 Å, each of intensity 1.5×10^{-3} Wm^{-2}.

The beam falls normally on an area 10^{-4} m^2 of a clean metallic surface of work function 1.9 eV. Assuming no loss of light energy (i.e. each capable photon emits one electron) calculate the number of photoelectrons liberated per second.

10 An isolated metal body is illuminated with monochromatic light and is observed to become charged to a steady positive potential 1.0 V with respect to the surrounding. The work function of the metal is 3.0 eV. Find the frequency of the incident light.

11 A monochromatic beam of electromagnetic waves is incident on the cathode of a photocell. Depict graphically, how does the following vary with change in frequency of incident radiation. (at constant intensity)

(i) Number of electrons emitted
(ii) Maximum kinetic energy of electrons
(iii) Stopping potential.

12. A point source of light of frequency $\nu > \nu_{Th}$ is placed at 2 m from the cathode of a photocell. The stopping potential is found to be V_0. If the distance of the light source is halved, state with reason what changes occur in

(i) stopping potential
(ii) photoelectric current and
(iii) maximum velocity of photoelectrons emitted.

13. The following graph shows the variation of stopping potential V_0 with the frequency ν of the incident radiation for two photosensitive metals X and Y.

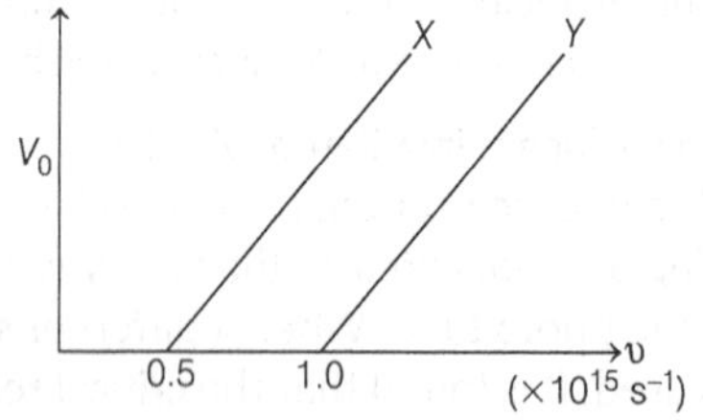

(i) Which of the metals has larger threshold wavelength?
(ii) Which metal gives out electrons, having larger kinetic energy, for the same wavelength of the incident radiation?

14 In photoelectric experiment the plot between anode potential and photoelectric current is shown.

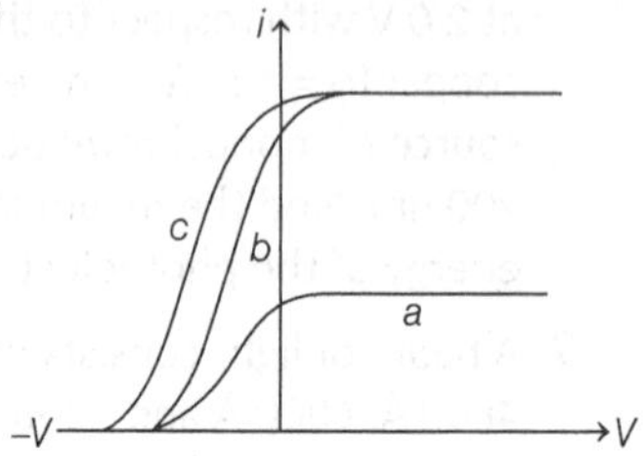

If frequencies and intensities corresponding to graph a, b and c are f_a, f_b, f_c and I_a, I_b, I_c respectively, then arrange them in ascending or descending order.

7.3 Matter Waves

1 Find the de-Broglie wavelength associated with a car of mass 2000 kg moving with velocity 30 m/s.

2 An electron is accelerated by a potential difference of 50V. Find the de-Broglie wavelength associated with it.

3 If λ_0 is the de Broglie wavelength for a proton accelerated through a potential difference of 100 V, then what will be de-Broglie wavelength for α-particle accelerated through the same potential difference?

4 What is the wavelength associated with thermal neutrons at 300K ? Mass of neutron $= 1.675 \times 10^{-27}$ kg.

5 Find the ratio of de-Broglie wavelength of molecules of hydrogen and helium which are at temperatures 27°C and 127°C respectively.

6 With what velocity must an electron travel, so that its momentum is equal to that of a photon with a wavelength of 5000 Å?
($h = 6.6 \times 10^{-34}$ J-s, $m_e = 9.1 \times 10^{-31}$ kg)

7 A photon and an electron have the same de-Broglie wavelength. Which one of these has greater kinetic energy?

7.4 Force due to Radiation

1 A plate of mass 10 gm is in equilibrium in air due to the force exerted by light beam on plate. Calculate power of beam if the plate is

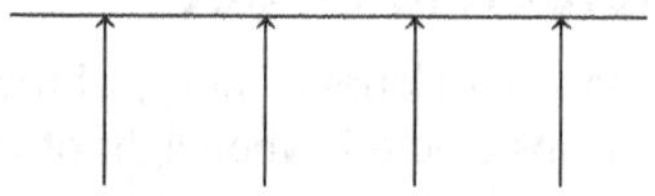

(i) perfectly absorbing (ii) perfectly reflecting

2 A beam of white light is incident normally on a plane surface absorbing 70% of the light and reflecting the rest. If the incident beam carries 30 W of power, find the force exerted by it on the surface.

3 A parallel beam of monochromatic light of wavelength 663nm is incident on a totally reflecting plane mirror. The angle of incidence is 60° and the number of photons striking the mirror per second is 5×10^{19}. Calculate the force exerted by the light beam on the mirror. ($h = 6.63 \times 10^{-34}$ J-s)

4 Find the radiation force experienced by a body exposed to radiation of intensity I assuming surface of body to be perfectly absorbing.

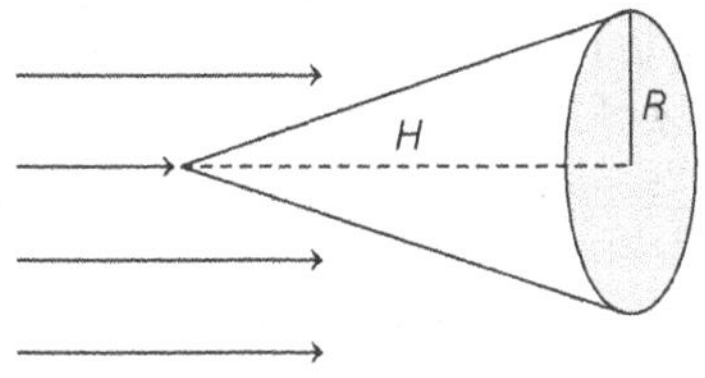

5 A laser gun emits a light pulse of duration $T = 0.1$ ms and energy $E = 10$ J. Find the mean pressure exerted by such a light pulse, when it is focussed into a spot of diameter $d = 10\ \mu m$ on a surface perpendicular to the beam and possessing a reflection coefficient $r = 0.5$.

6 A plane light wave of intensity $I = 0.60\ Wcm^{-2}$ falls on a plane mirror of reflection coefficient $r = 0.8$. The angle of incidence is $\theta = 45°$. Find the normal pressure exerted by light on that surface.

LEVEL 02 JEE Main/Advanced Level

1 How many photons are emitted by a laser source of 5×10^{-3} W operating at 632.2 nm in 2 s?
(a) 3.2×10^{16} (b) 1.6×10^{16}
(c) 8.4×10^{16} (d) None of these

2 Light of wavelength 5000 Å and intensity $39.8\ Wm^{-2}$ is incident on a metal surface. If only 1% photons of incident light emit photoelectrons, then the number of electrons emitted per second per unit area from the surface will be nearly
(a) 10^{18} (b) 10^{22} (c) 10^{24} (d) 10^{26}

3 10^{-3} W of 5000 Å light is directed on a photoelectric cell. If the current in the cell is $0.16\ \mu A$, the percentage of incident photons which produce photoelectrons, is
(a) 0.4% (b) 0.04% (c) 20% (d) 10%

4 Light of frequency 1.5 times the threshold frequency is incident on photosensitive material. If the frequency is halved and intensity is doubled, then the photocurrent becomes
(a) quadrupled (b) doubled
(c) halved (d) zero

5 A photon of energy $h\nu$ is absorbed by a free electron of a metal having work function $\phi < h\nu$
(a) the electron is sure to come out
(b) the electron is sure to come out with a kinetic energy $h\nu - \phi$
(c) either the electron does not come out or it comes out with a kinetic energy $h\nu - \phi$
(d) it may come out with a kinetic energy less than $h\nu - \phi$

6 If the frequency of light in a photoelectric experiment is doubled, the stopping potential will
(a) be doubled (b) be halved
(c) become more than double
(d) become less than double

7 The work function of a substance is 4.0 eV. The longest wavelength of light that can cause photoelectron emission from this substance is approximately
(a) 540 nm (b) 400 nm
(c) 310 nm (d) 220 nm

8 The maximum kinetic energy of photoelectrons emitted from a surface, when photons of energy 6 eV fall on it is 4 eV. The stopping potential in volts is
(a) 2 (b) 4
(c) 6 (d) 10

9 Photons of energy 6 eV are incident on a metal surface whose work function is 4 eV. The minimum kinetic energy of the emitted photoelectrons will be
(a) 0 eV (b) 1 eV
(c) 2 eV (d) 10 eV

10 When a point source of light is at a distance of 1m from a photocell, the cut-off voltage is found to be V. If the same source is placed at 2 m distance from photocell, the cut-off voltage will be
(a) V (b) $\frac{V}{2}$ (c) $\frac{V}{4}$ (d) $\frac{V}{\sqrt{2}}$

11 All electrons ejected from a surface by incident light of wavelength 200 nm can be stopped before travelling 1m against the direction of a uniform electric field of 4 N/C. The work function of the surface is
(a) 4 eV (b) 6.2 eV (c) 2 eV (d) 2.2 eV

12 Electromagnetic radiations described by the equation $E = 100\,[\sin(2 \times 10^{15})t + \sin(6.28 \times 10^{15})t]$ V/m are incident on a photosensitive surface having work function 1.5 eV. The maximum kinetic energy of photoelectrons will be
(a) 0.125 eV (b) 2.625 eV
(c) 4.125 eV (d) 6.125 eV

13 The work functions for tungsten and sodium are 4.5 eV and 2.3 eV, respectively. If the threshold wavelength for sodium is 5460 Å, the threshold wavelength for tungsten will be
(a) 5893 Å (b) 10683 Å (c) 2791 Å (d) 528 Å

14 If stopping potentials corresponding to wavelengths 4000 Å and 4500 Å are 1.3 V and 0.9 V, respectively, then the work function of the metal is
(a) 0.3 eV (b) 1.3 eV (c) 2.3 eV (d) 5 eV

15 When ultraviolet light of wavelength 100 nm is incident upon silver, a potential of 7.7 V is required to stop the photoelectrons from reaching the collector plate. The potential required to stop photoelectrons, when light of wavelength 200 nm is incident upon silver is
(a) 1.5 V (b) 1.85 V (c) 1.95 V (d) 2.37 V

16 Photons with energy 5 eV are incident on a cathode *C*, on a photoelectric cell. The maximum energy of the emitted photoelectrons is 2 eV. When photons of energy 6eV are incident on *C*, no photoelectrons will reach the anode *A* if the potential of *A* relative to *C* is
(a) 3 V (b) -3 V (c) -1 V (d) 4 V

17 Light of wavelength 330 nm falling on a piece of metal ejects electrons with sufficient energy which requires voltage V_0 to prevent them from reaching a collector. In the same setup, light of wavelength 220 nm, ejects electrons which require twice the voltage V_0 to stop them in reaching a collector. The numerical value of voltage V_0 is nearly
(a) $\frac{16}{15}$ V (b) $\frac{15}{16}$ V (c) $\frac{15}{8}$ V (d) $\frac{8}{15}$ V

18 Cut-off potentials for a metal in photoelectric effect for light of wavelength λ_1, λ_2 and λ_3 is found to be V_1, V_2 and V_3 volts. If V_1, V_2 and V_3 are in arithmetic progression, then λ_1, λ_2 and λ_3 will be in
(a) arithmetic progression (b) geometric progression
(c) harmonic progression (d) None of these

19 When a certain metallic surface is irradiated with monochromatic light wavelength λ, the stopping potential for photoelectric current is $3V_0$. When the same surface is irradiated with light of wavelength 2λ, the stopping potential is V_0. The threshold wavelength for the given surface is
(a) 4λ (b) 6λ (c) 8λ (d) $\frac{4\lambda}{3}$

20 Let K_1 be the maximum kinetic energy of photoelectrons emitted by a light of wavelength λ_1 and K_2 corresponding to λ_2. If $\lambda_1 = 2\lambda_2$, then
(a) $2K_1 = K_2$ (b) $K_1 = 2K_2$ (c) $K_1 < \frac{K_2}{2}$ (d) $K_1 > 2K_2$

21 Photoelectric emission is observed from a metallic surface for frequencies ν_1 and ν_2 of the incident light rays ($\nu_1 > \nu_2$). If the maximum values of kinetic energy of the photoelectrons emitted in the two cases are in the ratio of $1:k$, then the threshold frequency of the metallic surface is
(a) $\frac{\nu_1 - \nu_2}{k-1}$ (b) $\frac{k\nu_1 - \nu_2}{k-1}$ (c) $\frac{k\nu_2 - \nu_1}{k-1}$ (d) $\frac{\nu_2 - \nu_1}{k}$

22 Radiation of two photon energies twice and five times the work function of metal are incident successively on the metal surface. The ratio of the maximum velocity of photoelectrons emitted in the two cases will be
(a) 1 : 2 (b) 2 : 1
(c) 1 : 4 (d) 4 : 1

23 If the surface of a metal is successfully exposed to radiation of $\lambda_1 = 350$ nm and $\lambda_2 = 450$ nm the maximum velocity of photoelectrons will differ by a factor 2. The work function of this metal is
(a) 2.84×10^{-19} J (b) 1.6×10^{-19} J
(c) 3.9×10^{-19} J (d) 2.4×10^{-19} J

24 In a photoemissive cell, with exciting wavelength λ, the fastest electron has speed v. If the exciting wavelength is changed to $\frac{3\lambda}{4}$, the speed of the fastest emitted electrons will be
(a) $v\left(\frac{4}{3}\right)^{1/2}$ (b) $v\left(\frac{3}{4}\right)^{1/2}$
(c) less than $v\left(\frac{4}{3}\right)^{1/2}$ (d) greater than $v\left(\frac{4}{3}\right)^{1/2}$

25 Two identical photocathodes receive light of frequencies f_1 and f_2. If the velocities of the photoelectrons (of mass *m*) coming out are respectively v_1 and v_2, then
(a) $v_1 - v_2 = \left[\frac{2h}{m}(f_1 - f_2)\right]^{1/2}$
(b) $v_1^2 - v_2^2 = \frac{2h}{m}(f_1 - f_2)$
(c) $v_1 + v_2 = \left[\frac{2h}{m}(f_1 + f_2)\right]^{1/2}$
(d) $v_1^2 + v_2^2 = \frac{2h}{m}(f_1 + f_2)$

26 A surface irradiated with light $\lambda = 480$ nm gives out electrons with maximum velocity v m/s, the cut-off wavelength being 600 nm. The same surface would release electrons with maximum velocity $2v$ m/s, if it is irradiated by light of wavelength
(a) 325 nm (b) 360 nm (c) 384 nm (d) 300 nm

27 Two separate monochromatic light beams *A* and *B* of the same intensity (energy per unit area per unit time) are falling normally on a unit area of a metallic surface. Their wavelength are λ_A and λ_B respectively. Assuming that all the incident light is used in ejecting the photoelectrons, the ratio of the number of photoelectrons from beam *A* to that from *B* is

(a) $\frac{\lambda_A}{\lambda_B}$ (b) $\frac{\lambda_B}{\lambda_A}$ (c) $\left(\frac{\lambda_A}{\lambda_B}\right)^2$ (d) $\left(\frac{\lambda_B}{\lambda_A}\right)^2$

28 The work function of a certain metal is $\frac{hc}{\lambda_0}$. A monochromatic light of wavelength $\lambda < \lambda_0$ is incident such that the plate gains a total power *P*. If the efficiency of photoelectric emission is $\eta\%$ and all the emitted photoelectrons are captured by a hollow conducting sphere of radius *R* already charged to potential *V*, then neglecting any interaction between plate and the sphere, expression of potential of the sphere at time *t* is

(a) $V + \frac{100\,\eta\lambda Pet}{4\pi\varepsilon_0 Rhc}$ (b) $V - \frac{\eta\lambda Pet}{400\pi\varepsilon_0 Rhc}$

(c) V (d) $\frac{\lambda Pet}{4\pi\varepsilon_0 Rhc}$

29 When stopping potential is applied in an experiment on photoelectric effect, no photocurrent is observed. This means that

(a) the emission of photoelectrons is stopped
(b) the photoelectrons are emitted but are reabsorbed by the emitter metal
(c) the photoelectrons are accumulated near the collector plate
(d) the photoelectrons are dispersed from the sides of the apparatus

30 Monochromatic light with a frequency well above the cut-off frequency is incident on the emitter in a photoelectric effect apparatus. The frequency of the light is, then doubled while the intensity is kept constant. How does this affect the photoelectric current?

(a) The photoelectric current will increase.
(b) The photoelectric current will decrease.
(c) The photoelectric current will remain the same.
(d) None of the above

31 In photoelectric effect the frequency is doubled, keeping intensity and photometal unchanged. Then

(a) photocurrent is doubled
(b) maximum kinetic energy of photoelectrons is doubled
(c) maximum kinetic energy of photoelectrons increases but remains less than double kinetic energy
(d) maximum kinetic energy of photoelectrons becomes more than double kinetic energy.

32 The graph between the stopping potential V_0 and frequency (v) of incident photons for photocell is a straight line with a slope

(a) h (b) eh (c) $\frac{e}{h}$ (d) $\frac{h}{e}$

33 In a photoelectric experiment, the potential difference *V* that must be maintained between the illuminated surface and the collector, so as just to prevent any electron from reaching the collector is determined for different frequencies *f* of the incident illumination. The graph obtained is shown.The maximum kinetic energy of the electrons emitted at frequency f_1, is

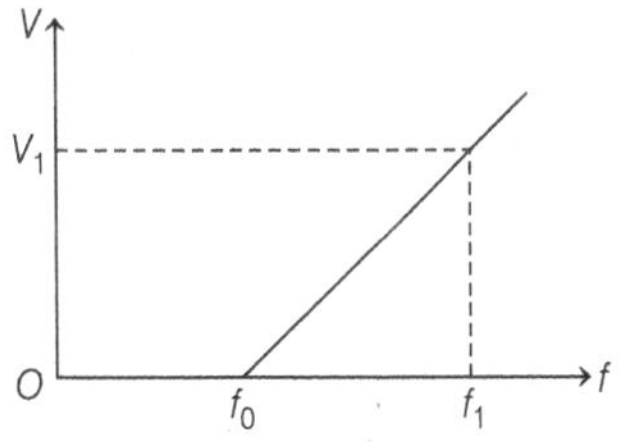

(a) hf_1 (b) $\frac{V_1}{(f_1 - f_0)}$

(c) $h(f_1 - f_0)$ (d) $eV_1 (f_1 - f_0)$

34 The stopping potential (V_0) *versus* frequency (ν) plot of a substance is shown in figure, the threshold wavelength is

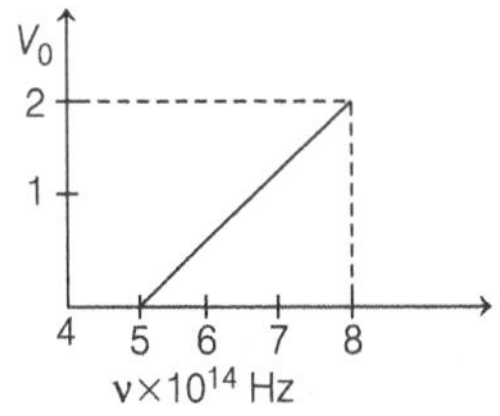

(a) 5×10^{14} m (b) 6000 Å
(c) 5000 Å
(d) can not be estimated from given data

35 Figure represents the graph of photocurrent *I versus* applied voltage (*V*). The maximum energy of the emitted photoelectrons is

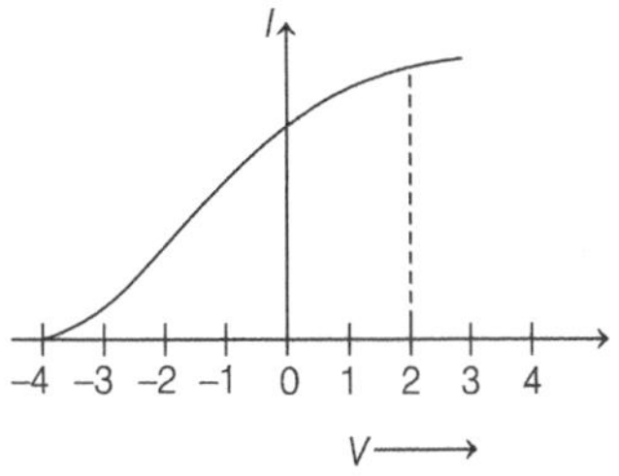

(a) 2 eV (b) 4 eV
(c) 0 eV (d) 3 eV

36 A photoelectric cell is connected to a source of variable potential difference V connected across it and the photoelectric current I is plotted against the applied potential difference. The graph in the broken line represents one for a given frequency and intensity of the incident radiation. If the frequency is increased and the intensity is reduced, the curve which now represents the situation is

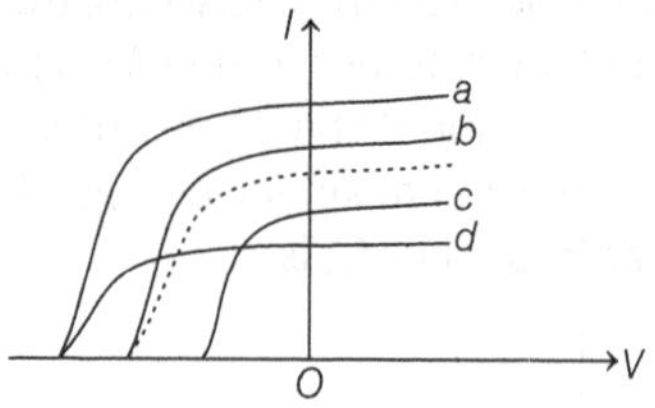

(a) a (b) b (c) c (d) d

37 In a photoelectric experiment, electrons are ejected from metals X and Y by light of intensity I and frequency f. The potential difference V required to stop the electrons is measured for various frequencies. If Y has a greater work function than X, which one of the following graphs best illustrates the expected results?

(a)
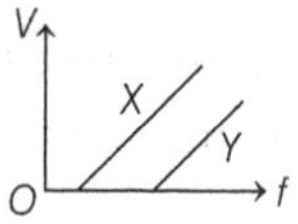

(b)
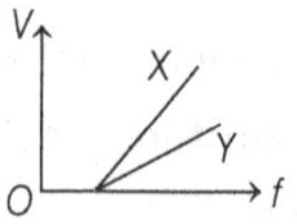

(c)
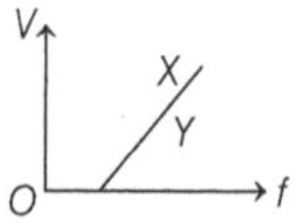

(d)
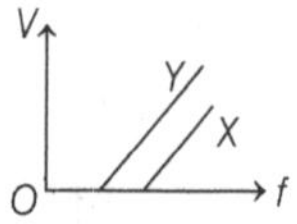

38 Photoelectric effect experiments are performed using three different metal plates p, q and r having work functions $\phi_p = 2.0$ eV, $\phi_q = 2.5$ eV and $\phi_r = 3.0$ eV, respectively.

A light beam containing wavelengths of 550 nm, 450 nm and 350 nm with equal intensities illuminates each of the plates. The correct I-V graph for the experiment is
[Take $hc = 1240$ eV-nm]

(a)
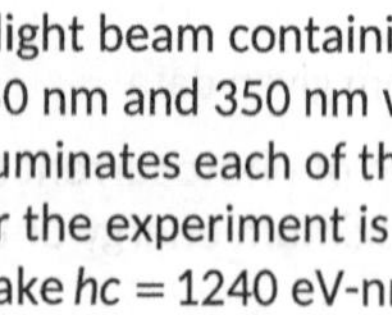

(b)
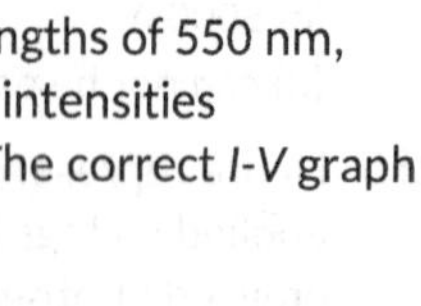

(c)
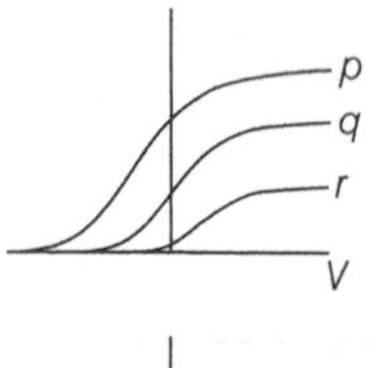

(d)
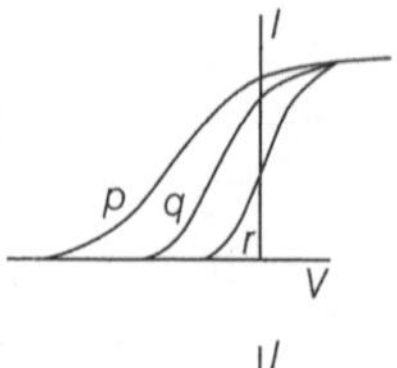

39. The equation $E = pc$ is valid

(a) for an electron as well as for a photon
(b) for an electron but not for a photon
(c) for a photon but not for an electron
(d) neither for an electron nor for a photon

40 A material particle with a rest mass m_0 is moving with a velocity of light c. Then, the wavelength of the de-Broglie wave associated with it is

(a) $\left(\frac{h}{m_0 c}\right)$ (b) zero (c) ∞ (d) $\left(\frac{m_0 c}{h}\right)$

41 If the momentum of an electron is changed by p_m, then the de-Broglie wavelength associated with it changes by 0.5%. The initial momentum of electron will be

(a) $\frac{p_m}{200}$ (b) $\frac{p_m}{100}$ (c) $200p_m$ (d) $100p_m$

42 The wavelength of an electron accelerated from rest through a potential difference of 150 V is of the order of

(a) 1000 Å (b) 100 Å
(c) 1 Å (d) 150 Å

43 The ratio of de-Broglie wavelength of a photon and an electron of mass m having the same energy E is

(a) $\sqrt{\frac{E}{2mc^2}}$ (b) $\sqrt{\frac{2mc^2}{E}}$ (c) $\sqrt{\frac{mc^2}{E}}$ (d) $\sqrt{\frac{mc^2}{2E}}$

44 Photoelectrons are liberated by ultraviolet light of wavelength 3000 Å from a metallic surface for which the photoelectric threshold wavelength is 4000 Å. Calculate the de-Broglie wavelength of electrons emitted with maximum kinetic energy.

(a) 12.07 Å (b) 25.70 Å
(c) 35.08 Å (d) 50.05 Å

45 An electron and a proton are accelerated through the same potential. If their masses are m_e and m_p respectively, then the ratio of their de-Broglie wavelength is

(a) 1 (b) $\frac{m_e}{m_p}$ (c) $\frac{m_p}{m_e}$ (d) $\sqrt{\frac{m_p}{m_e}}$

46 A particle of mass M at rest decays into two particles of masses m_1 and m_2, having non zero velocities. The ratio of the de-Broglie wavelengths of the particles, $\frac{\lambda_1}{\lambda_2}$ is

(a) $\frac{m_1}{m_2}$ (b) $\frac{m_2}{m_1}$ (c) 1 : 1 (d) $\sqrt{\frac{m_2}{m_1}}$

47 Proton, deuteron and α-particles are accelerated through the same potential difference. Then, the ratio of their de-Broglie wavelength is
(a) $1:\sqrt{2}:1$ (b) $1:1:1$
(c) $1:2:2\sqrt{2}$ (d) $2\sqrt{2}:2:1$

48 A proton, when accelerated through a potential difference of V volts, has a de-broglie wavelength λ associated with it. If an alpha particle is to have the same de-broglie wavelength λ, it must be accelerated through a potential difference of
(a) $\frac{V}{8}$ volts (b) $\frac{V}{4}$ volts (c) $4V$ volts (d) $8\,V$ volts

49 The wavelength of de-Broglie wave associated with a thermal neutron of mass m at absolute temperature T is given by (Here, k is the Boltzmann constant)
(a) $\frac{h}{\sqrt{2mkT}}$ (b) $\frac{h}{\sqrt{mkT}}$
(c) $\frac{h}{\sqrt{3mkT}}$ (d) $\frac{h}{2\sqrt{mkT}}$

50 To reduce de-Broglie wavelength of an electron from 100pm to 50pm, the required increase in energy will be
(a) 600 eV (b) 450 eV (c) 300 eV (d) 150 eV

51 Two photons having
(a) equal wavelengths have equal linear momenta
(b) equal energies have equal linear momenta
(c) equal frequencies have equal linear momenta
(d) equal linear momenta have equal wavelengths.

52 de-Broglie wavelength associated with the hydrogen atom moving with most probable velocity at 27°C is 1.26 Å. de-Broglie wavelength associated with helium atom moving with rms velocity at 51°C is
(a) 2.268 Å (b) 1.852 Å
(c) 0.5 Å (d) 0.7 Å

53 An electron of mass m and charge e initially at rest gets accelerated by a constant electric field E. The rate of change of de-Broglie wavelength of this electron at time t ignoring relativistic effects is
(a) $\frac{-h}{eEt^2}$ (b) $\frac{-eEt}{h}$ (c) $\frac{-mh}{eEt^2}$ (d) $\frac{-h}{eE}$

54 Two identical non relativistic particles move at right angles to each other, possessing de-Broglie wavelengths λ_1 and λ_2. Find the de-Broglie wavelength of each particle in the frame of their centre of mass.
(a) $\lambda_1+\lambda_2$ (b) $\frac{\lambda_1\lambda_2}{\sqrt{\lambda_1^2+\lambda_2^2}}$ (c) $\frac{\lambda_1\lambda_2}{\lambda_1+\lambda_2}$ (d) $\frac{2\lambda_1\lambda_2}{\sqrt{\lambda_1^2+\lambda_2^2}}$

55 The de-Broglie wavelength of a particle moving with a velocity 2.25×10^8 m/s is equal to the wavelength of a photon. The ratio of kinetic energy of the particle to the energy of the photon is (velocity of light is 3×10^8 m/s)
(a) $\frac{1}{8}$ (b) $\frac{3}{8}$ (c) $\frac{5}{8}$ (d) $\frac{7}{8}$

56 The radiation force experienced by body exposed to radiation of intensity I, assuming surface of body to be perfectly absorbing is

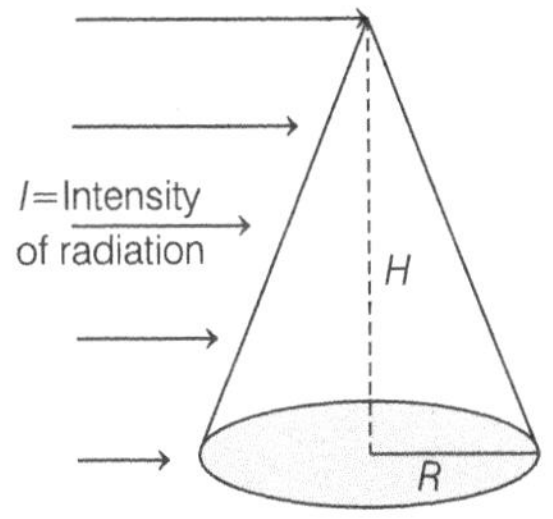

(a) $\frac{\pi R^2 I}{c}$ (b) $\frac{\pi RHI}{c}$ (c) $\frac{IRH}{2c}$ (d) $\frac{IRH}{c}$

57 If a parallel beam of light having intensity I is incident normally on a perfectly reflecting surface, the force exerted on the surface, equals F. When the surface is held at an angle θ, the force is
(a) $2F\tan\theta$ (b) $F\cos\theta$ (c) $F\cos^2\theta$ (d) $2F$

58 A parallel beam of light of intensity I is incident normally on a plane surface A which absorbs 50% of the incident light. The reflected light falls on B which is perfect reflector, the light reflected by B is again partly reflected and partly absorbed and this process continues. For all absorption by A, absorption coefficient is 0.5. The pressure experienced by A due to light is

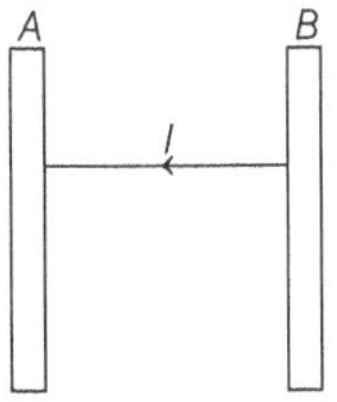

(a) $\frac{1.5I}{c}$ (b) $\frac{I}{c}$ (c) $\frac{3I}{2c}$ (d) $\frac{3I}{c}$

59 A parallel beam of photons of intensity I strike a plane surface at angle 45° to the surface. If plane surface have reflection coefficient 0.5, then pressure exerted by the beam on the surface (c is speed of light) is
(a) $\frac{3I}{4c}$ (b) $\frac{3I}{2c}$ (c) $\frac{I}{2\sqrt{2}c}$ (d) $\frac{3I}{2\sqrt{2}c}$

Multiple Choice(s) Correct Questions

1 Photoelectric effect supports quantum nature of light because
(a) there is a minimum frequency below which no photoelectrons are emitted
(b) the maximum kinetic energy of photoelectrons depends only on the frequency of light and not on its intensity
(c) even when the metal surface is faintly illuminated the photoelectrons leave the surface immediately
(d) electric charge of the photoelectrons is quantised.

2 Fig. shows a photo cell is illuminated by a monochromatic light. If the intensity is kept constant and the frequency of the incident light is increased, then the

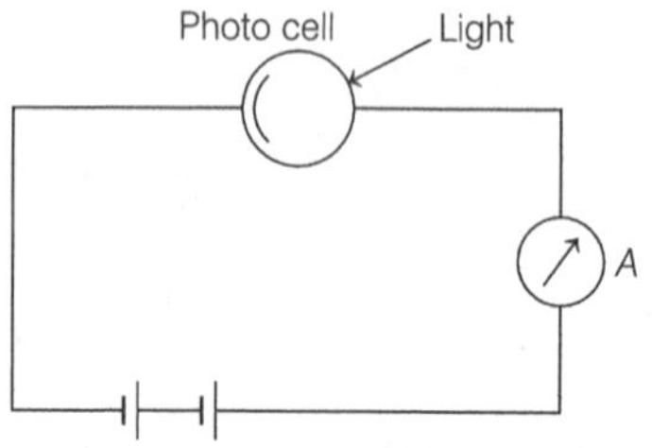

(a) photoelectric current in the circuit increases
(b) photoelectric current in the circuit decreases
(c) maximum kinetic energy of the photoelectrons increases
(d) photoelectric current in the circuit can be reduced to zero, when the polarity of the terminals is reversed.

3 When a monochromatic point source of light is at a distance of 0.2 m from a photoelectric cell, the cut-off voltage and the saturation current are respectively 0.6 V and 18.0 mA. If the same source is placed 0.6 m away from the photocell, then
(a) the stopping potential will be 0.2 V
(b) the stopping potential will be 0.6 V
(c) the saturation current will be 2.0 mA
(d) the saturation current will be 6.0 mA

4 Fig. shows the results of an experiment involving photoelectric effect. The graphs *A*, *B*, *C*, *D* related the light beam having different wavelengths.

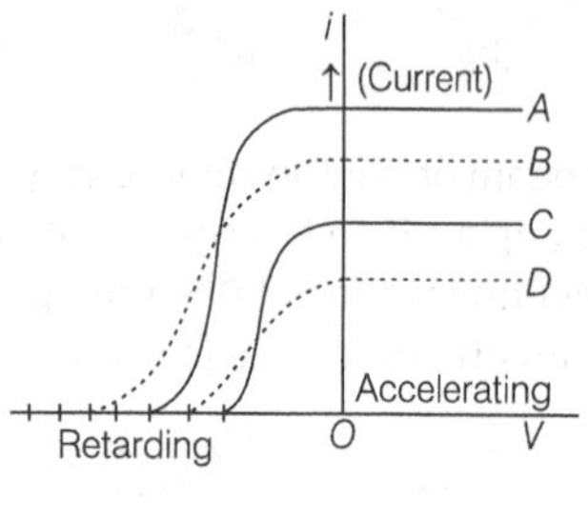

(a) Beam *B* has highest frequency
(b) Beam *C* has longest wavelength
(c) Beam *A* has the highest rate of photoelectric emission
(d) Photoelectrons ejected by beam *B* have the highest momentum

5 Photons of energy 4eV are incident on cathode. Electrons reaching the anode have kinetic energies varying from 5.5 eV to 7 eV.

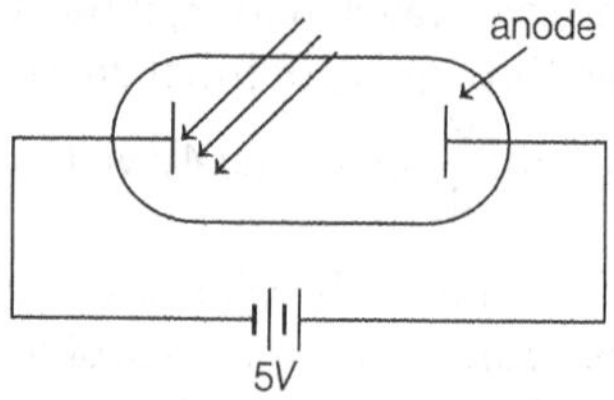

(a) The work function of the metal is 1.5eV
(b) Work function of the metal is 2 eV
(c) Current in the circuit is less than saturation current
(d) Current in the circuit is equal to saturation current

6 The graph between $\frac{1}{\lambda}$ and stopping potential *V* of three metals having work function ϕ_1, ϕ_2 and ϕ_3 in an experiment of photoelectric effect is plotted as shown in the figure. Which of the following statements is/are correct?

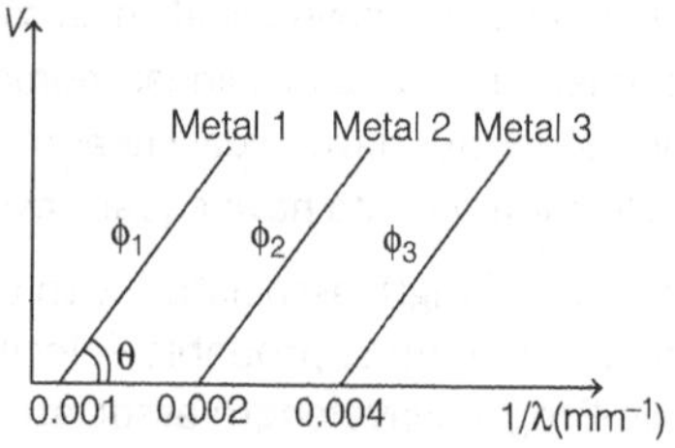

(a) Ratio of work function $\phi_1 : \phi_2 : \phi_3 = 4:2:1$
(b) $\tan\theta$ is inversely proportional to *e*, charge of electron
(c) Ratio of threshold wavelength $\lambda_1 : \lambda_2 : \lambda_3 = 4:2:1$
(d) The slope is independent of the nature of material.

7 Light of wavelength 496 nm is incident on a metal surface causing ejection of photoelectrons for which stopping potential is 1.5 V, then
(a) the work function of the surface is 1 eV
(b) de-Broglie wavelength of fastest photoelectron is 100 nm
(c) to move the fastest electron in a circle of radius 1 m, perpendicular magnetic field *B* required is 4.1×10^{-6} T.
(d) this fastest electron if strikes zinc target can produce X-rays

8 Light from a monochromatic source is incident normally on a small photosensitive surface of area S having work function ϕ. If power of the source is W and a is the distance between the source and S, then

(a) the number of photons striking the surface per unit time will be $\left(\frac{W\lambda S}{4\pi hca^2}\right)$

(b) the maximum energy of the emitted electrons will be $(hc-\lambda\phi)\frac{1}{\lambda}$

(c) the stopping potential needed to stop the most energetic photons will be $\frac{e}{\lambda}(hc-\lambda\phi)$

(d) photoemission occurs only if $0 \le \lambda \le \frac{hc}{\phi}$

9 In an experiment of photoelectric effect, the frequency and intensity of a light source are both doubled, then

(a) the saturation photocurrent remains almost the same

(b) the saturation photocurrent becomes doubled

(c) the maximum kinetic energy of the photoelectrons is doubled

(d) the stopping potential becomes more than double

10 Which of the following are not dependent on the intensity of the incident radiation in a photoelectric experiment?

(a) Amount of photoelectric current

(b) Stopping potential to reduce the photoelectric current to zero

(c) Work function of the surface

(d) Maximum kinetic energy of photoelectrons

11 Two electrons are moving with the same speed v. One electron enters a region of uniform electric field while the other enters a region of uniform magnetic field, then after sometime if the de-Broglie wavelengths of the two are λ_1 and λ_2, then select the possible option(s)

(a) $\lambda_1 = \lambda_2$ (b) $\lambda_1 > \lambda_2$

(c) $\lambda_1 < \lambda_2$ (d) $\lambda_1 > \lambda_2$ or $\lambda_1 < \lambda_2$

12 When photons of energy 4.25 *eV* strike the surface of a metal A, the ejected photoelectrons have maximum kinetic energy, T_A (expressed in eV) and de-Broglie wavelength λ_A. The maximum kinetic energy of photoelectrons liberated from another metal B by photons of energy 4.70 eV is $T_B = (T_A - 1.50 \text{ eV})$. If the de-Broglie wavelength of these photoelectrons is $\lambda_B = 2\lambda_A$, then

(a) the work function of A is 2.25 eV

(b) the work function of B is 4.20 eV

(c) $T_A = 2.00$ eV

(d) $T_B = 2.75$ eV

13 A parallel beam of radiation of intensity 10 W and of area of cross-section 1 cm^2 is falling on a plane surface at an angle 60° with normal to the surface. The surface is partially reflecting with reflection coefficient 0.5 and absorbing the remaining. Choose the correct option(s) of the following.

(a) Force on the surface normal to it is 2.5×10^{-12} N

(b) Force on the surface parallel to it is $\frac{2.5}{\sqrt{3}} \times 10^{-12}$ N

(c) Net force on the surface $= \frac{5}{\sqrt{3}} \times 10^{-12}$ N

(d) Net force on the surface acts at an angle 30° with normal to the surface

14 A sphere of radius r is exposed to a parallel beam of radiation of intensity I as shown in figure. Choose the correct option(s) of the following.

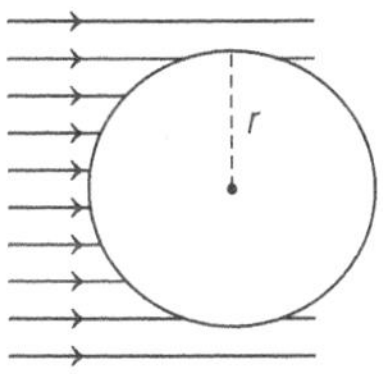

(a) If the surface of the sphere is completely reflecting, radiation force on the sphere is $\frac{2I\pi r^2}{c}$

(b) If surface of the sphere is completely absorbing, radiation force on the sphere is $\frac{I\pi r^2}{c}$

(c) If surface of the sphere is completely reflecting, radiation force on the sphere is $\frac{I\pi r^2}{c}$

(d) If surface of the sphere is partially reflecting with reflection coefficient 0.3 and absorbtion coefficient 0.7, the radiation force on the sphere is $\frac{1.7I\pi r^2}{c}$

Comprehension Based Questions

Comprehension-1

A mercury arc lamp provides 0.1 W of ultraviolet radiation at a wavelength of $\lambda = 2537$ Å only. The photo tube (cathode of photoelectric device) consists of potassium and has an effective area of 4 cm^2.The cathode is located at a distance of 1 m from the radiation source. The work function for potassium is $\phi_0 = 2.22$ eV.

1 According to classical theory, the radiation from arc lamp spreads out uniformly in space as spherical wave. What time of exposure to the radiation should be required for a potassium atom (radius 2Å) in the cathode to accumulate sufficient energy to eject a photoelectron?

(a) 352 s (b) 176 s

(c) 704 s (d) No time lag

2 To what saturation current does the flux of photons at the cathode corresponds if the photo conversion efficiency is 5%?

(a) 32.5 nA (b) 10.15 nA
(c) 65 nA (d) 3.25 nA

3 What is the cut-off potential V_0?

(a) 26.9 V (b) 2.69 V
(c) 1.35 V (d) 5.33 V

Comprehension-2

A photocell is operating in saturation mode with a photocurrent 4.8 μA, when a monochromatic radiation of wavelength 3000 Å and power 1 mW is incident. When another monochromatic radiation of wavelength 1650 Å and power 5 mW is incident, it is observed that the maximum velocity of photoelectron increases to two times. Assuming efficiency of photoelectron generation per incident photon to be same for both the cases.

4 What is threshold wavelength for the cell?

(a) 3100 Å (b) 4125 Å
(c) 5200 Å (d) 5000 Å

5 The saturation current in second case is

(a) 13 .34 μA (b) 20 μA
(c) 16 μA (d) 7 μA

6 The number of photons emitted per second by source in second case is

(a) 4.1×10^{13} (b) 4.1×10^{14}
(c) 4.1×10^{15} (d) 4.1×10^{16}

7 The efficiency of photoelectron generation per incident photon is

(a) 1.97% (b) 10.2%
(c) 7.3% (d) None of these

Comprehension-3

A metallic surface, when illuminated by light of frequency 8×10^{14} Hz and 12×10^{14} Hz, then electrons of maximum KE, 0.5 eV and 2.0 eV are emitted.

8 Work function of metal is

(a) 0.5 eV (b) 1.5 eV
(c) 2.5 eV (d) 3.5 eV

9 The value of Planck's constant is

(a) 6.0×10^{-34} J-s (b) 6.2×10^{-34} J-s
(c) 6.4×10^{-34} J-s (d) 6.6×10^{-34} J-s

10 de-Broglie wavelength of electron, when its energy is 0.5 eV

(a) 8.68 Å (b) 17.35 Å
(c) 21.25 Å (D) 24.54 Å

Comprehension-4

The circuit shown is placed in vacuum. Both the capacitors are identical and they have the same capacitance C. Light is incident on the left plate of the upper capacitor. When all the switches are open, then the *hf versus* KE_{max} is shown by the straight line (1). In all the cases, we are measuring the KE_{max}, when the electron reaches the opposite plate.

When only S_1 and S_2 are closed, the graph becomes (2). When only S_3 and S_4 are closed, then the graph becomes (3).

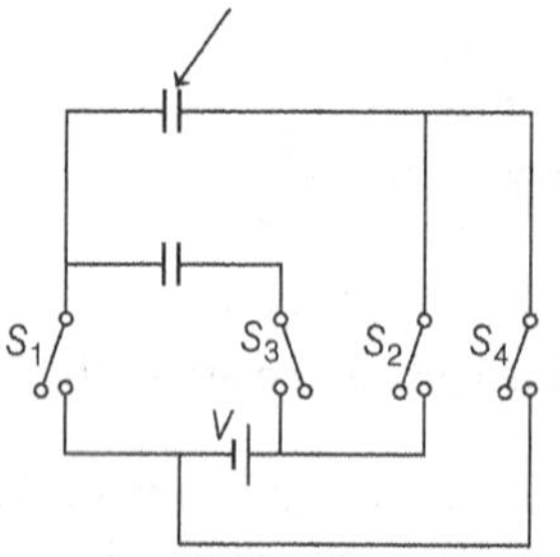

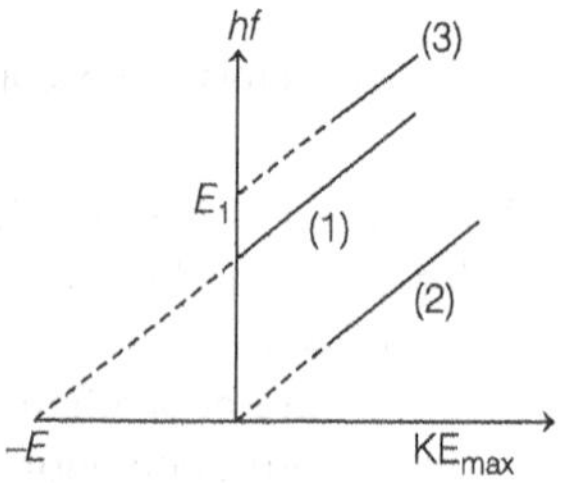

11 What is the work function of the cathode?

(a) E (b) E_1
(c) $E+E_1$ (d) None of these

12 What is the value of eV?

(a) E (b) E_1
(c) $E+E_1$ (d) None of these

13 What is the value of E_1?

(a) $3E$ (b) $\frac{3E}{2}$
(c) $\frac{E}{2}$ (d) None of these

Comprehension-5

A light of wavelength λ is incident on a metal sheet of work function $\phi = 2$ eV. The wavelength λ varies with time as $\lambda = 3000 + 40t$, where λ is in Å and t is in second. The power incident on metal sheet is constant at 100 W. This signal is switched on and off for time intervals of 2 min and 1 min respectively. Each time the signal is switched on, the λ start from initial value of 3000 Å. The metal plate is grounded and electron clouding is negligible. The efficiency of photoemission is 1%.
($hc = 12400$ eV-Å, 1 eV $= 1.6\times 10^{-19}$ J)

14 The time after which photoemission will stop is

(a) 120 s (b) 80 s
(c) 60 s (d) 180 s

15 The total number of photoelectrons ejected in one hour is

(a) 3.71×10^{17} (b) 3.71×10^{21}
(c) 3.71×10^{25} (d) 3.71×10^{7}

16 The variation of rate of emission *versus* time is

(a) 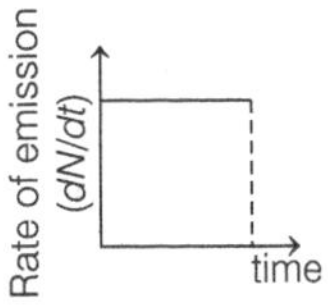

(b) 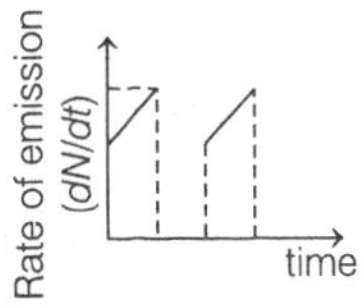

(c) 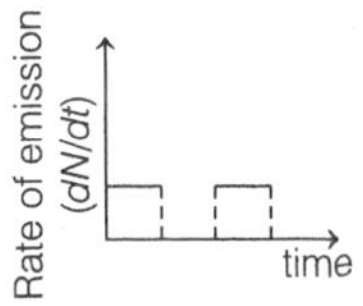

(d) 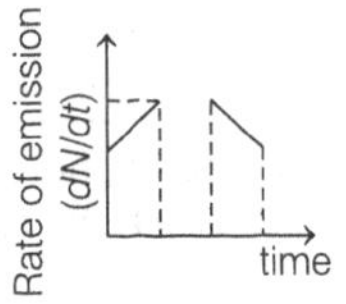

Comprehension-6

Two metallic plates *A* and *B*, each of area 5×10^{-4} m^2, are placed parallel to each other at a separation of 1 cm. Plate *B* carries a positive charge of 33.7×10^{-12} C. A monochromatic beam of light, with photons of energy 5 eV each, starts falling on plate *A* at $t = 0$, so that 10^{16} photons fall on it per square metre per second. Assume that one photoelectron is emitted for every 10^6 incident photons. Also assume that all the emitted photoelectrons are collected by plate *B* and the work function of plate *A* remains constant at the value 2 eV. Determine

17 the number of photoelectrons emitted up to $t = 10$ s,

(a) 5×10^6 (b) 5×10^7
(c) 5×10^8 (d) 5×10^9

18 the magnitude of the electric field between the plates *A* and *B* at $t = 10$ s,

(a) 500 N/C (b) 1000 N/C
(c) 2000 N/C (d) 3000 N/C

19 the kinetic energy of the most energetic photoelectron emitted at $t = 10$ s, when it reaches plate *B*. Neglect the time taken by the photoelectron to reach plate *B*. Take $\varepsilon_0 = 8.85 \times 10^{-12}$ C^2/N-m^2

(a) 3 eV (b) 13 eV (c) 20 eV (d) 23 eV

Comprehension-7

In a photoelectric effect setup, a point source of light of power 3.2×10^{-3} W emits monoenergetic photons of energy 5 eV. The source is located at a distance of 0.8 m from the centre of a stationary metallic sphere of work function 3 eV and of radius 8×10^{-3} m. The efficiency of photoelectrons emission is one for every 10^6 incident photons. Assume that the sphere is isolated and initially neutral and that the photoelectrons are instantly swept away after emission.

20 Calculate the number of photoelectrons emitted per second.

(a) 10^4 (b) 10^5
(c) 10^6 (d) 10^7

21 It is observed that the photoelectrons emission stops at a certain time *t* after the light source is switched on. Evaluate time *t*.

(a) 111.1 s (b) 50.2 s
(c) 40.5 s (d) 20.4 s

22 Find the ratio of the wavelength of incident light to the de-Broglie wavelength of the fastest photoelectron emitted.

(a) 56.18
(b) 156.18
(c) 186.18
(d) 286.04

Match the Columns Questions

1 Some quantities related to the photoelectric effect are mentioned under Column I and Column II. Match each quantity in Column I with the corresponding quantities in Column II on which it depends

Column I	Column II
A. Saturation current	1. Frequency of light
B. Stopping potential	2. Work function
C. de-Broglie wavelength of fastest photoelectron	3. Area of photosensitive plate
D. Force due to radiation falling on the photo plate.	4. Intensity of light (at constant frequency)
	5. None of these

2 In the experimental setup for a photocell, the wavelength of the light incident on the cathode is initially 0.6 times the threshold wavelength for the material of the cathode. Certain changes in the experiment setup are given in Column I and their possible effects are given in Column II.

Column I	Column II
A. The intensity of the incident light is doubled but the frequency remains unaltered	1. Saturation photocurrent remains the same
B. Both the intensity and wavelength of the incident light are doubled	2. Photocurrent falls to zero
C. The intensity of the incident light is doubled and its wavelength is made-half	3. Stopping potential increases
D. The intensity of the incident light remains the same and the wavelength is made-half	4. Saturation photocurrent increases

3 In the shown experimental setup to study photoelectric effect, two conducting electrodes are enclosed in an evacuated glass tube as shown. A parallel beam of monochromatic light, falls on photosensitive electrodes. The emf of battery shown is high enough such that all photoelectrons ejected from left electrode will reach the right electrode. Under initial conditions photoelectrons are emitted. As changes are made in each situation of Column I, match the statements in Column I with results in Column II.

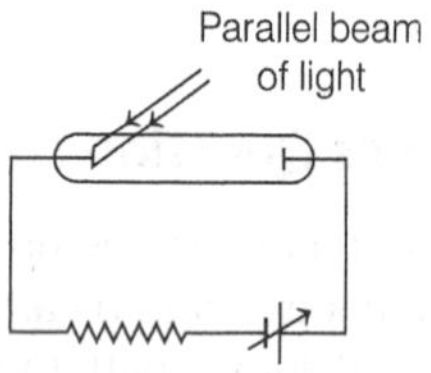

	Column I		Column II
A.	If frequency of incident light is increased keeping its intensity constant	1.	magnitude of stopping potential will increase
B.	If frequency of incident light is increased and its intensity is decreased	2.	current through circuit may stop
C.	If work function of photo sensitive electrode is increased	3.	maximum kinetic energy of ejected photoelectrons will increase
D.	If intensity of incident light is increased keeping its frequency constant.	4.	Saturation current will increase

4 In a photoelectric experimental arrangement, light of frequency f is incident on a metal target whose work function is $\phi = \frac{hf}{3}$ as shown, In Column I, KE of photoelectron is mentioned at various locations/instants and in Column II, the corresponding values. Match the entries of Column I with the entries of Column II.

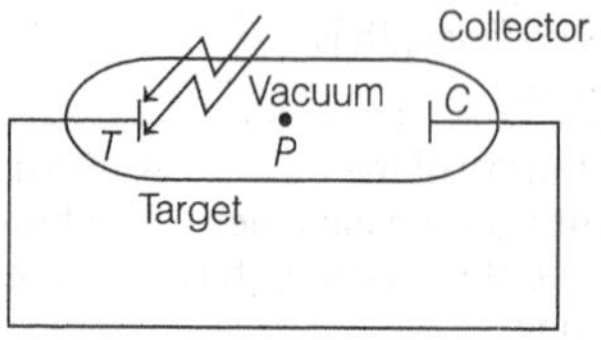

	Column I		Column II
A.	Maximum KE of photoelectrons just after emission from target	1.	zero
B.	KE of photoelectrons just after emission from target	2.	$\frac{hf}{3}$
C.	KE of photoelectron, when they are half-way between the target and collector	3.	$\frac{hf}{2}$
D.	KE of photoelectrons as they reach the collector	4.	$\frac{2hf}{3}$

5 In the shown experimental setup to study photoelectric effect, two conducting electrodes are enclosed in an evacuated glass tube as shown. A parallel beam of monochromatic radiation, falls on photosensitive electrode. Assume that for each photon incident, a photoelectron is ejected if its energy is greater than work function of electrode. Match the statements in Column I with corresponding graphs in Column II.

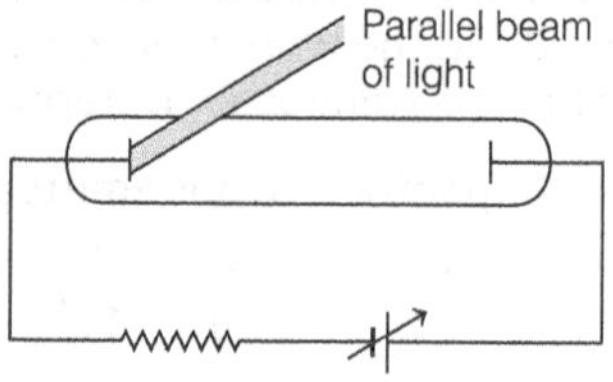

	Column I		Column II
A.	Saturation photocurrent (for same metal) *versus* intensity of radiation is represented by	1.	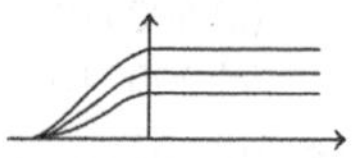
B.	Maximum kinetic energy of ejected photoelectrons *versus* frequency for electrodes of different work function is represented by	2.	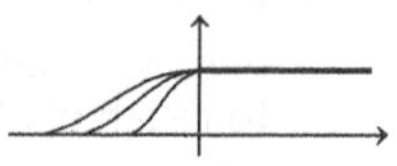
C.	Photocurrent *versus* applied voltage for different intensity of radiation (for same metal) is represented by	3.	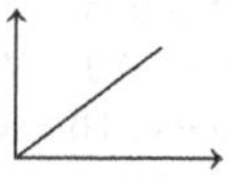
D.	Photocurrent *versus* applied voltage at constant intensity of radiation for electrodes of different work function.	4.	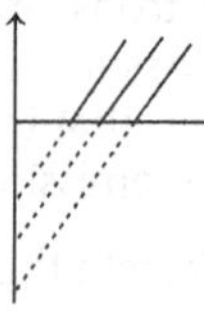

Numerical Value Questions

1 A parallel beam of uniform monochromatic light of wavelength 663 nm has an intensity of $90\ W/m^2$. Find the number of photons in $1\ mm^3$ of this radiation.

2 At $t = 0$, light of intensity 10^{12} photons/s-m^2 of energy 6 eV per photon start falling on a plate with work function 2.5 eV. If area of the plate is $2 \times 10^{-4}\ m^2$ and for every 10^5 photons one photoelectron is emitted, charge on the plate at $t = 25$ s is $n \times 10^{-15}$ C, find the value of n.

3 In the photoelectric experiment, if we use a monochromatic light, the photoelectric current *versus* voltage curve is as shown. If work function of the metal is 2 eV, estimate the power (in W) of light used. (Assume number of photoelectrons emitted are 10^{-3}% of number of photons incident on metal)

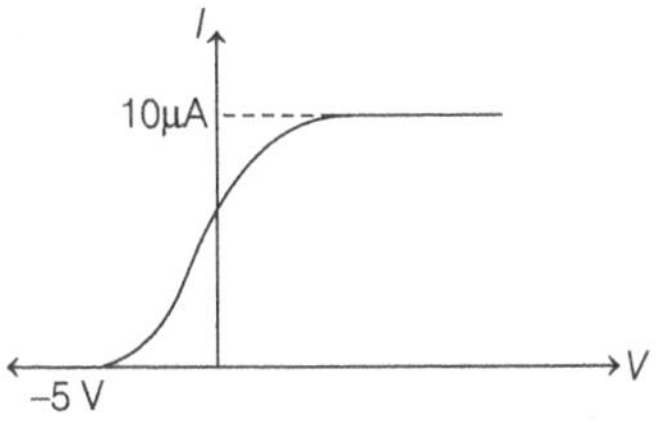

4 Flat aluminum electrode is illuminated by light with a wavelength of 83 nm. What is the maximum distance (in mm) from the electrode surface will a photoelectron move, if outside the electrode there is a retarding electric field of $E = 750$ V/m. Photoelectric threshold for aluminum is 332 nm. (Take $hc = 1245$ eV-nm)

5 A small piece of cesium metal (work function = 1.9 eV) is kept at a distance of 20 cm from a large metal plate having a charge density of $1.0 \times 10^{-9}\ Cm^{-2}$ on the surface facing the cesium piece. A monochromatic light of wavelength 400 nm is incident on the cesium piece. The ratio of maximum to minimum kinetic energy of the photoelectrons reaching the large metal plate is given by k. Then, find the nearest integral value of k. Neglect any change in electric field due to the small piece of cesium present.

6 The figure below shows a vacuum tube containing electrodes made of different metals, 1 and 2 whose work functions are ϕ_1 and ϕ_2. The electrodes are illuminated simultaneously. The maximum kinetic energy of photoelectrons reaching plate 2 is 1 eV and maximum kinetic energy of photoelectrons reaching plate 1 is 3 eV. Assume that photoelectron emitted from either plate do not interact with each other. $\phi_1 = 1.5$ eV and $\phi_2 = 0.7$ eV. Find wavelength (in nm) of the electromagnetic wave used.

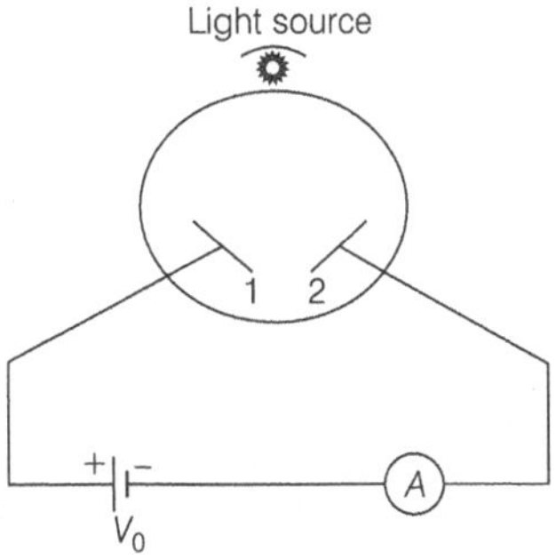

7 In an experiment on photoelectric effect, the separation between emitter and the collector plates is 10 cm. Plates are connected through an ammeter without any cell. A Magnetic field B exists parallel to the plates. The work function of the emitter is 2.39 eV and the light of wavelengths between 400 nm and 600 nm is incident on it. If minimum value of B for which the current registered by the ammeter is zero is $n \times 10^{-6}$ T. Then, find out value of n (Neglect any effect of space charge). (Assume emission of photoelectron to be randomly in every possible direction)

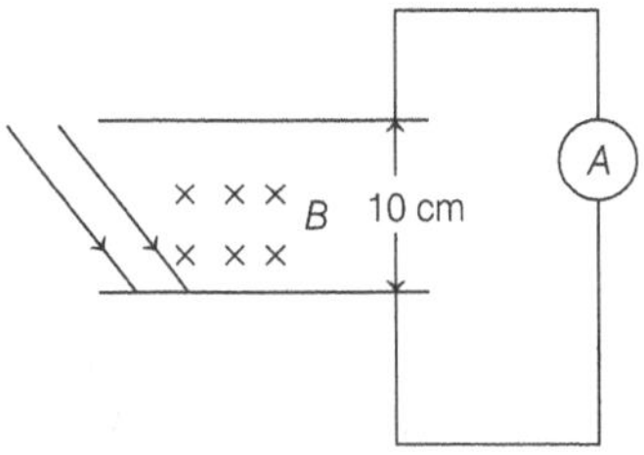

8 A light beam of wavelength 400 nm is incident on a metal plate of work function 2.2 eV. A particular electron absorbs a photon and makes some collisions before coming out of the metal. Assuming that 10% of the instantaneous energy is lost to the metal in each collision. Find the minimum number of collisions the electron can suffer before it becomes unable to come out of metal. (Use $hc = 12400$ eV-Å)

9 Figure shows the stopping potential *versus* the light frequency for a metal cathode used in a photoelectric effect experiment. Suppose this cathode is now illuminated with 6.63 μW of 300 nm light and that the efficiency of converting photons to photoelectrons is 10%. Take $h = 6.63 \times 10^{-34}$ J-s, $c = 3 \times 10^8\ ms^{-1}$.

What is the power (in multiple of 10^{-9} W) of emitted photoelectron beam assuming that on an average, each photoelectron emitted has energy $5K_{max}/6$. Assume that anode potential is sufficiently positive.

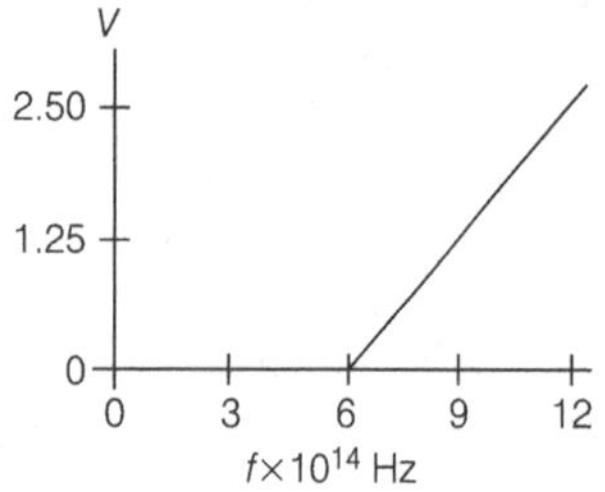

10 Three monochromatic sources having wavelengths 12.42 nm, 6.21 nm and 24.84 nm are placed close to each other in front of a converging lens such that equal powers from the three equal to 1mW each fall on a converging lens and then on a small spherical conductor of radius $r = 1$ mm and work function 62.1eV. (Assume 50% efficiency of emission and no change in effective value of work function due to photoelectric emission and potential rise) (Use hc = 1242 eV-nm) (All electrons emitted by the sphere are immediately removed by some non-electrical mechanism). At $t = 8$ s, switch S is closed, so that the sphere gets connected to the earth *via* a resistor of value 6.75 MΩ. Find the current (in A) flowing just after the switch is closed.

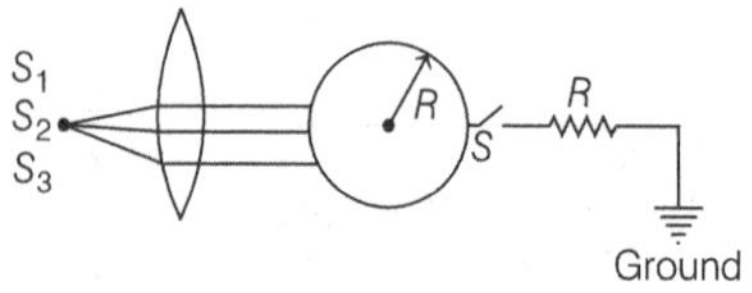

11 Neutrons in thermal equilibrium with matter at 27°C can be thought to behave like ideal gas. Assuming them to have a speed of v_{rms}, what is their de-Broglie wavelength λ (in nm)? Fill 156λ in the OMR sheet. Take $m_n = 1.69 \times 10^{-27}$ kg, $k = 1.44 \times 10^{-23}$ J/K, $h = 6.60 \times 10^{-34}$ J-s.

12 A totally reflecting, small plane mirror placed horizontally faces a parallel beam of light as shown in figure. The mass of the mirror is 20g. Assume that there is no absorption in the lens and that 30 % of the light emitted by the source goes through the lens. Find the power (in $x\,10^{8}$ W) of the source needed to support the weight of the mirror. Take $g = 10$ ms^{-2}.

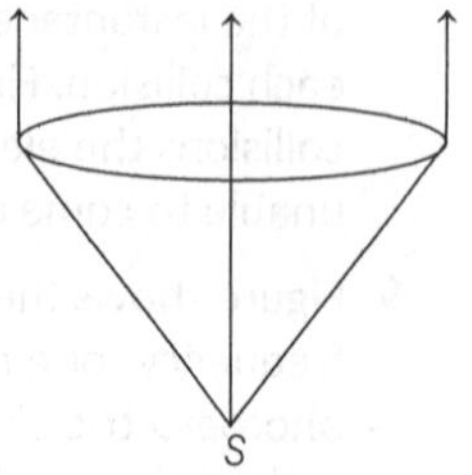

13 Light of intensity I is incident on a fixed plane surface at an angle 30° with the surface. If 50% light is reflected and remaining light is absorbed, then radiation pressure on the plate is $\frac{3I}{nc}$, then find n. (speed of light is c)

14 A point source of radiation of power P is placed on the axis of completely absorbing disc. The distance between the source and the disc is 2 times the radius of the disc.The force that light exerts on the disc is $\frac{P}{nc}$. Then, the value of x is

Previous Year's Questions

JEE Main

1 A convex lens of focal length 40 cm forms an image of an extended source of light on a photoelectric cell. A current I is produced. The lens is replaced by another convex lens having the same diameter but focal length 20 cm. The photoelectric current now is **[2024, 27 Jan Shift-I]**

(a) I (b) $4I$ (c) $\frac{I}{2}$ (d) $2I$

2 The threshold frequency of a metal with work function 6.63 eV is **[2024, 27 Jan Shift-II]**

(a) 16×10^{12} Hz (b) 1.6×10^{15} Hz
(c) 16×10^{15} Hz (d) 1.6×10^{12} Hz

3 The de-Broglie wavelength of an electron is the same as that of a photon. If velocity of electron is 25% of the velocity of light, then the ratio of KE of electron and KE of photon will be **[2024, 29 Jan Shift-I]**

(a) $\frac{8}{1}$ (b) $\frac{1}{8}$ (c) $\frac{1}{4}$ (d) $\frac{1}{1}$

4 In photoelectric effect **[2023, 8 April Shift-II]**

A. The photocurrent is proportional to the intensity of the incident radiation
B. Maximum Kinetic energy with which photoelectrons are emitted depends on the intensity of incident light.
C. Maximum KE with which photoelectrons are emitted depends on the frequency of incident light.
D. The emission of photoelectrons require a minimum threshold intensity of incident radiation.
E. Maximum KE of the photoelectrons is independent of the frequency of the incident light.

Choose the correct answer from the options given below:

(a) A and B only (b) B and C only
(c) A and C only (d) A and E only

5 The difference between threshold wavelengths for two metal surfaces A and B having work function $\phi_A = 9$ eV and $\phi_B = 4\cdot5$ eV in nm is {Given, $hc = 1242$ eV-nm) **[2023, 13 April Shift-I]**

(a) 264 (b) 276

(c) 540 (d) 138

6 A metallic surface is illuminated with radiation of wavelength λ, the stopping potential is V_0. If the same surface is illuminated with radiation of wavelength 2λ, the stopping potential becomes $V_0/4$. The threshold wavelength for this metallic surface will be **[2023, 11 April Shift-I]**

(a) 3λ (b) $\frac{3}{2}\lambda$

(c) $\frac{\lambda}{4}$ (d) 4λ

7 The work functions of aluminium and Gold are 4.1 eV and and 5.1 eV respectively. The ratio of the slope of the stopping potential *versus* frequency plot for gold to that of aluminium is **[2023, 6 April Shift-II]**

(a) 1.24 (b) 1.5

(c) 1 (d) 2

8 The variation of stopping potential (V_0) as a function of the frequency (ν) of the incident light for a metal is shown in figure. The work function of the surface is **[2023, 10 April Shift-II]**

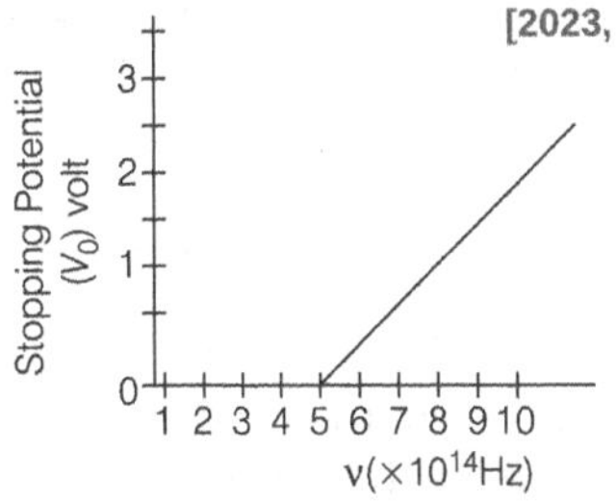

(a) 1.36 eV (b) 2.98 eV (c) 18.6 eV (d) 2.07 eV

9 Given below are two statements.

Statement I Out of microwaves, infrared rays and ultraviolet rays, ultraviolet rays are the most effective for the emission of electrons from a metallic surface.

Statement II Above the threshold frequency, the maximum kinetic energy of photoelectrons is inversely proportional to the frequency of the incident light. **[2023, 13 April Shift-II]**

In the light of the above statements, choose the correct answer from the options given below.

(a) Both Statement I and Statement II are false

(b) Both Statement I and Statement II are true

(c) Statement I is false but Statement II is true

(d) Statement I is true but Statement II is false

10 An atom absorbs a photon of wavelength 500 nm and emits another photon of wavelength 600 nm. The net energy absorbed by the atom in this process is $n \times 10^{-4}$ eV. The value of n is .... [Assume the atom to be stationary during the absorption and emission process] (Take, $h = 6.6 \times 10^{-34}$ J-s and $c = 3 \times 10^8$ m/s). **[2023, 13 April Shift-II]**

11 If the two metals A and B are exposed to radiation of wavelength 350 nm. The work functions of metals A and B are 4.8 eV and 2.2 eV. Then choose the correct option. **[2023, 31 Jan, Shift-II]**

(a) Both metals A and B will emit photoelectrons

(b) Metal B will not emit photoelectrons

(c) Both metals A and B will not emit photo electrons

(d) Metal A will not emit photoelectrons

12 The kinetic energy of an electron, α-particle and a proton are given as $4K$, $2K$ and K respectively. The de-Broglie wavelength associated with electron (λ_e), α-particle (λ_α) and the proton (λ_p) are as follows **[2023, 6 April Shift-I]**

(a) $\lambda_\alpha = \lambda_p > \lambda_e$ (b) $\lambda_\alpha < \lambda_p < \lambda_e$

(c) $\lambda_\alpha > \lambda_p > \lambda_e$ (d) $\lambda_\alpha = \lambda_p < \lambda_e$

13 A proton and an α-particle are accelerated from rest by 2V and 4V potentials, respectively. The ratio of their de-Broglie wavelength is **[2023, 12 April Shift-I]**

(a) 16 : 1 (b) 2 : 1

(c) 8 : 1 (d) 4 : 1

14 The de-Broglie wavelength of an electron having kinetic energy E is λ. If the kinetic energy of electron becomes $E/4$, then its de-Broglie wavelength will be **[2023, 15 April Shift-I]**

(a) $\frac{\lambda}{2}$ (b) $\frac{\lambda}{\sqrt{2}}$ (c) 2λ (d) $\sqrt{2}\lambda$

15 Given below are two statements: One is labelled as **Assertion (A)** and the other is labelled as **Reason (R)**

Assertion (A) The beam of electrons show wave nature and exhibit interference and diffraction.

Reason (R) Davisson Germer experimentally verified the wave nature of electrons.

In the light of the above statements, choose the most appropriate answer from the options given below : **[2023, 31 Jan, Shift-I]**

(a) Both A and R are correct but R is not the correct explanation of A

(b) A is correct but R is not correct

(c) A is not correct but R is correct

(d) Both A and R are correct and R is the correct explanation of A

16 The kinetic energy of emitted electron is E when the light incident on the metal has wavelength λ. To double the kinetic energy, the incident light must have wavelength [2022, 29 July Shift-I]

(a) $\frac{hc}{E\lambda - hc}$
(b) $\frac{hc\lambda}{E\lambda + hc}$
(c) $\frac{h\lambda}{E\lambda + hc}$
(d) $\frac{hc\lambda}{E\lambda - hc}$

17 A metal exposed to light of wavelength 800 nm and emits photoelectrons with a certain kinetic energy. The maximum kinetic energy of photoelectron doubles when light of wavelength 500 nm is used. The work function of the metal is

(Take, $hc = 1230$ eV-nm) [2022, 25 July Shift-I]

(a) 1.537 eV
(b) 2.46 eV
(c) 0.615 eV
(d) 1.23 eV

18 The electric field at a point associated with a light wave is given by

$$E = 200\,[\sin(6\times10^{15})t + \sin(9\times10^{15})t]\,\text{Vm}^{-1}$$

Given, $h = 4.14 \times 10^{-15}$ eVs

If this light falls on a metal surface having a work function of 2.50 eV, the maximum kinetic energy of the photoelectrons will be [2022, 29 June Shift-II]

(a) 1.90 eV
(b) 3.27 eV
(c) 3.60 eV
(d) 3.42 eV

19 Let K_1 and K_2 be the maximum kinetic energies of photo-electrons emitted when two monochromatic beams of wavelength λ_1 and λ_2, respectively are incident on a metallic surface. If $\lambda_1 = 3\lambda_2$, then [2022, 28 June shift-II]

(a) $K_1 > \frac{K_2}{3}$ (b) $K_1 < \frac{K_2}{3}$ (c) $K_1 = \frac{K_2}{3}$ (d) $K_2 = \frac{K_1}{3}$

20 A metal surface is illuminated by a radiation of wavelength 4500 Å. The ejected photo-electron enters a constant magnetic field of 2 mT making an angle of 90° with the magnetic field. If it starts revolving in a circular path of radius 2 mm, the work function of the metal is approximately. [2022, 26 June Shift-II]

(a) 1.36 eV
(b) 1.69 eV
(c) 2.78 eV
(d) 2.23 eV

21 The light of two different frequencies whose photonshave energies 3.8 eV and 1.4 eV, respectively, illuminate a metallic surface whose work function is 0.6 eV successively. The ratio of maximum speeds of emitted electrons for the two frequencies, respectively will be [2022, 24 June Shift-II]

(a) 1 : 1
(b) 2 : 1
(c) 4 : 1
(d) 1 : 4

22 With reference to the observations in photoelectric effect, identify the correct statements from below

(A) The square of maximum velocity of photoelectrons varies linearly with frequency of incident light.
(B) The value of saturation current increases on moving the source of light away from the metal surface
(C) The maximum kinetic energy of photo-electrons decreases on decreasing the power of LED (light emitting diode) source of light.
(D) The immediate emission of photo-electrons out of metal surface cannot be explained by particle nature of light/electromagnetic waves.
(E) Existence of threshold wavelength cannot be explained by wave nature of light/electromagnetic waves.

Choose the correct answer from the options given below : [2022, 27 July Shift-II]

(a) (A) and (B) only
(b) (A) and (E) only
(c) (C) and (E) only
(d) (D) and (E) only

23 Two streams of photons, possessing energies equal to five and ten times the work function of metal are incident on the metal surface successively. The ratio of maximum velocities of the photoelectron emitted, in the two cases respectively, will be [2022, 28 July Shift-II]

(a) 1 : 2
(b) 1 : 3
(c) 2 : 3
(d) 3 : 2

24 Let K_1 and K_2 be the maximum kinetic energies of photo-electrons emitted when two monochromatic beams of wavelength λ_1 and λ_2, respectively are incident on a metallic surface. If $\lambda_1 = 3\lambda_2$ then [2022, 28 June Shift-II]

(a) $K_1 > \frac{K_2}{3}$
(b) $K_1 < \frac{K_2}{3}$
(c) $K_1 = \frac{K_2}{3}$
(d) $K_2 = \frac{K_1}{3}$

25 Given below are two statements : One is labelled as Assertion (A) and the other is labelled as Reason (R).

Assertion (A) The photoelectric effect does not takes place, if the energy of the incident radiation is less than the work function of a metal.

Reason (R) Kinetic energy of the photoelectrons is zero, if the energy of the incident radiation is equal to the work function of a metal.

In the light of the above statements choose the most appropriate answer from the options given below. **[2022, 29 June Shift-I]**

(a) Both A and R are correct and R is the correct explanation of A

(b) Both A and R are correct but R is not the correct explanation of A

(c) A is correct but R is not correct

(d) A is not correct but R is correct

26 A parallel beam of light of wavelength 900 nm and intensity 100 Wm^{-2} is incident on a surface perpendicular to the beam. The number of photons crossing through area of 1 cm^2 perpendicular to the beam in one second is **[2022, 26 July Shift-I]**

(a) 3×10^{16} (b) 4.5×10^{16}

(c) 4.5×10^{17} (d) 4.5×10^{20}

27 An α-particle and a carbon 12 atom has same kinetic energy K. The ratio of their de-Broglie wavelengths $(\lambda_\alpha : \lambda_{C12})$ is **[2022, 27 June, Shift-I]**

(a) $1 : \sqrt{3}$ (b) $\sqrt{3} : 1$ (c) $3 : 1$ (d) $2 : \sqrt{3}$

JEE Advanced

1. When light of a given wavelength is incident on a metallic surface, the minimum potential needed to stop the emitted photoelectrons is 6.0 V. This potential drops to 0.6 V, if another source with wavelength four times that of the first one and intensity half of the first one is used. What are the wavelength of the first source and the work function of the metal, respectively? **(2022 Adv.)**

[Take, $\frac{hc}{e} = 1.24 \times 10^{-6}$ JmC^{-1}]

(a) 1.72×10^{-7} m, 1.20 eV

(b) 1.72×10^{-7} m, 5.60 eV

(c) 3.78×10^{-7} m, 5.60 eV

(d) 3.78×10^{-7} m, 1.20 eV

2. In a photoemission experiment, the maximum kinetic energies of photoelectrons from metals P, Q and R are E_P, E_Q and E_R, respectively, and they are related by $E_P = 2E_Q = 2E_R$. In this experiment, the same source of monochromatic light is used for metals P and Q while a different source of monochromatic light is used for the metal R. The work functions for metals P, Q and R are 4.0 eV, 4.5 eV and 5.5 eV, respectively. The energy of the incident photon used for metal R, in eV, is .... **(2021 Adv.)**

3. In a photoelectric experiment, a parallel beam of monochromatic light with power of 200 W is incident on a perfectly absorbing cathode of work function 6.25 eV. The frequency of light is just above the threshold frequency, so that the photoelectrons are emitted with negligible kinetic energy. Assume that the photoelectron emission efficiency is 100%. A potential difference of 500 V is applied between the cathode and the anode. All the emitted electrons are incident normally on the anode and are absorbed. The anode experiences a force $F = n \times 10^{-4}$ N due to the impact of the electrons. The value of n is .... (Take mass of the electron, $m_e = 9 \times 10^{-31}$ kg and eV= 1.6×10^{-19} J) **(2018 Adv.)**

4. In a historical experiment to determine Planck's constant, a metal surface was irradiated with light of different wavelengths. The emitted photoelectron energies were measured by applying a stopping potential. The relevant data for the wavelength (λ) of incident light and the corresponding stopping potential (V_0) are given below: **(2016 Adv.)**

λ (μm)	V_0 (Volt)
0.3	2.0
0.4	1.0
0.5	0.4

Given that $c = 3 \times 10^8$ ms^{-1} and $e = 1.6 \times 10^{-19}$ C, Planck's constant (in units of J-s) found from such an experiment is)

(a) 6.0×10^{-34}

(b) 6.4×10^{-34}

(c) 6.6×10^{-34}

(d) 6.8×10^{-34}

5. For photoelectric effect with incident photon wavelength λ, the stopping potential is V_0. Identify the correct variation(s) of V_0 with λ and $\frac{1}{\lambda}$. **(2015 Adv.)**

(a)
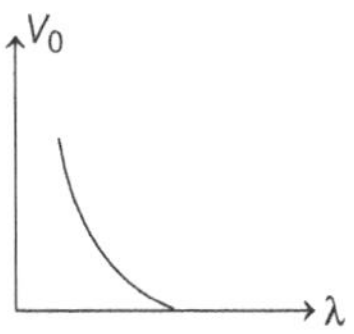

(b)
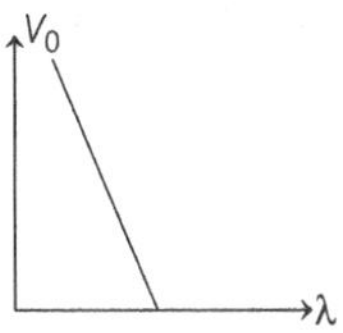

(c)
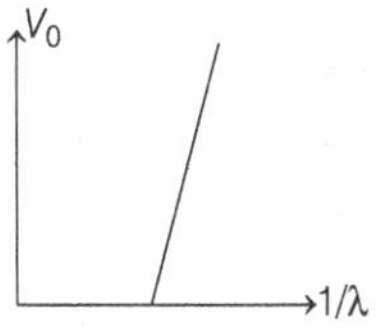

(d)
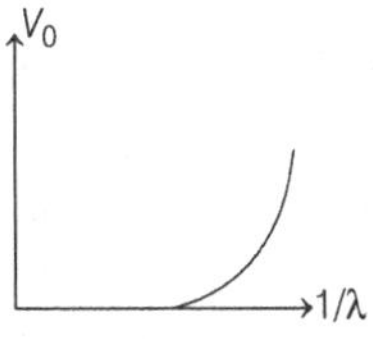

Answer Key

Level 1

7.1 Radiation from Source

1. 1.78×10^{19} 2. 5.76×10^{-11} A
3. 4.22×10^{21} photon/s-m^2

7.2 Photoelectric Effect

1. 1.6 eV 2. (a) 310 nm (b) 191 nm 3. 2222 Å
4. 0.34 V (increase) 5. 6λ 6. 1.9 eV
7. 1.91 eV, 4120 Å 8. 2 eV and 3.7 eV
9. 1.12×10^{12} 10. 9.7×10^{14} Hz
11.

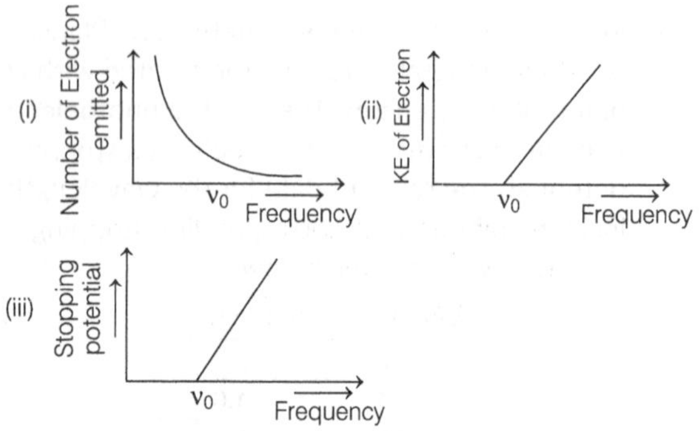

12. (i) No change in stopping potential
(ii) Photoelectric current will become four times
(iii) No change in maximum velocity of photoelectron emitted
13. (i) Metal X (ii) Metal X 14. $f_a = f_b < f_c$, $I_a < I_b = I_c$

7.3 Matter Waves

1. 1.1×10^{-38} m 2. 1.73 Å 3. $\dfrac{\lambda_0}{2\sqrt{2}}$ 4. 1.45 Å
5. $\sqrt{\dfrac{8}{3}}$ 6. 1450 m/s 7. photon

7.4 Force due to Radiation

1. (i) 3×10^7 W (ii) 1.5×10^7 W 2. 1.3×10^{-7} N
3. 5×10^{-8} N 4. $\dfrac{\pi R^2 I}{C}$ 5. 6.37×10^6 Nm^{-2}
6. 1.8×10^{-5} N/m^2

Level 2

Single Choice Correct Questions

1. (a)	2. (a)	3. (b)	4. (d)	5. (d)
6. (c)	7. (c)	8. (b)	9. (a)	10. (a)
11. (d)	12. (b)	13. (c)	14. (c)	15. (a)
16. (b)	17. (c)	18. (c)	19. (a)	20. (c)
21. (b)	22. (a)	23. (c)	24. (d)	25. (b)
26. (d)	27. (a)	28. (b)	29. (b)	30. (c)
31. (d)	32. (d)	33. (c)	34. (b)	35. (b)
36. (d)	37. (a)	38. (a)	39. (c)	40. (b)
41. (c)	42. (c)	43. (b)	44. (a)	45. (d)
46. (c)	47. (d)	48. (a)	49. (c)	50. (b)
51. (d)	52. (c)	53. (a)	54. (d)	55. (b)
56. (d)	57. (c)	58. (d)	59. (a)	

Multiple Choice(s) Correct Questions

1. (a, b, c)	2. (c, d)	3. (b, c)	4. (a,b,c,d)
5. (b, c)	6. (b, c, d)	7. (a, c)	8. (a, b, d)
9. (b, d)	10. (b, c, d)	11. (a,b,c,d)	12. (a, b, c)
13. (a,b,c,d)	14. (b, c)		

Comprehension Based Questions

1. (a)	2. (a)	3. (b)	4. (b)	5. (a)
6. (c)	7. (a)	8. (c)	9. (a)	10. (b)
11. (a)	12. (a)	13. (b)	14. (b)	15. (b)
16. (b)	17. (b)	18. (c)	19. (d)	20. (b)
21. (a)	22. (d)			

Match the Columns Questions

1. A $\rightarrow$ 1,3,4, B $\rightarrow$ 1, 2, C $\rightarrow$ 1, 2, D $\rightarrow$ 3, 4
2. A $\rightarrow$ 4, B $\rightarrow$ 2, C $\rightarrow$ 3, 4, D $\rightarrow$ 1, 3
3. A $\rightarrow$ 1, 3, B $\rightarrow$ 1,3, C $\rightarrow$ 2, D $\rightarrow$ 4
4. A $\rightarrow$ 4, B $\rightarrow$ 1,2,3,4, C $\rightarrow$ 2,3,4, D $\rightarrow$ 2,3,4
5. A $\rightarrow$ 3, B $\rightarrow$ 4, C $\rightarrow$ 1, D $\rightarrow$ 2

Numerical Value Questions

1. 1830	2. 8	3. 7	4. 15
5. 1	6. 400	7. 28.5	8. 4
9. 221	10. 80	11. 22	12. 1
13. 8	14. 20		

Previous Year's Questions

JEE Main

1. (a)	2. (b)	3. (b)	4. (c)	5. (d)
6. (a)	7. (c)	8. (d)	9. (d)	10. (4125)
11. (d)	12. (b)	13. (d)	14. (c)	15. (d)
16. (b)	17. (c)	18. (d)	19. (b)	20. (a)
21. (b)	22. (b)	23. (c)	24. (b)	25. (b)
26. (b)	27. (b)			

JEE Advanced

1. (a)	2. (6)	3. (24)	4. (b)
5. (a, c)			

SOLUTIONS

Level 1

7.1 Radiation from Source

1. Energy of one photon $= \frac{hc}{\lambda}$

$$= \frac{6.63\times10^{-34}\times3\times10^{8}}{590\times10^{-9}}$$

$$= 3.37\times10^{-19}\text{J}$$

Number of photons emitted per second $= \frac{P}{\frac{hc}{\lambda}}$

$$= \frac{10\times\frac{60}{100}}{3.37\times10^{-19}}$$

$$= 1.78\times10^{19}$$

2. Photocurrent $= \frac{P}{\frac{hc}{\lambda}}\times n\times e$

$$= \frac{663\times10^{-3}}{\frac{6.63\times10^{-34}\times3\times10^{8}}{540\times10^{-9}}}\times\frac{1}{5\times10^{9}}\times1.6\times10^{-19}$$

$$= 5.76\times10^{-11}\text{A}$$

3. I = Intensity of sunlight on earth $= \frac{P}{4\pi r^2}$

Energy of one photon $= \frac{hc}{\lambda}$

Photon flux $= \frac{I}{\frac{hc}{\lambda}} = \frac{P\lambda}{4\pi r^2 hc}$

$$= \frac{(3.9\times10^{26})(6000\times10^{-10})}{4\times3.14\times(1.49\times10^{11})^2\times6.63\times10^{-34}\times3\times10^{8}}$$

$= 4.22\times10^{21}$ photons/s-m^2

7.2 Photoelectric Effect

1. $K_{max} = \frac{hc}{\lambda} - W = \frac{1240}{350} - 1.9 = 1.6$ eV

2. (a) $\lambda_{Th} = \frac{hc}{W} = \frac{1240\text{ eV-nm}}{4\text{ eV}} = 310$ nm

(b) $$eV_s = \frac{hc}{\lambda} - W$$

$$\Rightarrow \quad e(2.5\text{ V}) = \frac{1240}{\lambda} - 4$$

$$\Rightarrow \quad \lambda = 191\text{ nm}$$

3. $W = \frac{hc}{\lambda_{Th}} = \frac{12400\text{ eV - Å}}{5000\text{ Å}} = 2.48$ eV

$$eV_s = \frac{hc}{\lambda} - W \quad \Rightarrow \quad e(3.1\text{ V}) = \frac{12400}{\lambda} - 2.48$$

$$\Rightarrow \quad \lambda = 2222\text{ Å}$$

4. $$eV_{s_1} = \frac{hc}{\lambda_1} - W \quad \text{...(i)}$$

$$eV_{s_2} = \frac{hc}{\lambda_2} - W \quad \text{...(ii)}$$

Subtracting Eq. (i) from (ii),

$$V_{s_2} - V_{s_1} = \frac{hc}{e}\left(\frac{1}{\lambda_2} - \frac{1}{\lambda_1}\right) = 0.34\text{ V}$$

5. $$e(5V_0) = \frac{hc}{\lambda} - W \quad \text{...(i)}$$

$$eV_0 = \frac{hc}{3\lambda} - W \quad \text{...(ii)}$$

Dividing the Eq. (i) by Eq. (ii)

$$5 = \frac{\frac{hc}{\lambda} - W}{\frac{hc}{3\lambda} - W} \quad \Rightarrow \quad W = \frac{hc}{6\lambda}$$

$$\lambda_{Th} = \frac{hc}{W} = \frac{hc}{\left(\frac{hc}{6\lambda}\right)} = 6\lambda$$

6. $$K_{max} = \frac{hc}{\lambda} - W$$

$$\frac{1}{2}mv_1^2 = \frac{hc}{\lambda_1} - W \quad \text{...(i)}$$

and $$\frac{1}{2}mv_2^2 = \frac{hc}{\lambda_2} - W \quad \text{...(ii)}$$

Dividing Eq. (i) by (ii),

$$\frac{v_1^2}{v_2^2} = \frac{\frac{hc}{\lambda_1} - W}{\frac{hc}{\lambda_2} - W} \quad \Rightarrow \quad \frac{(2v_2)^2}{v_2^2} = \frac{\frac{hc}{\lambda_1} - W}{\frac{hc}{\lambda_2} - W}$$

$$\Rightarrow \quad W = \frac{1}{3}\left(\frac{4hc}{\lambda_2} - \frac{hc}{\lambda_1}\right) = 1.9\text{ eV}$$

7. $$eV_s = \frac{hc}{\lambda} - W$$

$$\Rightarrow \quad e(0.6\text{ V}) = \frac{12400}{4950} - W$$

$$\Rightarrow \quad W = 1.91\text{ eV}$$

$$e(1.1\text{ V}) = \frac{12400}{\lambda} - 1.91$$

$$\Rightarrow \quad \lambda = 4120\text{ Å}$$

8. $K_{max} = \frac{hc}{\lambda} - \phi = \frac{1240}{200} - 4.5 = 1.7$ eV

Electrons emitted from cathode have kinetic energy ranging from 0 to 1.7eV. Now these electrons are accelerated through a potential difference of 2 V. So for electrons reaching anode,

$$K_{min} = 0 + 2 = 2 \text{ eV}$$

$$K_{max} = 1.7 + 2 = 3.7 \text{ eV}$$

9. $\lambda_{Th} = \dfrac{hc}{W} = \dfrac{12400}{1.9} = 6526 \text{ Å}$

Only wavelengths which are less than the threshold wavelength will cause photoelectric effect. So, photoelectrons will come out for wavelengths of 4000 Å, 4800 Å and 6000 Å.

Number of photoelectrons emitted per second

$$= \frac{IA}{\frac{hc}{\lambda}} \times n = \frac{IA\lambda n}{hc}$$

$$N = \frac{IAn\lambda_1}{hc} + \frac{IAn\lambda_2}{hc} + \frac{IAn\lambda_3}{hc}$$

$$= \frac{IAn}{hc}(\lambda_1 + \lambda_2 + \lambda_3)$$

$$= \frac{1.5 \times 10^{-3} \times 10^{-4} \times 1}{6.63 \times 10^{-34} \times 3 \times 10^{8}}(4000 + 4800 + 6000) \times 10^{-10}$$

$$= 1.12 \times 10^{12}$$

10. Potential of metal body will be steady, when it becomes equal to stopping potential

$$h\nu = W + eV_s$$

$$\Rightarrow \quad 6.63 \times 10^{-34}\,\nu = (3 + 1) + 1.6 \times 10^{-19}$$

$$\Rightarrow \quad \nu = 9.7 \times 10^{14} \text{ Hz}$$

11. (i) $n = \dfrac{IA}{h\nu} \quad \Rightarrow \quad n \propto \dfrac{1}{\nu}$ $\qquad \because \{I = \text{const.}\}$

So, graph will be hyperbola.

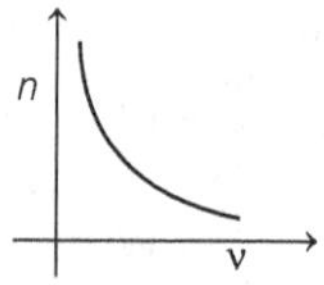

(ii) $K_{max} = h\nu - W$

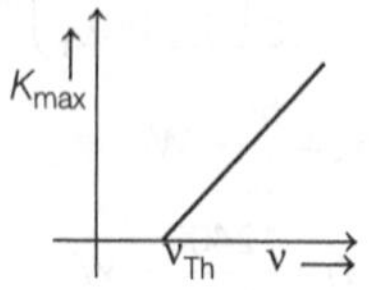

(iii) $V_s = \dfrac{1}{e}(h\nu - W)$

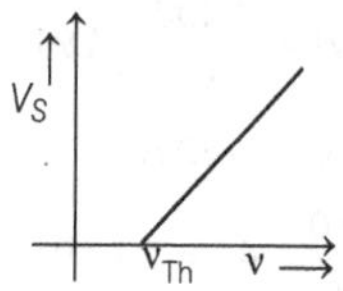

12. Intensity $= \dfrac{P}{4\pi r^2} \quad \Rightarrow \quad I \propto \dfrac{1}{r^2}$

When distance is halved, intensity will become four times.

(a) No change in stopping potential as stopping potential is independent of intensity.

(b) $i \propto I \quad \Rightarrow$ current will become four times.

(c) No change in K_{max} since K_{max} is independent of intensity.

13. (i) $\lambda_{Th} = \dfrac{c}{\nu_{Th}} \quad \Rightarrow \quad \lambda_{Th} \propto \dfrac{1}{\nu_{Th}}$

Metal *X* has lesser threshold frequency. So, it will have larger threshold wavelength.

(ii) $K_{max} = \dfrac{hc}{\lambda} - h\nu_{Th}$

Metal *X* has lesser threshold frequency. So, it will have larger kinetic energy of electrons.

14. $eV_s = h\nu - W$

Stopping potential is maximum for *c*. For *a* and *b* stopping potentials are equal. So, frequency of *c* will be maximum and frequency of *a* and *b* will be equal

$$f_c > f_a = f_b$$

$$I \propto i$$

Current for *b* and *c* are equal and maximum, so intensity of *b* and *c* will be equal and maximum

$$I_b = I_c > I_a$$

7.3 Matter Waves

1. $\lambda = \dfrac{h}{mv} = \dfrac{6.63 \times 10^{-34}}{2000 \times 30} = 1.1 \times 10^{-38} \text{ m}$

2. For an electron, $\lambda = \sqrt{\dfrac{150}{V}}\text{ Å} = \sqrt{\dfrac{150}{50}}\text{ Å} = 1.732 \text{ Å}$

3. $\lambda = \dfrac{h}{p} = \dfrac{1}{\sqrt{2mK}} = \dfrac{1}{\sqrt{2mqV}} \quad \Rightarrow \quad \dfrac{\lambda_1}{\lambda_2} = \sqrt{\dfrac{q_2 m_2}{q_1 m_1}}$

$$\Rightarrow \quad \frac{\lambda_\alpha}{\lambda_p} = \sqrt{\frac{em}{(2e)(4m)}}$$

$$\Rightarrow \quad \lambda_\alpha = \frac{\lambda_0}{2\sqrt{2}}$$

4. For thermal neutrons,

$$\lambda = \frac{h}{\sqrt{3mkT}} = \frac{6.63 \times 10^{-34}}{\sqrt{3 \times 1.675 \times 10^{-27} \times 1.38 \times 10^{-23} \times 300}}$$

$$= 1.45 \text{ Å}$$

5. For gas molecule, $\lambda = \dfrac{h}{\sqrt{3mkT}}$

$$\Rightarrow \quad \frac{\lambda_{H_2}}{\lambda_{He}} = \sqrt{\frac{m_{He}T_{He}}{m_{H_2}T_{H_2}}} = \sqrt{\frac{(4m)(400)}{(2m)(300)}} = \sqrt{\frac{8}{3}}$$

6. $mv = \dfrac{h}{\lambda} \quad \Rightarrow \quad 9.1 \times 10^{-31} v = \dfrac{6.6 \times 10^{-34}}{5000 \times 10^{-10}}$

$$\Rightarrow \quad v = 1450 \text{ m/s}$$

7. If m and v be mass and velocity of electron, then de-Broglie wavelength of electron

$$\lambda = \frac{h}{mv}$$

$$E_1 = \text{Energy of photon} = \frac{hc}{\lambda} = \frac{hc}{\left(\frac{h}{mv}\right)} = mvc$$

$$E_2 = \text{Kinetic energy of electron} = \frac{1}{2}mv^2 = mv\left(\frac{v}{2}\right)$$

Since, $c > \frac{v}{2} \Rightarrow E_1 > E_2$

7.4 Force due to Radiation

1. (i) For equilibrium of plate,

$$F_{\text{due to radiation}} = mg$$

$$\Rightarrow \frac{P}{c} = mg$$

$$\Rightarrow P = mgc = 10 \times 10^{-3} \times 10 \times 3 \times 10^8 = 3 \times 10^7 \text{ W}$$

(ii) $F_{\text{due to radiation}} = mg$

$$\Rightarrow \frac{2P}{c} = mg \Rightarrow P = \frac{mgc}{2} = 1.5 \times 10^7 \text{ W}$$

2. $F = a\left(\frac{P}{c}\right) + r\left(\frac{2P}{c}\right) = (a+2r)\frac{P}{c}$

$$= [0.7 + 2(0.3)]\frac{30}{3 \times 10^8} = 1.3 \times 10^{-7} \text{ N}$$

3. Change in momentum of one photon

$$= \frac{h}{\lambda}\cos\theta - \left(-\frac{h}{\lambda}\cos\theta\right) = \frac{2h}{\lambda}\cos\theta$$

$$F = n\left(\frac{2h}{\lambda}\cos\theta\right)$$

$$= (5 \times 10^{19})\left(\frac{2 \times 6.63 \times 10^{-34}}{663 \times 10^{-9}}\right)\cos 60^\circ$$

$$= 5 \times 10^{-8} \text{ N}$$

4. $F = \frac{IA_{\text{projected}}}{c} = \frac{I(\pi R^2)}{c}$

5. $I = \frac{E}{AT} = \frac{4E}{\pi d^2 T}$

$$F = a\left(\frac{IA}{c}\right) + r\left(\frac{2IA}{c}\right) = \frac{1.5IA}{c}$$

$$p = \frac{F}{A} = \frac{1.5I}{c} = \frac{1.5}{c}\left(\frac{4E}{\pi d^2 T}\right)$$

$$= \frac{1.5}{3 \times 10^8}\left[\frac{4 \times 10}{3.14 \times (10 \times 10^{-6})^2 (0.1 \times 10^{-3})}\right]$$

$$= 6.37 \times 10^{-6} \text{ Nm}^{-2}$$

6. $p = \frac{(1+r)I\cos^2\theta}{c} = \frac{(1+0.8)(0.6 \times 10^4)\cos^2 45^\circ}{3 \times 10^8}$

$$= 1.8 \times 10^{-5} \text{ Nm}^{-2}$$

Level 2

Single Choice Correct Questions

1. Number of photons emitted per second $= \frac{P}{\frac{hc}{\lambda}}$

Number of photons emitted $= \frac{P}{\left(\frac{hc}{\lambda}\right)} \times t$

$$= \frac{5 \times 10^{-3} \times 632.2 \times 10^{-9} \times 2}{6.63 \times 10^{-34} \times 3 \times 10^8}$$

$$= 3.2 \times 10^{16}$$

2. Number of electrons emitted per unit area per second

$$= \frac{P}{\left(\frac{hc}{\lambda}\right)} \times n = \frac{p\lambda n}{hc}$$

$$= \frac{39.8 \times 5000 \times 10^{-10}}{6.63 \times 10^{-34} \times 3 \times 10^8} \times \frac{1}{100} = 10^{18}$$

3. $i = \frac{P}{\frac{hc}{\lambda}} \times \frac{n}{100} \times e$

$$i = \frac{Pe\lambda n}{100hc}$$

$$\Rightarrow 0.16 \times 10^{-6} = \frac{10^{-3} \times 1.6 \times 10^{-19} \times 5000 \times 10^{-10} n}{100 \times 6.63 \times 10^{-34} \times 3 \times 10^8}$$

$$\Rightarrow n = 0.04\%$$

4. If the frequency is halved, frequency will become less than the threshold frequency. So, no photoelectrons will be emitted.

5. Electron may come out with a kinetic energy less than $h\nu - \phi$ as it may lose energy in internal collisions.

6. $V_s = \frac{1}{e}(hf - W)$

$$V'_s = \frac{1}{e}[h(2f) - W] = \frac{2}{e}(hf - W) + W$$

$$\Rightarrow V'_s = 2V_s + W$$

So, when frequency is doubled, stopping potential will become more than doubled.

7. $\lambda_{\text{Th}} = \frac{hc}{W} = \frac{1240}{4} = 310 \text{ nm}$

8. $K_{max} = eV_s \Rightarrow 4eV = eV_s \Rightarrow V_s = 4 \text{ V}$

9. Electrons emitted have kinetic energy ranging from 0 to K_{max}. So, minimum kinetic energy will be 0.

10. Cut-off voltage is independent of intensity.

11. $V_s = Ed = 4(1) = 4 \text{ V}$

$$W = \frac{hc}{\lambda} - eV_s = \frac{1240}{200} - 4 = 2.2 \text{ eV}$$

12. $E = E_0(\sin\omega_1 t + \sin\omega_2 t)$

$$f_1 = \frac{\omega_1}{2\pi} \text{ and } f_2 = \frac{\omega_2}{2\pi}$$

Maximum kinetic energy will be for higher frequency radiation,

$$E = hf_2 = 6.6\times10^{-34}\times\frac{6.28\times10^{15}}{2\times3.14} = 6.6\times10^{-19}\text{ J}$$

$$K_{max} = hf_2 - W = \frac{6.6\times10^{-19}}{1.6\times10^{-19}} - 1.5 = 2.625\text{ eV}$$

13. $\lambda_{Th} = \dfrac{hc}{W} \quad \Rightarrow \quad \dfrac{\lambda_1}{\lambda_2} = \dfrac{W_2}{W_2}$

$$\Rightarrow \quad \frac{\lambda_1}{5460} = \frac{2.3}{4.5} \quad \Rightarrow \quad \lambda_1 = 2791\text{ Å}$$

14. $\dfrac{hc}{\lambda} = eV_s + W \quad \Rightarrow \quad \dfrac{\lambda_2}{\lambda_1} = \dfrac{eV_{s_1} + W}{eV_{s_2} + W}$

$$\Rightarrow \quad \frac{4500}{4000} = \frac{e(1.3)+W}{e(0.9)+W}$$

$$\Rightarrow \quad W = 2.3\text{ eV}$$

15. $W = \dfrac{hc}{\lambda} - eV_s = \dfrac{1240}{100} - 7.7 = 4.7\text{ eV}$

$$eV_s = \frac{hc}{\lambda} - W \quad \Rightarrow \quad eV_s = \left(\frac{1240}{200} - 4.7\right)\text{eV}$$

$$\Rightarrow \quad V_s = 1.5\text{ V}$$

16. $W = h\nu - K_{max} = 5 - 2 = 3\text{ eV}$

$eV_s = h\nu - W = (6-3)\text{ eV} \quad \Rightarrow \quad V_s = 3\text{ V}$

The potential of anode relative to $C = -3$ V.

17. When light of wavelength 330 nm is used,

$$W = \frac{hc}{\lambda} - eV_s = \frac{1240}{330} - eV_0$$

When light of wavelength 220 nm is used,

$$W = \frac{1240}{220} - e(2V_0)$$

So, $\dfrac{1240}{330} - eV_0 = \dfrac{1240}{220} - e(2V_0)$

$$\Rightarrow \quad V_0 = \frac{62}{33} = 1.878\text{ V}$$

So, V_0 will be nearly $\dfrac{15}{8}$ V.

18. $V = \dfrac{1}{e}\left(\dfrac{hc}{\lambda} - W\right)$

V_1, V_2 and V_3 are in AP

$$\Rightarrow \quad 2V_2 = V_1 + V_3$$

$$\Rightarrow \quad 2\left[\frac{1}{e}\left(\frac{hc}{\lambda_2} - W\right)\right] = \frac{1}{e}\left(\frac{hc}{\lambda_1} - W\right) + \frac{1}{e}\left(\frac{hc}{\lambda_2} - W\right)$$

$$\Rightarrow \quad \frac{2}{\lambda_2} = \frac{1}{\lambda_1} + \frac{1}{\lambda_3}$$

So, λ_1, λ_2 and λ_3 are in HP

19.
$$\frac{hc}{\lambda} = W + e(3V_0) \quad \text{...(i)}$$

$$\frac{hc}{2\lambda} = W + eV_0 \quad \text{...(ii)}$$

Dividing Eq. (i) by (ii), we get

$$eV_0 = W$$

Substituting in Eq. (i),

$$\frac{hc}{\lambda} = W + 3W \quad \Rightarrow \quad W = \frac{hc}{4\lambda}$$

So, $\lambda_{Th} = \dfrac{hc}{W} = \dfrac{hc}{\left(\dfrac{hc}{4\lambda}\right)} = 4\lambda$

20. $K_1 = \dfrac{hc}{\lambda_1} - W = \dfrac{hc}{2\lambda_2} - W = \dfrac{1}{2}\left(\dfrac{hc}{\lambda_2} - W\right) - \dfrac{W}{2}$

$$\Rightarrow \quad K_1 = \frac{K_2}{2} - \frac{W}{2}$$

$$\Rightarrow \quad K_1 < \frac{K_2}{2}$$

21. $K_1 = h\nu_1 - h\nu_0$ and $K_2 = h\nu_2 - h\nu_0$

$$\Rightarrow \quad \frac{K_1}{K_2} = \frac{h(\nu_1 - \nu_0)}{h(\nu_2 - \nu_0)} = \frac{1}{K}$$

$$\Rightarrow \quad \nu_0 = \frac{K\nu_1 - \nu_2}{K - 1}$$

22.
$$\frac{1}{2}mv_1^2 = 2W - W = W \quad \text{...(i)}$$

$$\frac{1}{2}mv_2^2 = 5W - W = 4W \quad \text{...(ii)}$$

Dividing Eq. (i) by Eq. (ii), we get

$$\frac{v_1}{v_2} = \frac{1}{2}$$

23. $\dfrac{1}{2}mv_1^2 = \dfrac{hc}{\lambda_1} - W$ and $\dfrac{1}{2}mv_2^2 = \dfrac{hc}{\lambda_2} - W$

$$\frac{v_1^2}{v_2^2} = \frac{\dfrac{hc}{\lambda_1} - W}{\dfrac{hc}{\lambda_2} - W} \quad \Rightarrow \quad \frac{(2v_2)^2}{v_2^2} = \frac{\dfrac{hc}{\lambda_1} - W}{\dfrac{hc}{\lambda_2} - W}$$

$$\Rightarrow \quad W = \frac{1}{3}\left(\frac{4hc}{\lambda_2} - \frac{hc}{\lambda_1}\right) = 2.49\text{ eV} = 3.9\times10^{-19}\text{ J}$$

24. $\dfrac{1}{2}mv^2 = \dfrac{hc}{\lambda} - W$

When the wavelength is changed to $\dfrac{3\lambda}{4}$,

$$\frac{1}{2}mv'^2 = \frac{hc}{\left(\dfrac{3\lambda}{4}\right)} - W = \frac{4}{3}\left(\frac{hc}{\lambda} - W\right) + \frac{W}{3}$$

$$\Rightarrow \quad \frac{1}{2}mv'^2 = \frac{4}{3}\left(\frac{1}{2}mv^2\right) + \frac{W}{3} \quad \Rightarrow \quad v'^2 > \frac{4}{3}v^2$$

$$\Rightarrow \quad v' > \left(\frac{4}{3}\right)^{1/2} v$$

25. $$K_{max} = hf - W$$

$\Rightarrow$ $$\frac{1}{2}mv_1^2 = hf_1 - W \quad ...(i)$$

and $$\frac{1}{2}mv_2^2 = hf_2 - W \quad ...(ii)$$

Subtracting Eq. (ii) from (i), we get

$$v_1^2 - v_2^2 = \frac{2h}{m}(f_1 - f_2)$$

26. $$\frac{1}{2}mv^2 = \frac{hc}{\lambda_1} - \frac{hc}{\lambda_0} \quad ...(i)$$

$$\frac{1}{2}m(2v)^2 = \frac{hc}{\lambda_2} - \frac{hc}{\lambda_0} \quad ...(ii)$$

Solving Eqs. (i) and (ii), we get

$$\lambda_2 = \frac{\lambda_0\lambda_1}{4\lambda_0 - 3\lambda_1} = 300 \text{ nm}$$

27. $n = \dfrac{IA}{\left(\dfrac{hc}{\lambda}\right)} \times \eta \quad \Rightarrow \quad n \propto \lambda$

$\Rightarrow$ $$\frac{n_A}{n_B} = \frac{\lambda_A}{\lambda_B}$$

28. n = number of photoelectrons emitted in time t

$$n = \frac{P}{\left(\dfrac{hc}{\lambda}\right)} \times \frac{\eta}{100} \times t = \frac{\eta\lambda Pt}{100hc}$$

Potential of sphere $= \dfrac{k[q_0 + n(-e)]}{R} = \dfrac{kq_0}{R} - \dfrac{ke}{R}n$

$$= V - \frac{n\lambda Pet}{400\pi\varepsilon_0 Rhc}$$

29. The photoelectrons are emitted but are reabsorbed by the emitter metal.

30. The photoelectric current depends only on intensity.

31. $K = h\nu - W$

$K' = h(2\nu) - W = 2(h\nu - W) + W$

$\Rightarrow$ $$K' = 2K + W$$

$\Rightarrow$ $$K' > 2K$$

32. $V_0 = \dfrac{h}{e}\nu - \dfrac{W}{e}$

Comparing with $y = mx + c$, we get

Slope $= m = \dfrac{h}{e}$

33. Threshold frequency $= f_0$

$$K_{max} = hf - W = hf_1 - hf_0 = h(f_1 - f_0)$$

34. Threshold frequency $= 5 \times 10^{14}$ Hz

$$\lambda_{Th} = \frac{c}{\nu_{Th}} = \frac{3 \times 10^8}{5 \times 10^{14}} = 6000 \text{ Å}$$

35. From graph, stopping potential = 4 V

$$K_{max} = eV_s = 4 \text{ eV}$$

36. Due to increase in frequency, stopping potential will increase. Due to reduction in intensity, saturation current will decrease. So, graph will be *d*.

37. $V = \dfrac{h}{e}f - \dfrac{W}{e}$

Slope of graph is $\dfrac{h}{e}$, which will be same for both the metals

Y has greater work functon than *X*. So, threshold frequency of *Y* will be greater than *X*.

38. $V = \dfrac{1}{e}\left(\dfrac{hc}{\lambda} - W\right)$

$$V_p = \frac{1}{e}\left(\frac{1240}{350} - 2\right)\text{eV} = 1.54 \text{ V}$$

$$V_q = \frac{1}{e}\left(\frac{1240}{350} - 2.5\right)\text{eV} = 1.04 \text{ V}$$

$$V_r = \frac{1}{e}\left(\frac{1240}{350} - 3\right)\text{eV} = 0.54 \text{ V}$$

So, $$V_p > V_q > V_r$$

39. Equation $E = pc$ is valid only for a photon.

40. $m = \dfrac{m_0}{\sqrt{1 - \dfrac{v^2}{c^2}}}$

For particle, $v = c \quad \Rightarrow \quad m = \infty$

$$\lambda = \frac{h}{mv} = 0 \qquad \because (m = \infty)$$

41. $$p = \frac{h}{\lambda}$$

$\Rightarrow$ $$\frac{\Delta p}{p} \times 100 = \frac{\Delta\lambda}{\lambda} \times 100$$

$\Rightarrow$ $$\frac{p_m}{p} \times 100 = 0.5$$

$\Rightarrow$ $$p = 200\,p_m$$

42. For electron, $\lambda = \sqrt{\dfrac{150}{V}}$ Å $\quad \Rightarrow \quad \lambda = \sqrt{\dfrac{150}{150}} = 1$ Å

43. For photon, $E = \dfrac{hc}{\lambda_p} \quad \Rightarrow \quad \lambda_p = \dfrac{hc}{E}$

For electron, $\lambda_e = \dfrac{h}{\sqrt{2mE}}$

So, $$\frac{\lambda_p}{\lambda_e} = \sqrt{\frac{2mc^2}{E}}$$

44. $K_{max} = \dfrac{hc}{\lambda} - \dfrac{hc}{\lambda_0} = \dfrac{12400}{3000} - \dfrac{12400}{4000} = 1.03$ eV

de-Broglie wavelength for electron,

$$\lambda = \sqrt{\frac{150}{1.03}} = 12.07 \text{ Å}$$

45. $\lambda = \dfrac{h}{\sqrt{2mK}} \quad \Rightarrow \quad \lambda \propto \dfrac{1}{\sqrt{m}} \quad \Rightarrow \quad \dfrac{\lambda_e}{\lambda_p} = \sqrt{\dfrac{m_p}{m_e}}$

46. From linear momentum conservation

$$0 = m_1v_1 + m_2(-v_2) \Rightarrow m_1v_1 = m_2v_2$$

$$\frac{\lambda_1}{\lambda_2} = \frac{h/m_1v_1}{h/m_2v_2} = 1$$

47. $\lambda = \dfrac{h}{\sqrt{2mqV}} \Rightarrow \lambda \propto \dfrac{1}{\sqrt{mq}}$

$$\lambda_p : \lambda_d : \lambda_\alpha = \frac{1}{\sqrt{mq}} : \frac{1}{\sqrt{2mq}} : \frac{1}{\sqrt{4m(2q)}} = 2\sqrt{2} : 2 : 1$$

48. $\lambda = \dfrac{h}{\sqrt{2mqV}} \Rightarrow \dfrac{\lambda_p}{\lambda_\alpha} = \sqrt{\dfrac{m_\alpha q_\alpha V_\alpha}{m_p q_p V_p}}$

$$\Rightarrow \quad 1 = \sqrt{\frac{(4m)(2e)V_\alpha}{m(e)V}} \Rightarrow V_\alpha = \frac{V}{8}$$

49. Kinetic energy of neutron, $E = \dfrac{3}{2}kT$

$$\lambda = \frac{h}{\sqrt{2mE}} = \frac{h}{\sqrt{3mkT}}$$

50. de-Broglie wavelength of an electron $= \dfrac{h}{\sqrt{2mK}}$

$$\Rightarrow \quad 100 \times 10^{-12} = \frac{6.63 \times 10^{-34}}{\sqrt{2 \times 9.1 \times 10^{-31} K_1}}$$

$$\Rightarrow \quad K_1 = 150 \text{ eV}$$

$$\lambda = \frac{h}{\sqrt{2mK}} \Rightarrow \frac{\lambda_1}{\lambda_2} = \sqrt{\frac{K_2}{K_1}}$$

$$\Rightarrow \quad \frac{100}{50} = \sqrt{\frac{K_2}{K_1}} \Rightarrow K_2 = 4K_1$$

Increase in energy $= K_2 - K_1 = 4K_1 - K_1 = 3K_1 = 450$ eV

51. Linear momentum is vector. Two photons having equal wavelength will have same magnitude of linear momenta. But if they are travelling in different directions, then their linear momenta will be different.

52. For hydrogen atom moving with most probable velocity,

$$\lambda_1 = \frac{h}{mv} = \frac{h}{m\sqrt{\frac{2kT}{m}}} = \frac{h}{\sqrt{2mkT}}$$

For He atom moving with rms velocity,

$$\lambda_2 = \frac{h}{mv} = \frac{h}{m\sqrt{\frac{3kT}{m}}} = \frac{h}{\sqrt{3mkT}}$$

$$\frac{\lambda_1}{\lambda_2} = \sqrt{\frac{3}{2}\frac{m_2T_2}{m_1T_1}}$$

$$\Rightarrow \quad \frac{1.26}{\lambda_2} = \sqrt{\frac{3}{2}\frac{(4)\,324}{(1)\,300}} \Rightarrow \lambda_2 = 0.5 \text{ Å}$$

53. $v = u + at$

$$\Rightarrow \quad v = 0 + \left(\frac{eE}{m}\right)t = \frac{eEt}{m}$$

$$\lambda = \frac{h}{mv} = \frac{h}{eEt} \Rightarrow \frac{d\lambda}{dt} = -\frac{h}{eET^2}$$

54. $\mathbf{v}_{cm} = \dfrac{m_1\mathbf{v}_1 + m\mathbf{v}_2}{m+m} = \dfrac{\mathbf{v}_1 + \mathbf{v}_2}{2}$

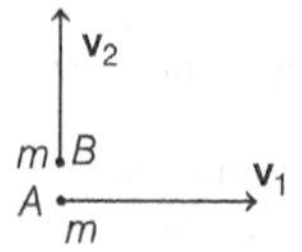

$$\mathbf{v}_{1cm} = \mathbf{v}_1 - \mathbf{v}_{cm} = \mathbf{v}_1 - \frac{\mathbf{v}_1 + \mathbf{v}_2}{2} = \frac{\mathbf{v}_1 - \mathbf{v}_2}{2}$$

$$|\mathbf{v}_{1,cm}| = \frac{1}{2}\sqrt{\mathbf{v}_1^2 + \mathbf{v}_2^2 - 2\mathbf{v}_1\mathbf{v}_2 \cos 90^\circ} = \frac{1}{2}\sqrt{\mathbf{v}_1^2 + \mathbf{v}_2^2}$$

So, required wavelength is

$$\lambda = \frac{h}{m|\mathbf{v}_{1,cm}|} = \frac{2h}{\sqrt{v_1^2 + v_2^2}}$$

$$= \frac{2h}{\sqrt{\left(\frac{h}{\lambda_1}\right)^2 + \left(\frac{h}{\lambda_2}\right)^2}} = \frac{2\lambda_1\lambda_2}{\sqrt{\lambda_1^2 + \lambda_2^2}}$$

55. $K_{particle} = \dfrac{1}{2}mv^2 = \dfrac{1}{2}\left(\dfrac{h}{\lambda v}\right)v^2 = \dfrac{hv}{2\lambda}$

$$\because \left\{\lambda = \frac{h}{mv} \Rightarrow m = \frac{h}{\lambda v}\right\}$$

$$K_{photon} = \frac{hc}{\lambda}$$

$$\frac{K_{particle}}{K_{photon}} = \frac{v}{2c} = \frac{2.25 \times 10^8}{2(3 \times 10^8)} = \frac{3}{8}$$

56.

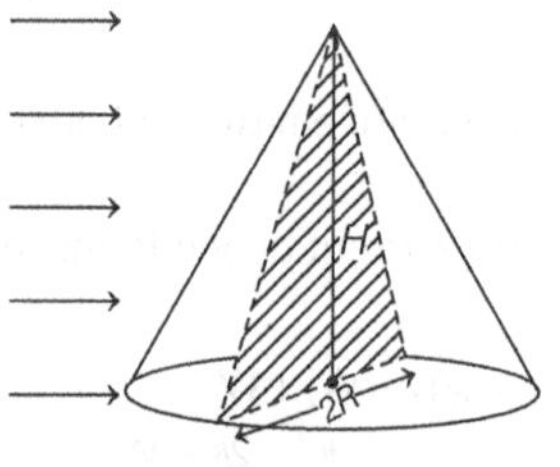

$$A_{projected} = \frac{1}{2}(2R)(H) = RH$$

$$F = \frac{IA_{projected}}{c} = \frac{IRH}{c}$$

57. For normal incidence, $F = \dfrac{2IA}{c}$

When the surface is held at angle θ,

$$F' = \frac{2IA\cos^2\theta}{c} = F\cos^2\theta$$

58. When light of intensity I is incident on A,

$$p_1 = a\left(\frac{I}{c}\right) + r\left(\frac{2I}{c}\right) = (0.5)\frac{I}{c} + (0.5)\left(\frac{2I}{c}\right) = \frac{1.5I}{c}$$

When light reflected by B is incident on A,

$$p_2 = \frac{1.5\,(0.5I)}{c}$$

So, total pressure experienced by A

$$= \frac{1.5I}{c} + \frac{1.5(0.5I)}{c} + \frac{1.5(0.5)^2 I}{c} + \ldots$$

$$= \frac{1.5I}{c}(1 + 0.5 + (0.5)^2 + \ldots \infty)$$

$$= \frac{1.5I}{c}\left(\frac{1}{1-0.5}\right) = \frac{3I}{c}$$

59. $P = \frac{I}{c}(r+1)\cos^2\theta = \frac{I}{c}(0.5+1)\cos^2 45° = \frac{3I}{4c}$

Multiple Choice(s) Correct Questions

1. a,b,c

2. Photoelectric current is independent of frequency of light.
$K_{max} = h\nu - W$, so K_{max} will increase on increasing frequency.
When the reverse voltage is equal to stopping potential, current in the circuit will become zero.

3. For a point source of light,

$$I = \frac{P}{4\pi r^2} \Rightarrow I \propto \frac{1}{r^2}$$

So, when distance is tripled, intensity will become $\frac{1}{9}$ times of original intensity.

$i \propto I \Rightarrow$ Saturation current will also become $\frac{1}{9}$ times

$\Rightarrow \; i = \frac{1}{9}(18\,\text{mA}) = 2\,\text{mA}$

Cut-off voltage is independent of intensity. So, cut-off voltage will be same.

4. Stopping potential is maximum for beam B. So, B has highest frequency and photoelectrons ejected by beam B have the highest kinetic energy and momentum.
Beam C has least stopping potential. So, it has least frequency and longest wavelength.
Saturation current is maximum for beam A. So, it has the highest rate of photoelectric emission.

5. At anode, $K_{max} = 7$ eV, $K_{min} = 5.5$ eV
At cathode, $K_{max} = 7 - 5 = 2$ eV

$$W = h\nu - K_{max} = 4 - 2 = 2\text{ eV}$$

$$K_{min} = 5.5 - 5 = 0.5\text{ eV}$$

Electrons having kinetic energy less than 0.5 eV are still not reaching anode. So, current in the circuit is less than saturation current.

6. (a) $\phi = \frac{hc}{\lambda_{th}}$

$\Rightarrow \quad \phi_1 : \phi_2 : \phi_3 = \frac{1}{\lambda_1} : \frac{1}{\lambda_2} : \frac{1}{\lambda_3} = 1 : 2 : 4$

(b) $V_s = \frac{hc}{e\lambda} - \frac{W}{e}$

$\Rightarrow$ Slope of graph $= \frac{hc}{e}$

$\Rightarrow \quad \tan\theta \propto \frac{1}{e}$

(c) $\lambda_1 : \lambda_2 : \lambda_3 = \frac{1}{0.001} : \frac{1}{0.002} : \frac{1}{0.004} = 4 : 2 : 1$

(d) Slope $= \frac{hc}{e}$, so slope is independent of the nature of material.

7. (a) $W = \frac{hc}{\lambda} - eV_s \quad \Rightarrow \quad W = \frac{1240}{496} - 1.5 = 1$ eV

(b) For fastest electron,

$$\lambda = \sqrt{\frac{150}{V}} = \sqrt{\frac{150}{1.5}} = 10\text{ Å}$$

(c) $R = \frac{\sqrt{2mqV}}{qB} \quad \Rightarrow \quad B = \sqrt{\frac{2mV}{qR^2}} = \sqrt{\frac{2 \times 9.1 \times 10^{-31} \times 1.5}{1.6 \times 10^{-19} \times (1)^2}}$

$$= 4.1 \times 10^{-6}\text{ T}$$

(d) X-rays have wavelength of the order of 1 Å.

So, $E = \frac{hc}{\lambda} = \frac{12400}{1} = 12.4$ keV

8. (a) $I = \frac{W}{4\pi a^2}$, $\quad P = IA = \frac{WS}{4\pi a^2}$

$$n = \frac{IA}{\left(\frac{hc}{\lambda}\right)} = \frac{W\lambda S}{4\pi hca^2}$$

(b) $K_{max} = \frac{hc}{\lambda} - \phi = \frac{hc - \lambda\phi}{\lambda}$

(c) $eV_s = \frac{hc - \lambda\phi}{\lambda} \quad \Rightarrow \quad V_s = \frac{hc - \lambda\phi}{e\lambda}$

(d) $\lambda \le \lambda_{Th} \quad \Rightarrow \quad \lambda \le \frac{hc}{\phi}$

9. (a) The saturation photocurrent is directly proportional to the intensity. So, when intensity is doubled, photocurrent also gets doubled.

(c) $K'_{max} = h(2\nu) - W = 2(h\nu - W) + W = 2K_{max} + W$
So, maximum kinetic energy will be more than doubled.

(d) $K_{max} = eV_s$
So, stopping potential will also become more than doubled.

10. (b, c, d)

11. Speed of the particle entering the magnetic field will not change because work done by magnetic force is zero. So, its wavelength will be λ_2 at any time.
Speed of particle entering electric field may increase, decrease or remain same depending on the direction of electric field.

So, $\quad \lambda_1 = \lambda_2, \lambda_1 < \lambda_2 \quad$ or $\quad \lambda_1 > \lambda_2$

12. For metal A, $W_A + T_A = 4.25$

and $\quad \lambda_A = \frac{h}{\sqrt{2mT_A}}$

For metal B, $W_B + T_B = 4.70$ and $\lambda_B = \dfrac{h}{\sqrt{2mT_B}}$

$$\lambda_B = 2\lambda_A$$

$$\Rightarrow \quad \frac{h}{\sqrt{2mT_B}} = 2\left(\frac{h}{\sqrt{2mT_A}}\right) \quad \Rightarrow \quad T_A = 4T_B$$

$$T_B = T_A - 1.50$$

$$\Rightarrow \quad T_B = 4T_B - 1.50 \quad \Rightarrow \quad T_B = 0.5 \text{ eV}$$

So, $T_A = 4T_B = 2$ eV, $W_A = 4.25 - T_A = 2.25$ eV

$$W_B = 4.70 - T_B = 4.20 \text{ eV}$$

13. (a)
$$F_N = \frac{IA}{c}(r+1)\cos\theta$$
$$= \frac{10 \times 1 \times 10^{-4}}{3 \times 10^8}(1 + 0.5)\cos 60°$$
$$= 2.5 \times 10^{-12} \text{ N}$$

(b)
$$F_T = \frac{IA}{c}(1 - r)\sin\theta$$
$$= \frac{10 \times 1 \times 10^{-4}}{3 \times 10^8}(1 - 0.5)\sin 60°$$
$$= \frac{2.5}{\sqrt{3}} \times 10^{-12} \text{ N}$$

(c) $F_{net} = \sqrt{F_N^2 + F_T^2} = \dfrac{5}{\sqrt{3}} \times 10^{-12}$ N

(d) $\tan\phi = \dfrac{F_T}{F_N} \quad \Rightarrow \quad \tan\phi = \dfrac{1}{\sqrt{3}} \quad \Rightarrow \quad \phi = 30°$

14. (a) Let O be the centre of the sphere and OZ be the line opposite to the incident beam. Consider a radius OP of the sphere making an angle θ with OZ. Rotate this radius about OZ to get a circle on the sphere. Change θ to $\theta + d\theta$ and rotate the radius about OZ to get another circle on the sphere. The part of circle between these circles is a ring of area $2\pi r^2 \sin\theta\, d\theta$. Consider a small part ΔA of this ring at P. Energy of light falling on this part in time Δt is $\Delta E = I\,\Delta t\,(\Delta A \cos\theta)$

The momentum of this light falling on ΔA is $\dfrac{\Delta E}{c}$ along QP. The light is reflected by the sphere along PR.

The change in momentum is
$$\Delta p = 2\frac{\Delta E}{c}\cos\theta = \frac{2}{c} I\,\Delta t\,(\Delta A \cos^2\theta)$$
(direction along **OP**)

The force on ΔA due to the light faling on it, is
$$\frac{\Delta p}{\Delta t} = \frac{2}{c} I\,\Delta A \cos^2\theta \quad \text{(direction along PO)}$$

The resultant force on the ring as well as on the sphere is along ZO by symmetry. The component of the force on ΔA along ZO
$$\frac{\Delta p}{\Delta t}\cos\theta = \frac{2}{c} I\,\Delta A \cos^3\theta \quad \text{(along ZO)}$$

The force acting on the ring is
$$dF = \frac{2}{c} I (2\pi r^2 \sin\theta\, d\theta)\cos^3\theta$$

The force on the entire sphere is
$$F = \int_0^{\pi/2} \frac{4\pi r^2 I}{c}\cos^3\theta \sin\theta\, d\theta = \frac{\pi r^2 I}{c}$$

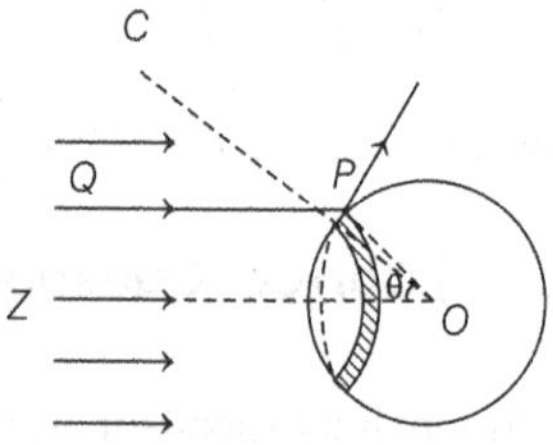

(b) If surface of sphere is completely absorbing,
$$F = \frac{IA_{projected}}{c} = \frac{I\pi r^2}{c}$$

Comprehension Based Questions

1. $I = \dfrac{P}{4\pi d^2}$

$$E = IA\,\Delta t \quad \Rightarrow \quad \Delta t = \frac{E(4\pi d^2)}{P(\pi r^2)}$$
$$= \frac{2.22 \times 1.6 \times 10^{-19} \times 4 \times (1)^2}{0.1 \times (2 \times 10^{-10})^2} = 355 \text{ s}$$

2. $i = \dfrac{IAen\lambda}{hc} = \dfrac{0.1 \times 4 \times 10^{-4} \times 1.6 \times 10^{-19} \times 0.05 \times 2537 \times 10^{-19}}{4\pi(1)^2 \times 6.6 \times 10^{-34} \times 3 \times 10^8}$

$$= 32.5 \text{ nA}$$

3. $V_0 = \dfrac{1}{e}\left(\dfrac{hc}{\lambda} - \phi_0\right) = \dfrac{1}{e}\left(\dfrac{12400}{2537} - 2.22\right)\text{eV} = 2.67 \text{ V}$

4. $K_1 = \dfrac{hc}{\lambda_1} - \dfrac{hc}{\lambda_0}$ and $K_2 = \dfrac{hc}{\lambda_2} - \dfrac{hc}{\lambda_0}$

$$K_2 = 4K_1 \quad \because (v_2 = v_1)$$
$$\Rightarrow \quad \frac{hc}{\lambda_2} - \frac{hc}{\lambda_0} = 4\left(\frac{hc}{\lambda_1} - \frac{hc}{\lambda_0}\right)$$
$$\Rightarrow \quad \lambda_0 = \frac{3\lambda_1\lambda_2}{4\lambda_2 - \lambda_1} = 4125 \text{ Å}$$

5. $i = \dfrac{Pen\lambda}{hc} \quad \Rightarrow \quad \dfrac{i_1}{i_2} = \left(\dfrac{P_1}{P_2}\right)\left(\dfrac{\lambda_1}{\lambda_2}\right)$

$$\Rightarrow \quad \frac{4.8}{i_2} = \frac{1}{5} \times \frac{3000}{1650} \quad \Rightarrow \quad i_2 = 13.2\,\mu\text{A}$$

6. $n_2 = \dfrac{P\lambda}{hc} = \dfrac{5 \times 10^{-3} \times 1650 \times 10^{-10}}{6.6 \times 10^{-34} \times 3 \times 10^8} = 4.16 \times 10^{15}$

7. $\eta = \dfrac{i_2 / e}{n_2} \times 100 = \dfrac{13.2 \times 10^{-6}}{1.6 \times 10^{-19} \times 4.16 \times 10^{15}} \times 100 = 1.97\%$

8.
$$h\nu = W + K_{max}$$
$$\Rightarrow \quad h(8 \times 10^{14}) = W + e(0.5) \quad \text{...(i)}$$
$$\text{and} \quad h(12 \times 10^{14}) = W + e(2) \quad \text{...(ii)}$$

Dividing Eq. (i) by (ii), we get

$$W = 2.5 \text{ eV}$$

9. Substituting value of W in Eq. (i),

$$h = \frac{3 \times 1.6 \times 10^{-19}}{8 \times 10^{14}} = 6.0 \times 10^{-34} \text{ J-s}$$

10. de-Broglie wavelength of an electron,

$$\lambda = \sqrt{\frac{150}{0.5}} \text{ Å} = 17.35 \text{ Å}$$

11. When all switches are open,

$$K_{max} = hf - W$$

$$\Rightarrow \quad -E = 0 - W \quad \Rightarrow \quad W = E$$

12. When only S_1 and S_2 are closed,

$$K_{max} = (hf - W) + eV$$

$$\Rightarrow \quad 0 = 0 - E + eV \quad \Rightarrow \quad eV = E$$

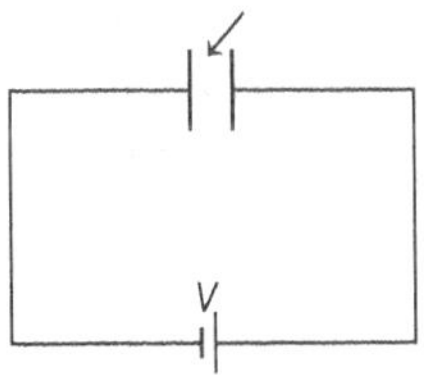

13. When only S_3 and S_4 are closed. Potential difference across each capacitor will be $\frac{V}{2}$.

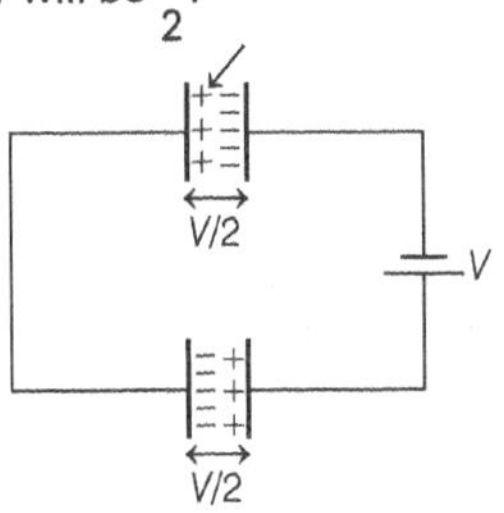

$$K_{max} = (hf - W) + e\left(-\frac{V}{2}\right)$$

$$\Rightarrow \quad 0 = E_1 - E - \frac{E}{2} \quad \Rightarrow \quad E_1 = \frac{3E}{2}$$

14. Photoemission will stop when

$$\lambda = \lambda_{Th}$$

$$\Rightarrow \quad 3000 + 40t = \frac{12400}{2} \quad \Rightarrow \quad t = 80 \text{ s}$$

15. For time interval $(0 \le t \le 80 \text{ s})$

$$\text{Number of electrons emitted} = \int_0^{80} \frac{P}{\left(\frac{hc}{\lambda}\right)} \eta \, dt$$

$$\Rightarrow \quad n_e = \int_0^{80} \frac{100(3000 + 40t)}{12400 \times 1.6 \times 10^{-19} \times 100} dt = 1.85 \times 10^{20}$$

Number of electrons emitted in one hour

$$= \left(\frac{60 \text{ min}}{3 \text{ min}}\right) \times n_e$$

$$= 20 \times 1.85 \times 10^{20} = 3.7 \times 10^{21}$$

16. $$\frac{dN}{dt} = \frac{P}{\left(\frac{hc}{\lambda}\right)} \eta = \frac{P\lambda\eta}{hc} = \frac{P(3000 + 40t)\,\eta}{hc}$$

So, when the signal is switched on, $\frac{dN}{dt}$ *versus* time graph will straight line with +ive slope and +ive y-intercept.

17. Number of photons incident on plate A upto $t = 10$ s

$$= 10^{16} \times 5 \times 10^{-4} \times 10 = 5 \times 10^{13}$$

Number of photoelectrons emitted

$$= 5 \times 10^{13} \times \frac{1}{10^6} = 5 \times 10^7$$

18. Charge on plate A,

$$q_A = (5 \times 10^7)(1.6 \times 10^{-19}) = 8 \times 10^{-12} \text{ C}$$

Charge on plate B,

$$q_B = 33.7 \times 10^{-12} - 8 \times 10^{-12} = 25.7 \times 10^{-12} \text{ C}$$

Electric field between the plates,

$$E = \frac{q_B - q_A}{2A\varepsilon_0} = 2000 \text{ N/C}$$

19. Potential difference between the plates,

$$V = Ed = 2000 \times 1 \times 10^{-2} = 20 \text{ V}$$

$$K_{max} = (h\nu - W) + eV = e(5 - 2) + e(20) = 23 \text{ eV}$$

20. I = Intensity of light source $= \frac{P}{4\pi d^2}$

Energy of one photon $= E = 5$ eV

Number of photoelectrons emitted

$$= \left(\frac{P}{4\pi d^2}\right)\frac{(\pi r^2)}{E} n$$

$$= \frac{3.2 \times 10^{-3}}{4\pi (0.8)^2} \frac{\pi (8 \times 10^{-3})^2}{5 \times 1.6 \times 10^{-19}} \times \left(\frac{1}{10^6}\right)$$

$$= 10^5$$

21. Photoelectrons emission will stop, when potential of the sphere becomes equal to stopping potential

$$eV_s = h\nu - W = 5 - 3 = 2 \text{ eV}$$

Charge on sphere at any time $t = 10^5 \times 1.6 \times 10^{-19} \times t$

$$= 1.6 \times 10^{-14} t$$

$$V = V_s$$

$$\Rightarrow \quad \frac{Kq}{R} = V_s$$

$$\Rightarrow \quad \frac{9 \times 10^9 \times 1.6 \times 10^{-14} t}{8 \times 10^{-3}} = 2$$

$$\Rightarrow \quad t = \frac{1000}{9} = 111.1 \text{ s}$$

22. $K_{max} = h\nu - W = 5 - 3 = 2$ eV

For incident light, $\frac{hc}{\lambda_1} = 5$ eV

$$\Rightarrow \quad \lambda_1 = \frac{hc}{(5 \text{ eV})} = \frac{12400}{5} = 2480 \text{ Å}$$

de-Broglie wavelength of the fastest electron,

$$\lambda_2 = \sqrt{\frac{150}{2}} = 8.67 \text{ Å}$$

$$\therefore \quad \frac{\lambda_1}{\lambda_2} = \frac{2480}{8.67} = 286.04$$

Match The Columns Questions

1. (A) Saturation current $= i = \frac{IA\eta e}{h\nu}$

   So, i depends on frequency, area of plate and intensity of light.

   (B) $V_s = \frac{1}{e}(h\nu - W)$

   Stopping potential depends on frequency and work function.

   (C) $\lambda = \frac{h}{\sqrt{2meV_s}}$

   So, λ depends on frequency and work function.

   (D) $F \propto \frac{IA}{c}$

   Force due to radiation depends on intensity and area of plate.

2. $\lambda = 0.6\lambda_{Th} \Rightarrow f = \frac{1}{0.6} f_{Th} = \frac{5}{3} f_{Th}$

   (A) Saturation photocurrnt $\propto$ intensity. So, when intensity is doubled, saturation photocurrent will also get doubled.

   (B) If wavelength gets doubled, wavelength will become more than the threshold wavelength and photocurrent will fall to zero.

   (C) If intensity is doubled, photocurrent increases. If wavelength is made-half, frequency will get doubled. So, stopping potential will increase.

   (D) If intensity remains the same, saturation photocurrent remains the same.

3. If frequency of incident light is increased, stopping potential and maximum kinetic energy of photoelectrons will increase.

   Saturation current is directly proportion to intensity of light.

   If work functon increase, threshold frequency increases. If frequency becomes less than threshold frequency, photoelectron emission will stop.

4. (A) Just after emission from metal target,

   $$K_{max} = hf - \phi = hf - \frac{hf}{3} = \frac{2hf}{3}$$

   (B) Electrons emitted from metal target have kinetic energy ranging from zero to K_{max}.

   (C) and (D) These electrons travel in vacuum without any accelerating voltage applied. So, their kinetic energy $K, 0 < K \le K_{max}$.

5. (A)-(3), (B)-(4), (C)-(1), (D)-(2)

Numerical Value Questions

1. $I = \frac{Nh\nu}{A\Delta t} = \frac{Nhc}{\lambda A \Delta t} \Rightarrow N = \frac{I\lambda A \Delta t}{hc}$

   Number of photons in 1 mm^3 volume,

   $$N = \frac{90 \times 663 \times 10^{-9} \times (1 \text{ mm}^2) \times \left(\frac{1 \text{ mm}}{c}\right)}{6.63 \times 10^{-34} \times 3 \times 10^8}$$

   $$\Rightarrow \quad N = \frac{90 \times 663 \times 10^{-9} \times 1 \times 10^{-6} \times 1 \times 10^{-3}}{6.63 \times 10^{-34} \times (3 \times 10^8)^2} = 1000$$

2. Number of photoelectrons emitted per second

   $$= 10^{12} \times 2 \times 10^{-4} \times \frac{1}{10^5} = 2000$$

   $n =$ Number of photoelectrons emitted upto $t = 25$ s

   $n = 2000 \times 25 = 5 \times 10^4$

   Charge on plate $= q = ne = 5 \times 10^4 \times 1.6 \times 10^{-19} = 8 \times 10^{-15}$ C

3. $E =$ Energy of one photon $= h\nu$

   $E = W + eV_s = 2\text{eV} + e(5\text{V}) = 7\text{eV}$

   Saturation current $= i = \frac{P\eta e}{E}$

   $$\Rightarrow \quad 10 \times 10^{-6} = P\left(\frac{10^{-3}}{100}\right)\frac{e}{(7\text{eV})}$$

   $$\Rightarrow \quad P = 7 \text{ W}$$

4. $E = \frac{hc}{\lambda} = \frac{1245}{83} = 15$ eV

   $$W = \frac{hc}{\lambda_{Th}} = \frac{1245}{332} = 3.75 \text{ eV}$$

   $$K_{max} = E - W = 15 - 3.75 = 11.25 \text{ eV}$$

   $$K_{max} = eV_s \Rightarrow 11.25\text{eV} = eV_s$$

   $$\Rightarrow \quad V_s = 11.25 \text{ V}$$

   $$V_s = Ed \Rightarrow 11.25 = 750d \Rightarrow d = 15 \text{ mm}$$

5. $K_{max} = \frac{hc}{\lambda} - W = \frac{1240}{400} - 1.9 = 1.2$ eV

   Electrons emitted from cesium surface have kinetic energy ranging from 0 to 1.2 eV.

   Electric field due to large metal plate

   $$= \frac{\sigma}{\varepsilon_0} = \frac{1 \times 10^{-9}}{8.85 \times 10^{-12}} = 113 \text{ V/m}$$

   $$V = Ed = 113 \times 0.2 = 22.6 \text{ V}$$

   Maximum KE of electron reaching the plate,

   $$K_1 = 1.2 + 22.6 = 23.8 \text{ eV}$$

   Minimum KE of electron reaching the plate,

   $$K_2 = 0 + 22.6 = 22.6 \text{ eV}$$

   $$\therefore \quad K = \left[\frac{K_1}{K_2}\right] = \left[\frac{23.8}{22.6}\right] = 1$$

6. When electrons emitted by plate 1 reach plate 2,

   $$K_{max} = \left(\frac{hc}{\lambda} - \phi_1\right) - eV_0$$

$$\Rightarrow \quad 1 = \frac{hc}{\lambda} - 1.5 - V_0 \quad ...(i)$$

When electrons emitted by plate 2 reach plate 1,

$$K_{max} = \left(\frac{hc}{\lambda} - \phi_2\right) + eV_0$$

$$\Rightarrow \quad 3 = \frac{hc}{\lambda} - 0.7 + V_0 \quad ...(ii)$$

Solving Eqs. (i) and (ii), we get

$$\frac{hc}{\lambda} = 3.1 \quad \Rightarrow \quad \lambda = \frac{1240}{3.1} = 400 \text{ nm}$$

7. Fastest photoelectron will correspond to wavelength of 400 nm

$$K_{max} = \frac{hc}{\lambda} - W = \frac{1240}{400} - 2.39 = 0.71 \text{ eV}$$

For the fastest electron emitted perpendicular to plate not to reach the collector plate,

$$r \le d$$

$$\Rightarrow \quad \frac{mv}{qB} \le d \quad \Rightarrow \quad \frac{\sqrt{2mK}}{qB} \le d \quad \Rightarrow \quad B_{min} = \frac{\sqrt{2mK}}{qd}$$

$$\Rightarrow \quad B_{min} = \frac{\sqrt{2 \times 9.1 \times 10^{-31} \times 0.71 \times 1.6 \times 10^{-19}}}{1.6 \times 10^{-19} \times 0.1}$$

$$= 28.5 \times 10^{-6} \text{ T}$$

8. $E = \frac{hc}{\lambda} = \frac{1240}{400} = 3.1 \text{ eV}$

Energy of electron after n collision $= E(0.9)^n$

Electron will be unable to come out of metal if

$$E(0.9)^n < 2.2$$

$$\Rightarrow \quad (0.9)^n < \left(\frac{2.2}{3.1}\right) \quad \Rightarrow \quad n > \frac{\log\left(\frac{22}{31}\right)}{\log (0.9)}$$

$$\Rightarrow \quad n > 3.25 \quad \Rightarrow \quad n_{min} = 4$$

9. $\frac{dn}{dt} = \frac{P}{\left(\frac{hc}{\lambda}\right)} \times n = \frac{6.63 \times 10^{-6} \times 300 \times 10^{-9}}{6.63 \times 10^{-34} \times 3 \times 10^{8}} \times \frac{10}{100} = 10^{12}$

$$K_{max} = \frac{hc}{\lambda} - h\nu_{th}$$

$$= \frac{6.63 \times 10^{-34} \times 3 \times 10^{8}}{300 \times 10^{-9}} - 6.63 \times 10^{-34} \times 6 \times 10^{14}$$

$$= 26.52 \times 10^{-20} \text{ J}$$

$$P = \left(\frac{dn}{dt}\right)\left(\frac{5}{6}K_{max}\right) = 10^{12} \times \frac{5}{6} \times 26.52 \times 10^{-20}$$

$$= 221 \times 10^{-9} \text{ W}$$

10. $E_1 = \frac{hc}{\lambda_1} = \frac{1242}{12.42} = 100 \text{ eV}$

$$E_2 = \frac{hc}{\lambda_2} = \frac{1242}{6.21} = 200 \text{ eV}$$

$$E_3 = \frac{hc}{\lambda_3} = \frac{1242}{24.84} = 50 \text{ eV}$$

λ_3 can't emit photoelectrons as $E_3 < W$.

$n =$ Number of photoelectrons emitted per second $= \frac{P}{e}\eta$

Number of electrons emitted in t time $= \frac{P\eta t}{E}$

$Q =$ Charge developed on sphere $= \frac{P\eta te}{E_1} + \frac{P\eta te}{E_2}$

$$= p\eta te\left[\frac{1}{E_1} + \frac{1}{E_2}\right]$$

$$\Rightarrow \quad Q = \frac{1 \times 10^{-3} \times \left(\frac{50}{100}\right) \times 8 \times 1.6 \times 10^{-19}}{1.6 \times 10^{-19}}\left[\frac{1}{100} + \frac{1}{200}\right]$$

$$= 6 \times 10^{-5} \text{ C}$$

Potential of sphere $= \frac{KQ}{r} = \frac{9 \times 10^{9} \times 6 \times 10^{-5}}{1 \times 10^{-3}} = 5.4 \times 10^{8}$ V

Current $= \frac{V}{R} = \frac{5.4 \times 10^{8}}{6.75 \times 10^{6}} = 80$ A

11. $\lambda =$ de-Broglie wavelength $= \frac{h}{\sqrt{3mkT}}$

$$= \frac{6.60 \times 10^{-34}}{\sqrt{3 \times 1.69 \times 10^{-27} \times 1.44 \times 10^{-23} \times 300}}$$

$$= \frac{6.6}{46.8} \times 10^{-9} \text{ m}$$

$$\therefore \quad 156\lambda = 156\left(\frac{6.6}{46.8}\right) = 22$$

12. Force on the mirror due to radiation $= \frac{2P}{c}$

For equilibrium of mirror,

$$F = mg \quad \Rightarrow \quad \frac{2}{c}(0.3P) = 20 \times 10^{-3} \times 10$$

$$\Rightarrow \quad P = \frac{20 \times 10^{-3} \times 10 \times 3 \times 10^{8}}{2 \times 0.3} = 10^{8} \text{ W}$$

13. $F_N = a\left[\frac{I(A\cos\theta)}{\frac{hc}{\lambda}}\right]\left(\frac{h}{\lambda}\cos\theta\right) + r\left[\frac{I(A\cos\theta)}{\frac{hc}{\lambda}}\right]\left(\frac{2h}{\lambda}\cos\theta\right)$

$$\Rightarrow \quad F_N = (1 + r)\frac{IA}{c}\cos^2\theta$$

Pressure $= \frac{F_N}{A} = (1 + r)\frac{I}{c}\cos^2\theta = (1 + 0.5)\frac{I}{c}\cos^2 60° = \frac{3I}{8c}$

So, $n = 8$

14. Number of photons striking per second $= N = \frac{IA}{h\nu}$

Consider a ring of radius x and width dx on the disc. Intensity on the ring due to source is

$$I = \frac{P}{4\pi r^2}$$

$$dA = 2\pi x \, dx$$

$$dA_{\perp} = (2\pi x\, dx)\cos\theta$$

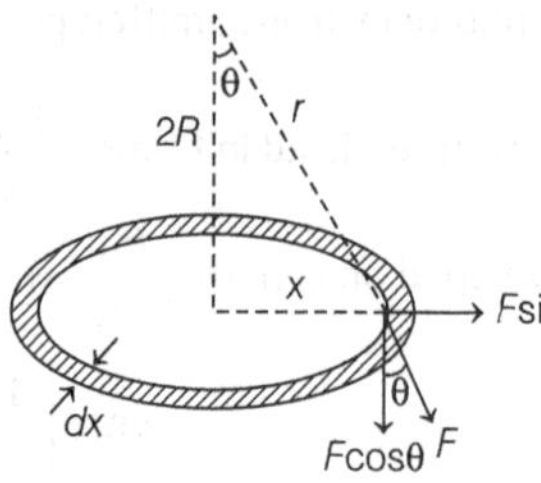

On a ring, only $F\cos\theta$ component will remain and $F\sin\theta$ will cancel out

$$\int dF = \int \left(\frac{IdA_{\perp}}{h\nu}\right)\left(\frac{h}{\lambda}\right)\cos\theta$$

$$\Rightarrow \quad F = \int_0^R \left[\frac{P}{4\pi(4R^2+x^2)}\right]\left[\frac{2\pi x\, dx\cos\theta}{\left(\frac{hc}{\lambda}\right)}\right]\left(\frac{h}{\lambda}\right)\cos\theta$$

$$\Rightarrow \quad F = \frac{P}{20c}$$

So, $n = 20$

Previous Year's Questions

JEE Main

1.

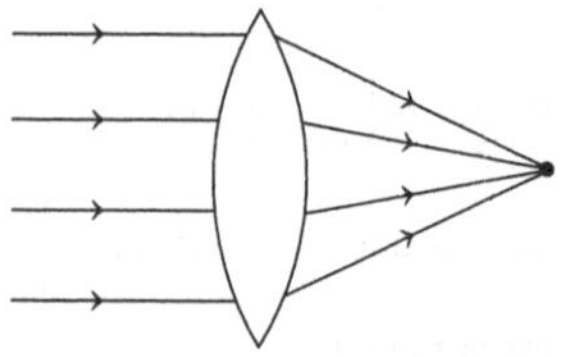

Intensity of image formed by lens does not depends on focal length of lens.

It only depends on diameter of lens.

As intensity remains same in both cases, so there is no change in photo current.

2. Given, work function

$$\phi = 6.68\text{ eV} = 6.68\times 1.6\times 10^{-19}\text{ V}$$

Work function

$$\phi = h\nu_0$$

$$\nu_0 = \frac{\phi}{h} = \frac{6.68\times 1.6\times 10^{-19}}{6.62\times 10^{-34}}$$

$$\nu_0 = 1.6\times 10^{15}\text{Hz}$$

3. For photon,

$$E_P = \frac{hc}{\lambda_P} \Rightarrow \lambda_P = \frac{hc}{E_p}$$

For electron,

$$\lambda_e = \frac{h}{m_e v_e} = \frac{hv_e}{2K_e}$$

$$v_e = 0.25c$$

$$\lambda_e = \frac{h\times 0.25c}{2K_e} = \frac{hc}{8K_e}$$

$$\lambda_P = \lambda_e$$

$$\frac{hc}{E_P} = \frac{hc}{8K_e} \Rightarrow \frac{K_e}{E_P} = \frac{1}{8}$$

4. In photoemission;

Intensity $\propto$ photocurrent

Maximum KE of emitted electrons depends on frequency of incident light.

Photoemission is possible only when frequency is greater than threshold frequency.

So statements A and C are correct.

5. Given, $\phi_A = 9$ eV, $\phi_B = 4.5$ eV

Threshold wavelength of metal surface, A

$$\lambda_A = \frac{1242}{\phi_A}\text{ nm} = \frac{1242}{9}\text{ nm}$$

Similarly, $\lambda_B = \dfrac{1242}{4.5}$

$$\lambda_B - \lambda_A = \frac{1240}{4.5} - \frac{1240}{9} = 275.55 - 137.77$$

$$= 137.78 \simeq 138\text{ nm}$$

6. Given, $E = \text{KE} + \phi_0$

Now, $\dfrac{hc}{\lambda} = eV_0 + \phi_0$ ... (i)

and $\dfrac{hc}{2\lambda} = \dfrac{eV_0}{4} + \phi_0$ ...(ii)

Eq. (ii) $\times$ 4

$$\frac{hc}{2\lambda}\times 4 = \left(\frac{eV_0}{4} + \phi_0\right)\times 4$$

$$\frac{2hc}{\lambda} = eV_0 + 4\phi_0$$

Putting value of $eV_0 = \dfrac{hc}{\lambda} - \phi_0$

$$\frac{2hc}{\lambda} = \frac{hc}{\lambda} - \phi + 4\phi_0$$

$$\frac{2hc}{\lambda} - \frac{hc}{\lambda} = 3\phi_0$$

$$\frac{hc}{\lambda} = 3\phi_0 \Rightarrow \frac{hc}{\lambda} = \frac{3hc}{\lambda_0}\left[\phi = \frac{hc}{\lambda_0}\right]$$

$$\frac{1}{\lambda} = \frac{3}{\lambda_0} \Rightarrow \lambda_0 = 3\lambda$$

Option (a) is correct.

7. Using $\text{KE}_{max} = eV_s = hf - \phi_0$

where, ϕ_0 = work function

V_s = Stopping potential

f = frequency

$$V_s = \frac{h}{e}f - \frac{\phi_0}{e}$$

Therefore, the slope m will be same for all graphs and will be independent of ϕ_0.

8. From Einstein's photoelectric equation,
we have, $eV_0 = h\nu - \phi$

$\Rightarrow \quad 0 = h\nu - \phi$

$\Rightarrow \quad \phi = h\nu = 6.6\times10^{-34}\times5\times10^{14} = 33\times10^{-20}$ J

$$= \frac{33\times10^{-20}}{1.6\times10^{-19}}\text{ eV} = 2.07\text{ eV}$$

9. Statement I correct (true) but Statement II is false.
⇒ Microwaves, infrared rays and ultraviolet rays.
Ultraviolet rays are the most effective for the emission of electron from metallic surface.

Option (d) is correct.

Explanation UV rays have maximum frequency hence are most effective for emission of electrons from the metallic surface.

$$KE_{max} = hf - hf_0$$

Thus, $KE_{max} \propto f$

10. $$E = E_1 - E_2 = hc\left(\frac{1}{\lambda_1} - \frac{1}{\lambda_2}\right)$$

$$E = 6.6\times10^{-34}\times3\times10^8\times10^9\left(\frac{1}{500} - \frac{1}{600}\right)$$

$$= 6.6\times10^{-20}\text{J} = 4.125\times10^{-1}\text{ eV}$$

$$= 4125\times10^{-4}\text{ eV}$$

11. Energy corresponding to incident radiation,

$$E = \frac{hc}{\lambda} = \frac{1240}{\lambda(\text{in nm})} = \frac{1240}{350}$$

$$E = 3.54\text{ eV}$$

Work function for metal-A,

$$\phi_A = 4.8\text{ eV}$$

and for metal-B, $\phi_B = 2.2$ eV

If energy of incident radiation is greater than work function of metal then photoelectron will emit. For metal-B, $E > \phi_B$ and for metal-A, $E < \phi_A$.

So, metal-A will not emit photoelectron but metal-B will emit.

12. According to de-broglie, momentum $p = \frac{h}{\lambda}$;

where h is planck's constant
and λ = wavelength

$$p = \sqrt{2mKE}$$

Now, $\lambda = \frac{h}{p} = \frac{h}{\sqrt{2m\,KE}}$

$$\lambda_e = \frac{h}{\sqrt{2m_eKE_e}} = \frac{h}{\sqrt{2m_e\times4K}} = \frac{h}{\sqrt{8m_eK}}$$

$$\lambda_p = \frac{h}{\sqrt{2m_pKE_p}}\frac{h}{\sqrt{2m_pK}}$$

$$\lambda_\alpha = \frac{h}{\sqrt{2m_\alpha KE_\alpha}} = \frac{h}{\sqrt{2m_\alpha\cdot2K}}$$

$$= \frac{h}{\sqrt{2\times4m_p\times2K}} = \frac{h}{\sqrt{16m_pK}}$$

Form above $\lambda_\alpha < \lambda_p < \lambda_e$

Option (b) is correct.

13. de-Broglie wavelength in given by

$$\lambda = \frac{h}{mv} = \frac{h}{\sqrt{2mq\Delta v}}$$

According to question,

$$\frac{\lambda_\alpha}{\lambda_p} = \sqrt{\frac{m_pv_pq_p}{m_\alpha v_\alpha q_\alpha}}$$

$$\Rightarrow \quad \frac{\lambda_\alpha}{\lambda_p} = \sqrt{\frac{1\times2\times1}{4\times4\times2}} = \frac{1}{4}$$

$$\Rightarrow \quad \lambda_p : \lambda_\alpha = 4:1$$

14. de-Broglie wavelength of electron in terms of kinetic energy K,

$$\lambda = \frac{h}{\sqrt{2mK}} \quad\Rightarrow\quad \lambda \propto \frac{1}{\sqrt{K}}$$

$$\therefore \quad \frac{\lambda_1}{\lambda_2} = \sqrt{\frac{K_2}{K_1}}$$

If $K_2 = \frac{E}{4}$ and $K_1 = E$ (Given in question)

$$\therefore \quad \frac{\lambda_1}{\lambda_2} = \sqrt{\frac{E/4}{E}} = \left(\frac{1}{4}\right)^{1/2} = \frac{1}{2}$$

or $\quad \lambda_2 = 2\lambda_1$

15. Davisson and Germer experiment is based on diffraction and it explain the wave nature of electron.

16. By the photoelectric equation,
Incident photon energy = Work function + Kinetic energy

$$\Rightarrow \quad \frac{hc}{\lambda} = \phi + E \quad \text{... (i)}$$

Now, when E is doubled,

$$\therefore \quad \frac{hc}{\lambda'} = \phi + 2E \quad \text{...(ii)}$$

Now, subtracting Eq. (i) from Eq. (ii),

Then, $\quad E = \frac{hc}{\lambda'} - \frac{hc}{\lambda}$

$$\Rightarrow \quad E = hc\left[\frac{1}{\lambda'} - \frac{1}{\lambda}\right]$$

$$\Rightarrow \quad \frac{E}{hc} = \frac{1}{\lambda'} - \frac{1}{\lambda}$$

$$\Rightarrow \quad \frac{1}{\lambda'} = \frac{E}{hc} + \frac{1}{\lambda} \quad\Rightarrow\quad \frac{1}{\lambda'} = \frac{E\lambda + hc}{hc\,\lambda}$$

$$\Rightarrow \quad \lambda' = \frac{hc\lambda}{E\lambda + hc}$$

17. Using Einstein's photoelectric equation,

$\frac{hc}{\lambda} = K_{max} + \phi_0$, we have,

$$\frac{hc}{800} = K + \phi_0 \quad \text{...(i)}$$

and $$\frac{hc}{500} = 2K + \phi_0 \quad \text{...(ii)}$$

Multiplying Eq. (i) by 2 and subtracting from Eq. (ii), we get

$$\frac{hc}{500}-\frac{2\times hc}{800}=(2K+\phi_0)-2(K+\phi_0)$$

$$\Rightarrow \quad \frac{hc}{100}\left(\frac{1}{5}-\frac{1}{4}\right)=-\phi_0$$

or $$-\phi_0=\frac{1230\text{ eV - nm}}{100\text{ nm}}\left(\frac{4-5}{5\times 4}\right)$$

$$\Rightarrow \quad \phi_0=0.615\text{ eV}$$

18. Given, $h=4.14\times 10^{-15}$ eV

$$=4.14\times 10^{-15}\times 1.6\times 10^{-19}\text{ J-s}$$
$$=6.624\times 10^{-34}\text{ J-s}$$

incident electric field,

$$E=200\,[\sin(6\times 10^{15})t+\sin(9\times 10^{15})t]\text{ Vm}^{-1}$$

So, $\omega_{max}=9\times 10^{15}$ rad/s

Frequency of largest energy photon,

$$f=\frac{\omega_{max}}{2\pi}=\frac{9\times 10^{15}}{2\pi}\text{ Hz}$$

Using Einstein's photoelectric equation, we have

$$K_{max}=hf-\phi_0$$
$$=\frac{6.624\times 10^{-34}\times 9\times 10^{15}}{2\pi\times 1.6\times 10^{-19}}-2.5$$
$$=5.93\times 10^{-34+15+19}-2.5$$
$$=5.93-2.5$$
$$=3.43\text{ eV}\simeq 3.42\text{ eV}$$

19. By Einstein's photoelectric equation, we have

$$K_{max}=\frac{hc}{\lambda}-\phi_0$$

So, in given situation,

$$K_1=\frac{hc}{\lambda_1}-\phi_0 \quad \text{...(i)}$$

and $$K_2=\frac{hc}{\lambda_2}-\phi_0 \quad \text{...(ii)}$$

Given $\lambda_1=3\lambda_2$, so from Eq. (i), We have

$$K_1=\frac{hc}{3\lambda_2}-\phi_0 \quad \text{...(iii)}$$

Multiply Eq. (iii) by 3 and subtracting from Eq. (ii), we get

$$K_2-3K_1=\left(\frac{hc}{\lambda_2}-\phi_0\right)-3\left(\frac{hc}{3\lambda_2}-\phi_0\right)$$

$$\Rightarrow \quad K_2-3K_1=2\phi_0 \quad \Rightarrow \quad 3K_1=K_2-2\phi_0$$

$$\Rightarrow \quad 3K_1<K_2 \quad \text{or} \quad K_1<K_2/3$$

20. Radius of circular path, $R=\frac{mv}{Bq} \Rightarrow v=\frac{RBq}{m}$

Kinetic energy of electron,

$$K=\frac{1}{2}mv^2=\frac{1}{2}m\left(\frac{RBq}{m}\right)^2$$
$$=\frac{1}{2}m\frac{R^2B^2q^2}{m^2}=\frac{R^2B^2q^2}{2m}$$
$$=\frac{(2\times 10^{-3})^2\times(2\times 10^{-3})^2(1.6\times 10^{-19})^2}{2\times 9.1\times 10^{-31}}$$

$$=2.25\times 10^{-19}\text{ J}=\frac{2.25\times 10^{-19}}{1.6\times 10^{-19}}\text{ eV}=1.4\text{ eV}$$

Energy of radiation,

$$E=\frac{hc}{\lambda}=\frac{6.62\times 10^{-34}\times 3\times 10^8}{4.5\times 10^{-7}}\text{ J}$$
$$=\frac{6.62\times 10^{-34}\times 3\times 10^8}{4.5\times 10^{-7}\times 1.6\times 10^{-19}}\text{ eV}$$
$$=2.76\text{ eV}$$

$\therefore$ Work function, $\phi=E-K=2.76-1.4=1.36$ eV

21. According to Einsteins's photoelectric equation,

$$\frac{1}{2}mv^2=E_{photon}-\phi,$$

For the first photon having energy $E_1=3.8$ eV,

$$\frac{1}{2}mv_1^2=E_1-\phi \quad \Rightarrow \quad \frac{1}{2}mv_1^2=3.8-0.6$$

$$\frac{1}{2}mv_1^2=3.2\text{ eV} \quad \text{...(i)}$$

Similarly, for the second photon,

$$E_2=1.4\text{ eV}$$

$$\therefore \quad \frac{1}{2}mv_2^2=E_2-\phi=1.4-0.6$$

$$\Rightarrow \quad \frac{1}{2}mv_2^2=0.8\text{ eV} \quad \text{...(ii)}$$

Dividing Eq. (i) by Eq. (ii), we get

$$\frac{\frac{1}{2}mv_1^2}{\frac{1}{2}mv_2^2}=\frac{3.2}{0.8} \quad \Rightarrow \quad \left(\frac{v_1}{v_2}\right)^2=(2)^2$$

$$\Rightarrow \quad \frac{v_1}{v_2}=\frac{2}{1} \quad \text{or} \quad v_1:v_2=2:1$$

22. According to Einstein's equation,

$$K_{max}=E-\phi, \quad \Rightarrow \quad \frac{1}{2}mv_{max}^2=hv-\phi \quad \text{...(i)}$$

Clearly, from above equation, v_{max}^2 varies linearly with v.

Threshold wavelength depends upon the work function and hence, nature of material.

23. According to Einstein's equation,

$$KE_{max}=hv-\phi,\ hv=KE_{max}+\phi$$

For 1st metal, $hv=5\phi$

Therefore, $5\phi=KE_1+\phi \quad \Rightarrow \quad KE_1=4\phi$ ... (i)

For IInd metal, $10\phi=KE_2+\phi$

$\Rightarrow \quad KE_2=9\phi$ ... (ii)

From Eqs. (i) and (ii), we get

$$\Rightarrow \quad \frac{KE_1}{KE_2}=\frac{4\phi}{9\phi} \quad \Rightarrow \quad \frac{\frac{1}{2}mv_1^2}{\frac{1}{2}mv_2^2}=\frac{4}{9}$$

$$\Rightarrow \quad \frac{v_1^2}{v_2^2}=\frac{4}{9};\ v_1:v_2=2:3$$

24. We know that

$$K_{max}=\frac{hc}{\lambda}-\phi_0$$

$\therefore \quad K_1 = \frac{hc}{\lambda_1} - \phi = \frac{hc}{3\lambda_2} - \phi$ ... (i)

and $\quad K_2 = \frac{hc}{\lambda_2} - \phi$ ... (ii)

From Eqs. (i) and (ii), we get

$$3K_1 = K_2 - 2\phi$$

Hence, $\quad K_1 < \frac{K_2}{3}$

25. The minimum energy required to eject electrons from a metal surface, must be equal to the work function of that metal. Thus, according to Einstein's photoelectric equation, kinetic energy of the emitted electrons is $KE = h\upsilon - \phi_0$

If $h\upsilon = \phi_0$, then KE = 0

26. Given, wavelength of parallel beam of light,

$$\lambda = 900 \text{ nm} = 9 \times 10^{-7} \text{ m}$$

Intensity of incident radiation,

$$I = 100 \text{ Wm}^{-2}$$

Area of surface, $A = 1 \text{ cm}^2 = 10^{-4} \text{m}^2$

$\therefore$ The energy of each photon,

$$E_1 = \frac{hc}{\lambda} = \frac{6.63 \times 10^{-34} \times 3 \times 10^8}{9 \times 10^{-7}} = 2.21 \times 10^{-19} \text{ J}$$

We know that, intensity of light wave,

$$I = \frac{P}{A}$$

$\Rightarrow \quad P = IA = 100 \times 10^{-4} = 10^{-2} \text{ W} = 10^{-2} \text{ J/s}$

$\therefore$ Total energy of light beam in one second, $E = P \times t$

$$= 10^{-2} \times 1 = 10^{-2} \text{ J}$$

$$\text{Number of photons} = \frac{\text{Total energy } (E)}{\text{Energy of one photon } (E_1)}$$

$$= \frac{10^{-2}}{2.21 \times 10^{-19}} = 4.5 \times 10^{16}$$

27. De-Broglie wavelength, $\lambda = \frac{h}{\sqrt{2mK}}$

For the same kinetic energy, $\lambda \propto \frac{1}{\sqrt{m}}$

$\therefore \quad \frac{\lambda_\alpha}{\lambda_c} = \sqrt{\frac{m_c}{m_\alpha}} = \sqrt{\frac{12}{4}} = \frac{\sqrt{3}}{1}$ or $\sqrt{3} : 1$

JEE Advanced

1. $\frac{hc}{\lambda} = \phi + 6$ (ϕ = work function) ...(i)

$$\frac{hc}{4\lambda} = \phi + 0.6 \quad \text{...(ii)}$$

Subtracting Eq. (i) from Eq. (ii),

$$\frac{3hc}{4\lambda} = 5.4 \text{ eV}$$

$\therefore \quad \phi = 1.2 \text{ eV}$

$\Rightarrow \quad \lambda = \frac{3}{4} \times \frac{6.63 \times 10^{-24} \times 3 \times 10^8}{5.4 \times 1.6 \times 10^{-19}} = 1.72 \times 10^{-7}$ m

2. For P and Q

$$E_1 - 4 = E_P \Rightarrow E_1 - 4.5 = E_Q$$

$$E_P = 2E_Q \Rightarrow E_1 - 4 = 2(E_1 - 4.5)$$

$$E_1 = 5 \text{ eV} \Rightarrow E_P = 1 \text{ eV}, E_Q = E_R = 0.5 \text{ eV}$$

For $\quad E_2 - 5.5 = 0.5 \Rightarrow E_2 = 6$ eV

3. $\therefore$ Power = nhf

(where, n = number of photons incident per second)

Since, KE = 0, hf = work-funcition W

$$200 = nW = n[6.25 \times 1.6 \times 10^{-19}]$$

$\Rightarrow \quad n = \frac{200}{1.6 \times 10^{-19} \times 6.25}$

As photon is just above threshold frequency KE_{max} is zero and they are accelerated by potential difference of 500 V.

$\therefore \quad KE_f = q\Delta V$

$$\frac{P^2}{2m} = q\Delta V \Rightarrow P = \sqrt{2mq\Delta V}$$

Since, efficiency is 100%, number of electrons emitted per second = number of photons incident per second.

As, photon is completely absorbed, force exerted

$= n(mV) = nP = n\sqrt{2mq\Delta V}$

$= \frac{200}{6.25 \times 1.6 \times 10^{-19}} \times \sqrt{2(9 \times 10^{-31}) \times 1.6 \times 10^{-19} \times 500} = 24$

4. $$\frac{hc}{\lambda} - \phi = eV_0$$

$$\frac{hc}{0.3 \times 10^{-6}} - \phi = 2e \quad \text{...(i)}$$

Similarly, $\quad \frac{hc}{0.4 \times 10^{-6}} - \phi = 1e$ ...(ii)

Subtracting Eq. (ii) from Eq. (i)

$$hc\left(\frac{1}{0.3} - \frac{1}{0.4}\right)10^6 = e$$

$\Rightarrow \quad hc\left(\frac{0.1}{0.12} \times 10^6\right) = e$

$$h = 0.64 \times 10^{-33} = 6.4 \times 10^{-34} \text{ J - s}$$

5. $eV_0 = \frac{hc}{\lambda} - W \Rightarrow V_0 = \left(\frac{hc}{e}\right)\left(\frac{1}{\lambda}\right) - \frac{W}{e}$

V_0 *versus* $\frac{1}{\lambda}$ graph is in the form $y = mx - c$

Therefore option (c) is correct.

Clearly, V_0 *versus* λ graph is not a straight line but V_0 decreases with increase in λ and V_0 becomes zero when $\frac{hc}{\lambda} = W$.

i.e. $\quad \lambda = \lambda_0 \quad$ (Threshold wavelength)

$\therefore$ Option (a) is also correct.

CHAPTER~08

ATOMS

LEVEL 01 Starter Level

8.1 Rutherford's Model

1 An α-particle of energy 5 MeV is scattered through 180° by a fixed uranium nucleus. What will be the distance of closest approach?

2 In Rutherford scattering experiment, what will be the correct angle for α scattering for an impact parameter $b = 0$?

3 In Rutherford scattering experiment, the number of α-particles scattered at 60° is 5×10^6. What will be the number of α-particles scattered at 120°?

8.2 Bohr's Model

1 If the radius of second Bohr orbit of hydrogen atom is r, then find the radius of the fourth Bohr orbit in Li^{2+}.

2 If an orbital electron of the hydrogen atom jumps from the ground state to higher energy state, its orbital speed reduces to half its initial value. If the radius of the electron orbit in the ground state is r, then find the radius of the new orbit.

3 In Bohr's model of hydrogen atom, what is the ratio of time periods of revolution of an electron corresponding to first excited state and ground state?

4 Calculate the value of acceleration of the electron in the first Bohr orbit in hydrogen atom (where, a_0 = Bohr radius, m = mass of an electron and $\hbar = \frac{h}{2\pi}$).

5 What is the angular momentum of an electron in Bohr's hydrogen atom whose potential energy is –6.8 eV?

6 The ionisation potential of a hydrogen like atom is 122.4 V. Find the value of its first excitation potential.

7 What is the binding energy of the electron in the first excited state of He^+?

8 A single electron orbits around a stationary nucleus of charge $+Ze$, where Z is a constant and e is the magnitude of electronic charge. It requires 47.2 eV to excite the electron from the second to the third Bohr orbit. Find

(i) the value of Z,

(ii) the energy required to excite the electron from the third to the fourth Bohr orbit,

(iii) the kinetic energy, potential energy and the angular momentum of the electron in the first Bohr orbit

9 In a hydrogen like atom, energy required to excite the electron from its first excited state to second excited state is 7.55 eV. Find the ionisation energy of the hydrogen like atom.

10 Find the kinetic energy, potential energy and total energy in the first and second orbit of hydrogen atom, if potential energy in first orbit is taken to be zero.

11 A small particle of mass m moves in such a way that the potential energy $U = ar^2$, where a is a constant and r is the distance of the particle from the origin. Assuming Bohr's model of quantisation of angular momentum and circular orbits, find the radius of nth allowed orbit.

8.3 Emission Spectrum

1 The wavelength of radiation emitted is λ_0, when an electron jumps from the third to the second orbit of hydrogen atom. For the electron jump from the fourth to the second orbit of the hydrogen atom, what will be the wavelength of radiation emitted?

2 Find the wavelength of the radiation required to excite the electron in Li^{++} from the first to the third

Bohr orbit. How many spectral lines are observed in the emission spectrum of the above excited system?

3 Find the largest and shortest wavelengths in the Lymen series for hydrogen. In what region of the electromagnetic spectrum does these wavelengths lie?

4 Calculate (a) the wavelength and (b) the frequency of the H_β line of the Balmer series for hydrogen.

5 The third line of Paschen series of an ion equivalent to hydrogen atom has wavelength of 273.5 nm.

Find the ground state energy of an electron of this ion.

6 Hydrogen atom in its ground state is excited by means of monochromatic radiation of wavelength 975 Å. How many different lines are possible in the resulting spectrum? Calculate the longest wavelength amongst them. You may assume the ionisation energy for H-atom as 13.6 eV.

7 The wavelength of the first member of the Balmer series in hydrogen spectrum is 6563 Å. Calculate the wavelength of second member of Brackett series in the same spectrum.

8 The wavelength of the first line of Lyman series for hydrogen is identical to that of the second line of Balmer series for some hydrogen like ion X.

Find the energies of first two levels of X. (Take, ground state binding energy of hydrogen atom = 13.6 eV)

9 A gas of hydrogen like atoms can absorb radiations of 68 eV. Consequently, the atoms emit radiations of only three different wavelengths. All the wavelengths are equal or smaller than that of the absorbed photon.

(a) Determine the initial state of the gas atoms.
(b) Identify the gas atoms.
(c) Find the minimum wavelength of the emitted radiations.

10 The energy levels of a hypothetical one electron atom are shown in the figure.

(i) Find the ionisation potential of this atom.
(ii) Find the short wavelength limit of the series terminating at $n = 2$
(iii) Find the excitation potential for the state $n = 3$
(iv) Find wave number of the photon emitted for the transition $n = 3$ to $n = 1$.
(v) What is the minimum energy that an electron will have, after interacting with this atom in the ground state, if the initial kinetic energy of the electron is 6 eV?
(vi) What is the minimum energy that an electron will have after interacting with this atom in the ground state, if the initial kinetic energy of the electron is 11 eV?

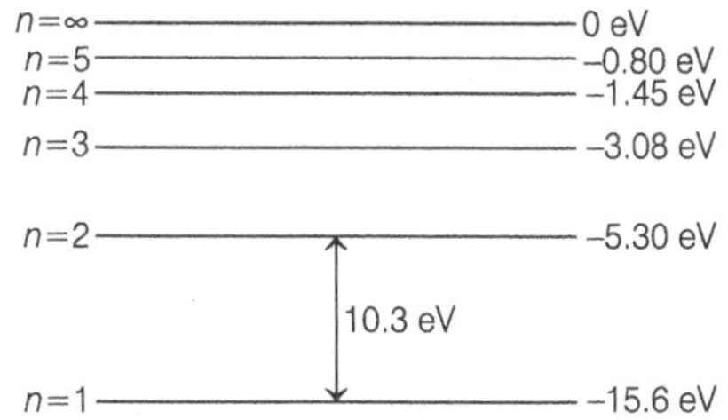

11. The hydrogen atom makes a transition from $n = 4$ to $n = 1$ state. Determine the recoil momentum of the H-atom in units of eV/c, where c = speed of light in vacuum.

8.4 Effect of Nucleus Motion

1 A positronium consists of an electron and a positron revolving about their common centre of mass. Calculate

(i) separation between the electron and positron in their first excited state.
(ii) energy of the electron in ground state.

2 A muon is an unstable elementary particle whose mass is $207\, m_e$ and whose charge is either $+e$ or $-e$. A negative muon (μ^-) can be captured by a nucleus to form a muonic atom. Suppose a proton captures a negative muon (μ^-), find

(i) the radius of first Bohr orbit and
(ii) the ionisation energy of the atom.

(Take mass of proton $m_p = 1836\, m_e$, where m_e is mass of electron).

8.5 Atomic Collisions

1 A neutron having kinetic energy K collides head on with H-atom at rest in ground state. What will be the types of collision possible, if

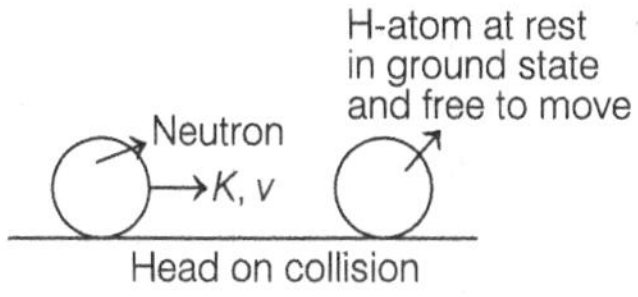

(a) $K = 14$ eV (b) $K = 20.4$ eV
(c) $K = 22$ eV (d) $K = 24.18$ eV

2. A He^+ ion is at rest and is in ground state. A neutron with initial kinetic energy K collides head on with the He^+ ion. Find minimum value of K, so that there can be an inelastic collision between these two particles.

LEVEL 02 JEE Main/Advanced Level

1 The Rutherford scattering of α-particles by atoms shows that
(A) the atom as a whole is positively charged
(B) the atom consists of uniformly distributed positive and negative charged particles
(C) there is no charged particle inside the atom
(D) the atom has a very small positively charged core at the centre

2 The diagram shows the paths of four α-particles, having the same energy, being scattered by the nucleus of an atom simultaneously. Which of these is/are not possible physically?

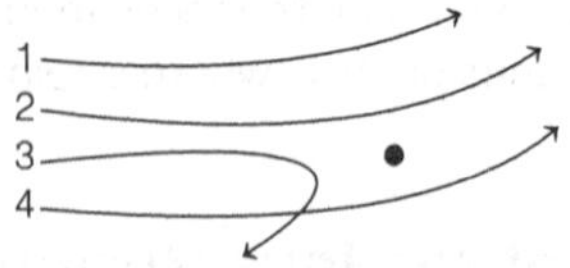

(a) 3 and 4 (b) 2 and 3
(c) 1 and 4 (d) 4 only

3 In a Rutherford scattering experiment when a projectile of charge z_1 and mass M_1 approaches a target nucleus of charge z_2 and mass M_2, the distance of closest approach is r_0. The energy of the projectile is
(a) Directly proportional to $M_1 \times M_2$
(b) Directly proportional to $z_1 z_2$
(c) Inversely proportional to z_1
(d) Directly proportional to mass M_1

4 In a head-on collision between an alpha particle and a gold nucleus, the distance of closest approach is 4×10^{-14} m. Calculate the energy of the α-particle in MeV
(a) 5.2 (b) 5.0
(c) 5.69 (d) 5.86

5 If in Rutherford's experiment, the number of particles scattered at 90° angle are 28 per min, then number of scattered particles at an angle 60° and 120° will be
(a) 112/min, 12.5/min (b) 100/min, 200/ min
(c) 50/min, 125.5/min (d) 117/min, 25/min

6 In which of the following systems will the radius of the first orbit be minimum?
(a) Hydrogen atom (b) Deuterium atom
(c) Singly ionised helium (d) Double ionised lithium.

7 Difference between nth and $(n+1)$th Bohr's radius of hydrogen atom is equal to $(n-1)$th Bohr's radius. The value of n is
(a) 1 (b) 2 (c) 3 (d) 4

8 The figure shows a graph between $\ln\left|\frac{A_n}{A_1}\right|$ and $\ln|n|$, where A_n is the area enclosed by the nth orbit in a hydrogen like atom. The correct curve is

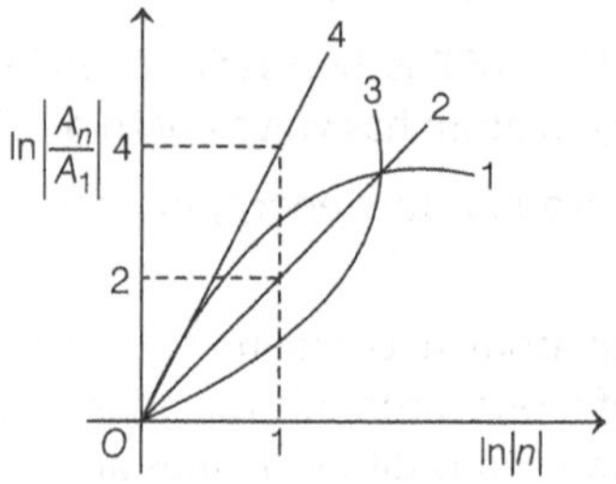

(a) 4 (b) 3 (c) 2 (d) 1

9 The velocity of an electron in the first orbit of H-atom is v. The velocity of an electron in the second orbit of He^+ is
(a) $2v$ (b) v (c) $\frac{v}{2}$ (d) $\frac{v}{4}$

10 The angular momentum of electron in hydrogen atom is proportional to
(a) $\sqrt{r}$ (b) $\frac{1}{r}$ (c) r^2 (d) $\frac{1}{\sqrt{r}}$

11 An electron in the ground state of hydrogen has an angular momentum L_1, and an electron in the first excited state of lithium has an angular momentum L_2
(a) $L_1 = L_2$ (b) $L_1 = 4L_2$
(c) $L_2 = 2L_1$ (d) $L_1 = 2L_2$

12 The ratio of the speed of an electron in the first Bohr orbit of hydrogen to the speed of light is equal to. Here e, h and c have their usual meanings in CGS system.
(a) $\frac{2\pi hc}{e^2}$ (b) $\frac{er^2 h}{2\pi c}$ (c) $\frac{e^2 c}{2\pi h}$ (d) $\frac{2\pi e^2}{hc}$

13 If an electron revolves around a proton, then its time period T is (R = radius of orbit)
(a) $\propto R^2$ (b) $\propto R^{3/2}$
(c) $\propto R^3$ (d) $\propto R$

14 The time period of the electron in the ground state of hydrogen atom is two times the time period of the electron in the first excited state of a certain hydrogen like atom (Atomic number Z). The value of Z is
(a) 2 (b) 3
(c) 4 (d) None of these

15 An electron in the $n = 2$ state of hydrogen like atom ($Z = 2$) makes transition to $n = 1$ state. The average life time of the excited state is 10^{-8} s. The number of revolutions performed by the electron before making the transition is

(a) 2.28×10^6 (b) 22.8×10^6
(c) 8.23×10^6 (d) 2.82×10^6

16 The ratio between total acceleration of the electron in singly ionised helium atom and doubly ionised lithium atom (Both in ground state) is

(a) $\frac{2}{3}$ (b) $\frac{4}{9}$ (c) $\frac{8}{27}$ (d) 1

17 Suppose, the electron in a hydrogen atom makes transition from $n = 3$ to $n = 2$ in 10^{-8} s. The order of the torque acting on the electron in this period is

(a) 10^{-34} N-m (b) 10^{-26} N-m
(c) 10^{-42} N-m (d) 10^{-8} N-m

18 Suppose the potential energy between electron and proton at a distance r is given by $-\frac{ke^2}{3r^3}$. Application of Bohr's theory to hydrogen atom in this case show that

(A) energy in the nth orbit is proportional to n^6
(B) energy is proportional to m^{-3} (m = mass of electron)

(a) Only (A) is correct.
(b) Only (B) is correct.
(c) Both (A) and (B) are correct.
(d) None are correct.

19 The attractive potential for an atom is given by $V = V_0 \ln \frac{r}{r_0}$, where V_0 and r_0 are constant and r is the radius of orbit. The radius r_n of the nth Bohr's orbit depends upon principal quantum number n as

(a) $r_n \propto \frac{1}{n^2}$ (b) $r_n \propto \frac{1}{n}$ (c) $r_n \propto n$ (d) $r_n \propto n^2$

20 An atom is placed in a uniform magnetic induction B such that plane normal to the electron orbit makes an angle of 30° with the magnetic induction. The torque acting on the orbiting electron in ground state is

(a) $\frac{ehB}{8\pi m}$ (b) $\frac{eh}{4\pi m}$ (c) $\frac{2eh}{3\pi m}$ (d) zero

21 Nth level of Li^{2+} has the same energy as the ground state energy of the hydrogen atom. If r_N and r_1 be the radius of the Nth Bohr orbit of Li^{2+} and first orbit radius of H-atom respectively, then the ratio $\frac{r_N}{r_1}$ is

(a) 9 (b) $\frac{1}{9}$
(c) 3 (d) None of these

22 A hydrogen atom in its ground state absorbs a photon of energy 10.2 eV and gets excited. The change in angular momentum of the electrons in this process is (in kg m^2/s) nearly

(a) 1×10^{-34}
(b) 2×10^{-34}
(c) 0.5×10^{-34}
(d) Cannot be determined

23 A hydrogen atom and a Li^{++} ion are both in the second excited state. If L_H and L_{Li} are their respective electronic angular momentum and E_H and E_{Li} their respective energies then,

(a) $L_H > L_{Li}$ and $|E_H| > |E_{Li}|$
(b) $L_H = L_{Li}$ and $|E_H| < |E_{Li}|$
(c) $L_H = L_{Li}$ and $|E_H| > |E_{Li}|$
(d) $L_H < L_{Li}$ and $|E_H| < |E_{Li}|$

24 The angular momentum of an electron in the hydrogen atom is $\frac{h}{\pi}$, where h is Planck's constant. The potential energy of this electron is

(a) –13.6 eV (b) –6.8 eV
(c) –3.4 eV (d) –27.2 eV

25 In a hydrogen atom, the binding energy of the electron in the nth state is E_n, then the frequency of revolution of the electron in the nth orbit is

(a) $\frac{2E_n}{nh}$ (b) $\frac{2E_n n}{h}$
(c) $\frac{E_n}{nh}$ (d) $\frac{E_n n}{h}$

26 The electron in a hydrogen atom makes a transition from an excited state to the ground state. Which of the following statements is true?

(a) Its kinetic energy increases and its potential and total energies decrease.
(b) Its kinetic energy decreases, potential energy increases and its total energy remains the same.
(c) Its kinetic and total energies decrease and its potential energy increases.
(d) Its kinetic, potential and total energies decrease.

27 A hydrogen atom makes a transition from $n = 2$ to $n = 1$ and emits a photon. This photon strikes a doubly ionised lithium atom in the excited state and completely removes the orbiting electron. The least quantum number for the excited state of the ion required for the process is

(a) 2 (b) 5
(c) 3 (d) 4

28 Of the following transitions in hydrogen atom, the one which gives an absorption line of highest frequency is

(a) $n = 1$ to $n = 2$ (b) $n = 3$ to $n = 8$
(c) $n = 2$ to $n = 1$ (d) $n = 8$ to $n = 3$

29 If the potential energy is taken zero at ground state of hydrogen atom in place of infinity, then

(i) total energy of atom will get changed.
(ii) binding energy of hydrogen atom in ground state will remain unchanged.
(iii) kinetic energy of electron in ground state will get changed.
(iv) energy of photon generated becuase of de-excitation of atom from first excited state will remain unchanged.

(a) Only (i) and (iv) are correct.
(b) Only (i), (ii) and (iv) are correct.
(c) Only (ii) and (iv) are correct.
(d) Only (i) and (ii) are correct.

30 Let the potential energy of a hydrogen atom in the ground state be zero. Then, its energy in the first excited state will be

(a) 10.2 eV (b) 13.6 eV
(c) 23.8 eV (d) 27.2 eV

31 The ratio of the binding energies of the hydrogen atom in the first and the second excited states is

(a) $\frac{1}{4}$ (b) 4 (c) $\frac{4}{9}$ (d) $\frac{9}{4}$

32 The first excitation potential of a hypothetical hydrogen like atom is 20 V. Find the third excitation potential of the atom

(a) 25 V (b) 30 V (c) 40 V (d) 60 V

33 In hydrogen and hydrogen like atoms, the ratio of difference of energies $E_{4n} - E_{2n}$ and $E_{2n} - E_n$ varies with its atomic number Z and n as

(a) $\frac{Z^2}{n^2}$ (b) $\frac{Z^4}{n^4}$ (c) $\frac{Z}{n}$ (d) $Z^0 n^0$

34 If R is the Rydberg's constant, the energy of the electron in the 1st excited state of hydrogen atom is

(a) $-\frac{Rc}{4h}$ (b) $-\frac{Rch}{4}$ (c) $-\frac{hc}{4R}$ (d) $-\frac{1}{4Rhc}$

35 An energy of 24.6 eV is required to remove one of the electrons from a neutral helium atom. The energy required to remove both the electrons from the neutral helium atoms is

(a) 79 eV (b) 51.8 eV
(c) 49.2 eV (d) 38.2 eV

36 In a transition to a state of excitation energy 10.19 eV, a hydrogen atom emits a 4890 Å photon. The binding energy of the initial state is

(a) 1.51 eV (b) 3.4 eV (c) 0.54 eV (d) 0.87 eV

37 If the difference of energies of an electron in the second and the fourth orbits of an atom is E, then the ionisation energy of that atom will be

(a) $\frac{36}{15}E$ (b) $\frac{16}{3}E$ (c) $\frac{15}{36}E$ (d) $\frac{3}{16}E$

38 If $n >> 1$, then the dependence of frequency (ν) of a photon, emitted as a result of transition of electron from nth orbit to $(n-1)$th orbit, on n will be

(a) $\nu \propto \frac{1}{n}$ (b) $\nu \propto \frac{1}{n^2}$ (c) $\nu \propto \frac{1}{n^3}$ (d) $\nu \propto \frac{1}{n^4}$

39 If the electron in a hydrogen atom jumps from the third orbit to the second orbit, the emitted radiation has wavelength (R = Rydberg constant)

(a) $\frac{36}{5R}$ (b) $\frac{5R}{36}$ (c) $\frac{6}{5R}$ (d) $\frac{5R}{6}$

40 If E_n and J_n are the magnitude of total energy and angular momentum of electron in the nth Bohr orbit respectively, then

(a) $E_n \propto J_n^2$ (b) $E_n \propto \frac{1}{J_n^2}$ (c) $E_n \propto J_n$ (d) $E_n \propto \frac{1}{J_n}$

41 According to Bohr model, magnetic field at centre (at the nucleus) of a hydrogen atom due to motion of electron in the nth orbit is proportional to

(a) $\frac{1}{n^3}$ (b) $\frac{1}{n^5}$ (c) n^5 (d) n^3

42 The longest wavelength that a singly ionised helium atom in its ground state will absorb is

(a) 912 Å (b) 304 Å (c) 606 Å (d) 1216 Å

43 A μ-meson (charge $= -e$, mass $= 207\, m_e$, where m is the mass of an electron) is captured by a proton (mass $= 1836\, m_e$) to form a hydrogen like 'mesonic' atom. μ-meson is in the state $n = 2$ of the atom. The wavelength of the photon emitted, when the mesonic atom drops to its ground state is

(a) 1315.2 nm (b) 135.2 nm
(c) 218.3 nm (d) 0.653 nm

44 In a hypothetical system, a particle of mass m and charge $-3q$ is moving around a very heavy particle having charge q. Assuming Bohr's model to be true to this system, the orbital velocity of mass m, when it is nearest to heavy particle is

(a) $\frac{3q^2}{2\varepsilon_0 h}$ (b) $\frac{3q^2}{4\varepsilon_0 h}$ (c) $\frac{3q}{2\varepsilon_0 h}$ (d) $\frac{3q}{4\varepsilon_0 h}$

45 In a hypothetical atom like that of hydrogen, the mass of the electrons is doubled. The energy E_0 and radius r_0 of the first Bohr orbit will be (a_0 = Bohr radius of hydrogen)

(a) $E_0 = -27.2$ eV, $r_0 = \frac{a_0}{2}$

(b) $E_0 = -27.2$ eV, $r_0 = a_0$

(c) $E_0 = -13.6$ eV, $r_0 = \frac{a_0}{2}$

(d) $E_0 = -13.6$ eV, $r_0 = a_0$

46 A particular H-like ion emits radiation of frequency 2.467×10^{15} Hz, when it makes a transition from $n = 2$ to $n = 1$. What will be the frequency of radiation in a transition from $n = 3$ to $n = 1$?

(a) 2.92×10^{15} Hz

(b) 1.54×10^{15} Hz

(c) 6.37×10^{15} Hz

(d) 3.34×10^{15} Hz

47 A spectral line results from the transition $n = 2$ to $n = 1$ in the single electron system given below. Which one of these will produce the shortest wavelength emission?

(a) H (b) He^+

(c) Li^{++} (d) Dueterium atom

48 Energy levels A, B and C of a certain atoms correspond to increasing values of energy, i.e. $E_A < E_B < E_C$. If $\lambda_1, \lambda_2, \lambda_3$ are the wavelengths of radiation corresponding to the transitions $C \to B$, $B \to A$ and $C \to A$ respectively, then

(a) $\lambda_1 = \lambda_2 = \lambda_3$ (b) $\lambda_3 = \frac{\lambda_1 \lambda_2}{\lambda_1 + \lambda_2}$

(c) $\lambda_3^2 = \lambda_1^2 + \lambda_2^2$ (d) None of these

49 An excited hydrogen atom emits a photon of wavelength λ in returning to the ground state. If R is the Rydberg's constant, then the quantum number n of the excited state is

(a) $\sqrt{\lambda R}$ (b) $\sqrt{\lambda R - 1}$

(c) $\sqrt{\frac{\lambda R}{\lambda R - 1}}$ (d) $\sqrt{\lambda R (\lambda R - 1)}$

50 An electron in hydrogen atom first jumps from second excited state to first excited state, and then from first excited state to ground state. Let the ratio of wavelength, momentum and energy of photons in the two cases be x, y and z, then select the wrong answer

(a) $z = \frac{1}{x}$ (b) $x = \frac{9}{4}$

(c) $y = \frac{5}{27}$ (d) $z = \frac{5}{27}$

51 Consider the following electronic energy level diagram of H-atom. Photons associated with shortest and longest wavelengths would be emitted from the atom by the transitions labelled

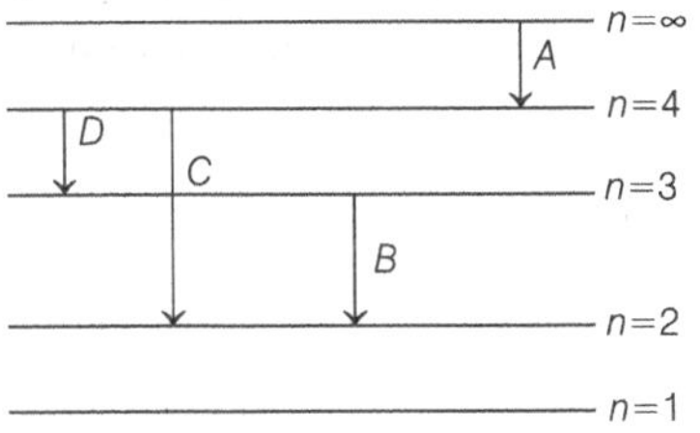

(a) D and C respectively (b) C and A respectively

(c) C and D respectively (d) A and C respectively

52 Imagine an atom made up of a proton and a hypothetical particle of double the mass of the electron but having the same charge as the electron. Apply the Bohr atom model and consider all possible transitions of this hypothetical particle to the first excited level. The longest wavelength photon that will be emitted has wavelength λ (given in terms of the Rydberg constant R for the hydrogen atom) equal to

(a) $\frac{9}{(5R)}$ (b) $\frac{36}{(5R)}$

(c) $\frac{18}{(5R)}$ (d) $\frac{4}{R}$

53 Assume that He obeys the Bohr theory exactly. Which of the following transitions in He will not give rise to a spectral line which has the same wavelength as some spectral line in the hydrogen spectrum?

(a) $n = 4$ to $n = 2$

(b) $n = 6$ to $n = 2$

(c) $n = 8$ to $n = 4$

(d) $n = 6$ to $n = 3$

54 Hydrogen atom emits blue light, when it changes from $n = 4$ energy level to $n = 2$ level. Which colour of the light would the atom emit, when it changes from $n = 5$ level to $n = 2$ level?

(a) Red (b) Yellow

(c) Green (d) Violet

55 In a sample of hydrogen like atoms all of which are in ground state, a photon beam containing photons of various energies is passed. In absorption spectrum, five dark lines are observed. The number of bright lines in the emission spectrum will be (Assume that all transitions take place)

(a) 5 (b) 10

(c) 15 (d) None of these

56 The figure indicates the energy level diagram of an atom and the origin of six spectral lines in emission (e.g. line number 5 arises from the transition from level B to A). Which of the following spectral lines will also occur in the absorption spectrum?

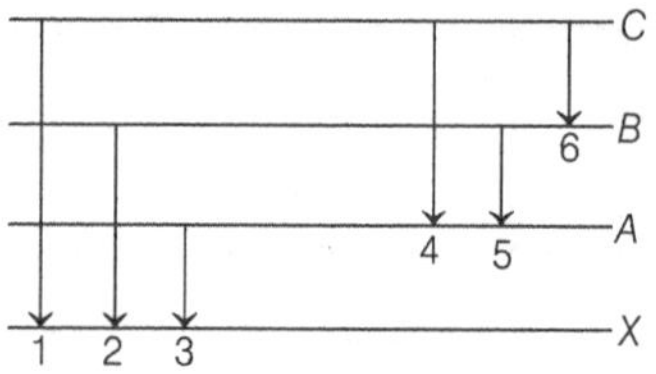

(a) 4,5,6 (b) 1,2,3,4,5,6
(c) 1,4,6 (d) 1,2,3

57 Electrons accelerated from rest by a potential difference of 12.75 V, are bombarded on a monoatomic hydrogen gas. Possible emission of spectral lines are

(a) first three Lyman lines, first two Balmer lines and first Paschen line
(b) first three Lyman lines only
(c) first two Balmer lines only
(d) None of the above

58 The shortest wavelength of the Brackett series of a hydrogen like atom (atomic number = Z) is the same as the shortest wavelength of the Balmar series of hydrogen atom. The value of Z is

(a) 2 (b) 3 (c) 4 (d) 6

59 The largest wavelength in the ultraviolet region of the hydrogen spectrum is 122 nm. The smallest wavelength in the infrared region of the hydrogen spectrum (to the nearest integer) is

(a) 802 nm
(b) 823 nm
(c) 1882 nm
(d) 1648 nm

60 The transition from the state $n = 4$ to $n = 3$ in a hydrogen like atom results in ultraviolet radiation. Infrared radiation will be obtained in the transition from

(a) $2 \rightarrow 1$ (b) $3 \rightarrow 2$
(c) $4 \rightarrow 2$ (d) $5 \rightarrow 4$

61 The electron in hydrogen atom in a sample is in nth excited state, then the number of different spectrum lines obtained in its emission spectrum will be

(a) $1 + 2 + 3 + \ldots\ldots + (n - 1)$
(b) $1 + 2 + 3 + \ldots\ldots + (n)$
(c) $1 + 2 + 3 + \ldots\ldots + (n + 1)$
(d) $1 \times 2 \times 3 \times \ldots\ldots \times (n - 1)$

62 The difference between the longest wavelength line of the Balmer series and shortest wavelength line of the Lyman series for a hydrogenic atom (Atomic number Z) equal to $\Delta\lambda$. The value of the Rydberg constant for the given atom is

(a) $\frac{5}{31} \frac{1}{\Delta\lambda \cdot Z^2}$ (b) $\frac{5}{36} \frac{Z^2}{\Delta\lambda}$
(c) $\frac{31}{5} \frac{1}{\Delta\lambda \cdot Z^2}$ (d) None of these

63 Radiations of wavelength λ are incident on hydrogen in the ground state. A fraction of these radiations is absorbed by these atoms. There are ten different waves in the emission spectrum of excited atoms. The λ will be

(a) 211 Å (b) 949 Å (c) 1211 Å (d) 821 Å

64 An electron in hydrogen atom after absorbing an energy photon jumps from energy state n_1 to n_2. Then, it returns to ground state after emitting six different wavelengths in emission spectrum.

The energy of emitted photons is either equal to, less than or greater than the absorbed photons. The n_1 and n_2 are

(a) $n_2 = 4, n_1 = 3$ (b) $n_2 = 5, n_1 = 3$
(c) $n_2 = 4, n_1 = 2$ (d) $n_2 = 4, n_1 = 1$

65 A sample of hydrogen atoms is in excited state (all the atoms). The photons emitted from this sample are made to pass through a filter through which light having wavelength greater than 800 nm can only pass. Only one type of photons are found to pass the filter. The sample's excited state initially is [Take, $hc = 1240$ eV-nm, ground state energy of hydrogen atom $= -13.6$ eV.]

(a) fifth excited state (b) fourth excited state
(c) third excited state (d) second excited state

66 An electron of mass m_e and charge $-e$ $(e > 0)$ moves in a closed orbit in a uniform magnetic field, B acting perpendicular to the plane of the orbit. If Bohr's quantisation rule for angular momentum were to be applied to this system, the minimum magnetic flux (of the applied magnetic field B) passing through the orbit equals

(a) zero (b) $\frac{h}{2e}$ (c) $\frac{h}{e}$ (d) None of these

67 The ratio of circumference of the circular orbit to the de-Broglie wavelength associated with the electron in the first excited state of hydrogen atom is

(a) 1 (b) 2
(c) 4 (d) 8

68 The de-Broglie wavelength of an electron in nth Bohr orbit of radius r_n (a_0 being the radius of the first Bohr orbit)

(a) $2\pi a_0$ (b) $2\pi n a_0$

(c) $2\pi n^2 a_0$ (d) $\frac{2\pi a_0}{n}$

69 In a hydrogen atom, the ratio of wavelength of first line of Lyman series to the de-Broglie wavelength of electron in the ground state in terms of Rydberg constant R and Bohr radius r is

(a) $\frac{2}{3\pi rR}$ (b) $\frac{8\pi}{3Rr}$

(c) $\frac{4}{3\pi rR}$ (d) None of these

70 When a stationary hydrogen atom emits a photon is going from $n = 5$ to $n = 1$, its recoil speed is about

(a) 60 m/s (b) 4 m/s

(c) 200 m/s (d) 0.4 km/s

71 A photon of energy 10.2 eV corresponds to light of wavelength λ_0. Due to an electron transition from $n = 2$ to $n = 1$ in a hydrogen atom, light of wavelength λ is emitted. If we take into account the recoil of the atom, when the photon is emitted

(a) $\lambda = \lambda_0$ (b) $\lambda < \lambda_0$

(c) $\lambda > \lambda_0$ (d) data insufficient

72 A stationary hydrogen atom of mass M emits a photon corresponding to the longest wavelength of Balmer series. The recoil velocity acquired by the atom is

(a) $\frac{Rh}{M}$ (b) $\frac{Rh}{4M}$ (c) $\frac{3}{4}\frac{Rh}{M}$ (d) $\frac{5}{36}\frac{Rh}{M}$

73 An electron with kinetic energy E eV collides with a hydrogen atom in the ground state. The collision will be elastic

(a) for all values of E (b) for $E < 10.2$ eV

(c) for $E < 13.6$ eV (d) only for $E < 3.4$ eV

74 A photon collides with a stationary hydrogen atom in ground state inelastically. Energy of the colliding photon is 10.2 eV. After a time interval of the order of microsecond, another photon collides with same hydrogen atom inelastically with an energy of 15 eV. What will be observed by the detector?

(a) One photon of energy 10.2 eV and an electron of energy 1.4 eV

(b) 2 photons of energy of 1.4 eV

(c) 2 photons of energy 10.2 eV

(d) One photon of energy 10.2 eV and another photon of 1.4 eV

75 Two hydrogen atoms in ground state are moving in opposite directions with the same speed and collide head on. The minimum kinetic energy of each hydrogen atom for the collision to be inelastic so, that both the atoms are excited is

(a) 13.6 eV (b) 10.2 eV

(c) 20.4 eV (d) 27.2 eV

76 Electrons in a sample of gas containing hydrogen like atom ($Z = 3$) are in fourth excited state. When photons emitted only due to transition from third excited state to second excited state are incident on a metal plate, photoelectrons are ejected. The stopping potential for these photoelectrons is 3.95 V. Now, if only photons emitted due to transition from fourth excited state to third excited state are incident on the same metal plate, the stopping potential for the emitted photoelectrons will be approximately equal to

(a) 0.85 V (b) 0.75 V

(c) 0.65 V (d) None of these

77 A monochromatic radiation of wavelength λ is incident on a sample containing He^+. As a result the Helium sample starts radiating. A part of this radiation is allowed to pass through a sample of atomic hydrogen gas in ground state. It is noticed that the hydrogen sample has started emitting electrons whose maximum kinetic energy is 37.4 eV. ($hc = 12400$ eV-Å) Then, λ is

(a) 275 Å (b) 243 Å

(c) 656 Å (d) 386 Å

Multiple Choice(s) Correct Questions

1 In Bohr model of the hydrogen atom, let R, v and E represent the radius of the orbit, speed of the electron and the total energy of the electron, respectively. Which of the following quantities are proportional to the quantum number n?

(a) vR (b) RE (c) $\frac{v}{E}$ (d) $\frac{R}{E}$

2 The magnitude of angular momentum, kinetic energy, velocity and frequency of an electron in a hydrogen atom corresponding to the quantum number n are L, K, v and f, respectively. Then, according to the Bohr's theory of hydrogen atom

(a) $K^{-1}Lf$ is constant for all the orbits.

(b) Kvf^{-1} is constant for all the orbits.

(c) $LK^{-1}v$ is proportional to n^2.

(d) $K^{-1}f$ is proportional to $1/n$.

3 Which of the following represent the velocity of electron in ground state in hydrogen atom. Here, r is the radius of first orbit of hydrogen atom?

(a) $\sqrt{\frac{e^2}{4\pi\varepsilon_0 mr}}$ (b) $\frac{h}{2\pi mr}$ (c) $\frac{h}{\pi mr}$ (d) $\frac{e^2}{2\varepsilon_0 h}$

4 An electron in a hydrogen atom makes a transition from $n = n_1$ to $n = n_2$. The time period of the electron in the initial state is eight times that in the final state. Then, the possible values of n_1 and n_2 are

(a) $n_1 = 4, n_2 = 2$ (b) $n_1 = 8, n_2 = 2$
(c) $n_1 = 8, n_2 = 1$ (d) $n_1 = 6, n_2 = 3$

5 Which of the following statements is (are) wrong for hydrogen atom?

(a) The rotational frequency of an electron in an orbit of radius r is proportional to the cube of the radius of the orbit.
(b) The linear momentum of the revolving electron is inversely proportional to the square root of the radius of the orbit.
(c) The total energy of the system is inversely proportional to the radius of the orbit.
(d) The magnetic moment of the electron is proportional to square of the radius of the orbit.

6 Negative charge is revolving around a fixed positive charge in a circular orbit. If the classical idea of an accelerating charge radiating energy is valid, then the negative charge will

(a) spiral towards the positive charge, with increasing kinetic energy
(b) spiral towards the positive charge with potential energy decreasing at a faster rate than increase in its kinetic energy.
(c) spiral away from the positive charge and finally escape from the binding of the positive charge
(d) revolve around the positive charge with increasing frequency of revolution.

7 Highly excited states for hydrogen like atoms (also called Rydberg states) with nuclear charge Ze are defined by their principal quantum number n, where $n >> 1$. Which of the following statement(s) is(are) true?

(a) Relative change in the radii of two consecutive orbitals does not depend on Z.
(b) Relative change in the radii of two consecutive orbitals varies as $\frac{1}{n}$
(c) Relative change in the energy of two consecutive orbitals varies as $\frac{1}{n^3}$
(d) Relative change in the angular momenta of two consecutive orbitals varies as $\frac{1}{n}$

8 In an electron transition inside a hydrogen atom, orbital angular momentum may change by

(a) h (b) $\frac{h}{\pi}$
(c) $\frac{h}{2\pi}$ (d) $\frac{h}{4\pi}$

9 When in a hydrogen atom an electron makes a transition from a higher state to a lower state

(a) angular momentum of the electron remains constant.
(b) its kinetic energy increases.
(c) its potential energy decreases.
(d) its de-Broglie wavelength decreases.

10. If potential energy in hydrogen atom with electron in ground state is taken to be 13.6 eV, then

(a) potential energy in the first excited state would be 34 eV
(b) total energy in the first excited state would be 37.4 eV
(c) kinetic energy in the first excited state would be 44.2 eV
(d) total energy in the ground state would be 27.2 eV

11 A hydrogen like atom of atomic number Z is in an excited state of quantum number $2n$. It can emit a maximum energy photon of 204 eV. It makes a transition to quantum state n, a photon of energy 40.8 eV is emitted, then

(a) $Z = 2$ (b) $Z = 4$
(c) $n = 1$ (d) $n = 2$

12 A hydrogen like atom is in excited quantum state n. From here, it can make transition to first excited state by successively emitting two photons of energies 10.2 eV and 17.00 eV, respectively. Alternatively the atom from the same state can make a transition to the second excited state by successively emitting two photons of energy 4.25 eV and 5.95 eV

(a) $n = 4$ (b) $n = 6$
(c) $Z = 3$ (d) $Z = 8$

13 A beam of ultraviolet light of all wavelengths passes through hydrogen gas at room temperature, in the x-direction. Assume that all photons emitted due to electron transitions inside the gas emerge in the y-direction. If A and B are the lights emerging from the gas in x and y-directions respectively, then

(a) some of the incident wavelengths will be absent in A.
(b) only those wavelengths will be present in B which are absent in A.
(c) B will contain some visible light.
(d) B will contain some infrared light.

14. Figure shows the energy level diagram of hydrogen like imaginary element X. ($hc = 1242$ eV-nm)

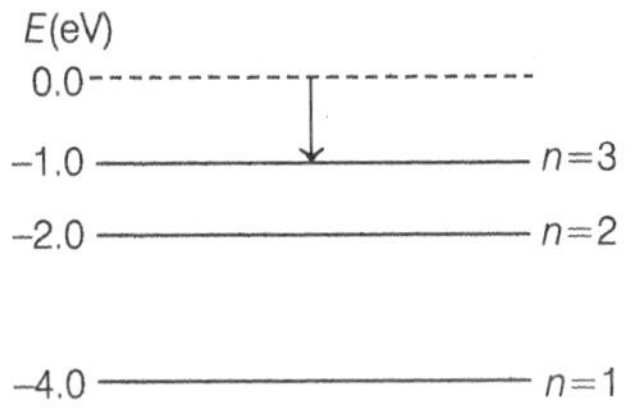

(a) The ionisation energy of element X is 4eV

(b) An atom in the ground state, absorbs a photon, comes to an excited state, then emits a photon with a wavelength of 1242 nm. The incident photon must have a wavelength of 414 nm.

(c) An atom in the ground state has a collision with an electron, then emits a photon with a wavelength of 1242 nm. The incident electron must have an energy of 3 eV.

(d) An atom in the ground state absorbs a photon, comes to an excited state then emits a photon with a wavelength of 1242 nm. The incident photon must have a wavelength of 1242 nm.

15 The figure shows electronic wave function for a hydrogen atom.

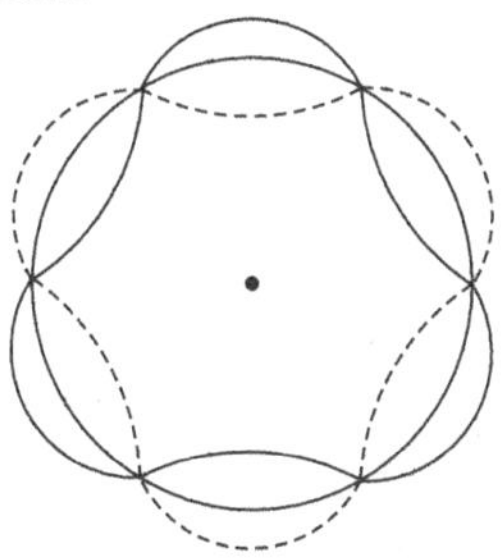

(a) The quantum number of this state is 6

(b) The wavelength of this electron is $6\pi r_0$ (r_0 is radius of ground state).

(c) It can go to ground state by emitting 3 different photons.

(d) On de-excitation it emits at least one line in infrared region of spectrum.

16. Suppose frequency of emitted photon is f_0, when electron of a stationary hydrogen atom jumps from a higher state m to a lower state n. If the atom is moving with a velocity v ($<< c$) and emits a photon of frequency f during the same transition, then which of the following statements are possible?

(a) f may be equal to f_0

(b) f may be greater than f_0

(c) f may be less than f_0

(d) f cannot be equal to f_0

17. A positronium atom consists of a positron and electron revolving around their common centre of mass. Then, as compared to hydrogen atom positronium atom has

(a) ground state energy half of hydrogen atom.

(b) Rydberg constant half of hydrogen atom.

(c) radius of first orbit of electron double that in case of hydrogen atom.

(d) velocity of electron in first orbit same as in case of hydrogen atom.

18. A free hydrogen atom in ground state is at rest. A neutron of kinetic energy K collides with the hydrogen atom. After collision hydrogen atom emits two photons in succession one of which has energy 2.55 eV. Assume that the hydrogen atom and neutron has same mass.

(a) Minimum value of K is 25.5 eV

(b) Minimum value of K is 12.75 eV

(c) The other photon has energy 10.2 eV

(d) The upper energy level is of excitation energy 12.75 eV

19 The radiation emitted, when an electron jumps from $n = 4$ to $n = 3$ in a lithium ion ($Z = 3$) falls on a metal surface to produce photoelectrons. When the photoelectrons with maximum kinetic energy are made to move perpendicular to a magnetic field of 2×10^{-4} T, it traces a circular path of radius $\sqrt{\frac{9.1}{1.6}}$ cm.

[Rhc = 13.6eV] (mass of electron $= 9.1 \times 10^{-31}$ kg)

(a) The wavelength of radiation falling on metal is 208 nm (nearly)

(b) The work function of metal is 2.75 eV

(c) The kinetic energy of photoelectrons is 6 eV

(d) The energy of incident photon is 5.95 eV

20 Energy liberated in the de-excitation of hydrogen atom from 3rd level to 1st level falls on a photocathode. Later when the same photocathode is exposed to a spectrum of some unknown hydrogen like gas, excited to 2nd energy level, it is found that the de-Broglie wavelength of the fastest photoelectrons, now ejected has decreased by a factor of 3. For this new gas, difference of energies of 2nd Lyman line and 1st Balmer line is found to be 3 times the ionisation potential of the hydrogen atom. Select the correct statement(s).

(a) The gas is lithium

(b) The gas is helium

(c) The work function of photocathode is 8.5 eV

(d) The work function of photocathode is 5.5 eV

Comprehension Based Questions

Comprehension-I

A gas sample of hydrogen like atoms has some atoms in the lowest (ground) energy level *A* and some atoms in a particular upper (excited) energy level *B* and there are no atoms in any other energy level. The atoms of the gas make transition to a higher level by absorbing monochromatic light of photon energy 2.7 eV. Subsequently, the atoms emit radiation of only six different photon energies. Some of the emitted photons have energy 2.7 eV. Some have energy more and some have less than 2.7 eV.

1 Principal quantum number of the initially excited level *B* is

(a) 2 (b) 3
(c) 4 (d) 5

2 Ionisation energy for the gas atoms is

(a) 1.6×10^{-19} J
(b) 2.3×10^{-18} J
(c) 1.3×10^{-18} J
(d) 2.6×10^{-19} J

3 Maximum and minimum energies of the emitted photons are respectively

(a) 2.2×10^{-18} J, 1.1×10^{-18} J
(b) 3.3×10^{-18} J, 2.2×10^{-18} J
(c) 1.1×10^{-18} J, 2.1×10^{-19} J
(d) 3.3×10^{-18} J, 2.2×10^{-19} J

Comprehension-2

A sample of hydrogen atom gas contains 100 atoms. All the atoms are excited to the same *n*th excited state. The total energy released by all the atoms is $\frac{4800}{49} Rch$ (where $Rch = 13.6$ eV) as they come to the ground state through various types of transitions, then

4 The maximum energy of the emitted photon

(a) $\frac{46}{49} Rch$ (b) $\frac{47}{49} Rch$
(c) $\frac{48}{49} Rch$ (d) None of these

5 The value of *n*

(a) 5 (b) 6
(c) 7 (d) 8

6 Maximum total number of photons that can be emitted by this sample

(a) 500 (b) 600
(c) 700 (d) 800

Comprehension-3

The figure above shown an energy level diagram for the hydrogen atom. Several transitions are marked as I, II, III, IV, V and VI. The diagram is only indicative and not to scale.

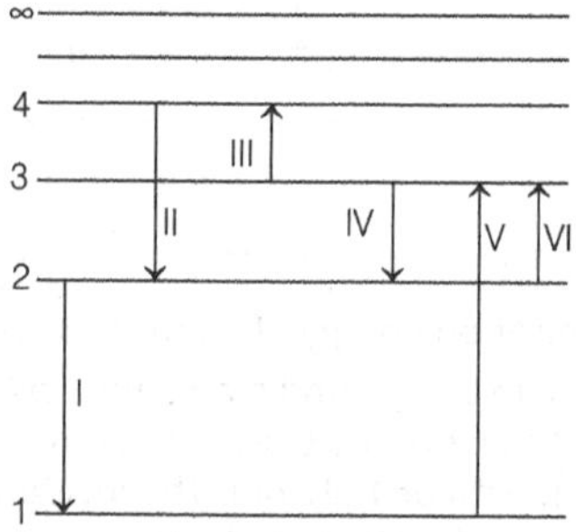

7 In which transition is a Balmer series photon absorbed?

(a) II (b) III (c) IV (d) VI

8 The wavelength of the radiation involved in transition II is

(a) 291 nm (b) 364 nm
(c) 487 nm (d) 652 nm

9 Which transition will occur, when a hydrogen atom is irradiated with radiation of wavelength 1025 Å?

(a) I (b) II (c) IV (d) V

Comprehension-4

Consider a hypothetical hydrogen like atom. The wavelength, in Å, for the spectral lines for transitions from $n = p$ to $n = 1$ are given by $\lambda = \frac{1500\, p^2}{p^2 - 1}$, where $p = 2, 3, 4, \ldots$

10 The wavelength of the most energetic photons in this series is

(a) 1300 Å (b) 1500 Å (c) 1800 Å (d) 2000 Å

11 The wavelength of the least energetic photons in this series is

(a) 1500 Å (b) 1800 Å (c) 2000 Å (d) 2200 Å

12 What is the ionisation potential of this element?

(a) 4.25 V (b) 6.50 V (c) 8.28 V (d) 9.75 V

Comprehension-5

An electron is orbiting in a circular orbit of radius *r* under the influence of a constant magnetic field of strength *B*. Assuming that Bohr's postulate regarding the quantisation of angular momentum holds good for this electron (charge of electron $= -e$ and mass of electron $= m$)

13 The kinetic energy of the electron in *n*th orbit is

(a) $\frac{nheB}{2\pi m}$ (b) $\frac{nheB}{\pi m}$ (c) $\frac{nheB}{4\pi m}$ (d) $\frac{nheB}{8\pi m}$

14 Potential energy of interaction between the magnetic moment of the orbital current due to the electron moving in its orbit and the magnetic field B is

(a) $\frac{nheB}{2\pi m}$ (b) $\frac{nheB}{\pi m}$ (c) $\frac{nheB}{4\pi m}$ (d) $\frac{nheB}{8\pi m}$

15 Total magnetic flux due to the magnetic field B passing through the nth orbit is

(a) $\frac{nh}{e}$ (b) $\frac{nh}{2e}$ (c) $\frac{nh}{4e}$ (d) $\frac{nh}{8e}$

Comprehension-6

Let us assume a different atomic model in which electron revolves around the nucleus (proton) at a separation r under the action of force which is different from electrostatic force of attraction. The potential energy between an electron and the proton due to this force is given by $U = -\frac{k}{r^4}$, where k is a constant.

16 The radius of nth Bohr's orbit is

(a) $\frac{\pi}{nh}\sqrt{km}$ (b) $\frac{2\pi}{nh}\sqrt{km}$

(c) $\frac{4\pi}{nh}\sqrt{km}$ (d) $\frac{8\pi}{nh}\sqrt{km}$

17 The velocity in the nth orbit is given by

(a) $\frac{nh}{8\pi^2 m\sqrt{km}}$ (b) $\frac{n^2h}{8\pi^2 m\sqrt{km}}$

(c) $\frac{nh^2}{4\pi^2 m\sqrt{km}}$ (d) $\frac{n^2h^2}{8\pi^2 m\sqrt{km}}$

18 The total energy of the electron in the nth orbit is given by

(a) $-\frac{n^4h^4}{128\pi^4 m^2 k}$ (b) $\frac{n^4h^4}{128\pi^4 m^2 k}$

(c) $\frac{n^4h^4}{256\pi^4 m^2 k}$ (d) $-\frac{n^4h^4}{256\pi^4 m^2 k}$

Comprehension-7

A monoenergetic beam of α-particles, each of them having kinetic E is incident on a sample of singly ionised Helium gas in ground state. The Helium gas in ground state. The Helium sample may start emitting radiation, since the kinetic energy of incident α-particle is sufficiently high. A part of this radiation (if any) is allowed to pass through atomic Hydrogen sample in ground state. A detector placed near the Hydrogen records both radiation and electrons. Assume all He^+ ions to be initially at rest.

19 If maximum kinetic energy of electrons intercepted by the detector is 27.2 eV, the minimum kinetic energy of α-particle must be

(a) 81.6 eV (b) 96.8 eV (c) 102 eV (d) 40.8 eV

20 If maximum kinetic energy of electrons intercepted by the detector is 27.2 eV, the KE of α-particle must be lower than

(a) 81.6 eV (b) 96.8 eV

(c) 102 eV (d) there is no upper limit

21 If no electrons are interpected by the detector, the energy of photons detected by it can be

(a) 10.2 eV (b) 40.8 eV

(c) 12.1 eV (d) None of these

Comprehension-8

The energy level scheme for the hypothetical one electron element Bansalium is shown in figure. The potential energy is taken to be zero for an electron at an infinite distance from the nucleus.

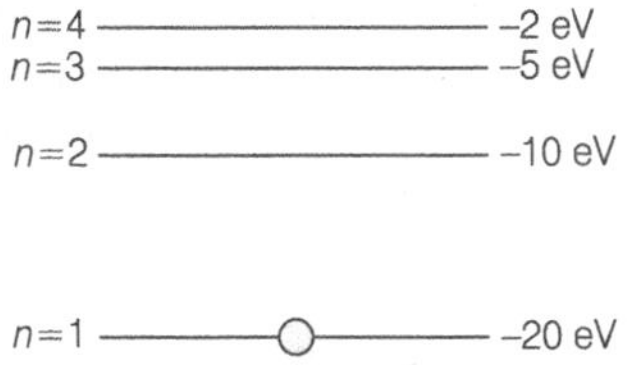

22 A sample of atoms of Bansalium are in all the 3 excited states shown above. What is the possible wavelength that can be emitted by atom in visible range?

(a) 414 nm (b) 620 nm

(c) 124 nm (d) 920 nm

23 If a Bansalium atom is in ground state, which of the following photons cannot excite the atom to a higher state?

(a) 10 eV (b) 15 eV (c) 18 eV (d) 12 eV

24 If photons emitted from Bansalium transitions $n = 4 \rightarrow n = 2$ and from $n = 2 \rightarrow n = 1$ will eject photoelectrons from an unknown metal but the photon emitted from the transition $n = 3 \rightarrow n = 2$ will not, what are the limits (maximum and minimum possible values) of the work function of the metal?

(a) 8 eV < ϕ < 10 eV (b) 5 eV < ϕ <10 eV

(c) 5 eV < ϕ < 8 eV (d) 5 eV < ϕ < 12 eV

Comprehension-9

A sample of hydrogen gas in its ground state is irradiated with photons of 10.2 eV energies. The radiation from the above sample is used to irradiate two other samples of excited ionised He^+ and excited ionised Li^{2+}, respectively. Both the ionised samples absorb the incident radiation.

25 How many spectral lines are obtained in the spectra of Li^{2+} ion?

(a) 10 (b) 15 (c) 20 (d) 17

26 Which is the smallest wavelength that will be observed in the spectra of Li^{2+} ion?

(a) 8.6 nm (b) 10.4 nm
(c) 12.8 nm (d) 14.6 nm

27 How many spectral lines are obtained in the spectra of He^+ ion?

(a) 2 (b) 4
(c) 6 (d) 8

28 Which is the smallest wavelength that will be observed in the spectra of He^+ ion?

(a) 24.3 nm (b) 28.8 nm
(c) 22.2 nm (d) 30.6 nm

Comprehension-10

Two hydrogen like atoms *A* and *B* are of different masses and each atom contains equal number of protons and neutrons. The difference in energies between the first Balmer lines emitted by *A* and *B* is 5.67 eV. When the atoms *A* and *B*, moving with the same velocity strike a heavy target they rebound with the same velocity. In this process atom *B* imparts twice momentum to the target than that of *A*.

29 Identify atom *A*

(a) H (b) D (c) He^{+1} (d) Li^{+2}

30. Identify atom/ion *B*

(a) H (b) D (c) He^{+1} (d) Li^{+2}

31. Find the wavelength of first Balmer line of *A*

(a) 550 nm (b) 450 nm (c) 750 nm (d) 656 nm

32. Find the wavelength of first Balmer line of *B*-

(a) 137 nm (b) 147 nm (c) 157 nm (d) 164 nm

33. The number of neutrons present in *A* and *B* are respectively

(a) $n_1 = 0$ and $n_2 = 1$ (b) $n_1 = 1$ and $n_2 = 2$
(c) $n_1 = 2$ and $n_2 = 3$ (d) $n_1 = 1$ and $n_2 = 3$

Comprehension-11

In a mixture of H-He^+ gas (He^+ is singly ionised He-atom), H-atoms and He^+ ions are excited to their respective first excited states. Subsequently, H-atoms transfer their total excitation energy to He^+ ions (by collisions). Assume that the Bohr model of atom is exactly valid.

34 The quantum number *n* of the state finally populated in He^+ ions is

(a) 2 (b) 3 (c) 4 (d) 5

35 The wavelength of light emitted in the visible region by He^+ ions after collisions with H-atoms is

(a) 650 nm (b) 560 nm
(c) 469 nm (d) 400 nm

36 The ratio of the kinetic energy of the $n = 2$ electron for the H-atom to that of He^+ ion is

(a) $\frac{1}{4}$ (b) $\frac{1}{2}$ (c) 1 (d) 2

Comprehension-12

When a particle is restricted to move along the *X*-axis between $x = 0$ and $x = a$, where *a* is of nanometer dimension, its energy can take only certain specific values. The allowed energies of the particle moving in such a restricted region, correspond to the formation of standing waves with nodes at its ends $x = 0$ and $x = a$. The wavelength of this standing wave is related to the linear momentum *p* of the particle according to the de-Broglie relation.

The energy of the particle of mass *m* is related to its linear momentum as $E = \frac{p^2}{2m}$. Thus, the energy of the particle can be denoted by a quantum number *n* taking values 1, 2, 3 ... ($n = 1$, called the ground state) corresponding to the number of loops in the standing wave. Use the model described above to answer the following question for a particle moving in the line $x = 0$ to $x = a$. Take, $h = 6.6. \times 10^{-34}$ J-s and $e = 1.6 \times 10^{-19}$ C.

37 The allowed energy for the particle for a particular value of *n* is proportional to

(a) a^{-2} (b) $a^{-3/2}$ (c) a^{-1} (d) a^2

38 If the mass of the particle is $m = 1.0 \times 10^{-30}$ kg and $a = 6.6$ nm, the energy of the particle in its ground state is closest to

(a) 0.8 meV (b) 8 meV
(c) 80 meV (d) 800 meV

39 The speed of the particle, that can take discrete values, is proportional to

(a) $n^{-3/2}$ (b) n^{-1}
(c) $n^{1/2}$ (d) n

Match the Columns Questions

1 Match the following.

	Column I		Column II
A.	Angular speed	1.	$\propto \frac{n^3}{Z^2}$
B.	Time period	2.	$\propto n$
C.	Angular momentum	3.	$\propto \frac{Z^2}{n^3}$
D.	Magnetic moment	4.	$\propto \frac{Z^3}{n^5}$
E.	Magnetic Field		

2 Match the following.

	Column I		Column II
A.	Binding energy of electron in doubly ionised lithium atom	1.	340 eV
B.	Energy that can remove electron from first excited state of triply ionised beryllium atom	2.	3.4 eV
C.	Ionisation energy of tetra ionised boron	3.	122.4 eV
D.	Energy obtained in assembling singly ionised helium atom so, that the atom can be in ground state or other excited states	4.	54.4 eV

3 The energy, the magnitude of linear momentum, magnitude of angular momentum and orbital radius of an electron in a hydrogen atom corresponding to the quantum number n are E, p, L and r, respectively.

Then according to Bohr's theory of hydrogen atom, match the expressions in Column I with statement in Column II.

	Column I		Column II
A.	Epr	1.	is independent of n
B.	$\frac{p}{E}$	2.	is directly proportional to n
C.	Er	3.	is inversely proportional to n
D.	pr	4.	is directly proportional to L

4. Match the following.

	Column I		Column II
A.	Ultraviolet light	1.	$n=6 \to n=3$
B.	Visible light	2.	$n=3 \to n=1$
C.	Infrared radiation	3.	$n=4 \to n=2$
D.	Microwave	4.	$n=7 \to n=6$
		5.	$n=5 \to n=4$

5. f_1 is maximum frequency of Lyman series, f_2 is minimum frequency Lyman series and f_3 is maximum frequency of Balmer series. Then, match Columns.

	Column I		Column II
A.	f_1	1.	greater than f_3
B.	f_2	2.	is negative
C.	$(f_2 - f_1)$	3.	less than f_2
D.	$(f_1 - f_2)$	4.	is equal to f_3

Numerical Value Questions

1 A Bohr hydrogen atom undergoes a transition $n=5 \to n=4$ and emits a photon of frequency ν. Frequency of circular motion of electron in $n=4$ orbit is ν_4. If the ratio $\frac{\nu}{\nu_4}$ is $\frac{N}{25}$, then find N.

2 The atoms of a hydrogen like gas are in a particular excited energy level. When these atoms de-excite, they emit photons of different energies. The maximum and minimum energies of emitted photons are $E_{max} = 204$ eV and $E_{min} = 10.5\overline{7}$ eV, respectively. Find the principal quantum number of initially excited energy level.

3 Photon with a wavelength $\lambda = 800$ Å knocks an electron from an atom of hydrogen in the ground state. Away from the atom the electron flies in a uniform electric field of intensity $E = 1000$ V/m. Electric field direction coincides with the velocity vector of the electron. Find the maximum distance (in μm) from the boundary of the field, where the electron is stopped. $\left(\text{Take, } \frac{hc}{e} = 12.42 \times 10^{-7}\right)$

4 A hydrogen atom in a state having a binding energy 0.85 eV makes a transition to a state of excitation energy 10.2 eV. Find the wavelength (in nm) of emitted photon. (Take, $hc = 1242$ eV-nm)

5 If the ratio of series limit wavelength of Balmer series to wavelength of the first line of Paschen series $x : 36$, then find x.

6 Determine the number of lines in Paschen series which have a wavelength greater than 1000 nm.

7 A gas containing hydrogen like ions with atomic number Z, emits photons in transition $(n+2) \to n$, where $n = Z$. These photons fall on a metallic plate and eject electrons having minimum de-Broglie wavelength λ of 5 Å. Find the value of Z, if the work function of metal is 4.2 eV.

8 An excited He^+ ion emits two photons in succession with wavelength 108.5 nm and 30.4 nm while making a transition to its ground state. Taking value of $hc = 1240$ eV-nm, find the quantum number of the excited state of He^+ ion.

9 A hydrogen atom at rest is in ground state. It is struck by a He^+ ion in first excited state. Assuming the collision to be head on and the mass of He^+ to be four times that of hydrogen atom, find the least value of kinetic energy (in eV) of incoming particle which can excite both the particles to second excited state.

10 In a hydrogen like atom, an electron is orbiting in an orbit having quantum number n. Its frequency of revolution is found to be 13.2×10^{15} Hz. Energy required to remove this electron from the orbit is 54.4 eV. In a time of 7 ns the electron jumps back to the orbit having quantum number $\frac{n}{2}$. If the average torque acted on the electron during the above process is $\beta \times 10^{-27}$ N-m, then find β.
(Given $\frac{h}{\pi} = 2.1 \times 10^{-34}$, frequency of revolution of electron in the ground state of H-atom is $v_0 = 6.6 \times 10^{15}$ Hz and ionisation energy of H-atom is $E_0 = 13.6$eV)

11 A neutron beam, in which each neutron has same kinetic energy, is passed through a sample of hydrogen like gas (but not hydrogen) in ground state. Due to collision of neutrons with the ions of the gas, ions are excited and then they emit photons. Six spectral lines are obtained in which one of the lines is of wavelength (6200/51) nm. What is the minimum possible value of kinetic energy (in eV) of the neutrons for this to be possible? The mass of neutron and proton can be assumed to be nearly same.

12 The electron in the ground state of hydrogen atom produces a magnetic field at the nucleus. This magnetic field depends on the value of many constants. If e is electronic charge, B is found to be proportional to e^n, then find n.

13 The peak emission from a black body at a certain temperature occurs at a wavelength of 6200 Å. On increasing its temperature, the total radiation emitted is increased 16 times. These radiations are allowed to fall on a metal surface. Photoelectrons emitted by the peak radiation at higher temperature can be brought to rest by applying a potential equivalent to the excitation potential corresponding to the transition for the level $n = 4$ to $n = 2$ in the Bohr's hydrogen atom. Find the work function (in eV) of the metal.

14 Electromagnetic waves of wavelength 1242 Å are incident on a metal of work function 2 eV. The target metal is connected to a 5 V cell, as shown. The electrons pass through hole A into a gas of hydrogen atoms in their ground state. Find the number of spectral lines emitted, when hydrogen atoms come back to their ground states after having been excited by the electrons. Assume all excitations in H-atoms from ground state only. ($hc = 12420$ eV-Å)

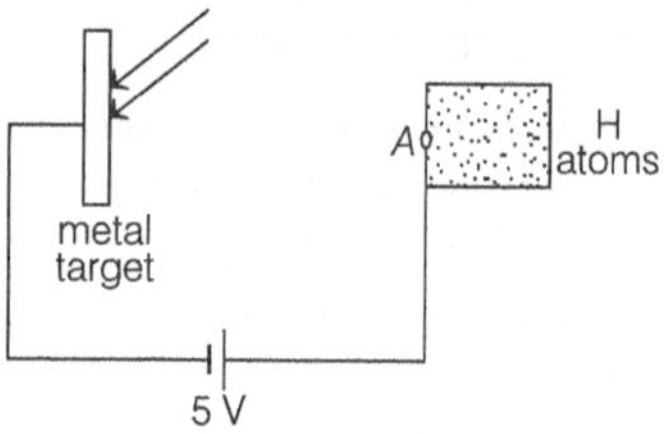

15 A monochromatic light source of frequency ν illuminates a metallic surface and ejects photoelectrons. The photoelectrons having maximum energy are just able to ionise the hydrogen atoms in ground state.
When the whole experiment is repeated with an incident radiation of frequency $\frac{5\nu}{6}$, the photoelectrons so emitted are able to excite the hydrogen atom beam which then emits a radiation of wavelength 1215 Å. Then, the frequency ν will be equal to $k \times 10^{15}$ Hz. The value of k is (consider nearest integer)

16 Radiation from hydrogen gas excited to first excited state is used for illuminating certain photoelectric plate. When the radiation from some unknown hydrogen like gas excited to the same level is used to expose the same plate, it is found that the de-Broglie wavelength of the fastest photoelectron has decreased 2.3 times. It is given that the energy corresponding to the longest wavelength of the Lyman series of the unknown gas is 3 times the ionisation energy of hydrogen gas (13.6 eV). Find the work function of photoelectric plate in eV. Take, $(2.3)^2 = 5.25$

Previous Year's Questions

JEE Main

1 The radius of third stationary orbit of electron for Bohr's atom is R. The radius of fourth stationary orbit will be **[2024, 27 Jan Shift-I]**

(a) $\frac{9}{16}R$ (b) $\frac{3}{4}R$
(c) $\frac{16}{9}R$ (d) $\frac{4}{3}R$

2 If Rydberg's constant is R, the longest wavelength of radiation in Paschen series will be $\frac{\alpha}{7R}$, where $\alpha = ...$.
[2024, 27 Jan Shift-II]

3 When a hydrogen atom going from $n = 2$ to $n = 1$ emits a photon, its recoil speed is $\frac{x}{5}$ m/s. Where $x =$ .... (Use, mass of hydrogen atom $= 1.6 \times 10^{-27}$ kg) **[2024, 29 Jan Shift-I]**

4 Given below are two statements:

Statement I Most of the mass of the atom and all its positive charge are concentrated in a tiny nucleus and the electrons revolve around it, is Rutherford's model.

Statement II An atom is a spherical cloud of positive charges with electrons embedded in it, is a special case of Rutherford's model. **[2024, 29 Jan Shift-II]**

In the light of the above statements, choose the **most appropriate** from the options given below

(a) Statement I is true but Statement II is false
(b) Both Statement I and Statement II are false
(c) Both Statement I and Statement II are true
(d) Statement I is false but Statement II is true

5 The radius of 2nd orbit of He^+ of bohr's model is r_1 and that of fourth orbit of Be^{3+} is represented as r_2. Now, the ratio $\frac{r_2}{r_1}$ is $x : 1$. The value of x is .... **[2023, 13 April Shift-I]**

6 The radius of fifth orbit of the Li^{++} is ...... $\times 10^{12}$ m.
Take: radius of hydrogen atom $= 0.51$ Å **[2023, 6 April Shift-I]**

7 Experimentally it is found that 12.8 eV energy is required to separate a hydrogen atom into a proton and an electron. So the orbital radius of the electron in a hydrogen atom $\frac{9}{x} \times 10^{-19}$ m. The value of the x is ....

($1 \text{ eV} = 1.6 \times 10^{-19}$ J, $\frac{1}{4\pi\varepsilon_0} = 9 \times 10^9$ Nm^2/C^2 and electronic charge $= 1.6 \times 10^{-19}$ C) **[2023, 6 April Shift-II]**

8 As per given figure A, B and C are the first, second and third energy levels of hydrogen atom, respectively. If the ratio of the two wavelengths $\left(\text{i.e. } \frac{\lambda_1}{\lambda_2}\right)$ is $\frac{7}{4n}$, then the value of n will be .... **[2023, 15 April Shift-I]**

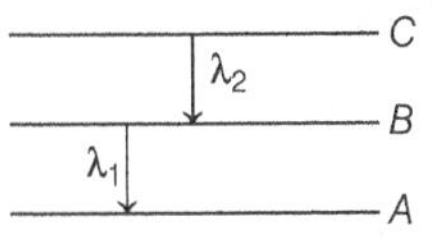

9 The wavelength of the radiation emitted is λ_0 when an electron jumps from the second excited state to the first excited state of hydrogen atom. If the electron jumps from the third excited state to the second orbit of the hydrogen atom the wavelength of the radiation emitted will be $\frac{20}{x}\lambda_0$. The value of x is ...... **[2023, 25 Jan Shift-I]**

10 If the binding energy of a ground state electron in a hydrogen atom is 13.6 eV , then the energy required to remove the electron from the second excited state of Li^{2+} will be $x \times 10^{-1}$ eV. The value of x is .... **[2023, 31 Jan Shift -II]**

11 If 917 Å be the lowest wavelength of Lyman series then the lowest wavelength of Balmer series will be .... Å. **[2023, 10 April Shift-II]**

12 The angular momentum for the electron in Bohr's orbit is L. If the electron is assumed to revolve in second orbit of hydrogen atom, then the change in angular momentum will be **[2023, 10 April Shift-I]**

(a) L (b) $\frac{L}{2}$
(c) Zero (d) $2L$

13 A 12.5 eV electron beam is used to bombard gaseous hydrogen at room temperature. The number of spectral lines emitted will be **[2023, 12 April Shift-I]**

(a) 1 (b) 3
(c) 2 (d) 4

14 An electron of a hydrogen like atom, having $Z = 4$, jumps from 4th energy state to 2nd energy state. The energy released in this process, will be (given, $Rch = 13.6$ eV)
where, $R =$ Rydberg constant, $c =$ Speed of light in vacuum and $h =$ Planck's constant **[2023, 1 Feb Shift-II]**

(a) 13.6 eV (b) 10.5 eV
(c) 40.8 eV (d) 3.4 eV

15 The energy levels of an atom is shown in figure.

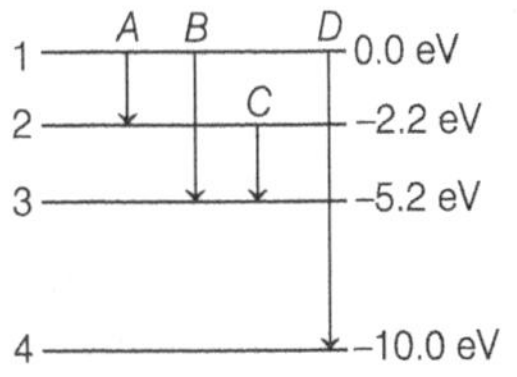

Which one of these transitions will result in the emission of a photon of wavelength 124.1 nm ?
(Given, $h = 6.62 \times 10^{-34}$ J-s) **[2023, 25 Jan Shift-II]**

(a) A (b) C (c) D (d) B

16 Speed of an electron in Bohr's 7th orbit for H-atom is 3.6×10^6 m/s. The corresponding speed of the electron in 3rd orbit, (in m/s) is **[2023, 30 Jan Shift-I]**

(a) 3.6×10^6 (b) 1.8×10^6
(c) 8.4×10^6 (d) 7.5×10^6

17 A photon is emitted in transition from $n = 4$ to $n = 1$ level in hydrogen atom. The corresponding wavelength for this transition is (given, $h = 4 \times 10^{-15}$ eV-s) **[2023, 24 Jan Shift-II]**

(a) 94.1 nm (b) 99.3 nm
(c) 974 nm (d) 941 nm

18 Find the ratio of energies of photons produced due to transition of an electron of hydrogen atom from its (i) second permitted energy level to the first level, and (ii) the highest permitted energy level to the first permitted level. **[2022, 29 July Shift-I]**

(a) 3 : 4 (b) 4 : 3
(c) 1 : 4 (d) 4 : 1

19 The momentum of an electron revolving in nth orbit is given by (Symbols have their usual meanings) **[2022, 25 July Shift-I]**

(a) $\frac{nh}{2\pi r}$ (b) $\frac{nh}{2r}$
(c) $\frac{nh}{2\pi}$ (d) $\frac{2\pi r}{nh}$

20 Given below are two statements :
Statement I In hydrogen atom, the frequency of radiation emitted when an electron jumps from lower energy orbit (E_1) to higher energy orbit (E_2), is given as $hf = E_1 - E_2$.

Statement II The jumping of electron from higher energy orbit (E_2) to lower energy orbit (E_1) is associated with frequency of radiation given as $f = (E_2 - E_1)/h$.
This condition is Bohr's frequency condition.
In the light of the above statements, choose the correct options. **[2022, 27 June Shift-II]**

(a) Both Statement I and Statement II are true.
(b) Both Statement I and Statement II are false.
(c) Statement I is true but Statement II is false.
(d) Statement I is false but Statement II is true.

21 A hydrogen atom is in ground state absorbs 10.2 eV of energy. The angular momentum of electron of the hydrogen atom will increase by the value of (Given, Planck's constant $= 6.6 \times 10^{-34}$ J-s) **[2022, 27 June Shift-I]**

(a) 2.10×10^{-34} J-s (b) 1.05×10^{-34} J-s
(c) 3.15×10^{-34} J-s (d) 4.2×10^{-34} J-s

22 The ratio for the speed of the electron in the 3rd orbit of He^+ to the speed of the electron in the 3rd orbit of hydrogen atom will be **[2022, 25 June Shift-I]**

(a) 1 : 1 (b) 1 : 2
(c) 4 : 1 (d) 2 : 1

23 In Bohr's atomic model of hydrogen, let K, P and E are the kinetic energy, potential energy and total energy of the electron, respectively. Choose the correct option when the electron undergoes transitions to a higher level. **[2022, 24 June Shift-II]**

(a) All K, P and E increase.
(b) K decreases, P and E increase.
(c) P decreases, K and E increase.
(d) K increases, P and E decrease.

24 $\sqrt{d_1}$ and $\sqrt{d_2}$ are the impact parameters corresponding to scattering angles 60° and 90° respectively, when an α-particle is approaching a gold nucleus. For $d_1 = x\, d_2$, the value of x will be .... **[2022, 29 June Shift-I]**

25 The radiation corresponding to $3 \rightarrow 2$ transition of a hydrogen atom falls on a gold surface to generate photoelectrons. These electrons are passed through a magnetic field of 5×10^{-4} T. Assume that the radius of the largest circular path followed by these electrons is 7 mm, the work-function of the metal is (Take, mass of electron $= 9.1 \times 10^{-31}$ kg) **[2021, 20 July Shift-I]**

(a) 1.36 eV (b) 1.88 eV
(c) 0.16 eV (d) 0.82 eV

26 A particular hydrogen like ion emits radiation of frequency 2.92×10^{15} Hz when it makes transition from $n = 3$ to $n = 1$. The frequency in Hz of radiation emitted in transition from $n = 2$ to $n = 1$ will be **[2021, 26 Aug Shift-I]**

(a) 0.44×10^{15} (b) 6.57×10^{15}
(c) 4.38×10^{15} (d) 2.46×10^{15}

27 The wavelength of the photon emitted by a hydrogen atom when an electron makes a transition from $n = 2$ to $n = 1$ state is **[2021, 25 Feb Shift-II]**

(a) 121.8 nm (b) 194.8 nm
(c) 490.7 nm (d) 913.3 nm

JEE Advanced

1. A hydrogen-like atom has atomic number Z. Photons emitted in the electronic transitions from level $n = 4$ to level $n = 3$ in these atoms are used to perform photoelectric effect experiment on a target metal. The maximum kinetic energy of the photoelectrons generated is 1.95 eV. If the photoelectric threshold wavelength for the target metal is 310 nm, the value of Z is ...... **(2023 Adv.)**

[Given : $hc = 1240$ eV-nm and $Rhc = 13.6$ eV, where R is the Rydberg constant, h is the Planck's constant and c is the speed of light in vacuum]

2. Which of the following statement(s) is(are) correct about the spectrum of hydrogen atom? **(2021 Adv.)**
   (a) The ratio of the longest wavelength to the shortest wavelength in Balmer series is 9/5.
   (b) There is an overlap between the wavelength ranges of Balmer and Paschen series.
   (c) The wavelengths of Lyman series are given by $\left(1+\frac{1}{m^2}\right)\lambda_0$, where λ_0 is the shortest wavelength of Lyman series and m is an integer.
   (d) The wavelength ranges of Lyman and Balmer series do not overlap.

3. A particle of mass m moves in circular orbits with potential energy $V(r) = Fr$, where F is a positive constant and r is its distance from the origin. Its energies are calculated using the Bohr model. If the radius of the particle's orbit is denoted by R and its speed and energy are denoted by v and E, respectively, then for the nth orbit (here h is the Planck's constant) **(2020 Adv.)**
   (a) $R \propto n^{1/3}$ and $v \propto n^{2/3}$ (b) $R \propto n^{2/3}$ and $v \propto n^{1/3}$
   (c) $E = \frac{3}{2}\left(\frac{n^2h^2F^2}{4\pi^2 m}\right)^{1/3}$ (d) $E = 2\left(\frac{n^2h^2F^2}{4\pi^2 m}\right)^{1/3}$

4. Consider a hydrogen-like ionised atom with atomic number Z with a single electron. In the emission spectrum of this atom, the photon emitted in the $n=2$ to $n=1$ transition has energy 74.8 eV higher than the photon emitted in the $n=3$ to $n=2$ transition. The ionisation energy of the hydrogen atom is 13.6 eV. The value of Z is .... **(2018 Adv.)**

5. A hydrogen atom in its ground state is irradiated by light of wavelength 970Å. Taking $hc/e = 1.237\times 10^{-6}$ eVm and the ground state energy of hydrogen atom as – 13.6 eV, the number of lines present in the emission spectrum is **(2016 Adv.)**

6. An electron in an excited state of Li^{2+} ion has angular momentum $\frac{3h}{2\pi}$. The de Broglie wavelength of the electron in this state is $p\pi a_0$ (where a_0 is the Bohr radius). The value of p is **(2015 Adv.)**

Answer Key

Level 1

8.1 Rutherford's Model

1. 10^{-12} cm 2. 180° 3. $\frac{5}{9}\times 10^6$

8.2 Bohr Model

1. $\frac{4r}{3}$ 2. $4r$ 3. 8 : 1 4. $\frac{\hbar}{m^2a_0^3}$

5. $\frac{h}{\pi}$ 6. 91.8 V 7. 13.6 eV

8. (i) 5 (ii) 16.53 eV
   (iii) 340 eV, – 680 eV, 1.06×10^{-34} kg-m^{2}s^{-1} 9. 54.4 eV

10.	K	U	E
First orbit	13.6 eV	0	13.6 eV
Second orbit	3.4 eV	20.4 eV	23.8 eV

11. $r = \left(\frac{n^2h^2}{8\,am\pi^2}\right)^{1/4}$

8.3 Emission Spectrum

1. $\frac{20}{27}\lambda_0$ 2. 11.4 mm, 3
3. $\lambda_{max} = 121.6$ nm, $\lambda_{min} = 91.2$ nm, ultraviolet (UV) region
4. (a) $\lambda = 4.9\times 10^{-7}$ m (b) 6.12×10^{14} Hz 5. – 54.4 eV
6. N=6, $\lambda_{max} = 18752$ Å 7. 26252 Å
8. – 54.4 eV, – 13.6 eV
9. (a) $n=3$ (b) $Z=6$ (c) 28.49 Å
10. (i) 15.6 eV (ii) 2340 Å (iii) 12.52 eV (iv) 1.009×10^7 m^{-1}
    (v) 6 eV (vi) 0.7 eV 11. 12.75 eV/c

8.4 Effect of Nucleus Motion

1. (i) 4.23 Å (ii) – 6.8 eV
2. 2.85×10^{-13} m, 2.53×10^3 eV

8.5 Atomic Collisioins

1. (a) elastic collision (b) elastic or perfectly inelastic collision
   (c) elastic or inelastic collision
   (d) elastic or inelastic or perfectly inelastic collision
2. 51 eV

Level 2

Single Choice Correct Questions

1. (d)	2. (d)	3. (b)	4. (c)	5. (a)
6. (d)	7. (d)	8. (a)	9. (b)	10. (a)
11. (c)	12. (d)	13. (b)	14. (c)	15. (c)
16. (c)	17. (b)	18. (c)	19. (c)	20. (a)
21. (c)	22. (a)	23. (b)	24. (b)	25. (a)
26. (a)	27. (d)	28. (a)	29. (b)	30. (c)
31. (d)	32. (a)	33. (d)	34. (b)	35. (a)
36. (d)	37. (b)	38. (c)	39. (a)	40. (b)
41. (b)	42. (b)	43. (d)	44. (a)	45. (a)
46. (a)	47. (c)	48. (b)	49. (c)	50. (b)
51. (c)	52. (c)	53. (d)	54. (d)	55. (c)
56. (d)	57. (a)	58. (a)	59. (b)	60. (d)
61. (b)	62. (c)	63. (b)	64. (c)	65. (c)
66. (b)	67. (b)	68. (b)	69. (a)	70. (b)
71. (c)	72. (d)	73. (b)	74. (a)	75. (b)
76. (b)	77. (b)			

Multiple Choice(s) Correct Questions

1. (a, c)	2. (a, b, c, d)	3. (a, b, d)	4. (a, d)
5. (a, d)	6. (a, b, d)	7. (a, b, d)	8. (b, c)
9. (b, c, d)	10. (a, b, d)	11. (b, d)	12. (b, c)
13. (a, c, d)	14. (a, b)	15. (b, c)	16. (a, b, c)
17. (a, b, c, d)	18. (a, c, d)	19. (a, b, d)	20. (b, c)

Comprehension Based Questions

1. (a)	2. (b)	3. (a)	4. (c)	5. (b)
6. (b)	7. (d)	8. (c)	9. (d)	10. (b)
11. (c)	12. (c)	13. (c)	14. (c)	15. (b)
16. (c)	17. (d)	18. (c)	19. (a)	20. (b)
21. (d)	22. (a)	23. (d)	24. (c)	25. (b)
26. (b)	27. (c)	28. (a)	29. (b)	30. (c)
31. (d)	32. (d)	33. (b)	34. (c)	35. (c)
36. (a)	37. (a)	38. (b)	39. (d)	

Match the Columns Questions

1. A → 3, B → 1, C → 2, D → 2, E → 4
2. A → 3, B → 1,3,4, C → 1, D → 2,4
3. A → 3, B → 2,4, C → 1, D → 1,4
4. A → 2, B → 3, C → 1, 5, D → 4
5. A → 1, B → 1, C → 2, D → 3,4

Numerical Value Questions

1. 18	2. 4	3. 1925	4. 487.06
5. 7	6. 4	7. 2	8. 5
9. 98.25	10. 15	11. 63.75	12. 7
13. 1.45	14. 6	15. 5	16. 3

Previous Year's Questions

JEE Main

1. (c)	2. (144)	3. (17)	4. (a)	5. (2)
6. (425)	7. (16)	8. (9.8)	9. (35)	10. (136)
11. (3668)	12. (a)	13. (b)	14. (c)	15. (c)
16. (c)	17. (b)	18. (a)	19. (a)	20. (d)
21. (b)	22. (d)	23. (b)	24. (3)	25. (d)
26. (d)	27. (a)			

JEE Advanced

1. (3)	2. (d)	3. (b,c)	4. (3)	5. (6)
6. (2)				

SOLUTIONS

Level 1

8.1 Rutherford's Model

1. $r_0 = \dfrac{(Ze)(2e)}{4\pi\varepsilon_0(E)} = \dfrac{2 \times 92(1.6 \times 10^{-19})^2 \times 9 \times 10^9}{5 \times 1.6 \times 10^{-13}}$

$$= 0.53 \times 10^{-14} \text{ m} \approx 10^{-12} \text{ cm}$$

2. Impact parameter $b \propto \cot\dfrac{\theta}{2}$

Here $b = 0$, hence, $\theta = 180°$

3. $N \propto \left[\dfrac{1}{\sin^4\theta/2}\right] \Rightarrow N_1 = 5 \times 10^6 \dfrac{(\sin 30°)^4}{(\sin 60°)^4} = \dfrac{5}{9} \times 10^6$

8.2 Bohr's Model

1. $r \propto \dfrac{n^2}{Z} \Rightarrow \dfrac{r_1}{r_2} = \left(\dfrac{n_1}{n_2}\right)^2 \dfrac{Z_2}{Z_1}$

$$\Rightarrow \quad \frac{r}{r_2} = \left(\frac{2}{4}\right)^2\left(\frac{3}{1}\right) \Rightarrow r_2 = \frac{4r}{3}$$

2. $v \propto \dfrac{1}{n} \Rightarrow \dfrac{v_1}{v_2} = \dfrac{n_2}{n_1}$

$$\Rightarrow \quad \frac{v}{v/2} = \frac{n_2}{1} \Rightarrow n_2 = 2$$

$$r \propto n^2 \Rightarrow \frac{r_1}{r_2} = \left(\frac{n_1}{n_2}\right)^2$$

$$\Rightarrow \quad \frac{r}{r_2} = \left(\frac{1}{2}\right)^2 \Rightarrow r_2 = 4r$$

3. $T \propto n^3 \Rightarrow \dfrac{T_1}{T_2} = \left(\dfrac{n_1}{n_2}\right)^3$

$$\Rightarrow \quad \frac{T_1}{T_2} = \left(\frac{2}{1}\right)^3 \Rightarrow T_1 : T_2 = 8 : 1$$

4. $mvr = \dfrac{nh}{2\pi} \Rightarrow mva_0 = \dfrac{h}{2\pi}$

$$\Rightarrow \quad v = \frac{h}{2\pi m a_0} = \frac{\hbar}{m a_0}$$

Acceleration of electron

$$= \frac{v^2}{r} = \left(\frac{\hbar}{m a_0}\right)^2 \frac{1}{a_0} = \frac{\hbar^2}{m^2 a_0^3}$$

5. $E = \dfrac{U}{2} = -\dfrac{6.8}{2} = -3.4 \text{ eV}$

$$E = -13.6\frac{Z^2}{n^2} = -3.4 \Rightarrow n = 2$$

Angular momentum $= \dfrac{nh}{2\pi} = 2\left(\dfrac{h}{2\pi}\right) = \dfrac{h}{\pi}$

6. Ionisation potential $= 122.4$ V

$$\Rightarrow \quad 122.4 = 13.6 \times \frac{Z^2}{1^2} \quad \text{...(i)}$$

First excitation potential $= E$

$$\Rightarrow \quad E = 13.6 \times Z^2\left[\frac{1}{1^2} - \frac{1}{2^2}\right] \quad \text{...(ii)}$$

From Eqs. (i) and (ii), we get

$$\Rightarrow \quad E = 91.8 \text{ V}$$

7. For He^+, $E_2 = -13.6 \times \dfrac{Z^2}{n^2} = -13.6 \times \dfrac{(2)^2}{(2)^2} = -13.6$ eV

Binding energy $= E_\infty - E_2 = 0 - (-13.6) = 13.6$ eV

8. (a) $\Delta E = 13.6Z^2\left[\dfrac{1}{n_1^2} - \dfrac{1}{n_2^2}\right]$

$$\Rightarrow \quad 47.2 = 13.6Z^2\left[\frac{1}{2^2} - \frac{1}{3^2}\right]$$

$$\Rightarrow \quad Z = 5$$

(b) $\Delta E = 13.6Z^2\left[\dfrac{1}{n_1^2} - \dfrac{1}{n_2^2}\right] = 13.6(5)^2\left[\dfrac{1}{3^2} - \dfrac{1}{4^2}\right] = 16.53$ eV

(c) $E_1 = -13.6\dfrac{Z^2}{n^2} = -13.6\dfrac{(5)^2}{(1)^2} = -340$ eV

$$K_1 = -E_1 = -(-340) \text{ eV} = 340 \text{ eV}$$

$$U_1 = 2E_1 = -680 \text{ eV}$$

$$L = \frac{nh}{2\pi} = \frac{1 \times 6.63 \times 10^{-34}}{2 \times 3.14} = 1.06 \times 10^{-34} \text{ kg-m}^2\text{/s}$$

9. $\Delta E = 13.6Z^2\left[\dfrac{1}{n_1^2} - \dfrac{1}{n_2^2}\right]$

$$\Rightarrow \quad 7.55 = 13.6Z^2\left[\frac{1}{2^2} - \frac{1}{3^2}\right]$$

$$\Rightarrow \quad Z = 2$$

$$E_1 = -13.6\frac{Z^2}{n^2} = -13.6\frac{(2)^2}{(1)^2} = -54.4 \text{ eV}$$

Ionisation energy $= E_\infty - E_1 = 0 - (-54.4) = 54.4$ eV

10. $E_1 = -13.6$ eV, $K_1 = 13.6$ eV, $U_1 = -27.2$ eV

$E_2 = -3.4$ eV, $K_2 = 3.4$ eV, $U_2 = -6.8$ eV

If potential energy in the first orbit is zero i.e., it has been increased by 27.2 eV. So, potential energy and total energy in all orbits will increase by 27.2 eV while kinetic energy will remain unchanged.

	U	E	K
First orbit	0	$-13.6 + 27.2 = 13.6$ eV	13.6 eV
Second orbit	$-6.8 + 27.2 = 20.4$ eV	$-3.4 + 27.2 = 23.8$ eV	3.4 eV

11. $F = -\frac{dU}{dr} = -2ar$

This force provides the centripetal force for circular motion of electron.

$$2ar = \frac{mv^2}{r} \quad \text{...(i)}$$

By quantisation of angular momentum,

$$mvr = \frac{nh}{2\pi} \quad \text{...(ii)}$$

Solving Eqs. (i) and (ii), we get

$$r = \left(\frac{n^2h^2}{8\pi^2 ma}\right)^{1/4}$$

8.3 Emission Spectrum

1. When electron jumps from the third orbit to the second orbit,

$$\frac{1}{\lambda_0} = R\left(\frac{1}{2^2} - \frac{1}{3^2}\right) \quad \text{...(i)}$$

When electron jumps from fourth to second orbit,

$$\frac{1}{\lambda} = R\left(\frac{1}{2^2} - \frac{1}{4^2}\right) \quad \text{...(ii)}$$

Solving Eqs. (i) and (ii), we get

$$\lambda = \frac{20}{27}\lambda_0$$

2.

$$\Delta E = 13.6Z^2\left[\frac{1}{n_1^2} - \frac{1}{n_2^2}\right]$$

$$= 13.6(3)^2\left[\frac{1}{1^2} - \frac{1}{3^2}\right] = 108.8 \text{ eV}$$

$$\Delta E = \frac{hc}{\lambda} \Rightarrow 108.8 = \frac{1240}{\lambda}$$

$$\Rightarrow \lambda = 11.39 \text{ nm}$$

When electron jumps back from $n = 3$ to $n = 1$,
Number of spectral lines $= {}^nC_2 = {}^3C_2 = 3$

3. For longest wavelength of Lyman series,

$$n_1 = 2, n_2 = 1$$

$$\Delta E = 13.6\left[\frac{1}{1^2} - \frac{1}{2^2}\right] = 10.2 \text{ eV}$$

$$\Delta E = \frac{hc}{\lambda} \Rightarrow 10.2 = \frac{1240}{\lambda}$$

$$\Rightarrow \lambda = 121.6 \text{ nm}$$

For shortest wavelength of Lyman series,

$$n_1 = \infty, n_2 = 1$$

$$\Delta E = 13.6\left[\frac{1}{1^2} - \frac{1}{(\infty)^2}\right] = 13.6 \text{ eV}$$

$$\Delta E = \frac{hc}{\lambda} \Rightarrow 13.6 = \frac{1240}{\lambda}$$

$$\Rightarrow \lambda = 91.2 \text{ nm}$$

4. (a) H_β line of Balmer series corresponds to the transition from $n = 4$ to $n = 2$ level.

$$\frac{1}{\lambda} = R\left(\frac{1}{n_2^2} - \frac{1}{n_1^2}\right)$$

$$\Rightarrow \frac{1}{\lambda} = (1.097 \times 10^7)\left(\frac{1}{2^2} - \frac{1}{4^2}\right)$$

$$\Rightarrow \lambda = 4.9 \times 10^{-7} \text{ m}$$

(b) $f = \frac{c}{\lambda} = \frac{3 \times 10^8}{4.9 \times 10^{-7}} = 6.12 \times 10^{14}$ Hz

5.

$$\frac{1}{\lambda} = RZ^2\left[\frac{1}{n_1^2} - \frac{1}{n_2^2}\right]$$

$$\Rightarrow \frac{1}{273.5 \times 10^{-9}} = (1.097 \times 10^7)\, Z^2\left(\frac{1}{3^2} - \frac{1}{6^2}\right)$$

$$\Rightarrow Z = 2$$

$$E_1 = -13.6\frac{Z^2}{n^2} = -13.6\frac{(2)^2}{(1)^2} = -54.4 \text{ eV}$$

6.

$$\frac{1}{\lambda} = R\left(\frac{1}{n_1^2} - \frac{1}{n_2^2}\right)$$

$$\Rightarrow \frac{1}{975 \times 10^{-10}} = 1.097 \times 10^7\left(\frac{1}{1^2} - \frac{1}{n^2}\right)$$

$$\Rightarrow n = 4$$

Number of different lines possible in the spectrum

$$= {}^nC_2 = {}^4C_2 = 6$$

Longest wavelength will be for the transition having least energy gap i.e., $n = 4$ to $n = 3$

$$\frac{1}{\lambda_{max}} = (1.097 \times 10^7)\left(\frac{1}{3^2} - \frac{1}{4^2}\right)$$

$$\Rightarrow \lambda_{max} = 18752 \text{ Å}$$

7. $\frac{1}{\lambda} = RZ^2\left[\frac{1}{n_2^2} - \frac{1}{n_1^2}\right]$

For first member of Balmer series,

$$n_1 = 3 \text{ and } n_2 = 2$$

$$\frac{1}{6563} = RZ^2\left[\frac{1}{2^2} - \frac{1}{3^2}\right] \quad \text{...(i)}$$

For second member of Brackett series,

$$n_1 = 6 \text{ and } n_2 = 4$$

$$\frac{1}{\lambda} = RZ^2\left[\frac{1}{4^2} - \frac{1}{6^2}\right] \quad \text{...(ii)}$$

For Eqs. (i) and (ii), we get

$$\lambda = 26252 \text{ Å}$$

8.

$$\frac{1}{\lambda_1} = \frac{1}{\lambda_2}$$

$$\Rightarrow R(1)^2\left[\frac{1}{1^2} - \frac{1}{2^2}\right] = RZ^2\left[\frac{1}{2^2} - \frac{1}{4^2}\right]$$

$$\Rightarrow Z = 2$$

$$E_1 = -13.6\frac{(2)^2}{(1)^2} = -54.4 \text{ eV}$$

$$E_2 = -13.6\frac{(2)^2}{(2)^2} = -13.6 \text{ eV}$$

9. (a) Number of different wavelengths $= {}^nC_2 = 3$

$$\Rightarrow \qquad n = 3$$

Therefore, the final excited state of the gas is $n = 3$. The initial state of the gas atoms is $n = 2$ as all the wavelengths are smaller and the energy will be greater.

(b) $\Delta E = 13.6Z^2\left[\frac{1}{2^2} - \frac{1}{3^2}\right] = 68 \quad \Rightarrow \quad Z = 6$

(c) The minimum wavelength corresponds to the transition

$n_1 = 3$ to $n_2 = 1$

$$\frac{1}{\lambda} = (1.097\times 10^7)(6)^2\left[\frac{1}{(1)^2} - \frac{1}{3^2}\right]$$

$$\Rightarrow \quad \lambda = 28.49 \text{ Å}$$

10. (i) Ionisation energy $= E_\infty - E_1 = 0 - (-15.6) = 15.6$ eV

Ionisation potential = 15.6 V

(ii) Short wavelength will correspond to transition with largest energy gap i.e., $n_1 = \infty$ to $n_2 = 2$

$$\Delta E = E_\infty - E_2 = 0 - (-5.30) = 5.30 \text{ eV}$$

$$\Delta E = \frac{hc}{\lambda} \quad \Rightarrow \quad 5.30 = \frac{12400}{\lambda}$$

$$\Rightarrow \quad \lambda = 2340 \text{ Å}$$

(iii) Excitation energy for state $n = 3$ is

$$\Delta E = E_3 - E_1 = -3.08 - (-15.6) = 12.52 \text{ eV}$$

(iv) For $n_1 = 3$ to $n_2 = 1$

$$\lambda = \frac{12400}{E_3 - E_1} = \frac{12400}{12\cdot 52} \text{ Å} = 990 \text{ Å}$$

$$\text{Wave number } \frac{1}{\lambda} = \frac{1}{990\times 10^{-10}\text{ m}} = 1.009\times 10^{-7} \text{ m}^{-1}$$

(v) Energy required to excite the electron in the ground state to $n = 2$ is 10.3 eV. Since, energy of incident electron is less than 10.3 eV, excitation of ground state electron doesn't take place. So, the incident electron won't interact with the atom and its energy will be 6 eV.

(vi) Energy of incident electron after excitation

$$= 11 - 10.3 = 0.7 \text{ eV}$$

11. $\Delta E_{4\to 1} = 13.6\cdot\left[\frac{1}{1^2} - \frac{1}{4^2}\right] = 12.75$ eV

Momentum of hydrogen atom = Momentum of photon

$$= \frac{\Delta E}{c} = 12.75 \text{ eV/c}$$

8.4 Effect on Nucleus Motion on Bohr Model

1. Mass of positron = Mass of electron $= m_e$

$$\text{Reduced mass} = \frac{m_1 m_2}{m_1 + m_2} = \frac{m_e m_e}{m_e + m_e} = \frac{m_e}{2}$$

(i) $r = (0.529 \text{ Å})\frac{n^2}{Z}\left(\frac{m_e}{\mu}\right) = (0.529 \text{ Å})\frac{(2)^2}{1}\frac{m_e}{(m_e/2)} = 4.23$ Å

(ii) $E = (-13.6 \text{ eV})\frac{Z^2}{n^2}\left(\frac{\mu}{m_e}\right) = -13.6\frac{(1)^2}{(1)^2}\left(\frac{m_e/2}{m_e}\right) = -6.8$ eV

2. $m_p = 1836m_e, m_\mu = 207m_e$

$$\mu = \frac{m_p m_\mu}{m_p + m_\mu} = 186m_e$$

(i) $r = (0.529 \text{ Å})\frac{n^2}{Z}\left(\frac{m_e}{\mu}\right) = \frac{0.529\times 10^{-10}}{186} = 2.84\times 10^{-13}$ m

(ii) $E_1 = (13.6 \text{ eV})\frac{Z^2}{n^2}\left(\frac{\mu}{m_e}\right) = (13.6 \text{ eV})(186) = 2.53\times 10^3$ eV

8.5 Atomic Collision

1. For collsion to be inelastic, H-atom must get excited. Let ΔE be the energy used to excite the H-atom. So,

$$\Delta E = \{10.2 \text{ eV}, 12.09 \text{ eV}, 12.75 \text{ eV}, \ldots\}$$

If the collision is perfectly inelastic, then using linear momentum conservation,

$$mv + 0 = mv' + mv'$$

$$\Rightarrow \qquad v' = \frac{v}{2}$$

$$\text{Energy loss} = \left(\frac{1}{2}mv^2 + 0\right) - \frac{1}{2}2m\left(\frac{v}{2}\right)^2 = \frac{1}{4}mv^2 = \frac{K}{2}$$

Maximum energy loss occurs in perfectly inelastic collisions.

So, $\Delta E_{max} = \frac{K}{2}$

(a) If $K = 14$ eV, $\Delta E_{max} = \frac{14}{2} = 7$ eV

This energy loss is not enough to excite the H-atom. So, collision has to be elastic.

(b) If $K = 20.4$ eV, $\Delta E_{max} = \frac{20.4}{2} = 10.2$ eV

So, if $\Delta E = 0 \quad \Rightarrow$ elastic collision

$\Delta E = \Delta E_{max} \quad \Rightarrow$ perfectly inelastic collision

(c) If $K = 22$ eV, $\Delta E_{max} = \frac{22}{2} = 11$ eV

So, if $\Delta E = 0 \quad \Rightarrow$ elastic collision

$\Delta E = 10.2 \text{ eV} < \Delta E_{max} \quad \Rightarrow$ inelastic collision

(d) If $K = 24.18$ eV, $\Delta E_{max} = \frac{24.18}{2} = 12.09$ eV

So, if $\Delta E = 0 \quad \Rightarrow$ elastic collision

$\Delta E = 10.2 \text{ eV} \quad \Rightarrow$ inelastic collision

$\Delta E = 12.09 \text{ eV} = \Delta E_{max} \quad \Rightarrow$ perfectly inelastic collision

2.

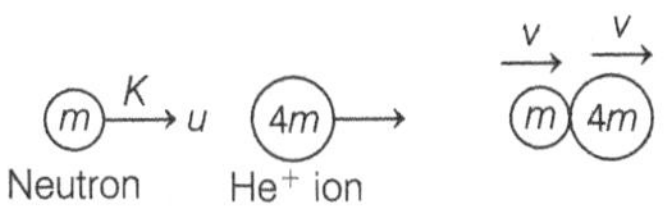

If collision is pefectly inelastic then, applying linear momentum conservation,

$$mu + 0 = 5mv$$

$$\Rightarrow \quad v = \frac{u}{5}$$

$$\text{Energy loss} = \Delta E_{max} = \frac{1}{2}mu^2 - \frac{1}{2}(5m)\left(\frac{u}{5}\right)^2 = \frac{2}{5}mu^2 = \frac{4K}{5}$$

For collision to be inelastic, electron in ground state of He^+ should excite to the first state.

$$\Delta E = E_2 - E_1 = 13.6(2)^2\left[\frac{1}{1^2} - \frac{1}{2^2}\right] = 40.8 \text{ eV}$$

So, $\frac{4K}{5} \le 40.8 \Rightarrow K \le 51 \text{ eV} \Rightarrow K_{min} = 51 \text{ eV}$

Level 2

Single Choice Correct Questions

1. Only one α-particle is deviated by an angle of 180°.
2. α-particles are scattered by the nucleus due to the force of repulsion between them and the nucleus.

   Trajectories of particles 1, 2, and 3 clearly indicate influence of force of repulsion. But the trajectory of particle 4 indicate influence of force of attraction, which is not possible.
3. At distance of closest approach, velocity of projectile becomes zero.

   $$\text{Energy, } E = \frac{1}{2}mu^2 + 0 = \frac{1}{4\pi\varepsilon_0}\frac{(z_1e)\times(z_2e)}{r} + 0$$

   E is directly proportional to Z_1Z_2.
4. $K = \frac{1}{4\pi\varepsilon_0}\frac{(Ze)(2e)}{d} = 9\times10^9\frac{(79e)(2e)}{4\times10^{-14}} = 5.69 \text{ MeV}$
5. $N \propto \left[\frac{1}{\sin^4\theta/2}\right]$

   $$\Rightarrow N_1 = 7\times\frac{1}{(\sin 30°)^4} = 112 \text{ and } N_2 = 7\times\frac{1}{(\sin 60°)^4} = 12.5$$
6. $r \propto \frac{n^2}{Z}$

   Z is maximum for Li^{2+}. So, its radius of first orbit will be minimum.
7. $r_n \propto n^2$

   $$r_{n+1} - r_n = r_{n-1}$$

   $$\Rightarrow (n+1)^2 - n^2 = (n-1)^2$$

   $$\Rightarrow n = 4$$
8. $\ln\left|\frac{A_n}{A_1}\right| = \ln\left|\frac{\pi r_n^2}{\pi r_1^2}\right| = \ln\left|\frac{n^4}{1^4}\right| = 4\ln|n| \quad (\because r_n \propto n^2)$

   So, graph of $\ln\left|\frac{A_n}{A_1}\right|$ *versus* $\ln|n|$ will be straight line of slope 4.
9. $v \propto \frac{Z}{n} \Rightarrow \frac{v_1}{v_2} = \left(\frac{Z_1}{Z_2}\right)\left(\frac{n_2}{n_1}\right)$

   $$\Rightarrow \frac{v}{v_2} = \left(\frac{1}{2}\right)\left(\frac{2}{1}\right) \Rightarrow v_2 = v$$
10. $L = mvr$

    $$\Rightarrow L \propto \left(\frac{Z}{n}\right)\left(\frac{n^2}{Z}\right) \Rightarrow L \propto n$$

    $$\Rightarrow L \propto \sqrt{r}$$
11. $L = \frac{nh}{2\pi}, L_1 = \frac{(1)h}{2\pi}, L_2 = \frac{(2)h}{2\pi}$

    So, $L_2 = 2L_1$
12. $$\frac{Ke^2}{r^2} = \frac{mv^2}{r} \quad \text{...(i)}$$

    $$mvr = \frac{(1)h}{2\pi} \quad \text{...(ii)}$$

    Solving Eqs. (i) and (ii), we get

    $$v = \frac{2\pi Ke^2}{h}$$

    So, $\frac{v}{c} = \frac{2\pi Ke^2}{ch}$

    In CGS system, $K = 1$
13. $T = \frac{2\pi R}{v} \Rightarrow T \propto \frac{n^2}{\left(\frac{1}{n}\right)} \Rightarrow T \propto n^3$

    $$\Rightarrow T \propto R^{3/2} \quad \left(\because R \propto n^2 \text{ and } v \propto \frac{1}{n}\right)$$
14. $T \propto \frac{n^3}{Z^2} \Rightarrow \frac{T_1}{T_2} = \left(\frac{n_1}{n_2}\right)^3\left(\frac{Z_2}{Z_1}\right)^2$

    $$\Rightarrow \frac{2T_2}{T_2} = \left(\frac{1}{2}\right)^3\left(\frac{Z_2}{1}\right)^2$$

    $$\Rightarrow Z_2 = 4$$
15. Velocity of electron, $v_n = (2.19\times10^6 \text{ m/s})\frac{Z}{n}$

    For $n = 2$, $v_2 = 1.095\times10^6$ m/s

    Radius of orbit, $r_n = (0.529\times10^{-10} \text{ m})\frac{n^2}{Z}$

    For $n = 2$, $r_2 = 2.116\times10^{-10}$ m

    $$\text{Frequency of revolution} = \frac{v_2}{2\pi r_2} = 8.23\times10^{14} \text{ s}^{-1}$$

    Number of revolutions = Frequency × Time

    $$= (8.23\times10^{14})(10^{-8}) = 8.23\times10^6$$
16. $v \propto \frac{Z}{n}$ and $r \propto \frac{n^2}{Z}$

    $$a = \frac{v^2}{r} \Rightarrow a \propto \frac{(Z/n)^2}{\left(\frac{n^2}{Z}\right)} \Rightarrow a \propto \frac{Z^3}{n^4}$$

    So, $\frac{a_1}{a_2} = \left(\frac{Z_1}{Z_2}\right)^3\left(\frac{n_2}{n_1}\right)^4 = \left(\frac{2}{3}\right)^3\left(\frac{1}{1}\right)^4 = \frac{8}{27}$

17. $\tau_{avg} = \dfrac{\Delta L}{\Delta t} = \dfrac{3\left(\frac{h}{2\pi}\right) - 2\left(\frac{h}{2\pi}\right)}{10^{-8}} = \dfrac{6.6 \times 10^{-34}}{2 \times 3.14 \times 10^{-8}}$

$\simeq 10^{-26}$ N-m

18. $U = -\dfrac{Ke^2}{3r^3}, \quad F = -\dfrac{dU}{dr} = -\dfrac{Ke^2}{r^4}$

$$\frac{Ke^2}{r^4} = \frac{mv^2}{r} \quad \text{...(i)}$$

$$mvr = \frac{nh}{2\pi} \quad \text{...(ii)}$$

From Eqs. (i) and (ii), we get

$$r = \frac{4\pi^2 e^2 Km}{n^2 h^2}$$

Total energy of electron,

$$E = K + U = \frac{1}{2}mv^2 - \frac{Ke^3}{3r^3}$$

$$= \frac{Ke^2}{2r^3} - \frac{Ke^2}{3r^3} = \frac{Ke^2}{6r^3}$$

Substituting the value of r, we get

$$E = \frac{n^6 h^6}{6(2\pi)^6 m^3 K^2 e^4}$$

So, $E \propto n^6$ and $E \propto m^{-3}$

19. $E = -\dfrac{dV}{dr} = -\dfrac{V_0}{r}$

$$eE = \frac{mv^2}{r}$$

$$\Rightarrow \quad \frac{eV_0}{r} = \frac{mv^2}{r} \quad \text{...(i)}$$

$$mvr = \frac{nh}{2\pi} \quad \text{...(ii)}$$

From Eqs. (i) and (ii), we get

$$r_n \propto n$$

20. Current due to orbiting electron $= \dfrac{q}{T} = \dfrac{e}{\left(\frac{2\pi r}{v}\right)} = \dfrac{ev}{2\pi r}$

Magnetic dipole moment,

$$M = i\pi r^2 = \left(\frac{ev}{2\pi r}\right)\pi r^2 = \frac{evr}{2} = \frac{e(mvr)}{2m} = \frac{nhe}{4\pi m}$$

Torque, $\tau = MB \sin\theta$

$$\Rightarrow \quad \tau = \left(\frac{nhe}{4\pi m}\right)B \sin 30^\circ \quad \Rightarrow \quad \tau = \frac{nheB}{8\pi m}$$

For ground state, $n = 1$

21. $E_N = E_1$

$$\Rightarrow \quad -13.6 \times \frac{(3)^2}{N^2} = -13.6 \times \frac{(1)^2}{(1)^2}$$

$$\Rightarrow \quad N = 3$$

$$r \propto \frac{n^2}{Z} \quad \Rightarrow \quad \frac{r_N}{r_1} = \left(\frac{N}{1}\right)^2\left(\frac{1}{3}\right) = 3$$

22. $E_2 - E_1 = 10.2$ eV

So, electron jumps from ground state to $n = 2$

$$L = \frac{nh}{2\pi}$$

$$\Delta L = 2\left(\frac{h}{2\pi}\right) - 1\left(\frac{h}{2\pi}\right) = \frac{h}{2\pi} \simeq 1 \times 10^{-34}$$

23. For second excited state, $n = 3$

$$L = \frac{nh}{2\pi} \quad \Rightarrow \quad L \propto n \quad \Rightarrow \quad L_H = L_{Li} \qquad (\because n_{Li} = n_H)$$

$$E \propto \frac{Z^2}{n^2} \quad \Rightarrow \quad |E_{Li}| > |E_H| \qquad (\because Z_{Li} > Z_H)$$

24. $L = \dfrac{nh}{2\pi} \quad \Rightarrow \quad \dfrac{h}{\pi} = \dfrac{nh}{2\pi} \quad \Rightarrow \quad n = 2$

$$E = -13.6\left(\frac{Z^2}{n^2}\right) = (-13.6 \text{ eV})\left[\frac{(1)^2}{(2)^2}\right] = -3.4 \text{ eV}$$

$$U = 2E = 2(-3.4 \text{ eV}) = -6.8 \text{ eV}$$

25. Kinetic energy of electron = Binding energy of electron

$$\Rightarrow \quad \frac{1}{2}mv^2 = E_n \quad \text{...(i)}$$

By quantisation of angular momentum

$$mvr = \frac{nh}{2\pi} \quad \text{...(ii)}$$

Dividing Eq. (i) by (ii), we get

$$\frac{v}{2\pi r} = \frac{2E_n}{nh} \quad \Rightarrow \quad f = \frac{2E_n}{nh}$$

26. $E_1 < E_2, U_1 < U_2$ and $K_1 > K_2$

27. Energy of photon $= E_2 - E_1$

$= -3.4 - (-13.6)$

$= 10.2$ eV

For removal of electron from Li^{2+},

$$10.2 \geq 13.6\frac{Z^2}{n^2}$$

$$\Rightarrow \quad n^2 \geq \frac{13.6 \times (3)^2}{10.2}$$

$$\Rightarrow \quad n_{min} = 4$$

28. For absorption line, electron should jump from lower state to higher state and energy gap is maximum for transition $n = 1$ to $n = 2$. Higher energy corresponds to higher frequency.

29. Total energy depends on the reference level chosen for zero potential energy. Kinetic energy, binding energy and energy gap between two states are independent of choice of zero potential energy.

30. $U_1 = 2E_1 = -27.2$ eV, $U'_1 = 0$

If potential energy in the ground state is taken zero, then potential energy increases by 27.2 eV in every orbit while kinetic energy remains unchanged. Hence, total energy will also increase by 27.2 eV in every orbit.

$$E_2 = -3.4 \text{ eV}$$

$$E'_2 = -3.4 + 27.2 = 23.8 \text{ eV}$$

31. Binding energy $= -E = (13.6\text{ eV})\left(\dfrac{Z^2}{n^2}\right)$

So, binding energy $\propto \dfrac{1}{n^2}$

For first excited state, $n = 2$

For second excited state, $n = 3$

$$\frac{E_2}{E_3} = \frac{(3)^2}{(2)^2} = \frac{9}{4}$$

32. First excitation potential $= 13.6Z^2\left[\dfrac{1}{1^2} - \dfrac{1}{2^2}\right] = 20$

$$\Rightarrow \quad 13.6Z^2 = \frac{80}{3}$$

Third excitation poential $= 13.6Z^2\left[\dfrac{1}{1^2} - \dfrac{1}{4^2}\right]$

$$= \left(\frac{80}{3}\right)\left(\frac{15}{16}\right) = 25\text{ V}$$

33. $E_n = -13.6\dfrac{Z^2}{n^2} \quad \Rightarrow \quad E_n \propto \dfrac{Z^2}{n^2}$

$$\frac{E_{4n} - E_{2n}}{E_{2n} - E_n} = \frac{\dfrac{Z^2}{(4n)^2} - \dfrac{Z^2}{(2n)^2}}{\dfrac{Z^2}{(2n)^2} - \dfrac{Z^2}{n^2}} = \frac{1}{4}$$

So, the ratio is independent of Z and n.

34. $E_n = \dfrac{-me^4}{8\varepsilon_0^2 n^2 h^2}$

Multiplying and dividing equation by hc

$$E_n = \frac{-me^4}{8\varepsilon_0^2 h^2}\left(\frac{1}{n^2}\right)\frac{hc}{hc} = -\frac{me^4}{8\varepsilon_0^2 h^3 c}\left(\frac{1}{n^2}\right)hc$$

$$= -\frac{Rhc}{n^2}, \text{ where } R = \frac{me^4}{8\varepsilon_0^2 h^3 c}$$

For first excited state, $n = 2$

$$E_2 = -\frac{Rhc}{(2)^2} = -\frac{Rhc}{4}$$

35. Energy required to remove an electron from He-atom $= 24.6$ eV

After removal of one electron, it becomes He^+ ion.

Ionisation energy of $He^+ = 13.6\dfrac{(2)^2}{(1)^2} = 54.4$ eV

Total energy required to remove both the electrons $= 24.6 + 54.4 = 79$ eV

36. Energy of emitted photon $= \dfrac{hc}{\lambda} = \dfrac{12400}{4890} = 2.54$ eV

Excitation energy is the energy to excite the atom to a level above the ground state. Therefore, the energy level is,

$$E_f = -13.6 + 10.19 = -3.41\text{ eV}$$

$$E_i - E_f = 2.54\text{ eV}$$

$$\Rightarrow \quad E_i - (-3.41\text{ eV}) = 2.54\text{ eV}$$

$$\Rightarrow \quad E_i = -0.87\text{ eV}$$

$\therefore$ Binding energy of initial state $= -E_i = 0.87$ eV

37. $E_4 - E_2 = E$

$$\Rightarrow \quad -RhcZ^2\left[\frac{1}{(4)^2} - \frac{1}{(2)^2}\right] = E$$

$$\Rightarrow \quad RhcZ^2 = \frac{16E}{3}$$

Ionisation energy $= -E_1 = -\left[-Rhc\dfrac{Z^2}{(1)^2}\right] = \dfrac{16E}{3}$

38. $h\nu = E_n - E_{n-1}$

$$\Rightarrow \quad \nu \propto \frac{1}{(n-1)^2} - \frac{1}{n^2} \quad \Rightarrow \quad \nu \propto \frac{n^2 - (n-1)^2}{(n-1)^2 n^2}$$

$$\Rightarrow \quad \nu \propto \frac{2n-1}{(n-1)^2 n^2} \quad \Rightarrow \quad \nu \propto \frac{2n}{n^2 n^2} \qquad (\because n >> 1)$$

$$\Rightarrow \quad \nu \propto \frac{1}{n^3}$$

39. $\dfrac{1}{\lambda} = R\left[\dfrac{1}{2^2} - \dfrac{1}{3^2}\right] \quad \Rightarrow \quad \lambda = \dfrac{36}{5R}$

40. $E_n \propto \dfrac{1}{n^2}, J_n \propto n$

So, $\quad E_n \propto \dfrac{1}{J_n^2}$

41. i = Current due to motion of electron $= qf = \dfrac{qv}{2\pi r}$

$$i \propto \frac{Z/n}{n^2/Z} \quad \Rightarrow \quad i \propto \frac{Z^2}{n^3}$$

Magnetic field $= B = \dfrac{\mu_0 i}{2r}$

$$\Rightarrow \quad B \propto \frac{i}{r} \quad \Rightarrow \quad B \propto \frac{Z^2/n^3}{n^2/Z} \quad \Rightarrow \quad B \propto \frac{Z^3}{n^5}$$

42. The longest wavelength will correspond to the transition having least energy gap i.e., $n = 1$ to $n = 2$

$$\Delta E = (13.6\text{ eV})\,Z^2\left[\frac{1}{n_1^2} - \frac{1}{n_2^2}\right] = (13.6\text{ eV})\,(2)^2\left[\frac{1}{1^2} - \frac{1}{2^2}\right]$$

$$= 40.8\text{ eV}$$

$$\Delta E = \frac{hc}{\lambda} \quad \Rightarrow \quad 40.8 = \frac{12400}{\lambda} \quad \Rightarrow \quad \lambda = 304\text{ Å}$$

43. Reduced mass $= \dfrac{m_1 m_2}{m_1 + m_2} = \dfrac{(1836m_e)(207m_e)}{1836m_e + 207m_e} = 186m_e$

$$E_n = -(13.6\text{ eV})\frac{Z^2}{n^2}\left(\frac{\mu}{m_e}\right)$$

$$E_2 - E_1 = (-13.6\text{ eV})\,(1)^2\left(\frac{186m_e}{m_e}\right)\left[\frac{1}{(2)^2} - \frac{1}{(1)^2}\right]$$

$$= 1897.2\text{ eV}$$

$$\Delta E = \frac{hc}{\lambda} \quad \Rightarrow \quad 1897.2 = \frac{1240}{\lambda} \quad \Rightarrow \quad \lambda = 0.653\text{ nm}$$

44. $\dfrac{1}{4\pi\varepsilon_0}\dfrac{(3q)\,q}{r^2}=\dfrac{mv^2}{r}$ ...(i)

$$mvr=\frac{nh}{2\pi}$$ ...(ii)

Solving Eqs. (i) and (ii), we get

$$v=\frac{3q^2}{2\varepsilon_0 nh}$$

When the particle is nearest to heavy particle, $n=1$

So, $$v=\frac{3q^2}{2\varepsilon_0 h}$$

45. If mass of electrons is doubled,

$E\propto m_e$, so energy will get doubled.

$r\propto\dfrac{1}{m_e}$, so radius will get halved.

46. $\Delta E=h\nu=RhcZ^2\left[\dfrac{1}{n_1^2}-\dfrac{1}{n_2^2}\right]$

$$\Rightarrow h(2.467\times10^{15})=RhcZ^2\left[\frac{1}{(1)^2}-\frac{1}{(2)^2}\right]$$ ...(i)

and $$h\nu=RhcZ^2\left[\frac{1}{(1)^2}-\frac{1}{(3)^2}\right]$$ ...(ii)

Dividing Eq. (ii) by Eq. (i), we get

$$\nu=2.92\times10^{15}\text{ Hz}$$

47. $\dfrac{1}{\lambda}=RZ^2\left[\dfrac{1}{n_1^2}-\dfrac{1}{n_2^2}\right]\Rightarrow\lambda\propto\dfrac{1}{Z^2}$

So, the shortest wavelength will be for element with highest atomic number i.e., Li^{2+}.

48. $E_{C\to A}=E_{C\to B}+E_{B\to A}$

$$\Rightarrow\frac{hc}{\lambda_3}=\frac{hc}{\lambda_1}+\frac{hc}{\lambda_2}$$

$$\Rightarrow\lambda_3=\frac{\lambda_1\lambda_2}{\lambda_1+\lambda_2}$$

49. $\dfrac{1}{\lambda}=R\left[\dfrac{1}{(1)^2}-\dfrac{1}{n^2}\right]\Rightarrow n=\sqrt{\dfrac{\lambda R}{\lambda R-1}}$

50. $\Delta E=$ Energy of photon

$$\Delta E_A=(13.6\text{ eV})\left[\frac{1}{2^2}-\frac{1}{3^2}\right]$$

$$\Delta E_B=(13.6\text{ eV})\left[\frac{1}{1^2}-\frac{1}{2^2}\right]$$

$$Z=\frac{\Delta E_A}{\Delta E_B}=\frac{5}{27}$$

$$x=\frac{\lambda_A}{\lambda_B}=\frac{\Delta E_B}{\Delta E_A}=\frac{1}{Z}=\frac{27}{5}$$

Momentum of photon, $p=\dfrac{\Delta E}{c}$

$$\Rightarrow\frac{p_A}{p_B}=\frac{\Delta E_A}{\Delta E_B}=Z$$

51. $\Delta E=\dfrac{hc}{\lambda}\Rightarrow\lambda\propto\dfrac{1}{\Delta E}$ and $\Delta E\propto\left[\dfrac{1}{n_1^2}-\dfrac{1}{n_2^2}\right]$

Energy gap is maximum for transition C. So, C will correspond to the shortest wavelength.

Energy gap is least for transition D. So, D will correspond to the longest wavelength.

52. Longest wavelength will correspond to the transition having least energy difference i.e., $n=3$ to $n=2$.

$$\Delta E\propto m$$

$$\frac{1}{\lambda}=R\left(\frac{m}{m_e}\right)\left[\frac{1}{2^2}-\frac{1}{3^2}\right]$$

$$\Rightarrow\frac{1}{\lambda}=R\left(\frac{2m_e}{m_e}\right)\left(\frac{5}{36}\right)$$

$$\Rightarrow\lambda=\frac{18}{5R}$$

53. For Hydrogen, $\dfrac{1}{\lambda_1}=R\left[\dfrac{1}{a^2}-\dfrac{1}{b^2}\right]$

For He^+, $\dfrac{1}{\lambda_2}=R(2)^2\left[\dfrac{1}{p^2}-\dfrac{1}{q^2}\right]$

$$\frac{1}{\lambda_1}=\frac{1}{\lambda_2}$$

$$\Rightarrow R\left[\frac{1}{a^2}-\frac{1}{b^2}\right]=4R\left[\frac{1}{p^2}-\frac{1}{q^2}\right]$$

$$\Rightarrow p=2a\text{ and }q=2b$$

So, p and q must be even integer.

54. As energy difference increases, wavelength decreases.

55. Since 5 dark lines are observed, electrons are excited to state $n=6$.

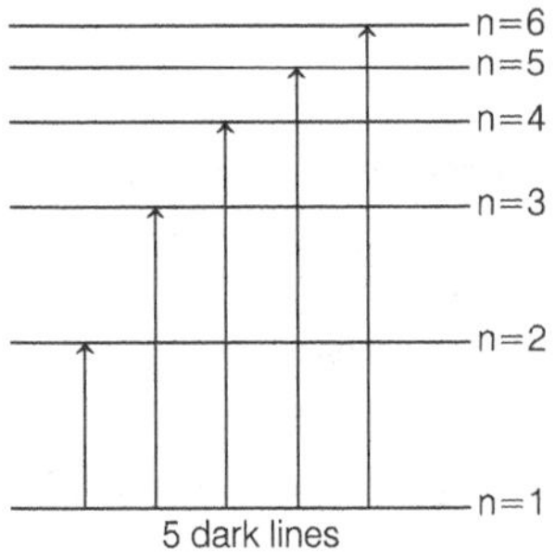

So, the number of bright lines $={}^6C_2=15$

56. Absorption lines are obtained, when electrons jump from ground state to excited states. Thus only lines 1, 2 and 3 are obtained in absorption spectrum.

57. $12.75=13.6\left[\dfrac{1}{1^2}-\dfrac{1}{n^2}\right]\Rightarrow n=4$

So, electrons are excited to state $n=4$.

So, during de-excitation, we will get 3 Lymen lines, 2 Balmer lines and one Paschen line.

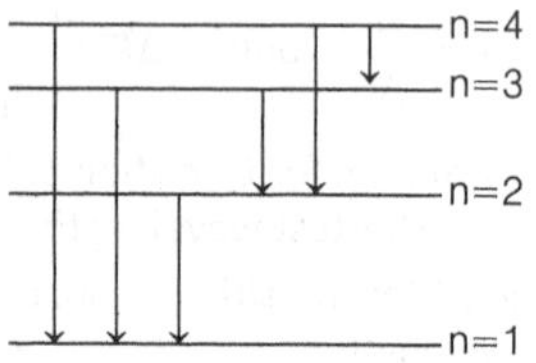

58. Shortest wavelength of the Brackett series,

$$\frac{1}{\lambda_1} = RZ^2\left[\frac{1}{4^2} - \frac{1}{(\infty)^2}\right]$$

Shortest wavelength of the Balmer series,

$$\frac{1}{\lambda_2} = R(1)^2\left[\frac{1}{(2)^2} - \frac{1}{(\infty)^2}\right]$$

$$\frac{1}{\lambda_1} = \frac{1}{\lambda_2}$$

$\Rightarrow$ $Z = 2$

59. Largest wavelength in UV region (Lymen series),

$$\frac{1}{122} = R\left[\frac{1}{(1)^2} - \frac{1}{(2)^2}\right] \quad ...(i)$$

Smallest wavelength in IR region (Paschen series),

$$\frac{1}{\lambda} = R\left[\frac{1}{3^2} - \frac{1}{(\infty)^2}\right] \quad ...(ii)$$

Dividing the two Eqs., we get

$$\lambda = 823.5 \text{ nm}$$

60. Infrared radiation has lesser energy compared to ultraviolet radiaion. So, a transition with energy difference less than the $n = 4$ to $n = 3$ transition will result in infrared radiation.

61. nth excited state means, $n = n + 1$

Number of lines in emission spectrum $= {}^{n+1}C_2$

$$= \frac{n(n+1)}{2} = 1 + 2 + 3 + \ldots + n$$

62. Longest wavelength of the Balmer series,

$$\frac{1}{\lambda_1} = RZ^2\left[\frac{1}{2^2} - \frac{1}{3^2}\right]$$

$$\Rightarrow \quad \lambda_1 = \frac{36}{5RZ^2}$$

Shortest wavelength of the Lymen series,

$$\frac{1}{\lambda_2} = RZ^2\left[\frac{1}{1^2} - \frac{1}{(\infty)^2}\right]$$

$$\Rightarrow \quad \lambda_2 = \frac{1}{RZ^2}$$

$$\lambda_1 - \lambda_2 = \frac{31}{5RZ^2} = \Delta\lambda$$

$$\Rightarrow \quad R = \frac{31}{5}\frac{1}{\Delta\lambda \cdot Z^2}$$

63. ${}^nC_2 = 10 \quad \Rightarrow \quad n = 5$

Thus electrons are excited to state $n = 5$.

$$\Delta E = (13.6 \text{ eV})\left[\frac{1}{1^2} - \frac{1}{5^2}\right] = 13.06 \text{ eV}$$

$$\Delta E = \frac{hc}{\lambda} \quad \Rightarrow \quad 13.06 = \frac{12400}{\lambda}$$

$$\Rightarrow \quad \lambda = 949.5 \text{ Å}$$

64. ${}^nC_2 = 6 \quad \Rightarrow \quad n = 4$

So, the final state be $n_2 = 4$

Since energy of emitted photons is either equal to less than or greater than the absorbed photons, lower state will $n_1 = 2$.

65. Through filter, only those photons will pass through whose energy is less than

$$E = \frac{1240}{800} = 1.55 \text{ eV}$$

From hydrogen's energy level diagram, we can easily identify that, when electron jumps from 3rd excited state (4th energy level) to 2nd excited state (3rd energy level), then photons of energy 1.55 eV have been emitted. So, the required initial energy level is the 3rd excited state.

66. $F = evB = \frac{mv^2}{r}$ ...(i)

$$mvr = \frac{nh}{2\pi} \quad ...(ii)$$

Solving Eqs. (i) and (ii), we get

$$r = \sqrt{\frac{nh}{2\pi eB}}$$

Magnetic flux, $\phi = B(\pi r^2) = B\pi\frac{nh}{2\pi eB} = \frac{nh}{2e}$

$$\phi_{min} = \frac{h}{2e} \quad (\because \text{For minimum flux, } n = 1)$$

67. de-Broglie wavelength, $\lambda = \frac{h}{mv} \quad \Rightarrow \quad mv = \frac{h}{\lambda}$

By quantisation of angular momentum,

$$mvr = \frac{nh}{2\pi}$$

$$\Rightarrow \quad \left(\frac{h}{\lambda}\right)r = \frac{nh}{2\pi}$$

$$\Rightarrow \quad 2\pi r = n\lambda$$

$$\Rightarrow \quad \frac{2\pi r}{\lambda} = n$$

For first excited state $n = 2$,

So, $\frac{2\pi r}{\lambda} = 2$

68. $2\pi r_n = n\lambda \quad \Rightarrow \quad \lambda = \frac{2\pi r_n}{n}$

$$\Rightarrow \quad \lambda = \frac{2\pi}{n}(n^2 a_0) = 2\pi n a_0$$

69. For first line of Lymen series,

$$\frac{1}{\lambda_1}=R\left[\frac{1}{1^2}-\frac{1}{2^2}\right] \Rightarrow \lambda_1=\frac{4}{3R}$$

de-Broglie wavelength of electron in ground state,

$$2\pi r=(1)\lambda_2 \Rightarrow \lambda_2=2\pi r$$

$$\frac{\lambda_1}{\lambda_2}=\frac{4/3R}{2\pi r}=\frac{2}{3\pi rR}$$

70. $\Delta E=$ Energy of photon $=13.6\left[\frac{1}{1^2}-\frac{1}{5^2}\right]=13.06$ eV

Momentum of photon = Momentum of hydrogen atom

$$\Rightarrow \quad \frac{\Delta E}{c}=mv$$

$$\Rightarrow \quad v=\frac{\Delta E}{mc}=\frac{13.06\times1.6\times10^{-19}}{1.67\times10^{-27}\times3\times10^{8}}=4 \text{ m/s}$$

71. Energy of photon emitted will be less than 10.2 eV as some energy will be taken by recoiled atom. So, $\lambda>\lambda_0$.

72. Longest wavelength of Balmer series will occur for the shortest transition i.e., from $n=3$ to $n=2$.

Momentum of photon $=\frac{h}{\lambda}=Rh\left[\frac{1}{2^2}-\frac{1}{3^2}\right]=\frac{5Rh}{36}$

Momentum of H-atom = Momentum of photon

$$\Rightarrow \quad Mv=\frac{5Rh}{36} \Rightarrow v=\frac{5Rh}{36M}$$

73. Minimum energy required for excitation is 10.2 eV in H-atom in ground state.

If $E<10.2$ eV, no excitation will take place and hence incident electron will not lose any energy and collision will be elastic.

74. First photon of energy 10.2 eV will excite the hydrogen atom from ground state to the first excited state. During de-excitation, a photon of energy 10.2 eV will be emitted.

Second photon of energy 15 eV will ionise the hydrogen atom (ionisation energy = 13.6 eV). So, the balance energy = 15 - 13.6 = 1.4 eV will be retained by the electron.

75. Let K be the kinetic energy of each hydrogen atom.

Maximum loss of energy occurs in perfectly inelastic collision.

From momentum conservation,

$$mu+m(-u)=2mv \Rightarrow v=0$$

$$\text{Loss in KE}=\left(\frac{1}{2}mu^2+\frac{1}{2}mu^2\right)-(0+0)=K+K=2K$$

For collision to be inelastic so that both the atoms are excited,

$$2K>(10.2+10.2)\text{ eV}$$

$$\Rightarrow \quad K_{min}=10.2\text{ eV}$$

76. When electrons de-excite from third excited state ($n=4$) to second excited state ($n=3$)

$$\Delta E_1=13.6(3)^2\left[\frac{1}{3^2}-\frac{1}{4^2}\right]=5.95\text{ eV}$$

$$E=W+eV_s$$

$$\Rightarrow \quad 5.95=W+3.95$$

$$\Rightarrow \quad W=2\text{ eV}$$

When electrons de-excite from fourth excited state ($n=5$) to third excited state ($n=4$),

$$\Delta E_2=13.6(3)^2\left[\frac{1}{4^2}-\frac{1}{5^2}\right]=2.75\text{ eV}$$

$$E=W+eV_s$$

$$\Rightarrow \quad 2.75=2+eV_s \Rightarrow V_s=0.75\text{ V}$$

77. Maximum energy of radiation incident on H-sample

= KE_{max} of electron + ionisation energy

= 37.4 + 13.6 = 51 eV

This energy corresponds to the transition $n\rightarrow4$ to $n\rightarrow1$ in He^+.

For electrons of He^+ in ground state to get excited to $n=4$,

$$\lambda=\frac{12400}{51}=243\text{ Å}$$

Multiple Choice(s) Correct Questions

1. Radius, $R\propto n^2$,

Speed of electron, $v\propto\frac{1}{n}$

Energy, $E\propto\frac{1}{n^2}$

(a) $vR\propto n$ (b) $RE\propto n^0$

(c) $\frac{v}{E}\propto n$ (d) $\frac{R}{E}\propto n^4$

2. $L\propto n,\quad K\propto\frac{1}{n^2},\quad v\propto\frac{1}{n},\quad f\propto\frac{1}{n^3}$

(a) $K^{-1}Lf\propto n^2(n)\left(\frac{1}{n^3}\right) \Rightarrow K^{-1}Lf=\text{constant}$

(b) $Kvf^{-1}\propto\frac{1}{n^2}\left(\frac{1}{n}\right)n^3 \Rightarrow Kvf^{-1}=\text{constant}$

(c) $LK^{-1}v\propto n(n^2)\left(\frac{1}{n}\right) \Rightarrow LK^{-1}v\propto n^2$

(d) $K^{-1}f\propto n^2\left(\frac{1}{n^3}\right) \Rightarrow K^{-1}f\propto\frac{1}{n}$

3.

$$\frac{1}{4\pi\varepsilon_0}\frac{e^2}{r^2}=\frac{mv^2}{r} \quad \text{...(i)}$$

$$mvr=\frac{nh}{2\pi} \quad \text{...(ii)}$$

From Eq. (i), $v=\sqrt{\frac{e^2}{4\pi\varepsilon_0 mr}}$

From Eq. (ii), $v=\frac{nh}{2\pi mr}$

From Eqs. (i) and (ii), $v=\frac{e^2}{2\varepsilon_0 hn}$

For ground state, $n=1$

4. $T \propto n^3 \Rightarrow \frac{T_1}{T_2} = \frac{n_1^3}{n_2^3}$

$\Rightarrow \frac{8T_2}{T_2} = \left(\frac{n_1}{n_2}\right)^3 \Rightarrow n_1 = 2n_2$

5. $r \propto n^2 \Rightarrow n \propto \sqrt{r}$

(a) $f \propto \frac{1}{n^3} \Rightarrow f \propto r^{-3/2}$

(b) $p = mv \propto \frac{1}{n} \Rightarrow p \propto \frac{1}{\sqrt{r}}$

(c) $E \propto \frac{1}{n^2} \Rightarrow E \propto \frac{1}{r}$

(d) $M = i\pi r^2 \Rightarrow M = ef\pi r^2$

$\Rightarrow M \propto \left(\frac{1}{n^3}\right)(n^2)^2 \Rightarrow M \propto n$

$\Rightarrow M \propto \sqrt{r}$

6. $K \propto \frac{1}{r}, \quad U \propto -\frac{1}{r}, \quad f \propto \frac{1}{r^{3/2}}$

7. (a) and (b) $r \propto \frac{n^2}{Z}$

$\therefore \frac{\Delta r}{r} = \frac{(n+1)^2 - n^2}{n^2} = \frac{2n+1}{n^2} \propto \frac{1}{n} \quad (\because n >> 1)$

(c) $E \propto \frac{Z^2}{n^2}$

$\therefore \frac{\Delta E}{E} = \frac{\frac{1}{n^2} - \frac{1}{(n+1)^2}}{\frac{1}{(n+1)^2}} = \frac{2n+1}{n^2} \propto \frac{1}{n} \quad (\because n >> 1)$

(d) $L = \frac{nh}{2\pi}, \quad L \propto n$

$\frac{\Delta L}{L} = \frac{(n+1) - n}{n} = \frac{1}{n}$

$\Rightarrow \frac{\Delta L}{L} \propto \frac{1}{n}$

8. $L = \frac{nh}{2\pi}$

$\Rightarrow \Delta L = (n_2 - n_1)\frac{h}{2\pi}$

9. $K \propto \frac{1}{r}, \quad U \propto -\frac{1}{r}$

$\lambda = \frac{2\pi r}{n}$

$\Rightarrow \lambda \propto \frac{n^2}{n} \Rightarrow \lambda \propto n$

When electron makes transition from higher state to lower state, kinetic energy increases and potential energy and de-Broglie wavelength decrease.

10. $E_1 = -13.6$ eV, $K_1 = -E_1 = 13.6$ eV,

$U_1 = 2E_1 = -27.2$ eV

If potential energy in ground state is taken to be 13.6 eV, then potential energy and total energy will increase in every state be 13.6 – (–27.2) = 40.8 eV while kinetic energy will remain unchanged.

$E'_1 = -13.6 + 40.8 = 27.2$ eV,

$K'_1 = 13.6$ eV; $U'_1 = 27.2$ eV

$E'_2 = -3.4 + 40.8 = 37.4$ eV, $K'_2 = 3.4$ eV,

$U'_2 = -6.8 + 40.8 = 34$ eV

11. $204 = 13.6Z^2\left[\frac{1}{1^2} - \frac{1}{(2n)^2}\right]$ ...(i)

$40.8 = 13.6Z^2\left[\frac{1}{n^2} - \frac{1}{(2n)^2}\right]$ ...(ii)

Solving Eqs. (i) and (ii), we get

$n = 2$ and $Z = 4$

12. $E_n - E_2 = 10.2 + 17 = 27.2$ eV ...(i)

$E_n - E_3 = 4.25 + 5.95 = 10.2$ eV ...(ii)

Subtracting Eq. (ii) from Eq. (i),

$E_3 - E_2 = 17$ eV

$\Rightarrow 13.6Z^2\left[\frac{1}{2^2} - \frac{1}{3^2}\right] = 17$

$\Rightarrow Z = 3$

$E_n - E_2 = 27.2$

$\Rightarrow 13.6Z^2\left[\frac{1}{2^2} - \frac{1}{n^2}\right] = 27.2$

$\Rightarrow n = 6$

13. Incident wavelengths travel in *X*-direction which are in UV region, which means they can excite an electron from $n = 1$ to higher levels. Hence some of the incident wavelengths will be absent in *A*.

Photons emerging due to transitions of electrons to their ground state contain visible region wavelengths if transitions are done into $n = 2$. If transition is done into $n > 2$, photons contain IR wavelengths.

14. (a) Ionisation energy $= E_\infty - E_1$

$= 0 - (-4) = 4$ eV

(b) $\Delta E = \frac{hc}{\lambda} = \frac{1242}{1242} = 1$ eV

$\Delta E = 1$ eV corresponds to transition from $n = 3$ to $n = 2$. So, electron is ground state must have been excited to $n = 3$.

$\lambda = \frac{hc}{E_3 - E_1} = \frac{1242}{3} = 414$ nm

(c) As calculated in option (b), electron in ground state must have been excited to $n = 3$.

$E_3 - E_1 = 3$ eV

Hence, incident electron must have energy more than 3 eV.

15. (a) $n = 3$

(b) $2\pi r_n = n\lambda$

$\Rightarrow 2\pi(n^2 r_0) = n\lambda$

$\Rightarrow \quad \lambda = 2\pi n r_0$

$\Rightarrow \quad \lambda = 2\pi(3) r_0 = 6\pi r_0$

(c) Number of photons $= {}^nC_2 = {}^3C_2 = 3$

16. When a stationary atom emits a photon, then energy of the emitted photon will be equal to the difference of the energy of the two levels involved in the transition. Hence, energy of emitted photon will be equal to $(E_m - E_n)$.

If a hydrogen atom is moving and a photon is emitted by it along the same direction in which it is moving, due to momentum of the emitted photon, the momentum of hydrogen atom will get decreased.

Therefore, energy of the emitted photon will be equal to $(E_m - E_n + \text{Loss in KE of hydrogen atom})$. Hence $f > f_0$.

But if the photon is emitted in a direction normal to the motion of the hydrogen atom, then the frequency of the emitted photon will be equal to f_0.

If the photon is emitted by the hydrogen atom in the direction opposite to its motion, then frequency of the emitted photon will be less than f_0.

17. $\mu = \text{Reduced mass} = \dfrac{m_e m_e}{m_e + m_e} = \dfrac{m_e}{2}$

(a) $E = (-13.6 \text{ eV}) \dfrac{Z^2}{n^2}\left(\dfrac{\mu}{m_e}\right)$

Here, $\mu = \dfrac{m_e}{2}$. So, ground state energy will be half of hydrogen atom.

(b) $R = \dfrac{e^4}{8\varepsilon_0^2 ch^3}\left(\dfrac{\mu}{m_e}\right)$

So, Rydberg constant will also be half of hydrogen atom.

(c) $r = (0.529 \text{ Å}) \dfrac{n^2}{Z}\left(\dfrac{m_e}{\mu}\right)$

So, radius of first orbit will be double of hydrogen atom.

(d) Velocity of electron $= \dfrac{e^2}{2\varepsilon_0 h}\left(\dfrac{Z}{n}\right)$

Velocity of electron is independent of mass.

18. $E_4 - E_2 = 2.55$ eV. So, electron in ground state must have been excited to state $n = 4$. During de-excitation other photon will correspond to transition $n = 2$ to $n = 1$. So, energy of other photon $= E_2 - E_1 = 10.2$ eV.

For perfectly inelastic collision,

$$mu + 0 = 2mv \quad \Rightarrow \quad v = \frac{u}{2}$$

$$\text{Loss in KE} = \frac{1}{2}mu^2 - \frac{1}{2}(2m)\left(\frac{u}{2}\right)^2 = \frac{1}{4}mu^2 = \frac{K}{2}$$

So, $\quad \dfrac{K}{2} \geq E_4 - E_1 \quad \Rightarrow \quad \dfrac{K}{2} \geq 12.75$ eV

$\Rightarrow \quad K \geq 25.5$ eV

Excitation energy for state $(n = 4) = E_4 - E_1 = 12.75$ eV

19. $R = \dfrac{\sqrt{2mK_{max}}}{qB} \quad \Rightarrow \quad K_{max} = \dfrac{q^2B^2R^2}{2m}$

$$\Rightarrow K_{max} = \frac{(1.6\times10^{-19})^2(2\times10^{-4})^2\left(\frac{9.1}{1.6}\times10^{-4}\right)}{2\times9.1\times10^{-31}} = 3.2 \text{ eV}$$

$$E = 13.6(3)^2\left[\frac{1}{3^2} - \frac{1}{4^2}\right] = 5.95 \text{ eV}$$

$$\lambda = \frac{hc}{E} = \frac{1240}{5.95} = 208.4 \text{ nm}$$

$$W = E - K_{max} = 5.95 - 3.20 = 2.75 \text{ eV}$$

20. $E_{3\to1} - E_{3\to2} = 3E_0 \quad \Rightarrow \quad E_{2\to1} = 3E_0$

$\Rightarrow \quad E_0 Z^2\left[\dfrac{1}{1^2} - \dfrac{1}{2^2}\right] = 3E_0 \quad \Rightarrow \quad Z = 2$

So, the gas is helium.

$$\Delta E_1 = E_0\left[\frac{1}{1^2} - \frac{1}{3^2}\right] = \frac{8E_0}{9}$$

$$\Delta E_2 = E_0(2)^2\left[\frac{1}{1^2} - \frac{1}{2^2}\right] = 3E_0$$

$$K_1 = \frac{8E_0}{9} - W \text{ and } K_2 = 3E_0 - W$$

$$\lambda = \frac{h}{\sqrt{2mK}} \quad \Rightarrow \quad K \propto \frac{1}{\lambda^2}$$

$\Rightarrow \quad \dfrac{K_1}{K_2} = \left(\dfrac{\lambda_2}{\lambda_1}\right)^2$

$$\lambda_2 = \frac{\lambda_1}{3} \quad \Rightarrow \quad K_2 = 9K_1$$

$\Rightarrow \quad 3E_0 - W = 9\left(\dfrac{8E_0}{9} - W\right)$

$\Rightarrow \quad W = \dfrac{5E_0}{8} = \dfrac{5\times13.6}{8} = 8.5$ eV

Comprehension Based Question

1. Number of different radiations = 6

$\Rightarrow \quad {}^nC_2 = 6 \quad \Rightarrow \quad n = 4$

So, the electrons must have been excited to state $n_f = 4$. Since, emitted photons have energy more and less than 2.7 eV, initial state must be $n_i = 2$.

2. $E_4 - E_2 = 2.7$ eV

$\Rightarrow \quad -\dfrac{E_1}{(4)^2} - \left[-\dfrac{E_1}{(2)^2}\right] = 2.7$

$\Rightarrow \quad E_1 = 14.4 \text{ eV} = 2.3\times10^{-18}$ J

3. $E_{max} = E_4 - E_1 = -\dfrac{E_1}{4^2} + E_1 = 13.5 \text{ eV} = 2.2\times10^{-18}$ J

$E_{min} = E_4 - E_3 = -\dfrac{E_1}{4^2} + \dfrac{E_1}{3^2} = 0.7 \text{ eV} = 1.1\times10^{-18}$ J

4. $100(E_{n+1} - E_1) = \dfrac{4800}{49}Rch \quad \Rightarrow \quad E_{n+1} - E_1 = \dfrac{48}{49}Rch$

So, the maximum energy of emitted photon will be $\dfrac{48}{49}Rch$.

5. $E_{n+1} - E_1 = \frac{48}{49}Rch \Rightarrow Rch\left[\frac{1}{1^2} - \frac{1}{(n+1)^2}\right] = \frac{48}{49}Rch$

$\Rightarrow \quad n = 6$

6. When electron jumps from 7th state to ground state, maximum number of emitted photons will be 6.

Maximum number of photons emitted by the sample

$$= 100 \times 6 = 600$$

7. Balmer series photon is absorbed, when lower state is $n = 2$.

8. For transition II, $\Delta E = E_4 - E_2 = 2.55$ eV

$$\Delta E = \frac{hc}{\lambda} \Rightarrow 2.55 = \frac{1242}{\lambda}$$

$\Rightarrow \quad \lambda = 487$ nm

9. $\Delta E = \frac{hc}{\lambda} = \frac{12400}{1025} = 12.09$ eV

For hydrogen atom,

$$E_3 - E_1 = 12.09 \text{ eV}$$

So, it will be transition V.

10. $\lambda = \frac{1500p^2}{p^2 - 1} \Rightarrow \frac{1}{\lambda} = \frac{1}{1500}\left(\frac{1}{1^2} - \frac{1}{p^2}\right)$

For most energetic photon, energy gap between the states should be maximum.

So, $p \rightarrow \infty$

$$\lambda = 1500 \text{ Å}$$

11. For least energetic photon, $p = 2$

$$\lambda = 2000 \text{ Å}$$

12. Ionisation enery $= \frac{hc}{\lambda} = \frac{12420}{1500} = 8.28$ eV

Ionisation potential = 8.28 V

13. $evB = \frac{mv^2}{r}$ ...(i)

$$mvr = \frac{nh}{2\pi} \quad \text{...(ii)}$$

Solving Eqs. (i) and (ii), we get

$$v = \sqrt{\frac{nheB}{2\pi m^2}} \text{ and } r = \sqrt{\frac{nh}{2\pi eB}}$$

$$\text{Kinetic energy} = \frac{1}{2}mv^2 = \frac{1}{2}m\left(\frac{nheB}{2\pi m^2}\right) = \frac{nheB}{4\pi m}$$

14. $T = \frac{2\pi r}{v} = \frac{2\pi m}{Be}$

Current, $i = \frac{e}{T} = \frac{e^2B}{2\pi m}$

Magnetic dipole moment, $M = i\pi r^2$

$$= \frac{e^2B}{2\pi m}\pi\left(\frac{nh}{2\pi eB}\right) = \frac{enh}{4\pi m}$$

$$\text{Potential energy} = MB = \left(\frac{enh}{4\pi m}\right)B = \frac{nhBe}{4\pi m}$$

15. $\phi = B\pi r^2 = B\pi\left(\frac{nh}{2\pi eB}\right) = \frac{nh}{2e}$

16. and 17. $F = -\frac{dU}{dr} = -\frac{4K}{r^5}$

$$\frac{4K}{r^5} = \frac{mv^2}{r} \quad \text{...(i)}$$

$$mvr = \frac{nh}{2\pi} \quad \text{...(ii)}$$

Solving Eqs. (i) and (ii), we get

$$r = \frac{4\pi}{nh}\sqrt{Km} \text{ and } v = \frac{n^2h^2}{8\pi^2 m\sqrt{Km}}$$

18. $K = \frac{1}{2}mv^2 = \frac{n^4h^4}{128\pi^4 m^2 K}$

$$U = -\frac{K}{r^4} = -\frac{n^4h^4}{256\pi^4 m^2 K}$$

$$E = K + U = \frac{n^4h^4}{256\pi^4 m^2 K}$$

19. Maximum energy of photons incident on H-sample

$$= 13.6 + 27.2 = 40.8 \text{ eV}$$

This corresponds to the transition $n = 2$ to $n = 1$ in He^+ sample. So, He^+ sample must have been excited to the first excited state. Since, mass of α-particle and He^+ ion is almost same, the α-particle transfers half of its kinetic energy to excitation energy (40.8 eV) for He^+ ion.

$$K_\alpha = 2 \times \text{(first excitation energy of } He^+\text{)}$$

$$= 2 \times 40.8 = 81.6 \text{ eV}$$

20. The kinetic energy of α-particle should not be, so large that it excites electron in He^+ to second excited state.

$$K_\alpha < 2 \times \text{second excitation energy of } He^+$$

$$K_\alpha < 2 \times 48.4$$

$$K_\alpha < 96.8 \text{ eV}$$

21. (d)

22. For transition $n \rightarrow 4$ to $n \rightarrow 3$,

$$\Delta E = E_4 - E_3 = -2 - (-5) = 3 \text{ eV}$$

$$\lambda = \frac{hc}{\Delta E} = \frac{1242}{3} = 414 \text{ nm}$$

Visible region is from 380-760 nm. So, wavelength of 414 nm belongs to visible region.

23.

$$\Delta E_{1\rightarrow 2} = E_2 - E_1 = 10 \text{ eV}$$

$$\Delta E_{1\rightarrow 3} = E_3 - E_1 = 15 \text{ eV}$$

$$\Delta E_{1\rightarrow 4} = E_4 - E_1 = 18 \text{ eV}$$

So, no excitation can take place for photon of energy 12 eV.

24.

$$\Delta E_{4\rightarrow 2} = E_4 - E_2 = 8 \text{ eV}$$

$$\Delta E_{2\rightarrow 1} = E_2 - E_1 = 10 \text{ eV}$$

$$\Delta E_{3\rightarrow 2} = E_3 - E_2 = 5 \text{ eV}$$

So, work function should be greater than 5 eV and lesser than 8 eV.

$$5 \text{ eV} < \phi < 8 \text{ eV}$$

25. Hydrogen sample on de-excitation will emit photons of energy 10.2 eV. These photons are absorbed by excited He^+ and excited Li^{2+} samples.

For hydrogen atom,

$$10.2 = E_1\left[\frac{1}{1^2}-\frac{1}{2^2}\right]$$

For He^+ ion, $$10.2 = E_1(2)^2\left[\frac{1}{n_1^2}-\frac{1}{n_2^2}\right]$$

For Li^{2+} ion, $$10.2 = E_1(3)^2\left[\frac{1}{a^2}-\frac{1}{b^2}\right]$$

On solving, we get

$$n_1 = 2, \quad n_2 = 4, \quad a = 3 \text{ and } b = 6$$

So, Li^+ had initially electron in state ($n_1 = 3$) and after absorbing photon of 10.2 eV gets excited to state ($n_2 = 6$). On de-excitation, number of spectral lines in Li^{2+}

$$= {}^6C_2 = 15$$

26. Smallest wavelength will correspond to transition having maximum energy gap i.e., $n_1 \to 6$ to $n_2 \to 1$.

$$\Delta E = 13.6(3)^2\left[\frac{1}{1^2}-\frac{1}{6^2}\right] = 119 \text{ eV}$$

$$\lambda = \frac{hc}{\Delta E} = \frac{1240}{119} = 10.4 \text{ nm}$$

27. For He^+, $n_1 = 2$ and $n_2 = 4$

So, He^+ had initially electron in state ($n_1 = 2$) and after absorbing photon of 10.2 eV gets excited to state ($n_2 = 4$). On de-excitation, number of spectral lines in $He^+ = {}^4C_2 = 6$

28. $$\Delta E_{max} = 13.6(2)^2\left[\frac{1}{1^2}-\frac{1}{4^2}\right] = 51 \text{ eV}$$

$$\lambda_{min} = \frac{hc}{\Delta E_{max}} = \frac{1240}{51} = 24.3 \text{ nm}$$

29. $$\Delta E_A = E_3 - E_2 = 13.6 Z_A^2\left[\frac{1}{2^2}-\frac{1}{3^2}\right]$$

$$\Delta E_B = E_3 - E_2 = 13.6 Z_B^2\left[\frac{1}{2^2}-\frac{1}{3^2}\right]$$

$$\Delta E_A - \Delta E_B = 5.67 \text{ eV}$$

Substituting values of ΔE_A and ΔE_B, we get

$$Z_B^2 - Z_A^2 = 3$$

Applying the law of conservation of momentum if p is the momentum imparted to target

$$m_A v = p - m_A v_1 \text{ and } m_B v = 2p - m_B v_1.$$

Here, $m_A = 2Z_A$ and $m_B = 2Z_B$ as they contain equal number of neutrons and protons. Hence,

$$2Z_A v = p - 2Z_A v_1$$

and $$2Z_B v = 2p - 2Z_B v_1$$

$$2Z_A(v + v_1) = p \quad \text{...(i)}$$

and $$2Z_B(v + v_1) = 2p \quad \text{...(ii)}$$

Dividing the two Eqs., we get

$$\frac{Z_A}{Z_B} = \frac{1}{2} \Rightarrow Z_B = 2Z_A$$

$$(2Z_A)^2 - Z_A^2 = 3 \Rightarrow Z_A = 1 \text{ and } Z_B = 2$$

So, atom A is deuterium

30. $Z_B = 2$, so ion is He^+.

31. $$\Delta E_A = 13.6(1)^2\left[\frac{1}{2^2}-\frac{1}{3^2}\right] = 1.88 \text{ eV}$$

$$\lambda = \frac{hc}{\Delta E_A} = \frac{1240}{1.88} = 656 \text{ nm}$$

32. $$\Delta E_B = 13.6(2)^2\left[\frac{1}{2^2}-\frac{1}{3^2}\right] = 7.56 \text{ eV}$$

$$\lambda = \frac{hc}{\Delta E_B} = \frac{1240}{7.56} = 164 \text{ nm}$$

33. Number of neutrons in $A = Z_A = 1$

Number of neutrons in $B = Z_B = 2$

34. Excitation energy transferred by H-atoms to He^+ ions

$$= E_2 - E_1 = 10.2 \text{ eV}$$

For He^+ ions,

$$10.2 = 13.6(2)^2\left[\frac{1}{2^2}-\frac{1}{n_2^2}\right]$$

$$\Rightarrow \quad n_2 = 4$$

35. For He^+ ions,

$$E_4 - E_3 = 13.6(2)^2\left[\frac{1}{3^2}-\frac{1}{4^2}\right] = 2.64 \text{ eV}$$

$$\lambda = \frac{hc}{E_4 - E_3} = \frac{1240}{2.64} = 469 \text{ nm}$$

36. $$K = 13.6\frac{Z^2}{n^2} \Rightarrow \frac{K_1}{K_2} = \left(\frac{Z_1}{Z_2}\right)^2 = \left(\frac{1}{2}\right)^2 = \frac{1}{4}$$

37.

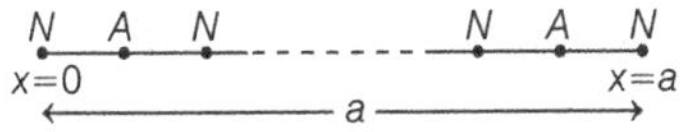

Figure shows the alternate nodes and antinodes in the region between $x = 0$ and $x = a$. In the nth node, there are n nodal points. The wavelength λ_n, of the stationary waves formed is therefore given by

$$n\left(\frac{\lambda_n}{2}\right) = a \Rightarrow \lambda_n = \frac{2a}{n}$$

Let p_n be the linear momentum of the particle. We are given that,

$$\lambda_n = \frac{h}{p_n} = \frac{h}{\sqrt{2mE_n}} \Rightarrow \frac{2a}{n} = \frac{h}{\sqrt{2mE_n}}$$

$$\Rightarrow \quad E_n = \frac{n^2h^2}{8ma^2}$$

For a given value of m, $E_n \propto a^{-2}$

38. $$E_n = \frac{n^2h^2}{8ma^2} = \frac{(1)^2(6.6\times10^{-34})^2}{8(1.0\times10^{-30})(6.6\times10^{-9})^2}$$

$$= 1.25\times10^{-21} \text{ J}$$

$$= 8 \text{ meV}$$

39. $$p_n = \frac{h}{\lambda_n} = \frac{nh}{2a}$$

$$\Rightarrow mv_n = \frac{nh}{2a} \Rightarrow v_n \propto n$$

Match the Columns Questions

1. $r \propto \frac{n^2}{Z}$, $v \propto \frac{Z}{n}$, $E \propto \frac{Z^2}{n^2}$

(A) Angular speed $= \omega = \frac{v}{r}$

$$\Rightarrow \omega \propto \frac{Z/n}{n^2} \Rightarrow \omega \propto \frac{Z^2}{n^3}$$

(B) $T = \frac{2\pi}{\omega} \Rightarrow T \propto \frac{1}{\omega} \Rightarrow T \propto \frac{n^3}{Z^2}$

(C) $L = \frac{nh}{2\pi} \Rightarrow L \propto n$

(D) $M = i\pi r^2 = \frac{e\omega}{2\pi}\pi r^2 = \frac{e\omega r^2}{2}$

$$M \propto \omega r^2 \Rightarrow M \propto \frac{Z^2}{n^3}\left(\frac{n^2}{Z}\right)^2 \Rightarrow M \propto n$$

(E) $B = \frac{\mu_0 i}{2r} = \frac{\mu_0}{2r}\left(\frac{\omega e}{2\pi}\right)$

$$B \propto \frac{\omega}{r} \Rightarrow B \propto \frac{Z^2/n^3}{n^2/Z} \Rightarrow B \propto \frac{Z^3}{n^5}$$

2. (A) Binding energy $= 13.6 \times \frac{Z^2}{n^2} = 13.6 \times \frac{(3)^2}{(1)^2} = 122.4$ eV

(B) $\Delta E = E_\infty - E_1 = 13.6(4)^2\left[\frac{1}{2^2} - \frac{1}{\infty^2}\right] = 54.4$ eV

Minimum energy required is 54.4 eV.

(C) Ionisation energy $= -E_1 = (13.6 \text{ eV})\frac{Z^2}{n^2}$

$$= (13.6 \text{ eV})\frac{(5)^2}{(1)^2} = 340 \text{ eV}$$

(D) For He^+ ion, $E = (13.6 \text{ eV})\frac{(2)^2}{n^2} = \frac{54.4 \text{ eV}}{n^2}$

For ground state, $E = 54.4$ eV

For $n = 2$, $E = 13.6$ eV

$n = 3$, $E = 6.04$ eV

$n = 4$, $E = 3.4$ eV

3. (A) $Epr = E(mv)r \propto \frac{Z^2}{n^2}\left(\frac{Z}{n}\right)\left(\frac{n^2}{Z}\right) \propto \frac{1}{n}$

(B) $\frac{p}{E} = \frac{mv}{E} \propto \frac{Z/n}{Z^2/n^2} \propto n$

$L = \frac{nh}{2\pi} \Rightarrow L \propto n$

So, $\frac{p}{E} \propto L$

(C) $Er \propto \left(\frac{Z^2}{n^2}\right)\left(\frac{n^2}{Z}\right) \propto n^0$

(D) $pr \propto \left(\frac{Z}{n}\right)\left(\frac{n^2}{Z}\right) \propto n$

Also, $pr \propto L$

4. (A) UV region corresponds to Lymen series. So, lower state should be $n = 1$.

(B) Visible region corresponds to Balmer series. So, lower state should be $n = 2$.

(C) Infrared region corresponds to Paschen and Brackett series. So, lower state should be $n = 3$ or $n = 4$.

(D) Microwave have less energetic photons than infrared. So, transition $n \to 7$ to $n \to 6$ will emit microwave.

5. Maximum frequency of Lymen series will correspond to largest transition i.e., $n \to \infty$ to $n \to 1$.

$$hf_1 = Rch\left[\frac{1}{1^2} - \frac{1}{\infty^2}\right] \Rightarrow f_1 = Rc$$

Minimum frequency of Lymen series will correspond to the shortest transition i.e., $n \to 2$ to $n \to 1$

$$hf_2 = Rch\left[\frac{1}{1^2} - \frac{1}{2^2}\right] \Rightarrow f_2 = \frac{3Rc}{4}$$

Maximum frequency of Balmer series will correspond to the largest transition i.e., $n \to \infty$ to $n \to 2$.

$$hf_3 = Rch\left[\frac{1}{2^2} - \frac{1}{\infty^2}\right] \Rightarrow f_3 = \frac{Rch}{4}$$

Numerical Value Questions

1. $E_n = -\frac{me^4}{8\varepsilon_0^2 h^2}\left(\frac{Z^2}{n^2}\right)$

So, $h\nu = \frac{me^4 Z^2}{8\varepsilon_0^2 h^2}\left[\frac{1}{4^2} - \frac{1}{5^2}\right] \Rightarrow \nu = \frac{me^4 Z^2}{8\varepsilon_0^2 h^3}\left(\frac{9}{16 \times 25}\right)$

Frequency, $\nu_4 = \frac{v}{2\pi r} = \left(\frac{Ze^2}{2\varepsilon_0 nh}\right)\frac{1}{2\pi}\left(\frac{\pi m Z e^2}{\varepsilon_0 h^2 n^2}\right) = \frac{Z^2 e^4 m}{4\varepsilon_0^2 n^3 h^3}$

$$\therefore \quad \frac{\nu}{\nu_4} = \frac{1}{8}\left(\frac{9}{16 \times 25}\right) \times 4(4)^3 = \frac{18}{25}$$

2. $E_{max} = E_n - E_1$

$$\Rightarrow \quad 204 = 13.6Z^2\left[\frac{1}{1^2} - \frac{1}{n^2}\right]$$

$$\Rightarrow \quad 15 = Z^2\left[\frac{1}{1^2} - \frac{1}{n^2}\right] \quad \text{...(i)}$$

$E_{min} = E_n - E_{n-1}$

$$\Rightarrow \quad 10.5\overline{7} = 13.6Z^2\left[\frac{1}{(n-1)^2} - \frac{1}{n^2}\right]$$

$$\Rightarrow \quad \frac{7}{9} = Z^2\left[\frac{1}{(n-1)^2} - \frac{1}{n^2}\right] \quad \text{...(ii)}$$

Solving Eqs. we get,

$n = 4$ and $Z = 4$

3. Energy of incident photon $= \frac{hc}{\lambda}$

$$= \frac{(12.42 \times 10^{-7} e)}{800 \times 10^{-10}} = 15.525 \text{ eV}$$

Kinetic energy of electron = 15.525 – 13.6 = 1.925 eV

Let the maximum distance be x.

$$e(1000)\,x = 1.925 \text{ eV}$$

$$\Rightarrow \quad x = 1925\,\mu\text{m}$$

4. Binding energy $= \frac{13.6}{n^2} = 0.85 \quad \Rightarrow \quad n = 4$

$$E_2 - E_1 = 10.2 \text{ eV}$$

So, $n = 2$ is the state of excitation energy 10.2 eV.

$$\lambda = \frac{hc}{E_4 - E_2} = \frac{1242}{2.55} = 487.06 \text{ nm}$$

5. Series limit wavelength of Balmer series,

$$\frac{1}{\lambda_1} = R\left[\frac{1}{2^2} - \frac{1}{(\infty)^2}\right] \quad \text{...(i)}$$

Wavelength of first line of Paschen series,

$$\frac{1}{\lambda_2} = R\left[\frac{1}{3^2} - \frac{1}{4^2}\right] \quad \text{...(ii)}$$

Dividing Eq. (ii) by Eq. (i), we get

$$\frac{\lambda_1}{\lambda_2} = \frac{7}{36}$$

6. $$\frac{1}{\lambda} = R\left[\frac{1}{n_1^2} - \frac{1}{n_2^2}\right]$$

$$\Rightarrow \quad \frac{1}{\lambda} = 1.097 \times 10^7\left[\frac{1}{3^2} - \frac{1}{n_2^2}\right]$$

$$\Rightarrow \quad \lambda = \frac{9n_2^2}{(n_2^2 - 9)(1.097 \times 10^7)}$$

$$\lambda > 1000 \times 10^{-9}$$

$$\Rightarrow \quad \frac{9n_2^2}{(n_2^2 - 9)(1.097 \times 10^7)} > 1000 \times 10^{-9}$$

$$\Rightarrow \quad 9n_2^2 > 10.97(n_2^2 - 9) \quad \Rightarrow \quad n_2 < 7.07$$

So, n_2 can be equal to 4, 5, 6, 7.

Therefore, number of lines = 4.

7. de-Broglie wavelength of electron $= \sqrt{\frac{150}{V}} = 5$

$$\Rightarrow \quad V = 6 \text{ V}$$

So, $K_{max} = e(6 \text{ V}) = 6$ eV

$$E = W + K_{max} = 4.2 + 6 = 10.2 \text{ eV}$$

$$E = 13.6Z^2\left[\frac{1}{Z^2} - \frac{1}{(Z+2)^2}\right] = 10.2$$

$$\Rightarrow \quad Z = 2$$

8. $E = \frac{hc}{\lambda_1} + \frac{hc}{\lambda_2} = \frac{1240}{108.5} + \frac{1240}{30.4} = 52.22$ eV

$$E = 13.6Z^2\left[\frac{1}{n_1^2} - \frac{1}{n_2^2}\right]$$

$$\Rightarrow \quad 52.22 = 13.6(2)^2\left[\frac{1}{1^2} - \frac{1}{n_2^2}\right]$$

$$\Rightarrow \quad n_2 = 5$$

9. 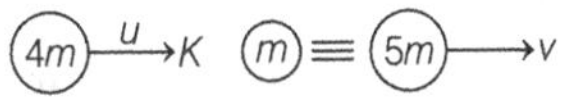

For perfectly inelastic collision,

$$4mu + 0 = 5mv \quad \Rightarrow \quad v = \frac{4u}{5}$$

$$\text{Loss in energy} = \frac{1}{2}(4m)u^2 - \frac{1}{2}(5m)\left(\frac{4u}{5}\right)^2$$

$$= \frac{1}{5}\left[\frac{1}{2}(4m)u^2\right] = \frac{K}{5}$$

Excitation energy for hydrogen $= E_3 - E_1 = 12.09$ eV

Excitation energy for $He^+ = E_3 - E_2 = 7.56$ eV

$$\frac{K}{5} > (12.09 + 7.56)$$

$$\Rightarrow \quad K_{min} = 98.25 \text{ eV}$$

10. $$f = \frac{v}{2\pi r} \propto \frac{Z^2}{n^3}$$

$$\frac{f_1}{f_2} = \left(\frac{Z_1}{Z_2}\right)^2\left(\frac{n_2}{n_1}\right)^3$$

$$\Rightarrow \quad \frac{6.6 \times 10^{15}}{13.2 \times 10^{15}} = \left(\frac{1}{Z}\right)^2\left(\frac{n}{1}\right)^3$$

$$\Rightarrow \quad \frac{Z^2}{n^3} = 2 \quad \text{...(i)}$$

$$E = E_0\frac{Z^2}{n^2} \quad \Rightarrow \quad 54.4 = 13.6\frac{Z^2}{n^2}$$

$$\Rightarrow \quad \frac{Z^2}{n^2} = 4 \quad \text{...(ii)}$$

Solving the two Eqs., we get

$$n = 2 \text{ and } Z = 4$$

Angular momentum, $L = \frac{nh}{2\pi}$

$$\text{Average torue} = \frac{\Delta L}{\Delta t} = \frac{\left(n - \frac{n}{2}\right)\frac{h}{2\pi}}{\Delta t}$$

$$= \frac{(2-1)\,2.1 \times 10^{-34}}{2 \times 7 \times 10^{-9}} = 15 \times 10^{-27} \text{ N-m}$$

11. $\Delta E = \frac{hc}{\lambda} = \frac{1240}{(6200/51)} = 10.2$ eV

For hydrogen like gas,

$$\Delta E = E_0 Z^2\left[\frac{1}{n_1^2} - \frac{1}{n_2^2}\right]$$

$$\Rightarrow \quad 10.2 = 13.6Z^2\left[\frac{1}{n_1^2} - \frac{1}{n_2^2}\right]$$

For hydrogen, $\Delta E = E_2 - E_1$

$$= 10.2 = 13.6\left[\frac{1}{1^2} - \frac{1}{2^2}\right]$$

So, we get $Z = 2, n_1 = 2$ and $n_2 = 4$

Number of lines $= {}^nC_2 = 6 \Rightarrow n = 4$

So, electrons in hydrogen like gas are excited to state $n = 4$.

For perfectly inelastic collision,

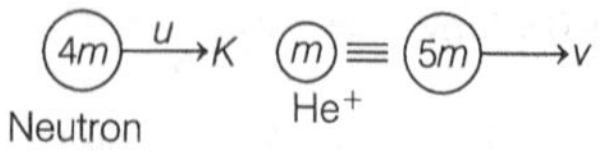

$$mu + 0 = 5mv \Rightarrow v = \frac{u}{5}$$

$$\text{Loss in energy} = \frac{1}{2}mu^2 - \frac{1}{2}(5m)\left(\frac{u}{5}\right)^2 = \frac{4}{5}\left(\frac{1}{2}mu^2\right) = \frac{4K}{5}$$

$$\frac{4K}{5} \geq E_4 - E_1 \Rightarrow \frac{4K}{5} \geq 13.6(2)^2\left[\frac{1}{1^2} - \frac{1}{(4)^2}\right]$$

$$\Rightarrow K_{min} = 63.75 \text{ eV}$$

12. $i = \frac{q}{T} = \frac{ev}{2\pi r}$, $v = \frac{e^2}{2\varepsilon_0 h}\left(\frac{Z}{n}\right)$ and $r = \frac{\varepsilon_0 h^2}{\pi m e^2}\frac{n^2}{Z}$

$$B = \frac{\mu_0 i}{2\pi r} = \frac{\mu_0 ev}{4\pi^2 r^2} = \frac{\mu_0 e}{4\pi^2}\left(\frac{e^2 Z}{2\varepsilon_0 hn}\right)\left(\frac{\pi^2 m^2 e^4 Z^2}{\varepsilon_0^2 h^4 n^4}\right)$$

$\Rightarrow B \propto e^7$

13. $E = \sigma T^4 \Rightarrow \frac{E_1}{E_2} = \left(\frac{T_1}{T_2}\right)^4$

$$\Rightarrow \frac{E_1}{16E_1} = \left(\frac{T_1}{T_2}\right)^4 \Rightarrow T_2 = 2T_1$$

$$\lambda_1 T_1 = \lambda_2 T_2 \Rightarrow (6200)\,T_1 = \lambda_2(2T_1)$$

$$\Rightarrow \lambda_2 = 3100 \text{ Å}$$

$$E = \frac{hc}{\lambda} = \frac{12400}{3100} = 4 \text{ eV}$$

$$K_{max} = \Delta E = 13.6\left[\frac{1}{2^2} - \frac{1}{4^2}\right] = 2.55 \text{ eV}$$

$$E = W + K_{max}$$

$$\Rightarrow 4 \text{ eV} = W + 2.55 \text{ eV} \Rightarrow W = 1.45 \text{ eV}$$

14. $E = \frac{hc}{\lambda} = \frac{12420}{1242} = 10 \text{ eV}$

$$K_{max} = (E - W) + \text{eV} = (10 - 2) \text{ eV} + e(5 \text{ V}) = 13 \text{ eV}$$

$$E_4 - E_1 = 12.75 \text{ eV}$$

$$E_5 - E_1 = 13.05 \text{ eV}$$

So, electrons in hydrogen can be excited from state $n = 1$ to $n = 4$.

On de-excitation, number of lines $= {}^4C_2 = 6$

15. $\Delta E = \frac{hc}{\lambda} \Rightarrow \Delta E = \frac{12400}{1215} = 10.2 \text{ eV}$

$$K_{max} = h\nu - W = 13.6 \text{ eV} \quad \text{...(i)}$$

$$K_{max} = h\left(\frac{5\nu}{6}\right) - W = 10.2 \text{ eV} \quad \text{...(ii)}$$

Solving Eqs. (i) and (ii), we get

$$W = 6.8 \text{ eV}, \; h\nu = 20.4 \text{ eV}$$

$$h\nu = 20.4 \text{ eV}$$

$$\Rightarrow \nu = \frac{20.4 \times 1.6 \times 10^{-19}}{6.6 \times 10^{-34}} = 4.94 \times 10^{15} \text{ Hz}$$

16. $10.2Z^2 = 3 \times 13.6 \Rightarrow Z = 2$

$$\lambda = \frac{h}{\sqrt{2mK}} \Rightarrow \frac{\lambda_1}{\lambda_2} = \sqrt{\frac{K_2}{K_1}} = 2.3$$

$$\Rightarrow K_2 = 5.25K_1 \quad \text{...(i)}$$

$$10.2 = W + K_1 \quad \text{...(ii)}$$

$$10.2(2)^2 = W + K_2 \quad \text{...(iii)}$$

Solving Eqs. (i), (ii) and (iii), we get

$$W = 3 \text{ eV}$$

and $K_1 = 7.2$ eV

Previous Year's Questions

JEE Main

1. In Bohr's atom (H-atom), radius of nth orbit is given by

$$R = \frac{Kn^2}{Z}$$

Let R' = radius of 4th orbit and

R = radius of 3rd orbit then,

$$\frac{R}{R'} = \frac{\frac{K(3)^2}{Z}}{\frac{K(4)^2}{Z}}$$

$$\frac{R}{R'} = \frac{9}{16} \Rightarrow R' = \frac{16}{9}R$$

2. $\frac{1}{\lambda} = R\left(\frac{1}{n_1^2} - \frac{1}{n_2^2}\right)$

For longest wavelength of Paschen series,

$$n_1 = 3 \text{ and } n_2 = 4$$

$$\therefore \frac{1}{\lambda_2} = R\left(\frac{1}{3^2} - \frac{1}{4^2}\right) = R\left(\frac{7}{144}\right)$$

$$\therefore \lambda_L = \frac{144}{7R} = \frac{\alpha}{7R} \quad \text{(given)}$$

$$\therefore \alpha = 144$$

3.

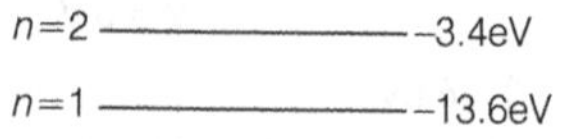

$$\Delta E = 10.2 \text{ eV}$$

$$\text{Recoil speed, } v = \frac{\Delta E}{mc} = \frac{10.2 \text{ eV}}{1.6 \times 10^{-27} \times 3 \times 10^8}$$

$$= \frac{10.2 \times 1.6 \times 10^{-19}}{1.6 \times 10^{-27} \times 3 \times 10^8}$$

$$v = 3.4 \text{ m/s} = \frac{17}{5} \text{ m/s} \Rightarrow x = 17$$

4. According to Rutherford model, an atom consists of positively particles concentrated at the centre known as nucleus.

The size of nucleus is very small as compared to the size of atom.

Thus, Statement I is true but Statement II is false.

5. We know that radius of nth orbit of H-atom is given as,

$$r_n = r_0 \times \frac{n^2}{Z}$$

For 2nd orbit of He^+, $Z = 2, n = 2$

$$\therefore \quad r_1 = r_0 \cdot \frac{2^2}{2} = 2r_0$$

$$\Rightarrow \quad r_1 = 2r_0 \quad \text{...(i)}$$

Similarly, for fourth orbit Be^{3-}

$$Z = 4, x = 4$$

$$\therefore \quad r_2 = r_0 \times \frac{4^2}{4} = 4r_0$$

$$\therefore \quad \frac{r_1}{r_2} = \frac{2r_0}{4r_0} = \frac{1}{2}$$

$$\Rightarrow \quad \frac{r_2}{r_1} = \frac{2}{1} = \frac{x}{1} \quad \text{[Given]}$$

$$\therefore \quad x = 2$$

6. $$r_n = \frac{0.51 n^2}{Z} \text{ Å}$$

for Li^{++}, $Z = 3$

$$r_5 = 0.51 \times \frac{25}{3} \times 10^{-10} \text{ m}$$

$$= 17 \times 25 \times 10^{-12} = 425 \times 10^{-12} \text{ m}$$

7. Using, $E = \frac{Ke^2}{2r}$

$$r = \frac{Ke^2}{2E}$$

Given, $E = 12.8 \text{ eV} = 12.8 \times e \text{ J}$

$$r = \frac{9 \times 10^9 \times e^2}{2 \times 12.8e} = \frac{9 \times 10^9 \times 1.6 \times 16^{-19}}{2 \times 12.8}$$

$$= \frac{9 \times 10^{-10}}{2 \times \frac{12.8}{1.6}} = \frac{9 \times 10^{-10}}{\frac{25.6}{1.6}} = \frac{9 \times 10^{-10}}{16} = \frac{9}{x} \times 10^{-10} \text{m}$$

$$x = 16$$

8. According to given situation,

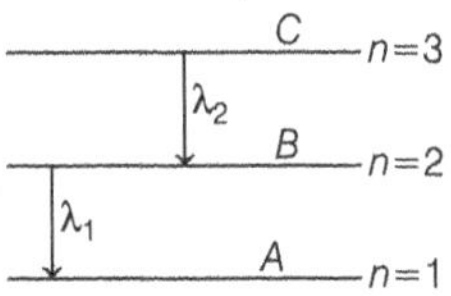

$$E_B - E_A = \frac{hc}{\lambda_1}$$

$$\Rightarrow \quad \frac{-13.6}{2^2} - \frac{(-13.6)}{1^2} = \frac{hc}{\lambda_1} \Rightarrow 10.2 = \frac{hc}{\lambda_1}$$

$$\Rightarrow \quad \frac{hc}{\lambda_1} = 10.2 \quad \text{...(i)}$$

Similarly, $E_C - E_B = \frac{hc}{\lambda_2}$

$$\Rightarrow \quad \frac{-13.6}{3^2} - \left(-\frac{13.6}{2^2}\right) = \frac{hc}{\lambda_2} \Rightarrow 13.6\left(\frac{1}{4} - \frac{1}{9}\right) = \frac{hc}{\lambda_2}$$

$$\Rightarrow \quad 13.6 \times \frac{5}{36} = \frac{hc}{\lambda_2} \Rightarrow 1.89 = \frac{hc}{\lambda_2}$$

$$\Rightarrow \quad \frac{hc}{\lambda_2} = 1.89 \quad \text{...(ii)}$$

On dividing Eqs. (ii) by Eq. (i), we get

$$\frac{\frac{hc}{\lambda_1}}{\frac{hc}{\lambda_2}} = \frac{10.2}{1.89} \Rightarrow \frac{\lambda_2}{\lambda_1} = 5.6$$

$$\Rightarrow \quad \frac{\lambda_1}{\lambda_2} = \frac{1}{5.6} = \frac{7}{4 \times 9.8} = \frac{7}{4n} \quad \text{[Given]}$$

$$\therefore \quad n = 9.8$$

9. According to first condition,

$$\frac{hc}{\lambda_0} = \frac{-13.6}{3^2} - \left(\frac{-13.6}{2^2}\right) \Rightarrow \frac{hc}{\lambda_0} = \frac{13.6 \times 5}{36} \quad \text{... (i)}$$

According to second condition,

$$\frac{hc}{\lambda'} = \frac{-13.6}{4^2} - \left(\frac{-13.6}{3^2}\right) = \frac{13.6}{9} - \frac{13.6}{16}$$

$$\frac{hc}{\lambda'} = \frac{13.6 \times 7}{16 \times 9} \quad \text{... (ii)}$$

On dividing Eq. (i) by Eq. (ii), we get

$$\frac{\frac{hc}{\lambda_0}}{hc/\lambda'} = \frac{13.6 \times 5}{36} \times \frac{16 \times 9}{13.6 \times 7}$$

$$\Rightarrow \quad \frac{\lambda'}{\lambda_0} = \frac{4}{7} = \frac{20}{35}$$

$$\Rightarrow \quad \lambda' = \frac{20}{35}\lambda_0 = \frac{20}{x}\lambda_0 \quad \text{[Given]}$$

$$\therefore \quad x = 35$$

10. Binding energy of an electron is negative of total energy in that state.

$$\text{BE} = -\text{Total energy}$$

$$= -\left(-13.6\frac{Z^2}{n^2}\right) = 13.6\frac{Z^2}{n^2} \text{ eV}$$

For Li^{++}, $Z = 3, n = 2 + 1 = 3$

$$\text{BE} = 13.6\frac{(3)^2}{(3)^2} = 13.6 \text{ eV} = 136 \times 10^{-1} \text{eV}$$

On comparing, $x = 136$

11. Given, lowest wavelength of Lyman series = 917 Å

For lowest wavelength of lyman series

$$\frac{1}{\lambda} = RZ^2\left(\frac{1}{1^2} - \frac{1}{\infty^2}\right) = RZ^2$$

For lowest wavelength of Balmer series,

$$\frac{1}{\lambda'} = RZ^2\left(\frac{1}{2^2} - \frac{1}{\infty^2}\right) = \frac{RZ^2}{4}$$

$$\Rightarrow \quad \lambda' = \frac{4}{RZ^2} = 4 \times 917 = 3668 \text{ Å}$$

12. Bohr's orbit is orbit of ground state of atom.

So, in first orbit angular momentum $L = \frac{h}{2\pi}$

In second orbit angular momentum $L' = \frac{2h}{2\pi}$

Hence, change in angular momentum is

$$\Delta L = L' - L = \frac{2h}{2\pi} - \frac{h}{2\pi} = \frac{h}{2\pi} \text{ or } L$$

13. Given, energy of the electron beam = 12.5 eV

According to Bohr's postulate, an electron makes jump to higher energy orbital if it absorbs a photon of energy equal to different between the energies of an excited state and the ground state. Assuming that collided electron takes energy equal to 10.2 eV or 12.09 eV from incoming electron beam. The maximum excited state is $n = 3$. So number of spectral lines is $\frac{3(3-1)}{2} = 3$.

14. The energy of an electron in nth orbit is given as

$$E_n = -Rhc\frac{Z^2}{n^2}$$

Electron is making an transition from 4th energy state to 2nd energy state, then energy released

$$\Delta E = E_4 - E_2 = -Rhc\frac{Z^2}{4^2} - \left(-Rhc\frac{Z^2}{2^2}\right)$$

$$\Rightarrow \quad \Delta E = Rhc\left(\frac{1}{2^2} - \frac{1}{4^2}\right)Z^2$$

For hydrogen like atom, $Z = 4$

$$\Delta E = 13.6\left(\frac{1}{4} - \frac{1}{16}\right) \times (4)^2 = 13.6 \times \left(\frac{3}{16}\right) \times (4)^2$$

$$\Rightarrow \quad \Delta E = 40.8 \text{ eV}$$

15. Given, wavelength of photon,

$$\lambda = 124.1 \text{ nm} = 1.24 \times 10^{-7} \text{ m}$$

$$h = 6.62 \times 10^{-34} \text{ J-s}$$

$\therefore$ Energy of photon,

$$E = \frac{hc}{\lambda} = \frac{6.62 \times 10^{-34} \times 3 \times 10^8}{1.24 \times 10^{-7}}$$

$$= 1.6 \times 10^{-18} \text{ J} = \frac{1.6 \times 10^{-18}}{1.6 \times 10^{-19}} = 10 \text{ eV}$$

Energy of photon in transition D,

$$E' = 0 - (-10) = 10 \text{ eV}$$

16. Speed of an electron in nth Bohr's orbit is given as,

$$v_n \propto \frac{1}{n}$$

$$\Rightarrow \quad \frac{v_7}{v_3} = \frac{3}{7} \Rightarrow \frac{3.6 \times 10^6}{v_3} = \frac{3}{7}$$

$$\Rightarrow \quad v_3 = \frac{7}{3} \times 3.6 \times 10^6$$

$$\Rightarrow \quad v_3 = 8.4 \times 10^6 \text{ ms}^{-1}$$

17. Energy released during transition from $n = 4$ to $n = 1$

$$\Delta E = \frac{-13.6}{4^2} - \left(-\frac{13.6}{1^2}\right)$$

$$= 13.6 - \frac{13.6}{4^2} = 13.6\left(1 - \frac{1}{16}\right)$$

$$= 12.75 \text{ eV} = 12.75 \times 1.6 \times 10^{-19} \text{ J}$$

Since, $\Delta E = \frac{hc}{\lambda}$

$$\Rightarrow \quad \lambda = \frac{hc}{\Delta E} = \frac{6.63 \times 10^{-34} \times 3 \times 10^8}{12.75 \times 1.6 \times 10^{-19}} \text{ m}$$

$$= 0.983 \times 10^{-7} \text{ m}$$

$$= 98.3 \times - 10^{-9} \text{ m}$$

$$= 98.3 \text{ nm}$$

18. We know that the energy of an electron in the nth orbit

$$E_n = \frac{-13.6}{n^2} \text{ eV}$$

(i) Energy of photon produced in transition from $n = 2$ to $n = 1$ energy level,

$$E_2 - E_1 = \left[\frac{-13.6}{4} - \left(\frac{-13.6}{1}\right)\right] = \frac{13.6}{4} \times 3 \text{ eV}$$

$$\Rightarrow \quad E_2 - E_1 = \frac{3}{4} \times 13.6 \text{ eV} \qquad \text{... (i)}$$

(ii) Energy of photon produced in transition from $n = \infty$ to $n = 1$ ($\because$ Highest energy level is $n = \infty$)

$$\Rightarrow \quad E_\infty - E_1 = \left[\frac{-13.6}{\infty} - \left(\frac{-13.6}{1}\right)\right] \text{eV}$$

$$= 13.6 \text{ eV} \qquad \text{...(ii)}$$

$\therefore$ From Eqs. (i) and (ii),

$$\frac{E_2 - E_1}{E_\infty - E_1} = \frac{\frac{3}{4} \times 13.6 \text{ eV}}{13.6 \text{ eV}} = \frac{3}{4} \text{ or } 3:4$$

19. We know that angular momentum

$$L = \frac{nh}{2\pi}$$

As, $L = mvr \Rightarrow mvr = \frac{nh}{2\pi}$

$$\Rightarrow \quad mv = \frac{nh}{2\pi r} \quad \text{or} \quad p = mv = \frac{nh}{2\pi r}$$

20. When an electron jumps from lower orbit (E_1) to higher orbit (E_2) it absorbs energy. If f be the frequency of absorbed photon, then

$$hf = E_2 - E_1 \Rightarrow f = (E_2 - E_1)/h$$

So, only statement II is correct.

21. Change in energy, $\Delta E = 10.2$ eV

If transition occurs from ground state i.e,

$n = 1$ to $n = 2$, then

change in momentum,

$$\Delta L = \frac{2h}{2\pi} - \frac{h}{2\pi} = \frac{h}{2\pi} = \frac{6.6 \times 10^{-34}}{2 \times \pi} = 1.05 \times 10^{-34} \text{ J-s}$$

22. Speed of electron in nth orbit is given as

$$v = \frac{e}{2\varepsilon_0 h}\left(\frac{Z}{n}\right) \quad \text{[Where, } Z = \text{atomic number]}$$

$$\Rightarrow \quad v \propto \frac{Z}{n}$$

$$\Rightarrow \quad \frac{v_{He^+}}{v_H} = \frac{Z_{He^+}}{Z_H} \times \frac{n_H}{n_{He^+}} \quad [\because Z_{He^+} = 2;\ Z_H = 1]$$

$$= \frac{2}{1} \times \frac{3}{3} = \frac{2}{1}$$

$\therefore\ v_{He^+} : v_H = 2:1$

23. Kinetic energy of electron in nth orbit,

$$K = \frac{kZe^2}{2r} = \frac{Ze^2}{8\pi\varepsilon_0 r}$$

$$\Rightarrow \quad K = \frac{Ze^2}{8\pi\varepsilon_0 r} \quad \text{...(i)}$$

Similarly, $P = -\frac{Ze^2}{4\pi\varepsilon_0 r}$ ...(ii)

And, $E = K + P = \frac{Ze^2}{8\pi\varepsilon_0 r} - \frac{Ze^2}{4\pi\varepsilon_0 r}$

$$E = -\frac{Ze^2}{8\pi\varepsilon_0 r} \quad \text{... (iii)}$$

When electron undergoes transitions to a higher energy level, then radius r of circular path of electron increases. Hence, from Eqs. (i), (ii) and (iii), we see that K decreases, P and E increase.

24.

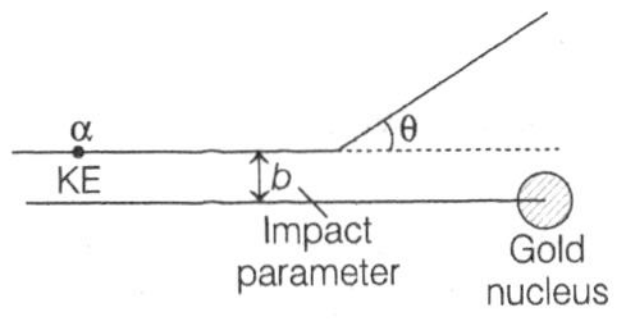

Impact parameter b is given by

$$b = \frac{Ze^2 \cdot \cot(\theta/2)}{4\pi\varepsilon_0 \cdot (KE_\alpha)} \quad \text{or} \quad b \propto \cot\frac{\theta}{2}$$

With given values, we get

$$\therefore \quad \frac{\sqrt{d_1}}{\sqrt{d_2}} = \frac{\cot(60°/2)}{\cot(90°/2)} = \frac{\cot 30°}{\cot 45°} \quad \text{or} \quad \frac{\sqrt{d_1}}{\sqrt{d_2}} = \frac{\sqrt{3}}{1}$$

$$\Rightarrow \quad d_1 = 3d_2$$

Hence, value of x is 3.

25. Energy of photon can be given as

$$E_p = 13.6\left[\frac{1}{n_1^2} - \frac{1}{n_2^2}\right] \text{eV}$$

Where, n_1= lower energy level

and n_2= higher energy level.

As per question, $n_1 = 2$, $n_2 = 3$

$$\therefore \quad E_p = 13.6\left[\frac{1}{(2)^2} - \frac{1}{(3)^2}\right] = 13.6\left[\frac{1}{4} - \frac{1}{9}\right]$$

$$= 13.6\left[\frac{9-4}{36}\right] = 1.89 \text{ eV}$$

For gold plate,

$$\phi = E_P - KE_{max} \quad \text{...(i)}$$

[Given, $B = 5\times10^{-4}$T, $r = 7$mm $= 7\times10^{-3}$m, $q = 1.6\times10^{-19}$C and $m = 9.1\times10^{-31}$ kg]

Therefore, velocity of photoelectrons will be

$$v = \frac{Bqr}{m} = \frac{5\times10^{-4}\times1.6\times10^{-19}\times7\times10^{-3}}{9.1\times10^{-31}}$$

$$= 6.15\times10^5 \text{ ms}^{-1}$$

Kinetic energy will be

$$\therefore \quad KE_{max} = \frac{1}{2}mv^2 = \frac{1\times9.1\times10^{-31}\times(6.15\times10^5)^2}{2\times1.6\times10^{-19}} \text{ eV}$$

$$= 1.075 \text{ eV}$$

From Eq. (i),

$$\phi = (1.89 - 1.075) \text{ eV} = 0.82 \text{ eV}$$

26. The frequency of the emitted radiation

$$f = RZ^2c\left(\frac{1}{n_2} - \frac{1}{n_1}\right)$$

For H-atom, $Z = 1$

So, for transition from $n = 3$ to $n = 1$,

$$f_1 = Rc\left(1 - \frac{1}{3^2}\right) \quad \text{...(i)}$$

Similarly for transition from $n = 2$ to $n = 1$,

$$f_2 = Rc\left(1 - \frac{1}{2^2}\right) \quad \text{...(ii)}$$

On dividing Eq. (i) by Eq. (ii), we get

$$\frac{f_1}{f_2} = \frac{Rc\left(1 - \frac{1}{9}\right)}{Rc\left(1 - \frac{1}{4}\right)} = \frac{\frac{8}{9}}{\frac{3}{4}} = \frac{32}{27}$$

Here, $f_1 = 2.92\times10^{15}$ Hz

$$\Rightarrow \quad \frac{2.92\times10^{15}}{f_2} = \frac{32}{27}$$

$$f_2 = \frac{27\times2.92\times10^{15}}{32} = 2.46\times10^{15} \text{ Hz}$$

27. Given, electron makes a transition from $n = 2$ to $n = 1$. From Bohr's hydrogen spectrum

$$\frac{1}{\lambda} = R\left[\frac{1}{n_f^2} - \frac{1}{n_i^2}\right]$$

$$\Rightarrow \quad \frac{1}{\lambda} = 1.097\times10^7\left[\frac{1}{1^2} - \frac{1}{2^2}\right]$$

$$= 1.097\times10^7\left[\frac{1}{1} - \frac{1}{4}\right] = \frac{3}{4}\times1.097\times10^7$$

$$\lambda = \frac{4}{3\times1.097\times10^7} = 1.215\times10^{-7}\text{m}$$

$$= 121.5\times10^{-9} \text{ m} \simeq 121.8 \text{ nm}$$

JEE Advanced

1. $\Delta E = E_4 - E_3$

$$\Rightarrow hv = 13.6Z^2\left(\frac{1}{9}-\frac{1}{16}\right) = 13.6 \times \frac{7}{9\times 16}(Z^2)$$

$\because$ $$(KE)_{max} = hv - \phi$$

$\Rightarrow$ $$1.95 = hv - \frac{1240}{310}$$

$\Rightarrow$ $$hv = 1.95 + 4$$

$\Rightarrow$ $$5.95 = 13.6 \times \frac{7}{9\times 16}(Z^2)$$

$$Z^2 = 9 \Rightarrow Z = 3$$

2. **For (a)** When the transition is from any level to $n = 2$, then photon emitted belong to Balmer series.

$\therefore$ For longest wavelength, transition occurs from $n = 3$ to $n = 2$.

$\therefore$ $$\frac{hc}{\lambda_{max}} = Rch\left[\frac{1}{2^2}-\frac{1}{3^2}\right]$$ and for shortest wavelength, transition occurs from $n = \infty$ to $n = 2$

$\therefore$ $$\frac{hc}{\lambda_{min}} = Rch\left[\frac{1}{2^2}-\frac{1}{\infty^2}\right]$$

$\therefore$ $$\frac{\lambda_{longest}}{\lambda_{shortest}} = \frac{9}{5}$$

For (b) $\lambda_{longest}$ of Balmer $= \frac{36}{5R}$

$\lambda_{shortest}$ of Paschen $= \frac{9}{R}$

Hence, these wavelength don't overlap.

For (c) $$\frac{1}{\lambda} = R\left[\frac{1}{1}-\frac{1}{m^2}\right]$$

Also, $$\frac{1}{\lambda_0} = R$$

$\therefore$ $$\frac{1}{\lambda} = \frac{1}{\lambda_0}\left[1-\frac{1}{m^2}\right] \Rightarrow \lambda = \frac{\lambda_0}{1-\frac{1}{m^2}}$$

For (d) $\lambda_{longest}$ of Lyman $= \frac{4}{3R}$, $\lambda_{shortest}$ of Balmer $= \frac{4}{R}$

Hence, that wavelength don't overlap.

3. $$|\text{Force}| = \left|-\frac{dV}{dr}\right| \Rightarrow F = \frac{mv^2}{r} \quad \text{... (i)}$$

$$mvr = \frac{nh}{2\pi} \quad \text{... (ii)}$$

From Eqs. (i) and (ii), we get

$\therefore$ $$F = \frac{m}{r}\left(\frac{nh}{2\pi mr}\right)^2 \qquad \left(\because v = \frac{nh}{2\pi mr}\right)$$

or $$F = \frac{mn^2h^2}{4\pi^2m^2r^3} \text{ or } F = \frac{n^2h^2}{4\pi^2mr^3}$$

$$r^3 \propto n^2 \qquad (\text{as } F = \text{constant})$$

$$r \propto n^{2/3}$$

$$v = \frac{nh}{2\pi mr}$$

$$v \propto \frac{n}{n^{2/3}} \text{ or } v \propto n^{1/3}$$

$\therefore$ $$KE = \frac{1}{2}mv^2 = \frac{Fr}{2}$$

$\because$ $$TE = PE + KE = Fr + \frac{Fr}{2}$$

$\Rightarrow$ $$\frac{3Fr}{2} = TE$$

or $$TE = E = \frac{3F}{2}\times\left(\frac{n^2h^2}{4\pi^2 rnF}\right)^{1/3} = \frac{3}{2}\left(\frac{n^2h^2F^2}{4\pi^2m}\right)^{1/3}$$

4. $$\Delta E_{2-1} = 13.6\times Z^2\left[1-\frac{1}{4}\right] = 13.6\times Z^2\left[\frac{3}{4}\right]$$

$$\Delta E_{3-2} = 13.6\times Z^2\left[\frac{1}{4}-\frac{1}{9}\right] = 13.6\times Z^2\left[\frac{5}{36}\right]$$

$\therefore$ $$\Delta E_2 = \Delta E_{3-2} + 74.8$$

$$13.6\times Z^2\left[\frac{3}{4}\right] = 13.6\times Z^2\left[\frac{5}{36}\right] + 74.8$$

$$13.6\times Z^2\left[\frac{3}{4}-\frac{5}{36}\right] = 74.8$$

$$Z^2 = 9$$

$\therefore$ $$Z = 3$$

5. Energy of incident light (in eV)

$$E = \frac{12375}{970} = 12.7 \text{ eV}$$

After excitation, let the electron jumps to nth state, then

$$\frac{-13.6}{n^2} = -13.6 + 12.7$$

Solving this equation, we get

$$n = 4$$

$\therefore$ Total number of lines in emission spectrum,

$$= \frac{n(n-1)}{2} = \frac{4(4-1)}{2} = 6$$

6. Angular momentum $= n\left(\frac{h}{2\pi}\right) = 3\left(\frac{h}{2\pi}\right)$

$\therefore$ $$n = 3$$

$$r_n \propto \frac{n^2}{z}$$

$\therefore$ $$r_3 = \frac{(3)^2}{3}(a_0) = 3a_0$$

Now, $$mv_3r_3 = 3\left(\frac{h}{2\pi}\right)$$

$\therefore$ $$mv_3(3a_0) = 3\left(\frac{h}{2\pi}\right) \text{ or } \frac{h}{mv_3} = 2\pi a_0$$

or $$\frac{h}{P_3} = 2\pi a_0 \qquad (\because P = mv)$$

or $$\lambda_3 = 2\pi a_0 \qquad \left(\lambda = \frac{h}{P}\right)$$

$\therefore$ Answer is 2.

CHAPTER~09

X-RAYS

LEVEL 01 Starter Level

9.1 Continuous X-Rays

1 An X- ray tube operates at 20 kV.

(i) Find the cut-off wavelength.

(ii) A particular electron loses 5% of its kinetic energy to emit an X-Ray photon at the first collision. Find the wavelength corresponding to this photon.

2 If the operating potential in an X -ray tube is increased by 0.1%, by what percentage does the cut-off wavelength decrease?

3 When 50 kV DC is applied across an X-ray tube, heat is produced in the target at the rate of 495 W.

Assuming that 1% of the energy of the incident electrons gets converted to X-rays, find

(a) the number of electrons striking the target per second

(b) the velocity of the incident electron

(c) the shortest wavelength of X-ray produced. Assume that the electrons are non-relativistic.

4 The distance between the cathode (filament) and the target in an X-ray tube is 1.5 m. If the cut-off wavelength is 30 pm, find the electric field between the cathode and the target.

9.2 Characteristics X-Rays

1 Calculate the value of a in the Moseley's equation $\sqrt{\nu} = a(Z-b)$ on the basis of the figure shown.

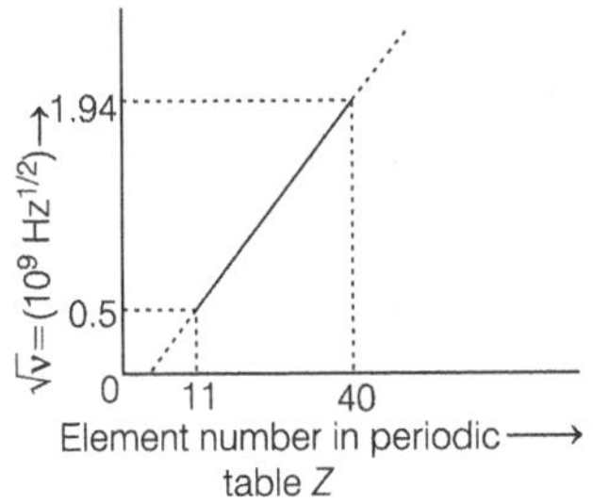

2 Find the constants a and b in Moseley's equation from the following data.

Element	Z	Wavelength of K_α X-ray
Mo	42	71 pm
Co	27	178.5 pm

3 Find the wavelength of the K_α line in copper (Z = 29), if the wavelength of the K_α line in iron (Z = 26) is known to be equal to 193 pm. (Take b = 1)

4 The K_α X-rays of aluminium (Z = 13) and zinc (Z = 30) have wavelengths 887 pm and 146 pm respectively. Use Moseley's law $\sqrt{\nu} = a(Z-b)$ to find the wavelength of the K_α X-ray of iron (Z = 26).

5 A cobalt target is bombarded with electrons and the wavelength of its characteristic spectrum are measured. A second, fainter, characteristic spectrum is also found because of an impurity in the target. The wavelength of the K_α lines are 178.9 pm (cobalt) and 143.5 pm (impurity). What is the impurity?

6 Characteristic X-rays of frequency 4.2×10^{18} Hz are emitted from a metal due to transition from L to K – shell. Find the atomic number of the metal using Moseley's law. Take Rydberg constant $R = 1.1 \times 10^7\ m^{-1}$.

7 The wavelength of K_αX-ray of tungsten is 21.3 pm. It takes 11.3 keV to knock out an electron from the L shell of a tungsten atom. What should be the minimum accelerating voltage across an X-ray tube having tungsten target which allows production of K_α X-ray ?

8 The K_α and K_β X-rays of molybdenum have wavelengths 0.71Å and 0.63 Å respectively. Find the wavelength of L_αX-ray of molybdenum.

9 Find the screening constant for the *L*-series of X-rays if it is known that X-rays with a wavelength 1.43 Å are emitted, when an electron in tungsten atom is transferred from M-layer to L-layer.

10 (i) Find which is K_α and K_β
(ii) Find which is K_α and L_α
(iii) Find in Z_1 and Z_2 which one is greater.

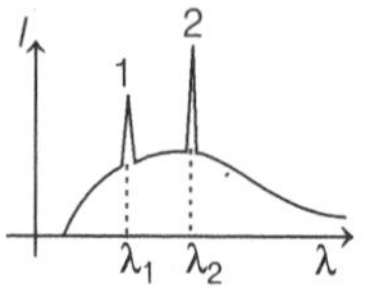

Figure for (i)

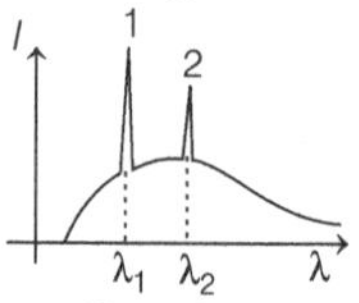

Figure for (ii)

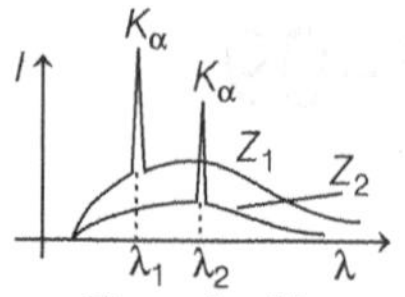

Figure for (iii)

11 When the voltage applied to an X-ray tube increased from $V_1 = 10\text{kV}$ to $V_2 = 20$ kV, the wavelength interval between the K_α line and the shortwave cut-off of the continuous X-ray spectrum increases by a factor $n = 3.0$. Find the atomic number of the element of which the tube's anticathode is made.

LEVEL 02 Advanced Level

1 The target used for production of X-ray beam must have
(a) high melting point and high atomic number
(b) high melting point and low atomic number
(c) low melting point and low atomic number
(d) low melting point and high atomic number

2 If the potential difference applied to the tube is doubled and the separation between the filament and the target is also doubled, the cut-off wavelength.
(a) will remain unchanged
(b) will be doubled
(c) will be halved
(d) will become four times the original

3 A potential difference of 20 kV is applied across an X-ray tube. Find the minimum wavelength of X-rays generated.
(a) 0.62 Å (b) 0.65Å
(c) 6.62 Å (d) 60.0Å

4 On increasing the operating voltage in a X-ray tube by 1.5 times, the shortest wavelength decreases by 26 pm. Find the original value of operating voltage.
(a) 10.9 kV (b) 12.9 kV
(c) 15.9 kV (d) 20.9 kV

5. X-rays are produced in an X-ray tube operating at a given accelerating voltage. The wavelength of the continuous X-rays have values from
(a) 0 to ∞
(b) λ_{min} to ∞, where $\lambda_{min} > 0$
(c) 0 to λ_{max}, where $\lambda_{max} < \infty$
(d) λ_{min} to λ_{max}, where $0 < \lambda_{min} < \lambda_{max} < \infty$

6. The potential difference applied to an X-ray tube is 5 kV and the current through it is 3.2 mA. Then, the number of electrons striking the target per second is
(a) 2×10^{16} (b) 5×10^{16} (c) 1×10^{17} (d) 4×10^{15}

7. The potential difference across the coolidge tube is 20kV and 10 mA current flows through the voltage supply. Only 0.5% of the energy carried by the electron striking the target is converted into X-rays. The power carried by X-ray is *P*.
(a) $P = 0.1$ W (b) $P = 1$ W
(c) $P = 2$ W (d) $P = 10$ W

8. The penetrating power of X-rays increases with the
(a) increase in its velocity (b) increase in its frequency
(c) increase in its intensity (d) decrease in its velocity

9. 50% of the X-ray coming from a coolidge tube is able to pass through a 0.1 mm thick aluminium foil. If the potential difference between the target and the filament is increased, the fraction of the X-ray passing through the same foiled will be
(a) 0% (b) < 50%
(c) 50% (d) > 50%

10. Cut-off wavelength of X-rays coming from a coolidge tube depends on
(a) target material
(b) accelerating voltage
(c) separation between the target and the filament
(d) temperature of filament

11. An X-ray tube is operated at 66 kV. Then, in the continuous spectrum of the emitted X-rays
(a) wavelengths 0.01 nm and 0.02 nm will both be present

(b) wavelengths 0.01 nm and 0.02 nm will both be absent

(c) wavelengths 0.01 nm will be present but wavelength 0.02 nm will be absent

(d) wavelength 0.01 nm will be absent but wavelength 0.02 nm will be present

12 Which of the following does not characterise X-rays?

(a) The radiation can ionise gases.

(b) It causes ZnS to fluorescence.

(c) Deflected by electric and magnetic fields.

(d) Have wavelengths shorter than ultraviolet rays.

13 The potential difference applied to an X-ray tube is V. The ratio of de-Broglie wavelength of electron to the minimum wavelength of X-ray is directly proportional to

(a) V (b) $V^{\frac{1}{2}}$

(c) $\frac{1}{\sqrt{V}}$ (d) independent of V

14 Electrons with de-Broglie wavelength λ fall on the target in an X-rays tube. The cut-off wavelength λ_0 of the emitted X-rays is

(a) $\lambda_0 = \frac{2mc\lambda^2}{h}$ (b) $\lambda_0 = \frac{2h}{mc}$

(c) $\lambda_0 = \frac{2m^2c^2\lambda^2}{h^2}$ (d) $\lambda_0 = \lambda$

15. When ultraviolet light is incident on a photocell, its stopping potential is V_0 and the maximum kinetic energy of the photoelectrons is K_{max}. When X-rays are incident on the same cell, then

(a) V_0 and K_{max} both increase

(b) V_0 and K_{max} decrease

(c) V_0 increases but K_{max} remains the same

(d) K_{max} increases but V_0 remains the same

16 Which of following is wrong in the context of X-ray generated from an X-ray tube?

(a) Wavelength of characteristic X-rays decreases, when the atomic number of the target increases

(b) Cut-off wavelength of the continuous X-rays depends on the atomic number of the target

(c) Intensity of the characteristic X-rays depends on the electrical power given to the X-ray tube

(d) Cut-off wavelength of the continuous X-rays depends on the energy of the electrons in the X-ray tube

17 Electrons with energy 80keV are incident on the tungsten target of an X-ray tube. K-shell electrons of tungsten have −72.5 keV energy. X-rays emitted by the tube contain only

(a) a continuous X-ray spectrum (Bremsstrahlung) with a minimum wavelength of ~ 0.155Å

(b) a continuous X-ray spectrum (Bremsstrahlung) with all wavelengths

(c) the characteristic X-ray spectrum of tungsten

(d) a continuous X-ray spectrum (Bremsstrahlung) with a minimum wavelength of ~ 0.155Å and the characteristic X-ray of tungsten

18 The K_α X-rays emission line of tungsten occurs at $\lambda = 0.021$ nm. The energy difference between K and L levels in this atom is about

(a) 0.51 MeV (b) 1.2 MeV

(c) 59 keV (d) 13.6 eV

19 The K, L and M energy levels of platinum lie roughly at 78, 12, and 3 keV respectively. The ratio of wavelength of K_α line to that of K_β line in X-ray spectrum is

(a) $\frac{22}{3}$ (b) $\frac{3}{22}$

(c) $\frac{22}{25}$ (d) $\frac{25}{22}$

20 If the frequencies of K_α, K_β and L_α X-rays for a material are ν_{K_α}, ν_{K_β} and ν_{L_α} respectively, then

(a) $\nu_{K_\alpha} = \nu_{K_\beta} + \nu_{L_\alpha}$ (b) $\nu_{L_\alpha} = \nu_{K_\alpha} + \nu_{K_\beta}$

(c) $\nu_{K_\beta} = \nu_{K_\alpha} + \nu_{L_\alpha}$ (d) None of these

21 The energy of a tungsten atom with a vacancy in L-shell is 11.3 keV. Wavelength of K_α photon for tungsten is 21.3 pm. If a potential difference of 62 kV is applied across the X-rays tube, following characteristic X-rays will be produced.

(a) K, L series (b) Only K_α and L series

(c) Only L series (d) None of these

22 In Moseley's law for characteristic X-rays is $\sqrt{\nu} = a(Z-b)$

(a) both a and b are independent of the material

(b) only a depends on material

(c) only b depends on material

(d) both of a and b depend on the material

23 A metal of atomic number Z is used as a target in coolidge tube. Let ν be the frequency of the K_α line. For which value of Z and ν, the plot is a straight line?

(a) ν vs Z (b) ν vs $\frac{1}{Z}$

(c) $\sqrt{\nu}$ vs Z (d) ν vs $\sqrt{Z}$

24 A K_α X-ray emitted from a sample has an energy of 7.46 keV. Of which element is the sample made?

(a) Calcium (Ca, Z = 20) (b) Cobalt (Co, Z = 27)

(c) Cadmium (Ca, Z = 48) (d) Nickel (Ni, Z = 28)

25 The wavelength of K_α X-rays produced by an X-rays tube is 0.76Å. The atomic number of the anode material of the tube is

(a) 31 (b) 41 (c) 51 (d) 61

26 K_α wavelength emitted by an atom of atomic number $Z = 11$ is λ. Find the atomic number for an atom that emits K_α radiation with wavelength 4λ

(a) $Z = 6$ (b) $Z = 4$ (c) $Z = 11$ (d) $Z = 44$

27 The wavelength of the K_α line for an element of atomic number 57 is λ. What is the wavelength of K_α line for the element of atomic number 29?

(a) λ (b) 2λ
(c) 4λ (d) 8λ

28. Frequency of the K_α X-ray for the element calcium (Ca, Z = 20) is 8.95×10^{17} Hz. Frequency of K_α X-ray for element cadmium (Cd, Z = 48) will be

(a) 5.47×10^{18} Hz (b) 6.31×10^{18} Hz
(c) 5.71×10^{17} Hz (d) 6.31×10^{17} Hz

29. If the K_α radiation of Mo (Z = 42) has a wavelength of 0.71 Å, find the wavelength of the corresponding radiation of Cu (Z = 29)

(a) 1Å (b) 2Å
(c) 1.52Å (d) 1.25Å

30 If the frequency of K_α X-ray emitted from element with atomic number 31 is f, then the frequency of K_α X-ray emitted from the element with atomic number 51 would be (assume that screening constant for K_α is 1)

(a) $\frac{5f}{3}$ (b) $\frac{51f}{31}$ (c) $\frac{9f}{25}$ (d) $\frac{25f}{9}$

31 In an X-ray experiment target is made up of copper (Z = 29) having some impurity. The K_α line of copper have wavelength λ. It was observed that another K_α line due to impurity have wavelength $\frac{784}{625}\lambda$. The atomic number of the impurity element is

(a) 22 (b) 23
(c) 24 (d) 26

32 X-rays emitted from a copper target and a molybdenum target are found to contain a line of wavelength 22.85 nm attributed to the K_α line of an impurity element. The K_α lines of copper (Z = 29) and molybdenum (Z = 42) have wavelength 15.42 nm and 7.12 nm respectively. The atomic number of the impurity element is

(a) 22 (b) 23
(c) 24 (d) 25

33 The wavelength of K_α X-rays of two metals A and B are $\frac{4}{1875R}$ and $\frac{1}{675R}$ respectively, where R is Rydberg constant. The number of elements lying between A and B according to their atomic numbers is

(a) 3 (b) 6 (c) 5 (d) 4

34 When 24.8 keV X-rays strike a material, the photoelectrons emitted from K-shell are observed to move in a circle of radius 23 mm in a magnetic field of 2×10^{-2} T. The binding energy of K-shell electrons is

(a) 6.2 keV (b) 5.4 keV
(c) 7.4 keV (d) 8.6 keV

35 According to Moseley's law, the ratio of the slopes of graph between $\sqrt{\nu}$ and Z for K_α and K_β is

(a) $\sqrt{\frac{32}{27}}$ (b) $\sqrt{\frac{27}{32}}$ (c) $\sqrt{\frac{33}{22}}$ (d) $\sqrt{\frac{22}{33}}$

36 The given graph shows the variation of $\sqrt{f}$ versus Z for characteristics X-rays. Lines 1, 2, 3, 4 shown in the graph corresponds to any one of K_α, K_β, L_α, L_β. Then, L_β is represented by

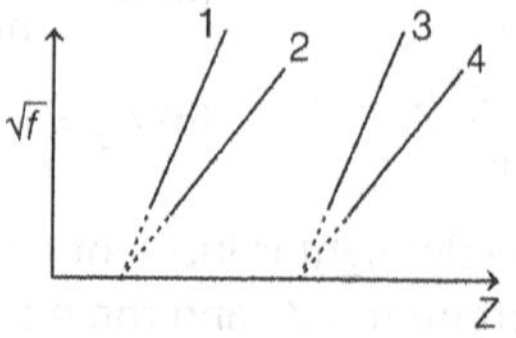

(a) line 1 (b) line 2 (c) line 3 (d) line 4

37 The intensity of X-rays from a Coolidge tube is plotted against wavelength λ as shown in the figure. The minimum wavelength found is λ_c and the wave length of the K_α line is λ_K. As the accelerating voltage is increased

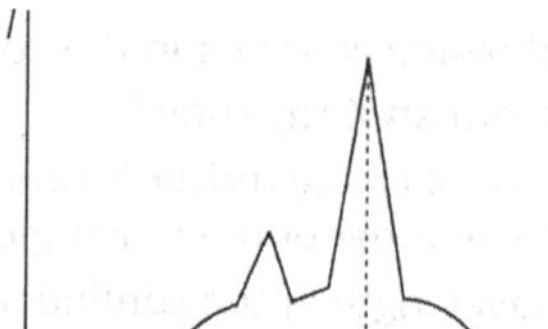

(a) $\lambda_K - \lambda_c$ increase (b) $\lambda_K - \lambda_c$ decreases
(c) λ_K increases (d) λ_K decreases

38 In X-ray tube, when the accelerating voltage V is doubled, the difference between the wavelength of K_α line and minimum wavelength of continuous X-ray spectrum

(a) remains constant (b) becomes less than half
(c) becomes half (d) becomes more than half

39. Figure shows the intensity-wavelength relations of X-rays coming from two different coolidge tubes. The solid curve represents the relation for the tube A in which the potential difference between the target and the filament is V_A and the atomic number of the target material is Z_A . These quantities are V_B and Z_B for the other tube. Then

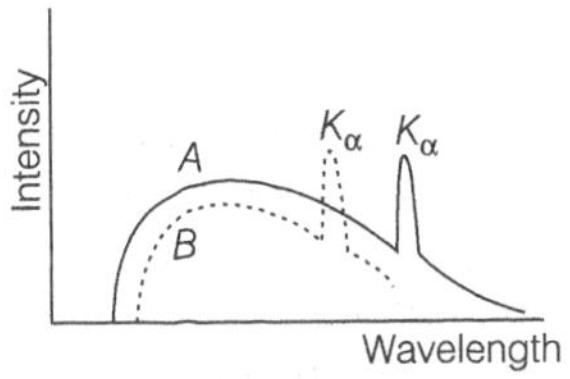

(a) $V_A > V_B, Z_A > Z_B$
(b) $V_A > V_B, Z_A < Z_B$
(c) $V_A < V_B, Z_A > Z_B$
(d) $V_A < V_B, Z_A < Z_B$

40 When an electron accelerated by potential difference V is bombarded on a specific metal, the emitted X-ray spectrum obtained is shown in figure. If the potential difference is reduced to $\frac{V}{3}$, the correct spectrum is

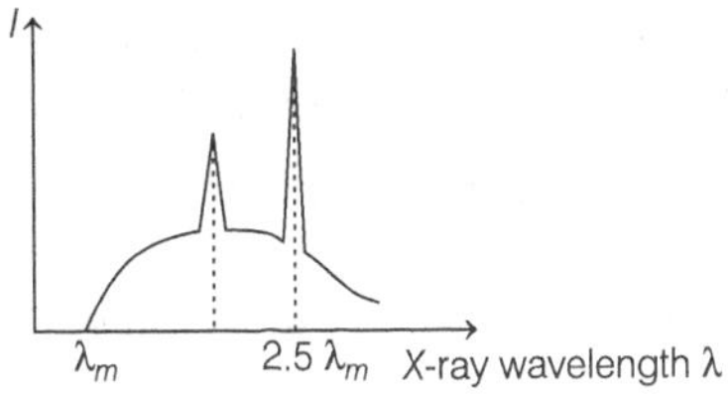

(a)
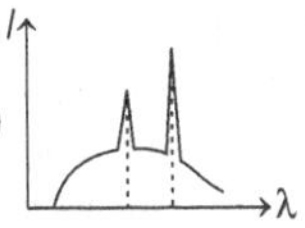

(b)
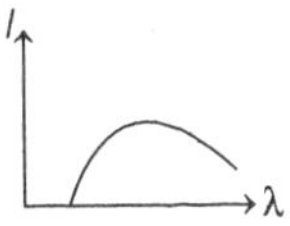

(c)
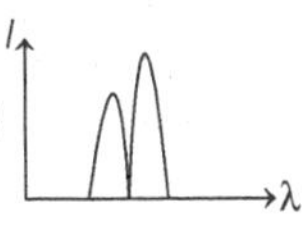

(d)
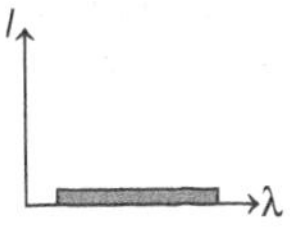

Multiple Choice(s) Correct Questions

1 In the Coolidge tube experiment, the short wavelength limit of the continuous X-ray spectrum is equal to 66.3 pm.

(a) Electrons accelerate through a potential of 12.75 kV in a Coolidge tube.
(b) Electrons accelerate through a potential of 18.75 kV in a Coolidge tube
(c) de-Broglie wavelength of the electrons reaching the anticathode is of the order of 10 pm.
(d) de-Broglie wavelength of the electrons reaching the anticathode is 0.01 Å.

2 In an X-ray tube the voltage applied is 20 kV. The energy required to remove an electron from L-shell is 19.9 keV. In the X-rays emitted by the tube ($hc = 12420$ eV-Å)

(a) minimum wavelength will be 62.1 pm
(b) energy of the characteristic X-rays will be equal to or less than 19.9 keV
(c) L_α X-ray may be emitted
(d) L_α X-ray will have energy 19.9 keV

3 If the accelerating voltage across an X-ray tube is doubled,

(a) the wavelength of characteristic lines are halved.
(b) the minimum wavelength of X-rays is halved
(c) the X-rays are probably becoming more penetrating
(d) the target metal will get heated up earlier.

4 In an X-ray tube, if the accelerating potential difference is increased then

(a) the frequency of characteristic X-rays of a material will get changed
(b) number of electron reaching the anode will change
(c) number of characteristic X-ray lines may increase
(d) the difference between λ_0 (minimum wavelength) and λ_{k_α} (wavelength of K_α X-ray) will increase.

5 Which of the following statements about X-rays is/are true?

(a) $E(K_\alpha) + E(L_\beta) = E(K_\beta) + E(M_\alpha) = E(K_\gamma)$
(b) For the harder X-rays, the intensity is higher than soft X-rays
(c) The continuous and the characteristic X-rays of same wavelengths differ only in the method of creation
(d) The cut-off wavelength λ_{min} depends only on the accelerating voltage applied between the target and the filament.

6 Figure shows the variation of frequency of a characteristic X-ray and atomic number.

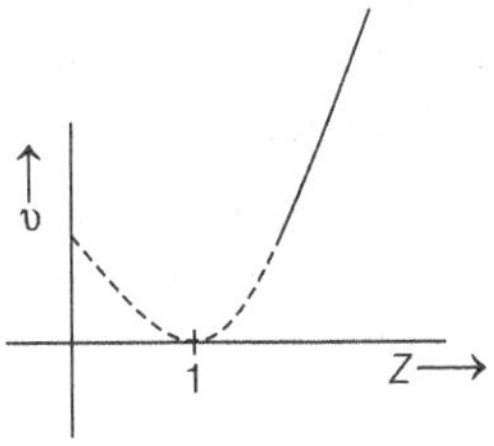

(a) The characteristic X-ray is K_α
(b) The characteristic X-ray is K_β
(c) The energy of photon emitted when this X-ray is emitted by a metal having $Z = 101$ is 204 keV
(d) The energy of photon emitted when this X-ray is emitted by a metal having $Z = 101$ is 102 keV

7 X-ray from a tube with a target A of atomic number Z shows strong K lines for target A and weak K lines for impurities. The wavelength of K_α lines is λ_z for target A and λ_1 and λ_2 for two impurities. If $\frac{\lambda_z}{\lambda_1} = 4$ and $\frac{\lambda_z}{\lambda_2} = \frac{1}{4}$. Screening constant of K_α lines to be unity.

Select the correct statement(s)

(a) The atomic number of first impurity is $2Z-1$

(b) The atomic number of first impurity is $2Z+1$

(c) The atomic number of second impurity is $\frac{Z+1}{2}$

(d) The atomic number of second impurity is $\frac{Z}{2}+1$

Comprehension Based Questions

Comprehension-I

The electric current in an X-ray tube (from the target to the filament) operating at 40 kV is 10 mA. Assume that on an average, 1% of the total kinetic energy of the electrons hitting the target is converted into X-rays.

1 What is the total power emitted as X-rays?

(a) 40 W (b) 400 W

(c) 4 W (d) 0.4 W

2 How much heat is produced in the target every second?

(a) 29.6 J (b) 396 J

(c) 3600 J (d) 360 J

3 Minimum wavelength of X-ray produced will be nearly

(a) 0.3 Å (b) 3 Å

(c) 30 Å (d) 300 Å

Comprehension-2

A tungsten target ($Z = 74$) is bombarded by electrons in an X-ray tube. The K, L and M atomic X-rays energy levels for tungsten are 69.5, 11.3 and 2.3 keV.

4 The minimum value of the accelerating potential that will permit the production of the characteristic K_β and K_α lines of tungsten

(a) 69.5 kV

(b) 58.2 kV

(c) 67.2 kV

(d) 11.3 kV

5 For the same accelerating potential, what is λ_{min}?

(a) 16.8 pm (b) 17.8 pm

(c) 18.8 pm (d) 19.8 pm

6 What is K_β wavelength?

(a) 16.5 pm (b) 17.5 pm

(c) 18.5 pm (d) 21.5 pm

7 What is K_α wavelength?

(a) 20.3 pm (b) 21.3 pm

(c) 22.3 pm (d) 23.3 pm

Comprehension-3

A 20 keV electron is brought to rest by undergoing two successive bremsstrahlung events, thus transferring its kinetic energy into the energy of two photons. The wavelength of second photon to be emitted is 130 pm greater, than the wavelength of the first photon to be emitted.

8 The wavelength of first photon emitted is

(a) 0.67 Å (b) 0.77 Å

(c) 0.87 Å (d) 0.97 Å

9 The wavelength of second photon emitted is

(a) 0.17 Å (b) 2.17 Å

(c) 3.17 Å (d) 5.17 Å

10 The energy of first photon emitted is

(a) 12.27 keV (b) 13.27 keV

(c) 14.27 keV (d) 15.27 keV

11 The energy of the second photon emitted is

(a) 7.73 keV (b) 6.73 keV

(c) 5.73 keV (d) 4.73 keV

Comprehension-4

The collector of the photocell (in photoelectric experiment) is made of tungsten while the emitter is of Platinum having work function of 10 eV. Monochromatic radiation of wavelength 124 Å and power 100 W is incident on emitter which emits photoelectrons with a quantum efficiency of 1%. The accelerating voltage across the photocell is of 10000 V (Use $hc = 12400$ eV-Å)

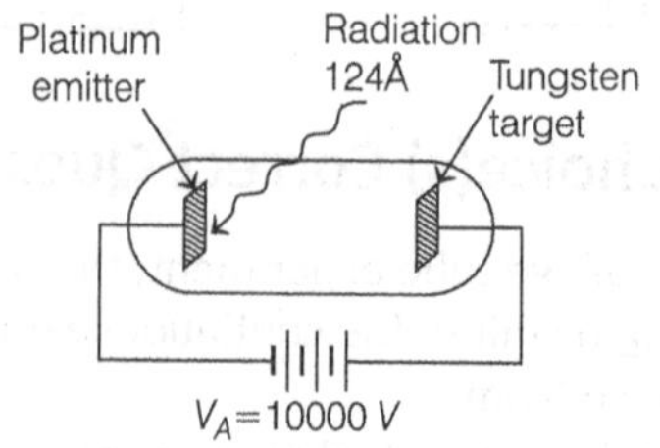

12 What is the power supplied by the accelerating voltage source?

(a) 100 W

(b) 10 W

(c) 0.1 W

(d) 1 W

13 The minimum wavelength of radiation coming from the tungsten target (collector) is

(a) 124 Å (b) 1.24 Å
(c) 1.23 Å (d) 12.3 Å

14 If the source of monochromatic radiation of wavelength 124 Å has an efficiency of 50% and the power of X-ray emitted by the tungsten target is 3W, the overall efficiency of the apparatus for X-ray production is

(a) 1% (b) 0.1%
(c) 1.5% (d) 0.67%

Match the Columns Questions

1 Match the following.

	Column I		Column II
A.	λ_{min} =	1.	high wavelength
B.	Hard X-rays	2.	large variety of wavelengths
C.	Soft X-rays	3.	$\frac{12400\,(Å)}{V\,(Volt)}$
D.	Continuous X-rays	4.	discrete wavelength
E.	Characteristic X-rays	5.	low wavelength

(Consider one to one matching)

2 Match the following.

	Column I		Column II
A.	β-rays	1.	Continuous energy distribution with dark lines in between
B.	γ-rays	2.	Continuous energy distribution with sharp peaks in between.
C.	Absorption spectrum of Hydrogen	3.	Continuous energy distribution
D.	X-rays	4.	Discrete energy distribution

3 Match the entries of Column I with the entries of Column II.

	Column I		Column II
A.	Characteristic X-ray	1.	Inverse process of photoelectric effect
B.	Photoelectric effect	2.	Emission of electrons
C.	Thermoionic emission	3.	Moseley's law
D.	Continuous X-ray	4.	Emission of radiations

4 Match the Column I with Column II.

	Column I		Column II
A.	Transition between two atomic energy levels	1.	Characteristic X-rays
B.	Electron emission from a material	2.	Photoelectric effect
C.	Moseley's law	3.	Hydrogen spectrum
D.	Change of photon energy into kinetic energy of electrons	4.	β-decay

5 Match the following.

	Column I		Column II
A.	Voltage applied to an X-ray tube is increased	1.	The average kinetic energy of the electrons decreases
B.	In photoelectric effect work function of target is increased	2.	The average kinetic energy of the electron increases
C.	Stopping potential decreases	3.	The cut-off wavelength decreases
D.	Wavelength of K_α X-ray is increased	4.	Atomic number of target material decreases

6 $\sqrt{v}$ *versus* Z graph for characteristic X-rays is as shown in figure. Match the following (assume screening constant for K_α and K_β is same and for L_α and L_β is same)

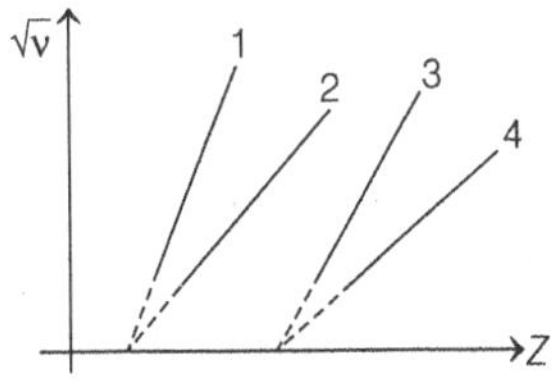

	Column I		Column II
A.	Line - 1	1.	L_α
B.	Line - 2	2.	L_β
C.	Line - 3	3.	K_α
D.	Line - 4	4.	K_β
		5.	Both K_α and L_β

Numerical Value Questions

1 An X-ray tube operated at a DC potential difference of 40 kV, produces heat at a rate of 3136 W. Assume that 2% of energy of the electron is converted into X-rays. If the number of electrons per second striking the target is $n \times 10^{17}$, then fill n in your OMR sheet.

2 If 10000 V is applied across an X-ray tube, if the ratio of de-Broglie wavelength of the incident electrons to the shortest wavelength of X-ray produced (e/m for electron is 1.8×10^{11} C kg^{-1}) is $n/10$, then n.

3 The wavelength of characteristic K_α line emitted by a hydrogen like element is 2.5 Å. Find the wavelength of the K_γ-line emitted by the same element (in Å). Assume the shielding effect to be same as of K_α.

4 A target element A is bombarded with electrons and the wavelengths of the characteristic spectrum are measured. A second characteristic spectrum is also obtained because of an impurity in the target. The wavelength of the K_α lines are 196 pm (element A) and 169 pm (impurity). The atomic number of element A is 27. Find the atomic number of the impurity.

5 An X-ray tube is working at a potential difference of 38.08 kV. The potential difference is decreased to half its initial value. It is found that difference of the wavelength of K_α X-rays and the most energetic continuous X-rays becomes 1/4 times of the difference prior to the change of voltage. Assuming K_α line is present in both cases, find the atomic number of the target element.
[Take Rch = 13.6 eV]

6 The K_α X-ray of molybdenum has wavelength 71 pm. If the energy of a molybdenum atoms with a K electron knocked out is 23.32 keV, what will be the energy (in keV) of this atom, when an L electron is knocked out? (hc = 1230 eV-nm)

7 How many elements are there in a row between those whose wavelengths of K_α lines are equal to 250 and 179 pm?

8 In a Coolidge tube the atomic number of target material is 41. A potential difference of 20 kV is applied across the tube. Let λ_K be K_α line produced by tube and λ_{min} be cut-off wavelength. Calculate $(\lambda_K - \lambda_{min})$ in the order of 10^{-12} m.

9 Intensity *versus* wavelength of X-rays are given for two different target elements. If number of protons in an atom of target element-1 is 37, then find the number of protons in atom of target element-2.

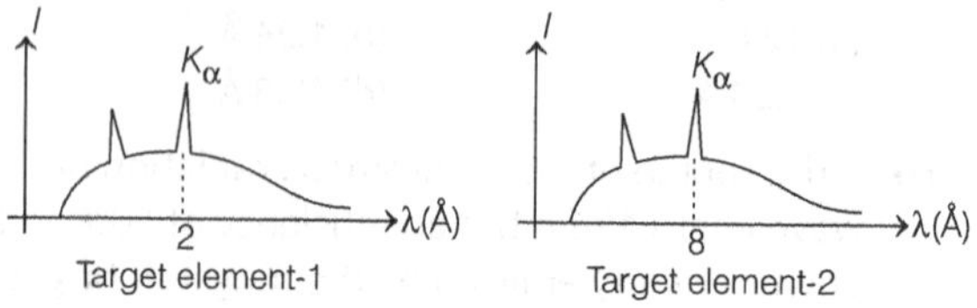

10 In the figure shown electromagnetic radiations of wavelength 200 nm are incident on the metallic plate A. The photoelectrons are accelerated by a potential difference 10 V. These electrons strike another metal plate B from which electromagnetic radiations are emitted. The minimum wavelength of the emitted photons is 100 nm. Find the work function (in eV) of the metal A. Use hc = 1240 eV-nm [Neglect work function of metal B]

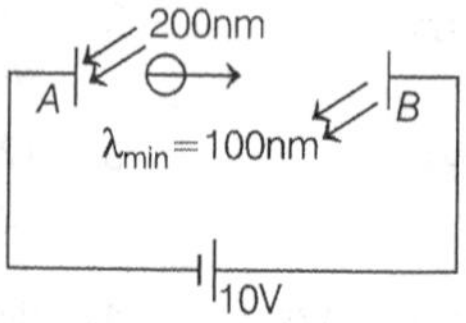

Previous Year's Questions

JEE Main

1 An electron having de-Broglie wavelength λ is incident on a target in a X-ray tube. Cut-off wavelength of emitted X-ray is **[2021, 20 July Shift-II]**

(a) Zero (b) $\frac{2m^2c^2\lambda^2}{h^2}$ (c) $\frac{2mc\lambda^2}{h}$ (d) $\frac{hc}{mc}$

2 An X-ray tube is operated at 1.24 million volt. The shortest wavelength of the produced photon will be **[2021, 24 Feb Shift-II]**

(a) 10^{-3} nm (b) 10^{-1} nm
(c) 10^{-2} nm (d) 10^{-4} nm

JEE Advanced

1 In an X-ray tube, electrons emitted from a filament (cathode) carrying current I hit a target (anode) at a distance d from the cathode. The target is kept at a potential V higher than the cathode resulting in emission of continuous and characteristic X-rays. If the filament current I is decreased to $\frac{I}{2}$, the potential difference V is increased to 2 V, and the separation distance d is reduced to $\frac{d}{2}$, then **(2020 Adv.)**

(a) the cut-off wavelength will reduce to half, and the wavelengths of the characteristic X-rays will remain the same
(b) the cut-off wavelength as well as the wavelengths of the characteristic X-rays will remain the same
(c) the cut-off wavelength will reduce to half, and the intensities of all the X-rays will decrease
(d) the cut-off wavelength will become two times larger, and the intensity of all the X-rays will decrease

2 If λ_{Cu} is the wavelength of K_α, X-ray line of copper (atomic number 29) and λ_{Mo} is the wavelength of the K_α, X-ray line of molybdenum (atomic number 42), then the ratio $\lambda_{Cu}/\lambda_{Mo}$ is close to **(2014 Adv.)**
(a) 1.99
(b) 2.14
(c) 0.50
(d) 0.48

Answer Key

Level 1

9.1 Continuous X-Rays

1. (i) 0.062 nm (ii) 1.24 nm
2. 0.1%
3. (a) 6.25×10^{16}, (b) 1.3×10^8 m/s (c) 0.248 Å
4. 27.7 kV/m

9.2 Characteristics of X-Rays

1. 4.97×10^7 $(Hz)^{1/2}$ 2. $a = 5.0 \times 10^7$ $(Hz)^{1/2}$ and $b = 1.37$
3. 153.86 pm 4. 198 pm 5. Zinc 6. 42
7. 69.5 kV 8. 5.6 Å 9. 6.25
10. (i) 1 is K_β and 2 is K_α (ii) 1 is K_α and 2 is L_α (iii) $Z_1 > Z_2$
11. 29

Level 2

Single Choice Correct Questions

1. (a)	2. (c)	3. (a)	4. (c)	5. (b)
6. (a)	7. (b)	8. (b)	9. (d)	10. (c)
11. (d)	12. (c)	13. (b)	14. (a)	15. (a)
16. (b)	17. (d)	18. (c)	19. (d)	20. (c)
21. (c)	22. (a)	23. (c)	24. (d)	25. (b)
26. (a)	27. (c)	28. (a)	29. (c)	30. (d)
31. (d)	32. (c)	33. (d)	34. (a)	35. (b)
36. (c)	37. (a)	38. (d)	39. (b)	40. (b)

Multiple Choice(s) Correct Questions

1. (b, c)	2. (a, b, c)	3. (b, c, d)	4. (c, d)
5. (a, c, d)	6. (a, d)	7. (a, c)	

Comprehension Based Questions

1. (c)	2. (b)	3. (a)	4. (a)	5. (b)
6. (c)	7. (b)	8. (c)	9. (b)	10. (c)
11. (c)	12. (a)	13. (c)	14. (a)	

Match the Columns Questions

1. $A \rightarrow 3, B \rightarrow 5, C \rightarrow 1, D \rightarrow 2, E \rightarrow 4$
2. $A \rightarrow 3, B \rightarrow 4, C \rightarrow 1, D \rightarrow 2$
3. $A \rightarrow 3,4, B \rightarrow 2, C \rightarrow 2, D \rightarrow 1,4$
4. $A \rightarrow 1,3, B \rightarrow 2,4, C \rightarrow 1, D \rightarrow 2$
5. $A \rightarrow 2,3, B \rightarrow 1,3, C \rightarrow 1, D \rightarrow 4$
6. $A \rightarrow 4, B \rightarrow 3, C \rightarrow 2, D \rightarrow 1$

Numerical Value Questions

1. (5)	2. (1)	3. (2)	4. (29)	5. (41)
6. (6)	7. (3)	8. (14)	9. (19)	10. (3.8)

Previous Year's Questions

JEE Main

1. (c) 2. (a)

JEE Advanced

1. (a, c) 2. (b)

SOLUTIONS

Level 1

9.1 Continuous X-Rays

1. (i) $\lambda_{min} = \frac{hc}{\Delta E} = \frac{1240 \text{ eV-nm}}{20 \times 10^3 \text{eV}} = 0.062 \text{ nm}$

(ii) $\Delta E = 20 \times 10^3 \times \frac{5}{100} = 10^3 \text{eV}$

$$\lambda = \frac{hc}{\Delta E} = \frac{1240 \text{ eV- nm}}{10^3 \text{eV}} = 1.24 \text{ nm}$$

2. $\lambda_{min} = \frac{hc}{eV} \Rightarrow \frac{\Delta\lambda}{\lambda} = -\frac{\Delta V}{V}$

$\Rightarrow \frac{\Delta\lambda}{\lambda} \times 100 = -\frac{\Delta V}{V} \times 100 = -(0.1\%) = 0.1\%$ decrease

3. (i) Heat produced per second $= \left(\frac{99}{100}\right)Vi$

$\Rightarrow \quad 495 = \left(\frac{99}{100}\right) \times 50 \times 10^3 \times i$

$\Rightarrow \quad i = 10 \text{ mA}$

Number of electrons striking the target per second

$$= \frac{i}{e} = \frac{10 \times 10^{-3}}{1.6 \times 10^{-19}} = 6.25 \times 10^{16}$$

(ii) $eV = \frac{1}{2}mv^2$

$\Rightarrow \quad 1.6 \times 10^{-19} \times 50 \times 10^3 = \frac{1}{2} \times 9.1 \times 10^{-31} v^2$

$\Rightarrow \quad v = 1.3 \times 10^8 \text{ m/s}$

(iii) $\lambda_{min} = \frac{hc}{eV} = \frac{12400 \text{ eV- Å}}{50 \times 10^3 \text{eV}} = 0.248 \text{ Å}$

4. $\Delta V = \frac{hc}{e\lambda_{min}} = \frac{6.63 \times 10^{-34} \times 3 \times 10^8}{1.6 \times 10^{-19} \times 30 \times 10^{-12}} = 41.4 \times 10^3 \text{V}$

Electric field, $E = \frac{\Delta V}{d} = \frac{41.4 \times 10^3}{1.5} = 27.6 \text{ kV/m}$

9.2 Characteristics X-Rays

1. $\sqrt{\nu} = a(Z - b)$

$\Rightarrow \quad 0.5 \times 10^9 = a(11 - b)$ ...(i)

and $\quad 1.94 \times 10^9 = a(40 - b)$ ...(ii)

Dividing Eq. (i) by (ii),

$$\frac{0.5}{1.94} = \frac{11 - b}{40 - b}$$

$\Rightarrow \quad b = 0.93$

Substituting value of b in Eq. (i), we get

$$a = 4.97 \times 10^7 (\text{Hz})^{1/2}$$

2. $\sqrt{\frac{c}{\lambda}} = a(Z - b)$

For Mo, $\sqrt{\frac{c}{71 \times 10^{-12}}} = a(42 - b)$ ...(i)

For Co, $\sqrt{\frac{c}{178.5 \times 10^{-12}}} = a(27 - b)$ ...(ii)

Dividing Eq. (i) by Eq. (ii), we get

$$\sqrt{\frac{178.5}{71}} = \frac{42 - b}{27 - b} \Rightarrow b = 1.37$$

Substituting value of b in Eq. (i), we get

$$a = 5.0 \times 10^7 (\text{Hz})^{1/2}$$

3. $\sqrt{\frac{c}{\lambda}} = a(Z - b)$

For copper, $\sqrt{\frac{c}{\lambda}} = a(29 - 1)$ ...(i)

For iron, $\sqrt{\frac{c}{193}} = a(26 - 1)$ ...(ii)

Dividing Eq. (ii) by (i), we get

$$\frac{\lambda}{193} = \left(\frac{25}{28}\right)^2$$

$\Rightarrow \quad \lambda = 153.86 \text{ pm}$

4. $\sqrt{\frac{c}{\lambda}} = a(Z - b)$

For aluminium, $\sqrt{\frac{c}{887 \times 10^{-12}}} = a(13 - b)$ ...(i)

For Zinc, $\sqrt{\frac{c}{146 \times 10^{-12}}} = a(30 - b)$ ...(ii)

Dividing Eq. (i) by Eq. (ii),

$$\sqrt{\frac{146}{887}} = \frac{13 - b}{30 - b}$$

$\Rightarrow \quad b = 1.39$

Substituting value of b in Eq. (i), we get

$$a = 5 \times 10^7$$

For iron, $\sqrt{\frac{3 \times 10^8}{\lambda}} = 5 \times 10^7 (26 - 1.39)$

$\Rightarrow \quad \lambda = 198 \text{ pm}$

5. $\sqrt{\frac{c}{\lambda}} = a(Z - b)$

For K_α, $b = 1$

For cobalt,

$$\sqrt{\frac{c}{178.9 \times 10^{-12}}} = a(27 - 1) \quad \text{...(i)}$$

For impurity,

$$\sqrt{\frac{c}{143.5 \times 10^{-12}}} = a(Z - 1) \quad \text{...(ii)}$$

Dividing Eq. (i) by (ii), we get

$$\sqrt{\frac{143.5}{178.9}} = \frac{26}{Z-1} \Rightarrow Z = 30$$

So, impurity is zinc.

6. $$\frac{1}{\lambda} = R(Z-b)^2\left(\frac{1}{n_1^2} - \frac{1}{n_2^2}\right)$$

For transition from L to K-shell, $b = 1$

So, $$\frac{c}{\lambda} = Rc(Z-1)^2\left(\frac{1}{n_1^2} - \frac{1}{n_2^2}\right)$$

$$\Rightarrow 4.2 \times 10^{18} = 1.1 \times 10^7 \times 3 \times 10^8 (Z-1)^2\left(\frac{1}{1^2} - \frac{1}{2^2}\right)$$

$$\Rightarrow Z = 42$$

7. $$E_L - E_K = \frac{hc}{\lambda_{K_\alpha}} = \frac{1240}{21.3 \times 10^{-3}} = 58.2 \text{ keV}$$

and $E_L = -11.3$ keV

So, $E_K = -58.2 - 11.3 = -69.5$ keV

Hence, energy required to knock out K-shell electron

$$= 0 - (-69.5) = 69.5 \text{ keV}$$

Accelerating voltage $= 69.5$ kV

8. $$E_{K_\beta} = E_{K_\alpha} + E_{L_\alpha}$$

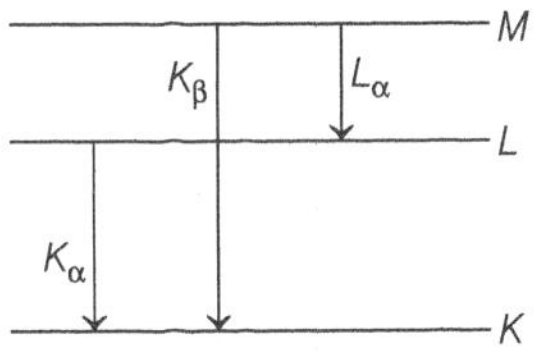

$$\Rightarrow \frac{hc}{0.63} = \frac{hc}{0.71} + \frac{hc}{\lambda_{L_\alpha}}$$

$$\Rightarrow \lambda_{L_\alpha} = 5.6 \text{ Å}$$

9. When electron jumps from M to L-shell, the first member of the L-series i.e. L_α line is given out. Its wavelength as given by Moseley's law is

$$\frac{1}{\lambda} = R(Z-b)^2\left(\frac{1}{n_1^2} - \frac{1}{n_2^2}\right)$$

$$\Rightarrow \frac{1}{1.43 \times 10^{-10}} = 1.097 \times 10^7 (74-b)^2\left[\frac{1}{2^2} - \frac{1}{3^2}\right]$$

$$\Rightarrow b = 6.25$$

10. (i) $E_{K_\beta} > E_{K_\alpha} \Rightarrow \lambda_{K_\beta} < \lambda_{K_\alpha}$

$\therefore$ 1 is K_β and 2 is K_α.

(ii) $E_{K_\alpha} > E_{L_\alpha} \Rightarrow \lambda_{K_\alpha} < \lambda_{L_\alpha}$

$\therefore$ 1 is K_α and 2 is L_α

(iii) $\frac{1}{\lambda} \propto (Z-1)^2$

So, one with higher atomic number has lesser wavelength.

$\therefore$ $Z_1 > Z_2$

11. Let wavelength of K_α line be λ_0

Cut-off wavelengths,

$$\lambda_1 = \frac{12400}{10 \times 10^3} = 1.24\text{Å}$$

and $$\lambda_2 = \frac{12400}{20 \times 10^3} = 0.62 \text{ Å}$$

$$\lambda_0 - \lambda_2 = 3(\lambda_0 - \lambda_1)$$

$$\Rightarrow \lambda_0 = \frac{3\lambda_1 - \lambda_2}{2} = 1.55 \text{ Å}$$

Using Moseley's law

$$\frac{1}{\lambda} = R(Z-1)^2\left[\frac{1}{n_1^2} - \frac{1}{n_2^2}\right]$$

$$\Rightarrow \frac{1}{1.55 \times 10^{-10}} = 1.097 \times 10^7 (Z-1)^2\left[\frac{1}{1^2} - \frac{1}{2^2}\right]$$

$$\Rightarrow Z = 29$$

Level 2

Single Choice Correct Questions

1. (a)

2. $\lambda_{min} \propto \frac{1}{V}$

3. $$\lambda_{min} = \frac{hc}{eV} = \frac{12400 \text{ eV-Å}}{20 \times 10^3 \text{eV}} = 0.62 \text{ Å}$$

4. $$\lambda = \frac{hc}{eV} \quad \text{...(i)}$$

and $$\lambda - 26 = \frac{hc}{(1.5 \text{ eV})} \quad \text{...(ii)}$$

Dividing Eq. (i) by Eq. (ii), we get

$$\frac{\lambda}{\lambda - 26} = \frac{3}{2}$$

$$\Rightarrow \lambda = 78 \text{ pm}$$

$$78 \times 10^{-12} = \frac{6.63 \times 10^{-34} \times 3 \times 10^8}{1.6 \times 10^{-19} \text{V}}$$

$$\Rightarrow V = 15.9 \text{ kV}$$

5. All wavelengths greater than cut-off wavelength (λ_{min}) are found.

6. $$n = \frac{i}{e} = \frac{3.2 \times 10^{-3}}{1.6 \times 10^{-19}} = 2 \times 10^{16}$$

7. Power drawn by the coolidge tube $= (20 \times 10^3 \text{V})(10 \times 10^{-3} \text{A})$
$= 200\text{W}$

Power of X-ray beam $= 200 \times \frac{0.5}{100} = 1$ W

8. Higher is the frequency, higher is the energy or penetrating power of X-rays.

9. If potential difference between the target and the filament is increased, energy of electrons incident on target metal will increase. Hence, X-rays photons emitted will be more energetic and will posses greater penetrating power.

10. $\lambda_{min} = \frac{hc}{eV}$

$\therefore$ Cut-off wavelength depends only on accelerating voltage.

11. $\lambda_{min} = \frac{hc}{eV} = \frac{1240\,\text{eV - nm}}{66 \times 10^3\,\text{eV}} = 0.018\text{ nm}$

So, all wavelengths greater than 0.018 nm will be present.

12. Photons are chargeless and hence not deflected by electric and magnetic fields.

13. de-Broglie wavelength of electron, $\lambda_e = \frac{h}{\sqrt{2meV}}$

Minimum wavelength of X-rays, $\lambda_{min} = \frac{hc}{eV}$

$$\therefore \quad \frac{\lambda_e}{\lambda_{min}} \propto V^{1/2}$$

14. de-Broglie wavelength of electron, $\lambda = \frac{h}{\sqrt{2meV}}$

$$\Rightarrow \quad eV = \frac{h^2}{2m\lambda^2}$$

Cut-off wavelength, $\lambda_0 = \frac{hc}{eV} = \frac{hc}{\left(\frac{h^2}{2m\lambda^2}\right)} = \frac{2mc\lambda^2}{h}$

15. X-rays photons are more energetic than ultraviolet light photons. Hence, stopping potential and maximum kinetic energy of photoelectrons will increase.

16. cut-off wavelength depends only on the accelerating voltage.

17. $\lambda_{min} = \frac{hc}{eV} = \frac{1240\,\text{eV}}{80 \times 10^3\,\text{eV}} = 0.155\text{ Å}$

Since, energy incident electrons is greater than the binding energy K-shell electron, K-shell electron will be knocked out. To fill vacancy in K-shell, electrons will jump from higher shells and hence, we get characteristic X-ray of tungsten.

18. $E_L - E_K = \frac{hc}{\lambda} = \frac{1240}{0.021} = 59\text{ keV}$

19. $\lambda_{K_\alpha} = \frac{hc}{E_K - E_L}$ and $\lambda_{K_\beta} = \frac{hc}{E_K - E_M}$

$$\therefore \quad \frac{\lambda_{K_\alpha}}{\lambda_{K_\beta}} = \frac{E_K - E_M}{E_K - E_L} = \frac{78-3}{78-12} = \frac{75}{66} = \frac{25}{22}$$

20.
$$E_K - E_L = h\nu_{K_\alpha}$$
$$E_K - E_M = h\nu_{K_\beta}$$
$$E_L - E_M = h\nu_{L_\alpha}$$
$$E_K - E_M = (E_K - E_L) + (E_L - E_M)$$
$$\Rightarrow \quad h\nu_{K_\beta} = h\nu_{K_\alpha} + h\nu_{L_\alpha}$$
$$\Rightarrow \quad \nu_{K_\beta} = \nu_{K_\alpha} + \nu_{L_\alpha}$$

21. $E_K - E_L = \frac{hc}{\lambda_{K_\alpha}} = \frac{1240}{21.3 \times 10^{-3}} = 58.22\text{ keV}$

$$E_L = 11.3\text{ keV}, E_K = 58.22 + 11.3 = 69.52\text{ keV}$$

Since, energy of incident electrons is less than E_K, K-shell electrons can't be knocked out. So, we will get only L-series of characteristic X-rays.

22. Both a and b are independent of the material.

23. $\sqrt{\nu} = a(Z-b)$

$\therefore$ $\sqrt{\nu}$ *versus* Z Plot is a straight line.

24. $\Delta E = (13.6\text{eV})(Z-1)^2\left[\frac{1}{n_1^2} - \frac{1}{n_2^2}\right]$

$$\Rightarrow \quad 7.46 \times 10^3 = 13.6(Z-1)^2\left[\frac{1}{1^2} - \frac{1}{2^2}\right]$$
$$\Rightarrow \quad Z = 28$$

25. $\sqrt{\frac{c}{\lambda}} = a(Z-b)$

For K_α, $a = \sqrt{\frac{3Rc}{4}}$ and $b = 1$

$$\therefore \quad \sqrt{\frac{c}{\lambda}} = \sqrt{\frac{3Rc}{4}}(Z-1) \Rightarrow \frac{1}{\lambda} = \frac{3R}{4}(Z-1)^2$$
$$\Rightarrow \quad \frac{1}{0.76 \times 10^{-10}} = \frac{3 \times 1.1 \times 10^7}{4}(Z-1)^2$$
$$\Rightarrow \quad Z = 41$$

26. $\sqrt{\frac{c}{\lambda}} = a(Z-b)$ ...(i)

$$\Rightarrow \quad \sqrt{\frac{c}{\lambda}} = a(11-1) \quad \text{...(ii)}$$

and $\sqrt{\frac{c}{4\lambda}} = a(Z-1)$ ...(iii)

Dividing Eqs. (ii) and (iii), we get

$$2 = \frac{10}{Z-1} \Rightarrow Z = 6$$

27. $\sqrt{\frac{c}{\lambda}} = a(Z-b)$

For $Z = 57$, $\sqrt{\frac{c}{\lambda}} = a(57-1)$ ...(i)

For $Z = 29$, $\sqrt{\frac{c}{\lambda'}} = a(29-1)$ ...(ii)

Dividing Eqs. (i) by (ii), we get

$$\frac{\lambda'}{\lambda} = \left(\frac{56}{28}\right)^2 \Rightarrow \lambda' = 4\lambda$$

28. $\sqrt{\nu} = a(Z-b)$

For calcium. $\sqrt{8.95 \times 10^{17}} = a(20-1)$ ...(i)

For cadmium, $\sqrt{\nu} = a(48-1)$ ...(ii)

Dividing Eq. (ii) by (i), we get

$$\frac{\nu}{8.95 \times 10^{17}} = \left(\frac{47}{19}\right)^2$$
$$\Rightarrow \quad \nu = 5.47 \times 10^{18}\text{Hz}$$

29. $\sqrt{\dfrac{c}{\lambda}} = a(Z-b)$

For Mo, $\sqrt{\dfrac{c}{0.71}} = a(42-1)$ ...(i)

For Cu, $\sqrt{\dfrac{c}{\lambda}} = a(29-1)$ ...(ii)

Dividing Eq. (i) by Eq. (ii), we get

$$\frac{\lambda}{0.71} = \left(\frac{41}{28}\right)^2 \Rightarrow \lambda = 1.52 \text{Å}$$

30. $\sqrt{f} = a(Z-b)$

For $Z = 31$, $\sqrt{f} = a(31-1)$ ...(i)

For $Z = 51$, $\sqrt{f'} = a(51-1)$ ...(ii)

Dividing Eq. (ii) by (i), we get

$$\frac{f'}{f} = \left(\frac{50}{30}\right)^2 \Rightarrow f' = \frac{25}{9}f$$

31. For copper, $\sqrt{\dfrac{c}{\lambda}} = a(29-1)$ ...(i)

For impurity, $\sqrt{\dfrac{c}{\left(\dfrac{784}{625}\lambda\right)}} = a(Z-1)$ ...(ii)

Dividing Eq. (ii) by Eq. (i), we get

$$\frac{Z-1}{28} = \sqrt{\frac{625}{478}} \Rightarrow Z = 26$$

32. $\sqrt{\dfrac{c}{\lambda}} = a(Z-b)$

For copper, $\sqrt{\dfrac{3\times10^8}{15.42\times10^{-9}}} = a(29-b)$ ...(i)

For molybdenum, $\sqrt{\dfrac{3\times10^8}{7.12\times10^{-9}}} = a(42-b)$ ...(ii)

Dividing Eq. (ii) by (i), we get

$$\sqrt{\frac{15.42}{7.12}} = \frac{42-b}{29-b} \Rightarrow b = 1.44$$

Substituting value of b in Eq. (i), we get

$$a = 5.06\times10^6$$

For impurity, $\sqrt{\dfrac{3\times10^8}{22.85\times10^{-9}}} = 5.06\times10^6(Z-1.44)$

$\Rightarrow$ $Z = 24$

33. $\dfrac{1}{\lambda} = R(Z-1)^2\left[\dfrac{1}{n_1^2} - \dfrac{1}{n_2^2}\right]$

For A, $\dfrac{1}{\left(\dfrac{4}{1875R}\right)} = R(Z_A-1)^2\left[\dfrac{1}{1^2} - \dfrac{1}{2^2}\right]$

$\Rightarrow$ $Z_A = 26$

For B, $\dfrac{1}{\left(\dfrac{1}{675R}\right)} = R(Z_B-1)^2\left[\dfrac{1}{1^2} - \dfrac{1}{2^2}\right] \Rightarrow Z_B = 31$

So, number of elements lying between A and B = 4

34. $R = \dfrac{\sqrt{2mK}}{qB}$

$\Rightarrow$ $23\times10^{-3} = \dfrac{\sqrt{2\times9.1\times10^{-31}K}}{1.6\times10^{-19}\times2\times10^{-2}}$

$\Rightarrow$ $K = 2.97\times10^{-15}$ J or 18.6 keV

$\therefore$ Binding energy $= E - K = 24.8 - 18.6 = 6.2$ keV

35. Slope $= a = \sqrt{Rc\left(\dfrac{1}{n_1^2} - \dfrac{1}{n_2^2}\right)}$

For K_α, $a_{K_\alpha} = \sqrt{Rc\left(\dfrac{1}{1^2} - \dfrac{1}{2^2}\right)} = \sqrt{\dfrac{3Rc}{4}}$

For K_β, $a_{K_\beta} = \sqrt{Rc\left(\dfrac{1}{1^2} - \dfrac{1}{3^2}\right)} = \sqrt{\dfrac{8Rc}{9}}$

$\therefore$ $\dfrac{a_{K_\alpha}}{a_{K_\beta}} = \sqrt{\dfrac{27}{32}}$

36. For a given value of Z, energy of K-series is more than L-series, also β-line has more energy as compared to α-line of L-series.

Hence, L_β will be represented by line 3.

37. As accelerating voltage is increased, λ_c decreases

So, $\lambda_K - \lambda_c$ increases.

38. $\Delta\lambda = \lambda_{K_\alpha} - \lambda_{\min} = \lambda_{K_\alpha} - \dfrac{hc}{eV}$

When accelerating voltage is doubled,

$$\Delta\lambda' = \lambda_{K_\alpha} - \frac{hc}{e(2V)} = \frac{1}{2}\left(\lambda_{K_\alpha} - \frac{hc}{eV}\right) + \frac{\lambda_{K_\alpha}}{2} = \frac{\Delta\lambda}{2} + \frac{\lambda_{K_\alpha}}{2}$$

So, difference in wavelengths will become more than half.

39. $\lambda_{\min} \propto \dfrac{1}{V}$

So, one with lesser $\lambda_{\min}$ will have greater accelerating voltage. Hence, $V_A > V_B$

For K_α, $\dfrac{1}{\lambda} \propto (Z-1)^2$

So, one with lesser wavelength will have greater atomic number. Hence, $Z_A < Z_B$.

40. If the potential difference is reduced to $\dfrac{V}{3}$, λ_m will increase to $3\lambda_m$. Hence, no characteristic X-rays will be obtained, only continous X-rays will be produced.

Multiple Choice(s) Correct Questions

1. (b) $\lambda_{\min} = \dfrac{hc}{eV}$

$\Rightarrow$ $66.3\times10^{-12} = \dfrac{6.63\times10^{-34}\times3\times10^8}{1.6\times10^{-19}\times V}$

$\Rightarrow$ $V = 18.75$ kV

(c) de-Broglie wavelength of electron,

$$\lambda = \frac{h}{\sqrt{2meV}} = \frac{6.63\times10^{-34}}{\sqrt{2\times9.1\times10^{-31}\times1.6\times10^{-19}\times18.75\times10^3}}$$

$$= 8.9 \text{ pm} \simeq 10 \text{ pm}$$

2. (a) $\lambda_{min} = \dfrac{hc}{eV} = \dfrac{12420}{20 \times 10^3} = 62.1$ pm

(b) Since, energy of incident electrons (20 keV) is greater than binding energy of *L*-Shell (19.9 keV), *L*-shell electron will be knocked out.

If vacancy in *L*-shell is filled by an electron jumping from $n = \infty$, energy of characteristic X-ray will be 19.9 keV. If vacancy in *L*-shell is filled by an electron from any other shell, energy of charateristic X-ray will be less than 19.9 keV.

(c) Since *L*-shell electron is knocked out, vacancy in *L*-shell may be filled by an electron jumping from *M*-shell. Hence, L_α may be emitted.

(d) Energy of L_α X-ray will be less than 19.9 keV.

3. (a) Wavelength of characteristic lines doesn't depend on accelerating voltage.

(b) $\lambda_{min} \propto \dfrac{1}{V}$, so minimum wavelength will be halved.

(c) X-rays photons will be more energetic and hence their penetrating power will increase.

(d) Energy of electrons incident on metallic target will get doubled. So, they will lose more energy on hitting the target and hence heat produced will be more.

4. Frequency of characteristic X-rays and number of electron reaching the anode are independent of the accelerating voltage.

Minimum wavelength (λ_0) will decrease and hence $\lambda_{K_\alpha} - \lambda_0$ will increase and number of characteristic X-ray lines may increase.

5. (a) $E(K_\alpha) + E(L_\beta) = (E_K - E_L) + (E_L - E_N) = E_K - E_N$

$E(K_\beta) + E(M_\alpha) = (E_K - E_M) + (E_M - E_N) = E_K - E_N$

$E(K_\gamma) = E_K - E_N$

(b) Harder X-rays have greater frequency than soft X-rays.

(c) Continous X-rays are produced when high speed electrons collide with a metallic target. These electrons slow down and loss in energy goes into heat and production of X-rays photons.

Characteristic X-rays are produced when vacancy created in one of the shells due to knocking out of electron is filled by an electron jumping from some higher shell.

(d) $\lambda_{min} \propto \dfrac{1}{V}$

6. $\sqrt{\nu} = a(Z - b) \Rightarrow \nu = a^2(Z - b)^2$

$\Rightarrow \quad 0 = a^2(1 - b)^2$

$\Rightarrow \quad b = 1$

So, characteristic X-rays is K_α.

For K_α, $a = \sqrt{\dfrac{3Rc}{4}}$ and $b = 1$

So, $\nu = \dfrac{3Rc}{4}(Z - 1)^2 = \dfrac{3 \times 1.097 \times 10^7 \times 3 \times 10^8}{4}(101 - 1)^2$

$= 2.47 \times 10^{19}$ Hz

Energy of photon, $E = h\nu = 6.63 \times 10^{-34} \times 2.47 \times 10^{19}$

$= 163.76 \times 10^{-16}$ J $= 102.35$ keV

7. $\sqrt{\dfrac{c}{\lambda}} = a(Z - b)$

For target *A*, $\sqrt{\dfrac{c}{\lambda_Z}} = a(Z - 1)$ ...(i)

For first impurity,

$\sqrt{\dfrac{c}{\lambda_1}} = a(Z_1 - 1)$ ...(ii)

For second impurity,

$\sqrt{\dfrac{c}{\lambda_2}} = a(Z_2 - 1)$ ...(iii)

Dividing Eq. (ii) by (i), we get

$\sqrt{\dfrac{\lambda_Z}{\lambda_1}} = \dfrac{Z_1 - 1}{Z - 1} \Rightarrow 2 = \dfrac{Z_1 - 1}{Z - 1}$

$\Rightarrow \quad Z_1 = 2Z - 1$

Dividing Eq. (iii) by (i), we get

$\sqrt{\dfrac{\lambda_Z}{\lambda_2}} = \dfrac{Z_2 - 1}{Z - 1} \Rightarrow \dfrac{1}{2} = \dfrac{Z_2 - 1}{Z - 1}$

$\Rightarrow \quad Z_2 = \dfrac{Z + 1}{2}$

Comprehension Based Questions

1. Power of X-rays $= (40 \times 10^3)(10 \times 10^{-3})\left(\dfrac{1}{100}\right) = 4$ W

2. Heat produced per second $= (40 \times 10^3)(10 \times 10^{-3})\left(\dfrac{99}{100}\right)$

$= 396$ J

3. $\lambda_{min} = \dfrac{hc}{eV} = \dfrac{12400}{40 \times 10^3} = 0.31$ Å.

4. For production of K_α and K_β, *K*-shell electron should be knocked out. So, energy required will be $E_K = 69.5$ keV.

5. $\lambda_{min} = \dfrac{hc}{eV} = \dfrac{12400 \text{ eV-Å}}{69.5 \times 10^3 \text{ eV}} = 0.178$ Å $= 17.8$ pm

6. For K_β, $\lambda = \dfrac{hc}{E_K - E_M} = \dfrac{12400}{67.2 \times 10^3} = 0.1845 = 18.5$ pm

7. For K_α, $\lambda = \dfrac{hc}{E_K - E_L} = \dfrac{12400}{58.2 \times 10^3} = 0.213$ Å $= 21.3$ pm

8. Let wavelength of first photon be λ pm.

$\dfrac{hc}{\lambda \times 10^{-12}} + \dfrac{hc}{(\lambda + 130) \times 10^{-12}} = 20 \times 10^3$ eV

$\Rightarrow \quad \dfrac{1}{\lambda} + \dfrac{1}{\lambda + 130} = \dfrac{20 \times 10^3 \times 1.6 \times 10^{-19} \times 10^{-12}}{6.63 \times 10^{-34} \times 3 \times 10^8}$

$\Rightarrow \quad \lambda = 87\text{pm} = 0.87$Å

9. Wavelength of second photon $= 130 + 87 = 217$ pm $= 2.17$ Å

10. $E_1 = \dfrac{hc}{\lambda_1} = \dfrac{1240}{87 \times 10^{-3}} = 14.25$ keV

11. $E_2 = \dfrac{hc}{\lambda_2} = \dfrac{1240}{217 \times 10^{-3}} = 5.71$ keV

12. Energy of one photon $= \frac{hc}{\lambda} = \frac{12400}{124} = 100$ eV

Number of photons incident per second $= \frac{P}{E} = \frac{100}{100e} = \frac{1}{e}$

Number of photoelectrons emitted per second $= \frac{1}{e} \times \frac{1}{100}$

Saturation photocurrent $= \frac{1}{e} \times \frac{1}{100} \times e = 0.01$ Å

Power supplied by the accelerating voltage $= Vi$

$$= 10 \times 10^3 (0.01)$$
$$= 100 \text{ W}$$

13. Energy of photoelectron reaching the collector

$$= K_{max} + eV$$
$$= (100 - 10) \text{ eV} + e(10 \times 10^3 \text{ V})$$
$$= 10.09 \times 10^3 \text{ eV}$$
$$\lambda_{min} = \frac{hc}{eV} = \frac{12400}{10.09 \times 10^3} = 1.23 \text{ Å}$$

14. Power provided by accelerating potential = 100 W

Power consumed by the source of 124Å $= \frac{100}{(0.5)} = 200$ W

Overall efficiency $= \frac{\text{Net power of X-ray}}{\text{Net power supplied}} \times 100$

$$= \frac{3 \text{ W}}{100 \text{ W} + 200 \text{ W}} \times 100 = 1\%$$

Match the Columns Questions

1. A → 3, B → 5, C → 1, D → 2, E → 4
2. A → 3, B → 4, C → 1, D → 2
3. A → 3, 4, B → 2, C → 2, D → 1, 4
4. A → 1, 3, B → 2, 4, C → 1, D → 2
5. (a) KE of electrons striking the target = eV

   So, if V increases, KE increases.

   Cut-off wavelength, $\lambda_{min} = \frac{12400}{V}$ Å

   So, if V increases, λ_{min} decreases.

   (b) $K_{max} = hf - W$

   So, if work function of target is increased in photoelectric effect, KE of photoelectrons emitted decreases.

   $$\lambda_{cutoff} = \frac{hc}{W}$$

   So, if W increases, $\lambda_{cut\text{-}off}$ decreases.

   (c) $K_{max} = eV_s$

   So, if stopping potential (V_s) decreases, then KE decreases.

   (d) $\frac{1}{\lambda} = \frac{3R}{4}(Z-1)^2$

   So, if λ increases, then Z decreases.
6. For a given value of Z, energy of K-series is more than L-series. Also β- line has more energy compared to α-line for a particular series.

Numerical Value Questions

1. Rate of heat production $= Vi \times \frac{98}{100} = 3136$

$$\Rightarrow \quad (40 \times 10^3) i \left(\frac{98}{100}\right) = 3136 \Rightarrow i = 0.08 \text{ A}$$

Number of electrons striking the target per second

$$= \frac{i}{e} = \frac{0.08}{1.6 \times 10^{-19}} = 5 \times 10^{17}$$

2. de-Broglie wavelength of electron,

$$\lambda = \frac{h}{\sqrt{2meV}}$$

Shortest wavelength of X-ray, $\lambda_o = \frac{hc}{eV}$

$$\therefore \quad \frac{\lambda}{\lambda_o} = \left(\frac{h}{\sqrt{2meV}}\right)\frac{eV}{hc} = \sqrt{\frac{eV}{2mc^2}}$$
$$= \sqrt{\frac{1.8 \times 10^{11} \times 10^4}{2 \times 9 \times 10^{16}}} = 0.1$$

3. $\frac{1}{\lambda} = R(Z-1)^2\left[\frac{1}{n_1^2} - \frac{1}{n_2^2}\right]$

For K_α, $\frac{1}{2.5} = R(Z-1)^2\left[\frac{1}{1^2} - \frac{1}{2^2}\right]$ ...(i)

For K_γ, $\frac{1}{\lambda} = R(Z-1)^2\left[\frac{1}{1^2} - \frac{1}{4^2}\right]$ ...(ii)

Dividing Eq. (i) by (ii), we get

$$\frac{\lambda}{2.5} = \frac{4}{5} \quad \Rightarrow \quad \lambda = 2 \text{ Å}$$

4. $\sqrt{\frac{c}{\lambda}} = a(Z-b)$

For element A, $\sqrt{\frac{c}{196}} = a(27-1)$ ...(i)

For impurity, $\sqrt{\frac{c}{169}} = a(Z-1)$ ...(ii)

Dividing Eq. (ii) by (i), we get

$$\frac{Z-1}{27-1} = \frac{14}{13} \quad \Rightarrow \quad Z = 29$$

5. Let cut-off wavelength be λ_c and K_α wavelength be λ_{K_α}.

$$\lambda_c = \frac{hc}{38.08 \times 10^3 \text{eV}}$$

When the potential difference is decreased to half, cut-off wavelength will become $2\lambda_c$.

$$\lambda_{K_\alpha} - 2\lambda_c = \frac{1}{4}(\lambda_{K_\alpha} - \lambda_c)$$
$$\Rightarrow \quad \lambda_{K_\alpha} = \frac{7\lambda_c}{3} = \frac{7hc}{(3 \times 38.03 \times 10^3) \text{eV}}$$

Using Moseley's law,

$$\frac{1}{\lambda_{K_\alpha}} = \frac{3R}{4}(Z-1)^2 \quad \Rightarrow \quad (Z-1)^2 = \frac{4}{3R\lambda_{K_\alpha}}$$

$$\Rightarrow \quad (Z-1)^2 = \frac{4(38.03\times 10^3 eV)}{7Rhc}$$

$$\Rightarrow \quad (Z-1)^2 = \frac{4\times 38.03\times 10^3}{7\times 13.6} \Rightarrow Z = 41$$

6. $E_K - E_L = \frac{hc}{\lambda_{K_\alpha}} = \frac{1230}{71\times 10^{-3}} = 17.32$ keV

$\therefore \quad E_L = E_K - 17.32 = 23.32 - 17.32 = 6$ keV

7. $\frac{1}{\lambda} = \frac{3R}{4}(Z-1)^2$

For $\lambda = 250$ pm, $\frac{1}{250\times 10^{-12}} = \frac{3}{4}\times 1.1\times 10^7 (Z_1 - 1)^2$

$\Rightarrow \quad Z_1 = 23$

For $\lambda = 179$ pm, $\frac{1}{179\times 10^{-12}} = \frac{3}{4}\times 1.1\times 10^7 (Z_2 - 1)^2$

$\Rightarrow \quad Z_2 = 27$

So, the number of elements between these two will be 3.

8. $\lambda_{min} = \frac{hc}{eV} = \frac{1240}{20\times 10^3} = 62\times 10^{-3}$nm $= 62$ pm

$$\frac{1}{\lambda} = \frac{3R}{4}(Z-1)^2$$

$$\Rightarrow \quad \frac{1}{\lambda_K} = \frac{3\times 1.097\times 10^7}{4}(41-1)^2$$

$\Rightarrow \quad \lambda_K = 76$ pm

$\therefore \quad \lambda_K - \lambda_{min} = 76 - 62 = 14$ pm

9. For K_α, $\frac{1}{\lambda} = \frac{3R}{4}(Z-1)^2$

For element 1, $\frac{1}{2} = \frac{3R}{4}(37-1)^2$ ...(i)

For element 2, $\frac{1}{8} = \frac{3R}{4}(Z-1)^2$ ...(ii)

Dividing Eq. (ii) by (i). we get

$$\frac{Z-1}{36} = \frac{1}{2} \Rightarrow Z = 19$$

10. For metal plate *B*,

$$\lambda_{min} = 100 \text{ nm}$$

Max. kinetic energy of electrons incident on plate *B*

$$= \frac{hc}{\lambda_{min}} = \frac{1240}{100} = 12.4 \text{ eV}$$

Max. kinetic energy of electrons emitted from plate *A*

$$= (12.4 - 10) \text{ eV} = 2.4 \text{ eV}$$

For plate *A*, $E = W + K_{max}$

$$\Rightarrow \quad \frac{1240}{200} = W + 2.4 \Rightarrow W = 3.8 \text{ eV}$$

Previous Year's Questions

JEE Main

1. Since, we know that de-Broglie wavelength of an electron can be given as

$$\lambda = \frac{h}{mv} \quad ...(i)$$

Also, we know that,

Kinetic energy, $K = \frac{p^2}{2m}$ ...(ii)

where, *p* is the linear momentum.

$\because$ Linear momentum,

$$p = \frac{h}{\lambda} \quad ...(iii)$$

From Eq. (ii) and Eq. (iii), we get

$$K = \frac{h^2}{2\lambda^2 m}$$

$$\Rightarrow \quad h\nu = \frac{h^2}{2\lambda^2 m} \quad \left\{\because K = h\nu = \frac{hc}{\lambda}\right\}$$

$$\Rightarrow \quad \frac{hc}{\lambda_C} = \frac{h^2}{2\lambda^2 m}$$

where, λ_C = cut off wavelength.

$$\Rightarrow \quad \lambda_C = \frac{2m\lambda^2 c}{h}$$

2. Given,

$$V = 1.24 \text{ million volt} = 1.24\times 10^6 \text{ volt}$$

Since, energy $(E) = eV$

$\therefore \quad E = 1.6\times 10^{-19}\times 1.24\times 10^6$ ...(i)

As we know that,

Energy of photon, $E = \frac{hc}{\lambda}$ ...(ii)

Here, Planck's constant,

$$h = 6.67\times 10^{-34} \text{ J-s},$$

c = speed of light in free space, $c = 3\times 10^8$ ms^{-1}

Equating Eqs. (i) and (ii), we get

$$1.6\times 10^{-19}\times 1.24\times 10^6 = \frac{6.67\times 10^{-34}\times 3\times 10^8}{\lambda}$$

$$\Rightarrow \quad \lambda = \frac{20.01\times 10^{-13}}{1.6\times 1.24} = 10.09\times 10^{-13} = 1.009\times 10^{-12}$$

$$\simeq 10^{-3}\times 10^{-9}\text{m} = 10^{-3} \text{ nm}$$

JEE Advanced

1. $\lambda \propto \frac{1}{V}$

So, when *V* double, then cut-off wavelength become half. Characteristic does not depend on voltage. When *I* is halved, then intensity will decrease.

2. (b) K_α transition takes place from $n_1 = 2$ to $n_2 = 1$

$$\therefore \quad \frac{1}{\lambda} = R(Z-b)^2\left[\frac{1}{(1)^2} - \frac{1}{(2)^2}\right]$$

For *K*-series, $b = 1$

$$\therefore \quad \frac{1}{\lambda} \propto (Z-1)^2$$

$$\Rightarrow \quad \frac{\lambda_{Cu}}{\lambda_{Mo}} = \frac{(z_{Mo}-1)^2}{(z_{Cu}-1)^2} = \frac{(42-1)^2}{(29-1)^2}$$

$$= \frac{41\times 41}{28\times 28} = \frac{1681}{784} = 2.14$$

CHAPTER~10

NUCLEI

LEVEL 01 Starter Level

10.1 Size of Nucleus

1 Calculate the radius of nucleus of $_{29}Cu^{64}$.

2 If radius of the $^{27}_{13}Al$ nucleus is estimated to be 3.6 fm, then find the radius of $^{125}_{52}Te$ nucleus.

3 Assuming the radius of a nucleus to be equal to $R = 1.3\,A^{1/3} \times 10^{-15}$ m, where A is its mass number, evaluate the density of nucleus. Take mass of one nucleon $= 1.67 \times 10^{-27}$ kg.

4 Two nuclei have mass numbers in the ratio 1 : 2. What is the ratio of their nuclear densities?

10.2 Binding Energy of Nucleus

1 A nucleus has a binding energy of 100 MeV. It further releases 10 MeV energy. Find the new binding energy of the nucleus.

2 Following data is available about 3 nuclei *P*, *Q* and *R*. Arrange them in decreasing order of stability.

	P	*Q*	*R*
Atomic mass number (*A*)	10	5	6
Binding Energy (MeV)	100	60	66

3 A nuclear reaction is given as $A + B \rightarrow C + D$. Binding energies of *A*, *B*, *C* and *D* are given as B_1, B_2, B_3 and B_4, respectively. Find the energy released in the reaction.

4 Calculate the binding energy of an α-particle from the following data. mass of ^1_1H atom = 1.007826 u, mass of neutron = 1.008665 u, mass of ^4_2He atom = 4.00260 u.

(Take 1 u=931 MeV/c^2)

5. Calculate the binding energy per nucleon of $^{40}_{20}Ca$ nucleus. [Given $m(^{40}_{20}Ca) = 39.962589$ u; m_n (mass of a neutron) = 1.008665 u, m_p (mass of a proton) = 1.007825 u]

6 Calculate the energy released when three α-particles combine to form a ^{12}C nucleus. The atomic mass of ^4_2He is 4.002603 u.

7 The positions of four different nuclei in the binding energy curve are shown in figure. Find *Q*-value for each of the following reactions.

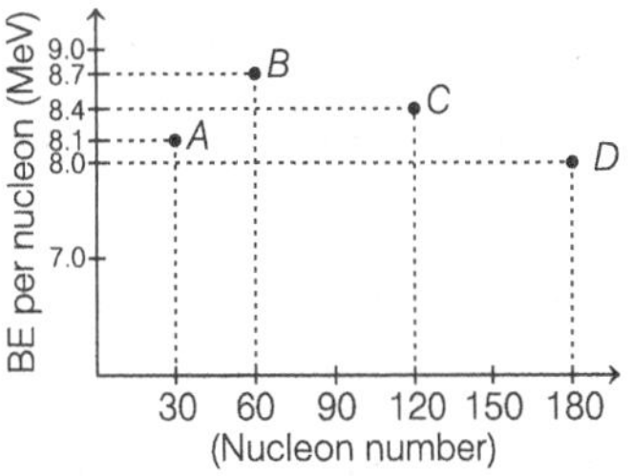

(a) $C \rightarrow 2B$ (b) $D \rightarrow B + C$ (c) $B \rightarrow 2A$

8 The binding energies per nucleon for deuteron ($_1H^2$) and helium ($_2He^4$) are 1.1 MeV and 7.0 MeV, respectively. Calculate the energy released, when two deuterons fuse to form a helium nucleus ($_2He^4$).

9 Find the energy required for separation of a Ne^{20} nucleus into two α-particles and a C^{12} nucleus if it is known that the binding energies per one nucleon in Ne^{20}, He^4 and C^{12} nuclei are equal to 8.03, 7.07 and 7.68 MeV, respectively.

10 Find the minimum kinetic energy of an α-particle to cause the reaction $^{14}N(\alpha, p)\,^{17}O$. The masses of ^{14}N, ^4He, ^1H and ^{17}O are respectively 14.00307 u, 4.00260 u, 1.00783 u and 16.99913u.

10.3 α-Decay, β-Decay and γ-Decay

1 A radioactive nucleus *A* undergoes a series of decays according to the following scheme

$$A \xrightarrow{\alpha} A_1 \xrightarrow{\beta} A_2 \xrightarrow{\alpha} A_3 \xrightarrow{\gamma} A_4$$

The mass number and atomic number of *A* are 180 and 72, respectively. What are these numbers for A_4?

2 How many α and β particles are emitted when uranium $({}_{92}U^{238})$ decays to lead $({}_{82}Pb^{206})$?

3 Consider the α-decay is given as ${}^{238}_{92}U \longrightarrow {}^{234}_{90}Th + {}^{4}_{2}He$. Given : atomic mass of ${}^{238}_{92}U = 238.05079$ u, atomic mass of ${}^{234}_{90}Th = 234.04363$ u, atomic mass of ${}^{4}_{2}He = 4.00260$ u, $1\ u = 931.5\ MeV/c^2$. Calculate
(i) the amount of energy released during the α-decay
(ii) kinetic energy of α-particle

4. A nucleus ${}^{23}_{10}Ne$ undergoes β^- decay and becomes ${}^{23}_{11}Na$. Calculate the maximum kinetic energy of electron emitted assuming that the daughter nucleus and anti-neutrino carry negligible kinetic energy atomic mass of ${}^{23}_{10}Ne = 22.994466$ u, atomic mass ${}^{23}_{11}Na = 22.989770$ u, $1\ u = 931.5\ MeV/c^2$.

5. Calculate the Q-value in the following decays :
(a) ${}^{19}O \to {}^{19}F + e^- + \bar{\nu}$ (b) ${}^{25}Al \to {}^{25}Mg + e^+ + n$

The atomic masses needed are as follows

${}^{19}O$	${}^{19}F$	${}^{25}Al$	${}^{25}Mg$
19.003576 u	18.998403 u	24.990432 u	24.985839 u

6 A neutron is absorbed by a ${}^{6}_{3}Li$ nucleus with the subsequent emission of an α-particle.
(i) Write the corresponding nuclear reaction.
(ii) Calculate the energy released, in MeV, in this reaction.

[Given mass $({}^{6}_{3}Li) = 6.015126$ u; mass (neutron) $= 1.0086654$ u; mass (α-particle) $= 4.0026044$ u and mass (triton) $= 3.0100000$ u.
[Take $1\ u = 931.5\ MeV/c^2$]

7 Identify the missing particle or nuclide in each of the following reactions?
(a) ? (n, p) ${}_{15}P^{32}$ (b) ? (p, α) ${}_{8}O^{16}$
(c) ${}_{4}Be^{9}$ (n, γ) ? (d) ${}_{7}N^{14}$ $(?, p)$ ${}_{6}C^{14}$

10.4 Nuclear Fission and Fusion

1 Assuming that 200 MeV of energy is released per fission of uranium atom, find the number of fissions per second required to release 1 kW power.

2 Consider the case of bombardment of U^{235} nucleus with a thermal neutron. The fission products are Mo^{95} and La^{139} and two neutrons. Calculate the energy released by one U^{235} nucleus. (Rest masses of the nuclides are $U^{235} = 235.0439$ u, ${}^{1}_{0}n = 1.0087$ u, $Mo^{95} = 94.9058$ u, $La^{139} = 138.9061$ u).

3 The U^{235} absorbs a slow neutron (thermal neutron) and undergoes a fission represented by

$${}_{92}U^{235} + {}^{1}_{0}n \longrightarrow {}_{92}U^{236} \longrightarrow {}_{56}Ba^{141} + {}_{36}Kr^{92} + 3\,{}_{0}n^{1} + E.$$ Calculate.

(i) the energy released E per fission.
(ii) the energy released, when 1 g of ${}_{92}U^{235}$ undergoes complete fission.

Given ${}_{92}U^{235} = 235.1175$ amu (atom), ${}_{56}Ba^{141} = 140.9577$ amu (atom); ${}_{36}Kr^{92} = 91.9264$ amu (atom); ${}_{0}n^{1} = 1.00898$ amu, $1\ u = 931.5\ MeV/c^2$

4 It is proposed to use the nuclear fusion reaction : ${}_{1}H^2 + {}_{1}H^2 \longrightarrow {}_{2}He^4$, in a nuclear reactor of 200 MW rating.
(a) Calculate the energy of the reaction
(b) If the energy from above reaction is used with a 25% efficiency in the reactor, how many grams of deuterium will be needed per day? the masses of ${}_{1}H^2$ and ${}_{2}He^4$ are 2.0141 u and 4.0026 u, respectively.

5. A star converts all its hydrogen to helium achieving 100% helium composition. It then converts helium to carbon via the reaction

$${}_{2}He^4 + {}_{2}He^4 + {}_{2}He^4 \longrightarrow {}_{6}C^{12} + 7.27\ MeV$$

The mass of the star is 5.0×10^{32} kg and it generates energy at the rate of 5×10^{30} W. How long will it take to convert all its helium to carbon?

LEVEL 02 JEE Main/Advanced Level

1 The ratio of radii of nuclei ${}_{13}Al^{27}$ and ${}_{52}X^{A}$ is 3 : 5. The number of neutrons in the nuclei of X will be
(a) 52 (b) 73
(c) 125 (d) 13

2 A nucleus disintegrates into two nuclear parts which have their velocities in the ratio of 2 : 1. The ratio of their nuclear sizes will be
(a) $3^{1/2} : 1$ (b) $1 : 2^{1/3}$ (c) $2^{1/3} : 1$ (d) $1 : 3^{1/2}$

3 The volume and mass of a nucleus are related as-
(a) $V \propto m^3$ (b) $V \propto 3\sqrt{m}$ (c) $V \propto m$ (d) $V \propto \dfrac{1}{m}$

4 Which of the following is a wrong description of binding energy of a nucleus?
(a) It is the energy required to break a nucleus into its constituent nucleons
(b) It is the energy made available when free nucleons combine to form a nucleus

(c) It is the sum of the rest mass energies of its nucleons minus the rest mass energy of the nucleus
(d) It is the sum of the kinetic energy of all the nucleons in the nucleus

5 Masses of nucleus, neutron and proton are M, m_n and m_p, respectively. If nucleus has been divided in to neutrons and protons, then
(a) $M = (A - Z)\, m_n + Z m_p$
(b) $M = Z m_n + (A - Z)\, m_p$
(c) $M < (A - Z)\, m_n + Z m_p$
(d) $M > (A - Z)\, m_n + Z m_p$

6 Find the binding energy of an α-particle from the following data. Mass of He nucleus = 4.001256 amu, Mass of proton = 1.007277amu, Mass of neutron = 1.00866 amu

(Take 1 amu = 931.5 MeV)
(a) 1850 MeV
(b) 296 MeV
(c) 28.52 MeV
(d) None of the above

7 If mass of proton = 1.008 amu and mass of neutron = 1.009 amu, then the binding energy per nucleon for ${}_4Be^9$ (mass = 9.012 amu) will be
(a) 7.727 MeV
(b) 8.672 MeV
(c) 6.727 MeV
(d) 60.542 MeV

8 The binding energies of the nuclei of ${}_2He^4$, ${}_3Li^7$, ${}_6C^{12}$ and ${}_7N^{14}$ are 28, 52, 90 and 98 MeV respectively. Which of these is most stable?
(a) ${}_2He^4$ (b) ${}_3Li^7$
(c) ${}_6C^{12}$ (d) ${}_7N^{14}$

9 The positions of ${}_1^2D$, ${}_2^4He$ and ${}_3^7Li$ are shown on the binding energy curve as shown in figure. The energy released in the fusion reaction.
${}_1^2D + {}_3^7Li \longrightarrow 2\,{}_2^4He + {}_0^1n$ will be closest to

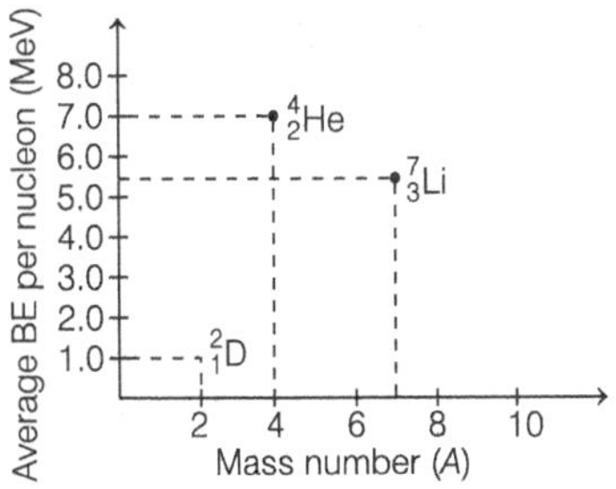

(a) 20 MeV (b) 16 MeV
(c) 8 MeV (d) 4 MeV

10. Binding energy per nucleon *versus* mass number curve for nuclei is shown in the figure. W, X, Y and Z are four nuclei as indicated on the curve. The process that would release energy is

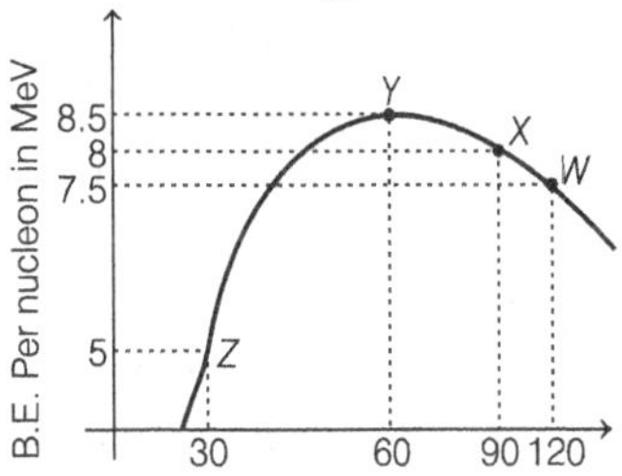

(a) $Y \rightarrow 2Z$ (b) $W \rightarrow X + Z$
(c) $W \rightarrow 2Y$ (d) $X \rightarrow Y + Z$

11 The nuclear binding energies of the elements P and Q are E_P and E_Q, respectively. Three nuclei of elements Q fuse to form one nucleus of element P. In this process the energy released is e. The correct relation between E_P, E_Q and e will be
(a) $E_Q = 3E_P + e$ (b) $E_Q = 3E_P - e$
(c) $E_P = 3E_Q + e$ (d) $E_P = 3E_Q - e$

12 Consider the nuclear reaction $X^{200} \longrightarrow A^{110} + B^{90}$. If the binding energy per nucleon for X, A and B are 7.4 MeV, 8.2 MeV and 8.1 MeV, respectively, then the energy released in the reaction will be
(a) 151 MeV (b) 200 MeV
(c) 190 MeV (d) 10 MeV

13 A heavy nucleus having mass number 200 gets disintegrated into two small fragments of mass number 80 and 120. If binding energy per nucleon for parent atom is 6.5 MeV and for daughter nuclei is 7 MeV and 8 MeV respectively, then the energy released in the decay will be
(a) 200 MeV (b) -220 MeV
(c) 220 MeV (d) 180 MeV

14 If the binding energy per nucleon in ${}_3Li^7$ and ${}_2He^4$ nuclei are 5.60 MeV and 7.06 MeV, respectively, then in the reaction $p + {}_3Li^7 \longrightarrow 2\,{}_2He^4$ energy of proton must be
(a) 39.2 MeV (b) 28.24 MeV
(c) 17.28 MeV (d) 1.46 MeV

15 A nuclear fission is represented by the following reaction $U^{236} \longrightarrow X^{111} + Y^{122} + 3n$

If the binding energies per nucleon of X^{111}, Y^{122} and U^{236} are 8.6 MeV, 8.5 MeV and 7.6 MeV respectively, then the energy released in the reaction will be
(a) 200 MeV (b) 202 MeV
(c) 195 MeV (d) 198 MeV

16 In the nuclear reaction ${}_1H^2 + {}_1H^2 \longrightarrow {}_0n^1 + {}_2He^3$, if the binding energy of deuteron is 2.23 MeV and the Q-value of the reaction is 3.27 MeV, then the binding energy of ${}_2He^3$ is

(a) 1.19 MeV (b) 7.73 MeV
(c) 4.46 MeV (d) None of these

17 The number of α and β^- emitted during the radioactive decay chain starting from ${}^{226}_{88}Ra$ and ending at ${}^{206}_{82}Pb$ is

(a) 3α and $6\beta^-$ (b) 4α and $5\beta^-$
(c) 5α and $4\beta^-$ (d) 6α and $6\beta^-$

18 To obtain an isotope of a radioactive atom the atom must emit

(a) one α and one β particle
(b) one α and 2β particles
(c) Two α and 2β particles
(d) one α and 4β particles

19 A nucleus with $Z = 92$ emits the following in a sequence. $\alpha, \beta^-, \beta^-, \alpha, \alpha, \alpha, \alpha, \alpha, \beta^-, \beta^-, \alpha, \beta^+, \beta^+, \alpha$. The Z of the resulting nucleus is

(a) 74 (b) 76
(c) 78 (d) 82

20 Consider α-particles, β-particles and γ-rays, each having an energy of 0.5 MeV. In increasing order of penetrating powers, the radiations are

(a) α, β, γ (b) α, γ, β
(c) β, γ, α (d) γ, β, α

21 When high energy α-particles (${}^4_2He$) pass through nitrogen gas, an isotope of oxygen is formed with the emission of particles named x. The nuclear reaction is ${}^{14}_7N + {}^4_2He \longrightarrow {}^{17}_8O + x$

What is the name of x?

(a) Electron (b) Proton
(c) Neutron (d) Positron

22 An element A decays into an element C by a two step process. $A \rightarrow B + He^4_2$ and $B \rightarrow C + 2e^0_{-1}$. Then,

(a) A and C are isotopes (b) A and C are isobars
(c) B and C are isotopes (d) A and B are isobars

23 When ${}_4Be^7$ transforms into ${}^7_3Li$, it does so by emitting

(a) an electron (b) a neutron
(c) a positron (d) a proton

24 A nuclear transformation is denoted by $X\,(n, \alpha)\,{}^7_3Li$. Which of the following is the nucleus of element X?

(a) ${}^{11}_4Be$ (b) ${}^9_5B$
(c) ${}^{10}_5B$ (d) ${}^{12}C_6$

25 A certain stable nuclide, after absorbing a neutron, emits a negative electron and then splits spontaneously into two α-particles. The original nuclide is

(a) ${}^8Be$ (b) ${}^7Be$
(c) ${}^7B$ (d) ${}^7Li$

26 Masses of two isobars ${}_{29}Cu^{64}$ and ${}_{30}Zn^{64}$ are 63.9298 amu and 63.9292 amu respectively. It can be concluded from these data that

(a) Both the isobars are stable
(b) Zn^{64} is radioactive, decaying to ${}_{29}Cu^{64}$ through β-decay
(c) ${}_{29}Cu^{64}$ is radioactive, decaying to Zn^{64} through γ-decay
(d) ${}_{29}Cu^{64}$ is radioactive, decaying to Zn^{64} through β-decay

27 Which of the following is a correct statement?

(a) Beta rays are same as cathode rays
(b) Gamma rays are high energy neutrons
(c) Alpha particles are singly ionized helium atoms
(d) Protons and neutrons have exactly the same mass

28 A free neutron decays to a proton but a free proton does not decay to a neutron. This is because

(a) Neutron is a composite particle made of a proton and an electron whereas proton is a fundamental particle.
(b) Neutron is an uncharged particle whereas proton is a charged particle
(c) Neutron has larger rest mass than the proton
(d) Weak forces can operate in a neutron but not in a proton

29 The nucleus of element X ($A = 220$) undergoes α-decay. If Q-value of the reaction is 5.5 MeV, then approximate kinetic energy of α-particle is

(a) 5.6 MeV (b) 5.4 MeV
(c) 4.9 MeV (d) 6.5 MeV

30 In an α-decay the kinetic energy of α-particle is 48 MeV and Q-value of the reaction is 50 MeV. The mass number of the mother nucleus is (Assume that daughter nucleus is in ground state)

(a) 96 (b) 100
(c) 104 (d) None of these

31 When ${}^6_3Li$ is bombarded with 4 MeV deuterons, one reaction that is observed is the formation of two α-particles, each with 13.2 MeV of energy. The Q-value for this reaction is

(a) 13.2 MeV (b) 26.4 MeV
(c) 22.4 MeV (d) 4 MeV

32 The emission of a gamma photon from a radioactive substance is associated with
(a) the transition of an orbiting electron
(b) de excitation of the nucleus
(c) breaking of an inter atomic bond
(d) None of the above

33 Masses of neutron, proton and electron are 1.0087 u, 1.0073 u and 0.0005 u, respectively. If a neutron decays into a proton and an electron, the energy released would be about
(a) 0.68 MeV (b) 0.84 MeV
(c) 0.75 MeV (d) 1.22 MeV

34. Mass of ${}^{7}_{4}Be$ atom = 7.016929 amu,
Mass of ${}^{7}_{3}Li$ atom = 7.016004 amu
${}^{7}_{4}Be$ undergoes electron capture at rest.
The energy of neutrinos is
(a) 0.2 MeV (b) 0.9 MeV
(c) 20 MeV (d) 28.6 MeV

35 Given that $M({}^{3}_{1}\text{H-atom}) = 3.016050$ amu,
$M({}^{3}_{2}\text{He-atom}) = 3.016030$ amu
Maximum energy of the electron emitted in the β-decay of ${}^{3}_{1}H$ is
(a) 18.6 keV (b) 0.186 keV (c) 186 keV (d) 186 MeV

36 The minimum frequency of γ-ray that causes a deuteron to disintegrate into a proton and a neutron is ($m_d = 2.0141$ amu, $m_p = 1.0078$ amu, $m_n = 1.0087$ amu)
(a) 2.7×10^{20} Hz (b) 5.4×10^{20} Hz
(c) 10.8×10^{20} Hz (d) 21.6×10^{20} Hz

37 An electron and a positron may annihilate one another producing two γ-ray photons of equal energy. The minimum energy of each of these photon is
(a) 8.2×10^{-14} MeV (b) 8.2×10^{-14} J
(c) 16.4×10^{-14} MeV (d) 16.4×10^{-14} J

38 If mass $U^{235} = 235.12142$ amu, mass of $U^{236} = 236.1205$ amu, mass of neutron $= 1.008665$ amu, then the energy required to remove one neutron from the nucleus of U^{236} is nearly about
(a) 75 MeV (b) 6.5 MeV (C) 1 eV (d) zero

39 Let F_{pp}, F_{pn} and F_{nn} denote the magnitude of the net force by a proton on a proton, by a proton on a neutron and by a neutron on a neutron, respectively. Neglect gravitational force. When the separation is 1 fm
(a) $F_{pp} > F_{pn} = F_{nn}$ (b) $F_{pp} = F_{pn} = F_{nn}$
(c) $F_{pp} > F_{pn} > F_{nn}$ (d) $F_{pp} < F_{pn} = F_{nn}$

40. According to binding energy per nucleon *versus* mass number curve, which is not correct?
(a) Two light nuclei fuse to form medium sized nuclei
(b) A heavy nucleus undergoes fission to form two medium sized nuclei
(c) Two medium sized nucleus fuse to form a heavy nucleus
(d) The peak of the curve corresponds to the most stable nucleus

41 Assuming that about 200 MeV of energy is released per fission of ${}_{92}U^{235}$ nuclei, then the mass of U^{235} consumed per day in fission reactor of power 1 MW will be approximately
(a) 10^{-2} g (b) 1 g (c) 100 g (d) 10000 g

42 In the fusion reaction, ${}_{1}H^{2} + {}_{1}H^{2} \longrightarrow {}_{2}He^{3} + {}_{0}n^{1}$
The masses of deutrons, helium and neutron expressed in amu are 2.015, 3.017 and 1.009, respectively. If 1 kg of deuterium undergoes complete fusion, find the amount of total energy released. 1 amu = 931 MeV/c^2
(a) 6×10^{13} J (b) 5.6×10^{13} J
(c) 9×10^{13} J (d) 0.9×10^{13} J

43 In a ${}_{92}U^{235}$ reactor, it takes 30 days to use up 2kg of fuel. If each fission gives 185 MeV of usable energy, then power output of reactor is
(a) 5.85×10^{7} W (b) 1.52×10^{14} W
(c) 5.07×10^{12} W (d) 3.82×10^{6} W

44 A nuclear reactor using U^{235} generates 250 MW of electrical power. The efficiency of the reactor is 25%. The thermal energy released per fission of U^{235} is 200 MeV. What is the amount of U^{235} used in the reactor per year?
(a) 3.84 kg (b) 38.44 kg (c) 384.4 kg (d) 3844 kg

45 Heavy water is used as moderator in a nuclear reactor. The function of the moderator is
(a) to control the energy released in the reactor
(b) to absorb neutrons and stop chain reaction
(c) to cool the reactor
(d) to slow down the neutrons to thermal energies

46 The rest mass of a deuteron ${}_{1}H^{2}$ is equivalent to an energy of 1876 MeV, the rest mass of a proton is equivalent to 939 MeV and that of a neutron is 940 MeV. A deuteron may disintegrate to a proton and a neutron if it
(A) emits a γ-ray photon of energy 2 MeV.
(b) captures a γ-ray photon of energy 2 MeV.
(c) emits a γ-ray photon of energy 3 MeV.
(d) captures a γ-ray photon of energy 3 MeV.

47. In the nuclear fusion reaction ${}_1^2\text{H} + {}_1^3\text{H} \longrightarrow {}_2^4\text{He} + n$, given that the repulsive potential energy between the two nuclei is ~ 7.7×10^{-14} J. The temperature at which the gases must be heated to initiate the reaction is nearly (Boltzmann constant $k = 1.38 \times 10^{-23}$ J/K)

(a) 10^5 K (b) 10^3 K (c) 10^9 K (d) 10^7 K

48. A star initially has 10^{40} deuterons. It produces energy via the processes

${}_1^2\text{H} + {}_1^2\text{H} \longrightarrow {}_1^3\text{H} + p$ and ${}_1^2\text{H} + {}_1^3\text{H} \longrightarrow {}_2^4\text{He} + n$

The masses of the nuclei are as follows,

$m({}_1^2\text{H}) = 2.014$ amu, $m({}_1^3\text{H}) == 3.016$ amu;
$m(p) = 1.007$ amu; $m(n) = 1.008$ amu;
$m({}_2^4\text{He}) = 4.001$ amu.

If the average power radiated by the star is 10^{16} W, the deuteron supply of the star is exhausted in a time of the order of

(a) 10^6 s (b) 10^8 s (c) 10^{12} s (d) 10^{16} s

49 Consider one of fission reactions of ${}^{235}\text{U}$ by thermal neutrons ${}_{92}^{235}\text{U} + \text{n} \rightarrow {}_{38}^{94}\text{Sr} + {}_{54}^{140}\text{Xe} + 2n$. The fission fragments are however unstable and they undergo successive β-decay until ${}_{38}^{94}\text{Sr}$ becomes ${}_{40}^{94}\text{Zr}$ and ${}_{54}^{140}\text{Xe}$ becomes ${}_{58}^{140}\text{Ce}$. The energy released in this process is

[Given $m({}^{235}\text{U}) = 235.439$ u, $m(n) = 1.00866$ u, $m({}^{94}\text{Zr}) = 93.9064$ u, $m({}^{140}\text{Ce}) = 139.9055$ u, 1 u = 931 MeV]

(a) 156 MeV (b) 208 MeV
(c) 456 MeV (d) 575.7 MeV

50. The following deuterium reactions and corresponding reaction energies are found to occur.

${}^{14}\text{N}(d, p)\,{}^{15}\text{N}, Q = 8.53$ MeV
${}^{15}\text{N}(d, \alpha)\,{}^{13}\text{C}, Q = 7.58$ MeV
${}^{13}\text{C}(d, \alpha)\,{}^{11}\text{B}, Q = 5.16$ MeV

The notation ${}^{14}\text{N}(d, p)\,{}^{15}\text{N}$ represents the reaction ${}^{14}\text{N} + d \rightarrow {}^{15}\text{N} + p$

${}_2^4\text{He} = 4.0026$ amu, ${}_1^2\text{H} = 2.014$ amu, ${}_1^1\text{H} = 1.0078$ amu, $n = 1.0087$ amu
(1 amu = 931 MeV)

The Q value of the reaction ${}^{11}\text{B}(\alpha, n)\,{}^{14}\text{N}$ is

(a) 0.5 eV (b) 0.5 MeV
(c) 0.05 MeV (d) 0.05 eV

51 Gold ${}_{79}^{198}\text{Au}$ undergoes β^- decay to an excited state of ${}_{80}^{198}\text{Hg}$. If the excited state decays by emission of a γ-photon with energy 0.412MeV, the maximum kinetic energy of the electron emitted in the decay is (This maximum occurs when the anti-neutrino has negligible energy. The recoil energy of the ${}_{80}^{198}\text{Hg}$ nucleus can be ignored. The masses of the neutral atoms in their ground states are 197.968225 u for ${}_{79}^{198}\text{Au}$ and 197.966752 u for ${}_{80}^{198}\text{Hg}$)

(a) 0.412 MeV (b) 1.371 MeV
(c) 0.960 MeV (d) 1.473 MeV

Multiple Choice(s) Correct Questions

1 Choose the correct statement(s)

(a) A β-particle is an electron which exists in the nucleus and comes out during β-decay
(b) A high energetic gamma ray can be converted into electron-positron pair near a heavy nucleus
(c) Nuclear forces binding proton with proton is greater than between neutron and neutron
(d) All lines of lyman series necessarily lie between 900 and 1500 Å

2. For nuclei having $A > 120$

(a) The binding energy of nucleus decreases as A increases
(b) The binding energy per nucleon decreases as A increases
(c) If the nucleus breaks into two roughly equal parts, energy is released
(d) If two nuclei fuse to form a bigger nucleus, energy is released

3. Let m_p be the mass of a proton, m_n the mass of neutron, M_1 the mass of a ${}_{10}^{20}\text{Ne}$ nucleus and M_2 the mass of a ${}_{20}\text{Ca}^{40}$ nucleus. Then,

(a) $M_2 = 2M_1$ (b) $M_2 > 2M_1$
(c) $M_2 < 2M_1$ (d) $M_1 < 10(m_n + m_p)$

4. Assume that the nuclear binding energy per nucleon $\left(\frac{B}{A}\right)$ *versus* mass number (A) is as shown in the figure. Use this plot to choose the correct choice(s) given below. Figure

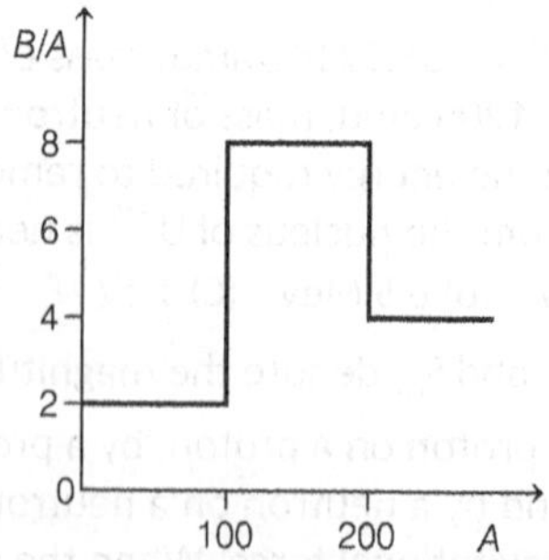

(a) Fusion of two nuclei with mass numbers lying in the range of $1 < A < 50$ will release energy
(b) Fusion of two nuclei with mass numbers lying in the range of $51 < A < 100$ will release energy

(c) Fission of a nucleus lying in the mass range of $100 < A < 200$ will release energy when broken into two equal fragments
(d) Fission of a nucleus lying in the mass range of $200 < A < 260$ will release energy when broken into two equal fragments

5 In an endoergic nuclear reaction an incoming particle collides with stationary nucleus
(a) Kinetic energy of incoming particle is greater than Q-value of reaction in ground frame
(b) Kinetic energy of incoming particle is equal to the Q-value of reaction in center of mass frame
(c) Linear momentum of particle-nucleus system is conserved
(d) Energy is released in the process

6 The heavier nuclie tend to have larger $\frac{N}{Z}$ ratio because
(a) a neutron is heavier than a proton
(b) a neutron is an unstable particle
(c) a neutron does not exert electric repulsion
(d) coulomb forces have longer range compared to the nuclear forces

7 Choose the correct statements from the following
(a) Like other light nuclei, the ${}_2He^4$ nuclei also have a low value of the binding energy per nucleon.
(b) The binding energy per nucleon decreases for nuclei with small as well as large atomic number.
(c) The energy required to remove one neutron from ${}_3Li^7$ to transform it into the isotope ${}_3Li^6$ is 5.6 MeV, which is the same as the binding energy per nucleon of ${}_3Li^6$.
(d) When two deuterium nuclei fuse together, they give rise to a tritium nucleus accompained by a release of energy.

8 Mark out the correct statement(s)
(a) In alpha decay, the energy released is shared between alpha particle and daughter nucleus in the form of kinetic energy and share of alpha particle is more than that of the daughter nucleus.
(b) In beta decay, the energy released is shared between electron and anti-neutrino.
(c) A nuclide undergoes α-decay, then all the α-particles emitted by that nuclide will have almost the same speed.
(d) A nuclide undergoes β-decay, then all the β-particles emitted by that nuclide may have widely different speeds.

9 In β-decay, the Q-value of the process is E. Then,
(a) KE of a β-particle cannot exceed E
(b) KE of anti-neutrino emitted lies between zero and E.
(c) N/Z ratio of the nucleus is altered
(s) Mass number (A) of the nucleus is altered.

10 During β-decay (beta minus), the emission of anti-neutrino particle is supported by which of the following statement (s)?
(a) Angular momentum conservation holds good in any nuclear reaction
(b) Linear momentum conservation holds good in any nuclear reaction
(c) The KE of emitted β-particle is varying continuously to a maximum value.
(d) None of the above

11 In the α-decay of U^{238} nucleus the energy released in the decay is Q. The U^{238} nucleus was initially stationary. Which of the following is (are) true?
(a) Ratio of KE of α-particle and Thorium nucleus is 117 : 2
(b) Ratio of KE of Thorium nucleus and α-particle is 1 : 234
(c) Momentum of α-particle is $\sqrt{\frac{234Qm_\alpha}{119}}$
(d) Recoil velocity of Thorium nucleus is $\sqrt{\frac{234Q}{119}\left(\frac{m_\alpha}{m_{Th}^2}\right)}$

12 Mark out the correct statement(s).
(a) For an exothermic reaction, if Q-value is +12.56 MeV and the KE of incident particle is 2.44 MeV, then the total KE of products of reaction is 15.00 MeV
(b) For an exothermic reaction, if Q value is +12.56 MeV and the KE of incident particle is 2.44 MeV, then the total KE of products of reaction is 12.56 MeV
(c) For an endothermic reaction, if we give the energy equal $|Q|$ value of reaction, then the reaction will be carried out.
(d) For an exothermic reaction, the BE per nucleon of products should be greater than the BE per nucleon of reactants.

13 Mark out the correct statement (s).
(a) In both fission and fusion processes, the mass of reactant nuclide is greater than the mass of product nuclide.
(b) In fission process, BE per nucleon of reactant nuclide is less than the binding energy per nucleon of product nuclide.
(c) In fusion process, BE per nucleon of reactant nuclide is less than the binding energy per nucleon of product nuclide.
(d) In fusion process, BE per nucleon of reactant nuclide is greater than the binding energy per nucleon of product nuclide.

14 The phenomenon of nuclear fission can be carried out both in a controlled and in an uncontrolled way. Out of the following, the correct statements vis-a-vis these phenomena are

(a) The fission energy released per reaction is much more than conventional nuclear reactions and one of the products of the reaction is that very particle which initiates the reaction.

(b) It is the "surface to volume" ratio of the sample of nuclear fuel used which determines whether or not the reaction would sustain itself as a "chain reaction".

(c) The "control rods" in a nuclear reactor must be made of a material that absorbs neutrons effectively

(d) The energy released per fission as well as energy released per unit mass of the fuel in nuclear fission are both greater than the corresponding quantities for nuclear fusion.

Comprehension Based Questions

Comprehension-I

In a nuclear fusion reactor, the reaction occurs in two stages.

(A) Two deuterium ($_1D^2$) nuclei fuse to form a tritium ($_1T^3$) nucleus with a proton as a by product. The reaction may be represented as D(D, *p*) T.

(B) A tritium nucleus fuses with another deuterium nucleus to form a helium ($_2He^4$) nucleus with a neutron as a by product. The reaction is represented as T(D, *n*) α.

Given, $m(_1D^2) = 2.014102$ u (atom), $m(_1T^3) = 3.016049$ u (atom), $m(_2He^4) = 4.002603$ u (atom), $m(_1H^1) = 1.007825$ u (atom), $m(_0n^1) = 1.008665$ u

1 The energy released in the second stage of fusion reaction, is

(a) 4.033 MeV (b) 17.580 MeV
(c) 40.33 MeV (d) 1.7580 MeV

2 The energy released in the combined reaction per deuterium, is

(a) 4.204 MeV (b) 5.204 MeV
(c) 6.204 MeV (d) 7.204 MeV

3 What percentage of the mass energy of the initial deuterium is released?

(a) 0.184% (B) 0.284% (c) 0.384% (d) 0.484%

Comprehension-2

Gold nucleus ($_{79}Au^{198}$) can decay into mercury nucleus ($_{80}Hg^{198}$) by two decay schemes shown in figure.

(i) It can emit a β-particle (β_1) and come to ground state by either emitting one γ ray (γ_1) or emitting two γ rays (γ_3 and γ_2)

(ii) It can emit one β-particle (β_2) and come to ground state by emitting γ_2 ray.

Atomic masses $_{79}Au^{198} = 197.9682$ amu, $_{80}Hg^{198} = 197.9662$ amu, 1 amu = 930 MeV/c^2

The energy levels of the nucleus are shown in figure.

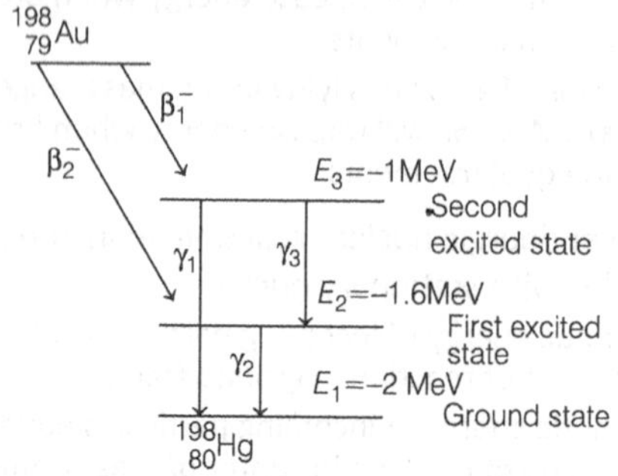

4 What is the maximum kinetic energy of emitted β_2 particles?

(a) 1.44 MeV (b) 0.59 MeV
(c) 1.86 MeV (d) 1.46 MeV

5 What is the maximum kinetic energy of emitted β_1 particles?

(a) 1.28 MeV (b) 0.77 MeV
(c) 1.86 MeV (d) 0.86 MeV

6 The wavelength of emitted γ-rays are in the order

(a) $\lambda_{\gamma_2} > \lambda_{\gamma_3} > \lambda_{\gamma_1}$ (b) $\lambda_{\gamma_3} > \lambda_{\gamma_2} > \lambda_{\gamma_1}$
(c) $\lambda_{\gamma_1} > \lambda_{\gamma_2} > \lambda_{\gamma_3}$ (d) $\lambda_{\gamma_3} = \lambda_{\gamma_2} > \lambda_{\gamma_1}$

Comprehension-3

A nucleus at rest undergoes α-decay emitting an α-particle of de-Broglie wavelength $\lambda = 5.76 \times 10^{-15}$ m. The mass of the daughter nucleus is 223.610 amu and that of α-particle is 4.002 amu.

7 The kinetic energy of α-particle is

(a) 0.01 MeV (b) 6.22 MeV
(c) 0.21 MeV (d) 0.31 MeV

8 The kinetic energy of daughter nucleus is

(a) 3.16 MeV (b) 4.16 MeV
(c) 5.16 MeV (d) 0.11 MeV

9 The mass of the parent nucleus in amu is

(a) 227.418 (b) 207.518 (c) 227.618 (d) 227.718

Comprehension-4

Consider the nuclear fission reaction $W \rightarrow X + Y$. Using the graph given, answer the following questions.

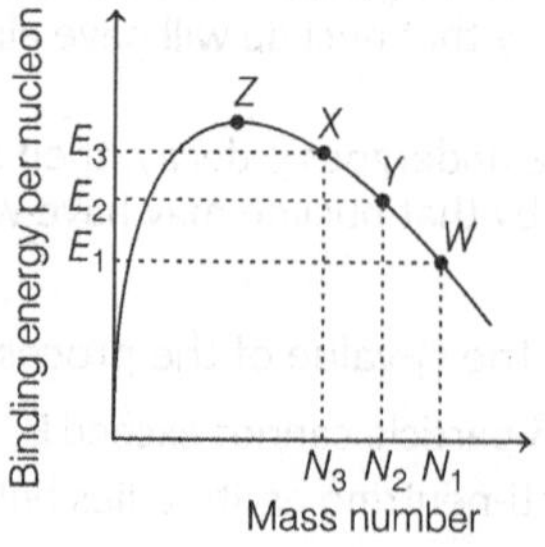

10 What is the Q-value of the reaction?

(a) $E_1N_1 - (E_2N_2 + E_3N_3)$ (b) $(E_2N_2 + E_3N_3 - E_1N_1)$
(c) $E_2N_2 + E_1N_1 - E_3N_3$ (d) $E_1N_1 + E_3N_3 - E_2N_2$

11 If M_W is the mass of W, M_X is mass of X and M_Y is mass of Y nucleus, choose correct statement

(a) $\frac{M_W}{N_1} > \frac{M_Y}{N_2} > \frac{M_X}{N_3}$ (b) $\frac{M_W}{N_1} < \frac{M_Y}{N_2} < \frac{M_X}{N_3}$
(c) $\frac{M_W}{N_1} < \frac{M_Y}{N_2} > \frac{M_X}{N_3}$ (d) $\frac{M_W}{N_1} > \frac{M_Y}{N_2} < \frac{M_X}{N_3}$

12 Which of the following graph might represent the relationship between atomic mass number (i.e., "atomic weight") and the total binding energy of the nucleus, for nuclei heavier than Z?

(a)
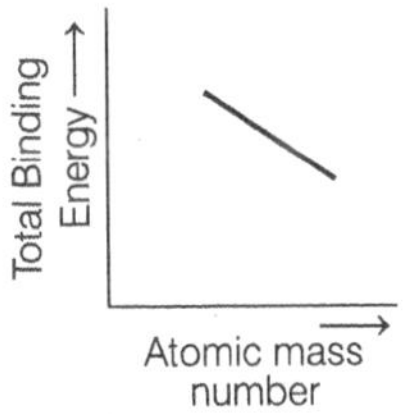

(b)
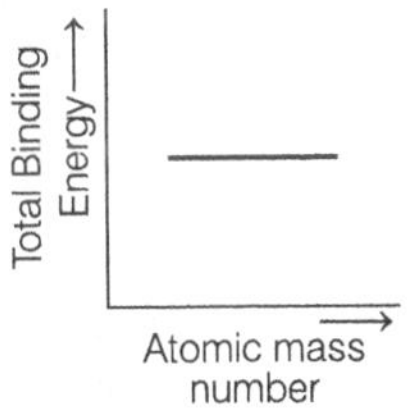

(c)
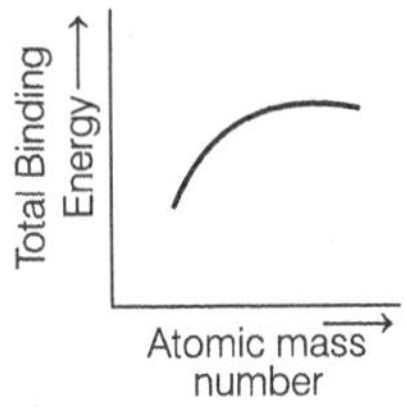

(d)
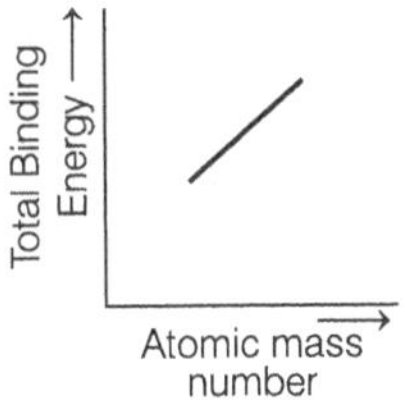

Comprehension-5

Nuclear reactions are performed for artificial transmutation of elements. There are two types of nuclear reactions, exoergic and endoergic. In exoergic reactions energy is released. In endoergic reactions energy has to supplied for the reaction proceed. In exoergic reactions nuclear energy is converted into kinetic energy. In endoergic reactions, energy input is required in the form of kinetic energy to be converted into nuclear binding energy. The minimum energy required for the reaction to take place is called threshold energy.

Consider the reaction$p + {}_1^3\text{H} \rightarrow {}_1^2\text{H} + {}_1^2\text{H}$.

Atomic masses are

$m({}_1^1\text{H-atom}) = 1.007825$ amu (u), $m({}_1^3\text{H-atom}) = 3.016049$ amu (u); $m({}_1^2\text{H-atom}) = 2.014102$ amu (u)

13 Protons are incident on ${}_1^3\text{H}$ at rest. The threshold energy for the reaction is

(a) 5.4 MeV (b) 10 MeV
(c) 2 MeV (d) 8 MeV

14. When ${}_1^3\text{H}$ are incident on protons, threshold energy is

(a) 10 MeV (b) 8 MeV
(c) 16 MeV (d) 20 MeV

15. Which of the following is true?

(a) Less energy is required for nuclear reaction if light part is at rest and heavy particle is incident
(b) More energy is required for nuclear reaction, when heavy particle is incident and light particle is at rest
(c) Threshold energy does not depend on which particle is at rest
(d) Threshold energy does not depend on Q-value of reaction

Comprehension-6

The two dominant forces in the nucleus of an atom are the electromagnetic force, which is the repulsive force among protons, and the strong force, which is attractive among protons and neutrons. Many of the things we observe in nuclei can be explained by a balance of these forces, combined with Pauli principle for the particles in the nucleus. For instance, most stable nuclei have somewhat more neutrons than protons, although non-massive stable nuclei have about the same number of neutrons as protons. Nuclear physicists say that these nuclei are in a valley of stability, so that $N \geq Z$,

where N is the number of neutrons and Z is the atomic number, and the symbol means that N is greater than or approximately equal to Z.

When the difference $N - Z$ is strongly positive, it is likely that a nucleus will decay by β-decay in which a neutron converts into a proton, an electron, and an anti-neutrino (which rarely interacts with matter).

When $N - Z$ is only slightly positive or even negative, then there are two likely modes of decay β^+ decay and K-capture. In β^+ decay (also called positron decay), a proton is converted into a neutron, a positron, and a neutrino.

In K-capture, an electron from orbital of the first shell (or K-shell, that is, the 1s orbital) combines with a nuclear proton to make a neutron and a neutrino. This often happens in nuclei in which positron decay is forbidden, for instance, because it is energetically unfavorable. K-capture is possible because there is some overlap of the first-shell orbital and the volume taken up the nucleus, that is, the first-shell orbital has a non-zero amplitude at the center of the nucleus.

16 Which of the following represents the K-capture decay of ${}^{56}\text{Ni}$?

(a) ${}^{56}\text{Ni} \rightarrow {}^{56}\text{Co} + e^+ + v$ (b) ${}^{56}\text{Ni} \rightarrow {}^{56}\text{Cu} + e^- + \bar{v}$
(c) ${}^{56}\text{Ni} \rightarrow {}^{56}\text{Co} + e^- + \bar{v}$ (d) ${}^{56}\text{Ni} + e^- \rightarrow {}^{56}\text{Co} + v$

17. What kind of nuclei would tend to undergo K-capture?

(a) Nuclei with many more neutrons than protons
(b) Nuclei with more protons than neutrons
(c) Nuclei with a deficit of electrons
(d) Nuclei with protons in low energy orbitals

18. Which of the following, if true, would explain why L-capture, the interaction of a nucleus with a second-shell electron, is extremely rare?

(a) The second-shell has greater energy than the first shell
(b) The second-shell has a vanishing amplitude in the nucleus
(c) The second-shell electrons are easily removed from the atom
(d) The second-shell electrons cannot be converted to positrons

Comprehension-7

A town has a population of 1 million. The average electric power needed per person is 300 W. A reactor is to be designed to supply power to this town. The efficiency with which thermal power is converted into electric power is aimed at 25%.

19 Assuming 200 MeV of thermal energy to come from each fission event on an average, the number of events that should take place every day.

(a) 2.24×10^{24} (b) 3.24×10^{24}
(c) 4.24×10^{24} (d) 5.24×10^{24}

20 Assuming the fission to take place largely through U^{235}, at what rate will the amount of U^{235} decrease (kg/day) ?

(a) 1.264 (b) 1.464 (c) 1.664 (d) 1.864

21 Assuming that uranium enriched to 3% in U^{235} will be used. How much uranium is needed per month(30 days)?

(a) 1064 kg (b) 1164 kg (c) 1264 kg (d) 1364 kg

Match the Columns Questions

1. In Column I consider each process just before and just after it occurs. Initial system is isolated from all other bodies. Consider all product particles (even those having rest mass zero) in the system. Match the system in Column I with the result they produce in Column II.

Column I	Column II
A. Spontaneous radioactive decay of an uranium nucleus initially at rest $^{238}_{92}U \rightarrow ^{234}_{90}Th + ^{4}_{2}He + \ldots$	1. Number of protons is increased
B. Fusion reaction of two hydrogen nuclei as given by reaction $^{1}_{1}H + ^{1}_{1}H \rightarrow ^{2}_{1}H + \ldots$	2. momentum is conserved
C. Fission of U^{235} nucleus initiated by a thermal neutron as given by reaction $n + ^{235}_{92}U \rightarrow ^{144}_{56}Ba + ^{89}_{36}Kr + 3^{1}_{0}n + \ldots$	3. Mass is converted to energy or vice versa
D. β^- decay (negative beta decay)	4. Charge is conserved

2. Match the following

Column I	Column II
A. β-decay	1. Charged particles are emitted having continuous energy till certain maximum value.
B. α-decay	2. Charged particles are emitted having discrete energies.
C. Photoelectric emission from a standard photoelectric effect experiment apparatus.	3. Angular momentum of emitting body is changed in process of emission
D. Photons of wavelength 90 nm pass through a sample of hydrogen gas in ground state.	4. If external factors change, the process of emission may stop
	5. Electronic configuration of the atom is changed in process of emission.

3. Q is the energy released in the decay, m_x is atomic mass of parent nucleus, m_y is atomic mass of daughter nucleus and m_e is mass of electron, then match the following

Column I	Column II
A. k-capture	1. $Q = (m_x - m_y)c^2$
B. β^--decay	2. $Q = (m_x - m_y - m_e)c^2$
C. β^+ decay	3. $Q = (m_x - m_y - 2m_e)c^2$
	4. $Q = (m_x - m_y + 2m_e)c^2$

4. Match the following

Column I	Column II
A. Energy of thermal neutrons	1. 0.025 eV
B. Energy of X-rays	2. 0.5 eV
C. Binding energy per nucleon	3. 3 eV
D. Photoelectric threshold of metal	4. 20 eV
	5. 10 keV
	6. 8 MeV

5. Match the following

Column I	Column II
A. Nuclear Fusion	1. Some matter converted into energy
B. Nuclear Fission	2. Generally occurs in nuclei having low atomic number.
C. β-decay	3. Generally occurs in nuclei having higher atomic number.
D. Exothermic	4. Essentially occurs reaction due to weak nuclear force.

Numerical Value Questions

1 Nucleus $_3A^7$ has binding energy per nucleon of 10 MeV. It absorbs a proton and its mass increases by $\frac{99}{100}$ times the mass of proton. Find the new binding energy (in MeV) of the nucleus so formed.

[Take, energy equivalent of proton = 930 MeV]

2 Binding energy per nucleon or a fixed nucleus X^A is 6 MeV. It absorbs a neutron moving with KE = 2 MeV, and converts into Y, emitting a photon of energy 1 MeV. If the binding Energy per nucleon of Y (in MeV) is found to be $\frac{nA-1}{A+1}$, find the value of n.

3 The binding energy per nucleon of $^{16}_{8}O$ is 7.97 MeV and that of $^{17}_{8}O$ is 7.75 MeV. Find the energy (in MeV) required to remove a neutron from $^{17}_{8}O$.

4 $_{92}U^{238}$ changes to $_{85}At^{210}$ by a series of α and β decays. Find the number of β-particles emitted.

5 In a nuclear reactor, ^{235}U undergoes fission liberating 200 MeV of energy. The reactor has a 10% efficiency and produces 1000 MW power. If the reactor is to function for 10 yr, the total mass of uranium required is 3.82×10^n kg, then find n.

6 A π^0 meson at rest decays into two photons of equal energy. If the wavelength (in m) of the photons is 1.8×10^{-n}, then find n. (The mass of the π^0 meson is 135 MeV/c^2)

7 The reaction $^7_3Li + ^1_1H \to ^7_4Be + ^1_0n$ is endothermic. Assuming that Li nuclei is free and at rest. What is the minimum kinetic energy (in MeV) of incident proton, so that this reaction occurs? Take Q-value of this reaction as – 1645 keV.

8 Consider the following nuclear reaction

$$^2_1D + ^2_1D \to ^3_1T + ^1_1P$$

Given that $m(^2_1D) = 2.01458$ amu, $m(^3_1T) = 3.01605$ amu, $m(^1_1P) = 1.00728$ amu.

Find the mass of deuterium $(_1D^2)$ (in kg) required per day in order to produce a power output of 10^9 W with 50% efficiency.

9 Consider a nuclear reaction $A + B \to C$. A nucleus A moving with kinetic energy of 5 MeV collides with a nucleus B moving with kinetic energy of 3 MeV and forms a nucleus C in excited state. Find the kinetic energy of nucleus C just after its formation if it is formed in a state with excitation energy 10.65 MeV. Take masses of nuclei of A, B and C as 25.0,10.0,34.995 amu. 1 amu = 930 MeV/c^2.

Previous Year's Questions

JEE Main

1 In a nuclear fission process, a high mass nuclide ($A \approx 236$) with binding energy 7.6 MeV/Nucleon dissociated into middle mass nuclides ($A \approx 118$), having binding energy of 8.6 MeV/Nucleon. The energy released in the process would be .... MeV.

[2024, 27 Jan Shift-I]

2 The atomic mass of $_6C^{12}$ is 12.000000 u and that of $_6C^{13}$ is 13.003354 u. The required energy to remove a neutron from $_6C^{13}$, if mass of neutron is 1.008665 u, will be **[2024, 27 Jan Shift-II]**

(a) 4.95 MeV (b) 62.5 MeV
(c) 49.5 MeV (d) 6.25 MeV

3 The explosive in a Hydrogen bomb is a mixture of $_1H^2$, $_1H^3$ and $_3Li^6$ in some condensed form. The chain reaction is given by **[2024, 29 Jan Shift-I]**

$$_3Li^6 + _0n^1 \longrightarrow _2He^4 + _1H^3$$
$$_1H^2 + _1H^3 \longrightarrow _2He^4 + _0n^1$$

During the explosion the energy released is approximately

[Given : M(Li) = 6.01690 amu, $M(_1H^2) = 2.01471$ amu, $M(_2He^4) = 4.00388$ amu, and 1 amu = 931.5 MeV]

(a) 12.64 MeV (b) 28.12 MeV
(c) 22.22 MeV (d) 16.48 MeV

4 Given below are two statements, one is labelled as Assertion (A) and the other is labelled as Reason (R).

Assertion (A) The binding energy per nucleon is practically independent of the atomic number for nuclei of mass number in the range 30 to 170.

Reason (R) Nuclear force is short ranged.

In the light of the above statements, choose the most appropriate answer from the options given below. **[2023, 13 April Shift-II]**

(a) Both A and R are true and R is the correct explanation of A
(b) Both A and R are true but R is not the correct explanation of A
(c) A is true but R is false
(d) A is false but R is true

5 Consider the following radioactive decays process

$$^{218}_{84}A \xrightarrow{\alpha} A_1 \xrightarrow{\beta^-} A_2 \xrightarrow{\gamma} A_3 \xrightarrow{\alpha} A_4 \xrightarrow{\beta^+} A_5 \xrightarrow{\gamma} A_6$$

The mass number and the atomic number of A_6 are given by **[2023, 24 Jan Shift-I]**

(a) 211 and 80 (b) 210 and 80
(c) 210 and 82 (d) 210 and 84

6 A nucleus with mass number 242 and binding energy per nucleon as 7.6 MeV breaks into two fragment each with mass number 121. If each fragment nucleus has binding energy per nucleon as 8.1 MeV, the total gain in binding energy is .... MeV. **[2023, 8 April Shift-I]**

7 Nucleus A having $Z = 17$ and equal number of protons and neutrons has 1.2 MeV binding energy per nucleon. Another nucleus B of $Z = 12$ has total 26 nucleons and 1.8 MeV binding energy per nucleons. The difference of binding energy of B and A will be .... MeV. **[2023, 1 Feb Shift-II]**

8 The energy released per fission of nucleus of ^{240}X is 200 MeV. The energy released, if all the atoms in 120 g of pure ^{240}X undergo fission is .... $\times 10^{25}$ MeV. (Given, $N_A = 6 \times 10^{23}$) **[2023, 24 Jan Shift-II]**

9 A nucleus disintegrates into two smaller parts, which have their velocities in the ratio 3 : 2. The ratio of their nuclear sizes will be $\left(\frac{x}{3}\right)^{\frac{1}{3}}$. The value of x is .... **[2023, 25 Jan Shift-II]**

10 A radioactive element $^{242}_{92}X$ emits two α-particles, one electron and two positrons. The product nucleus is represented by $^{234}_{P}Y$. The value of P is .... **[2023, 29 Jan Shift-I]**

11 For a nucleus $^{A}_{Z}X$ having mass number A and atomic number Z.

A. The surface energy per nucleon $(b_s) = -a_1 A^{2/3}$.
B. The Coulomb contribution to the binding energy, $b_c = -a_2 \frac{Z(Z-1)}{A^{4/3}}$
C. The volume energy, $b_v = a_3 A$
D. Decrease in the binding energy is proportional to surface area.
E. While estimating the surface energy, it is assumed that each nucleon interacts with 12 nucleons. (a_1, a_2 and a_3 are constants)

Choose the most appropriate answer from the options given below **[2023, 8 April Shift-I]**

(a) A, B, C, D only (b) C, D only
(c) B, C, E only (d) B, C only

12 Mass numbers of two nuclei are in the ratio of 4 : 3. Their nuclear densities will be in the ratio of **[2022, 26 July Shift-II]**

(a) 4 : 3 (b) $\left(\frac{3}{4}\right)^{1/3}$ (c) 1 : 1 (d) $\left(\frac{4}{3}\right)^{1/3}$

13 In the following nuclear reaction,

$$D \xrightarrow{\alpha} D_1 \xrightarrow{\beta^-} D_2 \xrightarrow{\alpha} D_3 \xrightarrow{\gamma} D_4$$

Mass number of D is 182 and atomic number is 74. Mass number and atomic number of D_4, respectively will be **[2022, 29 June Shift-II]**

(a) 174 and 71 (b) 174 and 69
(c) 172 and 69 (d) 172 and 71

14 Which of the following figures represents the variation of $\left(\frac{R}{R_0}\right)$ with $\ln A$ (If R = radius of a nucleus and A = its mass number)? **[2022, 25 June Shift-II]**

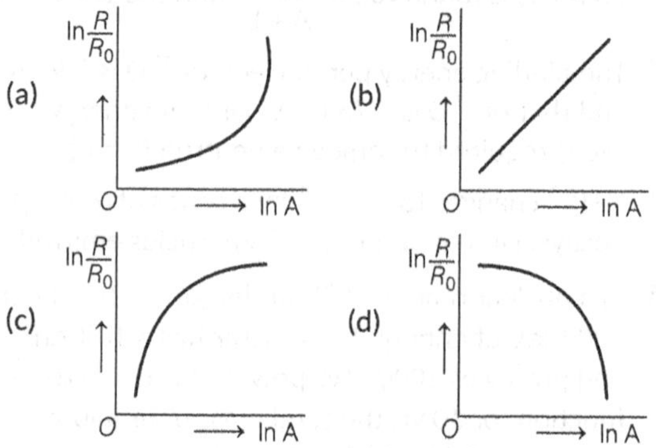

15 The decay of a proton to neutron is **[2021, 18 March Shift-II]**

(a) not possible as proton mass is less than the neutron mass
(b) possible only inside the nucleus
(c) not possible but neutron to proton conversion is possible
(d) always possible as it is associated only with β^+ decay

JEE Advanced

1. List-I shows different radioactive decay processes and List-II provides possible emitted particles match each entry in List-I with an appropriate entry from List-II, and choose the correct option.

List-I	List-II
(P) $^{238}_{92}U \rightarrow ^{234}_{91}Pa$	(1) One α-particle and one β^+-particle
(Q) $^{214}_{82}Pb \rightarrow ^{210}_{82}Pb$	(2) Three β^--particles and one α-particle
(R) $^{210}_{81}Tl \rightarrow ^{206}_{82}Pb$	(3) Two β^--particles and one α-particle
(S) $^{228}_{91}Pa \rightarrow ^{224}_{88}Ra$	(4) One α-particle and one β^--particle
	(5) One α-particle and two β^+-particles

(2023 Adv.)

Codes

	P	Q	R	S		P	Q	R	S
(a)	4	3	2	1	(b)	4	1	2	5
(c)	5	3	1	4	(d)	5	1	3	2

2. The binding energy of nucleons in a nucleus can be affected by the pairwise Coulomb repulsion. Assume that all nucleons are uniformly distributed inside the nucleus. Let the binding energy of a proton be E_b^p and the binding energy of a neutron be E_b^n in the nucleus.

Which of the following statement(s) is(are) correct? **(2022 Adv.)**

(a) $E_b^p - E_b^n$ is proportional to $Z(Z-1)$, where Z is the atomic number of the nucleus.

(b) $E_b^p - E_b^n$ is proportional to $A^{-\frac{1}{3}}$, where A is the mass number of the nucleus.

(c) $E_b^p - E_b^n$ is positive.

(d) E_b^p increases, if the nucleus undergoes a beta decay emitting a positron.

3. A heavy nucleus N, at rest, undergoes fission $N \rightarrow P + Q$, where P and Q are two lighter nuclei. Let $\delta = m_N - m_P - m_Q$, where m_P, m_Q and m_N are the masses of P, Q and N, respectively. E_P and E_Q are the kinetic energies of P and Q, respectively. The speeds of P and Q are v_P and v_Q, respectively. If c is the speed of light, which of the following statement(s) is(are) correct? **(2021 Adv.)**

(a) $E_P + E_Q = c^2\delta$

(b) $E_P = \left(\dfrac{m_P}{m_P + m_Q}\right)c^2\delta$

(c) $\dfrac{v_P}{v_Q} = \dfrac{m_Q}{m_P}$

(d) The magnitude of momentum for P as well as Q is $c\sqrt{2\mu\delta}$, where $\mu = \dfrac{m_P m_Q}{(m_P + m_Q)}$.

4. In a radioactive decay chain, $^{232}_{90}$Th nucleus decays to $^{212}_{82}$Pb nucleus. Let N_α and N_β be the number of α and β- particles respectively, emitted in this decay process. Which of the following statements is (are) true? **(2018 Adv.)**

(a) $N_\alpha = 5$ (b) $N_\alpha = 6$
(c) $N_\beta = 2$ (d) $N_\beta = 4$

5. The electrostatic energy of Z protons uniformly distributed throughout a spherical nucleus of radius R is given by

$$E = \frac{3}{5}\frac{Z(Z-1)e^2}{4\pi\varepsilon_0 R}$$

The measured masses of the particles neutron, $^1_1$H, $^{15}_7$N and $^{15}_8$O are 1.008665 u, 1.007825 u, 15.000109 u and 15.003065 u, respectively. Given that the radii of both the $^{15}_7$N and $^{15}_8$O nuclei are same, 1 u = 931.5 MeV/c^2 (c is the speed of light) and $e^2/(4\pi\varepsilon_0) = 1.44$ MeV fm. Assuming that the difference between the binding energies of $^{15}_7$N and $^{15}_8$O is purely due to the electrostatic energy, the radius of either of the nuclei is (1fm = 10^{-15} m) **(2016 Adv.)**

(a) 2.85 fm (b) 3.03 fm
(c) 3.42 fm (d) 3.80 fm

6. A fission reaction is given by $^{236}_{92}\text{U} \rightarrow {}^{140}_{54}\text{Xe} + {}^{94}_{38}\text{Sr} + x + y$, where x and y are two particles. Considering $^{236}_{92}$U to be at rest, the kinetic energies of the products are denoted by K_{Xe}, K_{Sr}, K_x (2 MeV) and K_y (2 MeV), respectively. Let the binding energies per nucleon of $^{236}_{92}$U, $^{140}_{54}$Xe and $^{94}_{38}$Sr be 7.5 MeV, 8.5 MeV and 8.5 MeV, respectively. Considering different conservation laws, the correct options is/are **(2015 Adv.)**

(a) $x = n, y = n, K_{Sr} = 129$ MeV, $K_{Xe} = 86$ MeV
(b) $x = p, y = e^-, K_{Sr} = 129$ MeV, $K_{Xe} = 86$ MeV
(c) $x = p, y = n, K_{Sr} = 129$ MeV, $K_{Xe} = 86$ MeV
(d) $x = n, y = n, K_{Sr} = 86$ MeV, $K_{Xe} = 129$ MeV

Direction (Q. NOs. 7-8) The mass of a nucleus $^A_Z X$ is less than the sum of the masses of $(A - Z)$ number of neutrons and Z number of protons in the nucleus. The energy equivalent to the corresponding mass difference is known as the binding energy of the nucleus. A heavy nucleus of mass M can break into two light nuclei of masses m_1 and m_2 only if $(m_1 + m_2) < M$. Also two light nuclei of masses m_3 and m_4 can undergo complete fusion and form a heavy nucleus of mass M' only if $(m_3 + m_4) > M'$. The masses of some neutral atoms are given in the table below

$^1_1$H	1.007825u	$^2_1$H	2.014102u
$^6_3$Li	6.01513u	$^7_3$Li	7.016004u
$^{152}_{64}$Gd	151.919803u	$^{206}_{82}$Pb	205.974455u
$^3_1$H	3.016050u	$^4_2$He	4.002603u
$^{70}_{30}$Zn	69.925325u	$^{82}_{34}$Se	81.916709u

(2013 Adv.)

7. The correct statement is
(a) The nucleus $^6_3$Li can emit an alpha particle.
(b) The nucleus $^{210}_{84}$Po can emit a proton.
(c) Deuteron and alpha particle can undergo complete fusion.
(d) The nuclei $^{70}_{30}$Zn and $^{82}_{34}$Se can undergo complete fusion.

8. The kinetic energy (in keV) of the alpha particle, when the nucleus $^{210}_{84}$Po at rest undergoes alpha decay, is
(a) 5316 (b) 5422 (c) 5707 (d) 5818

Answer Key

Level 1

10.1 Size of Nucleus

1. 4.8 fm 2. 6 fm 3. 1.8×10^{17} kg/m^3 4. 1 : 1

10.2 Binding Energy of Nucleus

1. 110 MeV 2. Stability order is Q > R > P
3. $(B_3+B_4)-(B_1+B_2)$ 4. 28.3 MeV 5. 8.547 meV
6. 7.27 MeV 7. (a) 36 MeV (b) 90 MeV (c) –36 MeV
8. 23.6 MeV 9. 11.88 MeV 10. 1.54 MeV

10.3 α-Decay, β-Decay and γ-Decay

1. 172 and 69 2. 8 alpha and 6 beta
3. (i) 4.25 MeV (ii) 4.18 MeV 4. 4.37 MeV
5. (a) 4.816 MeV (b) 3.254 MeV
6. (i) ${}_3Li^6 + {}_0n^1 \rightarrow {}_2He^4 + {}_1H^3 + Q$ (ii) 10.415 MeV
7. (a) ${}_{16}O^{32}$ (b) ${}_9F^{19}$ (c) ${}_4Be^{10}$ (d) ${}_0n^1$

10.4 Nuclear Fission and Fusion

1. 3.125×10^{13} 2. 207.9 MeV
3. (i) 200.57 MeV (ii) 22.84 MWh
4. (a) 23.83 MeV (b) 120.41 g/day 5. 1.85×10^8 years

Level 2

Single Choice Correct Questions

1. (b)	2. (b)	3. (c)	4. (d)	5. (c)
6. (c)	7. (c)	8. (c)	9. (b)	10. (c)
11. (c)	12. (a)	13. (c)	14. (c)	15. (c)
16. (b)	17. (c)	18. (b)	19. (c)	20. (a)
21. (b)	22. (a)	23. (c)	24. (c)	25. (d)
26. (d)	27. (a)	28. (c)	29. (b)	30. (b)
31. (c)	32. (b)	33. (b)	34. (b)	35. (a)
36. (b)	37. (b)	38. (b)	39. (d)	40. (c)
41. (b)	42. (c)	43. (a)	44. (c)	45. (d)
46. (d)	47. (c)	48. (c)	49. (d)	50. (c)
51. (c)				

Multiple Choice(s) Correct Questions

1. (b, d)	2. (b, c)	3. (c, d)	4. (b, d)
5. (a, b, c)	6. (c, d)	7. (b, c)	8. (a, b, c, d)
9. (a, b, c)	10. (a, b, c)	11. (a, c)	12. (a, d)
13. (a, b, c)	14. (a, b, c)		

Comprehension Based Questions

1. (b)	2. (d)	3. (c)	4. (d)	5. (d)
6. (a)	7. (b)	8. (d)	9. (c)	10. (b)
11. (a)	12. (c)	13. (a)	14. (c)	15. (b)
16. (d)	17. (b)	18. (b)	19. (b)	20. (a)
21. (c)				

Match the Columns Questions

1. A → 2, 3, 4; B → 2, 3, 4; C → 2, 3, 4; D → 1, 2, 3, 4
2. A → 1, 3, 5; B → 2, 5; C → 1, 4; D → 2,3,4,5
3. A → 1; B → 1; C → 3
4. A → 1; B → 5; C → 6, 4; D → 3
5. A → 1,2; B → 1, 3; C → 1, 4; D → 1, 2, 3

Numerical Value Questions

1. (79.3)	2. (6)	3. (4.23)	4. (7)	5. (4)
6. (14)	7. (1.88)	8. (1.32)	9. (2)	

Previous Year's Questions

JEE Main

1. (236)	2. (a)	3. (c)	4. (a)	5. (b)
6. (121)	7. (6)	8. (6)	9. (2)	10. (87)
11. (b)	12. (c)	13. (a)	14. (b)	15. (b)

JEE Advanced

1. (a)	2. (a, b, d)	3. (a, c, d)	4. (a, c,)
5. (c)	6. (a)	7. (c)	8. (a)

SOLUTIONS

Level 1

10.1 Size of Nucleus

1. $R = R_0 A^{1/3} = (1.2 \times 10^{-15})(64)^{1/3} = 4.8$ fm

2. $$R = R_o A^{1/3}$$
$$\Rightarrow \quad \frac{R_1}{R_2} = \left(\frac{A_1}{A_2}\right)^{1/3}$$
$$\Rightarrow \quad \frac{3.6}{R_2} = \left(\frac{27}{125}\right)^{1/3}$$
$$\Rightarrow \quad R_2 = 6 \text{ fm}$$

3. $$\text{Density} = \frac{\text{Mass}}{\text{Volume}} = \frac{A(1.67 \times 10^{-27})}{\frac{4}{3}\pi(1.3 \times 10^{-15} A^{1/3})^3}$$
$$= 1.8 \times 10^{17} \text{ kg/m}^3$$

4. Density of nucleus is independent of mass number. Density is constant for all nuclei.
So, ratio of nuclear densities will be 1 : 1.

10.2 Binding Energy of Nucleus

1. After releasing 10 MeV, it will become more stable and hence its binding energy will increase.
New binding energy = 100 + 10 = 110 MeV.

2. Stability $\propto$ Binding energy per nucleon.
$$\left(\frac{BE}{A}\right)_P = \frac{100}{10} = 10; \left(\frac{BE}{A}\right)_Q = \frac{60}{5} = 12$$
$$\left(\frac{BE}{A}\right)_R = \frac{66}{6} = 11$$
So, Stability order, $Q > R > P$

3. Energy released = Binding energy of products – Binding energy of reactants $= B_3 + B_4 - (B_1 + B_2)$

4. α-particle contains 2 protons and 2 neutrons
Mass defect, $\Delta m = [Zm_p + (A - Z)m_n] - M_{nucleus}$
$= [2(1.007826) + 2(1.008665)] - (4.00260)$
$= 0.030382$u
Binding energy $= \Delta mc^2 = (0.030382 \text{ u})(931 \text{ MeV/u})$
$= 28.3$ MeV

5. $\Delta m = [Zm_P + (A - Z)m_n] - M_{nucleus}$
$= [20(1.007825) + 20(1.008665)] - 39.962589$
$= 0.367211$ u
Binding energy $= \Delta mc^2 = (0.367211 \text{ u})(931 \text{ MeV/u})$
$= 341.87$ MeV
Binding energy per nucleon $= \frac{341.87}{40} = 8.547$ MeV

6. $\Delta m = 3$ (Mass of ${}^4_2$He nucleus) – Mass of ${}^{12}_6$C nucleus
$= 3$ (Mass of ${}^4_2$He nucleus $+ 2m_e$)
– (Mass of ${}^{12}_6$C nucleus $+ 6m_e$)
$= 3$ (Mass of ${}^4_2$He atom) – Mass of ${}^{12}_6$C atom
$= 3(4.002603) - 12 = 0.007809$ u
Energy released $= \Delta mc^2 = 0.007809 \times 931 = 7.27$ MeV

7. Q-value $= (BE)_{products} - (BE)_{reactants}$
(a) Q-Value $= 2(60 \times 8.7) - 120 \times 8.4 = 36$ MeV
(b) Q-Value $= (60 \times 8.7 + 120 \times 8.4) - 180 \times 8 = 90$ MeV
(c) Q-Value $= 2(30 \times 8.1) - 60 \times 8.7 = -36$ MeV

8. $2\,{}_1H^2 \longrightarrow {}^4_2He$
Energy released $= (BE)_{Products} - (BE)_{reactants}$
$= 4 \times 7.0 - 2(2 \times 1.1)$
$= 23.6$ MeV

9. ${}_{10}Ne^{20} \longrightarrow 2\,{}_2He^4 + {}^{12}_6C$
Energy required $= (BE)_{reactants} - (BE)_{Products}$
$= 20 \times 8.03 - (2 \times 4 \times 7.07 + 12 \times 7.68)$
$= 11.88$ MeV

10. ${}^{14}_7N + {}^4_2He \longrightarrow {}^{17}_8O + {}^1_1H$
$Q = (14.00307 + 4.00260 - 1.00783 - 16.99913)(931.5)$
$= -1.20$ MeV
Since, Q-value is negative, reaction is endothermic.
So, the minimum kinetic energy of α- particle to initiate the reaction will be
$$K_{min} = |Q|\left(\frac{m_\alpha}{m_N} + 1\right) = 1.20\left(\frac{4.00260}{14.00307} + 1\right) = 1.54 \text{ MeV}$$

10.3 α- Decay, β-Decay and γ -Decay

1. $${}^{180}_{72}A \xrightarrow{\alpha} {}^{176}_{70}A_1 \xrightarrow{\beta} {}^{176}_{71}A_2 \xrightarrow{\alpha} {}^{172}_{69}A_3 \xrightarrow{\gamma} {}^{172}_{69}A_4$$
For each α-decay, atomic number decreases by 2 and atomic mass number decreases by 4.
For each β-decay, atomic number increases by 1 and atomic mass number remains unchanged.
In γ-decay, both atomic number and atomic mass number remain unchanged.

2. Let number of α-Particles be n_1 and β -particles n_2
$$92 - n_1(2) + n_2(1) = 82$$
$$\Rightarrow \quad 2n_1 - n_2 = 10 \quad \text{...(i)}$$
$$238 - n_1(4) = 206$$
$$\Rightarrow \quad n_1 = 8 \quad \text{...(ii)}$$
Solving, we get $n_1 = 8$ and $n_2 = 6$

3. (i) $Q = \Delta mc^2 = (M_X - M_Y - M_{He})c^2$
$= (238.05079 - 234.04363 - 4.00260)\,931.5$
$= 4.25$ MeV

(ii) $\frac{K_\alpha}{K_Y} = \frac{m_Y}{m_\alpha} \Rightarrow K_\alpha = \left(\frac{m_Y}{m_Y + m_\alpha}\right)Q$

$= \left(\frac{234.04363}{234.04363 + 4.00260}\right)4.25 = 4.18$ MeV

4. Q-Value $= (M_X - M_Y)c^2$
$= (22.994466 - 22.989770)931.5$
$= 4.37$ MeV

Maximum kinetic energy of electron will be 4.37 MeV if daughter nucleus and anti-neutrino carry negligible kinetic energy.

5. (a) For β^- decay,
Q-value $= (M_X - M_Y)c^2 = (19.003576 - 18.998403)(931)$
$= 4.816$ MeV

(b) For β^+ decay
Q-value $= (M_X - M_Y - 2m_e)c^2$
$= (M_X - M_Y)c^2 - 2m_ec^2$
$= (24.990432 - 24.985839)(931) - 2\left(0.511\frac{\text{MeV}}{c^2}\right)c^2$
$= (4.276 - 1.022)$ MeV
$= 3.254$ MeV

6. (i) ${}^6_3\text{Li} + {}^1_0 n \longrightarrow {}^3_1\text{H} + {}^4_2\text{He} + Q$

(ii) Q-value
$= (M_{{}^6_3\text{Li}} + M_n - M_{{}^3_1\text{H}} - M_{{}^4_2\text{He}})c^2$
$= (6.015126 + 1.0086654 - 3.0100000 - 4.0026044)\,(931)$
$= 10.415$ MeV

7. (a) ${}^A_Z X + {}^1_0 n \longrightarrow {}^1_1 P + {}^{32}_{15} P$
$Z + 0 = 1 + 15 \Rightarrow Z = 16$
$A + 1 = 1 + 32 \Rightarrow A = 32$
So, X will be ${}^{32}_{16}$O.

(b) ${}^A_Z X + {}^1_1 p \longrightarrow {}^4_2\text{He} + {}^{16}_8\text{O}$
$Z + 1 = 2 + 8 \Rightarrow Z = 9$
$A + 1 = 4 + 16 \Rightarrow A = 19$
So, X will be ${}^{19}_9$F

(c) ${}^9_4\text{Be} + {}^1_0 n \longrightarrow {}^0_0\gamma + {}^A_Z X$
$4 + 0 = 0 + Z \Rightarrow Z = 4$
$9 + 1 = 0 + A \Rightarrow A = 10$
So, X ill be ${}^{10}_4$Be

(d) ${}^{14}_7\text{N} + {}^A_Z X \longrightarrow {}^1_1\text{P} + {}^{14}_6\text{C}$
$7 + Z = 1 + 6 \Rightarrow Z = 0$
$14 + A = 1 + 14 \Rightarrow A = 1$
So, X will ${}^1_0 n$.

10.4 Nuclear Fission and Fusion

1. Number of fission per second
$= \frac{1 \times 10^3}{200 \times 10^6 \times 1.6 \times 10^{-19}}$
$= 3.125 \times 10^{13}$

2. ${}^{235}_{92}\text{U} + {}^1_0 n \longrightarrow {}^{95}_{42}\text{Mo} + {}^{139}_{57}\text{La} + 2\,{}^1_0 n$
Q-Value $= (M({}^{235}_{92}\text{U}) - M({}^{95}_{42}\text{Mo}) - M({}^{139}_{27}\text{La}) - M({}^1_0 n))c^2$
$= (235.0439 - 94.9058 - 138.9061 - 1.0087)931$
$= 207.9$ MeV

3. (i) $E = (M({}^{235}_{92}\text{U}) - M({}^{141}_{56}\text{Ba}) - M({}^{92}_{36}\text{Kr}) - 2M({}^1_0 n))c^2$
$= [235.1175 - 140.9577 - 91.9264 - 2\,(1.00898)]931$
$= 200.57$ MeV

(ii) Energy released
$= \left(\frac{1}{235} \times 6.022 \times 10^{23}\right)(200.57 \times 10^6 \times 1.6 \times 10^{-19})$
$= 8.225 \times 10^{10}\,\text{J} = 22.84$ MWh

4. (a) Q-value $= [(2M({}^2_1\text{H}) - M({}^4_2\text{He}))c^2$
$= [2(2.0141)\,\text{u} - 4.0026\text{u})(931\ \text{MeV/u})$
$= 23.83$ MeV

(b) Let, x gm of deuterium be needed per day
Number of deuterium atoms $= \frac{x}{2} \times 6.022 \times 10^{23}$
Number of reactions $= \frac{1}{2}\left(\frac{x}{2} \times 6.022 \times 10^{23}\right)$
Energy produced per day $= (200 \times 10^6 \times 24 \times 3600)$ J
$200 \times 10^6 \times 24 \times 3600 = \frac{1}{2}\left(\frac{x}{2} \times 6.022 \times 10^{23}\right)$
$\times 23.83 \times 10^6 \times 1.6 \times 10^{-19} \times \frac{25}{100}$
$\Rightarrow x = 120.41$ gm

5. $E = \left(\frac{5 \times 10^{32}}{4 \times 10^{-3}} \times 6.022 \times 10^{23}\right)\left(\frac{1}{3}\right)(7.27 \times 10^6 \times 1.6 \times 10^{-19})$
$= 2.918 \times 10^{46}$ J
Time $= \frac{\text{Energy}}{\text{Power}} = \frac{2.918 \times 10^{46}}{5 \times 10^{30}} = 5.836 \times 10^{15}$ s
$= 1.85 \times 10^8$ yr

Level 2

Single Choice Correct Questions

1. $R = R_oA^{1/3}$
$\Rightarrow \frac{R_1}{R_2} = \left(\frac{A_1}{A_2}\right)^{1/3} \Rightarrow \frac{3}{5} = \left(\frac{27}{A}\right)^{1/3}$
$\Rightarrow A = 125$
Number of neutrons $= A - Z = 125 - 52 = 73$

2. $0 = M_1v_1 + M_2(-v_2)$

$\Rightarrow \quad \dfrac{v_1}{v_2} = \dfrac{M_2}{M_1}$

$R = R_0A^{1/3}$

$\Rightarrow \quad \dfrac{R_1}{R_2} = \left(\dfrac{A_1}{A_2}\right)^{1/3} = \left(\dfrac{M_1}{M_2}\right)^{1/3} = \left(\dfrac{v_2}{v_1}\right)^{1/3} = 1:2^{1/3}$

3. Density of a nucleus is constant.

So, $V \propto m$

4. (d)

5. Mass of nucleus is less than the sum of the masses of its constituents.

6. Binding Energy $= (2m_p + 2m_n - m_{He})c^2$

$= (2 \times 1.007277 + 2 \times 1.00866 - 4.001256)u \times 931$ MeV/u

$= 28.52$ MeV

7. Binding Energy $= (4m_p + 5m_n - m_{Be})c^2$

$= [4(1.008) + 5(1.009) - 9.012]u \times 931.5$ MeV

$= 60.547$ MeV

Binding energy per nucleon $= \dfrac{60.547}{9} = 6.727$ MeV

8. Binding energy per nucleon of ^4_2He, ^7_3Li, $^{12}_6C$ and $^{14}_7N$ are $\dfrac{28}{4}$MeV, $\dfrac{52}{7}$MeV, $\dfrac{90}{12}$MeV and $\dfrac{98}{14}$MeV respectively.

Binding energy per nucleon is maximum for $^{12}_6C$. So, $^{12}_6C$ is most stable.

9. Energy released $= (BE)_{products} - (BE)_{reactants}$

$= 2(7 \times 4) - (2 \times 1 + 7 \times 5.5) = 15.5$ MeV

10. (a) $Y \rightarrow 2Z$, $Q = 2(30 \times 5) - 60 \times 8.5 = -210$ MeV

(b) $W \rightarrow Y + Z$, $Q = [60(8.5) + 30(5)] - 120 \times 7.5 = -240$ MeV

(c) $W \rightarrow 2Y$, $Q = 2(60 \times 8.5) - 120 \times 7.5 = 120$ MeV

(d) $X \rightarrow Y + Z$, $Q = 60 \times 8.5 + 30 \times 5 - 90 \times 8 = -60$ MeV

Q-value is positive for $W \rightarrow 2Y$. So, it will be exothermic reaction.

11. $3Q \longrightarrow P$

Energy released $= e = (BE)_{products} - (BE)_{reactants}$

$\Rightarrow \quad e = E_P - 3E_Q \quad \Rightarrow \quad E_P = 3E_Q + e$

12. Energy released $= (BE)_{products} - (BE)_{reactants}$

$= (110 \times 8.2 + 90 \times 8.1) - 200 \times 7.4 = 151$ MeV

13. Energy released $= (BE)_{products} - (BE)_{reactants}$

$= (80 \times 7 + 120 \times 8) - 200 \times 6.5 = 220$ MeV

14. Energy of proton $= (BE)_{He} - (BE)_{Li}$

$= 2 \times 4 \times 7.06 - 7 \times 5.60$

$= 17.28$ MeV

15. Energy released $= (BE)_{products} - (BE)_{reactants}$

$= (111 \times 8.6 + 122 \times 8.5) - 236 \times 7.6$

$= 198$ MeV

16. Q-Value $= (BE)_{products} - (BE)_{reactants}$

$\Rightarrow \quad 3.27 = $ BE of $_2He^3 - 2 \times 2.23$

$\Rightarrow$ BE of $_2He^3 = 7.73$ MeV

17. Let number of α-particles be n_1 and β^--particle n_2.

$226 - n_1(4) = 206 \quad \Rightarrow \quad n_1 = 5$

$88 - 2n_1 + n_2(1) = 82 \quad \Rightarrow \quad n_2 = 4$

18. Isotopes have same atomic number. For each α-decay, atomic number decreases by 2 and for each β^--decay, atomic number increases by one.

19. Number of α-decay $= 8$

Number of β^--decay $= 4$

Number of β^+-decay $= 2$

New atomic number $= 92 - 8(2) + 4(1) - 2(1) = 78$

20. (a)

21. $^{14}_7N + ^4_2He \longrightarrow ^{17}_8O + ^A_ZX$

$7 + 2 = 8 + Z \quad \Rightarrow \quad Z = 1$

$14 + 4 = 17 + A \quad \Rightarrow \quad A = 1$

So, X is ^1_1P (Proton).

22. The first process is α-decay. So, A loses two protons.
The second process is β^--decay. So, C gains two protons.
Hence, atomic number Z is same for A and C and thus they are isotopes.

23. $_4Be^7 \longrightarrow ^7_3Li + ^A_ZX$

$4 = 3 + Z \quad \Rightarrow \quad Z = 1$

$7 = 7 + A \quad \Rightarrow \quad A = 0$

So, X is $^0_{+1}e$ (Positron)

24. $^A_ZX + ^1_0n \longrightarrow ^7_3Li + ^4_2He$

$Z + 0 = 3 + 2 \quad \Rightarrow \quad Z = 5$

$A + 1 = 7 + 4 \quad \Rightarrow \quad A = 10$

So, X will be $^{10}_5B$

25. $^A_ZX + ^1_0n \longrightarrow 2^4_2He + ^0_{-1}e$

$Z + 0 = 2(2) + (-1) \quad \Rightarrow \quad Z = 3$

$A + 1 = 2(4) + 0 \quad \Rightarrow \quad A = 7$

So, X will be ^7_3Li.

26. Expected atomic mass of Cu must be less than that of Zinc, but it is not. So, thats why Cu is radioactive and unstable and decays to Zn though β-decay.

27. (a) **28.** (c)

29. $\dfrac{K_\alpha}{K_Y} = \dfrac{m_Y}{m_\alpha}$ and $K_\alpha + K_Y = Q$

So, we get

$K_\alpha = \left(\dfrac{m_Y}{m_Y + m_\alpha}\right)Q = \left(\dfrac{216}{216 + 4}\right)5.5 = 5.4$ MeV

30. $K_\alpha = \left(\dfrac{A - 4}{A}\right)Q$

$\Rightarrow \quad 48 = \left(\dfrac{A - 4}{A}\right)50 \quad \Rightarrow \quad A = 100$

31. Q-Value $= K_\alpha - K_d = 2(13.2) - 4 = 22.4$ MeV

32. (b)

33. $E = \Delta mc^2 = [m_n - (m_P + m_e)]c^2$

$= (1.0087 - 1.0073 - 0.0005)\text{u} \times 931$ MeV/u

$= 0.0009 \times 931$ MeV $= 0.84$ MeV

34. ${}^7_4\text{Be} + {}^{0}_{-1}e \longrightarrow {}^7_3\text{Li} + \nu$

Energy of neutrinos $= (m_{\text{Be}} - m_{\text{Li}})c^2$

$= (7.016929 - 7.016004)\,u \times 931.5$ MeV/u

$= 0.9$ MeV

35. Q-Value $= (M_{{}^3_1\text{H}} - M_{{}^3_2\text{He}})c^2 = (3.016050 - 3.016030)$

$u \times 931.5$ MeV/u $= 0.0186$ MeV $= 18.6$ keV

If daughter nucleus and anti-neutrino carry negligible kinetic energy, then maximum energy of electron will be 18.6 keV.

36. $E = (m_P + m_n - m_d)c^2$

$= (1.0078 + 1.0087 - 2.0141)\text{u} \times 931.5$ MeV/u

$= 2.2356$ MeV

$$E = h\nu \Rightarrow \nu = \frac{E}{h} = \frac{2.2356 \times 10^6 \times 1.6 \times 10^{-19}}{6.6 \times 10^{-34}} = 5.4 \times 10^{20}\ \text{Hz}$$

37. $m_e = m_{\text{position}} = 0.000548$ u

Energy released $= \Delta mc^2$

$= (0.000548 + 0.000548)\text{u} \times 931.5$ MeV

$= 1.02$ MeV

So, energy of each γ-ray photon

$$= \frac{1.02 \times 10^6 \times 1.6 \times 10^{-19}}{2} = 8.2 \times 10^{-14}\ \text{J}$$

38. Energy required $= (M_{\text{U}235} + M_n - M_{\text{U}236})c^2$

$= (235.12142 + 1.008665 - 236.1205)\text{u} \times 931.5$ MeV/u

$= 8.9$ MeV $\simeq 6.5$ MeV

39. For separation of about 1 fm, nuclear force between the nucleons is significantly larger than electrostatic force and nuclear force is always attractive in nature. Nuclear force is independent of charge on nucleon.

Same nuclear force acts between proton and proton, neutron and proton, neutron and neutron. The repulsive electrostatic force acts only between two protons. So, net force exerted by one proton on another proton is reduced as electrostatic repulsion reduces net attractive force between the two protons.

So, $F_{PP} < F_{Pn} = F_{nn}$

40. (c)

41. Energy produced per day = Power × time

$= (10^6 \times 24 \times 60 \times 60)$ J

$$\text{Number of fissions per day} = \frac{10^6 \times 24 \times 60 \times 60}{200 \times 10^6 \times 1.6 \times 10^{-19}}$$

$= 2.7 \times 10^{21}$

$$\text{Mass of U}^{235}\text{ consumed per day} = \frac{2.7 \times 10^{21}}{6 \times 10^{23}} \times 235 = 1.05\ \text{gm}$$

42. Q-value $= (2M_d - M_{\text{He}} - M_n)c^2$

$= (2 \times 2.015 - 3.017 - 1.009)\,u \times 931$ MeV/u

$= 3.724$ MeV

Energy released

$$= \left(\frac{1}{2 \times 10^{-3}} \times 6 \times 10^{23}\right)\left(\frac{1}{2}\right)(3.724 \times 10^6 \times 1.6 \times 10^{-19})$$

$= 9 \times 10^{13}$ J

43. Number of fission reactions

$$= \frac{2 \times 10^3}{235} \times 6 \times 10^{23} = 5.1 \times 10^{24}$$

Energy produced $= 5.1 \times 10^{24} \times (185 \times 10^6 \times 1.6 \times 10^{-19})$

$= 1.509 \times 10^{14}$ J

$$\text{Power} = \frac{\text{Energy}}{\text{Time}} = \frac{1.509 \times 10^{14}}{30 \times 24 \times 3600} = 5.85 \times 10^7\ \text{W}$$

44. Energy generated in one year

= power × time

$= (250 \times 10^6) \times (365 \times 24 \times 3600)$

$= 7.884 \times 10^{15}$ J

Energy Obtained from one fission

$$= (200 \times 10^6 \times 1.6 \times 10^{-19}) \times \frac{25}{100} = 8 \times 10^{-12}\ \text{J}$$

$$\text{Number of fissions} = \frac{7.884 \times 10^{15}}{8 \times 10^{-12}} = 9.855 \times 10^{26}$$

Mass of U^{235} required per year

$$= \frac{9.855 \times 10^{26}}{6.023 \times 10^{23}} \times 235 = 384.4\ \text{kg}$$

45. (d)

46. Total rest mass energy of proton and neutron

$= 939 + 940 = 1879$ MeV

Rest mass energy of deuteron = 1876 MeV

$\Delta E = E_{p+n} - E_d = 1879 - 1876 = 3$ MeV

As $E_{p+n} > E_d$, a deuteron should capture a γ-ray photon of energy 3 MeV to disintegrate into a proton and a neutron.

47. Kinetic energy of gas molecules $= \frac{3}{2}KT$

To initiate the reaction.

$$\frac{3}{2}KT = 7.7 \times 10^{-14} \Rightarrow T \simeq 10^9\ \text{K}$$

48. Adding both the reactions, we get

$$3\,{}^2_1\text{H} \longrightarrow {}^4_2\text{He} + P + n$$

Q-value $= [3M({}^2_1\text{H}) - M({}^4_2\text{He}) - M_P - M_n]c^2$

$= (3 \times 2.014 - 4.001 - 1.007 - 1.008)\,u \times 931.5$ MeV/u

$= 24.219$ MeV

This is energy released by 3 deuterons.

Energy released by 10^{40} deuterons

$$= \frac{1}{3} \times 10^{40} \times 24.219 = 8.073 \times 10^{40}\ \text{MeV}$$

$$\text{Time} = \frac{\text{Energy}}{\text{Power}} = \frac{8.073 \times 10^{40} \times 10^6 \times 1.6 \times 10^{-19}}{10^{16}} \simeq 10^{12}\ \text{s}$$

49. The complete fission reaction is

$${}^{235}_{92}U + {}^{1}_{0}n \longrightarrow {}^{94}_{40}Zr + {}^{140}_{58}Ce + 2{}^{1}_{0}n + 6\,{}^{0}_{-1}e$$

$$Q = [m({}^{235}U) - m({}^{94}Zr) - m({}^{140}Ce) - m(n)]c^2$$

$$= (235.439 - 93.9064 - 139.9055 - 1.00866) \times 931$$

$$= 575.7 \text{ MeV}$$

50. The Q-value of the first reaction implies that

$${}^{14}N + d = {}^{15}N + p + 8.53 \text{ MeV}$$

Where ${}^{14}N$ represents the mass of ${}^{14}N$ nucleus in energy units. This can be rearranged to give

$${}^{14}N - {}^{15}N = p - d + 8.53 \text{ MeV} \quad ...(i)$$

Similarly, $${}^{15}N - {}^{13}C = \alpha - d + 7.58 \text{ MeV} \quad ...(ii)$$

$${}^{13}C - {}^{11}B = \alpha - d + 5.16 \text{ MeV} \quad ...(iii)$$

Adding Eqs. (i), (ii) and (iii), we get

$${}^{14}N - {}^{11}B = p + 2\alpha - 3d + 21.27 \text{ MeV}$$

$${}^{11}B(\alpha, n){}^{14}N = {}^{11}B - {}^{14}N + \alpha - n$$

$$= -(p + 2\alpha - 3d + 21.27\text{MeV}) + \alpha - n$$

$$= 3d - \alpha - p - n - 21.27 \text{ MeV}$$

Now, $3d - \alpha - p - n$

$$= (3 \times 2.014 - 4.0026 - 1.0078 - 1.0087) \text{ amu}$$

$$= 0.0229 \text{ amu}$$

$$Q = (0.0229 \times 931 - 21.27) \text{ MeV} = 0.05 \text{ MeV}$$

51. $\Delta m = (197.968225 - 197.966752)\,u \times 931.5$ MeV/u

$= 1.372$ MeV

Energy of γ-photon $= 0.412$ MeV

Maximum kinetic energy of electron

$$= 1.372 - 0.412 = 0.960 \text{ MeV}$$

Multiple Choice(s) Correct Questions

1. (b, d) **2.** (b, c)

3. (d) Mass of a nucleus is always less than the sum of masses of its constituent particles.

${}^{20}_{10}Ne$ is made up of 10 protons and 10 neutrons. Therefore, mass of ${}^{20}_{10}Ne$ nucleus

$$M_1 < 10(m_p + m_n)$$

(c) Also, heavier the nucleus, more is the mass defect.

$$20(m_p + m_n) - M_2 > 10(m_p + m_n) - M_1$$

Thus, $10(m_p + m_n) > M_2 - M_1$

$\Rightarrow$ $M_2 < M_1 + 10(m_p + m_n)$

Now since, $M_1 < 10(m_p + m_n)$

$\therefore$ $M_2 < 2M_1$

4. In fusion, two or more lighter nuclei combine to make a comparatively heavier nucleus. In fission, a heavy nucleus breaks into two or more comparatively lighter nuclei. Further, energy will be released in a nuclear process if total binding energy increases.

Hence, correct options are (b) and (d).

5. (a, b, c) **6.** (c, d)

7. (a) The ${}^{4}_{2}He$ nucleus is exceptionally stable and has a much higher value of BE per nucleon than that for most other light nuclei.

(b) This statement is correct but the reason of decrease in binding energy is different for the cases of smaller and larger values of A. The reason for the decrease in the BE per nucleon for nuclei with large A is that with an increase in the number of protons, the coulomb repulsion increases.

On the other hand, the decrease in the BE per nucleon for nuclei with small A is due to a surface effect, the nucleons at the surface being less strongly bounded than those in the interior.

(c) The energy required to remove one neutron (i.e. one nucleon) is the same as the binding energy per nucleon for a given isotope.

(d) To ensure both charge and mass number conservation, a proton must be produced as a by product of the reaction.

$${}^{2}_{1}D + {}^{2}_{1}D \longrightarrow {}^{3}_{1}T + {}^{1}_{1}P + Q$$

8. (a) $K_\alpha + K_Y = Q$ and $\dfrac{K_\alpha}{K_Y} = \dfrac{m_Y}{m_\alpha}$

$$K_\alpha > K_Y$$

$\because$ $\{m_Y > m_\alpha\}$

(b) $K_{e^-} + K_{\bar{\nu}} = Q$

(c) $K_\alpha = \left(\dfrac{A-4}{A}\right)Q \simeq Q$

(d) $K_\beta + K_{\bar{\nu}} = Q$

Energy released is randomly divided between β-particle and antineutrino. So, β-particles may have widely different speeds.

9. (a) $K_\beta + K_{\bar{\nu}} = E,$

So, KE of β-particle can't exceed E.

(b) Energy released is randomly divided between β-particle and anti-neutrino. So, KE of anti-neutrino lies between zero and E.

(c) A neutron converts into proton.

10. If the nuclear reaction involving β-decay is $n \longrightarrow p + e^{-1}$, the spins on two sides are not equals as all the three (neutron, proton and electron) have spins of $\pm\frac{1}{2}$. So, to conserve, spin angular momentum, some other particle must be emitted.

Through experiments it has been observed the direction of emitted electron and recoiling nuclei are almost never exactly opposite as required for linear momentum to be conserved.

During β-decay, the energy of electron is found to vary continuously from 0 to a maximum value (this maximum value is a characteristic of nuclide). To explain this experimental observation we also need some other particle.

11. (a) $\dfrac{K_\alpha}{K_{Th}} = \dfrac{m_{Th}}{m_\alpha} = \dfrac{234}{4} = \dfrac{117}{2}$

(c) $K_\alpha = \left(\dfrac{m_{Th}}{m_{Th} + m_\alpha}\right)Q = \left(\dfrac{234}{234 + 4}\right)Q = \dfrac{117Q}{119}$

$$p_\alpha = \sqrt{2m_\alpha K_\alpha} = \sqrt{\frac{234Qm_\alpha}{119}}$$

(d) $|p_{Th}| = |P_\alpha|$

$$\Rightarrow \quad m_{Th}v_{Th} = \sqrt{\frac{234Qm_\alpha}{119}}$$

$$\Rightarrow \quad v_{Th} = \sqrt{\frac{234Q}{119}\left(\frac{m_\alpha}{m_{Th}^2}\right)}$$

12. (a) For an exothermic reaction, $X + x \longrightarrow Y + y$

If K_i is the kinetic energy of incident particle x, then from energy conservation,

$$K_i + (m_x + M_X)c^2 = K_Y + K_y + (M_Y + m_y)c^2$$

$$\Rightarrow \quad K_Y + K_y = K_i + (m_x + M_X - M_Y - m_y)c^2$$

$$\Rightarrow \quad K_Y + K_y = K_i + Q$$

(c) For endothermic reaction to be carried out, minimum energy given to the reactant must be greater than $|Q|$ value of reaction.

(d) In any exothermic reaction, mass of products is less than the mass of reactants i.e., in product the nucleons are more tightly bound and hence have greater BE per nucleon as compared to BE per nucleon of reactants.

13. In general, fission and fusion processes are exothermic reactions, i.e., energy is released. Hence, mass of products must be less than mass of the reactant nuclide, and $\frac{BE}{A}$ of reactants $< \frac{BE}{A}$ of product nuclide.

14. The amount of energy released per unit mass of the fuel is much more for fusion than for fission. Hence, option -d is incorrect.

Comprehension Based Questions

1. 2nd stage of fusion reaction,

$$_1T^3 + {}_1D^2 \longrightarrow {}_2He^4 + {}_0n^1$$

Energy released $= [m({}_1T^3) + m({}_1D^2) - m({}_2He^4) - m(n)]c^2$

$= (3.016049 + 2.014102 - 4.002603 - 1.008665)$

$\text{u} \times 931$ MeV/u $= 17.580$ MeV

2. 1st stage of fusion reaction,

$$2\,{}_1D^2 \longrightarrow {}_1T^3 + {}_1P^1$$

Adding both the reactions, we get

$$3\,{}_1D^2 \longrightarrow {}_2He^4 + {}_0n^1 + {}_1P^1$$

Energy released $= [3m({}_1D^2) - m({}_2He^4) - m({}_0n^1) - m({}_1P^1))c^2$

$= [3 \times 2.014102 - 4.002603 - 1.008665 - 1.007825]$

$\text{u} \times 931$ MeV/u $= 21.611$ MeV

Energy released per deuterium $= \frac{21.611}{3} = 7.204$ MeV

3. % of the mass energy of the initial deuterium released

$$= \frac{7.204}{(2.014102 \times 931)} \times 100 = 0.384\%$$

4. Q-value $= \Delta mc^2 = [m({}_{79}Au^{198}) - m({}_{80}Hg^{198})]c^2$

$= (197.9682 - 197.9662)\text{u} \times 930$ MeV/u

$= 1.86$ MeV

Daughter nucleus is formed in the first excited state. It will jump to ground state by emitting a gamma ray photon of energy ΔE.

$$\Delta E = E_2 - E_1 = -1.6 - (-2) = 0.4 \text{ MeV/u}$$

Q-value $= K_{\beta_2} + \Delta E$

$$\Rightarrow \quad 1.86 = K_{\beta_2} + 0.4 \Rightarrow K_{\beta_2} = 1.46 \text{ MeV}$$

5. Q-value $= K_{\beta_1} + \Delta E$

$$\Rightarrow \quad 1.86 = K_{\beta_1} + [-1 - (-2)]$$

$$\Rightarrow \quad K_{\beta_1} = 0.86 \text{ MeV}$$

6. $\lambda = \frac{hC}{\Delta E} \Rightarrow \lambda \propto \frac{1}{\Delta E}$

For γ_1, $\Delta E = E_3 - E_1 = 1$ MeV

For γ_2, $\Delta E = E_2 - E_1 = 0.4$ MeV

For γ_3, $\Delta E = E_3 - E_2 = 0.6$ MeV

So, $\quad \lambda_{\gamma_2} > \lambda_{\gamma_3} > \lambda_{\gamma_1}$

7. $p_\alpha = \frac{h}{\lambda} = \frac{6.63 \times 10^{-34}}{5.76 \times 10^{-15}} = 1.15 \times 10^{-19}\text{kgms}^{-1}$

$$K_\alpha = \frac{p_\alpha^2}{2m_\alpha} = \frac{(1.15 \times 10^{-19})^2}{2(4.002 \times 1.66 \times 10^{-27})}$$

$= 9.95 \times 10^{-13}$ J

$= 6.22$ MeV

8. $\frac{K_\alpha}{K_Y} = \frac{m_Y}{m_\alpha}$

$$\Rightarrow K_Y = K_\alpha\left(\frac{m_\alpha}{m_Y}\right) = 6.22\left(\frac{4.002}{223.610}\right) = 0.11 \text{ MeV}$$

9. Q-value $= \Delta mc^2 = K_\alpha + K_Y$

$$\Rightarrow \quad (m_X - m_Y - m_\alpha)c^2 = K_\alpha + K_Y$$

$$\Rightarrow \quad (m_X - 223.610 - 4.002)\text{u} \times 931 \text{ MeV/u}$$

$= 6.22$ MeV $+ 0.11$ MeV

$$\Rightarrow \quad m_X = 227.618 \text{ amu}$$

10. $W \longrightarrow X + Y$

Q-value $= BE_{products} - BE_{reactants}$

$= (N_3E_3 + N_2E_2) - N_1E_1$

$= E_2N_2 + E_3N_3 - E_1N_1$

11. Heavier nuclei have larger mass per nucleon due to large number of neutrons.

12. For nuclei heavier than Z, binding energy per nucleon decreases but total binding energy will increase with atomic mass number.

13. Q-Value $= [m(p) + m({}_1^3H) - 2m({}_1^2H)]c^2$

$= (1.007285 + 3.016049 - 2(2.014102))u \times 931.5$ MeV

$= -4.033$ MeV

When protons are incident on ${}_1^3H$

$$K_{Th} = \left(1 + \frac{m({}_1^1H)}{m({}_1^3H)}\right)|Q| = \left(1 + \frac{1.007825}{3.016049}\right)4.033 = 5.4 \text{ MeV}$$

14. When ${}_1^3H$ are incident on protons,

$$K_{th} = \left[1 + \frac{m({}_1^3H)}{m({}_1^1H)}\right]|Q| = \left(1 + \frac{3.016049}{1.007825}\right)(4.033) = 16 \text{ MeV}$$

15. (b) **16.** (d)

17. According to the passage, K–capture happens under the same condition which promotes positron decay, that is, proton rich nuclei. That is to say, nuclei with more protons than neutrons have a negative $N - Z$ value.

18. According to the passage, the possibility of electron capture is non-zero, only if there is some overlap of the electron wave function and the nucleus. If the orbital has vanishing amplitude near the nucleus, the probability of capture is small.

19. Energy supplied per day = Power × time

$$= 300 \times 10^6 \times 24 \times 3600$$

Let number of events per day = n

$$n \times 200 \times 10^6 \times 1.6 \times 10^{-19} \times \frac{25}{100} = 300 \times 10^6 \times 24 \times 3600$$

$$\Rightarrow \quad n = 3.24 \times 10^{24}$$

20. Mass of $U^{235} = \frac{3.24 \times 10^{24}}{6.023 \times 10^{23}} \times 235 = 1264 \text{ gm} = 1.264 \text{ kg}$

21. $m = \frac{1.264 \times 30}{\left(\frac{3}{100}\right)} = 1264 \text{ kg}$

Match the Columns Questions

1. (A) In the given spontaneous radioactive decay, the number of protons remain constant and all conservation principles are obeyed.

(B) In fusion reaction of two hydrogen nuclei, a proton is decreased as positron shall be emitted in the reaction. All the three conservation principles are obeyed.

(C) In the given fission reaction, the number of protons remain constant and all conservation principles are obeyed.

(D) In beta negative decay, a neutron transform into a proton within the nucleus and the electron is ejected out.

2. (A) 1, 3, 5 (B) 2, 5
(C) 1, 4 (D) 2, 3, 4, 5

3. (A) ${}^A_Z X + {}^0_{-1} e \longrightarrow {}^A_{Z-1} Y + \nu$

$$Q = \Delta mc^2 = [((m_X - Zm_e) + m_e) - (m_Y - (Z-1)m_e)]c^2$$
$$= (m_X - m_Y)c^2$$

(B) ${}^A_Z X \longrightarrow {}^A_{Z+1} Y + {}^0_{-1} e + \overline{\nu}$

$$Q = \Delta mc^2$$
$$= [(m_X - Zm_e) - ((m_Y - (Z+1)m_e) + m_e)]c^2$$
$$= (m_X - m_Y)c^2$$

(C) ${}^A_Z X \longrightarrow {}^A_{Z-1} Y + {}^0_{-1} e + \nu$

$$Q = \Delta mc^2 = [(m_X - Zm_e) - ((m_Y - (Z-1)m_e) + m_e)]c^2$$
$$= (m_X - m_Y - 2m_e)c^2$$

4. A → 1, B → 5, C → 6, D → 3

5. A → 1, 2, B → 1, 3, C → 1, 4, D → 1, 2, 3

Numerical Value Questions

1. $\Delta m = m_p - \frac{99m_p}{100} = \frac{m_p}{100}$

$$Q = \Delta mc^2 = \left(\frac{m_p}{100}\right)c^2 = \frac{930}{100} = 9.3 \text{ MeV}$$

New binding energy = $7 \times 10 + 9.3 = 79.3$ MeV

2. Binding energy of $X = 6A$

Binding energy of $Y = 6A - 2 + 1 = 6A - 1$

Because absorption of energy decreases binding energy and release of energy increases binding energy.

In Y nucleus, there are $A + 1$ nucleons.

$\therefore$ Binding energy of Y per nucleon $= \frac{6A - 1}{A + 1}$

3. Energy required $= BE({}^{17}_8 O) - BE({}^{16}_8 O)$

$$= 17 \times 7.75 - 16 \times 7.97$$
$$= 4.23 \text{ MeV}$$

4. For each α-decay, atomic number decreases by 2 and atomic mass number decreases by 4. For each β^--decay, atomic number increases by 1. While atomic mass number remains unchanged.

Let number of α and β decays be n_1 and n_2 respectively.

$$238 - n_1(4) = 210 \quad \Rightarrow n_1 = 7$$
$$92 - n_1(2) + n_2 = 85 \Rightarrow n_2 = 7$$

5. Energy produced in 10 yr

$$= \text{Power} \times \text{Time}$$
$$= (1000 \times 10^6) \times (10 \times 365 \times 24 \times 3600)$$
$$= 3.15 \times 10^{17} \text{ J}$$

Input energy caused by fission

$$= \frac{\text{Output energy}}{\text{Efficiency}} = \frac{3.15 \times 10^{17}}{\left(\frac{10}{100}\right)} = 3.15 \times 10^{18} \text{ J}$$

Energy produced by one fission = 200 MeV

$$= 200 \times 10^6 \times 1.6 \times 10^{-19}$$
$$= 3.2 \times 10^{-11} \text{ J}$$

Therefore, no of fissions required

$$= \frac{\text{Total Energy}}{\text{Energy per fission}} = \frac{3.15 \times 10^{17}}{3.2 \times 10^{-11}} = 9.8 \times 10^{28}$$

Hence, mass of uranium required

$$= \frac{9.8 \times 10^{28}}{6.02 \times 10^{23}} \times 235 = 3.82 \times 10^7 \text{ gm} = 3.82 \times 10^4 \text{ kg}$$

6. Energy of each photon

$$= \frac{135}{2} \text{ MeV} = 67.5 \text{ MeV}$$

$$\lambda = \frac{hc}{E} = \frac{6.6 \times 10^{-34} \times 3 \times 10^8}{67.5 \times 10^6 \times 1.6 \times 10^{-19}} = 1.8 \times 10^{-14} \text{m}$$

7. $K_{Th} = \left(1 + \frac{m_P}{m_{Li}}\right)|Q| = \left(1 + \frac{1}{7}\right)(1645) = 1880 \text{ KeV}$

$$= 1.88 \text{ MeV}$$

8. Q-Value $= \Delta mc^2 = [2m(^2_1D) - m(^3_1T) - m(^1_1P)]c^2$

$= (2 \times 2.01458 - 3.01605 - 1.00728)\,u \times 931.5$ MeV/u

$= 5.43$ MeV

Energy produced per deuterium atom $= \dfrac{5.43}{2} = 2.715$ MeV

Energy required per day = Power × time

$= 10^9 \times 24 \times 3600 = 8.64 \times 10^{13}$ J

Energy input due to fusion

$= \dfrac{8.64 \times 10^{13}}{\left(\dfrac{50}{100}\right)} = 1.728 \times 10^{14}$ J

Number of deuterium atoms consumed

$= \dfrac{1.728 \times 10^{14}}{2.715 \times 10^6 \times 1.6 \times 10^{-19}} = 3.97 \times 10^{26}$

Mass of deuterium

$= \dfrac{3.97 \times 10^{26}}{6.02 \times 10^{23}} \times 2 = 1.32 \times 10^3$ gm $= 1.32$ kg

9. Q-value $= \Delta mc^2 = (m_A + m_B - m_C)c^2$

$= (25.0 + 10.0 - 34.995)\,u \times 930$ MeV/u

$= 4.65$ MeV

$KE_{Products} = KE_{Reactants} + Q\text{-value} - \Delta E_{Excitation}$

$\Rightarrow \quad KE_C = 5 + 3 + 4.65 - 10.65 = 2$ MeV

Previous Year's Questions

JEE Main

1. Given in the question,

$X^{236} \rightarrow 2X^{118}$

before after

Initially, $(BE)_i = 7.6$ MeV/nucleon

$= 7.6 \times 2.36$ MeV

Finally, $(BE)_f = 8.6$ MeV/nucleon

$= 2 \times 8.6 \times 118$ MeV

Heat released (Q) $= (BE)_f - (BE)_i$

$= 8.6 \times 2 \times 118 - 7.6 \times 236$

$= 2029.6 - 1793.6$

$= 236$ MeV

2. Given, ${}_6C^{12} = 12.000000\,u$

${}_6C^{13} = 13.003354\,u$

${}_0n^1 = 1.008665\,u$

Mass defect,

$\Delta M = [12.000000 + 1.008665] - 13.003354$

$= 0.005311\,u$

The required energy,

$\Delta E = 0.005311 \times 931.5$

$= 4.9471 \approx 4.95$ MeV

3. In given question,

${}_3Li^6 + {}_0n^1 \rightarrow {}_2He^4 + {}_1H^3$

${}_1H^2 + {}_1H^3 \rightarrow {}_2He^4 + {}_0n^1$

So net reaction is,

${}_3Li^6 + {}_1H^2 \rightarrow 2({}_2He^4)$

Energy released in process,

$Q = \Delta mc^2$

$Q = [m(Li) + m({}_1H^2) - 2\,m({}_2He^4)] \times 931.5$ MeV

$Q = [6.01690 + 2.01471 - 2 \times 4.00388] \times 931.5$ MeV

$Q = 22.216$ MeV

$Q = 22.22$ MeV

4. Both A and R are true.

⇒ For nuclei with atomic number 30 to 110 there is a saturation in nuclear force per nucleon as nucleons being added at large distance do not make much impact on the nuclear forces at a specific region.

5. In alpha (^4_2He) decay, mass number decreases by 4 units and charge number decreases by 2 units.

In β^- decay, mass number remains same but charge number increases by 1.

In β^+ decay, mass number remains same but charge number decreases by 1.

In γ-decay, there is no change in mass number or charge number.

$^{218}_{84}A \xrightarrow{\alpha} {}^{214}_{82}A_1 \xrightarrow{\beta^-} {}^{214}_{83}A_2 \xrightarrow{\gamma} {}^{214}_{83}A_3 \xrightarrow{\alpha}$

$^{210}_{81}Au \xrightarrow{\beta^+} {}^{210}_{80}A_5 \xrightarrow{\gamma} {}^{210}_{80}A_6$

6.

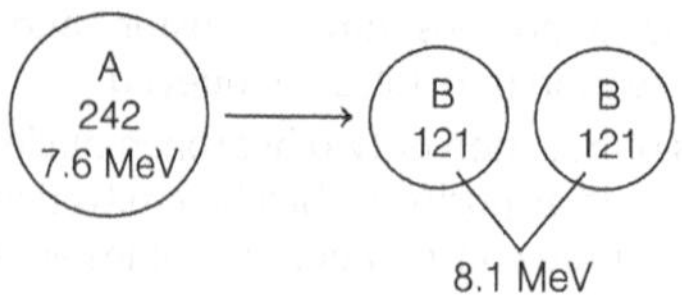

Total initial BE $= 242 \times 7.6 = 1839.2$ MeV

Total final BE $= 121 \times 2 \times 8.1 = 1960.2$

Gain in BE $= 1960.2 - 1839.2 = 121$ MeV

7. For nucleus A,

Number of proton, $Z = 17$ and number of neutrons, $N = 17$ (Given $Z = N$)

$A = Z + N = 17 + 17 = 34$

Binding energy per nucleon $= \dfrac{BE}{A} = 1.2$ MeV

$(BE)_A = 1.2 \times A = 1.2 \times 34 = 40.8$ MeV

For nucleus B,

Number of protons, $Z = 12$,

Number of nucleons, $A = 26$

$\dfrac{BE}{A} = 1.8$ MeV

$(BE)_B = 1.8 \times A = 1.8 \times 26 = 46.8$ MeV

Therefore, difference in binding energy of B and A is

$\Delta BE = BE_B - BE_A$

$\Rightarrow \quad \Delta BE = 46.8 - 40.8$

$\Rightarrow \quad \Delta BE = 6$ MeV

8. Molar mass of given isotope

$$(^{240}X) = 240\text{ g}$$

So, in 240 g number of nucleus present

$$= N_A = 6\times10^{23} \quad \text{(as given in question)}$$

$\therefore$ In 120 g, number of nucleus present

$$= N_A/2 = 3\times10^{23}$$

1 nucleus gives 200 MeV of energy in fission.

So, total energy obtained by fission of 120 g of ^{240}X will be

$$3\times10^{23}\times200 = 6\times10^{25} \approx 6\times10^{25}\text{ MeV}$$

9. When nucleus disintegrates into two smaller parts of masses m_1 and m_2, then according to conservation of linear momentum,

$$m_1v_1 - m_2v_2 = 0$$

$$\Rightarrow \frac{m_1}{m_2} = \frac{v_2}{v_1} = \frac{2}{3} \qquad \left[\because v_1 : v_2 = 3:2 \Rightarrow \frac{v_2}{v_1} = \frac{2}{3}\right]$$

$$\Rightarrow \frac{m_1}{m_2} = \frac{2}{3} \Rightarrow \frac{\rho_1 \text{vol}_1}{\rho_2 \text{vol}_2} = \frac{2}{3}$$

$$\Rightarrow \frac{\text{vol}_1}{\text{vol}_2} = \frac{2}{3} \qquad (\because \rho_1 = \rho_2)$$

$$\Rightarrow \frac{\frac{4}{3}\pi r_1^3}{\frac{4}{3}\pi r_2^3} = \frac{2}{3} \Rightarrow \left(\frac{r_1}{r_2}\right)^3 = \frac{2}{3}$$

$$\Rightarrow \left(\frac{r_1}{r_2}\right) = \left(\frac{2}{3}\right)^{1/3} = \left(\frac{x}{3}\right)^{1/3} \qquad \text{[Given]}$$

$$\therefore \quad x = 2$$

10. Given decay is

$$^{242}_{92}X \longrightarrow 2\,^4_2\text{He} + \beta^- + 2\beta^+ + {}^{234}_{P}Y$$

$$\Rightarrow {}^{242}_{92}X \longrightarrow 2\,^4_2\text{He} + {}^{0}_{-1}e + 2\,{}^{0}_{+1}e + {}^{234}_{P}Y$$

Conservation of charge number gives

$$92 = 4 - 1 + 2 + P \Rightarrow P = 87$$

11. For any nucleus ^A_ZX;

A. Surface energy per nucleon is proportional to total surface area divided by mass number.

$$\therefore \text{SE per nucleon} = -K_1\left(\frac{4\pi R^2}{A}\right) = -a_1\frac{A^{2/3}}{A} = -a_1A^{-1/3}$$

So, statement A is incorrect.

B. Coulomb's contribution is proportional to distance or radius.

So, Coulomb's contribution $\propto R$ or $A^{1/3}$.

So option B is incorrect.

C. Volume energy term is proportional to volume.

Volume energy $\propto R^3$ or volume energy $\propto (A^{1/3})^3$ or A

Hence, option C is correct.

D. As more BE means a smaller nucleus or a small surface area, decrease of BE must be proportional to surface area. Hence option D is correct.

E. Every nucleon can interact only with its nearby neighbours.

So option E is incorrect.

12. Nuclear density is independent of mass number of nuclei, hence option (c) is correct.

13. Reaction following conservation of mass number and conservation of charge number will be as follows

$$^{182}_{74}D \xrightarrow{^4_2\text{He}} {}^{178}_{72}D_1 \xrightarrow{^{0}_{-1}e} {}^{178}_{73}D_2$$

$$^{178}_{73}D_2 \xrightarrow{^4_2\text{He}} {}^{174}_{71}D_3^* \xrightarrow{\gamma = hf} {}^{174}_{71}D_4$$

So, product is $^{174}_{71}D_4$.

14. Radius of nucleus is given by

$$R = R_0A^{1/3} \Rightarrow \frac{R}{R_0} = A^{1/3}$$

$$\Rightarrow \ln\frac{R}{R_0} = \frac{1}{3}\ln A$$

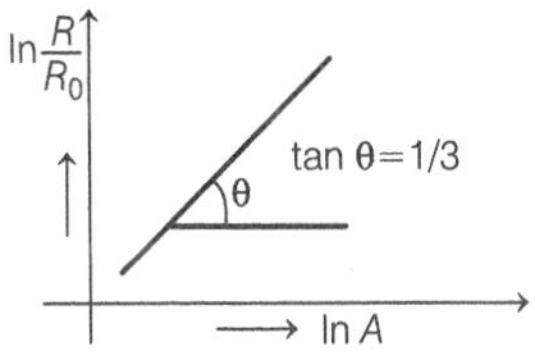

On comparing it with the equation of straight line $y = mx + c$, we get $m = \frac{1}{3}$ and $c = 0$

15. The decay of a proton to neutron is possible only inside the nucleus because the mass of proton is less than the mass of neutron. This mass difference is compensated with the binding energy of nucleus. This decay is not possible outside the nucleus because particle cannot be decayed into the greater mass.

JEE Advanced

1. In α-decays, mass number is decreased by 4 unit and atomic number is decreased by 2 units. In β^- decays, mass number remains unchanged but atomic number is increased by 1 unit. In β^+ decay, mass number remains unchanged but atomic number is decreased by 1 unit. Thus, using this, we find option (a) as correct one.

2. Total binding energy (without considering repulsions),

$$E_b = [Zm_p + (A-Z)m_n - m_x]c^2$$

where, ^A_ZX is the nuclei under consideration.

Now, considering repulsion :

Number of proton pairs $= {}^ZC_2$

$$\Rightarrow \text{This repulsion energy} \propto \frac{Z(Z-1)}{2}\times\frac{1}{4\pi\varepsilon_0}\frac{e^2}{R}$$

where, R is the radius of the nucleus.

$$\Rightarrow \quad E_b^p - E_b^n \propto Z(Z-1)$$

$\therefore$ There will be no repulsion term for neutrons.

Also, since $R = R_0A^{\frac{1}{3}} \Rightarrow E_b^p - E_b^n \propto A^{-\frac{1}{3}}$

Because of repulsion among protons,

$$E_b^p < E_b^n$$

Since, in β^+ decay, number of protons decrease

$\Rightarrow$ repulsion would decrease

$\Rightarrow E_b^p$ increases

3.

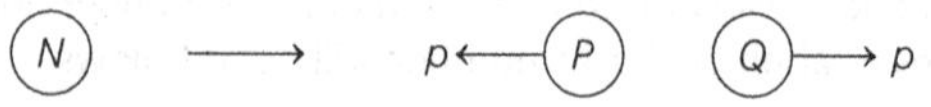

$$(p_{\text{total}}) = 0 \Rightarrow (p_{\text{total}})_f = 0$$

So, momentum of one nucleus is p in forward direction, then momentum of the other nucleus will be p in backwards direction.

Energy released $= (\Delta m)c^2 = \delta c^2 = \text{KE}_P + \text{KE}_Q$

$$\text{KE}_P = \frac{p^2}{2m_P}, \text{KE}_Q = \frac{p^2}{2m_Q}$$

$$\Rightarrow \quad \text{KE}_P : \text{KE}_Q = \frac{1}{m_P} : \frac{1}{m_Q} = m_Q : m_P$$

$$\text{KE}_P = \left(\frac{m_Q}{m_P + m_Q}\right)\delta c^2$$

$$\text{KE}_Q = \left(\frac{m_P}{m_P + m_Q}\right)\delta c^2$$

$$\text{KE}_P + \text{KE}_Q = \delta c^2$$

$$\frac{p^2}{2m_P} + \frac{p^2}{2m_Q} = \delta c^2 \Rightarrow p = c\sqrt{2\left(\frac{m_P m_Q}{m_P + m_Q}\right)\delta}$$

4. ${}^{232}_{90}\text{Th}$ is converting into ${}^{212}_{82}\text{Pb}$.

Change in mass number $(A) = 20$

$\therefore$ Number of α-particle emitted $= \frac{20}{4} = 5$

Due to 5 α-particles, Z will change by 10 units.

Since, given change is 8, therefore number of β-particles emitted is 2.

5. Electrostatic energy

= Binding energy of N – Binding energy of O

$= [[7M_H + 8M_n - M_N] - [8M_H + 7M_n - M_O]] \times c^2$

$= [-M_H + M_n + M_O\ M_N]c^2$

$= [-1.007825 + 1.008665 + 15.003065 - 15.000109] \times 93.15$

$= +3.5359$ MeV

$$\Delta E = \frac{3}{5} \times \frac{1.44 \times 8 \times 7}{R} = 3.5359$$

$$R = \frac{3 \times 1.44 \times 14}{5 \times 3.5359} = 3.42 \text{ fm}$$

6. From conservation laws of mass number and atomic number, we can say that $x = n$, $y = n$

$$(x = {}^1_0n, y = {}^1_0n)$$

$\therefore$ Only (a) and (d) options may be correct.

From conservation of momentum, $|P_{xe}| = |P_{sr}|$

$$K = \frac{p^2}{2m} \Rightarrow K \propto \frac{1}{m} \Rightarrow \frac{K_{sr}}{K_{xe}} = \frac{m_{xe}}{m_{sr}}$$

$\therefore$ $K_{sr} = 129$ MeV, $K_{xe} = 86$ MeV

NOTE There is no need of finding total energy released in the process.

7. (a) ${}_3\text{Li}^6 \rightarrow {}_2\text{He}^4 + {}_1\text{H}^2$

$$\Delta m = [M_{Li} - M_{He} - M_{H^3}]$$
$$= [6.01513 - 4.002603 - 2.01410]$$
$$= -0.001573 \text{ u}$$

Δm is negative so reaction is not possible.

(b) ${}_{84}\text{Po}^{210} \rightarrow {}_{83}\text{Bi}^{209} + {}_1\text{P}^1$

Δm is negative so reaction is not possible.

(c) ${}_1\text{H}^2 + {}_2\text{He}^4 \rightarrow {}_3\text{Li}^6$

Δm is positive so reaction is possible.

(d) ${}_{30}\text{Zn}^{70} + {}_{34}\text{Se}^{82} \rightarrow {}_{64}\text{Gd}^{152}$

Δm is negative so reaction is not possible.

8. ${}_{84}\text{Po}^{210} \longrightarrow {}_2\text{He}^4 + {}_{82}\text{Pb}^{206}$

Mass defect $\Delta m = (m_{Po} - M_{He} - m_{Pb}) = 0.005818$ u

$\therefore$ $Q = (\Delta m)(931.48)$ MeV

$= 5.4193$ MeV $= 5419$ keV

From conservation of linear momentum,

$$p_{Pb} = p_\alpha$$

$\therefore$ $\sqrt{2m_{Pb}k_{Pb}} = \sqrt{2m_\alpha k_\alpha}$

or $\frac{k_\alpha}{k_{Pb}} = \frac{m_{Pb}}{m_\alpha} = \frac{206}{4}$

$\therefore$ $k_\alpha = \left(\frac{206}{206 + 4}\right)(k_{\text{total}})$

$= \left(\frac{206}{210}\right)(5419)$

$= 5316$ keV

CHAPTER~11

RADIOACTIVITY

LEVEL 01 Starter Level

11.1 Radioactivity Decay Law

1 The decay constant of a radioactive substance is $1.8 \times 10^{-4}\ s^{-1}$.
(a) What is the half-life?
(b) What is the average life?
(c) How much time will it take for 25% of this substance to decay? [ln (4/3) = 0.288]

2 A radioactive isotope X has a half-life of 3 s. Initially a given sample of this isotope contains 8000 atoms. Calculate (a) its decay constant, (b) the time t_1 when 1000 atoms of the isotope X remain in the sample, and (c) the number of decays per second in the sample at $t = t_1$.

3 The half-life of radium is about 1600 yr. In how much time will 1 g of radium
(a) reduce to 100 mg (b) lose 100 mg?

4 A sample of radioactive element has a mass of 10 gm at an instant $t = 0$. What is the mass of this element in the sample after two mean lives?

5 At a given instant there are 25% undecayed radioactive nuclei in a sample. After 10 s the number of undecayed nuclei reduces to 12.5%. Calculate
(a) mean life of the nuclei, and
(b) the time in which the number of undecayed nuclei will further reduce to 6.25% of the reduced number

6 At any instant the ratio of the amount of radioactive substances is 2: 1. If their half-lives be respectively 12 h and 16 h, then after two days, what will be the ratio of the substances?

7 How many beta-particles are emitted during one hour by 1.0 μg of Na^{24} radionuclide whose half-life is 15 h?

8 Knowing the decay constant λ, of a nucleus, find the probability of decay of the nucleus during the time from 0 to t.

11.2 Activity

1 The decay constant for the radioactive nuclide ^{64}Cu is $1.516 \times 10^{-5}\ s^{-1}$. Find the activity of a sample containing 1 μg of ^{64}Cu. Atomic weight of copper = 63.5 g/mol.

2 Calculate the mass in grams of a radioactive sample Pb^{214} having an activity of one microcurie and a half-life of 26.8 min.

3 A freshly prepared radioactive source of half-life 2h emits radiation of intensity which is 64 times the permissible safe level. What is the minimum time after which it would be possible to work safely with this source?

4 The activity of a radioactive source at $t = 0$ was 1600 Bq and at $t = 8$ s it was 100 Bq. What will be the activity observed at $t = 6$ s?

5 A certain sample of a radioactive material decays at the rate of 500 per second at a certain time. The count rate falls to 200 per second after 50 min.
(a) What is the decay constant of the sample?
(b) What is its half-life? [ln (2.5) = 0.916]

6 At the initial moment the activity of a certain radionuclide total 650 particles per minute. What will be the activity of the preparation after half of its half-life period?

11.3 Radioactive Dating

1 In an ore containing uranium, the ratio of U^{238} to Pb^{206} nuclei is 3. Calculate the age of the ore, assuming that all the lead present in the ore is the final stable product of U^{238}. Take the half-life of U^{238} to be 4.5×10^9 yr.

2 The age of a rock containing lead and uranium is equal to 1.5×10^9 yr. The uranium is decaying into lead with half-life equal to 4.5×10^9 yr.

Find the ratio of lead to uranium present in the rock, assuming initially no lead was present in the rock. (Given, $2^{1/3} = 1.259$)

3. When charcoal is prepared from a living tree, it shows a disintegration rate of 15.3 disintegrations of ^{14}C per gram per minute. A sample from an ancient piece of charcoal shows ^{14}C activity to be 12.3 disintegrations per gram per minute. How old is this sample?

Half-life of ^{14}C is 5730 yr. $\ln\left(\frac{15.3}{12.3}\right) = 0.218$

11.4 Disintegration with Successive Production

1 A factory produces a radioactive substance A at a constant rate R which decays with a decay constant λ to form a stable substance B.

Assuming the production of A starts at $t = 0$, at any time t find

(i) the number of nuclei of A and

(ii) number of nuclei of B,

(iii) also find out the maximum number of nuclei of A present at any time during its formation.

2 Nuclei of a radioactive element A are being produced at a constant rate α. The element has a decay constant λ. At time $t = 0$, there are N_0 nuclei of the element.

(a) Calculate the number N of nuclei of A at time t.

(b) If $\alpha = 2N_0\lambda$, calculate the number of nuclei of A after one half-life of A, and also the limiting value of N as $t \to \infty$.

11.5 Simultaneous Decay

1 A radioactive nucleus can decay by two different processes. The half-life for the first process is t_1 and that for the second process is t_2. Find the effective half-life t of the nucleus.

2 The mean lives of a radioactive substance are 1600 and 400 yr for α-emission and β-emission, respectively. Find out the time during which three fourth of a sample will decay, if it is decaying both by α-emission and β-emission simultaneously.

11.6 Sequential Decay

1 A radioactive substance A having N_0 active nuclei at $t = 0$, decays to another radioactive substance B with decay constant λ_1. B further decays to a stable substance C with decay constant λ_2. Find the number of nuclei of A, B and C after time t.

2 A radioactive nucleus X decays to a nucleus Y with a decay constant $\lambda_X = 0.1\ s^{-1}$. Y further decays to a stable nucleus Z with a decay constant $\lambda_Y = \frac{1}{30}\ s^{-1}$.

Initially, there are only X nuclei and their number is $N_0 = 10^{20}$. The population of the Y nucleus as a function of time is given by $N_Y(t) = \frac{N_0\lambda_X}{\lambda_X - \lambda_Y}\{e^{-\lambda_Y t} - e^{-\lambda_X t}\}$. Find the time at which N_Y is maximum and determine the populations X and Z at that instant.

3 Suppose, the daughter nucleus in a nuclear decay is itself radioactive. Let λ_p and λ_d be the decay constants of the parent and the daughter nuclei. Also, let N_p and N_d be the number of parent and daughter nuclei at time t. Find the condition for which the number of daughter nuclei becomes constant.

LEVEL 02 JEE Advanced Level

Single Choice Correct Questions

1 The half-life of ^{215}At is 100 μs. The time taken for the radioactivity of a sample of ^{215}At to decay to 1/16th of its initial value is

(a) 400 μs (b) 6.3 μs (c) 40 μs (d) 300 μs

2 A radioactive source has a half-life of 20 days. During a period of 60 days fraction of the atoms that have decayed would be

(a) 100% (b) 87.5%
(c) 64% (d) 50%

3 Three fourths of the active nuclei present in a radioactive sample decay in 3/4 s. The half-life of the sample is

(a) 1 s (b) 0.5 s
(c) 0.75 s (d) 0.375 s

4 A radioactive sample decays by 63% of its initial value in 10 s. It would have decayed by 50 % of its initial value in

(a) 7 s (b) 14 s
(c) 5 s (d) 1.4 s

5 A fraction f_1 of a radioactive sample decays in one mean life, and a fraction f_2 decays in one half-life.
(a) $f_1 > f_2$ (b) $f_1 < f_2$
(c) $f_1 = f_2$
(d) May be (a), (b) or (c) depending on the values of the mean life and half-life.

6 The fraction of the initial number of active nuclie which remain undecayed after half of a half-life of the radioactive sample is
(a) $\frac{1}{4}$ (b) $\frac{1}{2\sqrt{2}}$ (c) $\frac{1}{\sqrt{2}}$ (d) $\sqrt{2}-1$

7 The half-life of the radioactive radon is 3.8 days. The time, at the end of which 1/20th of the radon sample will remain undecayed, is (given $\log_{10} e = 0.4343$)
(a) 3.8 days (b) 16.5 days
(c) 33 days (d) 76 days

8 Half-life of radium is 1620 yr. How many radium nuclei decay in 5 h in 5 gm radium? (Atomic weight of radium = 223)
(a) 9.1×10^{12} (b) 3.23×10^{15}
(c) 1.72×10^{20} (d) 3.3×10^{17}

9 ${}^{221}_{87}Ra$ is a radioactive substance having half-life of 4 days. Find the probability that a nucleus undergoes decay after two half-lives
(a) 1 (b) $\frac{1}{2}$
(c) $\frac{3}{4}$ (d) $\frac{1}{4}$

10 The probability that particular nucleus of ${}^{38}Cl$ will undergo β-decay in time interval 10^{-3} s (the half-life of ${}_{38}Cl$ is 37.2 min) is
(a) 3.1×10^{-7} (b) 2.25×10^{-6}
(c) 3.36×10^{-5} (d) 1.73×10^{-7}

11. A radioactive sample contains 0.1 kg each of two substances X and Y with half-lives 4 s and 8 s, respectively. Their atomic masses are in the ratio 1 : 2. The amount of substances X and Y after an interval of 16 s is
(a) 2.5×10^{-3} kg, 5×10^{-2} kg
(b) 2.5×10^{-3} kg, 5×10^{-1} kg
(c) 6.25×10^{-3} kg, 2.5×10^{-2} kg
(d) 6.25×10^{-3} kg, 2.5×10^{-1} kg

12. A radioactive substance is dissolved in a liquid and the solution is heated. The activity of the solution
(a) is smaller than that of element
(b) is greater than that of element
(c) is equal to that of element
(d) will be smaller or greater depending upon whether the solution is weak or concentrated.

13. A sample of radio-nuclide contains 10^{18} atoms. The half-life of the material is 2.0 days, then the activity of a sample is
(a) 3.5×10^{12} Bq (b) 4×10^{11} Bq
(c) 8×10^{12} Bq (d) 4×10^{12} Bq

14 Plutonium has atomic mass 210 and a decay constant equal to $5.8 \times 10^{-8}\ s^{-1}$. The number of α-particles emitted per second by 1 mg of plutonium is (Avogadro's constant $= 6.0 \times 10^{23}$)
(a) 1.7×10^9 (b) 1.7×10^{11}
(c) 2.9×10^{11} (d) 3.4×10^9

15 The ratio of molecular mass of two radioactive substance is $\frac{3}{2}$ and the ratio of their decay constant is $\frac{4}{3}$. Then, the ratio of their initial activity per mole will be
(a) 2 (b) $\frac{8}{9}$ (c) $\frac{4}{3}$ (d) $\frac{9}{8}$

16 The activity of a sample reduces from A_0 to $\frac{A_0}{\sqrt{3}}$ in one hour. The activity after 3 h more will be
(a) $\frac{A_0}{3\sqrt{3}}$ (b) $\frac{A_0}{9}$ (c) $\frac{A_0}{9\sqrt{3}}$ (d) $\frac{A_0}{27}$

17 The count rate of activity of a radioactive sample of a very large population decreased from 1024 to 128 in 3 min. Then, the rate of disintegration at the end of 5 min is
(a) 96 (b) 64 (c) 48 (d) 32

18 The mean life time of a radionuclide, if its activity decreases by 4 % for every 1h, would be (product is non-radioactive, i.e. stable)
(a) 25 h (b) 1.042 h (c) 2 h (d) 30 h

19 The activity of a certain radionuclide decreases to 15% of its original value in 10 days. Find its half-life. [ln (0.15) = −1.9].
(a) 3.00 days (b) 3.50 days
(c) 3.65 days (d) 3.8 days

20 The count rate from 100 cm^3 of a radioactive liquid is c. Some of this liquid is now discarded. The count rate of the remaining liquid is found to be $c/10$ after three half-lives. The volume of the remaining liquid, in cm^3, is
(a) 20 (b) 40 (c) 60 (d) 80

21. A 280 days old radioactive substance show an activity of 6000 dps, 140 days later its activity becomes 3000 dps. What was its initial activity?
(a) 20000 dps (b) 24000 dps
(c) 12000 dps (d) 6000 dps

22 The radioactivity of a given sample of whisky due to tritium (half-life 12.5 yr) was found to be only 3% of that measured in a recently purchased bottle marked 7 years old. The sample must have been prepared about

(a) 220 yr back (b) 300 yr back
(c) 400 yr back (d) 70 yr back

23 The activity of a sample of radioactive material is A_1 at time t_1 and A_2 at time t_2 $(t_2 > t_1)$. Its mean life is T.

(a) $A_1 t_1 = A_2 t_2$ (b) $\frac{A_1 - A_2}{t_2 - t_1} =$ constant
(c) $A_2 = A_1 e^{(t_1 - t_2)/T}$ (d) $A_2 = A_1 e^{(t_1 / Tt_2)}$

24 The radioactivity of a sample is R_1 at time T_1 and R_2 at time T_2. If the half-life of the specimen is T, number of atoms that have disintegrated in time $(T_2 - T_1)$ is proportional to

(a) $(R_1 T_1 - R_2 T_2)$ (b) $(R_1 - R_2) T$
(c) $\frac{(R_1 - R_2)}{T}$ (d) $(R_1 - R_2)(T_1 - T_2)$

25 Two radioactive samples of different elements (half-lives t_1 and t_2, respectively) have same number of nuclei at $t = 0$. The time after which their activities are same is

(a) $\frac{t_1 t_2}{0.693\,(t_2 - t_1)} \ln \frac{t_2}{t_1}$ (b) $\frac{t_1 t_2}{0.693} \ln \frac{t_2}{t_1}$
(c) $\frac{t_1 t_2}{0.693\,(t_2 + t_1)} \ln \frac{t_2}{t_1}$ (d) None of these

26 A radioactive material of half-life T was produced in a nuclear reactor at different instants, the quantity produced second time was twice of that produced first time. If now their present activities are A_1 and A_2 respectively, then their age difference equals

(a) $\frac{T}{\ln 2}\left|\ln \frac{A_1}{A_2}\right|$ (b) $T\left|\ln \frac{A_1}{A_2}\right|$
(c) $\frac{T}{\ln 2}\left|\ln \frac{A_2}{2A_1}\right|$ (d) $T\left|\ln \frac{A_2}{2A_1}\right|$

27 The half-life of ^{131}I is 8 days. Given a sample of ^{131}I at time $t = 0$, we can assert that

(a) no nucleus will decay before $t = 4$ days
(b) no nucleus will decay before $t = 8$ days
(c) all nuclei will decay before $t = 16$ days
(d) a given nucleus may decay at any time after $t = 0$

28 Consider the following statements.

Assertion (A) An isolated radioactive atom may not decay at all whatever be its half-life.

Reason (R) Radioactive decay law is statistical.

Of these statements

(a) Both A and R are true and R is the correct explanation of A.
(b) Both A and R are true but R is not a correct explanation of A.
(c) A is true but R is false.
(d) A is false but R is true.

29 A radioactive nucleus X decays to a stable nucleus Y. Then, the graph of rate of formation of Y against time t will be

(a)
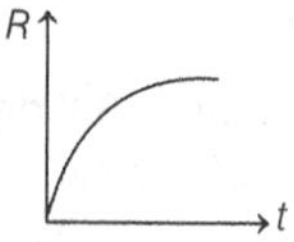

(b)
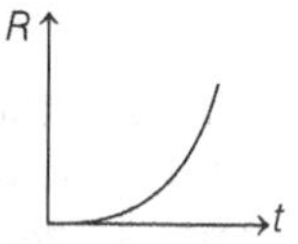

(c)
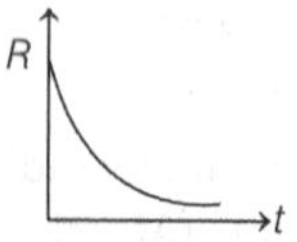

(d)
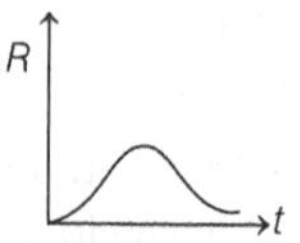

30 A radioactive sample consists of two distinct species having equal number of atoms initially. The mean life time of one species is τ and that of the other is 5τ. The decay products in both cases are stable. A plot is made of the total number of radioactive nuclei as a function of time. Which of the following figures best represents the form of this plot?

(a)
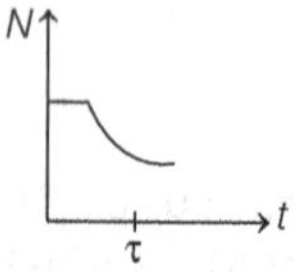

(b)
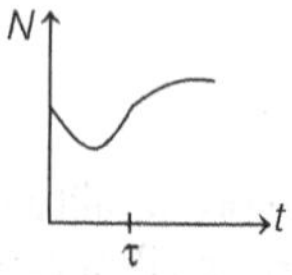

(c)
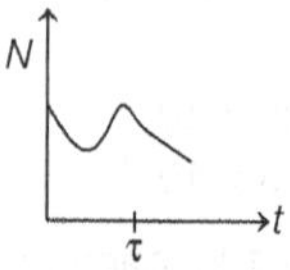

(d)
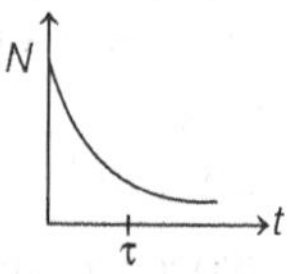

31 The half-life period of a radioactive element X is same as the mean life time of another radioactive element Y. Initially both of them have the same number of atoms. Then,

(a) X and Y have the same decay rate initially
(b) X and Y decay at the same rate always
(c) Y will decay at a faster rate than X
(d) X will decay at a faster rate than Y

32 Two radioactive sources A and B of half-lives of 1 h and 2 h respectively, initially contain the same number of radioactive atoms. At the end of two hours, their rates of disintegration are in the ratio of

(a) 1 : 4 (b) 1 : 3
(c) 1 : 2 (d) 1 : 1

33 There are two radioactive substances A and B. Decay constant of B is twice that of A. Initially, both have equal number of nuclei. After n half-lives of A, rate of disintegration of both become equal. The value of n is

(a) 1 (b) 2
(c) 4 (d) All of these

34 Two radioactive material X_1 and X_2 have decay constants 10λ and λ, respectively. If initially they have the same number of nuclei, then the ratio of the number of nuclei of X_1 to that of X_2 will be $\frac{1}{e}$ after a time

(a) $\frac{1}{10\lambda}$ (b) $\frac{1}{11\lambda}$
(c) $\frac{11}{10\lambda}$ (d) $\frac{1}{9\lambda}$

35 Two radioactive samples X and Y having half-life 3 yr and 2 yr, respectively have been decaying for many years. Today both samples have equal number of atoms. The number of atoms in the sample X will be twice of the number of atoms in the sample Y after

(a) $\frac{6}{5}$ yr (b) $\frac{5}{6}$ yr
(c) 6 yr (d) 2 yr

36 Half-life of a radioactive substance A is two times the half-life of another radioactive substance B. Initially, the number of A and B are N_A and N_B, respectively. After three half-lives of A, number of nuclei of both are equal. Then, the ratio $\frac{N_A}{N_B}$ is

(a) $\frac{1}{4}$ (b) $\frac{1}{8}$ (c) $\frac{1}{3}$ (d) $\frac{1}{6}$

37 Radioactive isotopes X and Y have half-lives of 4 days and 16 days, respectively. The total activity of their mixture is 1 curie at certain time. The activity reduces by 50% in 8 days. Determine the ratio $\left(\frac{N_X}{N_Y}\right)$ of their initial number of atoms.

(a) $\frac{2}{\sqrt{2}-1}$ (b) $\frac{\sqrt{2}-1}{2}$
(c) $2(\sqrt{2}-1)$ (d) None of these

38 A radioactive element X converts into another stable element Y. Half-life of X is 2 h. Initially, only X is present. After time t, the ratio of atoms of X and Y is found to be 1 : 4, then t in hours is

(a) 2 (b) 4
(c) between 4 and 6 (d) 6

39 There are two radio nuclei A and B. A is an alpha emitter and B a beta emitter. Their disintegration constants are in the ratio of 1 : 2. What should be the ratio of number of atoms of A and B at any time t so, that probabilities of getting alpha and beta particles are same at that instant?

(a) 2 : 1 (b) 1 : 2 (c) e (d) e^{-1}

40 Samples of two radioactive nuclides, X and Y, each have equal activity A_0 at time $t = 0$. X has a half-life of 24 yr and Y a half-life of 16 yr. The samples are mixed together. What will be the total activity of the mixture at $t = 48$ yr?

(a) $\frac{A_0}{2}$ (b) $\frac{A_0}{4}$ (c) $\frac{3A_0}{16}$ (d) $\frac{3A_0}{8}$

41 An isotope of potassium $^{40}_{19}K$ has a half-life of 1.4×10^9 yr and decays to Argon $^{40}_{18}Ar$ which is stable. A sample of rock taken from the moon contains both potassium and argon in the ratio $\frac{1}{7}$. Age of the rock is

(a) 2.8×10^9 yr (b) 3.5×10^9 yr
(c) 4.2×10^9 yr (d) 8.2×10^{10} yr

42 Half-lives of two isotopes X and Y of a material are known to be 2×10^9 yr and 4×10^9 yr, respectively. If a planet was formed with equal number of these isotopes, estimate the current age of the planet, given that currently the material has 20% of X and 80% of Y by number.

(a) 2×10^9 yr (b) 4×10^9 yr
(c) 6×10^9 yr (d) 8×10^9 yr

43 A certain radioactive material can undergo three different types of decay, each with a different decay constant 2λ, 3λ and 6λ. Then, the effective decay constant λ_{eff} is

(a) 11λ (b) 7λ (c) 4λ (d) λ

44 A radioactive material has a mean life 1620 yr and 520 yr for α and β emissions, respectively. The material decays by simultaneous α and β emissions. What is the time in which (1/4)th of material is intact?

(a) 4675 yr (b) 720 yr (c) 545 yr (d) 324 yr

45 A sample of radioactive material decays simultaneously by two processes A and B with half-lives $\frac{1}{2}$ and $\frac{1}{4}$ h, respectively. For first half an hour it decays with the process A, next one hour with the process B and for further half an hour with both A and B. If originally there were N_0 nuclei, find the number of nuclei after 2 h of such decay.

(a) $\frac{N_0}{(2)^8}$ (b) $\frac{N_0}{(2)^4}$ (c) $\frac{N_0}{(2)^6}$ (d) $\frac{N_0}{(2)^5}$

46 A radioactive substance is being produced at a constant rate of 10 nuclei/s. The decay constant of the substance is $\frac{1}{2}\ s^{-1}$. After what time, the number of radioactive nuclei will become 10? Initially there are no nuclei present. Assume decay law holds for the sample.

(a) 2.45 s (b) log (2) s (c) 1.386 s (d) $\frac{1}{\ln(2)}$ s

47 A radioactive isotopes is being produced at a constant rate X. Half-life of substance is Y. After some time the number of radioactive nuclei become constant. The value of this constant is

(a) $\frac{XY}{\ln(2)}$ (b) XY (c) $(\ln 2)\, XY$ (d) $\frac{X}{Y}$

48 A radioactive nucleus is being produced at a constant rate α per second. Its decay constant is λ. If N_0 are the number of nuclei at time $t = 0$, then maximum number of nuclei possible are

(a) $\frac{\alpha}{\lambda}$ (b) $N_0 \frac{\alpha}{\lambda}$ (c) N_0 (d) $\frac{\lambda}{\alpha} + N_0$

49 A certain radio-nuclide starts getting produced at a constant rate $= 10^4\ s^{-1}$ by some mechanism at a certain moment $t = 0$. At this moment, there are already 10^5 number of radio-nuclides present in the sample. The mean life of the radio-nuclide is 20 s. At $t = 40$ s, what will be $\frac{dN}{dt}$, rounded to the nearest whole number? [Given that, $e^2 = 7.4$]

(a) – 375 /s (b) +676 /s
(c) – 676 /s (d) + 762 /s

50 In a certain nuclear reactor, a radioactive nucleus is being produced at a constant rate = 1000/s. The mean life of the radio-nuclide is 40 min. At steady state, the number of radio-nuclide will be

(a) 4×10^4 (b) 24×10^4
(c) 24×10^5 (d) 24×10^6

51 In the above question, if there were 20×10^5 radio-nuclide at $t = 0$, then the graph of N vs t is

(a)
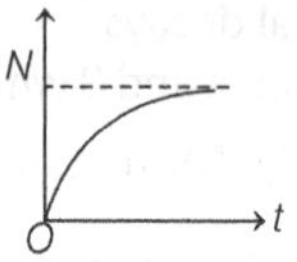

(b)
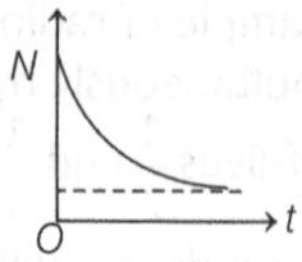

(c)
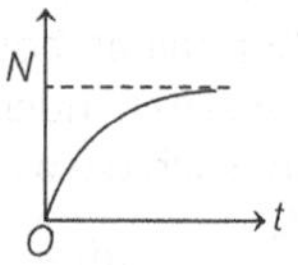

(d)
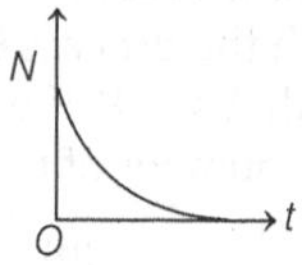

52 Nuclei of radioactive element A are produced at rate t^2 at any time t. The element A has decay constant λ. Let N be the number of nuclei of element A at any time t. At time $t = t_0$, $\frac{dN}{dt}$ is minimum. N is

(a) $\frac{\lambda t_0^2 - 2t_0}{\lambda^2}$ (b) $\frac{\lambda t_0^2 - t_0}{\lambda^2}$

(c) $\frac{\lambda t_0^2 - 2t_0}{\lambda}$ (d) $\frac{\lambda t_0^2 - t_0}{\lambda}$

53

	A	$\xrightarrow{\lambda}$	B	$\xrightarrow{2\lambda}$	C
$t = 0$	N_0		0		0
t	N_1		N_2		N_3

The ratio of N_1 to N_2, when N_2 is maximum is

(a) at no time this is possible

(b) 2 (c) $\frac{1}{2}$ (d) $\frac{\ln 2}{2}$

54.

	A	$\xrightarrow{\lambda_1}$	B	$\xrightarrow{\lambda_2}$	C
$t = 0$	N_0		0		0
t	N_1		N_2		N_3

In the above radioactive decay, C is stable nucleus. Then,

(a) number of nuclei of B will first increase and then decrease.

(b) rate of decay of A will first increase and then decrease.

(c) if $\lambda_2 > \lambda_1$, then activity of B will always be higher than activity of A.

(d) if $\lambda_1 >> \lambda_2$, then number of nucleus of C will always be less than number of nucleus of B.

Multiple Choice(s) Correct Questions

1 For a certain radioactive substance, it is observed that after 4 h, only 6.25% of the original sample is left undecayed. If follows that

(a) the half-life of the sample is 1 h.

(b) the mean life of the sample is $\frac{1}{\ln 2}$ h.

(c) the decay constant of the sample is $\ln(2)\ h^{-1}$.

(d) after a further 4 h, the amount of the substance left over would by only 0.39% of the original amount.

2 Two radioactive nuclei A and B are present in equal numbers to begin with. Three days later, number of nuclei of A are 3 times number of nuclei of B. Choose the correct statement(s).

(a) $\lambda_B - \lambda_A = \frac{\ln 3}{3\ \text{days}}$ (b) $\lambda_A - \lambda_B = \frac{\ln 3}{3\ \text{days}}$

(c) the ratio of activity rate of A and B after 3 days is 3.

(d) the ratio of activity rate of A and B after 3 days is less than 3.

3 Two radioactive nuclei A and B are initially in the ratio 1 : 4. Also, initial activities of the nuclei are in the ratio 1 : 8. Given that, half-life of A is 2 yr, choose the correct alternatives.
(a) Half-life of nuclei B is 1 yr
(b) At $t = 4$ yr, activities of A and B are equal.
(c) At $t = 6$ yr, ratio of number of nuclei of A to that of B is 2 : 1.
(d) Fraction of nuclei decayed in one mean life for A and B are f_1 and f_2, respectively, $f_1 > f_2$.

4 At $t = 0$, a sample of radio-nuclide A has the same decay rate as a sample of radio-nuclide B has at $t = 60$ min. The disintegration constants of A and B are λ_A and λ_B, respectively, with $\lambda_A < \lambda_B$.
(a) The half-life of radio-nuclide A is greater than that of B.
(b) At $t = 60$ min, number of atoms in sample of material A is greater than that of sample B.
(c) The two samples will never have the same decay rate simultaneously.
(d) After some time, the two samples will have the same decay rate simultaneously for an instant.

5. $_{92}U^{235}$ is α (Alpha) active. Then, in a large quantity of the element
(a) The probability of a nucleus disintegrating during one second is lower in the first half-life and greater in the fifth half-life.
(b) The probability of a nucleus disintegrating during one second remains constant for all time.
(c) More than half of U^{235} will remain even after the average life.
(d) The energy of the emitted α particle is less than the disintegration energy of the U^{235} nucleus.

6 The graph in figure shows how the count rate A of a radioactive source as measured by a Geiger counter varies with time t. [Assume, ln 12 = 2.6]

Which of the following quantities can be obtained from the above graph?

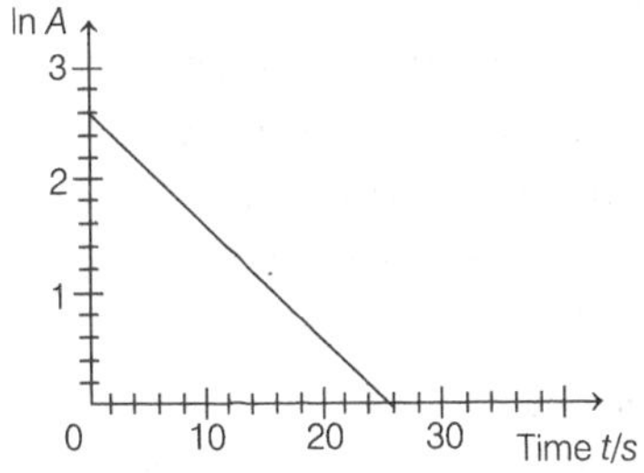

(a) Initial activity
(b) Initial number of active nuclei
(c) Type of radioactive decay
(d) Q-value of the decay reaction

7 The half-life of a radioactive sample can be experimentally found by the following method. A pure radioactive sample A decays into B by a decay.

$A \rightarrow B + \alpha$

N_A and N_B are measured at different times and $\dfrac{N_B}{N_A}$ is plotted against time. If time interval is much less than half-life,
(a) graph is straight line with negative slope.
(b) graph is straight line with positive slope.
(c) graph has slope whose magnitude is the disintegration constant.
(d) graph has slope whose magnitude is the reciprocal of disintegration constant.

8 A large population of radioactive nucleus starts disintegrating at $t = 0$. At time t, if $N =$ number of parent nuclei present, $D =$ the number of daughter nuclei present and $R =$ rate at which the daughter nuclei are produced, then the correct representation will be

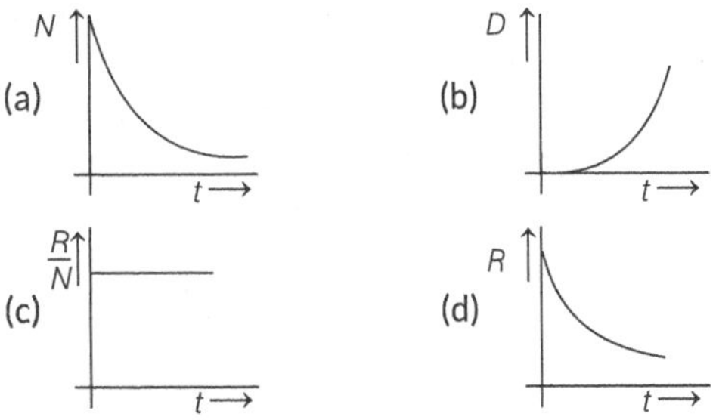

9 In a decay process A decays to B, $A \rightarrow B$. Two graphs of number of nuclei of A and B *versus* time is given then,

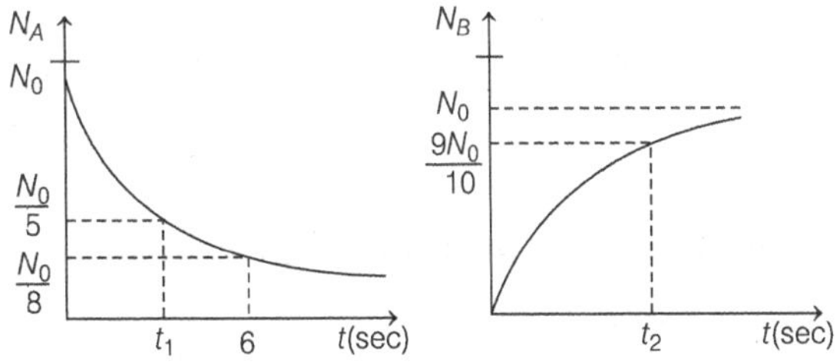

(a) $t_2 - t_1 = 4$ (b) $t_2 - t_1 = 2$
(c) $t_1 = 2\log_2 5$ (d) $t_2 = \log_2 100$

10 A radio-nuclide decays with a constant λ. Let $A = \log\left|\dfrac{dN}{dt}\right|$, where $\left|\dfrac{dN}{dt}\right|$ is the number of radioactive decay acts taking place per second. Suppose, the experiment starts at $t = 0$ and the curve between A and t is shown in the adjacent figure.

Now, choose the correct statement(s) from the following.

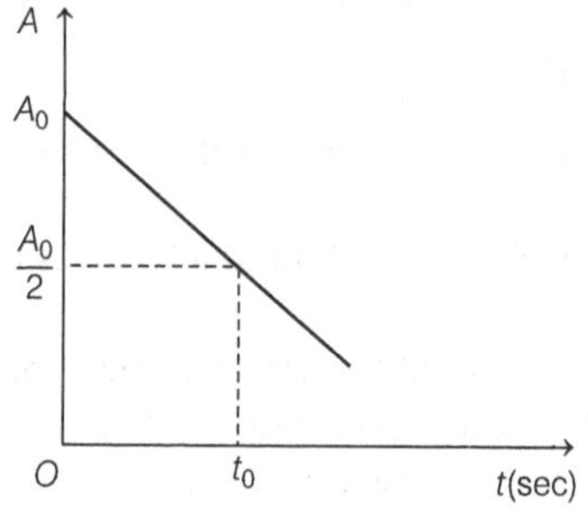

(a) Decay constant of the radioactive sample is $\frac{A_0}{2t_0}$.

(b) Number of radioactive nuclei at the start of the experiment was $\frac{t_0}{A_0}e^{A_0}$.

(c) Number of radioactive nuclei after half-life is $\frac{t_0}{A_0}e^{A_0}$.

(d) Half-life of radioactive sample is t_0.

11 A nucleus A (parent) decays into B (daughter) with half-life T_1 and B decays into C with half-life T_2. Graph is drawn between number of atoms/activity *versus* time. Select the correct graph(s).

(a) 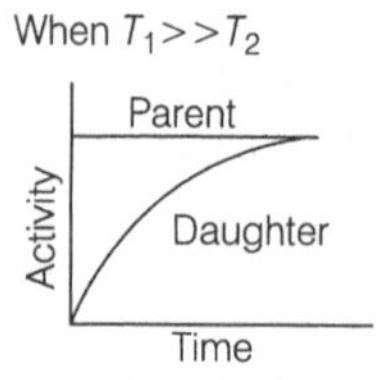

(b) 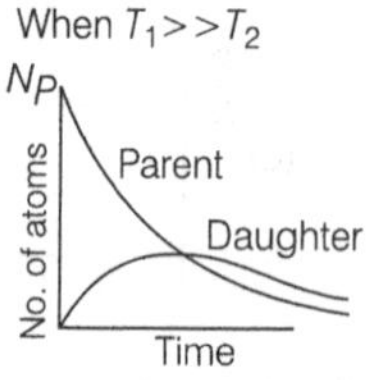

(c) 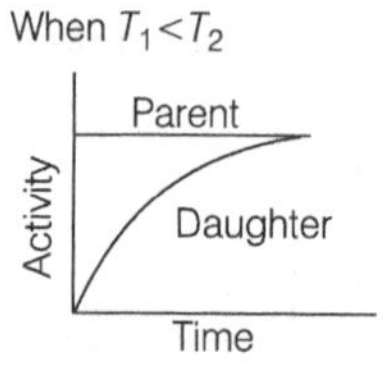

(d) 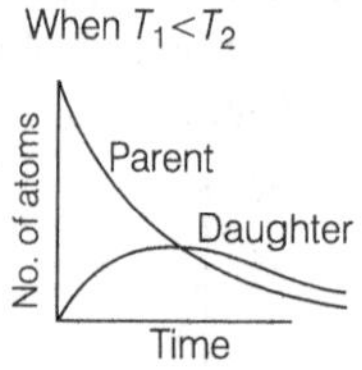

Comprehension Based Questions

Comprehension-I

$^{64}_{29}Cu$ can decay by β^- or β^+ emission, or electron capture. It is known that $^{64}_{29}Cu$ has a half-life of 12.8 h with 40% probability of β^- decay, 20% probability of β^+ decay and 40% probability of electron capture. The mass of $^{64}_{29}Cu$ is 63.92977 amu while $^{64}_{30}Zn$ is 63.92914 amu and $^{64}_{28}Ni$ is 63.92796 amu.

1 What is the half-life for electron capture?
(a) 5.12 h (b) 32 h
(c) 2.56 h (d) 16 h

2 What is the Q-value of β^- decay?
(a) 0.587 MeV (b) 0.077 MeV
(c) 1.686 MeV (d) 0.666 MeV

3 If initially there was 10^{22} atoms of $^{64}_{29}Cu$, what is the initial rate at which energy is being produced due to β^+ decay?
(a) 5.8×10^4 W (b) 3.2×10^3 W
(c) 8.4×10^2 W (d) 1.6×10^4 W

Comprehension-2

The radio-nuclide ^{56}Mn is being produced in a cyclotron at a constant rate P by bombarding a manganese target with deuterons. ^{56}Mn has a half-life of 2.5 h and the target contains large number of only the stable manganese isotope ^{55}Mn. The reaction that produces ^{56}Mn is

$$^{55}Mn + d \longrightarrow {}^{56}Mn + p$$

After being bombarded for a long time, the activity of ^{56}Mn becomes constant equal to $13.86\times10^{10}\ s^{-1}$. (Use ln 2 = 0.693, Avogadro number $=6\times10^{23}$, atomic weight of ^{56}Mn = 56 gm/mol).

4 At what constant rate P, ^{56}Mn nuclei are being produced in the cyclotron during the bombardment?
(a) 2×10^{11} nuclei/s
(b) 13.86×10^{10} nuclei/s
(c) 9.6×10^{10} nuclei/s
(d) 6.93×10^{10} nuclei/s

5 After the activity of ^{56}Mn becomes constant, number of ^{56}Mn nuclei present in the target, is equal to
(a) 5×10^{11}
(b) 20×10^{11}
(c) 1.2×10^{14}
(d) 1.8×10^{15}

6 After a long time bombardment, number of ^{56}Mn nuclei present in the target depends upon
(A) the number of ^{56}Mn nuclei present at the start of the process
(B) half-life of the ^{56}Mn
(C) the constant rate of production P
(a) All (A), (B) and (C) are correct
(b) only (A) and (B) are correct
(c) only (B) and (C) are correct
(d) only (A) and (C) are correct

Comprehension-3

A radioactive with decay constant λ is being produced in a nuclear reactor at a rate q_0t per second, where q_0 is a positive constant and t is the time. During each decay, E_0 energy is released. The production of radio-nuclide starts at time $t = 0$.

7 Which differential equation correctly represents the above process?

(a) $\frac{dN}{dt}+\lambda N=q_0 t$ (b) $\frac{dN}{dt}-\lambda N=q_0 t$

(c) $\frac{dN}{dt}+q_0 t=\lambda N$ (d) $\frac{dN}{dt}+q_0 t=-\lambda N$

8 Instantaneous power developed at time t due to the decay of the radio-nuclide is

(a) $\left(q_0 t-\frac{q_0}{\lambda}+\frac{q_0}{\lambda}e^{-\lambda t}\right)E_0$

(b) $\left(q_0 t+\frac{q_0}{\lambda}-\frac{q_0}{\lambda}e^{-\lambda t}\right)E_0$

(c) $\left(q_0 t+\frac{q_0}{\lambda}+\frac{q_0}{\lambda}e^{-\lambda t}\right)E_0$

(d) $\left(q_0 t-\frac{q_0}{\lambda}-\frac{q_0}{\lambda}e^{-\lambda t}\right)E_0$

9 Average power developed in time t due to the decay of the radio-nuclide is

(a) $\left(\frac{q_0 t}{2}-\frac{q_0}{\lambda}+\frac{q_0}{\lambda^2 t}-\frac{q_0}{\lambda^2 t}e^{-\lambda t}\right)E_0$

(b) $\left(\frac{q_0 t}{2}+\frac{q_0}{\lambda}+\frac{q_0}{\lambda^2 t}-\frac{q_0}{\lambda^2 t}e^{-\lambda t}\right)E_0$

(c) $\left(\frac{q_0 t}{2}-\frac{q_0}{\lambda}+\frac{q_0}{\lambda^2 t}+\frac{q_0}{\lambda^2 t}e^{-\lambda t}\right)E_0$

(d) $\left(\frac{q_0 t}{2}+\frac{q_0}{\lambda}+\frac{q_0}{\lambda^2 t}+\frac{q_0}{\lambda^2 t}e^{-\lambda t}\right)E_0$

Match the Columns Questions

1. Match the following

	Column I		Column II
A.	1 Rutherford	1.	1 dps
B.	1 Becquerel	2.	3.7×10^{10} dps
C.	1 Curie	3.	10^6 dps
D.	Activity of 1 g of Ra^{226}	4.	10^{10} dps

2 Figure shows activities A of three different radioactive material samples (labelled as I, II and III) *versus* time. Using the given information, correctly match the requisite parameter in the left Column with the options given in right Column. Consider only their natural decay as the cause of rate of change of number of parent nuclei

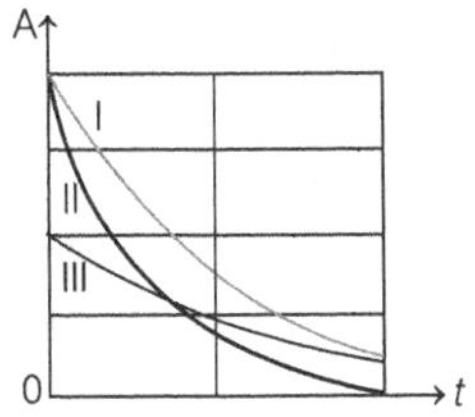

	Column I		Column II
A.	Disintegration constant (λ) has maximum value for the material of sample.	1.	I
B.	Half-life is maximum for the material of the sample.	2.	II
C.	Initially if samples of all three materials have same number of atoms, then number of parent atoms of which of the sample will be maximum at any later time.	3.	III
D.	Suppose all the materials decay by emitting α-particles of same energy and initially all three samples contain same amount (in gm) of the materials. Till the end of time span equal to their respective half-lives, maximum energy is radiated by the sample.	4.	It is not possible to compare with the help of data available.

3 Consider two radioactive nuclei A and B. Both convert into a stable nucleus C. Nucleus A converts into C after emitting two α-particles and three β-particles. Nucleus B converts into C after emitting one α-particle and five β-particles. At time $t=0$, number of nuclei of A are $4N_0$ and that of B are N_0. Half-life of A (in conversion of A into C) is 1 min and of that B (in conversion of B into C) is 2 min. Initially number of nuclei of C are zero. Then, match the following table

	Column I		Column II
A.	The difference between atomic number of A and that of B is	1.	6
B.	The difference between mass number of A and that of B is	2.	4
C.	If at an instant number of nuclei of A are equal to number of nuclei of B, then at the same instant the ratio between number of nuclei of C and number of nuclei of B is	3.	18
D.	The time t at which rate of disintegrations of A are equal to that of B in minutes is	4.	2
		5.	0.25

4. Match the following

	Column I		Column II
A.	Binding energy per nucleon for middle order of elements is	1.	spin of nucleon
B.	Nuclear force depends on	2.	200 MeV

	Column I		Column II
C.	In nuclear fission energy released is about	3.	temperature, pressure
D.	The radioactive decay rate is not affected by	4.	8 MeV
		5.	Number of neutrons
		6.	Charge of nucleons
		7.	2 MeV
		8.	26.6 MeV

Numerical Value Questions

1 A radioactive sample contains two radio-nucleoids A and B having decay constant $\lambda\, h^{-1}$ and $2\lambda\, h^{-1}$. Initially 25% of total decay comes from A. How long (in h) will it take before 75% of total decay comes from A? [Take, $\lambda = \ln 3$]

2. The nuclei of two radioactive isotopes of same substance A^{236} and A^{234} are present in the ratio 4 : 1 in an ore obtained from Mars. Their half-lives are 30 min and 60 min, respectively. Both isotopes are alpha emitters and the activity of the isotope with half-life 30 min is one Rutherford. Calculate after how much time (in min) their activities will become identical.

3 A radioactive sample contains two different types of radioactive nuclei. A with half-life 5 days and B with half-life 30 days. Initially, the decay rate of the A-type nuclei is 64 times that of B-type nuclei. Find the number of days after which their decay rates will be equal.

4 A radioactive material decays by β-particle emission. During the first 2 s of a measurement, $n\beta$-particles are emitted and in the next 2 s 0.75 $n\beta$-particles are emitted. Calculate the mean life of this material (in s) to the nearest whole number. ($\ln 3 = 1.0986$ and $\ln 2 = 0.6931$).

5 A laboratory stock solution is prepared with an initial activity due to ^{24}Na of 2.5 mCi/ml, and 10 ml of the stock solution is diluted (at $t_0 = 0$) to a working solution whose total volume is 250 ml. After 30 h, a 5 ml sample of the working solution is monitored with a counter. What is the measured activity (in μCi)? Given that half-life of ^{24}Na is 15 h.

6 Equal masses of two samples of charcoal A and B are burnt separately and the resulting carbon dioxide are collected in two vessels. The radioactivity of ^{14}C is measured for both the samples. The gas from the charcoal A gives 2100 counts per week and gas from the charcoal B gives 1400 counts per week.

Find the age difference (in yr) between two samples. Half-life of $^{14}C = 5730$ yr and $\left[\ln\left(\frac{3}{2}\right) = 0.4055\right]$

7. In a slow reaction, heat is being evolved at a rate about 10 mW in a liquid. If the heat were being generated by the decay of ^{32}P, a radioactive isotope of phosphorus that has half-life of 14 days and emits only beta-particles with a mean energy of 700 keV, estimate the number of ^{32}P atoms in the liquid. Express your answer in form of $A \times 10^{16}$ and fill A in OMR sheet. [Take, $\ln 2 = 0.675$]

8 A radioactive sample decays with a mean life of 20 ms. A capacitor of capacitance 100 μF is charged to some potential and then the plates are connected through a wire of resistance R. What should be the value of R (in ohm) so that, the ratio of the charge on the capacitor to the activity of the radioactive sample remain constant in time?

9. A small quantity of solution containing Na^{24} radio-nuclide (half-life 15 hours) of activity 1.0 microcurie is injected into the blood of a person. A sample of the blood of volume 1 cm^3 taken after 5 h shows an activity of 296 disintegrations per minute. Determine the total volume (in litre) of blood in the body of the person. Assume that the radioactive solution mixes uniformly in the blood of the person. (1 curie $= 3.7 \times 10^{10}$ disintegrations per second, $2^{1/3} = 1.25$)

10 The element Curium $_{96}Cm^{248}$ has a mean life of 10^{13} s. Its primary decay modes are spontaneous fission and α-decay, the former with a probability of 8% and the latter with a probability of 92%. Each fission releases 200 MeV of energy. The masses involved in α-decay are as follows. Atomic masses of atoms are $_{96}Cm^{248} = 248.072220$ u, $He^4 = 4.002603$ u and $Pu^{244} = 244.064100$ u. (1 u = 931 MeV/c^2). If the power output from a sample of 10^{20} Cm atoms is 3.3×10^{-n} W. then find n.

Previous year's Questions

JEE Main

1 Two radioactive elements A and B initially have same number of atoms. The half life of A is same as the average life of B. If λ_A and λ_B are decay constants of A and B respectively, then choose the correct relation from the given options. **[2023, 11 April Shift-I]**

(a) $\lambda_A = 2\lambda_B$ (b) $\lambda_A \ln 2 = \lambda_B$
(c) $\lambda_A = \lambda_B$ (d) $\lambda_A = \lambda_B \ln 2$

2 Substance A has atomic mass number 16 and half-life of 1 day. Another substance B has atomic mass number 32 and half-life of $1/2$ day.
If both A and B simultaneously start undergo radioactivity at the same time with initial mass 320 g each, how many total atoms of A and B combined would be left after 2 days. **[2023, 29 Jan Shift-II]**

(a) 1.69×10^{24} (b) 6.76×10^{24}
(c) 3.38×10^{24} (d) 6.76×10^{23}

3 If a radioactive element having half-life of 30 min is undergoing beta decay, the fraction of radioactive element remains undecayed after 90 min, will be **[2023, 29 Jan Shift-I]**

(a) $\frac{1}{16}$ (b) $\frac{1}{8}$ (c) $\frac{1}{2}$ (d) $\frac{1}{4}$

4 A radioactive nucleus decays by two different process. The half-life of the first process is 5 min and that of the second process is 30 s, The effective half-life of the nucleus is calculated to be $\alpha/11$ s, The value of α is .... **[2023, 30 Jan Shift-II]**

5 The activity of a radioactive material is 6.4×10^{-4} curie. Its half-life is 5 days. The activity will become 5×10^{-6} curie after **[2022, 27 July Shift-II]**

(a) 7 days (b) 15 days (c) 25 days (d) 35 days

6 The disintegration rate of a certain radioactive sample at any instant is 4250 disintegrations per minute. 10 minutes later, the rate becomes 2250 disintegrations per minute. The approximate decay constant is (Take, $\log_{10} 1.88 = 0.274$) **[2022, 26 July Shift-I]**

(a) $0.02\ \text{min}^{-1}$ (b) $2.7\ \text{min}^{-1}$
(c) $0.063\ \text{min}^{-1}$ (d) $6.3\ \text{min}^{-1}$

7 A radioactive nucleus can decay by two different processes. Half-life for the first process is 3.0 h while it is 4.5 h for the second process. The effective half-life of the nucleus will be **[2022, 26 June Shift-II]**

(a) 3.75 h (b) 0.56 h (c) 0.26 h (d) 1.80 h

8 The half-life period of a radioactive substance is 60 days. The time taken for 7/8 th of its original mass to disintegrate will be **[2022, 28 July Shift-I]**

(a) 120 days (b) 130 days
(c) 180 days (d) 20 days

9 Following statements related to radioactivity are given below

(A) Radioactivity is a random and spontaneous process and is dependent on physical and chemical conditions.
(B) The number of un-decayed nuclei in the radioactive sample decays exponentially with time.
(C) Slope of the graph of $\log_e$ (number of undecayed nuclei) *versus* time represents the reciprocal of mean life time (τ).
(D) Product of decay constant (λ) and half-life time ($T_{1/2}$) is not constant.

Choose the most appropriate answer from the options given below. **[2022, 28 June Shift-II]**

(a) (A) and (B) only (b) (B) and (D) only
(c) (B) and (C) only (d) (C) and (D) only

10 The half-life of a radioactive substance is 5 yr. After x years a given sample of the radioactive substance gets reduced to 6.25% of its initial value of x is .... **[2022, 29 June Shift-II]**

11 Two radioactive materials A and B have decay constants 25λ and 16λ, respectively. If initially they have the same number of nuclei, then the ratio of the number of nuclei of B to that of A will be e after a time $\frac{1}{a\lambda}$. The value of a is .... **[2022, 29 July Shift-II]**

12 A radioactive sample has an average life of 30 ms and is decaying. A capacitor of capacitance 200 μF is first charged and later connected with resistor R. If the ratio of charge on capacitor to the activity of radioactive sample is fixed with respect to time, then the value of R should be .... Ω. **[2021, 27 July Shift-I]**

13 Some nuclei of a radioactive material are undergoing radioactive decay. The time gap between the instances when a quarter of the nuclei have decayed and when half of the nuclei have decayed is given as (where, λ is the decay constant) **[2021, 25 July Shift-I]**

(a) $\frac{1}{2}\frac{\ln 2}{\lambda}$ (b) $\ln\frac{(3/2)}{\lambda}$ (c) $\frac{2\ln 2}{\lambda}$ (d) $\frac{\ln 2}{\lambda}$

14 There are 10^{10} radioactive nuclei in a given radioactive element. Its half-life time is 1min. How many nuclei will remain after 30 s? ($\sqrt{2} = 1.414$) **[2021, 27 Aug Shift-I]**

(a) 2×10^{10} (b) 7×10^{9}
(c) 10^{5} (d) 4×10^{10}

15 At time $t = 0$, a material is composed of two radioactive atoms A and B, where $N_A(0) = 2N_B(0)$. The decay constant of both kind of radioactive atoms is λ. However, A disintegrates to B and B disintegrates to C. Which of the following figures represents the evolution of $N_B(t)/N_B(0)$ with respect to time t?

$$\begin{bmatrix} N_A(0) = \text{Number of } A \text{ atoms at } t = 0 \\ N_B(0) = \text{Number of } B \text{ atoms at } t = 0 \end{bmatrix}$$

[2021, 26 Aug Shift-II]

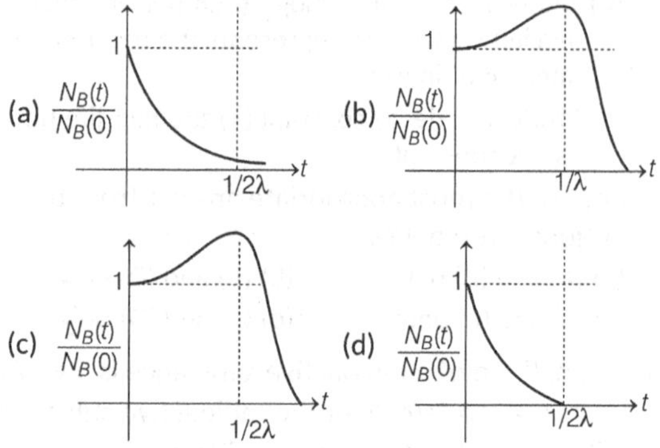

16 Consider the following statements. **[2021, 27 July Shift-II]**

A. Atoms of each element emit characteristics spectrum.

B. According to Bohr's postulate, an electron in a hydrogen atom, revolves in a certain stationary orbit.

C. The density of nuclear matter depends on the size of the nucleus.

D. A free neutron is stable but a free proton decay is possible.

E. Radioactivity is an indication of the instability of nuclei.

Choose the correct answer from the options given below.

(a) A, B, C, D and E (b) A, B and E

(c) B and D (d) A, C and E

17 If f denotes the ratio of the number of nuclei decayed (N_d) to the number of nuclei at $t = 0$ (N_0), then for a collection of radioactive nuclei, the rate of change of f with respect to time is given as **[2021, 27 July Shift-I]**

[λ is the radioactive decay constant]

(a) $-\lambda(1-e^{-\lambda t})$ (b) $\lambda(1-e^{-\lambda t})$

(c) $\lambda e^{-\lambda t}$ (d) $-\lambda e^{-\lambda t}$

18 For a certain radioactive process, the graph between $\ln R$ and t (sec) is obtained as shown in the figure. Then, the value of half-life for the unknown radioactive material is approximately **[2021, 20 July Shift-II]**

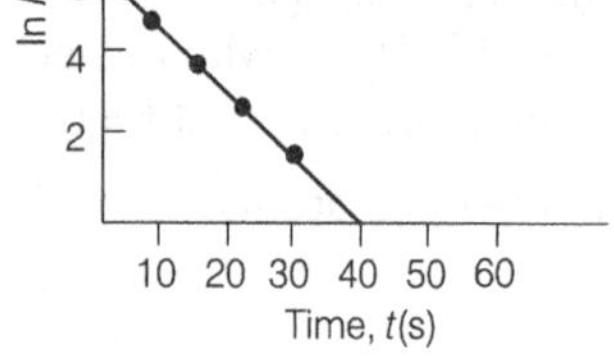

(a) 9.15 s (b) 6.93 s

(c) 2.62 s (d) 4.62 s

19 A radioactive material decays by simultaneous emission of two particles with half-lives of 1400 yr and 700 yr, respectively. What will be the time after the which one-third of the material remains ? [Take, $\ln 3 = 1.1$] **[2021, 20 July Shift-I]**

(a) 1110 yr (b) 700 yr

(c) 340 yr (d) 740 yr

20 A radioactive sample is undergoing α-decay. At any time t_1, its activity is A and another time t_2, the activity is $A/5$. What is the average life time for the sample? **[2021, 26 Feb Shift-II]**

(a) $\frac{\ln 5}{t_2 - t_1}$ (b) $\frac{t_1 - t_2}{\ln 5}$

(c) $\frac{t_2 - t_1}{\ln 5}$ (d) $\frac{\ln(t_2 + t_1)}{2}$

JEE Advanced

1. In a radioactive decay process, the activity is defined as $A = -dN/dt$, where $N(t)$ is the number of radioactive nuclei at time t. Two radioactive sources, S_1 and S_2 have same activity at time $t = 0$. At a later time, the activities of S_1 and S_2 are A_1 and A_2, respectively. When S_1 and S_2 have just completed their 3rd and 7th half-lives, respectively, the ratio A_1/A_2 is .... **(2023 Adv.)**

2. A heavy nucleus Q of half-life 20 min undergoes α-decay with probability of 60% and β-decay with probability of 40%. Initially, the number of Q nuclei is 1000. The number of α-decays of Q in the first one hour is **(2021 Adv.)**

(a) 50 (b) 75

(c) 350 (d) 525

3. ^{131}I is an isotope of Iodine that decays into an isotope of Xenon with a half-life of 8 days. A small amount of a serum labelled with ^{131}I is injected into the blood of a person. The activity of the amount of ^{131}I injected was 2.4×10^5 Becquerel (Bq). It is known that the injected serum will get distributed uniformly in the blood stream in less than half an hour. After 11.5 h, 2.5 ml of blood is drawn from the person's body, and gives an activity of 115 Bq. The total volume of blood in the person's body, in litres is approximately (you may use $e^x \approx 1 + x$ for $|x| << 1$ and $\ln 2 \approx 0.7$). **(2017 Adv.)**

4. An accident in a nuclear laboratory resulted in deposition of a certain amount of radioactive material of half-life 18 days inside the laboratory. Tests revealed that the radiation was 64 times more than the permissible level required for safe operation of the laboratory. What is the minimum number of days after which the laboratory can be considered safe for use? **(2016 Adv.)**
   (a) 64 (b) 90
   (c) 108 (d) 120

5. For a radioactive material, its activity A and rate of change of its activity R are defined as $A = -\frac{dN}{dt}$ and $R = -\frac{dA}{dt}$, where $N(t)$ is the number of nuclei at time t. Two radioactive source P(mean life τ) and Q (mean life 2τ) have the same activity at $t = 0$. Their rate of change of activities at $t = 2\tau$ are R_P and R_Q, respectively. If $\frac{R_P}{R_Q} = \frac{n}{e}$, then the value of n is **(2015 Adv.)**

Answer Key

Level 1

11.1 Radioactivity Decay Law

1. (a) 64.17 mm (b) 92 min (c) 1600 s
2. (a) 0.231 s^{-1} (b) 9 s (c) 231 s^{-1}
3. (a) 5,315 yr (b) 243.2 yr
4. 1.35 gm
5. (a) 14.43 s (b) 40 s
6. 1 : 1
7. 1.13×10^{15} β-particles
8. $1 - e^{-\lambda t}$

11.2 Activity

1. 3.88 Ci
2. 3.05×10^{-14} g
3. 12 h
4. 200 Bq
5. (a) $3.05 \times 10^{-4} s^{-1}$ (b) 38 mins
6. 460 particles/min

11.3 Radioactive Dating

1. 1.868×10^9 year
2. 0.259
3. 1800 year

11.4 Disintegration with Successive Production

1. (i) $N = \frac{R}{\lambda}(1 - e^{-\lambda t})$ (ii) $\frac{R}{\lambda}(\lambda t - 1 + e^{-\lambda t})$ (iii) $\frac{R}{\lambda}$
2. (a) $N = \frac{R}{\lambda}[\alpha - (\alpha - \lambda N_0)e^{-\lambda t}]$ (b) $3N_0/2,\ 2N_0$

11.5 Simultaneous Decay

1. $\frac{t_1 t_2}{t_1 + t_2}$
2. 443.52 years

11.6 Sequential Decay

1. $N_1 = N_0 e^{-\lambda_1 t},\ N_2 = \frac{\lambda_1 N_0}{\lambda_2 - \lambda_1}(e^{-\lambda_1 t} - e^{-\lambda_2 t}),\ N_3 = N_0 - (N_1 + N_2)$
2. $t = 16.5$ s, $N_x = 1.92 \times 10^{19},\ N_z = 2.3 \times 10^{19}$
3. $\lambda_p N_p = \lambda_d N_d$

Level 2

Single Choice Correct Questions

1. (a)	2. (b)	3. (d)	4. (a)	5. (a)
6. (c)	7. (b)	8. (b)	9. (c)	10. (a)
11. (c)	12. (c)	13. (d)	14. (b)	15. (c)
16. (a)	17. (d)	18. (a)	19. (c)	20. (d)
21. (b)	22. (d)	23. (c)	24. (b)	25. (a)
26. (c)	27. (d)	28. (a)	29. (c)	30. (d)
31. (c)	32. (d)	33. (a)	34. (d)	35. (c)
36. (b)	37. (b)	38. (c)	39. (a)	40. (d)
41. (c)	42. (d)	43. (a)	44. (c)	45. (a)
46. (c)	47. (a)	48. (a)	49. (b)	50. (c)
51. (c)	52. (a)	53. (b)	54. (a)	

Multiple Choice(s) Correct Questions

1. (a,b,c,d) 2. (a, d) 3. (a, c) 4. (a, c)
5. (b, d) 6. (a, b) 7. (b, c) 8. (a, c)
9. (b, c, d) 10. (a, c) 11. (a, d)

Comprehension Based Questions

1. (b) 2. (a) 3. (b) 4. (b) 5. (d) 6. (c) 7. (a) 8. (a) 9. (a)

Match the Columns

1. A → 3; B → 1; C → 2; D → 2
2. A → 2; B → 3; C → 3, 4; D → 4
3. A → 2; B → 2; C → 3; D → 1
4. A → 4; B → 1; C → 2; D → 3

Numerical Value Questions

1. 2 2. 180 3. 36 4. 7
5. 125 6. 3353 7. 16 8. 200
9. 6 10. 5

Previous Year's Questions

JEE Main

1. (d)	2. (c)	3. (b)	4. (300)	5. (d)
6. (c)	7. (d)	8. (c)	9. (c)	10. (20)
11. (9)	12. (150)	13. (b)	14. (b)	15. (c)
16. (b)	17. (c)	18. (d)	19. (d)	20. (c)

JEE Advanced

1. (16) 2. (d) 3. (5) 4. (c) 5. (2)

SOLUTIONS

Level 1

11.1 Radioactivity Decay Law

1. (a) $T_{1/2} = \frac{\ln 2}{\lambda} = \frac{0.693}{1.8 \times 10^{-4}} = 3850 \text{ s} \simeq 64 \text{ min}$

(b) $T_{avg} = \frac{1}{\lambda} = \frac{1}{1.8 \times 10^{-4}} = 5555.5 \text{ s} \simeq 92 \text{min}$

(c) $t = \frac{1}{\lambda}\ln\left(\frac{N_0}{N}\right)$

$\Rightarrow \quad t = \frac{1}{1.8 \times 10^{-4}}\ln\left(\frac{N_0}{\left(\frac{3N_0}{4}\right)}\right)$

$\Rightarrow \quad t = 1600 \text{ s}$

2. (a) $T_{1/2} = 3 \text{ s} = \frac{\ln 2}{\lambda} \quad \Rightarrow \quad \lambda = 0.231 \text{ s}^{-1}$

(b) $N = \frac{N_0}{2^n} \quad \Rightarrow \quad 1000 = \frac{8000}{2^n} \quad \Rightarrow \quad n = 3$

So, $t_1 = 3T_{1/2} = 3(3) = 9 \text{ s}$

(c) $-\frac{dN}{dt} = \lambda N = (0.231)(1000) = 231 \text{ s}^{-1}$

3. $T_{1/2} = \frac{\ln 2}{\lambda} = 1600 \quad \Rightarrow \quad \lambda = \frac{\ln 2}{(1600 \text{ yr})}$

(a) $t = \frac{1}{\lambda}\ln\left(\frac{m_0}{m}\right)$

$\Rightarrow \quad t = \frac{1600}{\ln 2}\ln\left(\frac{1}{100 \times 10^{-3}}\right) = 5315 \text{ yr}$

(b) $t = \frac{1}{\lambda}\ln\left(\frac{m_0}{m}\right)$

$\Rightarrow \quad t = \frac{1600}{\ln 2}\ln\left(\frac{1}{900 \times 10^{-3}}\right) = 243.2 \text{ yr}$

4. $t = 2T_{avg} = 2\left(\frac{1}{\lambda}\right) = \frac{2}{\lambda}$

$m = m_0 e^{-\lambda t} = 10e^{-\lambda\left(\frac{2}{\lambda}\right)} = \frac{10}{e^2} = 1.35 \text{ gm}$

5. (a) In 10 s, number of undecayed nuclei goes from 25% to 12.5%. So, half-life of sample would be 10 s.

$T_{1/2} = \frac{\ln 2}{\lambda} = 10 \quad \Rightarrow \quad \lambda = \frac{\ln 2}{10}$

$T_{mean} = \frac{1}{\lambda} = \frac{10}{\ln 2} = 14.43 \text{ s}$

(b) $N = \frac{N_0}{2^n}$

$\Rightarrow \quad \frac{6.25}{100}N_0 = \frac{N_0}{2^n}$

$\Rightarrow \quad n = 4$

So, $\quad t = nT_{1/2} = 4(10) = 40 \text{ s}$

6. In 2 days,

Number of half-lives of first substance $= \frac{48}{12} = 4$

Number of half-lives of second substance $= \frac{48}{16} = 3$

After n half-lives, $N = \frac{N_0}{2^n}$

$\therefore \quad N_1 = \frac{(N_0)_1}{2^4} \quad \text{and} \quad N_2 = \frac{(N_0)_2}{2^3}$

So, $\frac{N_1}{N_2} = \frac{(N_0)_1}{(N_0)_2} \times \frac{2^3}{2^4} = \left(\frac{2}{1}\right)\left(\frac{8}{16}\right) = 1:1$

7. $N_o = \frac{1 \times 10^{-6}}{24} \times 6 \times 10^{23} = 2.5 \times 10^{16}$

$T_{1/2} = \frac{\ln 2}{\lambda} = 15 \quad \Rightarrow \quad \lambda = \frac{\ln 2}{15}$

Number of β-particles emitted in one hour

$= N_o(1 - e^{-\lambda t})$

$= 2.5 \times 10^{16}\left(1 - e^{-\left(\frac{\ln 2}{15}\right)1}\right)$

$= 1.13 \times 10^{15}$

8. Number of nuclei decayed $= N_o(1 - e^{-\lambda t})$

Probability of decay of a nucleus $= \frac{N_0(1 - e^{-\lambda t})}{N_0} = 1 - e^{-\lambda t}$

11.2 Activity

1. Number of nuclei in 1 μg of ^{64}Cu

$= N = \frac{1 \times 10^{-6}}{63.5} \times 6.02 \times 10^{23}$

Activity $= \lambda N = 1.516 \times 10^{-5}\left(\frac{1 \times 10^{-6}}{63.5} \times 6.02 \times 10^{23}\right)$

$= 14.37 \times 10^{10}$ dps

$= 3.88$ curie $\quad [\because 1 \text{ curie} = 3.7 \times 10^{10} \text{ dps}]$

2. Activity $= \lambda N = 1\mu\text{Ci}$

$\Rightarrow \quad \left(\frac{\ln 2}{T_{1/2}}\right)N = 1 \times 10^{-6} \times 3.7 \times 10^{10}$

$\Rightarrow \quad N = \frac{1 \times 10^{-6} \times 3.7 \times 10^{10} \times (26.8 \times 60)}{\ln 2}$

$\Rightarrow \quad N = 8.58 \times 10^7$

Mass of sample $= \frac{N}{N_A} \times M = \frac{8.58 \times 10^7}{6.02 \times 10^{23}} \times 214$

$= 3.05 \times 10^{-14}$ gm

3. Let initial activity be A_0,

Activity at permissible safe level $= \frac{A_0}{64}$

After n half-lives, $A = \frac{A_0}{2^n}$

$$\Rightarrow \quad \frac{A_0}{64} = \frac{A_0}{2^n} \quad \Rightarrow \quad n = 6$$

$$t = nT_{1/2} = 6(2) = 12\text{ h}$$

4. $A = \frac{A_0}{2^n} \quad \Rightarrow \quad 100 = \frac{1600}{2^n}$

$$\Rightarrow \quad n = 4$$

$$\therefore \quad t = nT_{1/2} \quad \Rightarrow \quad 8 = 4T_{1/2}$$

$$\Rightarrow \quad T_{1/2} = 2\text{ s}$$

At, $t = 6$ s, $t = nT_{1/2}$

$$\Rightarrow \quad 6 = n(2) \quad \Rightarrow \quad n = 3$$

$$\Rightarrow \quad A = \frac{A_0}{2^n} = \frac{1600}{2^3} = 200\text{ Bq}$$

5. (a) $t = \frac{1}{\lambda}\ln\left(\frac{A_0}{A}\right)$

$$\Rightarrow \quad 50 \times 60 = \frac{1}{\lambda}\ln\left(\frac{500}{200}\right)$$

$$\Rightarrow \quad \lambda = \frac{\ln(2.5)}{3000} = \frac{0.916}{3000} = 3.05 \times 10^{-4}\text{ s}^{-1}$$

(b) $T_{1/2} = \frac{\ln 2}{\lambda} = \frac{0.693}{3.05 \times 10^{-4}} = 2272\text{ s} \simeq 38\text{min}$

6. $t = \frac{1}{2}T_{1/2} = \frac{1}{2}\left(\frac{\ln 2}{\lambda}\right)$

$$A = A_0 e^{-\lambda t} = 650 e^{-\lambda\frac{1}{2}\left(\frac{\ln 2}{\lambda}\right)} = \frac{650}{\sqrt{2}} = 460\text{ particles per minute}$$

11.3 Radioactive dating

1.

	$U^{238} \longrightarrow$	Pb^{206}
$t = 0,$	N_0	0
$t = t,$	N	$N_0 - N$

$$\frac{N}{N_0 - N} = 3 \quad \Rightarrow \quad N = \frac{3N_0}{4}$$

$$t = \frac{1}{\lambda}\ln\left(\frac{N_0}{N}\right) = \frac{T_{1/2}}{\ln 2}\ln\left(\frac{N_0}{\frac{3N_0}{4}}\right)$$

$$= 4.5 \times 10^9\left(\frac{2\ln 2 - \ln 3}{\ln 2}\right)$$

$$= 1.868 \times 10^9\text{ yr}$$

2. Number of half-lives $= n = \frac{t}{T_{1/2}} = \frac{1.5 \times 10^9}{4.5 \times 10^9} = \frac{1}{3}$

	$U \longrightarrow$	Pb
$t = 0,$	N_0	0
$t = t,$	N	$N_0 - N$

$$\therefore \quad \frac{N_0 - N}{N} = \frac{N_0}{N} - 1 = 2^n - 1 = 2^{\frac{1}{3}} - 1 = 1.259 - 1 = 0.259$$

3. $t = \frac{1}{\lambda}\ln\left(\frac{A_0}{A}\right) = \frac{T_{1/2}}{\ln 2}\ln\left(\frac{A_0}{A}\right) = \frac{5730}{\ln 2}\ln\left(\frac{15.3}{12.3}\right)$

$$= \frac{5730 \times 0.218}{0.693} = 1802\text{ yr}$$

11.4 Disintegration with Successive Production

1. (i) For A, $\frac{dN}{dt} = R - \lambda N$

$$\Rightarrow \quad \int_0^N \frac{dN}{R - \lambda N} = \int_0^t dt$$

$$\Rightarrow \quad -\frac{1}{\lambda}[\ln(R - \lambda N)]_0^N = [t]_0^t$$

$$\Rightarrow \quad N = \frac{R}{\lambda}(1 - e^{-\lambda t})$$

(ii) Number of nuclei of A produced in t time $= Rt$

Number of nuclei of A decayed in t time $= Rt - N$

$\therefore$ Number of nuclei of B at time $t = Rt - N$

$$= Rt - \frac{R}{\lambda}(1 - e^{-\lambda t})$$

$$= \frac{R}{\lambda}(\lambda t - 1 + e^{-\lambda t})$$

(iii) Number of nuclei A will be maximum when

$$\frac{dN}{dt} = R - \lambda N = 0 \quad \Rightarrow \quad N = \frac{R}{\lambda}$$

2. (a) $\frac{dN}{dt} = \alpha - \lambda N$

$$\Rightarrow \quad \int_{N_0}^N \frac{dN}{\alpha - \lambda N} = \int_0^t dt$$

$$\Rightarrow \quad \frac{[\ln(\alpha - \lambda N)]_{N_0}^N}{(-\lambda)} = [t]_0^t$$

$$\Rightarrow \quad N = \frac{1}{\lambda}[\alpha - (\alpha - \lambda N_0)e^{-\lambda t}]$$

(b) Given, $\alpha = 2N_0\lambda$ and $t = T_{1/2} = \frac{\ln 2}{\lambda}$

$$N = \frac{1}{\lambda}\left[2N_0\lambda - (2N_0\lambda - \lambda N_0)e^{-\lambda\left(\frac{\ln 2}{\lambda}\right)}\right]$$

$$= \frac{3N_0}{2}$$

As $t \to \infty$, $N = \frac{1}{\lambda}[2N_0\lambda - (2N_0\lambda - \lambda N_0)e^{-\infty}] = 2N_0$

11.5 Simultaneous Decay

1. $\lambda = \lambda_1 + \lambda_2$

$$\Rightarrow \quad \frac{\ln 2}{t} = \frac{\ln 2}{t_1} + \frac{\ln 2}{t_2}$$

$\Rightarrow \quad \frac{1}{t} = \frac{1}{t_1} + \frac{1}{t_2}$

$\Rightarrow \quad t = \frac{t_1 t_2}{t_1 + t_2}$

2. For simultaneous decay,

$\lambda = \lambda_1 + \lambda_2$

$\Rightarrow \quad \lambda = \frac{1}{T_1} + \frac{1}{T_2}$

$\Rightarrow \quad \lambda = \frac{1}{1600} + \frac{1}{400} = \frac{1}{320}$ per yr

$$t = \frac{1}{\lambda}\ln\left(\frac{N_0}{N}\right) = 320\ln\left[\frac{N_0}{\left(\frac{N_0}{4}\right)}\right] = 320\ln 4 = 443.52 \text{ yr}$$

11.6 Sequential Decay

1. $A \xrightarrow{\lambda_1} B \xrightarrow{\lambda_2} C$

$t = 0$	N_0	0	0
$t = t$	N_1	N_2	N_3

Here, N_1, N_2 and N_3 are the nuclei of A, B and C at any time t

For A, $\quad N_1 = N_0 e^{-\lambda_1 t}$

For B, $\quad \frac{dN_2}{dt} = \lambda_1 N_1 - \lambda_2 N_2$

$\Rightarrow \quad \frac{dN_2}{dt} + \lambda_2 N_2 = \lambda_1 N_0 e^{-\lambda_1 t}$

This is a linear differential equation with integrating factor of $e^{\lambda_2 t}$.

$$e^{\lambda_2 t}\frac{dN_2}{dt} + e^{\lambda_2 t}\lambda_2 N_2 = \lambda_1 N_0 e^{-\lambda_1 t} e^{\lambda_2 t}$$

$\Rightarrow \quad \int d(N_2 e^{\lambda_2 t}) = \lambda_1 N_0 \int e^{-\lambda_1 t} e^{\lambda_2 t} dt$

$\Rightarrow \quad N_2 e^{\lambda_2 t} = \lambda_1 N_0 \frac{e^{(\lambda_2 - \lambda_1)t}}{\lambda_2 - \lambda_1} + c$

To find c,

At $t = 0$, $N_2 = 0$,

$$0 = \frac{\lambda_1 N_0}{\lambda_2 - \lambda_1} + c \quad \Rightarrow \quad c = \frac{\lambda_1 N_0}{\lambda_1 - \lambda_2}$$

Substituting value of c, we get

$$N_2 = \frac{\lambda_1 N_0}{\lambda_2 - \lambda_1}(e^{-\lambda_1 t} - e^{-\lambda_2 t})$$

For C,

$N_1 + N_2 + N_3 = N_0$

$\Rightarrow \quad N_3 = N_0 - (N_1 + N_2)$

2. $N_Y = \frac{N_0 \lambda_X}{\lambda_X - \lambda_Y}(e^{-\lambda_Y t} - e^{-\lambda_X t})$

For N_Y to be maximum,

$$\frac{dN_Y}{dt} = \frac{N_0 \lambda_X}{\lambda_X - \lambda_Y}[e^{-\lambda_Y t}(-\lambda_Y) - e^{-\lambda_X t}(-\lambda_X)] = 0$$

$\Rightarrow \quad \lambda_X e^{-\lambda_X t} = \lambda_Y e^{-\lambda_Y t}$

$\Rightarrow \quad t = \left(\frac{1}{\lambda_X - \lambda_Y}\right)\ln\left(\frac{\lambda_X}{\lambda_Y}\right) = 15\ln 3 = 16.5 \text{ s}$

At $t = 16.5$ s, $N_X = N_0 e^{-\lambda_X t}$

$= 10^{20} \times e^{-(0.1)(16.5)}$

$= 1.92 \times 10^{19}$

$N_Y = \frac{N_0 \lambda_X}{\lambda_X - \lambda_Y}(e^{-\lambda_Y t} - e^{-\lambda_X t})$

$= \frac{10^{20}(0.1)}{0.1 - \frac{1}{30}}\left(e^{-\frac{1}{30}(16.5)} - e^{-0.1(16.5)}\right)$

$= 5.778 \times 10^{19}$

$N_X + N_Y + N_Z = N_0$

$\Rightarrow \quad N_Z = N_0 - N_X - N_Y$

$= 10^{20} - 1.92 \times 10^{19} - 5.778 \times 10^{19}$

$= 2.3 \times 10^{19}$

3. For daughter nucleus, $\frac{dN_d}{dt} = \lambda_p N_p - \lambda_d N_d$

For N_d to become constant, $\frac{dN_d}{dt} = 0$

$\Rightarrow \quad \lambda_p N_p - \lambda_d N_d = 0$

$\Rightarrow \quad \lambda_p N_p = \lambda_d N_d$

Level 2

Single Choice(s) Correct Questions

1. $N = \frac{N_0}{2^n}$

$\Rightarrow \quad \frac{N_0}{16} = \frac{N_0}{2^n} \Rightarrow n = 4$

$t = nT_{1/2} = 4(100\,\mu\text{s}) = 400\,\mu\text{s}$

2. $n = \frac{t}{T_{1/2}} = \frac{60}{20} = 3$

After n half-lives, $N = \frac{N_0}{2^n} = \frac{N_0}{2^3} = \frac{N_0}{8}$

% of atoms decayed $= \frac{N_0 - N}{N_0} \times 100 = 87.5\%$

3. After n half-lives, $N = \frac{N_0}{2^n}$

$\Rightarrow \quad N_0 - \frac{3N_0}{4} = \frac{N_0}{2^n} \quad \Rightarrow \quad n = 2$

$t = nT_{1/2} \quad \Rightarrow \quad \frac{3}{4} = 2T_{1/2}$

$\Rightarrow \quad T_{1/2} = \frac{3}{8} = 0.375 \text{ s}$

4. $N = N_0 e^{-\lambda t}$

$\Rightarrow \quad N_0 - 0.63N_0 = N_0 e^{-\lambda(10)}$

$\Rightarrow \quad e^{-10\lambda} = 0.37 = e^{-1}$

$\Rightarrow \qquad \lambda = 0.1\ s^{-1}$

$$T_{1/2} = \frac{\ln 2}{\lambda} = \frac{0.693}{0.1} = 7\ s$$

5. $T_{mean} > T_{1/2}$

$\therefore \qquad f_1 > f_2$

6. $n = \dfrac{t}{T_{1/2}} = \dfrac{\frac{1}{2}T_{1/2}}{T_{1/2}} = \dfrac{1}{2}$

$$N = \frac{N_0}{2^n} = \frac{N_0}{2^{1/2}} = \frac{N_0}{\sqrt{2}}$$

Fraction of nuclei undecayed $= \dfrac{N}{N_0} = \dfrac{1}{\sqrt{2}}$

7. $t = \dfrac{1}{\lambda}\ln\left(\dfrac{N_0}{N}\right) = \left(\dfrac{T_{1/2}}{\ln 2}\right)\ln\left(\dfrac{N_0}{\left(\dfrac{N_0}{20}\right)}\right) = \dfrac{3.8\ln 20}{\ln 2} = 16.5$ days

8. $N_0 = \left(\dfrac{m}{M}\right)N_A = \dfrac{5}{223}\times 6.02\times 10^{23} = 1.34\times 10^{22}$ nuclei

$$T_{1/2} = \frac{0.693}{\lambda} = 1620\times 365\times 24$$

$\Rightarrow \quad \lambda = 4.88\times 10^{-8}\ h^{-1}$

Number of nuclei decayed in 5 h $= N_0(1 - e^{-\lambda t})$

$$= 1.34\times 10^{22}(1 - e^{-4.88\times 10^{-8}\times 5})$$
$$= 3.23\times 10^{15}$$

9. After 2 half-lives, $N = \dfrac{N_0}{2^2} = \dfrac{N_0}{4}$

Number of nuclei decayed in 2 half-lives $= N_0 - \dfrac{N_0}{4} = \dfrac{3N_0}{4}$

Probability that a nucleus undergoes decay $= \dfrac{\frac{3N_0}{4}}{N_0} = \dfrac{3}{4}$

10. $T_{1/2} = \dfrac{0.693}{\lambda} = 37.2\times 60$

$\Rightarrow \qquad \lambda = 3.1\times 10^{-4}\ s^{-1}$

Probability of nucleus to decay $= 1 - e^{-\lambda t}$

$$= 1 - e^{-3.1\times 10^{-4}\times 10^{-3}}$$
$$= 3.1\times 10^{-7}$$

11. Number of half-lives, $n = \dfrac{t}{T_{1/2}}$

For X, $n_1 = \dfrac{16}{4} = 4,$

$$m_1 = \frac{m_0}{2^n} = \frac{0.1}{2^4} = 6.25\times 10^{-3}\ kg$$

For Y, $n_2 = \dfrac{16}{8} = 2,$

$$m_2 = \frac{m_0}{2^n} = \frac{0.1}{2^2} = 2.5\times 10^{-2}\ kg$$

12. Activity is not affected by change in temperature.

13. $\lambda = \dfrac{\ln 2}{T_{1/2}} = \dfrac{0.693}{2\times 24\times 3600} = 4\times 10^{-6}$

Activity $= \lambda N = (4\times 10^{-6})\times 10^{18} = 4\times 10^{12}$ Bq

14. $N = \dfrac{m}{M}\times N_A = \dfrac{1\times 10^{-3}}{210}\times 6.0\times 10^{23} = 2.85\times 10^{18}$

Number of α-particles emitted per second $= \lambda N$

$$= 5.8\times 10^{-8}\times 2.85\times 10^{18} = 1.7\times 10^{11}$$

15. A = Activity per mole $= \lambda N_A$

$\therefore \qquad \dfrac{A_1}{A_2} = \dfrac{\lambda_1}{\lambda_2} = \dfrac{4}{3}$

16. $\lambda t = \ln\left(\dfrac{A_0}{A}\right)$

In 1 hour, $\lambda(1) = \ln\left[\dfrac{A_0}{\left(\dfrac{A_0}{\sqrt{3}}\right)}\right] \quad \Rightarrow \quad \lambda = \dfrac{1}{2}\ln 3$

After 3 h, $\lambda(3) = \ln\left(\dfrac{A_0}{A}\right)$

$\Rightarrow \qquad \left(\dfrac{1}{2}\ln 3\right)3 = \ln\left(\dfrac{A_0}{A}\right)$

$\Rightarrow \qquad A = \dfrac{A_0}{3\sqrt{3}}$

17. $A = \dfrac{A_0}{2^n} \quad \Rightarrow \quad 128 = \dfrac{1024}{2^n} \quad \Rightarrow \quad n = 3$

$t = nT_{1/2} \quad \Rightarrow \quad 3 = 3T_{1/2} \quad \Rightarrow \quad T_{1/2} = 1\text{min}$

At the end of 5 min,

$t = nT_{1/2} \quad \Rightarrow \quad 5 = n(1) \quad \Rightarrow \quad n = 5$

$$A = \frac{A_0}{2^n} = \frac{1024}{2^5} = 32$$

18. $\dfrac{dN}{dt} = -0.04\ N$

Comparing it with the standard equation,

$$\lambda = 0.04\ h^{-1}$$

$$T_{mean} = \frac{1}{\lambda} = \frac{1}{0.04} = 25\ h$$

19. $\lambda t = \ln\left(\dfrac{A_0}{A}\right)$

$\Rightarrow \qquad \lambda(10) = \ln\left(\dfrac{A_0}{0.15A_0}\right)$

$\Rightarrow \qquad \lambda(10) = 1.9$

$\Rightarrow \qquad \lambda = 0.19$ per day

$$T_{1/2} = \frac{0.693}{\lambda} = \frac{0.693}{0.19} = 3.65\ \text{days}$$

20. Let, volume of the remaining liquid $= V$

Initial activity of the remaining liquid $= \left(\dfrac{c}{100}\right)V$

After 3 half-lives,

$$A = \frac{A_0}{2^3} \Rightarrow \frac{c}{10} = \frac{\left(\frac{c}{100}\right)V}{8} \Rightarrow V = 80 \text{ cc}$$

21. Activity goes from 6000 dps to 3000 dps in 140 days
So, half-life of sample will be 140 days.
In 280 days, there will be 2 half-lives.

$$\therefore \quad A = \frac{A_0}{2^n}$$

$$\Rightarrow \quad 6000 = \frac{A_0}{2^2}$$

$$\Rightarrow \quad A_0 = 24000 \text{ dps}$$

22. $A = \frac{A_0}{2^n} \Rightarrow 0.03A_0 = \frac{A_0}{2^n} \Rightarrow n \simeq 5$

So, age of sample $= 5T_{1/2} + 7$
$= 5(12.5) + 7 \simeq 70$ yr

23. $A_1 = A_0 e^{-\lambda t_1}$ and $A_2 = A_0 e^{-\lambda t_2}$

$$\therefore \quad \frac{A_2}{A_1} = e^{\lambda(t_1 - t_2)}$$

$$\Rightarrow \quad A_2 = A_1 e^{\frac{(t_1 - t_2)}{T}} \qquad \because \left\{\lambda = \frac{1}{T}\right\}$$

24. $R_1 = \lambda N_1$, $R_2 = \lambda N_2$
Number of atoms disintegrated in time $(T_2 - T_1)$

$$= N_1 - N_2 = \frac{R_1 - R_2}{\lambda} = \frac{(R_1 - R_2)T}{\ln 2} \propto (R_1 - R_2)T$$

25. $R_1 = R_2$

$$\Rightarrow \quad \lambda_1 N_1 = \lambda_2 N_2$$

$$\Rightarrow \lambda_1 N_0 e^{-\lambda_1 t} = \lambda_2 N_0 e^{-\lambda_2 t}$$

$$\Rightarrow \quad t = \frac{1}{\lambda_1 - \lambda_2}\ln\left(\frac{\lambda_1}{\lambda_2}\right)$$

Substituting $\lambda_1 = \frac{0.693}{t_1}$ and $\lambda_2 = \frac{0.693}{t_2}$, we get

$$t = \frac{t_1 t_2}{0.693(t_2 - t_1)}\ln\left(\frac{t_2}{t_1}\right)$$

26. Given, $N_1 = N_0$, $N_2 = 2N_0$

$$t_1 = \frac{1}{\lambda}\ln\left(\frac{\lambda N_0}{A_1}\right)$$

$$t_2 = \frac{1}{\lambda}\ln\left(\frac{\lambda(2N_0)}{A_2}\right)$$

Hence, $t_2 - t_1 = \frac{1}{\lambda}\ln\left(\frac{A_2}{2A_1}\right) = \frac{T}{\ln 2}\ln\left(\frac{A_2}{2A_1}\right) \qquad \because \left\{T = \frac{\ln 2}{\lambda}\right\}$

27. A given nucleus may decay at any time after $t = 0$.

28. (a)

29. $X \xrightarrow{\lambda} Y$

$$\frac{dY}{dt} = \lambda N \Rightarrow R = \lambda N_0 e^{-\lambda t}$$

So, rate of formation of Y will exponentially decrease with time.

30. $\lambda_1 = \frac{1}{\tau}$, $\lambda_2 = \frac{1}{5\tau}$,

$$N = N_0 e^{-\lambda t}$$

$$N = N_1 + N_2 = N_0 e^{-t/\tau} + N_0 e^{-t/5\tau}$$

For each species, the number of radioactive nuclei are decreasing exponentially with time. So, when both species are taken together, total number of nuclei will also decrease exponentially with time.

31. Half-life of X = Mean life of Y

$$\Rightarrow \quad \frac{0.693}{\lambda_X} = \frac{1}{\lambda_Y} \Rightarrow \lambda_X = 0.693\lambda_Y$$

So, $\lambda_Y > \lambda_X$

Hence, Y will decay at faster rate than X.

32. In 2 h,

Number of half-lives of $A = \frac{2}{1} = 2$

Number of half-lives of $B = \frac{2}{2} = 1$

So, $N_A = \frac{N_0}{2^2} = \frac{N_0}{4}$; $N_B = \frac{N_0}{2^1} = \frac{N_0}{2}$

Rate of disintegration $= R = \lambda N$

$$\therefore \quad \frac{R_A}{R_B} = \left(\frac{\lambda_A}{\lambda_B}\right)\left(\frac{N_A}{N_B}\right) = \left(\frac{\frac{0.693}{1}}{\frac{0.693}{2}}\right)\left(\frac{\frac{N_0}{4}}{\frac{N_0}{2}}\right) = 1:1$$

33. $\lambda_B = 2\lambda_A$

Number of half-lives, $n = \frac{t}{T_{1/2}} = \frac{\lambda t}{\ln 2}$

$$\Rightarrow \quad n \propto \lambda$$

$$\therefore \quad \frac{n_A}{n_B} = \frac{\lambda_A}{\lambda_B}$$

$$\Rightarrow \quad n_B = 2n_A = 2n$$

Rate of disintegration, $R = \lambda N = \frac{\lambda N_0}{2^n}$

Given, $R_A = R_B \Rightarrow \frac{\lambda_A N_0}{2^n} = \frac{\lambda_B N_0}{2^{2n}}$

$$\Rightarrow \quad 2^n = 2 \Rightarrow n = 1$$

34. $N_1 = N_0 e^{-10\lambda t}$, $N_2 = N_0 e^{-\lambda t}$

$$\therefore \quad \frac{N_1}{N_2} = \frac{N_0 e^{-10\lambda t}}{N_0 e^{-\lambda t}} = e^{-9\lambda t}$$

Given, $\frac{N_1}{N_2} = \frac{1}{e}$

$$\Rightarrow \quad e^{-9\lambda t} = e^{-1} \Rightarrow t = \frac{1}{9\lambda}$$

35. In t time, number of half-lives of $X = \frac{t}{3}$

Number of half-lives of $Y = \frac{t}{2}$

Given, $N_1 = 2N_2 \Rightarrow \frac{N_0}{2^{t/3}} = 2\left(\frac{N_0}{2^{t/2}}\right) \qquad \because \left\{N = \frac{N_0}{2^n}\right\}$

$$\Rightarrow \quad t = 6 \text{ yr}$$

36. Three half-lives of A is equivalent to six half-lives of B.

Given, $N'_A = N'_B$

$$\Rightarrow \quad \frac{N_A}{2^3} = \frac{N_B}{2^6} \quad \Rightarrow \quad \frac{N_A}{N_B} = \frac{1}{8}$$

37. Initial activity,

$$\lambda_X N_X + \lambda_Y N_Y = 1\text{ Ci} \quad \text{...(i)}$$

Activity after 8 days,

$$\lambda_X\left(\frac{N_X}{2^2}\right) + \lambda_Y\left(\frac{N_Y}{2^{1/2}}\right) = 0.5\text{ Ci} \quad \text{...(ii)}$$

Dividing Eqs. (i) by (ii), we get

$$\frac{N_X}{N_Y} = 2(\sqrt{2}-1)\frac{\lambda_Y}{\lambda_X}$$

$$\frac{\lambda_Y}{\lambda_X} = \frac{T_X}{T_Y} = \frac{4}{16} = \frac{1}{4}$$

So, $$\frac{N_X}{N_Y} = 2(\sqrt{2}-1)\left(\frac{1}{4}\right) = \frac{\sqrt{2}-1}{2}$$

38.

	X	$\longrightarrow$	Y
$t = 0,$	N_0		0
$t = t$	N		$N_0 - N$

$$\frac{N_X}{N_Y} = \frac{N}{N_0 - N} = \frac{1}{4}$$

$$\Rightarrow \quad N = \frac{N_0}{5}$$

After 2 half-lives, $N = \frac{N_0}{2^2} = \frac{N_0}{4}$

After 3 half-lives, $N = \frac{N_0}{2^3} = \frac{N_0}{8}$

So, $2T_{1/2} < t < 3T_{1/2}$

$\Rightarrow \quad 2(2) < t < 3(2) \quad \Rightarrow \quad 4 < t < 6$

39. $\frac{\lambda_A}{\lambda_B} = \frac{1}{2}$

Probabilities of getting α and β-particles are same.

Thus, rate of disintegration are equal

$\therefore \quad \lambda_A N_A = \lambda_B N_B \quad \Rightarrow \quad \frac{N_A}{N_B} = \frac{\lambda_B}{\lambda_A} = 2:1$

40. In 48 yr,

Number of half-lives of $A = \frac{48}{24} = 2$

Number of half-lives of $B = \frac{48}{16} = 3$

Activity of mixture after 48 yr $= \frac{A_0}{2^2} + \frac{A_0}{2^3} = \frac{3A_0}{8}$

41.

	${}^{40}_{19}\text{K}$	$\longrightarrow$	${}^{40}_{18}\text{Ar}$
$t = 0,$	N_0		0
$t = t,$	N		$N_0 - N$

Given, $\frac{N}{N_0 - N} = \frac{1}{7} \quad \Rightarrow \quad N = \frac{N_0}{8}$

After n half-lives, $N = \frac{N_0}{2^n} = \frac{N_0}{8} \quad \Rightarrow \quad n = 3$

So, age of the rock $= 3T_{1/2} = 3(1.4 \times 10^9) = 4.2 \times 10^9$ yr

42. n half-lives of Y are equivalent to $2n$ half-lives of X.

$$N_X = \frac{N_0}{2^{2n}}, \quad N_Y = \frac{N_0}{2^n}$$

Given, $$\frac{N_X}{N_Y} = \frac{20}{80} \quad \Rightarrow \quad \frac{\frac{N_0}{2^{2n}}}{\frac{N_0}{2^n}} = \frac{1}{4} \quad \Rightarrow \quad n = 2$$

So, current age of planet $= 2 \times$ half-life of Y

$= 2(4 \times 10^9) = 8 \times 10^9$ yr

43. $\lambda_{\text{eff}} = \lambda_1 + \lambda_2 + \lambda_3 = 2\lambda + 3\lambda + 6\lambda = 11\lambda$

44. $\lambda = \lambda_1 + \lambda_2 = \frac{1}{1620} + \frac{1}{520} = 2.54 \times 10^{-3}\text{ yr}^{-1}$

$\therefore \quad T_{1/2} = \frac{\ln 2}{\lambda} = 272.8$ yr

After n half-lives, $N = \frac{N_0}{2^n}$

$\Rightarrow \quad \frac{N_0}{4} = \frac{N_0}{2^n} \Rightarrow n = 2$

$t = nT_{1/2} = 2(272.8) = 545$ yr

45. After first half an hour,

$$N = \frac{N_0}{2^1} = \frac{N_0}{2}$$

Next one hour is equivalent to 4 half-lives of B.

So, after next one hour, $N = \frac{\frac{N_0}{2}}{2^4} = \frac{N_0}{2^5}$

For further half an hour,

$$\frac{1}{T_{1/2}} = \frac{1}{T_A} + \frac{1}{T_B}$$

$$\Rightarrow \quad \frac{1}{T_{1/2}} = \frac{1}{\left(\frac{1}{2}\right)} + \frac{1}{\left(\frac{1}{4}\right)}$$

$$\Rightarrow \quad T_{1/2} = \frac{1}{6}\text{ h}$$

Number of half-lives $\frac{t}{T_{1/2}} = \frac{\frac{1}{2}}{\frac{1}{6}} = 3$

$$\therefore \quad N = \frac{\frac{N_0}{2^5}}{2^3} = \frac{N_0}{2^8}$$

46. $$\frac{dN}{dt} = 10 - \frac{1}{2}N$$

$$\Rightarrow \quad \int_0^N \frac{dN}{20 - N} = \frac{1}{2}\int_0^t dt$$

$$\Rightarrow \quad N = 20(1 - e^{-t/2})$$

Given, $N = 10 = 20(1 - e^{-t/2}) \quad \Rightarrow \quad t = 2\ln 2 = 1.386$ s

47. Half-life $= Y = \frac{\ln 2}{\lambda} \quad \Rightarrow \quad \lambda = \frac{\ln 2}{Y}$

$$\frac{dN}{dt} = X - \lambda N$$

When number of nuclei becomes constant,

$$\frac{dN}{dt}=0$$

$$\Rightarrow \quad X-\lambda N=0$$

$$\Rightarrow \quad X-\left(\frac{\ln 2}{Y}\right)N=0$$

$$\Rightarrow \quad N=\frac{XY}{\ln 2}$$

48. $\frac{dN}{dt}=\alpha-\lambda N$

Number of nuclei will be maximum when

$$\frac{dN}{dt}=0$$

So, $\alpha-\lambda N=0 \quad \Rightarrow \quad N=\frac{\alpha}{\lambda}$

49. $T_{mean}=\frac{1}{\lambda}=20 \quad \Rightarrow \quad \lambda=\frac{1}{20}s^{-1}$

$$\frac{dN}{dt}=\alpha-\lambda N$$

$$\Rightarrow \quad \int_{N_0}^{N}\frac{dN}{\alpha-\lambda N}=\int_0^t dt$$

$$\Rightarrow \quad N=\frac{1}{\lambda}[\alpha-(\alpha-\lambda N_0)e^{-\lambda t}]$$

So, $\frac{dN}{dt}=(\alpha-\lambda N_0)e^{-\lambda t}$

At $t=40$ s, $\frac{dN}{dt}=\left(10^4-\frac{1}{20}\times 10^5\right)e^{-\left(\frac{1}{20}\right)40}$

$$=\frac{1}{2}\times 10^4\times\frac{1}{e^2}=676\ s^{-1}$$

50. $T_{mean}=\frac{1}{\lambda}=40\times 60$

$$\Rightarrow \quad \lambda=\frac{1}{2400}s^{-1}$$

$$\frac{dN}{dt}=1000-\left(\frac{1}{2400}\right)N$$

At steady state, $\frac{dN}{dt}=0$

$$\Rightarrow 1000-\left(\frac{1}{2400}\right)N=0$$

$$\Rightarrow \quad N=24\times 10^5$$

51. $N=\frac{1}{\lambda}[\alpha-(\alpha-\lambda N_0)e^{-\lambda t}]$

So, N will exponentially increase with time.

52. $\frac{dN}{dt}=t^2-\lambda N$

For $\frac{dN}{dt}$ to be minimum, $\frac{d}{dt}\left(\frac{dN}{dt}\right)=0$

$$\Rightarrow \quad 2t-\lambda\left(\frac{dN}{dt}\right)=0$$

$$\Rightarrow \quad 2t_0-\lambda(t_0^2-\lambda N)=0$$

$$\Rightarrow \quad N=\frac{\lambda t_0^2-2t_0}{\lambda^2}$$

53. $\frac{dN_2}{dt}=\lambda N_1-(2\lambda_1)N_2$

N_2 will be maximum when $\frac{dN_2}{dt}=0$

$$\Rightarrow \quad \lambda N_1-2\lambda N_2=0$$

$$\Rightarrow \quad \frac{N_1}{N_2}=2$$

54. $\frac{dN_2}{dt}$ = production rate–decay rate $=\lambda_1 N_1-\lambda_2 N_2$

Initially, production rate of B is higher than its decay rate. So, number of nuclei of B will first increase. As number of nuclei of B go on increasing, decay rate becomes more than production rate. So, now number of nuclei of B will decrease.

Rate of decay of A will keep decreasing as number of nuclei of A will keep decreasing.

Initial activity of A is $\lambda_1 N_0$ while initial activity of B is 0. So, statement of option (c) is wrong.

At $t\longrightarrow\infty$, $N_1=0$, $N_2=0$ and $N_3=N_0$

So, statement of option (d) is also wrong.

Multiple Choices Correct Questions

1. After n half-lives, $N=\frac{N_0}{2^n}$

$$\Rightarrow \quad \frac{6.25}{100}N_0=\frac{N_0}{2^n} \quad \Rightarrow \quad 2^n=16 \quad \Rightarrow \quad n=4$$

$$t=nT_{1/2} \quad \Rightarrow \quad 4=4T_{1/2} \quad \Rightarrow \quad T_{1/2}=1\text{ h}$$

Half-life, $T_{1/2}=\frac{\ln 2}{\lambda}=1 \quad \Rightarrow \quad \lambda=(\ln 2)\text{h}^{-1}$

Mean life, $T_{mean}=\frac{1}{\lambda}=\frac{1}{\ln 2}$ h

After further 4h, $N=\frac{N_0}{2^8}=0.0039N_0$

$\therefore$% amount of substance left $=\frac{N}{N_0}\times 100=0.39\%$

2. For A, λ_A (3 days) $=\ln\left(\frac{N_0}{N_A}\right)$ ...(i)

For B, λ_B(3 days) $=\ln\left(\frac{N_0}{N_B}\right)$ ...(ii)

Subtracting Eq. (i) from Eq. (ii),

$$(\lambda_B-\lambda_A)\text{ (3 days)}=\ln\left(\frac{N_A}{N_B}\right)$$

$$\Rightarrow \quad \lambda_B-\lambda_A=\frac{\ln 3}{3\text{ days}} \qquad \{\because N_A=3N_B\}$$

Activity rate of A, $R_A=\lambda_A N_A$

Activity rate of B, $R_B=\lambda_B N_B$

$\therefore \quad \frac{R_A}{R_B} = \left(\frac{\lambda_A}{\lambda_B}\right)\left(\frac{N_A}{N_B}\right) = 3\left(\frac{\lambda_A}{\lambda_B}\right)$

$\frac{R_A}{R_B} < 3 \qquad \{\because \lambda_A < \lambda_B\}$

3. (a) $\frac{(R_0)_A}{(R_0)_B} = \left(\frac{\lambda_A}{\lambda_B}\right)\left(\frac{(N_0)_A}{(N_0)_B}\right) = \frac{1}{8}$

$\frac{\lambda_A}{\lambda_B}\left(\frac{1}{4}\right) = \frac{1}{8} \quad \Rightarrow \quad \frac{\lambda_A}{\lambda_B} = \frac{1}{2}$

Let, half-lives of A and B be t_A and t_B, respectively.

$\frac{t_A}{t_B} = \frac{\lambda_B}{\lambda_A} \quad \Rightarrow \quad \frac{2}{t_B} = 2 \quad \Rightarrow \quad t_B = 1 \text{ yr}$

(b) 4 yr is equivalent to 2 half-lives of A and 4 half-lives of B.

$$\frac{R_A}{R_B} = \frac{\lambda_A}{\lambda_B}\left(\frac{N_A}{N_B}\right) = \frac{\lambda_A}{\lambda_B}\frac{\frac{(N_0)_A}{2^2}}{\frac{(N_0)_B}{2^4}} = \frac{1}{2}\left(\frac{1}{4}\right)(4) = \frac{1}{2}$$

(c) 6 yr is equivalent to 3 half-lives of A and 6 half-lives of B.

$$\frac{N_A}{N_B} = \frac{\frac{(N_0)_A}{2^3}}{\frac{(N_0)_B}{2^6}} = \left(\frac{1}{4}\right)(8) = 2:1$$

(d) $f_2 > f_1 \quad \because \{\lambda_B > \lambda_A\}$

4. (a) Half-life $\propto \frac{1}{\lambda}$

So, $\quad T_A > T_B \qquad \{\because \lambda_A < \lambda_B\}$

(b) At $t = 0$, $R_A = \lambda_A (N_0)_A$

At $t = 60$, $R'_A = \lambda_A N_A$, $R'_B = \lambda_B N_B$

$R_A = R'_B$

$\Rightarrow \quad \lambda_A (N_0)_A = \lambda_B N_B$

Number of nuclei of A decreases with time.

So, $\quad N_A < (N_0)_A$

$\Rightarrow \quad \lambda_A N_A < \lambda_A (N_0)_A$

$\lambda_A N_A < \lambda_B N_B$

Since, $\lambda_B > \lambda_A$, we can't decide whether $N_A > N_B$, $N_A < N_B$ or $N_A = N_B$.

(c) $\lambda_A N_A < \lambda_B N_B$. So, they will never have the same decay rate simultaneously.

5. (b) The probability of a nucleus disintegrating during one second is equal to decay constant which remains constant for all time.

(d) Energy released in α-decay is shared by both the daughter nucleus and α-particle.

6. $\quad y = mx + c$

$\Rightarrow \quad \ln A = -\left(\frac{2.6}{26}\right)t + 2.6$

$\Rightarrow \quad \ln A = -(0.1)t + 2.6$

$\Rightarrow \quad A = e^{2.6} e^{-(0.1)t}$

$\Rightarrow \quad A = 12 e^{-(0.1)t}$

So, initial activity $= 12$, $\lambda = 0.1$

$A_0 = \lambda N_0 \quad \Rightarrow \quad 12 = (0.1) N_0 \quad \Rightarrow \quad N_0 = 120$

7. $N_A = N_0 e^{-\lambda t}$, $N_B = N_0(1 - e^{-\lambda t})$

So, $\quad \frac{N_B}{N_A} = e^{\lambda t} - 1$

If $t << T$, then $\quad \frac{N_B}{N_A} = 1 + \lambda t - 1 \qquad \{\because e^x = 1 + x \text{ for small } x\}$

$\Rightarrow \quad \frac{N_B}{N_A} = \lambda t$

8. $N = N_0 e^{-\lambda t}$, $D = N_0(1 - e^{-\lambda t})$

$R = -\frac{dN}{dt} = -N_0 e^{-\lambda t}(-\lambda)$

$\Rightarrow \quad R = N_0 \lambda e^{-\lambda t}$

$\therefore \quad \frac{R}{N} = \frac{N_0 \lambda e^{-\lambda t}}{N_0 e^{-\lambda t}} = \lambda$

9. At $t = 6$, $N_A = \frac{N_0}{2^n} = \frac{N_0}{8} \quad \Rightarrow \quad n = 3$

So, $\quad t = nT_{1/2} = 6$

$\Rightarrow \quad 3T_{1/2} = 6$

$\Rightarrow \quad T_{1/2} = 2 \text{ s}$

$\therefore \quad \lambda = \frac{\ln 2}{T_{1/2}} = \frac{\ln 2}{2}$

At $t = t_1$, $\lambda t = \ln\left(\frac{N_0}{N}\right) \quad \Rightarrow \quad \left(\frac{\ln 2}{2}\right)t_1 = \ln\left[\frac{N_0}{\left(\frac{N_0}{5}\right)}\right]$

$\Rightarrow \quad t_1 = 2\log_2 5$

$N_B = N_0(1 - e^{-\lambda t})$

$\Rightarrow \quad \frac{9N_0}{10} = N_0\left[1 - e^{-\left(\frac{\ln 2}{2}\right)t_2}\right]$

$\Rightarrow \quad t_2 = \log_2 100$

$\therefore \quad t_2 - t_1 = \log_2 100 - 2\log_2 5 = \log_2\left(\frac{100}{25}\right) = 2$

10. (a) $\quad y = mx + c$

$\Rightarrow \quad A = -\left(\frac{A_0 - \frac{A_0}{2}}{t_0}\right)t + A_0$

$\Rightarrow \quad A = -\frac{A_0}{2t_0}t + A_0$

$\Rightarrow \quad \log\left|\frac{dN}{dt}\right| = -\frac{A_0}{2t_0}t + A_0$

$\Rightarrow \quad \frac{dN}{dt} = e^{A_0} e^{-\left(\frac{A_0}{2t_0}\right)t}$

Comparing with $A = A_0 e^{-\lambda t}$, we get

$\lambda = \frac{A_0}{2t_0}$, Initial activity $= e^{A_0}$

(b) Initial activity $= \lambda N_0 = e^{A_0}$

$$\Rightarrow \qquad N_0 = \frac{2t_0 e^{A_0}}{A_0}$$

(c) Number of nuclei after one half-life $= \frac{N_0}{2} = \frac{t_0 e^{A_0}}{A_0}$

11. (a) $T_1 >> T_2 \quad \Rightarrow \quad \lambda_1 << \lambda_2$

So, parent nuclei decay at very slow rate and therefore activity of parent nuclei will be almost constant.

(d) $T_1 < T_2 \quad \Rightarrow \quad \lambda_1 > \lambda_2$

$$N_1 = N_P e^{-\lambda_1 t}$$

$$\frac{dN_2}{dt} = \lambda_1 N_1 - \lambda_2 N_2$$

So, number of nuclei of parent will decrease exponentially with time while number of nuclei of daughter will first increase and then decrease.

Comprehension Based Questions

1. Half-life of sample $= \frac{\ln 2}{\lambda_{avg}} = 12.8$ h

For electron capture, $\lambda = (0.40)\lambda_{avg}$

Half-life for electron capture $= \frac{\ln 2}{(0.40)\lambda_{avg}}$

$$= \frac{12.8}{0.4} = 32 \text{ h}$$

2. Q-value $= \Delta mc^2 = [m(^{64}_{29}\text{Cu}) - m(^{64}_{30}\text{Zn})]c^2$

$$= (63.92977 - 63.92914)\text{u} \times 931.5 \text{ MeV/u}$$

$$= 0.587 \text{ MeV.}$$

3. For β^+ decay,

Q-value $= [m(^{64}_{29}\text{Cu}) - m(^{64}_{28}\text{Ni}) - 2m_e]c^2$

$$= (63.92977 - 63.92796)\text{u} \times 931.5 \text{ MeV/u} - 2(0.511) \text{ MeV}$$

$$= 0.664 \text{ MeV}$$

$$\lambda = \frac{20}{100} \times \lambda_{avg} = (0.2)\left(\frac{\ln 2}{12.8 \times 3600}\right)$$

$$\left|\frac{dN}{dt}\right| = \lambda N_0 = \frac{(0.2)(0.693)}{12.8 \times 3600} \times 10^{22} = 3 \times 10^{16} \text{ Nuclei/s}$$

Initial rate at which energy is produced $= \left|\frac{dN}{dt}\right| Q$

$$= 3 \times 10^{16} \times (0.664 \times 10^6 \times 1.6 \times 10^{-19})$$

$$= 3.2 \times 10^3 \text{ W}$$

4. $$\frac{dN}{dt} = P - \lambda N = 0$$

$$\Rightarrow \qquad P = \lambda N = 13.86 \times 10^{10} \text{ s}^{-1}$$

5. $$\lambda N = 13.86 \times 10^{10}$$

$$\Rightarrow \qquad \left(\frac{0.693}{2.5 \times 3600}\right) N = 13.86 \times 10^{10}$$

$$\Rightarrow \qquad N = 1.8 \times 10^{15}$$

6. After a long time, $N = \frac{P}{\lambda}$

7. $$\frac{dN}{dt} = \text{production rate} - \text{decay rate}$$

$$\Rightarrow \qquad \frac{dN}{dt} = q_0 t - \lambda N$$

$$\Rightarrow \qquad \frac{dN}{dt} + \lambda N = q_0 t$$

8. $$\frac{dN}{dt} + \lambda N = q_0 t$$

Solving differential equation, we get

$$N = q_0\left[\frac{t}{\lambda} - \frac{1}{\lambda^2}(1 - e^{-\lambda t})\right]$$

Instantaneous power,

$$P = \frac{dN}{dt}E_0 = (\lambda N)E_0 = \left(q_0 t - \frac{q_0}{\lambda} + \frac{q_0}{\lambda}e^{-\lambda t}\right)E_0$$

9. Average power, $P_{avg} = \frac{\int_0^t P\,dt}{\int_0^t dt} = \frac{\int_0^t \left(q_0 t - \frac{q_0}{\lambda} + \frac{q_0}{\lambda}e^{-\lambda t}\right)E_0\,dt}{\int_0^t dt}$

$$= \left(\frac{q_0 t}{2} - \frac{q_0}{\lambda} + \frac{q_0}{\lambda^2 t} - \frac{q_0}{\lambda^2 t}e^{-\lambda t}\right)E_0$$

Match the Columns Questions

1. A $\rightarrow$ 3, B $\rightarrow$ 1, C $\rightarrow$ 2, D $\rightarrow$ 2

2. (a) Activity of the sample II becomes half in minimum time. Hence, it has maximum disintegration constant.

(b) Activity of the sample III takes maximum time to become half, therefore it has maximum half-life.

(c) Since, half-life of the sample III is maximum, number of parent atoms of sample III will be maximum at any time.

(d) It can't be compared without information about atomic weight as energy radiated will depend upon number of atoms, not upon amount of substance.

3. (a) $^{A_1}_{Z_1}\text{A} \longrightarrow {}^{A}_{Z}\text{C} + 2\,{}^4_2\text{He} + 3\,{}^0_{-1}e$

$$Z_1 = Z + 2(2) + 3(-1) = Z + 1$$

$$^{A_2}_{Z_2}\text{B} \longrightarrow {}^{A}_{Z}\text{C} + 2\,{}^4_2\text{He} + 5\,{}^0_{-1}e$$

$$Z_2 = Z + 2 + 5(-1) = Z - 3$$

$$\therefore \qquad Z_1 - Z_2 = (Z+1) - (Z-3) = 4$$

(b) $A_1 = A + 2(4) = A + 8$

$$A_2 = A + 4$$

$$\therefore \quad A_1 - A_2 = 4$$

(c) $N_A = N_B \quad \Rightarrow \quad \frac{4N_0}{2^{2n}} = \frac{N_0}{2^n} \quad \Rightarrow \quad n = 2$

So, after 2 half-lives of B,

$$N_A = \frac{4N_0}{2^{2(2)}} = \frac{N_0}{4}, \qquad N_B = \frac{N_0}{2^2} = \frac{N_0}{4}$$

$$N_C = \left(4N_0 - \frac{N_0}{4}\right) + \left(N_0 - \frac{N_0}{4}\right) = \frac{18N_0}{4}$$

$$\therefore \qquad \frac{N_C}{N_B} = \frac{\frac{18N_0}{4}}{\frac{N_0}{4}} = 18$$

(d) $R_A = R_B \Rightarrow \lambda_A N_A = \lambda_B N_B$

$$\Rightarrow \left(\frac{\ln 2}{1\text{min}}\right)\left(\frac{4N_0}{2^{2n}}\right) = \left(\frac{\ln 2}{2\text{min}}\right)\left(\frac{N_0}{2^n}\right)$$

$$\Rightarrow \quad n = 3$$

So, $\quad t = nT_{1/2} = 3(2) = 6\text{min}$

4. (A) – 4, B – 1, C – 2, D – 3

Numerical Value Questions

1. Let initial amount of A and B be N_1 and N_2, respectively.
Since, 25% of the decay comes from A,

$$\lambda N_1 = \frac{25}{100}(\lambda N_1 + 2\lambda N_2) \Rightarrow N_2 = \frac{3N_1}{2}$$

After time t,

$$\lambda N_1 e^{-\lambda t} = \frac{75}{100}(\lambda N_1 e^{-\lambda t} + 2\lambda N_2 e^{-2\lambda t})$$

$$\Rightarrow N_1 e^{-\lambda t} = 6N_2 e^{-2\lambda t} \Rightarrow e^{\lambda t} = 9 \quad \left\{\because N_2 = \frac{3N_1}{2}\right\}$$

$$\Rightarrow \lambda t = 2\ln 3 \Rightarrow t = 2 \quad \because \{\lambda = \ln 3\}$$

2. Let initial amount of A^{236} and A^{234} be $4N_0$ and N_0, respectively.
After n half-lives of A^{234},

$$R_1 = R_2 \Rightarrow \lambda_1 N_1 = \lambda_2 N_2$$

$$\Rightarrow \left(\frac{\ln 2}{30}\right)\frac{4N_0}{2^{2n}} = \left(\frac{\ln 2}{60}\right)\frac{N_0}{2^n}$$

$$\Rightarrow \quad n = 3$$

So, $t = nT_{1/2} = 3(60) = 180\text{min}$

3. Let initial decay rate of A and B be $64R_0$ and R_0, respectively.
After time t, $\quad R_A = R_B$

$$\Rightarrow (64R_0)e^{-\lambda_A t} = R_0 e^{-\lambda_B t}$$

$$\Rightarrow e^{(\lambda_A - \lambda_B)t} = 64$$

$$\Rightarrow t = \frac{6\ln 2}{\lambda_A - \lambda_B} = \frac{6\ln 2}{\frac{\ln 2}{5} - \frac{\ln 2}{30}} = 36 \text{ days}$$

4. $\lambda t = \ln\left(\frac{N_0}{N}\right)$

For $t = 0$ to $t = 2$

$$\lambda(2) = \ln\left(\frac{N_0}{N_0 - n}\right) \quad \text{...(i)}$$

For $t = 0$ to $t = 4$

$$\lambda(4) = \ln\left(\frac{N_0}{N_0 - n - 0.75n}\right)$$

$$\Rightarrow \lambda(4) = \ln\left(\frac{N_0}{N_0 - 1.75n}\right) \quad \text{...(ii)}$$

Dividing Eqs. (i) by (ii), we get

$$N_0 = 4n$$

So, $\lambda(2) = \ln\left(\frac{4n}{4n-3}\right) \Rightarrow \lambda = \frac{2\ln 2 - \ln 3}{2}$

Mean life, $T_{avg} = \frac{1}{\lambda} = \frac{2}{2\ln 2 - \ln 3} = 6.95 \simeq 7$

5. Initial activity of 5 mL sample $= \frac{2.5 \times 10}{250} \times 5 = 0.5\text{ mCi}$

Number of half-lives $= \frac{30}{15} = 2$

After n half-lives, $A = \frac{A_0}{2^n}$

$$\Rightarrow A = \frac{0.5}{2^2}\text{mCi} = 0.125\text{ mCi} = 125\ \mu\text{Ci}$$

6. The activity of sample A is 2100 counts per week. After a certain time t, its activity will be reduced to 1400 counts per week. This is because a fraction of the active ^{14}C nuclei will decay in time t. So, the sample B must be a time t older than the sample

$$A = A_0 e^{-\lambda t} \Rightarrow 1400 = 2100e^{-\lambda t}$$

$$\Rightarrow t = \frac{\ln\left(\frac{3}{2}\right)}{\lambda} = \left[\frac{\ln\left(\frac{3}{2}\right)}{\ln 2}\right] t_{1/2} = \left(\frac{0.4055}{0.693}\right)(5730) = 3353 \text{ yr}$$

7. Rate at which heat is being evolved $= 10 \times 10^{-3}$W

$$\Rightarrow \left(\frac{dN}{dt}\right)E_0 = 10 \times 10^{-3}$$

$$\Rightarrow \lambda N E_0 = 10 \times 10^{-3}$$

$$\Rightarrow \left(\frac{0.675}{14 \times 24 \times 3600}\right) N(700 \times 10^3 \times 1.6 \times 10^{-19}) = 10 \times 10^{-3}$$

$$\Rightarrow N = 16 \times 10^{16}$$

8. The charge on capacitor at any time, $\quad q = q_0 e^{-\frac{t}{RC}}$

Activity of sample at any time,

$$A = A_0 e^{-\frac{A}{\tau}}, \text{ where } \tau = \text{Mean life}$$

$$\therefore \frac{q}{A} = \frac{q_0}{A_0} e^{-t\left(\frac{1}{RC} - \frac{1}{\tau}\right)}$$

It will be independent of t, if $\frac{1}{RC} - \frac{1}{\tau} = 0$

$$\Rightarrow RC = \tau$$

$$\Rightarrow R(100 \times 10^{-6}) = 20 \times 10^{-3}$$

$$\Rightarrow R = 200\Omega$$

9. Let the total volume of blood $= V$ litre
Initial activity of 1 cm^3 sample

$$= \frac{1 \times 10^{-3}}{V} \times 1 \times 10^{-6} \times 3.7 \times 10^{10} = \frac{37}{V}$$

Number of half-lives $= \frac{5}{15} = \frac{1}{3}$

Activity of 1 cm^3 sample after 5 h $= \frac{296}{60}$ dps

$$\Rightarrow \frac{\frac{37}{V}}{2^{1/3}} = \frac{296}{60}$$

$$\Rightarrow V = \frac{7.5}{2^{1/3}} = \frac{7.5}{1.25} = 6\text{ L}$$

10. The α-decay is represented as,

$$^{248}_{96}\text{Cm} \longrightarrow ^{244}_{94}\text{Pu} + ^{4}_{2}\text{He}$$

$$Q\text{-value} = \Delta mc^2 = [m(^{248}_{96}\text{Cm}) - m(^{244}_{94}\text{Pu}) - m(^{4}_{2}\text{He})]c^2$$

$$= (248.07220 - 244.064100 - 4.002603)u \times 931 \text{ MeV/u}$$

$$= 5.118 \text{ MeV}$$

α-decay has 92% probability and fission has 8% probability.

So, total energy released

$$= 0.92 \times 10^{20} \times 5.118 + 0.08 \times 10^{20} \times 200$$

$$= 20.71 \times 10^{20} \text{ MeV}$$

$$\text{Power output} = \frac{\text{Total energy released}}{\text{Mean life}}$$

$$= \frac{20.71 \times 10^{20} \times 10^6 \times 1.6 \times 10^{-19}}{10^{13}}$$

$$= 3.3 \times 10^{-5} \text{ W}$$

Previous Year's Questions

JEE Main

1. Given,

	A	B	T-half life
$t = 0$	N_0	N_0	$\tau \rightarrow$ avg life

$T_A = \tau_B$

Now, $\frac{\ln(2)}{\lambda_A} = \frac{1}{\lambda_B}$

$$\lambda_A = \lambda_B \ln 2$$

2. Mass number of $A = 16$

Mass number of $B = 32$

Initial mass of A = Initial mass of $B = 320$ g

So, Number of moles of $A = \frac{320}{16} = 20$

Number of moles of $B = \frac{320}{32} = 10$

Initial number of atoms of A present in sample $= 20N_A$

Initial number of atoms of B present in sample $= 10N_A$

Now, half-life of A is 1 day and half-life of B is $\frac{1}{2}$ day.

Following is decay scheme;

For A, $20N_A \xrightarrow{\text{1 day}} 10N_A \xrightarrow{\text{1 day}} 5N_A$

For B, $10N_A \xrightarrow{\text{1/2 day}} 5N_A \xrightarrow{\text{1/2 day}} 2.5N_A \xrightarrow{\text{1/2 day}} 1.25\,N_A \longrightarrow 0.625\,N_A$

Total number of A and B left after 2 days.

$$= 5N_A + 0.625N_A = 5.625N_A$$

$$= 5.625 \times 6.022 \times 10^{23}$$

$$= 33.8 \times 10^{23} = 3.38 \times 10^{24}$$

3. Decay scheme is as shown,

$$N_0 \xrightarrow{\text{30 min}} \frac{N_0}{2} \xrightarrow{\text{30 min}} N_0/4 \xrightarrow{\text{30 min}} N_0/8$$

4. When a radioactive nucleus decays by two different process such that its half-life in the first process is T_1 and half-life of second process is T_2, then its effective half-life (T) is given as,

$$\frac{1}{T} = \frac{1}{T_1} + \frac{1}{T_2}$$

$$\Rightarrow \quad T = \frac{T_1 T_2}{T_1 + T_2}$$

Here, $T_1 = 5\text{min} = 60 \times 5 \text{ s} = 300 \text{ s}$ and $T_2 = 30$ s

$$\therefore \quad T = \frac{300 \times 30}{300 + 30}$$

$$= \frac{300 \times 30}{330} = \frac{300}{11} \text{ s} = \frac{\alpha}{11} \text{ s} \qquad \text{(given)}$$

$$\therefore \quad \alpha = 300$$

5. We know,

$$R = R_0 e^{-\lambda t}$$

Also, $R_0 = 6.4 \times 10^{-4}$ curie

$R = 5 \times 10^{-6}$ curie

$$\therefore \quad 5 \times 10^{-6} = 6.4 \times 10^{-4} e^{-\lambda t} \qquad \text{...(i)}$$

We know,

$$t_{1/2} = \frac{\ln 2}{\lambda} \Rightarrow 5 = \frac{\ln 2}{\lambda}$$

$$\Rightarrow \quad \lambda = \frac{\ln 2}{5}$$

Putting $\lambda = \left(\frac{\ln 2}{5}\right)$ in Eq. (i),

$$5 \times 10^{-6} = 6.4 \times 10^{-4} e^{-\left(\frac{\ln 2}{5}\right)t}$$

$$\Rightarrow \quad e^{\left(+\frac{\ln 2}{5}\right)t} = \frac{6.4 \times 10^{-4}}{5 \times 10^{-6}}$$

$$\Rightarrow \quad e^{\left(\frac{\ln 2}{5}\right)t} = \frac{64}{5 \times 10 \times 10^{-2}}$$

$$\Rightarrow \quad e^{\left(\frac{\ln 2}{5}\right)^t} = \frac{64 \times 100}{50}$$

$$\Rightarrow \quad e^{\left(\frac{\ln 2}{5}\right)^t} = 128$$

On taking log on both the sides, we get

$$\frac{(\ln 2)t}{5} \ln e = \ln 128$$

$$\Rightarrow \quad \frac{(\ln 2)t}{5} = \ln 2^7 \Rightarrow \frac{t}{5} \ln 2 = 7 \ln 2$$

$$\Rightarrow \quad t/5 = 7 \Rightarrow t = 35 \text{ days}$$

6. $A_0 = 4250$ disintegration / min

$\Rightarrow$ After 10 min, disintegration rate of radioactive sample,

$A = 2250$ disintegration / min

We know that,

$$A = A_0 e^{-\lambda t} \qquad \text{...(i)}$$

$$2250 = 4250e^{(-\lambda\times10)}$$

$$\Rightarrow \quad e^{-10\lambda} = \frac{2250}{4250}$$

$$\Rightarrow \quad e^{-10\lambda} = \frac{9}{17}$$

$$\Rightarrow \quad e^{10\lambda} = \frac{17}{9}$$

On taking log both sides, we get

$$\log_e e^{10\lambda} = \ln\frac{17}{9}$$

$$\Rightarrow \quad 10\lambda = \ln(1.89) = 0.636$$

$$\Rightarrow \quad \lambda = 0.063 = 0.063\ \text{min}^{-1}$$

7. Given, half-life for the first process, $(T_{1/2})_1 = 3$ h and half-life for the second process, $(T_{1/2})_2 = 4.5$ h

$$\lambda_{eff} = \lambda_1 + \lambda_2$$

$$\frac{\ln_2}{(T_{1/2})_{eff}} = \frac{\ln_2}{(T_{1/2})_1} + \frac{\ln_2}{(T_{1/2})_2}$$

$$\Rightarrow \quad \frac{1}{(T_{1/2})_{eff}} = \frac{1}{(T_{1/2})_1} + \frac{1}{(T_{1/2})_2} = \frac{1}{3} + \frac{1}{4.5} = \frac{3+2}{9} = \frac{5}{9}$$

$$\therefore \quad (T_{1/2})_{eff} = \frac{9}{5}\text{ h} = 1.8\text{ h}$$

8. Time taken for 7/8 disintegrates or 1/8 remains

$$\frac{N_0}{8} = N_0\left(\frac{1}{2}\right)^n \quad \Rightarrow \quad \left(\frac{1}{2}\right)^3 = \frac{1}{8}$$

$$\Rightarrow \quad n = 3 \text{ half-live}$$

$\therefore$ Time taken $= 3\times60 = 180$ days

9. According to radioactive decay law,

$$N = N_0e^{-\lambda t}$$

So, option (b) is correct.

$$\Rightarrow \quad \log_e N = \log_e N_0 - \lambda t$$

On comparing it with equation of straight line, we get

$$y = mx + c$$

$$m = \frac{1}{\lambda} \quad \Rightarrow \quad m = \tau$$

So, option (c) is correct.

Again, $\lambda T_{1/2} = \frac{\ln 2}{T_{1/2}}.T_{1/2} = \ln 2$, which is constant.

So, option (d) is incorrect.

10. Given, $T_{1/2} = 5$ yr

After x year, $N = 6.25\%$ of N_0

$$\Rightarrow \quad N = \frac{N_0}{16}$$

$$\frac{N}{N_0} = \frac{1}{16} = \left(\frac{1}{2}\right)^4 \quad \text{... (i)}$$

We know that $\frac{N}{N_0} = \left(\frac{1}{2}\right)^n \quad \Rightarrow \quad n = 4$

So, total time $x = 4$ half-life

$$\Rightarrow \quad x = 4\times5\text{ yr} = 20\text{ yr}$$

11. For radioactive material A, $\lambda_1 = 25\lambda$ For radioactive material B, $\lambda_2 = 16\lambda$

$$N = N_0e^{-\lambda t}$$

$$\Rightarrow \quad \frac{N_B}{N_A} = \frac{e^{-\lambda_2 t}}{e^{-\lambda_1 t}} = e^{-\lambda_2 t}.e^{\lambda_1 t}$$

$$e' = e^{(\lambda_1-\lambda_2)t} \quad \Rightarrow \quad (\lambda_1 - \lambda_2)t = 1$$

$$\Rightarrow \quad t = \frac{1}{\lambda_1 - \lambda_2} = \frac{1}{25\lambda - 16\lambda} = \frac{1}{9\lambda}$$

Compare with $\frac{1}{a\lambda}$ we obtain, $a = 9$

12. We know that

$$q = q_0\,e^{-\frac{t}{RC}} \quad \text{...(i)}$$

Where, RC is the time constant of RC- circuit.

At time t, activity A is given by

$$A = A_0e^{-\lambda t} \quad \text{...(ii)}$$

Where, $A_0 =$ initial activity

and $\lambda =$ decay constant.

On dividing Eqs. (i) and (ii), we get

$$\frac{q}{A} = \frac{q_0e^{-\frac{t}{RC}}}{A_0e^{-\lambda t}}$$

$$\Rightarrow \quad 1 = \frac{e^{-\frac{t}{RC}}}{e^{-\lambda t}} \quad \Rightarrow \quad e^{-\lambda t} = e^{-\frac{t}{RC}}$$

Taking log on both sides of above equation, we get

$$\ln(e^{-\lambda t}) = \ln\left(e^{-\frac{t}{RC}}\right)$$

$$\Rightarrow \quad -\lambda t = -\frac{t}{RC}$$

$$\Rightarrow \quad \lambda = \frac{1}{RC}$$

$$\Rightarrow \quad R = \frac{1}{\lambda C}$$

$$\Rightarrow \quad R = \frac{30\times10^{-3}}{200\times10^{-6}}$$

$$\Rightarrow \quad R = 150\ \Omega$$

13. The formula of radioactivity,

$$N = N_0e^{-\lambda t}$$

Case I $\frac{3N_0}{4} = N_0e^{-\lambda t_1}; \ln\frac{3}{4} = -\lambda t_1$ ...(i)

Case II $\frac{N_0}{2} = N_0e^{-\lambda t_2}; \ln\frac{1}{2} = -\lambda t_2$ ...(ii)

On subtracting Eq. (ii) from Eq. (i), we get

$$\ln\frac{3}{4} - \ln\frac{1}{2} = \lambda(t_2 - t_1)$$

Therefore,

$$t_2 - t_1 = \frac{\ln\frac{3\times2}{4\times1}}{\lambda} = \frac{\ln(3/2)}{\lambda}$$

14. Initial $N_0 = 10^{10}$

Half-life, $t_{1/2} = 1 \text{ min} = 60 \text{ s}$

Time, $t = 30 \text{ s}$

We know that

$$\frac{N}{N_0} = \left(\frac{1}{2}\right)^n = \left(\frac{1}{2}\right)^{\frac{t}{t_{1/2}}}$$

$$\frac{N}{10^{10}} = \left(\frac{1}{2}\right)^{30/60} = \left(\frac{1}{2}\right)^{1/2} = \frac{1}{\sqrt{2}}$$

$\Rightarrow \quad N \approx 7 \times 10^9$

15. Given, at time $t = 0$,

$$N_A(0) = 2N_B(0)$$

Decay constant is same for both radioactive atoms as λ.

For

$A \to B$, $\dfrac{dN_B(t)}{dt} = \lambda N_A(t) - \lambda N_B(t)$

Substituting $N_A(0)e^{-\lambda t}$ for $N_A(t)$ in above expression, we get

$$\frac{dN_B(t)}{dt} = \lambda N_A(0)e^{-\lambda t} - \lambda N_B(t)$$

$$= 2\lambda N_B(0)e^{-\lambda t} - \lambda N_B(t)$$

$$\Rightarrow \frac{dN_B(t)}{dt} + \lambda N_B(t) = 2\lambda N_B(0)e^{-\lambda t}$$

On multiplying both sides by $e^{\lambda t}$, we get

$$e^{\lambda t}\left[\frac{dN_B(t)}{dt} + \lambda N_B(t)\right] = 2\lambda N_B(0)e^{-\lambda t} \times e^{\lambda t}$$

$$\Rightarrow \frac{d}{dt}[N_B(t)e^{\lambda t}] = 2\lambda N_B(0)$$

On integrating both sides, we get

$$[N_B(t)e^{\lambda t}] = 2\lambda N_B(0)t + C \quad \text{... (i)}$$

Putting $t = 0$ in above expression, we get

$$[N_B(0)e^{\lambda \times 0}] = 2\lambda N_B(0) \times 0 + C$$

$$\Rightarrow C = N_B(0)$$

Putting the value of C in Eq. (i), we get

$$[N_B(t)e^{\lambda t}] = 2\lambda N_B(0)t + N_B(0) \quad \text{...(ii)}$$

$$\Rightarrow N_B(t) = N_B(0)[1 + 2\lambda t]e^{-\lambda t}$$

$$\Rightarrow \frac{N_B(t)}{N_B(0)} = [1 + 2\lambda t]e^{-\lambda t}$$

As, $N_B(t) = N_B(0)[1 + 2\lambda t]e^{-\lambda t}$

$$\Rightarrow N_B(t) = C[1 + 2\lambda t]e^{-\lambda t} \quad \text{...(iii)}$$

The maximum value of $N_B(t)$ is obtained at

$$\frac{dN_B(t)}{dt} = 0$$

From Eq. (ii),

$$\frac{dN_B(t)}{dt} = -\lambda C[1 + 2\lambda t]e^{-\lambda t} + 2C\lambda e^{-\lambda t} = 0$$

Solving the above expression,

$$t = \frac{1}{2\lambda} \text{ s}$$

Thus, maximum value of function will be at $t = \dfrac{1}{2\lambda}$ s.

16. **Statement A** is true, because atom of each element emits characteristics spectrum.

Statement B is true,

$\because$ According to Bohr's postulates,

$mvr = \dfrac{nh}{2\pi}$ and due to this reason, the electron resides into orbits of specific radius called stationary orbits.

Statement C is false, because density of nucleus is constant.

Statement D is false because a free neutron is unstable which decays into proton, electron and anti-neutrino.

Statement E is true because unstable nucleus shows radioactivity.

So, we can say that radioactivity is the instability of nuclei.

17. According to law of radioactive decay,

$$N = N_0 e^{-\lambda t} \quad \text{...(i)}$$

According to question, $N_d = N_0 - N$ ...(ii)

$\therefore$ From Eqs. (i) and (ii), we get

$$N_d = N_0 - N_0 e^{-\lambda t}$$

$$\Rightarrow N_d = N_0(1 - e^{-\lambda t})$$

$$\Rightarrow \frac{N_d}{N_0} = 1 - e^{-\lambda t}$$

$$\Rightarrow f = 1 - e^{-\lambda t} \quad \text{...(iii)}$$

On differentiating Eq. (iii), we get

$$\frac{df}{dt} = \lambda e^{-\lambda t}$$

18. According to law of radioactive decay,

$$R = R_0 e^{-\lambda t} \quad \text{...(i)}$$

$$\Rightarrow \ln R = \ln R_0 + \ln e^{-\lambda t}$$

$$\Rightarrow \ln R = \ln R_0 - \lambda t \quad \text{...(ii)}$$

So, for a given graph between $\ln R$ and t, $-\lambda$ is slope.

According to above graph given in question at

$$t = 0, \ln R = 6$$

$\therefore$ Eq. (ii) becomes,

$$\ln R_0 = 6 \quad \text{...(iii)}$$

and at $t = 40$ s, $\ln R = 0$

$\therefore$ Eq. (ii) becomes $\lambda = \dfrac{\ln R_0}{t} = \dfrac{\ln R_0}{40}$ ...(iv)

From Eqs. (iii) and (iv), we get

$$\lambda = \frac{6}{40} \quad \text{...(v)}$$

$\because$ We know that

Half-life, $t_{1/2} = \dfrac{0.693}{\lambda}$ ...(vi)

$\therefore$ From Eq. (v) and (vi), we get

$$t_{1/2} = \frac{0.693 \times 40}{6}$$

$$\Rightarrow t_{1/2} = 4.62 \text{ s}$$

19. The given situation can be shown as

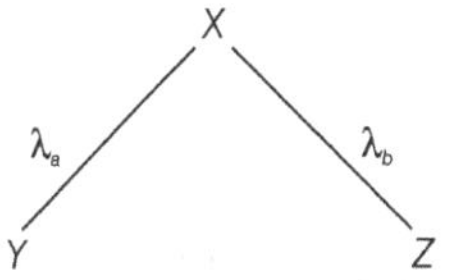

Here, radioactive material X decays into two particles Y and Z with their respective decay constant, λ_a and λ_b. It means that

$$\because \quad \lambda = \frac{\ln 2}{t_{1/2}}$$

Where, $t_{1/2}(a) = 700$ yr

and $t_{1/2}(b) = 1400$ yr

$$\lambda_a = \frac{\ln 2}{700} \text{yr}^{-1} \quad \text{and} \quad \lambda_b = \frac{\ln 2}{1400} \text{yr}^{-1}$$

$$\because \quad \lambda_{\text{total}} = \lambda_a + \lambda_b$$

$$= \left(\frac{\ln 2}{700} + \frac{\ln 2}{1400}\right) \text{yr}^{-1}$$

$$= \ln 2\left(\frac{1}{700} + \frac{1}{1400}\right) = \left(\frac{3\ln 2}{1400}\right) \text{yr}^{-1}$$

Suppose, the initial number of radioactive nuclei was N_0.

$$\therefore \quad N = N_0 e^{-\lambda t}$$

$$\Rightarrow \quad \frac{N_0}{3} = N_0 e^{-\lambda t} \quad \text{or} \quad \frac{N_0}{3} = N_0 e^{-\lambda_{\text{total}}\, t}$$

$$\Rightarrow \quad \frac{1}{3} = e^{-\lambda_{\text{total}}\, t}$$

Taking log on both the sides of above equation, we get

$$\ln\left(\frac{1}{3}\right) = \ln(e^{-\lambda_{\text{total}}\, t}) \Rightarrow \ln\left(\frac{1}{3}\right) = -\lambda_{\text{total}}\, t$$

$$\Rightarrow \quad 1.1 = \frac{3 \times 0.693}{1400} \times t$$

$$\Rightarrow \quad t \approx 740 \text{ yr}$$

20. Given, activity of radioactive element at time t_1,

$$A_1 = A$$

and at time t_2, $A_2 = A/5$

As we know that,

activity at any time $(A) = A_0 e^{-\lambda t}$

Where, A_0 is activity at time $t = 0$.

$$\therefore \quad A = A_0 e^{-\lambda t_1} \quad \text{...(i)}$$

$$\text{and} \quad A/5 = A_0 e^{-\lambda t_2} \quad \text{...(ii)}$$

On dividing Eq. (i) by Eq. (ii), we get

$$\frac{A}{A/5} = \frac{e^{-\lambda t_1}}{e^{-\lambda t_2}} \Rightarrow 5 = e^{-\lambda t_1 + \lambda t_2}$$

Taking log on both sides, we get

$$\ln 5 = \lambda (t_2 - t_1) \ln e$$

$$\Rightarrow \quad \ln 5 = \lambda (t_2 - t_1) \quad [\because \ln e = 1]$$

$$\Rightarrow \quad \lambda = \ln 5 / (t_2 - t_1)$$

Also, average life, $\tau = \frac{1}{\lambda} \Rightarrow \tau = \frac{t_2 - t_1}{\ln 5}$

JEE Advanced

1. nth half-life $= \frac{A_0}{2^n}$

$$\frac{A_1}{A_2} = \frac{\frac{A_0}{2^3}}{\frac{A_0}{2^7}} = 2^4 = 16$$

2. Out of 1000 nuclei of Q, 60% may go α-decay

$\Rightarrow$ 600 nuclei may have α-decay

$$\lambda = \frac{\ln 2}{t_{1/2}} = \frac{\ln 2}{20}$$

$$t = 1 \text{ h} = 60 \text{ min}$$

Using, $N = N_0 e^{-\lambda t} = 600 \times e^{-\frac{\ln 2}{20} \times 60}$

$$N = 75$$

$\Rightarrow$ 75 nuclei are left after one hour

So, number of nuclei decayed $= 600 - 75 = 525$

3. Let V is total blood in ml.

After 11.5 h, activity in 2.5 ml of blood is 115 Bq. Hence activity in V ml of blood would be,

$$R = \frac{115}{2.5V} = 46V$$

Here R is the activity

Using the equation, $R = R_0 e^{-\lambda t}$

we have, $46V = 2.4 \times 10^5 e^{-\frac{\ln 2}{8} \times \frac{11.5}{24}}$ $\quad (\ln 2 = 0.7)$

$$\text{or} \quad V = \frac{2.4 \times 10^5}{46\, e^{0.042}} = \frac{2.4 \times 10^5}{46(1 + 0.042)}$$

$$\approx 5 \times 10^3 \text{ ml} \quad \text{or} \quad V = 5\text{L}$$

4. Using the relation, $R = R_0 \left(\frac{1}{2}\right)^n$

Here, R is activity of radioactive substance, R_0 initial activity and n is number of half lives.

$$1 = 64\left(\frac{1}{2}\right)^n$$

Solving we get, $n = 6$

Now, $t = n(T_{1/2}) = 6(18 \text{ days}) = 108$ days

5. Let initial activity of both is A_0.

Then after time t, $A = A_0 e^{-\lambda t}$

$$R = \frac{-dA}{dt} = \lambda A_0 e^{-\lambda t} \quad \text{...(i)}$$

For P, $\lambda = \frac{1}{\tau}$ and for Q, $\lambda = \frac{1}{2\tau}$ and $t = 2\tau$

Substituting in equation (i), we have

$$\frac{R_P}{R_Q} = \frac{(A_0/\tau)e^{-(2\tau/\tau)}}{(A_0/2\tau)e^{-(2\tau/2\tau)}} = \frac{2}{e}$$

$$\therefore \quad n = 2$$

CHAPTER~12

SEMICONDUCTORS

LEVEL 01 Starter Level

12.1 Extrinsic Semiconductor

1 A silicon specimen is made into a *p*-type semiconductor by doping, on an average, one indium atom per 5×10^7 silicon atoms. If the number density of atoms in the silicon specimen is 5×10^{28} atoms m^{-3}, then what will be the number of acceptor atoms in silicon per cubic centimeter?

2 In a pure silicon ($n_i = 10^{16}$ /m^3) crystal at 300 K, 10^{21} atoms of phosphorus are added per cubic meter. What will be the new hole concentration?

3 Suppose a pure Si crystal has 5×10^{28} atoms/m^3 at room temperature. It is doped by 1 ppm concentration of pentavalent As. Calculate the number of electrons and holes. Given $n_i = 1.5 \times 10^{16}$ /m^3

4 If the ratio of the concentration of electrons to that of holes in a semiconductor is $\frac{7}{5}$ and the ratio of current is $\frac{7}{4}$, then what is the ratio of their drift velocities?

5 Mobilities of electrons and holes in a sample of intrinsic germanium at room temperature are $0.36\ m^2V^{-1}s^{-1}$ and $0.18\ m^2V^{-1}s^{-1}$, respectively. The electron and hole densities are 4.5×10^{20} /m^3 and 1.5×10^{19} /m^3, respectively.

(a) Is the semiconductor *n*-type or *p*-type?

(b) What will be the electrical conductivity of germanium?

6 In the energy band diagram of a material shown below, the open circles and filled circles denote holes and electrons respectively. What is the type of the material?

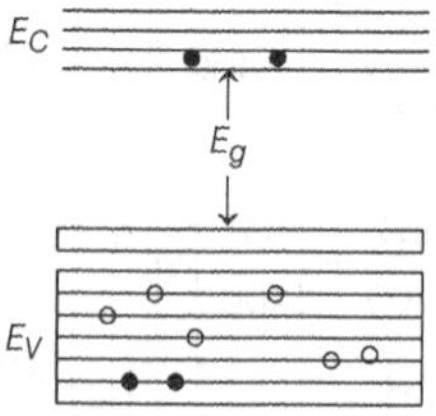

7 The electrical conductivity of a semiconductor increases when electromagnetic radiation of wavelength shorter than 2480 nm, is incident on it. What is the band gap for the semiconductor?

8 The energy gap of silicon is 1.14 eV. What will be the maximum wavelength at which silicon starts energy absorption? ($h = 6.62 \times 10^{-34}$ Js; $c = 3 \times 10^8$ ms^{-1})

9 A *p-n* photodiode is fabricated from a semiconductor with a band gap of 2.5 eV. What is the maximum wavelength of signal it can detect?

12.2 *p-n* Junction Diode

1 A potential barrier of 0.50 V exists across a *p*-*n* junction. If the depletion region is 5.0×10^{-7} m wide, what is the intensity of the electric field in this region?

2 Of the diodes shown in the following diagrams, which are forward biased and which are reverse biased?

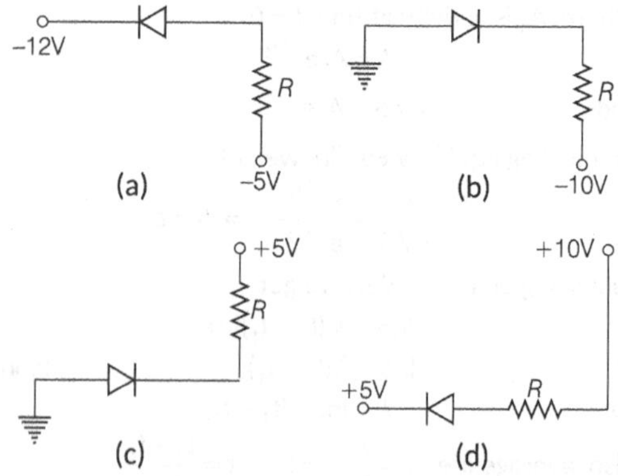

3 If the forward voltage in a semiconductor diode is changed from 0.5 V to 0.7 V, then the forward current changes by 1.0 mA. What will be the forward resistance of diode junction?

4 In a reverse biased diode when the applied voltage changes by 1 V, the current is found to change by 0.5 μA. What is the reverse bias resistance of the diode?

5 Consider the junction diode is ideal. What is the value of current in the figure?

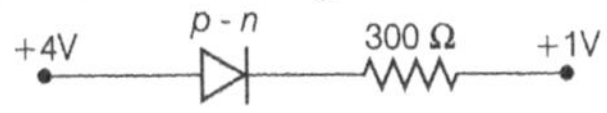

6 What will be the current through an ideal *p-n* junction shown in the following circuit diagram?

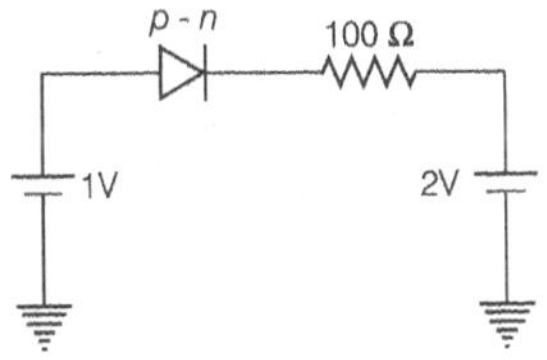

7 Figure shows a diode connected to an external resistance and an emf. Assuming that the barrier potential developed in diode is 0.5 V, obtain the value of current in the circuit in milli ampere.

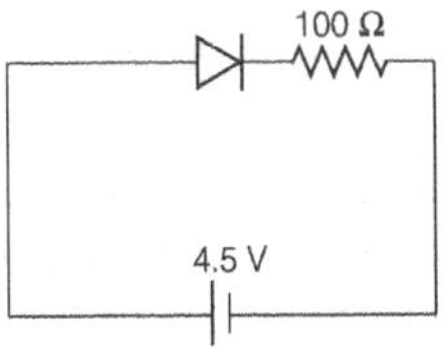

8 The diode shown in the circuit is a silicon diode. What will be the potential difference between the points *A* and *B*?

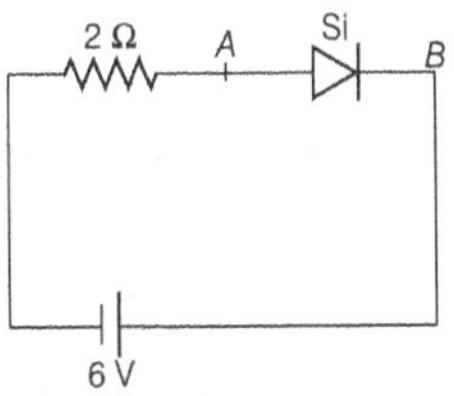

9 In the network shown, what is the current flowing through the battery of negligible internal resistance?

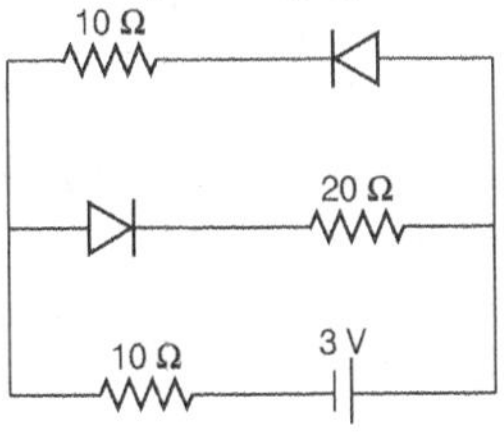

10 Assuming the diodes to be of silicon with forward resistance zero, what is the current *I* in the following circuit?

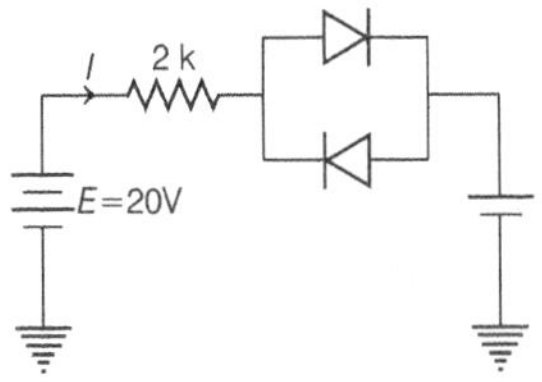

11 What are the currents flowing in each of the following circuits?

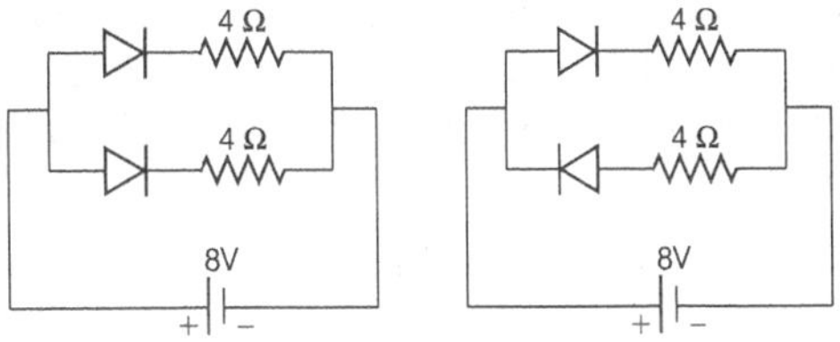

(a) (b)

12 In the following circuit of *p-n* junction diodes D_1, D_2 and D_3 are ideal then find *i*.

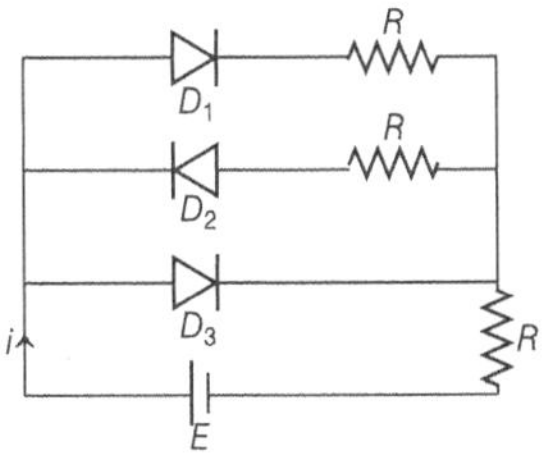

13 A Zener diode has a contact potential of 1 V in the absence of biasing. It undergoes Zener breakdown for an electric field of 10^6 V-m^{-1} at the depletion region of *p-n* junction. If the width of the depletion region is 2.5 μm, what should be the reverse biased potential for the Zener breakdown to occur?

14 A Zener diode, having breakdown voltage equal to 15V, is used in a voltage regulator circuit shown in figure. What is the current through the diode?

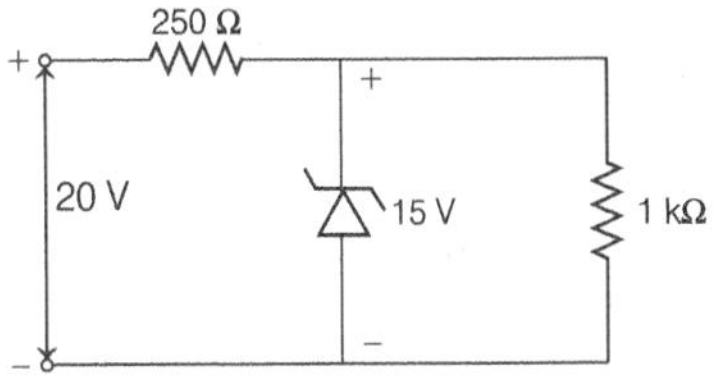

12.3 Rectifier

1 If a full wave rectifier circuit is operating from 50Hz mains, what will be the fundamental frequency in the ripple?

2 The output current versus time curve of a rectifier is shown in the figure. What is the average value of the output current in this case?

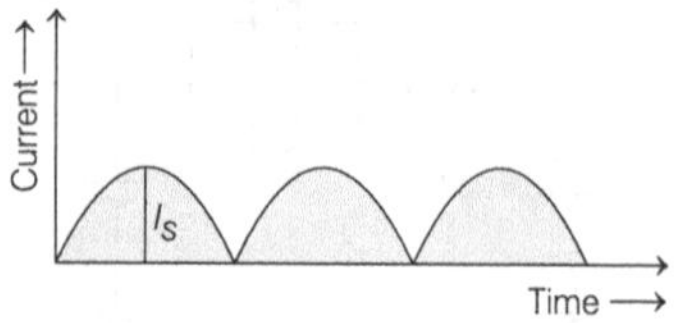

3 What is the average value of output direct current in a half wave rectifier?

4 The peak voltage in the output of a half-wave diode rectifier fed with a sinusoidal signal without filter is 10V. What is the DC component of the output voltage?

5 What is the maximum efficiency of full wave rectifier?

12.4 Logic Gates

1 In the following combinations of logic gates, what are the outputs?

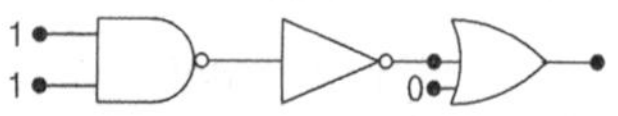

(a)

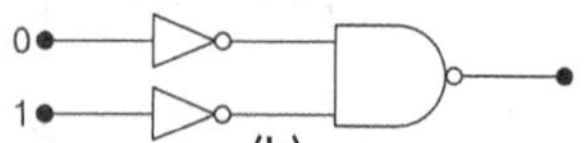

(b)

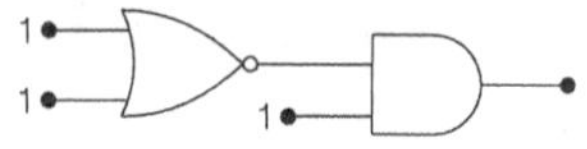

(c)

2 What is the output of the combination of the gates shown in the figure?

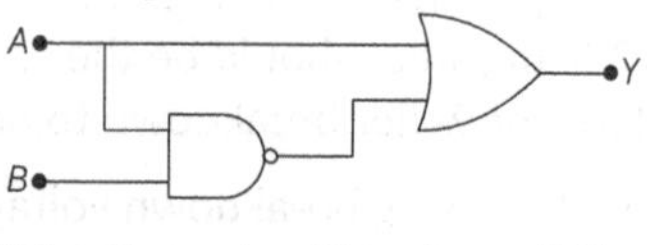

3 What will be the output Y, when all three inputs are (a) high (b) low?

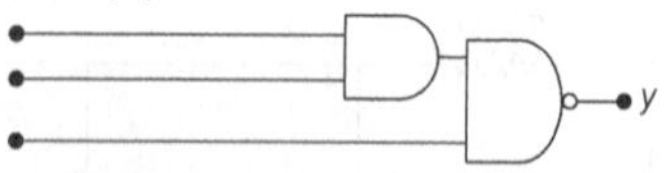

4 Which gate is produced by the combination of the following gates?

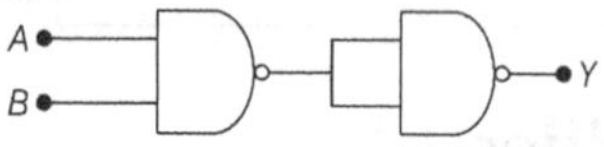

5 The following circuit is equivalent to which gate?

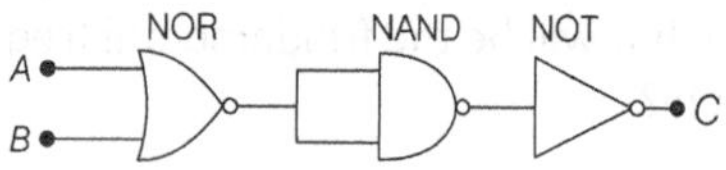

6 The combination of gates shown below produces which gate?

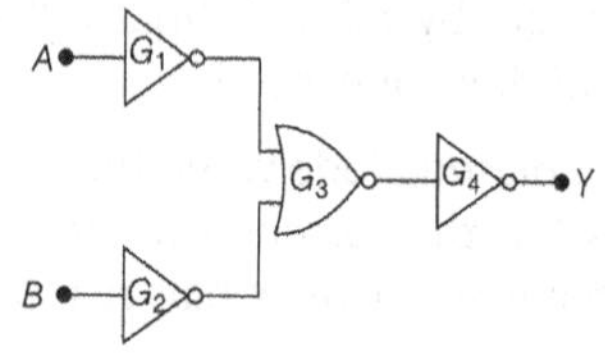

7 The figure shows two NAND gates followed by a NOR gate. The system is equivalent to which logic gate?

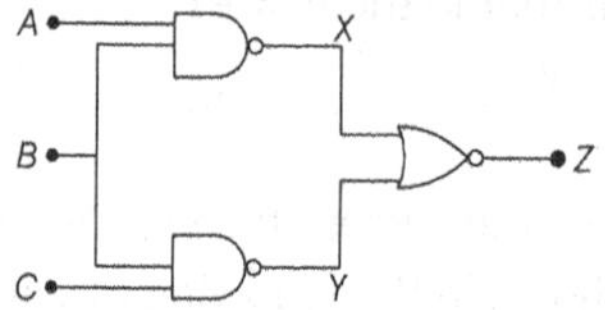

8 The given figure shows the wave forms for two inputs A and B and that for the output Y of a logic circuit. The logic circuit corresponds to which gate?

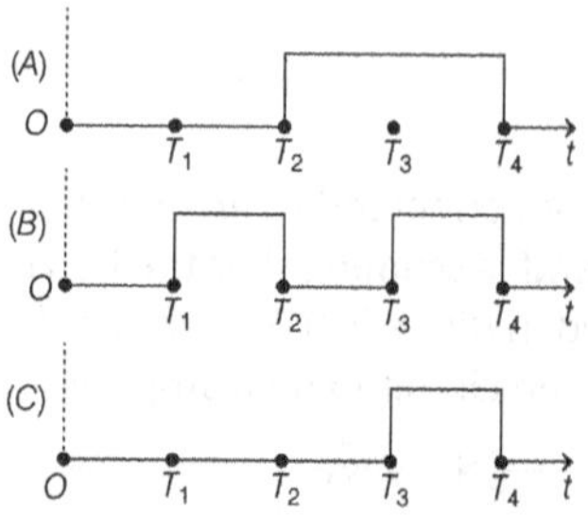

9 In a given circuit as shown the two input waveforms A and B are applied simultaneously. Draw the resultant waveform Y.

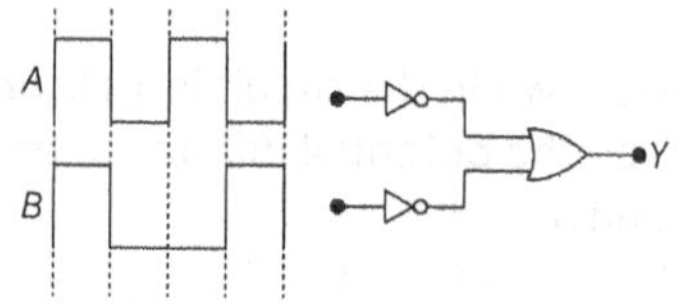

10 In the following circuit, draw the truth table.

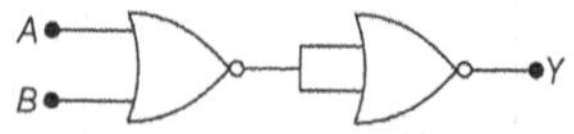

11 The given figure represents a combination of gates, write the truth table for this.

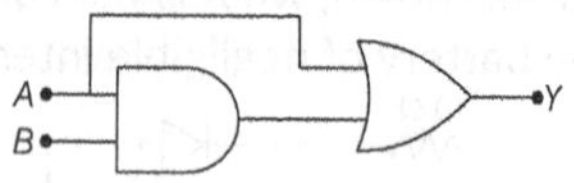

12 Draw the truth table for the following logic circuit.

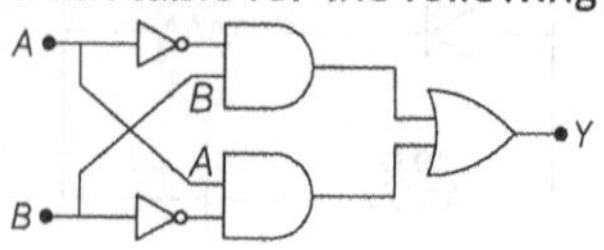

LEVEL 02 JEE Main Level

1 If N_p and N_e be the numbers of holes and conduction electrons in an extrinsic semiconductor, then

(a) $N_p > N_e$
(b) $N_p = N_e$
(c) $N_p < N_e$
(d) $N_p > N_e$ or $N_p < N_e$ depending on the nature of impurity

2 A Ge specimen is doped with Al. The concentration of acceptor atoms is $\sim 10^{21}$ atoms/m^3. Given that the intrinsic concentration of electron hole pairs is $\sim 10^{19}$ /m^3, the concentration of electron in the specimen is

(a) 10^{17} /m^3 (b) 10^{15} /m^3
(c) 10^{4} /m^3 (d) 10^{2} /m^3

3 Pure Si at 500 K has equal number of electron (n_e) and hole (n_h) concentrations of 1.5×10^{16} m^{-3}. Doping by indium increases n_h to 4.5×10^{22} m^{-3}. The doped semiconductor is of

(a) *n*-type with electron concentration $n_e = 2.5 \times 10^{23}$ m^{-3}
(b) *p*-type having electron concentration $n_e = 5 \times 10^{9}$ m^{-3}
(c) *n*-type with electron concentration $n_e = 5 \times 10^{22}$ m^{-3}
(d) *p*-type with electron concentration $n_e = 2.5 \times 10^{10}$ m^{-3}

4 The contribution in the total current flowing through a semiconductor due to electrons and holes are $\frac{3}{4}$ and $\frac{1}{4}$ respectively. If the drift velocity of electrons is $\frac{5}{2}$ times that of holes at this temperature, then the ratio of concentration of electrons and holes is

(a) 6 : 5 (b) 5 : 6
(c) 3 : 2 (d) 2 : 3

5 In semiconductor the concentration of electrons and holes are 8×10^{18} /m^3 and 5×10^{18} /m^3 respectively. If the mobilities of electrons and holes are 2.3 m^2 /volt-s and 0.01 m^2 /volt-s respectively, then then semiconductor is

(a) *n*-type and its resistivity is 0.34 ohm-metre
(b) *p*-type and its resistivity is 0.034 ohm-metre
(c) *n*-type and its resistivity is 0.034 ohm-metre
(d) *p*-type and its resistivity is 3.40 ohm-metre

6 A potential difference of 2V is applied between the opposite faces of a Ge crystal plate of area 1 cm^2 and thickness 0.5 mm. If the concentration of electrons in Ge is 2×10^{19} /m^3 and mobilities of electrons and holes are 0.36 m^2 /volt-s and 0.14 m^2 /volt-s respectively, then the current flowing through the plate will be

(a) 0.25 A (b) 0.45 A (c) 0.56 A (d) 0.64 A

7 The temperature coefficient of resistance of a semiconductor

(a) is always positive
(b) is always negative
(c) is zero
(d) may be positive or negative or zero

8 Wires *P* and *Q* have the same resistance at ordinary (room) temperature. When heated, resistance of *P* increases and that of *Q* decreases. We conclude that

(a) *P* and *Q* are conductors of different materials
(b) *P* is *n*-type semiconductor and *Q* is *p*-type semiconductor
(c) *P* is semiconductor and *Q* is conductor
(d) *P* is conductor and *Q* is semiconductor

9 A strip of copper and another of germanium are cooled from room temperature to 80 K. the resistance of

(a) Each of these decreases
(b) Copper strip increases and that of germanium decreases
(c) Copper strip decreases and that of germanium increases
(d) Each of the above increases

10 Although carbon, silicon and germanium have same lattice structure and four valence electrons each, their band structure leads to the energy gaps as

(a) E_g(Si) < E_g(Ge) < E_g(C)
(b) E_g(C) > E_g(Si) > E_g(Ge)
(c) E_g(Ge) > E_g(Si) > E_g(C)
(d) E_g(Si) = E_g(Ge) = E_g(C)

11 The typical ionisation energy of a donor in silicon is

(a) 10.0 eV (b) 1.0 eV
(c) 0.1 eV (d) 0.001 eV

12 The energy gap between conduction band and the valence band is of the order of 0.7 eV. Then, it is

(a) an insulator (b) a conductor
(c) a semiconductor (d) an alloy

13 The band gap in germanium and silicon in eV respectively are

(a) 0.7, 1.1 (b) 1.1, 0.7
(c) 1.1, 0 (d) 0, 1.1

14 Which of the energy band diagrams shown in the figure corresponds to that of a semiconductor?

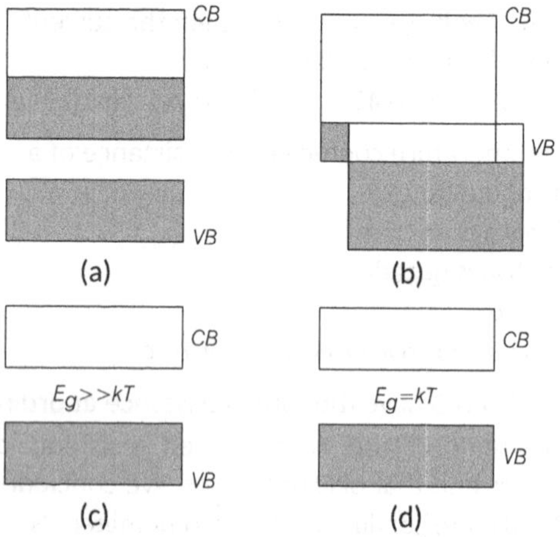

15 Which of the following statements is true for an *n*-type semiconductor?

(a) The donor level lies closely below the bottom of the conduction band.
(b) The donor level lies closely above the top of the valence band
(c) The donor level lies at the halfway mark of the forbidden energy gap
(d) None of the above

16 The energy band diagrams for three semiconductor samples of silicon are as shown. We can then assert that

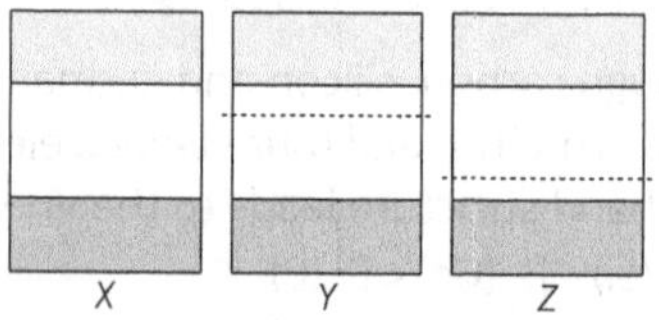

(a) Sample *X* is undoped while samples *Y* and *Z* have been doped with a third group and a fifth group impurity respectively
(b) Sample *X* is undoped while both samples *Y* and *Z* have been doped with a fifth group impurity
(c) Sample *X* has been doped with equal amounts of third and fifth group impurities while samples *Y* and *Z* are undoped
(d) Sample *X* is undoped while samples *Y* and *Z* have been doped with a fifth group and a third group impurity respectively

17 The width of forbidden gap in silicon crystal is 1.1 eV. When the crystal is converted in to a *n*-type semiconductor the distance of Fermi level from conduction band is

(a) greater than 0.55 eV (b) equal to 0.55 eV
(c) lesser than 0.55 eV (d) equal to 1.1 eV

18 A *p-n* photodiode is made of a material with a band gap of 2.0 eV. The minimum frequency of the radiation that can be absorbed by the material is nearly

(a) 10×10^{14} Hz (b) 5×10^{14} Hz
(c) 1×10^{14} Hz (d) 20×10^{14} Hz

19 An electron-hole pair is formed when light of maximum wavelength 6000 Å is incident on the semiconductor. What is the band gap energy of the semiconductor? ($h = 6.62 \times 10^{-34}$ J-s)

(a) 3.31×10^{-19} J (b) 3.07×10^{-19} J
(c) 2.07×10^{-19} J (d) 2.07 J

20 A *p*-type semiconductor has acceptor levels 57 meV above the valence band. The maximum wavelength of light required to create a hole is (Planck's constant $h = 6.6 \times 10^{-34}$ J-s)

(a) 57Å (b) 57×10^{-3} Å
(c) 217100 Å (d) 11.61×10^{-33} Å

21 The depletion layer in the *p-n* junction region is caused by

(a) Drift of holes
(b) Diffusion of charge carriers
(c) Migration of impurity ions
(d) Drift of electrons

22 Within depletion region of *p-n* junction diode

(a) *p*-side is positive and *n*-side is negative
(b) *p*-side is negative and *n*-side is positive
(c) Both sides are positive or both negative
(d) Both sides are neutral

23 The electrical resistance of depletion layer is large because

(a) It has no charge carriers
(b) It has a large number of charge carriers
(c) It contains electrons as charge carriers
(d) It has holes as charge carriers

24 In the middle of the depletion layer of reverse biased *p-n* junction, the

(a) electric field is zero
(b) potential is maximum
(c) electric field is maximum
(d) potential is zero

25 In a junction diode, the direction of diffusion current is
(a) From *n*-region to *p*-region
(b) From *p*-region to *n*-region
(c) From *n*-region to *p*-region if the junction is forward baised and *vice versa* if it is reverse baised
(d) From *p*-region to *n*-region if the junction is forward baised and *vice-versa* if it is reversed baised

26 The dominant mechanism for motion of charge carriers in forward and reverse biased silicon *p*-*n* junctions are
(a) drift in forward bias, diffusion in reverse bias
(b) diffusion in forward bias, drift in reverse bias
(c) diffusion in both forward and reverse bias
(d) drift in both forward and reverse bias

27 When forward bias is applied to a *p*-*n* junction, then what happens to the potential barrier V_B and the width of charge depleted region x?
(a) V_B increases, x decreases
(b) V_B decreases, x increases
(c) V_B increases, x increases
(d) V_B decreases, x decreases

28 On increasing the reverse bias to a large value in a *p*-*n* junction, diode current
(a) increases slowly (b) remains fixed
(c) suddenly increases (d) decreases slowly

29 Consider the following statements A and B and identify the correct choice of the given answers.
A. The width of the depletion layer in a *p*-*n* junction diode increases in forward bias.
B. In an intrinsic semiconductor the fermi energy level is exactly in the middle of the forbidden gap
(a) A is true and B is false (b) Both A and B are false
(c) A is false and B is true (d) Both A and B are true

30 A Si and a Ge diode has identical physical dimensions. The band gap in Si is larger than that in Ge. An identical reverse bias is applied across the diodes
(a) The reverse current in Ge is larger than that in Si
(b) The reverse current in Si is larger than that in Ge
(c) The reverse current is identical in the two diodes
(d) The relative magnitude of the reverse currents cannot be determined from the given data only

31 A semiconductor X is made by doping a germanium crystal with arsenic ($Z = 33$). A second semiconductor Y is made by doping germanium with indium ($Z = 49$). The two are joined end to end and connected to a battery as shown. Which of the following statements is correct

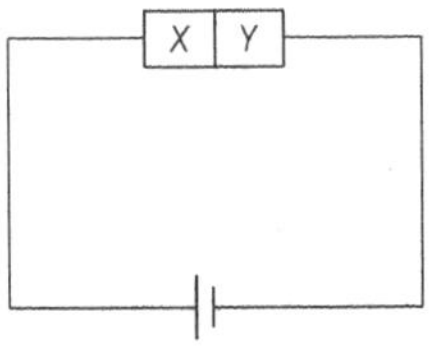

(a) X is *p*-type, Y is *n*-type and the junction is forward biased
(b) X is *p*-type, Y is *p*-type and the junction is forward biased
(c) X is *p*-type, Y is *n*-type and the junction is reverse biased
(d) X is *n*-type, Y is *p*-type and the junction is reverse biased

32 In the case of forward biasing of *p*-*n* junction, which one of the following figures correctly depicts the direction of flow of carriers?

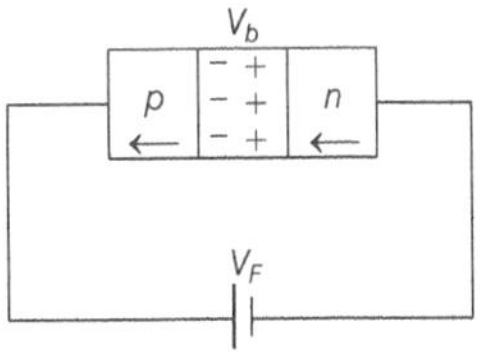

(a)

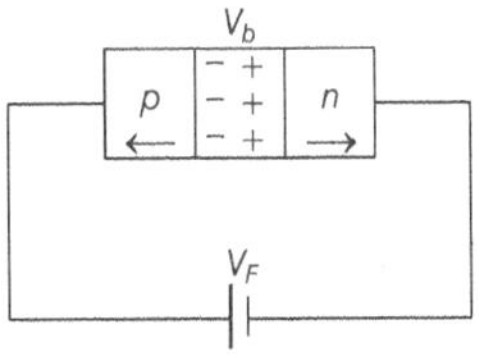

(b)

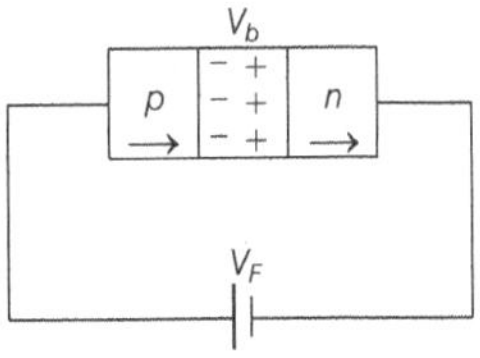

(c)

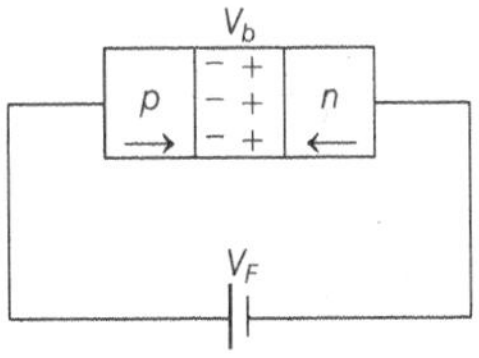

(d)

33 The depletion layer in a silicon diode is 1 μm wide and its knee potential is 0.6 V, then the electric field in the depletion layer will be
(a) 0.6 Vm^{-1} (b) $6 \times 10^4 \text{ Vm}^{-1}$
(c) $6 \times 10^5 \text{ Vm}^{-1}$ (d) Zero

34 Two identical *p*-*n* junctions are connected in series in three different ways as shown below to a battery. The potential drop across the *p*-*n* junctions are equal in

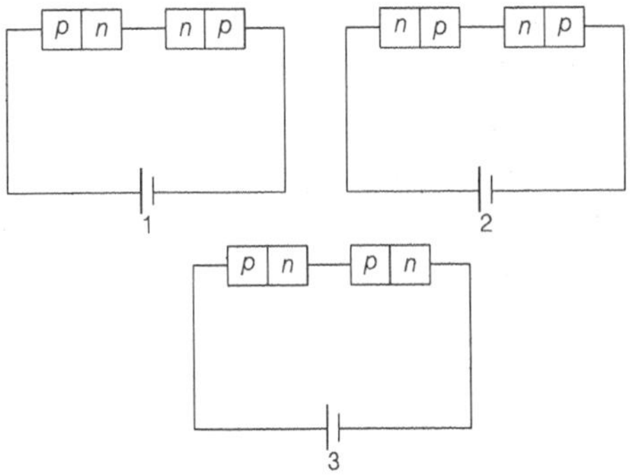

(a) circuits 2 and 3
(b) circuits 1 and 2
(c) circuits 1 and 3
(d) None of the circuit

35 A *p*-*n* junction in series with a resistance of 5 kΩ is connected across a 50 V DC source. If the forward bias resistance of the junction is 50 Ω bias current is

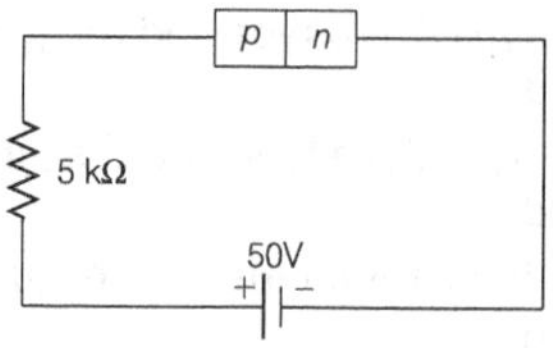

(a) 8.8 mA (b) 1 mA
(c) 2 mA (d) 9.9 mA

36 In a forward biased *p*-*n* junction diode, the potential barrier in the depletion region is of the form

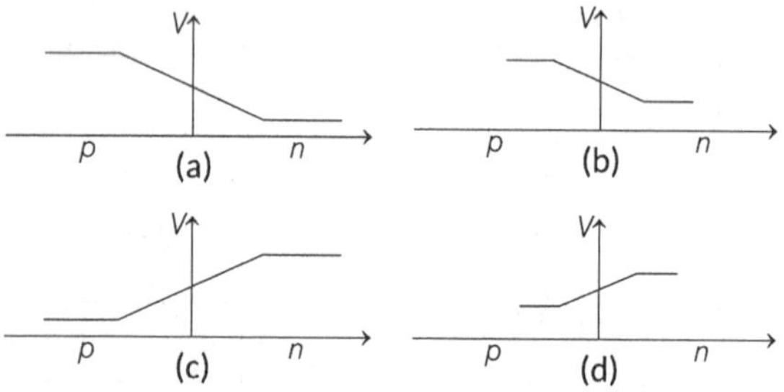

37 The approximate ratio of resistances in the forward and reverse bias of the *pn*-junction diode is
(a) $10^2 : 1$ (b) $10^{-2} : 1$
(c) $1 : 10^{-4}$ (d) $1 : 10^4$

38 When the forward bias voltage of a diode is changed from 0.6 V to 0.7 V, the current changes from 5 mA to 15 mA. Then its forward bias resistance is
(a) 0.01 Ω (b) 0.1 Ω
(c) 10 Ω (d) 100 Ω

39 The reverse bias in a junction diode is changed from 8 V to 13 V then the value of the current charges from 40μA to 60 μA. The resistance of junction diode will be
(a) 2×10^5 Ω (b) 2.5×10^5 Ω
(c) 3×10^5 Ω (d) 4×10^5 Ω

40 When a silicon *pn* junction is in forward biased condition with series resistance, it has knee voltage of 0.6 V. Current flow in it is 5 mA, when *pn* junction is connected with 2.6 V battery, the value of series resistance is
(a) 100 Ω (b) 200 Ω
(c) 400 Ω (d) 500 Ω

41 The *i*-*V* characteristic of a *p*-*n* junction diode is shown below. The approximate dynamic resistance of the *P*-*N* junction when a forward bias of 2 volt is applied

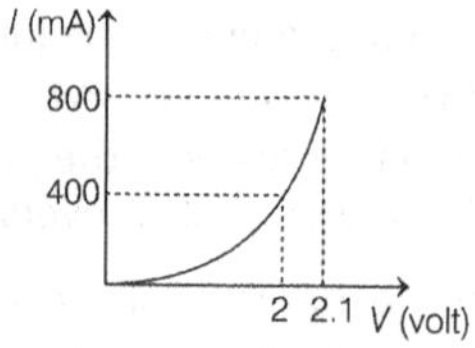

(a) 1 Ω (b) 0.25 Ω
(c) 0.5 Ω (d) 5 Ω

42 A junction diode has a resistance of 25 Ω when forward biased and 2500 Ω when reverse biased. The current in the diode, for the arrangement shown will be

(a) $\frac{1}{15}$ A (b) $\frac{1}{7}$ A (c) $\frac{1}{25}$ A (d) $\frac{1}{480}$ A

43 What is the current through an ideal *pn*-junction diode shown in figure below

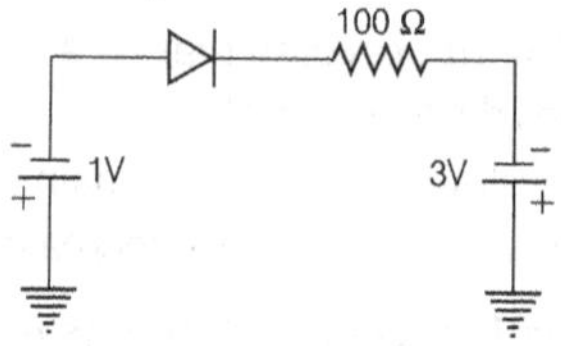

(a) Zero (b) 10 mA
(c) 20 mA (d) 50 mA

44 In the circuit, if the forward voltage drop for the diode is 0.5 V, the current will be

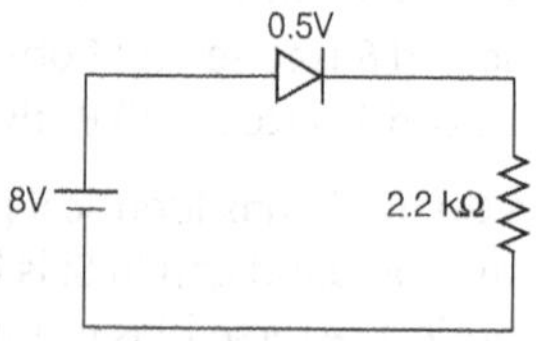

(a) 3.4mA (b) 2 mA (c) 2.5 mA (d) 3 mA

45 A source of 8V drives the diode in figure. through a current-limiting resistor of 100 ohm. Then the magnitude of the slope load line on the *I*-*V* characteristics of the diode is

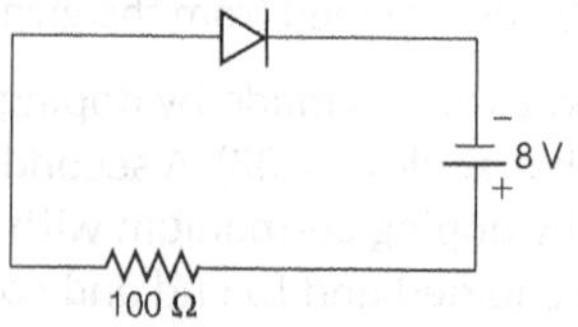

(a) 0.01 (b) 100 (c) 0.08 (d) 12.5

46 For the given circuit of *pn*-junction diode, which of the following statement is correct

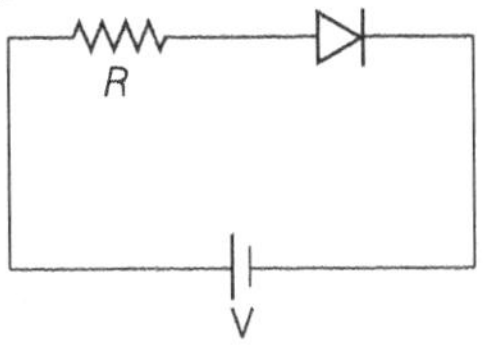

(a) In forward biasing the voltage across R is V
(b) In forward biasing the voltage across R is $2V$
(c) In reverse biasing the voltage across R is V
(d) In reverse biasing the voltage across R is $2V$

47 The junction diode in the following circuit requires a minimum current of 1mA to be above the knee point (0.7 V) of its *I-V* characteristic curve. The voltage across the junction diode is independent of current above the knee point. If V_B = 4V, then the maximum value of R so that the voltage is above knee point will be

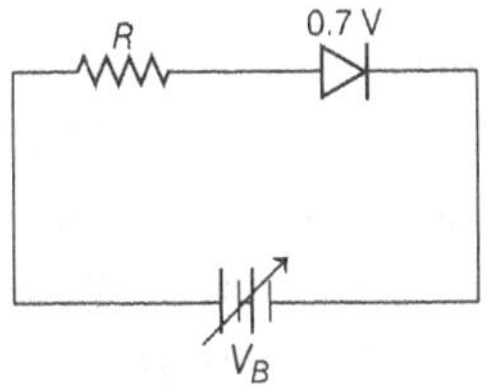

(a) 3.3 kΩ (b) 4.0 kΩ (c) 4.7 kΩ (d) 6.6 kΩ

48 The diode used in the circuit shown in the figure has a constant voltage drop of 0.5 V at all currents and a maximum power rating of 100 mW. What should be the value of the resistor R, connected in series with the diode for obtaining maximum current?

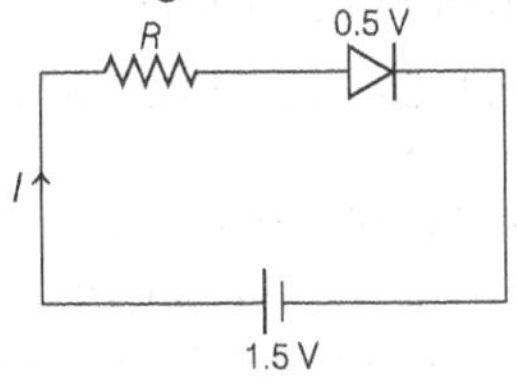

(a) 1.5 Ω (b) 5 Ω (c) 6.67 Ω (d) 200 Ω

49 The circuit shown in the figure contains two diodes each with a forward resistance of 50 Ω and with infinite backward resistance. If the battery is 6V, the current through the 100 Ω resistance (in ampere) is

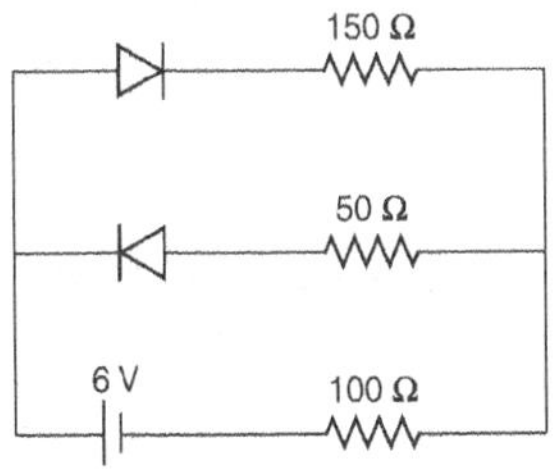

(a) Zero (b) 0.02 (c) 0.03 (d) 0.036

50 In the following circuit find i_1 and i_2

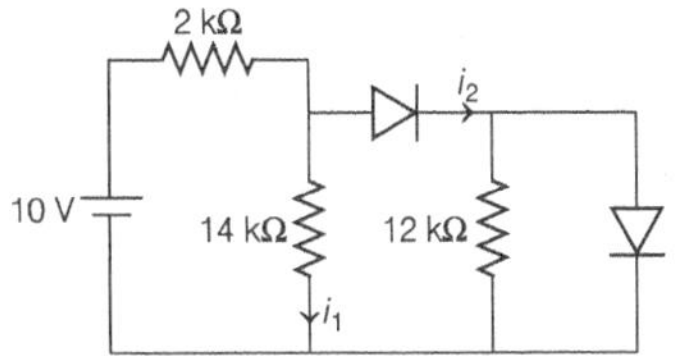

(a) 0, 0 (b) 5 mA, 5 mA
(c) 5 mA, 0 (d) 0, 5 mA

51 In the given circuit

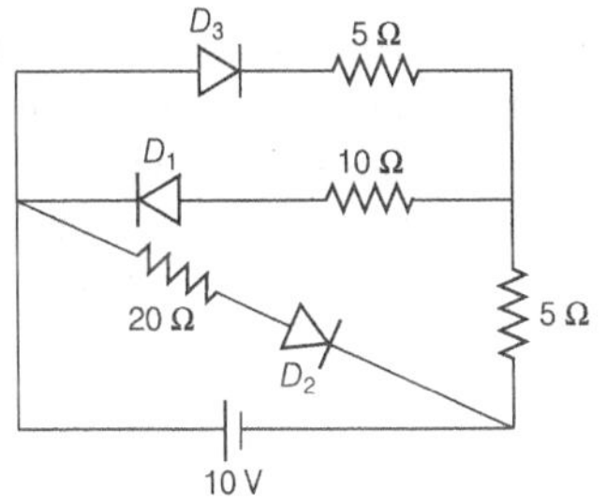

The current through the battery is
(a) 0.5 A (b) 1 A
(c) 1.5 A (d) 2 A

52 In the following circuit the equivalent resistance between A and B is

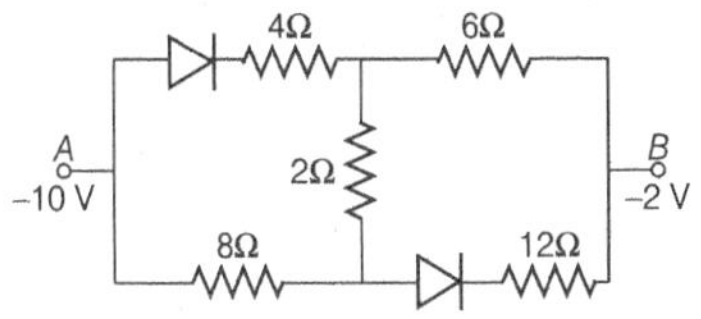

(a) $\frac{20}{3}$ Ω (b) 10 Ω
(c) 16 Ω (d) 20Ω

53 In the following circuits *pn*-junction diodes D_1, D_2 and D_3 are ideal. For the following potentials of A and B, the correct increasing order of resistance between A and B will be

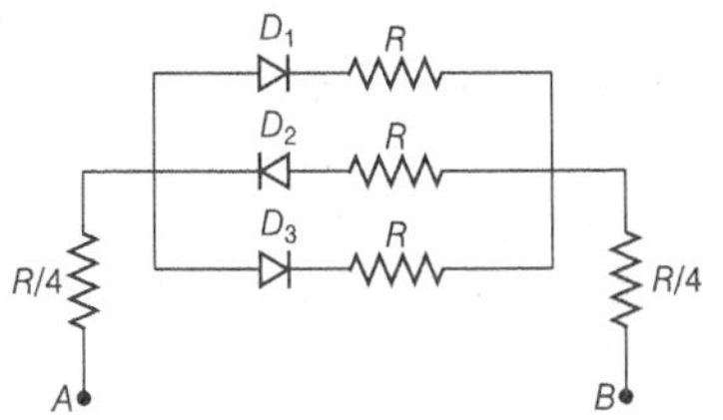

(i) −10V, −5V (ii) −5V, −10V
(iii) −4V, −12 V
(a) (i) < (ii) < (iii) (b) (iii) < (ii) < (i)
(c) (ii) = (iii) < (i) (d) (i) = (iii) < (ii)

54 Ge and Si diodes conduct at 0.3V and 0.7 V respectively. In the following figure if Ge diode connection is reversed, the value of V_0 changes by

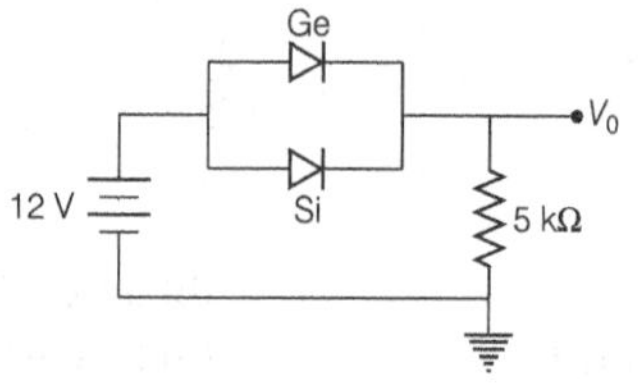

(a) 0.2 V (b) 0.4 V (c) 0.6 V (d) 0.8 V

55 Two identical capacitors *A* and *B* are charged to the same potential *V* and are connected in two circuits at $t = 0$, as shown in figure. The charge on the capacitors at time $t = CR$ are respectively

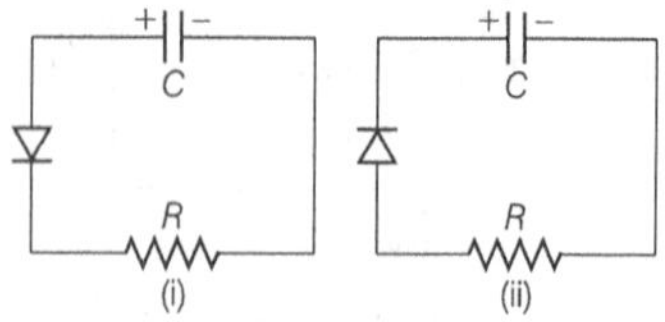

(a) VC, VC (b) $\frac{VC}{e}, VC$ (c) $VC, \frac{VC}{e}$ (d) $\frac{VC}{e}, \frac{VC}{e}$

56 A junction diode is connected to a 10 V source and $10^3\,\Omega$ rheostat as shown in figure. The slope of load line on the characteristic curve of diode will be

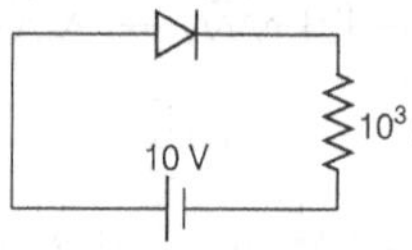

(a) 10^{-2} AV^{-1} (b) 10^{-3} AV^{-1}
(c) 10^{-4} AV^{-1} (d) 10^{-5} AV^{-1}

57 Zener breakdown takes place if
(a) doped impurity is low (b) doped impurity is high
(c) less impurity in *n*-part (d) less impurity in *p*-type

58 Zener diode is used as
(a) Half wave rectifier (b) Full wave rectifier
(c) AC voltage stabilizer (d) DC voltage stabilizer

59 Avalanche breakdown is due to
(a) Collision of minority charge carrier
(b) Increase in depletion layer thickness
(c) Decrease in depletion layer thickness
(d) None of the above

60 If a Zener diode ($V_z = 5$V and $I_z = 10$ mA) is connected in series with a resistance and 20 V is applied across the combination, then the maximum resistance one can use without spoiling zener action is
(a) 20 kΩ (b) 15 kΩ (c) 10 kΩ (d) 1.5 kΩ

61 In the circuit given the current through the zener diode is

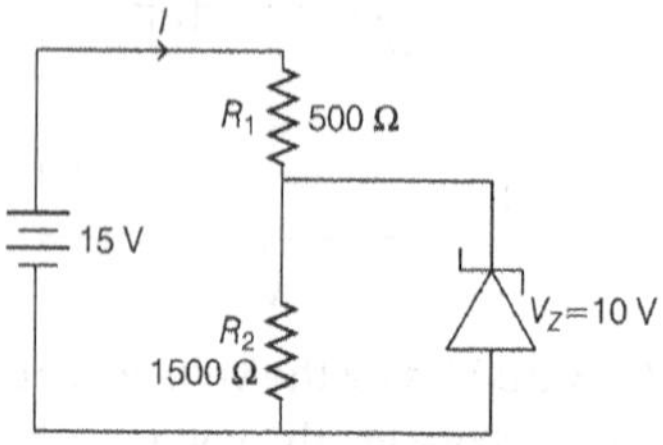

(a) 10 mA (b) 6.67 mA
(c) 5 mA (d) 3.33 mA

62 From the circuit shown below, the maximum and minimum values of Zener diode current are

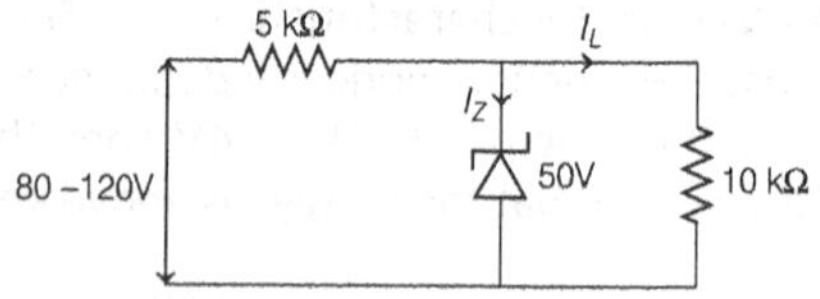

(a) 6mA, 5mA (b) 14mA, 5mA
(c) 9 mA, 1mA (d) 3mA, 2mA

63 Consider the following statement *A* and *B* and identify the correct choice of the given answers
(A) A Zener diode is always connected in reverse bias to use it as a voltage regulator.
(B) The potential barrier of a *p-n* junction lies between 0.1 to 0.3 approximately
(a) *A* and *B* are correct
(b) *A* and *B* are wrong
(c) *A* is correct but *B* is wrong
(d) *A* is wrong but *B* is correct

64 Avalanche breakdown in a *p-n* junction diode is due to
(a) sudden shift of Fermi level
(b) increase in the width of forbidden gap
(c) sudden increase of impurity concentration
(d) cumulative effect of increased electron collision and creation of added electron-hole pairs

65 If in a *p-n* junction diode, a square input signal of 10 V is applied as shown

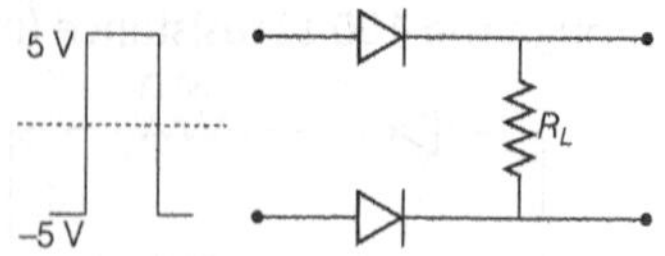

Then, the output signal across R_L will be

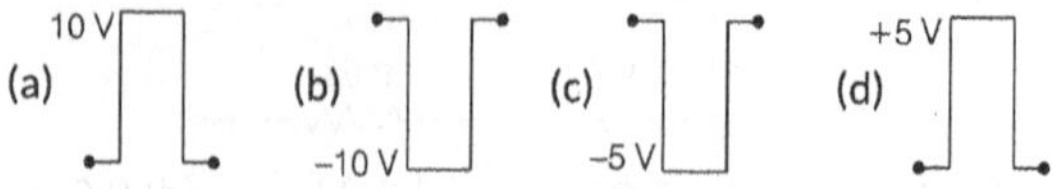

66 The output in the circuit of figure is taken across a capacitor. It is as shown in figure

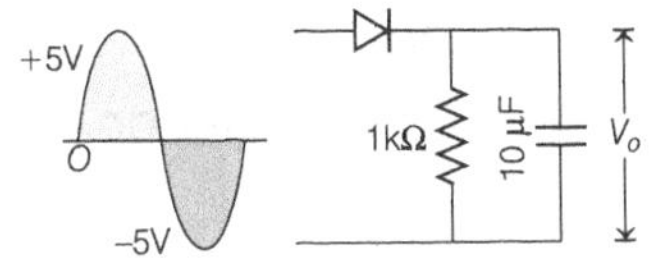

(a) 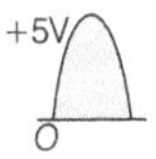

(b) 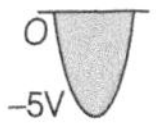

(c) 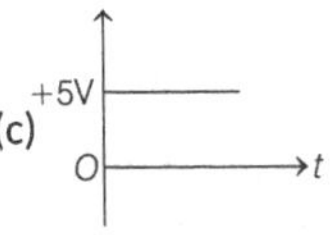

(d) 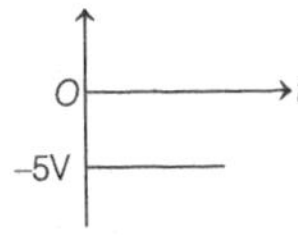

67 A waveform shown when applied to the following circuit will produce which of the following output waveform? Assuming ideal diode configuration and $R_1 = R_2$

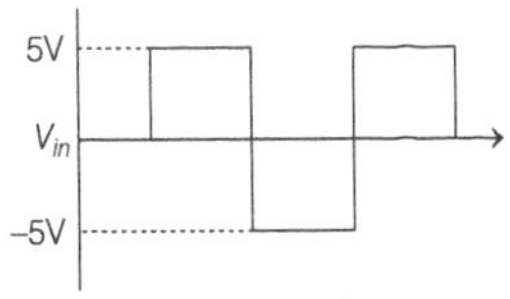

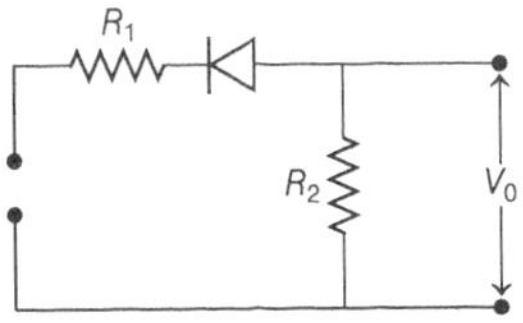

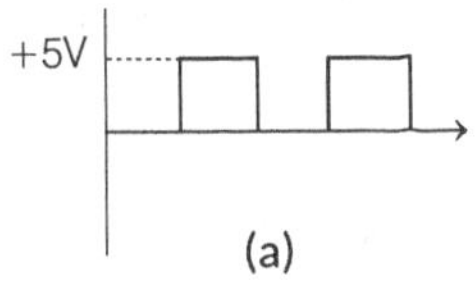

(a)

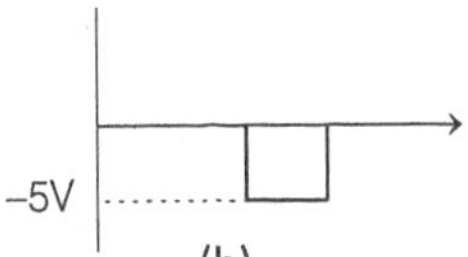

(b)

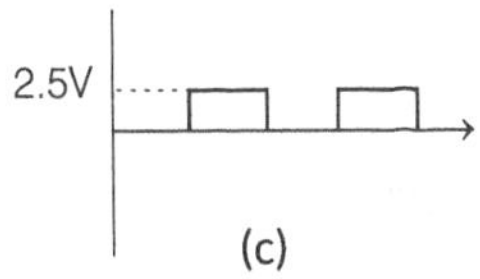

(c)

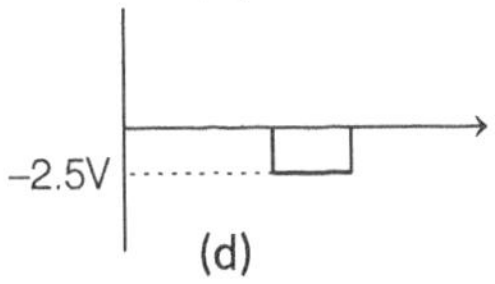

(d)

68 In the circuit shown in figure the maximum output voltage V_0 is

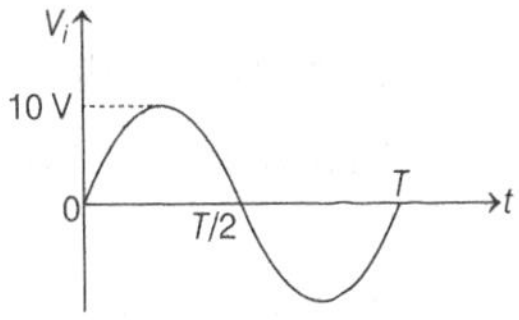

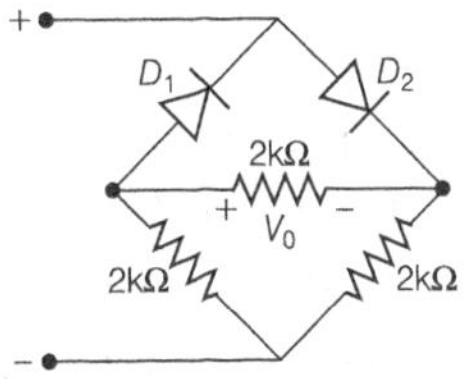

(a) 0 V (b) 5 V (c) 10 V (d) $\frac{5}{\sqrt{2}}$ V

69 A diode is connected to 220 V (rms) AC in series with a capacitor as shown in figure. The voltage across the capacitor is

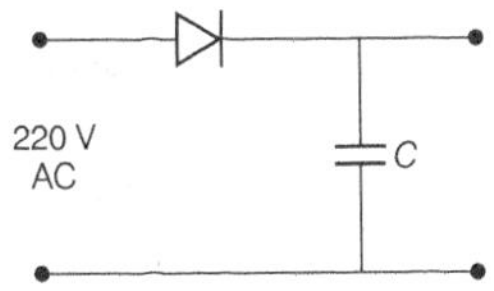

(a) 220 V (b) 110 V (c) 311.1 V (d) $\frac{220}{\sqrt{2}}$ V

70 A *p-n* junction (*D*) shown in the figure can act as a rectifier. An alternating current source (*V*) is connected in the circuit. The current (*I*) in the resistor (*R*) can be shown

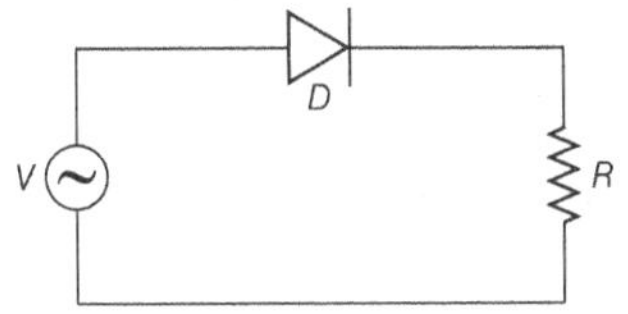

(a) 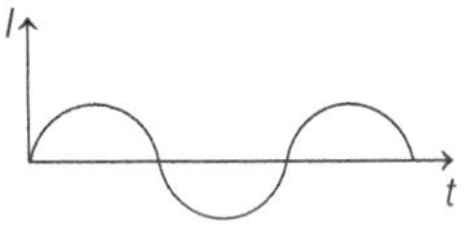

(b) 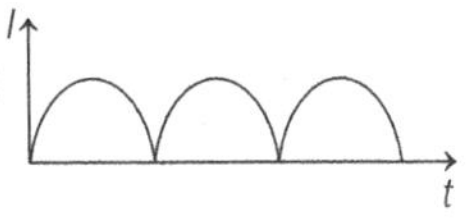

(c) 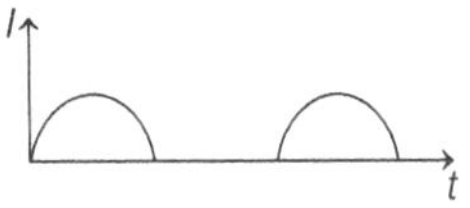

(d) 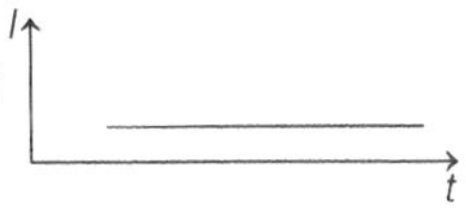

71 The output wave form of full wave rectifier is

(a) 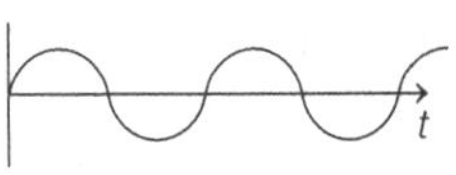

(b) 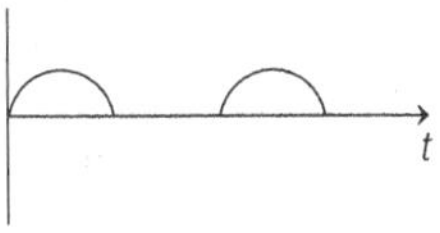

(c) 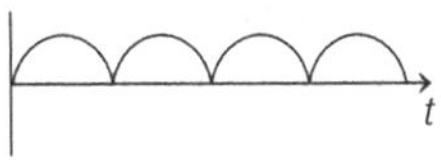

(d) 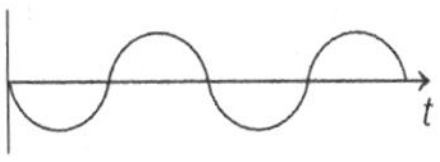

72 In the half wave rectifier circuit operating from 50 Hz mains frequency, the fundamental frequency in the ripple would be

(a) 25 Hz (b) 50 Hz
(c) 70.7 Hz (d) 100 Hz

73 A full-wave rectifier circuit with an AC input is shown

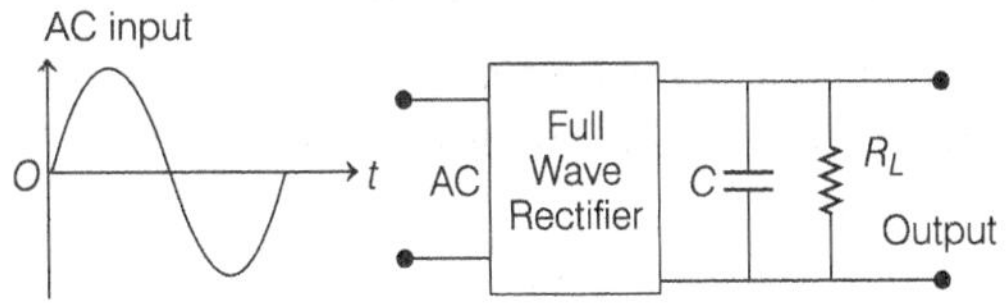

The output voltage across R_L is represented as

(a) 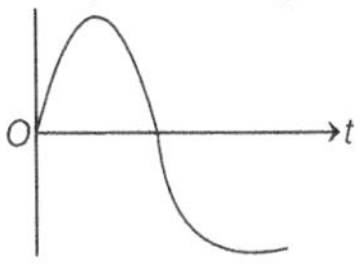

(b) 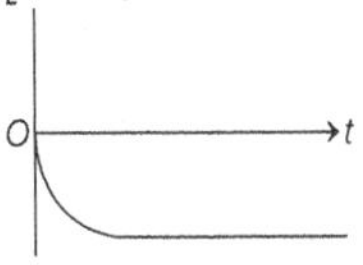

(c) 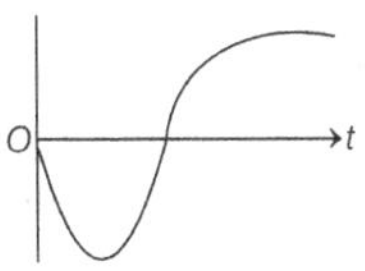

(d) 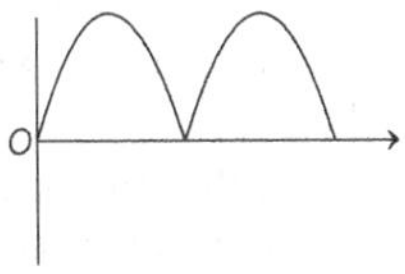

74 A full wave rectifier circuit along with the input and output voltages is shown in the figure

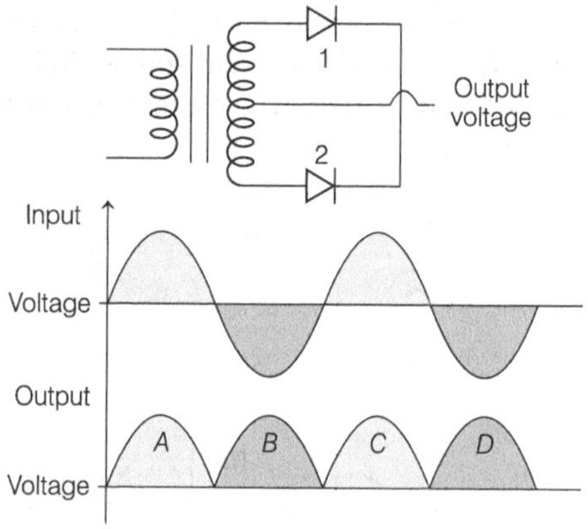

The contribution to output voltage from diode-2 is

(a) A, C (b) B, D (c) B, C (d) A, D

75 A silicon diode has a threshold voltage of 0.7 V. If an input voltage given by 2 sin(πt) is supplied to a half wave rectifier circuit using this diode, the rectified output has a peak value of

(a) 2 V (b) 1.4 V (c) 1.3 V (d) 0.7 V

76 In the diagram, the input is across the terminals *A* and *C* and the output is across the terminals *B* and *D*, then the output is

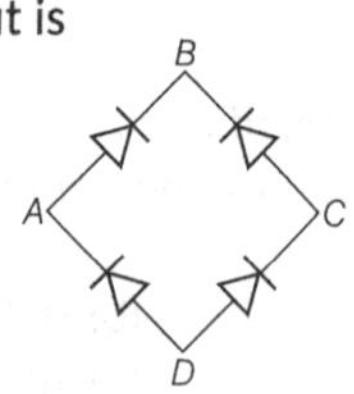

(a) zero (b) same as input

(c) full wave rectifier (d) half wave rectifier

77 In the circuit given below, $V(t)$ is the sinusoidal voltage source, voltage drop $V_{AB}(t)$ across the resistance is

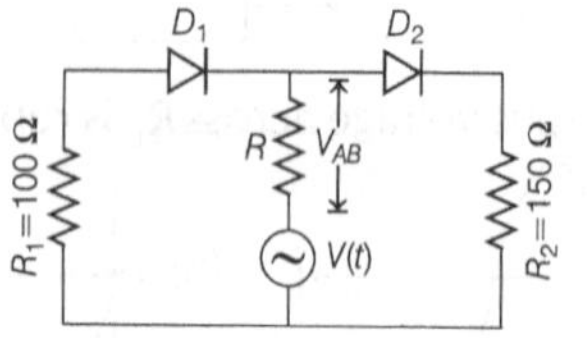

(a) is half wave rectified

(b) is full wave rectified

(c) has the same peak value in the positive and negative half cycles

(d) has different peak values during positive and negative half cycle

78 The value of DC voltage in half wave rectifier in converting AC voltage $V = 100 \sin(314\,t)$ into DC is

(a) 100 V (b) 50 V (c) 32 V (d) 0 V

79 For given electric voltage signal DC value is

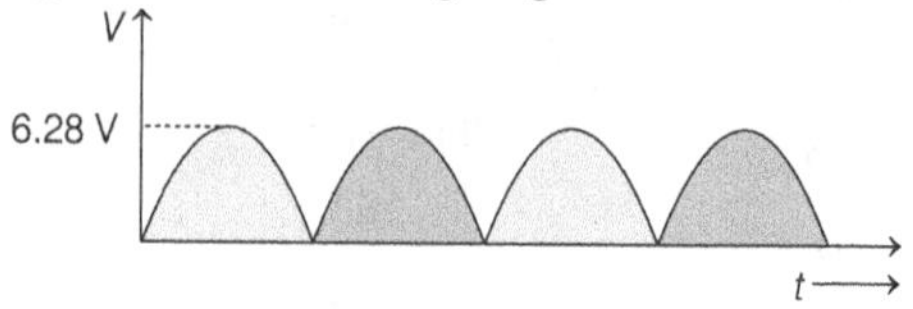

(a) 6.28 V (b) 3.14 V (c) 4 V (d) 0 V

80 A sinusoidal voltage of peak value 200 volt is connected to a diode and resistor in the circuit figure, so that halfwave rectification occurs. If the forward resistance of the diode is negligible compared to *R*, the RMS voltage (in volt) across *R* is approximately

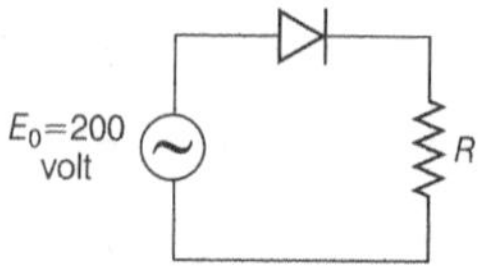

(a) 200 (b) 100 (c) $\frac{200}{\sqrt{2}}$ (d) 280

81 In the given diagram, input voltage is V_i and output across R_L is V_0. Frequency of output voltage (V_0) will be

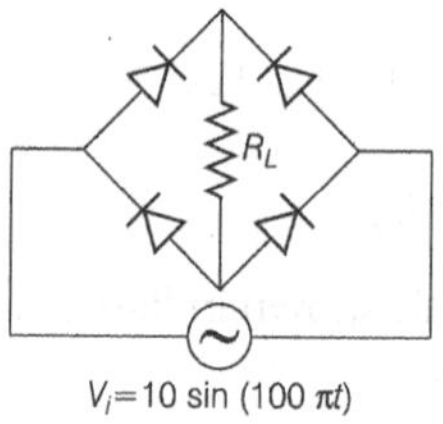

(a) 50 Hz (b) 100 Hz (c) 150 Hz (d) 25 Hz

82 What will be the input of *A* and *B* for the Boolean expression $\overline{(A+B)} \cdot \overline{(A \cdot B)} = 1$

(a) 0, 0 (b) 0, 1 (c) 1, 0 (d) 1, 1

83 Which of the following logic gate is a universal gate?

(a) OR (b) NOT (c) AND (d) NOR

84 Digital circuit can be made by repetitive use of this gate

(a) AND (b) OR

(c) NOT (d) NAND

85 When the two inputs of a NAND gate are shorted, the resulting gate is

(a) NOR (b) OR

(c) NOT (d) AND

86 Given below are symbols for some logic gates. The XOR gate and NOR gate respectively are

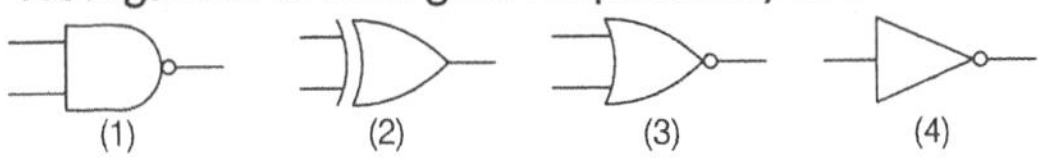

(a) 1 and 2 (b) 2 and 3 (c) 3 and 4 (d) 1 and 4

87 The following logic circuit represents

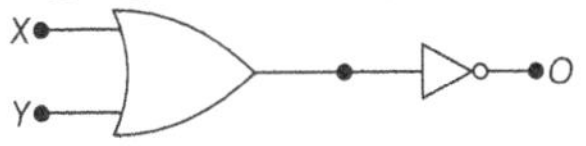

(a) NAND gate with output $O = \overline{X} + \overline{Y}$
(b) NOR gate with output $O = \overline{X + Y}$
(c) NAND gate with output $O = \overline{X \cdot Y}$
(d) NOR gate with output $O = \overline{X} \cdot \overline{Y}$

88 The output Y of the logic circuit shown in figure is best represented as

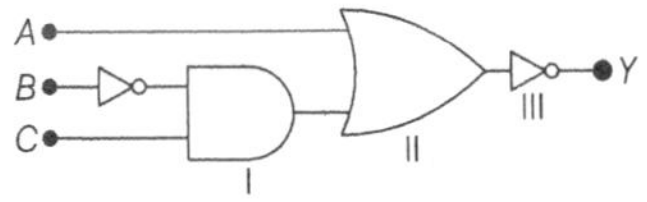

(a) $\overline{A} + \overline{B \cdot C}$ (b) $A + \overline{B} \cdot C$
(c) $\overline{A + B \cdot C}$ (d) $\overline{A + \overline{B} \cdot C}$

89 Output W is given by

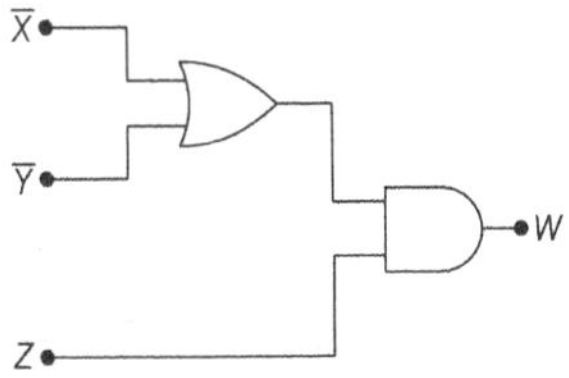

(a) $(\overline{X \cdot Y}) \cdot Z$ (b) $(X + Y)\,Z$
(c) $(X + Y)\,\overline{Z}$ (d) $\overline{X} \cdot \overline{Y} + \overline{Z}$

90 The diagram of a logic circuit is given below.

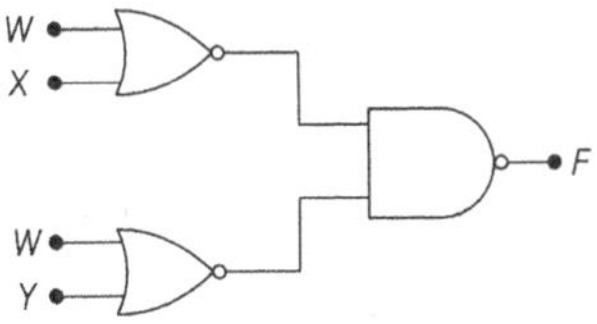

The output F of the circuit is given by
(a) $W \cdot (X + Y)$ (b) $W \cdot (X \cdot Y)$
(c) $W + (X \cdot Y)$ (d) $W + (X + Y)$

91 To get an output 1 from the circuit shown in the figure, the input must be

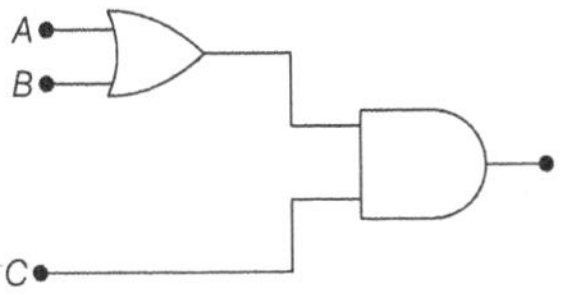

(a) $A = 0, B = 1, C = 0$ (b) $A = 1, B = 0, C = 0$
(c) $A = 1, B = 0, C = 1$ (d) $A = 1, B = 1, C = 0$

92 In the circuit given A, B and C are inputs and Y is the output

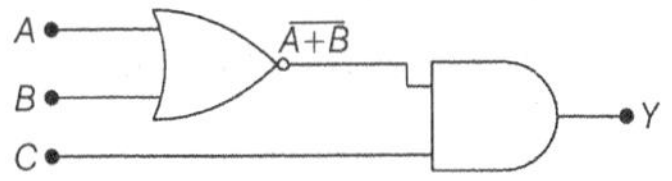

The output of Y is
(a) high for all the high inputs
(b) high for all the low inputs
(c) high only when $A = 0, B = 0, C = 1$
(d) low for all low inputs

93 Figure gives a system of logic gates. From the study of truth table, it can be found that to produce a high output (1) at R we must have

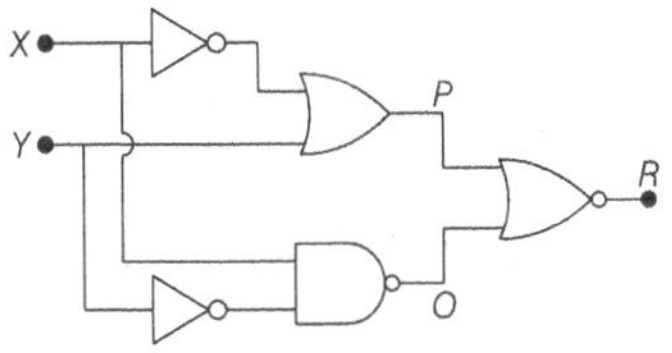

(a) $X = 0, Y = 1$ (b) $X = 1, Y = 1$
(c) $X = 1, Y = 0$ (d) $X = 0, Y = 0$

94 Select the outputs Y of the combination of gates shown below for inputs $A = 1, B = 0$; $A = 1, B = 1$ and $A = 0, B = 0$ respectively

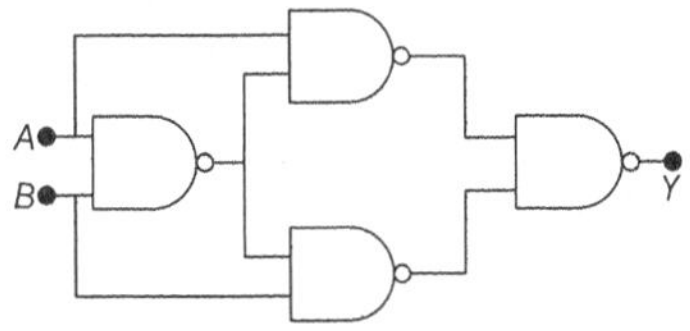

(a) (0 1 1) (b) (0 0 1) (c) (1 0 0) (d) (1 1 1)

95 The circuit diagram shows a logic combination with the states of output X, Y and Z given for inputs P, Q, R and S all at state 1. When inputs P and R change to state 0 with inputs Q and S still at 1, the states of outputs X, Y and Z change to

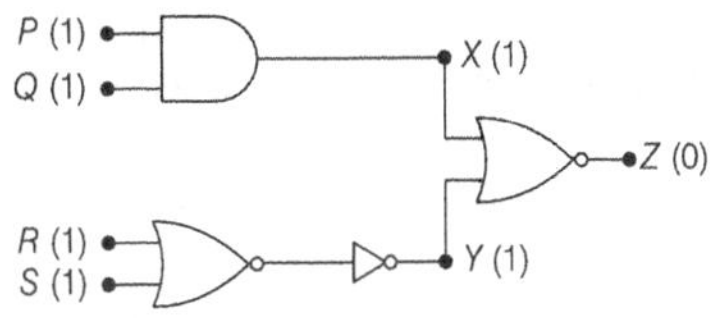

(a) 1, 0, 0 (b) 1, 1, 1 (c) 0, 1, 0 (d) 0, 0, 1

96 In circuit in following fig. the value of Y is

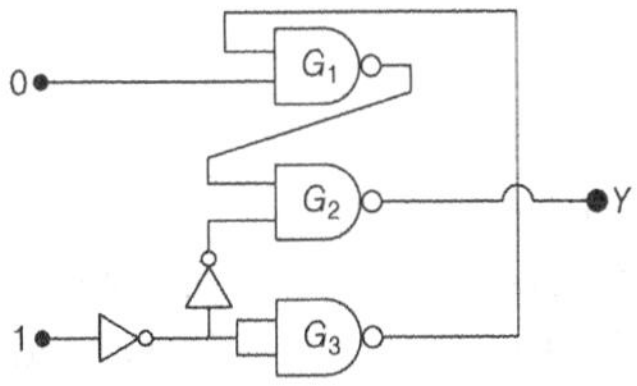

(a) 0
(b) 1
(c) fluctuates between 0 and 1
(d) indeterminate as the circuit can't be realised

97 The output of an OR gate is connected to both the inputs of a NAND gate. The combination will serve as a
(a) OR gate (b) NOT gate
(c) NOR gate (d) AND gate

98 The combination of gates shown below yields

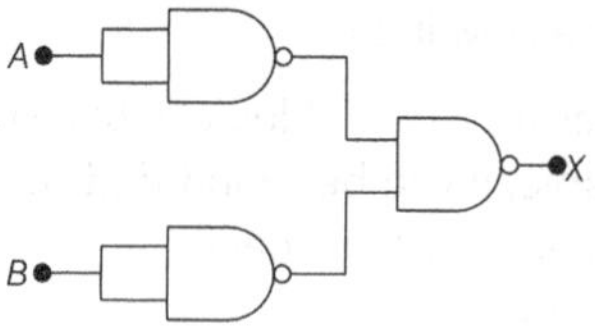

(a) OR gate (b) NOT gate
(c) XOR gate (d) NAND gate

99 The following configuration of gate is equivalent to figure.

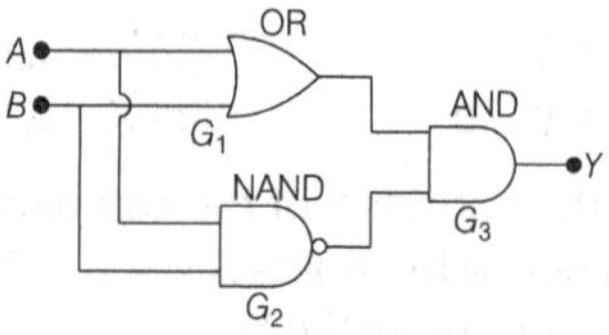

(a) NAND (b) XOR
(c) OR (d) None of these

100 Identify the operation performed by the circuit given in the figure.

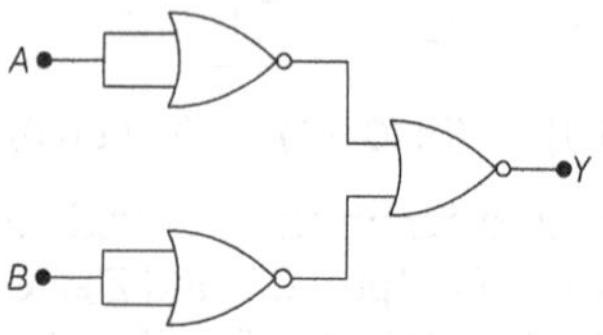

(a) NOT (b) AND (c) OR (d) NAND

101 The following figure shows a logic gate circuit with two inputs A and B and the output C. The voltage waveforms of A, B and C are as shown below

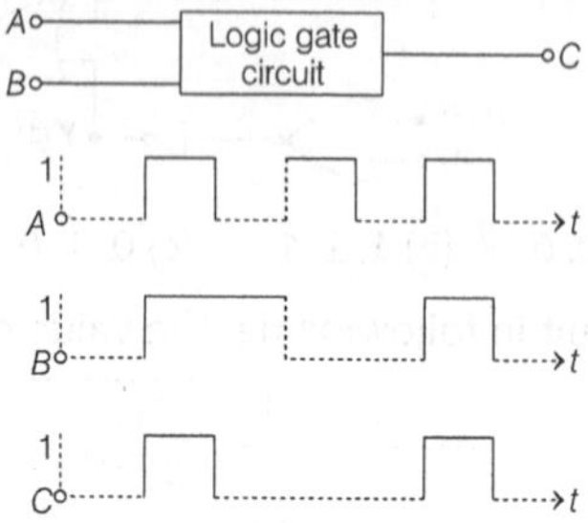

The logic circuit gate is
(a) AND gate (b) NAND gate
(c) NOR gate (d) OR gate

102 The real time variation of input signals A and B are as shown below. If the inputs are fed into NAND gate, then select the output signal from the following

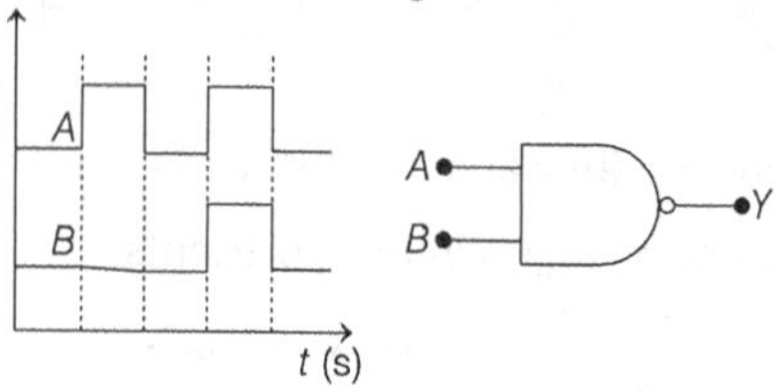

(a) 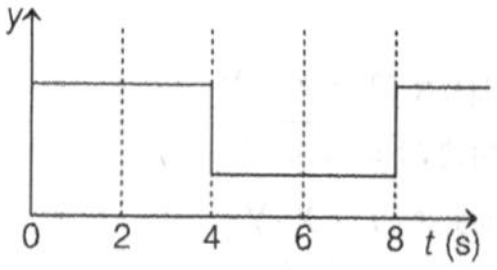

(b) 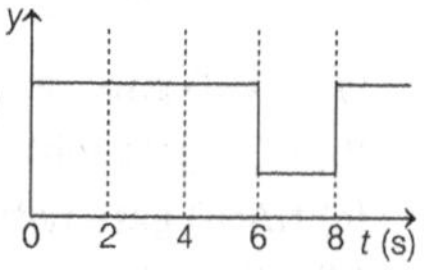

(c) 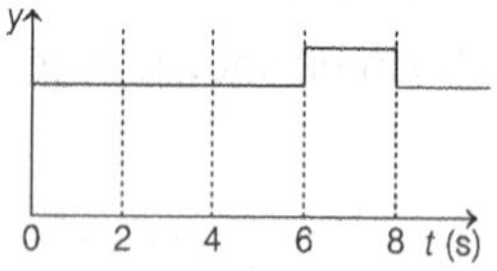

(d) 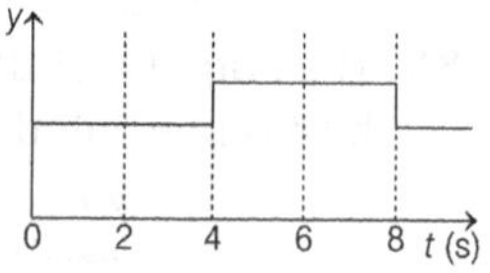

103 For this truth table

A	B	Y
0	0	1
0	1	0
1	0	0
1	1	1

Which logic expression is correct?
(a) $Y = \overline{A}B + \overline{AB}$ (b) $Y = \overline{A}\,\overline{B} + A\overline{B}$
(c) $Y = \overline{A}\,\overline{B} + \overline{AB}$ (d) $Y = \overline{A}\,\overline{B} + AB$

104 In the adjacent circuit, A and B represent two inputs and C represents the output. The circuit represents

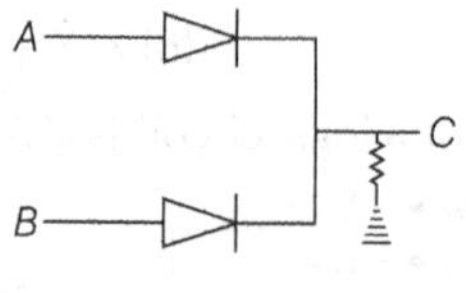

(a) NOR gate (b) AND gate
(c) NAND gate (d) OR gate

Previous Year's Questions

JEE Main

1 Which of the following circuits is reverse-biased?
[2024, 27 Jan Shift-I]

(a) 

(b) 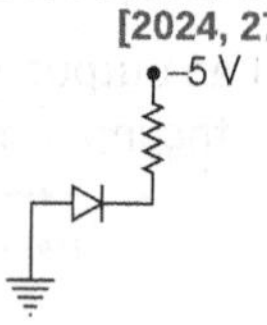

(c) 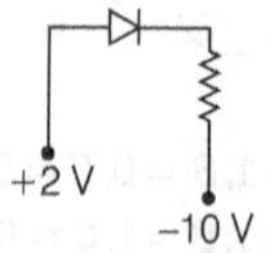

(d) 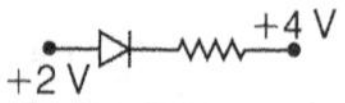

2 The truth table of the given circuit diagram is

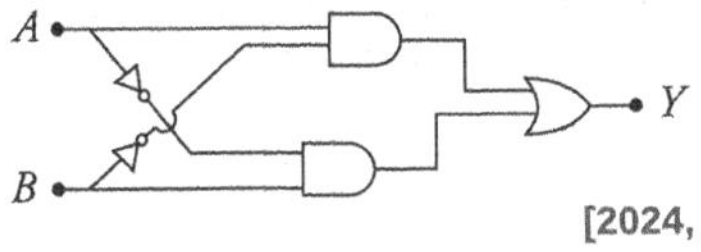

[2024, 27 Jan Shift-II]

(a)

A	B	Y
0	0	0
0	1	0
1	0	0
1	1	1

(b)

A	B	Y
0	0	1
0	1	1
1	0	1
1	1	0

(c)

A	B	Y
0	0	1
0	1	0
1	0	0
1	1	1

(d)

A	B	Y
0	0	0
0	1	1
1	0	1
1	1	0

3 In the given circuit, the breakdown voltage of the Zener diode is 3.0 V. What is the value of I_z?

[2024, 29 Jan Shift-I]

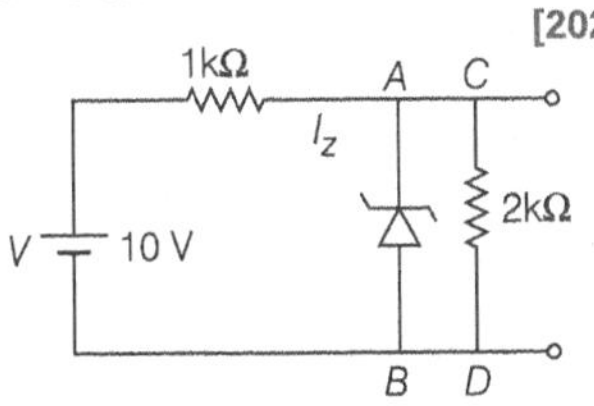

(a) 5.5 mA (b) 3.3 mA (c) 10 mA (d) 7 mA

4 The truth table for this given circuit is

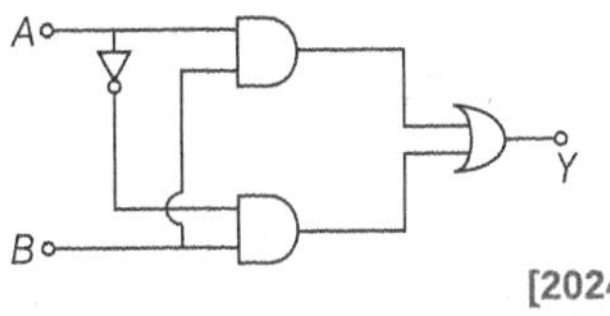

[2024, 29 Jan Shift-II]

(a)

A	B	Y
0	0	0
0	1	1
1	0	0
1	1	1

(b)

A	B	Y
0	0	1
0	1	0
1	0	1
1	1	0

(c)

A	B	Y
0	0	1
0	1	1
1	0	1
1	1	0

(d)

A	B	Y
0	0	0
0	1	0
1	0	0
1	1	1

5 The resistivity (ρ) of semiconductor varies with temperature. Which of the following curve represents the correct behaviour? [2023, 6 April Shift-I]

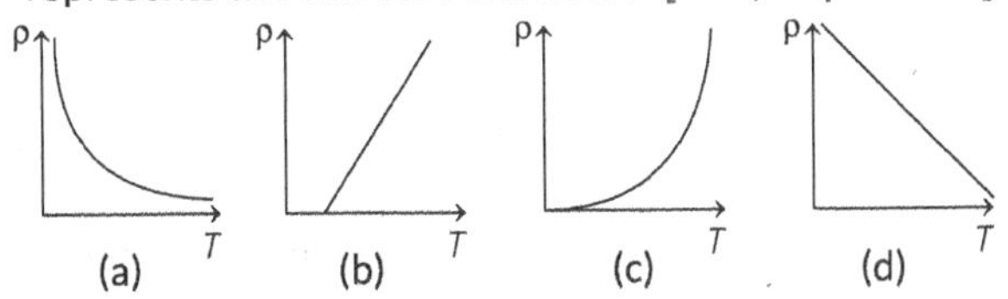

(a) (b) (c) (d)

6 A zener diode of power rating 1.6 W is to be used as voltage regulator. If the zener diode has a breakdown of 8 V and it has to regulate voltage fluctuating between 3 V and 10 V. The value of resistance R_8 for safe operation of diode will be

[2023, 10 April Shift-I]

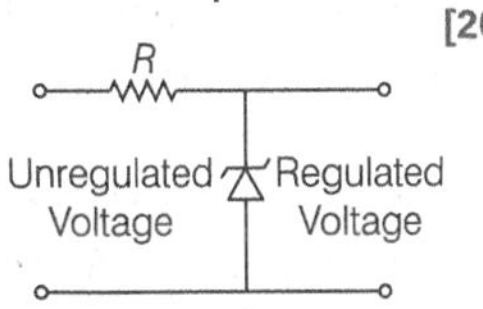

(a) 13.3 Ω (b) 10 Ω (c) 13 Ω (d) 12 Ω

7 If each diode has a forward bias resistance of 25 Ω in the below circuit. [2023, 10 April Shift-II]

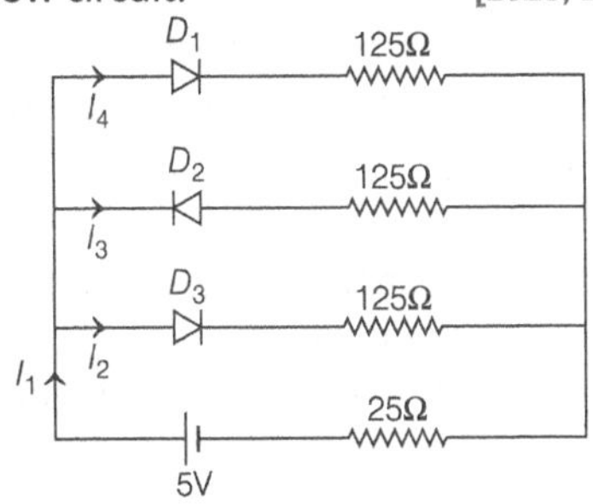

Which of the following options is correct

(a) $\frac{I_1}{I_2} = 1$ (b) $\frac{I_2}{I_3} = 1$

(c) $\frac{I_3}{I_4} = 1$ (d) $\frac{I_1}{I_2} = 2$

8 Given below are two statements

One is labelled as Assertion A and the other is labelled as Reason R.

Assertion (A) Photodiodes are preferably operated in reverse bias condition for light intensity measurement.

Reason (R) The current in the forward bias is more than the current in the reverse bias for a *p-n* junction diode.

In the light of the above statements, choose the correct answer from the options given below.

[2023, 24 Jan Shift-I]

(a) Both A and R are true and R is the correct explanation of A.
(b) Both A and R are true but R is not the correct explanation of A.
(c) A is true but R is false.
(d) A is false but R is true.

9 **Statement I** When a Si sample is doped with Boron, it becomes *p*-type and when doped by Arsenic it becomes *n*-type semiconductor such that *p*-type has excess holes and *n*-type has excess electrons.

Statement II When such *p*-type and *n*-type semiconductors are fused to make a junction, a current will automatically flow which can be detected with an externally connected ammeter.

In the light of above statements, choose the most appropriate answer from the options given below.

[2023, 25 Jan Shift-II]

(a) Statement I is correct but Statement II is incorrect

(b) Statement I is incorrect but Statement II is correct

(c) Both Statement I and Statement II are incorrect

(d) Both Statement I and Statement II are correct

10 Which one of the following statement is not correct in the case of light emitting diodes?

A. It is a heavily doped *p-n* junction.

B. It emits light only when it is forward biased.

C. It emits light only when it is reverse biased.

D. The energy of the light emitted is equal to or slightly less than the energy gap of the semiconductor used.

Choose the correct answer from the options given below **[2023, 29 Jan Shift-I]**

(a) B (b) C

(c) A (d) C and D

11 Choose the correct statement about zener diode. **[2023, 1 Feb Shift-II]**

(a) It works as a voltage regulator in reverse bias and behaves like simple *p-n* junction diode in forward bias.

(b) It works as a voltage regulator only in forward bias.

(c) It works as a voltage regulator in forward bias and behaves like simple *p-n* junction diode in reverse bias.

(d) It works as a voltage regulator in both forward and reverse bias.

12 Match List I with List II

	List I		List II
A.	Intrinsic semiconductor	I.	Fermi-level near the valence band
B.	*n*-type semiconductor	II.	Fermi-level in the middle of valence and conduction band
C.	*p*-type semiconductor	III.	Fermi-level near the conduction band
D.	Metals	IV.	Fermi-level inside the conduction band

Choose the correct answer from the options given below : **[2023, 1 Feb, Shift-I]**

(a) A-I, B-II, C-III, D-IV

(b) A-III, B-I, C-II, D-IV

(c) A-II, B-III, C-I, D-IV

(d) A-II, B-I, C-III, D-I

13 For the following circuit and given inputs *A* and *b*, choose the correct option for **[2023, 13 April Shift-I]**

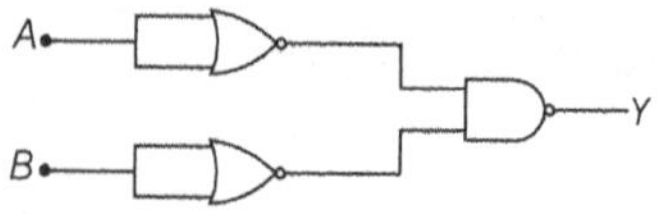

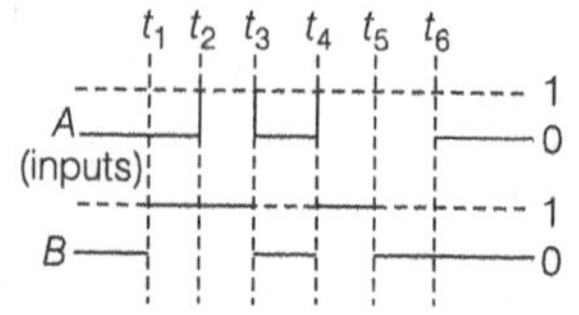

(a)

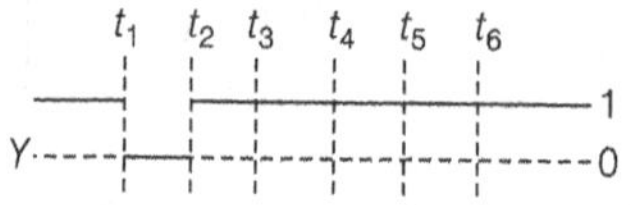

(b)

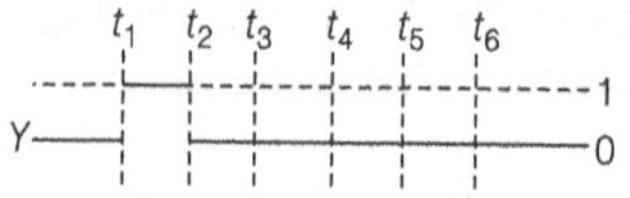

(c)

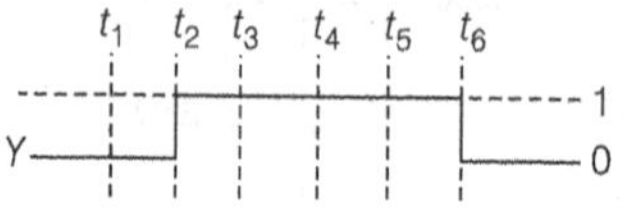

(d)

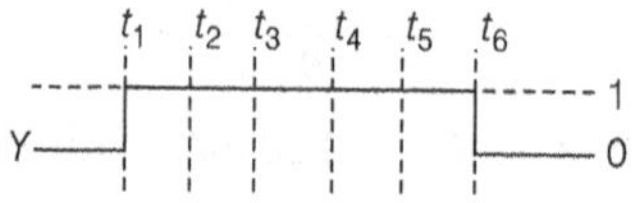

14 The output from a NAND gate havign inputs *A* and *B* given below will be, **[2023, 13 April Shift-II]**

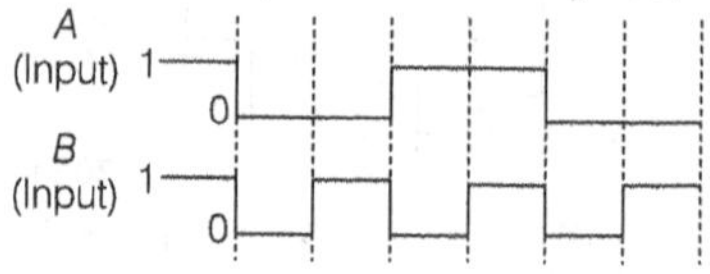

(a)

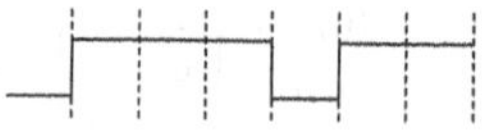

(b)

(c)

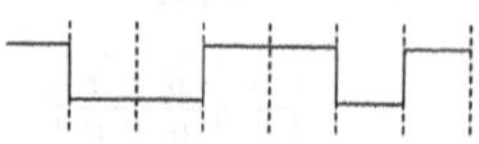

(d)

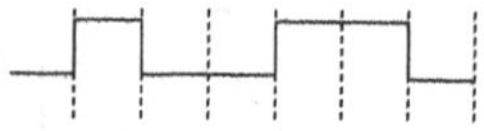

15 The logic gate equivalent of the given circuit diagram is **[2023, 24 Jan Shift-II]**

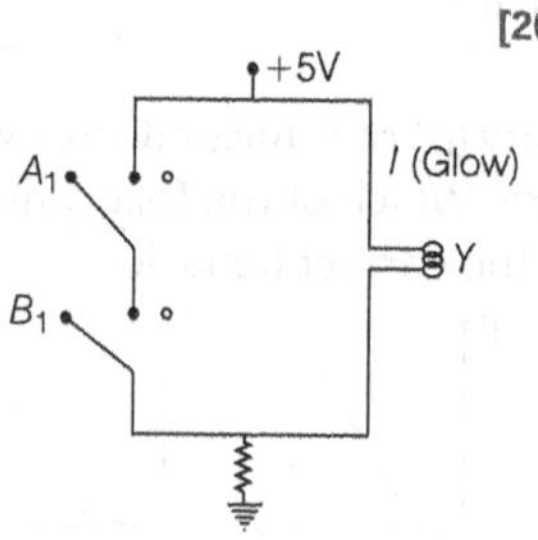

(a) NAND (b) AND (c) NOR (d) OR

16 For the given logic gates combination, the correct truth table will be **[2023, 29 Jan Shift-II]**

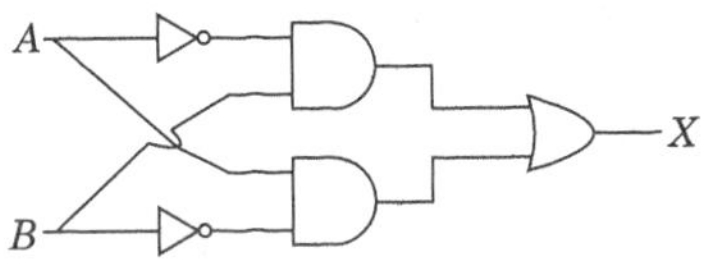

(a)

A	B	X
0	0	1
0	1	0
1	0	1
1	1	0

(b)

A	B	X
0	0	1
0	1	0
1	0	0
1	1	0

(c)

A	B	X
0	0	0
0	1	1
1	0	1
1	1	1

(d)

A	B	X
0	0	0
0	1	1
1	0	1
1	1	0

17 The output Y for the inputs A and B of circuit is given by **[2023, 30 Jan Shift-II]**

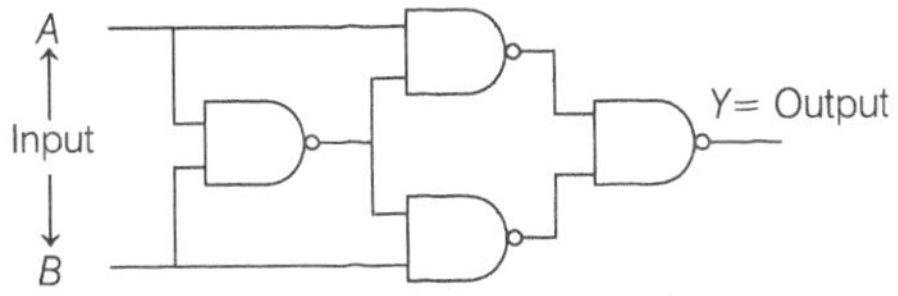

Truth table of the shown circuit is

(a)

A	B	Y
0	0	0
0	1	1
1	0	1
1	1	0

(b)

A	B	Y
0	0	1
0	1	1
1	0	1
1	1	0

(c)

A	B	Y
0	0	0
0	1	1
1	0	1
1	1	1

(d)

A	B	Y
0	0	1
0	1	0
1	0	0
1	1	1

18 The photodiode is used to detect the optical signals. These diodes are preferably operated in reverse biased mode because **[2022, 25 June, Shift-I]**

(a) fractional change in majority carries produce higher forward bias current

(b) fractional change in majority carriers produce higher reverse bias current

(c) fractional change in minority carriers produce higher forward bias current

(d) fractional change in minority carriers produce higher reverse bias current.

19 For using a multimeter to identify diode from electrical components, choose the correct statement out of the following about the diode **[2022, 28 June Shift-I]**

(a) It is two terminal device which conducts current in both directions.

(b) It is two terminal device which conducts current in one direction only.

(c) It does not conduct current gives initial deflection which decays to zero.

(d) It is three terminal device which conducts current in one direction only between central terminal and either of the remaining two terminals.

20 Identify the solar cell characteristics from the following options **[2022, 28 July Shift-I]**

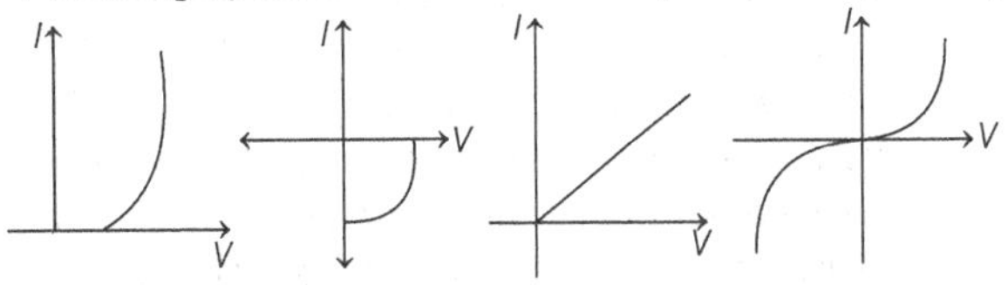

(a) (b) (c) (d)

21 A 8 V Zener diode along with a series resistance R is connected across a 20 V supply (as shown in the figure). If the maximum Zener current is 25 mA, then the minimum value of R will be .... Ω. **[2022, 29 July Shift-II]**

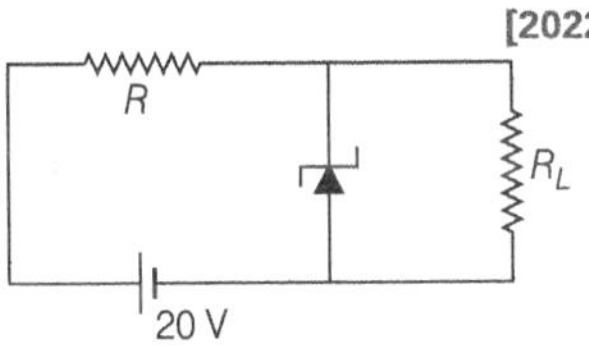

22 If the potential barrier across a p-n junction is 0.6 V. Then, the electric field intensity in the depletion region having the width of 6×10^{-6} m, will be .... $\times 10^{5}$ N/C. **[2022, 29 June Shift-I]**

23 In the circuit shown below, maximum Zener diode current will be ......mA. **[2022, 26 July Shift-I]**

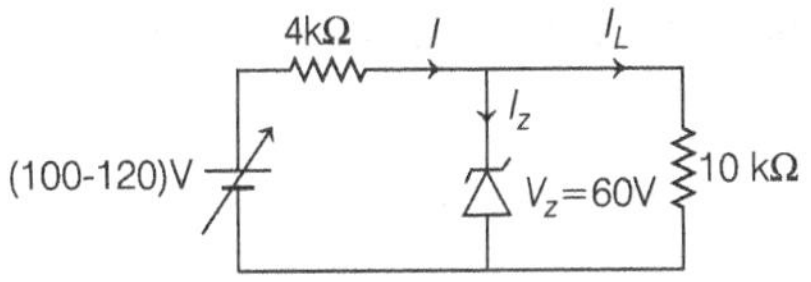

24 As per the given circuit, the value of current through the battery will be .... A. **[2022, 26 June Shift-I]**

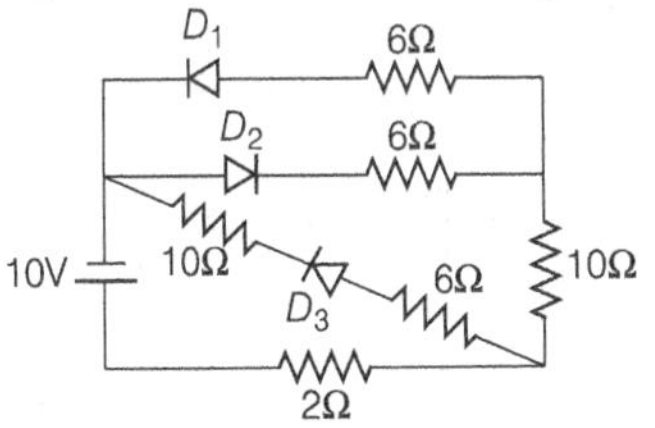

25 The cut-off voltage of the diodes (shown in figure) in forward bias is 0.6 V. The current through the resistor of 40 Ω is .... mA. **[2022, 27 June Shift-II]**

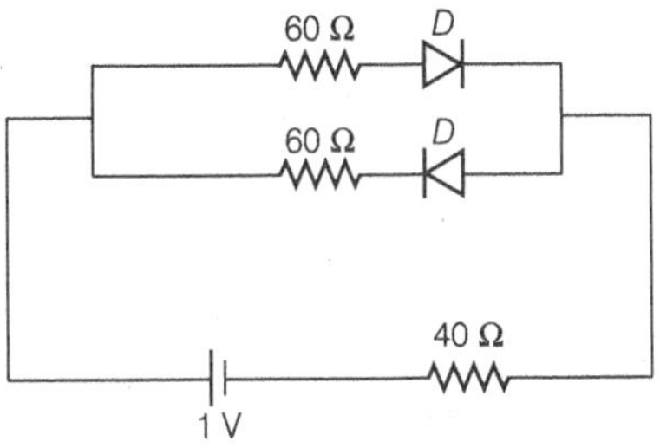

26 The circuit diagram used to study the characteristics curve of a zener diode is connected to variable power supply (0 – 15 V) as shown in figure. A zener diode with maximum potential $V_z = 10$ V and maximum power dissipation of 0.4 W is connected across a potential divider arrangement. The value of resistance R_p connected in series with the zener diode to protect it from the damage is .... Ω.
[2022, 30 June Shift-I]

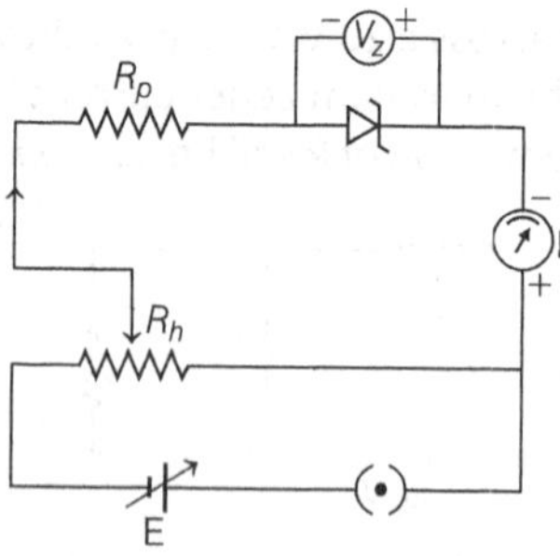

27 The energy band gap of semiconducting material to productive violet (wavelength = 4000 Å) LED is .... eV. (Round off to the nearest integer)
[2022, 25 July, Shift-I]

28 Identify the correct logic gate for the following output (Y) of two inputs A and B. **[2022, 27 June Shift-I]**

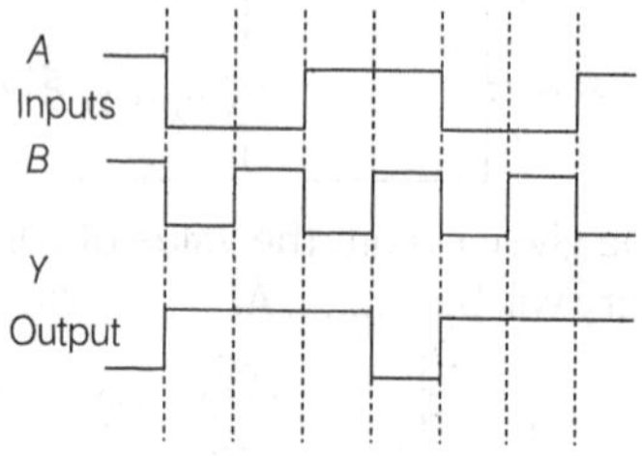

(a)
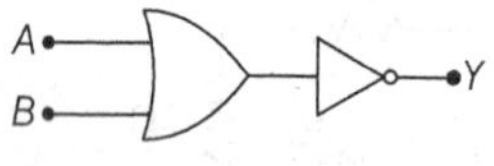
(b)
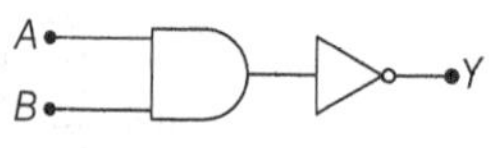
(c)
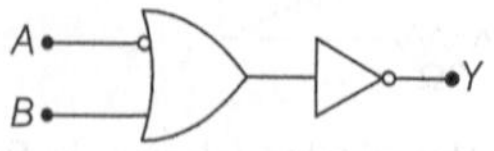
(d)
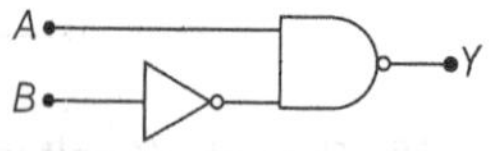

29 A logic gate circuit has two inputs A and B and output Y. The voltage waveforms of A, B and Y are shown below. **[2022, 27 July Shift-I]**

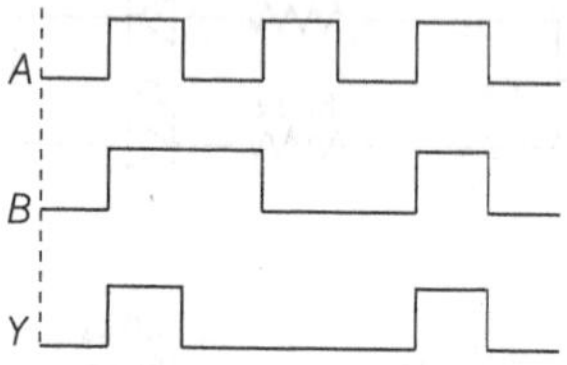

The logic gate circuit is
(a) AND gate (b) OR gate (c) NOR gate (d) NAND gate

30 In the following logic circuit, the sequence of the inputs A, B are (0, 0), (0,1), (1, 0) and (1, 1). The output Y for this sequence will be **[2021, 31 Aug Shift-I]**

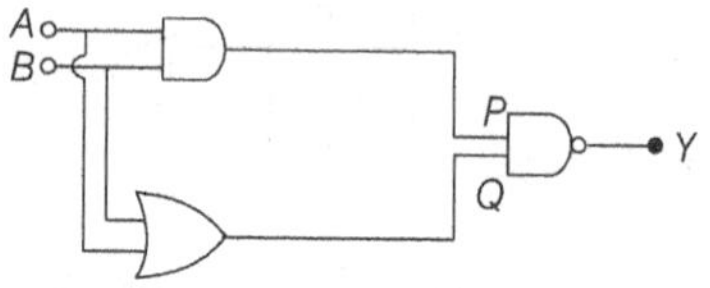

(a) 1, 0, 1, 0 (b) 0, 1, 0, 1
(c) 1, 1, 1, 0 (d) 0, 0, 1, 1

31 If V_A and V_B are the input voltages (either 5V or 0V) and V_0 is the output voltage then the two gates represented in the following circuit (A) and (B) are
[2021, 31 Aug Shift-II]

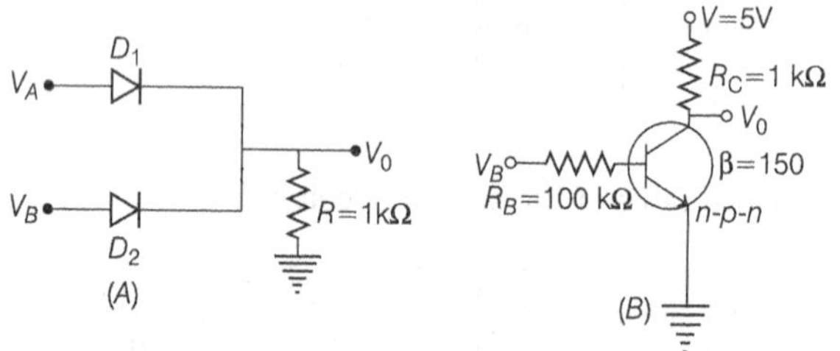

(a) AND and OR gate
(b) OR and NOT gate
(c) NAND and NOR gate
(d) AND and NOT gate

32 Four NOR gates are connected as shown in figure. The truth table for the given figure is
[2021, 26 Aug Shift-II]

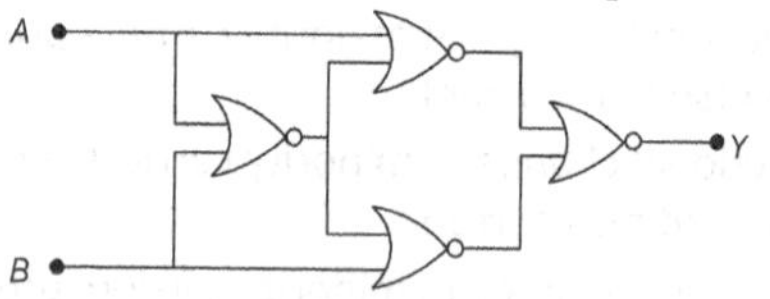

(a)

A	B	Y
0	0	1
0	1	0
1	0	1
1	1	0

(b)

A	B	Y
0	0	0
0	1	1
1	0	1
1	1	0

(c)

A	B	Y
0	0	0
0	1	1
1	0	0
1	1	1

(d)

A	B	Y
0	0	1
0	1	0
1	0	0
1	1	1

33 Identify the logic operation carried out by the given circuit.
[2021, 26 Aug Shift-I]

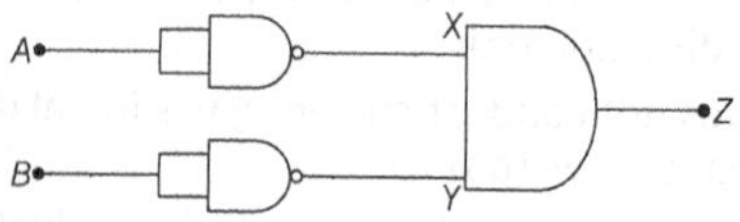

(a) OR (b) AND
(c) NOR (d) NAND

34 Identify the logic operation carried out. **[2021, 25 July Shift-I]**

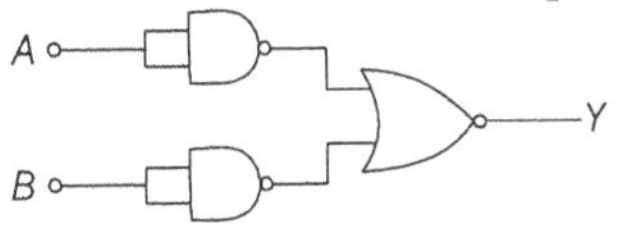

(a) OR (b) AND
(c) NOR (d) NAND

35 The output of the given combination gates represents **[2021, 17 March Shift-I]**

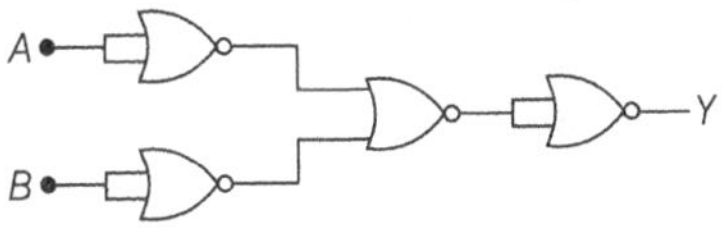

(a) XOR gate (b) NAND gate
(c) AND gate (d) NOR gate

36 The following logic gate is equivalent to **[2021, 16 March Shift-II]**

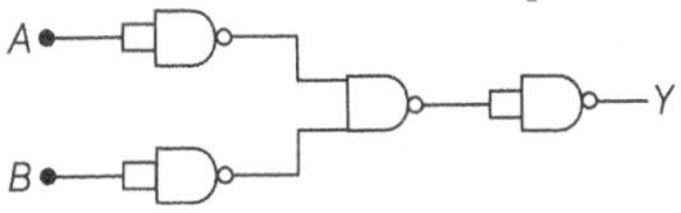

(a) NOR Gate (b) OR Gate
(c) AND Gate (d) NAND Gate

37 Draw the output signal Y in the given combination of gates **[2021, 26 Feb Shift-II]**

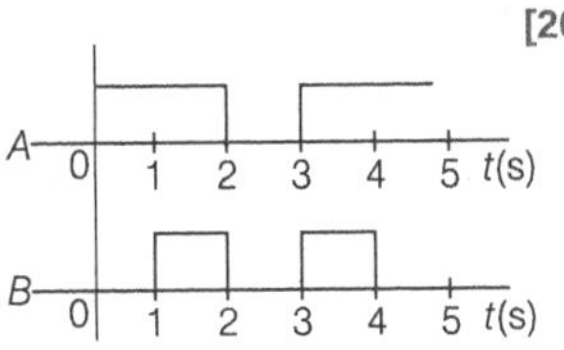

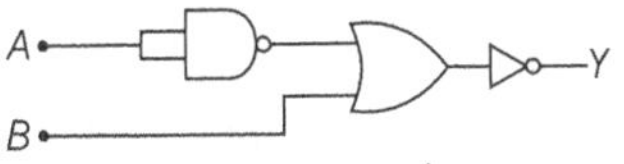

(a) 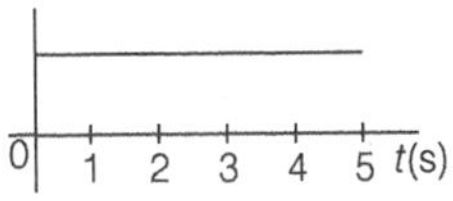

(b) 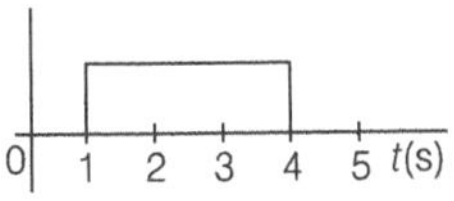

(c) 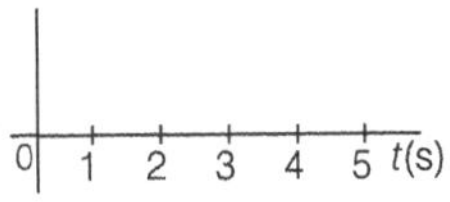

(d) 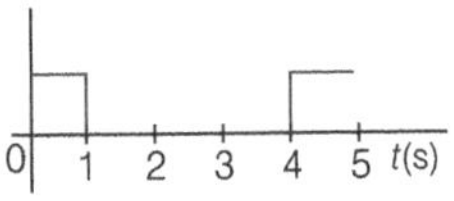

38 The truth table for the followng logic circuit is **[2021, 25 Feb Shift-II]**

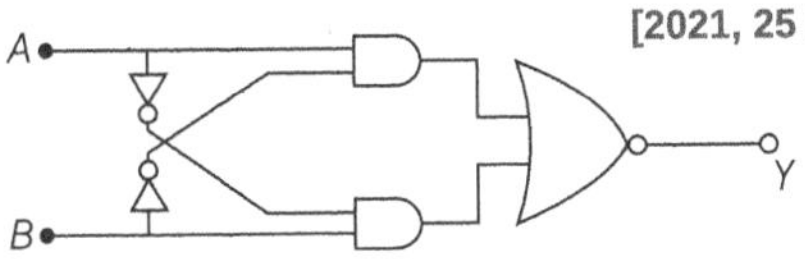

(a)

A	B	Y
0	0	0
0	1	1
1	0	1
1	1	0

(b)

A	B	Y
0	0	1
0	1	0
1	0	0
1	1	0

(c)

A	B	Y
0	0	0
0	1	0
1	0	1
1	1	0

(d)

A	B	Y
0	0	0
0	1	1
1	0	0
1	1	1

39

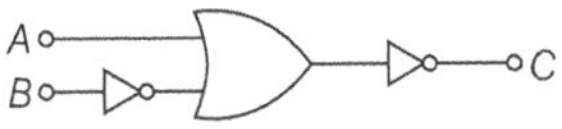

The logic circuit shown above is equivalent to **[2021, 24 Feb Shift-II]**

(a) 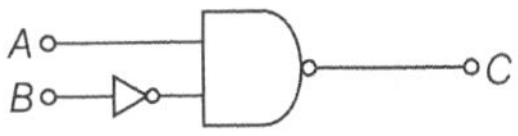 (b) 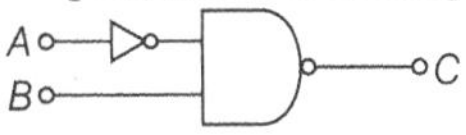

(c) 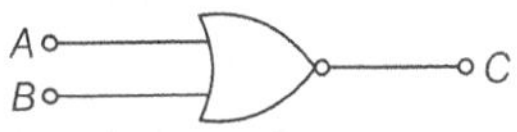 (d) 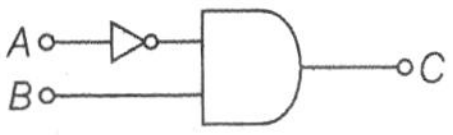

40 In the logic circuit shown in the figure, if input A and B are 0 to 1 respectively, the output at Y would be x. The value of x is .... **[2021, 16 March Shift-I]**

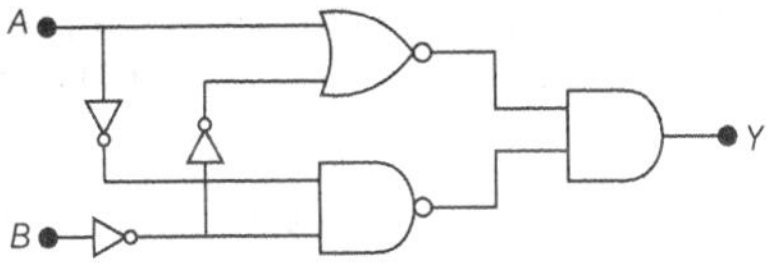

41 Choose the correct waveform that can represent the voltage across R of the following circuit, assuming the diode is ideal one. **[2021, 31 Aug Shift-I]**

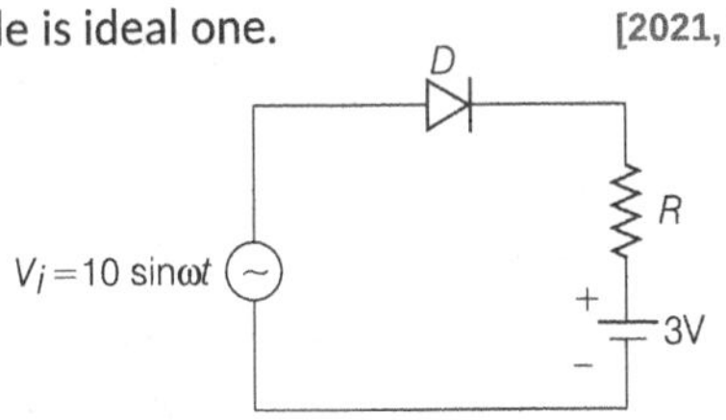

(a) 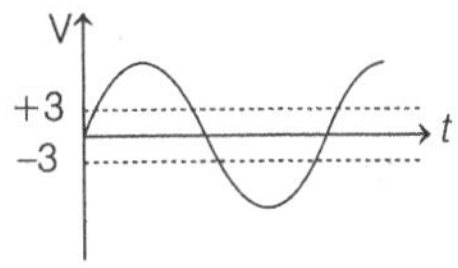 (b) 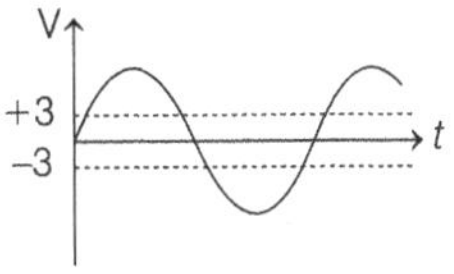

(c) 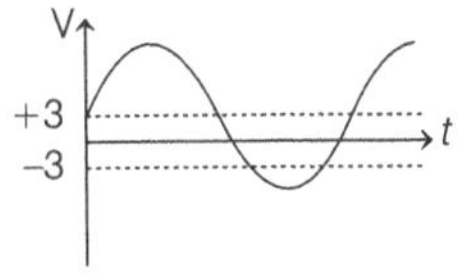 (d) 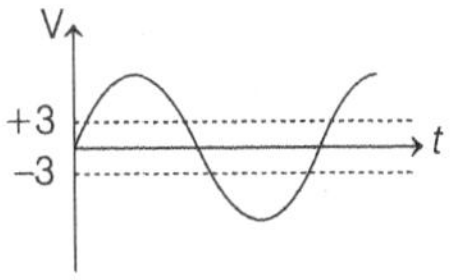

42 Consider a situation in which reverse biased current of a particular p-n junction increases when it is exposed to a light of wavelength ≤ 621 nm. During this process, enhancement in carrier concentration takes place due to generation of hole-electron pairs. The value of band gap is nearly **[2021, 22 July Shift-II]**

(a) 2 eV (b) 4 eV (c) 1 eV (d) 0.5 eV

43 For the circuit shown below, calculate the value of I_z. **[2021, 20 July Shift-I]**

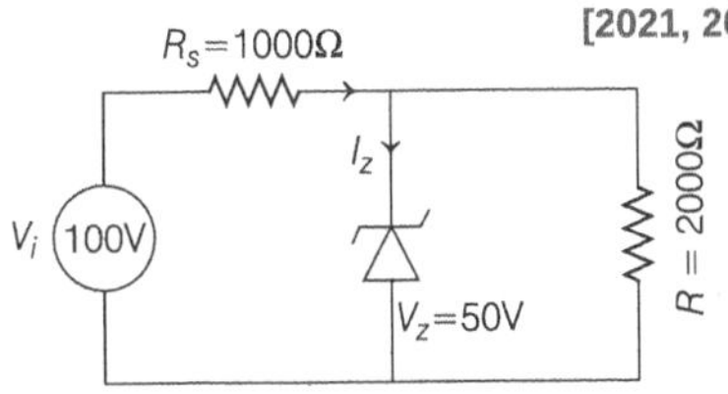

(a) 25 mA (b) 0.15 A (c) 0.1 A (d) 0.05 A

Answer Key

Level 1

12.1 Extrinsic Semiconductor

1. 1.0×10^{15} atoms cm^{-3}
2. 10^{11} per m^3
3. $n_e = 5 \times 10^{22}/m^3$, $n_h = 4.5 \times 10^9/m^3$
4. 5 : 4
5. (a) *n*-type (b) 26.35 S/m
6. *p*-type semiconductor
7. 0.5 eV
8. 10888 Å
9. 4960Å

12.2 *p-n* Junction Diode

1. 1.0×10^6 V/m
2. (a) Forward biased (b) Forward biased (c) Reverse biased (d) Forward biased
3. 200 Ω
4. 2×10^6 Ω
5. 10^{-2} A
6. Zero
7. 40 mA
8. 6V
9. 0.15 A
10. 10 mA
11. 4 A, 2 A
12. *E/R*
13. 2.5 V
14. 5 mA

12.3 Rectifier

1. 100 Hz
2. $\frac{2I_0}{\pi}$
3. $\frac{I_0}{\pi}$
4. $\frac{10}{\pi}$V
5. 81.2 %

12.4 Logic Gates

1. 1, 1, 0
2. $A + \overline{A \cdot B}$
3. (a) 0 (b) 1
4. AND gate
5. NOR gate
6. NAND gate
7. AND gate
8. AND gate

9. 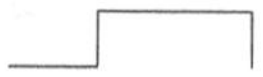

10.

A	B	Y
0	0	0
0	1	1
1	0	1
1	1	1

11.

A	B	Y
0	0	0
0	1	0
1	0	1
1	1	1

12.

A	B	Y
0	0	0
0	1	1
1	0	1
1	1	0

Level 2

Single Choice Correct Questions

1. (d)	2. (a)	3. (b)	4. (a)	5. (a)
6. (d)	7. (b)	8. (d)	9. (c)	10. (b)
11. (c)	12. (c)	13. (a)	14. (d)	15. (a)
16. (d)	17. (c)	18. (b)	19. (a)	20. (c)
21. (b)	22. (b)	23. (a)	24. (a)	25. (b)
26. (b)	27. (d)	28. (c)	29. (c)	30. (c)
31. (d)	32. (d)	33. (c)	34. (a)	35. (d)
36. (d)	37. (d)	38. (c)	39. (b)	40. (c)
41. (b)	42. (b)	43. (c)	44. (a)	45. (a)
46. (a)	47. (a)	48. (b)	49. (b)	50. (d)
51. (c)	52. (c)	53. (c)	54. (b)	55. (b)
56. (b)	57. (b)	58. (c)	59. (a)	60. (d)
61. (d)	62. (c)	63. (c)	64. (d)	65. (d)
66. (c)	67. (d)	68. (b)	69. (d)	70. (c)
71. (c)	72. (b)	73. (b)	74. (b)	75. (c)
76. (c)	77. (d)	78. (c)	79. (c)	80. (c)
81. (b)	82. (a)	83. (d)	84. (d)	85. (c)
86. (b)	87. (b)	88. (d)	89. (a)	90. (c)
91. (c)	92. (c)	93. (c)	94. (c)	95. (c)
96. (a)	97. (c)	98. (a)	99. (b)	100. (b)
101. (a)	102. (b)	103. (d)	104. (d)	

Previous Year's Questions

JEE Main

1. (d)	2. (d)	3. (a)	4. (a)	5. (a)
6. (b)	7. (d)	8. (b)	9. (a)	10. (b)
11. (a)	12. (c)	13. (*)	14. (a)	15. (a)
16. (d)	17. (a)	18. (d)	19. (b)	20. (b)
21. (480)	22. (1)	23. (9)	24. (1)	25. (4)
26. (125)	27. (3)	28. (b)	29. (a)	30. (c)
31. (b)	32. (d)	33. (c)	34. (b)	35. (b)
36. (a)	37. (d)	38. (b)	39. (d)	40. (0)
41. (*)	42. (a)	43. (a)		

SOLUTIONS

Level 1

12.1 Extrinsic Semiconductor

1. Number density of atoms in silicon specimen $= 5 \times 10^{28}$ atoms/m^2 $= 5 \times 10^7$ silicon atoms, so total number of indium atoms doped per atoms, so total number of indium atoms doped per cm^3 of silicon will be $n = 5 \times 10^{22}/$ $5 \times 10^7 = 10^{15}$ atoms cm^{-3}

2. By using mass action law $n_i^2 = n_e n_h$

$$\Rightarrow \quad n_h = \frac{n_i^2}{n_e} = \frac{(10^{16})^2}{10^{21}} = 10^{11} \text{ per m}^3$$

3. The number density of donor atoms,

$$N_d = \frac{5 \times 10^{28} / \text{m}^3}{10^6} = 5 \times 10^{22} \text{ atoms/m}^3$$

[As 1 ppm = 1 part per million $= \frac{1}{10^6}$]

Each donor atom contributes one free electron. So

$$n_e = N_d = 5 \times 10^{22} / \text{m}^3$$

By using mass action law $n_i^2 = n_e\, n_h$

$$\Rightarrow \quad n_h = \frac{n_i^2}{n_e} = \frac{(1.5 \times 10^{16})^2}{5 \times 10^{22}} = 4.5 \times 10^9/\text{m}^3$$

4. $I = n_e A v_d \Rightarrow \frac{I_e}{I_h} = \frac{n_e \times (v_d)_e}{n_h \times (v_d)_h}$

Here, $\frac{n_e}{n_h} = \frac{7}{5}, \frac{I_e}{I_h} = \frac{7}{4}$

$$\frac{7}{4} = \frac{7}{5} \times \frac{(v_d)_e}{(v_d)_h} \quad \Rightarrow \quad \frac{(v_d)_e}{(v_d)_h} = \frac{5}{7} \times \frac{7}{4} = \frac{5}{4}$$

5. (a) n-type semiconductor as $n_e > n_h$

(b) $\sigma = e(n_e\mu_e + n_h\mu_h) = 1.6 \times 10^{-19}\,[4.5 \times 10^{20} \times 0.36 + 1.5 \times 10^{19} \times 0.18] = 26.35$ S/m

6. p-type semiconductor

7. $E_g = h\nu = \frac{hc}{\lambda} = \left(\frac{6.63 \times 10^{-34} \times 3 \times 10^8}{2480 \times 10^{-9} \times 1.6 \times 10^{-19}}\right) = 0.5$ eV

8. $\lambda = \frac{hc}{E} = \frac{6.62 \times 10^{-34} \times 3 \times 10^8}{(1.14 \times 1.6 \times 10^{-19})} = 10{,}888$ Å

9. $E = \frac{hc}{\lambda} \quad \Rightarrow \quad \lambda = \frac{12400}{E(eV)} = \frac{12400}{2.5} = 4960$ Å

This is the maximum wavelength i.e., the signals having wavelength greater than this value are not detected by photodiode.

12.2 p-n Junction Diode

1. $E = \frac{V}{d} = \frac{0.5}{5 \times 10^{-7}} = 10^6$ V/m

2. (a) Forward biased (b) Forward biased (c) Reverse biased (d) Forward biased

3. Forward resistance $= \frac{\Delta V}{\Delta I} = \frac{0.7 - 0.5}{1.0 \times 10^{-3}} = 200\ \Omega$

4. Reverse resistance $= \frac{\Delta V}{\Delta I} = \frac{1}{0.5 \times 10^{-6}} = 2 \times 10^6\ \Omega$

5. $I_f = \frac{4 - 1}{300} = \frac{1}{100} = 10^{-2}$ A

6. The diode is in reverse biasing so current through it is zero.

7. $I_f = \frac{4.5 - 0.5}{100} = \frac{4}{100}$ A = 40 mA

8. In the given condition diode is in reverse biasing so it acts as open circuit. Hence potential difference between A and B is 6V.

9. The upper junction diode is forward biased and middle junction diode is reverse biased. So, effective resistance of circuit = 10 + 10 = 20 Ω.

$$I = \frac{3}{20} = 0.15 \text{ A}$$

10. Total resistance in the circuit = 2 kΩ,

E = 20V

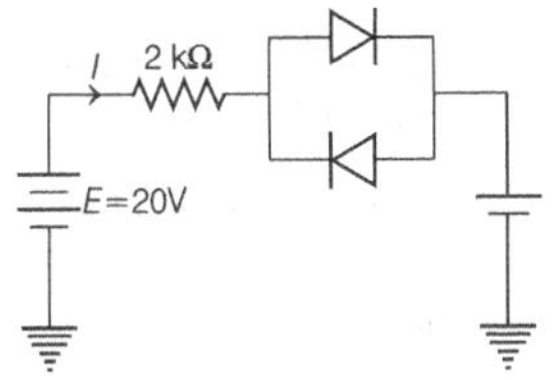

$\therefore$ The current $= \frac{20}{2000} = \frac{1}{100}$ A = 10 mA

11. In circuit A, both (p-n) junction diode act as forward biased. Hence, current flows in circuit A,

Total resistance R is given by

$$\frac{1}{R} = \frac{1}{4} + \frac{1}{4}$$

$$\Rightarrow \quad \frac{1}{R} = \frac{2}{4} \quad \Rightarrow \quad R = 2\Omega$$

According to Ohm's law

$$V = I_A R \quad \Rightarrow \quad 8 = I_A \times 2 \quad \Rightarrow \quad I_A = 4 \text{ A}$$

In circuit B, lower p-n junction diode is reverse biased. Hence, no current will flow but upper diode is forward biased, so current can flow through it

$$V = I_B R$$

$$\Rightarrow \quad 8 = I_B \times 4 \quad \Rightarrow \quad I_B = 2 \text{ A}$$

12. Diodes D_1 and D_3 are forward biased and D_2 is reverse biased so the circuit can be redrawn as follows

$$\Rightarrow \quad i = \frac{E}{R}$$

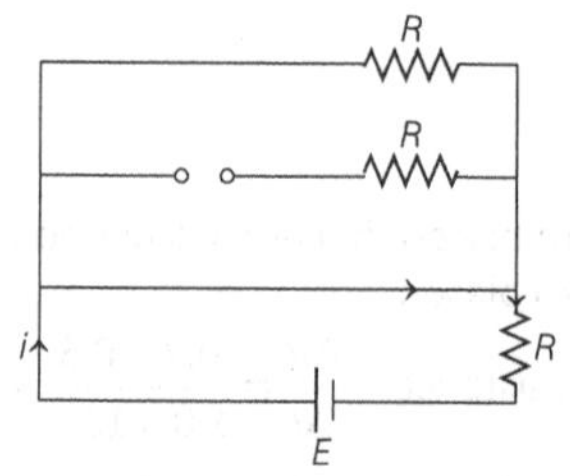

13. Reverse biased potential for the Zener breakdown

$$V_r = Ed = 10^6 \times 2.5 \times 10^{-6} = 2.5 \text{ volt}$$

14. Voltage across Zener diode is constant

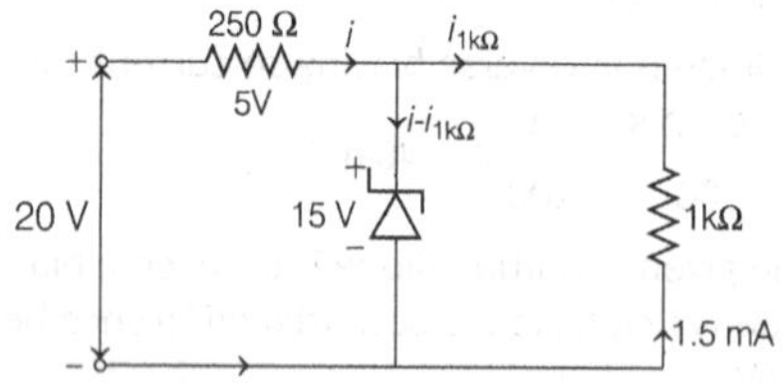

$$i_{2k\Omega} = \frac{15 \text{ volt}}{1\,k\Omega} = 15 \text{ mA}$$

$$i_{250\,\Omega} = \frac{(20-15)\text{V}}{250\,\Omega} = \frac{5\text{V}}{250\,\Omega} = \frac{20}{1000}\text{ A} = 20 \text{ mA}$$

$$\therefore \quad i_{\text{zener diode}} = (20-15) = 5 \text{ mA}$$

12.3 Rectifier

1. For full wave rectifier, ripple frequency $= 2 \times$ input frequency $= 2 \times 50 = 100$ Hz
2. The average value of output in a full wave rectifier $= \frac{2I_0}{\pi}$.
3. The average value of output direct current in a half wave rectifier

$$= \text{(average value of current over a cycle)/2}$$

$$= \frac{\left(\frac{2I_0}{\pi}\right)}{2} = \frac{I_0}{\pi}.$$

4. In half wave rectifier $V_{DC} = \frac{V_0}{\pi} = \frac{10}{\pi}$
5. Efficiency of a rectifier is given by

$$\eta = \frac{\text{DC}}{\text{AC}} = \frac{\text{power output}}{\text{power input}}$$

For full wave rectifier, DC power output

$$= I_{DC}^2 \times R_L = \left(\frac{2I_0}{\pi}\right)^2 \times R_L$$

$$\text{AC input power} = I_{rms}^2 (r_f + R_L) = \left(\frac{I_0}{\sqrt{2}}\right)^2 (r_f + R_L)$$

$$\therefore \text{ Rectifier efficiency } \eta = \frac{\left(\frac{2I_0}{\pi}\right)^2 R_L}{\left(\frac{I_0}{\sqrt{2}}\right)^2 (r_f + R_L)} = \frac{0.812\,R_L}{r_f + R_L}$$

η will be maximum, if r_f is negligible as compared to R_L.
Maximum rectified efficiency = 81.2%.

12.4 Logic Gates

1. (A) Output of NAND gate 0 and output of NOT is 1. The output of OR gate is 1.
   (B) Output of NOT gate is 1 and of other NOT gate is 0. The output of NAND gate is 1.
   (C) Output of NOR gate is 0 and output of AND gate is 0.
2. The input of OR gate is A and $\overline{(A \cdot B)}$. Hence $Y = A + \overline{(A \cdot B)}$.
3. $Y = \overline{(A \cdot B) \cdot C}$

   (a) If $A = 1, B = 1, C = 1$, then $Y = \overline{(1 \cdot 1) \cdot 1} = 0$

   (b) If $A = 0, B = 0, C = 0$, then $Y = \overline{(0 \cdot 0) \cdot 0} = 1$
4. From circuit $Y = \overline{\overline{A \cdot B}} = A \cdot B$

   This is an output of an AND gate.
5. The output of NOR gate gives $y' = \overline{A+B}$

   The output of NAND gate gives

$$y'' = \overline{(\overline{A+B}) \cdot (\overline{A+B})}$$

$$= \overline{\overline{(A+B)}} + \overline{\overline{(A+B)}}$$

$$= (A+B) + (A+B) = A+B$$

   The output of NOT gate, $y = \overline{A+B}$

   It is a Boolean expression for NOR gate
6. NAND gate

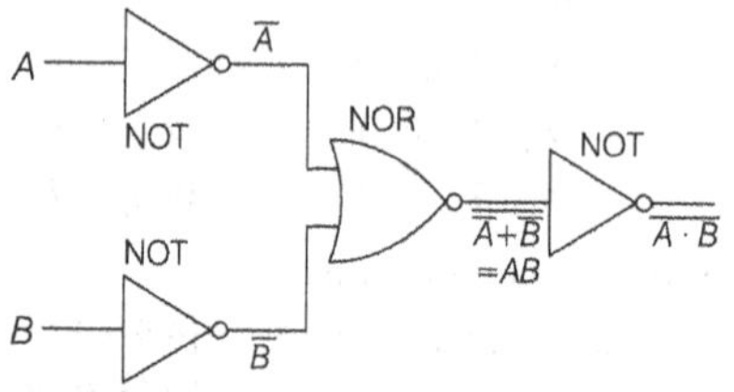

7. AND gate

   The truth table of the circuit is given

A	B	C	$X = \overline{AB}$	$Y = \overline{BC}$	$Z = \overline{X+Y}$
0	0	0	1	1	0
1	0	0	1	1	0
0	0	1	1	1	0
1	0	1	1	1	0
0	1	0	1	1	0
1	1	0	0	1	0
0	1	1	1	0	0
1	1	1	0	0	1

Output Z of single three input gate is that of AND gate

8. From the given waveforms, the following truth table can be made

Time interval	Inputs A	B	Output Y
$0 \rightarrow T_1$	0	0	0
$T_1 \rightarrow T_2$	0	1	0
$T_2 \rightarrow T_3$	1	0	0
$T_3 \rightarrow T_4$	1	1	1

This truth table is equivalent to AND gate

9. (1 = high, 0 = low)
Input to A is in the sequence, 1,0,1,0
Input to B is in the sequence, 1, 0, 0, 1
Sequence is inverted by NOT gate
Thus inputs to OR gate become 0, 1, 0, 1 and 0, 1, 1, 0.
Output of OR gate becomes 0, 1, 1, 1 which is drawn as

10. Boolean expression of the given circuit is
$Y = \overline{\overline{A+B}+\overline{A+B}} = A+B$

11. $Y = A + A \cdot B$

12. $Y = \overline{A} \cdot B + A \cdot \overline{B}$

Level 2

Single Choice(s) Correct Questions

1. $N_P > N_e$ for p-type semiconductor
$N_P < N_e$ for n-type semiconductor

2. $n_i^2 = n_h n_e \Rightarrow (10^{19})^2 = 10^{21} \times n_e \Rightarrow n_e = 10^{17}/\text{m}^3$

3. $n_i^2 = n_e\, n_h \Rightarrow (1.5 \times 10^{16})^2 = n_e\,(4.5 \times 10^{22})$
$$\Rightarrow \quad n_e = 0.5 \times 10^{10} = 5 \times 10^9$$
$$n_h = 4.5 \times 10^{22}$$
$n_h >> n_e$, Semiconductor is p-type and $n_e = 5 \times 10^9\ \text{m}^{-3}$

4. As we know, current density $J = nqv$
$$\Rightarrow \quad J_e = n_e q v_e \text{ and } J_h = n_h q v_h$$
$$\frac{j_e}{J_h} = \frac{n_e}{n_h} \times \frac{v_e}{v_n} \quad \Rightarrow \quad \frac{3/4}{1/4} = \frac{n_e}{n_h} \times \frac{5}{2}$$
$$\Rightarrow \quad \frac{n_e}{n_h} = \frac{6}{5}$$

5. $n_e = 8 \times 10^{18}/\text{m}^3,\ n_h = 5 \times 10^{18}/\text{m}^3,$
$$\mu_e = 2.3 \frac{\text{m}^3}{\text{volt} - \text{sec}},\ \mu_h = 0.01 \frac{\text{m}^3}{\text{volt} - \text{sec}}$$
$$\because \quad n_e > n_h$$
so semiconductor is n type
$$\text{Also conductivity } \sigma = \frac{1}{\text{Resistivity } (\rho)} = e\,(n_e \mu_e + n_h \mu_h)$$
$$\Rightarrow \quad \frac{1}{\rho} = 1.6 \times 10^{-19}\,[8 \times 10^{18} \times 2.3 + 5 \times 10^{18} \times 0.01]$$
$$\rho = 0.34\ \Omega\text{m}$$

6. $\sigma = ne(\mu_e + \mu_h) = 2 \times 10^{19} \times 1.6 \times 10^{-19}\,(0.36 + 0.14)$
$$= 1.6\ \Omega\text{m}^{-1}$$
$$R = \rho \frac{l}{A} = \frac{l}{\sigma A} = \frac{0.5 \times 10^{-3}}{1.6 \times 10^{-4}} = \frac{25}{8}\ \Omega$$
$$\therefore \quad i = \frac{V}{R} = \frac{2}{25/8} = \frac{16}{25}\ \text{A} = 0.64\ \text{A}$$

7. The temperature co-efficient of resistance of a semiconductor is always negative.

8. Conductor has positive temperature coefficient of resistance but semiconductor has negative temperature coefficient of resistance.

9. Germanium is semiconductor, whereas copper is conductor. For conductors, $R \propto \Delta t$
For semiconductors, $\quad R \propto \dfrac{1}{\Delta t}$
Hence, when both are cooled, then resistance of copper decreases whereas that of germanium increases.

10. $E_g\,(\text{C}) > E_g(\text{Si}) > E_g(\text{Ge})$

11. When donor impurity (+5 valence) is added to a pure silicon (+4 valence), the +5 valence donor atom sits in the place of +4 valence silicon atom. So it has a net additional +1 electronic charge. The four valence electrons form covalent bond and get fixed in the lattice. The fifth electron (with net −1 electronic charge) can be approximated to revolve around + 1 additional charge. The situation is like the hydrogen atom for which energy is given by $E = -\dfrac{13.6}{n^2}$ eV.
For the case of hydrogen, the permittivity was taken as ε_0. However, if the medium has a permittivity ε_r, relative to ε_0, then $E = -\dfrac{13.6}{\varepsilon_r^2 n^2}$ eV.
For Si, $\varepsilon_r = 12$ and for $n = 1, E \simeq 0.1$ eV

12. It is a semiconductor,
For Ge, $\Delta E_g = 0.72$ eV
For Si, $\Delta E_g = 1.1$ eV

13. (*a*)

14. Diagram ((d) represents semiconductor because in semiconductor the forbidden energy gap between valence and conduction band is equal to the energy corresponding to room temperature.

15. The donor level is found only in n-type semiconductors. The donor level lies closely below the bottom of the conduction band.

16. In sample X no impurity level seen, so it is undoped. In sample Y impurity energy level lies below the conduction bond so it is doped with fifth group impurity.
In sample Z, impurity energy level lies above the valence band so it is doped with third group impurity

17. (*c*)

18. p-n photodiode is a semiconductor diode that produces a significant current when illuminated. It is reversed biased but is operated below the breakdown voltage.
Energy of radiation = band gap energy

i.e., $h\nu = 2.0 \text{ eV}$ or $\nu = \dfrac{2.0 \times 1.6 \times 10^{-19}}{6.6 \times 10^{-34}} \approx 5 \times 10^{14}$ Hz

19. Band energy gap, $E = \dfrac{hc}{\lambda} = \dfrac{6.62 \times 10^{-34} \times 3 \times 10^{8}}{6000 \times 10^{-10}}$

$= 3.31 \times 10^{-19}$ J

20. $E = \dfrac{hc}{\lambda} \Rightarrow \lambda = \dfrac{hc}{E} = \dfrac{6.6 \times 10^{-34} \times 3 \times 10^{8}}{57 \times 10^{-3} \times 1.6 \times 10^{-19}} = 217100$ Å

21. Due to the large concentration of electrons in *n*-side and holes in *p*-side, they diffuse from their own side to other side. Hence depletion region produces

22. In a *p-n* junction diode, electrons in conduction band on *n*-type side travel across the junction and leave the positively ionized impurity atoms unneutralised. Consequently, there is positively charged region adjacent to the junction in *n*-type material. On *p*-type side the electrons which have traversed the boundary recombine with positive holes in the valence band and form a layer of unneutralised negatively ionised trivalent impurity atoms making a negatively charged region as shown in figure.

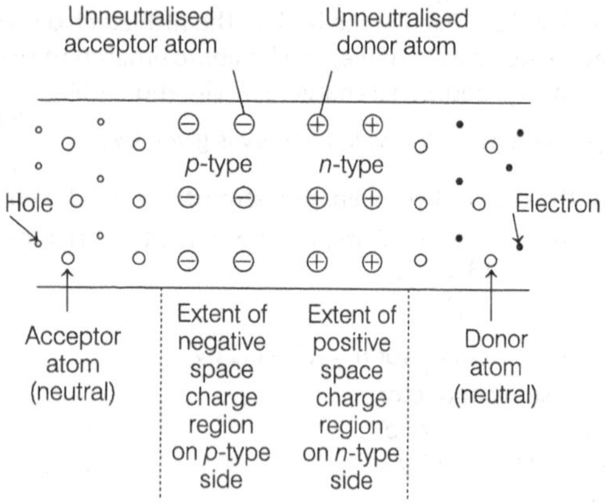

The region around the junction is called charge depletion region or space charge region. Hence, within the depletion region, *p*-side is negative and *n*-side is positive.

23. Depletion layer consists of mainly stationary ions.

24. Due to the reverse biasing the width of depletion region increases and current flowing through the diode is almost zero. In this case electric field is almost zero at the middle of the depletion region.

25. In a *p-n* junction, the direction of diffusion current is from *p*-region to *n*-region only.

26. In forward biasing the diffusion current increases and drift current remains constant so not current is due to the diffusion. In reverse biasing diffusion becomes more difficult so net current (very small) is due to the drift

27. In forward biasing both V_B and x decrease

28. Under normal reverse voltage, a very little reverse current flows through a *p-n* junction.

However, if the reverse voltage attains a high value, the junction may breakdown with sudden rise in reverse current. If reverse voltage is increased continuously, the kinetic energy of electrons (minority carriers) may become high enough to knock out electrons from the semiconductor atoms. At this stage breakdown of the junction occurs characterised by a sudden rise of reverse current and a sudden fall of the resistance of barrier region. This may destroy the junction permanently.

29. In forward biasing of *pn* junction diode width of depletion layer decreases. In intrinsic semiconductor fermi energy level is exactly in the middle of the forbidden gap

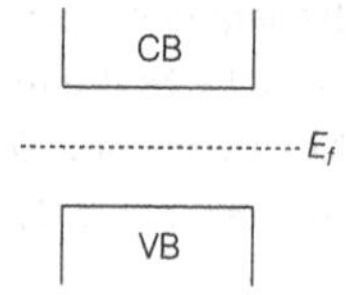

30. The reverse current is identical in two diodes if the identical reverse bias is applied across the diodes.

31. Arsenic has five valence electrons, so it is a donor impurity. Hence *X* becomes *n*-type semiconductor.

Indium has only three outer electrons, so it is an acceptor impurity. Hence *Y* becomes *p*-type semiconductor. Also *n*(*i.e.*, *X*) is connected to positive terminal of battery and *p* (*i.e.*, *Y*) is connected to negative terminal of battery so *p-n* junction is reverse biased.

32. Positive charge (i.e., holes) should move in the direction of current and negative charge (i.e., electrons) should move opposite to the direction of current.

33. $E = -\dfrac{dV}{dr} = \dfrac{0.6}{10^{-6}} = 6 \times 10^{5}\ \text{Vm}^{-1}$

34. In circuit 2, each *p-n* junction is reverse biased, some current will flow giving equal potential difference across each *p-n* junction diode. In circuit 3, each *p-n* junction is forward biased, hence same current flows, giving same potential difference across *p-n* junctions.

35. Total resistance = 50 + 5000 = 5050 Ω

$\therefore$ Forward current $i = \dfrac{50}{5050} = \dfrac{1}{101} = 9.9$ mA

36. In a forward biased *p-n* junction, the applied potential is opposite to the junction barrier potential V_B. The consequence of this is the effective barrier potential reduces. Hence, the graph (d) is correctly shown.

37. Resistance in forward biasing $R_{fr} \approx 10\Omega$ and resistance in reverse biasing $R_{R\omega} = 10^{5}\Omega$

$\Rightarrow \dfrac{R_{fr}}{R_{R\omega}} = \dfrac{1}{10^{4}}$

38. Forward biased resistance

$\dfrac{\Delta V}{\Delta I} = \dfrac{0.7 - 0.6}{(15-5) \times 10^{-3}} = \dfrac{0.1}{10 \times 10^{-3}} = 10\Omega$

39. $R_e = \dfrac{\Delta V}{\Delta I} = \dfrac{(13-8)}{(60-40) \times 10^{-6}} = 2.5 \times 10^{5}\ \Omega$

40.

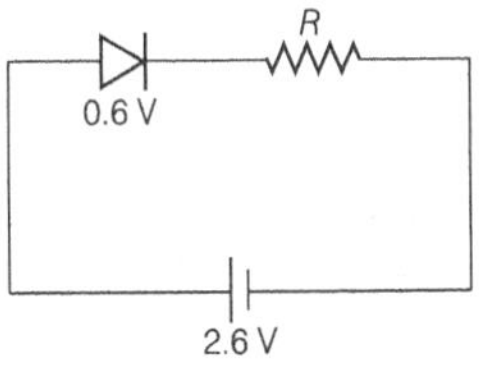

$$R = \frac{(2.6 - 0.6)}{5 \times 10^{-3}} = 400\,\Omega$$

41. The current at 2V is 400 mA and at 2.1 V it is 800 mA. The dynamic resistance in this region

$$R = \frac{\Delta V}{\Delta i} = \frac{(2.1 - 2)}{(800 - 400) \times 10^{-3}} = \frac{1}{4} = 0.25\,\Omega$$

42. For forward bias, $I = \frac{V}{R} = \frac{5}{25 + 10} = \frac{5}{35} = \frac{1}{7}$ A

43. The potential of n-side is more negative than that of p-side, hence diode is in forward biasing from circuit

resultant potential is 2V

$$\therefore \qquad I = \frac{2}{100} = 20 \text{ mA}$$

44. When diode is forward biased, then there is a small voltage drop across it, $i = \frac{V - V'}{R}$

Given, $V = 8$ volt, $V' = 0.5$ volt, $R = 2.2\text{ k}\Omega = 2.2 \times 10^3\,\Omega$

$$\therefore \qquad i = \frac{8 - 0.5}{2.2 \times 10^3} = \frac{7.5 \times 10^3}{2.2} = 3.4 \times 10^{-3}\text{ A}$$

$$\Rightarrow \qquad i = 3.4\text{ mA}$$

45. If i is the current in the diode and V is voltage drop across it, then for given figure voltage equation is

$$i \times 100 + V = 8$$

$$\Rightarrow \qquad i = -\frac{1}{100}V + \frac{8}{100}$$

$$\Rightarrow \qquad i = -(0.01)V + 0.08$$

Thus the slope of i-V graph $= \frac{1}{R_L} = 0.01$

46. In forward biasing, resistance of pn junction diode is zero, so whole voltage appears across the resistance.

47. $V_B = V_{knee} + IR$ or $4 = 0.7 + 10^{-3}R$

or $R = 3.3/10^{-3} = 3.3 \times 10^3\,\Omega$

48. Current through circuit,

$$I = \frac{P}{V} = \frac{100 \times 10^{-3}}{0.5} = 0.2\text{ V}$$

Voltage drop across $R = 1.5 - 0.5 = 1.0$ V

Hence, $R = 1/0.2 = 5\Omega$

49. In circuit the upper diode junction is forward biased and the lower diode junction is reverse biased. Thus there will be no conduction across lower diode junction.

Now the total resistance of circuit $= 100 + 150 + 50 = 300\,\Omega$

Current in $100\Omega = \frac{6}{300} = 0.02$ A

50. The equivalent circuit can be redrawn as

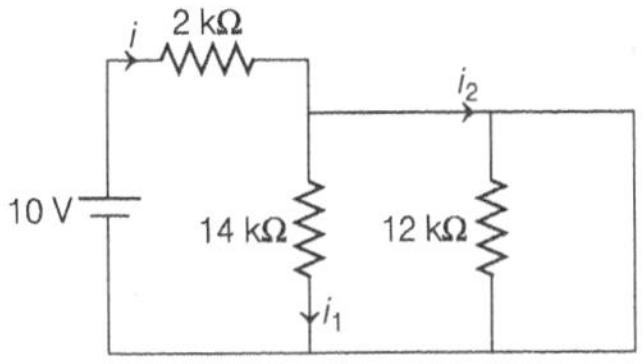

From figure it is clear that 14 kΩ and 12 kΩ have been short-circuited.

So current drawn from the battery $i = i_2 = \frac{10}{2} = 5$ mA and

$i_1 = 0$.

51. In the given circuit, diode D_1 is reverse biased, so it will not conduct. Diodes D_2 and D_3 are forward biased, so they will conduct. The corresponding equivalent circuit is as shown in the figure

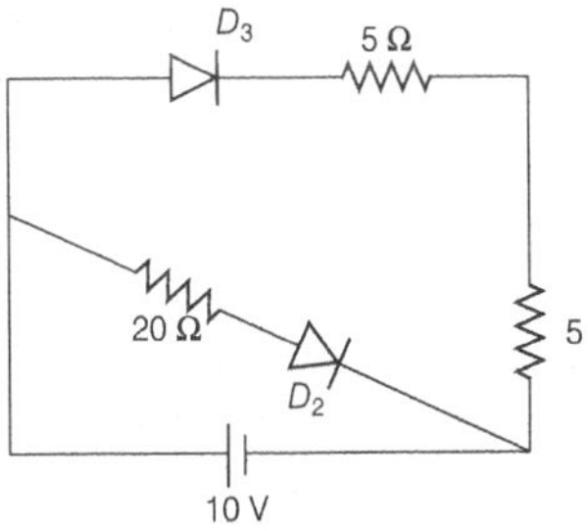

The equivalent resistance of the circuit is

$$R_{eq} = \frac{(5+5) \times 20}{(5+5) + 20} = \frac{10 \times 20}{10 + 20} = \frac{200}{30} = \frac{20}{3}\,\Omega$$

Current through the battery,

$$I = \frac{10\text{ V}}{\frac{20}{3}\,\Omega} = 1.5\text{ A}$$

52. According to the given figure A is at lower potential $w.r.t.$ B. hence both diodes are in reverse biasing, so equivalent circuit can be redrawn as follows

⇒ Equivalent resistance between A and B

$$R = 8 + 2 + 6 = 16\,\Omega$$

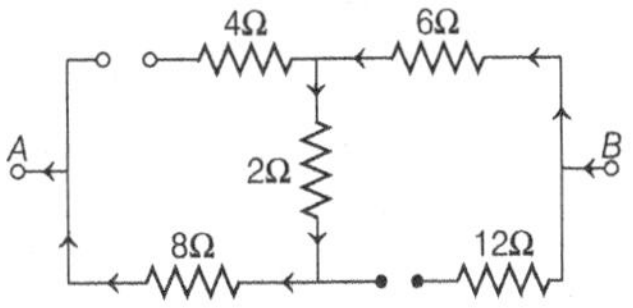

53. (i) $V_A = -10$ V and $V_B = -5$ V

Diodes D_1 and D_3 are reverse biased and D_2 is forward biased

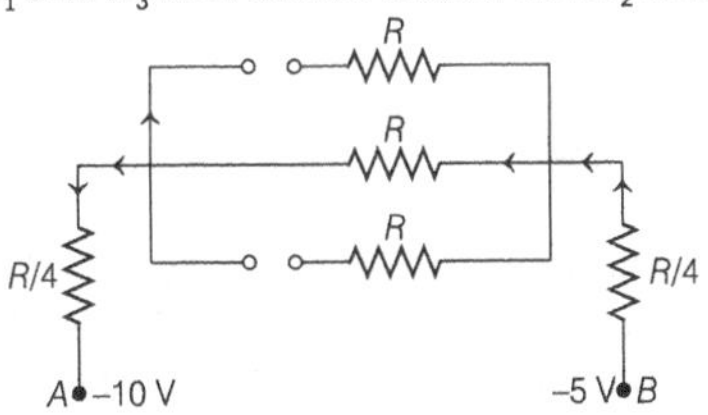

(ii) When $V_A = -5$ V and $V_B = -10$ V

Diode D_2 is reverse biased while D_1 and D_3 are forward biased

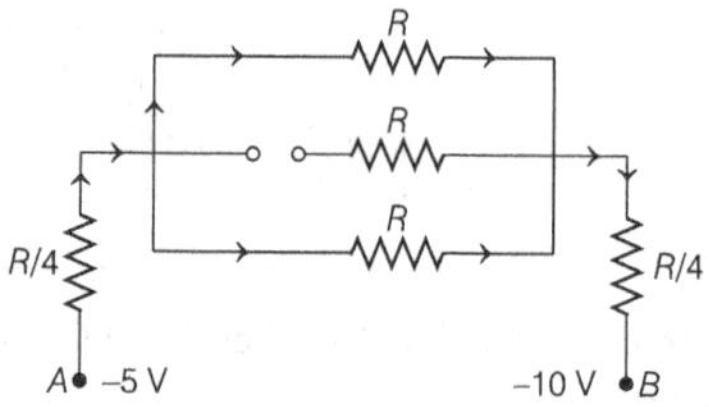

$$\Rightarrow \quad R_{AB} = \frac{R}{4} + \frac{R}{2} + \frac{R}{4} = R$$

(iii) In this case equivalent resistance between A and B is also R

Hence (ii) = (iii) < (i)

54. Consider the case when Ge and Si diodes are connected as show in the given figure.

Equivalent voltage drop across the combination Ge and Si diode = 3.0 V

$$\Rightarrow \quad \text{Current } i = \frac{12 - 0.3}{5\,\text{k}\Omega} = 2.34 \text{ mA}$$

$\therefore$ Output voltage $V_0 = Ri = 5\text{k}\Omega \times 2.34 \text{ mA} = 11.7$ V

Now consider the case when Ge diode connection is reversed. In this case voltage drop across the diode's combination = 0.7 V

$$\Rightarrow \quad \text{Current } i = \frac{12 - 0.7}{5\,\text{k}\Omega} = 2.26 \text{ mA}$$

$$\therefore \quad V_0 = iR = 2.26 \text{ mA} \times 5\text{k}\Omega = 11.3 \text{ V}$$

Hence charge in the value of $V_0 = 11.7 - 11.3 = 0.4$ V

55. Time $t = CR$ is known as time constant. It is time in which charge on the capacitor decreases to $\frac{1}{e}$ times of its initial charge (steady state charge).

In figure (i) p-n junction diode is in forward bias, so current will flow the circuit i.e. charge on the capacitor decreases and in time t it becomes $Q = \frac{1}{e}(Q_0)$; where $Q_0 = CV$

$$\Rightarrow \quad Q = \frac{CV}{e}$$

In figure (ii) p-n junction diode is in reverse bias, so no current will flow through the circuit. Hence charge on capacitor will not decay and it remains same, i.e. CV after time t.

56. If V is the voltage across the junction and I is the circuit current, then $V + IR = E$ or $I = \frac{E}{R} - \frac{V}{R} = -\frac{V}{R} + \frac{E}{R}$

$$\text{Slope of load line} = -\frac{1}{R} = \frac{1}{1000} = 10^{-3} \text{ AV}^{-1}$$

57. Zener breakdown can occur in heavily doped diodes. In lightly doped diodes the necessary voltage is higher, and avalanche multiplication is then the chief process involved.

58. For a wide range of values of load resistance, the current in the zener diode may change but the voltage across it remains unaffected. Thus the output voltage across the zener diode is a regulated voltage.

59. At high reverse voltage, the minority charge carriers acquire very high velocities. These by collision break down the covalent bonds, generating more carriers. This mechanism is called Avalanche breakdown.

60. Voltage available across load resistance

$$R = 20 - 5 = 15 \text{ V}$$

Resistance of load,

$$R = \frac{15}{10 \times 10^{-3}} = 1.5 \times 10^3 = 1.5 \text{ k}\Omega$$

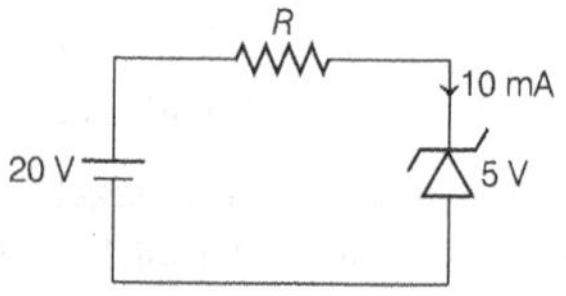

61. Given circuit, $V_{R_2} = 10$ V and $R_2 = 1500\,\Omega$

$$I_{R_2} = \frac{10}{1500} \text{ A} = 6.67 \text{ mA}$$

$$I_{R_1} = \frac{5}{500} = 10 \text{ mA}$$

$$\therefore \quad I_2 = 10 - 6.67 = 3.33 \text{ mA}$$

62. $$I_{max} = \frac{120 - 50}{5} - \frac{50}{10} = 9 \text{ mA}$$

$$I_{min} = \frac{80 - 50}{5} - \frac{50}{10} = 1 \text{ mA}$$

63. When Zener diode is forward biased, it behaves like ordinary diode and when reverse biased, it will be a voltage stabilizer. Also, at room temperature, the voltage across the depletion layer for silicon is about 0.6-0.7 V and for germanium is about 0.3-0.35V. Hence, statement A is correct but statement B is incorrect.

64. At high reverse voltage, due to high electric field, the minority charge carriers, while crossing the junction acquire very high velocities. These by collision breaks down the covalent bonds generating more carriers. A chain reaction is established giving rise to high current. This mechanism is called avalanche breakdown.

65. For $V_i < 0$, the diode is reverse biased and hence offer infinite resistance, so circuit would be like as shown in Fig. (2) and $V_0 = 0$.

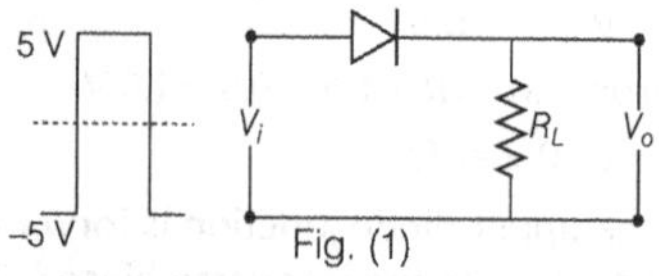

Fig. (1)

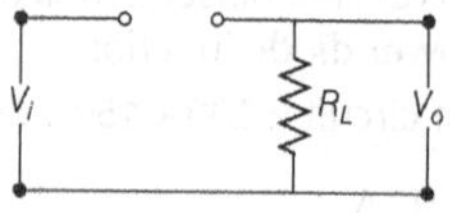

Fig. (2)

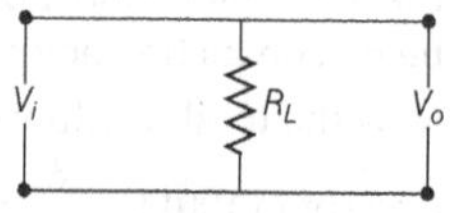

Fig. (3)

For $V_i > 0$, the diode is forward biased and circuit would be as shown in Fig. (3) and $V_0 = V_i$.

Hence, the option (d) is correct.

66. As RC time constant of the capacitor is quite large ($\tau = RC = 10 \times 10^3 \times 10 \times 10^{-6} = 0.1$ s), it will not discharge appreciably. Hence voltage remains nearly constant.

67. The *p-n* junction will conduct only when it is forward biased, *i.e.* when –5V is fed to it, so it will conduct only for 3rd quarter part of signal shown and when it conducts potential drop 5 V will be across both the resistors, so output voltage across R_2 is 2.5 V.

$$\therefore \qquad V_0 = -2.5 \text{ V}$$

68. For the positive half cycle of input the resulting network is shown below

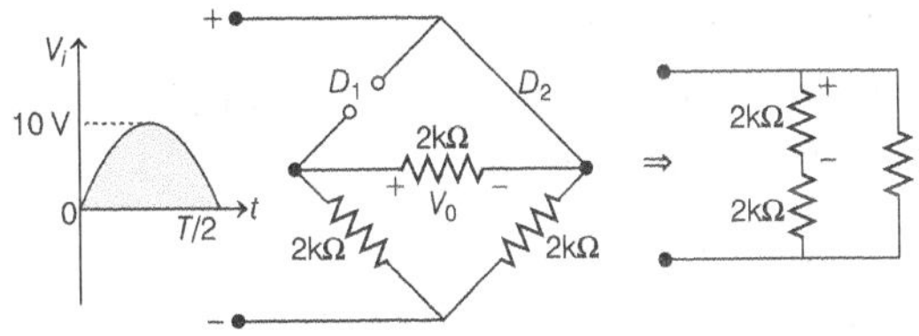

$$\Rightarrow \qquad (V_0)_{max} = \frac{1}{2}(V_i)_{max} = \frac{1}{2} \times 10 = 5 \text{ V}$$

69. The diode D will conduct for positive half cycle of AC of supply because this is forward biased. For negative half cycle of AC supply, this is reverse biased and does not conduct. So output would be half wave rectified and for half wave rectified output

$$V_{rms} = \frac{V_0}{2} = \frac{200\sqrt{2}}{2} = \frac{200}{\sqrt{2}}$$

70. The given circuit works is half wave rectifier. In this circuit, we will get current through R when *p-n* junction diode is forward biased and no current when *p-n* junction is reversed biased. Thus the current through resistance will be shown by graph (c).

71. (c)

72. In half wave rectifier, we get the output only in one half cycle of input AC therefore, the frequency of the ripple of the output is same as that of input AC i.e., 50 Hz.

73. (*b*)

74. In the positive half cycle of input AC signal diode D_1 is forward biased and is reverse biased so in the output voltage signal, A and C are due to D_1. In negative half cycle of input AC signal D_2 conducts, hence output signals B and D are due to D_2.

75. Peak value of rectified output voltage = peak value of input voltage – barrier voltage = 2 – 0.7 = 1.3 V

76. The given circuit is full wave rectifier.

77. In positive half cycle one diode is in forward biasing and other is in reverse biasing while in negative half cycle their polarity reverses, and direction of current is opposite through R for positive and negative half cycles so output is not rectified.

Since, R_1 and R_2 are different hence the peaks during positive half and negative half of the input signal will be different.

78. In the half wave rectifier, the value of DC voltage in one cycle is given by

$$V_{DC} = \frac{V_0}{\pi} = \frac{100}{3.14} = 31.8 \text{ V} \approx 32 \text{ V}$$

79. $V_{DC} = V_{AC} = \dfrac{2V_0}{\pi} = \dfrac{2 \times 6.28}{3.14} = 4$ V

80. If half wave rectifier the output voltage is the rms voltage $= \dfrac{V_0}{\sqrt{2}} = \dfrac{200}{\sqrt{2}}$

81. Frequency of input voltage $= \dfrac{\omega}{2\pi} = \dfrac{100\pi}{2\pi} = 50$ Hz

The given circuit is full wave rectifier

So the frequency of output voltage $= 2 \times 50 = 100$ Hz

82. The given Boolean expression can be written as

$$Y = \overline{(A+B)} \cdot \overline{(A \cdot B)} = (\overline{A} \cdot \overline{B}) \cdot (\overline{A} + \overline{B})$$
$$= (\overline{A}\overline{A}) \cdot \overline{B} + (\overline{B} \cdot \overline{B})\overline{A} = \overline{A} \cdot \overline{B} + \overline{A} \cdot \overline{B} = \overline{A} \cdot \overline{B}$$

A	B	Y
0	0	1
1	0	0
0	1	0
1	1	0

83. NOR gates are considered as universal gates, because all the gates like AND, OR, NOT can be obtained by using only NOR gates.

84. We know the repetitive use of NAND and NOR gate gives digital circuits.

85. The circuit diagram of a NAND gate when its two inputs are shorted, is given as NAND = AND + NOT

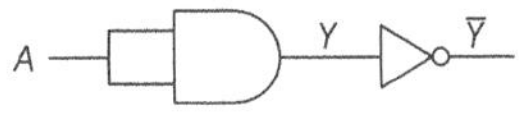

The truth table of the logic gate is given as

A	Y	$\overline{Y}$
0	1	0
1	1	0

Hence, if the input is zero then output is 1 and when input is 1 than output is zero.

So, the resulting gate is NOT gate.

86. (*b*)

87. NOR gate with output $O = \overline{X + Y}$

88. At logic gate, the Boolean expression is $\overline{B} \cdot C = Y'$

At logic gate II, the Boolean expression is $A + (\overline{B} \cdot C) = Y''$

At logic gate III, the Boolean expression is $\overline{A + (\overline{B} \cdot C)} = Y$

89. We can realise the combination as shown below.

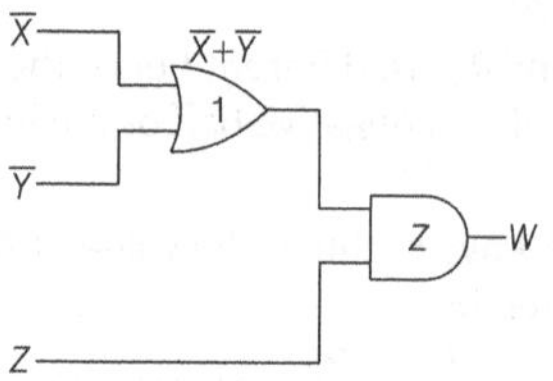

Gate-1 is OR gate while gate-2 is AND gate.

Output of OR gate, $W_1 = \overline{X} + \overline{Y}$

Thus, output of AND gate, $W = W_1 \cdot Z = (\overline{X} + \overline{Y}) \cdot Z$

$= \overline{(X \cdot Y)} \cdot Z \qquad [\because \overline{X} + \overline{Y} = \overline{X \cdot Y}]$

90.
$$F = (W + X) \cdot (W + Y)$$
$$= W \cdot W + W \cdot Y + W \cdot X + X \cdot Y$$
$$= W + W \cdot Y + W \cdot X + X \cdot Y \qquad [\because W \cdot W = W]$$
$$= W \cdot (1 + Y) + W \cdot X + X \cdot Y$$
$$= W \cdot (1 + X) + X \cdot Y \qquad [\because (1 + Y) = 1]$$
$$= W + X \cdot Y \qquad [\because (1 + X) = 1 \text{ and } W \cdot 1 = W]$$

91. We can realise the gate circuit as

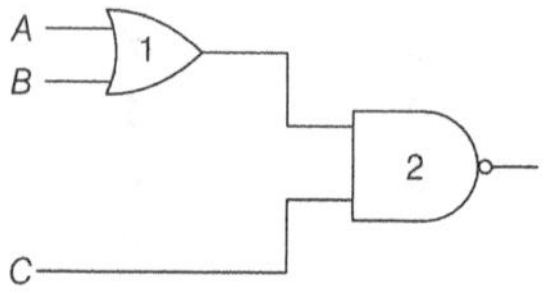

Output of gate 1, $Y_1 = A + B$

Output of gate 2, $Y_2 = \overline{Y_1 \cdot C} = \overline{(A + B) \cdot C}$

(a) If $A = 0, B = 1, C = 0$, then $Y_2 = \overline{(0 + 1) \cdot 0} = \overline{1 \cdot 0} = 0$

(b) If $A = 1, B = 0, C = 0$, then $Y_2 = \overline{(1 + 0) \cdot 0} = \overline{1 \cdot 0} = 0$

(c) If $A = 1, B = 0, C = 1$, then $Y_2 = \overline{(1 + 0) \cdot 1} = \overline{1 \cdot 1} = 1$

(d) If $A = 1, B = 1, C = 0$, then $Y_2 = \overline{(1 + 1) \cdot 0} = \overline{1 \cdot 0} = 0$

92.

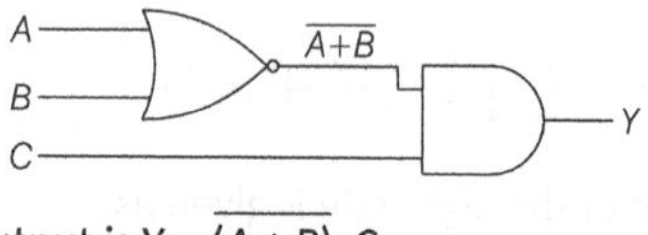

The output is $Y = \overline{(A + B)} \cdot C$

The truth table of the given circuit is as shown in the table

A	B	C	$\overline{A+B}$	$Y = \overline{(A+B)} \cdot C$
0	0	0	1	0
0	0	1	1	1
0	1	0	0	0
0	1	1	0	0
1	0	0	0	0
1	0	1	0	0
1	1	0	0	0
1	1	1	0	0

93.

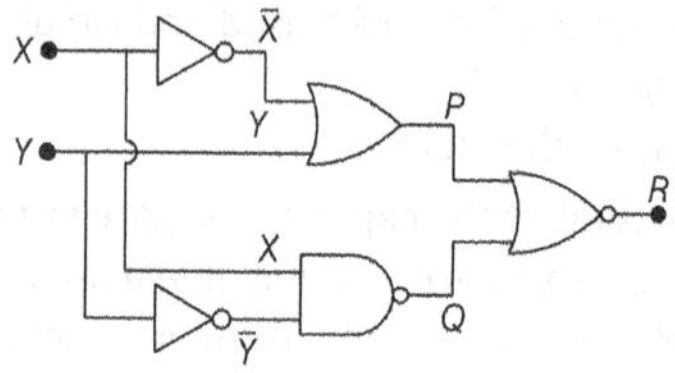

The truth table can be written as

X	Y	$\overline{X}$	$\overline{Y}$	$P = \overline{X} + Y$	$Q = \overline{X \cdot \overline{Y}}$	$R = \overline{P + Q}$
0	1	1	0	1	1	0
1	1	0	0	1	1	0
1	0	0	1	0	0	1
0	0	1	1	1	1	0

Hence $X = 1, Y = 0$ gives output $R = 1$

94. $Y = \overline{\overline{(A \cdot \overline{(A \cdot B)})} \cdot \overline{(B \cdot \overline{(A \cdot B)})}} = A \cdot \overline{(A \cdot B)} + B \cdot \overline{(A \cdot B)}$

$= A \cdot (\overline{A} + \overline{B}) + B \cdot (\overline{A} + \overline{B})$

$= A \cdot \overline{A} + A \cdot \overline{B} + \overline{A} \cdot B + B \cdot \overline{B}$

$= A \cdot \overline{B} + \overline{A} \cdot B$

When $A = 1, B = 0$ then $Y = 1 \cdot \overline{0} + \overline{1} \cdot 0 = 1$

When $A = 1, B = 1$ then $Y = 1 \cdot \overline{1} + \overline{1} \cdot 1 = 0$

When $A = 0, B = 0$ then $Y = 0 \cdot \overline{0} + \overline{0} \cdot 0 = 0$

95.

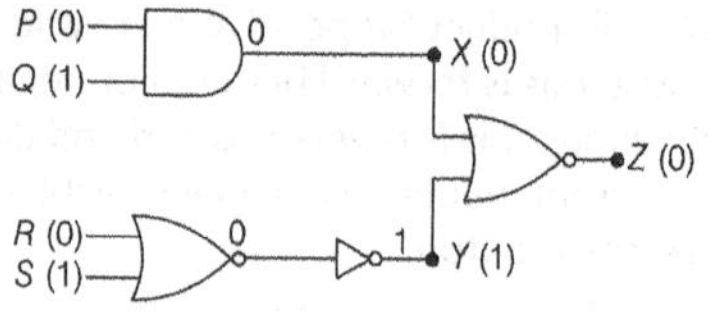

Output X, Y and Z changes to 0, 1, 0.

96. Lower NOT gate inverts input to zero. NOT gate from NAND gate inverts this output to 1. Upper NAND gate converts this input 1 and input 0 to 1. Thus $A = 1$ and $B = 1$ become inputs of NAND gate giving final output as zero. Choice A is correct

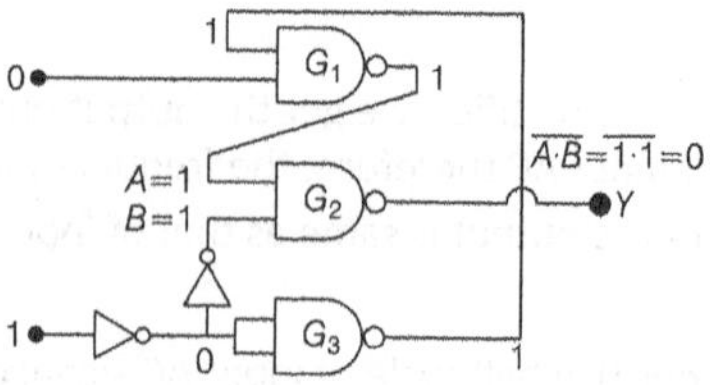

97. $Y' = A + B$

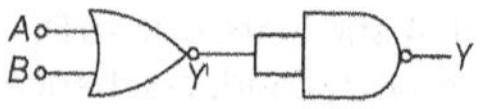

And $Y = \overline{Y'} = \overline{A + B}$ i.e, out of a NOR gate.

98. Truth table for given combination is

A	B	X
0	0	1
1	0	1
0	1	0
1	1	1

This comes out to be truth table of OR gate.

99. Output of $G_1 = (A + B)$

Output of $G_2 = \overline{A \cdot B}$;

Output of $G_3 = (A + B) \cdot \overline{(A \cdot B)}$ which give XOR gate.

100. The output of the circuit is,

$$Y = \overline{\overline{A} + \overline{B}} = \overline{\overline{A}} \cdot \overline{\overline{B}} = A \cdot B \qquad [\because \overline{\overline{A}} = A \text{ and } \overline{\overline{B}} = B]$$

which is the output of an AND gate.

101. From truth table it is clear that output is high only when both inputs are high. The Boolean expression.

Which satisfies the output of this logic gate is $C = A \cdot B$, which is for AND gate.

102. From real time variation of input signals, we can from truth table for A and B and conclude output from NAND gate.

Inputs		Output
A	B	Y
0	0	1
1	0	1
0	0	1
1	1	0
0	0	1

From output, we can show real time variation of output signal as below.

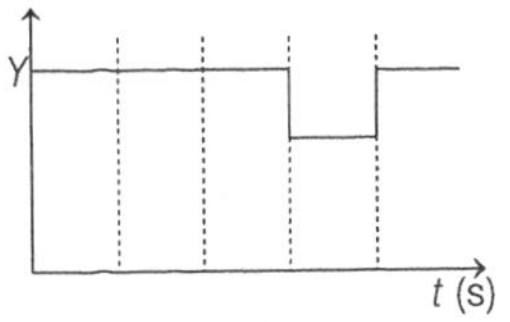

103. (*d*)

104. Given, *A* and *B* are inputs and *C* is output. Assume that some voltage is applied across *AB*.

If the voltage is positive, then diode corresponding to *A* will be ON and the other diode will be OFF

$\Rightarrow \qquad C = A$

If the voltage is negative then diode corresponding to *B* will be ON and the other diode will be OFF

$\Rightarrow \qquad C = B$

Therefore, we can say that $C = A$ or B. Therefore, it acts like OR gate. So the correct option is (d).

Previous Year's Questions

JEE Main

1. A diode is said to be in reverse biased when *p*-side is connected to less voltage than *n*-side. i.e.

$$V_p - V_n = 2 - 4 = -2(-\text{ve})$$

So, diode is in reverse bias.

Hence, circuit is in reverse bias.

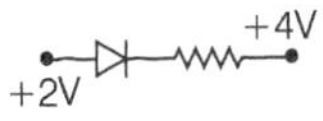

2.

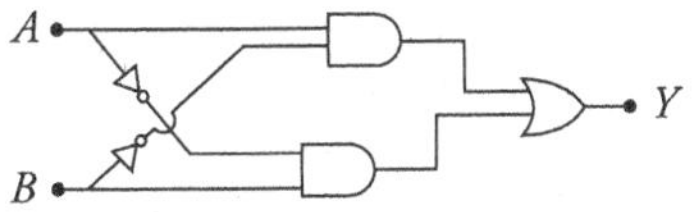

$$Y = A\overline{B} + \overline{A}B$$

	B	$A\overline{B}$	$\overline{A}B$	Y
0	0	0	0	0
0	1	0	1	1
1	0	1	0	1
1	1	0	0	0

3.

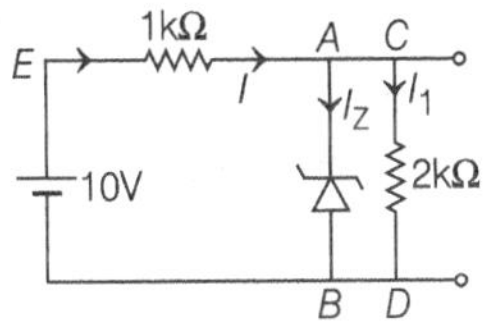

Given in question, $V_Z = 3.0$ V

Let potential at $B = 0$ V

Let potential at $E, V_E = 10$ V

$$V_C = V_A = 3\text{ V}$$

$$I_Z + I_1 = I,$$

$$I_Z = I - I_1$$

$$I = \frac{10 - 3}{1000} = \frac{7}{1000}\text{A}$$

$$I_1 = \frac{V_C - V_D}{2\text{k }\Omega} = \frac{3 - 0}{2000}\text{A}$$

$$I_Z = \frac{7 - 1.5}{1000} = 5.5\text{ mA}$$

4. The given circuit is

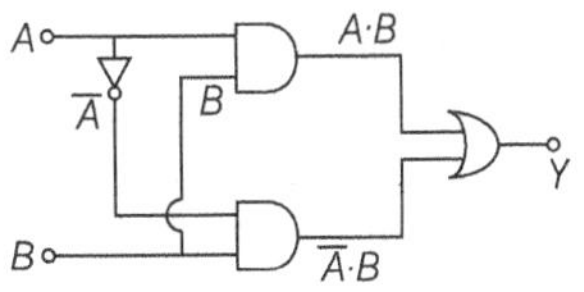

$$\therefore \quad Y = AB + \overline{A}B = B \cdot (A + \overline{A}) = B$$

$\therefore$ Truth table will be

A	B	Y = B
0	0	0
0	1	1
1	0	0
1	1	1

5. A semiconductor starts conducting more as the temperature increases. It means resistance decreases with increase in temperature. So, if temp increases its resistivity decreases.

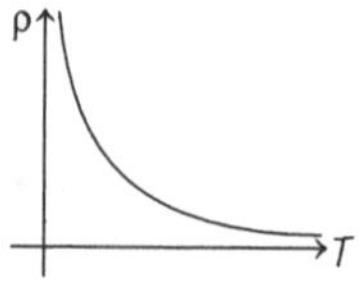

Also, $\rho = \dfrac{m}{ne^2\tau}$

as temperature increases, τ decreases but n increases and n is dominant over τ, thus reducing overall resistivity of the semiconductor.

6.

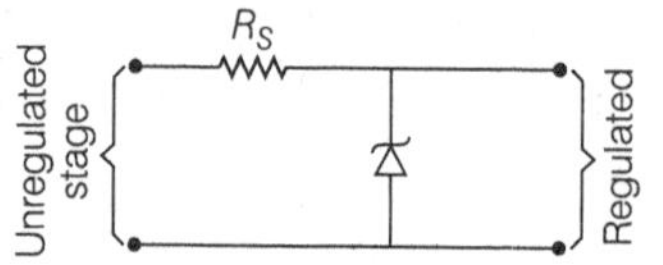

Power rating of zener = 1.6 W

Max voltage across zener = 8 V

Using $P = VI$; for zener diode,

$$I = \frac{P}{V} = \frac{1.6}{8} = 0.2\text{ A}$$

Hence, for safe operation 2V (excess voltage of 10 V) potential drop must occur in series resistor R_S.

For R_S, $V = 2$ V, $I = 0.2$ A

Using, $V = IR$,

$$R = \frac{2}{0.2} = 10\Omega$$

7. Given, forward bias resistance

$$(r) = 25\ \Omega$$

Diode D_2 is in reverse biased, thus $I_3 = 0$.

Since, resistance in each branch is same

Thus, $I_2 = I_4$

From KCL,

$$I_2 + I_4 + I_3 = I_1 \Rightarrow 2I_2 = I_1 \Rightarrow \frac{I_1}{I_2} = 2$$

8. A photodiode is operated in reverse bias because photocurrent is more significant in reverse bias as compared to the forward bias.

9. When Si is doped with trivalent impurities like Boron, then a *p*-type semiconductor is formed. In *p*-type semiconductor, excess number of holes are found because holes are majority carrier in *p*-type semiconductor.

When Si is doped with pentavalent impurities (like Arsenic), then an *n*-type semiconductor is formed.

In *n*-type semiconductor, excess no. of electrons are found because these are majority carrier. Thus, statement I is correct.

When *p*-type semiconductor and *n*-type semiconductor are fused to make a junction, a potential barrier is produced across the junction which stops the flow of current.

Thus, no current is detected by externally connected ammeter.

Hence, statement II is incorrect.

10. An LED is a heavily doped *p-n* junction. When an electron transits from conduction band to valence band in forward bias, it emits energy which is nearly equal to the energy gap in form of visible radiation.

So, an LED cannot be used in reverse bias.

11. Zener diode is a reverse biased heavily doped *p-n* junction diode. It is operated in breakdown region. Zener diode is designed to operate in the reverse breakdown voltage continuously without being damaged.

12. The highest energy level that an electron can occupy at the absolute zero temperature is known as the fermi level. The fermi level lies between the valence band and conduction band because at absolute zero temperature, the electrons are all in the lowest energy state.

In intrinsic semiconductor, fermi level is between the two bands.

In *p*-type, fermi level is closer to valence band.

In *n*-type, fermi level is closer to conduction band.

In metal, fermi level is inside conduction band.

Thus, correct sequence is

A - II, B- III, C - I, D- IV.

13.

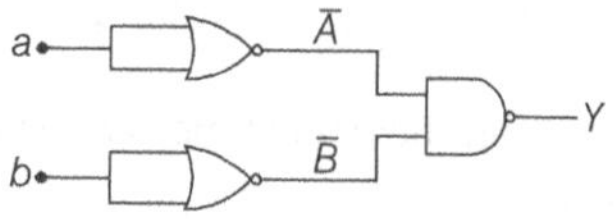

$$Y = \overline{(\bar{A} \cdot \bar{B})} = \bar{\bar{A}} + \bar{\bar{B}} = A + B = \text{output of OR gate}$$

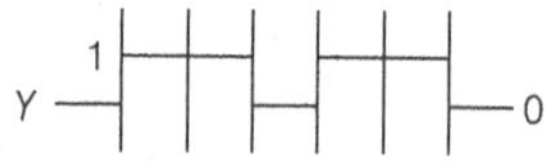

14. We know that output of NAND gate is high only when one or both input are low (zero) and low when both inputs are high (1). Thus, option (a) is correct.

15. Circuit will not work when both *A* and *B* are closed.

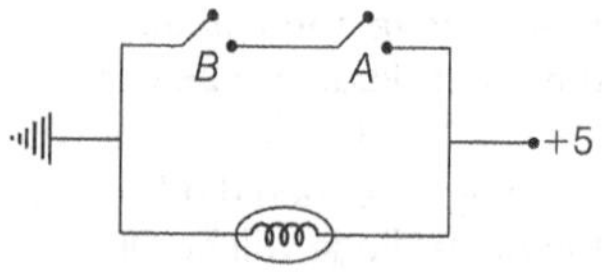

So above circuit is logic equivalent of NOT + AND = NAND

16.

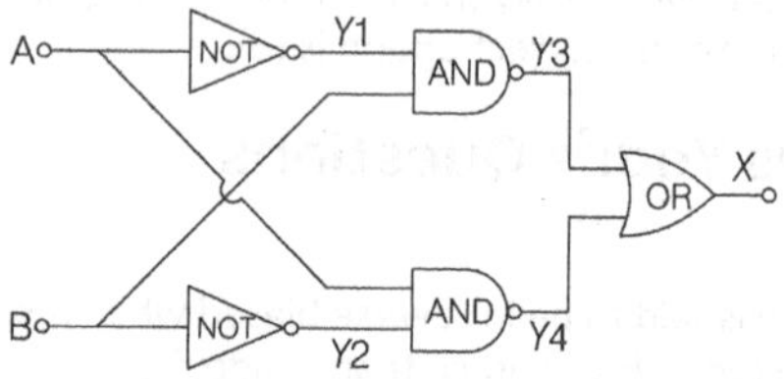

Truth table of above gate is

A	B	Y_1	Y_2	Y_3	Y_4	X
0	0	1	1	0	0	0
1	0	0	1	0	1	1
0	1	1	0	1	0	1
1	1	0	0	0	0	0

17. The logic circuit diagram is given as

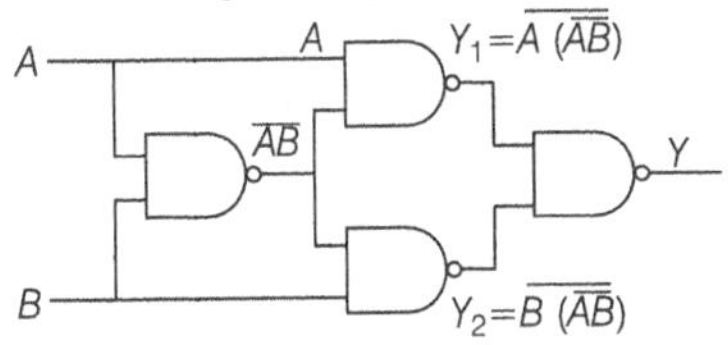

Output is given by, $Y = \overline{Y_1 \cdot Y_2}$ ...(i)

Where, $Y_1 = \overline{A(\overline{AB})} = \overline{A} + \overline{\overline{AB}} = \overline{A} + AB$

Similarly, $Y_2 = \overline{B} + AB$

$\therefore$ From Eq. (i), we get

$$Y = \overline{(\overline{A} + AB)(\overline{B} + AB)}$$
$$= \overline{(\overline{A} + AB)} + \overline{(\overline{B} + AB)}$$
$$= (\overline{\overline{A}} \cdot \overline{AB}) + (\overline{\overline{B}} \cdot \overline{AB})$$
$$= (A \cdot (\overline{A} + \overline{B})) + (B \cdot (\overline{A} + \overline{B}))$$
$$= A\overline{A} + A\overline{B} + B\overline{A} + B\overline{B}$$
$$= A\overline{B} + B\overline{A}$$

$\therefore$ Truth table for the given logic gate is

A	B	$\overline{A}$	$\overline{B}$	$Y = A\overline{B} + B\overline{A}$
0	0	1	1	0
0	1	1	0	1
1	0	0	1	1
1	1	0	0	0

18. Photodiode is used in reverse bias because very small change in minority charge carriers produces high value of reverse bias current.

19. Diode is two terminal device which conducts current in forward bias only. It will not conduct in reverse bias.

20. I-V characteristics of solar cell is as shown below.

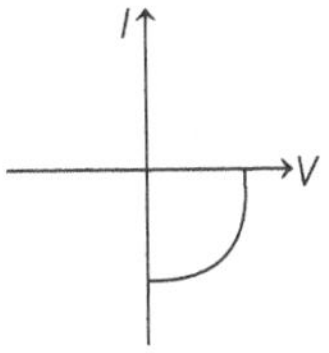

21. The circuit diagram for the given situation is shown below.

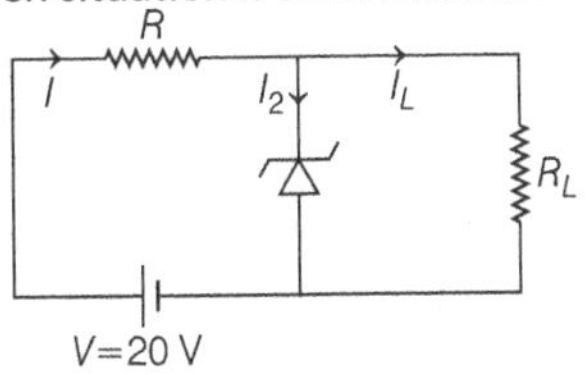

$V_Z = 8\text{V}$

$$I = \frac{V - V_Z}{R} = \frac{20 - 8}{R}$$

$$\Rightarrow \quad I = \frac{12}{R}\text{ A}$$

$$\therefore \quad (I_Z)_{max} = I$$

$$\Rightarrow 25 \times 10^{-3} = \frac{12}{R}$$

$$\Rightarrow \quad R = \frac{12}{25 \times 10^3} = 480\ \Omega$$

22. We know that

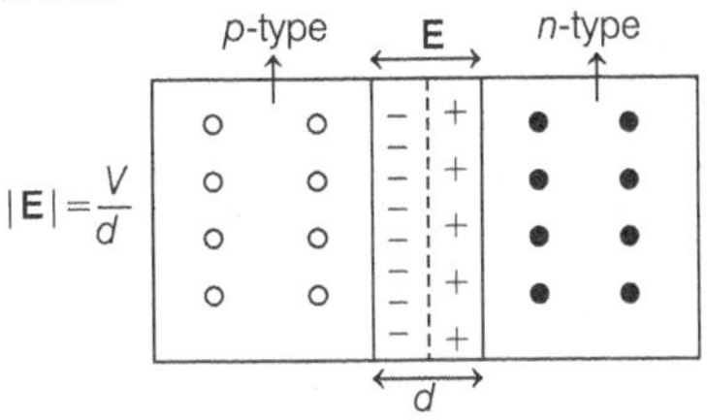

$$\Rightarrow \quad |\mathrm{E}| = \frac{0.6}{6 \times 10^{-6}}\text{N/C}$$

$$\Rightarrow \quad |\mathrm{E}| = 1 \times 10^5\text{ N/C}$$

23. The given circuit diagram is represented as

For maximum zener diode current

$$\therefore \quad I = \frac{120 - V_Z}{R} = \frac{120 - 60}{4 \times 10^3} = 15 \times 10^{-3}\text{A} = 15\text{ mA}$$

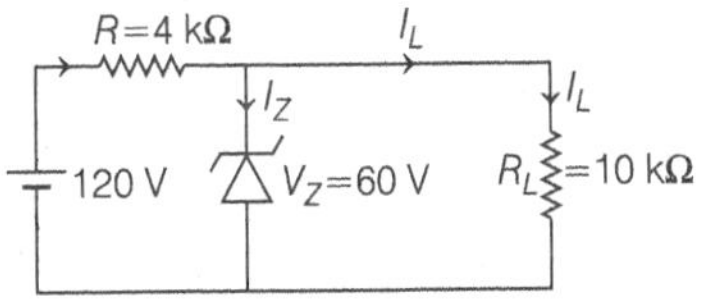

$$I_L = \frac{V_L}{R_L} = \frac{V_Z}{R_L} \qquad (\because V_L = V_Z)$$

$$= \frac{60}{10 \times 10^3} = 6 \times 10^{-3}\text{ A} = 6\text{ mA}$$

$\therefore$ Zener diode current,

$$I_Z = I - I_L = 15 - 6 = 9\text{ mA}$$

24. In the given circuit, the diode D_1 and D_3 are forward biased, while D_2 is reverse biased. Hence, no current flows from D_2. The resultant circuit can be represented as,

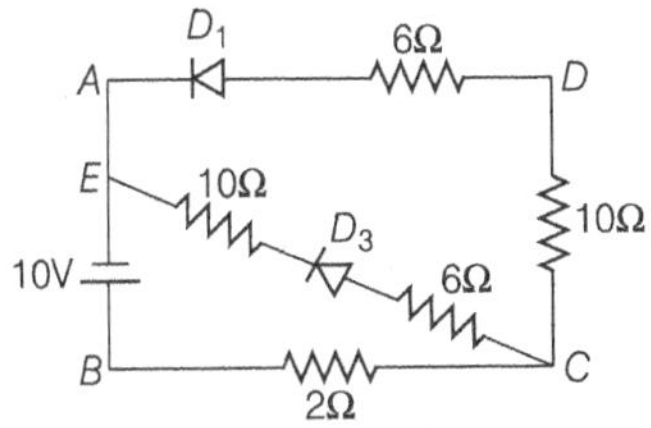

The resultant resistance over the loop, $AECDA$

$$\frac{1}{R'} = \frac{1}{16} + \frac{1}{16} \Rightarrow R' = \frac{16}{2} = 8\ \Omega$$

The effective resistance is $R = 8 + 2 = 10\ \Omega$

$\therefore$ Current through circuit, $I = \frac{V}{R} = \frac{10}{10} = 1\text{ A}$

25. Here, diode in upper branch is in forward biasing and diode in lower branch is in reverse biasing.

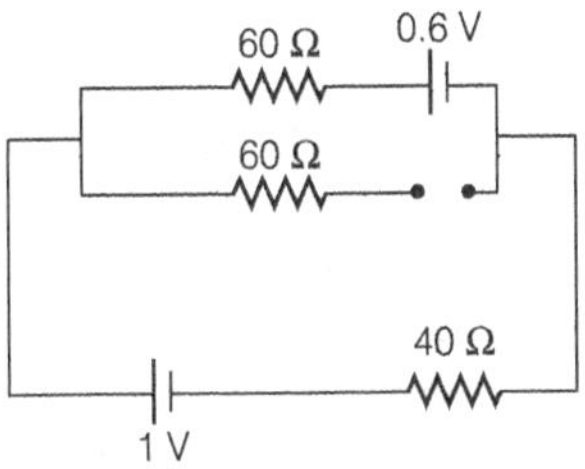

$$R_{eq} = 60 + 40 = 100\Omega$$

$$V_{net} = 1 - 0.6 = 0.4\text{ V}$$

$$\text{So, } i = \frac{V_{net}}{R_{eq}} = \frac{0.4}{100}\text{A} = 4\text{ mA}$$

26. $\because$ Power, $P_{ZM} = I_{ZM} V_z$

$$I_{ZM} = \frac{P_{ZM}}{V_z} = \frac{0.4}{10} = 0.04 \text{ A}$$

So, $$R_p = \frac{E_{max} - V_z}{I_{ZM}} = \frac{15-10}{0.04} = \frac{5}{0.04} = 125\ \Omega$$

27. $\because$ Given, $\lambda = 4000$ Å

$$E(\text{eV}) = \frac{12400}{\lambda(\text{Å})} = \frac{12400}{4000} \simeq 3 \text{ eV}$$

28. We have truth table as shown

A	B	Y
0	0	1
0	1	1
1	0	1
1	1	0

Which resembles to NAND gate, so correct option is (b).

29. From the given input and output waveforms, we observe that output Y is high only when both the inputs A and B are individually high. This is possible only in AND gate.

30. Given, logic inputs are given as

$(A, B) = (0, 0), (0,1), (1, 0)$ and $(1, 1)$

And the logic circuit is drawn as

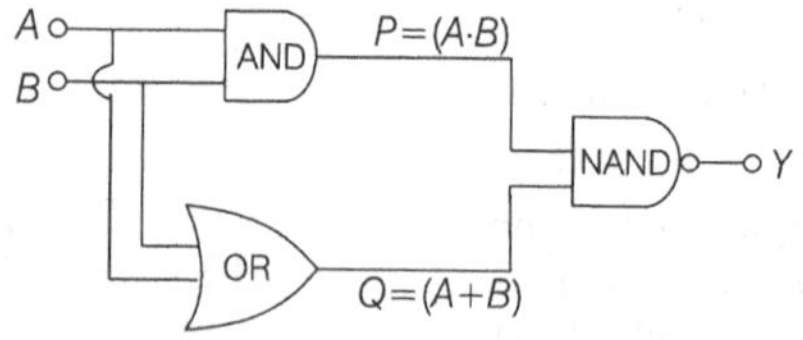

Output of the given logic circuit is given as

$Y = \overline{AB \cdot (A+B)} = \overline{AB} + \overline{(A+B)}$ [using de-Morgan's theorem]

$= (\bar{A} + \bar{B}) + \bar{A} \cdot \bar{B} = \bar{A} + \bar{B} + \bar{A}\bar{B}$

Now, by using truth table for above logic circuit

A	B	$\bar{A}$	$\bar{B}$	$\bar{A}\,\bar{B}$	P	Q	Y
0	0	1	1	1	0	0	1
0	1	1	0	0	0	1	1
1	0	0	1	0	0	1	1
1	1	0	0	0	1	1	0

31. In figure A, V_A and V_B are two input voltages (either 5 V or 0 V)

When, $V_A = 0, V_B = 0$

Both D_1 and D_2 are OFF, so $V_0 = 0$,

When, $V_A = 1$ i.e. 5 V, $V_B = 0$ i.e. 0 V

D_1 is ON but D_2 is OFF

So, $V_0 = 1$ i.e. 5 V

When, $V_A = 0$ i.e. 0 V, $V_B = 1$ i.e. 5 V

D_1 is OFF and D_2 is ON

So, $V_0 = 1$ i.e. 5 V.

Similarly, when $V_A = V_B = 1$

Both D_1 and D_2 are ON

So, $V_0 = 1$ i.e. 5 V.

We get the final truth table on the basis of inputs and their corresponding output.

A	B	Y
0	0	0
0	1	1
1	0	1
1	1	1

$\therefore$ The given circuit (A) is an OR gate.

In figure B, it is a transistor in common emitter configuration which gives high output at low input and low output at high input.

Hence, this circuit behaves as NOT Gate.

32. Given, logic circuit can be drawn as shown below.

The expression for output is

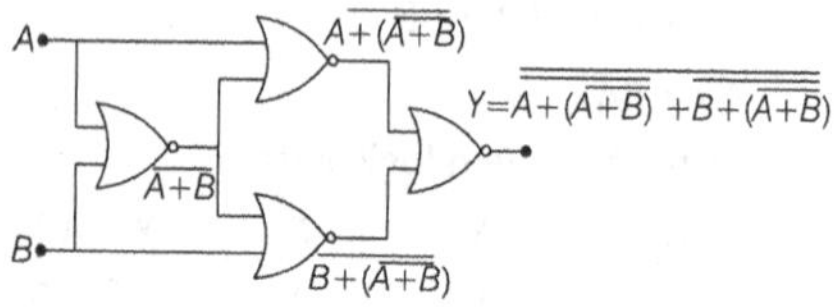

$= \overline{A + \overline{(A+B)}} \cdot \overline{B + \overline{(A+B)}}$

(Using de-Morgan's theorem,

$\overline{x+y} = \bar{x} \cdot \bar{y}$

$\Rightarrow \quad Y = (A + \overline{A+B}) \cdot (B + \overline{A+B})$

Draw the truth table for the logic circuit is shown below

A	B	A+B	$\overline{A+B}$	$A+\overline{A+B}$	$B+\overline{A+B}$	Y
0	0	0	1	1	1	1
0	1	1	0	0	1	0
1	0	1	0	1	0	0
1	1	1	0	1	1	1

33. The given circuit can be drawn as

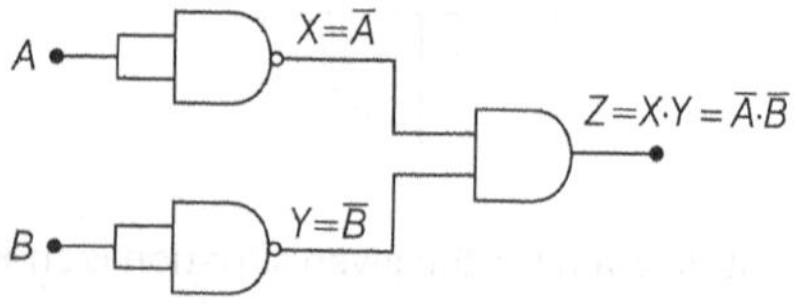

The output, $Z = \bar{A} \cdot \bar{B} = \overline{A+B}$ (Using de-Morgan theorem)

This is the expression of a NOR gate. So, the logic operation carried out by the given circuit is NOR.

34. By using de-Morgan's theorem,

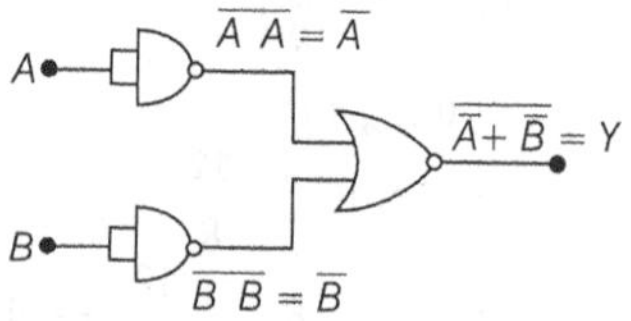

$Y = \overline{\bar{A} + \bar{B}}$

$= \bar{\bar{A}} \cdot \bar{\bar{B}} = A \cdot B$

So, the given circuit perform AND operation.

35. We can find the output of given combination of gates using Boolean algebra.

Consider the given figure

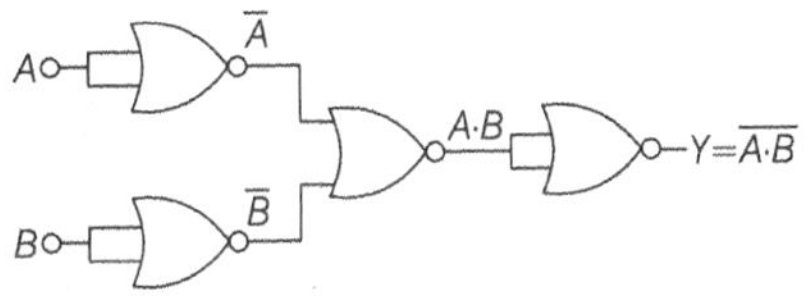

The output $Y=\overline{A\cdot B}$

which is the expresssion for NAND gate.

36. Let us consider the given logic circuit and solve it using Boolean algebra.

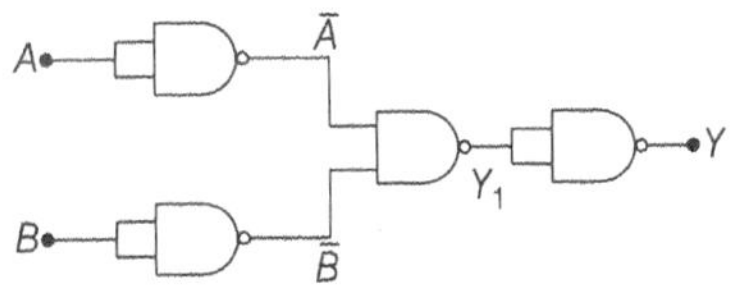

Here, $Y_1=\overline{\bar{A}\cdot\bar{B}}=\bar{\bar{A}}+\bar{\bar{B}}=A+B$

$\therefore \quad Y=\bar{Y}_1=\overline{A+B}$

which is an expression for NOR Gate.

37. According to the given figure signals are

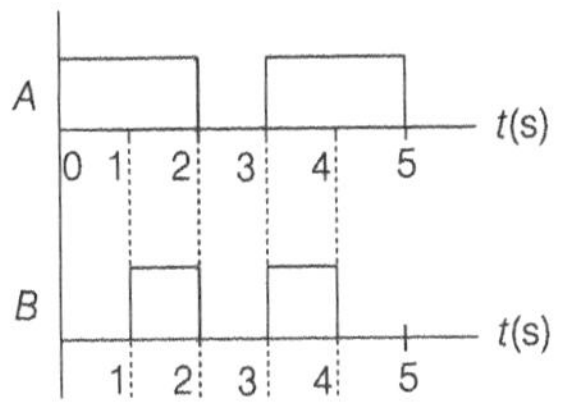

The output of given circuit diagram is

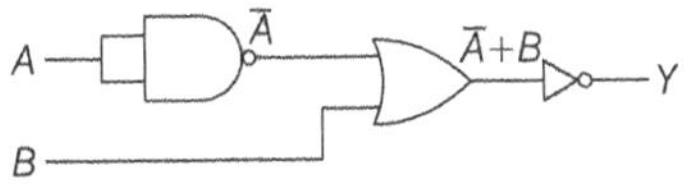

By using concept of de-Morgan's law,

$$Y=\overline{\bar{A}+B}=A\cdot\bar{B}$$

Truth table of given signals is

Time interval	A	B	$\bar{B}$	$A\bar{B}$
(0-1)s	1	0	1	1
(1-2)s	1	1	0	0
(2-3)s	0	0	1	0
(3-4)s	1	1	0	0
(4-5)s	1	0	1	1

Hence, output signal is,

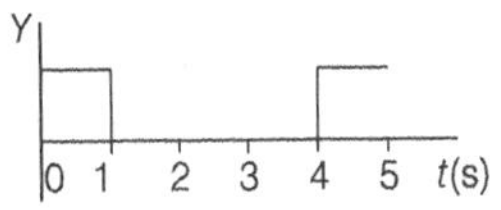

38. Here A and B be the input and

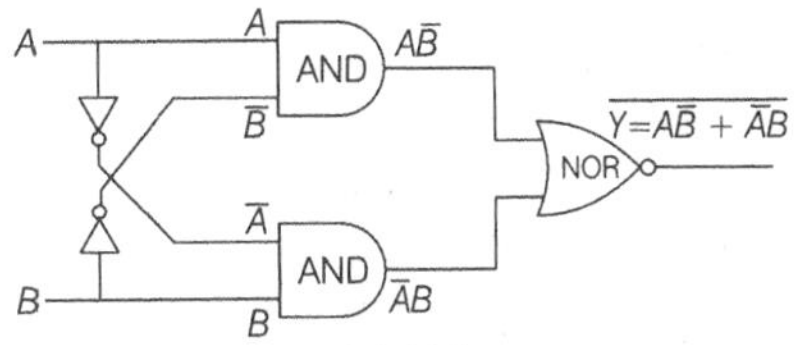

$\because \quad Y=\overline{A\bar{B}+\bar{A}B}=\overline{A\bar{B}}\cdot\overline{\bar{A}B}$

$=(\bar{A}+\bar{\bar{B}})\cdot(\bar{\bar{A}}+\bar{B})$

$=(\bar{A}+B)(A+\bar{B})$

$=\bar{A}A+\bar{A}\bar{B}+AB+B\bar{B}$

$=0+\bar{A}\bar{B}+AB+0$

$=AB+\bar{A}\bar{B}$

According to the truth table

A	B	$\bar{A}$	$\bar{B}$	AB	$\bar{A}\bar{B}$	$Y=AB+\bar{A}\bar{B}$
0	0	1	1	0	1	1
0	1	1	0	0	0	0
1	0	0	1	0	0	0
1	1	0	0	1	0	1

39. The logic circuit is given as

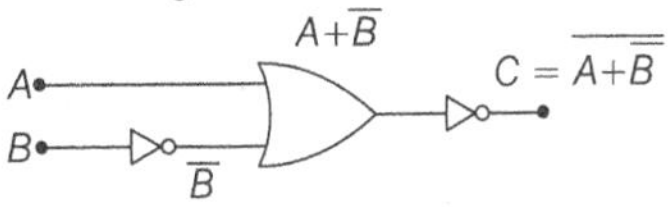

By using De-morgan's theorem,

$$C=\overline{A+\bar{B}}=\bar{A}\cdot\bar{\bar{B}}=\bar{A}\cdot B$$

This relation can be shown by the circuit drawn below

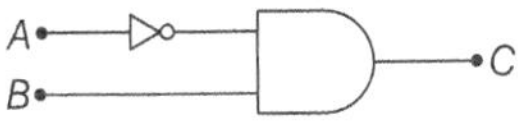

Hence, correct option is (d).

40. Consider the figure given in the question and solve it using Boolean identities.

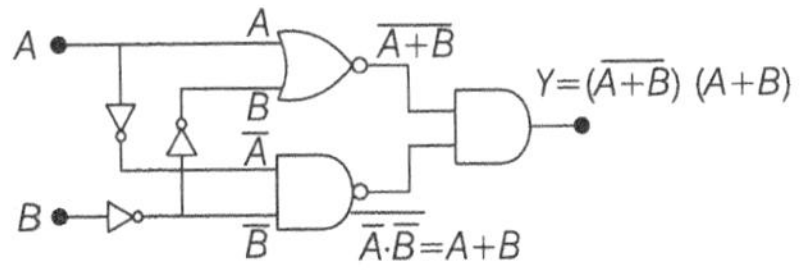

Now, put the value of A and B in the output, we get

$$Y=\overline{(0+1)}(0+1)$$

$\Rightarrow \quad Y=\bar{1}\cdot 1=0$

41. According to given circuit diagram,

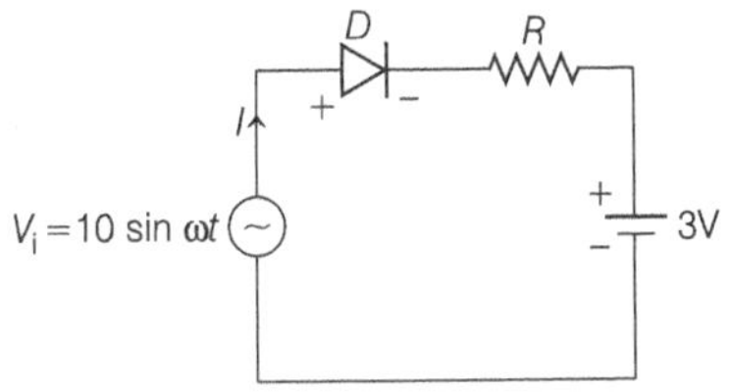

Let I current is flowing through the circuit.

$\therefore$ Kirchhoff's voltage loop equation will be

$$10\sin\omega t - IR - 3 = 0$$

$$\Rightarrow \quad IR = V = 10\sin\omega t - 3$$

$\therefore$ At time, $t = 0, V = 0 - 3 = -3V$ ...(i)

$$t = \frac{T}{4}, V = 10\sin\left(\frac{2\pi}{T}\right)\cdot\frac{T}{4} - 3$$

$$= 10 - 3 = 7\text{ V} \quad \text{...(ii)}$$

$t = T/2$ to T, diode is in reverse bias.

$\therefore$ $V = 0$ ...(iii)

We see that at $t = 0, V = -3$

and $T/2 \le t \le T, V = 0$

No graph matches these conditions.

42. Given, $\lambda = 621 \times 10^{-9}$ m

As we know that

$$E = \frac{hc}{\lambda}\text{ J}$$

$$\Rightarrow \quad E = \frac{hc}{\lambda e}\text{ eV} \quad \text{...(i)}$$

$$E = \frac{6.63 \times 10^{-34} \times 3 \times 10^{8}}{621 \times 10^{-9} \times 1.6 \times 10^{-19}}$$

$$= 0.02014 \times 10^{2} = 2.014\text{ eV} \simeq 2\text{eV}$$

43. Consider the given figure and draw the direction of current as follows

$\therefore$ Current, $I = \dfrac{V_i - V_z}{R_s}$

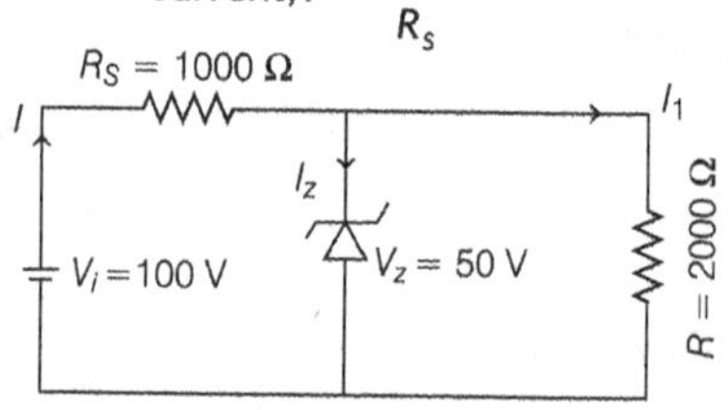

$$\Rightarrow \quad I = \frac{100 - 50}{1000} = 50\text{ mA} \quad \text{...(i)}$$

[$\because$ Resistance and Zener diode are in parallel, therefore voltages across them are same]

and current, $I_1 = \dfrac{50}{2000} = 25$ mA ...(ii)

By using Kirchhoff 's current law,

$$\because \quad I = I_1 + I_z$$

$$\Rightarrow \quad I_z = I - I_1 \quad \text{...(iii)}$$

From Eq. (i) and (ii) and, we get

$$\Rightarrow \quad I_z = (50 - 25)\text{ mA}$$

$$I_z = 25\text{ mA}$$